FAMILY LAW

SIXTH EDITION

William P. Statsky

FAMILY LAW

SIXTH EDITION

William P. Statsky

DELMAR
CENGAGE Learning

Australia • Brazil • Japan • Korea • Mexico • Singapore • Spain • United Kingdom • United States

DELMAR
CENGAGE Learning™

Family Law, Sixth Edition
William P. Statsky

Vice President, Careers & Computing:
Dave Garza

Director of Learning Solutions: Sandy Clark

Senior Acquisitions Editor: Shelley Esposito

Director, Development-Career and Computing:
Marah Bellegarde

Senior Product Development Manager:
Larry Main

Senior Product Manager: Melissa Riveglia

Editorial Assistant: Diane Chrysler

Senior Market Development Manager:
Erin Brennan

Senior Brand Manager: Kristin McNary

Senior Production Director: Wendy Troeger

Production Manager: Mark Bernard

Senior Content Project Manager:
Betty L. Dickson

Art Director: Riezebos Holzbaur Group

Senior Technology Project Manager: Joe Pliss

Media Editor: Deborah Bordeaux

Cover Image Credits:

Family sunset
© Losevsky Photo and Video/shutterstock

Structure of crosswalk with couple
© Peter Zurek/shutterstock

Pillars of Law and Information at the
United States Supreme Court
© Brandon Bourdages/shutterstock

Court of Appeals Courtroom 2
© Davidgn/Dreamstime.com

For product information and technology assistance, contact us at
Cengage Learning Customer & Sales Support, 1-800-354-9706
For permission to use material from this text or product,
submit all requests online at **www.cengage.com/permissions**
Further permissions questions can be emailed to
permissionrequest@cengage.com

Library of Congress Control Number: 2012952052

ISBN-13: 978-1-4354-4074-6

ISBN-10: 1-4354-4074-9

Loose-leaf Edition:

ISBN-13: 978-1-337-41376-3

ISBN-10: 1-337-41376-3

Delmar
Executive Woods
5 Maxwell Drive
Clifton Park, NY 12065
USA

Cengage Learning is a leading provider of customized learning solutions with office locations around the globe, including Singapore, the United Kingdom, Australia, Mexico, Brazil, and Japan. Locate your local office at **www.cengage.com/global**

Cengage Learning products are represented in Canada by Nelson Education, Ltd.

To learn more about Delmar, visit **www.cengage.com/delmar**

Purchase any of our products at your local bookstore or at our preferred online store **www.cengagebrain.com**

Notice to the Reader
Publisher does not warrant or guarantee any of the products described herein or perform any independent analysis in connection with any of the product information contained herein. Publisher does not assume, and expressly disclaims, any obligation to obtain and include information other than that provided to it by the manufacturer. The reader is expressly warned to consider and adopt all safety precautions that might be indicated by the activities described herein and to avoid all potential hazards. By following the instructions contained herein, the reader willingly assumes all risks in connection with such instructions. The publisher makes no representations or warranties of any kind, including but not limited to, the warranties of fitness for particular purpose or merchantability, nor are any such representations implied with respect to the material set forth herein, and the publisher takes no responsibility with respect to such material. The publisher shall not be liable for any special, consequential, or exemplary damages resulting, in whole or part, from the readers' use of, or reliance upon, this material.

Printed in Mexico
Print Number: 02   Print Year: 2019

For my own domestic relations:

Pat, Jess, Gabe, Randy, Carlie, Ava, Hailey, Ryder, Myles, Kaia, Joe, Brenda, Rich, Milosc, Moxie, and Rainy

By the Same Author

For all publications by William Statsky, see:

www.statsky.blogspot.com

....

The California Paralegal: Essential Rules, Documents, and Resources. Clifton Park, N.Y.: Delmar Cengage Learning, 2008 (with S. Sandberg)

Case Analysis and Fundamentals of Legal Writing, 4th ed. St. Paul: West Group, 1995 (with J. Wernet)

Essentials of Paralegalism, 5th ed. Clifton Park, N.Y.: Delmar Cengage Learning, 2010

Torts: Personal Injury Litigation, 5th ed. Clifton Park, N.Y.: Delmar Cengage Learning, 2011

Essentials of Torts, 3d ed. Clifton Park, N.Y.: Delmar Cengage Learning, 2012

Family Law: The Essentials, 2d ed. Clifton Park, N.Y.: Delmar Cengage Learning, 2004

The Florida Paralegal: Essential Rules, Documents, and Resources. Clifton Park, N.Y.: Delmar Cengage Learning, 2009 (with B. Diotalevi & P. Linquist)

Inmate Involvement in Prison Legal Services: Roles and Training Options for the Inmate as Paralegal. Chicago: American Bar Association, Commission on Correctional Facilities and Services, 1974

Introduction to Paralegalism: Perspectives, Problems, and Skills, 7th ed. Clifton Park, N.Y.: Delmar Cengage Learning, 2009

Legal Desk Reference. St. Paul: West Group, 1990 (with B. Hussey, M. Diamond, & R. Nakamura)

The Legal Paraprofessional as Advocate and Assistant: Training Concepts and Materials. New York: Center on Social Welfare Policy and Law, 1971 (with P. Lang)

Legal Research and Writing: Some Starting Points, 5th ed. Clifton Park, N.Y.: Delmar Cengage Learning, 1999

Legal Thesaurus/Dictionary: A Resource for the Writer and Computer Researcher. St. Paul: West Group, 1985

Legislative Analysis and Drafting, 2d ed. St. Paul: West Group, 1984

The New York Paralegal: Essential Rules, Documents, and Resources. Clifton Park, N.Y.: Delmar Cengage Learning, 2009 (with R. Sarachan)

The Ohio Paralegal: Essential Rules, Documents, and Resources. Clifton Park, N.Y.: Delmar Cengage Learning, 2008 (with K. Reed & B. Moore)

Paralegal Employment: Facts and Strategies for the 1990s, 2d ed. St. Paul: West Group, 1993

Paralegal Ethics and Regulation, 2d ed. St. Paul: West Group, 1993

The Pennsylvania Paralegal: Essential Rules, Documents, and Resources. Clifton Park, N.Y.: Delmar Cengage Learning, 2009 (with J. DeLeo & J. Geis)

The Texas Paralegal: Essential Rules, Documents, and Resources. Clifton Park, N.Y.: Delmar Cengage Learning, 2009 (with L. Crossett)

Rights of the Imprisoned: Cases, Materials, and Directions. Indianapolis, Ind.: Bobbs-Merrill Company, 1974 (with R. Singer)

What Have Paralegals Done? A Dictionary of Functions. Washington, D.C.: National Paralegal Institute, 1973

Contents in Brief

Contents

CHAPTER 2

Ethics in a Family Law Practice   43

CHAPTER 5

CHAPTER 7

Divorce Grounds and Procedure   241

CHAPTER 8

Spousal Support, Property Division, and the Separation Agreement

CHAPTER 9

CHAPTER 10

Child Support   421

CHAPTER 14

The Legal Status of Children   541

CHAPTER 15

Adoption   558

CHAPTER 16

The New Science of Motherhood 594

CHAPTER 17

APPENDIX A

Say it isn't true. A recent *New York Times* story reported that a well-known divorce attorney was giving out pens to prospective clients that said, "Sue Someone You Love." This is not the image the legal profession wishes to project to the public. Yet newspapers, magazines, blogs, and talk shows do seem to give the impression that our society is in a litigation frenzy: "Son Sues to Divorce His Mother," "Wife Demands Half of Husband's Medical Practice in Divorce Settlement," "Surrogate Mother Refuses to Turn Over Baby," "Live-In Lover Seeks Palimony," "Facebook Divorces on the Rise."

Our goal in this book is to sort through the headlines to find an accurate picture of the state of family law today and the role of the attorney-paralegal team within it. We are living in an era of great change in the practice of family law. The primary focus of the family-law practitioner is no longer adultery and who gets the kids.

No-fault divorce has made marriage relatively easy to dissolve. The women's movement has helped bring about major shifts in determining what property can be split after a divorce and how to split it. Same-sex marriage is no longer a distant maybe. The country has declared war on the "deadbeat" parent who fails to pay child support. Major new enforcement mechanisms have been designed to find these parents and make them pay. To the surprise of many, courts have come to the aid of some unmarried fathers seeking to undo the adoption of their children. Science and technology have unleashed new concepts of motherhood and parentage. The law has not been able to keep pace with the scientific revolution taking place in the test tube and in the womb.

In short, there is a lot to talk about! It's a fascinating time to study family law.

CHAPTER FORMAT

Each chapter includes features designed to assist students in understanding the material:

- A Chapter Outline at the beginning of each chapter provides a preview of the major topics discussed in the chapter.
- Chapter Objectives, also at the beginning of each chapter, present a more detailed listing of the themes and skills covered in the chapter.
- Exhibits and tables are used extensively to clarify concepts and present detailed information in an organized chart form.
- Assignments that ask students to apply concepts to particular fact situations are included in the chapters. The assignments cover critical skills such as analysis, investigation, interviewing, and drafting.
- Key terms are printed in boldface type the first time they appear in the chapter. A list of key terms also appears at the end of each chapter to help students review important terminology introduced in that chapter.
- Each key term is also defined in the margin next to the text to which the terms are relevant.
- At the end of most chapters, there is an outline of Paralegal Roles related to the material in the chapter that cross-references the broader array of paralegal roles covered elsewhere in the book.

- At the end of most chapters, there is a Check the Cite exercise in which the student is sent to a specific case found on the Internet that is relevant to the material covered in the chapter.

- At the end of every chapter, there is a Project assignment in which the student is asked to use Internet sources to develop a particular theme related to the chapter.

- Following each project assignment there is an exercise called Ethics in a Family Law Practice, which asks the student to read a fact situation and identify ethical problems that may exist. These exercises build on the principles of ethics covered in Chapter 2.

- At the end of most chapters, there is a Writing Sample assignment in which the student is asked to draft a family-law document that could be developed into a writing sample when searching for employment.

- A Summary at the end of each chapter provides a concise review of the main concepts discussed.

- Each chapter has Review Questions covering the major themes in the chapter.

- Helpful Websites are added at the end of each chapter to provide additional materials on the topics of the chapter.

CHANGES IN THE SIXTH EDITION

New chapter features include:
- Chapter Objectives. At the beginning of each chapter, there is an outline of the themes and skills covered in the chapter.

- Paralegal Roles. An outline of paralegal tasks related to the subject-matter of the chapter.

- Check the Cite. A link to a particular court opinion found on the Internet and questions about that case in relationship to the subject-matter of the chapter.

- Chapter Project. An Internet assignment to research a particular chapter topic in greater depth, keyed to the law of your state.

- Writing Sample. An assignment that can become the basis of a writing sample to place in one's portfolio when looking for employment.

- Review Questions. A comprehensive list of questions that review all the major topics covered in the chapter.

In addition to updating the law, new coverage in each chapter includes the following:
- Chapter 1. A major section on the constitutional underpinnings of many of the changes that have occurred in family law.

- Chapter 1. The impact of social media (e.g., Facebook) on the practice of family law.

- Chapter 1. Paralegal roles outside the traditional law office, such as government paralegals in child-support cases and freelance paralegals offering family-law services.

- Chapter 2. Collaborative law as a form of limited-scope representation.

- Chapter 2. The ethical problems of identifying the client in family-law cases when multiple family members are involved in a case.

- Chapter 2. Ethical responsibilities when attempting to interact with a witness on Facebook or MySpace.
- Chapter 2. Ethical problems involving interactive software programs in family-law cases.
- Chapter 3. Software used in family-law cases during the intake stage of the case.
- Chapter 4. Postnuptial agreements.
- Chapter 4. The ethical dilemma a family-law attorney can face when a client wishes to sign a disadvantageous premarital agreement.
- Chapter 4. The distinction between procedural and substantive fairness in premarital agreements.
- Chapter 5. The major state and federal constitutional issues in same-sex marriage cases.
- Chapter 5. Antinepotism policies as a restraint on marriage.
- Chapter 6. New immigration rules on sham marriages, sometimes called green-card marriages.
- Chapter 7. Historical background on divorce law and procedure.
- Chapter 7. Strategic and substantive roles of fault principles in no-fault cases.
- Chapter 7. The relationship between religious law (e.g., Islamic Sharia) and civil family law in our courts.
- Chapter 8. The defense of mutual mistake in challenges to separation agreements involving funds in the Madoff Ponzi scheme.
- Chapter 8. The divisibility of public pensions.
- Chapter 9. Virtual visitation in child-custody cases.
- Chapter 10. The liability of stepparents and coparents for child support.
- Chapter 10. The three-pony rule in the calculation of child support.
- Chapter 10. The right of an indigent to state-paid counsel in child-support cases.
- Chapter 12. The sexual-harassment suit against President (then Governor) Bill Clinton.
- Chapter 12. The law requiring accommodations for women who need to express breast feeding at work.
- Chapter 12. The controversy surrounding mandatory-arrest and mandatory-prosecution laws in domestic-violence cases and the defendant's right of confrontation in such cases when the victim refuses to testify.
- Chapter 13. The constitutional status of nonmarital children.
- Chapter 13. How a court resolves conflicting presumptions of paternity.
- Chapter 13. Paternity by estoppel.
- Chapter 13. Different requirements for citizenship of a nonmarital child born abroad to a citizen mother as opposed to a citizen father.
- Chapter 14. Free speech and search-and-seizure constitutional rights of students.
- Chapter 15. Adoption of embryos.
- Chapter 16. The octomom and abuse of infertility treatments.
- Chapter 16. Posthumous birth and posthumous conception.

- Chapter 17. Domestic tort claims brought in divorce actions.
- Chapter 17. Tortious interference with custody.
- Chapter 17. Intrafamily crimes.
- Appendix B. Computer-generated reports in divorce cases.
- Appendix D. Fifty-state links to family law.

TEACHING AIDS AND SUPPLEMENTS

The text is accompanied by the following support materials designed to assist students in learning and instructors in teaching.

PARALEGAL COURSEMATE

Family Law, Sixth Edition, has a Paralegal CourseMate available.

Paralegal CourseMate includes:
* an interactive eBook, with highlighting, note-taking, and search capabilities
* interactive teaching and learning tools, including:

- Quizzing
- Case studies
- Chapter objectives
- Flashcards
- Web links
- Crossword puzzles
- PowerPoint® presentations
- State-specific supplements
- And more!

* Engagement Tracker, a first-of-its-kind tool that monitors student engagement in the course.

State-specific supplements are available for California, Florida, New York, and Texas. These supplements are keyed to each chapter in the text and point out state-specific information when it differs from the text's discussion.

To learn more about this resource and access free demo CourseMate resources, go to www.cengagebrain.com and search by this book's ISBN (9781435440746). To access CourseMate materials that you have purchased, go to login.cengagebrain.com, enter your access code, and create an account or log into your existing account.

INSTRUCTOR'S MANUAL

The Instructor's Manual and Test Bank by the author of the text have been greatly expanded to incorporate changes in the text and to provide comprehensive teaching support. The Instructor's Manual provides answers to many of the text assignments and all of the end-of-chapter review questions. The test bank includes a variety of questions in multiple choice, true/false, short answer, fill-in, and matching. A test bank answer key is also included.

**INSTRUCTOR
RESOURCES**

INSTRUCTOR RESOURCES

Spend less time planning and more time teaching. With Delmar Cengage Learning's Instructor Resources to Accompany Family Law, preparing for class and evaluating students have never been easier!

This invaluable instructor CD-ROM allows you "anywhere, anytime" access to all of your resources.

- The **Instructor's Manual** contains various resources for each chapter of the book.

- The **Computerized Testbank** in ExamView makes generating tests and quizzes a snap. With many questions and different styles to choose from, you can create customized assessments for your students with the click of a button. Add your own unique questions and print rationales for easy class preparation.

- Customizable **PowerPoint® Presentations** focus on key points for each chapter.

(PowerPoint® is a registered trademark of the Microsoft Corporation.)

To access additional course materials (including CourseMate), please go to login.cengage.com, then use your SSO (single sign on) login to access the materials.

Web**TUTOR**™

WEBTUTOR™

The WebTutor™ supplement allows you, as the instructor, to take learning beyond the classroom. This online courseware is designed to complement the text and benefit students and instructors alike by helping to better manage your time, prepare for exams, organize your notes, and more. WebTutor™ allows you to extend your reach beyond the classroom.

WEB PAGE

Come visit our website at http://www.paralegal.delmar.cengage.com/, where you will find valuable information such as hot links and sample materials to download, as well as other Delmar Cengage Learning products.

SUPPLEMENTS AT-A-GLANCE

SUPPLEMENT:	WHAT IT IS:	WHAT'S IN IT:
Paralegal CourseMate CourseMate	Online interactive teaching and learning tools and an interactive eBook. Go to **login.cengage.com** to access.	Interactive teaching and learning tools, including: • Quizzing • Case studies • Chapter objectives • Flashcards • Weblinks • Crossword puzzles • PowerPoints® presentations • State-specific supplements • Interactive eBook • Engagement tracker
Online Instructor Companion Site	Resources for the instructor accessible via Cengage Single Sign On.	• Instructor's Manual with answers to most test assignments and test bank with answer key • Computerized Testbank in ExamView, with many questions and styles to choose from to create customized assessments for your students • PowerPoint® presentations
Instructor Resources CD-ROM INSTRUCTOR RESOURCES	Resources for the instructor, available on CD-ROM	• Instructor's Manual with answers to text questions and test bank and answer key • Computerized Testbank in ExamView, with many questions and styles to choose from to create customized assessments for your students • PowerPoint® presentations
WebTutor™ WebTUTOR™	WebTUTOR™ supplemental courseware is the best way to use the Internet to turn everyone in your class into a front-row student. It complements Cengage Learning paralegal textbooks by providing interactive reinforcement that helps students grasp complex concepts. WebTUTOR™ allows you to know quickly what concepts your students are or aren't grasping.	• Automatic and immediate feedback from quizzes and exams • Online exercises that reinforce what students have learned • Flashcards • Greater interaction and involvement through online discussion forums

Please note that the Internet resources are time-sensitive and URL addresses may change or be deleted.

ACKNOWLEDGMENTS

A word of thanks to the reviewers who made valuable suggestions for improving the text:

Eric Baime
Brandman University
West Palm Beach, FL

Mary Conwell
Edison State College
Fort Myers, FL

Kimberly Murphy
Sanford-Brown College
Fenton, MO

Ellen Sheffer
Carmel & Naccasha Law Firm
San Luis Obispo, CA

1

Introduction to Family Law and Practice

CHAPTER OUTLINE

CHAPTER OBJECTIVES

After completing this chapter, you should be able to:

- Identify the major themes of family law in the twenty-first century.
- Understand how the practice of family law interacts with other areas of the law.
- List the major terminology changes in family law.
- State the tests used by a court when a family law is challenged as

- a violation of due process or equal protection.
- Understand the impact of social media on the practice of family law.
- List the variety of roles paralegals can have in various family-law offices and settings.
- Identify the dangers of bias in the practice of family law.

- Understand the dangers of dealing with volatile clients in the practice of family law.
- Know the main legal-research sources of family law and where they can be found online and on the shelves of a law library.

FAMILY LAW IN THE TWENTY-FIRST CENTURY

family law
The body of law that defines relationships, rights, and duties in the formation, ongoing existence, and dissolution of marriage and other family units.

marriage
The legal union of two persons as spouses with designated rights and obligations to each other.

Family law consists of legal principles that govern marital and nonmarital families. The principles cover rights and duties as these units are created, maintained, and dissolved. More specifically, family law is the body of law that defines relationships, rights, and duties in the formation, ongoing existence, and dissolution of **marriage** and other family units.

Marriage is the cornerstone of family law and for centuries this law has been relatively unchanged. Not so in recent decades. The world of our grandparents was dramatically different from today's world:

> [U]ntil a generation ago there was a social consensus as to what marriage meant. Marriage was permanent and monogamous; children were automatic, essential, and central; husbands earned money and made decisions; wives stayed home taking care of house, children, and husband. The legal system reinforced the social norms for marriage. Now the clarity and unity of the domestic picture is gone. Only a small percentage of American families still have all the characteristics associated with the traditional nuclear family ideal. In place of a single socially approved ideal we have compelling demands for autonomy and privacy, and multiple models of intimacy: single parents, working wives, house husbands, homosexual [marriage], living-together arrangements without marriage, serial marriage, stepchildren, [and surrogate parents]. The changes are legion, and their message is clear: the destruction of traditional marriage as the sole model for adult intimacy is irreversible.[1]

Indeed, we live in a society that sometimes appears to be in a state of perpetual change. One scholar maintains that "marriage has changed more in the past 30 years than in the previous 3,000."[2] A recent survey came to the provocative conclusion that 39 percent of Americans feel that marriage is obsolete.[3] Another survey found that just under half of young Americans do not believe that the government should be in the business of issuing marriage licenses.[4] According to Justice Scalia of the U.S. Supreme Court, a "cultural war" is underway as society debates whether we have gone too far, or not far enough.[5]

Courts and legislatures have not always been able to fit traditional family-law principles into this environment of debate and change. New principles have been—and still are—needed. One of the central themes in this book will be how family law has evolved in response to the shifting boundary lines in how people choose to live together.

Five important developments in family law are a product of this turmoil. They have shaped our recent history and will continue to play major roles in the twenty-first century. The following is an overview of these developments, which we will be studying along with traditional principles of family law.

EQUALITY OF THE SEXES: THE STRUGGLE CONTINUES

unity of person
The legal identity of a wife subsumed into the legal identity of the husband. Also called doctrine of oneness or spousal-unity rule.

There was a time in our history when a wife could not make her own will or bring a lawsuit in her own name. Without the consent of her husband, there was relatively little that she could do. Two centuries ago, the greatest legal scholar of the day, Blackstone, declared that "the very being or legal existence of a woman was suspended during the marriage, or at least was incorporated and consolidated into that of her husband."[6] Indeed, in the eyes of the law, the husband and wife were one person, and that person was the husband. This legal rule had several names: **unity of person**, doctrine of oneness, and spousal-unity rule. Carried to its logical extreme, the rule meant that a wife could not sue her husband (the suit would be the equivalent of the husband suing himself) and that a husband could not be convicted of raping his wife (the conviction would be for the equivalent of the husband raping himself).

Much progress has been made in abandoning a theory of the law based on male dominance. To a large extent, the law has equalized the legal status of husbands and wives. Some changes, however, have had unintended consequences that have served to perpetuate inequality. For example, no-fault divorce (which we will study in Chapter 7) gave both spouses an equal right to end a marriage without having to prove adultery, cruelty, or other marital misconduct. Yet some have argued that this reform removed a substantial bargaining chip for wives on the issues of money and custody, particularly in the case of long-term marriages. A husband did not have to bargain so hard to get out of the marriage if a divorce was now relatively easy to obtain. Also, for many couples, the standard of living of the ex-husband increases after divorce, while that of the ex-wife decreases.[7] Some feminists say that "equality" has actually led to a diminution of women's rights. A Columbia law professor and author of *The Illusion of Equality* has argued that "[e]quality is being applied with a vengeance against women."[8]

Furthermore, it is important to keep in mind that reforms in the law do not always translate into changes in human behavior. Not that long ago, for example, a court was asked to interpret a marital agreement between a Mr. and Mrs. Spires that contained the following provisions:

Mrs. Spires:

- may not withdraw any money from the bank without Mr. Spires's express permission
- may not "attempt to influence the status/intensity" of any relationship that Mr. Spires may have "with other individuals outside of the marriage unless the husband verbally requests input from the wife"
- may not "dispute" Mr. Spires in public "on any matter"
- must "conduct herself in accordance with all scriptures in the Holy Bible applicable to marital relationships germane to wives and in accordance with the husband's specific requests"
- must maintain a sexual relationship that "remains spontaneous and solely with the husband"
- must "carry out requests of the husband in strict accordance, i.e., timeliness, sequence, scheduling, etc."
- may not receive any loan or gift without first obtaining Mr. Spires's permission.[9]

The date the parties entered this agreement was not 1791 or 1891, but 1991. Although the court eventually declared the agreement to be unenforceable (for reasons we will cover elsewhere in the book), the fact that such a case had to be litigated close to the beginning of the twenty-first century suggests that not everyone in society accepts the legal principle of equality between the sexes. Fortunately, most do accept it. Nevertheless, anyone engaged in the practice of family law must be prepared to find serious discrepancies between the laws on the books and the reality of how people conduct their lives. These discrepancies will continue to generate considerable business for family-law practices.

INCREASED FEDERALIZATION OF FAMILY LAW

The U.S. Constitution has specific enumerated powers that are the responsibility of the U.S. (federal) government, e.g., raising armies and regulating patents. Family-law matters are *not* among these enumerated powers. Under the Tenth Amendment, the "powers not delegated to the United States by the Constitution, nor prohibited by it to the States, are reserved to the States respectively, or to the people." Hence, family law is substantially within the responsibility of state law. As Chief Justice William Rehnquist of the U.S. Supreme Court has said, the law of domestic relations "has been left to the states from time immemorial."[10] Congress, federal courts, and federal administrative agencies have historically played relatively minor roles in family law. When parties want a divorce, for example, they go to a state court, not to a federal court.

Although state law continues to dominate the field, federal law is becoming increasingly important. Here are some examples:

- Competent legal representation in a divorce settlement must include advice on how federal tax laws affect alimony and property division.
- Competent representation also requires providing advice on the impact of our federal bankruptcy laws.
- The legalization of abortion occurred through an interpretation by a federal court (the U.S. Supreme Court) of the federal Constitution.
- Major changes in the state law of paternity have been due to interpretations of the federal Constitution.
- Interstate child-custody disputes are now substantially regulated by federal statutes such as the Parental Kidnapping Prevention Act.
- Congress has passed laws that have led to substantial changes in the enforcement of child-support obligations, perhaps the most dramatic inroad of federal law into state law. Child support is still governed by state law, but Congress has told states that if they want to receive specified federal funds (e.g., grants for public assistance), they need to pass specified state laws designed to increase collection of child support from delinquent parents. All states have made such changes.

When federal laws such as these bring about a change in an area of the law once controlled mainly by state law, we refer to the change as the **federalization** of that area of the law. If the federal law consists of interpretations of the U.S. Constitution by the U.S. Supreme Court and by other federal courts, we refer to the change as the **constitutionalization** of that area of the law. Of course, state family law has not been swallowed up by federalization or constitutionalization. The bulk of family law today is still written by state legislatures and state courts. Yet, the role of federal law in family law is significant and is increasing. Not everyone is happy with this trend, as we will see.

CONTRACT DIMENSION OF FAMILY LAW

A great deal of family law is governed by the **status** of the participants. *Status* is a legal term that means a bundle of legal rights and obligations that are imposed by law, often without regard to the consent or contract desires of the persons involved. For example, once parties are married, they cannot agree on their own to dissolve their marriage so that they can marry someone else. Spouses cannot divorce themselves. They need a court order of divorce. Nor can they agree that either or both will have additional spouses. A basic requirement of the law is that people have one spouse at a time. The parties cannot agree (contract) between themselves to divorce on their own or to turn their relationship into a multiple marriage by adding more spouses. The *status* of marriage would trump such contractual desires. Phrased another way, such contracts are unenforceable because of the duties and obligations imposed by the status of marriage.

Yet, there is still considerable room for the parties to enter agreements (contracts) about their marriage so long as they do not tamper with basic rights and obligations that are central to the status of marriage. In fact, a relatively recent major development in family law has been a substantial increase in the capacity of parties to enter enforceable contracts that help define their rights and obligations. When we study **premarital agreements**, for example, we will see a greater willingness of the courts to allow the parties to enter contracts that define important components of the marriage they are about to enter, particularly in the area of finances. To an increasing degree, marriage is viewed as an economic partnership that is subject to some mutual modification, rather than as an eternal union of love benevolently presided over by the husband. Again, there are still limits on what parties can accomplish by contract. Courts will not approve (enforce) everything the parties agree to do.

federalization
Changes in state law that result from (a) laws written by the federal legislature (Congress) and (b) interpretations of the U.S. Constitution by federal courts.

constitutionalization
Changes in state law that result from interpretations of the U.S. Constitution by the U.S. Supreme Court and other federal courts.

status
A person's legal condition in which rights and obligations are imposed by law, often without regard to the consent or contract desires of the person involved.

premarital agreement
A contract by persons about to be married that can cover (1) financial and related matters once the marriage occurs and (2) spousal support, property division, and related matters in the event of death, separation, divorce, or annulment. Also called prenuptial agreement ("prenup") or antenuptial agreement.

It is sometimes said that in every marriage there is a third party—the state—that imposes rights and obligations on the spouses. This is still true, although we have begun to see more flexibility in what the parties are allowed to do by contract. This trend is even greater in family units created as alternatives to marriage, as we will see when we study contract cohabitation and domestic partnership.

SCIENCE AND LAW

Scientific breakthroughs have created substantial challenges for family law. Nowhere is this more evident than in the modern science of motherhood. New ways to create babies have given us the reality of multiple parents: "Reproductive technology has made it possible for one person to supply an egg, another to fertilize it, a third to gestate it and a fourth and fifth to be deemed the parents."[11] This reality has forced legislatures and courts to redefine traditional areas of the law and to confront new categories of disputes. For example, who is the legal parent when a surrogate mother changes her mind about turning the baby over to the couple that provided the embryo for the child?

DEREGULATION OF SEXUALITY

At one time society imposed severe restrictions on intimate conduct. The law contained numerous examples of crimes related to sexuality, such as the sale of contraceptives, homosexual conduct between adults, and abortion. Although all restrictions on sexuality have not been eliminated, they have been substantially reduced when adults are involved. In the dramatic case of *Lawrence v. Texas* that decriminalized private homosexual conduct between adults, the U.S. Supreme Court said that "[l]iberty presumes an autonomy of self that includes . . . certain intimate conduct."[12] Although there is a segment of society that wants to maintain—and, indeed, increase—government regulation of sexual behavior and other "intimate conduct," the law is moving in the other direction.

As family law continues into the twenty-first century, these are some of the major themes that will continue to demand the attention of courts and legislatures, and, therefore, will be part of the family-law practices where attorneys and paralegals serve the needs of clients.

THE NEW TERMINOLOGY OF FAMILY LAW

One of the consequences of changes in family law over recent decades has been the development of new terminology to describe some of the participants and procedures that make up family law. Here are some examples:
New Terminology
(older terms in parentheses)

- dissolution (divorce)
- spousal support (alimony)
- maintenance (alimony)
- nonmarital child (illegitimate child, out-of-wedlock child, bastard)
- caregiver (custodian)
- parenting plan, parenting schedule, parenting functions, parental responsibility, residential schedule (custody, visitation, access to the child)

Some of the changes in terminology are cosmetic. Others have a more substantial purpose, such as emphasizing responsibilities rather than rights, downplaying an emphasis on morality, and toning down rhetoric that can contribute to the hostility that some family-law disputes can engender. A major goal is to move away from terminology that encourages parties to view themselves as "winners" or "losers" so that there can be a greater focus on an amicable resolution of conflict, particularly when children are involved.

Not all states use the new terminology. Indeed, you are likely to find that some states use both the old and the new terminologies at the same time. This is inevitable as courts apply prior decisions (**precedents**) to current facts. The prior decisions, of course, use the old terminology. In this book, we will be examining both the old and the new terminologies.

precedent
A prior decision covering a similar issue that can be used as a standard or guide in a later case.

SCOPE OF FAMILY LAW

To work in an office where family law is practiced, you need compassion, flexibility, skill, and, above all, an ability to handle a wide diversity of problems. While many cases are straightforward, some are not. A veteran attorney observed that a family-law practice requires everyone "to become an expert in many fields of law and not just one."[13] In this sense, the specialty of family law requires one to be a generalist.

Let's examine this diversity using an example. Assume that you are a paralegal working for Karen Smith, an attorney in your state. One of the clients of the office is Susan Miller, who lives out of state. The attorney receives the following e-mail message from Ms. Miller:

2/7/13

Karen Smith:

I am leaving the state in a week to live with my mother in your state. She will help me move everything so that we can start a new life. I must see you as soon as I arrive. Yesterday my husband called from his business. He threatened me and the three children. I will bring the twins with me. I don't know where my oldest boy is. He is probably with his father getting into more trouble.

Susan Miller

The checklist below lists many of the questions that are potentially relevant to the case of Susan Miller. Most of the technical terms in this list will be defined in subsequent chapters. Our goal here is simply to demonstrate that the scope of the law covered in a family-law practice can be very broad.

One final word before we begin the overview. Some state bar associations have **specialty certification** programs for attorneys who practice family law. At least one state (Texas) also has a certification specialty for paralegals in family law.[14] Certification requires meeting designated qualifications, such as experience in the specialty, and passing an exam in the law of the specialty. Most attorneys and paralegals, however, do not have specialty certification, either because the state does not offer it or because of a perception that it is not needed.

specialty certification
Recognition of competency in a particular area of law.

Areas of Law Often Covered in a Family Law Practice: The Example of *Miller v. Miller*

Criminal Law

- Has Mr. Miller committed a crime? What kind of threats did he make? Did he assault his wife and children? Has domestic violence been committed?

- Even if her husband has committed a crime, would it be wise for Ms. Miller to ask the district attorney to investigate and prosecute the case?

- Has Mr. Miller failed to support his family? If so, is the nonsupport serious enough to warrant state or federal criminal action against him?

- Is there any danger of further criminal acts by Mr. Miller? If so, what can be done, if anything, to prevent such acts from occurring? Can Ms. Miller obtain a restraining or protective order to keep her husband away?

- Is Ms. Miller subject to any penalties for taking the children out of state?

Divorce/Separation/Annulment Law

- What does Ms. Miller want?

- Does Ms. Miller know what her husband wants to do?

- Does Ms. Miller have grounds for a divorce?

- Does Ms. Miller have grounds for an annulment? (Were the Millers validly married?)

- Does Ms. Miller have grounds for a legal separation?

- Does Mr. Miller have grounds for a divorce, annulment, or legal separation against his wife?

Child Custody Law

- Does Ms. Miller want sole physical and sole legal custody of all three children? Is she the natural (genetic) mother of all three? Is Mr. Miller their natural father? Are there any paternity problems? Will Mr. Miller want custody? What is the lifestyle of the parent or parents seeking custody? Is joint physical custody or joint legal custody an option?

- If Ms. Miller does not want a divorce, annulment, or legal separation, how can she obtain custody of the children?

- Does Ms. Miller want anyone else to be given temporary or permanent custody of any of the children (e.g., a relative)? Could such a person make a claim for custody *against* Ms. Miller?

- If she wants custody, has Ms. Miller jeopardized her chances of being awarded custody by taking the twins out of state?

- Which custody law applies: The custody law of the state where Mr. Miller lives, the state where Ms. Miller has now moved to, or the state where the children live?

Support Law

- Is Mr. Miller supporting his wife? Is she supporting him?

- Is Mr. Miller supporting the three children? Is Ms. Miller supporting them? Do the children have any special medical or school needs? If so, are these needs being met?

- Are the children now covered under Mr. Miller's health insurance policy? Is Ms. Miller covered? Is there a danger that the policy will be changed? Who has the authority under the policy to change the beneficiaries?

- Can Ms. Miller obtain a court order forcing Mr. Miller to support her and the children while she is deciding whether she wants to terminate the marital relationship?

- If Ms. Miller files for divorce, annulment, or legal separation, can she obtain a temporary support order while the case is in progress?

- If Ms. Miller files for divorce, annulment, or legal separation and loses, can she still obtain a support order for separate maintenance against Mr. Miller?

- Does Mr. Miller have assets (personal property or real property) against which a support order can be enforced? Is there a danger that he might try to hide these assets? Is there a danger he might try to give the assets to persons he controls, for example, by transferring title to their names? If so, can this be prevented?

- If Mr. Miller cannot be relied upon for support and Ms. Miller cannot work, does Ms. Miller qualify for public assistance such as Temporary Assistance for Needy Families (TANF)?

- Is Mr. Miller supporting any other children, such as from a previous marriage? If so, how would this affect his duty to support the three children he has with Ms. Miller?

Contract/Agency Law

- In his business, has Mr. Miller entered into any contracts for which Ms. Miller could be found liable if he fails to perform the contracts?

- While she is living apart from her husband, can Ms. Miller enter into contracts with merchants for the purchase of food, clothing, furniture, medical care, prescriptions, transportation, and other necessities (called "necessaries") and make *him* pay for them? Can she use his credit?

- Can Mr. Miller obligate Ms. Miller on any of his current or future debts?

- Has Ms. Miller ever worked for Mr. Miller or otherwise acted as his agent?

- Has Mr. Miller ever worked for Ms. Miller or otherwise acted as her agent?

- Have the Millers' children (particularly the oldest child) entered into any contracts under their own names? If so, who is liable for such contracts? Can they be canceled (disaffirmed)?

Real Property Law and Personal Property Law

- Do either or both of the Millers own any real property (e.g., land)? If so, how is the real property owned? How is title held? Individually? As tenants by the entirety? As community property?

- Who provided the funds for the purchase of this property? Were the funds earned during the marriage or did any of the funds come from monies either of the Millers brought into the marriage?

- What rights does Ms. Miller have in Mr. Miller's separate property?

- What rights does Mr. Miller have in Ms. Miller's separate property?

- What is Mr. Miller's income? Can his wages be garnished?

- Does Mr. or Ms. Miller have a pension plan from prior or present employment? Can one spouse (or ex-spouse) obtain rights in the pension plan of the other spouse (or ex-spouse)?

- What other personal property exists (e.g., cars, bank accounts, stocks, bonds, furniture)? Who owns this property? With what funds was it purchased?

Corporate Law/Business Law

- What kind of business does Mr. Miller have? Is it a corporation? A partnership? A sole proprietorship? If the parties separate and obtain a divorce, will Ms. Miller be entitled to a share of the business as part of the division of marital property? The same questions apply to any business owned by Ms. Miller.

- What are the assets and liabilities of the business?

Bankruptcy Law

- Is there a danger that Mr. Miller or his business might go into bankruptcy? If so, how would this affect Ms. Miller's rights to support and to her share of the marital property? How would it affect Mr. Miller's duty of child support? The same questions apply to any business owned by Ms. Miller.

Tort Law

- Has Mr. Miller committed any torts against Ms. Miller (e.g., assault, fraud, conversion, intentional infliction of emotional distress)?
- Has Ms. Miller committed any torts against Mr. Miller?
- Can one spouse sue another in tort?
- Have Millers' children (particularly the oldest) damaged any property or committed any torts for which the parents might be liable?

Civil Procedure Law

- If a court action is brought (e.g., for divorce, custody, separate maintenance), what court would have jurisdiction? A court in this state? A court in the state where Mr. Miller resides?
- How can service of process be made?
- If Ms. Miller sues and obtains a judgment in this state, can it be enforced in another state?

Evidence Law

- What factual claims will Ms. Miller be making (e.g., that Mr. Miller has hidden money or other assets that could be used to support the family)?
- What testimonial evidence (oral statements of witnesses) exists to support Ms. Miller's claims?
- How much of this evidence is admissible in court?
- What documentary evidence should be obtained (e.g., marriage license, birth certificates, records of purchases)?
- Whose depositions should be taken?
- What claims will Mr. Miller make against Ms. Miller? What evidence is he likely to use to support these claims? What objections can be made to this evidence?

Juvenile Law

- Can a dependency or child-neglect petition be brought against Mr. Miller? Against Ms. Miller?
- Why is Ms. Miller upset about her eldest son? Has he committed an act of delinquency or other status offense?
- Is the Millers' oldest child a Person in Need of Supervision (PINS), a Child in Need of Supervision (CHINS), or a Child in Need of Protection and Services (CHIPS)?
- If the Millers' oldest child has damaged anyone else's property, can a parent be financially responsible for the damage?

Tax Law

- Have Mr. Miller and his wife filed joint tax returns in the past?
- Are any refunds due (or money owed) on past returns?
- In a property settlement following a divorce or separation, what would be the most advantageous settlement for Ms. Miller from a tax perspective?

- What arrangement might Mr. Miller seek in order to obtain the best tax posture for him? What is negotiable? What will he be willing to give up to obtain his tax objectives? Will he, for example, cooperate in allowing Ms. Miller to have sole physical custody and sole legal custody of the children in exchange for her cooperation in ensuring that his alimony payments are deductible?

Estate Law

- Do the Millers have their own wills? If so, who are the beneficiaries? If there is no divorce, can Mr. Miller leave Ms. Miller out of his will entirely?
- Who receives the Millers' property if they die without a will while they are separated or after a divorce?
- Does Mr. Miller have any life insurance policies on which Ms. Miller or the children are beneficiaries? If so, is he allowed to change these beneficiaries?

Social Security

- When will Mr. Miller be eligible for social security? Can Ms. Miller be eligible for social security through his earnings if she is not eligible independently?
- How do social security benefits affect support obligations?

Professional Responsibility/Ethics

- Is Mr. Miller represented by counsel? If so, can we contact Mr. Miller directly, or must all communications to him be made through his attorney? If he is not yet represented, are there limitations on what we can and cannot say to him?
- If Ms. Miller can find her eldest son, can she simply take him away from her husband when the latter is not present? If this would be illegal, what is the ethical obligation of an attorney whose client is about to do something illegal?

Miscellaneous

- Can Mr. Miller be forced to pay attorney fees that Ms. Miller will incur in her legal disputes with him?
- Can Ms. Miller be forced to pay Mr. Miller's attorney fees?

———————

The purpose of this book is to examine questions such as these that could arise in a client's case. More specifically, the purpose is to equip you to raise, and to help answer, such questions that could arise in your state.

CONSTITUTIONAL LAW

INTRODUCTION

As indicated, a good deal of family law has been changed because of constitutional law rulings of the courts, particularly interpretations of the federal Constitution by the U.S. Supreme Court. We will be covering these changes in later chapters. Here, our goal is simply to provide a refresher on some basic constitutional principles that provide a background for understanding the changes.

Family law consists of a vast array of rules found in the statutes of the legislature and in the **common law** opinions of the courts. The rules cover (a) what

common law
Judge-made law in the absence of controlling statutory law or other higher law. (See glossary for additional meanings.)

can and cannot be done in family relationships and (b) the steps that must be followed to do what is allowed. The rules can range from gender requirements on who can enter the state of marriage to residency requirements on when a court can hear a paternity case. Eventually, almost every rule is challenged by persons who believe that the rule wrongly restricts what they want to do because, they assert, the restriction is unconstitutional. The argument is that the restriction violates the state constitution, the federal (U.S.) Constitution, or both constitutions.

When a court agrees to hear such a challenge, it will use its power of **judicial review** to determine the constitutionality of the rule, including its power to invalidate the rule if the court concludes that it violates the constitution. In this book, we will examine family-law challenges that have been based on state constitutions and on the federal (U.S.) Constitution. For now, our focus will be the two major *federal* challenges based on the U.S. Constitution: due process of law (DPL) and equal protection of law (EPL).

judicial review
The power of a court to determine the constitutionality of a statute or other law, including the power to refuse to enforce it if the court concludes that it violates the constitution.

DUE PROCESS OF LAW (DPL)

The Fourteenth Amendment to the U.S. Constitution provides that no state shall "deprive any person of life, liberty or property, without due process of law."[15] The phrase **due process of law** means both procedural due process and substantive due process:

- **Procedural due process (PDP).** The constitutional requirement that the government provide fair procedures, such as adequate notice and an opportunity to be heard whenever the government seeks to deprive someone of life, liberty, or property.

- **Substantive due process (SDP).** The constitutional requirement that the government avoid arbitrary and capricious actions that deprive someone of life, liberty, or property regardless of how fair the government is in the procedures that lead to the actions.

The focus of SDP is the *content* of what the government is doing (e.g., terminate parental rights). The focus of PDP is the *method* or steps used by the government to implement that content (e.g., provide a hearing and attorney representation).

due process of law (DPL)
Both procedural due process and substantive due process.

procedural due process (PDP)
The constitutional requirement that the government provide fair procedures, such as notice and an opportunity to be heard whenever the government seeks to deprive someone of life, liberty, or property.

substantive due process (SDP)
The constitutional requirement that the government avoid arbitrary and capricious actions that deprive someone of life, liberty, or property regardless of how fair the government is in the procedures that lead to the actions.

Procedural Due Process (PDP)

To comply with PDP, the government must provide fair procedures when it deprives someone of life, liberty, or property. What are these procedures? The answer depends on the seriousness of what is being removed (deprived) by the government. If, for example, the government is taking away a poor person's welfare check, terminating the parental rights of a parent, or expelling a student from public school (all very serious deprivations), then the procedures must include notice of the reasons for the government action and an opportunity to contest the deprivations at a hearing, including the right to have attorney representation at the hearing. The failure to provide these procedures is a violation of PDP.

Substantive Due Process (SDP)

Most of the due-process challenges against family-law restrictions have alleged SDP. When a court must decide if a family-law restriction violates SDP, it goes through the following steps:

- First, the court must determine whether the restriction is of a **fundamental right** (e.g., the right to marry) or is a restriction of a nonfundamental right (e.g., the right to adopt a child). To determine the constitutionality of any restriction, the court applies a test or standard. The test is called a *level of scrutiny* and it is different for fundamental rights and nonfundamental rights.

fundamental right
A right that (a) is specifically guaranteed in the U.S. Constitution, (b) is implicit in the concept of ordered liberty, or (c) is deeply rooted in the nation's history and tradition.

strict scrutiny
The standard used to determine if a restriction or a classification complies with due process or equal protection (and is therefore constitutional). Under this standard, the restriction or the classification must be narrowly tailored to serve a compelling state interest.

narrowly tailored
No more than needed to maintain the effectiveness of a goal; no broader than absolutely necessary.

compelling state interest
An interest that is of the highest order; an interest that has a clear justification in the necessities of national or community life.

rational basis
The standard used to determine if a restriction or a classification complies with due process or equal protection (and is therefore constitutional). Under this standard, the restriction or the classification must be reasonably related to a legitimate state purpose. Also called rational relation.

reasonably related
Logically connected (pertaining to any means used to achieve a goal that is reasonably likely to be successful).

legitimate state purpose
Any government objective that the state has the authority to pursue, such as to provide for public safety.

classification
(1) A group the government treats differently from another group, in that the government discriminates for or against that group. (2) The government's different treatment of one group over another. (3) The identification of property as either separate property or marital property (or community property).

equal protection of law (EPL)
The constitutional requirement that the government treat one group or class the same as it treats another group or class in like circumstances. Shortened to *equal protection*.

suspect class
A class based on race, national origin, or alienage. Alienage is the condition of being an alien. (An alien is a person who was born outside the United States, is still a subject of a foreign nation, and has not been naturalized in the United States.)

quasi-suspect class
A class based on gender or on a child's legitimacy.

intermediate scrutiny
The standard used to determine if a classification complies with equal protection (and is therefore constitutional). Under this standard, the classification must be substantially related to serve an important state interest. Also called heightened scrutiny or elevated scrutiny.

The test for the constitutionality of a restriction of a fundamental right is much higher (and more difficult for a state to meet) than if the restriction is of a nonfundamental right.

- Because there are two tiers of rights (fundamental rights and nonfundamental rights), the analysis of whether a restriction violates SDP is called a *two-tier analysis*. If the restriction is of a fundamental right, then it must pass the test of **strict scrutiny** to be valid. This test is met if the restriction is **narrowly tailored** to serve a **compelling state interest**. If the restriction is of a nonfundamental right, then it must pass the broader (and easier to meet) **rational-basis** test to be valid (also called rational-relation test). This test is met if the restriction is **reasonably related** to a **legitimate state purpose**.

If a government restriction does not meet these tests, the restriction violates SDP. Exhibit 1-1 summarizes these principles. We will come back to them in greater detail later when we examine specific family-law restrictions, such as those relating to the right to marry.

EQUAL PROTECTION OF LAW (EPL)

To classify something means to divide it into groups or classes. The word **classification** (or class) has different meanings in the law. In divorce, for example, it refers to the identification of property as either separate property or marital property. In constitutional law, classification often means a group that the government treats differently from another group, discriminating either for or against that group. The question we are addressing here is whether a classification violates the **equal protection of law (EPL)**, often shortened to *equal protection*.

EPL is the constitutional requirement that the government treat one group the same as it treats another group *in like circumstances*. If two groups are similarly situated, the government must treat them the same. The origin of this rule is the Equal Protection Clause of the Fourteenth Amendment to the U.S. Constitution, which provides that no state shall "deny to any person within its jurisdiction the equal protection of the laws."[16] An example of discrimination that violates EPL would be a rule that allows ex-wives, but not ex-husbands, to obtain alimony in a divorce.

Not all classifications, however, violate EPL. "Equal protection does not require that all persons be dealt with identically."[17] It is not a violation of EPL, for example, for the government to require males, but not females, to register for the draft. To determine whether a particular discrimination violates the EPL, we must examine (a) the kind of discrimination involved and (b) the *reason* the government believes the discrimination is needed. Here are the steps that a court would take in an EPL case:

- First, it would determine which of four categories the discrimination fits into: (1) discrimination involving a fundamental right, (2) discrimination involving a suspect class, (3) discrimination involving a quasi-suspect class, or (4) every other kind of discrimination.

- If the discrimination involves a fundamental right or involves a **suspect class** (a class based on race, national origin, or alienage), then it must pass the test of *strict scrutiny*. As we have seen, this test is met if the discrimination is *narrowly tailored* to meet a *compelling state interest*.

- If the discrimination involves a **quasi-suspect class** (a class based on gender or on a child's legitimacy), then it must pass the test of **intermediate scrutiny**. This test is met if the classification is *substantially* related to serve an *important* state interest. Intermediate scrutiny is also called heightened scrutiny or elevated scrutiny.

EXHIBIT 1-1 Constitutional Challenges to Family Law Restrictions Based on Substantive Due Process (SDP)

Substantive Due Process (SDP): The constitutional requirement that the government avoid arbitrary and capricious actions that deprive someone of life, liberty, or property regardless of how fair the government is in the procedures that lead to the deprivation.

Guideline: Whether a family-law restriction violates SDP depends on whether the restriction is (1) of a fundamental right or (2) of a nonfundamental right. The highest test or level of scrutiny is used to determine whether a restriction on a fundamental right violates SDP (the test is strict scrutiny). A broader and easier-to-meet test is used to determine whether a restriction on a nonfundamental right violates SDP (the test is rational basis).

Kind of Right the Restriction Interferes with	Definition	Examples	Test, Standard, or Level of Scrutiny Used by Court to Decide if the Restriction Violates SDP	Definition
Fundamental Right	A right that is (a) specifically guaranteed in the U.S. Constitution, (b) implicit in the concept of ordered liberty, or (c) deeply rooted in the nation's history and tradition.	Family Law Examples: • Right to marry • Right of a couple to use contraceptives • Right to direct the education and upbringing of one's children • Right to an abortion without undue burden Other Examples: • Right to vote • Right to interstate travel	*Strict Scrutiny:* The restriction on the fundamental right must be *narrowly tailored* to serve a *compelling state interest.* Also phrased as *necessary* to serve a compelling state interest.	*Narrowly Tailored:* No more than needed to maintain the effectiveness of a goal; no broader than absolutely necessary. *Compelling State Interest:* An interest that is of the highest order; an interest that has a clear justification in the necessities of national or community life.
Nonfundamental Right	Any right that is not a fundamental right	Family Law Examples: • Right of adults to engage in homosexual conduct in private • Right of grandparents to have a relationship with their grandchildren Other Examples: • Right to use a public park • Right to buy a boat	*Rational Basis:* The restriction on the nonfundamental right must be reasonably related to a *legitimate state purpose.*	*Reasonably Related:* Logically connected (pertaining to any means used to achieve a goal that is reasonably likely to be successful). *Legitimate State Purpose:* Any government objective that the state has the authority to pursue, such as to provide for public safety.

© Cengage Learning 2013

- If the discrimination does not fit into any of these three categories (fundamental right, suspect class, or quasi-suspect class), then it must pass the broader (and easier to meet) *rational-basis* test to be valid. (This test is also called a rational-relation test.) This test is met if the classification is *reasonably related* to a *legitimate state purpose.*
- Because there are three tiers of rights, the analysis of whether a restriction violates EPL is called a *three-tier analysis.* The first tier is a classification that impacts fundamental rights or a suspect class (the same test applies to both). The second tier is a classification that impacts a quasi-suspect class. The third tier is every other kind of classification, i.e., one that does not involve a fundamental right, a suspect class, or a quasi-suspect class.

Exhibit 1-2 summarizes these principles. We will examine them in greater detail later.

EXHIBIT 1-2   Constitutional Challenges to Family Law Restrictions Based on Equal Protection of Law (EPL)

Equal Protection of Law (EPL): The constitutional requirement that the government treat one group or class the same as it treats another group or class in like circumstances.

Guideline: Whether a family-law classification violates EPL depends on whether the discrimination involves (1) a fundamental right, (2) a suspect class, (3) a quasi-suspect class, or (4) any other class. The highest test is used to determine the constitutionality of a classification involving a fundamental right or a suspect class (the test is strict scrutiny for both). Broader and easier-to-meet tests are used when the classification involves a quasi-suspect class (the test is intermediate scrutiny) and when the classification involves any other group (the test is rational basis).

Kind of Classification Involved	Definition	Example	Test Used by Court to Decide if the Discrimination Violates EPL	Definitions
• Classification involving *a fundamental right* or • Classification involving a *suspect class*	*Fundamental Right:* A right that is (a) specifically guaranteed in the U.S. Constitution, (b) implicit in the concept of ordered liberty, or (c) deeply rooted in the nation's history and tradition. *Suspect Class:* A class based on race, national origin, or alienage	Family Law Example: • A statute allowing same-race couples to marry but not mixed-race couples Other Example: • A statute allowing U.S. citizens to receive welfare benefits but denying such benefits to noncitizens in the country	*Strict Scrutiny:* The classification must be narrowly tailored to serve a compelling state interest. Also phrased as necessary to serve a *compelling state interest.*	*Narrowly Tailored:* No more than needed to maintain the effectiveness of a goal; no broader than absolutely necessary. *Compelling State Interest:* An interest that is of the highest order; an interest that has a clear justification in the necessities of national or community life.
• Classification involving a *quasi-suspect class*	*Quasi-Suspect Class:* A class based on gender or on a child's legitimacy	Family Law Example: • A statute that allows women to receive alimony but not men • A statute that allows children of married couples to inherit from their parents but not the illegitimate children of their parents Other Example: • A statute that allows men to be drafted, but not women	*Intermediate Scrutiny* (also called heightened scrutiny or elevated scrutiny): The classification must be substantially related to serve an important state interest.	
• Discrimination that does NOT involve a fundamental right, a suspect class, or a quasi-suspect class			*Rational Basis:* The classification must be reasonably related to a legitimate state purpose.	

© Cengage Learning 2013

STATE CONSTITUTIONS

Keep in mind that this overview has focused on *federal* law, which is based on the U.S. Constitution. Each state has its own constitution. Some of the states have provisions similar to those in the U.S. Constitution. States also have many very different provisions. It is quite possible for a state court to conclude that its state constitution requires a family-law restriction to meet a higher standard of scrutiny than what would be allowed under the U.S. Constitution. For example, sex-based discrimination will be upheld under the U.S. Constitution if it meets the standard of intermediate scrutiny. A state, however, can set the bar higher than the federal Constitution and rule that its own *state* constitution requires sex-based discrimination to meet the standard of strict scrutiny for it to be allowed within the state. In this book, we will examine some of these differences as they affect family-law issues.

PRACTICING FAMILY LAW IN THE AGE OF ELECTRONIC EXHIBITIONISM

Computers have affected the practice of family law in a number of important ways beyond the fact that computers sit on the desks of every attorney, paralegal, and secretary in the office. As we will see later in this chapter, a great deal of legal research in family law can be done online on fee-based sites and on free sites (see also Appendix D). In Chapter 9, we will discuss virtual visitation (e-visitation) in which the custodial parent allows the other parent to visit the children through programs such as Skype that allow real-time communication over the Internet. In Chapter 15, we will discuss how the Internet has been successfully used by persons seeking to adopt a child or by adoptees seeking to reconnect with their biological parents.

There is also a darker side to the Internet. Run the search "Facebook ruined my marriage" on search engines such as Google or Bing. You will find, for example, that spouses in shaky marriages have been using social media as a source of evidence of marital wrongs. As one blogger recently commented, "Facebook may not be good for your marriage, but it might be good for your divorce."[18]

Family-law attorneys are also making use of social media. According to the president of the American Academy of Matrimonial Lawyers, an organization of family-law attorneys, "In just about every case now, to some extent, there is some electronic evidence. . . . It has completely changed our field."[19] By one estimate, 81 percent of the members of the Academy "have used or faced evidence plucked from Facebook, MySpace, Twitter, and other social-networking sites, including YouTube and LinkedIn, over the past five years."[20] A Denver attorney commented, "You're finding information that you just never get in the normal discovery process—ever. People are just blabbing things all over Facebook. People don't yet quite connect what they're saying in their divorce cases is completely different from what they're saying on Facebook. It doesn't even occur to them that they'd be found out."[21] Another attorney points out that battles over infidelity often become uglier when the parties are confronted with damaging text messages. "It's much different than rumors running around about a husband at dinner with a babe in the back booth," he said. "It's in the spouse's face. They read it over and over again. It's harsh and hurtful."[22]

It is now becoming part of standard procedure for family-law attorneys to advise clients "about the location and preservation of evidence in the family's 'digital vault.' The location and preservation of this digital evidence to support a client's case requires a new skill set. Family-law attorneys must know how to economically and effectively locate, preserve, collect, review, and utilize electronically stored information (ESI)."[23] Bar associations now offer seminars for attorneys on how to locate and make tactical use of Word documents, PDF files, e-mail posts, text messages, browsing history, and activity on social networks such as Facebook. When parties are in litigation, the discovery of this material (**e-discovery**) can be critical. Furthermore, the parties cannot simply erase or delete their online data. They could be sanctioned by a court and be subject to a tort suit for **spoliation**.

e-discovery
The discovery of data found in e-mails, spreadsheets, databases, and other digital formats. Also called *electronic data discovery (EDD)*.

spoliation
Intentionally destroying, altering, or concealing evidence.

The country's fascination with the Internet, particularly the urge to tell the world about oneself on a social network, has been described by one family-law attorney as "electronic exhibitionism."[24] Here are some examples of how this trend has affected the practice of family law:

- A New York attorney says that she routinely asks the court for a court order to seize and copy the hard drives of the spouses of her clients in order to collect evidence of financial resources for property division and information relevant to child custody.

- An attorney for the wife in a divorce case hires a **forensic** investigator (sometimes called an e-forensic investigator) to retrieve bank records and other files that spouses tried to delete from their computer.

- A husband suspected his wife of having an affair. He secretly installed a program called PC Pandora (www.pcpandora.com) that took snapshots of every site visited and every e-mail sent over the Internet. He discovered that she was romantically involved with the parent of a classmate of their son.

- Every day the secretary of a Louisiana family-law attorney browses MySpace and Facebook to search for useful information. In one case, the firm won "shared custody for the father after finding his wife had posted sexually explicit comments on her boyfriend's MySpace page. In another case, a husband's credibility was questioned because, on his MySpace page, he said he was single and looking."

- A wife introduced evidence that her husband went on a dating site (match.com) and declared that he was single and childless, even though he was seeking primary custody of the child he had with his soon-to-be ex-wife.

- A father seeking legal custody introduced records he subpoenaed from a gaming site (WorldofWarcraft.com), which indicated that the mother of their child was online playing the game at the time she testified that she was unable to attend a school event of their child. The records showed that on some days the mother played for 10 hours.

- A teenager's mother accused her ex-husband of not adequately supervising their daughter. He disputed this—until the daughter posted photos on her Facebook page showing her and friends playing drinking games at her father's house.

- A mother denied in court that she smoked marijuana, but on her Facebook page she had pictures of herself partying and smoking pot.

- A mother introduced into evidence the fact that her husband forced their son to "defriend" her on Facebook.

- A woman sought an annulment on the grounds of bigamy, suspecting that her husband was married in Europe at an earlier time. He denied this. On his computer, she found a wedding photo of him and another woman (in a bridal gown) exchanging vows in front of a minister.

- As a result of Facebook's practice of recommending friends, a woman received a routine request to be the friend of another woman, both of whom, Facebook said, were probably connected to a certain man. Unknown to Facebook and to the two women, the connection the women had was the fact that they were both currently married to the man! At the time he married his second wife, the man had not divorced his first. He is now facing a charge of bigamy.

Cell phones, smart phones, Global Position System receivers, and E-ZPass records are also sources of electronic evidence. "We had one woman," reports a New York attorney, "who said her husband was beating her, and we found the

forensic
Pertaining to the use of scientific techniques to discover and examine evidence. See glossary for additional definitions.

E-ZPass records showing her crossing the George Washington Bridge at the precise time she said she was being beaten."[25]

Unfortunately, the Internet also allows parties to continue their bitterness after a divorce has been concluded. For example, a father who is upset about a child-custody decision might create a blog in order to air his hostility toward his ex-wife about the children. Enraged spouses have uploaded videos on YouTube describing the alleged unfairness of the other side's divorce tactics. (For an example, type "Tricia Walsh-Smith" into www.youtube.com.) In a recent case, a judge ordered an ex-husband to stop attacking his ex-wife on his Facebook page and to post an apology on the page for his past attacks.

To confront these online realities, many family-law attorneys have standard advice for their clients.

- One divorce attorney says that she includes a confidentiality clause in every separation agreement that prohibits both spouses from publishing even fictional accounts of their marriage.

- Another attorney regularly advises his clients to change all their passwords and privacy settings to prevent their spouses from being able to gain access to their sites during (and after) the divorce. If this process is too cumbersome, he advises them to close or shut down their Internet pages. This approach, however, does not always work. In a recent custody dispute, a judge ordered the parties to exchange each other's passwords for their Facebook and dating websites to allow mutual opportunity for discovery of evidence relevant to their dispute.

Some paralegals in family-law practices are frequently assigned the task of trolling the Internet for evidence (or leads to evidence) on their clients and opponents. If a father tells the court that his child-support payments are too high, a paralegal may search for online photos of him driving his new Audi. If a parent seeking sole custody denies that she drinks, a paralegal may search for photos of her in her apartment partying with a drink in her hand. Such evidence is not always verifiable or admissible in court. But attorneys have found that they can sometimes gain bargaining leverage by simply suggesting that the evidence exists.

PARALEGAL ROLES IN FAMILY LAW CASES

The media (particularly in television dramas) often give a distorted view of a family-law practice, and indeed, of attorneys in general. The practice of law is not an endless series of confessions and concessions that are pried loose from opponents. Every attorney does not spend all day engaged in the kind of case that makes front-page news. It is rare for the legal system to become the spectacle—some would say the circus—that the occasional high-profile case leads us to believe is common in the practice of law. While excitement and drama can be part of the legal system, they are not everyday occurrences. What is common is painstaking and meticulous hard work. This reality is almost never portrayed in the media.

Nevertheless, it is true that the day-to-day work of paralegals in a family-law practice can expose them to intense emotions and occasional drama. In many ways, paralegals who work in family law are unique, as indicated by the following comments from an experienced paralegal:

> Perhaps in no other area of the law can paralegals have such substantive impact than in family-law matters. From the moment the client seeks an attorney's services to the conclusion of the attorney's representation, paralegals can and do have real impact. Not only can they prepare most, if not all, pleadings under the direction of their supervising attorney, but they often

become the client's most frequent contact during an extremely traumatic time in the client's life. Whether the matter involves a divorce, child custody, or paternity action, post-judgment support modification, or adoption, the paralegal develops a close bond with the client.[26]

We will now take a more specific look at the possible range of paralegal responsibilities in a family-law practice. Keep in mind, however, that no two paralegals will have identical job descriptions. According to veteran paralegal Yasmin Spiegel, "Your skills and interests, as well as the degree of trust and communication between you and your boss, will determine the tasks that you will be assigned."[27] Nevertheless, it is possible to list some of the commonly performed tasks of many paralegals.[28] (See Exhibit 1-3.) Following this list of tasks, we will hear more from Yasmin Spiegel as she provides a flesh-and-bones perspective of life in the trenches. (See Exhibit 1-4.) Paralegal tasks will also be presented at the end of most of the remaining chapters in this book.

Although some definitions will be provided in the following descriptions, definitions of the major family-law terms will be provided in the glossary and in later chapters, where they will be covered in depth.

EXHIBIT 1-3   Examples of Paralegal Roles in Family Law
(divorce litigation)

New Clients

- Screen prospective family-law clients who telephone the office seeking information about the law firm.
- Help identify problems that can be referred to others, e.g., to government agencies that provide public assistance.
- Schedule appointment for the prospective client with the attorney.
- Conduct a **conflicts check** on a prospective client to make sure that the law firm would not have a **conflict of interest** that would disqualify the law firm from representing the client (e.g., because the firm once represented the spouse of the prospective client).
- After the attorney has accepted the person as a client, either (a) attend the initial interview of the client conducted by the attorney or (b) conduct the initial interview of the client.
- Open a case file for the new client.
- Maintain contact with the client by (a) keeping the client apprised of the status of the case, (b) answering client questions that do not involve giving legal advice, and (c) referring legal questions to the attorney.
- Set up the calendar or **tickler** system covering all-important dates that must be monitored throughout the case.
- Help the client assemble needed documents, e.g., marriage certificate, divorce decree on prior marriage (if any), proof of residences, birth certificates of children, pay stubs, prior year tax returns, copies of deeds, and medical records on the health of client and children.
- Prepare chronology (**timeline**) of relevant events, e.g., tasks and time spent raising the children.
- Draft letters for the client to sign authorizing the release of confidential information on the client, e.g., medical records, tax returns, and employment records.

Commencement of Action

- Conduct follow-up interviews with the client to obtain information needed for the drafting of the petition, summons, and accompanying affidavits.
- Prepare the first draft of the petition, summons, and accompanying affidavits.

---

conflicts check
A determination of whether a conflict of interest exists that might disqualify a law office from representing a client or from continuing the representation.

conflict of interest
Divided loyalties that actually or potentially harm (or disadvantage) someone who is owed undivided loyalty.

tickler
A system designed to provide reminders of important dates.

timeline
A chronological presentation of significant events, often organized as a straight-line diagram.

- Prepare special orders as needed (e.g., ordering the parties not to take the children out of the state, ordering the parties not to sell or otherwise transfer marital assets).
- Arrange for service of process of the pleadings and discovery documents.
- Maintain and update the tickler systems to monitor due dates such as the date when the defendant must respond to the petition and the date when interrogatories must be answered.
- Prepare **stipulations** covering agreements between the parties on facts, procedures, or plans.

Financial Data

- Assist the client in compiling an inventory of the personal and business financial data on the assets and liabilities of the client and the client's spouse.
- Prepare financial **affidavits** on these data.
- Assist the client in preparing **financial statements**, e.g., monthly income-and-expense sheet.
- Prepare a report that compares the inventory of assets and liabilities identified by the client and the inventory of assets and liabilities asserted by his or her spouse.
- Classify real property and personal property as (a) separate property or (b) as marital or community property.
- Help the client trace the source of funds used to purchase specific property.
- Hire experts as needed to assemble financial data, e.g., accountant and financial adviser.
- Hire an appraiser to assess the value of real property in which either spouse has an interest.
- Hire a business appraiser to assess the value of any business in which either spouse has an interest.
- Hire an appraiser to assess the value of any other valuable personal property (e.g., cars, jewelry).
- Hire and monitor the work of a private investigator.

Support Needs

- Assist the client in compiling financial data on the day-to-day living needs and expenses of (a) the client, (b) the children, and (c) other dependents.
- Prepare affidavits of these support needs pending the outcome of the case.
- Obtain child-support worksheets and assist the client in filling them out.
- Calculate **arrearages** of child support, if any.

Temporary Orders

- Interview the client and others to obtain information relevant to requests for temporary orders from the court on (a) child custody, (b) child support, (c) spousal support, (d) payment of attorney fees (including paralegal fees), and (e) maintaining the status quo on marital property.
- Determine the amount of child support based on the state's formula for calculating child support.
- Document any special needs of children that will be the basis of child support beyond what the formula requires.
- Prepare a draft of the pleadings needed for temporary orders.
- Arrange for the service of the pleadings for temporary orders.

Settlement

- Assemble and organize the package of documents and other materials that the attorney will need for the negotiation sessions.
- Be available to obtain additional facts and materials that the attorney may need during negotiation sessions.
- Draft proposed settlement offers.
- Draft stipulations reached during settlement negotiations.

(continued)

stipulation
An agreement between opposing parties about a particular matter. The verb is *stipulate*.

affidavit
A written statement containing facts, claims, or other legal positions given under oath or affirmation.

financial statement
A report covering the assets (e.g., income, investments) and debts of a person or business as of a particular date or over a designated period. A financial accounting or balance sheet.

arrearages
Payments that are due but have not been made. Also called arrears.

discovery

1. Devices used by parties to force information from each other before trial to aid in trial preparation. Examples of such devices include interrogatories and depositions. 2. Devices used by parties to force information from each other after trial to aid in the enforcement of the trial judgment.

interrogatories

("rogs") A discovery device in which one party sends written questions to another party.

protective order

A court order directing a person to refrain from doing something such as harming or harassing another. Also called order of protection.

deposition

A discovery device in which one party questions another (or questions the other party's witness), usually outside the courtroom.

subpoena

A command to appear at a certain time and place.

subpoena duces tecum

A command that a witness appear at a certain time and place and bring specified things such as documents or jewelry.

request for production (RFP)

A discovery device in which one party requests that another party provide access to documents or other tangible things for copying or inspection. The device also includes a request to enter the party's land.

request for admission (RFA)

A discovery device in which one party sends a request to another party that the latter agree that a certain fact or legal conclusion is true so that there will be no need to present proof or arguments about such matters during the trial.

independent medical examination (IME)

A discovery device in which a party obtains a court order for a professional examination of a person whose physical or mental condition is in controversy.

alternative dispute resolution (ADR)

A method or procedure for resolving a legal dispute without litigating it in a court or administrative agency. ADR methods include mediation, arbitration, and Med-Arb.

mediation

A method of alternative dispute resolution (ADR) in which the parties avoid litigation by submitting their dispute to a neutral third person (the mediator) who helps the parties resolve their dispute; he or she does not render a decision resolving it for them.

EXHIBIT 1-3   *(continued)*

- Draft other settlement documents, e.g., releases.
- Draft proposed parenting plan.
- Draft separation agreement or property-division agreement.
- Draft proposed temporary and final orders based on settlement agreements.

Discovery

- Prepare and distribute the **discovery** documents that are subject to automatic disclosure to the opposing party. ("Automatic" means that the documents must be sent without a request for them.)
- Prepare and monitor a checklist of the automatic-disclosure documents that the other side must provide.
- Draft proposed stipulations on discovery.
- Draft **interrogatories** to the opponent. Arrange for their distribution.
- Enter due dates for responses in the office tickler system.
- Digest and index the responses to the interrogatories when they are received.
- Identify interrogatories (or other discovery requests) sent by the opponent that could be the basis of objection or of a **protective order**.
- Draft responses to interrogatories sent by the opponent.
- Draft **deposition** notices and **subpoenas**.
- Draft **subpoena duces tecum** identifying documents or other things the deponent should bring to the deposition.
- Coordinate the hiring of court reporters or providers of other recording systems (e.g., video) for the deposition.
- Help draft deposition questions for the attorney conducting the deposition.
- Assemble a folder of documents the attorney will use at the deposition.
- Help prepare client for his or her deposition by the opponent (e.g., role play a question-and-answer session with the client).
- Attend the deposition and take notes.
- Order the deposition transcripts.
- Digest and index deposition transcripts.
- Maintain a database for all discovery data.
- Draft other discovery demands to be submitted to the opponent, e.g., **requests for production (RFPs)** and **requests for admissions (RFAs)**.
- Enter due dates for responses to RFPs and RFAs in the office tickler system.
- Help prepare the client's responses to other discovery demands sent to the client.
- Digest and index responses to other discovery devices.
- Accompany the client to **independent medical examinations (IMEs)**.

ADR (Alternative Dispute Resolution)

- Provide the client with information on **alternative dispute resolution (ADR)** options or requirements.
- Help schedule **mediation** or other ADR sessions.
- When the client must attend ADR (e.g., mandatory mediation), help prepare client for these ADR sessions.
- Prepare proof of the client's attendance at ADR sessions.

Trial Preparation

- Using the Internet and other resources, research the availability of expert witnesses (e.g., check their credentials and fees).
- Coordinate meetings between attorney and proposed expert witnesses.
- Assist in preparing witnesses for trial.
- Research the credentials of the proposed expert witnesses for the other side.
- Perform legal research, particularly on procedural issues.
- Organize documents that will be used to **impeach** opposing witnesses.
- Compile the **trial notebook**.
- Order exhibits (e.g., blow-ups of receipts and pie charts of expenses).
- Draft the list of exhibits.
- Assemble and organize trial exhibits.
- Prepare needed trial subpoenas for witnesses and arrange for their service. File **proof of service**.
- Prepare affidavits of **court costs** and attorney fees (detailing specific tasks performed by attorneys and paralegals on the case) that must be submitted to the court.
- Draft and file requests to set court hearings.
- Help prepare the client for trial.
- Ensure that the client, witnesses, and office personnel have the address of the court and are aware of dress requirements and other etiquette norms that must be observed in the courtroom.
- Prepare documents for the **pretrial conference**, such as the case status statement.
- Draft the case management report.

Trial

- Drive the client to court, if necessary.
- Attend the trial to provide general assistance to the trial attorney.
- Compile a list of exhibits submitted into evidence.
- Take notes on the testimony of witnesses.
- Draft the proposed decree of dissolution, order, and other documents to be submitted to the court.

Post-Trial

- Draft a motion for a new trial.
- Order a transcript of the trial.
- Draft a notice of appeal.
- Read the transcript to identify testimony and rulings the attorney wishes to highlight in the **appellate brief**.
- File the appeal documents in court and arrange for them to be served on opposing counsel.
- Assemble the documents the attorney will need for the settlement conference with the appellate judge.
- Assemble the documents that the attorney will need for oral argument.
- Draft the letter to the client providing instructions on what he or she needs to do as a result of the final judgment.
- Draft the documents needed for the enforcement or **execution of judgment**, e.g., **garnishment** of wages.
- Draft the instruments needed for the transfer of assets pursuant to the final judgment.
- Coordinate the filing and recording of transfer instruments.

impeach
To challenge; to attack the credibility of.

trial notebook
A collection of documents, arguments, and strategies that an attorney plans to use during a trial.

proof of service
A sworn statement or other evidence that service of process on a party has been accomplished. Also called certificate of service and return of service.

court costs
Charges or fees (paid to and imposed by the court) that are directly related to litigation in that court.

pretrial conference
A meeting of the attorneys and the judge (or magistrate) before the trial to attempt to narrow the issues, secure stipulations, make a final effort to settle the case without a trial, and cover other preliminary matters. Also called a trial management conference.

appellate brief
A document submitted (filed) by a party to an appellate court (and served on an opposing party) in which arguments are presented as to why the appellate court should affirm (approve), reverse, or otherwise modify what a lower court has done.

execution of judgment
The process of carrying out or satisfying the judgment of a court. Using a *writ of execution*, a court officer (e.g., a sheriff) is commanded to seize the property of the losing litigant, sell it, and pay the winning litigant out of the proceeds.

garnishment
A court proceeding by a creditor to force a third party in possession of the debtor's property (e.g., wages) to turn the property over to the creditor to satisfy the debt.

EXHIBIT 1-4   Family Law for Paralegals: An Insider's View
by Yasmin Cogswell Spiegel

The role of a paralegal in a family-law practice is exciting and varied. Whereas all areas of law can be interesting, the opportunities for client contact, full involvement, and case responsibility in family law make it a truly satisfying area of specialty. Family law affords tremendous scope for helping people in a very basic change in their lives. With the divorce rate at roughly 50 percent, there are few families who haven't been touched in some way by the problems and trauma of a court action. Our job as paralegals can be to smooth the way through this difficult time for the client, making the experience kinder, easier to understand, more efficient, and, hopefully, less expensive. Divorce is not the only area covered in family law. Adoption, grandparent visitation issues, and emancipation of minors also come under this topic. . . .

The teamwork between attorney and paralegal is crucial to the success of a paralegal working in family law. Your skills and interests, as well as the degree of trust and communication between you and your boss, will determine the tasks that you will be assigned. If there is good communication and rapport between you as team members, the clients will come to rely on both of you in handling the case, and your participation will be invaluable.

In my office the attorney conducts the initial interview with the client. This is primarily done to establish the attorney/client bond, which is crucial to the successful processing of the case. Any general questions the client has about the dissolution process, as well as discussion of strategy, fees, and expectations, are done at this stage. If there is an immediate need for temporary orders, such as restraining orders or temporary custody or support, the attorney will begin the information gathering process by taking detailed notes on the client's situation.

The initial interview is usually concluded by inviting me into the office to be introduced as the "paralegal who will be assisting me with your case." This gives me the authority to contact the client on behalf of the attorney to gather more detailed information, and to answer the client's questions as to general procedure. I find that the clients are, for the most part, pleased to know that a paralegal will be working on their case. I am usually more accessible than the attorney to answer their questions or to convey information, and they are billed at a lower rate for my time.

It is often my responsibility to draft the opening documents. These include the summons, petition, and related pleadings. With the recent adoption of income-and-expense forms, this job has become quite critical. The forms are complicated, and in some instances intimidating; clients often need a lot of assistance in filling them out. Often I find that our women clients don't understand that the forms are meant to demonstrate "need" for support. They spend all their time trying to make their income on the form come out even with their expenses, but that is often impossible. It is often my job to tell them that if they don't show the court any evidence of the need for support, the judge won't order any. I am also responsible for drafting mediation counseling stipulations, property declarations, and even orders to show cause and motions for *pendente lite* relief [relief granted during the litigation, pending the final outcome of the case]. I rely on notes from the attorney as well as my own interviews with the client to obtain the facts necessary to create the pleadings. The attorney then reviews the documents for accuracy and obtains the signature of the client. When the documents are filed, I see that the papers are served on the client's spouse and keep the client informed of subsequent developments.

Discovery plays an important role in family law. Over the years my office has developed a set of family-law interrogatories on our computer that can be modified and used to flush out the details of marital property and separate property. For the property division between the spouses, all real property and pension plans must be appraised for their value. This is also the responsibility of the paralegal. Building a strong working relationship with various legal support personnel (such as appraisers, actuaries, deposition reporters, mediation and rehabilitation counselors, process servers, and photocopy services) is essential. These people trust and respect my role as a professional and as a representative of my office; they often go out of their way to assist us in emergencies because of the relationship we have built over the years.

Preparing and arranging the service of deposition notices is another important part of family-law practice, which falls within the scope of the paralegal's responsibility. After the transcript of the deposition comes back from the reporter, it is my job to index and summarize it for the attorney's use in trial preparation. Comparing the bank account dates, numbers, and balances, as well as other descriptions of property, with the opposing party's previous descriptions is an important part of establishing the full extent of a marital or separate property interest and achieving an appropriate division.

Child custody and visitation is often the most traumatic aspect of a family-law case. Parents who are separating are often terrified of what the effect of the separation will be on their children, and are frequently afraid that dividing their households will result in a loss of closeness and opportunities for quality parenting time. Fortunately, courts lean heavily in favor of joint custody whenever feasible. Mediation counseling programs have been set up to assist parents in working out arrangements for custody and visitation with the assistance of trained facilitators. The agreements are then presented as stipulations to the court. Wherever possible, a judge will not hear a motion for custody or visitation until the parties have been to mediation. This is practical and beneficial because the mediation session is often the first time that the parties have been able to sit down and actually *listen* to each other since their problems began. It also provides a beginning for the future cooperation that they will have to achieve to be separated parents with children in common. It is my job as paralegal to prepare the mediation counseling stipulation, to see that it is signed by all parties and attorneys, to make sure that it is filed with the court, and then to arrange contact between the mediator and the parties.

If the parties are unable to settle their disputes (and we try very hard to settle every family-law case without the necessity of a trial), I draft a *trial brief* setting out the facts, the history of the case, the contested and uncontested issues, our proposal for division of property, and a memorandum setting forth the applicable law. Updated income-and-expense statements and property declarations must be filed along with the trial brief, and any appraisals or actuarial analyses of pension funds must also be updated as of the time of trial.

Before the day of the trial, I contact the client to make sure that he or she is psychologically prepared to attend, and make arrangements with the client for last-minute prepping by the attorney. I organize the file to make all exhibits and necessary documents finger-tip accessible to the attorney trying the case. I subpoena any witnesses who may be needed. It is difficult to get a firm court date because of case congestion, and the client must be assisted in dealing with the resulting anxiety and inconvenience. If the case does go to trial, I sometimes go along to help my boss keep organized with respect to the documents, to take notes on the areas of inquiry to be explored, to run emergency errands, and to keep the witnesses organized.

When the judgment is prepared, (a) by stipulation in the form of a marital settlement agreement or (b) by reducing a decision by the trial court to judgment form, I often draft the first document for review by the attorney and client. Keeping track of dates, such as deadlines for appeal and eligibility for final judgment, is also my responsibility. Some of my wrap-up details include preparing transfer deeds and notifying the ex-spouse's pension plan of the other ex-spouse's interest in the plan that was ordered by the court.

As the family-law case progresses, a paralegal becomes intimately familiar with the client's life and affairs. You are in a unique position to offer comfort and guidance to people in deep transition. While the legal professional's role should never be confused with that of a therapist or psychiatrist, your positive attitude and sensitivity to the client's situation can make a big difference in how he or she experiences the adjustment to what amounts to an entirely new life. Over the past six years in a practice, predominantly devoted to family law, I have watched hundreds of clients pass through this difficult change in their lives, heal their wounds, and create more successful and satisfying lifestyles. This is a very rewarding part of my job.

Although I have had to skip over many areas of a paralegal's responsibilities in the area of family law, I have tried to give you a sense of some of the duties that a paralegal may have. Your particular tasks will be assigned by the attorney. Short of giving the client legal advice and appearing as his or her representative in court, there is tremendous scope for the utilization of paralegals in a family-law practice.

The Journal (Sacramento Valley Paralegal Association, June 1986). Reprinted with permission of Yasmin Cogswell Spiegel.

OTHER FAMILY LAW ROLES

FREELANCERS IN FAMILY LAW

Family law is a popular area of law for freelance paralegals. These are persons who have their own businesses; they operate as independent contractors rather than as employees of law offices. There are two main categories of individuals that a freelancer might serve: attorneys or the general public.

- Attorneys. Freelancers who serve attorneys receive specific jobs or assignments from attorneys in different law offices, e.g., to summarize the transcript of a divorce deposition or to file an adoption petition in court. Attorney supervision of the freelancer is required even though he or she may work out of a home office.

- General public. Freelancers who serve the general public do not work under attorney supervision. They sell what are called self-help services directly to the public. (See Chapter 2 for a discussion of self-help services.) State laws restrict the services that freelancers can provide and what they can call themselves. In some states, for example, they cannot call themselves paralegals if they do not work under attorney supervision. Also, they run the risk of being charged with the unauthorized practice of law (UPL) if they perform services that only attorneys are allowed to perform. We will cover these UPL limitations in Chapter 2.

Success as a freelancer in family law depends to a very large extent on the experience of the paralegal. It is relatively rare for someone to go into business as an independent without years of prior experience as an employee of a law office.

GOVERNMENT PARALEGAL

Family-law paralegals are also in demand in government. For example, every state has child-support enforcement agencies (called IV-D agencies) and most of them use paralegals in their work helping custodial parents collect child support. The following is an example of the duties of a child-support paralegal in West Virginia.

Duties of a Government Paralegal (Child Support Enforcement)

- Maintain records of all cases before counsel, including briefs submitted, rulings, and opinions and all cases appealed to the Supreme Court of Appeals.
- Schedule court hearing dates and coordinate attorney schedules.
- Keep abreast of changes in agency or departmental laws, rules, and regulations, as well as in state, federal, and local laws relating to child-support enforcement.
- Collect and summarize information from books and periodicals for review by a responsible supervisor or attorney.
- Research basic statistical work in the compilation of reports involving the activities of the division/section/unit.
- Compose correspondence to inquiries where considerable knowledge of child-support policy, procedures, and guidelines is required.
- Answer telephone, screen calls, and place outgoing calls.
- Screen mail and respond to routine correspondence.
- Schedule appointments and make travel arrangements and reservations for a supervisor.
- Attend meetings with or on behalf of a supervisor to take notes or deliver basic information.
- Take and transcribe dictation, or transcribe from dictation equipment.
- Type and assist in the preparation of briefs and legal documents.
- Compose form letters, routine correspondence, and factual reports requiring judgment and originality.
- Gather, request, and/or provide factual information, requiring reference to a variety of sources.
- Maintain bookkeeping records for grants, contract- or state-appropriated funds, and/or related departmental accounts.[29]

We will cover the work of child-support enforcement agencies in greater detail in Chapter 10.

COURT APPOINTED SPECIAL ADVOCATE (CASA)

In most states, paralegals and other nonattorneys can provide volunteer advocacy services in cases involving children in the court system. The volunteers are called **court appointed special advocates (CASAs)**. A CASA might be appointed to act as a **guardian ad litem (GAL)**. Paralegals who are CASAs devote several hours a week of their volunteer time to the CASA program, where the focus is on children in abuse and neglect cases, particularly children in the foster care system. Typically, a CASA volunteer will be assigned one case with duties such as the following:

- Conduct an independent investigation by (a) reviewing all pertinent documents and records and (b) interviewing the child, parents, social workers, foster parents, teachers, therapists, daycare providers, and other relevant persons to determine the facts and circumstances of the child's situation.

court appointed special advocate (CASA)
A volunteer appointed by the court to undertake special assignments pertaining to children in the court system.

guardian ad litem (GAL)
A special guardian (often, but not always, an attorney) appointed by the court to appear in court proceedings on behalf of a person who is a minor, is insane, or is otherwise incapacitated.

- Seek cooperative solutions by acting as a facilitator among conflicting parties to achieve resolution of problems and to foster positive steps toward achieving permanence for the child.

- Appear at all hearings to advocate for the child's best interests and provide testimony when necessary.

- Make recommendations for specific, appropriate services for the child and the child's family, and advocate for necessary services.

- Monitor implementation of case plans and court orders, checking to see that court-ordered services are provided in a timely manner and that review hearings are held in accordance with the law.

- Inform the court of important developments, including an agency's failure to provide services or the family's failure to participate.[30]

CASAs are not substitutes for attorneys, social workers, or other child welfare personnel. A CASA cannot give **legal advice** or engage in the **practice of law**. The CASA's role is to be an independent voice for the child, helping the judge to better understand the child's needs.

CASAs undergo training conducted by the local CASA program. Training requirements vary from program to program, but an average course is approximately 30 hours. Volunteers learn about courtroom procedure from judges, lawyers, social workers, court personnel, and others. They also learn effective advocacy techniques for children, and cover topics relating to child sexual abuse, early childhood development, and adolescent behavior.[31]

legal advice
The application of laws or legal principles to the facts of a particular person's legal problem.

practice of law
Using legal skills to assist a specific person in resolving his or her specific legal problem.

ASSESSING YOUR OWN BIASES

Work in family law is not for the faint of heart: "One of the worst kept secrets in legal practice is the toll that domestic relations work can take on a lawyer's staff, resources, and psyche."[32] The unfolding of client cases can be emotionally draining. The client's world may be falling apart in a tumult of pain, anger, and confusion. Someone once said that in a criminal-law practice, you deal with bad people at their best, and in a family-law practice, you deal with good people at their worst.[33]

Inevitably, you will have personal feelings about a particular case. A client's objective or personality might give you a sense of discomfort or unease. The question is whether those feelings will become the basis of a **bias**, which is a prejudice or predisposition to think and to act in a certain way. How would you answer the following question: "Am I objective enough that I can assist a person even though I have a personal distaste for what that person wants to do or what that person has done?" Many of us would quickly answer "yes" to this question. We all like to feel that we are levelheaded and not susceptible to letting our prejudices interfere with the job we are asked to accomplish. Many of us, however, are unaware of how strongly our personal likes and dislikes may affect us.

bias
Prejudice for or against something or someone. A predisposition, inclination, or tendency to think or act in a certain way. A danger of prejudgment.

ASSIGNMENT 1.1

In the following cases, to what extent might an individual be hampered in delivering legal services because of personal reactions toward the client? Identify *potential* bias.

a. Mr. Smith, a client of your office, is being sued by his estranged wife for custody of their two small children. Mr. and Mrs. Smith live separately, but Mr. Smith has had custody of the children during most of their lives while Mrs. Smith has been in the hospital. Mrs. Smith has charged that Mr. Smith often yells at the children, leaves them with neighbors and day-care centers for most of the day, and is an alcoholic. Your investigation reveals that Mrs. Smith will probably be able to prove all these allegations in court.

(continued)

b. Mrs. Jones is being sued by Mr. Jones for divorce on the ground of adultery. Mrs. Jones is the client of your office. Thus far, your investigation has revealed that there is considerable doubt over whether Mrs. Jones did in fact commit adultery. During a recent conversation with Mrs. Jones, however, she tells you that she is a prostitute.

c. Jane Anderson is seeking an abortion. She is not married. The father of the child wants to prevent her from having the abortion. Jane comes to your office for legal help. She wants to know what her rights are. You belong to a church that believes abortion is murder. You are assigned to work on the case.

d. Paul and Victor are a gay couple who want to adopt Sammy, a six-month-old baby whose parents recently died in an automobile accident. Sammy's maternal grandmother is not able to adopt him because of her age and health. She opposes the adoption by Paul and Victor because she does not approve of their sexual orientation. Paul and Victor are clients of your office in their petition for adoption. You agree with the grandmother's position, but have been assigned to work on the case.

e. Tom Donaldson is a client of your office. His former wife claims that he has failed to pay court-ordered alimony payments and that the payments should be increased because of her needs and his recently improved financial status. Your job is to help Tom collect a large volume of records concerning his past alimony payments and his present financial worth. You are the only person in the office who is available to do this record gathering. It is clear, however, that Tom does not like you. On a number of occasions, he has indirectly questioned your ability.

objectivity
The state of being dispassionate; the absence of a bias.

Having analyzed the fact situations in Assignment 1.1, do you still feel the same about your assessment of your own **objectivity**? Clearly, we cannot simply wish our personal feelings away or pretend that they do not exist. There are no absolute rules or techniques that apply to every situation you will be asked to handle. Nor are the following admonitions very helpful: "Be objective," "be dispassionate," "don't get personally involved," "control your feelings." Such admonitions are too general, and when viewed in the abstract, they may appear to be unnecessary, because we want to believe that we are always objective, dispassionate, detached, and in control.

We must recognize that there are facts and circumstances that arouse our emotions and tempt us to impose our own value judgments. Perhaps if we know where we are vulnerable, we will be in a better position to prevent our reactions from interfering with our work. It is not desirable for you to be totally dispassionate and removed. A paralegal who is cold, unfeeling, and incapable of empathy is not much better than a paralegal who self-righteously scolds a client. It is not improper for a paralegal to express sympathy, surprise, and perhaps even shock at what unfolds in the client's life story. If these feelings are genuine, and if they would be normal reactions to the situation at a given moment, then they should be expressed. The problem is how to draw the line between expressing these feelings and reacting so judgmentally that you interfere with your ability to communicate with the client, now and in the future. Again, there are no absolute guidelines. As you gain experience in the art of dealing with people, you will develop styles and techniques that will enable you to avoid crossing that line. But first you must acknowledge how easy it is to cross the line.

Some paralegals apply what is called the "stomach test." If your gut tells you that your personal feelings about the case are so intense that you may not be able to do a quality job for the client, you need to take action.[34] Talk with your supervisor. You may have some misunderstandings about the case that your supervisor can clear up. You may be able to limit your role in the case, or be reassigned to other cases. Without breaching client confidentiality (see Chapter 2), contact your local paralegal association to try to talk with other paralegals who have handled similar situations. They may be able to give you some guidance.

Attorneys often take unpopular cases involving clients who have said or done things that run the gamut from politically incorrect to socially reprehensible. As professionals, attorneys are committed to the principle that *everyone* is entitled to representation. Paralegals should have this same commitment. But attorneys and paralegals are human beings. No one can treat every case identically. In the final analysis, you need to ask yourself whether your bias is so strong that it might interfere with your ability to give the needs of the client 100 percent of your energy and skill. If so, you have an obligation not to work on the case.

Ethical concerns also dictate this result. As we will see in Chapter 2, attorneys have an ethical obligation to avoid a conflict of interest. Such a conflict exists when an attorney has divided loyalties. An obvious example is an attorney who represents both sides in a legal dispute. A less obvious example is an attorney whose personal feelings could interfere with his or her obligation to give a client vigorous representation. The attorney's personal feelings should not be in conflict with a client's legitimate need for undiluted advocacy. Is the attorney going to be loyal to his or her personal feelings and values, or to the client's cause? Clients should not be subjected to such conflicts of loyalty. When a conflict of this kind exists, the attorney has an ethical obligation not to take the case. The same ethical concerns apply to paralegals. There should be no interference with anyone's inclination to give the client total commitment.

ASSIGNMENT 1.2

a. Think about your past and present contacts with people who have irritated you the most. Make a specific list of what bothered you about these people. Suppose that you are working in a law office where a client did one of the things on your list. Could you handle such a case?

b. In the relationships among a husband, wife, and child, many things can be done that would be wrong (i.e., illegal, immoral, improper) according to your personal system of values. Make a list of the five things that could be done by a husband, wife, or child to another family member (e.g., husband to wife, child to parent) that would be most offensive to your sense of values. Assume that a client in the office where you work has done one of these five things and is being challenged in court by someone because of it. Your office is defending the client against this challenge. What difficulties do you see for yourself in being able to assist this client?

VIOLENCE IN A FAMILY LAW PRACTICE

Unfortunately, violence must be one of the concerns of a family-law practice. In Chapter 10, for example, we will see that special measures must be taken to protect a mother from violence once she asserts a claim for child support against a father. In Chapter 12, we will examine other dimensions of domestic violence.

Violence can also be directed at family-law offices. At a conference of attorneys, a speaker asked a group of about 120 experienced family-law attorneys if anyone in the room had experienced violence or threats of violence in their practice. Almost all the attorneys in the room raised their hands. One woman told the group, "Just yesterday, I [learned that] my client and I were in grave danger."[35] Many attorneys are upgrading their office security systems; some acknowledge that when interviewing a new client, they consciously assess whether taking the case might pose personal risks to anyone in the office.

Family court personnel are also concerned. Violence has erupted in the corridors of some courthouses and occasionally in the courtroom itself. In a recent case, a San Jose man fighting for custody of his three children shot and wounded three deputies. Abe Gorenfeld is a family-law court commissioner. At his retirement party, he pointed to the "bullet hole still visible in the ceiling outside his fifth-floor courtroom where a woman fired her pistol at her soon-to-be ex-husband and missed."[36] Many courthouses now have elaborate security systems at their entrances. Some courts, however, have been slow to add such security. One court did not do so until a bailiff discovered a gun in the lunch box of an estranged husband sitting in a courtroom.

Of course, violence is not an everyday occurrence in family-law offices and courthouses. Many paralegals rarely if ever witness extreme behavior of this kind. Yet out-of-control, angry, frustrated citizens exist in our society. We all should be aware of the reality that volatile emotions may be close to the surface in families undergoing disintegration. Individuals who perceive themselves as victims are sometimes capable of lashing out against anyone involved in what they irrationally feel is an unresponsive legal system. Caution is the order of the day.

FAMILY LAW SOURCES

In this section, we will cover some of the fundamentals of the law library from the viewpoint of the family-law practitioner. The many different sources of family law are outlined in Exhibit 1-5.

Because there is so much law, and because a good deal of it changes, no one—including an experienced judge—can be expected to know all the family law of

---

EXHIBIT 1-5   Sources of Family Law

PRIMARY AUTHORITY

Primary authority is any law that a court could rely on in reaching its decision. The main primary authorities are constitutions, statutes, court opinions, court rules (rules of court), and administrative regulations. Primary authorities exist at the federal, state, and local levels of government.

State and Local Law Sources

- *State constitution:* The state constitution is the highest state law, to which all other state laws must conform.

- *Statutes of the state legislature:* Most states have family codes that cover a broad range of family-law topics, such as divorce and adoption. The statutes on family law may be scattered throughout the statutory code of your state legislature, although in many states, a large number of these statutes are collected in several volumes or titles, often appearing under the heading of "domestic relations," "families," or "family law." (See Appendix A for more about using statutory codes.) Many states have enacted *uniform laws* (e.g., Uniform Parentage Act, Uniform Marriage and Divorce Act). Uniform laws are laws that were proposed to state legislatures in areas where uniformity is deemed appropriate. Each state can adopt, modify, or reject the proposals. Once a uniform law is accepted by a state (often with modifications), it becomes a statute of that state.

- *State court opinions interpreting the state constitution, state statutes, and state administrative regulations.*

- *State court opinions creating and interpreting common law. Common law* has several meanings, the principal of which is judge-made law in the absence of controlling statutory law or other higher law. If a problem exists for which there is no governing statute, a court may have the authority to create common law to solve that problem.

- *State court rules (also called rules of court) governing the mechanics of litigation before a particular court.* They cover many of the procedural aspects of divorces, annulments, adoptions, etc. The rules often contain standard forms that are either required or recommended.

- *State administrative regulations of agencies that carry out statutes:* For example, the agency that administers child-support enforcement laws.

- *Local law:* A major example is a zoning ordinance on single-family residences.

Federal Law Sources

- *U.S. Constitution.* The federal Constitution is the nation's highest law, to which all other federal and state laws must conform in areas covered by the U.S. Constitution.
- *Federal statutes.* For example, a statute of Congress that requires states to enact specific child-support enforcement laws as a condition for receiving federal grants.
- *Federal court opinions interpreting federal laws.*
- *Federal regulations.* For example, a regulation of the Internal Revenue Service on how marital status affects tax liability.
- *International law.* For example, the Hague Convention on the Civil Aspects of International Child Abduction.

SECONDARY AUTHORITY

- *Secondary authority* is any nonlaw that a court could rely on in reaching its decision. The major examples of secondary authorities are legal periodicals, legal encyclopedias, and legal treatises. Secondary sources are sometimes used by the courts to help them interpret primary authority. In this sense, secondary authorities influence family law and can be included as a source of family law.

© Cengage Learning 2013

a particular state. In a child-support case, for example, the question is not so much, "What is the law of child support?" as it is "What is the law of child support *today*?" Understanding general principles is helpful as a starting point, but more is usually needed in the actual practice of law. The ticket of admission to current law is the law library, both traditional and online.

Fortunately, most of the primary authority mentioned in Exhibit 1-5 is available online for free. See Appendix D for the sites linking to this material in your state. See also Family Law Online section on page 35.

SAMPLE PROBLEM

To examine some of the family-law sources more closely, let us assume that you work in a law office representing a client who signed a surrogate motherhood contract. She agreed to be artificially inseminated with the semen of a man who is not her husband and to allow the child to be adopted at birth by this man and his wife. Problems have arisen in this arrangement, however. Your supervisor asks you to do some legal research on surrogacy contracts. In Chapter 16, we will study such contracts in greater detail. For now, our goal is simply to give you an overview of some of the law books you might consult when researching a family-law case such as this.

STARTING WITH PRIMARY AUTHORITY

One possible starting point is to go directly to law books containing or indexing primary authority.

STATUTES To find out if there are any statutes on surrogacy, check the index of your state statutory code. It might lead you to such statutes. For an example, see Exhibit 1-6. For a summary of techniques to use when trying to find statutory law, see Appendix A. For the site that contains the statutory code of your state, see Appendix D.

COURT OPINIONS Exhibit 1-7 gives an example of a page from a regional reporter volume containing *Doe v. Attorney General*, a court opinion on the legality of surrogate motherhood contracts. The opinion in Exhibit 1-7 is from a hard copy—that is, it comes from a traditional volume that you take from the shelves. Such opinions can also be found online in fee-based services such as Westlaw, LexisNexis, and Loislaw. The opinions are often also available via free resources such as a state court website (see Appendix D) and Google Scholar. See Exhibit 1-8 for the steps to use to find family-law court opinions using Google Scholar.

EXHIBIT 1-6 Example of a Family Law Statute: *Michigan Compiled Laws Annotated,* §§ 772.851 and 772.855 (1993)

772.851. Short title

This act shall be known and may be cited as the "surrogate parenting act".
P.A. 1988, No. 199, § 1, Eff. Sept. 1, 1988.

722.855. Contracts; void and unenforceable

A surrogate parentage contract is void and unenforceable as contrary to public policy.
P.A. 1988, No. 199, § 5, Eff. Sept. 1, 1988.

Reprinted from *Michigan Compiled Laws Annotated* with permission of Thomson Reuters. (To find these statutes online, see www.legislature.mi.gov.)

Example of a Statutory Code Volume ▶

STARTING WITH SECONDARY AUTHORITY

Another option is to start with secondary authority. This approach is often valuable when you are doing research in an area of the law that is new to you. Secondary authority will not only give you leads to primary authority, but also often give you background information about the law. This background can be tremendously helpful in providing basic terminology and general understanding. Here are some of the main secondary authorities:

LEGAL ENCYCLOPEDIAS A legal encyclopedia is a multivolume set of books that summarizes almost every major legal topic. The two most important national legal encyclopedias are:

- *American Jurisprudence, 2d* (WestGroup) *(Am. Jur. 2d)* (available in bound volumes and online via Westlaw and LexisNexis)
- *Corpus Juris Secundum* (WestGroup) *(C.J.S.)* (available in bound volumes and online via Westlaw)

Here are some examples of family-law topics covered in these legal encyclopedias:

Abduction and Kidnapping	Divorce and Separation
Abortion and Birth Control	Domestic Abuse and Violence
Adoption	Family Planning
Annulment	Guardian and Ward
Breach of Promise to Marry	Husband and Wife
Children Out of Wedlock	Infants
Community Property	Marriage
Desertion and Nonsupport	Parent and Child

Exhibit 1-9 contains a page from a volume of *American Jurisprudence, 2d,* on surrogate motherhood. Exhibit 1-10 contains a page from a volume of *Corpus Juris Secundum* on the same topic. In addition to these national encyclopedias, some states have their own encyclopedias covering the law of that particular state, e.g., *California Jurisprudence*; *Florida Jurisprudence, 2d*; *Michigan Law and Practice, 2d ed.*

EXHIBIT 1-7 Sample Page from a Regional Reporter Volume Containing a Family Law Court Opinion: *Doe v. Attorney General*, 487 N.W.2d 484 (Mich. Ct. App. 1992)

DOE v. ATTORNEY GENERAL Mich. **484**
Cite as 487 N.W.2d 484 (Mich.App. 1992)

194 Mich.App. 432

Jane DOE, John Doe, Rena Roe, Richard Roe, Carol Coe, Carl Coe, Paula Poe, and Nancy Noe, Plaintiffs-Appellants,

v.

ATTORNEY GENERAL, Defendant-Appellee.

Docket No. 113775.

Court of Appeals of Michigan.

Submitted March 20, 1990, at Detroit.

Decided June 1, 1992, at 9:10 A.M.

Released for Publication August 28, 1992.

Infertile couples and prospective surrogate mothers brought action for declaratory judgment against state Attorney General regarding constitutionality of Surrogate Parenting Act. The Circuit Court, Wayne County, John H. Gillis, Jr., J., granted summary disposition for the Attorney General, and plaintiffs appealed. The Court of Appeals, Holbrook, P.J., held that: (1) case or controversy existed concerning constitutionality of statute, giving court jurisdiction for declaratory judgment; (2) state had compelling interests sufficient to warrant governmental intrusion into protected area of privacy in matter of procreation; and (3) surrogate parentage contract involving voluntary relinquishment after conception of female's parental rights to child, is void and unenforceable.

Affirmed in part and reversed in part.

Murphy, J., concurred and filed opinion.

1. Declaratory Judgment ⚸ 124

"Case or controversy" existed, for purposes of declaratory judgment, despite agreement as to interpretation of statute, where attorney for infertile couples and prospective surrogate mothers later informed trial court that he misunderstood agreement with state con-

cerning constitutionality of interpretation of Surrogate Parenting Act. M.C.L.A. §722.851 et seq.; U.S.C.A. Const. Amends. 5, 14; MCR 2.605(A).

2. Constitutional Law ⚸ 82(10), 274(5)

Due process clauses of State and Federal Constitutions, together with penumbral rights emanating from specific guarantees of the Bill of Rights, protect individual decisions in matters of childbearing from unjustified intrusion by the state. U.S.C.A. Const. Amends. 5, 14.

American Civil Liberties Union Fund of Michigan by Robert A. Sedler, Elizabeth L. Gleicher and Paul J. Denenfeld, Detroit, for plaintiffs-appellants.

Frank J. Kelley, Atty. Gen., Gay Secor Hardy, Sol. Gen., and A. Michael Leffler and Vincent J. Leone, Asst. Attys. Gen., for defendant-appellee.

Before HOLBROOK, P.J., and MURPHY and JANSEN, JJ.

HOLBROOK, Presiding Judge.

In this action for a declaratory interpretation of the Surrogate Parenting Act, M.C.L. § 722.851 *et seq.;* M.S.A. § 25.-248(151) *et seq.,* plaintiffs appeal as of right from an order of the Wayne Circuit Court granting defendant's motion for summary disposition for failure to state a claim. We affirm in part and reverse in part.

Plaintiffs are infertile couples and prospective surrogate mothers. In their suit, filed on August 4, 1988, plaintiffs assert that if the Surrogate Parenting Act were interpreted as being an outright ban on surrogacy contracts for pay, the statute would deny them their constitutionally protected privacy rights and would offend the Due Process and Equal Protection Clauses of the state and federal constitutions. . . .

Caption (parties, their litigation status, docket number, dates, etc.)

Syllabus (summary of the entire opinion)

Headnote (summary of a portion of the opinion). At the top, you find Key Topic and Number "Declaratory Judgment 124." You can take this key topic and number to any West digest to try to find additional cases.

Headnote (summary of a portion of the opinion). At the top, you find Key Topic and Numbers "Constitutional Law 82(10)" and "274(5)". You can take them to any West digest to try to find additional cases.

Attorneys who litigated the case

Name of judge who wrote the opinion

The body of the opinion begins.

Reprinted from *North Western Reporter 2d* with permission of Thomson Reuters. (To find this case online, see Exhibit 1-8.)

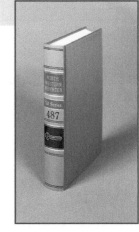

Example of a regional reporter volume ▶

EXHIBIT 1-8 **Finding Family Law Court Opinions Using Google Scholar**

GOOGLE SCHOLAR

- Go to scholar.google.com
- Select "Legal documents"
- There are three ways to find cases once you are in "Legal documents":
  (1) Enter a topic in the search box (e.g., "surrogate mother")
  (2) If you know the name of a case, enter it in the search box (e.g., "Doe v. Attorney General")
  (3) If you know the citation of a case, enter it in the search box (e.g., "487 N. W.2d 484")

OTHER FREE SOURCES OF ONLINE OPINIONS

- www.findlaw.com/casecode
- www.lexisone.com
- findacase.com
- www.justia.com
- openjurist.org
- www.plol.org
- www.law.stanford.edu/library/research
- www.ll.georgetown.edu/guides/freelowcost.cfm
- www.law.cornell.edu/states/listing.html

© Cengage Learning 2013

Example of an *Am. Jur. 2d* volume ▼

EXHIBIT 1-9 **Example of a Discussion of a Family Law Topic from a Volume of *American Jurisprudence, 2d*: 59 Am. Jur. 2d § 3 (1987)**

59 Am Jur 2d   PARENT AND CHILD   § 4

§ 3.   — "Surrogate mother"

The surrogate mother arrangement is an arrangement between a surrogate mother and a husband and wife, whereby the surrogate mother agrees to be artificially inseminated with the husband's semen, bear a child, and relinquish all rights regarding that child to the husband and wife. They agree to pay the costs of the surrogate mother's pregnancy and to accept the child at birth. In addition, they may agree to pay the surrogate mother a fee in excess of the costs of bearing a child.[22] The legality and enforceability of a surrogate mother arrangement is questionable.[23]

Reprinted from *American Jurisprudence, 2d* with permission of Thomson Reuters.

LEGAL TREATISES A *legal treatise* is a book written by a private individual (or a public official writing as a private citizen) that provides an overview, a summary, or a commentary on a legal topic. Exhibit 1-11 contains a page from a widely used legal treatise on family law, Homer H. Clark's *The Law of Domestic Relations in the United States* (2d ed., 1987). If the legal treatise contains very practical material such as litigation techniques and standard forms, it is often also called a formbook or a practice manual.

LEGAL PERIODICALS A legal periodical is a pamphlet on legal topics that is issued at regular intervals (e.g., quarterly). Many legal periodicals are published by law schools, such as the one in Exhibit 1-12 from the *Marquette Law Review*.

EXHIBIT 1-10   Example of a Discussion of a Family Law Topic from a Volume of *Corpus Juris Secundum:* 2 C.J.S. § 25 (1972, Supp. 1994)

2 C.J.S.

ADOPTION OF PERSONS §§ 24-25

§ 25. In General

While an adoption relationship cannot ordinarily be created by private contract, contracts for the adoption of persons are usually not considered as opposed to public policy and in some circumstances such a contract may be treated as an adoption and enforced with consequences equivalent to a formal adoption. . . .

While surrogate parenting agreements in which the surrogate mother receives payment for bearing and surrendering the baby to the natural father and his wife for adoption have been prohibited,[29.5] such surrogate parenting agreements which compensate the surrogate mother have been given legal effect.[29.10]

A contractual provision in a surrogate parenting agreement purporting to terminate the parental rights of the surrogate mother does not conform to statutory prerequisites for termination and is invalid and unenforceable.[29.15]

Example of a *C.J.S.* volume ▶

Reprinted from *Corpus Juris Secundum* with permission of Thomson Reuters.

Example of a legal treatise ▼

EXHIBIT 1-11   Example of a Page from a Legal Treatise on Family Law: Homer H. Clark, *The Law of Domestic Relations in the United States* § 21.9, pp. 669–670 (2d ed. 1987)

§ 21.9   **Adoption—The Surrogate Mother Contract**

If the soundness of the solutions to legal problems varied directly with the number of words devoted to the problems and with the number of persons engaged in producing the words, we would need to have no fears about being able to cope with the difficulties created by surrogate mother contracts.[1] The legal and nonlegal output on the subject has been enormous[2] and will doubtless continue at the same rate until some other fascinating and unanswerable question appears. Unfortunately, however, the ability to solve legal problems probably varies inversely with the number of words expended. Generally acceptable methods of dealing with these contracts therefore do not seem likely to be devised.

Reprinted from *The Law of Domestic Relations in the United States 2d* with permission of Thomson Reuters.

ANNOTATIONS An *annotation* is a note or commentary on something. The word also refers to the extensive research papers in:

- *American Law Reports, First Series (A.L.R.)*
- *American Law Reports, Second Series (A.L.R.2d)*
- *American Law Reports, Third Series (A.L.R.3d)*
- *American Law Reports, Fourth Series (A.L.R.4th)*
- *American Law Reports, Fifth Series (A.L.R.5th)*
- *American Law Reports, Sixth Series (A.L.R.6th)*

- *American Law Reports, Federal (A.L.R. Fed.)*
- *American Law Reports, Federal, Second Series (A.L.R. Fed. 2d)*

All eight sets are sometimes referred to collectively as *American Law Reports* or *ALRs*. Many very useful annotations are available in these sets, such as this one: James Rigelhaupt, Annotation, *Attorney's Liability for Negligence in Cases Involving Domestic Relations*, 78 ALR 3d 255 (1977). Exhibit 1-13 contains an example of an annotation on surrogacy from *A.L.R.4th.*

Example of a legal periodical ▼

EXHIBIT 1-12 Example of a Page from a Legal Periodical Article on Family Law: 76 *Marquette Law Review* 675 (1993)

SURROGATE GESTATOR: A NEW AND HONORABLE PROFESSION

JOHN DWIGHT INGRAM

I. INTRODUCTION

In recent decades, sex without reproduction has become common and widely accepted, and more recently medical science has made it increasingly possible to have reproduction without sex. The former is much more enjoyable than the latter for most of us and, while it does entail some moral and legal issues, is a great deal less complex than the latter.[1] A major cause of the complexity of the issues associated with noncoital reproduction is that, while "science [tends to] look . . . forward to anticipate new and unforeseen possibilities, the law looks backward, drawing its support from precedent."[2] Our society seems to first develop and perfect medical and scientific techniques, and only later consult experts in ethics and law to determine if we *should* be doing that which in fact we already *are* doing. Meanwhile, we try to resolve disputes arising from new reproductive technologies by using "old legal codes of paternity, maternity, baby-selling, adoption, and contracts."[3]

Reprinted with permission from *Marquette Law Review.*

Example of an *A.L.R.4th* volume ▼

EXHIBIT 1-13 Example of a Page from an Annotation of Family Law: 77 *A.L.R.4th 70* (1990)

ANNOTATION

VALIDITY AND CONSTRUCTION OF SURROGATE PARENTING AGREEMENT

by

Danny R. Veilleux, J.D.

I. Preliminary Matters

§ 1. Introduction

[a] Scope

This annotation collects and analyzes the reported cases in which the courts have construed or considered the validity of a surrogate parenting agreement. For the purposes of this annotation, the "surrogate parenting" or "surrogacy" agreement refers to a contract in which the natural or "surrogate" mother, for a fee, agrees to conceive a child through artificial insemination with the sperm of the natural father, to bear and deliver the child to the natural father, and to terminate all of her parental rights subsequent to the child's birth. Although the parties to a surrogacy agreement generally anticipate the eventual adoption of the child by the natural father's wife, this annotation will discuss all surrogacy agreements, regardless of whether they contain any provisions concerning such adoption. Moreover, the surrogate mother's husband, or the natural father's wife, assuming either parent is married, may be a party to the surrogacy agreements included within the scope of this annotation.

Reprinted from *American Law Reports 4th* with permission of Thomson Reuters.

FAMILY LAW ONLINE

It is possible to obtain a great deal of information online that is relevant to a family-law practice. In addition to research into court opinions, statutes, and other primary authorities, a law firm often must do factual research. An example of factual research would be the attempt to uncover personal and business assets that an estranged spouse may be trying to hide.

Three major fee-based online databases, for which the firm pays a subscription fee, are Westlaw (www.westlaw.com), LexisNexis (www.lexis.com), and Loislaw (estore.loislaw.com). In addition, you can obtain a great deal of free material on the Internet. (See Exhibit 1-8 for sites that will give you free access to court opinions.) Greater caution is needed when using free sites than when using the fee-based ones. In general, the fee-based sites are more comprehensive, current, and user-friendly than the free sites. The latter, however, are becoming increasingly reliable, particularly those run by the government itself. (See comprehensive links to federal, state, local, and tribal governments and laws at www.usa.gov.)

Exhibit 1-14 presents examples of government sites that are relevant to a family-law practice. See also the Helpful Websites section at the end of each chapter in the book.

SKILLS ASSIGNMENTS

To help you develop the ability to perform paralegal tasks, 12 categories of skills assignments are presented in various chapters of this book. Your instructor will decide which of these assignments you will complete. Some of the instructions

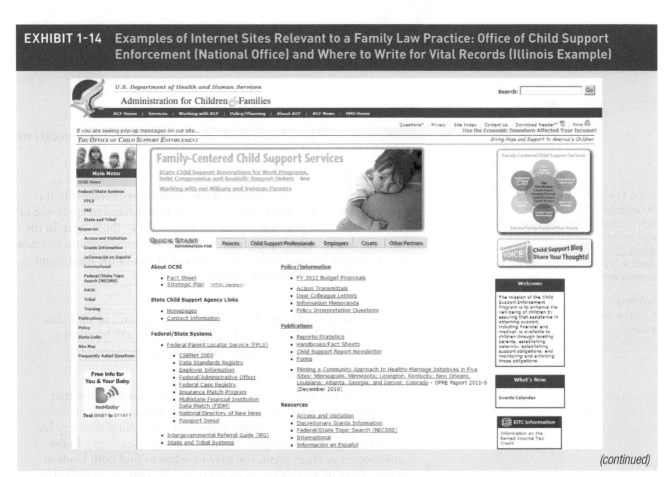

EXHIBIT 1-14 Examples of Internet Sites Relevant to a Family Law Practice: Office of Child Support Enforcement (National Office) and Where to Write for Vital Records (Illinois Example)

(continued)

U.S. Department of Health and Human Services, Administration for Children & Families, The Office of Child Support Enforcement (www.acf.hhs.gov/programs/cse).

EXHIBIT 1-14 *(continued)*

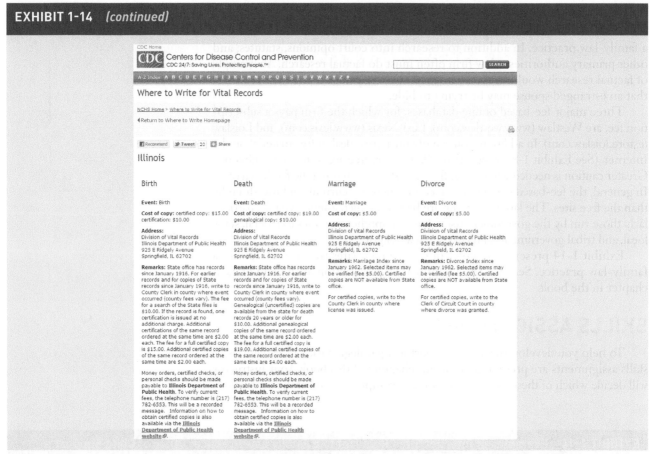

Centers for Disease Control and Prevention, *Where to Write for Vital Records. Example:* Illinois (www.cdc.gov/nchs/w2w/illinois.htm). All other states (www .cdc.gov/nchs/w2w.htm).

for these assignments are found in Appendix A. The categories of assignments are as follows:

1. *Legal analysis assignment*

   There are two main kinds of **legal analysis** assignments in this book. In the first, you are given a set of facts and asked to apply one or more of the legal principles discussed in the text to those facts. In the second, you are asked to apply the **holding** of a court opinion to a new set of facts. A holding is the court's answer to one of the legal issues the court has resolved in the opinion.

2. *State code assignment*

   A great deal of family law is found in the statutes of your state statutory code. In the state code assignment, you will be asked to determine what your state code says about a particular topic.

3. *Court opinion assignment*

   Two of the major categories of court opinions are those that interpret statutes and those that create and interpret *common law*, which is judge-made law in the absence of controlling statutory law or other higher law (see glossary for additional meanings). In the court-opinion assignment, you may be asked to find both kinds of court opinions written by state courts in your state on a family-law issue.

legal analysis
The application of one or more rules to the facts of a client's case in order to answer a legal question that will help (1) avoid a legal dispute, (2) resolve a legal dispute that has arisen, or (3) prevent a legal dispute from becoming worse.

holding
A court's answer to one of the legal issues in a case.

4. *Complaint drafting assignment*

    In this assignment, you will be asked to draft a complaint (called a petition in some states) that would be acceptable in your state on a specific family-law controversy.

5. *Agreement drafting assignment*

    Agreements are often used in a family-law practice by parties who wish to define an aspect of their relationship or to avoid litigation. In this assignment, you will be asked to draft such agreements.

6. *Checklist formulation assignment*

    In this assignment, you will examine a statute or common-law principle and design a checklist of questions that an interviewer would ask (or that an investigator would pursue) to help determine whether that statute or common-law principle applies.

7. *Investigation strategy assignment*

    This assignment asks you to formulate a plan for gathering new facts or for substantiating facts that you already have on a family-law problem.

8. *Interview assignment*

    In this assignment, you will role-play an interviewer conducting a legal interview on a hypothetical (i.e., assumed) set of facts in a family-law case.

9. *Interrogatory assignment*

    In this assignment, you will draft a set of interrogatories, which are questions sent to an opposing party in litigation to help your side prepare for trial.

10. *Flowchart assignment*

    This assignment requires the presentation of a step-by-step outline of a particular legal procedure in your state.

11. *Systems assignment*

    In the systems assignment, you will contact someone who now works in a family-law office to determine what system(s) the office uses to accomplish some aspect of client service.

12. *Writing sample*

    At the end of each chapter, an idea is presented on a topic that you could write about and use as a writing sample when looking for employment upon graduation.

The general instructions for most of these assignments are found in Appendix A of the book. Within each assignment, you will find specific instructions. In addition, you will be referred to Appendix A, where you will find general instructions for that category of assignment.

■ PROJECT

This project will require you to use the Internet to compile a list of some of the major family-law publications and resources for your state. For leads to begin the search, see the Helpful Websites section at the end of the chapter. Other leads can be found in Appendix D.

Family Law of Your State

(a) What is the name of the statutory code containing the statutes of your legislature? If more than one code exists, list each one. (See Appendix D.)

(b) In this code, find any statute on divorce. Quote and cite the first line from this statute that mentions the word *divorce*.

(c) Go to the Internet site of the state courts in your state. (See Appendix D.) Find the court rules of any civil court in your state that hears divorce cases. Quote from any court rule that uses the word *divorce*.

(d) What is the name of the regional reporter that contains the court opinions of the highest state court in your state? To find out, (1) type the following search in Google, Bing, or Yahoo: map of regional reporters, or (2) type the phrase "regional reporter" and the name of your state (e.g., "regional reporter" Indiana).

(e) In this question, you will use Google Scholar to find court opinions on divorce written by your state courts. Follow these steps:

-Go to Google Scholar (scholar.google.com)
-In the search box, type "divorce" and the name of your state
-Select "Legal documents"
-Click the search button
-Scroll down the results until you find opinions written by state courts in your state

Give the citation of any two opinions written by different state courts in your state that cover divorce. For each opinion, include the name of the opinion, the reporter in which it is found, the court that wrote the opinion, and the date of the opinion. Briefly describe the facts of each opinion. (If Google Scholar does not lead you to such opinions, try the links in Exhibit 1-8.)

(f) Run this search in Google, Bing, or Yahoo: West digest aa (substitute the name of your state for aa). What are the names of the digests (published by WestGroup) that will give small-paragraph summaries of court opinions in your state?

(g) The topics in the WestGroup digests are arranged alphabetically by digest topics. Over 450 topics cover all of the law found in court opinions. Each topic is assigned a number (for example, 134 Divorce, 205 Husband and Wife). Run this search in Google, Bing, or Yahoo: West digest topic outline "family law". It should lead you to sites that list all the numbered topics (store.westlaw .com/pdf/wln2/L-352461.pdf). Twelve of the major family-law topics are Abortion and Birth Control, Adoption, Child Custody, Child Support, Children Out-of-Wedlock, Divorce, Husband and Wife, Incest, Infants, Marriage, Parent and Child, and Protection of Endangered Persons. What is the topic number for each of these 12 topics? (You have already been told the answers for Divorce and Husband and Wife.)

(h) Go to the online catalog of the library of Congress (catalog.loc.gov). Do a search for the word *divorce* and your state (e.g., California divorce, Florida divorce), or do the same search with the phrase "family law" (e.g., California "family law" and Florida "family law"). From these two searches, select any five legal treatises written within the last 10 years. For each treatise, give its author, title, and date of publication. Do not use the same author more than once (i.e., the five treatises you select should have different authors).

(i) Most law schools have online catalogs. To find the law schools in your state, run this search in Google, Bing, or Yahoo: "law school" aa (substitute the name of your state for aa). At the site, go to the law library page of the school. Select its online catalog. (If it does not have one, pick another school in the state.) Repeat question h for this catalog. The five legal treatises you select should be different from the ones you selected in question h.

(j) In this question, you will use Google Scholar to find law review articles that contain the name of your state and the word *divorce* (e.g., New York divorce and Alaska divorce). Follow these steps:

-In the search box, type "divorce" and the name of your state
-Select "Articles"
-Click the search button

Give the citation of any two law review articles that contain the word "divorce" and the name of your state in the title of the articles. (The results of the search may give you only the first page of the article, which is all you need for this assignment. Reading the full article may require payment of a fee.)

(k) Run this search in Google, Bing, or Yahoo: blog "family law" aa (substitute the name of your state for aa). List any blogs that cover the family law of your state. For each blog, provide the web address and a description of the information that the site contains.

■ ETHICS IN A FAMILY LAW PRACTICE

It is an ethical obligation of every legal professional to help extend legal services to persons in society who cannot afford to pay private attorneys. Every state has pro bono programs that provide free legal services to persons with family-law problems. While you are in school, you may not be able to devote time to pro bono work, but you should know how to find out what pro bono opportunities are available in the area of family law so that you can consider donating time at a later date. To find this information, run the following search in Google, Bing, or Yahoo: aa "pro bono" "family law" (substitute the name of your city and state for aa in the search, e.g., Cleveland, Ohio "pro bono" "family law"). Many of the links will direct you to organizations seeking pro bono help from attorneys. Determine if the websites of such organizations indicate that they also appreciate pro bono help from paralegals. Locate two different organizations in the state that accept pro bono help from paralegals in the area of family law. Give the names of the organizations, their street and web addresses, and the kind of assistance that paralegals can provide to their clients.

SUMMARY

Family law is the body of law that defines relationships, rights, and duties in the formation, ongoing existence, and dissolution of marriage and other family units. Some of the major trends in the development of family law are equality of the sexes, increased federalization of family law, expanding role of contracts, scientific advances in childbearing, and deregulation of sexuality. To accommodate changes in family law, many states are using newer terminology that better reflects the values that underlie the changes.

Someone working in a family-law practice may encounter legal problems in a wide variety of areas in addition to basic family law. These other areas include criminal law, contract law, agency law, real property law, personal property law, corporate law, business law, bankruptcy law, tort law, civil procedure law, evidence law, juvenile law, tax law, estate law, Social Security law, and ethics law.

Courts are often asked to review the constitutionality of family laws. At the federal level, the major challenges are those that allege a violation of due process of law and equal protection of the laws. The two categories of due process are procedural due process (PDP) and substantive due process (SDP). PDP requires fair procedures before the government can restrict life, liberty, or property. SDP requires the government to avoid arbitrary or capricious actions that deprive someone of life, liberty, or property. Interferences with fundamental rights must meet the test of strict scrutiny. Interferences with nonfundamental rights must meet the rational-basis test. Challenges that allege a violation of equal protection

must meet the test of strict scrutiny (fundamental rights, suspect class), intermediate scrutiny (quasi-suspect class), or rational basis (all other categories). Social media sites such as Facebook have provided family-law attorneys with new avenues to evidence that can be used in negotiation and litigation.

Paralegals in family law perform many functions, such as interviewing clients, drafting temporary orders and other court pleadings, preparing financial statements, preparing clients and witnesses for hearings and trials, maintaining case files, and assisting in discovery and trial. Paralegals also use family-law skills in government employment and freelance work. Volunteer work is also possible as a Court Appointed Special Advocate (CASA).

Because the cases handled in a family-law practice can be emotionally charged, the need for professionalism and objectivity is paramount, particularly if the office is representing a client who has done something that clashes with an employee's personal values. Violence is an ongoing concern in family law. Perhaps more than in any other area of law practice, there is a potential for violence among family members, and sometimes between parties and opposing counsel.

The primary sources of family law are constitutions, statutes, court opinions, court rules (rules of court), and administrative regulations. Secondary authorities such as legal treatises can also be important for a family-law practitioner. Many family-law attorneys are able to use the Internet to find information that is relevant to the legal disputes of their clients.

KEY TERMS

family law	judicial review	legitimate state purpose
marriage	due process of law	classification
unity of person	procedural due process	equal protection of law
federalization	substantive due process	suspect class
constitutionalization	fundamental right	quasi-suspect class
status	strict scrutiny	intermediate scrutiny
premarital agreement	narrowly tailored	e-discovery
precedent	compelling state interest	spoliation
specialty certification	rational basis	forensic
common law	reasonably related	conflicts check

conflict of interest	subpoena duces tecum	execution of judgment
tickler	request for production (RFP)	garnishment
timeline	request for admission (RFA)	court appointed special advocate (CASA)
stipulation	independent medical examination (IME)	guardian ad litem (GAL)
affidavit	alternative dispute resolution (ADR)	legal advice
financial statement	mediation	practice of law
arrearages	impeach	bias
discovery	trial notebook	objectivity
interrogatories	proof of service	legal analysis
protective order	court costs	holding
deposition	pretrial conference	
subpoena	appellate brief	

REVIEW QUESTIONS

1. What is family law?

2. What are five major developments that are affecting the practice of family law in the twenty-first century?

3. What are some of the changes in family-law terminology and why have such changes been made?

4. When working on family-law cases, what are some major areas of law that could be involved?

5. What are the two categories of due-process challenges to family-law rules under the U.S. Constitution, and how would a court resolve the challenges?

6. What are the three categories of equal-protection challenges to family-law rules under the U.S. Constitution, and how would a court resolve the challenges?

7. How have social media sites on the Internet affected the practice of family law?

8. What are some of the major roles that paralegals play in the practice of family law?

9. What is the role of a CASA?

10. What is a bias and when can a paralegal's bias affect performance on case assignments?

11. To what extent is violence a concern in the practice of family law?

12. What are the main categories of primary authority in family law? Where can you find such authority?

13. What secondary authorities can be important in a family-law practice?

HELPFUL WEBSITES

Roles of Paralegals in Family Law and Other Areas of Practice

- www.lawcost.com/paras.htm#family
- www.lectlaw.com/files/pap01.htm
- www.paralegals.org/associations/2270/files/Paralegal_Responsibilities_v.pdf
- www.cobar.org/index.cfm/ID/106/subID/23108/CLAS
- www.cobar.org/repository/Inside_Bar/Paralegal/Paralegal%20Guidelines/FamilyLaw.pdf
- www.caparalegal.org/index.php/duties-skills
- www.helium.com/items/2153754-what-a-paralegal-should-know-about-family-law

Research Guides to Family Law

- www.ll.georgetown.edu/guides/familylaw.cfm

- www.justia.com/family
- www.hg.org/family.html
- www.enotes.com/family-law-reference
- www.abanet.org/family/familylaw/home.html
- topics.law.cornell.edu/wex/table_divorce
- www.catalaw.com/cattopics/Family.shtml
- library.law.umn.edu/researchguides/familylaw.html
- www.kcll.org/researchhelp/researchguides/familylaw/index.html
- www.divorcelawinfo.com
- www.expertlaw.com/library/family_law
- divorcesupport.about.com/cs/legalities/index.htm
- www.law.arizona.edu/Library/Research/Guides/familylaw/default.cfm
- law.syr.edu/academics/center-and-institutes/family-law-and-social-policy/research-guides-and-resources

Societal Changes and Family Law

- ncfmr.bgsu.edu
- www.census.gov (type "family" in the search box)
- quod.lib.umich.edu/m/mfr/4919087.0005.105?rgn=main;view=fulltext
- blogs.census.gov/censusblog/2011/05/how-many -trips-do-we-take-down-the-aisle.html

Social Media and the Family Law Client

- burtonhunteresq.blogspot.com/2011/03 /social-media-tips-for-family-law-client.html

Google/Bing/Yahoo Searches

(on these search engines, run the following searches, substituting your state for "aa")

- "family law" aa
- divorce aa
- "family law" bias aa
- paralegal roles aa
- "family law" violence aa
- "family law" research aa
- constitution "family law" aa
- paralegal jobs "family law" aa
- "family law" social media aa
- freelance paralegal "family law" aa
- Facebook divorce aa

ENDNOTES

Note: All or most of the court opinions in these endnotes can be read online. To do so, go to Google Scholar (scholar .google.com), select "Legal documents," and in the search box, enter the cite (e.g., "539 U.S. 558") or the name of the case (e.g., "Lawrence v. Texas") that is given in the endnote.

1 Marjorie Maguire Shultz, *Contractual Ordering of Marriage: A New Model for State Policy*, 70 Cal. L. Rev. 204, 207 (Mar. 1982).

2 Claudia Dreifus, *Where Have You Gone, Norman Rockwell? A Fresh Look at the Family* (interview with Dr. Stephanie Coontz), N.Y. Times, Jun. 14, 2005, at D3 (www.nytimes .com/2005/06/14/science/14conv.html).

3 *The Decline of Marriage and the Rise of New Families* (Pew Research Center Publications, Nov. 18, 2010) (pewresearch.org/pubs/1802 /decline-marriage-rise-new-families).

4 Harry D. Krause & David D. Meyer, *Family Law in a Nutshell* 16 (5th ed. 2007).

5 *Lawrence v. Texas*, 539 U.S. 558, 602 (dissent) (2003).

6 Quoted in *Warren v. State*, 255 Ga. 151, 154, 336 S.E.2d 221, 223 (1985).

7 Lenore Weitzman, *The Divorce Revolution* 382 (1985).

8 Elizabeth Gleick, *Hell Hath No Fury*, Time Magazine, Oct. 7, 1996. (www.time.com/time/magazine/article /0,9171,985269,00.html).

9 *Spires v. Spires*, 743 A.2d 186 (D.C. 1999).

10 *Santosky v. Kramer*, 455 U.S. 745, 769 (1982)(dissent).

11 Ruth Padawer, *Who Knew I Was Not the Father?* N.Y. Times, Nov. 17, 2009 (www.nytimes.com/2009/11/22/magazine /22Paternity-t.html?pagewanted=1&ref=magazine). A version of this article appeared on page MM38 of the New York edition.

12 *Lawrence v. Texas*, supra note 5 at 562.

13 John Greenya, *Family Affairs: Seven Experts in Family Law Discuss Their Experiences*, 9 Washington Lawyer 23, 31 (Nov./Dec. 1994).

14 www.tbls.org/cert.

15 U.S. Const. amend. XIV, § 1 (www.usconstitution.net /const.html).

16 U.S. Const. amend. XIV, § 1 (www.usconstitution.net /const.html).

17 *Baxtrom v. Herold*, 383 U.S. 107, 111 (1966).

18 Stephanie Rabiner, *Facebook Divorce: Evidence from Wall Posts* (Feb. 9, 2011) (blogs.findlaw.com/law_and_life /2011/02/facebook-divorce-evidence-from-wall-posts .html).

19 Brad Stone, *Tell-All PCs and Phones Transforming Divorce*, N.Y. Times, Sept. 15, 2007, at A1 (www.nytimes.com /2007/09/15/business/15divorce.html).

20 Leanne Italie, *Divorce Lawyers: Facebook Tops in Online Evidence in Court*, Jun. 29, 2010. (www.usatoday.com/tech /news/2010-06-29-facebook-divorce-N.htm).

21 Ibid.

22 Laura Holson, *Text Messages: Digital Lipstick on the Collar*, N.Y. Times, Dec. 9, 2009, at A1. (www.nytimes.com/2009 /12/09/us/09text.html).

23 William Hamilton & Wendy Akbar, *E-Discovery in the Age of Facebook, Twitter, & the Digital Family*, 33 Family Advocate 16 (Fall 2010).

24 Carolyn Davis, *Divorce Facebook Style*, The Philadelphia Enquirer (Jul. 12, 2010) (www.aaml.org/sites/default/files /Divorce,%20Facebook%20style.pdf).

25 Nadine Brozan, *Divorce Lawyers' New Friend: Social Networks*, N.Y. Times, May 13, 2011 (www.nytimes.com/2011/05/15 /fashion/weddings/divorce-lawyers-new-friend-social -networks.html?_r=1).

26 Beverly Ann Miller and Sherryll Babboni-Stripp, *The Role of the Legal Assistant in Family Matters*, 74 Michigan Bar Journal 54 (Jan. 1995). (The phrase *legal assistant* was changed to *paralegal* in the quote.)

27 Yasmin Spiegel, *Family Law for Paralegals*, 6 The Journal 7 (Sacramento Valley Paralegal Association, Jun. 1986).

28 See also State Bar of Texas, *Attorney's Guide to Practicing with Legal Assistants* (1986) and Colorado Bar Association Legal

Assistant Committee, *Duties . . . of the Family Law Legal Assistant* (1986).

[29] West Virginia Child Support Paralegal (9519) (run this search in Google, Bing, or Yahoo: West Virginia child support paralegal).

[30] CASA, *Volunteer Commitment Top Ten List* (www.casaforchildren.org/site/c.mtJSJ7MPIsE/b.5406005/k.3C2D/Volunteer_Commitment_Top_Ten_List.htm).

[31] William Statsky and Lynn Crossett, *The Texas Paralegal: Essential Rules, Documents, and Resources,* 49 (Cengage 2010).

[32] Jennifer J. Rose, *The Ten Commandments of Family Law . . . ,* 39 Practical Lawyer 85 (Jan. 1993).

[33] *The Volokh Conspiracy* (Mar. 11, 2011) (volokh.com/2011/03/10/in-criminal-court-you-see-bad-people-at-their-best-in-family-court-you-see-good-people-at-their-worst).

[34] Shari Caudron, *Crisis of Conscience,* 12 Legal Assistant Today 73, 75 (Sept./Oct. 1994).

[35] A.P. Roth, *Dangerous Divorces,* California Lawyer 23, 24 (Feb. 1994).

[36] Deborah Belgum, *82-Year-Old Jurist Bows Out . . . ,* Los Angeles Times, Jan. 6, 1997, at B1 (articles.latimes.com/1997-01-06/local/me-15922_1_family-law-cases).

Ethics in a
Family Law
Practice

CHAPTER OUTLINE

CHAPTER OBJECTIVES

After completing this chapter, you should be able to:

- Recognize the major ethical violations that can be committed in a family-law office so that you can assist the office in avoiding them.
- Know when an attorney-client relationship is formed.
- Understand the ethical dangers of attorney websites.
- Understand the ethical obligation to be competent.
- Explain the relationship between unethical incompetence and legal malpractice.
- Know the ethical obligations of an attorney engaged in limited-scope representation, including collaborative law.

- Explain the ethical limitations of attorney fees in a family-law case.
- State the criteria used by courts to award paralegal fees in family-law cases.
- Know whether an attorney can pay someone for a client referral.
- Explain the ethical duty of diligence.
- Identify when an attorney is allowed to reveal client confidences.
- List the major conflicts of interest that an attorney can have in a family-law practice.
- State the attorney's ethical duty in safeguarding client property.
- Define the anticontact rule.

- Understand when an attorney can or must withdraw from a case.
- State the attorney's duty to be truthful and to disclose adverse authority.
- Describe ethical issues that can arise when "friending" someone on a social-network site such as Facebook.
- State the main ethical duty when you are notarizing a document.
- Explain ethical duties when soliciting clients or advertising services.
- Explain the ethical consequences of inadequate supervision of paralegals.
- Understand the obligations of attorneys when working with self-represented persons.

INTRODUCTION

ethics
Rules that embody standards of behavior to which members of an occupation, profession, or other organization are expected to conform.

Ethics are rules that embody standards of behavior to which members of an occupation, a profession, or other organization are expected to conform. An ethics survey in one state revealed that 25 percent of all grievances filed against attorneys involved family-law cases.[1] This figure was almost double the percentage for every other area of practice. An uncomfortably large number of family-law clients eventually turn on their own attorneys with charges of unethical conduct: "The intensely personal and very emotional tone of many family-law proceedings undoubtedly contributes to the fact that family-law practitioners are on the receiving end of a disproportionately high percentage of professional grievances filed against lawyers."[2]

Many of the ethical rules we will be discussing in this chapter are based on the *Model Rules of Professional Conduct*. The *Model Rules* were written by the American Bar Association (ABA). Although the ABA publishes ethical rules, it does not discipline attorneys for unethical conduct. The ABA rules are not binding on any attorney unless the rules are adopted by the state court where the attorney practices. Attorney conduct is regulated by the state court, often in collaboration with the state bar association. The role of the ABA is to *propose* ethical rules for consideration by the various states. A state is free to adopt, modify, or reject the ethical rules recommended by the ABA. In view of the prestige of the ABA, many states have adopted its proposals with little change. The rules referenced in this chapter (e.g., Rule 1.1) will be the Model Rules. For the full text of the Model Rules, see the Helpful Websites section at the end of the chapter.

Exhibit 2-1 summarizes the major ethical standards that should guide a paralegal working in a family-law office. These standards are based on the Model Rules.

metadata
Data about data. Data about a computer document that are hidden within the document itself (e.g., earlier versions of the document).

EXHIBIT 2-1 Refresher Checklist of Ethical Guidelines for Paralegals in a Family Law Practice

1. *Disclosure of status.* Be sure that everyone with whom you come in contact knows that you are not an attorney. Do not allow people to assume that you are an attorney, which is likely when they learn you work in a law office.

2. *Accepting cases.* Do not "accept" a family-law case. You can tell someone what kinds of cases the office handles, but you cannot tell someone that the office will take his or her case.

3. *Setting fees.* Do not "set" a fee. You can tell someone what the attorney initial consultation fee is, but when questioned further about fees, you need to say that fees need to be discussed with the attorney.

4. *Sharing fees.* Do not accept a part of the fee of a particular client even if the attorney offers it to you. Attorneys cannot share (split) fees of particular clients with nonattorneys.

5. *Referring clients.* Do not accept anything of value for referring a case to your office. Something of value can include increased salary, a bonus, time off, a promotion, etc.

6. *Confidentiality.* Do not discuss the facts of a case with anyone outside the office (including your spouse) without permission from your supervisor.

7. *Confidentiality.* Before sending documents prepared on a computer (or filing them in court), remove the **metadata**. The latter can contain confidential information.

8. *Confidentiality.* When sending messages or documents over the Internet (e.g., as e-mail attachments) know how to **encrypt** them if your supervisor deems this precaution to be necessary.

9. *Conflict of interest.* Let your supervisor know immediately if in your prior employment (or volunteer activities) you worked for other law offices with clients who have any connection or relationship with clients of the law office where you now work. Your supervisor must determine if such connections create a **conflict of interest**.

10. *Conflict of interest.* Avoid romantic or financial relationships with opposing clients, relatives of opposing clients, or attorneys of opposing clients.

11. *Conflict of interest.* Understand how the office performs its **conflicts check** on every prospective family-law client so that the office can avoid cases that would create a conflict of interest.

12. *Conflict of interest.* Let your supervisor know if a client has offered you a gift. If the gift requires the preparation of a document, the document may have to be prepared by an attorney who does not work in your office.

13. *Competence.* If you do not know how to perform an assigned task, let your supervisor know that you need additional training or a different assignment.

14. *Competence.* Never stop learning more about the substantive and procedural law that pertains to the family-law tasks you are assigned. Competence is accomplished mainly through self-study and through **continuing legal education (CLE)**.

15. *Communication with other side.* Do not communicate with an opponent in a case unless you have the permission of your supervisor and your opponent's attorney.

16. *Communication with other side.* If the other side is proceeding **pro se** (without representation) and your supervisor allows you to communicate with him or her, you must not give the impression that you are **disinterested**. He or she must know that you work for the other side.

17. *Solicitation.* Do not initiate contacts with anyone (in person, by e-mail, or by phone) in order to encourage him or her to hire your law office unless the person already has a relationship with the law office. (You can, however, recommend your office if someone asks you for a recommendation.)

18. *Unauthorized practice of law.* Never answer a question about how the law applies to the facts of a particular person's situation even if you are certain that you know the correct answer to the question. You can provide legal information (comments about the law in general) but not **legal advice** (comments relevant to the particular facts of an individual).

19. *Unauthorized practice of law.* Avoid performing any task in the office without attorney supervision, even if you have performed the task before and know how to perform it.

20. *Commingling.* Do not deposit client funds (e.g., proceeds of the sale of a home that is part of a property division) into the same account that the law office uses for rent, salaries, or other office expenses. Avoid **commingling**.

21. *Misconduct.* Do not notarize a signature unless you were present and saw the signer place his or her signature on the document.

22. *Misconduct.* Do not lie or otherwise misrepresent facts (e.g., do not pretend to be a stranger in order to obtain information from someone in an office or on an Internet social media site).

23. *Misconduct.* Do not pad your timesheets by stating that you performed a task you did not perform or spent time on a task that you did not spend.

24. *Misconduct.* Do not tell anyone how to hide assets so that the assets will not be available for property division, spousal support, or child support.

25. *Misconduct.* Do not tell anyone how to avoid a **subpoena** or other legal **process**.

encrypt
Convert text into a code that renders it incomprehensible until it is reconverted to a readable format by an authorized recipient.

conflict of interest
Divided loyalties that actually or potentially harm (or disadvantage) someone who is owed undivided loyalty.

conflicts check
A determination of whether a conflict of interest exists that might disqualify a law office from representing a client or from continuing the representation.

continuing legal education (CLE)
Training in the law (usually short term) that a person receives after completing his or her formal legal training.

pro se
(on one's own behalf) Appearing for or representing oneself; not using an attorney. Also called pro per (in propria persona).

disinterested
Not working for one side or the other in a controversy; not deriving benefit if one side of a dispute wins or loses; objective.

legal advice
The application of laws or legal principles to the facts of a particular person's legal problem.

commingling
Mixing together (e.g., mixing separate property with marital property, mixing client funds with funds needed to run an office).

subpoena
A command to appear at a certain time and place.

process
The means (e.g., a summons, writ, or other court order) used by the court to acquire or exercise its power or jurisdiction over a person.

FORMATION OF THE ATTORNEY-CLIENT RELATIONSHIP

meritorious

Having merit; having a reasonable basis for believing that a person's claim or defense will succeed.

letter of nonengagement

A letter sent by an attorney to a prospective client explicitly stating that the attorney will not be representing this person.

statute of limitations

A law stating that civil or criminal actions are barred if not brought within a specified period of time. The action is time-barred.

time-barred

Prevented or barred from bringing a civil or criminal action because of the passage of a designated period of time without commencing the action.

When an attorney first meets with a prospective client, one of his or her first concerns is whether to accept the case. The attorney may reject a case for a number of reasons, such as (a) the belief that the prospective client does not have a **meritorious** case, (b) the presence of a conflict of interest (see the discussion on page 56), or (c) the likelihood that the office would not be able to collect its fees and costs of representation. Once the office decides not to take the case, it should send out a **letter of nonengagement** to avoid or refute a later claim by a prospective client that the office was going to provide representation. Initial contacts with the office may have involved a meeting and some phone calls without a clear indication of whether the attorney was going to take the case. As time passes, the matter can become ugly if the **statute of limitations** has run out so that a claim can no longer be asserted. The attorney does not want to be blamed for the fact that the claim is now **time-barred**. Sending a letter of nonengagement helps prove that the attorney never had an ethical or professional duty to act on the case before the claim was barred by the statute of limitations because the attorney never agreed to provide representation.

The test of whether an attorney-client relationship has been formed is whether a reasonable person would interpret the attorney's conduct as an agreement to provide legal services to a specific person. It does not depend on whether a retainer agreement or letter of engagement was signed. The test is not whether the attorney wanted or intended to become someone's attorney. The test is how a reasonable person would interpret what the attorney did. In the absence of clear evidence of nonengagement, attorneys can find themselves in an unwanted and unintended attorney-client relationship.

> *Harry Davis is an attorney. He meets Mary Patterson at a party. They have never met before. When Mary finds out that Harry is an attorney, she tells him that she recently separated from her husband, Kevin Patterson, and that she suspects he is starting to hide the assets they accumulated during the marriage. Harry tells her that she could get copies of bank statements and close any joint accounts with her husband. He also answers her questions about her custody rights. During the conversation, Harry is called away, but before he leaves the party, he gives Mary his card. Nothing else is said.*

Is Harry Mary's attorney? Has an attorney-client relationship been formed? The question is critical because if such a relationship exists, Harry has ethical duties pertaining to confidentiality and conflict of interest. He must treat what Mary told him as confidential and he would not be allowed to represent Mary's husband in the divorce, even if she later hires someone else to represent her in the divorce.

Did Harry become Mary's attorney at the party? He gave her legal advice along with his business card after she gave him details about her legal problem. On the other hand, they never signed an agreement or discussed fees. As indicated, however, a formal agreement and fees are not essential to forming an attorney-client relationship. As of the time of the party, if a reasonable person in Mary's position would believe that Harry agreed to provide legal services, then the attorney-client relationship exists. It can always be ended (see the discussion of withdrawal on page 64), but once it is formed, serious consequences can result if the attorney does not act properly before it is ended.

Some prospective clients shop around for an attorney on the phone, in person, by e-mail, or through attorney websites. While doing so, they may give information about their cases to the attorneys they contact. Until a formal attorney-client relationship is entered, preferably in writing, attorneys must use great care to make clear that they are not providing representation. Websites create a particular cause for concern. When you go to the website of an attorney, you will often see statements that caution visitors that no attorney-client relationship is created simply by reason of the fact that the site is visited or that an e-mail query is sent to the attorney through a link on the site. Before allowing a visitor to send an e-mail question, cautious attorneys make visitors click "yes" to the question, "Do you understand that the receipt of your e-mail does not in and of itself create an attorney-client relationship between us?"

Here is what the American Bar Association says about websites and the attorney-client relationship:

> Websites have become a common means by which lawyers communicate with the public. Lawyers must not include misleading information on websites, must be mindful of the expectations created by the website, and must carefully manage inquiries invited through the website. Websites that invite inquiries may create a prospective client-lawyer relationship.[3] (Rule 1.18)

COMPETENCE

Attorneys have an ethical obligation to represent their clients competently (Rule 1.1). A classic example of an incompetent family-law attorney is one who accepts more cases than his or her office can handle. As a consequence, the law is not adequately researched, filing deadlines are missed, etc. Such an attorney is practicing law unethically.

Attorneys must be **competent**, which means using the knowledge and skill that are reasonably necessary to represent a particular client. The amount of knowledge and skill that is needed depends on the complexity of the case. A great deal may be needed when representing a wife in a divorce case where the issue is the disputed valuation of a husband's partially vested pension or his partnership interest in a foreign business. Relatively less is required for a garden-variety, **uncontested** divorce case in which the parties have no children and no assets. This does not mean that every attorney handling uncomplicated cases is competent. In fact, a number of attorneys have been charged with incompetence in part because of a failure to hire additional attorney or paralegal help for a high-volume caseload. The skill of managing a caseload is a component of competence.

How do ethical attorneys become competent? They draw on the general principles of analysis learned in law school. They take the time they need to prepare themselves. They spend time in traditional and online law libraries. They talk with their colleagues. They do not accept cases that are beyond the capacity of present staff. An attorney who fails to take these steps is acting unethically if his or her knowledge and skill are not what is reasonably necessary to represent a particular client.

Attorneys in a family-law practice must also make sure that their paralegals are competent. Steps to insure that this occurs include the following:

- Supervising every task performed by paralegals.
- Encouraging paralegals to attend continuing legal education (CLE) programs relevant to their assigned tasks on family-law cases.
- Encouraging paralegals to engage in self-study, e.g., by occasionally going to court to sit in on divorce and other family-law cases and reading online material on the family law of the state (see Appendix B).

Victory is not the measure of competence. Competent attorneys can lose cases. There is nothing unethical about losing a case if the attorney used the knowledge and skill reasonably needed to represent a client who lost.

Clients, particularly family-law clients, often seek reassurances about their case. Responding to this anxiety can sometimes be delicate, especially when dealing with clients who have unreasonable expectations about the outcome of their case. Everyone in the law firm, paralegals included, must avoid saying

competent
Using the knowledge and skill that are reasonably necessary to represent a particular client. The noun is *competency*. (See the glossary for an additional definition.)

uncontested
Unchallenged; without opposition or dispute.

anything that could be interpreted as guaranteeing a particular result. For example, compare the following statements:

- "The court will grant you full custody."
- "While we can never predict what a court will do, we have good arguments that we will use to try to persuade the court to grant you full custody."

The first statement can be interpreted as a warranty that the client will be given full custody. If this result does not occur, the attorney might lose a breach-of-contract or breach-of-warranty suit brought by the client. In such a suit, the attorney cannot raise the defense that he or she competently represented the client in the custody dispute. A guarantee, once established, is measured by the result promised, not by whether reasonable knowledge and skill were used. The second statement properly avoids promising a result.

ETHICAL INCOMPETENCE AND LEGAL MALPRACTICE

Two major consequences can result when an attorney is incompetent. First, the attorney might be disciplined for unethical conduct pursuant to the rules of ethics. The discipline can lead to sanctions such as a reprimand and disbarment. Second, the attorney might be sued for **legal malpractice**, which is the failure of an attorney to exercise the skills commonly applied by attorneys in the same area of practice under the same circumstances. The essence of legal malpractice is professional negligence by an attorney. The ethics case and the malpractice case are separate proceedings, although the same conduct might be the basis of both.

The three major errors most commonly committed by family-law attorneys are as follows:

- *Failure to know the law or to apply it properly.* According to the claims statistics of one legal-malpractice insurance company, "A failure to know or apply the law is almost three times more likely to occur in family law than in other areas of practice."[4]
- *Failure to follow client instructions.* Clients often win a case based on this kind of error when the attorney has failed to document everything that the client was told and that the client told the attorney. In the absence of such documentation, courts tend to side with the client when the client alleges that the attorney went against the client's instructions.
- *Failure to obtain client consent or to provide the client with needed information about the case.*

To the extent that errors are based on communication problems, paralegals have an important role to play. Once a case commences, the person in the office to whom the client speaks most often is usually the paralegal. The paralegal will be providing information on the status of the case and relaying messages back and forth between attorney and client. Every such contact with the client should be noted in the file, indicating the date of the contact and the specifics of what was said. These notes can become important evidence in a legal-malpractice action in which the client and the attorney disagree about what instructions were given, when they were given, and what the client did in response.

Legal malpractice requires proof of actual harm.

John Hamilton represents Mary Smith in her divorce action against her husband, Ed Smith. Hamilton tells Mary that she is not entitled to a share of a business that Ed started during the marriage. It cannot be part of the property division. A year later, Mary suspects that Hamilton was incorrect in this advice and sues him for legal malpractice.

To win this case, Mary has the burden of proving that the divorce advice Hamilton gave her about the business fell below the standard of skill that is

legal malpractice
The failure of an attorney to exercise the skills commonly applied by attorneys in the same area of practice under the same circumstances.

commonly applied by attorneys in the same area of practice under the same circumstances. She must *also* prove that this incompetence caused her actual harm. This is done by proving that she was legally entitled to a share of the business as part of the property division in the divorce case. If she is unable to prove causation, then she lost nothing by Hamilton's incompetent advice and the legal-malpractice claim fails.

In the *ethics* case against Hamilton, there is no requirement that his conduct caused actual harm, although such harm is often asserted. Attorneys can be disciplined for unethical conduct if they fail to use the knowledge and skill that are reasonably necessary to represent a particular client—even if this failure does not lead to actual loss by a client.

Can a paralegal in a family-law practice be sued for negligence? Yes. Every person is personally liable for negligence that causes harm. The paralegal's supervisor can also be liable for the paralegal's negligence. Under the doctrine of **respondeat superior**, an employer is responsible for the conduct of employees while they are acting within the scope of employment.

LIMITED-SCOPE REPRESENTATION

Most attorney services consist of a mix or bundle of tasks, such as legal advice on the grounds for divorce, investigation of marital assets, document preparation, document review, document filing, legal research, negotiation, and court representation. Collectively, these tasks are called **bundled legal services**. Suppose, however, that a client does not want the full range of attorney services. The client might be representing him or herself (pro se) but would like the attorney to perform specific tasks, such as reviewing a separation agreement the client has prepared or drafting a letter that the client wants to send to the employer of his or her spouse. Attorneys who agree to provide discrete task representation of this kind are providing **unbundled legal services**. (Charging for such services is called *task-based billing*, *unit billing*, or *project billing*.) Increasingly, clients are turning to the Internet to locate attorneys willing to provide unbundled services.

The main ethical danger in providing unbundled legal services is that the client does not have a clear understanding of the limited nature of the representation (Rule 1.2). A nightmare example is the attorney who agrees to review a document prepared by a pro se client who believes, wrongly, that the attorney will also file a court claim based on that document. The client then loses the claim when it is not filed before the statute of limitations expires. Attorneys have an ethical obligation to take all reasonable steps to avoid such misunderstandings on the limited scope of representation in unbundled cases.

In some states, documents filed in court that were prepared by an attorney must state the attorney's name on the document. In such states, a client who hires an attorney for the limited purpose of drafting a divorce complaint, for example, cannot allow the court to believe that the client drafted it.

COLLABORATIVE LAW

Collaborative law is an example of limited-scope representation because of its emphasis on **alternative dispute resolution (ADR)**. Collaborative law is a method of practicing law in which the attorneys and parties seek to resolve their family-law differences without litigation. It is limited because the collaborative law attorneys do not litigate. It is alternative because of its emphasis on mediation and other alternatives to litigation.

Each party hires his or her own attorney who practices collaborative law. A four-way agreement is then reached in which the parties consent to the limited role of their attorneys. To encourage settlement, the agreement provides that the attorneys will refuse to continue representing the parties if litigation becomes necessary because ADR has failed to resolve the disputes. The parties must find other attorneys if the case goes to trial. The collaborative law

respondeat superior
An employer is responsible for the conduct of employees while they are acting within the scope of employment.

bundled legal services
All tasks needed to represent a client on a legal matter; all-inclusive legal services.

unbundled legal services
Discrete task representation, as opposed to providing services on all tasks needed by a client on a legal matter.

collaborative law
A method of practicing law in which the attorneys and parties seek to resolve their family-law differences without litigation. To encourage settlement, the attorneys refuse to continue representing the parties if litigation becomes necessary; the parties must find other attorneys if the case goes to trial. Collaborative law is a form of limited-scope representation and alternative dispute resolution (ADR).

alternative dispute resolution (ADR)
A method or procedure for resolving a legal dispute without litigating the dispute in a court or administrative agency. ADR methods include mediation, arbitration, and Med-Arb.

attorneys, therefore, do not have a financial incentive to drag the dispute into litigation in order to increase their hourly fees. When collaborative law is successful, the role of the court is limited to reviewing the agreements reached by the parties. Courts often approve such agreements.

Most states say that practicing collaborative law is ethical so long as clients give informed consent to the restriction on litigation in a collaborative law practice. A client who hires a collaborative law attorney may not understand the litigation restriction and may not realize that he or she could hire other attorneys who are not subject to this restriction.

> Obtaining the client's informed consent requires that the lawyer communicate adequate information and explanation about the material risks of and reasonably available alternatives to the limited representation. The lawyer must provide adequate information about the rules or contractual terms governing the collaborative process, its advantages and disadvantages, and the alternatives. The lawyer also must assure that the client understands that, if the collaborative law procedure does not result in settlement of the dispute and litigation is the only recourse, the collaborative lawyer must withdraw and the parties must retain new lawyers to prepare the matter for trial.[5]

The most troublesome ethical question is whether the four-way agreement, not to be litigation attorneys, places an attorney under a contractual commitment to an opposing party. This was the concern of one of the few bar associations to take the position that practicing collaborative law is unethical.[6] Most state bars (and the American Bar Association) disagree. It is true that it is unethical for an attorney to represent a party if the representation will be "materially limited" by the attorney's responsibilities to a "third person" (Rule 1.7[b]). In this instance, the third person is the opposing party to whom the attorney has made a contractual commitment to cease providing services to the attorney's own client if ADR collapses and litigation becomes necessary. If, however, a client gives informed consent to the arrangement, the ethical objection is eliminated. The contractual agreement to withdraw from the case places no limits on the attorney's duty to provide competent and vigorous representation prior to the time litigation becomes necessary. This is the view of most bar associations. They also do not believe that the agreement to withdraw interferes with the attorney's independent judgment of whether litigation is needed.

Collaborative law will not work in every family-law case. The parties must be willing and able, through their attorneys, to engage in robust negotiation in order to reach a settlement of all the issues involved. Some spouses might be pressured into agreeing to try collaborative law without fully understanding what it entails. If there is a serious power imbalance between the husband and wife or if one of the spouses has committed domestic violence in the past and the other spouse feels that the threat of violence still exists, collaborative law may not work. At a minimum, the parties must be strong enough to engage in the necessary give-and-take. Although the client's attorney will take the lead in the negotiations, the client must believe in the process and not feel threatened by it.

FEES

REASONABLE FEE

Attorney fees must be reasonable (Rule 1.5). There is no absolute rule on when a fee in the area of family law is excessive and therefore unreasonable. A number of factors must be considered: the amount of time and labor involved, the complexity of the matter, the experience and reputation of the attorney, the customary fee in the locality for the same kind of case, etc. The basis or rate of the fee should be communicated to the client, preferably in writing, before or soon after the attorney starts to work on the case. This is often done in the contract called an attorney-client fee agreement.

CONTINGENT FEE

Most attorneys in family law charge an hourly fee for tasks that they perform and a lower hourly fee for tasks performed by their paralegals. Hourly fees are paid regardless of whether the attorney achieves the objectives sought by the client. A **contingent fee** is very different. It is paid only if the case is successfully resolved by litigation or settlement.

Serious ethical problems can arise if contingent fees are charged in family-law cases.

> *Tom hires an attorney to obtain a divorce from his wife. The fee will be $25,000 if the divorce is granted. No fee is due if it is not granted.*

Such a fee is unethical and is against **public policy**. In this example, assume that a glimmer of hope arises that the husband and wife might reconcile. Note the pressure on the attorney. The attorney's interest (obtaining the $25,000) could conflict with the interest of the client (the possibility of reconciliation). This conflict might lead the attorney to discourage a reconciliation or to set up roadblocks to it. Reconciliation obviously removes the possibility of the divorce from occurring.

In family-law cases, therefore, contingent fees are unethical if the fee is dependent (1) on securing a divorce, (2) on the amount of alimony or support obtained, or (3) on the amount of property settlement obtained in lieu of alimony or support. This is so even if the client wants to pay by contingent fee. Hence, the following fees would be unethical under this rule:

- The attorney will receive a designated fee *if* the divorce is granted.
- The attorney will receive a designated fee *if* the court issues an alimony or support order above a specified dollar amount per month.
- The attorney will receive a designated fee *if* the court issues a property division or settlement order that is in place of (in lieu of) an alimony or support order.

Some states have limited exceptions to this prohibition on contingent fees in family-law cases. For example, although a state will forbid a contingent fee when a client is seeking *future* support, the state might allow it if the client is hiring an attorney to collect **arrearages**, or past-due obligations. A contingent fee to collect support arrearages of an ex-spouse will not exert pressure on the attorney to block a reconciliation. The marriage is already dissolved. Rule 1.5 of the Model Rules of the American Bar Association does not prohibit "a contract for a contingent fee for legal representation in connection with the recovery of post-judgment balances due under support, alimony or other financial orders."[7]

contingent fee
A fee that is paid only if the case is successfully resolved by litigation or settlement. (The fee is also referred to as a *contingency*.)

public policy
The principles inherent in the customs, morals, and notions of justice that prevail in a state; the foundation of public laws; the principles that are naturally and inherently right and just.

arrearages
Payments that are due but have not been made. Also called arrears.

ASSIGNMENT 2.1

(1) Dan and Elaine were divorced in 2011. The divorce decree ordered Dan to pay $350 a month in child support for their daughter, which he has faithfully paid. A year later, Elaine goes to an attorney to seek help in obtaining an increase in child support to $500 a month. Is there any policy reason against the attorney taking this case for a fee of 20 percent of everything a court orders Dan to pay above $350 a month? (See General Instructions for the Legal-Analysis Assignment in Appendix A.)

(2) Paulene Adams hires an attorney to help her establish the paternity of a child she says she had with Tom Canter. They are not married. The attorney will charge her $2,000 if he wins a court judgment establishing Tom as the father. If such a judgment is not obtained, no fee will be paid. Is the fee ethical? (See General Instructions for the Legal-Analysis Assignment in Appendix A.)

FEE-SPLITTING

fee-splitting

Giving a nonlawyer part of the fee of a particular client. The latter is often done as payment for making a referral of the client. Also called fee-sharing. (See glossary for an additional meaning.)

Next, we examine the problem of **fee-splitting** with a nonattorney (also called fee-sharing). It is unethical for an attorney to share the fee of a particular client with a nonattorney. For example, if a paralegal does particularly outstanding work on the divorce case of a client, the attorney cannot reward the paralegal by paying him or her a portion of the fee that the attorney charged the client. Of course, a law firm uses client fees to pay paralegal salaries and benefits such as a bonus and retirement plan. Such payments, however, are ethical because they are not paid out of particular client fees.

PARALEGAL FEES IN FAMILY LAW CASES

paralegal fee

A fee that an attorney can collect for the nonclerical work of his or her paralegal on a client case.

As indicated, most attorneys charge a client **paralegal fees** for the work done on the client's case by the attorney's paralegal. The following case briefly reviews the standards a court uses when awarding paralegal fees. It also acknowledges the important role that paralegals play in the practice of family law.

CASE

McMackin v. McMackin
651 A.2d 778 (1993)
Family Court of Delaware

Background: *The attorney fees of the husband and wife in this divorce case include work performed by the paralegals of the attorneys. Under Delaware law, a court "after considering the financial resources of both parties may order a party to pay all or part of" the other party's attorney fees (Delaware Code Annotated, title 13, § 1515) (delcode.delaware.gov/title13/c015/index.shtml). An award of attorney fees can include paralegal fees if the standards for awarding paralegal fees are met. After reviewing the standards, the court must decide how the fees are to be paid in view of the income of the husband and wife.*

OPINION OF THE COURT

Crompton, Judge

The following is my decision regarding attorney's fees in the above-captioned matter. I have reviewed Affidavits for Fees submitted by counsel for both James H. McMackin (hereinafter "Husband") and Marianne C. McMackin (hereinafter "Wife"). Wife's total attorney's fees, paralegal fees and costs amount to $12,785.50. Husband's total attorney fees, paralegal fees and costs are $9,768.35....

The United States Supreme Court has found that the term "attorney's fee" refers not only to the work performed by members of the Bar but also to reasonable fees for the work product of an attorney, which includes the work of paralegals, law clerks and recent law graduates at market rates for their services (*Missouri v. Jenkins,* 491 U.S. 274 [1989]).

The definition of a legal assistant or paralegal was defined in *ABA By-Laws,* § 21-12 (1986) as follows:

Persons who, although not members of the legal profession, are qualified through education, training, or work experience, are employed or retained by a lawyer, law office, governmental agency, or other entity in a capacity or function which involves the performance, under the direction and supervision of an attorney, of specifically delegated substantive legal work, which work, for the most part, requires a sufficient knowledge of legal concepts such that, absent that legal assistant, the attorney would perform the task.

Paralegal fees are not a part of the overall overhead of a law firm. Paralegal services are billed separately by attorneys, and these legal assistants have the potential for greatly decreasing litigation expenses and, for that matter, greatly increasing the efficiency of many attorneys. By permitting paralegal fees, the danger of charging these fees off as the attorney's work is hopefully extinguished. By the same token, the danger of charging off a secretary's services as those of a paralegal is very real and present, thereby mandating that certain information be provided by the supervising attorney before paralegal fees can be awarded by this Court in the future. Those criteria are as follows:

1. The time spent by the person in question on the task;

2. The hourly rate as charged to clients (will vary based on expertise and years of experience);

3. The education, training or work experience of the person which enabled him or her to acquire sufficient knowledge of legal concepts. The Court recognizes that not all those who work in a paralegal capacity have a

(continued)

paralegal degree or license, but many of these people do possess expertise, which should be recognized in family-law matters;

4. The type of work involved in detail. The work must *not* be purely clerical or secretarial in nature. Such work would fall under costs and may not be charged as paralegal fees at the market rate. The task must contain substantive legal work under the direction or supervision of an attorney such that if the assistant were not present, the work would be performed by the attorney and not a secretary. However, the assistant may not do work that only an attorney is allowed to do under the rules of practice and ethics. Substantive legal work which may be performed by legal assistants and billed at the market rate includes, but is not limited to, such activities as:

   (a) Factual investigation, including locating and interviewing witnesses;

   (b) Assistance with depositions, interrogations and document production;

   (c) Compilation of statistical and financial data;

   (d) Checking legal citations;

   (e) Correspondence with clients/opposing counsel/courts; and

   (f) Preparing/reviewing/answering petitions and other pleadings.

Applying the above standards to the two affidavits received in the matters sub judice, it is evident that both of them contain the required information. Both affidavits clearly comply with all four criteria previously discussed. For example, they describe the time spent by the paralegal, the hourly rate, and the education training or work experience of the paralegal. The type of affidavit submitted by Husband's counsel is exactly what this Court expects when reviewing fees. The affidavit of Wife's counsel leaves a bit to be desired in that it merely attaches invoices sent to the client. These invoices are very difficult to read and should be consolidated into one document with a separate affidavit attached by the paralegal. Husband's affidavit complies in every respect, but Wife's affidavit is certainly within the guidelines. Both attorneys have described in detail the type of work performed by the paralegal. This work includes such activities as reviewing depositions, preparing subpoenas, reviewing discovery, assisting in preparing Rule 52(d) Submissions, conferences with clients and correspondence. Clearly the type of work involved is that which would normally have been prepared or accomplished by the attorney and not a secretary. . . .

Husband has stated in his answer to Wife's Motion for Counsel Fees that he has no cash available to pay her fees. It is my opinion that his substantial income of approximately $82,000 per year versus Wife's income of approximately $35,600 per year mandates that he pay 60% of her fees or $7,671.30. This amount is to be added to the lump sum which Husband owes to Wife and is to be paid at the same time.

IT IS SO ORDERED.

PAYMENT FOR REFERRALS

An attorney cannot give someone any form of compensation or payment for referring clients to the attorney. With few exceptions, a "lawyer shall not give anything of value to a person for recommending the lawyer's services." "Lawyers are not permitted to pay others for channeling professional work" (Rule 7.2[b]).

> *Alice Davis is a paralegal who works for the law firm of Sullivan and Sullivan. For every divorce client that Alice refers to the firm, she will receive one extra day a year in vacation time.*

Alice is receiving something of value—added vacation time—for referring business to an attorney. This is unethical even if the client consents to this payment to the paralegal.

DILIGENCE AND UNWARRANTED DELAY

Attorneys have an ethical duty to be diligent in the representation of their clients. It is unethical for an attorney to use **dilatory** tactics that cause unwarranted delay in representing a client. An attorney must act with reasonable diligence and promptness (Rule 3.2).

dilatory
Causing delay, usually without merit or justification.

Angry clients often complain that attorneys keep clients in the dark about what is happening and take forever to complete a case: "He never answers my calls"; "It took months to file the case in court"; "She keeps telling me that everything is fine, but nothing ever gets done." Such complaints do not necessarily indicate dilatory tactics or other unethical behavior by the attorney. Events may be beyond the control of the attorney. For example, the court calendar may be crowded or the other side may not be responding. Yet this does not excuse a lack of regular communication with clients to keep them reasonably informed about the status of their cases. Other explanations for a lack of diligence and promptness, however, are more serious and probably indicate unethical conduct. Here are some examples:

- The attorney is disorganized. The law office has not developed adequate systems to process its large volume of family-law cases. The delays are due to careless mistakes and a lack of skill.

- The attorney is taking many more cases than the office can handle. Cases are taking much longer to process than they should take. Additional personnel should be hired to do the needed work, or new cases should not be accepted.

- The office fails to designate backup attorneys to handle ongoing cases of attorneys who are away on vacation or are otherwise unavailable because of pressing work on other cases. As a result, work on some cases stagnates during such periods.

- The attorney is trying to "wear the opponent down" with unnecessary motions and stalling tactics that are not required for competent representation on the merits of the case.

CONFIDENTIALITY

confidential

Pertaining to information that others do not have a right to receive.

Information is **confidential** if others do not have a right to receive it. The ethical rule of confidentiality in a law office is summarized in Exhibit 2-2.

The confidentiality rule applies to *all* information relating to the representation of a client, whatever its source. The prohibition is not limited to so-called secrets or matters explicitly communicated in confidence. Here are some examples of unethical breaches of confidentiality:

- At home, a paralegal tells her husband that J. K. Thompson is one of the new divorce clients in the office where the paralegal works. (The identity of a client should not be disclosed to anyone.)

EXHIBIT 2-2   Rule on Confidentiality in a Law Office

Attorneys, paralegals, and other employees of a law office may not disclose information relating to the representation of a client unless:

1. the client consents to the disclosure; or

2. the attorney reasonably believes the disclosure is necessary (a) to prevent reasonably certain death or substantial bodily harm, or (b) to prevent the client from committing a crime or fraud that is reasonably certain to result in substantial injury to the financial interests of another and in furtherance of which the client has used or is using the attorney's services; or

3. the attorney needs to make the disclosure in order to collect a fee from the client or to respond to a claim (e.g., a legal-malpractice claim) by the client against the attorney. (Rule 1.6)

© Cengage Learning 2013

- In an elevator crowded with strangers, a paralegal tells her supervisor that the adoption notice in the Smith case came in today's mail. (Confidential information should not be discussed in public places where strangers can hear what is being said.)
- In an attorney's office, a client file is left open on the desk, where child-custody documents are visible to and are glanced at by an electrician who is in the office repairing a light fixture. (Extra care is needed to prevent strangers from seeing anything in documents that contain confidential information.)

The confidentiality rule is designed to encourage clients to discuss their cases fully and frankly with the law office they have hired, including providing information that may be embarrassing or legally damaging. Arguably, clients would be reluctant to tell the office everything if they had to worry about whether an attorney, a paralegal, or anyone else in the office might reveal the information to others.

Many law offices communicate with clients by e-mail. Some offices store documents on smartphones and on digital record-keeping services that are "in the cloud" (i.e., stored offsite on a computer company's servers). Of course, client information should never be mentioned on any open social networks such as Facebook. Yet, even "private" or restricted online communications are vulnerable to hacking and other unauthorized access. Cautious attorneys warn clients about the dangers of online communication and obtain written client permission to use any of them. Precautions such as *encryption* (placing text in a code readable only by authorized recipients) are also highly recommended, and in some instances, required.

Confidentiality can also be breached by sending inappropriate *metadata*. When you send someone a document online (e.g., a memo created by Microsoft Word that *you* send as an attachment to an e-mail message), you are sending more than the data that will be read on the screen when the document is opened. Digital documents also contain metadata, which are data about data. They could consist of hidden information about the document, such as the text or language you used in earlier drafts of the document or "margin" comments on the strengths and weaknesses of your client's position. It may be helpful for *you* to be able to read these earlier drafts and comments, but recipients of the document should not be able to read them, particularly opposing attorneys to whom you send the documents! Yet, they can read them if they know how to locate the metadata in what you send. Hence, before you send a document online, you need to find out how to erase the document's metadata. (For guidance, run the search "removing metadata" in Google, Bing, or Yahoo.)

Careless online disclosure of confidential information can also occur when the wrong addressee is typed into the address bar of an e-mail program. Most e-mail programs allow you to accept a suggested addressee after you type the first few letters of a person's e-mail address. When in a hurry, you may hit the *send* button before realizing that the addressee the program suggested was not the person you wanted.

A great fear of law office personnel is that the wrong person will obtain material that should be protected by ethics, by the **attorney-client privilege**, or by the **work-product rule**. This can have devastating consequences. For example, if a stranger overhears a confidential communication by a client to the attorney or to the attorney's paralegal, a court might rule that the attorney-client privilege has been waived on the theory that it is inconsistent to let a stranger or any third party hear what you claim was confidential. Media celebrity Martha Stewart was confronted with this reality when a court ruled in her trial that she had waived the attorney-client privilege covering the

attorney-client privilege

A client or a client's attorney can refuse to disclose any confidential (private) communication between them if the purpose of the communication was to facilitate the provision of legal services to the client.

work-product rule

Notes, working papers, memoranda, or similar things prepared by or for an attorney in anticipation of litigation are not discoverable by an opponent—absent a showing of substantial need. They are protected by privilege. Also called attorney work product.

contents of an e-mail with her attorney when Stewart sent a copy of the e-mail to her daughter.

In some situations, however, it is proper for a law office to breach confidentiality. For example:

> *An attorney represents a husband in a bitter divorce case against his wife. During a meeting at the law firm, the husband shows the attorney a gun and says he is going to use it to kill his wife later the same day.*

In this example, can the attorney tell the police what the husband said? Yes. It is not unethical for an attorney to reveal information about a client if the attorney reasonably believes the disclosure is necessary to prevent the client from committing a criminal act that could lead to someone's reasonably certain death or substantial bodily harm. (See Exhibit 2-2 for other examples.)

CONFLICT OF INTEREST

As indicated in Exhibit 2-1, a conflict of interest is divided loyalty that actually or potentially harms (or disadvantages) someone who is owed undivided loyalty (Rule 1.7). Assume, for example, that a salesman does part-time work selling the same kind of products of two competing companies. The salesman has a conflict of interest. How can he serve these two masters with the same degree of loyalty? How does he divide his customers between the two companies? There is an obvious danger that he will favor one over the other. The fact that he may try to be fair in his treatment of both companies does not eliminate the conflict of interest. The *potential* exists for one of the companies to be disadvantaged. It may be that the two companies are aware of the problem and are not worried; they consent to his working for both of them with full knowledge of the risks. This does not mean that there is no conflict of interest; it simply means that the affected parties are willing to take the risks involved in the conflict. As we shall see, consent can be a valid defense to some (but not all) conflict-of-interest charges. Consent, however, does not mean that there was no conflict of interest.

In a family-law practice, a number of conflicts of interest can arise:

- Multiple representation
- Former client/present adversary
- Law firm disqualification
- Identity of the client
- Business transactions with a client
- Gifts from a client
- Loaning money to a client
- Sex with a client
- Bias

MULTIPLE REPRESENTATION

> *Bob and Patricia Fannan are separated, and they both want a divorce. They are contesting who should have sole custody of the children and how the marital property should be divided. Mary Franklin, Esq., is an attorney that Bob and Patricia know and trust. They decide to ask Franklin to represent both of them in the divorce.*

In this case, Franklin has a conflict of interest due to **multiple representation**. How can she give her undivided loyalty to both sides? They have **adverse interests**, which simply means different goals or claims. On the custody

multiple representation
Representing more than one side in a legal matter or controversy. Also called *joint representation* and *common representation*.

adverse interest
A goal or claim of one person that is different from or opposed to the goal or claim of another.

question, for example, how can Franklin vigorously argue that Bob should have sole custody, and at the same time vigorously argue that Patricia should have sole custody? A client is entitled to the *independent professional judgment* of an attorney, particularly in a **contested** case where the parties are disputing a factual or legal issue. How can Franklin act independently for two different people who are at odds with each other? Franklin's commitment to be fair and objective in giving her advice to the parties will not solve the difficulty. Her role as attorney is to be a *partisan advocate* for the client. It is impossible for Franklin to play this role for two clients engaged in such a dispute. A clear conflict of interest exists. In every state, it would be unethical for Franklin to represent both Bob and Patricia in this case even if both parties consent to the multiple representation. Consent would not be a defense against a conflict-of-interest charge when the parties have the kind of adverse interests that Bob and Patricia have.

Suppose, however, that the divorce case involved different facts:

> *Jim and Mary Smith are separated, and they both want a divorce. They have been married only a few months. There are no children and no marital assets to divide. George Davidson, Esq., is an attorney that Jim and Mary know and trust. They decide to ask Davidson to represent both of them in the divorce.*

Can Davidson ethically represent both sides here? Some states *will* allow him to do so, on the theory that there are no adverse interests between the parties; hence, the potential for harm in multiple representation is almost nonexistent. Other states, however, disagree. They frown on multiple representation even in so-called **friendly divorces** of this kind. The divorce may have been "friendly" when granted, but years later one of the ex-spouses may attack the attorney for having had a conflict of interest. When reminded that both parties consented to the multiple representation, the ex-spouse will inevitably respond by saying, "I didn't understand what I was being asked to consent to."

Ethical problems involving multiple representation are not limited to divorces. When we study adoption in Chapter 15, we will see that attorneys are sometimes hired to facilitate the adoption among the various parties. Facilitation, however, is different from representation. A facilitator performs tasks such as connecting (bringing together) a birth mother and the parties who want to adopt the child (the prospective adoptive parents). Disputes can arise between birth mothers and prospective parents. They can have adverse interests. It is, therefore, unethical for an attorney to *represent* the birth mother as well as the prospective parents.

FORMER CLIENT/PRESENT ADVERSARY

Jessica Winters, Esq., represented Gregory Noonan in his divorce action against his former wife, Eileen Noonan. In this action, Eileen received custody and alimony. Five years later, Eileen wants to reopen the case in order to obtain more alimony. Winters no longer represents Gregory, who now has a different attorney. Eileen hires Winters in her action for increased alimony.

A former client is now an **adversary**. Winters once represented Gregory; she now represents a party who is suing Gregory. Without the **informed consent** of the former client (Gregory), it is unethical for Winters to "switch sides" and represent Eileen against him. Consent is needed (1) when the second case is the same as the first one or when the two are substantially related, and (2) when the former client and the present client have **materially** adverse interests in the current case (Rule 1.9[a]).

The necessity of consent is not limited to cases in which the same sets of parties are involved. Without Gregory's consent, it would be equally unethical

contested
Challenged; opposed or disputed.

friendly divorce
A divorce proceeding in which the husband and wife are not contesting the dissolution of the marriage or anything related thereto. An uncontested divorce.

adversary
An opponent. (See glossary for an additional meaning.)

informed consent
Agreement to let something happen after obtaining a reasonable explanation of the benefits and risks involved.

material
Serious and substantial. (See glossary for an additional meaning.)

for Winters to represent one of his children who later sues the father for support to force him to pay college expenses. Such an action would be substantially related to the original divorce action.

Why is this so? If the cases are the same or are substantially related, the likelihood is strong that the attorney will use information learned in the first case to the detriment of the former client in the second case. Winters undoubtedly found out a good deal about Gregory when she represented him in the divorce case. She might now be able to use this information *against* him in Eileen's attempt to increase her alimony or in his child's attempt to force him to pay college expenses.

ASSIGNMENT 2.2

Is there a conflicts problem in any of the following cases? (See General Instructions for the Legal-Analysis Assignment in Appendix A.)

(1) Irene Farrell is an attorney who helped Bill and Gail Davis, a married couple, set up a business. Two months later, Bill and Gail separate. Gail asks Farrell to represent her in the divorce.

(2) Ted Harris is an attorney who represents Jim O'Toole in a negligence case in which Jim is seeking damages for injuries he suffered in an automobile collision. A year after the negligence case is over, Jim's wife asks Harris to represent her in her divorce against Jim.

(3) Bob Richards makes an appointment with Alex Jacobs, an attorney, to discuss the possibility of Jacobs representing him in his divorce against his wife, Lena Richards. They discuss fees, the grounds for divorce, and Bob's prospects of obtaining sole custody of their child. Bob decides not to hire Jacobs. Instead, he hires Dan Henderson, Esq., to represent him. Lena hires Jacobs to represent her in the divorce.

LAW FIRM DISQUALIFICATION

Two years ago, John Farrell, Esq., represented the father in a custody dispute with the child's grandmother (the mother of the father's ex-wife). The father won the case, but the grandmother was awarded limited visitation rights. The grandmother now wants to sue the father for failure to abide by the visitation order. She asks John Farrell to represent her. (The father is now using a different law firm.) John declines because of a conflict of interest, but he sends her to his law partner down the corridor.

If an attorney is disqualified from representing a client because of a conflict of interest, every attorney in the *same law firm* is also disqualified unless the client being protected by this rule consents to the representation. In the Farrell example, the *father* would have to consent to the representation of the grandmother by the partner or, indeed, by John Farrell himself. The disqualification of the partner and the entire law firm is called an **imputed disqualification**. It occurs when an attorney causes another attorney or law firm to be disqualified. In effect, John Farrell's knowledge about the father is imputed (i.e., attributed) to the partner and everyone else in the firm.

A paralegal can also cause the imputed disqualification of a law firm. This situation most commonly arises when the paralegal switches jobs. For example:

Claire Anderson is a paralegal at the firm of Lawrence Burton, Esq. Her sole assignment is to work on the Vickers divorce case. The firm represents Sam Vickers. One of Anderson's tasks is to make an inventory of all of Sam Vickers's assets. Sam's wife, Karen Vickers, is represented by Edward Walsh, Esq. Before this case comes to

imputed disqualification

All attorneys in the same firm are ineligible to represent a client because one of the attorneys or other employees in the firm has a conflict of interest with that client. Also called vicarious disqualification.

trial, Anderson quits her job with Burton and becomes a paralegal with Walsh, who immediately assigns her to the Vickers case. When Burton finds out that Anderson has performed substantial work on the Vickers case, he makes a motion in court to disqualify Walsh from continuing to represent Karen Vickers.

Claire Anderson is **tainted**. (Any attorney, paralegal, or other employee who creates a conflict of interest is deemed to be tainted.) Will the motion to disqualify Walsh be granted? Yes, if the paralegal reveals any information about the Vickers case to Walsh, her new employer. Suppose, however, that there is no evidence that the paralegal revealed anything about the case. How would the court decide the disqualification motion?

In most states, the court will handle the motion by asking two questions: (1) Did the paralegal obtain confidences and secrets about the case while at the first firm? (2) Did the paralegal reveal any of these confidences and secrets about the case at the second firm? To help answer these questions, the court will use two **presumptions**:

- **Conclusive presumption**. If the paralegal did *any* work on the case in the first firm, a conclusive presumption is raised that the paralegal obtained confidences and secrets about the case. (A conclusive presumption is an assumption or inference of fact that a party will not be allowed to try to disprove. A conclusive presumption is also called an irrebuttable presumption.) No evidence can be introduced to show that the paralegal did not obtain confidences and secrets. For example, the paralegal will not be allowed to testify that he or she did no more than carry the file back and forth between attorneys in the office. Such evidence is inadmissible because the presumption is conclusive that confidences and secrets about the case were obtained at the first firm if it is established that the paralegal did any work on the case.

- **Rebuttable presumption**. Once it is established that confidences and secrets were obtained at the first firm, the next question is whether any of these confidences or secrets were revealed at the second firm. Another presumption helps answer this question, but this time the presumption is rebuttable. (A rebuttable presumption is an assumption or inference of fact that a party will be allowed to disprove or rebut.) The rebuttable presumption here is that the confidences and secrets were revealed by the paralegal at the second firm. (See Exhibit 2-3.)

How can the attorney at the second firm rebut this presumption that the confidences and secrets were shared? By proving that he or she set up a **Chinese Wall** around the paralegal at the second firm.

A Chinese Wall is a series of steps taken to prevent a tainted employee (e.g., attorney or paralegal) from having any contact with the case of a particular client because of the conflict of interest the employee has created in that case. A tainted employee shielded or screened by a Chinese Wall becomes a *quarantined* employee. The steps can include making sure that the employee never works on

tainted
Having or causing a conflict of interest.

presumption
An assumption or inference that a certain fact is true once another fact is established. The presumption is *conclusive* if a party is not allowed to introduce evidence to show that the assumption is false. The presumption is *rebuttable* if a party is allowed to introduce evidence to show that the assumption is false.

conclusive presumption
An assumption or inference of fact that a party will not be allowed to try to disprove.

rebuttable presumption
An assumption or inference of fact that a party will be allowed to try to disprove (rebut) but that will be treated as true if it is not disproved.

Chinese Wall
Steps taken to prevent a tainted employee (e.g., attorney or paralegal) from having any contact with the case of a particular client because of the conflict of interest the employee has created in that case. A tainted employee shielded by a Chinese Wall becomes a quarantined employee.

EXHIBIT 2-3 Presumptions When a Paralegal Switches Jobs		
Paralegal does some work on a case at the first firm. =	This creates an irrebuttable presumption that the paralegal obtained confidences and secrets about the case at the first firm. +	It also creates a rebuttable presumption that the paralegal shared (revealed) those confidences and secrets about the case at the second firm.

the case at the new firm, ordering the employee not to say anything about the case to any employee of the new firm, instructing all others in the firm to refrain from discussing the case with the employee, and physically storing the file on the case in a section of the office away from the employee. If a paralegal with a conflict of interest is effectively screened from the case in this manner, most states will not impose an imputed disqualification on the paralegal's new employer.

IDENTITY OF THE CLIENT

In most family-law cases, it is clear who the client is. There is no doubt who is entitled to the attorney's zealous advocacy and undivided loyalty. In some cases, however, this is not clear. The attorney may interact with multiple family members who do not always have the same interests. Each may need (now or eventually) independent legal advice. Consider the following cases:

- Family members contact an attorney about an aging parent, seeking advice on ways to protect the parent's health and assets. In some instances, the elderly person may be the one who comes to the attorney accompanied by relatives such as the person's children, all of whom are the person's potential heirs.

- A client asks an attorney to draft a will in which he makes provisions for his wife and children. After the client dies, some of the deceased's relatives contact the attorney with questions about the will. The surviving spouse has heard that she has a right to reject what the deceased provided for her in the will and instead select (elect) a percentage of the deceased's will. She asks the attorney about this option. The attorney also suspects that some of the deceased's children have disagreements about the estate.

- For years, a man has physically abused his wife and children. In a recent incident, the police arrest the man and a prosecution begins. The wife and one of the children call an attorney and ask the attorney to represent the husband/father in the criminal case (which the prosecution is refusing to drop). The wife and children, anxious to have the scandal disappear, tell the attorney that they will pay all attorney fees.

- A pregnant woman agrees to allow a couple to adopt her child upon birth. The parties have been brought together by an attorney hired by the proposed adoptive parents, a married couple. A week after the child is born (but before the adoption is final), the married couple separate and file for divorce. The birth mother calls the attorney and asks if she can cancel the adoption. The soon-to-be ex-wife tells the attorney that she wants to adopt the child as a single person. The soon-to-be ex-husband tells the attorney that he wants to adopt the child with a woman he met online who has agreed to marry him.

Each of these situations involves persons who have actual or possible conflicting interests. In later chapters, we will discuss the substantive law that governs these situations, such as the right of a surviving spouse to elect against the will. Here, our concern is with the ethical landmine that can exist when the same attorney interacts with different family members. The temptation of the attorney is to try to satisfy everyone so that the case does not fall apart. Yet the ethical obligation of the attorney is to avoid giving legal advice to persons who do not have the same interests. Providing multiple advice of this kind is almost always a conflict of interest. Once the attorney has identified who the client is, everyone else should be told in writing that the attorney does not represent them and that they should obtain their own attorneys.

BUSINESS TRANSACTIONS WITH A CLIENT

> *Paul Kelly, Esq., is Ed Johnson's attorney in a divorce case. Johnson owns a cleaning business for which Kelly does some of the legal work. Johnson offers to allow Kelly to buy a 30 percent interest in the business. Kelly would continue as Johnson's attorney.*

Assume that the business runs into difficulties and Johnson considers bankruptcy. He goes to Kelly for advice on bankruptcy law. Kelly has dual concerns: to give Johnson competent legal advice, and to protect his own 30 percent interest in the business. Bankruptcy may be good for Johnson but disastrous for Kelly's investment, or vice versa. How can Kelly give Johnson independent professional advice when the advice may go against Kelly's own interest?

This is not to say, however, that it is always unethical for an attorney to enter a business transaction with a client. If certain strict conditions are met, it can be proper. Three conditions must be met: (1) the terms of the transaction are "fair and reasonable" and are clearly explained to the client in writing, (2) the client has an opportunity to consult with another attorney on the advisability of entering the transaction, and (3) the client gives his or her written consent to entering the transaction (Rule 1.8). In our example, Johnson must be given the chance to consult with an attorney other than Kelly on the advisability of letting Kelly buy a 30 percent interest in the business; Kelly must give Johnson a clear, written explanation of their business relationship; Johnson must consent in writing; and the relationship must be fair and reasonable to Johnson.

GIFTS FROM A CLIENT

> *William Stanton, Esq., has been the family attorney of the Tarkinton family for years. At Christmas, Mrs. Tarkinton gave Stanton an expensive computer and told Stanton to change her will so that Stanton's daughter would receive funds to cover her college education.*

Generally, attorneys are allowed to accept a gift from a client. If, however, a document must be prepared to carry out the gift, it is unethical for the attorney to prepare that document. Note the conflict. It would be in Mrs. Tarkinton's interest to have the will written so that a set or maximum sum is identified for this gift as well as a cutoff date for its use. Stanton would probably want the will drafted so that there is no maximum amount stated and no cutoff date. Suppose his daughter obtains a bachelor's degree and then wants to go to graduate school. If the language of the will is vague (and no time limits are inserted), an argument could be made that the gift covers both undergraduate and graduate work. Other questions could arise as well (e.g., does the gift cover room and board at college, and what if the daughter does not go to college until after she marries and raises her own children?). It is in Stanton's interest to draft the will to benefit his daughter under all these contingencies. This may not be in Mrs. Tarkinton's interest.

Because of this conflict, an attorney cannot prepare a document such as a will, trust, or contract that results in any substantial gift from a client to the attorney or to the attorney's children, spouse, parents, or siblings. If a client wants to make such a gift, another attorney, who is not part of the same law firm, must prepare the document. There is, however, one exception. If the client-donor is related to the person receiving the gift, the attorney can prepare the document (Rule 1.8[c]).

There does not appear to be any ethical problem in taking the gift of the expensive computer from Mrs. Tarkinton. No documents are involved.

LOANING MONEY TO A CLIENT

Henry Harris, Esq., is Barbara Atkinson's attorney in a divorce action against her husband in which the main dispute is over the property division. While the case is pending, Harris agrees to lend Atkinson living expenses and court filing fees.

It can be a conflict of interest for an attorney to give financial assistance to a client in connection with current or planned litigation. A loan covering litigation expenses, however, is an exception to this rule. Such a loan is ethical. In our example, the main difficulty is the loan to cover the client's living expenses. Suppose that the husband makes an offer to settle the case with Barbara. There is a danger that Harris's advice will be colored by the fact that he has a financial interest in Barbara—he wants to have his loan for living expenses repaid. The offer to settle from the husband may not be enough to cover the loan. Should he advise Barbara to accept the offer? It may be in Barbara's interest to accept the offer, but not in the attorney's own interest. Such divided loyalty is the essence of a conflict of interest. Hence, the loan of living expenses is unethical. As indicated, however, an exception exists for a loan to cover the expenses of litigation, such as filing fees and other court costs. It is not unethical for an attorney to lend the client money to cover such expenses (Rule 1.8[e]).

SEX WITH A CLIENT

One of the more dramatic examples of a conflict of interest is the attorney who develops a romantic relationship with a current client, particularly a sexual relationship. Family-law clients often seek an attorney when they are most vulnerable. It is inappropriate for the attorney to take advantage of this vulnerability. An attorney with a physical or emotional interest in a client will be looking for ways to increase that interest and to inspire a reciprocal interest from the client. This pressure is not what the client needs. The attorney's own need could cloud the duty to put the client's welfare first. The only way to maintain professional independence is for attorneys—and their paralegals and other employees as well—to avoid these kinds of relationships with current clients. When the case is over and they cease being clients, such relationships are less likely to constitute a conflict of interest.

The American Bar Association prohibits sexual relations between attorney and client, even if it is consensual, unless the sexual relationship began before the attorney-client relationship began (Rule 1.8[j]). Surprisingly, however, only a few states specifically mention this subject in their codes of ethics, and those that do are hesitant to impose prohibitions. In the Florida ethics code, for example, sexual conduct is prohibited only if it can be shown that the conduct "exploits or adversely affects the client."[8] In the California ethics code, a member of the bar shall not:

(B) (1) Require or demand sexual relations with a client incident to or as a condition of any professional representation; or

(2) Employ coercion, intimidation, or undue influence in entering into sexual relations with a client; or

(3) Continue representation of a client with whom the member has sexual relations if such sexual relations cause the member to perform legal services incompetently. . . .

(C) Paragraph (B) shall not apply to . . . ongoing consensual sexual relationships which predate the initiation of the lawyer-client relationship.[9]

New York is particularly concerned about sexual relations between clients and family-law attorneys. Although all New York attorneys must not require or demand sex in exchange for legal work, only attorneys engaged "in domestic relations" cases are prohibited from beginning a sexual relationship during the representation.[10]

BIAS

On how **bias** in an attorney or paralegal can be a conflict of interest, see "Assessing Your Own Biases" in Chapter 1. In our **adversary system** (where disputes are resolved by advocates arguing before a neutral decision maker), clients are entitled to vigorous representation within the bounds of law and ethics. If an attorney or paralegal has strong personal feelings that go against what a client is trying to accomplish, there is a likelihood—not a guarantee—that the feelings will interfere with the ability to provide vigorous representation. If there is interference, it is unethical to continue (Rule 8.4). In New York, attorneys are cautioned that they "should decline employment if the intensity of personal feelings . . . may impair effective representation of a prospective client."[11]

SAFEKEEPING OF PROPERTY

An attorney shall hold client property separate from the attorney's own property (Rule 1.15). Every family-law office has an account that is used to pay items such as salaries, rent, and other office expenses. Client funds must not be placed in this account; client funds *must* be kept in separate accounts (Rule 1.15). The *commingling* of funds is unethical no matter how accurate the records are regarding who owns the amounts in the account. In a commingled account, the danger is simply too great that client funds will be used for nonclient purposes. This is extremely important for paralegals to know, as they are sometimes placed in charge of bookkeeping records in a law firm. Their supervising attorney may tell them that "it's OK to put everything in a single account." Doing something unethical, however, is never OK.

ANTICONTACT RULE

If attorney A knows that an opposing party is represented by attorney B, then attorney A cannot communicate with that party about the case unless attorney B consents to the communication (Rule 4.2). If an attorney knows that an opposing party is not represented, that attorney must not give this party the impression that the attorney is *disinterested* (uninvolved) in the case (Rule 4.3). This is called the **anticontact rule**. Someone is disinterested if he or she is not working for one side or the other in a controversy and will not derive any benefit if either side wins or loses.

> *Dan and Theresa Kline have just separated and are thinking about a divorce. Each claims the marital home. Theresa hires Thomas Darby, Esq., to represent her. Darby calls Dan to ask if Dan is willing to settle the case.*

It is unethical for Darby to contact Dan about the case if Darby knows that Dan has his own attorney. The same would be true of efforts to contact Dan made by paralegals or other employees of Darby. The communication must be with Dan's attorney. Only the latter can give Darby permission to communicate with Dan. If Dan does not have an attorney, Darby can talk with Dan, but he must not allow Dan to be misled about Darby's role. Dan must be made to understand that Darby works for the other side. It would be unethical for Darby to say anything that would suggest that he is disinterested. The only advice Darby can ethically give Dan in such a situation is to obtain his own attorney.

The anticontact rule also covers electronic communication. The rule is violated if a represented party is contacted (without permission) by e-mail or through social-network sites such as Facebook, LinkedIn, or MySpace. (See Ethics Online section on page 65.)

bias
Prejudice for or against something or someone. A predisposition, inclination, or tendency to think or to act in a certain way. A danger of prejudgment.

adversary system
A method of resolving a legal dispute whereby the parties (alone or through their advocates) argue their conflicting claims before a neutral decision maker.

anticontact rule
An advocate should not contact an opposing party without permission of the latter's attorney. If the party is unrepresented, the advocate must not convey the impression that the advocate is disinterested (uninvolved).

WITHDRAWAL

Attorneys are not required to take every case. Furthermore, once attorneys begin a case, they are not obligated to stay with a client until the case is over. If, however, the attorney has been appointed or assigned to the case by a judge, or if the case has already begun in court, the permission of the court must usually be obtained before withdrawal is ethical.

There are circumstances in which an attorney must not accept a case or must withdraw from a case:

- The representation of the client would violate the law (e.g., the attorney is asked for advice on how to defraud the Internal Revenue Service on an alimony deduction).
- The representation of the client would violate ethical rules (e.g., the attorney discovers he or she has a conflict of interest with the client that cannot be cured by consent).
- The client fires the attorney.
- The attorney's physical or mental condition has deteriorated (e.g., alcohol problems, depression due to grief) to the point where the attorney's ability to represent the client has been materially impaired. (Rule 1.16)

An attorney has the option of withdrawing if the client insists on an objective that the attorney considers "repugnant" (e.g., the client wants to pursue custody litigation solely to harass the other parent) or "imprudent" (e.g., the client insists that a motion be refiled if the attorney concludes that the refiling would be an obvious waste of time and likely to incur the anger of the court).

Withdrawal, if allowed, must be done reasonably. An attorney should not abruptly withdraw on the eve of an important hearing or on the day before the client's cause of action dies because of the expiration of the statute of limitations. Before the attorney withdraws, the client will need a reasonable amount of time to find other representation.

FALSE STATEMENTS/FAILURE TO DISCLOSE

An attorney must not knowingly (1) make false statements of "material fact or law" to a court or other tribunal, (2) fail to tell a court or other tribunal about legal authority that the attorney knows is "directly adverse" to the attorney's client, or (3) offer evidence the attorney knows is false (Rule 3.3). One of the reasons the legal profession is held in low esteem by the general public is the perception that attorneys do not always comply with these requirements.

The implications of subsection 3 of the rule are particularly startling.

Karen Singer and Bill Carew are attorneys opposing each other in a bitter divorce case involving a large sum of money. Singer knows about a very damaging but obscure case that goes against her client. Because of sloppy research, Carew does not know about it. Singer never mentions the case and it never comes up during the litigation.

Singer may pay a price for her silence. She is subject to sanctions for a violation of her ethical obligation of disclosure under Rule 3.3(2).

MISCONDUCT

An attorney shall not commit a criminal act that reflects adversely on the fitness of the attorney. Nor shall an attorney engage in any conduct involving dishonesty, fraud, or misrepresentation (Rule 8.4). Conduct of an attorney that constitutes a crime (e.g., stealing a client's property) can lead to criminal prosecution by the state and to ethical discipline by the bar association. If the state decides not to prosecute, discipline for ethical misconduct under Rule 8.4 is still possible if the bar association (and the supervising court) determines that the attorney engaged in dishonesty, fraud, or misrepresentation.

ETHICS ONLINE: FRAUDULENT "FRIENDING"

Assume that a Pennsylvania family-law attorney conducts a **deposition** of a witness in preparation for a trial. (A witness answering questions in a deposition is being **deposed**.) Assume further that the testimony of this witness is **adverse** (harmful or unfavorable) to the attorney's client. While deposing this witness, the attorney learns that the witness has Facebook and MySpace pages. The attorney would like to find out what is on these pages. Their content might be usable to **impeach** (challenge) the witness if she later testifies in the trial itself. To enter someone's Facebook or MySpace page, you seek permission by asking to become a friend of that person. The attorney wants to ask his paralegal or another third party to "friend" the witness without revealing that the paralegal or third person works for the attorney. Is this ethical? The attorney is not sure. He is also not sure if communicating with the witness would violate the anticontact rule since the witness is unrepresented. To help resolve these ethical questions, the attorney decides to ask the local bar association for an opinion on whether it is ethical. (Most bar associations provide this service for its members.) The following opinion is the response of the ethics committee. The attorney is referred to in the opinion as the "inquirer" who is asking the committee for ethics advice.

deposition
A discovery device in which one party questions another (or questions the other party's witness), usually outside the courtroom.

deposed
Asked questions in a deposition.

adverse
Opposed to; harmful, unfavorable.

impeach
To challenge; to attack the credibility of.

OPINION | **The Philadelphia Bar Association Professional Guidance Committee Opinion 2009-02 (March 2009)**

The inquirer deposed an 18-year-old woman (the "witness"). The witness is not a party to the litigation, nor is she represented. Her testimony is helpful to the party adverse to the inquirer's client.

During the course of the deposition, the witness revealed that she has "Facebook" and "MySpace" accounts. Having such accounts permits a user like the witness to create personal "pages" on which he or she posts information on any topic, sometimes including highly personal information. Access to the pages of the user is limited to persons who obtain the user's permission, which permission is obtained after the user is approached online by the person seeking access. The user can grant access to his or her page with almost no information about the person seeking access, or can ask for detailed information about the person seeking access before deciding whether to allow access.

The inquirer believes that the pages maintained by the witness may contain information relevant to the matter in which the witness was deposed, and that could be used to impeach the witness's testimony should she testify at trial. The inquirer did not ask the witness to reveal the contents of her pages, either by permitting access to them online or otherwise. He has, however, either himself or through agents, visited Facebook

and MySpace and attempted to access both accounts. When that was done, it was found that access to the pages can be obtained only by the witness's permission, as discussed in detail above.

The inquirer states that based on what he saw in trying to access the pages, he has determined that the witness tends to allow access to anyone who asks (although it is not clear how he could know that), and states that he does not know if the witness would allow access to him if he asked her directly to do so.

The inquirer proposes to ask a third person, someone whose name the witness will not recognize, to go to the Facebook and MySpace websites, contact the witness and seek to "friend" her, to obtain access to the information on the pages. The third person would state only truthful information, for example, his or her true name, but would not reveal that he or she is affiliated with the lawyer or the true purpose for which he or she is seeking access, namely, to provide the information posted on the pages to a lawyer for possible use antagonistic to the witness. If the witness allows access, the third person would then provide the information posted on the pages to the inquirer who would evaluate it for possible use in the litigation.

(continued)

The inquirer asks the Committee's view as to whether the proposed course of conduct is permissible under the Rules of Professional Conduct, and whether he may use the information obtained from the pages if access is allowed. Several Pennsylvania Rules of Professional Conduct (the "Rules") are implicated in [may apply or be relevant to] this inquiry.

Rule 5.3. Responsibilities Regarding Nonlawyer Assistants provides in part that,

> With respect to a nonlawyer employed or retained by or associated with a lawyer: . . .
>
> (c) a lawyer shall be responsible for conduct of such a person that would be a violation of the Rules of Professional Conduct if engaged in by a lawyer if:
>
> (1) the lawyer orders or, with the knowledge of the specific conduct, ratifies the conduct involved; . . .

Since the proposed course of conduct involves a third person, the first issue that must be addressed is the degree to which the lawyer is responsible under the Rules for the conduct of that third person. The fact that the actual interaction with the witness would be undertaken by a third party who, the committee assumes, is not a lawyer does not insulate the inquirer from ethical responsibility for the conduct.

The Committee cannot say that the lawyer is literally "ordering" the conduct that would be done by the third person. That might depend on whether the inquirer's relationship with the third person is such that he might require such conduct. But the inquirer plainly is procuring the conduct, and, if it were undertaken, would be ratifying it with full knowledge of its propriety or lack thereof, as evidenced by the fact that he wisely is seeking guidance from this Committee. Therefore, he is responsible for the conduct under the Rules even if he is not himself engaging in the actual conduct that may violate a rule. (Of course, if the third party is also a lawyer in the inquirer's firm, then that lawyer's conduct would itself be subject to the Rules, and the inquirer would also be responsible for the third party's conduct under Rule 5.1, dealing with responsibilities of Partners, Managers and Supervisory Lawyers.)

Rule 8.4 [on] misconduct provides in part that, "It is professional misconduct for a lawyer to (a) violate or attempt to violate the Rules of Professional Conduct, knowingly assist or induce another to do so, or do so through the acts of another; . . . (c) engage in conduct involving dishonesty, fraud, deceit or misrepresentation; . . ."

Turning to the ethical substance of the inquiry, the Committee believes that the proposed course of conduct contemplated by the inquirer would violate Rule 8.4(c) because the planned communication by the third party with the witness is deceptive. It omits a highly material fact, namely, that the third party who asks to be allowed access to the witness's pages is doing so only because he or she is intent on obtaining information and sharing it with a lawyer for use in a lawsuit to impeach the testimony of the witness. The omission would purposefully conceal that fact from the witness for the purpose of inducing the witness to allow access, when she may not do so if she knew the third person was associated with the inquirer and the true purpose of the access was to obtain information for the purpose of impeaching her testimony.

The fact that the inquirer asserts he does not know if the witness would permit access to him if he simply asked in forthright fashion does not remove the deception. The inquirer could test that by simply asking the witness forthrightly for access. That would not be deceptive and would of course be permissible. Plainly, the reason for not doing so is that the inquirer is not sure that she will allow access and wants to adopt an approach that will deal with her possible refusal by deceiving her from the outset. In short, in the Committee's view, the possibility that the deception might not be necessary to obtain access does not excuse it.

The possibility or even the certainty that the witness would permit access to her pages to a person not associated with the inquirer who provided no more identifying information than would be provided by the third person associated with the lawyer does not change the Committee's conclusion. Even if, by allowing virtually all would-be "friends" onto her Facebook and MySpace pages, the witness is exposing herself to risks like that in this case, excusing the deceit on that basis would be improper. Deception is deception, regardless of the victim's wariness in her interactions on the Internet and susceptibility to being deceived. The fact that access to the pages may readily be obtained by others who either are or are not deceiving the witness, and that the witness is perhaps insufficiently wary of deceit by unknown Internet users, does not mean that deception at the direction of the inquirer is ethical.

The inquirer has suggested that his proposed conduct is similar to the common—and ethical—practice of videotaping the public conduct of a plaintiff in a personal injury case to show that he or she is capable of performing physical acts he claims his injury prevents. The Committee disagrees. In the video situation, the videographer simply follows the subject and films him as he presents himself to the public. The videographer does not have to ask to enter a private area to make the video. If he did, then similar issues would be confronted, as for example, if the videographer took a hidden camera and gained access to the inside of a house to make a video by presenting himself as a utility worker.

(continued)

Rule 4.1 (Truthfulness in Statements to Others) provides in part that, "In the course of representing a client a lawyer shall not knowingly (a) make a false statement of material fact or law to a third person. . . ." The Committee believes that in addition to violating Rule 8.4c, the proposed conduct constitutes the making of a false statement of material fact to the witness and therefore violates Rule 4.1 as well. Furthermore, since the violative conduct would be done through the acts of another third party, this would also be a violation of Rule 8.4a.

The Committee is aware that there is controversy regarding the ethical propriety of a lawyer engaging in certain kinds of investigative conduct that might be thought to be deceitful. For example, the New York Lawyers' Association Committee on Professional Ethics, in its Formal Opinion No. 737 (May, 2007), approved the use of deception, but limited such use to investigation of civil right or intellectual property right violations where the lawyer believes a violation is taking place or is imminent, other means are not available to obtain evidence and rights of third parties are not violated.

Elsewhere, some states have seemingly endorsed the absolute reach of Rule 8.4. In *People v. Pautler*, 47 P. 3d 1175 (Colo. 2002), for example, the Colorado Supreme Court held that no deception whatever is allowed, saying,

> Even noble motive does not warrant departure from the rules of Professional Conduct. . . . We reaffirm that members of our profession must adhere to the highest moral and ethical standards. Those standards apply regardless of motive. Purposeful deception by an attorney licensed in our state is intolerable, even when undertaken as a part of attempting to secure the surrender of a murder suspect. . . . Until a sufficiently compelling scenario presents itself and convinces us our interpretation of Colo. RPC 8.4(c) is too rigid, we stand resolute against any suggestion that licensed attorneys in our state may deceive or lie or misrepresent, regardless of their reasons for doing so. (The opinion can be found at www.cobar.org/opinions/opinion.cfm?opinionid=627&courtid=2.)

The Oregon Supreme Court in *In Re Gatti*, 8 P3d 966 (Ore 2000), ruled that no deception at all is permissible, by a private or a government lawyer, even rejecting proposed carve-outs for government or civil rights investigations, stating,

> The Bar contends that whether there is or ought to be a prosecutorial or some other exception to the disciplinary rules is not an issue in this case. Technically, the Bar is correct. However, the issue lies at the heart of this case, and to ignore it here would be to leave unresolved a matter that is vexing to the Bar, government lawyers, and lawyers in the private practice of law. A clear answer from this court regarding exceptions to the disciplinary rules is in order. As members of the Bar ourselves—some of whom have prior experience as government lawyers and some of whom have prior experience in private practice—this court is aware that there are circumstances in which misrepresentations, often in the form of false statements of fact by those who investigate violations of the law, are useful means for uncovering unlawful and unfair practices, and that lawyers in both the public and private sectors have relied on such tactics. However, . . .[f]aithful adherence to the wording of [the analog of Pennsylvania's Rule 8.4], and this court's case law does not permit recognition of an exception for any lawyer to engage in dishonesty, fraud, deceit, misrepresentation, or false statements. In our view, this court should not create an exception to the rules by judicial decree." (The opinion can be found at www.publications.ojd.state.or.us/S45801.htm.)

Following the *Gatti* ruling, Oregon's Rule 8.4 was changed. It now provides:

> (a) It is professional misconduct for a lawyer to: . . .
>   (3) engage in conduct involving dishonesty, fraud, deceit or misrepresentation that reflects adversely on the lawyer's fitness to practice law.
>
> (b) Notwithstanding paragraphs (a) (1), (3) and (4) and Rule 3.3(a) (1), it shall not be professional misconduct for a lawyer to advise clients or others about or to supervise lawful covert activity in the investigation of violations of civil or criminal law or constitutional rights, provided the lawyer's conduct is otherwise in compliance with these Rules of Professional Conduct. "Covert activity," as used in this rule, means an effort to obtain information on unlawful activity through the use of misrepresentations or other subterfuge. "Covert activity" may be commenced by a lawyer or involve a lawyer as an advisor or supervisor only when the lawyer in good faith believes there is a reasonable possibility that unlawful activity has taken place, is taking place or will take place in the foreseeable future.

Iowa has retained the old Rule 8.4, but adopted a comment interpreting the Rule to permit the kind of exception allowed by Oregon.

The Committee also refers the reader to two law review articles collecting other authorities on the issue. See *Deception in Undercover Investigations: Conduct Based v. Status Based Ethical Analysis*, 32 Seattle Univ. L. Rev.123 (2008), and *Ethical Responsibilities of Lawyers for*

(continued)

OPINION (continued)

Deception by Undercover Investigators and Discrimination Testers: An Analysis of the Provisions Prohibiting Misrepresentation under Model Rules of Professional Conduct, 8 Georgetown Journal of Legal Ethics 791 (Summer 1995).

Finally, the inquirer also requested the Committee's opinion as to whether or not, if he obtained the information in the manner described, he could use it in the litigation. The Committee believes that issue is beyond the scope of its charge. If the inquirer disregards the views of the Committee and obtains the information, or if he obtains it in any other fashion, the question of whether or not the evidence would be usable either by him or by subsequent counsel in the case is a matter of substantive and evidentiary law to be addressed by the court.

The Committee also considered the possibility that the proposed conduct would violate Rule 4.3 (Dealing with Unrepresented Person), which provides in part that

(a) In dealing on behalf of a client with a person who is not represented by counsel, a lawyer shall not state or imply that the lawyer is disinterested. . . .

(c) When the lawyer knows or reasonably should know that the unrepresented person misunderstands the lawyer's role in the matter the lawyer should make reasonable efforts to correct the misunderstanding.

Since the witness here is unrepresented, this rule addresses the interactions between her and the inquirer. However, the Committee does not believe that this rule is implicated by this proposed course of conduct. Rule 4.3 was intended to deal with situations where the unrepresented person with whom a lawyer is dealing knows he or she is dealing with a lawyer, but is under a misapprehension as to the lawyer's role or lack of disinterestedness. In such settings, the rule obligates the lawyer to insure that unrepresented parties are not misled on those matters. One might argue that the proposed course here would violate this rule because it is designed to induce the unrepresented person to think that the third person with whom she was dealing is not a lawyer at all (or lawyer's representative), let alone the lawyer's role or his lack of disinterestedness. However, the Committee believes that the predominating issue here is the deception discussed above, and that that issue is properly addressed under Rule 8.4.

CAVEAT: The foregoing opinion is advisory only and is based upon the facts set forth above. The opinion is not binding upon the Disciplinary Board of the Supreme Court of Pennsylvania or any other Court. It carries only such weight as an appropriate reviewing authority may choose to give it.

ASSIGNMENT 2.3

Tom and Gail Owen have been married for 20 years. Gail contacts an attorney to seek advice about a divorce. Gail suspects that Tom is having an affair with Rachel Adams and that there are pictures of Tom and Rachel on Rachel's Facebook page. Gail says that she has tried to enter Rachel's Facebook page, but it is restricted to friends and Gail did not want to ask Rachel for permission to friend her. At the conclusion of the interview, the attorney asks her paralegal to find out what is on the Facebook page of Rachel Adams. Discuss the paralegal's options in completing this assignment. What can the paralegal do ethically and what would be unethical?

FALSE NOTARIZATION

affidavit
A written statement containing facts, claims, or other legal positions given under oath or affirmation.

Documents must sometimes be notarized in a family-law case. An example is an **affidavit** that must be filed in court. Unfortunately, paralegals who are also notaries are sometimes asked by their supervisors to notarize documents that should not be notarized. In fact, when paralegals are sued, the most common reason is false notarization of a signature. A signature should never be notarized unless the notary personally watches the person sign the document. A supervisor who is pressed by deadlines might ask the notary to notarize a document that the client signed earlier without the notary watching the signing. The attorney might say that the attorney saw the signing or that the document is simply one of many minor documents that still require a notary's seal. "The client is out of town and we must file the document by the end of the day today," says the frantic attorney to the paralegal. This pressure should be resisted. False notarization is illegal.

Closely related are **attestation clauses** in documents stating that you saw (witnessed) someone sign the document or perform other tasks related to the validity of the document. Do not sign a clause saying you witnessed something being performed or executed unless you actually did witness it.

attestation clause
A clause in a document stating that you saw (witnessed) someone sign a document or perform other tasks related to the validity of the document.

SOLICITATION

There are two main ways that attorneys seek to be hired by prospective clients in their **solicitation** efforts:

1. In-person, live telephone, or **real-time** electronic contact. Solicitation of clients through such contact is unethical if the attorney's goal is to seek fees or other financial benefit ("**pecuniary** gain") unless the contact is with (a) another attorney or (b) someone with whom the attorney has a family, close personal, or prior professional relationship.

2. Written, recorded, or standard (not real-time) electronic contact. Solicitation of clients through such contact is ethical unless (a) the attorney knows that the prospective client does not want to be solicited, (b) the solicitation involves coercion, duress, or harassment, or (c) the solicitation is untruthful or misleading. (Rule 7.3)

solicitation
An appeal or request for clients or business. (See glossary for an additional meaning.)

real time
Occurring now; happening as you are watching; able to respond immediately or within milliseconds.

pecuniary
Relating to money. (A pecuniary interest is a financial interest.)

People in family distress are sometimes so distraught that they are not in a position to evaluate their need for legal services. They should not be subjected to pressures from an attorney who shows up wanting to be hired, particularly if the attorney is not a relative, close friend, or has never represented them in the past. Such in-person solicitation of clients is unethical if the attorney has a monetary or other financial goal such as generating fees.

Frank Ellis, Esq., stands outside the office of a marriage counselor and gives a business card to any depressed, angry, or otherwise distraught husband or wife coming out of the office after a therapy session. The card says that Ellis is an attorney specializing in divorce cases.

Ellis's way of looking for prospective divorce clients is pejoratively referred to as **ambulance chasing**. There is no indication that Ellis is related to any of the people coming out of the therapy sessions, nor that he has any prior professional relationship with them, e.g., as former clients. Ellis appears to have one goal, which is pecuniary: finding a source of fees. His conduct is therefore unethical.

This kind of solicitation would also be improper for the attorney's paralegals or other employees whom he sends out to try to "drum up business."

ambulance chasing
Approaching accident victims (or anyone else who might have a legal problem or claim) to encourage them to hire a particular attorney. If the attorney uses someone else to do the soliciting, the latter is called a *runner*. If this other person uses deception or fraud in the solicitation, he or she is sometimes called a *capper* or a *steerer*.

ADVERTISING

An attorney must not engage in false or misleading advertising in the newspaper, on television, on the Internet, or in other media (Rule 7.2). One of the ways in which the public can be misled is by advertising that creates unjustified expectations of the results the attorney will be able to obtain in the case. The following ad, for example, would be unethical:

"If you are owed more than $5,000 in child support, we will collect it for you."

SUPERVISION IN A LAW OFFICE

Attorneys act unethically if they do not properly supervise paralegals and other nonattorneys working in the office. Such supervision must include "appropriate instruction" on the ethical rules governing an attorney's conduct (Rule 5.3). Paralegals who function without proper supervision are engaged in the **unauthorized practice of law (UPL)**.

Thomas Monroe, Esq., has a busy family-law practice consisting of himself and a part-time secretary who recently quit. He decides to hire Alex Ogden, a paralegal who recently graduated from a paralegal program. Ogden did not take a family-law course in school and has never worked in this area of the law. Monroe gives him the files of all current divorce cases and asks him to "read through them to get an idea of the kind of cases we handle in this office." Since Ogden arrived, Monroe has spent a great deal of time in court. Ogden is often alone in the office. During these times, divorce clients call with questions about their cases. Ogden takes these calls and answers the questions as best he can, based on whatever information he finds in the files and on his general understanding of family law. Here are examples of questions he has answered:

- *"When is the date of my next hearing?"*
- *"Have you received the appraisal from my husband's lawyer?"*
- *"Can I sue my ex-husband for the slanderous things he has been saying about me to our daughter?"*

Monroe is unethically failing to supervise his paralegal. Indeed, there seems to be almost no supervision at all. An attorney cannot hire a paralegal and then disappear. Employees must be given needed on-the-job training and supervision. According to one expert in the field, overdelegation of tasks without supervision can be a serious problem, "[e]specially in the domestic relations area, where paralegals are extensively utilized. . . . I have seen attorneys allow their paralegals to do all of the client's work except for court appearances. There are situations where the client never once met or talked to an attorney."[12] The potential for ethical violations and legal-malpractice claims in such offices is high.

One of the dangers of having unsupervised employees is that they might give clients *legal advice*, which is the application of laws or legal principles to the facts of a particular person's legal problem. This is unethical even if the advice is correct. The first two examples of questions Ogden answered (on the date of a hearing and the receipt of an appraisal) do not call for legal advice. They are simply factual questions that do not require the application of law to the facts of a particular client's legal problem. The opposite is true of the last example. Ogden would be providing legal advice if he tells a client whether her husband can be sued for slander.

It is appropriate to give someone *legal information*, which is general information about the law (e.g., "Our state has specific guidelines on how much child support a parent must pay"). The line is crossed when you cover the facts of a specific person's legal problem (e.g., "Under the guidelines, your remarriage will not affect the amount of child support you were initially ordered to pay"). Once you discuss specific facts, you are probably providing legal advice. Here is how the American Bar Association distinguishes between legal information and legal advice:

> Although the line between legal information and legal advice is blurry, there are important differences between the two. Anyone can sell or give you legal information. On the other hand, only a licensed lawyer can give you legal advice. Legal information is supposed to be general and not based on a specific set of facts. Legal advice is provided by a trained lawyer who uses his or her knowledge of the law to tell you how the law applies to your specific circumstances. When you get legal advice from a lawyer, you also enter

unauthorized practice of law (UPL)

1. Assistance on a legal matter provided by a person who does not have a license to practice law or other special authorization to provide that assistance. 2. Engaging in legal tasks without attorney supervision and/or without special authorization to engage in such tasks.

into an "attorney-client relationship" with the lawyer. This gives you certain legal protections. For example, the lawyer cannot tell someone else what you said without your permission. [The attorney-client privilege prevents this.] Your lawyer can't advise or represent someone whose position or interests will conflict with yours. [This would be a conflict of interest.] You do not have these protections when you get legal information from someone.[13]

MY SISTER'S DIVORCE

Most people are fascinated by family law and almost always have a question or two that they would like to ask someone. Once your relatives, friends, neighbors, and acquaintances find out that you work in a family-law office, you will probably become a target of inquiries. Inevitably, while talking to someone in a social gathering, you will find yourself being asked about child-support rights or about "my sister's divorce." Be careful. If you answer a legal question about the facts of a particular person's case, you are giving legal advice and may be engaging in the unauthorized practice of law. It makes no difference whether you answer the question correctly or incorrectly. Nor is it relevant that your advice is free. Nonattorneys cannot give legal advice on matters that ultimately require resolution by a court. There are some areas, such as social security, where you do not have to be an attorney to answer legal questions. This is rarely true in family law.

It may be awkward for you to decline to answer legal questions, especially when they cover topics on which you may be more knowledgeable than some attorneys. People you know may not appreciate being told that they should consult an attorney for legal questions that they are asking you. Yet this is the proper response. Do not risk misleading someone and being charged with the unauthorized practice of law. There are many self-help books and Internet sites that provide information about the law. If you are aware of some good ones (see Appendix D for legal sites covering your state), there is nothing wrong with referring the questioner to them. This is quite different from telling someone what laws apply to particular facts. Of course, you can also suggest that the person contact your law office for legal assistance.

SELF-HELP AND UPL

We turn now to a different component of UPL. Thus far, we have discussed UPL involving traditional employees employed by attorneys, particularly when the attorneys fail to provide them with adequate supervision. Here we cover UPL committed by nonattorneys who are not employees of attorneys.

FREELANCERS

As we saw in Chapter 1, there are nonattorney freelancers who sell self-help services directly to the public. The freelancers do not work for and are not supervised by attorneys. The buyers of self-help services are persons who, although representing themselves, would like some assistance in their self-representation effort. A freelancer, for example, might:

- sell a do-it-yourself divorce kit containing legal forms
- type the legal forms for the buyer

The nonattorneys providing such services have different titles, such as paralegal, independent paralegal, or legal document preparer. (In a few states, however, the paralegal title cannot be used if the nonattorney does not have attorney supervision.)

Some traditional attorneys are worried by the large number of nonattorneys who are providing these services. A recent management seminar of the American Bar Association on "nonlegal vendors" commented on the "shrinking legal monopolies" once enjoyed by the legal profession: "There's been a permanent shift to self-representation in the majority of divorce proceedings in states such as California" where "increased competition from nonlawyer entities" have "blurred distinctions between legal and nonlegal work."[14]

Nonattorneys can sell self-help services so long as they do not mislead anyone into thinking they are attorneys and do not provide legal advice by selecting the forms for a buyer or by helping the buyer fill them out. Providing legal information or generalized legal instructions to the public at large is not the same as providing legal advice, nor is it the **practice of law**. Kits on divorcing yourself, suing your landlord, incorporating a business, etc., are illegal only when legal advice is provided along with the kits. Buyers must make their own decisions on which forms to use and how to use them. When the nonattorney types the forms, the language used on them must come exclusively from the client.

practice of law
Using legal skills to assist a specific person in resolving his or her specific legal problem.

INTERACTIVE COMPUTER PROGRAMS

Courts have struggled with interactive Internet or computer software programs that are designed to help individuals engage in many legal activities such as drafting pleadings for their uncontested divorces (e.g., www.completecase .com). The question-and-answer format of these programs allows documents to be selected and prepared in response to the specific facts typed in by the users. Some courts have said that this is the equivalent of providing personal assistance on a person's specific legal problem and hence is the practice of law. Most courts, however, have disagreed, on the theory that the website or software is nothing more than the equivalent of a more detailed, user-friendly, how-to book or kit. The do-it-yourself divorce sites are careful to point out that they cannot give legal advice. They make referrals to attorneys whenever a standard question cannot be answered by standardized answers. If, however, the site has human interaction with the user by making corrections and suggestions based on the answers provided by the user, there is a danger that a court will rule that the program is more than a mere self-help service and that the human interaction turns the transaction into the unauthorized practice of law.

As expected, many traditional attorneys are hostile toward computer-driven self-help services. A well-known family-law attorney argues that they delude and exploit people: "It's like the sick person who calls the doctor and the doctor says 'cough on the phone, I'll tell you what's wrong with you.'"[15]

ASSISTING IN THE UPL

Sometimes a nonattorney who sells law-related kits or other legal material will hire an attorney to help him or her prepare or implement the kits or materials without having the attorney provide day-to-day supervision.

Sam Grondon is a nonattorney who sells Do-It-Yourself Divorce Kits. A kit contains all the forms for a divorce in the state, plus written instructions on how to use the forms. Phillis Unger, a local attorney, writes the kits and obtains a royalty from Sam on every sale. She never talks to any buyers of the kits. Most customers make their purchases by mail without talking to Sam. A few customers go to Sam's house to buy the kits. Occasionally, Sam will answer questions to help these buyers decide which forms they need to file and how to fill them out. If he does not know the answer, he calls Phillis for help.

It is unethical for an attorney to aid a nonattorney in UPL (Rule 5.5). Has Phillis done this? Yes, but only with respect to the customers who come to Sam's home and receive in-person instruction on selecting and filling out the forms. Such activity is UPL. By being available on the phone to answer Sam's questions, Phillis is assisting Paul's UPL. It is proper for a nonattorney to sell how-to-do-it material and to give written instructions on using the material so long as the instructions are not directed at a particular person. An attorney acts unethically to the extent that he or she is associated with or profits from a nonattorney who improperly provides legal advice.

ASSIGNMENT 2.4

You are a paralegal working at the law office of David Smith, Esq. Your first assignment is to draft a divorce petition for the case of *Harris v. Harris,* which is to be heard the next day. Your office represents Elaine Harris in her divorce action against her husband, Paul Harris. You never took family law in school. After Smith gives you this assignment, he leaves for the day and asks you to bring the petition to him in court tomorrow. You do the best you can. On your way to court, you see a woman crying on the steps of the court. As you pass by, you give her one of Smith's business cards and tell her that she may want to contact Smith if she has any family legal problems. Inside the building, you see a man standing alone next to a phone booth. He looks like the photo of Paul Harris that is in the file. You ask him if he is Paul Harris, and he says that he is. You tell him that you represent his wife and you ask him if he is going to contest the divorce. After he tells you that his wife is lying about his assets, you walk away. What ethical problems do you see? (See the General Instructions for the Legal-Analysis Assignment in Appendix A.)

◾ PARALEGAL ROLES

- For an overview of paralegal roles in family-law cases, see Exhibits 1-3 and 1-4 in Chapter 1.
- For all financial issues covered in Chapter 2 (e.g., entering a business transaction with a client), a paralegal may be asked to help collect documents and facts outlined in:
  - the checklist in Exhibit 3-1 of Chapter 3
  - the interrogatories in Appendix C
- Conflicts Specialists. In larger firms, some paralegals (often called conflicts specialists) have more specific ethics duties. They may carry out these duties full time or in combination with traditional paralegal duties on cases in the office.

Examples of Duties:

- Maintain a database that contains the names of (a) all clients that the office represents or has represented in the past and (b) all persons who have had significant relationship with such clients, e.g., name of spouse of client (maiden name, for women), names of parent and subsidiary corporations of client, and names of client's business partners and associates.

- For each prospective client, search the conflicts database to determine whether personal, business, or other connections exist between the prospective client and current or past clients.
- If such connections exist, bring them to the attention of the supervising attorney who will determine whether a conflict of interest exists.
- When a new attorney is hired, examine a list of the prior clients of this attorney and identify possible conflicts between clients on this list and the current and former clients of the new office. Bring all possible conflicts to the attention of the supervising attorney.
- When a new paralegal is hired, examine a list of the prior client cases the paralegal worked on in prior employment and identify possible conflicts between clients on this list and the current and former clients of the new office. Bring all possible conflicts to the attention of the supervising attorney.

◾ CHECK THE CITE

In the divorce case of Norman Mailer ("a writer of substantial acclaim"), his wife made a motion to disqualify Norman's attorney. What was the reason for the motion? How did the appellate court rule on the motion? Why did the court say that this was a close case? *Mailer v. Mailer*, 390 Mass. 371, 455 N.E.2d 1211 (Mass. 1983). To read the opinion online: (1) Run a citation search ("455 N.E.2d 1211") in the Legal Documents database of Google Scholar (scholar.google.com). (2) Run a citation search ("455 N.E.2d 1211") or a case name and state search ("Mailer v. Mailer" Massachusetts) in the general search engine of Google, Bing, or Yahoo. (Other sites that can be used to try to find a case online include www.findlaw.com/casecode, www.plol.org, findacase.com, and law.justia.com.)

■ PROJECTS

Project 2.1

In Google, Bing, or another general search engine, run the following search: aa "collaborative law" (substitute the name of your state for aa in the search). Write a short essay in which you compare at least two collaborative law offices in your state. Describe how these offices operate. In what ways are they similar and different in how they pursue the goals of collaborative law?

Project 2.2

Ted is a paralegal who works for Edward Davis, Esq. Davis has a caseload of over 100 divorces. Ted feels overwhelmed because he constantly receives calls from clients asking him legal questions and wanting to know the status of their cases. Davis is almost always in court and hence is not available to supervise Ted. Examine the three ethical codes of the major national associations of paralegals and legal assistants. Quote rules and guidelines from these codes that might be relevant to potential ethical problems in the Davis office. The three codes are as follows:

- National Association of Legal Assistants, *NALA Code of Ethics and Professional Responsibility* (www.nala.org/code.aspx)
- National Federation of Paralegal Associations, *Model Code of Ethics and Professional Responsibility* (www.paralegals.org) (Under "Positions and Issues" click "Ethics")
- NALS The Association for Legal Professionals, *NALS Code of Ethics* (www.nals.org/aboutnals/code)

■ WRITING SAMPLE

Write a memo to your supervisor on the ethical obligations in your state of an attorney whose client is charged with domestic violence against his spouse and children, a charge that the attorney believes is true. In Google, Bing, or Yahoo, run this search: aa "domestic violence" (for aa substitute the name of your state). Also run searches such as: "ethical responsibilities of an attorney who represents a spouse suspected of domestic violence" (without the quotation marks). For more leads, run this search in the Articles database of Google Scholar (scholar.google.com): aa ethics attorney "domestic violence" (for aa, substitute the name of your state). Cite sources in the following order of priority: your state code of ethics, opinions of state courts and bar associations in your state, the American Bar Association's Model Rules, and ethics opinions from other states. (See General Instructions for the Writing Sample in Appendix A.)

SUMMARY

Ethics are rules that embody standards of behavior to which members of an occupation, profession, or other organization are expected to conform. Ethical duties can arise when an attorney-client relationship is formed, which sometimes can occur without the attorney intending to form such a relationship, particularly on the Internet. It is unethical for an attorney to fail to have the knowledge and skill that are reasonably necessary to represent a particular client. Some unethical incompetence can be the basis of a legal-malpractice action if the client can prove actual harm. It is ethical to provide limited-scope representation (including collaborative law) if the client understands and consents to the limited scope of the services. It is unethical for an attorney to charge an unreasonable fee or to charge a contingent fee if the fee is dependent on securing a divorce, the amount of alimony or support obtained, or the amount of property settlement in lieu of alimony or support. It is unethical to share part of a particular fee with a nonattorney. Paralegal fees can be collected for the nonclerical work of a paralegal. An attorney cannot give something of value for a client referral. Attorneys must avoid dilatory tactics that cause unwarranted delay. All information pertaining to a case must be kept confidential. There are exceptions, however, such as when the attorney reasonably believes the disclosure is necessary to prevent reasonably certain death or substantial bodily harm.

Conflicts of interest must be avoided in situations involving multiple representation, representing someone against a person who was once a client, job switches, multiple family members contacting the attorney, business transactions with a client, gifts from a client, loans to a client, romantic relationships with a client, and bias because of personal preferences and belief systems.

Attorneys have an ethical duty to safeguard client property such as by avoiding commingling of client and office funds. The anticontact rule requires an office not to contact an opposing party without permission of the latter's attorney. Unrepresented parties must not be led to believe that the office is disinterested. In some cases, an attorney must withdraw from a case; in others, attorneys have the option to withdraw. The attorney must not make false statements to a tribunal; fail to disclose certain information to the tribunal; or engage in any conduct involving dishonesty, fraud, or misrepresentation (including the use of deception to obtain information on social media); or falsely notarize a document. Some forms of solicitation are improper, such as in-person contact with strangers in order to generate fees. Advertising must be truthful. An attorney has an ethical obligation to give proper supervision to paralegals. Caution is needed to avoid giving legal advice when friends and relatives find out that a paralegal works in a family-law office. Nonattorneys offering self-help veer into the unauthorized practice of law if they give legal advice to their clients in cases that require a license to practice law. Attorneys must not aid nonattorneys in the unauthorized practice of law.

KEY TERMS

ethics	unbundled legal services	presumption
metadata	collaborative law	conclusive presumption
encrypt	alternative dispute resolution (ADR)	rebuttable presumption
conflict of interest	contingent fee	Chinese Wall
conflicts check	public policy	bias
continuing legal education (CLE)	arrearages	adversary system
pro se	fee-splitting	anticontact rule
disinterested	paralegal fee	deposition
legal advice	dilatory	deposed
commingling	confidential	adverse
subpoena	attorney-client privilege	impeach
process	work-product rule	affidavit
meritorious	multiple representation	attestation clause
letter of nonengagement	adverse interest	solicitation
statute of limitations	contested	real time
time-barred	friendly divorce	pecuniary
competent	adversary	ambulance chasing
uncontested	informed consent	unauthorized practice of law (UPL)
legal malpractice	material	practice of law
respondeat superior	imputed disqualification	
bundled legal services	tainted	

REVIEW QUESTIONS

1. What are ethics?
2. Why are many family-law attorneys charged with unethical conduct?
3. What is the authority of the *Model Rules of Professional Conduct*?
4. What are the main ethical guidelines for paralegals in a family-law practice?
5. How are most attorney-client relationships entered?
6. How can an attorney-client relationship be entered without the attorney intending to form such a relationship?
7. How is it possible to create an attorney-client relationship through website interaction?
8. What is attorney competence?
9. What steps can an attorney take to increase the competence of his or her paralegals?
10. How can an attorney avoid giving a guarantee to a client?
11. What is the relationship between ethical incompetence and legal malpractice?
12. What are the three major errors committed by family-law attorneys that have led to legal-malpractice suits?
13. What role do paralegals play in avoiding errors based on communication problems?
14. What is limited-scope representation and when is it ethical for an attorney to provide it?
15. What is the distinction between bundled and unbundled legal services?
16. What is collaborative law and when is it ethical to practice it?
17. How is a reasonable fee determined?

18. When are contingent fees ethical and unethical in family-law cases?
19. What is fee-splitting?
20. When will a court grant paralegal fees in a family-law case?
21. Can an attorney pay for client referrals?
22. What is the attorney's ethical duty regarding diligence and delay?
23. What is confidential information?
24. When is it ethical for an attorney to divulge confidential information?
25. What is a conflict of interest?
26. When is multiple representation unethical?
27. When is consent needed to represent a client against a former client?
28. What is imputed disqualification?
29. How does a court determine if an office should be disqualified because of a paralegal's prior employment?
30. In what kind of family-law case must the attorney make clear who the client is?
31. When is a business transaction with a client a conflict of interest?
32. When is taking a gift from a client a conflict of interest?
33. When is a loan to a client a conflict of interest?
34. How do different states determine if sex with a client is a conflict of interest?
35. How can bias constitute a conflict of interest?
36. What is unethical commingling?
37. What is the anticontact rule?
38. When must an attorney withdraw from a case and when is withdrawal at the option of the attorney?
39. What is the attorney's duty on truthfulness and disclosure of adverse authority?
40. In what ways can it be unethical to obtain information from online social networks?
41. What is false notarization?
42. When is solicitation ethical and unethical?
43. In what ways can advertising be unethical?
44. What are the consequences of failing to provide proper supervision of paralegals?
45. When do nonattorneys offering self-help services engage in the unauthorized practice of law?
46. In what ways does an attorney behave unethically in assisting a nonattorney in the unauthorized practice of law?
47. What are some of the functions of a conflicts specialist?

HELPFUL WEBSITES

Ethical Rules in Your State

(See also Appendix D)
- www.abanet.org/cpr/links.html
- www.hricik.com/StateEthics.html
- www.law.cornell.edu/ethics
- www.law.cornell.edu/ethics/listing.html
- www.sunethics.com/other_states.htm

Guides to Legal Ethics on the Internet

- www.findlaw.com/01topics/14ethics/index.html
- www.virtualchase.com/topics/ethics.shtml
- lawlibguides.seattleu.edu/ethics
- www.findlaw.com/01topics/14ethics/index.html
- law.lexisnexis.com/infopro/zimmermans/disp.aspx?z=1623
- law.duke.edu/lib/researchguides/legale
- www.ethicsandlawyering.com

- www.legalethics.com
- www.freivogelonconflicts.com

ABA Model Rules of Professional Conduct

- www.law.cornell.edu/ethics/aba
- www.americanbar.org (click Model Rules of Professional Conduct)

ABA Model Code (prior version of ABA Model Rules)

- www.law.cornell.edu/ethics/aba/mcpr/MCPR.HTM

ABA Ethics Opinions

- www.abanet.org/cpr/pubs/ethicopinions.html

Bounds of Advocacy of the American Academy of Matrimonial Lawyers

- www.aaml.org (under Library, select "Bounds of Advocacy" in the search box)

International Academy of Collaborative Professionals

• www.collaborativepractice.com

A Basic Guide for Paralegals: Ethics, Confidentiality, and Privilege

• www.cfpainc.com/legalethics.html

State–by–State "Report Card" on the Adequacy of Attorney Discipline

• www.halt.org/news-a-publications/report-cards/2006
  -lawyer-discipline-report-card

Google/Bing/Yahoo Searches

(on these search engines, run the following searches, substituting your state for "aa")

• attorney ethics aa
• paralegal ethics aa
• family law ethics aa
• solicitation attorney aa
• confidentiality attorney aa
• Chinese Wall attorney aa

• collaborative law aa
• attorney fees aa
• conflict of interest attorney aa
• unauthorized practice of law aa
• legal malpractice aa

ENDNOTES

[1] *Report: Lawyer Discipline, Washington State Bar News* 37 (Aug. 1993).

[2] Kathleen Hogan, *Not-So-Innocent Bystanders*, 33 Family Advocate 4 (Fall 2010) (apps.americanbar.org/abastore /products/books/toc/51311003302_toc.pdf).

[3] American Bar Association Standing Committee on Ethics and Professional Responsibility, *Formal Opinion 10-457* (Aug. 5, 2010) (www.americanbar.org/content/dam/aba /migrated/cpr/pdfs/10_457.authcheckdam.pdf).

[4] Dan Pinnington, *Family Law: Increasingly a Risky Business* (American Bar Association, Law Practice Today, Jul. 2005) (apps.americanbar.org/lpm/lpt/articles/mgt07051.html).

[5] American Bar Association Standing Committee on Ethics and Professional Responsibility, *Formal Opinion 07-447* (Aug. 9, 2007) (netfiles.uiuc.edu/r-ferrer/Visitation Schedule/ADR/ABA%20Ethics%20Opinion1.pdf).

[6] Ethics Committee of the Colorado Bar Association, *Ethics Opinion 115* (Feb. 24, 2007) (www.cobar.org [enter "collaborative law 115" in the search box]).

[7] American Bar Association Model Rules of Professional Responsibility, Rule 1.5, Comment 6 (www.americanbar .org/groups/professional_responsibility/publications /model_rules_of_professional_conduct/rule_1_5_fees /comment_on_rule_1_5.html).

[8] Rule 4-8.4 (i), *Florida Rules of Professional Conduct* (2002) (www.floridabar.org/divexe/rrtfb.nsf/FV/0B6C8E5CDCA4 64D685257172004B0FBD).

[9] Rule 3-120, *California Rules of Professional Conduct* (rules .calbar.ca.gov/Rules/RulesofProfessionalConduct /CurrentRules/Rule3120.aspx).

[10] Rule 1.8 (j) (1) (iii), *New York Rules of Professional Conduct* (2009) (www.nysba.org/Content/NavigationMenu /ForAttorneys/ProfessionalStandardsforAttorneys /NYRulesofProfessionalConduct4109.pdf).

[11] *New York Lawyer's Code of Professional Responsibility*, Ethical Consideration 2–30 (2005) (www.law.cornell.edu/ethics /ny/code).

[12] Stacey Hunt, *Attorney Supervision of Paralegals*, Recap 10 (California Alliance of Paralegal Associations, Fall 1998).

[13] Legal Information vs. Legal Advice (www.abanet.org /legalservices/findlegalhelp/faq_legalinfo.cfm) (emphasis added).

[14] Rachel Zahorsky, *As Nonlawyer Vendors, Would-Be Clients Take on More Legal Tasks, How Can Practitioners Get Ahead?* www. ABAJournal.com (Aug. 5, 2011).

[15] Dee McAree, *Online Divorce Services Spark Debate*, National Law Journal (Jul. 22, 2003) (www.zsa.ca/zsa .php?fuseaction=main.featured_articles_item&id=251).

The available CourseMate for this text has an interactive eBook and interactive learning tools, including flash cards, quizzes, and more. To learn more about this resource and access free demo CourseMate resources, go to **www.cengagebrain.com** and search for this book. To access CourseMate materials that you have purchased, go to **login.cengagebrain.com**.

CHAPTER OUTLINE

CHAPTER OBJECTIVES

After completing this chapter, you should be able to:

- Know when a family history is needed in a family-law case.

- Understand the reasons a client is not always sure what he or she wants.

- Know the major guidelines for interviewing clients in a family-law case.

- List the major documents that often need to be collected.

- Know the kinds of information that should be obtained in order to determine if the client's case creates a conflict of interest.

- Identify the emergency concerns that may need to be addressed immediately.

- Know the facts that need to be obtained about the marriage, the children, prior marriages,

contracts about the marriage, expenses, insurance, family assets and debts, and business assets and debts.

- Identify some of the major roles of paralegals in legal interviewing and the compilation of a family history.

INTRODUCTION

Many family-law clients go through life-changing events that bring them to a law office. Competent representation of such clients can require an enormous amount of fact gathering. Often the office must compile the equivalent of a life history of the client and the client's family. This history can have social, psychological, spiritual, and financial dimensions—each of which can involve numerous detailed facts. In this chapter, we introduce some of the essential factual building blocks for compiling this history through interviewing and investigation.

Some attorneys will ask a new client to fill out a lengthy questionnaire on his or her married life. The client might be asked to write a detailed narrative or autobiography that describes major events of the marriage, wrongs or improprieties committed by both spouses, strengths and weaknesses of each as a marital partner and as a parent, changes in each spouse's standard of living before and during the marriage, contributions each spouse made to the raising of the children, circumstances of separations, etc.

Not every office will compile this life history at one time. In addition to asking the client to fill out a questionnaire, there may be an extended interview early in the case and then a series of involved follow-up interviews on different aspects of the case as it unfolds. In some offices, however, the compilation of a comprehensive life history begins as soon as it is clear that the case:

- will be contested (disputed)
- will raise complex factual issues
- will involve relatively large sums of money and other property

Before we begin our introduction to comprehensive fact gathering, we will explore some sensitive dimensions of legal interviewing in a family-law practice.

WHAT DOES THE CLIENT WANT?

Recently, a veteran family-law paralegal was asked what her greatest challenges were in this specialty. She responded as follows:

> The greatest challenges are in dealing with the people. We see the best in people, the worst, and everything in between. Different clients need different levels and types of support from their legal team. Sometimes it takes several interactions with a client and some wrong turns to figure out their needs and expectations.[1]

A number of assumptions can be made about many clients with family-law problems, particularly new clients:

- They are not sure what they want.
- They change their minds about what they want.
- They are not aware of all the legal and nonlegal options available to them.
- The legal problem they tell you about involves other legal problems that they are not aware of and that even you may not be aware of at the outset.

Suppose that a client walks into the office and tells the attorney, "I want a divorce." The following observations *might* be possible about the client:

- The client has an incorrect understanding of what a divorce is.
- The client says she wants a divorce because she thinks this is the only legal remedy available to solve her problem. If the client knew that other remedies existed (e.g., annulment, judicial separation, a support order, a restraining order), she would consider these options.

- What really troubles the client is that her husband beats their children. A divorce is the only way she thinks she can stop it.
- The client does not want a divorce. She is being pressured by her husband to institute divorce proceedings. He has threatened her with violence if she refuses.
- If the client knew that marriage or family counseling was available, she would consider using it before taking the drastic step of going to a law office for a divorce.

If any of these observations is correct, think of how damaging it would be for someone in the law office to take out the standard divorce forms and quickly fill them out immediately after the client says, "I want a divorce." This response would not be appropriate until an attorney first probes beneath the statement to determine what in fact is on the client's mind. The danger exists that the client might be steered in the direction of a divorce because no other options are presented to her. No one takes the time to help her express the ideas, intentions, and desires that are lurking beneath the seemingly clear statement, "I want a divorce."

This is not to say that the office must be prepared to psychoanalyze every client or that it must always distrust what the client initially says. It is rather a recognition of the fact that *most people are confused about the law and make requests based upon misinformation as to what courses of action are available to solve problems.* Furthermore, a client's ability to communicate may be substantially limited because of the emotional crisis that prompted the visit to a law office. Common sense tells us to avoid taking all statements at face value. An important part of an attorney's obligation, therefore, is to present options for the client to consider. (Only an attorney can present the options because they involve legal advice, or the application of law to the specific facts of a person's legal problem.) Clients may not know what they want until the options are carefully explained.

ASSIGNMENT 3.1

For each of the following statements made by a client, what areas do you think would be reasonable to probe to determine if the statement is an accurate reflection of what the client wants? What misunderstandings do you think the client might have? What further questions would you ask to be sure that you have identified what the client wants?

a. "I want to commit my husband to a mental institution."

b. "I can't control my teenage son anymore. I want him placed in a juvenile home."

c. "I want to put my baby daughter up for adoption."

INTERVIEWING GUIDELINES

This section outlines additional sensitivity guidelines for conducting a client interview in a family-law case. They cover the times when a paralegal is conducting the interview, usually a follow-up interview after the attorney has accepted the case, discussed options, agreed on fees, and obtained the basic facts.

1. A primary objective of the interview is to establish a relationship of confidence and trust with the client. Initial contacts can be crucial. All aspects of highly sensitive information must be explored as the office compiles a family history. Any hesitancy on the part of the client can substantially interfere with this task. The client needs to feel that he or she is working with a competent professional who treats the case as extremely important and who is keenly sensitive to the predicaments, embarrassments, defeats, angers, and frustrations that are part of and that underlie the client's narrative.

2. Set aside an adequate amount of time to conduct the interview. You do not want to be rushed. Try to avoid taking calls during the interview. Do not handle or look at any electronic devices (e.g., iPhone) during the interview even if the client decides to use his or her own devices.

3. Dress conservatively and professionally.

4. Clear away open files and papers of other clients. You do not want to violate their confidentiality by allowing a stranger to see anything in their files. Confidentiality is another reason to avoid taking calls during the interview. A client in the office should not be able to hear you discuss the cases of other clients on the phone.

5. Make sure the client is comfortable. Offer coffee or water. Have a supply of tissues available.

6. At the beginning of the interview, give the client your business card that states your name, title, street address, e-mail address, and phone number. Repeat your name even if you provided it at an earlier date when you first met the client. You should assume that clients will not remember the names of everyone they meet in a law office.

7. Make sure the client knows that you are not an attorney. It is usually not enough to tell the client that you are a "paralegal" or a "legal assistant." In addition to stating your title, use the word "nonattorney" or the phrase "I am not an attorney," so that there will be no misunderstanding. Also point out that you will be working closely with the attorney handling the case.

8. Prepare the client for what will happen during the interview. Explain that you may need to meet with the client more than once. Let the client know that you will be taking detailed notes because you consider everything the client says about the case to be important and you want to obtain an accurate account of the case.

9. Maintain eye contact as much as possible even though you are taking notes.

10. Use great sensitivity in obtaining facts from the client. You will be hearing a large number of highly personal facts about the client's life. Think of how you would feel if you were revealing such facts about yourself to a stranger. Think of how you would want this other person to react to what you are revealing. At such a vulnerable time, clients need understanding and compassion. (For a discussion of the sensitivity required when interviewing a woman who has been a victim of domestic violence, see Exhibit 12-3 at the end of Chapter 12.)

11. Listen attentively. The best way to build rapport with a client is to demonstrate that you are listening to everything the client is saying. A useful technique of attentive listening is to repeat back a portion of what the client has just told you. Not only does this tend to assure the client that you have been listening, but it also often triggers the client's memory to provide more detail or explanation. Another active-listening technique is to refer back to something the client said as the basis of a new question (e.g., "Earlier you said that you rarely used the vacation home. Could you tell me more about the vacation home?").

12. Encourage the client to do most of the talking. If you receive a one- or two-word answer, ask the client to explain the answer in greater detail.

13. Encourage the client to express his or her feelings whenever this might be helpful in obtaining underlying facts (e.g., "How did you feel when your husband told you that your daughter wanted to live with him?").

14. Interpret the client's body language. Sitting posture, eye contact (or its absence), and facial expressions are nonverbal communications that can indicate levels of trust, interest, and confusion. Be ready to make adjustments in the way you are phrasing or sequencing questions so that you and the client are working together on the same plane of clarity and trust. Also be aware of your own body language. You do not want your gestures or mannerisms to indicate anything other than the highest level of professionalism and respect.

15. Take your notes in the language of the client. Use quotation marks for important language (e.g., client said she is "certain the father is unable to raise the children on his own"). Avoid extensive paraphrasing in which you restate what the client said in your own words.

16. Never talk down to or criticize a client.

17. Avoid disparaging comments about the opposing attorney or about the client's spouse.

18. Do not give *legal advice*, which is the application of the law to the facts of a specific person's legal problem. If the client asks you a legal question, say that you are not permitted to give legal advice but that you would be glad to bring the question to the attorney's attention. This response is necessary even when you know the answer and when your good relationship with the client makes it awkward to pull back. When you answer a legal question by giving legal advice, you are probably engaging in the unauthorized practice of law (UPL). (See Chapter 2.)

19. Clients will often ask you what their chances of success are. The only appropriate answer you can give is that every case is different and that the office will do the best it can. Never give a client any reason to believe that you think the client will win, even if you do have this belief. An expression of confidence in the outcome of a case might be interpreted as guarantee. A client may have a breach-of-contract action against the office for failure to deliver what a court later interprets was a promised or guaranteed result.

20. Let the client know how to reach you if he or she thinks of other relevant information after the interview is concluded.

21. Make mental notes on the client's personality. Here is how one attorney described this aspect of the interview: "Assess the client's personality" and whether the office "can work with this person. Watch for red flags or danger signals, including the client who is emotionally distraught or vengeful; is inconsistent with the story or avoids answering questions; has unrealistic objectives; suggests use of improper influence or other unethical or illegal conduct; rambles, wanders off the subject, or constantly interrupts you"; tells the office "how to run the case; has already discharged or filed disciplinary complaints against other lawyers; has a personality disorder; or is flirtatious."[2] In your report or memorandum to your supervisor on the interview, be sure to include your observations and assessments relevant to concerns such as these. They, of course, would never be mentioned to the client.

FAMILY HISTORY CHECKLIST

The inclination of a cautious office is to be comprehensive about facts. The items in the checklist of Exhibit 3-1 aim for such comprehensiveness.[3] Yet a checklist is no more than a starting point. Effective interviewers are willing to add questions to a checklist even if they do not appear to be directly on point. Relevant facts have a way of materializing from seemingly irrelevant lines of inquiry. Sometimes you do not know what you are looking for until you find it.

EXHIBIT 3-1   Checklist for Compiling a Family History

I. BASIC INFORMATION

- Client's name.
- Street address.
- E-Mail address(es).
- Social security number.
- Facebook and other social media address(es).
- Phone number, residence.
- Phone number, business.
- Cell number(s).
- Same information as above for client's spouse.
- Date of marriage (DOM).
- Date of separation (DOS).
- How did the client select this law office? Referral?
- Is the spouse represented by an attorney? If so, when was the attorney retained? Who is paying for his or her services? What is the attorney's name, address, phone number, e-mail address, web address, and fax number?

  - *If the spouse is represented by an attorney, all contacts with the spouse must be through that attorney. (See anticontact rule in Chapter 2.)*

II. DOCUMENTS CLIENT SHOULD BRING TO THE LAW OFFICE

- Marriage license.
- Prior divorce or annulment decree with this or other spouse(s).
- Powers of attorney the client and spouse have given each other.
- Premarital agreement.

EXHIBIT 3-1 *(continued)*

- Documents client was given prior to signing the premarital agreement.
- Other written agreements between client and spouse entered prior to and during the marriage, e.g., child-custody agreements.
- Federal, state, and local tax returns (last five years).
- Net worth statements (financial statements) of client, spouse, or business (e.g., financial statement filed when applying for a loan).
- Tax assessments or bills.
- Deeds to property the client or spouse obtained as a gift or that was purchased prior to the marriage.
- Deeds to property the client or spouse obtained as a gift or that was purchased during the marriage.
- Recent pay stubs of client and spouse.
- Business formation records (e.g., articles of incorporation, partnership agreement, board of director minutes).
- Recent bank statements for all personal and business accounts of client and spouse.
- Recent securities statements (e.g., mutual fund report).
- Recent statements from pension fund.
- Loan or refinancing applications made by client or spouse.
- Recent major bills (e.g., mortgage, tuition, rent).
- Credit reports on client, spouse, or business from TransUnion, Experian, Equifax, or other credit information company.
- Wills and codicils to wills.
- Trusts.
- Medical records of client on major current ailments.
- Police records if relevant to domestic violence committed during the marriage or since the separation.
- Separation agreement the parties have signed or drafts of such an agreement the parties considered.
- Birth certificates of children.
- Court documents on litigation in which the client, the spouse, or both were parties.
- Client's résumé.
- Spouse's résumé.

III. CONFLICT-OF-INTEREST INFORMATION

- Client's maiden name (if a woman).
- Other names used by client.
- Has this office ever represented the client before?
- Has this office ever represented any relatives of the client?
- Has this office ever represented any business associates of the client?
- Names of other attorneys the client has contacted about this case.
- Names of attorneys who have represented the client on any other matter in the past.
- Spouse's full name.
- Other names used by spouse.
- Has this office ever represented the spouse before?
- Has this office ever had any contact with the spouse before?

• If the client does not have any of these documents, ask the client if he or she thinks they exist and, if so, where they might be obtained. For some documents, the client may be asked to sign a form giving the office authorization to obtain a copy of the document.

• Before a law office accepts a case, it must do a conflicts check to determine whether a conflict of interest would prevent the office from representing the prospective client (e.g., because the office once represented an opponent of the prospective client). (See Chapter 2.)

• There is a danger that if a person once contacted the office about the marriage, the office might be precluded from representing that person's spouse even if the person eventually hires another attorney. Some communications with an attorney can create an attorney-client relationship regardless of whether the attorney is hired. (See Chapter 2.)

- Has this office ever represented any relatives of the spouse?
- Has this office ever represented any business associates of the spouse?
- Details of all contacts the spouse has had with the office in the past (e.g., a general inquiry about a legal matter during the marriage).
- Names of other attorneys who have represented the spouse on any matter in the past.

IV. EMERGENCY CONCERNS

- If court proceedings have already been initiated by the client or spouse, what are the next court dates on which the client is required to make an appearance or to file pleadings?
- Does the client think there is a danger that the spouse will remove the children out of state?
- Is the spouse abusing the client or the children?
- Does the client think there is a danger the spouse will give away marital assets?
- Does the client think there is a danger the spouse will conceal marital assets?
- Does the client's spouse know that the client is seeking legal services? If not, is there a danger of a hostile reaction when this becomes known (e.g., domestic violence)?
- While waiting for a court date on the divorce case, do the client and children have immediate support needs?
- Is the client suffering emotional trauma? (Provide referral list of psychologists, other counselors, or support agencies.)
- Did the parties have joint credit cards or joint charge cards?
- Did the client cosign or guarantee a loan secured by the spouse?
- Is the client or spouse currently pregnant? Due date? What prenatal care is underway?
- If a divorce occurs, could there be immigration consequences if the client, the spouse, and/or the children are not citizens?

V. BACKGROUND

- How long has the client lived at current address?
- How many consecutive months has the client been a resident of this county?
- Address of the most recent three prior residences of the client and the dates at each residence.
- Client's date of birth.
- Client's place of birth.
- Client's race.
- Client's social security number.
- Client's present occupation(s) and length of time in this field. Business address, phone/cell number(s), e-mail address(es), web address, and fax number.
- Prior occupations of the client.
- Highest grade of school or college completed. Date(s) completed.
- Client's religious affiliation and extent of involvement.
- Length of time spouse has lived at current residence.
- Number of consecutive months spouse been a resident of this county.
- Addresses of the most recent three prior residences of spouse and the dates at each residence.
- Spouse's date of birth.
- Spouse's place of birth.
- Spouse's race.
- Spouse's social security number.
- Spouse's present occupation(s) and length of time in this field.

*Sidebar notes:*

- *Protective orders may be needed if there is a danger of violence or of a change in the status of marital property such as by selling it or moving it out of the state. (See Chapter 8.)*
- *A motion for temporary support and attorney fees may be needed pending the outcome of the case— pendente lite—while the litigation is going on. (See Chapter 8.)*
- *Some attorneys advise their clients to cancel all joint credit or charge accounts, apply for an account in his or her own name, and notify lenders to cancel future loans for which the client provided earlier authorization. (See Chapter 8.)*
- *Length of residence may be important to establish the court's in rem jurisdiction (through domicile) and to establish venue. (See Chapter 7.)*
- *Race and religious practices may become relevant in child-custody issues, although custody decisions cannot be based solely on race. (See Chapter 9.)*

(continued)

EXHIBIT 3-1 *(continued)*

- Business address of spouse, phone/cell number(s), e-mail address(es), web address, and fax number.
- Prior occupations of the spouse.
- Highest grade of school or college completed. Date(s) completed.
- Spouse's religious affiliation and extent of involvement.

VI. MARITAL FACTS

Marriage

- Date of current marriage.
- Place where marriage ceremony occurred.
- Date on marriage license/certificate.
- Compliance with blood tests or other formalities required to obtain the license.
- Name and address of person who performed marriage ceremony.
- Names and addresses of witnesses to the marriage ceremony.
- [If doubt exists on whether the parties are married] Facts that would lead others to believe the parties were married (e.g., whether they used the same last name, whether they introduced each other to others as "my husband" and "my wife").

  • *The belief of others as to whether the parties are married could be relevant to whether a common-law marriage was formed (in states that allow such marriages). (See Chapter 5.)*

- At the time of the marriage, did either party have a prior marriage that was not ended by divorce or death?
- How old were the client and spouse when they married?
- Are they related to each other by blood (e.g., cousins) or by marriage (e.g., in-laws)?
- Were both parties able to perform all marital functions upon marriage?
- Did both parties go through the marriage ceremony with the full and free intention to become husband and wife?
- When the parties went through the marriage ceremony, did either lie about or misrepresent important facts that would have led to a cancellation of the ceremony if the facts were known (e.g., a willingness to have children)?

  • *These questions are relevant to whether grounds for an annulment (e.g., nonage or fraud) might exist. (See Chapter 6.)*

Children

- For each child born to the marriage, state his or her full name, date of birth, place of birth, current address, prior addresses, length of time child has spent at current address and at each prior address, adults with whom the child has lived since birth, past sources of support, current sources of support, and the child's desire and ability to attend college.
- For each child to whom the client or the spouse was an adoptive parent, guardian, or stepparent, state the child's full name, date of birth, place of birth, current address, prior addresses, length of time child has spent at current address and at each prior address, adults with whom the child has lived since birth, past sources of support, current sources of support, and the child's desire and ability to attend college. Also state the names and addresses of the birth parents and the circumstances of the child's coming into the family.
- Have any of the children been emancipated?

  • *A child who is emancipated is legally independent of his or her parent or legal guardian. (See Chapter 14.)*

Prior Marriages

- If client was ever married before, state the name of each former spouse; his or her current or last known address; the date, place, and circumstances of each marriage; how each marriage was terminated; the names of all children born, adopted, or who otherwise lived with the family during this marriage; and how these children are (or were) supported.
- If the spouse of the client has a prior marriage or marriages, state the name of each former spouse; his or her current or last known address; the date, place, and circumstances of each marriage; how each marriage was terminated; the names of all children born, adopted, or who otherwise lived with the family during this marriage; and how these children are (or were) supported.

- Known sources of support (employment, family business) of former spouses.
- Outstanding debts or obligations owed to or by former spouses (e.g., alimony, child support, property division). Was there a court order?

Deterioration of Marriage

- Does the client want the divorce? Why or why not?
- Does the client's spouse want the divorce? Why or why not?
- When did the marriage start to deteriorate? State the circumstances.
- For what length of time have the parties had marital difficulties?
- What is the date of the last sexual relations with spouse?
- Has there been domestic violence or the threat of such violence? State the circumstances.
- Are the parties now separated?
- If the parties are separated, state the date the separation began, who initiated it, the reason the client thinks the separation occurred, and the reason the spouse thinks the separation occurred.
- Where have each party and the children lived since the separation? Include the dates.
- How have each party and the children been supported since the separation?
- Have the parties ever separated in the past?
- If the parties have ever separated in the past, for each separation, state the dates involved, who initiated the separation, the reason the client thinks the separation occurred, the reason the spouse thinks the separation occurred, where each party and the children lived during the separation, how each party and the children were supported during the separation, and the circumstances of the end of the separation leading to a resumption of the marital relationship.
- Does the client think there is a realistic chance of reconciliation? Why or why not?
- Does the spouse think there is a realistic chance of reconciliation? Why or why not?
- Have the parties ever attempted marital counseling? If so, who initiated each effort and to what extent was the effort successful?
- Who was the marital counselor? How was he or she paid?
- Does either party now want to try marital counseling? Why or why not?

- *Because of no-fault divorce, facts on who caused the breakdown of the marriage (marital fault) are generally not relevant to whether a divorce will be granted, but may be relevant to spousal support and child custody in some states. (See Chapters 7 to 9.)*

VII. PRIOR CONTRACTS

Premarital Agreement

- Do the parties have a premarital agreement?
- If a premarital agreement exists, what date was it signed?
- List the names and addresses of the attorneys, if any, who represented either party during the negotiation and drafting of the premarital agreement.
- What other individuals were consulted in the creation of the agreement (e.g., accountant, financial planner, business associate, friend, or relative).
- Describe the nature of the disclosure the spouse gave the client concerning the spouse's financial assets and worth before the client signed the agreement.
- Describe the nature of the disclosure the client gave the spouse concerning the client's financial assets and worth before the spouse signed the agreement.
- What rights did each side waive in the agreement (e.g., right of support)?
- Summarize the major provisions in the agreement for the client and for the spouse in the event of a divorce.
- Summarize the major provisions in the agreement for the client and for the spouse upon the death of either during the marriage.
- What is the location of the original agreement?

- *The validity of a premarital agreement may depend, in part, on whether there was full disclosure of each other's assets and liabilities prior to signing the premarital agreement. (See Chapter 4.)*

(continued)

EXHIBIT 3-1 *(continued)*

Separation Agreement

- Have the parties discussed or entered a separation agreement?
- What date was the agreement signed?
- Were the parties already separated when the agreement was signed?
- List the names and addresses of the attorneys, if any, who represented either party during the negotiation and drafting of the separation agreement.
- Summarize the major provisions in the agreement on support, custody, and property division.
- What is the location of the original agreement?

Other Agreements

- Have the client and spouse entered employment agreements with each other at a place of business? If so, state the details of the agreement(s).
- Has either spouse lent the other money?
- If lending has taken place, describe the major terms of the agreement (e.g., interest charged). What is the present status of the loan? What amounts have been repaid?
- Where are the loan documents kept?
- List the names and addresses of the attorneys, if any, who represented either party during the negotiation and drafting of the loan agreement.
- Give the details of any other postnuptial agreement between the parties.
- Has the client's spouse ever borrowed money from a relative of the client? Describe the circumstances and present status of the loan.
- Has the client ever borrowed money from a relative of his or her spouse? Describe the circumstances and present status of the loan.

- *Agreements between spouses during the marriage are called postnuptial agreements. (See Chapter 4.)*

VIII. ITEMIZED EXPENSES

(Where relevant, state whether the expense is for client only or for children only. Use monthly figures where appropriate. To obtain a monthly figure for an expense incurred less frequently than monthly, add the total spent for that item for the year and divide by 12.)

- Mortgage (state if payments include taxes and insurance).
- Rent.
- Real property taxes.
- Homeowner association fees.
- Utilities: gas/oil.
- Utilities: electric.
- Utilities: water and sewer.
- Water softener.
- Telephones (landline, cell, other).
- Internet service provider.
- Maintenance of house.
- Maintenance of swimming pool.
- Gardener.
- Groceries.
- Restaurants.
- Clothes: purchase.
- Clothes: maintenance (tailor, laundry, etc.).
- Shoes.

- Maid.
- Cleaning service.
- Baby-sitter.
- Day care center.
- School expenses: tuition.
- School expenses: books and supplies.
- School expenses: tutoring.
- School expenses: transportation.
- School expenses: after-school programs.
- School expenses: miscellaneous.
- Extracurricular lessons: music, dance, sports, theater, etc.
- Equipment maintenance: music, sports, etc.
- Summer camp.
- Visitation expenses when child visits noncustodial parent (transportation, phone calls, meals, etc.).
- Car: payments.
- Car: gas.
- Car: maintenance.
- Car: registration.
- Car: tolls.
- Car: automobile club dues.
- Insurance premium: house.
- Insurance premium: car.
- Insurance premium: life.
- Insurance premium: dental.
- Insurance premium: health.
- Insurance premium: disability.
- Insurance premium: umbrella.
- Health costs not covered by insurance for medical doctors, dentists, orthodontists, homeopathic/ holistic practitioners, prescription and nonprescription drugs, glasses and eye care, and other medical-related costs.
- Hairdresser.
- Haircuts.
- Toiletries and cosmetics.
- Pets: veterinarian.
- Pets: food and supplies.
- Entertainment.
- Cable TV access.
- Vacation.
- Computer supplies.
- Camera supplies.
- Contribution: church/synagogue.
- Contribution: other charity.
- Newspaper/magazine subscriptions.
- Allowances for child.
- Membership: country club.

(continued)

EXHIBIT 3-1   *(continued)*

- Other memberships (e.g., gym).
- Cost of gifts (birthdays, holidays, etc.).
- Payments to IRA or other retirement fund.
- Accountant/tax preparer fees.
- Court-ordered payments of child support or alimony from a prior marriage.
- Miscellaneous expenses.

IX. HEALTH INFORMATION

- Current health of client.
- Current health of spouse.
- Current health of children.
- Physical and mental health history of client (covering periods before marriage, during marriage, and since separation): major problems, names and addresses of treating physicians or counselors, dates of hospitalizations or other major treatments, diagnosis for future, etc.
- Physical and mental health history of spouse (covering periods before marriage, during marriage, and since separation): major problems, names and addresses of treating physicians or counselors, dates of hospitalizations or other major treatments, diagnosis for future, etc.
- Physical and mental health history of each child: major problems, names and addresses of treating physicians or counselors, dates of hospitalizations or other major treatments, diagnosis for future, etc.

- *The health facts can be relevant to many issues (e.g., future medical expenses, need for alimony, ability to care for a child, capacity to understand agreements signed before and during the marriage). (See Chapters 4, 6, 8, 9, and 10)*

X. WILLS AND TRUSTS

Wills

- Wills in existence (client's separate will, spouse's separate will, joint will, etc.). Address the following topics for each will:
- Date signed/executed.
- Name and address of attorney who prepared the will.
- Names and addresses of witnesses.
- Name and address of initial executor and of alternate/successor executor.
- Guardian for minor children.
- Primary beneficiaries (who receives what).
- Remainder beneficiaries.
- Codicils or amendments (state the reasons for changes, dates executed, summary of changes).
- Names and addresses of witnesses.
- Location of original instruments.

Trusts

- Kinds of trusts in existence (testamentary trust, inter vivos trust, etc.). Address the following topics for each trust:
- Date signed/executed.
- Name and address of attorney who prepared the trust.
- Names and addresses of witnesses.
- Name and address of initial trustee and of alternate/successor trustee.
- Description of assets/property (principal) to go in the trust.
- Lifetime beneficiaries.
- Remainder beneficiaries.

- Amendments (state the reasons for changes, dates executed, summary of changes).
- Location of original instruments.

XI. REARING AND CUSTODY OF CHILDREN

- Names of natural (birth) children, adopted children, stepchildren, and other children living with client or spouse. Address the following topics for each child:
- Age.
- Location of birth certificate.
- Names and addresses of natural parents.
- Who should have custody according to the client? Cover the client's views on the options of sole physical custody, joint physical custody, sole legal custody, and joint legal custody.
- Who should have custody according to the client's spouse? Cover the spouse's views on the options of sole physical custody, joint physical custody, sole legal custody, and joint legal custody.
- What are the strengths and weaknesses of the client as a parent?
- What are the strengths and weaknesses of spouse as a parent?

    - *All of these topics will be relevant to a court's decision on child custody. (See Chapter 9.)*

- Career responsibilities and goals of the client and how they affect availability of client to care for the child.
- Career responsibilities and goals of the spouse and how they affect availability of spouse to care for the child.
- Does either client or spouse expect to move to another area in the future? If so, why? How will the move affect visitation opportunities of the noncustodial parent?

    - *Disputes over child relocation are called move-away cases. (See Chapter 9.)*

- What relatives of the client are in the area who are available to help client with child care?
- What relatives of the spouse are in the area who are available to help spouse with child care?
- What is the child's relationship with other children in the home?
- List court actions or orders to date, e.g., paternity, child support, guardianship, adoption, and juvenile delinquency (include dates, courts and agencies involved, attorneys for parties, reasons court action was initiated, outcome/decision of court, major events since court actions or orders occurred).
- Police involvement, e.g., misconduct by child, abuse of child by others (include dates, enforcement agencies involved, reasons police became involved, action taken by police, major events since police involvement occurred).
- Has child protective services investigated the home? If so, state the circumstances.
- Regarding the religious activities of child, describe role of each parent.
- Regarding major school events (teacher conferences, assembly performances, etc.), describe role of each parent.

    - *All of these factors are relevant to a court's custody decision based on the best interests of the child. (See Chapter 9.)*

- Regarding homework (assistance provided, checking for completion, etc.), describe role of each parent.
- Regarding after-school activities at home, at friend's house, at playground (amount of supervision, transportation provided, etc.), describe role of each parent.
- Regarding sports (transportation provided, attendance at games, etc.), describe role of each parent.
- Regarding medical and dental appointments, describe role of each parent.
- Regarding birthdays, describe role of each parent.
- Regarding vacations, describe role of each parent.
- Regarding discipline at home, describe role of each parent.
- Regarding other major events in child's life, describe role of each parent.
- Describe the attitude of the child toward each parent. Where would child like to live?

    - *Courts will consider the wishes of a child, depending upon the age of the child. (See Chapter 9.)*

- Describe the client's efforts to encourage child to have a positive or a negative attitude about spouse.

(continued)

EXHIBIT 3-1 *(continued)*

- Describe the spouse's efforts to encourage child to have a positive or a negative attitude about client.
- Describe the child's awareness of client's romantic relationships with others since separation from the spouse. What is its impact on the child?
- Describe the child's awareness of spouse's romantic relationships with others since separation from the client. What is its impact on the child?
- What third parties exist who might be witnesses to the home environment (e.g., neighbors, relatives, teachers, day care providers, clergy, counselors, friends)?

- *When a child is hostile to one of the parents, some courts might consider evidence of parental alienation syndrome. (See Chapter 9.)*

XII. BUSINESS INTERESTS

- For any and all businesses in which client or spouse had (or has) an ownership interest (solely owned by client, solely owned by spouse, jointly owned), address the following topics:
- Name of business. Description of its products or services.
- Address, phone, e-mail, website.
- Legal status of business (partnership, corporation, limited liability company, business trust, sole proprietorship, other).
- Addresses and other contact information of all major branches or sub-entities.
- Names and addresses of accountants or others responsible for compiling and storing financial records of the business.
- Date the business was created or entered.
- Source of funds used to start the business.
- Source of funds used to develop the business.
- Distribution of profits.
- Location of accounts in which profits are or were deposited, and the ownership of these accounts.
- Most recent financial statement for the business. Who prepared it? Where is the statement located?
- Nature and extent of business debt, losses, or liabilities.
- Location of business tax returns for prior years and names of persons who prepared them.
- Partnership: kind (family, limited, general, etc.).
- Partnership: profit and loss history.
- Partnership: percentage interest of client and of spouse.
- Partnership: names of other partners.
- Partnership: provisions for sale of a partner's interest.
- Partnership: provisions for termination.
- Corporation: kind (public, closely held, etc.).
- Corporation: state of incorporation.
- Corporation: names and addresses of incorporators.
- Corporation: total issued shares. Kinds of shares.
- Corporation: profit and loss history.
- Corporation: number and kind of shares owned by client or spouse.
- Corporation: names of officers of corporation.
- Corporation: names of officers and of members of board of directors.
- Corporation: provisions for sale of stock.
- Corporation: provisions for dissolution.
- Limited liability company: percentage owned by client and spouse.
- Limited liability company: other owners or principals and their roles.

- Limited liability company: profit-and-loss history.
- Sole proprietorship: profit-and-loss history.
- Other business entities: description, method of operation, profit-and-loss history.

XIII. EMPLOYMENT HISTORY

(Answer separately for client and for spouse.)

- Name, address, e-mail, website of employer. Cover the following topics for the current employer and for each prior employer for the last 10 years:
- Occupation or profession.
- Dates employed.
- Title and responsibilities.
- Name of supervisor.
- Compensation history. Methods of payment (periodic salary, commission, deferred compensation, dividends, etc.).
- Salary: gross.
- Salary: net.
- Deferred salary or other compensation.
- Bonus availability. Other incentive plans.
- Cost-of-living adjustments.
- Benefits: pension (defined-benefit plan, defined-contribution plan, other).
- Benefits: deferred-savings plan, profit-sharing plan, stock options.
- Benefits: life insurance (names of beneficiaries, amount of cash surrender value).
- Benefits: health insurance (persons covered).
- Benefits: dental insurance (persons covered).
- Benefits: disability insurance.
- Benefits: vacation.
- Benefits: sick leave.
- Benefits: severance pay.
- Benefits: union.
- Benefits: perks (payment of membership fees at clubs or professional associations, company car, company yacht, recreational facilities, entertainment allowance, sports tickets, other).
- Expense account: details.

XIV. EDUCATION

(Answer separately for client, spouse, and each child.)

- Education: highest grade or degree achieved, dates, institutions attended, special training received (e.g., certificates), etc.
- How was the education financed?
- What are future education/training plans?
- Assess mental ability to pursue further education/training.
- Assess potential interference (e.g., health, transportation, cost, need to care for others).

XV. CONTRIBUTIONS TO CAREER ENHANCEMENT

- Before the parties were married, did either contribute to the career enhancement of the other? Explain.
- During the marriage, did the client or spouse enhance his or her own career, such as by obtaining education or training?

(continued)

EXHIBIT 3-1 *(continued)*

- How did one spouse contribute to the enhancement of the other's career during the marriage (e.g., took a job to support the family, used personal funds to help pay for the other's education, agreed to assume all child-raising and household chores while the other pursued education)?
- Did one spouse postpone his or her own career enhancement during the marriage so that the other's career could be enhanced?

XVI. REAL PROPERTY

- What is the ownership of real property (solely owned by client, solely owned by spouse, jointly owned, ownership with others)? Address the following topics for each real property:
- Legal status (joint tenancy, tenancy by the entirety, tenancy in common, fee simple, landlord-tenant interest, other).
- How is legal title held?
- Nature of the real property (residence, vacation, time-share, business, rental property, vacant land, other).
- Location/address.
- Persons currently using/benefiting from the real property.
- Original cost and date of purchase.
- Name and address of seller.
- Source of funds used to purchase.
- Amount owed on the property. Name and address of creditor/mortgagee.
- Source of funds used to pay ongoing debt.
- Current fair market value of property. Amount of the most recent written appraisal.
- If acquired by gift, list the name and address of the donor. Circumstances of the gift: To whom was the gift made? What is the relationship between donor and donee (recipient)?
- If acquired by inheritance, list the name and address of the decedent transferor. Circumstances of the inheritance: To whom was the inheritance given? What is the relationship between transferor and transferee (recipient)?
- Improvements made to property. Dates and sources of funds used.
- Sources of funds used to pay insurance covering the property.
- Sources of funds used to pay taxes on the property.

XVII. STOCKS, BONDS, AND OTHER ACCOUNTS

Address the following topics for each separately owned item:
- Stocks: names of corporations.
- Stocks: name of owner(s) as shown on stock certificate.
- Stocks: number of shares.
- Stocks: approximate value.
- Stocks: certificate numbers.
- Stocks: dates acquired.
- Stocks: cost of shares.
- Stocks: source of funds used to purchase.
- Bonds: name of corporations or obligors.
- Bonds: name of owner(s) as shown on bond certificate.
- Bonds: dates acquired.
- Bonds: bond numbers.
- Bonds: face amount at maturity. Maturity date.

In a property division, most courts will try to find ways to "compensate" the spouse who sacrificed his or her own education or career so that the other spouse could obtain an education or career. (See Chapter 8.)

Although the law office should determine who has legal title to all property, the distribution of property upon divorce is usually not dependent on the identity of the title holder. More important is knowing when the property interest was acquired and whether the property is marital or community property (as opposed to separate property), regardless of who holds title. (See Chapter 8.)

- Bonds: approximate present value.
- Bonds: interest rate.
- Bonds: coupons attached.
- Bonds: cost of bond.
- Bonds: source of funds used to purchase.
- Other. For each of the following, state the kind of instrument, owner(s), beneficiaries, issuing banks or institutions, dates opened and renewed, amount to open, maturity dates, interest earned, penalties, source of funds used to open, and current balance.
- Certificates of deposit.
- Money market accounts.
- Mutual funds.
- IRA accounts.
- 401(k) account.
- Keogh plan.
- Checking accounts.
- Savings accounts.
- Christmas club accounts.
- Other financial accounts or instruments.
- Safe deposit box (banks or institutions holding, dates opened, number of box, persons authorized to enter, contents).

XVIII. OTHER PERSONAL PROPERTY

Address the following topics for each item of personal property with a fair market value of over $100:

- Ownership (solely owned by client, solely owned by spouse, jointly owned, owned with others).
- Nature of the property (e.g., furniture, jewelry, precious metal, antique, art, china, fur, car, boat, sporting equipment, coin collection, stamp collection, airplane, pet, other).
- Location/address.
- Persons currently using/benefiting from property.
- Original cost and date of purchase.
- Name and address of seller.
- Source of funds used to purchase.
- Amount owed on the property. Name and address of creditor/mortgagee.
- Source of funds used to pay ongoing debt.
- Current fair market value of property (method of valuation, e.g., written appraisal).
- If acquired by gift, name and address of the donor. Circumstances of gift. To whom was the gift made? Relationship between donor and donee (recipient).
- If acquired by inheritance, name and address of the deceased transferor. Circumstances of gift. To whom was the inheritance made? Relationship between transferor and transferee (recipient).
- Improvements made to property. Dates and sources of funds used.
- Sources of funds to pay insurance covering the property.

XIX. INSURANCE

(For each category of insurance, provide as much of the following information as is relevant to the kind of insurance involved: insurance company, policy number, date taken out, beneficiaries, whether beneficiaries are irrevocable [can they be changed?], face amount, amount of premium, source of funds used to pay premiums, date premiums are due, assignability of policy, loans against policy, and other features of the insurance.)

- Life insurance.
- Health insurance.

(continued)

EXHIBIT 3-1 *(continued)*

- Fire/homeowner insurance on residence or vacation home.
- Title insurance.
- Vehicle insurance.
- Boat insurance.
- Disability insurance.
- General liability insurance.
- Commercial property insurance.
- Product liability insurance.
- Business interruption insurance.
- Other insurance.

XX. MISCELLANEOUS INCOME

(For each source of income listed below not otherwise covered in the checklist thus far, state name and address of payor, who receives it [client, spouse, children], dates of receipt, source of the funds, and reason payments are/were/will be made.)

- Social security income (client, spouse).
- Unemployment compensation income (client, spouse).
- Workers' compensation income (client, spouse).
- Income from veterans benefits (client, spouse).
- Public assistance, e.g., TANF, Temporary Assistance for Needy Families.
- Anticipated tax refund (client, spouse).
- Income from annuity (client, spouse).
- Income from trusts (client, spouse).
- Income from alimony/maintenance obligation (client, spouse).
- Income from book or patent royalties (client, spouse).
- Income from rental property (client, spouse).
- Interest income from personal loans (client, spouse).
- Gift from client to spouse.
- Gift from spouse to client.
- Other income (client, spouse).

XXI. CLAIMS (INSURANCE/COURT)

- Has the client or spouse filed, or does either expect to file, a claim against an insurance company, e.g., a claim arising out of a recent automobile accident? State the circumstances.
- Is the client or spouse awaiting recovery from an insurance claim or court judgment? If so, state the circumstances.
- Does the client or spouse anticipate filing a civil court action in the future? If so, state the circumstances (e.g., what damages will probably be sought?).
- Is the client or spouse currently the plaintiff in a civil action? If so, state the circumstances.
- For each insurance or court claim, explain whether the recovery will cover a loss of income or other property that was lost or interfered with during the marriage.

• Anticipated court damage awards may be marital property that can be divided upon divorce, depending on whether the amount received is personal to the victim (e.g., pain and suffering) or is designed to replace income that would have been earned during the marriage. (See Chapter 8.)

XXII. FREQUENTLY OVERLOOKED ASSETS

(For each asset listed below, state who owns the asset, dates it was acquired, resources used to acquire it, current method of valuing it, and expiration restrictions.)

- Frequent flier points.
- Hotel discount program based on accumulated points.

- Credit card cash or discount program based on accumulated points.
- Department store discount program based on accumulated points.
- Unused season tickets; the right to purchase season tickets at a discount.
- Accumulated equity in a car lease.
- Expected medical reimbursement.
- Unused sick leave.
- Lottery tickets purchased during the marriage that may produce winnings in the future.

XXIII. LIABILITIES

(Address the following topics for each liability listed: nature of debt or other kind of liability, name and address of creditor, names of debtor, loan number, date debt was incurred, source of funds in the past and currently used to pay the debt, reason debt was incurred, original amount of the debt, amount outstanding, date and amount of next payment, whether client or spouse can increase the amount of the debt on his or her own.)

- Mortgage on primary residence.
- Mortgage on second home or vacation home.
- Mortgage on business property.
- Other mortgages.
- Mechanic's lien.
- Credit cards.
- Charge cards.
- Car loan.
- Boat loan.
- Student loan.
- Loan against cash value of life insurance policy.
- Loan from a friend.
- Other notes or loans.
- Court judgment for money in which the client or spouse is or will be a defendant or may otherwise be responsible for the judgment and thereby become a judgment debtor. State the circumstances.
- Bankruptcy payments (e.g., under a Chapter 13 bankruptcy).

XXIV. TAX RETURNS

(Provide the following information on each of the returns listed below for the last three years the returns were filed: gross income, taxable income, taxes due, source of funds used to pay the taxes, accountant or attorney who helped prepare the return, extent to which the client or spouse was involved in the preparation of the return, location of a copy of the return. Provide the same information if an amended return was filed for any of the returns.)

- Federal income tax return.
- Federal corporate (or other business) tax return.
- State income tax return.
- State corporate (or other business) tax return.
- City or other local tax return.
- City or other local corporate (or other business) tax return.
- Gift tax return.
- Estate tax return.
- Returns filed abroad.
- Other returns.

- *Under the innocent spouse doctrine, a spouse may be able to avoid liability for delinquent taxes that result from a tax return prepared by the other spouse. (See Chapter 11.)*

(continued)

EXHIBIT 3-1 *(continued)*

XXV. ASSETS OF THE CHILDREN

- List any real or personal property the children own (over $100 in value) in their own name or jointly with another, e.g., cash, securities, land.
- How was this property acquired? Gift (by whom)? Inheritance (from whom)? Purchase by child?
- Who controls this property? A guardian or custodian? A trustee?
- Has the client, the spouse, or anyone else used or consumed any of this property?
- When will the child have unrestricted access to this property?

XXVI. PROFESSIONAL PERSONS HIRED OR CONSULTED

(For each of the following persons, state the name and address, dates hired or consulted, whether hired or consulted by client or spouse, fees paid, fees due, and the kinds of financial or other records this person now possesses.)

- Attorneys.
- Accountants.
- Real estate agents or brokers.
- Insurance agents.
- Bankers.
- Stockbrokers.
- Clergy.
- Doctors.
- Others.

XXVII. NEXT STEPS

(The client needs clear instructions on what further steps he or she should take.)

- Locate documents identified during the interview as important (e.g., copies of tax returns).
- Cancel joint accounts with spouse.
- Take photos of the contents of the house.
- Start keeping a journal on the behavior of the spouse, interactions with the children, expenses, etc.

© Cengage Learning 2013

The checklist in Exhibit 3-1 is not the only place in the book where there are guidelines on fact gathering. Throughout many of the remaining chapters, you will find interviewing and investigation checklists that pertain to specific issues under discussion in a chapter. (See also the interrogatories in Appendix C and the technique of fact particularization discussed in Appendix A prior to the general instructions for the investigation and interviewing assignments.)

ASSIGNMENT 3.2

Your instructor will play the role of a new client in the office where you work as a paralegal. Assume that you have been asked to conduct a comprehensive interview of this client in order to compile a family history. The client is a spouse in a marriage where there are substantial personal and business assets over which the spouses are expected to have bitter disputes. They are also expected to contest the custody of their two minor children. The marriage was the second marriage for both parties. To date, the client has not been asked to bring anything to the interview. You must let the client know what you want him or her to bring to you in subsequent meetings.

Everyone in the class will play the role of interviewer. Raise your hand when you have questions. Everyone should ask numerous questions in this potentially complex case. (You do not have to follow the outline of questions in Exhibit 3-1 in the chapter.) Take detailed notes on the questions and answers, regardless of who asks the questions. Do not limit your notes to the answers to the questions you ask.

If you feel that another student failed to elicit sufficient detail on a question, re-ask the question in your own way to try to obtain greater detail.

After the interview, prepare a detailed report (sometimes called an *intake memorandum*) on what you learned from the interview. Use headings for different categories of data. Choose an overall organization for the report that you feel would best facilitate reading. The format of the beginning of the report should be as follows:

INTER-OFFICE MEMORANDUM
TO: [name of your instructor]
FROM: [your name]
DATE: [date(s) of the interview]
RE: Comprehensive Interview of [name of client]

(See General Instructions for the Interview Assignment in Appendix A.)

SOFTWARE

Many law offices use special software to record the basic facts obtained during client interviews. See Exhibit 3-2 for an example.

EXHIBIT 3-2 Example of Software Used for the Intake of New Family Law Clients

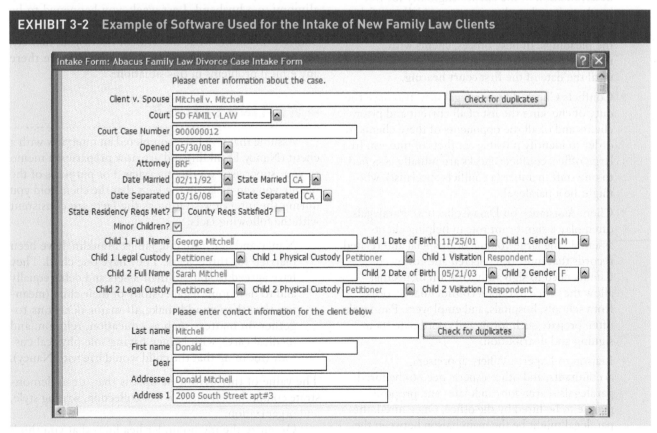

■ PARALEGAL ROLES

- For an overview of paralegal roles in family-law cases, see Exhibits 1-3 and 1-4 in Chapter 1.

- In addition to the large number of documents and facts outlined in Chapter 3 that paralegals help an office to collect for a case, see the list of documents and facts sought in the interrogatories on financial assets in Appendix C.

- Interviewing. Depending on the kind of office where the client is seeking legal services, paralegal interviewing and data collection duties can vary considerably. In private law offices, the attorney conducts the initial interview (sometimes with the paralegal present taking notes) that establishes the attorney-client relationship, sets fees, and collects basic facts. Very often a paralegal is then assigned the task of conducting follow-up interviews with the client to complete the family history. Because of the volume of data required, the paralegal tends to form a close working relationship with the client. In some publicly funded law offices (e.g., a legal aid society), paralegals can have a much larger role. They may be asked to make a preliminary determination of the client's eligibility for free legal services (based on income guidelines of the office), interview the client, and start preparing the pleadings. In busy offices, clients with relatively simple cases may not see an attorney until the date of the first court hearing.

- Conflicts Check. The paralegal may also have the duty of checking the list of all current and prior clients and of all the opponents of these clients in order to identify possible conflicts of interest. In a large office, conflicts checks are initially assigned to one staff member (a conflicts specialist), who might be a paralegal.

- Client Assistance on Data Collection. Paralegals often play a significant role in helping clients assemble the large volume of financial and related records that must be collected and reviewed. Clients need to sign authorization forms that allow the office to obtain confidential records from schools, hospitals, and employers. Paralegals often prepare such forms and coordinate their signing and distribution.

- Liaison to Experts. Where appraisers, accountants, and other experts need to be hired, paralegals search for candidates and propose people to be hired by the office. Once hired, the paralegal might be the main liaison between the office and the experts.

■ PROJECT

Some family-law attorneys post an online interview form or checklist that they ask prospective clients to fill out or be ready to discuss. Find three such forms or checklists on the Internet. How do they compare with each other (discuss relative strengths and weaknesses) and how do they compare with Exhibit 3-1 in this chapter? What items would you add to Exhibit 3-1 based on what you learned online? To find the interview forms or checklists, run the following searches in Google, Bing, or Yahoo:

family law interview
family law checklist
divorce interview

You can also add the name of your state to the search terms, but you are not limited to the interview forms used in your state.

■ ETHICS IN A FAMILY LAW PRACTICE

You are a paralegal working at the law office of Smith and Smith. You have referred a client to the firm. The client is a close friend of yours. During an interview, the client asks you whether a wife is ever obligated to pay alimony to a husband. Last week, you happened to be discussing the same topic with your attorney supervisor. You tell the client what the attorney told you, namely, that either spouse can be liable for alimony. Are there any ethical problems in this situation?

■ WRITING SAMPLE

Assume that you have completed an interview with a client (Nancy Franklin) and are now preparing a memo to your supervisor on the interview. For purposes of the memo, you can make up the facts that the client told you during the interview so long as the facts are consistent with the following facts:

Nancy and her husband, James Franklin, have been married for three years. They have one child. They have agreed to split all their assets and debts equally and to have joint legal custody of their child (meaning that they would make all major decisions together on matters such as education, religion, and medical care), with Nancy having sole physical custody (meaning that the child would live with Nancy).

The value of this writing sample is that it can demonstrate comprehensiveness of fact collection, writing style, and organization.

Organize the memo under headings that you think will make it easy for a busy attorney to read. Again, you will make up all of the facts for your memo (e.g., what the assets and debts are, Nancy's wishes on custody, and how much visitation she wants the father to have) consistent with the outline above. You do not need to know any law to conduct this interview. The heading and first line of your memo will be as follows:

Interview Memo

TO: Helen Foley, Esq.

FR: Your name

Date: Today's date

RE: Interview of Nancy Franklin
2014-Div-Franklin

You have asked me to interview Nancy Franklin to determine the assets and debts of the parties and the client's wishes on custody and visitation.

(See General Instructions for the Writing Sample in Appendix A.)

Note: If you do use this as a writing sample when searching for a job, tell prospective employers that it is based on a hypothetical—not a real—case. You do not want anyone to think that you have violated confidentiality by revealing the facts of a client's case.

SUMMARY

In light of the potential complexity of a family-law case, a law office may want to compile a comprehensive family history, particularly in contested cases that involve complex fact issues and relatively large sums of money or other property. The history is collected primarily by legal interviewing and investigation. Because clients are not always sure of what they want, sensitivity is needed in providing explanations and options. Often clients are confused about the law. Guidelines in conducting a client interview include having uninterrupted time to conduct the interview, preserving confidentiality, listening attentively, and avoiding legal advice and outcome guarantees.

The client is told what documents he or she should bring to the office. Any emergency concerns (e.g., physical safety) should be dealt with soon after the client arrives.

To compile a family history, facts are collected on the marriage and its deterioration, prior contracts between the spouses, expenses, health history, wills and trusts, children, businesses, employment history, education and training, contributions each made to the education and career of the other, real and personal property, insurance, debts and liabilities, tax returns, assets of the children, and professionals either has consulted.

REVIEW QUESTIONS

1. In what ways do attorneys obtain facts that will be needed to represent a client in a family-law case?

2. When is a family-law attorney most likely to want a detailed family history of a client?

3. What concerns must an attorney have when determining what a client wants?

4. What are some of the techniques for conducting an interview attentively and with sensitivity?

5. What steps should an attorney take to preserve client confidentiality during an interview?

6. What misunderstanding about the paralegal's role should a paralegal avoid when interviewing a client?

7. What is legal advice and why should a paralegal avoid giving it?

8. How can an interviewer avoid giving guarantees during an interview?

9. What observations for a supervisor should the interviewer be making of the client's personality during the interview?

10. What documents should a client be asked to bring to interviews?

11. What information does an office need in order to avoid a conflict of interest?

12. What emergency concerns should be inquired into at the outset of a client interview?

13. What are the main categories of facts that make up a family history?

HELPFUL WEBSITES

Interviewing a Family Law Client

- www.jsrp.com/Interview_Form.pdf
- www.busby-lee.com/pdf/Client-Info-Sheet(Divorce).pdf
- www.tinamhall.com/Forms/CLIENT _INFORMATION_SHEET_-_FAMILY_LAW.pdf
- www.familylawsoftware.com/resources /SampleScreens_ClientWeb1.htm

The Anxious Family Law Client

- winattrial.com/Calming%20Down%20the%20 Anxious%20Family%20Law%20Client.htm

Interviewing: Selected Articles

- www.rongolini.com/Interviewing.html

Basics of Legal Interviewing

- courses.washington.edu/civpro03/resources /interviewing.doc

Attentive Listening

- www.businesslistening.com/listening_skills-3.php
- everyonenegotiates.com/attentive-listening-skills.php

Google/Bing/Yahoo Searches

(on these search engines, run the following searches)
- intake memo
- attentive listening
- "kinds of questions"
- "legal interviewing"
- interviewing clients
- "difficult clients"

ENDNOTES

[1] *My Specialty: Divorce Law*, 27 Paralegal Today 27 (Apr./Jun. 2010).

[2] James Feldman, *That First Contact Is Crucial*, 12 Family Advocate 6 (Summer 1990).

[3] Some of the checklist questions are based on Form 4, *Affidavit* [on financial resources] (Supreme Court of the United States, 2003) (www.gpo.gov/fdsys/pkg/USCODE -2004-title28/pdf/.pdf); *A History for Your Attorney*, 15 Family Advocate 12 (Summer 1992); *What Your Lawyer Needs to Know*, 15 Family Advocate 28 (Summer 1992); Louis Brown, *A Family Legal Information Check List*, 3 Practical Lawyer 60 (no. 6, Oct. 1957); Leo Barrett, *The Initial Interview with a Divorce Client*, 23 Practical Lawyer 75 (no. 4, Jun. 1977); Louis Brown, *Manual for Periodic Checkup* (1983); Allan Chay & Judith Smith, *Legal Interviewing in Practice* (1996).

Premarital, Postnuptial, and Cohabitation Agreements

CHAPTER OUTLINE

CHAPTER OBJECTIVES

After completing this chapter, you should be able to:

- Define the four major kinds of agreements that can be entered by persons in intimate relationships: cohabitation agreement, premarital agreement, postnuptial agreement, and separation agreement.

- Identify some of the major reasons couples enter premarital agreements.

- Know what can be included in a premarital agreement.

- State the requirements for a valid premarital agreement.

- Distinguish between procedural and substantive fairness.

- Conduct an interview and an investigation to uncover facts that would be relevant to the validity of a premarital agreement.

- Know the malpractice dilemma faced by an attorney who represents the financially weaker party in a premarital agreement.

- Know what can be included in a postnuptial agreement.

- Know what can be included in a cohabitation agreement.

- State the holding and impact of *Marvin v. Marvin* on the law of cohabitation.

- List the remedies that are possible in cohabitation cases that agree with *Marvin v. Marvin*.

- Know why many courts are reluctant to provide remedies for cohabitants other than an action for breach of an express contract.

KINDS OF AGREEMENTS

There are four major kinds of agreements that can be entered by persons in an intimate relationship: cohabitation, premarital, postnuptial, and separation. See Exhibit 4-1. The parties using these agreements may be about to enter the intimate relationship, may already be in it, or may want to end it. Our main focus in this chapter will be premarital and cohabitation agreements.

EXHIBIT 4-1 Kinds of Agreements Made between Persons in an Intimate Relationship

Kind of Agreement	Definition	Example
Cohabitation Agreement	A contract by persons in an intimate relationship who are not married to each other (and who intend to stay unmarried indefinitely) that covers financial and related matters while they are living together and upon the end of the relationship by death or separation.	Ed and Claire meet at a bank where they work. After dating several years, they decide to live together. Although they have a child, they do not want to be married. They enter an agreement that specifies what property is separately owned and how they will divide property purchased with joint funds if the relationship ends. The agreement is an example of a cohabitation agreement.
Premarital Agreement (also called prenuptial agreement ["prenup"] or antenuptial agreement)	• A contract by persons about to be married that can cover (1) financial and related matters once the marriage occurs and (2) spousal support, property division, and related matters in the event of death, separation, divorce, or annulment. • The Uniform Premarital Agreement Act (§ 1) defines it as "an agreement between prospective spouses made in contemplation of marriage and to be effective upon marriage."	Jim and Mary want to marry. Each has a child from a prior marriage. Before the wedding, they enter an agreement that makes clear what property each brings to the marriage and will remain separate property. The agreement states that neither will have any rights in this separate property; it will go to the children from their prior marriages. In addition, the agreement states that all income earned by a party during the marriage shall be the separate property of that party and therefore shall not be divided as marital or community property in the event of a divorce. The agreement is an example of a premarital agreement.
Postnuptial Agreement ("postnup," "midnup")	A contract between married persons that covers financial and related matters between them. They may have no intention of separating. If they have this intention, the contract is commonly called a separation agreement.	• While happily married, George and Helen enter an agreement whereby George lends Helen $5,000 at 5 percent interest. She is to make monthly payments of $300. (For this loan, George uses money he recently inherited from his mother.) The agreement is an example of a postnuptial agreement. • While happily married, George and Helen decide to amend their premarital agreement by changing some of its terms. The new agreement is also an example of a postnuptial agreement. • After Jim and Mary separate, they reconcile. They enter a reconciliation agreement that covers issues that they want clarified. The reconciliation agreement is another example of a postnuptial agreement.

EXHIBIT 4-1 (continued)

Kind of Agreement	Definition	Example
Separation Agreement (also called marital settlement agreement) Because the separation agreement is entered during the marriage, it is sometimes referred to as a postnuptial agreement, although when separation is contemplated, the more common term is "separation agreement."	A contract by married persons who have separated (or who are about to separate) that can cover support, custody, property division, and other terms of their separation and divorce.	Sam and Jessica have separated. In anticipation of their divorce, they enter an agreement that specifies how their marital property will be divided, who will have custody of their children, and what their support obligations will be. Later they will ask the divorce court to approve this agreement. The agreement is an example of a separation agreement.

© Cengage Learning 2013

PREMARITAL AGREEMENTS

INTRODUCTION

Not all states define a premarital agreement in the same way. In general, a premarital agreement is a contract by persons about to be married that can cover (1) financial and related matters once the marriage occurs and (2) spousal support, property division, and related matters in the event of death, separation, divorce, or annulment. The agreement is also called a prenuptial agreement ("prenup") and an antenuptial agreement. Of course, the marriage itself is a contract. A premarital agreement is a contract that helps define some of the major terms of the marriage contract.

Why, you might ask, would two individuals about to enter the blissful state of marriage discuss such matters as "who gets what" if they ever divorce? According to one family-law attorney, "The typical young couple starting out does not need" a prenuptial agreement. "For the middle-aged couple or older couple who has accumulated significant assets, it can be appropriate."[1] Other attorneys are more emphatic about who needs a prenup. "If you're going to get married and you don't want a prenuptial," exclaims a New York attorney, "you need to see a psychiatrist, not a lawyer."[2]

Needs and emotions, however, are not always in accord. Raising the "P" word ("prenuptial") during an engagement can sometimes be unsettling. When former Beatle Paul McCartney separated from Heather Mills, "legal experts estimated that he could lose up to a quarter of his $1 billion fortune because he reportedly felt that asking her to sign a prenup was unromantic."[3]

Here are some of the categories of persons most likely to enter premarital agreements:

- They are older.
- They have substantial property that was acquired independently of each other.
- They have an independent interest in a business, particularly a family-run business.
- They have prior marriages.
- They have children and perhaps grandchildren from prior relationships.

At least one spouse in 22 percent of currently married couples is in his or her second marriage; another 6 percent have a spouse in a third marriage.[4] Such individuals may want to make clear that the new spouse is not to have any claim on designated property or that the children of the former marriage will have first claim to property acquired before the new marriage.

"It's a prenuptial agreement silly! I'm asking you to *marry* me!"

Source: Mark Hannabury, 90 Case and Comment 34 (Mar.–Apr. 1985). Reprinted with permission.

Another large category of couples favoring premarital agreements are young professionals, particularly those in their early thirties, with separate careers. Although the women's movement of the 1980s and 1990s did not crusade in favor of premarital agreements, the "protect yourself" message of the movement helped increase the popularity of premarital agreements among brides-to-be. Finally, the high divorce rate has made more and more young couples aware of the need for preplanning for the possible crisis of separation and dissolution. One preplanning tool that might prevent divorces from becoming protracted and emotionally brutal is the premarital agreement.

WHAT CAN AND CANNOT BE INCLUDED

In most states, parties have considerable flexibility on what they can include in a premarital agreement. Valid agreements allow the parties to waive or limit many of the rights that state law gives them upon divorce or death. Here are examples of what happens without a premarital agreement (which we will examine in greater detail later) and the changes such agreements can make:

- In most states, the salary or other income earned by either spouse becomes marital property, which can be divided in the event of a divorce. A husband, for example, could not say that his soon-to-be ex-wife is not entitled to any of the wages he earned during the marriage. A valid premarital agreement, however, can change this result. The parties can decide to treat salaries and other income as the separate property of the spouse who earned it so that it would not become divisible marital property upon divorce.

- In most states, a surviving spouse has a right to elect to receive a designated portion (called an **elective share**) of the estate of a deceased spouse even if the latter's will gives the survivor considerably less or nothing at all. A valid premarital agreement can change this result. The parties can waive the right of election so that the will of a deceased spouse cannot be overridden by the surviving spouse.

elective share
The percentage of a deceased spouse's estate that the surviving spouse can choose (elect) to receive despite what the will of the deceased spouse provided for the surviving spouse. Also called statutory share, forced share.

Here is the scope of what is allowed in states that have adopted the **Uniform Premarital Agreement Act (UPAA)**:

Uniform Premarital Agreement Act (UPAA)

A model statute adopted by many states that governs the legality of premarital agreements.

Uniform Premarital Agreement Act § 3

(a) Parties to a premarital agreement may contract with respect to:

    (1) the rights and obligations of each of the parties in any of the property of either or both of them whenever and wherever acquired or located;

    (2) the right to buy, sell, use, transfer, exchange, abandon, lease, consume, expend, assign, create a security interest in, mortgage, encumber, dispose of, or otherwise manage and control property;

    (3) the disposition of property upon separation, marital dissolution, death, or the occurrence or nonoccurrence of any other event;

    (4) the modification or elimination of spousal support;

    (5) the making of a will, trust, or other arrangement to carry out the provisions of the agreement;

    (6) the ownership rights in and disposition of the death benefit from a life insurance policy;

    (7) the choice of law governing the construction of the agreement; and

    (8) any other matter, including their personal rights and obligations, not in violation of public policy or a statute imposing a criminal penalty.

(b) The right of a child to support may not be adversely affected by a premarital agreement.[5]

ASSIGNMENT 4.1

What restrictions exist in your state on what a premarital agreement can and cannot do? (See the General Instructions for the State Code and the Court Opinion Assignments in Appendix A.)

Note the admonition in section 3(a)(8) of the UPAA that the premarital agreement must not violate statutes or **public policy**. The latter consists of the principles inherent in the customs, morals, and notions of justice that prevail in a state. For example, the parties cannot agree that neither will ever bring a divorce action or any other suit against the other. It is against public policy to discourage the use of the courts in this way, as legitimate grievances might go unheard. Let's take a closer look at specific clauses that may or may not violate statutes or public policy.

public policy

The principles inherent in the customs, morals, and notions of justice that prevail in a state; the foundation of public laws; the principles that are naturally and inherently right and just.

Spousal-Support Clause

At one time, many courts considered spousal-support clauses to be against public policy because they *facilitated* (or encouraged) *divorce*. The thinking was that divorce planning before marriage might incline a party to seek a divorce if he or she knew what funds or other property would be available upon divorce, particularly, of course, if the financial terms upon divorce were favorable.

Today, most modern courts no longer place such limitations on premarital agreements. In the era of no-fault divorce, terminating a marriage is no longer difficult. There is less pressure from society to keep marriages together at all costs. A spouse who wants a divorce can obtain one with relative ease and probably does not need the inducement of a favorable premarital agreement to end the marriage. Hence, most (but by no means all) courts uphold clauses in premarital agreements that provide a designated amount of spousal support (alimony) or, indeed, that provide for no spousal support in the event of a divorce. These courts will allow parties to waive spousal support.

public charge

An individual who is primarily dependent on the government for subsistence, as demonstrated by either the receipt of public cash assistance for income maintenance or institutionalization for long-term care at government expense.

Suppose, however, that a divorce occurs and, because of changed circumstances between the time the agreement was signed and the time of the divorce, one of the spouses is about to become a **public charge**—that is, in need of public assistance. As it turned out, the spouse made a bad bargain if he or she agreed in the premarital agreement to waive spousal support in the event of a divorce. Later, when we discuss the issue of fairness, we will see that most courts will refuse to enforce the no-support clause in such circumstances. To prevent a spouse from becoming destitute or a public charge, a court can force the other spouse to provide spousal support despite the no-support clause in the premarital agreement. Here is how the UPAA states this rule:

> If a provision of a premarital agreement modifies or eliminates spousal support and such modification or elimination causes one party to the agreement to be eligible for support under a program of public assistance at the time of separation or marital dissolution, a court, notwithstanding the terms of the agreement, may require the other party to provide support to the extent necessary to avoid such eligibility.[6]

When we study the *Barry Bonds* case later in the chapter, we will examine another rule on the enforceability of spousal-support clauses in premarital agreements when both spouses are not represented by independent counsel.

Death Clause

As indicated earlier, most states give a surviving spouse the right to an *elective share* of his or her deceased spouse's estate. The elective share (also called a statutory share or forced share) is a percentage of a deceased spouse's estate that the surviving spouse can choose (elect) to receive despite what the will of the deceased spouse provided for the surviving spouse. The right to an elective share is designed to prevent a deceased spouse from disinheriting the surviving spouse by a will (see Chapters 8 and 12).

In premarital agreements, parties often give up (waive) their right to an elective share in each other's estates. (The waiver is sometimes called a death clause.) The agreement might say that a surviving spouse will receive a specified amount (e.g., $100,000) upon the death of the other spouse in lieu of the elective share.

Life-Insurance Clause

A common clause found in premarital agreements commits a spouse to purchase and fund a life insurance policy of a designated amount with the other spouse as the beneficiary.

Property-Division Clause

property division

The allocation and distribution of property between spouses (or ex-spouses) after a legal separation or divorce. Also called property settlement, property distribution.

Premarital agreements can spell out what property belongs to each spouse during the marriage and upon its termination. Key to the enforceability of clauses on **property division** is whether there was adequate disclosure to each other of the property that each owned at the time they signed the premarital agreement. We will examine this issue later under the heading of financial disclosure.

Retirement-Benefits Clause

Premarital agreements sometimes provide that each party waives any rights that either has in the retirement benefits of the other, e.g., a 401(k) plan. (See Chapter 8 for a discussion of such plans.) There is some doubt as to the legality of such clauses under federal law. A *married* person (a "spouse") may be able to waive such rights but it is not clear that someone contemplating marriage (a fiancée or fiancé) can do so. In light of this uncertainty, the premarital agreement should have a clause requiring both parties within a short time *after* they are married to sign waiver forms approved by the administrator of the pension or retirement plan.

Child-Support Clause

Parents have an equal duty to support their children pursuant to child-support guidelines that mandate the minimum amount of support each parent must provide (see Chapter 10). A premarital agreement can specify child-support amounts that are higher than the minimum, but it cannot have a support clause that goes below the minimum. Furthermore, a clause that purports to absolve one of the parents from contributing to child support is unenforceable.

Child-Custody Clause

Courts take great care in making child-custody decisions based on what is in the best interests of the child (see Chapter 9). The desires of both parents are taken into consideration, but what they want is not controlling. Hence, a clause in a premarital agreement on child custody is never binding on a court.

Debts Clause

Debts that a spouse brings into the marriage are the debts of that spouse alone. Individual debts do not become joint debts simply because of the marriage. Individual debts can be considerable, particularly for recent graduates of undergraduate and professional schools. It is not uncommon for such individuals to enter the marriage with over $200,000 in school debts. To prevent later misunderstandings (e.g., "You said you would help me pay my school loans"), the premarital agreement might include a clause that specifies what debts are being brought into the marriage and who is responsible for them. To protect the nondebtor, the clause could say that "any assistance on the other's debt does not constitute an agreement to assume joint responsibility for the debt."

Lifestyle Clauses

Some premarital agreements try to regulate very specific and sensitive aspects of the marriage relationship. Examples:

- who will perform what household chores
- how often sexual relations will occur
- whether the children are to be vegetarian
- how much time the couple will spend with the in-laws
- whose career will take priority in the event that one of the spouses is laid off from work
- what night the husband can watch football with his friends
- how long a spouse will work until retirement
- how much weight a wife can gain (with a fine of $500 per excess pound!)[7]

In 2012, a widely publicized clause in the premarital agreement of Priscilla Chan and the billionaire founder of Facebook, Mark Zuckerberg, stated that they would have at least one date night a week that would be 100 minutes away from his apartment or office.

Although such clauses are not illegal, their practical effect is questionable, as it is unlikely that a court would become involved in enforcing terms of this nature. (Most "jurisdictions will not enforce agreements with respect to personal services rendered during marriage."[8]) Yet some family-law attorneys still recommend that these lifestyle clauses be included in the premarital agreement in order to clarify expectations and help prevent future marital bickering or tension.

Remaining-Childless Clause

Occasionally, a clause in a premarital agreement will assert that the parties will always use birth control so that they will remain childless. Such a clause is often insisted upon by an older man (who already had children from a prior marriage) about to marry a younger woman. There is considerable doubt about the legality of such a clause because one of the purposes of marriage is to have children.[9] Furthermore, if the clause is violated and a child is born, the violation would have no effect on the obligation of both parents to support the child. Yet an attorney might want to include the clause, again to clarify expectations while candidly acknowledging to the client that a court is unlikely to enforce it.

Confidentiality Clause

A feature of some confessional television and having-my-say social media is the ex-spouse (often the ex-wife) telling the world about the horrors of a former marriage. (See the stories on electronic exhibitionism in Chapter 1.) To try to head off such exposés, the premarital agreement may require the parties to maintain confidentiality about what occurs in the marriage they are about to enter. Although difficult to enforce in the age of the Internet, the clause is often sought by well-to-do and powerful clients.

The confidentiality clause could also cover what is in the premarital agreement itself. A client may be reluctant to place financial data in the agreement without such a clause.

Automatic-Termination Clause

The parties can agree that the terms of the premarital agreement will automatically terminate or expire after a designated number of years (e.g., five) if the parties are still married at that time. This will force the now-married couple to renegotiate the terms of their relationship. (See the discussion below on postnuptial agreements.) Wealthy clients rarely agree to such **sunset** clauses. Attorneys for a less-wealthy client may try to negotiate it into the agreement on the theory that the client would probably do better in a new agreement or, if a new agreement cannot be reached, in a divorce settlement in the event that a divorce occurs.

Severability Clause

A **severability clause** states that if any single portion of the agreement is found to be invalid, the remaining valid provisions of the agreement should still be carried out. Something is **severable** if it can be removed without destroying what remains. (The opposite of severable is *essential* or *indispensable*.) The purpose of the clause is to prevent anyone from arguing that the parties intended the entire agreement to be canceled if any part of it cannot be performed because of the invalidity of that part.

VALID CONTRACT

A premarital agreement is an example of a **contract**, which is a legally enforceable agreement. It is an **executory contract** because performing the terms of the contract will take place in the future (after the marriage is entered). The traditional requirements or elements of most contracts are offer, acceptance, and **consideration**. (Consideration is something of value that is exchanged between parties.) The consideration for the premarital agreement is the mutual promise of the parties to enter the marriage. In most states, however, the premarital agreement is enforceable without proof of consideration.

Like all contracts, the parties to a premarital agreement must have the **capacity** to enter a contract. Someone who is underage or mentally incompetent, for

---

sunset
Automatic termination or expiration.

severability clause
A clause in an agreement that provides that if any part of the agreement is declared to be invalid, the remaining valid portions of the agreement should be carried out.

severable
Removable without destroying what remains. Something is severable when what remains after it is taken away has legal force and can survive without it. The opposite of severable is essential or indispensable.

contract
A legally enforceable agreement. The elements of most contracts are offer, acceptance, and consideration. Some contracts must be in writing.

executory contract
A contract in which the parties bind themselves to future activity. A contract that is not yet fully completed or performed.

consideration
Something of value that is exchanged between parties. It can be an act, a forbearance (not performing an act), a promise to perform an act, or a promise to refrain from performing an act.

capacity
The legal power to do something such as enter a contract or a relationship. Also called legal capacity. (See glossary for an additional meaning.)

example, cannot form a valid contract. Contracts must be entered voluntarily. Fraud and duress can invalidate the contract, as we will see. The **statute of frauds** requires some categories of contract to be in writing. Many states have this requirement for premarital agreements.

Although there are similarities between premarital agreements and commercial contracts, there are also some important differences. A singular characteristic of most commercial contracts is that the parties are allowed to treat each other at **arm's length**, as if they are strangers, both looking out solely for their own self-interests. This is not entirely true of couples engaged to be married. Both parties must make a full financial disclosure to each other before signing the premarital agreement and both must be given the opportunity to consult with his or her own attorney or other advisers on whether to sign it. Most states do not say that an engaged couple is in a **fiduciary relationship**, requiring loyalty and fair treatment. Yet the couple cannot treat each other as strangers; **overreaching** (taking unfair advantage of another's naiveté or other vulnerability, especially by deceptive means) is frowned upon. Note, however, that many states say that a *married* couple does have a fiduciary relationship with each other, as we will see when we discuss postnuptial agreements.

We need to examine some of these themes more closely.

Voluntary

The agreement must be **voluntary**, meaning that it must proceed from a free and unconstrained will. A court will not enforce an agreement that a party was forced to sign or that is the product of **duress**, which is the unlawful use of force or threats that overcome a person's will so that he or she does something he or she does not want to do. In most cases, it is not duress for a party to threaten to call off the engagement if the other party does not sign the premarital agreement. This is not an unlawful threat.

> *Leo and Helen are engaged to be married. Leo's attorney drafts a premarital agreement and Leo tells Helen he will cancel the engagement if she does not sign it. She signs it and they marry. Five years later, they separate. In the divorce proceeding, Leo asks the court to enforce the premarital agreement. Helen argues that the agreement is invalid because it was the product of duress.*

Helen will lose her argument if at the time she signed the agreement, she was an intelligent woman, had an adequate or good command of the English language, was given full disclosure of Leo's finances, and had adequate time to consult her own attorney or other advisers. She may have felt pressure to sign, but the pressure was not unlawful if she had the information she needed (or the opportunity to obtain it) and proceeded to sign of her own free will. The result might be different if Helen was still learning English, had limited life experience, was pregnant or in poor health, and was presented with the agreement for the first time on the day of the wedding with hundreds of guests (many from out of town) about to file into church.

To help **rebut** the charge of duress, some attorneys recommend that the premarital agreement be presented to the other party at least three months before the marriage.

Fraud

Fraud is an intentionally false statement of fact that is **material**, made to induce reliance, and results in harm because of the reliance. If, for example, a party lies about what he or she owns in order to obtain the consent of the other party to the premarital agreement, the agreement will not be enforced. The false statement must be material, meaning that it was important enough to influence the decision to sign.

---

statute of frauds
A law requiring some contracts (e.g., one that cannot be performed within a year of its making) to be in writing and signed by the party to be charged by the contract.

arm's length
Pertaining to how parties would treat each other if they were strangers looking out for their own self-interests with no confidential or other relationship between them that would cause one to expect the other to provide a special advantage or to act with fairness.

fiduciary relationship
The relationship that exists when one party (called the fiduciary) owes another loyalty, candor, and fair treatment. The fiduciary is required to act in the interest of and for the benefit of the other. Also called a confidential relationship.

overreaching
Taking unfair advantage of another's naiveté or other vulnerability, especially by deceptive means.

voluntary
By choice; proceeding from a free and unconstrained will.

duress
The unlawful use of force or threats that overcome the will so that a person does something he or she does not want to do. Illegal coercion.

rebut
To attack, dispute, or refute.

fraud
An intentionally false statement of fact that is material and is made to induce reliance by the plaintiff, and that results in harm because of the reliance.

material
Important enough to influence the decision that was made. (See glossary for an additional meaning.)

waiver
The relinquishment or giving up of a right or privilege because of an explicit rejection of it or because of a failure to take appropriate steps to claim it at the proper time.

FINANCIAL DISCLOSURE

Before you give up (waive) something in a premarital agreement, you must know what it is that you are giving up. For a **waiver** of property rights to make sense, the parties must make a fair and reasonable disclosure of their financial resources to each other. The disclosure must cover assets and debts or liabilities.

States differ on how much disclosure is fair and reasonable. Some insist on a full and frank disclosure. In other states, it is enough to provide a general picture of one's financial worth. Once the general picture is provided, the other party has a duty to make inquiries or to consult with experts in order to obtain more financial details. Careful attorneys, however, will always try to provide maximum disclosure in order to rebut a later claim by a spouse that he or she did not know the scope of the other spouse's wealth when the premarital agreement was signed. Such attorneys will not only list all assets but will also state the estimated or actual value of each asset, being careful to avoid undervaluation.

Often the agreement includes a clause that says full disclosure has been made. This clause, however, is not always controlling, particularly if it can be shown that the party was tricked or unduly coerced into signing the agreement.

Finally, although the right to receive financial disclosure is critical to the validity of a premarital agreement, the right can be waived in most states. Parties can agree to a clause saying that whatever the other party has disclosed is sufficient or that no disclosure is needed.

FAIRNESS AND UNCONSCIONABILITY

There are two kinds of fairness:

- **Procedural fairness.** Full financial disclosure, adequate opportunity to consult with others, voluntariness, and the absence of duress and fraud. Informed consent.
- **Substantive fairness.** Equitable in the sense that the terms are satisfactory and reasonable.

The focus of procedural fairness is the *process* the parties went through when they entered the premarital agreement. Was it open, voluntary, and informed? The focus of substantive fairness is the *content* of the agreement itself. Was it a good deal for both parties? All states require procedural fairness for premarital agreements. Most states do not require that they meet the test of substantive fairness so long as there was procedural fairness.

Procedural Fairness

Cautious attorneys advise their clients to give their prospective spouses sufficient time to study and think about the premarital agreement before signing. Waiting until the morning of the wedding to bring up the subject of a premarital agreement is not wise, particularly if the parties have substantially different education and business backgrounds. The more immature a person is in age and in worldly matters, the more time he or she needs to consider the agreement and to consult with independent experts or friends who are able to explain (1) the present and future financial worth of the prospective spouse and (2) the waivers asked for in the premarital agreement.

Substantive Fairness

At one time, society viewed women as vulnerable and in need of special protection. There was almost a presumption that a woman's prospective husband would try to take advantage of her through the premarital agreement. Courts that took this view tended to scrutinize such agreements to make sure they were procedurally *and* substantively fair to the prospective bride. The agreement had to be free of coercion and deception, and also had to be equitable in the sense of being a reasonably good deal under the circumstances.

The women's movement has helped change this perspective. Today, there is a greater degree of equality between the sexes. Consequently, if a woman makes a bad bargain in a premarital agreement, most courts are inclined to force her to live with it so long as:

- it was voluntarily entered,
- there was no duress or fraud,
- there was adequate disclosure of the identity and value of the other's assets and debts, and
- there was an opportunity to seek advice from independent counsel, financial advisers, or others.

In short, procedural fairness is all that is required. An agreement will not be struck down simply because there is an inequality in what each party receives. A wife cannot undo the agreement because of "buyer's remorse" or a wish that a better deal had been agreed to. Of course, the same is true of men of modest means who later regret signing premarital agreements with relatively wealthy women.

In a few states, if the terms of the agreement are not fair (substantive fairness), the court will presume that the other party concealed assets and failed to make a complete financial disclosure (procedural fairness), requiring this party to overcome the presumption by proving that the disclosure was adequate. This gives the disadvantaged party a procedural advantage. He or she does not have to prove that the disclosure was inadequate; the other party has the burden of proving that it was adequate.

The rule that procedural fairness is enough to enforce a premarital agreement is subject to a major exception. As we have seen, if the terms of the agreement leave a spouse in such poverty that he or she is likely to become a public charge when the other spouse seeks to enforce it, most courts will step in and require enough spousal support to avoid this result.

Unconscionability

Premarital agreements must not be **unconscionable**, which means shocking the conscience by heavily favoring one side due to the absence of meaningful choice and the highly unequal bargaining positions of the parties. One court defined unconscionability as "the absence of meaningful choice on the part of one party due to one-sided contract provisions, together with terms which are so oppressive that no reasonable person would make them and no fair and honest person would accept them."[10] All unconscionable agreements are also characterized by procedural unfairness. In effect, a party is practically railroaded into accepting very little and giving up a great deal in a highly pressurized take-or-leave environment.

unconscionable
Shocking the conscience by heavily favoring one side due to the absence of meaningful choice and the highly unequal bargaining positions of the parties.

Second Glance

When a court must decide whether an agreement is unconscionable, it examines two time frames: (a) when the agreement was signed (before the marriage) and (b) when an attempt is made to enforce it (often after a divorce action is filed). First, the court will want to know if the agreement was unreasonable and shockingly one-sided at the time it was signed. Second, when a party seeks to enforce the agreement, the court will want to know if its terms will leave the spouse destitute and a public charge. An agreement may have been reasonable at the time it was signed, but because of changed circumstances (e.g., health problems), the terms may now be substantially inadequate to

second-glance doctrine
To help determine the validity of a document that a party wants to enforce, a court will examine changed circumstances since the time the document was entered (executed). Also called the second-look rule.

provide for the ex-spouse's even minimal support needs. Examining a document after it was entered in order to determine whether changed circumstances affect its enforceability is referred to as the **second-glance doctrine**.

Norm and Irene enter a premarital agreement in which they waive all rights they have in each other's separate property. In the event of a divorce, the agreement provides that Norm will pay Irene support of $500 a month for two years. A year before the parties divorce, Irene is diagnosed with cancer. She will need substantially more than $500 a month for support. Norm has resources to pay her more than what the premarital agreement provides. If he does not do so, Irene will need public assistance.

To avoid this result, most courts will disregard the spousal-support clause in the premarital agreement and order Norm to pay Irene additional support as part of the divorce proceedings. The enforceability of this part of the agreement will be judged as of the date of separation or divorce, not the date the agreement was signed.

ASSIGNMENT 4.2

a. Jim and Mary are about to be married. Mary is a wealthy actress. Jim is a struggling artist. Both agree that it would be a good idea to have a premarital agreement. Mary suggests that Jim make an appointment to visit her tax preparer, whom Mary will instruct to give Jim a complete understanding of her assets. Laughing, Jim replies, "Not necessary. I'm insulted at the suggestion, my love." A year after the marriage, the parties divorce. Mary seeks to enforce the premarital agreement, which provides that Jim waives spousal support and is not entitled to any of Mary's property in the event of a divorce. Jim argues that the agreement is unenforceable. Discuss whether he is correct. (See General Instructions for the Legal-Analysis Assignment in Appendix A.)

b. Do women have enough equality in today's society that they should be forced to live with agreements that, in hindsight, they should not have made? Is it more demeaning to a woman to rescue her from a poorly bargained agreement or to force her to live in drastically poorer economic circumstances because of the premarital agreement she signed?

☑ INTERVIEWING AND INVESTIGATION CHECKLIST

Factors Relevant to the Validity of the Premarital Agreement (C = client; D = defendant/spouse)

LEGAL INTERVIEWING QUESTIONS

1. On what date did you begin discussing the premarital agreement?
2. Whose idea was it to have an agreement?
3. On what date did you first see the agreement?
4. Who wrote the agreement?
5. Did you read the agreement? If so, how carefully?
6. Did you understand everything in the agreement?
7. Describe in detail what you thought was in the agreement.
8. Did you sign the agreement? If so, why?

9. Were any changes made in the agreement? If so, describe the circumstances, the nature of each change, who proposed it, etc.
10. Do you recall anything said during the discussions about the agreement that was different from what was eventually written down?
11. Was anyone present at the time you discussed or signed the agreement?
12. Where is the agreement kept? Were you given a copy at the time you signed?
13. Before you signed the agreement, did you consult with anyone (e.g., attorney, accountant, relative)?

14. If you did consult with anyone, describe that person's relationship, if any, with D? Friend of D? Business associate of D?

15. What were you told by the individuals with whom you consulted? Did they think it was wise for you to sign the agreement? Why or why not?

16. How old were you when you signed the agreement? How old was D?

17. How much did you know about D's background before you agreed to marry D? What generally did you think D's wealth and standard of living were?

18. How did you obtain this information?

19. While you were considering the premarital agreement, describe what you specifically knew about the following: D's bank accounts (e.g., savings, checking, trust), insurance policies, home ownership, business property, salary, investments (e.g., stocks, bonds), rental income, royalty income, inheritances (recent or expected), cars, planes, boats, etc.

20. What did you know about D's debts and other liabilities? How did you obtain the knowledge?

21. When did you find out that at the time you signed the agreement D owned (_____)? (Insert items

in parentheses that C learned about only after the agreement was signed.)

22. Do you think you were given an honest accounting of all D's assets at the time you signed? Why or why not?

23. Do you think the agreement you signed was fair to you and to the children you and D had? Why or why not?

POSSIBLE INVESTIGATION TASKS

- Obtain copies of the premarital agreement and of drafts of the agreement, if any, reflecting changes.

- Contact and interview anyone who has knowledge of, or was present during, the discussions and/or signing of the agreement.

- Try to obtain bank records, tax records, etc., that would help identify the wealth and standard of living of D and of C at the time they signed the premarital agreement.

- Prepare an inventory of every asset that C *thought* D owned at the time the agreement was signed, and an inventory of every asset your investigation has revealed D *in fact* owned at the time of the signing.

INDEPENDENT COUNSEL

The preferred practice is for each party to a premarital agreement to have independent counsel. If one of them cannot afford to pay an attorney, the other should offer to provide funds for this purpose.

What happens if a party signs a premarital agreement without the benefit of independent counsel? Is it strong evidence that the agreement could not have been voluntarily entered? The celebrated case of *In re Marriage of Bonds* answers this question. A multimillionaire baseball player, Barry Bonds, entered a premarital agreement with his prospective wife, Sun Bonds. Paragraph 10 of the agreement provided:

> 10. CONTROL AND EARNINGS OF BOTH HUSBAND AND WIFE DURING MARRIAGE. We agree that all the earnings and accumulations resulting from the other's personal services, skill, efforts and work, together with all property acquired with funds and income derived therefrom, shall be the separate property of that spouse.

This clause meant that Sun Bonds would have no marital rights in Barry Bonds's baseball salary, clearly the largest asset in the coming marriage. She did not have independent counsel when she signed the agreement.

The case arose in California, a **community-property** state in which each spouse has a 50 percent interest in marital property such as a spouse's salary, regardless of which spouse earned the salary. A valid premarital agreement can change this rule. If the *Bonds* case had arisen in a **common-law property** state, the same issue would have had to be decided. The question before the court would still be whether the absence of independent counsel rendered the premarital agreement involuntary and therefore unenforceable.

community property
Property in which each spouse has a 50 percent interest because it was acquired during the marriage other than by gift, will, or intestate succession (inheritance) to only one of the spouses.

common-law property
Property acquired during the marriage in a state other than a community-property state. (Older definition: property acquired during the marriage that is owned by the spouse who earned it or who has title to it.)

CASE

In re Marriage of Bonds
24 Cal. 4th 1, 5 P.3d 815 (2000)
Supreme Court of California

Background: *At the time Barry Bonds married Susann (Sun) Bonds, he was earning $106,000 a year with the Pittsburgh Pirates. At the time of his divorce, he was earning millions a year with the San Francisco Giants. Before they married, they signed a premarital agreement prepared by Barry's counsel in which Sun waived any interest in his earnings during the marriage. Sun Bonds did not have independent counsel and she argued that the agreement was invalid because she did not sign it voluntarily. The trial court found that Sun entered the agreement voluntarily with a full understanding of its terms. Sun appealed to the Court of Appeal, which reversed and directed a retrial on the issue of voluntariness. Barry has now appealed to the California Supreme Court. He is the petitioner; Sun is the respondent.*

Decision on Appeal: *The Court of Appeal is reversed. There is substantial evidence that Sun Bonds signed voluntarily despite the lack of independent counsel.*

OPINION OF THE COURT

Chief Justice GEORGE delivered the opinion of the court: . . .

Sun and Barry met in Montreal in the summer of 1987 and maintained a relationship during ensuing months through telephone contacts. In October 1987, at Barry's invitation, Sun visited him for 10 days at his home in Phoenix, Arizona. In November 1987, Sun moved to Phoenix to take up residence with Barry and, one week later, the two became engaged to be married. In January 1988, they decided to marry before the commencement of professional baseball's spring training. On February 5, 1988, in Phoenix, the parties entered into a written premarital agreement in which each party waived any interest in the earnings and acquisitions of the other party during marriage. [The agreement was signed in the office of Barry's attorney, Leonard Brown. Sun did not have an attorney when she signed. After the signing, Barry and Sun flew to Las Vegas, and were married the following day.]

Each of the parties then was 23 years of age. Barry, who had attended college for three years and who had begun his career in professional baseball in 1985, had a contract to play for the Pittsburgh Pirates. His annual salary at the time of the marriage ceremony was approximately $106,000. Sun had emigrated to Canada from Sweden in 1985, had worked as a waitress and bartender, and had undertaken some training as a cosmetologist, having expressed an interest in embarking upon a career as a makeup artist for celebrity clients. Although her native language was Swedish, she had used both French and English in her employment, education, and personal relationships when she lived in Canada. She was unemployed at the time she entered into the premarital agreement. . . .

[The trial court concluded that Barry had demonstrated by clear and convincing evidence that the agreement and its execution were free from the taint of fraud, coercion, or undue influence and that Sun entered the agreement with full knowledge of the property involved and her rights therein. The court of appeal reversed, concluding that the trial court erred in failing to give proper weight to the circumstance that Sun was not represented by independent counsel. Barry has now appealed to the Supreme Court.]

Pursuant to Family Code section 1615, a premarital agreement will be enforced unless the party resisting enforcement of the agreement can demonstrate . . . that he or she did not enter into the contract voluntarily. . . . *Black's Law Dictionary* defines "voluntarily" as "Done by design. . . . Intentionally and without coercion" (Black's Law Dict. (6th ed. 1990) p. 1575). The same source defines "voluntary" as "Proceeding from the free and unrestrained will of the person. Produced in or by an act of choice. Resulting from free choice, without compulsion or solicitation. The word, especially in statutes, often implies knowledge of essential facts" (Ibid.) The *Oxford English Dictionary* defines "voluntarily" as "[o]f one's own free will or accord; without compulsion, constraint, or undue influence by others; freely, willingly" (19 *Oxford English Dict.* [2d ed. 1989] p. 753.). . . .

[A number of factors are relevant to the issue of voluntariness in addition to the presence or absence of independent counsel. A court should examine whether the evidence indicates coercion or lack of knowledge and consider] the impact upon the parties of such factors as

- the coercion that may arise from the proximity of execution of the agreement to the wedding, or from surprise in the presentation of the agreement;

- the presence or absence of independent counsel or of an opportunity to consult independent counsel;

- inequality of bargaining power in some cases indicated by the relative age and sophistication of the parties;

- whether there was full disclosure of assets; and

- the parties' understanding of the rights being waived under the agreement or at least their awareness of the intent of the agreement. . . .

The trial court determined that there had been no coercion. . . . Several witnesses, including Sun herself, stated that she was not threatened. The witnesses were unanimous in observing that Sun expressed no reluctance to sign the agreement, and they observed in addition that she appeared calm, happy, and confident as she participated in discussions of the agreement. [Barry's attorney, Leonard Brown,] testified that Sun had indicated a desire at their first meeting to enter into the agreement, and that during the discussion preceding execution of the document, she stated that she understood the agreement. As the trial court determined, although the wedding between Sun and Barry was planned for the day following the signing of the agreement, the wedding was impromptu—the parties had not secured a license or a place to be married, and the few family members and close friends who were invited could have changed their plans without difficulty. (For example, guests were not arriving from Sweden.) In view of these circumstances, the evidence supported the inference, drawn by the trial court, that the coercive force of the normal desire to avoid social embarrassment or humiliation was diminished or absent. Finally, Barry's testimony that the parties early in their relationship had discussed their desire to keep separate their property and earnings, in addition to the testimony of Barry and [his attorney] that they had met with Sun at least one week before the document was signed to discuss the need for an agreement, and the evidence establishing that Sun understood and concurred in the agreement, constituted substantial evidence to support the trial court's conclusion that Sun was not subjected to the type of coercion that may arise from the surprise and confusion caused by a last-minute presentation of a new plan to keep earnings and property separate during marriage. . . .

Brown testified that [he] informed Sun that he represented Barry and that therefore it might be in her best interest to have her own attorney. She declined. Brown testified that at the February 5, 1988, session he explained the basics of community property law, telling Sun that she would be disavowing the protection of community property law by agreeing that income and acquisitions during marriage would be separate property. He informed her of her right to separate counsel, and told both parties that the agreement did not have to be signed that day. He again informed Sun that he represented Barry. He testified that Sun stated that it was not necessary for her to have counsel, and that she said she understood how the contract affected her interests under the community property law. . . . Sun did not forgo separate legal advice out of ignorance. Instead, she declined to invoke her interests under the community property law because she agreed, for her own reasons, that Barry's and her earnings and acquisitions after marriage should be separate property. . . .

[The] basic purport of the agreement—that the parties would hold their earnings and accumulations during marriage as separate property, thereby giving up the protection of marital property law— was a relatively simple concept that did not require great legal sophistication to comprehend and that was, as the trial court found, understood by Sun. Finally, we observe that the evidence supports the inference that Sun was intrepid rather than a person whose will is easily overborne. She emigrated from her homeland at a young age, found employment and friends in a new country using two languages other than her native tongue, and in two years moved to yet another country, expressing the desire to take up a career and declaring to Barry that she "didn't want his money." These circumstances support the inference that any inequality in bargaining power—arising primarily from the absence of independent counsel who could have advised Sun not to sign the agreement or urged Barry to abandon the idea of keeping his earnings separate—was not coercive. . . .

Family Code section 1615 places on the party seeking to avoid a premarital agreement the burden of demonstrating that the agreement was involuntary. The trial court determined that Sun did not carry her burden, and we believe that its factual findings in support of this conclusion are supported by substantial evidence.

The judgment of the Court of Appeal is reversed. . . .

ASSIGNMENT 4.3

a. Assess the voluntariness of the premarital agreement in the fact situations in (i)–(iv) below. Assume in each instance that the parties did not have independent counsel. How would the *Bonds* case apply to each?

   (i) Harry presented Linda with the premarital agreement for the first time at the jewelry store where they were buying a ring the day before the wedding. Immediately after the wedding, they were scheduled to begin an expensive honeymoon cruise.

   (ii) Sam presented Mary with the premarital agreement for the first time two weeks before the wedding, just after Mary's elderly and frail parents arrived for the wedding from abroad.

   (iii) When Diane signed the premarital agreement, she was a pregnant teenager, anxious about the legitimacy of her child. Her husband-to-be and the father of the child, Bill, was an older man.

   (iv) The spouse preparing the premarital agreement was an attorney. The spouse of this attorney was a paralegal.

b. Should the law *require* each party to have his or her own independent counsel in order for the premarital agreement to be valid?

c. Do you think that there should be a difference between determining the voluntariness of a confession in a criminal case and the voluntariness of a premarital agreement in a civil case? Why or why not?

DO NOT SIGN THE AGREEMENT!

Assume there is a substantial disparity between the wealth of the parties to a premarital agreement, and that the financially weaker party is being asked to waive all or substantially all of the property rights normally accorded spouses. An attorney representing the weaker party is in a potentially vulnerable position. It is easy to say that the attorney should fight hard and bargain for better terms for the client. If, however, the wealthy party insists on no changes and if the attorney's client is prepared to go along and sign the agreement, there is not much that the attorney can do.

To be sure, the attorney needs to provide clear explanations of what the client is giving up. This, however, may not be enough to prevent the client from suing the attorney for legal malpractice years later when the premarital agreement is being enforced and the full brunt of the agreement is felt. Inevitably, the client says that she (it is usually a woman) did not understand the terms of the agreement and was not given proper advice by her attorney.

To protect themselves in such situations, some attorneys feel that they need to advise their clients in writing *not* to sign the agreement. Another strategy is to withdraw from the representation. If the attorney feels that the client is relatively immature and not capable of handling the intense emotional pressure she is under, the ultimate step of self-protection that the attorney can take is to formally withdraw from representing the client.

It is not much consolation to say that the premarital agreement might eventually be attacked on grounds such as unconscionability. It can take years to bring such litigation. Furthermore, if such litigation is brought, the chances of winning it are hurt when it is brought out that the agreement was signed against the advice of the party's own attorney. She understood that it was a bad deal because her attorney told her not to sign it or because he withdrew from representing her. Yet she went ahead and signed anyway.

DRAFTING GUIDELINES

At the end of this section on premarital agreements, you will find a sample premarital agreement. See also the drafting guidelines in the following checklist.

☑ PREMARITAL AGREEMENTS: A CHECKLIST OF DRAFTING GUIDELINES

Ensuring the Enforceability of a Premarital Agreement (FH = future husband; FW = future wife)

Although all the steps listed in this checklist may not be required in your state, they will help ensure the enforceability of the agreement. This checklist assumes that the attorney drafting the agreement represents the future husband (FH), who is going to enter the marriage with considerably more wealth than the future wife (FW).

PREPARATION

- Research the requirements for premarital agreements in the state, e.g., whether they must be subscribed (signed), acknowledged (affirmed as a genuine document), notarized (affirmed as having an authentic signature), or recorded (deposited with an official office or body such as a county clerk's office).

- Determine if FH and FW have any expectation of moving to another state during the marriage. If so, research the requirements for premarital agreements in such state(s) in order to ensure that the premarital agreement would be valid there in the event that they do move. (Even if there is a move, however, the parties can designate the state whose law will govern the agreement. See below.)

- Weeks (and, if possible, months) before the marriage, notify the FW when the agreement will be prepared and that she should obtain independent counsel.

- The greater the disparity in the age, wealth, education, and business experience of the FH and FW, the more time the FW should be given to study the agreement.

- Have the FW sign a statement acknowledging that she has been advised to hire independent counsel and that the FH will provide funds for such hiring if needed.

- Have the FW sign a statement acknowledging that she has been told that the persons hired by the FH represent the FH and do not represent the FW.

- Make sure the FW is old enough to have the legal capacity to enter a valid contract in the state.

- Determine whether the FW has ever been treated for mental illness or if any question could be raised about the FW's current mental health for purposes of understanding the agreement. If needed, assist the FW in selecting a mental health professional who is qualified to issue a certificate or affidavit of competency following an evaluation.

- Prepare a list of all currently owned assets of FH with the exact or approximate value of each asset. Use market value (what it could be sold for in an open market), not book value (the amount stated on the books). (Include real property, jewelry, household furnishings, stocks, bonds, other securities, and cash.) This list should be referred to in the agreement; shown to the FW, to her independent counsel, and to her other advisers; and attached to the agreement.

- Have the FW (and her independent counsel and other advisers) sign a statement acknowledging receipt of this list.

- Prepare a list of all known future assets that FH expects to acquire during the marriage, with the exact or approximate market value of each asset. (Include future employment contracts, options, and anticipated purchases.) This list should be referred to in the agreement; shown to the FW, to her independent counsel, and to her other advisers; and attached to the agreement.

- Have the FW (and her independent counsel and other advisers) sign a statement acknowledging receipt of this list.

- Prepare a list of all current debts or other liabilities of FH. This list should be referred to in the agreement; shown to the FW, to her independent counsel, and to her other advisers; and attached to the agreement.

- Have the FW (and her independent counsel and other advisers) sign a statement acknowledging receipt of this list.

- Hire an accountant to prepare a financial statement on the FH's assets and liabilities. This statement should be referred to in the agreement; shown to the FW, to her independent counsel, and to her other advisers; and attached to the agreement.

- Have the FW (and her independent counsel and other advisers) sign a statement acknowledging receipt of this financial statement.

- Obtain copies of recent personal tax returns, business tax returns, existing contracts of employment, deeds, purchase agreements, credit card bills, pension reports, and brokerage reports. Make a list of these documents. The documents and the list should be referred to in the agreement; shown to the FW, to her independent counsel, and to her other advisers; and attached to the agreement. (Note: to preserve confidentiality of sensitive financial data, the participants might acknowledge reading such lists and documents but not have them attached to the premarital agreement.)

- Have the FW (and her independent counsel and other advisers) sign a statement acknowledging the receipt of the list and the availability of these documents.

- Verify the accuracy of the names, addresses, and relationships of every individual to be mentioned in the premarital agreement.

- Once a year, contact FH to determine whether proposed changes in the agreement are needed because of changed circumstances.

PARTICIPANTS AND THEIR ROLES

- The FH's attorney, financial adviser, and other experts who have any communication with the FW should make clear to the FW (a) that they represent the FH only, (b) that FW should not rely on them to protect the interests of the FW, and (c) that FW should seek independent counsel or other advice.

- If needed, suggestions should be made to the FW about where she can find independent counsel and other experts who have never had any business or social dealings with the FH.

- If needed, funds should be made available to the FW to hire independent counsel or other experts.

- If no independent counsel of the FW is used, representatives of the FH will explain the terms of the agreement to the FW. When doing so, they should again remind the FW that their sole role is to protect the best interests of the FH, not the FW.

- If English is the second language of the FW, arrange for a translator to be present. Encourage the FW to select this translator.

- There should be at least two witnesses present who will observe the execution of the agreement. (Paralegals are sometimes asked to act as witnesses to such documents.)

- The agreement should contain a clause stating that when the agreement was negotiated, discussed, and signed, neither party was under the influence of alcohol, prescribed medication, or any drug that would affect their ability to understand the rights granted and waived in the agreement.

CONTENT OF THE AGREEMENT

- State the reasons the parties are entering the agreement.

- Include a separate list of the names, addresses, and titles, if any, of every individual who helped the FW prepare and/or understand the agreement.

- State whether the assets of the FH and of the FW that are now separate property will remain separate property during the marriage.

- State whether the appreciation (i.e., increase in value) of separate property during the marriage will constitute separate property.

- List FH's existing children, other relatives, or friends and specify what assets, if any, they will be given (to the exclusion of FW) during the marriage or upon the termination of the marriage.

- List FW's existing children, other relatives, or friends and specify what assets, if any, they will be given (to the exclusion of FH) during the marriage or upon the termination of the marriage.

- List the documents that were shown to, read by, and understood by FW (e.g., lists of the assets, lists of debts, copies of tax returns, and financial statements). State which of these documents are attached to the agreement.

- Include a statement that the FW acknowledges receipt of details regarding FH's assets and liabilities, that this disclosure is comprehensive, that FW has had sufficient time to study these details and consult with others about them, and that the FW is fully satisfied that this disclosure adequately apprises her of FH's financial condition.

- Briefly summarize the major property and support rights that FW and FH would have upon dissolution of a marriage or upon the death of either *in the absence of a premarital agreement* (e.g., the right to an equitable share in all marital property, the right to alimony, and the right to elect against the will of a deceased spouse). Then include a statement that the parties understand that by signing the premarital agreement, they are waiving these rights.

(continued)

☑ PREMARITAL AGREEMENTS: A CHECKLIST OF DRAFTING GUIDELINES (*continued*)

- State whether there is specific business or nonbusiness property that FH will have the right to manage and dispose of without the consent or participation of FW.

- State whether FW will own and be entitled to the death benefits of specific life insurance policies.

- Indicate which state's law will govern the interpretation and enforcement of the agreement.

- State whether arbitration will be used if FW and FH have disagreements over the agreement and whether the arbitrator's findings can be appealed. If an arbitrator is to be used, state how he or she will be chosen and compensated.

- State the method FH and FW will use to modify or terminate the agreement during the marriage.

- Do not ask for a waiver of disclosure of assets.

- Do not ask for a waiver of mutual support during the marriage.

- Do not ask for a waiver of child support.

- Do not ask for a waiver of the right to seek custody or visitation.

- Do not specify a date on which the prospective marriage will be dissolved.

- State that if either party provides financial or other help to the other to pursue his or her education during the marriage, that the help shall be considered gifts without expectation of repayment.

- If the parties are of child-bearing age, do not state that either or both will not have children.

- State that each party will keep the contents of the agreement confidential.

- State what documents, if any, the parties will be obligated to sign or obtain within a specified time after they are married (e.g., a waiver of rights in each other's retirement benefits, a life insurance policy, or an amendment to an existing will or trust).

- Include a severability clause stating that if any specific clause in the agreement is found to be invalid, the intent of the parties is to have the remainder of the agreement enforced.

SIGNING THE AGREEMENT

- Videotape the signing session, particularly while FW is explaining (a) why she is signing; (b) whom she relied upon for advice in accepting the terms of the agreement; (c) her understanding of FH's present and future assets; (d) her understanding of what she is waiving in the agreement; and (e) if she does not have independent counsel, why she chose not to have such counsel.

- FH and FW should sign every page of the agreement.

- The signatures should be notarized.

- Any changes or corrections to the agreement should be dated and signed by the parties in the margin next to the change.

RECORDKEEPING

- Keep copies of the agreement and all of the attachments (also called schedules attached to the agreement).

- Keep copies of all documents that were changed before the final agreement was signed. They may be needed to help prove the state of mind of the participants.

- Store these documents indefinitely. They may not be needed until decades later when the parties separate or when one of them dies and the agreement is enforced or challenged.

ASSIGNMENT 4.4

a. Pretend you are about to be married. Draft a premarital agreement for you and your future spouse. Assume that you are substantially more wealthy than your spouse-to-be. You can make up facts about the financial affairs and interests of your spouse-to-be and yourself. Number each clause of the agreement separately and consecutively. Try to anticipate as many difficulties as possible that could arise during the marriage and state in the agreement how you want them resolved. (See General Instructions for the Agreement-Drafting Assignment in Appendix A.)

b. After your instructor makes note of the fact that you have drafted an agreement, you will be asked to exchange agreements with another member of the class. You are to analyze the agreement written by your classmate. Go through each numbered clause in the agreement and determine all possible legal problems that might be raised according to the standards identified in this chapter. When you cannot apply a standard, in whole or in part, because you need more facts, simply list the factual questions to which you would like answers and state how they might be relevant to the validity of the clause in question. (See General Instructions for the Legal-Analysis Assignment in Appendix A.)

SAME-SEX PARTNERS

In states where same-sex couples can marry (see Chapter 5), they have the same right to enter premarital agreements as opposite-sex couples. In states that allow **civil unions** and **domestic partnerships,** same-sex couples about to enter such a union or partnership can also enter agreements (called civil-union agreements or domestic-partnership agreements) that will define their support and property rights in the same manner as the premarital agreements of opposite-sex couples.

EXAMPLE OF A PREMARITAL AGREEMENT

Exhibit 4-2 contains an example of a premarital agreement. Margin comments are provided to highlight important themes in the clauses. For terms you do not understand in the clauses, consult the glossary at the end of the book.

civil union
A same-sex legal relationship of unmarried individuals who have the same state benefits and responsibilities as individuals in a marriage.

domestic partnership
A same-sex or opposite-sex legal relationship of unmarried individuals who are emotionally and financially interdependent and who have some of the same state benefits and responsibilities as individuals in a marriage.

EXHIBIT 4-2   Example of a Premarital Agreement

PREMARITAL AGREEMENT

This premarital agreement is made [date], between [name of future husband], of [address], [city], County, [state] and [future wife], of [address], [city], County, [state].

RECITALS

A. The parties have represented to each other that each is single and legally free to marry.

B. The parties presently contemplate marriage to each other, such marriage to be solemnized in the near future.

C. The parties have fully and completely disclosed the nature and approximate value of all of their presently existing assets, liabilities, and income to each party's satisfaction on their respective schedules attached to this agreement.

D. Each party recognizes that certain interests, rights, and claims may accrue to each of them in the property and interests of the other as a result of their marriage.

E. The parties desire to define and agree to certain obligations arising out of their marriage to each other and to fix, limit, and determine the interest, rights, and claims that may accrue to each of them in the property and estate of the other by reason of their marriage to each other and to accept the provisions of this agreement in lieu of and in full discharge, settlement, and satisfaction of any and all interest, rights, and claims that otherwise each might or could have under the law, in and to the property and estate of the other, in the event of the parties' separation or dissolution of marriage.

F. Each party enters into this prenuptial agreement with full knowledge of the extent and approximate present value of all the property and estate of the other, and of all the rights and privileges in and to such property and estate that may be conferred by law upon each in the property and estate of the other by virtue of their marriage but for the execution of this agreement, to each party's satisfaction.

G. Future husband has had the benefit of independent legal advice, prior to the execution of this agreement, from _____, Esq., of [city], [state].

H. Future wife has had the benefit of independent legal advice, prior to the execution of this agreement, from _____, Esq., of [city], [state].

In consideration of the matters described above, and of the mutual benefits and obligations set forth in this agreement, the parties agree as follows:

SECTION ONE. DISCLOSURE OF FACTS

The parties acknowledge that, to their mutual satisfaction, each has had the opportunity to ascertain, has been informed by a full and frank disclosure by the other, and is fully acquainted with and aware of the approximate assets, liabilities, income, and general financial circumstances of the other; that each has ascertained and weighed all of the facts, conditions, and circumstances likely

- *A recital is a preliminary statement in a document covering its background or purpose.*

- *Clauses D, E, and F point out that the parties know that valuable legal rights accrue to married couples. The clauses also state that the parties realize that a valid premarital agreement can eliminate or otherwise modify these rights. The clauses help rebut a later claim that either of the parties did not realize what the agreement changed or waived.*

- *One of the strongest arguments for the validity of a premarital agreement is the fact that both sides had independent counsel advising them.*

(continued)

EXHIBIT 4-2 *(continued)*

to influence his or her judgment in all matters embodied here; that each has given due consideration to all such matters and questions, and clearly understands and consents to all the provisions contained here; and that each has had the opportunity to have, or has in fact had, the benefit and advice of independent counsel of his or her own choice and is willing to accept the provisions of this agreement in lieu of all other rights each may have.

SECTION TWO. EFFECT OF AGREEMENT

A. After the solemnization of the marriage between the parties, each of them will separately retain all rights in his or her own property now owned and more fully set forth in schedules attached to this agreement (collectively referred to in this agreement as "property"). Each party will have the absolute and unrestricted right to dispose of their separate property free from any claim that may be made by the other by reason of their marriage and with the same effect as if no marriage has been consummated between them.

B. The schedules list the property of future husband and future wife, respectively, as that property is now constituted. Each party will separately retain all rights to the property in its present form and in any form that is traceable to it, including any appreciation in the value of the property as a direct or indirect result of the contribution or efforts of either party or due to market factors, except as may be provided to the contrary in this agreement.

C. Any property either party acquires after the marriage, except for such property that has been specifically excepted in this agreement and that has not been commingled with joint or otherwise marital property, will be divided between the parties upon separation or divorce as provided in this agreement. The further effects of this agreement are more specifically set forth and detailed in the following provisions.

SECTION THREE. RELEASE OF MARITAL RIGHTS

Except as otherwise stated in this agreement, the parties waive, relinquish, and release any and all claims and rights either may have ever had, presently has, or may in the future acquire, with respect to the property listed on the other party's attached schedule, including any property that is traceable and acquired, in whole or in part, from the proceeds derived from the property and any appreciation or accretion in its value attributable, directly or indirectly, to the efforts or contributions of either party, or due to market factors. This provision will apply whether the claims and rights arise as a result of the parties' separation or the dissolution of marriage.

SECTION FOUR. PARTIES' UNDERSTANDING OF RIGHTS WAIVED

The parties intend that the disposition of the property referred to in this agreement be deemed a disposition of this property that would fully satisfy any claims either party may have against the other, including each party's rights to equitable distribution under [cite statute].

SECTION FIVE. GENERAL STATEMENT OF INTENTIONS

While in no way limiting or restricting the understanding of the parties, or the provisions or effect of this agreement, the parties generally state their intentions for this agreement as follows:

A. While the parties fully intend to commit themselves to achieving a successful long-term marriage, each party is personally aware of the practicalities and realities of life, together with the time and the financial and emotional cost involved in the unfortunate event of a legal proceeding concerning the parties' separation or dissolution. Each party intends by entering into this agreement to minimize the time and financial and emotional cost involved in the event of a future separation or dissolution of marriage between them.

B. Future husband has children from his prior marriage. Future wife has children from her prior marriage. While acknowledging that each is assuming a new status and relationship relative to the other's children, the parties intend by entering into this agreement to provide that each will continue to be responsible for any parental or legal obligations of support each may have with respect to his or her own children and in no event will either

Financial disclosure of assets and liabilities is critical for a valid agreement. Throughout the agreement there are references to attachments that are included to the agreement. The attachments—also called schedules—provide this financial disclosure.

Property that a person brings into the marriage is separate property, not marital or community property. (See Chapter 8.) The schedules will list this property to prevent later misunderstandings.

In some states, the appreciation (increase in value) of separate property is considered marital or community property. The agreement wants to change this result. Appreciation of separate property will be separate property. (See Chapter 8.)

This agreement is written for a couple in a common-law property state that divides property upon divorce on the basis of an equitable distribution. The same clause could be written if the parties were in a community property state. (See Chapter 8.)

Once the marriage occurs, the parties are going to become stepparents to each other's children from prior marriages. They want to make clear that they do not intend to obligate themselves for the child support of their stepchildren. (See Chapter 10.)

party be responsible, now or in the future, for any such parental or legal obligations of support with respect to the other party's children.

C. The parties each have retirement plans, either through their employer or self-procured. The parties intend by entering into this agreement that neither party will acquire any rights at any time, in any form or nature, to the other's retirement benefits.

SECTION SIX. RIGHTS TO SEPARATE PROPERTY

Each party will retain sole ownership, enjoyment, control, and power of disposal of all the property listed on his or her respective schedule, and all increments to that property, free and clear of any interest, rights, or claims of the other except as may be otherwise set forth in this agreement.

SECTION SEVEN. PROPERTY ACQUIRED DURING MARRIAGE

Nothing contained in this agreement will be construed to preclude any rights either party may have in the event of the parties' separation or dissolution of marriage in those assets that are acquired during the marriage and not otherwise specifically exempted or excepted by any other provision contained in this agreement.

SECTION EIGHT. WAIVER OF SPOUSAL SUPPORT

The parties represent that each is presently employed. Future husband is employed by _____, and future wife is employed by _____. Both future husband and future wife are entering the marriage financially independent and self-sufficient. If the parties separate or the marriage is dissolved, each party understands and agrees to waive, relinquish, and release the other from any duty or obligation to support the other in any fashion or manner. No claim or demand for such support may be made. If a separation or dissolution of marriage is sought by either party, and it appears that the financial circumstances of either party has changed to such a degree that such party can sufficiently demonstrate that he or she would be left without a means of support, destitute or a public charge, or at a standard of living far below that which the party enjoyed before the marriage, as a result of this agreement, then in that event, the party who is not left in any of the foregoing circumstances agrees to provide support for the other in an amount not to exceed $ _____ per month, for a period not to exceed _____ years.

SECTION NINE. INSURANCE

If the parties separate or the marriage contemplated is dissolved, the parties mutually agree that neither will be responsible for maintaining any policy of insurance for the benefit of the other, including, but not limited to, health, life, and automobile insurance.

SECTION TEN. PROPERTY RIGHTS UPON DEATH

The parties understand that this agreement makes no provision for apportionment of property rights in the event of either party's death. Each of the parties agrees to prepare and execute a last will and testament to resolve any such issue that may arise in this regard.

SECTION ELEVEN. DEDICATION OF INCOME

The parties specifically make no delineation as to the precise use of their income, except to state that it is their general intention to pool their income for their mutual benefit, for the purpose of maintaining their agreed-upon lifestyle, and for the accumulation of marital assets. For purposes of this provision, retirement income will not be deemed income but will instead be deemed separate property.

SECTION TWELVE. NONINCURRENCE OF DEBT

The parties represent that neither has incurred any debt, charge, obligation, or liability for which the other is or may become liable, nor will either party incur such debt, charge, obligation, or liability without first providing the other with reasonable notice and obtaining the other's written consent. Each party agrees to indemnify and hold the other harmless of loss, expenses (including reasonable attorney fees), and damages in the event that a claim is made on the other arising out of or in connection with a breach by either party of this paragraph.

This clause may not be enough to waive rights to retirement plans. As indicated earlier in Chapter 4, the waiver may have to occur after the marriage is entered. Sections 17 and 27 of the agreement state that the parties will cooperate in creating (executing) any documents that are needed once the marriage occurs.

Section 7 says that the parties do not intend to make any changes in how the state divides marital or joint property if there is a divorce and if the parties cannot agree (in a separation agreement) on how it should be divided.

If there is a separation or divorce, Section 8 waives spousal support (alimony) unless one of the parties faces a drastically lower standard of living or needs public assistance. In such circumstances, the agreement lists a specific amount of money for a specific number of years. Note, however, that a court is not bound by this limitation if it determines that more support for a longer period is needed. (See Chapter 8.)

Section 12 makes clear that the debts the parties bring into the marriage are separate debts and that neither intends to make gifts to the other that would help pay for the other's debts. Nor will either incur joint debts without written consent.

(continued)

EXHIBIT 4-2   *(continued)*

SECTION THIRTEEN. EQUITABLE DISTRIBUTION

The parties acknowledge and understand that each enters into the marriage with the same approximate total value of assets. The parties further acknowledge and understand that they intend to pool their financial resources in a joint effort to acquire various and, at present, undetermined assets (such as real estate and securities) in addition to other marital assets. In the event of the parties' separation or marriage dissolution, each agrees that all such acquired property will be distributed amicably between them or, in the event the parties cannot agree, liquidated with the net proceeds derived from the liquidation to be evenly distributed between them. "Net proceeds" are the sales price or total liquidated value of any asset less any and all liens and encumbrances, together with any actual gains tax, realtor's or broker's commissions, attorney fees and any other reasonable and necessary costs of the liquidation.

SECTION FOURTEEN. FULL DISCLOSURE

The parties acknowledge and represent to each other that they have made a full, fair, and complete disclosure to the other of the nature and approximate value of their assets, liabilities, and income as presently constituted in accordance with their attached respective schedules, and that each accepts those disclosures. The parties represent and acknowledge that based upon the foregoing representations, each knowingly, voluntarily, and without undue pressure, waives further discovery relative to the nature and value of the other's assets, liabilities, and income.

SECTION FIFTEEN. INHERITANCES OR GIFTS FROM THIRD PARTIES

Notwithstanding any provision contained in this agreement to the contrary, any and all property acquired during the marriage by either party by way of gift or inheritance from a third party will be deemed the separate property of the party acquiring it including, but not limited to, any income or profits, increments, accretions, or increases in value of such assets at any time, whether due to market conditions or the services, skills, or efforts of either party, and that all such property will be kept separate and not commingled with joint or otherwise marital property. To the extent that any such property is commingled or not kept separate from marital property, it will be deemed joint property. Any assets acquired by the parties jointly during the marriage by way of gift or inheritance from a third party shall be deemed joint property acquired during the marriage, the distribution of which, in the event of the parties' separation or dissolution of marriage, is governed by Section 13 of this agreement.

SECTION SIXTEEN. INTERSPOUSAL TRANSFERS, DEVISES, AND BEQUESTS

Notwithstanding any provision of this agreement to the contrary, any other rights acquired by either party by virtue of any transfer or conveyance of property between the parties during their lifetime, or by devises or bequests made by either party for the benefit of the other pursuant to a last will and testament, will not be limited or restricted.

SECTION SEVENTEEN. WAIVER OF RIGHT TO SHARE IN RETIREMENT BENEFITS

The parties relinquish any claim either may have to all retirement benefits titled in the other party's individual name. Both parties agree to execute all documents necessary to give full force and effect to this provision.

SECTION EIGHTEEN. ATTORNEY FEES

In the event of any court proceeding concerning their marital relationship or the dissolution of their marriage, each party will be responsible for the payment of his or her own attorney fees and all ancillary costs incurred in connection with any such proceeding.

SECTION NINETEEN. TIMING OF EXECUTION

This agreement is being executed in sufficient time prior to the scheduled wedding date of _____. The parties acknowledge that each had sufficient opportunity prior to executing this agreement to consult with counsel, to reschedule the wedding date if necessary, and to not proceed with the marriage, but each agrees that the timing of the execution of this agreement relative to their wedding date has no effect on his or her decision to execute this agreement. Each party further waives his or her right to argue that he or she had insufficient time to make an informed and calculated decision to execute it. The parties further represent that this agreement has been discussed between them for a period of [number] [days or weeks or months] prior to the date of executing this agreement, and it is only as a result of their deliberations and thoughtful consideration of the provisions contained in this agreement that it is being executed at this time.

- *Section 13 states that in the event of a divorce, if the parties cannot agree on how their marital property should be divided, the division should be equal.*

- *Section 14 says that the financial disclosures are adequate and that further disclosure (discovery) is waived.*

- *Section 15 says that property from a gift or inheritance to one spouse is the separate property of that spouse unless that property is mixed (commingled) with their joint assets. If the gift or inheritance is to both parties, it is marital or joint property. (See Chapter 8.)*

- *A court would not be bound by Section 18 if it concluded that one of the spouses could not finance private counsel on his or her own. It could order the other spouse to provide funds for this purpose despite what Section 18 says.*

- *Section 19 addresses the problem of a party claiming that the pressures of wedding arrangements prevented his or her from calmly and thoroughly studying the agreement before deciding to sign it.*

SECTION TWENTY. VOLUNTARY EXECUTION

This agreement has been executed by each of the parties free from persuasion, fraud, undue influence, or economic, physical, or emotional duress of any kind asserted by the other party or by other persons.

SECTION TWENTY-ONE. INDEPENDENT COUNSEL

The parties acknowledge that each has procured and has been advised as to all aspects of this agreement by independent counsel of his or her own choice and that each understands that he or she has the right to seek additional advice of counsel and of others but has expressly waived that right. Each party is satisfied that he or she has freely negotiated the contents of this agreement free from the persuasion of the other or of any third party.

SECTION TWENTY-TWO. INCORPORATION OF AGREEMENT

This agreement may be offered in evidence in any proceeding instituted by either of the parties in any court of competent jurisdiction in which a determination of the status of the parties' relationship is sought and may, subject to the approval of the court, be incorporated in any order or judgment rendered in that action.

SECTION TWENTY-THREE. VALIDITY AND ENFORCEABILITY OF AGREEMENT

The parties further agree that this agreement is valid and enforceable in any action that may subsequently be commenced by either party that may require the use of this agreement as evidence to demonstrate the parties' understanding of any issues addressed in this agreement.

SECTION TWENTY-FOUR. SEVERABILITY

Should any provision of this agreement be held invalid or unenforceable by any court of competent jurisdiction, all other provisions will nonetheless continue in full force and effect.

SECTION TWENTY-FIVE. MODIFICATION OR WAIVER

No modification or waiver of any terms of this agreement will be valid unless in writing and executed by the parties.

SECTION TWENTY-SIX. GOVERNING LAW

The laws of [state] will govern the execution and enforcement of this agreement.

SECTION TWENTY-SEVEN. NECESSARY DOCUMENTS

Each party must, on the request of the other, execute, acknowledge, and deliver any instruments appropriate or necessary to carry into effect the intentions and provisions of this agreement.

SECTION TWENTY-EIGHT. CONSIDERATION

The consideration for this agreement is the mutual promises contained in this agreement and the marriage about to be solemnized. If the marriage does not take place, this agreement shall be void.

SECTION TWENTY-NINE. ENTIRE AGREEMENT

This agreement contains the entire agreement and understanding of the parties, and no representations or promises have been made except those set forth in this agreement.

SECTION THIRTY. BINDING EFFECT

This agreement is binding on and inures to the benefit of the parties and their respective heirs, executors, and administrators.

SECTION THIRTY-ONE. EFFECTIVE DATE OF AGREEMENT

This agreement shall become effective upon the date the parties are married.

Dated: _____

_____

[Name and Signature of Party]

_____

[Name and Signature of Party]

- *Undue influence is improper persuasion, coercion, force, or deception that substitutes the will of one person for the free will of another.*
- *Section 21 is being extra cautious. It says the parties consulted their own independent attorneys and that each waives any right they have to seek additional advice.*

(continued)

EXHIBIT 4-2 *(continued)*

Witnesses:

_____

_____

Notary Public:

_____ (Seal)

My commission expires _____

This instrument was prepared by [name], of [address], [city], [county], [state].

[Attach schedules]

Reprinted from 9B *American Jurisprudence Legal Forms 2d*, § 139:19 (May 2011) with permission of Thomson Reuters.

POSTNUPTIAL AGREEMENTS

postnuptial agreement

A contract by married persons that covers financial and related matters between them. The parties may have no intention of separating. If they have this intention, the agreement is commonly called a separation agreement.

separation agreement

A contract by married persons who have separated (or who are about to separate) that can cover support, custody, property division, and other terms of their separation and divorce.

unity of person

The legal identity of a wife was subsumed into the legal identity of the husband. Also called doctrine of oneness, spousal-unity rule.

As we saw in Exhibit 4-1 at the beginning of the chapter, a **postnuptial agreement** (also called a postnup or a midnup) is a contract made between married parties that covers financial and related matters between them. They may have no intention of separating. If they have this intention, the contract is commonly called a **separation agreement**. Keep in mind, however, that in some states the separation agreement is also referred to as a postnuptial agreement.

As pointed out in Chapter 1, there was a time when a wife could not enter a valid contract with her husband. Through the common-law rule of **unity of person**, the legal identity of a wife was subsumed into the legal identity of the husband. The husband and wife were one person and that person was the husband. Hence, for a wife to enter a contract with her husband was the equivalent of the husband contracting with himself. This rule no longer exists. Today, a wife has her own independent legal identity and can enter contracts such as postnuptial agreements with her husband. Furthermore, spouses can sue each other for breach of these contracts.

Postnuptial contracts, like premarital agreements, can designate what each spouse would receive upon the death of one of them or in the event of a divorce. In addition, here are some specific purposes of such agreements:

- Update or change the premarital agreement.
- Revoke the premarital agreement entirely.
- Ratify the premarital agreement after a child is born to help rebut a potential claim that the pregnant spouse-to-be acted under undue pressure or duress because of the pregnancy when she signed the premarital agreement.
- Change (or purchase) a life insurance policy with a commitment to keep it funded and to designate one of them as the beneficiary.
- Clarify what will be done with a large inheritance given to one of the spouses during the marriage.
- Specify the terms of a reconciliation after the parties begin living together after a separation.
- Set the terms of a financial transaction between the spouses such as a plan to form a business partnership together or a loan to one spouse from the personal (separate) funds of the other spouse.
- Specify how the funds will be distributed from the sale of a business that one spouse began before the marriage and that both spouses ran during the marriage.

Of course, not all married couples enter postnuptial agreements in such circumstances. One family-law attorney comments, "Postnups, like prenups, aren't everybody's idea of problem solving. Skeptics say even mentioning a marital contract is asking for trouble. How do you sit down with your spouse and say, 'I just got a bonus and I'd like to keep it all. Can we sign an agreement?' Who's going to feel good about that? It's kind of tacky."[11]

Despite this concern, however, postnuptial agreements are becoming increasingly popular, particularly in times of economic uncertainty when both spouses have separate financial lives. A fair number of husbands and wives have their own individual businesses and manage their own finances. As one journalist noted, "It is impossible to know how many couples are signing postnuptial agreements, since they are drafted by private lawyers and usually not reviewed by the courts unless they are challenged. But lawyers who specialize in family and matrimonial law say the demand has been growing."[12] There are spouses who appreciate the level of security provided by postnuptial agreements that spell out some of the major financial terms that will govern their marriage as it moves forward.

The requirement of procedural fairness discussed earlier for premarital agreements also applies to postnuptial agreements. They must be entered voluntarily by both spouses without duress or undue influence. Full financial disclosure is essential. A court, for example, is unlikely to enforce a postnuptial agreement in which the wife is to enter a business arrangement with her husband who will control all the finances and deny his wife access to the financial information that will allow her to make an informed decision about the agreement.

Some postnuptial agreements, however, are not enforceable even if they are entered voluntarily and with informed consent. For example, one spouse cannot enter a contract to support the other spouse. Spouses already have a duty of mutual support. A promise of support would not meet the contract requirement of consideration, which is something of value (e.g., a promise) that is exchanged. You are not receiving something of value if you already have what is being promised. For the same reason, an agreement to provide standard household services is not backed by consideration. Spouses already have a duty to provide such services to each other. Furthermore, clauses on child custody and child support are treated the same in premarital and postnuptial agreements. Such clauses do not restrict the court's right to make an independent decision of what support and custody needs will best serve the interests of a child.

In a recent case on the legality of a postnuptial agreement, the wife agreed not to file for divorce in exchange for her husband's agreement to make the marital home her exclusive nonmarital (i.e., separate) property if she ever does file for divorce. The court upheld this agreement on the ground that her agreement to refrain from filing for divorce (a forbearance) was sufficient consideration for his agreement to make the home her separate property.[12a]

Although most states will enforce postnuptial agreements for valid purposes, there remains a lingering concern that one of the spouses is being taken advantage of. According to one family-law attorney, "If you look at the agreements, they're almost always to increase the rights of the wealthier partner and decrease the rights of the less wealthy one."[13] The tendency of the court is to scrutinize the agreements carefully to make sure that procedural fairness existed when they were entered.

Some states go even further and will not enforce postnuptial agreements in the absence of substantive fairness as well. In these states, married couples have a *fiduciary relationship* with each other, unlike unmarried couples and unlike most strangers. Persons in a fiduciary relationship owe each other loyalty, candor, and fair treatment. By definition, therefore, a court in these states will scrutinize the terms of a postnuptial agreement to ensure that they are fair to both parties.

ASSIGNMENT 4.5

In a famous postnup case, a married couple (Jamie and Frank McCourt) had a dispute over the terms of their postnuptial agreement and the ownership of the Los Angeles Dodgers. The couple were married and living in Massachusetts when they entered the postnuptial agreement. After purchasing the Dodgers, they decided to move to California (a community-property state). One of the objectives of the postnuptial agreement was to try to shield some of their assets from creditors. Do a search (McCourt Dodgers postnup) in Google, Bing, or Yahoo on the controversy.

a. What dispute did Jamie and Frank have about the postnup and the ownership of the Dodgers?

b. How has the dispute been resolved thus far? What decisions have been made by the courts?

c. What could the attorneys have done to prevent the dispute?

COHABITATION AGREEMENTS

In 1950, married couples were present in 78 percent of American households. In 2010, the percentage was 47 percent, dropping below 50 percent for the first time.[14] Approximately 6.7 million unmarried couples live together, including 620,000 same-sex couples.[15] The "number of unmarried couples living together has roughly doubled each decade since 1970, increasing overall by about 1000 percent."[16] At one time, the inclination of society was to punish couples who lived together without being married. (They were "living in sin" or what the church calls "public concubinage.") **Adultery** and **fornication** were crimes, even though they were not often prosecuted. Today the environment is dramatically different. The predominant value in the nation is privacy in how couples choose to live their lives together. This is not to say that anything goes, but the shift is substantially toward the elimination of restrictions.

Parties have different reasons for living in a marriage-like relationship without marrying:

- They may want to live together to find out if they are sufficiently compatible for marriage.

- They may not believe in marriage. (In a recent national survey, 39 percent of respondents said that they believed marriage was obsolete.[17])

- The parties may not be eligible to marry (e.g., they are a same-sex couple living in a state that does not allow such marriages).

- One of the parties might be receiving alimony from a prior marriage and does not want to jeopardize its continuation; the terms of the divorce might provide that the alimony would end if the recipient remarried.

- One of the parties might be receiving public assistance of some kind that would end or be reduced if the recipient marries.

Whatever the reason, the number of couples living together continues to grow.

Cohabitation means living together in an intimate (usually sexual) relationship. This definition, of course, would also cover husbands and wives, although the word *cohabitation* is most often used in reference to unmarried persons living together in an intimate relationship. Hence, the most common definition of cohabitation is living together as (or like) husband and wife without being married, or living together in an intimate relationship in the manner of a husband and wife. Parties who are cohabiting are called **cohabitants**. (Texas refers to the relationship as "nonmarital conjugal cohabitation."[18])

In this section, we will examine the **cohabitation agreement**, which is a contract by persons in an intimate relationship who are not married to each other (and who intend to stay unmarried indefinitely). The contract covers financial and related matters while living together and upon the end of the cohabitation by death or separation.

adultery
Voluntary sexual intercourse between a married person and someone other than his or her spouse. (See glossary for an expanded meaning.)

fornication
Voluntary sexual intercourse between unmarried persons.

cohabitation
Living together in an intimate (usually sexual) relationship in the manner of a husband and wife. A de facto husband and wife relationship. The verb is *cohabit*. Although a married couple cohabits, the word *cohabitation* is more often used in reference to unmarried couples.

cohabitants
Two persons living together in an intimate (usually sexual) relationship.

cohabitation agreement
A contract by persons in an intimate relationship who are not married to each other (and who intend to stay unmarried indefinitely) that covers financial and related matters while they are living together and upon the end of the relationship by death or separation.

CONSIDERATION

First, let's look at contract law in general. As we saw earlier, a contract is a legally enforceable agreement, and most contracts consist of the three elements: offer, acceptance, and consideration. Not all consideration, however, will qualify. Compare the following two situations:

> *Case I. Jim contacts a cleaning service and hires Mary as a maid for his house. She receives weekly compensation plus room and board. For a three-month period, Jim fails to pay Mary's wages, even though she faithfully performs all of her duties. During this period, Jim seduces Mary and they have a brief affair. After the affair ends, Mary sues Jim for breach of contract due to nonpayment of wages for cleaning services.*

> *Case II. Barbara is a prostitute. Sam hires Barbara for an evening but refuses to pay her fee the next morning. Barbara sues Sam for breach of contract due to nonpayment of the fee.*

The result in Case II is clear. Barbara cannot sue Sam for breach of contract. A contract for sex is not enforceable in court. Sam promised to pay money for sex. Barbara promised and provided sexual services. This was the consideration for the bargain. But sex for hire is illegal in most states. In fact, fornication is still a crime in some states (usually if it is "open and notorious") even if no payment is involved. There cannot be a valid contract when the consideration is payment for sexual services. Most states refer to payment for sexual services as **meretricious**, which means pertaining to prostitution or unlawful sexual relations. (Washington State is an exception. Payment for sex is not legal in Washington State, but the state does not use the word *meretricious* to describe unlawful sexual relations.[19])

The result in Case I should also be clear. Mary has a valid claim for breach of contract. Her agreement to have a sexual relationship with Jim is incidental and, therefore, irrelevant to her right to collect compensation that is due her as a maid. She did not sell sexual services to Jim. There is no indication in the facts that the parties bargained for sexual services or that she engaged in sex in exchange for anything from Jim (e.g., continued employment, a raise in pay, lighter work duties). The sex they had with each other is a *severable* part of their relationship and should not affect her main claim. As we have seen, something is severable when what remains after it is removed has legal force and can survive without it.

There are two ways to determine whether something is severable. First, the parties might explicitly state that it is severable, such as by inserting a severability clause in their agreement. Second, if no such explicit agreement exists, we ask whether the parties would probably have carried out the rest of what happened if the questionable part did not exist. In Case I, we can say that the cleaning services would have been paid for even if a sexual relationship had not developed between Jim and Mary. Hence, the sexual relationship was severable. In Case II, we can say that the payment would not have been made if sexual services had not been provided. Thus, sex was not a severable part of the arrangement; it was an essential part.

Now we come to a more difficult case:

> *Dan and Helen met in college. They soon started living together. They moved into an apartment, pooled their resources, and had children. They never married. Twenty years after they entered this relationship, they decide to separate. Helen now sues Dan for a share of the property acquired during the time they lived together.*

The fact that Dan and Helen never married does not affect their obligation to support their children, as we shall see in Chapter 10. But what about Dan and Helen themselves? They cohabited and never married. They built a relationship, acquired property together, and helped each other over a long period of time. Do they have any support or property rights in each other now that they have separated?

meretricious

1. Pertaining to prostitution or unlawful sexual relations. 2. Vulgar or tawdry. 3. In Washington State, a meretricious relationship means a stable, marital-like relationship where both parties cohabit with knowledge that a lawful marriage between them does not exist.

For years, the law has denied any rights to an unmarried person who makes financial claims based upon a period of cohabitation. The traditional reasons for this denial are as follows:

- To grant financial or property rights to unmarried persons would treat them as if they were married. Our laws favor the institution of marriage. To recognize unmarried relationships would denigrate marriage and discourage people from entering it.

- Most states have abolished **common-law marriage**, as we will see in Chapter 5. The preference of the law is for **ceremonial marriages**. To allow substantial financial rights to be awarded upon the termination of an unmarried relationship would be the equivalent of giving the relationship the status of a common-law marriage.

- Sexual relations are legal and morally acceptable within marriage. If the law recognizes unmarried cohabitation, then illicit sex is being condoned.

MARVIN v. MARVIN

In 1976, the important case of *Marvin v. Marvin* was decided in California.[20] This case held that parties living together would not be denied a remedy in court upon their separation solely because they never married. Although the case was widely discussed in the media, most states have *not* followed all of the holdings in *Marvin*. As we will see, many states agree with the holding in *Marvin* on express contracts, but not all of its other holdings.

The parties in *Marvin v. Marvin* lived together for seven years without marrying. The plaintiff was Michelle Marvin (formerly Michelle Triola) and the defendant was Lee Marvin, a famous actor. They never married, but Michelle changed her last name to Marvin. She alleged that she and Lee Marvin had entered an oral agreement (1) that he would support her and (2) that while "the parties lived together they would combine their efforts and earnings and would share equally any and all property accumulated as a result of their efforts whether individual or combined." She further alleged that she agreed to give up her career as a singer in order to devote herself full time to the defendant as a companion, homemaker, housekeeper, and cook. During the seven years that they were together, the defendant accumulated in his name more than $1 million in property. When they separated, she sued for her share of this property.

The media viewed her case as an alimony action between two unmarried "ex-pals" and dubbed it a **palimony** suit. The word has come to mean support payments ordered after the end of a nonmarital relationship if the party seeking support was induced to initiate or stay in the relationship by a promise of support or if ordering support is otherwise equitable. Although *Marvin v. Marvin* centered on the issue of support, the broader topics of loans, expense-sharing, and other property agreements were also involved in the case.

One of the first hurdles for the plaintiff in *Marvin* was the problem of "meretricious sexual services." The defendant argued that even if a contract did exist (which he denied), it was unenforceable because it involved an illicit relationship. The parties were not married but were engaging in sexual relations. The court, however, ruled that

> [A] contract between nonmarital partners is unenforceable only *to the extent* that it *explicitly* rests upon the immoral and illicit consideration of meretricious sexual services.... The fact that a man and woman live together without marriage, and engage in a sexual relationship, does not in itself invalidate agreements between them relating to their earnings, property, or expenses.... [Adults] "who voluntarily live together and engage in sexual relations are ... as competent as any other persons to contract respecting their earnings and property rights."[21]

The agreement will be invalidated only if sex is an express or explicit condition of the relationship. If the sexual aspect of their relationship is *severable* from

common-law marriage
A marriage entered without license or traditional ceremony by persons who (a) agree to marry, (b) live together as husband and wife, and (c) hold themselves out as married. A marriage of two people who have not gone through a ceremonial marriage. Called "informal marriage" in Texas.

ceremonial marriage
A marriage that is entered in compliance with statutory requirements (e.g., obtaining a marriage license, having the marriage performed by an authorized person before witnesses). A marriage other than a common-law marriage.

palimony
Support payments ordered after the end of a nonmarital relationship (a) if the party seeking support was induced to initiate or stay in the relationship by a promise of support or (b) if ordering support is otherwise equitable.

their agreements or understandings on earnings, property, and expenses, the agreements or understandings will be enforced. An example of an *unenforceable* agreement would be a promise by a man to provide for a woman in his will in exchange for her agreeing to live with him for the purpose of bearing his children through unprotected sexual relations between them. This agreement is *explicitly* based on a sexual relationship. Thus, sex in such a case cannot be separated from the agreement and is *not* severable.

The next problem faced by the plaintiff in *Marvin* was the theory of *recovery*. Married parties have financial rights in each other because of their *marital status*, which gives rise to duties imposed by law. What about unmarried parties? The *Marvin* court suggested several theories of recovery (**remedies**) for such individuals:

- Express contract
- Implied-in-fact contract
- Implied-in-law contract (quasi contract)
- Implied trust; constructive trust
- Partnership
- Joint venture

remedy
1. The means by which a right is enforced or the violation of a right is prevented, compensated for, or otherwise redressed.
2. To correct. The plural is *remedies*.

Before we examine these theories, two points must be emphasized. First, as indicated earlier, most states do not agree with *Marvin* that all of these remedies should be available to unmarried couples when they separate. States are very reluctant to grant rights to unmarried couples in a way that would undermine the strong preference for *ceremonial marriage*. Many states will agree with the express-contract theory, but not the implied-contract theories. The fear is that opening the door to allow implied-contract theories can present huge problems of proof, encourage litigation, and create substantial uncertainty that could have been avoided if the parties had entered an express contract, or, indeed, a marriage. It is too easy for a cohabitant to fabricate or exaggerate a claim after the cohabitation has ended, particularly after one of the cohabitants dies and the claim is made against his or her estate. Second, all of the theories will be to no avail if it can be shown that meretricious sexual services were at the heart of the relationship and cannot be separated (are not severable) from the other aspects of the relationship.

EXPRESS CONTRACT

An **express contract** is an agreement or contract whose terms are explicitly stated by the parties. Express contracts can be oral or written. An example of the latter is a written cohabitation agreement. As we saw in Exhibit 4-1, this is a contract by persons in an intimate relationship who are not married to each other (and who intend to stay unmarried indefinitely) that covers financial and related matters while they are living together and upon the end of the relationship by death or separation. A few states have enacted laws on the enforceability of cohabitation agreements. For example, a statute in Minnesota provides that the parties can enforce the property and financial terms of the agreement if the agreement is in writing and is signed by the parties.[22] However, most states that enforce cohabitation agreements do not require them to be in writing.

express contract
An agreement or contract whose terms are explicitly stated by the parties.

Unfortunately, most cohabitants (persons living together in an intimate relationship) do not have an express contract such as a cohabitation agreement. Without a written express contract, it can be extremely difficult (although not impossible) to prove what agreements the parties reached on financial matters during the cohabitation.

Next we will examine some of the more controversial theories of recovery endorsed by the court in the *Marvin* case. These theories are not as widely accepted in other states as the express-contract theory.

IMPLIED-IN-FACT CONTRACT

There are two kinds of implied contracts: implied-in-fact contracts and implied-in-law contracts.

An **implied-in-fact contract** is a contract that is not created by an express agreement between the parties but is inferred as a matter of reason and justice from their conduct and the surrounding circumstances. The contract exists when it is reasonable to conclude that the parties had a **tacit** understanding that they were bound by a contract, even though the terms of the contract were never expressly discussed. Consider the following example:

> *Someone delivers bottled milk to your door daily, which you never ordered. You consume the milk every day, place the empty bottles at the front door, exchange greetings with the delivery person, never demand that the deliveries stop, etc.*

At the end of the month when you receive the bill for the milk, you will not be able to hide behind the fact that you never expressly ordered the milk. Under traditional contract principles, you have entered an "implied contract" to buy the milk, which is as binding as an express contract. Unless the state has enacted special laws to change these principles, you must pay for the milk.

In the case of unmarried individuals living together, we must similarly determine whether an implied contract existed.

> *Sally and Frank are an unmarried couple. After 20 years together, they separate. Sally now sues Frank for an equal share of the income from the rental properties purchased while they lived together. The funds for the first two properties came from Frank alone. The funds for all the other properties came from the rents earned from the initial properties and from later property purchases. All the properties were placed in Frank's name only. They never discussed sharing rental income. Sally performed all bookkeeping services, collected the rents, and paid bills for the all properties. She never took a salary. Both Sally and Frank always told everyone that they were "a team" who worked together "like a pair of gloves."*

There was no express contract to share rental income. Was there an implied-in-fact contract to do so? A court would have to determine if it is reasonable to conclude from their conduct that they were entering an agreement to share the rental income. Is it reasonable to conclude that the intent of Sally and Frank was that she would be exchanging her financial and support services for such a share? Did both sides expect "compensation" in some form to be provided for what each did? If so, an implied-in-fact contract existed, which can be as enforceable as an express contract.

Most courts are reluctant to imply a contract of compensation for personal services. The thinking is that when parties in an intimate relationship provide personal services for each other, their intent usually is to do so without expectation of payment. If asked why certain services were provided, the likely response is that it was convenient or gratifying to do so. The "case law of cohabitation makes it clear that courts will not order compensation for services performed by one partner that can be characterized as part of the ordinary give-and-take of a shared life."[23]

Another objection to implied contracts is that they might be used as a backdoor route to the equivalent of a *common-law marriage* in states that have abolished such marriages. As we will see in Chapter 5, strong policy reasons have prompted most states to abolish common-law marriages. Attorneys are always looking for strategies to get around laws that are not helpful to their clients. The states do not want implied-contract claims to be such a strategy.

IMPLIED-IN-LAW CONTRACT (QUASI CONTRACT)

Another *Marvin* theory is **implied-in-law contract** (also called *quasi contract*), which is an obligation created by law to avoid **unjust enrichment**. Although an implied-in-law contract is referred to as a contract, it is a legal fiction to use the word "contract" because it does not involve an express or implied agreement.

---

implied-in-fact contract
A contract that is not created by an express agreement between the parties but is inferred as a matter of reason and justice from their conduct and the surrounding circumstances. A contract that is manifested by conduct and circumstances rather than by words of agreement. A contract that a reasonable person would infer exists, even though there is no express agreement.

tacit
Understood without being openly stated; implied by silence or conduct.

implied-in-law contract
An obligation created by the law to avoid unjust enrichment in the absence of an express or implied contract creating this obligation. Also called quasi contract.

unjust enrichment
The receipt of a benefit in the form of goods or services from another when, in fairness and equity, the recipient should provide restitution for the goods or compensation for the services even though there was no express or implied promise to do so. The amount the recipient should pay for services is called quantum meruit, the reasonable value of the services provided.

The doctrine of implied-in-law contract is simply a device designed by the courts to prevent unjust enrichment. The latter occurs when someone receives a benefit in the form of goods or services from another when, in fairness and equity, the recipient should provide restitution for the goods and compensation for the services, even though there was no express or implied promise to do so. (When the benefit provided is services, the amount the recipient should pay is called **quantum meruit**, the reasonable value of the services provided.) An example might be a doctor who provides medical care to an unconscious motorist on the road. The doctor can recover the reasonable cost of medical services under the theory of an implied-in-law contract, even though the motorist never expressly or impliedly asked for such services. Another example might be a man who arranges for a foreign woman to come to this country to live in his home and provide domestic services. Assume there was no express or implied understanding between them that she would be paid. If what she provided was not meretricious, the law might obligate him to pay the reasonable value of her services (quantum meruit), less the value of any support she received from him during the time they were together. The court's objective would be to avoid unjust enrichment. A court might reach a similar result when unmarried cohabitants separate.

quantum meruit

"As much as he deserves." An award of the reasonable value of services provided despite the absence of an express or implied agreement to pay for the services.

CONSTRUCTIVE TRUST

A **trust** is a property arrangement or device involving three parties:

- the creator of the trust (called the settlor or trustor),
- the person who holds legal title to the property (called the trustee), and
- the person who is to benefit from the property (called the beneficiary or cestui que trust); the beneficiary has a **beneficial interest** in the property.

The property itself is called the *corpus*. A trust comes into existence when the creator transfers legal title of the corpus to the trustee who holds it for the benefit of the beneficiary.

At times, the law will imply the existence of a trust even if the parties did not intend to create one. It is called a **constructive trust**. It comes into existence by **operation of law** rather than (or even despite) what the parties intended. A constructive trust is imposed as an **equitable remedy** to prevent unjust enrichment by someone who has improperly obtained property through fraud, duress, abuse of confidence, or other wrongful conduct.

> *Tim and Sandra, an unmarried cohabiting couple, decide to buy a house. The funds for the house come from an inheritance from Sandra's father. Without telling Sandra, Tim places the title to the house in his name only, although he had told her that he would put it in their joint names. After the couple separate, Tom refuses to acknowledge Sandra's interest in the house. He sells the house and keeps the proceeds for himself.*

On such facts, a court will impose a constructive trust on the funds for Sandra's benefit. She will be entitled to all or most of the proceeds from the sale. A theory of constructive trust might also be possible if Sandra contributed valuable services rather than money toward the purchase of the property. A court would have to decide what her interest in the property should be in light of the nature and value of these services.

In our example, Tim obtained the property wrongfully—he lied about whose name would be on the title. Suppose that the inheritance from Sandra's father was the house itself and that when she was given the house, she became concerned that some of her future creditors might be able to reach the house. Therefore, she and Tim decided to place the title of the house in Tim's name alone as a device to shield the house from her creditors (or at least to make it more difficult for them to reach the house). After Tim and Sandra separate, Tim sells the house and keeps the proceeds. Here again, the law will impose a trust

trust

A device or arrangement by which its creator (the settlor or trustor) transfers property (the corpus) to a person (the trustee) who holds legal title for the benefit of another (the beneficiary or cestui que trust).

beneficial interest

A right to a benefit from property or an estate as opposed to the legal ownership of that property or estate.

constructive trust

A trust created by operation of law to prevent unjust enrichment by someone who has improperly obtained property through fraud, duress, abuse of confidence, or other wrongful conduct.

operation of law

The means by which legal consequences are imposed by law, regardless of (or even despite) the intent of the parties involved.

equitable remedy

A form of relief (e.g., injunction, specific performance, or constructive trust) that may be available when remedies at law (e.g., damages) are not adequate.

on the proceeds by operation of law in order to avoid unjust enrichment. Because, however, Tim did not obtain title wrongfully (Sandra wanted the house to be in his name alone), the trust that will be imposed is called a **resulting trust**. This trust is an equitable remedy designed to carry out the original intent of the parties as to who was supposed to have the benefit of the property despite who held legal title.

The following two cases, *Hewitt v. Hewitt* and *Watt v. Watt*, are examples of the contrasting points of view among courts of different states on whether unmarried cohabitants should be given support or other financial rights upon the termination of the cohabitation. The *Watts* case says no. *Hewitt v. Hewitt* is more inclined to adopt the approach of *Marvin v. Marvin*.

CASE

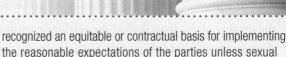

Hewitt v. Hewitt
77 Ill. 2d 49, 394 N.E.2d 1204, 3 A.L.R. 4th 1 (1979)
Supreme Court of Illinois

Background: *Victoria Hewitt met Robert Hewitt in college. When she became pregnant, he told her they were husband and wife and that no formal ceremony was necessary. He said he would "share his life, his future, his earnings, and his property" with her. They announced to their parents that they were married and held themselves out as husband and wife. She helped him in his education and business. During fifteen years together, they had three children. They never entered a ceremonial marriage. (Since 1905 Illinois has not allowed parties to enter a common law marriage, which is a marriage entered by intent and by openly living together as husband and wife, but without going through a ceremonial marriage.) Upon their separation, she sued him for "an equal share of the profits and properties accumulated" while together. Her theories of recovery included express contract, implied contract, constructive trust, and unjust enrichment. The circuit court dismissed her complaint. She appealed. The lower appellate court reversed and ruled that she could sue him for violating an express oral contract. Robert then appealed. The case is now on appeal before the Supreme Court of Illinois.*

Decision on Appeal: *Judgment for Robert. It is against public policy in Illinois to enforce property rights of unmarried cohabitants.*

OPINION OF THE COURT

Justice UNDERWOOD delivered the opinion of the court: . . .

In finding that plaintiff's complaint stated a cause of action on an express oral contract, the appellate court adopted the reasoning of the California Supreme Court in the widely publicized case of Marvin v. Marvin (1976), 18 Cal. 3d 660, 134 Cal. Rptr. 815, 557 P.2d 106, . . . We are aware, of course, of the increasing judicial attention given the individual claims of unmarried cohabitants to jointly accumulated property, and the fact that the majority of courts considering the question have

recognized an equitable or contractual basis for implementing the reasonable expectations of the parties unless sexual services were the explicit consideration. . . .

The issue of unmarried cohabitants' mutual property rights, however, . . . cannot appropriately be characterized solely in terms of contract law, nor is it limited to considerations of equity or fairness as between the parties to such relationships. There are major public policy questions involved in determining whether, under what circumstances, and to what extent it is desirable to accord some type of legal status to claims arising from such relationships. Of substantially greater importance than the rights of the immediate parties is the impact of such recognition upon our society and the institution of marriage. Will the fact that legal rights closely resembling those arising from conventional marriages can be acquired by those who deliberately choose to enter into what have heretofore been commonly referred to as "illicit" or "meretricious" relationships encourage formation of such relationships and weaken marriage as the foundation of our family-based society? In the event of death shall the survivor have the status of a surviving spouse for purposes of inheritance, wrongful death actions, workmen's compensation, etc.? And still more importantly: What of the children born of such relationships? What are their support and inheritance rights and by what standards are custody questions resolved? What of the sociological and psychological effects upon them of that type of environment? Does not the recognition of legally enforceable property and custody rights emanating from nonmarital cohabitation in practical effect equate with the legalization of common law marriage at least in the circumstances of this case? And, in summary, have the increasing numbers of unmarried cohabitants and changing mores of our society . . . reached the point at which the general welfare of the citizens of this State is best served by a return to something resembling the judicially created common law marriage our legislature outlawed in 1905?

Illinois' public policy regarding agreements such as the one alleged here was implemented long ago in *Wallace v. Rappleye* (1882), 103 Ill. 229, 249, where this court said: "An agreement in consideration of future illicit cohabitation between the plaintiffs is void." This is the traditional rule. . . . It is true, of course, that cohabitation by the parties may not prevent them from forming valid contracts about independent matters, for which it is said the sexual relations do not form part of the consideration. *Restatement of Contracts* secs. 589, 597 (1932). . . .

The real thrust of plaintiff's argument here is that we should abandon the rule of illegality because of certain changes in societal norms and attitudes. It is urged that social mores have changed radically in recent years, rendering this principle of law archaic. It is said that because there are so many unmarried cohabitants today the courts must confer a legal status on such relationships. . . . If this is to be the result, however, it would seem more candid to acknowledge the return of varying forms of common law marriage than to continue displaying the naiveté we believe involved in the assertion that there are involved in these relationships contracts separate and independent from the sexual activity, and the assumption that those contracts would have been entered into or would continue without that activity. . . .

[J]udicial recognition of mutual property rights between unmarried cohabitants would, in our opinion, clearly violate the policy of our recently enacted Illinois Marriage and Dissolution of Marriage Act . . . "[to] strengthen and preserve the integrity of marriage and safeguard family relationships." (Ill. Rev. Stat. 1977, ch. 40, par. 102.) We cannot confidently say that judicial recognition of property rights between unmarried cohabitants will not make that alternative to marriage more attractive by allowing the parties to engage in such relationships with greater security. . . . The policy of the Act gives the State a strong continuing interest in the institution of marriage and prevents the marriage relation from becoming in effect a private contract terminable at will. This seems to us another indication that public policy disfavors private contractual alternatives to marriage. . . .

[W]e believe that these questions are appropriately within the province of the legislature, and that, if there is to be a change in the law of this State on this matter, it is for the legislature and not the courts to bring about that change. We accordingly hold that plaintiff's claims are unenforceable for the reason that they contravene the public policy, implicit in the statutory scheme of the Illinois Marriage and Dissolution of Marriage Act, disfavoring the grant of mutually enforceable property rights to knowingly unmarried cohabitants.

Appellate court reversed; circuit court affirmed.

CASE

Watts v. Watts
137 Wis. 2d 506, 405 N.W.2d 303 (1987)
Supreme Court of Wisconsin

Background: *Sue Watts alleges that she quit her job and abandoned her career in exchange for James Watts' promise to take care of her. For twelve years, they raised a family and worked in a family business together. They never married. (Common law marriages are not allowed in Wisconsin.) When the relationship deteriorated, she sued him in circuit court for her share of the property they had accumulated. Among her legal theories were breach of an express or implied contract and unjust enrichment. The circuit court dismissed the case, arguing that the legislature, not the court, should provide relief to parties who have accumulated property in nonmarital cohabitation relationships. The case is now on appeal before the Supreme Court of Wisconsin.*

Decision on Appeal: *Reversed. The court does not have to wait until the legislature acts. Sue Watts should be allowed to bring her claims against James.*

OPINION OF THE COURT

Justice ABRAHAMSON delivered the opinion of the court: . . .

Nonmarital cohabitation does not render every agreement between the cohabiting parties illegal. . . . The plaintiff alleges that during the parties' relationship, and because of her domestic and business contributions, the business and personal wealth of the couple increased. Furthermore, the plaintiff alleges that she never received any compensation for these contributions to the relationship and that the defendant indicated to the plaintiff both orally and through his conduct that he considered her to be his wife and that she would share equally in the increased wealth.

The plaintiff asserts that since the breakdown of the relationship the defendant has refused to share equally with her the wealth accumulated through their joint efforts or to compensate her in any way for her contributions to the relationship. . . . [H]er claim . . . is that she and the defendant had a contract to share equally the property accumulated during their relationship. The essence of the complaint is that the parties had a contract, either an express or implied in fact contract, which the defendant breached. . . .

The defendant appears to attack the plaintiff's contract theory on three grounds. First, the defendant apparently asserts that the court's recognition of plaintiff's contract claim for a share of the parties' property contravenes the Wisconsin Family

(continued)

CASE • Watts v. Watts (continued)

Code. Second, the defendant asserts that the legislature, not the courts, should determine the property and contract rights of unmarried cohabiting parties. Third, the defendant intimates that the parties' relationship was immoral and illegal and that any recognition of a contract between the parties or plaintiff's claim for a share of the property accumulated during the cohabitation contravenes public policy.

The defendant rests his argument that judicial recognition of a contract between unmarried cohabitants for property division violates the Wisconsin Family Code on *Hewitt v. Hewitt,* 77 Ill. 2d 49, 394 N.E.2d 1204, 3 A.L.R. 4th 1 (1979). In *Hewitt* the Illinois Supreme Court concluded that judicial recognition of mutual property rights between unmarried cohabitants would violate the policy of the Illinois Marriage and Dissolution Act because enhancing the attractiveness of a private arrangement contravenes the Act's policy of strengthening and preserving the integrity of marriage. The Illinois court concluded that allowing such a contract claim would weaken the sanctity of marriage, put in doubt the rights of inheritance, and open the door to false pretenses of marriage. . . .

The defendant has failed to persuade this court that enforcing an express or implied in fact contract between these parties would in fact violate the Wisconsin Family Code. The Family Code, chs. 765–68, Stats. 1985–86, is intended to promote the institution of marriage and the family. We find no indication, however, that the Wisconsin legislature intended the Family Code to restrict in any way a court's resolution of property or contract disputes between unmarried cohabitants.

The defendant also urges that if the court is not willing to say that the Family Code proscribes contracts between unmarried cohabiting parties, then the court should refuse to resolve the contract and property rights of unmarried cohabitants without legislative guidance. The defendant asserts that this court should conclude, as the *Hewitt* court did, that the task of determining the rights of cohabiting parties is too complex and difficult for the court and should be left to the legislature. We are not persuaded by the defendant's argument. Courts have traditionally developed principles of contract and property law through the case-by-case method of the common law. While ultimately the legislature may resolve the problems raised by unmarried cohabiting parties, we are not persuaded that the court should refrain from resolving such disputes until the legislature gives us direction. . . .

We turn to the defendant's third point, namely, that any contract between the parties regarding property division contravenes public policy because the contract is based on immoral or illegal sexual activity. . . . Courts have generally refused to enforce contracts for which the sole consideration is sexual relations, sometimes referred to as "meretricious" relationships. See *In Matter of Estate of Steffes,* 95 Wis. 2d 490, 514, 290 N.W.2d 697 (1980), citing *Restatement of Contracts,* Section 589 (1932). Courts distinguish, however, between contracts that are explicitly and inseparably founded on sexual services and those that are not. This court, and numerous other courts, have concluded that "a bargain between two people is not illegal merely because there is an illicit relationship between the two so long as the bargain is independent of the illicit relationship and the illicit relationship does not constitute any part of the consideration bargained for and is not a condition of the bargain." *Steffes,* supra, 95 Wis. 2d at 514, 290 N.W.2d 697.

While not condoning the illicit sexual relationship of the parties, many courts have recognized that the result of a court's refusal to enforce contract and property rights between unmarried cohabitants is that one party keeps all or most of the assets accumulated during the relationship, while the other party, no more or less "guilty," is deprived of property which he or she has helped to accumulate. See e.g., *Marvin v. Marvin,* 18 Cal. 3d 660, 682, 134 Cal. Rptr. 815, 830, 557 P.2d 106, 121 (1976).

The *Hewitt* decision, which leaves one party to the relationship enriched at the expense of the other party who had contributed to the acquisition of the property, has often been criticized by courts and commentators as being unduly harsh. Moreover, courts recognize that their refusal to enforce what are in other contexts clearly lawful promises will not undo the parties' relationship and may not discourage others from entering into such relationships. *Tyranski v.Piggins,* 44 Mich. App. 570, 577, 205 N.W.2d 595 (1973). A harsh, per se rule that the contract and property rights of unmarried cohabiting parties will not be recognized might actually encourage a partner with greater income potential to avoid marriage in order to retain all accumulated assets, leaving the other party with nothing.

In this case, the plaintiff has alleged many facts independent from the parties' physical relationship which, if proven, would establish an express contract or an implied in fact contract that the parties agreed to share the property accumulated during the relationship. The plaintiff has alleged that she quit her job and abandoned her career training upon the defendant's promise to take care of her. A change in one party's circumstances in performance of the agreement may imply an agreement between the parties. *Steffes,* supra, 95 Wis. 2d at 504, 290 N.W.2d 697; *Tyranski, supra,* 44 Mich. App. at 574, 205 N.W.2d at 597. In addition, the plaintiff alleges that she performed housekeeping, childbearing, childrearing, and other services related to the maintenance of the parties' home, in addition to various services for the defendant's business and her own business, for which she received no compensation. Courts have recognized that money, property, or services (including housekeeping or childrearing) may constitute adequate consideration independent of the parties' sexual relationship to support an agreement to share or transfer property. See *Tyranski,* supra, 44 Mich. App. at 574, 205 N.W.2d at 597; *Steffes,* supra 95 Wis. 2d at 501, 290 N.W.2d 697.

[Until recently, the prevailing view was that services performed in the context of a "family or marriage relationship" were presumed gratuitous. However, that presumption was rebuttable. In *Steffes,* we held the presumption to be irrelevant where the plaintiff can show either an express or implied agreement to pay for those services, even where the plaintiff has rendered them "with a sense of affection, devotion and duty." Id. 95 Wis. 2d at 503, 290 N.W.2d at 703–704.]

According to the plaintiff's complaint, the parties cohabited for more than twelve years, held joint bank accounts, made joint purchases, filed joint income tax returns, and were listed as husband and wife on other legal documents. Courts have held that such a relationship and "joint acts of a financial nature can give rise to an inference that the parties intended to share equally." *Beal v. Beal,* 282 Or. 115, 122, 577 P.2d 507, 510 (1978). The joint ownership of property and the filing of joint income tax returns strongly implies that the parties intended their relationship to be in the nature of a joint enterprise, financially as well as personally.

Having reviewed the complaint and surveyed the law in this and other jurisdictions, we hold that the Family Code does not preclude an unmarried cohabitant from asserting contract and property claims against the other party to the cohabitation. We further conclude that public policy does not necessarily preclude an unmarried cohabitant from asserting a contract claim against the other party to the cohabitation so long as the claim exists independently of the sexual relationship and is supported by separate consideration. Accordingly, we conclude that the plaintiff in this case has pleaded the facts necessary to state a claim for damages resulting from the defendant's breach of an express or an implied in fact contract to share with the plaintiff the property accumulated through the efforts of both parties during their relationship. . . . [W]e do not judge the merits of the plaintiff's claim; we merely hold that she be given her day in court to prove her claim. . . .

The plaintiff's [next] theory of recovery involves unjust enrichment. Essentially, she alleges that the defendant accepted and retained the benefit of services she provided knowing that she expected to share equally in the wealth accumulated during their relationship. She argues that it is unfair for the defendant to retain all the assets they accumulated under these circumstances and that a constructive trust should be imposed on the property as a result of the defendant's unjust enrichment. . . .

As part of his general argument, the defendant claims that the court should leave the parties to an illicit relationship such as the one in this case essentially as they are found, providing no relief at all to either party. For support, the defendant relies heavily on *Hewitt v. Hewitt,* supra, to argue that courts should provide no relief whatsoever to unmarried cohabitants until the legislature provides specifically for it.

As we have discussed previously, allowing no relief at all to one party in a so-called "illicit" relationship effectively provides total relief to the other, by leaving that party owner of all the assets acquired through the efforts of both. Yet it cannot seriously be argued that the party retaining all the assets is less "guilty" than the other. Such a result is contrary to the principles of equity. Many courts have held, and we now so hold, that unmarried cohabitants may raise claims based upon unjust enrichment following the termination of their relationships where one of the parties attempts to retain an unreasonable amount of the property acquired through the efforts of both. . . .

In summary, we hold that the plaintiff's complaint has stated a claim upon which relief may be granted. . . . Accordingly, we reverse the judgment of the circuit court, and remand the cause to the circuit court for further proceedings consistent with this opinion.

ASSIGNMENT 4.6

a. Why did the *Hewitt* court rule that it should not provide a remedy for unmarried cohabitating couples? Why did the *Watts* court rule that a remedy should be provided for them?

b. The *Watts* court referred to the decision of the *Hewitt* court as "unduly harsh." Do you agree? Which opinion do you think was correctly decided, *Hewitt* or *Watts*?

c. Assume that James Watts died without leaving a will while he still had a good relationship with Sue Watts. Would she be able to claim a share of his estate as one of his heirs?

Other theories of possible recovery that might work for some unmarried cohabitants include partnership and joint venture.

PARTNERSHIP

A **partnership** is a voluntary association of two or more persons to place their resources in a jointly owned business or enterprise, with a proportional sharing of profits and losses. A court might find that an unmarried couple entered the equivalent of a partnership and thereby acquired rights and obligations in the property involved in the partnership.

partnership

A voluntary association of two (or more) persons to place their resources in a jointly owned business or enterprise, with a proportional sharing of profits and losses.

joint venture
A business or profit-seeking activity of two or more persons who each participate and control the activity (or who have the right of participation and control).

JOINT VENTURE

A **joint venture** is a business or profit-seeking activity of two or more persons who each participate and control the activity (or who have the right of participation and control). A court might use the joint-venture theory to cover enterprises entered into by two unmarried individuals while living together (e.g., the purchase of a rental property). Once a joint venture is established, the parties have legally enforceable rights in the fruits of their endeavors.

ASSIGNMENT 4.7

a. Tom and George are gay. They live together. George agrees to support Tom while the latter completes engineering school, at which time Tom will support George while the latter completes law school. After Tom obtains his engineering degree, however, he leaves George. George now sues Tom for the amount of money that would have been provided as support while George attended law school. What result? (See General Instructions for the Legal-Analysis Assignment in Appendix A.)

b. Rich and Diane enter an elaborate cohabitation agreement in a state where such agreements are often enforced. The agreement makes clear that sexual relations are not the consideration of the agreement. One of the clauses in the agreement is that Diane will be given a bequest of $200,000 in Rich's will if Rich and Diane are still together upon the death of Rich. During the period that Rich and Diane lived together, Rich was married to Mary, from whom he has been separated for 10 years. Rich and Mary never divorced. Rich dies while still living with Diane. Diane now wants to enforce the cohabitation agreement against the Rich's estate, including the clause giving $200,000 to her. Mary appears and contests this clause. What result? (See the General Instructions for the Legal-Analysis Assignment in Appendix A.)

c. Richard and Lea have lived together for 10 years without being married. This month, they separated. They never entered a formal contract, but Lea says that they had an informal understanding that they would equally divide everything acquired during their relationship together. Lea sues Richard for half of all property so acquired. You work for the law firm that represents Lea. Draft a set of interrogatories for Lea that will be sent to Richard in which you seek information that would be relevant to Lea's action. (See General Instructions for the Interrogatories Assignment in Appendix A.)

✔ INTERVIEWING AND INVESTIGATION CHECKLIST

Factors Relevant to the Property Rights of Unmarried Couples

LEGAL INTERVIEWING QUESTIONS

1. When and how did the two of you meet?

2. When did you begin living together?

3. On what dates did you live together?

4. What changes, if any, had to be made in your personal, social, or business lives in order to start living together?

5. Why did the two of you decide to start living together? What exactly did you say to each other about your relationship at the time?

6. Did you discuss the living arrangement together? If so, what was said?

7. Do the two of you have a sexual relationship together? If so, when did it begin?

8. What was said or implied about the sexual relationship between you? Was there an express or implied understanding that either of you would provide sex in exchange for other services, for money, or for other property?

9. If sexual relations had not been a part of your relationship, would you have still lived together?

10. Were the two of you "faithful" to each other? Did either of you ever date others? Explain.

11. What was your understanding about the following matters: rent, house purchase, house payments, furniture payments, food, clothing, medical bills, health insurance, and household chores?

12. Describe the extent to which you both maintained separate financial lives. Describe the extent to which you had a joint or communal financial life. For example, did you agree to keep separate or joint bank accounts? Why?

13. What other commitments were made, if any? For example, was there an agreement on providing support, making a will, giving each other property or shares in property?

14. What discussions occurred, if any, about having children together?

15. Did you ever discuss marriage? If so, what was said by both of you on the topic?

16. What did you give up in order to live with him or her? Was this understood by both of you? How do you know?

17. What did he or she give up in order to live with you? Was this understood by both of you? How do you know?

18. What other promises were made or implied between you? Why were they made?

19. Is there a way for you to substantiate the existence of any of these promises, agreements, or understandings? Were any commitments put in writing? Explain.

20. How did you introduce each other to other people?

21. What understanding did other people have of the nature of your relationship together? How did they come to this understanding?

22. Did either of you have a separate business before or during the cohabitation? If so, explain how the business was financed and run.

23. Did either of you have a jointly run business before or during the cohabitation? If so, how it was financed and run?

24. Have either of you received compensation from the other or from a business that was solely or jointly run? If so, explain.

25. What were your roles in the house? How were these roles decided upon? Through agreement? Explain.

26. Did he or she ever pay you for anything you did? Did you ever pay him or her? Explain the circumstances.

27. If no payment was ever made, was payment expected in the future? Explain.

28. Did you use each other's money for any purpose? If so, explain the circumstances. If not, why not?

29. Did you ever feel pressured or coerced by any aspect of your relationship together? If so, explain.

30. Did you ever feel you were cheated or taken advantage of by any aspect of your relationship together? If so, explain.

POSSIBLE INVESTIGATION TASKS

- Obtain copies of bank statements, deeds for property acquired while the parties were together, loan applications, tax returns, etc.
- Interview persons who knew the parties.
- Contact professional housekeeping companies to determine the going rate for housekeeping services.

EXAMPLE OF A COHABITATION AGREEMENT

EXHIBIT 4-3 Example of a Cohabitation Agreement

COHABITATION AGREEMENT

Intention of the Parties

1. _____ and _____ declare that they are not married to each other, but they are living together under the same roof, and by this agreement intend to protect and define each other's rights pertaining to future services rendered, earnings, accumulated property and furnishings, and other matters that may be contained herein.

2. It is expressly set forth herein that the consent of either party to cohabit sexually with the other is not a consideration, either in whole or in part, for the making of this agreement.

3. It is further expressly set forth herein that the general purpose of this agreement is that the earnings, accumulations, and property of each party herein shall be the separate property of the person who earns or acquires said property, and shall not be deemed community property, joint property, or common law property, or otherwise give the non-earning or non-acquiring party an interest in same.

Representations to the Public

4. It is agreed that should either or both of the parties to this agreement represent to the public, in whatever manner, that they are husband and wife, that said representation shall be for social convenience only, and shall in no way imply that sexual services are a consideration for any part of this agreement, nor shall it imply that sexual cohabitation is taking place.

Property, Earnings, and Accumulations

5. It is agreed that all property of any nature or in any place, including but not limited to the earnings and income resulting from the personal services, skill, effort, and work of either party to this agreement, whether acquired before or during the term of this agreement, or acquired by either one of them by purchase, gift, or inheritance during the said term, shall be the separate property of the respective party, and that neither party shall have any interest in, and both parties hereby waive any right or interest he or she may have in the property of the other.

- *In the statement of intention in clause 2, the parties want to make clear that their sexual relationship is not the essence of their relationship and of their agreement. If it was, a court could declare the agreement to be invalid.*

- *If parties hold themselves out to be husband and wife, a court might conclude that they have entered a common-law marriage if such marriages are allowed in the state where they live or where they spend significant time. (See Chapter 5.) See, however, clause 17, in which they explicitly disclaim an intent to enter a common-law marriage.*

(continued)

EXHIBIT 4-3 *(continued)*

Services Rendered

6. It is agreed that whatever household, homemaking, or other domestic work and services that either party may contribute to the other or to their common domicile shall be voluntary, free, and without compensation, and each party agrees that work of this nature is done without expectation of monetary or other reward from the other party.

- *Note that clause 6 does not cover business or professional services they render to each other. Such services are covered in clauses 11 to 13.*

Debts and Obligations

7. It is agreed that all debts and obligations acquired by either party which is to the benefit of that party shall be the debt or obligation of that party only, and that the other shall not be liable for same. Should one party be forced to pay a debt rightfully belonging to and benefiting the other, the other promises to reimburse, indemnify, and hold harmless the one who has paid said debt or obligation. Those debts and obligations, which are to the benefit of both parties, such as utilities, garbage, Internet, telephone service, rent, and renter's insurance shall be paid in such sums and in such proportion by each party as shall be mutually agreeable.

Money Loaned

8. All money, with the exception of mortgage or rent payments, transferred by one party to the other, either directly or to an account, obligation, or purchase of the other, shall be deemed a loan to the other, unless otherwise stated in writing. This shall include such things as down payments on a home or vehicle and deposits in either party's separate bank account.

Rented Premises

9. It is agreed that should the parties share rented premises, said rented premises shall "belong" to the person who first rented the same, and should the parties separate, the second one shall leave taking only such belongings as he or she owned prior to moving in or purchased while living together. If the parties both rent the premises from the beginning, then it is agreed that they will have a third person flip a coin to see who "owns" the premises, and the winner will have the option to remain while the loser leaves.

Rent or Mortgage

10. It is agreed that the parties may split the rent or mortgage payments in whatever proportion they choose, each contributing such sum as is mutually agreeable. It is also agreed that if one party contributes to the mortgage payment of a premises belonging to or being purchased in the name of the other party, that such contribution shall be deemed rent only, and shall be non-refundable and shall not create in the person who is living in the premises owned or being purchased by the other, any interest in said property or in the equity therein.

Business Arrangements

11. It is agreed that should one party hereto contribute services, labor, or effort to a business enterprise belonging to the other, that the party contributing said services, labor, or effort shall not acquire by reason thereof any interest in, ownership of, or claim to said business enterprise, nor shall said person be compensated in any way for said services, labor, or effort, unless the terms of said compensation are expressly agreed to by both parties.

12. Should the parties share services, labor, or effort in a jointly owned business enterprise the relative interests of each party shall be apportioned according to a separate partnership agreement, or, if there is no express agreement, then in proportion that each contributed thereto.

13. It is agreed that the business known as _____ is the individual and separate business of [*Name of Owner*], and is not to be deemed a jointly owned business of both parties.

Separate Accounts

14. In conformity with the intentions of the parties set forth herein, both parties agree to maintain separate bank accounts, insurance accounts (except "renter's" insurance to insure the contents of an apartment, house, etc., which the parties may jointly hold), tax returns, credit accounts, credit union accounts, medical accounts, automobile registration and ownership, and deeds to property, and to make all purchases of personal property, including furniture, appliances, records, books,

works of art, stereo equipment, etc., separate, in order to avoid confusion as to the ownership of same, and also in order to avoid nullifying the general intent of this agreement.

Duration of This Agreement

15. This agreement shall remain in effect from the date the parties start cohabiting until either party leaves or removes himself or herself from the common domicile with the intention not to return, or until they marry, or until they make a new written agreement that is contrary to the terms of this agreement.

Attorney Fees and Costs

16. Each party agrees to act in good faith with the provisions of this agreement, and should one party breach the agreement or fail to act in good faith therewith, such party agrees to pay to the other such attorney fees and costs as may be reasonable in order to properly enforce the provisions herein.

No Common Law Marriage Intended

17. Even though the parties hereto are cohabiting under the same roof and may give the appearance of being married, or from time to time represent to the public that they are husband and wife, they do not intend by such acts to acquire the status of common law marriage, and expressly state herein that this is not an agreement to marry, that they are not now married, and that they understand they are not married to each other during the term of this agreement.

Waiver of Support

18. Both parties waive and relinquish any and all rights to alimony, spousal support, or other separate maintenance from the other in the event of a termination of their living together arrangement.

Dated: _____

_____
[*Name and Signature of Party*]

_____
[*Name and Signature of Party*]

Witnesses:

_____

_____

Notary Public:

_____(Seal)

My commission expires _____

Reprinted from William Mulloy, *West's Legal Forms* § 3.54, pp. 225–29 (2d ed., West Group, 1983) with permission of Thomson Reuters.

■ PARALEGAL ROLES

- For an overview of paralegal roles in family-law cases, see Exhibits 1-3 and 1-4 in Chapter 1.
- For all financial issues covered in this chapter, a paralegal may be asked to help collect documents and facts outlined in:
  - the checklist in Exhibit 3-1 of Chapter 3
  - the interrogatories in Appendix C
- The interviewing and investigation checklist in this chapter also covers fact-finding roles of paralegals.

- Give client a list of all documents he or she should bring to the office pertaining to the premarital, postnuptial, or cohabitation agreement.
- Conduct extensive follow-up interview of client to identify all facts on the circumstances of the agreement.
- Schedule follow-up meetings of client with attorney to discuss client objectives for the negotiation and drafting of the agreement.

- Research the background of potential accountants, appraisers, or other experts who may be hired to prepare a financial statement of current assets and liabilities for disclosure to the other party to the agreement.
- Compile exhibits or documents the attorney will need for the negotiation of the agreement with opposing counsel.
- Prepare a memorandum that details the terms that the attorney has negotiated with opposing counsel.
- Label, date, and file each draft of the agreement as it is changed during client discussions and negotiations with opposing counsel.
- Compile and label financial statements and other disclosure documents that will become attachments to the agreement.
- Prepare a first draft of the agreement, using prior agreements of the same kind as a starting point.
- Read the draft of the agreement proposed by opposing counsel, noting discrepancies from negotiated terms.
- Schedule the execution of the agreement.
- Note on calendar the dates by which further forms, affidavits, or agreements must be executed (e.g., filing of form to waive pension rights for the cohabitation agreement). Monitor compliance of these events.

■ CHECK THE CITE

Mary Alessandro Hardee is a legal assistant who developed a romantic relationship with and eventually married Jay Hardee, a client of the office where Mary worked. The office was representing Jay on his second divorce. At the time Mary and Jay signed a premarital agreement, her assets totaled $48,200; Jay's totaled $1,536,642. Some years later they divorced. During the divorce, what position did each party take on the effect of the premarital agreement? How did the court rule on their positions? Read *Hardee v. Hardee*, 348 S.C. 84, 558 S.E.2d 264 (2001). To read the opinion online: (1) Run a citation search ("558 S.E.2d 264") in the Legal Documents database of Google Scholar (scholar.google.com). (2) Run a citation search ("558 S.E.2d 264") or a case name and state search ("Hardee v. Hardee" South Carolina) in the general search engines of Google, Bing, or Yahoo. (Other sites that can be used to try to find the *Hardee* case online include www.findlaw.com/casecode, www.plol.org, findacase.com, and law.justia.com.)

■ PROJECT

(a) In Google, Bing, or Yahoo, run the following searches: aa "prenuptial agreement" or aa "antenuptial agreement" or aa "premarital agreement" (substitute the name of your state for aa in the search, e.g., Florida "premarital agreement").

Write an essay on the requirements for premarital agreements in your state. You must cite and quote from a minimum of five different sources that you find on the Internet. At least three of these sources should be statutes, court opinions, or other laws.

(b) In Google, Bing, or Yahoo, run the following search: aa "cohabitation agreement" (substitute the name of your state for aa in the search, e.g., California "cohabitation agreement"). Write an essay on the requirements for cohabitation agreements in your state. You must cite and quote from a minimum of five different sources that you find on the Internet. At least three of these sources should be statutes, court opinions, or other laws.

■ ETHICS IN A FAMILY LAW PRACTICE

You are a paralegal working at the law office of Paul Smith, Esq. Alice Henderson has asked the firm to write a cohabitation agreement for her and her boyfriend, Fred Lincoln. Both Alice and Fred come to the firm's office. Paul Smith describes the agreement that he has drafted for them, telling them that it is a standard agreement considered fair to both parties. Alice and Fred are happy with the agreement and sign it. Any ethical problems?

■ WRITING SAMPLE

Find two relatives or friends who would agree to let you interview them. Tell them you want them to pretend that they are Helen Smith and Sam Jones and have decided to move in together. They can make up answers to all of your questions. Tell them to assume the following facts: They are not married and do not intend to become married. They would like to enter a contract that spells out their rights and responsibilities. Specifically, they want to make clear that the house in which they will live belongs to Helen even though Sam will be doing extensive remodeling work on it. They each have separate bank accounts and one joint account. They want to make clear that only the funds in the joint account belong to both of them equally. Next year they hope to have or adopt a child. In either event, they want the contract to specify that the child will be given the surname "Smith-Jones," a combination of their own last names. Before you interview them, prepare a checklist of topics that you want them to discuss with you, such as how they will pay for everyday expenses and what separate property they will each initially bring with them to the house. To prepare the checklist, review all the material in this chapter on cohabitation agreements and check online for additional ideas for topics that a couple should discuss and cover in such an agreement. (Examples of additional topics: making wills, duration of the contract, education and religion of children) Take notes on what they tell you and draft the cohabitation agreement for them. (See General Instructions for the Agreement-Drafting Assignment and for the Writing Sample in Appendix A.)

SUMMARY

The four main kinds of agreements parties enter before and after marriage are cohabitation agreement, premarital agreement, postnuptial agreement, and separation agreement. A premarital agreement is a contract by persons about to be married that can cover (1) financial and related matters once the marriage occurs and (2) spousal support, property division, and related matters in the event of death, separation, divorce, or annulment. In most states, the agreement can waive spousal support so long as one of the spouses is not left destitute at the time it is enforced. Some clauses may necessitate further action after the marriage, e.g., waiver of retirement benefits. In general, courts are not receptive to enforcing lifestyle clauses that cover personal services during the marriage. To be valid, most states require procedural fairness (full financial disclosure, opportunity to consult with others, voluntariness, and the absence of duress and fraud), but most states do *not* require substantive fairness (meaning equitable terms that are satisfactory and reasonable). Most courts will not enforce the agreement if it is unconscionable at the time a party tries to enforce it. "Unconscionable" means shocking the conscience by heavily favoring one side due to the absence of meaningful choice and to the highly unequal bargaining positions of the parties. Independent counsel for each party is not required, although each must be given the opportunity to consult such counsel.

A postnuptial agreement is a contract by married persons that covers financial and related matters between them. The parties may have no intention of separating. If they have this intention, the agreement is commonly called a separation agreement. The requirement of procedural fairness applies to postnuptial agreements. Some states also require substantive fairness because of the fiduciary relationship that exists between spouses.

A cohabitation agreement is a contract by persons in an intimate relationship who are not married to each other (and who intend to stay unmarried indefinitely) that covers financial and related matters while living together and upon the end of the relationship by death or separation. Valid consideration is required; the consideration cannot be meretricious (pertaining to prostitution or unlawful sexual relations). The sexual aspect of the relationship, if any, must be severable from the rest of the agreement. Most states are reluctant to enforce a cohabitation agreement unless the parties have entered an express agreement, preferably in writing. If the aggrieved party cannot establish the existence of an express cohabitation contract, other theories some courts will entertain to avoid the unfairness of one of the parties walking away from the relationship with nothing include implied-in-fact contract, implied-in-law contract (quasi contract), constructive trust, partnership, and joint venture.

KEY TERMS

cohabitation agreement	voluntary	cohabitation agreement
premarital agreement	duress	meretricious
postnuptial agreement	rebut	common-law marriage
separation agreement	fraud	ceremonial marriage
elective share	material	palimony
Uniform Premarital Agreement Act (UPAA)	waiver	remedy
	procedural fairness	express contract
public policy	substantive fairness	implied-in-fact contract
public charge	unconscionable	tacit
property division	second-glance doctrine	implied-in-law contract
sunset	community property	unjust enrichment
severability clause	common-law property	quantum meruit
severable	civil union	trust
contract	domestic partnership	beneficial interest
executory contract	postnuptial agreement	constructive trust
consideration	separation agreement	operation of law
capacity	unity of person	equitable remedy
statute of frauds	adultery	resulting trust
arm's length	fornication	partnership
fiduciary relationship	cohabitation	joint venture
overreaching	cohabitants	

REVIEW QUESTIONS

1. What are the four main categories of agreements that persons in an intimate relationship can enter?
2. What is a premarital agreement?
3. Why do couples enter premarital agreements?
4. What does the Uniform Premarital Agreement Act say about what can be included in a premarital agreement?
5. What is meant by public policy?
6. Why did the law once forbid spousal-support clauses?
7. When will a court not enforce a spousal-support clause?
8. What is an elective share and can it be waived?
9. What difficulty might exist when parties waive retirement benefits in a premarital agreement and how can this difficulty be resolved?
10. Can child support be waived?
11. Can the parties decide who will have custody of the children?
12. How are debts sometimes handled?
13. What are lifestyle clauses and do courts enforce them?
14. Can the agreement commit the parties to remain childless?
15. What is a confidentiality clause?
16. What is the effect of a sunset clause?
17. What is the function of a severability clause?
18. What is a contract? When is a contract executory?
19. What are the requirements for a valid contract?
20. In what ways are commercial contracts and premarital agreements treated differently in the law?
21. When is an agreement voluntary?
22. What is duress?
23. What is fraud?
24. What is the obligation to provide financial disclosure?
25. What is the distinction between procedural fairness and substantive fairness?
26. Do courts require substantive fairness in premarital agreements?
27. When is an agreement unconscionable?
28. What is the second-glance doctrine?
29. Is each party required to have independent counsel?
30. Why did the *Bonds* case hold that the premarital agreement was voluntary even though both sides did not have independent counsel?
31. What dilemma does an attorney face when he or she represents the less well-to-do party who is being asked to sign (and is willing to sign) a premarital agreement that substantially favors the better-off party?
32. What are some of the major drafting guidelines that will help ensure the enforceability of the premarital agreement?
33. What is a postnuptial agreement?
34. Why were postnuptial agreements once illegal?
35. What are some of the reasons couples enter postnuptial agreements?
36. When are postnuptial agreements valid?
37. What is cohabitation?
38. What is a cohabitation agreement?
39. What consideration for the cohabitation agreement would be invalid?
40. What did the *Marvin* case hold?
41. What is palimony?
42. What remedies did the *Marvin* court say were possible?
43. Why do most courts disfavor remedies other than an action for breach of an express contract?
44. What is an implied-in-fact contract?
45. What is an implied-in-law contract?
46. What is quantum meruit?
47. What is a trust?
48. When does something happen by operation of law?
49. What is an equitable remedy?
50. What is the distinction between a constructive trust and a resulting trust?
51. When could a partnership be a remedy for a cohabitant?
52. What is a joint venture?

HELPFUL WEBSITES

Premarital Agreements

- www.expertlaw.com/library/family_law/prenuptial_agreements.html
- www.bankrate.com/brm/prenup.asp
- www.prenuptialagreements.org
- family.findlaw.com/marriage/marriage-resources/le19_4_1.html

Uniform Premarital Agreement Act (UPAA)

- www.prenupdoc.com/premarital_agreements
_around_the_world_usa/index.html
- www.prenupdoc.com/premarital_agreements
_around_the_world_usa/statuatory_text_upaa.html

Postnuptial Agreements

- marriage.about.com/od/agreements/a/postnuptial.htm
- maritalmediation.com/postnuptial-agreements
- en.wikipedia.org/wiki/Postnuptial_agreement

Cohabitation Agreements

- www.equalityinmarriage.org/bmagreements.html
- en.wikipedia.org/wiki/Cohabitation_agreement
- www.palimony.com
- family.findlaw.com/marriage/living-together
/le18_6_1.html

Legal Forms

- www.legalforms.com
- www.formdepot.com
(type "premarital" in the search box)

Jewish Law

- www.jlaw.com/Articles/antenuptial_agreement4
.html

Videos of Attorneys Describing Agreements

- www.youtube.com

(in the search box, run the following searches: "premarital agreement," "postnuptial agreement," "cohabitation agreements," and "separation agreements")(the attorneys in these videos want to be hired, but in the process, some of them give excellent short overviews of the law governing the agreements in their states)

Google/Bing/Yahoo Searches

(on these search engines, run the following searches, substituting your state for "aa")
- "premarital agreement" aa
- "antenuptial agreement" aa
- "separation agreement" aa
- meretricious aa
- "Marvin v. Marvin" aa
- "postnuptial agreement" aa
- "cohabitation agreement" aa
- palimony aa
- "unjust enrichment" aa

ENDNOTES

Note: All or most of the court opinions in these endnotes can be read online. To do so, go to Google Scholar (scholar.google.com), select "Legal Documents," and in the search box, enter the cite (e.g., "5 P.3d 815") or name of the case (e.g., "In re Marriage of Bonds") that is given in the endnote.

[1] Pamila Yip, *To Have and to Hold*, San Jose Mercury News, Jan. 26, 2003, at 3F.

[2] David Rovella, *Pre-Nups No Longer Just for the Wealthy*, National Law Journal 9/6/99, at A1.

[3] Kerry Hannon, *Planning for Love and Money*, U.S. News & World Report, 56 (Jul. 16, 2006) (www.usnews.com/usnews/biztech/articles/060716/24prime.htm).

[4] Rose Kreider, *How Many Trips Do We Take Down the Aisle?* U.S. Census Bureau, (May 18, 2011) (blogs.census.gov/censusblog/2011/05/how-many-trips-do-we-take-down-the-aisle.html).

[5] Uniform Premarital Agreement Act (www.law.upenn.edu/bll/archives/ulc/fnact99/1980s/upaa83.htm).

[6] Id at § 6(b). See also Connecticut General Statutes, § 46b-36g (search.cga.state.ct.us/dtsearch_pub_statutes.html).

[7] Geoffrey Gray, *With This Ring (and This Contract), I Thee Wed*, New York, 51 (Mar. 26, 2006) (nymag.com/relationships/features/16470). Jan Hoffman, *The Rich; How They Keep It*, N.Y. Times, 102 (Nov. 19, 1995) (www.nytimes.com/1995/11/19/magazine/the-rich-how-they-keep-it.html).

[8] *In re Marriage of Bonds*, 24 Cal. 4th 1, 25, 5 P.3d 815, 830 (2000), quoting Katharine Silbaugh, Marriage Contracts and the Family Economy (1998) 93 N.W.U. L.Rev. 65, 123 (1998).

[9] Jill Brooke, *A Promise to Love, Honor and Bear No Children*, N.Y. Times, Oct. 13, 2002, at ST1 (www.nytimes.com/2002/10/13/style/a-promise-to-love-honor-and-bear-no-children.html).

[10] *Holler v. Holler* 364 S.C. 256, 269, 612 S.E.2d 469, 476 (S.C. App., 2005).

[11] Susan Berfield, *Does Your Marriage Need a Postnup?* Business Week, 80 (Apr. 16, 2007) (www.businessweek.com/magazine/content/07_16/b4030091.htm).

[12] Tamar Lewin, "Among Nuptial Agreements, Post- Has Now Joined Pre-," N.Y. Times, Jul. 7, 2001. (www.nytimes.com/2001/07/07/us/among-nuptial-agreements-post-has-now-joined-pre.html).

[12a] *In re Marriage of Tabassum and Younis*, 377 Ill. App. 3d 761, 881 N.E.2d 396 (Ill. App. 2007).

[13] *Among Nuptial Agreements*, supra note 12.

[14] Sabrina Tavernise, *Married Couples Are No Longer Majority*, Census Finds, N.Y. Times, May 26, 2011, at A22 (www.nytimes.com/2011/05/26/us/26marry.html).

[15] U.S. Bureau of the Census, *Increase in Opposite-Sex Cohabiting Couples from 2009 to 2010* . . . (2010) (www.census.gov/population/www/socdemo/Inc-Opp-sex-2009-to-2010.pdf).

[16] Harry D. Krause and Davis D. Meyer, *Family Law* (5th ed. 2007).

[17] *The Decline of Marriage and the Rise of New Families* (Pew Research Center Publications, Nov. 18, 2010) (pewsocialtrends.org/2010/11/18/the-decline-of-marriage-and-rise-of-new-families/1).

[18] Vernon's Texas Statutes and Codes Annotated, Family Code, § 1.108 (1997) (www.statutes.legis.state.tx.us/Docs/FA/htm/FA.1.htm).

[19] The state defines a meretricious relationship as a stable, marital-like relationship where both parties cohabit with knowledge that a lawful marriage between them does not exist. *Connell v. Francisco*, 127 Wash. 2d 339, 346, 898 P.2d 831, 833 (1995).

[20] 18 Cal. 3d 660, 557 P.2d 106, 134 Cal. Rptr. 815 (1976).

[21] 18 Cal. 3d at 669, 670, 674, 557 P.2d at 112, 113, 116, 134 Cal. Rptr. at 821, 822, 825 (emphasis in original).

[22] Minnesota Statutes § 513.075 (1980) (www.revisor.mn.gov/statutes/?year=2010&id=513.075).

[23] Ann Estin, *Unmarried Partners and the Legacy of Marvin v. Marvin*, 76 Notre Dame Law Review 1381, 1400 (2001).

Traditional Marriage and Alternatives

CHAPTER OUTLINE

CHAPTER OBJECTIVES

After completing this chapter, you should be able to:

- Explain when an action for breach of promise to marry (or for inducing a breach) can be brought.
- Explain whether actions for fraud and intentional infliction of emotional distress can be brought for breaching a promise to marry.
- Know when gifts must be returned upon the breaking of an engagement.
- Know when restraints on marriage are enforceable.
- Understand what is meant by a fundamental right and what the *Zablocki* and *Loving* cases said about restrictions on this right.
- List the times when a person is likely to want to know if he or she is married.

- Distinguish between ceremonial and common-law marriages.
- State the technical or procedural requirements states often impose for ceremonial marriages and the consequences of violating them.
- Know when a proxy marriage is allowed.
- Define civil unions and domestic partnerships.
- State the two parts of the Defense of Marriage Act (DOMA).
- Know the impact of DOMA and full faith and credit.
- Explain the state and federal constitutional issues involved when a state bans same-sex marriage.

- Explain how a covenant marriage is entered and terminated.
- List the requirements for a common-law marriage.
- State why common-law marriages are disfavored.
- Know how a conflict-of-laws issue is resolved in a state where common-law marriage cannot be entered.
- Explain what happens when an impediment is removed.
- Identify the elements of a putative marriage.
- Explain marriage by estoppel and de facto marriage.

LEGAL ISSUES PRIOR TO MARRIAGE

Before we examine the question of who can enter a marriage and the availability of alternatives to marriage, we will explore three important issues that can arise when a planned marriage does not occur. First, can someone be sued for failing to fulfill a promise to marry? If so, what is the theory of the suit—what is the **cause of action**? Second, if both parties agree to call off the marriage, what happens to engagement and wedding gifts that have already been exchanged? Finally, we need to look at the related problem of whether a promise not to marry is enforceable.

BREACH OF PROMISE TO MARRY

Over 100,000 engagements are broken each year. This can be a costly experience. In some cities, "traditional weddings can cost as much as $50,000 or $100,000, and as the wedding day approaches, less and less of the expense of the event can be recovered if the event is canceled." In New York City, for example, many caterers and hotels charge for services and rooms that cannot be rebooked when canceled with less than six months' notice.[1] Faced with such costs, some victims of broken engagements sue for breach of contract or, more specifically, for breach of promise to marry.

In a minority of states, one person can sue another for breach of promise to marry. Such suits are called **heart-balm actions** because they are based on the loss of love and relationship—on a broken heart. (In Chapter 17, we will examine more of these actions, such as alienation of affections and seduction.) The main remedy available in such actions is **compensatory damages**. This is an amount of money that will restore an injured party to his or her position prior to the injury or other loss. Examples of such losses are payments to buy a trousseau, rent a hall, and purchase rings. Damages for humiliation and mental anguish are also allowed.

The remedy of **specific performance** (ordering the carrying out of the contract as promised) is not available. No court would force parties to enter a marriage that one of the parties no longer wants. At one time, **expectation damages** (money to compensate for the loss of what was reasonably anticipated from a contract that was not performed) were allowed. Today, however, this is no longer the case. The **aggrieved** party cannot be compensated for a loss of the lifestyle he or she would have enjoyed if the marriage had occurred. **Punitive damages** can be awarded if the party breaching the promise to marry acted out of **malice** (e.g., wanting to humiliate the other party or recklessly disregarding the upheaval and pain that the breach would cause).

As indicated, however, not all states allow heart-balm actions such as breach of promise to marry. The states that have abolished such actions have done so by what is called a **heart-balm statute**. Such statutes were enacted for a number of reasons. The emotions involving a refusal to marry are usually so personal, intense, and possibly bitter that a court did not appear to be a proper setting to handle them. Furthermore, people should be allowed to correct their mistakes without fear of a lawsuit. As one judge said, the "courtroom scene" should not be "transposed into a grotesque marketplace whose wares would be the exposure of heart-rending episodes of wounded pride, which should be best kept private rather than public."[2] Courts were also afraid of being flooded with breach-of-promise lawsuits, particularly by unscrupulous "gold diggers and blackmailers" who use the threat of publicity to force a settlement.[3]

---

cause of action

1. A legally acceptable reason for bringing a suit. A rule that constitutes a legal theory for bringing a suit. 2. The facts that give a person a right to judicial relief. When you state a cause of action, you list the facts that give you a right to judicial relief against the wrongdoer.

heart-balm action

An action based on the loss of love and relationships—on a broken heart (e.g., breach of promise to marry, alienation of affections, and seduction).

compensatory damages

Money paid to restore an injured party to his or her position prior to the injury or other loss.

specific performance

A remedy for breach of contract that forces the wrongdoing party to complete the contract as promised.

expectation damages

Money to compensate for the loss of what was reasonably anticipated from a contract that was not performed.

aggrieved

Injured or wronged and thereby entitled to a remedy.

punitive damages

Damages that are added to actual or compensatory damages in order to punish malicious, outrageous, or reckless conduct and to deter similar conduct in the future. Also called exemplary damages, smart money, vindictive damages.

malice

1. The intent to inflict injury or other wrongful harm. 2. Reckless disregard of what is right. 3. Animosity or ill will.

heart-balm statute

A statute that abolishes heart-balm actions.

CASE

Stanard v. Bolin
88 Wash. 2d 614, 565 P.2d 94 (1977)
Supreme Court of Washington

Background: *During their courtship, the defendant assured the plaintiff that he was worth in excess of $2 million, that he was planning to retire in two years, and that the two of them would then travel. He promised plaintiff that she would never have to work again and that he would see to the support of her two teenage sons. He also promised that the plaintiff's mother would never be in need. After he proposed, the parties found a suitable home for their residence and signed the purchase agreement as husband and wife. At the insistence of the defendant, the plaintiff placed her home on the market for sale and sold most of her furniture at a public auction. The parties set the wedding date, reserved a church, and hired a minister to perform the service. Dresses for the plaintiff, her mother, and the matron of honor were ordered, and a reception was arranged at a local establishment. The parties began informally announcing their plans to a wide circle of friends. After the wedding date was set, the plaintiff's employer hired another person and asked the plaintiff to assist in teaching the new employee the duties of her job. A month before the wedding, the defendant informed the plaintiff that he would not marry her. This came as a great shock to the plaintiff and caused her to become ill and to lose sleep and weight. She sought medical advice and was treated by her physician. The plaintiff also had to take her home off the market and repurchase furniture at a cost in excess of what she received for her older furniture. In addition, the plaintiff had to cancel all wedding plans and reservations, return wedding gifts, and explain to her friends, family, and neighbors what had happened. The plaintiff sued the defendant for breach of promise to marry. The trial court ruled for the defendant. The plaintiff is now appealing before the Supreme Court of Washington.*

Decision on Appeal: *The trial court is reversed. The plaintiff should be allowed to sue for breach of promise, although there are limitations on the kind of damages that can be awarded.*

OPINION OF THE COURT

Justice HAMILTON delivered the opinion of the court.

This appeal presents the question of whether the . . . action for breach of promise to marry should be abolished. . . . When two persons agree to marry, they should realize that certain actions will be taken during the engagement period in reliance on the mutual promises to marry. Rings will be purchased,

wedding dresses and other formal attire will be ordered or reserved, and honeymoon plans with their attendant expenses will be made. . . . When the plans to marry are abruptly ended, it is certainly foreseeable that the party who was unaware that the future marriage would not take place will have expended some sums of money and will suffer some forms of mental anguish, loss to reputation, and injury to health. We do not feel these injuries should go unanswered merely because the breach-of-promise-to-marry action may be subject to abuses; rather, an attempt should be made to eradicate the abuses from the action.

One major abuse of the action is allowing the plaintiff to bring in evidence of the defendant's wealth and social position . . . under the theory that the plaintiff should be compensated for what she or he has lost by not marrying the defendant. [We do not believe these damages are justified in light of modern society's concept of marriage, which is a coming together out of love, not in order to secure property. Hence damages] for loss of expected financial and social position should no longer be recoverable under the breach-of-promise-to-marry actions. This means that evidence of the defendant's wealth and social position becomes immaterial in assessing the plaintiff's damages.

Other damages subject to criticism are those damages given for mental anguish, loss to reputation, and injury to health. It is argued that these injuries are "so vague and so little capable of measurement in dollars that they give free rein to the jury's passions, prejudices and sympathies." See Homer Clark, *The Law of Domestic Relations in the United States* 12 (1968). This argument has little merit, for it places no faith in the jury's ability to evaluate objectively the evidence regarding plaintiff's injuries and render a just verdict. If a jury's verdict is tainted by passion or prejudice, or is otherwise excessive, the trial court and the appellate court have the power to reduce the award or order a new trial. See *Hogenson v. Service Armament Co.*, 77 Wash. 2d 209, 461 P.2d 311 (1969). Lack of ability to quantify damages in exact dollar amounts does not justify abolishing the breach-of-promise-to-marry action. In her complaint plaintiff alleged that she had suffered pain, impairment to health, humiliation, and embarrassment as a result of the defendant's breach of his promise to marry. If this is true . . . , she is entitled to compensation for these injuries. . . .

The judgment of the trial court is reversed. . . .

ASSIGNMENT 5.1

a. Give (i) specific examples of evidence of damages you think the plaintiff will try to introduce at the new trial and (ii) specific examples of evidence of damages she will be forbidden to introduce.

b. Do you agree with the result reached by the court in *Stanard?* Why or why not? Is marriage a property transaction today? Should expectation damages be awarded in such cases?

ASSIGNMENT 5.2

Assume that you live in a state where heart-balm actions can be brought. Dan asks Carol to marry him. Carol says yes. The date is set for the wedding. Two weeks before the wedding, Carol learns that Dan has just married Linda. At the time Dan was engaged to Carol, Carol was already married to Bill, but Dan did not know this. Carol was in the process of divorcing Bill and hoped the divorce would be finalized before her marriage to Dan. Carol wanted to wait until the divorce was final before telling Dan about the prior marriage and divorce. Dan did not learn about any of this until after his marriage to Linda. When Carol's divorce to Bill became final, she sues Dan for breach of promise to marry. Should Carol be allowed to bring this action? Why or why not? (See General Instructions for the Legal-Analysis Assignment in Appendix A.)

☑ INTERVIEWING AND INVESTIGATION CHECKLIST

For States That Allow Suits for Breach of Promise to Marry (C = client; D = defendant) (This checklist covers breach of promise to marry and gifts. Gifts are examined later in the chapter.)

LEGAL INTERVIEWING QUESTIONS

1. On what date did you and D first agree to be married?

2. Where were you at the time of this agreement? Were you in this state? If not, what state?

3. How old were you at the time? How old was D?

4. What specific language did D use when D agreed (promised) to marry you? What specific language did you use when you accepted? (Try to obtain exact quotations.)

5. Who were the first persons you told? Did you and D tell them together?

6. Was a date set for a wedding? If so, what date? If not, why not?

7. What preparations were made for the wedding (e.g., church selected or caterer ordered)?

8. Did D send you any letters ("love letters") about the engagement? Did you send D any? What promises, if any, were made in the letters?

9. Did D ever repeat his or her promise to marry you? If so, under what circumstances?

10. What other actions did D take to indicate to you that D wanted to marry you? How much time did you spend together? Did you live together? (Where? How long?) Did you talk about children? Did you meet each other's parents?

11. When did you first learn that D no longer wished to marry you? What specifically was said and done?

12. What reason did D give?

13. What did you say or do when you learned about this? Did you give any indication to D that you did not want to marry D? Were you angry? How were your feelings expressed?

14. Was there anything about your life prior to the time that D promised to marry you that D did not know but that D now feels you should have revealed, e.g., information about a prior marriage, your age, or your prior sex life?

15. What expenses did you incur to prepare for the wedding (e.g., clothes, church, rings)?

16. Were you employed before the engagement? Did you leave your job? Did the cancellation of the marriage affect your job?

17. Describe your standard of living before the cancellation (e.g., kind of dwelling, car, travel, entertainment interests).

18. Describe D's standard of living.

19. If D had married you, describe what you think your financial standing and standard of living would have been.

20. Describe the effect of D's breach of promise on your physical and mental health (e.g., did you lose any sleep, were there any special mental problems?).

21. When D broke the promise to marry you, who knew about it? Was there any publicity?

22. Were you humiliated? If so, describe the reasons why.

23. Since D broke the engagement, have you dated others? When they find out about the broken engagement, what is their reaction? Do you think your chances of marrying in the future are diminished because of D's breach of promise?

24. Did you have sexual relations with D? Were you seduced by D? Did D impregnate you? (If so, inquire into pregnancy problems, abortion, miscarriage, delivery, etc.)

25. Do you have any reason to believe at the time D promised to marry you that D never intended to fulfill this promise? Explain.

26. Do you have any reason to believe D wanted to hurt you? Explain.

27. Could D say that you never loved D?

28. Did D ever give you any gifts?

29. For each gift received, describe the gift, the date you were told about it, and what was said when it was given. Specify whether the gift was received before or after the engagement.

30. Has D ever given you gifts on special occasions such as birthdays; holidays such as Easter, Christmas, or Chanukah; or on recognition days such as the day you won a race or other prize? Describe the circumstances of all such gifts.

31. When did each gift come into your possession?

32. Answer questions 28–31 for any gifts you gave D.

33. Did you or D receive any shower gifts or wedding gifts from others before the engagement was broken? Explain.

POSSIBLE INVESTIGATION TASKS

- Try to contact people who may have heard about D's promise to marry C. Obtain witness statements.

- Locate all letters from D to C.

- Locate all receipts of expenses resulting from wedding preparations. If not available, help C contact merchants and others to whom money was paid in order to obtain new receipts or copies.

- Obtain financial records, e.g., bank statements, to show C's financial worth and standard of living before the engagement was broken. Try to obtain the same kind of records for D.

- Obtain medical records to document the physical and mental strain C experienced when D broke the promise to marry (e.g., hospital records, doctor bills).

- Determine the kind of publicity, if any, that accompanied the news that D broke the engagement (e.g., newspaper clippings).

- Attempt to determine whether D had broken any other marriage engagements.

- Draft an inventory of every gift connected with D's relationship with C. For each gift, identify the donor (the giver), donee (the recipient), date of the gift, kind and value of the gift, circumstances surrounding the gift, present location of the gift, etc.

INDUCING A BREACH OF PROMISE TO MARRY

In the commercial world, it is a tort to induce a person to break a contract with someone else. It is called **interference with contract relations**. For example, company X persuades company Y to break Y's contract with company Z so that Y can enter a contract with X. Company Z has a tort action against company X for interfering with Z's contract relations with Y. Suppose that Jim and Mary are engaged to be married. Mary's mother is opposed to the marriage and persuades Mary to break her promise to marry Jim. Can Jim sue Mary's mother for interference with contract relations by inducing a breach of Mary's promise to marry him? Most states would say no, even in states that allow actions for breach of promise to marry. Courts do not want to discourage relatives from advising against what they consider to be a bad match. Indeed, relatives have a privilege to provide such advice in order to protect those close to them.

interference with contract relations

Intentionally encouraging or provoking a breach of contract between two other persons. Also called tortious interference with contractual relations.

FRAUD

If a heart-balm statute exists, some plaintiffs have tried to get around it by bringing an action for **fraud** rather than for breach of promise to marry. The action would be for fraudulently inducing someone to enter a marriage. Fraud is

fraud

An intentionally false statement of fact that is material and is made to induce reliance by the plaintiff, and that results in harm because of the reliance. Also called deceit, misrepresentation.

an intentionally false statement of fact that is material, made to induce reliance by the plaintiff, and results in harm because of the reliance.

Elements of the Tort of Fraud
(Sometimes called deceit or misrepresentation)

- There must be a false statement of present fact by the defendant (D).
- The D must know that it is false.
- The D must intend that the plaintiff (P) rely upon the statement (this element is called **scienter**, the intent to deceive).
- The P must rely on the statement of the D and be reasonable in so relying.
- The P must suffer harm due to the reliance.

scienter
Intent to deceive or mislead.

Here is an example of how a fraud cause of action might arise out of a broken engagement.

Don tells Phyllis that he wants to marry her. At the time he makes this statement of fact, it is false because Don has never wanted to marry Phyllis. He knows he is lying. Don's goal—his intention—is to obtain a loan of $25,000 from her. He knows that without a marriage proposal, she will refuse. Phyllis, however, believes that Don wants to marry her and she lends him the money in reliance on his promise of marriage. Soon thereafter, she learns that he never wanted to marry her and that he has spent the money she lent him. Her reliance on his promise has led to the harm of losing $25,000.

Or suppose that Don falsely promises to marry Phyllis in order to persuade her to give up her virginity to him. Assume that Phyllis and Don live in a state that has abolished the breach-of-promise-to-marry cause of action. Can Phyllis overcome this obstacle by suing Don for fraud? The answer depends on whether the legislature intended the heart-balm statute to eliminate both causes of action even though the act may specifically mention only the breach-of-promise action. Some states allow the fraud action. Others have said that the heart-balm statute eliminates both the breach-of-promise and the fraud action.

INTENTIONAL INFLICTION OF EMOTIONAL DISTRESS

intentional infliction of emotional distress
Intentionally causing severe emotional distress by extreme or outrageous conduct.

Another tort action some plaintiffs have tried to bring is **intentional infliction of emotional distress**. The plaintiff must convince a court that the heart-balm statute does not bar this action as well. If this can be done, the next step is to prove that he or she was the victim of particularly shocking conduct by the defendant. For example, a man knows that his fiancée is emotionally unstable because she is a former mental patient. He proposes marriage for the sole purpose of humiliating her by changing his mind just after she makes elaborate, public, and expensive wedding plans. A state might conclude that this is sufficiently outrageous and shocking conduct. A more common change-of-mind case, on the other hand, would probably not be enough for this tort, no matter how upset the jilted party becomes. The behavior of the culprit must shock the conscience.

We will return to the tort of intentional infliction of emotional distress in Chapter 12 when we discuss the allegation that President (then Governor) Clinton committed this tort and in Chapter 17 when we study the case of *Hakkila v. Hakkila*, which resolved the question of whether this tort could be brought against a spouse in a divorce action.

GIFTS

gift
The voluntary delivery of something with the present intent to transfer title and control, for which no payment or consideration is made. The person making the gift is the donor. The person receiving it is the donee.

consideration
Something of value that is exchanged between parties. It can be an act, a forbearance (not performing an act), a promise to perform an act, or a promise to refrain from performing an act.

donor
The person who gives a gift.

A **gift** is a voluntary delivery of something with the present intent to transfer title and control, for which no payment or consideration is made. (**Consideration** is something of value that is exchanged.) The two parties in a gift are the **donor** (the giver) and the **donee** (the recipient). There are two main categories of gifts: testamentary and inter vivos. A **testamentary gift** is a gift made in a will. Donors of testamentary gifts can always change their minds before they die by changing their will. Our primary concern in this chapter is the **inter vivos gift**, which is a gift that is given while the donor is living. It is not commonly known that once an inter vivos gift is made, it is **irrevocable**; the donor cannot revoke the gift and reclaim it from the donee. The one exception in some states is an inter vivos gift made while the donor knows that death is near ("impending death"). In these states, an inter vivos gift made in view of impending death is **revocable**.

Irrevocable Gifts

For a gift to be irrevocable, all of the elements of a gift must be present:

Elements of an Irrevocable Gift

- There must be a delivery of the property. (For some kinds of property, delivery is accomplished by a symbolic act such as giving the donee the key to the property, e.g., a key to a safe deposit box.)
- The transfer must be voluntary.
- The donor must intend to relinquish title and control of or dominion over what is given.
- There must be no consideration such as a cash payment for the gift.
- The donor must intend that the gift take effect immediately; there must be a present intention to give an unconditional gift.
- The donee must accept the gift.

If Pat says to Bill, "I'll give you my car next year," no gift has taken place. There was no intent that an immediate transfer occur. There was also no delivery. Similarly, no gift has been made if Pat says to Bill, "Maybe I'll let you keep the pen you borrowed." There was no intent by Pat to relinquish her title and dominion over the pen now. This is so even though Bill already had possession of the pen.

Conditional Gifts

Suppose that Pat says to Bill, "I'll give you this desk if it rains tomorrow." No gift has occurred because a condition exists that must be fulfilled before the gift becomes effective (i.e., it must rain tomorrow). There is no present intention to relinquish title and dominion.

In the context of a wedding engagement, the general rule is that gifts given in contemplation of marriage are conditional gifts, meaning that they are subject to a condition—the occurrence of the marriage. The gifts are not irrevocable if the condition is not met due to a cancellation of the marriage. With some exceptions, most states allow the donor to force the return of such conditional gifts. Examine the following sequence of events:

January 1, 2013:	Mary and Bob meet.
January 2, 2013:	On a date at a restaurant, Bob gives Mary a bracelet.
February 13, 2013:	Mary and Bob become engaged; he gives her an engagement ring. The marriage date will be in eight months.
March 26, 2013:	This is Mary's birthday; Bob gives Mary a new car.
June 5, 2013:	Bob and Mary change their minds about marriage.

Assume that Bob now wants the bracelet, ring, and car back. When Mary refuses, Bob sues her, contending in court that the elements of a gift were not met when he gave Mary the items because he intended that she keep them only if they married. Will a court infer this condition of marriage? The answer depends on Bob's intention

---

donee
The person who receives a gift.

testamentary gift
A gift made in a will.

inter vivos gift
A gift that takes effect while the donor is living.

irrevocable
Not capable of being revoked, canceled, or recalled.

revocable
Susceptible of being revoked, canceled, or recalled.

at the time he gave each of the items to Mary. The court must turn the clock back to the dates when the gifts were given and determine intention at those times.

When the bracelet was given, the parties were not engaged. A jury might conclude that Bob's intent was to please Mary, but not necessarily to win her hand in marriage. The bracelet was given the day after they met, when marriage was probably not on his mind. If so, the bracelet was a courting gift (called a gift of pursuit). It is unlikely, therefore, that a court would rule that the gift of the bracelet was conditional and force Mary to return it. On the other hand, the facts show that a month and a half after the bracelet was given, the parties became engaged. This short time period does raise the possibility, however slight, that marriage was on Bob's mind when he gave Mary the bracelet (i.e., that the gift was conditional).

The birthday gift of the car is the most troublesome item. Again, the central issue is Bob's intent at the time he gave her the car. Mary would argue that no condition of marriage was attached to the gift. She would say that a birthday gift would have been given whether or not they were engaged. Bob would argue that the extraordinary cost of a new car is persuasive evidence that it would not have been given as a birthday gift unconnected with the impending marriage. This is a strong argument.

ASSIGNMENT 5.3

What further facts would you seek in order to assess whether the car was a gift in the case of Bob and Mary above? (See General Instructions for the Investigation-Strategy Assignment in Appendix A.)

Engagement Rings

What about the engagement ring? When the decision to break the engagement is mutual, most courts say that a condition of marriage was implied, and therefore, the ring must be returned. Suppose, however, that one of the parties unilaterally breaks the engagement without any plausible reason or justification. This person is considered to be at fault. Must the ring be returned in such a case? Some courts will order the return of the ring if the person receiving it (the donee) is the one who broke the engagement without justification, but not if he or she is the "innocent" party. Most courts, however, will order the return of the ring regardless of who was at fault.

Of course, websites have been created to try to cash in on the predicament faced by no-longer-engaged couples. For example, one site (www.idonowidont .com) is designed to be a clearinghouse for the sale of engagement rings that are no longer suitable for their original purpose because of the breakup.

ASSIGNMENT 5.4

Roy and Brooke have been dating for months. Roy is a football player who is often on the road. While away at a game just before Valentine's Day, Roy sends Brooke a proposal of marriage along with a $76,000 ring. Brooke refuses the proposal and will not return the ring. Does she have to return it? (See the General Instructions for the Legal-Analysis Assignment in Appendix A.)

Third-Party Gifts

Third parties (e.g., relatives and friends) often give wedding gifts. When the marriage does not take place, these parties can force a return of the gifts because courts almost always will conclude that such gifts were conditional. In a few states, however, they may have trouble getting the gifts back. Earlier we saw that heart-balm statutes abolished the cause of action for breach of promise to marry. Some of these statutes are worded so broadly that courts might interpret them to mean that *any* cause of action growing out of a broken engagement will not be allowed, including a cause of action to obtain the return of conditional gifts.

ASSIGNMENT 5.5

Examine the following sequence of events:

February 13, 2014:	Jim says to Bob, "Please introduce me to Joan. I want to meet her because I know that she is the girl I want to spend the rest of my life with." Bob does so. Jim is so happy that he gives Bob a gold wristwatch and says to him, "I want you to have this. Thanks for being my friend. I want you to wear this watch to my wedding someday."
March 1, 2014:	Joan brings Jim home to meet her mother. When the evening is over, Jim gives Joan's mother an expensive family Bible.
June 23, 2014:	Jim loans Joan $1,000 to pay the medical bill of her youngest brother, giving her one year to pay back the loan without interest.
July 23, 2014:	Joan pays back the $1,000.
September 5, 2014:	They agree to marry. The wedding date is to be February 18, 2015. On the day that they agree to marry, Jim gives Joan a diamond bracelet, saying, "I want you to have this no matter what happens."
December 14, 2014:	They both agree to break the engagement.

Jim asks Bob for the wristwatch back. Bob refuses. Jim asks Joan's mother for the Bible back. The mother refuses. Jim asks Joan for one month's interest at 10 percent on the $1,000 loan and also asks for the bracelet back. Joan refuses both requests.

a. Assume that the law office where you work represents Jim. Conduct a legal interview of Jim. (See General Instructions for the Interview Assignment in Appendix A.)

b. Can Jim obtain the wristwatch from Bob, the Bible from the mother, and the interest and bracelet from Joan? (See General Instructions for the Legal-Analysis Assignment in Appendix A.)

c. Draft a complaint against Joan in which Jim seeks the return of the bracelet and one month's interest. (See General Instructions for the Complaint-Drafting Assignment in Appendix A.)

d. Prepare a flowchart of the steps necessary to litigate the matter raised in the complaint that you drafted in (c) above. (See General Instructions for the Flowchart Assignment in Appendix A.)

Unjust Enrichment

The theory of recovery we have been discussing thus far is the existence of a conditional gift. An alternative theory of recovery available in some states is **unjust enrichment**. When allowed, this remedy is used when someone has received a benefit that was not intended as a gift and that should be returned or for which compensation should be paid.

unjust enrichment
The receipt of a benefit in the form of goods or services from another when, in fairness and equity, the recipient should provide restitution for the goods or compensation for the services even though there was no express or implied promise to do so. The amount the recipient should pay for services is called quantum meruit, the reasonable value of the services provided.

RESTRAINT OF MARRIAGE

restraint of marriage

A condition in a contract or gift that a benefit will be lost upon marriage or remarriage.

What happens if a contract or gift contains a condition that a benefit will be lost if a marriage or remarriage occurs? Such a condition is called a **restraint of marriage**. The law looks with disfavor on attempts to limit the right to marry, even with the consent of the person subject to the limitation. Not all restrictions, however, are invalid. A distinction must be made between a general restraint on marriage and a reasonable limitation on marriage.

General Restraint

A general restraint on marriage is a total or near-total prohibition against marriage and is unenforceable. For example:

- In exchange for a large sum of money to be given to her by her father, Mary agrees never to marry.
- As John goes off to war, Jane says, "It is you that I want to marry. Even if you don't want to marry me, even if you marry someone else, even if you die, I promise you that I will never marry anyone else as long as I live." John leaves without promising to marry Jane.

Mary's father cannot sue her to hold her to her agreement never to marry, nor can Jane be sued by John for breach of her promise should she marry someone other than him. People may decide on their own never to marry, but no court will force them to abide by that decision.

The John/Jane agreement is unenforceable for another reason. For a contract to exist, there must be consideration (something of value that is exchanged between the parties). Jane's consideration was her promise never to marry anyone but John. John, however, gave no consideration in exchange. Hence, Jane's promise is unenforceable because she received no consideration; there was no contract to breach.

Reasonable Limitation

A reasonable limitation on marriage is one that (1) is a partial rather than a general prohibition, (2) serves what the court feels is a useful purpose, and (3) is not otherwise illegal. Consider the following situations:

- Jim enters a contract in which he promises that he will never marry a woman who is not of his religious faith.
- Mary enters a contract in which she promises never to marry anyone who has a criminal record.
- Jill enters a contract in which she promises that she will not marry before she turns eighteen, and that she will obtain the permission of her parents if she decides to marry between the ages of 18 and 21.
- Linda enters a contract in which she promises that she will not marry until she completes her college education.

Assume that Jim, Mary, Jill, and Linda received consideration from a relative (e.g., cash) in exchange for their promises. Are the promises enforceable? If Jim, Mary, Jill, and Linda later decide to marry contrary to their promises, can they be forced through litigation to return whatever consideration they received as a remedy for their breach of promise? Not all states answer this question in the same way, but generally the answer is yes. The restraints on marriage to which they agreed are enforceable.

All of the restraints in the examples are partial: They do not totally prohibit marriage or come near such a total prohibition. All of the restraints arguably serve a useful purpose: to protect a person or to preserve a valuable tradition or culture. There is no illegality evident in any of the restraints (e.g., no one is being asked to refrain from marriage in order to engage in adultery or fornication). Hence, all of the restraints could be considered reasonable limitations on one's right to marry and are enforceable in most states.

Thus far, we have been examining *contracts* that restrain marriage. Suppose, however, that the attempted restriction on marriage came as a condition attached to a *gift* (inter vivos or testamentary) rather than through a contract. For example:

- In Bob's will, he promises to give $100,000 to Fran "so long as she remains unmarried." When Bob dies, Fran is not married. She is given the **bequest** of $100,000. One year later, Fran marries. Bob's estate brings a suit against Fran to have the money returned.

- John has a deed drafted that states, "I convey all my property to my widowed sister, Joan, to be owned and used by her until she remarries, at which time all remaining property shall go to the Red Cross."

bequest
A gift of personal property in a will. (In some states, a bequest can be a gift of personal property or real property in a will.)

In theory, the same rules on marriage restrictions apply to such gifts as apply to contracts. It should be noted, however, that some courts are more inclined to find the restrictions to be reasonable (and hence enforceable) when the restriction is attached to a gift than when it is embodied in a contract.

In the Bob/Fran will case, Fran might have an additional argument in her favor. The condition in the will is that the $100,000 bequest will be made to Fran "so long as she remains unmarried." The condition does not say she must remain unmarried forever. A reasonable interpretation of the will is that she must remain unmarried up until the time the will takes effect—when he dies. Under this interpretation, Fran met the condition because her marriage occurred after Bob died.

ASSIGNMENT 5.6

Closely examine each of the following situations. Determine which restraints on marriage, if any, are enforceable. Give specific reasons you think the restraint is or is not enforceable. (See General Instructions for the Legal-Analysis Assignment in Appendix A.)

a. John is married to Brenda. John enters a contract with Brenda's father stating that if children are born from the marriage and if Brenda dies before John, John will never remarry. In exchange, John is given the father's large farm to live on rent-free for life. Children are born, and Brenda does die first. John marries Patricia. Brenda's father then sues to evict John from the farm. Does John have a defense to this suit?

b. Joan enters a contract with her aunt stating that she will not have children before she turns 21. In exchange, Joan is given a sum of money when she signs the contract. Before she turns 21, Joan has a baby (out of wedlock). The aunt sues Joan for breach of contract. Does Joan have a defense?

c. Fred enters a contract with his father in which the father agrees to pay for Fred's entire medical education if Fred agrees to marry a doctor or a medical student if he decides to marry. When Fred becomes a doctor, he marries Sue, an electrician. The father sues Fred for the cost of the medical education. Does Fred have a defense?

d. Bill and Jean live together, but do not wish to marry each other. They enter a contract by which Jean promises to continue to live with Bill, to care for him, and to help raise their child in the event that they have a child. Bill agrees to place $500 per month in a bank account for Jean so long as she carries out her promise. Jean cannot receive the money until Bill dies. Also, if she marries before Bill dies, she forfeits the right to all the money in the account. After living with Bill for 20 years (and remaining childless), Jean leaves him to marry Tom. Can Jean sue Bill to recover $120,000 (plus interest), the amount in the account at the time she married Tom?

nepotism

Favoritism shown to relatives. A rule against nepotism is called an antinepotism rule.

marriage

The legal union of two persons as spouses with designated rights and obligations to each other.

fundamental right

A right that (a) is specifically guaranteed in the U.S. Constitution, (b) is implicit in the concept of ordered liberty, or (c) is deeply rooted in the nation's history and tradition.

Antinepotism

In Chapter 12, we will learn that discrimination on the basis of marital status is often illegal as violation of civil rights. For example, it is illegal for a bank to deny credit solely because the applicant is not married.

Nepotism is favoritism shown to relatives. Suppose that an employer has an *antinepotism* policy that forbids its employees to be married to each other. Under this policy, if one employee marries another employee, one or both must be terminated. Is this policy an unenforceable restriction on marriage? Most courts have said that the policy is reasonable because it (1) avoids spousal quarrels in the workplace, (2) avoids the appearance of favoritism if a spouse has supervisory authority over his or her spouse, and (3) cuts down on scheduling problems when, for example, the spouses seek the same vacation dates.

Antinepotism policies do not discriminate on the basis of marital status. They do not say that only single persons can be employed. The restriction is against marrying a particular person—someone who works for the same employer. Although not all states agree with the conclusion that antinepotism policies are enforceable, most states do.

INTRODUCTION TO MARRIAGE

> Marriage is a coming together for better or for worse, hopefully enduring and intimate to the degree of being sacred. It is an association that promotes a way of life, not causes; a harmony in living, not political faiths; a bilateral loyalty, not commercial or social projects. Yet it is an association for as noble a purpose as any involved in our prior decisions. *Griswold v. Connecticut*, 381 U.S. 479, 486 (1965) (Douglas, J.).

We now begin our examination of the law governing the formation of **marriage**—the legal union of two persons as spouses with designated rights and obligations to each other. Fifty-one percent of adults in America are married; 50 years ago, the number was 72 percent.[4] The marriage rate has declined in part because of the large number of couples living together without marrying. (See Chapter 4.) Considerable diversity exists among those that do marry. Although most couples are men and women in their first marriage, an increasing number are in their second and third marriages. (In a recent cartoon, a confused minister accidentally asked the bride, "Do you take this man to be your first husband?"[5]) Gender diversity also exists among the population of married couples as more states authorize same-sex marriage. (In another cartoon, a minister in a conservative state solemnly proclaims, "I now pronounce you husband and wife of the opposite sex."[6])

In the remainder of the chapter, we will explore the formation of marriage. We will also examine marriage-like relationships that have some, but not always all, the attributes of a marriage.

FUNDAMENTAL RIGHT

As individuals, we have different categories of rights. The highest category is a **fundamental right**. The right to marry is such a right. A fundamental right is a right that (a) is specifically guaranteed in the U.S. Constitution, (b) is implicit in the concept of ordered liberty, or (c) is deeply rooted in the nation's history and tradition. Marriage falls into the third category—a right that is deeply rooted in the nation's history and tradition. According to the U.S. Supreme Court, "The freedom to marry has long been recognized as one of the vital personal rights essential to the orderly pursuit of happiness by free men."[7]

In *Zablocki v. Redhail*, the U.S. Supreme Court said that only "reasonable regulations that do not significantly interfere with decisions to enter into the marital relationship may legitimately be imposed."[8] In *Zablocki*, the court held that a restriction based on child-support payments was not reasonable. A state could not require an unmarried person to prove compliance with current child-support obligations before being allowed to obtain a marriage license. In *Loving v. Virginia*, the Court held that the state could not ban mixed-race marriages.[9] A law against **miscegenation** impermissibly burdens the fundamental right to marry and is a denial of equal protection of the laws.

We will have more to say about when restrictions on the right to marry (particularly gender restrictions) are constitutional. For now, we simply establish the starting point of the analysis, namely that marriage is a fundamental right.

miscegenation
Marriage between persons of different races.

AM I MARRIED?: HOW THE MARRIAGE ISSUE IS RAISED

A client is not likely to walk into a law office and ask, "Am I married?" The existence of a marriage becomes an issue when the client is trying to obtain some other objective, such as seeking:

- a divorce (you can't divorce someone to whom you are not married). Sometimes "people discover that their marriage is invalid only when filing for divorce."[10]
- pension benefits as the surviving spouse of a deceased employee.
- social security benefits as the surviving spouse of a deceased worker.
- workers' compensation death benefits as the surviving spouse of an employee fatally injured on the job.
- assets as the spouse of a deceased person who died **intestate** (i.e., without leaving a valid will).
- recovery for the **wrongful death** of a spouse.
- assets under a clause in a will that gives property "to my wife" or "to my husband."
- an **elective share** of a deceased spouse's estate (this share can be selected—elected—in place of what is provided for the surviving spouse in the will of the deceased spouse).
- entrance into the United States (or avoidance of deportation) as a result of being married to a U.S. citizen.
- the **marital-communications privilege** (the right of spouses not to testify and to prevent each other from testifying about confidential communications between them during the marriage).

intestate
(1) Pertaining to someone who dies without a valid will. (2) A person who dies without a valid will.

wrongful death
A death caused by a tort or other wrong.

elective share
The percentage of a deceased spouse's estate that the surviving spouse can choose (elect) to receive despite what the will of the deceased spouse provided for the surviving spouse. Also called statutory share, forced share.

marital-communications privilege
A person can refuse to testify and can prevent his or her spouse or ex-spouse from testifying as to any confidential communications made between them during the marriage. Also called marital privilege, husband–wife privilege.

In all of these examples, the seeking party must establish that he or she is a spouse, i.e., that a marriage existed or exists.

CEREMONIAL AND COMMON LAW MARRIAGES

There are two main kinds of marriage:

- **Ceremonial marriage.** A marriage that is entered in compliance with statutory requirements (e.g., obtaining a marriage license, having the marriage performed by an authorized person before witnesses). Also called formal marriage and statutory marriage.
- **Common-law marriage.** A marriage that is entered without license or traditional ceremony by persons who (a) agree to marry, (b) live together as husband and wife, and (c) hold themselves out as married. A marriage of two people who have not gone through a ceremonial marriage. Called an "informal marriage" in Texas.

Although most states have abolished common-law marriage, the law governing such marriages must still be understood as we will see later in the chapter.

Both ceremonial and common-law marriages are the result of contracts that the parties have entered. It is often said, however, that there are three parties in every marriage: the two spouses and the state. The state is always present because of its regulatory power over who can enter a marriage, what can and cannot be done in a marriage, and how a marriage can be terminated. As we saw in Chapter 4, parties are allowed to control many aspects of a marriage, but the state remains a powerful enforcer of marriage basics.

CEREMONIAL MARRIAGE

The hallmark of a ceremonial marriage is compliance with statutory requirements such as obtaining a license. These requirements have not always existed. For most of Western history, marriage was a private contract between two families that did not require the permission or involvement of the state or of the church. For 16 centuries, society's main ecclesiastical authority (the Roman Catholic Church) accepted the validity of marriages that were based solely on the couple's exchange of marital vows; however,

> In 1215, the church decreed that a 'licit' marriage must take place in church. But people who married illicitly had the same rights and obligations as a couple married in church: their children were legitimate; the wife had the same inheritance rights; the couple was subject to the same prohibitions against divorce. Not until the sixteenth century did European states begin to require that marriages be performed under legal auspices. In part, this was an attempt to prevent unions between young adults whose parents opposed their match.[11]

Although the American colonies required marriages to be registered, common-law marriages were widely accepted as valid until the latter part of the nineteenth century, when many (but by no means all) states decreed that only ceremonial marriages would be recognized as valid.

TECHNICAL/PROCEDURAL REQUIREMENTS

We need to distinguish between (a) technical or procedural requirements for marriage (e.g., obtaining a marriage license, having witnesses to the ceremony) and (b) the essential requirements for marriage that pertain to the intent to marry and the capacity to marry (e.g., being of minimum age, having no serious mental disability). Most of the essential requirements will be discussed in Chapter 6 when we cover annulment. For now, our focus is on the technical/procedural requirements for a ceremonial marriage.

Not all states have the same technical/procedural requirements. (See Appendix D for a link to the requirements for your state.) Here are the technical/procedural requirements most often found in statutory codes:

- Marriage license (a marriage license is required; in some states, both parties must apply for the license in person).
- Ceremony performed by an authorized person, known as the **officiant** (e.g., a member of the clergy, a judge, or other designated person).
- Witnesses to the ceremony.
- Marriage declaration (during the ceremony, before the officiant and witnesses, the parties must indicate that they take each other as husband and wife).
- Waiting period between the time the marriage license is obtained and the wedding.
- Recording of the marriage by the officiant in a designated government office (e.g., county clerk) following the ceremony (the process is called **recordation**).

officiant
One who leads or performs a ceremony, often a religious service.

recordation
Filing a document with a government body so that it becomes part of the official record.

Some states require a blood test or other medical reports to determine the presence of venereal disease, sickle cell disease, or rubella, although such requirements are becoming less common. Florida offers a substantial discount on the cost of the marriage license if the couple agrees to take a premarital preparation course, but the course is not required.[12] In a few states, parties who wish their marriage to be private can choose what is called a **confidential marriage**. Such marriages have fewer technical/procedural requirements (e.g., no witnesses are needed) and information about the marriage that is recorded in a government office is not available to the general public.[13]

Solemnization means the formal steps taken in a public ceremony in order to enter into a status or contract. In most states, all that is required to solemnize a marriage is for the parties to declare in the presence of the clergy member, judge, or other officiant that they take each other as husband and wife. Some states do not require a ceremony. New York, for example, allows a couple to become married by a written contract (called a *marriage by contract*) signed before two witnesses and acknowledged by a judge.[14] In Colorado, no officiant is needed; the couple can solemnize their own marriage (sometimes referred to as a *self-solemnization*).[15]

States impose different time periods for the marriage license. It may be good for 60 days in one state, whereas in another state it may expire if the parties are not married within 90 days after the license is issued. There might be an additional waiting period for persons who wish to marry after having obtained a divorce decree. In one state, a license can be used in any county of the state, whereas in another state the parties may have to be married in the county where they obtained the license.

VIOLATING TECHNICAL/PROCEDURAL REQUIREMENTS

In Chapter 6, we will examine whether a marriage can be annulled if it is entered in violation of one of the technical/procedural requirements (e.g., the officiant did not have proper authorization to marry the parties). In general, such violations are not grounds for annulment, although there are some exceptions, as we will see.

SURNAMES

There is no requirement that one party take the other's surname. In some states, parties are given specific notice that marriage does not automatically change anyone's name. Although it is traditional for women to take their husband's last name, there is nothing to prevent a woman from keeping her own name or using a hyphenated name consisting of the surnames of both spouses. The husband-to-be also has the option of keeping his own name, taking his wife's name, or using a hyphenated name. We will have more to say about change-of-name laws in Chapters 7, 9, and 12.

PROXY MARRIAGE

Is physical presence of the bride and groom at the ceremony a requirement for a ceremonial marriage? You might think so, but most states allow a **proxy marriage**, in which the ceremony takes place with one or both parties being absent (e.g., the groom is overseas in the military). A third-party agent must be given the authority (usually in writing) to act on behalf of the missing party or parties during the ceremony.

Immigration officials are often suspicious of proxy marriages. The concern is that an American citizen is entering a proxy marriage with someone who lives

confidential marriage
A ceremonial marriage entered with fewer technical/procedural requirements and greater privacy than a traditional ceremonial marriage.

solemnization
Formal steps taken in a public ceremony in order to enter a status or contract. The verb is *solemnize*.

proxy marriage
A ceremonial marriage in which agents ("stand-ins") take the place of one or both of the prospective spouses because of their absence at the ceremony.

abroad solely to qualify that person for an entry status as the spouse of a citizen. It may not succeed. Immigration law provides:

> The term *spouse*, *wife*, or *husband* does not include a spouse, wife, or husband by reason of any marriage ceremony where the contracting parties thereto are not physically present in the presence of each other, unless the marriage shall have been consummated.[16]

Note, however, that a proxy marriage with a foreign bride or groom might be valid under *state* law even if the immigration authorities do not recognize it for purposes of entry into the country.

POSTHUMOUS MARRIAGE

Proxy marriages occur in the absence of one or both spouses. Suppose that one of the would-be spouses is no longer alive. Can you marry a dead person? Not in America. Some European countries, however, do allow posthumous marriages. In France, for example, anyone "wishing to marry a dead person must send a request to the president, who then forwards it to the justice minister, who sends it to the prosecutor in whose jurisdiction the surviving person lives. If the prosecutor determines that the couple planned to marry before the death and if the parents of the deceased approve, the prosecutor sends a recommendation back up the line. The president, if so moved, eventually signs a decree allowing the marriage."[17]

ASSIGNMENT 5.7

Go to your state statutory code and identify all of the technical or procedural requirements for entering a ceremonial marriage (e.g., obtaining a license, paying a fee). (See General Instructions for the State-Code Assignment in Appendix A.)

ABM: ANYTHING BUT MARRIAGE

We turn now to the law governing same-sex marriage. To understand this law, we first need to look at the ABM (anything but marriage) movement and DOMA, the Defense of Marriage Act.

The most controversial issue in family law—other than abortion—is whether same-sex couples should be allowed to marry. In the 1990s, the momentum toward recognizing such marriages gained strength. To offset that momentum, a major strategy of some conservatives was to pass laws that granted a new legal status to same-sex couples. In the new status, the couples would enjoy many of the benefits of marriage but would not be married. The strategy was ABM: anything but marriage (sometimes called EBM: everything but marriage).

The newly created ABM status had different names, and in some states was made available to both opposite-sex and same-sex couples:

- **Civil union.** A same-sex legal relationship in which the individuals in the relationship have some or all of the same state benefits and responsibilities as individuals in a marriage.

- **Domestic partnership.** A same-sex or opposite-sex legal relationship of unmarried individuals who are emotionally and financially interdependent and who have some of the same state benefits and responsibilities as individuals in a marriage.

Other terms include *reciprocal beneficiary relationship* and *designated beneficiary*. Wisconsin has two categories of domestic partnerships: limited purpose domestic partnerships (for state employees) and domestic partnerships for the general public. Some of the ABM laws were passed by the state legislature and apply to the entire state. Others were passed by counties, cities, or other local units of government and apply only within the boundaries of the locality covered. (See Exhibit 5-2 later in the chapter.)

Because a civil union or domestic partnership is a legal status, formal steps are required to enter it and to terminate it. Here are some of the requirements that are often imposed by law to enter the status (the references to domestic partnership can also apply to civil unions):

- Both are at least 18 years old.
- Both are mentally competent to consent to a civil contract and neither is acting under force or duress.
- Neither is married to or legally separated from any other person and neither is in another domestic partnership.
- Neither is related to each other by blood or marriage in a degree of closeness that would constitute grounds for annulment of a marriage.
- Each acknowledges being in a committed relationship of mutual caring and support for each other and both are jointly responsible for each other's common welfare.

Another requirement might be that the parties have shared a residence or been financially interdependent for a designated period of time, e.g., three months. If the status is restricted to same-sex couples, the parties must declare that they are in such a relationship. If the status is available to opposite-sex couples, special restrictions might apply. For example, in California, domestic partnerships are not open to opposite-sex couples unless one partner is at least 62 years old.

In most states, the new status is entered by filing a document (e.g., Declaration of Domestic Partnership) with a government official (e.g., the county clerk). No solemnization ceremony is required. In relatively uncomplicated cases, the status can be terminated by filing a corresponding document (e.g., Notice of Termination of Domestic Partnership) with the same official. A court filing to terminate may be needed if the parties have children or acquired a designated amount of assets or debts during the relationship.

The marriage-like benefits bestowed on couples in the new status vary. The most common benefits include:

- Allowing your partner to be a covered person on your health insurance policy.
- Receiving workers' compensation benefits when a partner is injured on the job.
- Being able to bring a lawsuit for the wrongful death of your partner.
- Being allowed to visit a partner in a hospital and to make medical decisions for an incapacitated partner.
- Filing joint state tax returns.
- Receiving a portion of the estate of a partner who dies intestate (without a valid will).

Many large businesses and associations have decided on their own to grant some domestic-partnership benefits to their employees. The most important of these benefits is coverage of the partner on the group health insurance policy of the business or association.

DEFENSE OF MARRIAGE ACT (DOMA)

FULL-FAITH-AND-CREDIT CONTROVERSY

Of course, not all states joined the movement to create new relationships for same-sex couples who are not allowed to marry. Opponents of the ABM status felt that it legitimated immoral conduct and was an uncomfortable step in the direction of full recognition of same-sex marriage.

In 1993, the Hawaii Supreme Court reached the surprising conclusion that the denial of same-sex marriage is presumed to be unconstitutional and sent the case back to the lower court for further proceedings.[18] This decision made international news. Many gay activists were ecstatic. Could this be the breakthrough they had hoped for? The ongoing Hawaii litigation sounded like it might lead to a lifting of the ban on same-sex marriage. To say that conservatives in Hawaii and in the nation were alarmed would be an understatement.

The fear of opponents in other states was that if Hawaii eventually authorized same-sex marriage, other states might be forced to recognize such marriages within their own state. Here is how this could happen. Assume that State X allows same-sex marriage but State Y does not:

Ted and Bob marry in State X. They then move to State Y, where they continue to live together. Bob dies. Ted now goes to a court in State Y and asks for a share of Bob's estate as his spouse.

Or:

After Ted and Bob move to State Y, they decide to separate. They go to a Y state court and ask for a divorce and an order dividing their marital property.

In either event, the Y state court must decide whether to recognize the marriage entered in State X. What law does the Y state court apply? Its own (where same-sex marriage is illegal) or that of State X (where same-sex marriage is allowed)? This is a **conflict-of-laws** question. As we will see later in this chapter and in Chapter 6, the traditional conflict-of-law rule is as follows:

Conflict of Laws and the Validity of a Marriage

The validity of a marriage is determined by the law of the state in which the marriage was entered or contracted. Another state will recognize that marriage unless to do so would violate a strong public policy of the state asked to recognize it.

Under this rule, State Y would be required to recognize the same-sex marriage entered in State X unless State Y determined that to do so would violate a strong public policy of State Y. In our example, we said that same-sex marriages are not allowed in State Y. A State Y court would have to decide if recognizing such a marriage from another state would violate the strong public policy of State Y. If the answer was yes, State Y would not consider giving Ted a share of Bob's estate or allowing Ted and Bob to divorce in State Y.

The problem is further compounded by the **Full Faith and Credit (FFC)** Clause of the U.S. Constitution that requires states to recognize (give full faith and credit to) each other's official decisions. Assume that Ted and Bob have a judgment from a court in State X that declares their marriage legal under the law of State X. Would other states be required to give FFC (that is, to recognize) the judgment of this State X court?

This was the unanswered question that troubled many states in 1993 when Hawaii appeared to be on the verge of recognizing same-sex marriage. While the Hawaii case was still in litigation, however, the Hawaii legislature and voters overwhelmingly approved a constitutional amendment that gave the legislature the authority to limit marriage to opposite-sex couples. The legislature then passed such a statute. This made the Hawaii litigation **moot** and the case was dismissed.

Opponents of same-sex marriage across the country expressed a collective sigh of relief. There was no longer a possibility that their state might be forced to recognize (give FFC to) a Hawaiian same-sex marriage. But if Hawaii came this close, what if another state actually authorized such marriages? (As of 1993, no state had done so.) Rather than wait, over 35 state legislatures enacted statutes banning same-sex marriages and making clear that it is against the state's strong public policy to recognize such marriages entered in other states. A story in the *New York Times* on this development was titled "Fearing a Toehold for Gay Marriages, Conservatives Rush to Bar the Door."[19]

conflict of laws
An inconsistency between the laws of different legal systems such as two states or two countries.

full faith and credit (FFC)
The obligation of one state to recognize and enforce the legal decisions of another state. The obligation is based on the U.S. Constitution, which provides that "Full Faith and Credit shall be given in each State to the public Acts, Records, and judicial Proceedings of every other State." Article IV, § 1.

moot
Pertaining to a nonexistent controversy where the issues have ceased to exist from a practical point of view. (See glossary for an additional meaning.)

At the federal level, Congress passed, and President Bill Clinton signed, the **Defense of Marriage Act (DOMA)**, which said that a state is not required to give FFC to a same-sex marriage entered in another state:

> No State . . . shall be required to give effect to any public act, record, or judicial proceeding of any other State . . . respecting a relationship between persons of the same sex that is treated as a marriage under the laws of such other State . . . or a right or claim arising from such relationship.[20]

If a state wants to recognize another state's same-sex marriage, it can, but DOMA says that this recognition is not required. DOMA does not say that same-sex marriages are illegal. It simply provides that one state cannot be forced to recognize such a marriage if another state ever allows one. The state statutes declaring that it is against the state's strong public policy to recognize out-of-state same-sex marriages became known as **mini-DOMAs** or baby-DOMAs.

DOMA is a statute that carves out an exception to the FFC requirement of the U.S. Constitution. Can a statute change the constitution in this way? We do not yet have a definitive answer to this question. The U.S. Supreme Court might eventually rule that DOMA (and the mini-DOMAs) are unconstitutional. At the present time, we do not know whether any legislature has the constitutional power to limit the scope of the FFC clause of the U.S. Constitution in the way that DOMA does. We will eventually find out, now that there are states that authorize same-sex marriage (see discussion on page 166). When a same-sex couple enters a valid marriage in a state such as Massachusetts and moves to another state seeking recognition and enforcement of their marriage, the other state might say that DOMA gives it the right to refuse. This will eventually require the U.S. Supreme Court to decide whether DOMA is constitutional.

Of course, there is another way that this controversy could be resolved. If the U.S. Supreme Court one day rules that the ban on same-sex marriage violates the U.S. Constitution (see discussion on page 166) then every state must allow and recognize these marriages. Such a ruling would invalidate all of the mini-DOMAs so that the federal DOMA rule on interstate recognition of same-sex marriages would become irrelevant.

Defense of Marriage Act (DOMA)
A federal statute that says (1) one state is not required to give full faith and credit to a same-sex marriage entered in another state (28 U.S.C. § 1738C) and (2) for federal purposes, only opposite-sex marriage is recognized (1 U.S.C. § 7).

mini-DOMA
A statute of a state declaring that its strong public policy is not to recognize any same-sex marriage that might be validly entered in another state.

FEDERAL DEFINITION OF MARRIAGE

The federal DOMA did more than declare that states did not have to recognize the same-sex marriages of other states. It also said that for all federal purposes, marriage is defined as the legal union of only opposite-sex couples:

> In determining the meaning of any Act of Congress, or of any ruling, regulation, or interpretation of the various administrative bureaus and agencies of the United States, the word "marriage" means only a legal union between one man and one woman as husband and wife, and the word "spouse" refers only to a person of the opposite sex who is a husband or a wife.[21]

This part of DOMA did not ban same-sex marriages. It has no effect on states that might want to interpret their own law as allowing same-sex marriage. It simply says that for purposes of administering *federal* laws such as social security, immigration, and federal income tax, same-sex marriages are not recognized. There are over 1,000 federal benefits and rights that are granted to married couples. Same-sex couples are not eligible for them even if they are validly married in a state that authorizes same-sex marriage. For example, married same-sex couples are not eligible for surviving-spouse benefits under social security and cannot file a joint federal income tax return. Such couples can file a joint *state* tax return as spouses, but they must file two individual *federal* tax returns because DOMA says only opposite-sex marriage is recognized for federal purposes.

DOMA's nonrecognition of opposite-sex marriage has been challenged in court, and some lower federal courts have ruled that this part of DOMA is unconstitutional as a denial of equal protection. Other lower courts have reached the opposite conclusion. This is another issue that awaits a final resolution by the U.S. Supreme Court.

With this background, we turn now to the states that have allowed same-sex marriage and to the challenges that have been raised to the states that ban it.

SAME-SEX MARRIAGE

INTRODUCTION

In 2010, there were 646,464 same-sex couples in the United States. Of this number, 137,729 checked "husband" or "wife" on their census forms.[22] This reflects the dramatic change in the law of marriage since 2003 when the first state, Massachusetts, allowed same-sex couples to marry.

A same-sex marriage, where allowed, is a ceremonial marriage. All of the technical/procedural requirements discussed earlier (e.g., obtaining a license) must be complied with. Similarly, the relevant grounds for annulment discussed in the next chapter (e.g., bigamy, nonage, and sham marriage) fully apply to same-sex marriages.

Here, our discussion of same-sex marriage will center on two major themes:

- State law. How have states reached their individual decisions on whether state law allows same-sex marriage?

- Federal law. Does a state that bans same-sex marriage violate the U.S. Constitution?

The regulation of marriage consists of a mixture of state and federal law. As we examine same-sex marriage, the following general principles will guide our discussion of the state-federal regulatory mix.

SAME-SEX MARRIAGE: GENERAL PRINCIPLES

- *State law.* State governments have laws that define marriage and that specify who can enter them. These laws must comply with the provisions of the state's own constitution on individual rights. For example, if the Massachusetts legislature passes a statute on marriage, that statute must not violate the constitution of the Commonwealth of Massachusetts.

- *State law.* States have come to different conclusions as to whether same-sex couples can marry under state law. They have reached these conclusions by different routes:

  - State constitutions in some states prohibit same-sex marriage. State constitutions in other states allow it.

  - State statutes in some states prohibit same-sex marriage. State statutes in other states allow it.

  - In some states, voters have decided through the initiative and referendum process whether to allow same-sex marriage in the state. These votes have resulted in changes in the state's constitution and/or statutes.

- *Federal law.* The federal government also has a role in marriage law. The federal Constitution (U.S. Constitution) establishes minimum standards for certain individual rights. Every state statute and every provision of a state constitution must be consistent with (must not violate) the federal Constitution. This is so because of the **Supremacy Clause** of the U.S. Constitution.

Supremacy Clause

The clause in the U.S. Constitution (art. VI, cl. 2) that has been interpreted to mean that when valid federal law conflicts with state law, federal law controls.

- *State and federal law.* Although a state constitution must meet the minimum standards of the federal Constitution, it is possible for a state constitution to provide more rights than the federal Constitution. Here is an example:

  - Federal courts have ruled that the U.S. Constitution does not require the appointment of counsel (at government expense) in every civil case in which a poor person is sued for failure to pay child support.

  - A state court in a particular state might rule that under its state constitution, the appointment of counsel (at government expense) for poor persons *is* required in every civil child-support case.

  Hence, on the issue of appointed counsel in child-support cases, a state constitution could provide greater individual rights than the federal Constitution.

- *State and federal law.* Now let's examine the interrelationship between state and federal constitutional law on the issue of same-sex marriage. As indicated, states differ on whether their state constitutions will allow same-sex marriage. The U.S. Supreme Court has not yet ruled on whether the U.S. Constitution allows a state to ban same-sex marriage. Lower federal courts have ruled on this question (see the discussion below), but not the U.S. Supreme Court. In view of this gap in the law, keep the following principles in mind:

  - If the U.S. Supreme Court never rules on same-sex marriage, the states that allow it can continue to allow it and the states that ban it can continue to ban it.

  - If the U.S. Supreme Court does issue a ruling and concludes that a state's ban on same-sex marriage does not violate the U.S. Constitution, then the states that allow same-sex marriage can continue to allow it and the states that ban it can continue to ban it.

  - If the U.S. Supreme Court rules that a state's ban on same-sex marriage violates the U.S. Constitution, then every state must allow same-sex couples to marry.

  Under the second scenario, a state constitution that allows same-sex marriage would be providing an individual right that is not provided by the federal Constitution. The state constitution would be providing greater individual rights than the federal Constitution.

- *Will the U.S. Supreme Court rule that the ban on same-sex marriage violates the U.S. Constitution?* We have some clues on what the U.S. Supreme Court might eventually decide. Before we look at these clues, we need to examine the two clauses of the U.S. Constitution that are most likely to be the basis of whatever the court decides: the Due Process Clause and the Equal Protection Clause of the Fourteenth Amendment. When the Court decides that a state ban is either allowed or not allowed, the Court may be applying one or both of these clauses. Therefore we will take a close look at each clause. Our overview will involve two questions: What does the clause cover, and what level of scrutiny or standard of review will a court use to decide if the clause has been violated?

- *Due process.* We begin with due process. The Due Process Clause in the Fourteenth Amendment of the U.S. Constitution provides that no state shall "deprive any person of life, liberty, or property, without due process of law."[23] There are two components of due process:

  - **Procedural due process (PDP).** The constitutional requirement that the government provide fair procedures such as adequate notice and an opportunity to be heard whenever the government seeks to deprive someone of life, liberty, or property.

procedural due process (PDP)
The constitutional requirement that the government provide fair procedures such as notice and an opportunity to be heard whenever the government seeks to deprive someone of life, liberty, or property.

substantive due process (SDP)
The constitutional requirement that the government avoid arbitrary and capricious actions that deprive someone of life, liberty, or property regardless of how fair the government is in the procedures that lead to the deprivation.

- **Substantive due process (SDP).** The constitutional requirement that the government avoid arbitrary and capricious actions that deprive someone of life, liberty, or property regardless of how fair the government is in the procedures that lead to the deprivation.

Our primary concern here is SDP.

- *Substantive due process (SDP).* There are two categories of SDP rights: fundamental rights and nonfundamental rights.

  - Fundamental rights: A right that is (a) specifically guaranteed in the U.S. Constitution, (b) implicit in the concept of ordered liberty, or (c) deeply rooted in the nation's history and tradition. An example is the right to marry.

  - Nonfundamental rights: Any right that is not a fundamental right. An example is the right to adopt a child.

- *Substantive due process (SDP): standards of review.* When a right is restricted by the state and is challenged as a violation of SDP, the court must apply a test to determine its constitutionality. The test is called the *standard of review.* The standard differs based on the nature of the right being restricted and on the nature of the restriction itself.

  - If the state passes a law that bans or substantially restricts a fundamental right, the standard of review is called **strict scrutiny**. Under this test, the state must justify the law by showing that it is narrowly tailored to serve a compelling state interest. If the state cannot do so, the law is struck down as a violation of SDP.

  - If the state passes a law that merely regulates a fundamental right but does not ban or substantially restrict it, the standard of review is called minimal scrutiny, or more commonly, **rational basis**. Under this test, the state must justify the law by showing that it is reasonably related to a legitimate state purpose. An example is a law that requires persons who want to marry to obtain a marriage license. If the state is pursuing a legitimate purpose (e.g., to have accurate records of the citizenry) and if the license law is reasonably related to this purpose, then the law does not violate SDP.

  - If the state restricts a nonfundamental right in any way (by banning it, by substantially restricting it, or by merely regulating it), the standard of review is rational basis.

- *Substantive due process (SDP): banning or substantially restricting same-sex marriage.* Now let's apply these principles to same-sex marriage. We want to know if a state law that bans or substantially restricts same-sex marriage violates SDP under the U.S. Constitution. Keep in mind that we are still focusing on the Due Process Clause of the Fourteenth Amendment of the U.S. Constitution. We will cover the Equal Protection Clause shortly.

  - If a court decides that same-sex couples have a fundamental right to marry, then strict scrutiny applies. A state law banning or substantially restricting same-sex marriage will be held to violate SDP unless the state can show that the law is narrowly tailored to serve a compelling state interest. (If a state law merely regulates, but does not ban or substantially restrict a fundamental right, the standard of review is rational basis, not strict scrutiny.)

strict scrutiny
The government's action must be narrowly tailored to serve a compelling state interest.

rational basis
The government's action must be reasonably related to a legitimate state purpose. Also called minimal scrutiny or rational relation.

- If a court decides that same-sex marriage is a nonfundamental right, then rational basis (minimal scrutiny) applies. Any state law restricting same-sex marriage will be upheld if the law is reasonably related to a legitimate state interest.

We do not yet know which of these two levels of scrutiny the U.S. Supreme Court will choose. Later we will see how lower federal courts have handled this issue, but a final resolution of the issue awaits a decision of the U.S. Supreme Court.

- *Substantive due process (SDP): a third level of scrutiny?* Some scholars have suggested that the U.S. Supreme Court might use a *third* level of scrutiny to determine the constitutionality of the ban on same-sex marriage, one that is roughly in between strict scrutiny and minimal scrutiny. This level has been called "rational basis with bite" or "rational basis plus," meaning that something more than a rational basis will have to be shown to justify the ban, but something less than full strict scrutiny.[24]

- *Lawrence v. Texas.* In 2003, the U.S. Supreme Court decided the landmark case of *Lawrence v. Texas*, which struck down a Texas statute that made it a crime for consenting same-sex adults to commit sodomy in private. Writing for the majority, Justice Kennedy held that such laws violated SDP. The focus of the opinion was the liberty interest protected by the Due Process Clause of the Fourteenth Amendment. (States cannot deprive persons of "life, liberty, or property without due process of law.") Although many in society condemn homosexual conduct as immoral, the Court said that the liberty interest enjoyed by every individual cannot be dictated by anyone's moral code. (The "fact that the governing majority in a State has traditionally viewed a particular practice as immoral is not a sufficient reason for upholding a law prohibiting the practice."[25]) Justice Kennedy used very broad language in concluding that "liberty presumes an autonomy of self that includes freedom of thought, belief, expression, and certain intimate conduct. The instant case involves liberty of the person both in its spatial and more transcendent dimensions." The Court held that Texas had no justification for criminalizing conduct that occurs within these dimensions: "The Texas statute furthers no legitimate state interest which can justify its intrusion into the personal and private life of the individual."[26]

- *Lawrence v. Texas: implications for same-sex marriage.* In the majority opinion of *Lawrence*, Justice Kennedy wanted to make clear that that striking down criminal laws against private sexual conduct of same-sex couples was not a ruling that the ban on same-sex marriage should also be struck down. The *Lawrence* case, he said, "does not involve whether the government must give formal recognition to any relationship that homosexual persons seek to enter."[27] In dissent, Justice Scalia bitterly attacked Kennedy's opinion. Scalia said that laws can and should be based on moral choices. He gave the examples of laws "against bigamy, same-sex marriage, adult incest, prostitution, masturbation, adultery, fornication, bestiality, and obscenity." Every one of these laws, said Scalia "is called into question by today's decision."[28] In Scalia's mind, therefore, if the logic and rationale of *Lawrence* is applied to same-sex marriage, the ban against same-sex marriage would be held to violate SDP.

- *Lawrence v. Texas: levels of scrutiny.* It is important to point out that Justice Kennedy did not discuss the two traditional levels of scrutiny (strict scrutiny and minimal scrutiny - rational basis) that are commonly applied in SDP cases. As indicated, this has led some to speculate that in cases involving sexual intimacy, the Court might be developing a new standard or level of scrutiny such as rational basis with bite or rational basis plus. Despite the dissent of Justice Scalia in *Lawrence*, we do not know whether the U.S. Supreme Court will eventually decide if the ban on same-sex marriage is constitutional. Only if it does so will we know what kind of scrutiny the Court will use.

- *Equal protection.* Next, we examine equal protection. The Equal Protection Clause in the Fourteenth Amendment of the U.S. Constitution provides that no state shall "deny any person within its jurisdiction the equal protection of the laws."[29]

- *Equal protection and due process.* Due process and equal protection are closely related. In general, the major distinction is as follows:

  - Due process (particularly substantive due process [SDP]). If the government decrees that everyone must do something or that everyone is forbidden from doing something, the constitutionality of the government's action is judged by due process.

  - Equal protection. If the government says that only some groups can do something or that only some groups are forbidden from doing something, the constitutionality of the government's action is judged by equal protection of law (EPL).

- *Equal protection: discrimination and classification.* In the broadest sense of the word, **discrimination** simply means treating things or people differently depending on the group they are in. Another word for group is *class*. The word **classification** means a group that the government treats differently from another group in that the government discriminates for or against that group.

- *Equal protection.* **Equal protection of law (EPL)** is the constitutional requirement that the government treat one group or class the same as it treats another group or class in like circumstances. Four questions must be asked in this area of the law:

  - Has the government created a classification by treating one group or class differently from another?

  - Are the groups or classes similarly situated?

  - What justification does the government have for the different treatment?

  - Is this justification constitutionally adequate?

The most important question is the fourth. A court answers this question by applying one of three levels of scrutiny, depending on the kind of classification that is involved.

- *Equal protection: three levels of scrutiny.* When we discussed SDP, we saw that the court used different levels of scrutiny depending on whether the government was depriving someone of fundamental rights. Levels of scrutiny are also part of a court's analysis when deciding if the government has violated equal protection.

  - Strict scrutiny. If the classification by the government involves a fundamental right or a **suspect class**, the government must justify the classification by showing that the different treatment is *narrowly tailored to serve a compelling state interest.*

discrimination

Treating things or people differently depending on which group they are in. Differential treatment.

classification

(1) A group the government treats differently from another group in that the government discriminates for or against that group. (2) The government's different treatment of one group over another. (See glossary for an additional meaning.)

equal protection of law (EPL)

The constitutional requirement that the government treat one group or class the same as it treats another group or class in like circumstances. Shortened to equal protection.

suspect class

A class based on race, national origin, or alienage. Alienage is the condition of being an alien. (An alien is a person who was born outside the United States, is still a subject of a foreign nation, and has not been naturalized in the United States.)

- **Intermediate scrutiny.** If the classification by the government involves a **quasi-suspect class**, the government must justify the classification by showing that the different treatment is *substantially related to serve an important state interest*.

- Minimal scrutiny (rational basis). If the classification by the government does not involve a fundamental right, a suspect class, or a quasi-suspect class, the government must justify the classification by showing that the different treatment is *reasonably related to a legitimate state purpose*.

intermediate scrutiny

The government's action must be substantially related to serve an important state interest. Also called heightened scrutiny, elevated scrutiny.

quasi-suspect class

A class based on gender or on a child's legitimacy.

- *Equal protection: same-sex marriage.* Is a law that bans or substantially restricts same-sex marriage a violation of EPL? Under such a law, the state would be treating opposite-sex couples and same-sex couples differently. Does this different treatment (discrimination) violate EPL? The U.S. Supreme Court has not yet answered this question, although lower federal courts have answered it, as we will see.

- *State and federal law.* A reminder that the discussion thus far about due process and equal protection has pertained to the federal (U.S.) Constitution. State constitutions have their own provisions and may apply different standards of review and levels of scrutiny. We will now take a closer look at this state law.

DOES THE BAN VIOLATE STATE LAW?

The Early Decisions

Between 2003 and 2009, the highest state courts in Massachusetts, California, Connecticut, and Iowa ruled that the ban on same-sex marriage violated their state constitutions. These early decisions are summarized in Exhibit 5-1. Because each court was applying its own state constitution, it was free to make its own decision on what level of scrutiny to apply. Federal courts decide what level of scrutiny to apply under the U.S. Constitution. State courts decide what level of scrutiny to apply under the state constitution.

EXHIBIT 5-1 Lifting the Ban on Same-Sex Marriage: The Early Decisions

MASSACHUSETTS: 2003

- *Decision.* In 2003, Massachusetts became the first state to recognize same-sex marriage in a 4-3 decision of the Massachusetts Supreme Judicial Court, *Goodridge v. Department of Public Health.*[30]

- *Law Applied to Reach Its Decision.* The constitution of the Commonwealth of Massachusetts. Barring an individual from the protections, benefits, and obligations of civil marriage solely because that person would marry a person of the same sex violated the state constitution.

- *Standard of Review (Level of Scrutiny Applied).* Rational basis. There is no need to decide if the ban on same-sex marriage meets the test of strict scrutiny because the ban does not meet the broader rational-basis test.

Application of Standard.

- The proponents of the ban argued that the ban furthered the goal of providing the optimal setting to raise children. The court, however, said that there is no rational relationship between the ban and this goal because there is no evidence that the ban will increase the number of couples who choose opposite-sex marriage in order to have and raise children.

- It is not rational to penalize children by denying marital benefits to their same-sex parents.

- There is no reasonable relationship between the ban and the protection of public health, safety, or general welfare. The ban, therefore, is impermissibly based on private prejudice against homosexuals.

EXHIBIT 5-1 *(continued)*

CALIFORNIA: 2008

- *Decision.* In May of 2008, the California Supreme Court ruled in the 4–3 decision of *In re Marriages* that same-sex marriage could not be banned.[31]

- *Law Applied to Reach Its Decision.* The California constitution. The privacy and due process provisions of the state constitution guarantee the fundamental right of marriage to all couples without regard to their sexual orientation.

- *Standard of Review (Level of Scrutiny Applied).* Strict scrutiny because the ban infringed the fundamental right to marry.

- *Later History.* In November of 2008, the voters nullified this decision by passing Proposition 8, which amended the constitution to provide that "[o]nly marriage between a man and a woman is valid or recognized in California." Between the date of the court decision and the date of the passage of the proposition, 18,000 same-sex couples married in the state. Proposition 8 did not affect the validity of these marriages. In 2010, a federal trial court (U.S. District Court in San Francisco) in *Perry v. Schwarzenegger* ruled that Proposition 8 violated the Due Process Clause and the Equal Protection Clause of the U.S. Constitution.[32] In the 2012 decision of *Perry v. Brown,* a three-judge panel of the federal appeals court (U.S. Court of Appeals for the Ninth Circuit) affirmed the trial court decision that Proposition 8 violated the U.S. Constitution, but for a different reason. The trial court held (1) that same-sex couples had a fundamental right to marry under the Due Process Clause of the U.S. Constitution and (2) that the ban on same-sex marriage violated the Equal Protection Clause of the U.S. Constitution. The appeals court, however, avoided the broad question of whether same-sex couples had a right to marry under the U.S. Constitution. Instead, it reached the narrower conclusion that the state had no legitimate reason to take away the right to marry that same-sex couples enjoyed prior to the passage of Proposition 8. Without a legitimate reason, the Equal Protection Clause does not allow the targeting of a disfavored group by depriving it of a right they already enjoyed.[33]

CONNECTICUT: 2008

- *Decision.* In 2008, the Supreme Court of Connecticut recognized same-sex marriage in the 4–3 decision of *Kerrigan v. Commissioner of Public Health.*[34]

- *Law Applied to Reach Its Decision.* The Connecticut constitution. Restricting civil marriage to heterosexual couples violates the equal protection rights of same-sex couples under the state constitution.

- *Standard of Review (Level of Scrutiny Applied).* Heightened or intermediate level of scrutiny because sexual orientation is a quasi-suspect classification. There is no need to decide whether same-sex marriage is a fundamental right requiring a stricter standard of review. Under intermediate scrutiny, the government must show that the challenged legislative enactment is substantially related to an important governmental interest. It failed to do so.

Application of Standard.

- The ban against same-sex marriage discriminates on the basis of sexual orientation.

- The ban is not substantially related to the government purpose of promoting uniformity and consistency with the law of other states. The government has not explained why this is an important government purpose.

- The ban is not substantially related to the government purpose of preserving the traditional definition of marriage as a union between one man and one woman. It is not enough that the ban has been in existence for a long time and that many voters and legislators have strong personal convictions that the ban should exist.

- The ban is not substantially related to the government purpose of privileging and regulating procreative conduct because ending the ban "in no way" undermines the interest of the state in regulating procreative conduct of opposite-sex couples.

IOWA: 2009

- **Decision.** In 2009, the Supreme Court of Iowa recognized same-sex marriage in the 7–0 decision of *Varnum v. Brien*.[35]

- **Law Applied to Reach Its Decision.** The Iowa constitution. The statute limiting civil marriage to a union between a man and a woman violated equal protection rights of same-sex couples seeking marriage licenses.

- **Standard of Review (Level of Scrutiny Applied).** Heightened or intermediate level of scrutiny because sexual orientation is a quasi-suspect classification.

Application of Standard.

- Protecting traditional marriage between a man and woman is not an important governmental objective.

- The ban on same-sex marriage is not substantially related to the government goal of ensuring an optimal environment for raising children. The ban is *over-inclusive* because not all same-sex couples want to raise children and it is *under-inclusive* because it did not forbid same-sex couples from raising children.

- The ban is not substantially related to the government goal of promoting procreation. The link between the ban and increased procreation is far too tenuous to withstand heightened scrutiny.

- The ban is not substantially related to the government goal of promoting stability in opposite-sex relationships.

- The ban is not substantially related to the government goal of conserving state resources.

- Religious opposition to same-sex marriage cannot be a government interest supporting the ban. The government can have no religious views or preferences.

- **Later History.** After the *Varnum* decision was rendered, three of the seven justices were on the ballot in the next judicial retention election in what is usually a routine approval by the voters. In a stunning rebuke, all three were voted out of office: "Conservative groups angered by the unanimous same-sex marriage decision spent heavily to convince voters to throw out then-Chief Justice Marsha Ternus and Justices David Baker and Michael Streit during retention elections in 2010. . . . [T]here was some talk among conservatives of impeaching the remaining four."[36]

© Cengage Learning 2013

Other States

Other states have also changed their marriage law by allowing same-sex marriage. Some of the changes occurred by legislation and others by a combination of court opinion and legislation.

VERMONT In 2009, Vermont passed a statute that allowed same-sex marriage. The governor vetoed the bill. The veto was overridden by the legislature and the bill became law. Earlier, the state had allowed same-sex couples to enter civil unions.

DISTRICT OF COLUMBIA In 2010, the District of Columbia passed a statute that allowed same-sex marriage.

NEW HAMPSHIRE In 2010, New Hampshire passed a statute that allowed same-sex marriage.

NEW YORK In 2011, New York passed a statute that allowed same-sex marriage.

WASHINGTON STATE   In 2012, Washington State passed a statute that allowed same-sex marriage.

MARYLAND AND MAINE   In 2012, Maryland and Maine became the first states to allow same-sex marriage by popular vote of the electorate. Up until 2012, states lifting the ban had done so by court decision or by statute.

———————————

For many purposes, Native American tribes are considered sovereign nations with the right to pass their own laws. Several tribal councils have passed laws authorizing same-sex marriage. Examples include Coquille Nation in Coos Bay, Oregon,[37] and Suquamish Nation, Seattle, Washington.[38]

The Argument against Same-Sex Marriage

The argument is often made that there is no need to decide whether the banning of same-sex marriage requires the highest standard of review (strict scrutiny) because the justifications for the ban do not even meet the lowest standard of review (rational basis). Before we look at a case that makes this argument, we should look at the contrary argument, namely, that there is a rational basis for a state legislature to impose the ban.

Argument That There Is a Rational Basis for Banning Same-Sex Marriage

(The following analysis is an edited version of one of the dissenting opinions in *Goodridge v. Department of Public Health*, the Massachusetts decision holding that the ban on same-sex marriage violated the state constitution.[39])

· ·

The question is whether a conceivable rational basis exists on which the legislature could conclude that continuing to limit the institution of civil marriage to members of the opposite sex furthers the legitimate purpose of ensuring, promoting, and supporting an optimal social structure for the bearing and raising of children. We must assume that the legislature (1) might conclude that the institution of civil marriage has successfully and continually provided this structure over several centuries; (2) might consider and credit studies that document negative consequences that too often follow children either born outside of marriage or raised in households lacking either a father or a mother figure, and scholarly commentary contending that children and families develop best when mothers and fathers are partners in their parenting; and (3) would be familiar with many recent studies that variously (a) support the proposition that children raised in intact families headed by same-sex couples fare as well on many measures as children raised in similar families headed by opposite-sex couples; (b) support the proposition that children of same-sex couples fare worse on some measures; or (c) reveal notable differences between the two groups of children that warrant further study.

We must also assume that the legislature would be aware of the critiques of the methodologies used in virtually all of the comparative studies of children raised in these different environments, cautioning that the sampling populations are not representative, that the observation periods are too limited in time, that the empirical data are unreliable, and that the hypotheses are too infused with political or agenda driven bias. A 2001 report criticized forty-nine studies on same-sex parenting as suffering from flaws in formulation of hypotheses, use of experimental controls, use of measurements, sampling and statistical testing, and finding false negatives.

Taking all of this available information into account, the legislature could rationally conclude that a family environment with married opposite-sex parents remains the optimal social structure in which to bear children, and that the raising of children by same-sex couples, who by definition cannot be the two sole biological parents of a child and cannot provide children with a parental authority figure of each gender, presents an alternative structure for child rearing that has not yet proved itself beyond reasonable scientific dispute to be as optimal as the biologically based marriage norm. This family structure raises the prospect of children lacking any parent of their own gender. For example, a boy raised by two lesbians as his parents has no male parent. Contrary to the suggestion that concerns about such a family arrangement is based on "stereotypical" views about the differences between sexes, concern about such an arrangement remains rational. It is, for example, rational to posit that the child himself might invoke gender as a justification for the view that neither of his parents "understands" him, or that they "don't know what he is going through," particularly if his disagreement or dissatisfaction involves some issue pertaining to sex. Given that same-sex couples raising children is a very recent phenomenon, the ramifications of an adolescent child having two parents but not one of his or her own gender have yet to be fully realized and cannot yet even be tested in significant numbers. Working from the assumption that a recognition of same-sex marriages will increase the number of children experiencing this alternative, the legislature could conceivably conclude that declining to recognize same-sex marriages remains prudent until empirical questions about its impact on the upbringing of children are resolved.

The fact that the state currently allows same-sex couples to adopt, does not affect the rationality of this conclusion. The eligibility of a child for adoption presupposes that at least one of the child's biological parents is unable or unwilling, for some reason, to participate in raising the child. In that sense, society has "lost" the optimal setting in which to raise that child—it is simply not available. In these circumstances, the principal and overriding consideration is the "best interests of the child," considering his or her unique circumstances and the options that are available for that child. The objective is an individualized determination of the best environment for a particular child, where the normative social structure—a home with both the child's biological father and mother—is not an option. That such a focused determination may lead to the approval of a same-sex couple's adoption of a child does not mean that it would be irrational for a legislator, in fashioning statutory laws that cannot make such individualized determinations, to conclude generally that being raised by a same-sex couple has not yet been shown to be the absolute equivalent of being raised by one's married biological parents.

That the state does not preclude different types of families from raising children does not mean that it must view them all as equally optimal and equally deserving of state endorsement and support. For example, single persons are allowed to adopt children, but the fact that the legislature permits single-parent adoption does not mean that it has endorsed single parenthood as an optimal setting in which to raise children or views it as the equivalent of being raised by both of one's biological parents. The same holds true with respect to same-sex couples—the fact that they may adopt children means only that the legislature has concluded that they may provide an acceptable setting in which to raise children who cannot be raised by both of their biological parents. The legislature may rationally permit adoption by same-sex couples yet harbor reservations as to whether parenthood by same-sex couples should be affirmatively encouraged to the same extent as parenthood by the heterosexual couple whose union produced the child.

Similarly, while the fact that our laws have evolved to include a strong affirmative policy against discrimination on the basis of sexual orientation, have decriminalized intimate adult conduct, and have abolished the legal distinctions between marital and nonmarital children, may well be a reason to celebrate a more open and humane society, they ought not

be the basis on which to conclude that there is no longer a rational basis for the current marriage law. To conclude the latter based on the former threatens the process of social reform in a democratic society. States must be free to experiment in the realm of social and civil relations, incrementally and without concern that a step or two in one direction will determine the outcome of the experiment as a matter of law. If they are not, those who argue "slippery slope" will have more ammunition than ever to resist any effort at progressive change or social experimentation, and will be able to put the lie to the arguments of the proponents of such efforts, that an incremental step forward does not preordain a result which neither the people nor their elected representatives may yet be prepared to accept.

In addition, the legislature could conclude that redefining the institution of marriage to permit same-sex couples to marry would impair the state's interest in promoting and supporting heterosexual marriage as the social institution that it has determined best normalizes, stabilizes, and links the acts of procreation and child rearing. While same-sex couples argue that they only want to take part in the same stabilizing institution, the legislature conceivably could conclude that permitting their participation would have the unintended effect of undermining to some degree marriage's ability to serve its social purpose.

So long as marriage is limited to opposite-sex couples who can at least theoretically procreate, society is able to communicate a consistent message to its citizens that marriage is a (normatively) necessary part of their procreative endeavor; that if they are to procreate, then society has endorsed the institution of marriage as the environment for it and for the subsequent rearing of their children; and that benefits are available explicitly to create a supportive and conducive atmosphere for those purposes. If society proceeds similarly to recognize marriages between same-sex couples who cannot procreate, it could be perceived as an abandonment of this claim, and might result in the mistaken view that civil marriage has little to do with procreation: just as the potential of procreation would not be necessary for a marriage to be valid, marriage would not be necessary for optimal procreation and child rearing to occur. In essence, the legislature could conclude that the consequence of such a policy shift would be a diminution in society's ability to steer the acts of procreation and child rearing into their most optimal setting.

Proponents of same-sex marriage brush aside this concern by asserting that permitting same-sex couples to marry will not diminish the validity or dignity of opposite-sex marriage, that marriage will continue to be a vibrant and revered institution. Whether a court might be correct in this assumption is irrelevant. What is relevant is that such predicting is not the business of the courts. A rational legislature, given the evidence, could conceivably come to a different conclusion, or could at least harbor rational concerns about possible unintended consequences of a dramatic redefinition of marriage.

(continued)

Argument That There Is a Rational Basis for Banning Same-Sex Marriage (*continued*)

There is no question that many same-sex couples are capable of being good parents, and should be (and are) permitted to be so. The policy question that a legislator must resolve is a different one, and turns on an assessment of whether the marriage structure proposed by same-sex couples will, over time, if endorsed and supported by the state, prove to be as stable and successful a model as the one that has formed a cornerstone of our society since colonial times, or prove to be less than optimal, and result in consequences, perhaps now unforeseen, adverse to the state's legitimate interest in promoting and supporting the best possible social structure in which children should be born and raised. Given the critical importance of civil marriage as an organizing and stabilizing institution of society, it is eminently rational for the legislature to postpone making fundamental changes to it until such time as there is unanimous scientific evidence, or popular consensus, or both, that such changes can safely be made.

There is no reason to believe that legislative processes are inadequate to effectuate legal changes in response to evolving evidence, social values, and views of fairness on the subject of same-sex relationships. Deliberate consideration of, and incremental responses to rapidly evolving scientific and social understanding is the norm of the political process—that it may seem painfully slow to those who are already persuaded by the arguments in favor of change is not a sufficient basis to conclude that the processes are constitutionally infirm.

The advancement of the rights, privileges, and protections afforded to homosexual members of our community in the last three decades has been significant, and there is no reason to believe that that evolution will not continue. Changes of attitude in the civic, social, and professional communities have been even more profound. Thirty years ago, *The Diagnostic and Statistical Manual*, the seminal handbook of the American Psychiatric Association, still listed homosexuality as a mental disorder. Today, the American Psychoanalytic Association and many other psychiatric, psychological, and social science organizations have called for an end of the ban on same-sex marriage. A body of experience and evidence has provided the basis for change, and that body continues to mount. The legislature is the appropriate branch, both constitutionally and practically, to consider and respond to it. It is not enough that we as judges might be personally of the view that we have learned enough to decide what is best. So long as the question is at all debatable, it must be the legislature that decides. The marriage statute thus meets the requirements of the rational basis test.

While the state constitution protects matters of personal liberty against government incursion as zealously, and often more so, than does the federal constitution, this case is not about government intrusions into matters of personal liberty. It is not about the rights of same-sex couples to choose to live together, or to be intimate with each other, or to adopt and raise children together. It is about whether the state must endorse and support their choices by changing the institution of civil marriage to make its benefits, obligations, and responsibilities applicable to them. While the courageous efforts of many have resulted in increased dignity, rights, and respect for gay and lesbian members of our community, the issue presented here is a profound one, deeply rooted in social policy, that must, for now, be the subject of legislative, not judicial, action.

DOES THE BAN VIOLATE FEDERAL LAW?

Many states have applied state law to resolve the question of whether same-sex marriage is allowed in their state. Federal courts have addressed different aspects of the issue with respect to federal law, but not many federal cases have said directly whether the U.S. Constitution prohibits states from banning same-sex marriage. *Perry v. Schwarzenegger* of the U.S. District Court in San Francisco is an exception. It answers the question of whether the ban violates the Due Process Clause and the Equal Protection Clause of the U.S. Constitution. The court held that the ban that the voters approved in Proposition 8 violates both clauses. On appeal, the U.S. Court of Appeals for the Ninth Circuit affirmed the District Court's holding that the ban violated the U.S. Constitution, but did so on the narrower ground that the state had no legitimate reason to take away the right to marry that same-sex couples enjoyed prior to the passage of Proposition 8. (See the California entry in Exhibit 5-1.) The Ninth Circuit did not disagree with the due process and equal protection conclusions of the District Court. It simply did not address those conclusions.

The District Court case of *Perry v. Schwarzenegger* is presented here because of the comprehensive way in which it covers the federal due process and equal protection arguments.

CASE

Perry v. Schwarzenegger
704 F. Supp. 2d 921 (2010)
United States District Court, Northern District of California

Background: *Until 2008, same-sex couples in California were able to enter domestic partnerships, but not marriages. That changed in 2008 when the California Supreme Court ruled that the ban on same-sex marriage violated the state constitution. (In re Marriage Cases, 183 P.3d 384 (California 2008)). Approximately 18,000 same-sex couples were married in the state after the ban was lifted. The voters, however, reinstated the ban when it passed Proposition 8, which amended the California Constitution by restricting marriage to couples of the opposite-sex. Opponents of Proposition 8 have now brought this suit in a federal court on the ground that the proposition violates the U.S. Constitution. The plaintiffs are the opponents of the proposition; the defendants are the proponents of the proposition.*

Decision of District Court: *The provision in the California Constitution limiting marriage to opposite-sex couples violates the Due Process Clause and the Equal Protection Clause of the Fourteenth Amendment of the U.S. Constitution.*

OPINION OF THE COURT:

Chief Judge Vaughn R. Walker delivered the opinion of the court.

Plaintiffs challenge a November 2008 voter-enacted amendment to the California Constitution ("Proposition 8" or "Prop 8"). Cal. Const. Art. I, § 7.5. In its entirety, Proposition 8 provides: "Only marriage between a man and a woman is valid or recognized in California." Plaintiffs allege that Proposition 8 deprives them of due process and of equal protection of the laws contrary to the Fourteenth Amendment. . . .

Plaintiffs are two couples. Kristin Perry and Sandra Stier reside in Berkeley, California, and raise four children together. Jeffrey Zarrillo and Paul Katami reside in Burbank, California. Plaintiffs seek to marry their partners and have been denied marriage licenses by their respective county authorities on the basis of Proposition 8. . . .

CONCLUSIONS OF LAW

Plaintiffs challenge Proposition 8 under the Due Process and Equal Protection Clauses of the Fourteenth Amendment. Each challenge is independently meritorious, as Proposition 8 both unconstitutionally burdens the exercise of the fundamental right to marry and creates an irrational classification on the basis of sexual orientation.

DUE PROCESS

The Due Process Clause provides that no "State [shall] deprive any person of life, liberty, or property, without due process of law." U.S. Const. Amend. XIV, § 1. Due process protects individuals against arbitrary governmental intrusion into life, liberty or property. See *Washington v. Glucksberg*, 521 U.S.

702, 719–720 (1997). When legislation burdens the exercise of a right deemed to be fundamental, the government must show that the intrusion withstands strict scrutiny. *Zablocki v. Redhail*, 434 U.S. 374, 388 (1978).

THE RIGHT TO MARRY PROTECTS AN INDIVIDUAL'S CHOICE OF MARITAL PARTNER REGARDLESS OF GENDER

The freedom to marry is recognized as a fundamental right protected by the Due Process Clause. . . . *Zablocki*, 434 U.S. at 384 ("The right to marry is of fundamental importance for all individuals."). . . . The parties do not dispute that the right to marry is fundamental. The question presented here is whether plaintiffs seek to exercise the fundamental right to marry; or, because they are couples of the same sex, whether they seek recognition of a new right.

To determine whether a right is fundamental under the Due Process Clause, the court inquires into whether the right is rooted "in our Nation's history, legal traditions, and practices." *Glucksberg*, 521 U.S. at 710. Here, because the right to marry is fundamental, the court looks to the evidence presented at trial to determine: (1) the history, tradition and practice of marriage in the United States; and (2) whether plaintiffs seek to exercise their right to marry or seek to exercise some other right.

Marriage has retained certain characteristics throughout the history of the United States. Marriage requires two parties to give their free consent to form a relationship, which then forms the foundation of a household. The spouses must consent to support each other and any dependents. The state regulates marriage because marriage creates stable households, which in turn form the basis of a stable, governable populace. The state respects an individual's choice to build a family with another and protects the relationship because it is so central a part of an individual's life. . . .

Never has the state inquired into procreative capacity or intent before issuing a marriage license; indeed, a marriage license is more than a license to have procreative sexual intercourse. "[I]t would demean a married couple were it to be said marriage is simply about the right to have sexual intercourse." *Lawrence v. Texas*, 539 U.S. 558, 567 (2003). The Supreme Court recognizes that, wholly apart from procreation, choice and privacy play a pivotal role in the marital relationship. See *Griswold v. Connecticut*, 381 U.S. 479, 485–486 (1965).

Race restrictions on marital partners were once common in most states but are now seen as archaic, shameful or even bizarre. When the Supreme Court invalidated race restrictions in *Loving v. Virginia*, 388 U.S. 1 (1967), the definition of the right to marry did not change. Instead, the Court recognized that race restrictions, despite their historical prevalence, stood in stark

(continued)

CASE • Perry v. Schwarzenegger (continued)

contrast to the concepts of liberty and choice inherent in the right to marry.

The marital bargain in California (along with other states) traditionally required that a woman's legal and economic identity be subsumed by her husband's upon marriage under the doctrine of coverture; this once-unquestioned aspect of marriage now is regarded as antithetical to the notion of marriage as a union of equals. As states moved to recognize the equality of the sexes, they eliminated laws and practices like coverture that had made gender a proxy for a spouse's role within a marriage. Marriage was thus transformed from a male-dominated institution into an institution recognizing men and women as equals. Yet, individuals retained the right to marry; that right did not become different simply because the institution of marriage became compatible with gender equality.

The evidence at trial shows that marriage in the United States traditionally has not been open to same-sex couples. The evidence suggests many reasons for this tradition of exclusion, including gender roles mandated through coverture, social disapproval of same-sex relationships, and the reality that the vast majority of people are heterosexual and have had no reason to challenge the restriction. The evidence shows that the movement of marriage away from a gendered institution and toward an institution free from state-mandated gender roles reflects an evolution in the understanding of gender rather than a change in marriage. The evidence did not show any historical purpose for excluding same-sex couples from marriage, as states have never required spouses to have an ability or willingness to procreate in order to marry. Rather, the exclusion exists as an artifact of a time when the genders were seen as having distinct roles in society and in marriage. That time has passed.

The right to marry has been historically and remains the right to choose a spouse and, with mutual consent, join together and form a household. Race and gender restrictions shaped marriage during eras of race and gender inequality, but such restrictions were never part of the historical core of the institution of marriage. Today, gender is not relevant to the state in determining spouses' obligations to each other and to their dependents. Relative gender composition aside, same-sex couples are situated identically to opposite-sex couples in terms of their ability to perform the rights and obligations of marriage under California law. Gender no longer forms an essential part of marriage; marriage under law is a union of equals.

Plaintiffs seek to have the state recognize their committed relationships, and plaintiffs' relationships are consistent with the core of the history, tradition and practice of marriage in the United States. Perry and Stier seek to be spouses; they seek the mutual obligation and honor that attend marriage, Zarrillo and Katami seek recognition from the state that their union is "a coming together for better or for worse, hopefully enduring, and intimate to the degree of being sacred." *Griswold,* 381 U.S. at 486. Plaintiffs' unions encompass the historical purpose and form of marriage. Only the plaintiffs' genders relative to one another prevent California from giving their relationships due recognition.

Plaintiffs do not seek recognition of a new right. To characterize plaintiffs' objective as "the right to same-sex marriage" would suggest that plaintiffs seek something different from what opposite-sex couples across the state enjoy—namely, marriage. Rather, plaintiffs ask California to recognize their relationships for what they are: marriages.

DOMESTIC PARTNERSHIPS DO NOT SATISFY CALIFORNIA'S OBLIGATION TO ALLOW PLAINTIFFS TO MARRY

Having determined that plaintiffs seek to exercise their fundamental right to marry under the Due Process Clause, the court must consider whether the availability of Registered Domestic Partnerships fulfills California's due process obligation to same-sex couples. . . . California has created two separate and parallel institutions to provide couples with essentially the same rights and obligations. Cal. Fam. Code § 297.5(a). Domestic partnerships are not open to opposite-sex couples unless one partner is at least sixty-two years old. Cal. Fam. Code § 297(b)(5)(B). Apart from this limited exception—created expressly to benefit those eligible for benefits under the Social Security Act—the sole basis upon which California determines whether a couple receives the designation "married" or the designation "domestic partnership" is the sex of the spouses relative to one another. Compare Cal. Fam. Code §§ 297-299.6 (domestic partnership) with §§ 300-536 (marriage). No further inquiry into the couple or the couple's relationship is required or permitted. Thus, California allows almost all opposite-sex couples only one option—marriage—and all same-sex couples only one option—domestic partnership.

The evidence shows that domestic partnerships do not fulfill California's due process obligation to plaintiffs for two reasons. First, domestic partnerships are distinct from marriage and do not provide the same social meaning as marriage. Second, domestic partnerships were created specifically so that California could offer same-sex couples rights and benefits while explicitly withholding marriage from same-sex couples. . . .

The evidence at trial shows that domestic partnerships exist solely to differentiate same-sex unions from marriages. A domestic partnership is not a marriage; while domestic partnerships offer same-sex couples almost all of the rights and responsibilities associated with marriage, the evidence shows that the withholding of the designation "marriage" significantly disadvantages plaintiffs. The record reflects that marriage is a culturally superior status compared to a domestic partnership. California does not meet its due process obligation to allow plaintiffs to marry by offering them a substitute and inferior institution that denies marriage to same-sex couples.

PROPOSITION 8 IS UNCONSTITUTIONAL BECAUSE IT DENIES PLAINTIFFS A FUNDAMENTAL RIGHT WITHOUT A LEGITIMATE (MUCH LESS COMPELLING) REASON

Because plaintiffs seek to exercise their fundamental right to marry, their claim is subject to strict scrutiny. *Zablocki,* 434 U.S. at 388. That the majority of California voters supported Proposition 8 is irrelevant, as "fundamental rights may not be submitted to [a] vote; they depend on the outcome of no elections." *West Virginia State Board of Education v. Barnette,* 319 U.S. 624 (1943). Under strict scrutiny, the state bears the burden of producing evidence to show that Proposition 8 is narrowly tailored to a compelling government interest. *Carey v. Population Services International,* 431 U.S. 678, 686 (1977). . . .

As explained in detail in the equal protection analysis, Proposition 8 cannot withstand rational basis review. Still less can Proposition 8 survive the strict scrutiny required by plaintiffs' due process claim. The minimal evidentiary presentation made by proponents does not meet the heavy burden of production necessary to show that Proposition 8 is narrowly tailored to a compelling government interest. Proposition 8 cannot, therefore, withstand strict scrutiny. Moreover, proponents do not assert that the availability of domestic partnerships satisfies plaintiffs' fundamental right to marry; proponents stipulated that "[t]here is a significant symbolic disparity between domestic partnership and marriage." Accordingly, Proposition 8 violates the Due Process Clause of the Fourteenth Amendment.

EQUAL PROTECTION

The Equal Protection Clause of the Fourteenth Amendment provides that no state shall "deny to any person within its jurisdiction the equal protection of the laws." U.S. Const. Amend. XIV, § 1. Equal protection is "a pledge of the protection of equal laws." *Yick Wo v. Hopkins,* 118 U.S. 356 (1886). The guarantee of equal protection coexists, of course, with the reality that most legislation must classify for some purpose or another. See *Romer v. Evans,* 517 U.S. 620 (1996). When a law creates a classification but neither targets a suspect class nor burdens a fundamental right, the court presumes the law is valid and will uphold it as long as it is rationally related to some legitimate government interest. . . .

The court defers to legislative (or in this case, popular) judgment if there is at least a debatable question whether the underlying basis for the classification is rational. . . . Even under the most deferential standard of review, however, the court must "insist on knowing the relation between the classification adopted and the object to be attained." *Romer,* 517 U.S. at 632. . . . The court may look to evidence to determine whether the basis for the underlying debate is rational. *Plyler v. Doe,* 457 U.S. 202 (1982) (finding an asserted interest in preserving state resources by prohibiting undocumented children from attending public school to be irrational because "the available evidence suggests that illegal aliens underutilize public services, while contributing their labor to the local economy and tax money to the state fisc"). The search for a rational relationship, while quite deferential, "ensure[s] that classifications are not drawn for the purpose of disadvantaging the group burdened by the law." *Romer,* 517 U.S. at 633. The classification itself must be related to the purported interest. *Plyler,* 457 U.S. at 220 ("It is difficult to conceive of a rational basis for penalizing [undocumented children] for their presence within the United States," despite the state's interest in preserving resources).

Most laws subject to rational basis easily survive equal protection review, because a legitimate reason can nearly always be found for treating different groups in an unequal manner. . . . Yet, to survive rational basis review, a law must do more than disadvantage or otherwise harm a particular group. *United States Department of Agriculture v. Moreno,* 413 U.S. 528 (1973).

SEXUAL ORIENTATION OR SEX DISCRIMINATION

Plaintiffs challenge Proposition 8 as violating the Equal Protection Clause because Proposition 8 discriminates both on the basis of sex and on the basis of sexual orientation. Sexual orientation discrimination can take the form of sex discrimination. Here, for example, Perry is prohibited from marrying Stier, a woman, because Perry is a woman. If Perry were a man, Proposition 8 would not prohibit the marriage. Thus, Proposition 8 operates to restrict Perry's choice of marital partner because of her sex. But Proposition 8 also operates to restrict Perry's choice of marital partner because of her sexual orientation; her desire to marry another woman arises only because she is a lesbian.

The evidence at trial shows that gays and lesbians experience discrimination based on unfounded stereotypes and prejudices specific to sexual orientation. Gays and lesbians have historically been targeted for discrimination because of their sexual orientation; that discrimination continues to the present. As the case of Perry and the other plaintiffs illustrates, sex and sexual orientation are necessarily interrelated, as an individual's choice of romantic or intimate partner based on sex is a large part of what defines an individual's sexual orientation. Sexual orientation discrimination is thus a phenomenon distinct from, but related to, sex discrimination.

Proponents argue that Proposition 8 does not target gays and lesbians because its language does not refer to them. In so arguing, proponents seek to mask their own initiative. Those who choose to marry someone of the opposite sex—heterosexuals—do not have their choice of marital partner restricted by Proposition 8. Those who would choose to marry someone of the same sex—homosexuals—have had their right to marry eliminated by an amendment to the state constitution. Homosexual conduct and identity together define what it means to be gay or lesbian. Indeed, homosexual conduct and attraction are constitutionally protected and integral parts of what makes someone gay or lesbian. *Lawrence,* 539 U.S. at 579. . . .

(continued)

CASE • Perry v. Schwarzenegger (continued)

Proposition 8 targets gays and lesbians in a manner specific to their sexual orientation and, because of their relationship to one another, Proposition 8 targets them specifically due to sex. Having considered the evidence, the relationship between sex and sexual orientation and the fact that Proposition 8 eliminates a right only a gay man or a lesbian would exercise, the court determines that plaintiffs' equal protection claim is based on sexual orientation, but this claim is equivalent to a claim of discrimination based on sex.

STANDARD OF REVIEW

As presently explained in detail, the Equal Protection Clause renders Proposition 8 unconstitutional under any standard of review. Accordingly, the court need not address the question whether laws classifying on the basis of sexual orientation should be subject to a heightened standard of review.

Although Proposition 8 fails to possess even a rational basis, the evidence presented at trial shows that gays and lesbians are the type of minority strict scrutiny was designed to protect. *Massachusetts Board of Retirement v. Murgia,* 427 U.S. 307, 313 (1976) (noting that strict scrutiny may be appropriate where a group has experienced a "'history of purposeful unequal treatment' or been subjected to unique disabilities on the basis of stereotyped characteristics not truly indicative of their abilities") (quoting *San Antonio Independent School District v. Rodriguez,* 411 U.S. 1, 28 (1973)). Proponents admit that "same-sex sexual orientation does not result in any impairment in judgment or general social and vocational capabilities."

The court asked the parties to identify a difference between heterosexuals and homosexuals that the government might fairly need to take into account when crafting legislation. Proponents pointed only to a difference between same-sex couples (who are incapable through sexual intercourse of producing offspring biologically related to both parties) and opposite-sex couples (some of whom are capable through sexual intercourse of producing such offspring). Proponents did not, however, advance any reason why the government may use sexual orientation as a proxy for fertility or why the government may need to take into account fertility when legislating. Consider, by contrast, *City of Cleburne v. Cleburne Living Center,* 473 U.S. 432, 444 (1985) (Legislation singling out a class for differential treatment hinges upon a demonstration of "real and undeniable differences" between the class and others); see also *United States v. Virginia,* 518 U.S. 515, 533 (1996) ("Physical differences between men and women . . . are enduring"). No evidence at trial illuminated distinctions among lesbians, gay men and heterosexuals amounting to "real and undeniable differences" that the government might need to take into account in legislating.

The trial record shows that strict scrutiny is the appropriate standard of review to apply to legislative classifications based on sexual orientation. All classifications based on sexual orientation appear suspect, as the evidence shows that California would rarely, if ever, have a reason to categorize individuals based on their sexual orientation. Here, however, strict scrutiny is unnecessary. Proposition 8 fails to survive even rational basis review.

PROPOSITION 8 DOES NOT SURVIVE RATIONAL BASIS

Proposition 8 cannot withstand any level of scrutiny under the Equal Protection Clause, as excluding same-sex couples from marriage is simply not rationally related to a legitimate state interest. One example of a legitimate state interest in not issuing marriage licenses to a particular group might be a scarcity of marriage licenses or county officials to issue them. But marriage licenses in California are not a limited commodity, and the existence of 18,000 same-sex married couples in California shows that the state has the resources to allow both same-sex and opposite-sex couples to wed. . . .

Proponents put forth several rationales for Proposition 8, which the court now examines in turn: (1) reserving marriage as a union between a man and a woman and excluding any other relationship from marriage; (2) proceeding with caution when implementing social changes; (3) promoting opposite-sex parenting over same-sex parenting; (4) protecting the freedom of those who oppose marriage for same-sex couples; (5) treating same-sex couples differently from opposite-sex couples; and (6) any other conceivable interest.

PURPORTED INTEREST #1: RESERVING MARRIAGE AS A UNION BETWEEN A MAN AND A WOMAN AND EXCLUDING ANY OTHER RELATIONSHIP

Proponents first argue that Proposition 8 is rational because it preserves: (1) "the traditional institution of marriage as the union of a man and a woman"; (2) "the traditional social and legal purposes, functions, and structure of marriage"; and (3) "the traditional meaning of marriage as it has always been defined in the English language." These interests relate to maintaining the definition of marriage as the union of a man and a woman for its own sake.

Tradition alone, however, cannot form a rational basis for a law. . . . The "ancient lineage" of a classification does not make it rational. *Heller v. Doe,* 509 U.S. 312, 327 (1993). Rather, the state must have an interest apart from the fact of the tradition itself.

The evidence shows that the tradition of restricting an individual's choice of spouse based on gender does not rationally further a state interest despite its "ancient lineage." Instead, the evidence shows that the tradition of gender restrictions arose when spouses were legally required to adhere to specific gender roles. California has eliminated all legally mandated gender roles except the requirement that a marriage consist of one man and one woman. Proposition 8 thus enshrines in the California Constitution a gender restriction that the evidence shows to be nothing more than an artifact of a foregone notion that men and women fulfill different roles in civic life.

The tradition of restricting marriage to opposite-sex couples does not further any state interest. Rather, the evidence shows that Proposition 8 harms the state's interest in equality, because it mandates that men and women be treated differently based only on antiquated and discredited notions of gender.

Proponents' argument that tradition prefers opposite-sex couples to same-sex couples equates to the notion that opposite-sex relationships are simply better than same-sex relationships. Tradition alone cannot legitimate this purported interest. Plaintiffs presented evidence showing conclusively that the state has no interest in preferring opposite-sex couples to same-sex couples or in preferring heterosexuality to homosexuality. Moreover, the state cannot have an interest in disadvantaging an unpopular minority group simply because the group is unpopular. *Moreno,* 413 U.S. at 534.

The evidence shows that the state advances nothing when it adheres to the tradition of excluding same-sex couples from marriage. Proponents' asserted state interests in tradition are nothing more than tautologies and do not amount to rational bases for Proposition 8.

PURPORTED INTEREST #2: PROCEEDING WITH CAUTION WHEN IMPLEMENTING SOCIAL CHANGES

Proponents next argue that Proposition 8 is related to state interests in: (1) "[a]cting incrementally and with caution when considering a radical transformation to the fundamental nature of a bedrock social institution"; (2) "[d]ecreasing the probability of weakening the institution of marriage"; (3) "[d]ecreasing the probability of adverse consequences that could result from weakening the institution of marriage"; and (4) "[d]ecreasing the probability of the potential adverse consequences of same-sex marriage."

Plaintiffs presented evidence at trial sufficient to rebut any claim that marriage for same-sex couples amounts to a sweeping social change. Instead, the evidence shows beyond debate that allowing same-sex couples to marry has at least a neutral, if not a positive, effect on the institution of marriage and that same-sex couples' marriages would benefit the state. Moreover, the evidence shows that the rights of those opposed to homosexuality or same-sex couples will remain unaffected if the state ceases to enforce Proposition 8.

The contrary evidence proponents presented is not credible. Indeed, proponents presented no reliable evidence that allowing same-sex couples to marry will have any negative effects on society or on the institution of marriage. The process of allowing same-sex couples to marry is straightforward, and no evidence suggests that the state needs any significant lead time to integrate same-sex couples into marriage. . . . The evidence shows that allowing same-sex couples to marry will be simple for California to implement because it has already done so; no

change need be phased in. California need not restructure any institution to allow same-sex couples to marry.

Because the evidence shows same-sex marriage has and will have no adverse effects on society or the institution of marriage, California has no interest in waiting and no practical need to wait to grant marriage licenses to same-sex couples. Proposition 8 is thus not rationally related to proponents' purported interests in proceeding with caution when implementing social change.

PURPORTED INTEREST #3: PROMOTING OPPOSITE-SEX PARENTING OVER SAME-SEX PARENTING

Proponents' largest group of purported state interests relates to opposite-sex parents. Proponents argue Proposition 8:(1) promotes "stability and responsibility in naturally procreative relationships"; (2) promotes "enduring and stable family structures for the responsible raising and care of children by their biological parents"; (3) increases "the probability that natural procreation will occur within stable, enduring, and supporting family structures"; (4) promotes "the natural and mutually beneficial bond between parents and their biological children"; (5) increases "the probability that each child will be raised by both of his or her biological parents"; (6) increases "the probability that each child will be raised by both a father and a mother"; and (7) increases "the probability that each child will have a legally recognized father and mother."

The evidence supports two points which together show Proposition 8 does not advance any of the identified interests: (1) same-sex parents and opposite-sex parents are of equal quality, and (2) Proposition 8 does not make it more likely that opposite-sex couples will marry and raise offspring biologically related to both parents.

The evidence does not support a finding that California has an interest in preferring opposite-sex parents over same-sex parents. Indeed, the evidence shows beyond any doubt that parents' genders are irrelevant to children's developmental outcomes. Moreover, Proposition 8 has nothing to do with children, as Proposition 8 simply prevents same-sex couples from marrying. Same-sex couples can have (or adopt) and raise children. When they do, they are treated identically to opposite-sex parents under California law. Even if California had an interest in preferring opposite-sex parents to same-sex parents—and the evidence plainly shows that California does not—Proposition 8 is not rationally related to that interest, because Proposition 8 does not affect who can or should become a parent under California law.

To the extent California has an interest in encouraging sexual activity to occur within marriage (a debatable proposition in light of *Lawrence v. Texas,* 539 U.S. at 571) the evidence shows Proposition 8 to be detrimental to that interest. Because of Proposition 8, same-sex couples are not permitted to engage in sexual activity within marriage. Domestic partnerships, in which sexual activity is apparently expected, are separate from marriage and thus codify California's encouragement of

(continued)

CASE • Perry v. Schwarzenegger (continued)

non-marital sexual activity. Cal. Fam. Code §§ 297-299.6. To the extent proponents seek to encourage a norm that sexual activity occur within marriage to ensure that reproduction occur within stable households, Proposition 8 discourages that norm because it requires some sexual activity and child-bearing and child-rearing to occur outside marriage.

Proponents argue Proposition 8 advances a state interest in encouraging the formation of stable households. Instead, the evidence shows that Proposition 8 undermines that state interest, because same-sex households have become less stable by the passage of Proposition 8. The inability to marry denies same-sex couples the benefits, including stability, attendant to marriage. Proponents failed to put forth any credible evidence that married opposite-sex households are made more stable through Proposition 8. The only rational conclusion in light of the evidence is that Proposition 8 makes it less likely that California children will be raised in stable households.

None of the interests put forth by proponents relating to parents and children is advanced by Proposition 8; instead, the evidence shows Proposition 8 disadvantages families and their children.

PURPORTED INTEREST #4: PROTECTING THE FREEDOM OF THOSE WHO OPPOSE MARRIAGE FOR SAME-SEX COUPLES

Proponents next argue that Proposition 8 protects the First Amendment freedom of those who disagree with allowing marriage for couples of the same sex. Proponents argue that Proposition 8:(1) preserves "the prerogative and responsibility of parents to provide for the ethical and moral development and education of their own children"; and (2) accommodates "the First Amendment rights of individuals and institutions that oppose same-sex marriage on religious or moral grounds."

These purported interests fail as a matter of law. Proposition 8 does not affect any First Amendment right or responsibility of parents to educate their children. . . . Californians are prevented from distinguishing between same-sex partners and opposite-sex spouses in public accommodations, as California antidiscrimination law requires identical treatment for same-sex unions and opposite-sex marriages. *Koebke v. Bernardo Heights Country Club,* 36 Cal. 4th 824 (2005). The evidence shows that Proposition 8 does nothing other than eliminate the right of same-sex couples to marry in California. Proposition 8 is not rationally related to an interest in protecting the rights of those opposed to same-sex couples because, as a matter of law, Proposition 8 does not affect the rights of those opposed to homosexuality or to marriage for couples of the same sex.

To the extent proponents argue that one of the rights of those morally opposed to same-sex unions is the right to prevent same-sex couples from marrying, as explained presently those individuals' moral views are an insufficient basis upon which to enact a legislative classification.

PURPORTED INTEREST #5: TREATING SAME-SEX COUPLES DIFFERENTLY FROM OPPOSITE-SEX COUPLES

Proponents argue that Proposition 8 advances a state interest in treating same-sex couples differently from opposite-sex couples by: (1) "[u]sing different names for different things"; (2) "[m]aintaining the flexibility to separately address the needs of different types of relationships"; (3) "[e]nsuring that California marriages are recognized in other jurisdictions"; and (4) "[c]onforming California's definition of marriage to federal law."

Here, proponents assume a premise that the evidence thoroughly rebutted: rather than being different, same-sex and opposite-sex unions are, for all purposes relevant to California law, exactly the same. The evidence shows conclusively that moral and religious views form the only basis for a belief that same-sex couples are different from opposite-sex couples. The evidence fatally undermines any purported state interest in treating couples differently; thus, these interests do not provide a rational basis supporting Proposition 8.

In addition, proponents appear to claim that Proposition 8 advances a state interest in easing administrative burdens associated with issuing and recognizing marriage licenses. Under precedents such as *Craig v. Boren,* "administrative ease and convenience" are not important government objectives. 429 U.S. 190, 198 (1976). Even assuming the state were to have an interest in administrative convenience, Proposition 8 actually creates an administrative burden on California because California must maintain a parallel institution for same-sex couples to provide the equivalent rights and benefits afforded to married couples. Domestic partnerships create an institutional scheme that must be regulated separately from marriage. Compare Cal. Fam. Code §§ 297-299.6 with Cal. Fam. Code §§ 300-536. California may determine whether to retain domestic partnerships or eliminate them in the absence of Proposition 8; the court presumes, however, that as long as Proposition 8 is in effect, domestic partnerships and the accompanying administrative burden will remain. Proposition 8 thus hinders rather than advances administrative convenience.

PURPORTED INTEREST #6: THE CATCHALL INTEREST

Finally, proponents assert that Proposition 8 advances "[a]ny other conceivable legitimate interests identified by the parties, amici, or the court at any stage of the proceedings." But proponents, amici and the court, despite ample opportunity and a full trial, have failed to identify any rational basis Proposition 8 could conceivably advance. Proponents, represented by able and energetic counsel, developed a full trial record in support of Proposition 8. The resulting evidence shows that Proposition 8 simply conflicts with the guarantees of the Fourteenth Amendment.

Many of the purported interests identified by proponents are nothing more than a fear or unarticulated dislike of same-sex couples. Those interests that are legitimate are unrelated to the classification drawn by Proposition 8. The evidence shows that, by every available metric, opposite-sex couples are not better than their same-sex counterparts; instead, as partners, parents and citizens, opposite-sex couples and same-sex couples are equal. Proposition 8 violates the Equal Protection Clause because it does not treat them equally.

A PRIVATE MORAL VIEW THAT SAME-SEX COUPLES ARE INFERIOR TO OPPOSITE-SEX COUPLES IS NOT A PROPER BASIS FOR LEGISLATION

In the absence of a rational basis, what remains of proponents' case is an inference, amply supported by evidence in the record, that Proposition 8 was premised on the belief that same-sex couples simply are not as good as opposite-sex couples. Whether that belief is based on moral disapproval of homosexuality, animus towards gays and lesbians or simply a belief that a relationship between a man and a woman is inherently better than a relationship between two men or two women, this belief is not a proper basis on which to legislate. . . . *Palmore v. Sidoti,* 466 U.S. 429, 433 (1984) ("[T]he Constitution cannot control [private biases] but neither can it tolerate them").

The evidence shows that Proposition 8 was a hard-fought campaign and that the majority of California voters supported the initiative. The arguments surrounding Proposition 8 raise a question similar to that addressed in *Lawrence v. Texas,* when the Court asked whether a majority of citizens could use the power of the state to enforce "profound and deep convictions accepted as ethical and moral principles" through the criminal code. 539 U.S. at 571. The question here is whether California voters can enforce those same principles through regulation of marriage licenses. They cannot. California's obligation is to treat its citizens equally, not to "mandate [its] own moral code." Id. (citing *Planned Parenthood of Southeastern Pa. v. Casey,* 505 U.S. 833, 850 (1992)). "[M]oral disapproval, without any other asserted state interest," has never been a rational basis for legislation. *Lawrence,* 539 U.S. at 582 (O'Connor, J, concurring). Tradition alone cannot support legislation. . . .

Proponents' purported rationales are nothing more than post-hoc justifications. While the Equal Protection Clause does not prohibit post-hoc rationales, they must connect to the classification drawn. Here, the purported state interests fit so poorly with Proposition 8 that they are irrational, as explained above. What is left is evidence that Proposition 8 enacts a moral view that there is something "wrong" with same-sex couples.

The evidence at trial regarding the campaign to pass Proposition 8 uncloaks the most likely explanation for its passage: a desire to advance the belief that opposite-sex couples are morally superior to same-sex couples. The campaign relied heavily on negative stereotypes about gays and lesbians and focused on protecting children from inchoate threats vaguely associated with gays and lesbians. . . .

At trial, proponents' counsel attempted through cross-examination to show that the campaign wanted to protect children from learning about same-sex marriage in school. . . . Transcript 132:25-133:3 (proponents' counsel to Katami: "But the fact is that what the Yes on 8 campaign was pointing at, is that kids would be taught about same-sex relationships in first and second grade; isn't that a fact, that that's what they were referring to?"). The evidence shows, however, that Proposition 8 played on a fear that exposure to homosexuality would turn children into homosexuals and that parents should dread having children who are not heterosexual. . . .

Moral disapproval alone is an improper basis on which to deny rights to gay men and lesbians. The evidence shows conclusively that Proposition 8 enacts, without reason, a private moral view that same-sex couples are inferior to opposite-sex couples. *Romer,* 517 U.S. at 634 ("[L]aws of the kind now before us raise the inevitable inference that the disadvantage imposed is born of animosity toward the class of persons affected"). Because Proposition 8 disadvantages gays and lesbians without any rational justification, Proposition 8 violates the Equal Protection Clause of the Fourteenth Amendment.

CONCLUSION

Proposition 8 fails to advance any rational basis in singling out gay men and lesbians for denial of a marriage license. Indeed, the evidence shows Proposition 8 does nothing more than enshrine in the California Constitution the notion that opposite-sex couples are superior to same-sex couples. Because California has no interest in discriminating against gay men and lesbians, and because Proposition 8 prevents California from fulfilling its constitutional obligation to provide marriages on an equal basis, the court concludes that Proposition 8 is unconstitutional. . . .

ASSIGNMENT 5.8

The court in *Perry v. Schwarzenegger* said that "the evidence shows beyond any doubt that parents' genders are irrelevant to children's developmental outcomes." How would the dissenting opinion in the *Goodridge* case in Massachusetts (presented just before *Perry*) respond to this comment?

Exhibit 5-2 summarizes the positions taken by various governments on same-sex marriage and their alternatives.

EXHIBIT 5-2 Formalized Same-Sex Relationships

STATES THAT ALLOW MARRIAGE OR OTHER RELATIONSHIPS

State	Same-Sex Relationship Allowed	More Information about This Relationship in the State
California	domestic partnership	Domestic Partners Registry www.sos.ca.gov/dpregistry
Connecticut	civil union, marriage	Department of Public Health www.ct.gov/dph/cwp/view.asp?A=3294&Q=427720
Colorado	designated beneficiaries	Colorado Bar Association www.cobar.org/index.cfm/ID/21614
Delaware	civil union	State of Delaware delaware.gov/CivilUnions
District of Columbia	marriage	Superior Court Marriage Bureau www.dccourts.gov/dccourts/superior/family/marriage.jsp
Hawaii	civil union	Department of Health hawaii.gov/health/vital-records/vital-records/civilunion/index.html
Illinois	civil union	Equality Illinois www.eqil.org/civil.html
Iowa	marriage	State of Iowa www.iowa.gov/tax/taxlaw/ssmarriage.pdf
Maine	marriage domestic partnership	www.maine.gov (enter "marriage" in the search box) (also "domestic partnership")
Maryland	marriage	State of Maryland www.maryland.gov (enter "same-sex marriage" in search box)
Massachusetts	marriage	Commonwealth of Massachusetts www.mass.gov/portal (enter "same-sex marriage" in search box)
Nevada	domestic partnership	Nevada Secretary of State nvsos.gov/index.aspx?page=274
New Hampshire	marriage, civil union	New Hampshire Government www.nh.gov (enter "civil union" in search box)
New Jersey	civil union	Department of Health and Senior Services www.state.nj.us/health/vital/civilunion_apply.shtml
New York	marriage	Office of the City Clerk www.cityclerk.nyc.gov/ html/marriage/same_sex_couples.shtml
Oregon	domestic partnership	State of Oregon www.oregon.gov (enter "domestic partner" in search box)
Rhode Island	civil union	State of Rhode Island www.ri.gov (enter "civil union" in search box)
Vermont	marriage, civil union	Vermont Secretary of State www.sec.state.vt.us/municipal/civil_mar.htm
Washington	marriage	Washington State Government access.wa.gov (enter "same-sex marriage" in search box)
Wisconsin	domestic partnership	State Law Library wilawlibrary.gov/topics/familylaw/domesticpartner.php

Cities and Counties That Have Domestic Partnership Registries

Arkansas
Eureka Springs

Arizona
Phoenix, Tucson

California
Berkeley, Beverly Hills, Cathedral City, Davis, Laguna Beach, Long Beach, Los Angeles, Marin County, Oakland, Palm Springs, Palo Alto, Petaluma, Sacramento, San Francisco, Santa Barbara, Santa Monica, West Hollywood

Colorado
Boulder, Denver

Connecticut
Hartford

Florida
Broward, Key West, Miami Beach, Miami-Dade County, West Palm Beach

Georgia
Athens-Clarke County, Atlanta, Fulton

Iowa
Iowa City

Illinois
Cook County, Oak Park, Urbana

Kansas
Lawrence

Louisiana
New Orleans

Massachusetts
Boston, Brewster, Brookline, Cambridge, Nantucket, Provincetown

Maine
Portland

Michigan
Ann Arbor

Minnesota
Duluth, Edina

Minneapolis
St. Paul

Missouri
Columbia, Kansas City, St. Louis

North Carolina
Carrboro, Chapel Hill

New York
Albany, East Hampton, Ithaca, New York City, Rockland, Suffolk County, Rochester, Southampton, Westchester

Ohio
Cleveland, Cleveland Heights

Oregon
Ashland, Eugene, Multnomah County

Pennsylvania
Philadelphia, Pittsburgh

Texas
Travis County

(continued)

EXHIBIT 5-2 (continued)

Cities and Counties That Have Domestic Partnership Registries
Utah
Salt Lake City
Washington
Lacey, Olympia, Seattle, Tumwater
Wisconsin
Dane County, Madison, Milwaukee
Other Countries Where Same-Sex Marriage Is Legal   **(in the entire country or in parts of the country)**
Argentina, Belgium, Brazil, Canada, Iceland, Mexico, Netherlands, Norway,   Portugal, South Africa, Spain, Sweden
(Note: Marriage alternatives are common in some countries. In France, for example, there are two civil unions for every three marriages. French civil unions can be used for opposite-sex and same-sex couples.)

© Cengage Learning 2013

TRANSSEXUALS

transsexual

(1) A person who has undergone a sex-change operation. (2) A person who wants to be considered by society as having a gender of the opposite sex.

Suppose that one of the parties seeking to marry is a **transsexual** (an individual who has had a sex-change or reassignment surgery). Could a transsexual, born a man but now a woman, marry a man? Could a transsexual, born a woman but now a man, marry a woman? Most courts in states that limit marriage to opposite-sex couples would not permit such marriages, arguing that both parties to the marriage must have been born members of the opposite sex. A Texas case considered the related issue of whether a transsexual man ("Christie") who underwent sex reassignment surgery could be considered the surviving spouse of a recently deceased male patient. He and Christie had previously gone through a ceremonial marriage. The Texas Court of Appeals held that "Christie cannot be married to another male" and, therefore, cannot be a surviving spouse.[40] Kansas reached a similar result when it ruled that a man's marriage to J'Noel, a post-operative male to female transsexual, was void, and only the man's son could share in his father's estate after he died intestate.

> [We] recognize that J'Noel has traveled a long and difficult road. J'Noel has undergone electrolysis, thermolysis, tracheal shave, hormone injections, extensive counseling, and reassignment surgery. Unfortunately, after all that, J'Noel remains a transsexual, and a male for purposes of marriage under [the Kansas code]. We are not blind to the stress and pain experienced by one who is born a male but perceives oneself as a female. We recognize that there are people who do not fit neatly into the commonly recognized category of male or female, and to many life becomes an ordeal. However, the validity of J'Noel's marriage . . . is a question of public policy to be addressed by the legislature and not by this court.[41]

Although this is the majority view, there are a few courts that have taken the opposite position and have allowed transsexuals to marry in such cases.[42] Some of these courts say that gender is determined by current anatomy so that sex reassignment surgery and hormone treatment can qualify a person born male to be considered female for purposes of spousal support based on her marriage to a man.

Note that a court in a child-custody case might decide that a transsexual can be awarded custody of a child if the award is determined to be in the best interests of the child. Proof of the gender is not a requirement for an adult seeking custody. We will examine custody issues in Chapter 9.

ADULT ADOPTION

In Chapter 15, we will discuss the issue of whether one adult can adopt another adult. In states where this is allowed, some unmarried same-sex couples have used adult adoption as a method of achieving similar legal consequences to those they could have achieved in a marriage if they had lived in a state that allowed same-sex marriage. For example, in a parent–child relationship, the child can inherit from a parent who dies intestate, visit a parent in the hospital without restrictions, make-end-of life decisions for a terminally ill parent, and sue for the wrongful death of a parent. A major drawback to this strategy is the predicament the parties face in the event that they separate. Parents and children cannot divorce each other. Undoing a valid adoption is very difficult, if not impossible.

COVENANT MARRIAGE

To enter a conventional or standard marriage all that is required are (a) compliance with the technical/procedural requirements we discussed earlier in the chapter (e.g., witnesses and a waiting period) and (b) the intent and capacity requirements (e.g., being old enough) that we will discuss in the next chapter. To dissolve a conventional marriage in the era of no-fault divorce (discussed in Chapter 7), all that is required in most states is for one spouse to declare that the parties are no longer compatible or that their differences are irreconcilable; there is no need to prove who was at fault in the collapse of the marriage.

Many people are alarmed at the high incidence of divorce in America. In a few states, reformers have argued that one way to reduce the divorce rate is to increase the requirements for entering and for dissolving a marriage. Hence, they created the **covenant marriage**. This is a form of ceremonial marriage (a) that is entered upon proof of premarital counseling and a promise to seek marital counseling when needed during the marriage and (b) that is dissolved upon separation for a designated period or upon proof of marital fault such as adultery. Three states allow covenant marriages: Louisiana, Arkansas, and Arizona.

Note the differences between covenant and conventional marriages. No state requires parties seeking to enter a conventional marriage to undergo premarital counseling or to promise to seek marital counseling if the need arises during the marriage. (Florida offers a discount on the marriage license if the couple takes a premarital counseling course, but does not require the course.) Living separate and apart is a ground for divorce of conventional marriages (see Chapter 7) and of covenant marriages, but the period of time the couple must live separate and apart is often considerably longer for covenant marriages.

It is important to note, however, that the few states that have enacted covenant-marriage laws do *not* require every couple contemplating marriage to go through a covenant marriage. A two-tiered marriage system exists in these states. Couples are given a choice between a covenant marriage and a conventional marriage. If they choose the latter, they do not need to comply with the additional requirements for entering and dissolving their marriage. These requirements apply only if they choose the covenant marriage.

Proponents of covenant marriage argue that premarital counseling will better prepare the parties for handling the difficulties that marriage can entail. Furthermore, when such difficulties do in fact arise in the marriage, marital counseling may be able to help resolve the difficulties. The result could be a reduction in the divorce rate.

covenant marriage
A form of ceremonial marriage (a) that is entered upon proof of premarital counseling and a promise to seek marital counseling when needed during the marriage and (b) that is dissolved upon separation for a designated period or upon proof of marital fault. Also called high-test marriage.

Proponents also hope that if a man wants to choose a conventional marriage, his fiancée might ask him why he wants a marriage that is so easy to get out of. This frank discussion may lead to a decision to cancel the marriage or at least to postpone it until they have more serious discussions about the institution of marriage. Through such discussions, potentially weak marriages might be avoided.

The components of covenant marriage are the same or similar in Louisiana, Arkansas, and Arizona: mandatory premarital counseling, agreement to seek marital counseling if needed, and limited grounds for divorce. In Louisiana, the first state to create this option, a couple that selects a covenant marriage must submit an affidavit from a therapist, minister, or other member of the clergy that he or she has given premarital counseling on the "nature and purpose" of marriage. The couple must also sign a statement that says:

> We do solemnly declare that marriage is a covenant between a man and a woman who agree to live together as husband and wife for so long as they both may live. We have chosen each other carefully and disclosed to one another everything which could adversely affect the decision to enter into this marriage. We have received premarital counseling on the nature, purposes, and responsibilities of marriage. We have read the Covenant Marriage Act, and we understand that a Covenant Marriage is for life. If we experience marital difficulties, we commit ourselves to take all reasonable efforts to preserve our marriage, including marital counseling. With full knowledge of what this commitment means, we do hereby declare that our marriage will be bound by Louisiana law on Covenant Marriages and we promise to love, honor, and care for one another as husband and wife.[43]

The acknowledgement that the marriage will last "as long as they both may live" does not mean that divorce has been abolished. Divorce is possible, but only on specified grounds, most of which are fault-based. In Louisiana, the grounds are adultery, a sentence of death or imprisonment for a felony, abandonment of the matrimonial domicile for a year, physical or sexual abuse, and living separate and apart continuously without reconciliation for a period of two years. Fault or a two-year separation is *not* required to dissolve a conventional Louisiana marriage. Such a marriage can be dissolved simply by showing that the parties have lived separate and apart for a designated period of time.

Will covenant marriages reduce the rate of divorce? It is too early to tell. One study of Louisiana marriages over an eight-year period concluded that "covenant couples have only a little over half the odds (.55) of divorce or separation that standard couples have."[44] Yet the study concluded that this result was due more to the religious views of the couple (particularly the wife) than to the covenant marriage itself. Furthermore, only a very small number of couples chose covenant marriages in the state (about 2 percent). Nevertheless, many states are exploring the possibility of creating their own covenant-marriage option. States are uneasy about reintroducing fault into the law of divorce, but want to remain open to policy changes that might reduce the divorce rate.

ASSIGNMENT 5.9

a. Explain why you think it is a good or bad idea for every state to force couples to choose between conventional and covenant marriages.

b. Explain why you think it is a good or bad idea for every state to abolish conventional marriages and to require every marriage to be a covenant marriage.

COMMON-LAW MARRIAGE

INTRODUCTION

A *common-law marriage* is a marriage entered without license or traditional ceremony by persons who (a) agree to marry, (b) live together as husband and wife, and (c) hold themselves out as married. In short, it is a marriage of two people who have not gone through a ceremonial marriage. (In Texas, a common-law marriage is called an "informal marriage.") The marriages of couples who enter a common-law marriage are as valid as the marriages of couples who enter a ceremonial marriage. To end a common-law marriage, for example, one of the parties must die, or they both must go through a divorce proceeding in the same manner as any other married couple seeking to dissolve a marriage.[45] Common-law marriages are not allowed in every state. In fact, most states have abolished them. Some states have abolished them as of certain dates as you will see later in Exhibit 5-3.

Even in states that have abolished common-law marriages, however, it is important to know something about them for the following reasons:

1. Parties may enter a common-law marriage in a state where such marriages are valid and then move to another state that has abolished such marriages. Under conflict-of-laws principles, as we shall see, the second state may have to recognize the marriage as valid. In our highly mobile society, parties who live together should be aware that if they travel through states that recognize common-law marriages for vacations or for other temporary purposes, one of the parties might later try to claim that they entered a common-law marriage in such a state.

2. It may be that your state once recognized common-law marriages as valid, but then, as of a certain date, abolished all such marriages for the future. A number of people may still live in your state who entered valid common-law marriages before the law was changed, and hence, their marriages are still valid.

Requirements for Common-Law Marriage

In states that recognize common-law marriages, it is not enough that the parties lived together, even for an extended period of time. The following elements must be established:

- Capacity. The parties must have **capacity** to marry. (For example, they must be of age and not be already married to someone else. Some states impose a minimum age to enter a common-law marriage [e.g., 18] that is higher than the age required to enter a ceremonial marriage.) Capacity is the legal power to do something.

- Present intent and agreement. There must be a present intent to marry and a present agreement to enter a marital relationship. It is not enough for the couple to discuss marriage in the future. The intent and agreement to become husband and wife to each other must be **in praesenti**—undertaken at present. (Some states require an **express** agreement; others allow the agreement to be inferred from the manner in which the man and woman relate to each other.)

- Cohabitation. The parties must actually live together as husband and wife (i.e., there must be **cohabitation**). In some states, cohabitation must include sexual relations. In other states, however, living openly together as husband and wife is sufficient even if the relationship was never consummated, particularly if illness prevented **consummation**. (Note that consummation is never a requirement for a valid ceremonial marriage.)

capacity
The legal power to do something such as enter a contract or a relationship. Also called legal capacity.

in praesenti
At present; now.

express
Explicitly stated, rather than merely implied or inferred.

cohabitation
Living together in an intimate (usually sexual) relationship in the manner of a husband and wife. A de facto husband and wife relationship. The verb is *cohabit*. Although a married couple cohabits, the word *cohabitation* is more often used in reference to unmarried couples.

consummation
Sexual intercourse for the first time, particularly between spouses. (See glossary for an additional meaning.)

holding out
Taking steps that will allow others to believe that something exists such as a legal status.

clear and convincing evidence
A standard of proof that is met when the evidence demonstrates that the existence of a disputed fact is much more probable than its nonexistence. This standard is stronger than preponderance of the evidence but not as strong as beyond a reasonable doubt.

preponderance of the evidence
A standard of proof that is met when the evidence establishes that it is more likely than not that the facts are as alleged. Also called fair preponderance of evidence.

power of attorney (see page 191)
(1) A document that authorizes another to act as one's agent or attorney in fact. (An attorney in fact is one authorized to act in place of or for another, often in a business transaction. An attorney in fact may or may not be an attorney at law.) (2) The authority itself.

- Holding out. There must be an openness about the relationship; the parties must make representations to the world that they are husband and wife. This is referred to as **holding out**. The holding-out requirement functions as a major deterrent of fraudulent claims that a common-law marriage was entered. (See Interviewing and Investigation Checklist on page 191.)

A popular misconception about common-law marriages is that the parties must live together for seven years before the marriage becomes legal. In most states that recognize common-law marriage, there is no time requirement.

Courts are generally reluctant to find that a common-law marriage exists. During America's pioneer days, there may have been a need for common-law marriage because of the scarcity of officials to perform ceremonial marriages. This, of course, is no longer true today. More importantly, common-law marriages are disfavored (even in states where they are legal) because it is relatively easy to fabricate a claim that the parties married by common-law, particularly after one of them has died. As one court said of a common-law marriage, "It tends to weaken the public estimate of the sanctity of the marriage relation. It puts in doubt the certainty of the rights of inheritance. It opens the door to false pretenses of marriage and the imposition on estates of suppositious [fraudulent] heirs."[46]

Although millions of adults live together in an intimate relationship, their goals or intent is not always clear. In many relationships, neither party may want a marriage, although in some, one of the adults may have this intention or hope. Most states require strong evidence (**clear and convincing evidence** rather than just a **preponderance of the evidence**) that the parties had the intent to marry before concluding that a common-law marriage was entered. According to one court, the "mutual understanding or consent must be conveyed with such a demonstration of intent and with such clarity on the part of the parties that marriage does not creep up on either of them and catch them unawares. One cannot be married unwittingly or accidentally."[47]

Another reason common-law marriages are disfavored is the fact that there is no public record of the marriage. It is important for society to have accurate records on its various populations in order to identify needs, allocate resources, and provide protection. This goal is hampered if a large segment of the population is married without the state knowing about it. (Some states allow couples to register their common-law marriage with the county, but few couples do so.) Also, bypassing the technical requirements for a ceremonial marriage defeats other government objectives. Blood tests, for example, help prevent the spread of certain diseases and waiting periods discourage hasty marriages. None of these goals can be achieved with a common-law marriage.

ASSIGNMENT 5.10

Paul and Fran live in a state that recognizes common-law marriage. They become engaged. The wedding will take place in eight months. Three months after the engagement, Paul dies in an automobile accident.

a. Is Fran the widow of Paul for purposes of inheritance and state government benefits such as Social Security?

b. Consider the same facts, except that Paul died after he became engaged to George in a state where same-sex marriage is valid. (See the General Instructions for the Legal-Analysis Assignment in Appendix A.)

☑ INTERVIEWING AND INVESTIGATION CHECKLIST

Factors Relevant to the Formation of a Common Law Marriage between C (Client) and D (Defendant)

LEGAL INTERVIEWING QUESTIONS

1. On what date did you first meet D?

2. When did the two of you first begin talking about living together? Describe the circumstances. Where were you? Who said what, etc.?

3. Did you or D ever discuss with anyone else your plans to live together? If so, with whom and what was said?

4. On what date did you actually move in together? How long have you been living together? (Obtain precise dates.)

5. Have you and D had sexual relations? If so, when was the first time?

6. In whose name was the lease to the apartment or the deed to the house in which you lived?

7. Do you have separate or joint bank accounts? If joint, what names appear on the account?

8. Who pays the rent or the mortgage?

9. Who pays the utility bills?

10. Who pays the food bills?

11. Since you have been living together, have you filed separate or joint tax returns?

12. Other than everyday purchases, what did the two of you purchase with joint funds?

13. What attitudes have you both expressed to each other about marriage in general? For example, did either of you feel that there was a difference between commitment and marriage?

14. Did you and D have a written or oral agreement that you and D were going to be married? What precise language did you both use when you discussed marriage?

15. Why didn't you and D have a marriage ceremony?

16. Did you ever introduce each other as "my husband" or "my wife"? If so, to whom? Name the specific individuals.

17. Name any relatives, neighbors, business associates, friends, etc., who think of you and D as husband and wife. State why each thinks so.

18. Did you and D ever discuss making individual or joint wills? Do you have them? What attorneys, if any, did you contact?

19. Did either of you give each other a **power of attorney** for business or healthcare? If so, what are the details?

20. Did you and D ever separate for any period of time? If so, describe the circumstances.

21. Did you and D have or adopt children? If so, what is the surname of the children?

22. On insurance policies, is either of you the beneficiary? How is the premium paid?

23. During your life with D, what other indications exist that the two of you treated each other as husband and wife?

24. Have the two of you ever spent significant time on vacation or for any other reason in the District of Columbia or in any of the following states: Alabama, Colorado, Georgia, Idaho, Iowa, Kansas, Montana, New Hampshire, Ohio, Oklahoma, Pennsylvania, Rhode Island, South Carolina, Texas, or Utah? (These states recognize or have recognized common-law marriage. See Exhibit 5-3.) If so, describe the circumstances. How long were you there? Did you discuss your relationship while there? Etc.

POSSIBLE INVESTIGATION TASKS

- Obtain copies of leases or deeds.
- Obtain copies of bills, receipts, tax returns, etc., to determine how the names of C and D appear on them.
- Obtain copies of any written agreements between C and D.
- Interview anyone C indicates would think of C and D as husband and wife.
- Obtain birth certificates of children, if any.

EXHIBIT 5-3 States That Allow Common Law Marriage

States	Requirements for Common Law Marriage Established by Case or Statute
Alabama	Case: (1) Capacity; (2) present, mutual agreement to permanently enter the marriage relationship to the exclusion of all other relationships; and (3) public recognition of the relationship as a marriage and public assumption of marital duties and cohabitation. *Watson v. Bowden*, 38 So. 3d 93 (Ala. Civ. App., 2009).
Colorado	Case: A common-law marriage is established by the mutual consent or agreement of the parties to be husband and wife, followed by a mutual and open assumption of a marital relationship. *People v. Lucero*, 747 P.2d 660, 663 (Colo., 1987). Statute: (1) A common law marriage entered into on or after September 1, 2006, shall not be recognized as a valid marriage in this state unless, at the time the common law marriage is entered into: (a) Each party is eighteen years of age or older; and (b) The marriage is not prohibited, as provided in section 14-2-110. C.R.S.A. § 14-2-109.5.

(continued)

EXHIBIT 5-3 (continued)

States	Requirements for Common Law Marriage Established by Case or Statute
District of Columbia	Case: In the District of Columbia, when a man and woman who are legally capable of entering into the marriage relation, mutually agree, in words of the present tense, to be husband and wife, and consummate their agreement by cohabiting as husband and wife, a "common law marriage" results. *U.S. Fidelity & Guaranty Co. v. Britton,* 269 F.2d 249 (C.A. D.C. 1959).
Georgia (allowed only for marriages entered before 1997)	Case: In order for there to be a "common law marriage," the three essential elements of marriage . . . must be met all at one time: (1) the parties must be able to contract, (2) there must be an actual contract, and (3) there must be consummation according to law. *Brown v. Brown,* 234 Ga. 300, 215 S.E.2d 671 (Ga. 1975). Statute: No common law marriage shall be entered into in this state on or after January 1, 1997. Otherwise valid common law marriages entered into prior to January 1, 1997, shall . . . be recognized in this state. Ga. Code Ann., § 19-3-1.1.
Idaho (allowed only for marriages entered before 1996)	Case: In order to demonstrate the existence of a common law marriage, the evidence must show that the parties were both capable of giving consent, and did in fact consent, to the common law marriage at its inception. The parties must assume the rights, duties and obligations of marriage. The parties' consent may be either expressed or implied by their conduct. If consent is implied, the best and most common, although not exclusive, method of proving consent is to show cohabitation, general reputation in the community as husband and wife, and holding oneself out as married. From such evidence, the court may infer that, at the outset, mutual consent was present. *Wilkins v. Wilkins,* 137 Idaho 315, 320, 48 P.3d 644, 649 (Idaho, 2002). Statute: (1) . . . Marriage created by a mutual assumption of marital rights, duties or obligations shall not be recognized as a lawful marriage. (2) The provisions of subsection (1) of this section requiring the issuance of a license and a solemnization shall not invalidate any marriage contract in effect prior to January 1, 1996, created by consenting parties through a mutual assumption of marital rights, duties or obligations. I.C. § 32-201.
Iowa	Case: The elements and conditions necessary to establish the existence of a common law marriage [are] . . . intent and agreement in praesenti as to marriage on the part of both parties together with continuous cohabitation and public declaration that they are husband and wife; [there must be] a general and substantial "holding-out" or open declaration thereof to the public by both parties thereto. *In re Dallman's Estate,* 228 N.W.2d 187, 189 (Iowa 1975).
Kansas	Case: The basic elements essential in establishing the existence of such marriage relationship are: (1) capacity of the parties to marry, (2) a present marriage agreement, and (3) a holding out of each other as husband and wife to the public. *Sullivan v. Sullivan,* 196 Kan. 705, 709, 413 P.2d 988, 992 (Kan. 1966). Statute: (b) The state of Kansas shall not recognize a common law marriage contract if either party to the marriage contract is under 18 years of age. K.S.A. 23-101.
Montana	Case: Under our common law, such a marriage is established when a couple: (1) is competent to enter into a marriage, (2) mutually consents and agrees to a common law marriage, and (3) cohabits and is reputed in the community to be husband and wife. *Snetsinger v. Montana University System,* 325 Mont. 148, 156, 104 P.3d 445, 451 (Mont., 2004).
New Hampshire (effective only at death for purposes of inheritance and death benefits)	Case: [T]he status of "common law" spouse obtains only as to the survivor of two people who had cohabited and acknowledged each other as husband and wife, and who had been generally reputed as such, for a period of three years and until the decease of one of them. *Joan S. v. John S.,* 121 N.H. 96, 98, 427 A.2d 498, 499 (N.H., 1981). Statute: Persons cohabiting and acknowledging each other as husband and wife, and generally reputed to be such, for the period of 3 years, and until the decease of one of them, shall thereafter be deemed to have been legally married. N.H. Rev. Stat. § 457:39.

States	Requirements for Common Law Marriage Established by Case or Statute
Ohio (allowed only for marriages entered before October 1991)	Case: An agreement of marriage in praesenti when made by parties competent to contract, accompanied and followed by cohabitation as husband and wife, they being so treated and reputed in the community and circle in which they move, establishes a valid marriage at common law. . . . *Fitzgerald v. Mayfield,* 584 N.E.2d 13, 17 (Ohio App. 4 Dist., 1990). Statute: R.C. § 3105.12.
Oklahoma (the law is unclear as to whether they are allowed only for marriages entered before November 1998)	Case: To constitute a valid "common law marriage," it is necessary that there should be an actual and mutual agreement to enter into a matrimonial relation, permanent and exclusive of all others, between parties capable in law of making such a contract, consummated by their cohabitation as man and wife, or their mutual assumption openly of marital duties and obligations. A mere promise of future marriage, followed by illicit relations, is not, in itself, sufficient to constitute such marriage. *Brooks v. Sanders,* 190 P.3d 357, 358 (Okla. Civ. A p. Div. 4, 2008).
Pennsylvania (allowed only for marriages entered before 2005)	Case: In Pennsylvania, a common law marriage is a marriage by express agreement of the parties without ceremony, and usually without a witness, and verba de praesenti [words of present intention], uttered with the purpose of establishing a relation of husband and wife. However, common law marriage will still be recognized without use of verba de praesenti, where the intention of the parties as expressed by their words, is that they were married. While cohabitation and reputation alone will not suffice to establish a common law marriage, they are relevant factors which a court may consider in determining whether the parties have entered into a common law marriage. *Cann v. Cann,* 632 A.2d 322, 325 (Pa. Super., 1993). Statute: No common law marriage contracted after January 1, 2005, shall be valid. Nothing in this part shall be deemed or taken to render any common law marriage otherwise lawful and contracted on or before January 1, 2005, invalid. 23 Pa.C.S.A. § 1103.
Rhode Island	Case: Such a marriage "can be established by clear and convincing evidence that the parties seriously intended to enter into the husband-wife relationship . . . and that their conduct was of such a character as to lead to a belief in the community that they were married. . . . The requisite intent and belief may be demonstrated by "inference from cohabitation, declarations, reputation among kindred and friends, and other competent circumstantial evidence." *Fravala v. City of Cranston ex rel. Baron,* 996 A.2d 696, 703 (R.I., 2010).
South Carolina	Case: A common law marriage is formed when two parties contract to be married. No express contract is necessary; the agreement may be inferred from the circumstances. The fact finder is to look for mutual assent: the intent of each party to be married to the other and a mutual understanding of each party's intent. Consideration is the participation in the marriage. *Callen v. Callen,* 620 S.E.2d 59, 62 (S.C., 2005). Statute: A common law marriage hereinafter entered into by a person under the age of 16 is void ab initio. Code 1976 § 20-1-100.
Texas (common-law marriage is called informal marriage in Texas)	Statute: (a) [T]he marriage of a man and woman may be proved by evidence that . . . the man and woman agreed to be married and after the agreement they lived together in this state as husband and wife and there represented to others that they were married. . . . (c) A person under 18 years of age may not: (1) be a party to an informal marriage. . . . V.T.C.A., Family Code § 2.401. Note: A couple in an informal marriage has the option of filing (registering) a Declaration of Informal Marriage in the county clerk's office. V.T.C.A., Family Code § 2.402.
Utah	Statute: (1) A marriage which is not solemnized according to this chapter shall be legal and valid if a court or administrative order establishes that it arises out of a contract between a man and a woman who: (a) are of legal age and capable of giving consent; (b) are legally capable of entering a solemnized marriage under the provisions of this chapter; (c) have cohabited; (d) mutually assume marital rights, duties, and obligations; and (e) who hold themselves out as and have acquired a uniform and general reputation as husband and wife. U.C.A. 1953 § 30-1-4.5.

Two situations remain to be considered: conflict of laws and impediment removal.

CONFLICT OF LAWS

choice of law

A selection of which law to apply when a case involves the law of more than one legal system, such as two states or two countries.

As we have seen, a conflict of laws exists when a court is being asked to apply inconsistent laws of two different legal systems such as two different states or countries. In such cases, the court must make a **choice of law**. Let's look at two examples:

- Case #1. Bill and Pat live in State X, where common-law marriages are legal. They enter such a marriage. Then they move to State Y, where common-law marriages have been abolished. They could have entered a ceremonial marriage in State Y, but they did not do so because they did not want a ceremonial marriage and they knew that their marriage was valid in State X. Bill is injured on the job and dies in State Y. Pat claims workers' compensation benefits as the "wife" of Bill. Will State Y recognize Pat as married to Bill?

- Case #2. Ed and Mary are both 14 years of age living in State A. Fourteen is the minimum age to marry in State A. They enter a valid ceremonial marriage in State A. They then move to State B where the minimum age to marry is 16. (If they had tried to marry in State B, their marriage would not have been valid.) Ed is injured on the job and dies in State B. He is 15 at the time of death. Mary claims workers' compensation benefits as the "wife" of Ed. Will State B recognize Mary as married to Ed?

domicile

The place where a person has been physically present with the intent to make that place a permanent home (or with no intent to make any other place a permanent home); the place to which one intends to return when away.

domiciliary

One who is domiciled in a particular place.

domiciliary state

The state where one has a domicile.

In Case #1, the conflict of law is over the validity of common-law marriages: State X recognizes them; State Y does not. In Case #2, the conflict of law is over the minimum age to marry: States A and B have different minimum ages to marry. The couples are now domiciled in a state that would not recognize their marriage if entered there. (**Domicile** is the place where a person has been physically present with the intent to make that place a permanent home. A **domiciliary** is a person domiciled in a particular place. The state where someone is domiciled is called the **domiciliary state**.) The current domiciliary state in Case #1 is State Y; the current domiciliary state in Case #2 is State B. The issue in both cases is whether the domiciliary state will recognize the marriage entered in another state.

Earlier in the chapter, we discussed the general conflict-of-law rule on the validity of marriage:

Conflict of Laws and the Validity of a Marriage

The validity of a marriage is determined by the law of the state in which the marriage was entered or contracted. Another state will recognize that marriage unless to do so would violate a strong public policy of the state asked to recognize it.

Under this general rule:

- Case #1. State Y will recognize as valid the marriage of Bill and Pat that was entered in State X unless State Y determines that recognizing common-law marriages violates the strong public policy of State Y.

- Case #2. State B will recognize as valid the marriage of Ed and Mary that was entered in State A unless State B determines that recognizing underage marriages violates the strong public policy of State B.

We will study this general rule (and the meaning of strong public policy) in Chapter 6 on annulment. For now, here is how the general rules would apply to our two cases:

- Case #1. Most domiciliary states would recognize as valid common-law marriages that were entered in other states. It is not against the strong public policy of most domiciliary states to recognize out-of-state common-law marriages even if such marriages cannot be entered in the domiciliary state.

- Case #2. Not all states agree on whether to recognize a marriage in which the parties were of age in the state where they entered the marriage but would not be of age if they had entered it in the domiciliary state. Some states would consider it against their strong public policy to recognize such marriages. Other states disagree and would recognize it.

Again, we will return to these themes in Chapter 6.

IMPEDIMENT REMOVAL

In 1989, Ernestine enters a valid ceremonial marriage with John. They begin having marital troubles and separate, but do not divorce. In 1995, Ernestine and Henry begin living together. They cohabit and hold each other out as husband and wife in a state where common-law marriages are valid. (They do not enter a ceremonial marriage.) Except for the existence of the 1989 marriage to John, it is clear that Ernestine and Henry would have a valid common-law marriage. In 2001, John obtains a divorce from Ernestine. Henry and Ernestine continue to live together in the same manner as they have since 1995. In 2009, Henry dies on the job. Ernestine claims death benefits under workers' compensation as his surviving "wife." Was she married to Henry in 2009?

Until 2001, a serious **impediment** existed to their being able to marry: Ernestine was already married to someone else. An impediment is a legal obstacle that prevents the formation of a valid marriage or other contract. When Ernestine's marriage to John was dissolved by the divorce in 2001, the impediment was removed. The issue is (1) whether Ernestine and Henry would be considered to have entered a valid common-law marriage at the time the impediment was removed, or (2) whether at that time they would have had to enter a *new* common-law marriage agreement, express or implied. In most states, a new agreement would not be necessary. An earlier agreement to marry (by common law) will carry forward to the time the impediment is removed so long as the parties have continued to live together openly as husband and wife. Accordingly, Ernestine automatically became the wife of Henry when the impediment of the prior marriage was removed because she and Henry continued to live together openly as husband and wife after that time. As one court explains:

> It is not to be expected that parties once having agreed to be married will deem it necessary to agree to do so again when an earlier marriage is terminated or some other bar to union is eliminated.[48]

In the states that reach this conclusion, it makes no difference that either or both of the parties knew of the impediment at the time they initially agreed to live as husband and wife.

impediment
A legal obstacle that prevents the formation of a valid marriage or other contract.

ASSIGNMENT 5.11

Examine the following sequence of events:

- Ann and Rich meet in State Y where they agree to live together as husband and wife forever. They do not want to go through a marriage ceremony, but they agree to be married and openly represent themselves as such. State Y, however, does not recognize common-law marriages.
- Rich accepts a job offer in State X, where common-law marriages are legal, and they both move there.
- After three years in State X, Rich and Ann move back to State Y. One year later Rich dies in State Y. In his will, he leaves all his property "to my wife." Ann is not mentioned by name in his will.
- From the time they met until the time of Rich's death, they lived together as husband and wife, and everyone who knew them thought of them as such.

Can Ann claim anything under the will? State Y provides tax benefits to "widows." Can Ann claim these benefits? (See the General Instructions for the Legal-Analysis Assignment in Appendix A.)

ASSIGNMENT 5.12

State Y does not recognize common-law marriages. Vivian and Tom begin living together in State Y in 1995 and continuously do so until Tom's death in 2004. During this time, pursuant to mutual agreement, they cohabited and held themselves out as husband and wife, but never went through a marriage ceremony. They purchased real property in their joint names as husband and wife. On four different occasions, they went on vacation fishing trips to a resort in State X, where they registered as husband and wife, held themselves out as such, and lived together during their stay. Two trips in 1997 were of three days' duration each. Two other trips were of seven days' duration each, one in 1998 and one in 1999. State X recognizes common-law marriages. Were the parties married in 2004? (See General Instructions for the Legal-Analysis Assignment in Appendix A.)

ASSIGNMENT 5.13

What is the feminist argument in favor of allowing common-law marriages? (In Google, Bing, Yahoo, or other search engine, run this search: feminist common-law marriage.)

PUTATIVE MARRIAGE

putative spouse

A person who believes in good faith that he or she entered (and cohabitated in) a valid marriage even though an impediment made the marriage invalid. The marriage with such a spouse is called a putative marriage.

In some states, courts will treat unmarried parties as **putative spouses** for purposes of providing limited rights such as the right to receive support and the right to inherit from the other putative spouse. A putative spouse is a person who believes he or she entered a valid marriage even though there was an impediment that made the marriage unlawful. The marriage is referred to as a putative marriage. Here is how one court described it:

A putative marriage is one which has been contracted in good faith and in ignorance of some existing impediment on the part of at least one of the contracting parties. Three circumstances must occur to constitute this species of marriage: (1) There must be **bona fides**. At least one of the parties must have been ignorant of the impediment, not only at the time of the marriage, but must also have continued ignorant of it during his or her life. (2) The marriage must be duly solemnized. (3) The marriage must have been considered lawful in the estimation of the parties or of that party who alleges the bona fides.[49]

bona fides
Good faith. The absence of wrongful intent or desire to take inappropriate advantage of someone.

An example of a putative marriage is a woman who goes through a marriage ceremony in good faith and does not find out until after her "husband" dies that he never even tried to obtain a divorce from his first wife, who is still alive. In the few states that recognize putative marriages, such a woman would be given some protection (e.g., she would be awarded the reasonable value of the services she rendered or a share of the property the parties accumulated during the relationship). Note, however, that only the innocent party can benefit from the putative marriage. If the woman had died first in our example, her bigamist "husband" could not claim benefits as her putative spouse.

A putative spouse can collect Social Security as the widow or widower of his or her deceased putative spouse if the applicant for benefits "in good faith went through a marriage ceremony" that resulted "in a purported marriage," which "but for a legal impediment not known to the applicant at the time of such ceremony, would have been a valid marriage."[50]

States differ on whether putative marriages require cohabitation. (Common-law marriages do require it.) Most states do not require cohabitation for putative marriages. States that have adopted the Uniform Marriage and Divorce Act do require it as you can see from the definition of putative spouse in § 209 of the Act:

> Any person who has cohabited with another to whom he is not legally married in the good faith belief that he was married to that person is a putative spouse until knowledge of the fact that he is not legally married terminates his status and prevents acquisition of further rights. A putative spouse acquires the rights conferred upon a legal spouse, including the right to maintenance following termination of his status. . . .

Good faith is measured by a **subjective standard**. The test is whether the innocent party actually believed that the marriage was valid. The test is not whether a reasonable person would have believed it was valid. Reasonableness is an **objective standard**. The test is not objective; it is subjective.

subjective standard
A standard by which something is measured by what a particular person actually knew, felt, or did.

objective standard
A standard by which something is measured by comparing (1) what a person actually knew, felt, or did with (2) what a reasonable person would have known, felt, or done under the same circumstances.

estopped
Prevented from asserting a right or a defense because it would be unfair or inequitable to allow the assertion. The noun is estoppel.

marriage by estoppel
A relationship that is recognized as a marriage because a party is prevented from asserting the invalidity of the marriage even though grounds for its invalidity may exist.

MARRIAGE BY ESTOPPEL

In Chapter 7, we will discuss invalid marriages that are treated as valid because one of the parties is **estopped** (prevented) from asserting the invalidity of the marriage. In the absence of someone who can challenge the validity of the marriage, the marriage is treated as valid—it is a **marriage by estoppel**. This is a relationship that is recognized as a marriage because a party is prevented from asserting the invalidity of the marriage even though grounds for its invalidity may exist. Here is an example:

> Ted is married to Alice. Ted goes to another state and obtains an invalid divorce from Alice. Ted then marries Helen. Some years later, Helen files a divorce action against Ted seeking alimony and attorney fees. Ted's defense is that he was never legally married to Helen because his marriage to Alice was not terminated by a valid divorce.

On these facts, Ted will be prevented from raising this defense because he is the one who procured the "divorce" that was invalid. He will not be allowed to take inconsistent positions. Ted took advantage of the "divorce" to Alice by marrying Helen. It is inconsistent and unfair to allow him to try to undo the marriage to Helen. Hence the marriage to Helen is treated as valid because there is no one who can challenge its validity. If Ted could challenge it, a court would rule that the marriage to Helen is invalid because it was entered at a time when he was still married to Alice. But because Ted cannot raise this challenge, the marriage to Helen becomes a marriage by estoppel. Hence Helen has the right to go to court and seek a divorce (including alimony, attorney fees, and other spousal rights) from the man whom the court will treat as her legal husband.

DE FACTO MARRIAGE

de facto marriage

(a marriage in fact) A relationship of a cohabiting couple that is recognized as a marriage for limited purposes even though the relationship does not meet the requirements of a ceremonial, common-law, or putative marriage, although the couple has acted in a marriage-like manner.

Assume that a couple lives together for an extended period but never had a ceremonial marriage, never held themselves out as husband and wife, and never had a good-faith belief that they were married. After years of being together, one of them dies. Does the survivor have any rights? There was no common-law marriage because the couple did not meet the holding-out requirement for such marriages. There was no putative marriage because neither had a good-faith belief that they were married. The couple had what is sometimes called a **de facto marriage**, a marriage in fact as opposed to a legal marriage. A de facto marriage is a relationship that is recognized as a marriage for limited purposes even though the relationship does not meet the requirements of a ceremonial, common-law, or putative marriage, although the couple has acted in a marriage-like manner. A few states recognize de facto marriages. For example, if one of the cohabitants dies on the job, the surviving cohabitant might be given workers' compensation benefits as the "spouse" of the deceased. Most states, however, do not recognize de facto marriages and will not grant marital benefits to cohabitants in such relationships.

On whether one of the parties could obtain benefits under the theories discussed in *Marvin v. Marvin* (e.g., breach of a cohabitation agreement), see Chapter 4.

There is another meaning of de facto marriage in some states. The phrase is sometimes applied to cases in which a man is paying alimony to his ex-wife and asks a court to end his alimony obligation because his ex-wife is cohabiting with another man and living in a marriage-like relationship. Her relationship with this other man is referred to as a de facto marriage. In some states, this is sufficient to end the ex-husband's alimony obligation. In West Virginia, for example, a statute provides as follows:

> In the discretion of the court, an award of spousal support may be reduced or terminated upon specific written findings by the court that since the granting of a divorce and the award of spousal support a de facto marriage has existed between the spousal support payee and another person.[51]

We will examine this issue in Chapter 8.

THE STRUGGLE TO FIND A REMEDY

Sometimes a court will stretch a legal definition in order to cover facts that call out for a remedy even though traditional legal concepts do not seem to fit. In New York City, for example, rent-control laws limit the right of a landlord to evict "the surviving spouse of the deceased tenant or some other member of the deceased tenant's family who has been living with the tenant."[52] In a highly publicized case, the New York State Court of Appeals ruled that a man whose male lover died of AIDS was a "family" member of the deceased within the meaning of this law and therefore was entitled to remain in the apartment. The two men had never married and had no traditional family relationship.

It is not true that courts will bend every legal definition in order to find a way to reach a decision that is appropriate. Many people come away from the legal system without relief if the facts of their case do not fit within the elements of a traditional remedy. Yet the themes of Chapters 4 and 5 in this book demonstrate that family law is continually evolving. Legislatures and courts are often receptive to the creation of new legal relationships and of retooling some of the old legal relationships to accommodate the rich diversity of how people in our society form families. This is aptly demonstrated by the expanding contractual rights of unmarried cohabitants discussed in Chapter 4 and by the willingness of many states to allow the formal same-sex relationships that we have discussed in this chapter.

■ PARALEGAL ROLES

- For an overview of paralegal roles in family-law cases, see Exhibits 1-3 and 1-4 in Chapter 1.
- For financial issues covered in Chapter 5, a paralegal may be asked to help collect documents and facts outlined in:
  - the checklist in Exhibit 3-1 of Chapter 3
  - the interrogatories in Appendix C
- The interviewing and investigation checklists in Chapter 5 also cover fact-finding roles of paralegals.
- Do a records research for past divorces or annulments in order to determine whether prior marriages were properly terminated so that a current client can apply for social security or other benefits that require the existence of a valid current marriage.
- Investigate facts that are relevant to issues involving breach of promise to marry, common-law marriage, putative marriage, marriage by estoppel, and de facto marriage.
- Obtain the paperwork needed for a covenant marriage, a civil union, or a domestic partnership.
- Do a survey of the academic literature on issues such as the social development of children raised in families run by same-sex couples.
- Assist attorneys in locating and screening potential parties who will bring a test case to challenge a right denied to a same-sex couple.

■ CHECK THE CITE

The U.S. Supreme Court held in *Turner v. Safley* that the restriction on marriage imposed on inmates was unconstitutional. What was the restriction and why was it held unconstitutional? See *Turner v. Safley*, 482 U.S. 78, 107 S. Ct. 2254 (1987). To read the opinion online: (1) Run a citation search ("482 U.S. 78") in the Legal documents database of Google Scholar (scholar.google.com); (2) Run a citation search ("482 U.S. 78") or a case name ("Turner v. Safley") in the general search engines of Google, Bing, or Yahoo.

■ PROJECT

Exhibit 5-2 lists places where formalized same-sex relationships are allowed. Use the Internet to find:

(1) The definition of marriage in any three states that allow same-sex marriages.
(2) The definition of domestic partnership or civil union in any three states that allow either relationship.
(3) The definition of domestic partnership or civil union in any three cities or counties that allow either relationship.
(4) The definition of marriage in any foreign country that allows same-sex marriage.

■ ETHICS IN A FAMILY LAW PRACTICE

Mary and Ted live in Louisiana. They want to enter a covenant marriage. They visit Rev. Sharon Fox for the required premarital counseling. Reverend Fox is also a part-time paralegal. The couple spends two hours with Rev. Fox. She uses over half this time answering questions from Ted and Mary about the grounds for the divorce of a covenant marriage, the kind of testimony that will be admissible in court to prove marital fault, and the court that can grant such a divorce. Reverend Fox does the best she can to answer these questions. Any ethical problems?

■ WRITING SAMPLE

Polygamy (having more than one spouse at the same time) is illegal in every state. Write a memorandum in which you apply *Lawrence v. Texas*, 539 U.S. 558 (2003) to whether the ban on polygamous marriage violates the U.S. Constitution. To read *Lawrence v. Texas* online: (1) Go to Google Scholar (scholar.google.com) and enter the search "539 U.S. 558" in the Legal documents database. (2) Run a citation search ("539 U.S. 558") or a case name ("Lawrence v. Texas") in the general search engines of Google, Bing, or Yahoo. (See General Instructions for the Writing Sample in Appendix A.)

SUMMARY

Most states do not allow the heart-balm action of breaching a promise to marry. Nor do they allow suits for inducing someone to breach this promise. States differ on whether they also prohibit a tort action for fraud based on the breach. For states that do allow an action for breach of promise to marry, recovery is limited to compensatory and punitive damages. Expectation damages are not allowed. If the breach is particularly shocking, the tort of intentional infliction of emotional distress might have been committed.

When a planned marriage does not occur, conditional gifts (those dependent on the marriage occurring) must be returned. This is also true of engagement rings except in the few states where the ring does not have to be returned to the person who broke the engagement without justification. This person is not entitled to have the ring returned to him or her. A contract that imposes a total or a near total prohibition on marriage is an unenforceable, general restraint on marriage. On the other hand, contracts that impose reasonable limitations on one's right to marry can be enforceable. Most states enforce antinepotism job rules that forbid married employees from working together for the same employer.

Marriage is a fundamental right. The two major categories of marriage are ceremonial and common-law marriages. Ceremonial marriages must comply with technical or procedural requirements such as obtaining a marriage license and observing a waiting period. There is no requirement that either party take the surname of the other party when the marriage occurs. In most states, the failure to comply with some of the technical or procedural requirements does not invalidate the marriage. Most states allow proxy marriages when the bride, groom, or both is not present for the marriage ceremony.

Civil unions and domestic partnerships seek to give same-sex couples (and some opposite-sex couples) all or some of the state rights and responsibilities that apply to married couples. The Defense of Marriage Act (DOMA) is a federal statute that says (1) one state is not required to give full faith and credit to a same-sex marriage entered in another state and (2) for federal purposes, only opposite-sex marriage is recognized. Many states have passed mini-DOMAs that say they will not enforce a same-sex marriage entered in another state. States differ on whether their state law allows same-sex marriage. Lower federal courts have reached different conclusions on whether a state's ban of same-sex marriage is a violation of the U.S. Constitution. Most states will not allow a trans-sexual to marry someone whose birth gender is the same as the gender of his or her partner. Where adult adoption is allowed, a same-sex couple might try to use adoption to achieve some of the legal results denied them in states that have banned same-sex marriage.

A covenant marriage is a form of ceremonial marriage (a) that is entered upon proof of premarital counseling and a promise to seek marital counseling when needed during the marriage and (b) that is dissolved upon separation for a designated period or upon proof of marital fault. It is more difficult to dissolve a covenant marriage than a conventional one.

In states where common-law marriages are allowed, the requirements are the legal capacity to marry, a present intent and agreement to enter a marital relationship, living together as husband and wife (cohabitation), and an openness about living together as husband and wife (holding out). Under conflict-of-laws rules, the validity of a marriage is governed by the state in which it was entered or contracted. Therefore, if a couple enters a valid common-law marriage in a state where it is valid but moves to a state where such marriages have been abolished, the latter state will recognize the marriage as valid unless recognition would violate its strong public policy.

Occasionally, an impediment exists to an otherwise valid common-law marriage (e.g., one of the parties is still married to someone else). If the impediment is removed while the parties are still openly living together, a valid common-law marriage will be established as of the date of the removal. In most states, a new agreement to enter a common-law marriage is not needed when the impediment is removed.

A putative spouse is a person who reasonably believed in good faith that he or she entered (and cohabitated in) a valid marriage even though there was an impediment that made the marriage unlawful. The putative spouse can obtain some of the benefits of the resulting marriage (called a putative marriage) despite the impediment. A marriage by estoppel is a relationship that is recognized as a marriage because a party is prevented from asserting the invalidity of the marriage even though grounds for its invalidity may exist. A de facto marriage is a relationship of a cohabiting couple that is recognized as a marriage for limited purposes, even though the relationship does not meet the requirements of a ceremonial, common-law, or putative marriage, despite the fact that the couple has acted in a marriage-like manner.

KEY TERMS

cause of action
heart-balm action
compensatory damages
specific performance
expectation damages
aggrieved
punitive damages
malice
heart-balm statute
interference with contract relations
fraud
scienter
intentional infliction of emotional
    distress
gift
consideration
donor
donee
testamentary gift
inter vivos gift
irrevocable
revocable
unjust enrichment
restraint of marriage
bequest
nepotism
marriage
fundamental right

miscegenation
intestate
wrongful death
elective share
marital-communication privilege
ceremonial marriage
common law marriage
officiant
recordation
confidential marriage
solemnization
proxy marriage
civil union
domestic partnership
conflict of laws
full faith and credit (FFC)
moot
Defense of Marriage Act (DOMA)
mini-DOMA
Supremacy Clause
procedural due process (PDP)
substantive due process (SDP)
strict scrutiny
rational basis
discrimination
classification
equal protection of law (EPL)
suspect class

intermediate scrutiny
quasi-suspect class
transsexual
covenant marriage
capacity
in praesenti
express
cohabitation
consummation
holding out
clear and convincing evidence
preponderance of the
    evidence
power of attorney
choice of law
domicile
domiciliary
domiciliary state
impediment
putative spouse
bona fides
subjective standard
objective standard
estopped
marriage by estoppel
de facto marriage

REVIEW QUESTIONS

1. What is a cause of action?

2. What is a heart-balm action?

3. What is the distinction between compensatory and expectation damages? How do they differ from punitive damages?

4. What is specific performance?

5. What is an action for breach of promise to marry and why have many states abolished the action?

6. What is a heart-balm statute?

7. What was the holding in *Stanard v. Bolin*?

8. Why is it unlikely that someone can be successfully sued for inducing another to break his or her promise to marry?

9. What are the elements of fraud?

10. When can a fraud action be brought in a state that has a heart-balm statute?

11. What is scienter?

12. Under what circumstances can a breach of promise to marry be the basis of an action for intentional infliction of emotional distress?

13. When is a gift irrevocable?

14. What is the distinction between an inter vivos and a testamentary gift?

15. When is a gift conditional?

16. When do wedding gifts have to be returned after an engagement is broken?

17. When do engagement rings have to be returned?

18. What is unjust enrichment?

19. What is a restraint of marriage?

20. What is the difference between a general restraint and a reasonable limitation on marriage?

21. What is a bequest?

22. Do antinepotism policies at work constitute an unenforceable restraint on marriage?

23. What is a fundamental right?

24. What did *Zablocki v. Redhail* and *Loving v. Virginia* hold?

25. Under what circumstances is a client likely to face the question of whether he or she is married?

26. What does intestate mean?

27. What is a wrongful death?
28. What is an elective share?
29. What is the marital-communications privilege?
30. What is the distinction between a ceremonial and a common-law marriage?
31. What is the distinction between intent and capacity requirements and technical/procedural requirements for marriage?
32. What technical/procedural requirements often apply to ceremonial marriages?
33. What is a confidential marriage?
34. How are marriages solemnized?
35. Is there an obligation for one person to take the other's surname upon marriage?
36. In general, can a violation of a technical/procedural requirement be a ground for annulment?
37. What is a proxy marriage?
38. Can a person be married posthumously?
39. What is the ABM movement?
40. What is a civil union? What is a domestic partnership?
41. What is the full-faith-and-credit controversy?
42. How does the federal Defense of Marriage Act (DOMA) resolve the controversy?
43. What is a mini-DOMA?
44. What is the federal definition of marriage?
45. How has state constitutional law affected the right of same-sex couples to marry?
46. How does federal constitutional law affect a state's ban on same-sex marriage?
47. What are the levels of scrutiny for challenges based on violations of due process and equal protection?
48. What did *Lawrence v. Texas* decide and how does it affect the right of same-sex couples to marry?
49. What is the argument that the ban on same-sex marriage passes the rational basis test?
50. What did *Perry v. Schwarzenegger* decide?
51. What are the marriage rights of a transsexual?
52. Can adult adoption be a substitute for marriage?
53. What is a covenant marriage?
54. What are the requirements for a common-law marriage?
55. What is meant by capacity?
56. When is something done in praesenti?
57. How is holding out accomplished?
58. Why are common-law marriages disfavored?
59. What is the distinction between clear and convincing evidence and preponderance of the evidence?
60. What is a conflict of laws?
61. What is meant by domicile? What is a domiciliary? What is a domiciliary state?
62. What is the conflict-of-laws general rule on the validity of marriages?
63. What is an impediment?
64. What happens when an impediment to a valid common-law marriage is removed?
65. What is a putative spouse?
66. What is the distinction between a subjective and an objective standard?
67. What is marriage by estoppel?
68. What is a de facto marriage and when is it recognized?

HELPFUL WEBSITES

Heart-Balm Actions

- heartbalmlaws.uslegal.com/breach-of-promise-to-marry
- en.wikipedia.org/wiki/Breach_of_promise
- www.ilga.gov/legislation/ilcs/ilcs3.asp?ActID=2022&ChapterID=57

Conditional Gifts

- www.jud.ct.gov/lawlib/Notebooks/Pathfinders/Marry.PDF
- en.wikipedia.org/wiki/Engagement_ring
- www.nolo.com/legal-encyclopedia/returning-engagement-ring-30198.html

Marriage Requirements in All States

- topics.law.cornell.edu/wex/table_marriage
- usmarriagelaws.com/search/united_states/index.shtml
- marriage.about.com/cs/marriagelicenses/a/usmarlaws.htm
- www.1800bride2b.com/articles/marriagelaws_chart.htm

Same-Sex Marriage

- www.ncsl.org/default.aspx?tabid=16430
- www.hrc.org/issues/marriage
- www.lambdalegal.org/publications/nationwide-status-same-sex-relationships

Common Law Marriage

- www.buddybuddy.com/common.html
- www.unmarried.org/common-law-marriage-fact -sheet.html
- topics.law.cornell.edu/wex/table_marriage
- www.ncsl.org/issues-research/human-services /common-law-marriage.aspx

Domestic Partnerships and Civil Unions

- en.wikipedia.org/wiki/Domestic_partnership
- www.hrc.org/issues/pages/civil-unions
- www.unmarried.org

Marriage by Proxy

- marriagebyproxy.com
- en.wikipedia.org/wiki/Proxy_marriage

Covenant Marriage

- www.covenantmarriage.com

Gay & Lesbian Advocates & Defenders

- www.glad.org

National Organization for Marriage

- www.nationformarriage.org

Google/Bing/Yahoo Searches

(on these search engines, run the following searches, substituting your state for "aa")

- "heart balm" aa
- "conditional gift" aa
- civil union aa
- DOMA aa
- "covenant marriage" aa
- "putative marriage" aa
- "de facto marriage" aa
- "breach of promise to marry" aa
- "restraint of marriage" aa
- "domestic partnership" aa
- "same-sex marriage" aa
- "common law marriage" aa
- "marriage by estoppel" aa

ENDNOTES

Note: All or most of the court opinions in these endnotes can be read online. To do so, go to Google Scholar (scholar .google.com), select "Legal documents," and in the search box, enter the cite (e.g., "368 N.Y.S.2d 980") or name of the case (e.g., *Friedman v. Geller*) that is given in the endnote.

[1] Keith Bradsher, *Modern Tale of Woe: Being Left at the Altar*, N.Y. Times, Mar. 7, 1990, at B8 (www.nytimes .com/1990/03/07/garden/left-at-the-altar-modern-tale-of -woe.html?pagewanted=all&src=pm).

[2] *Friedman v. Geller*, 368 N.Y.S.2d 980, 983 (Civil Court, City of New York 1975).

[3] W. Page Keeton et al., *Prosser and Keeton on the Law of Torts* 929 (5th ed. 1984).

[4] Vera Cohn et al., *Barely Half of U.S. Adults Are Married—A Record Low* (Pew Research Center, 2011) (www.pewsocialtrends.org/2011/12/14 /barely-half-of-u-s-adults-are-married-a-record-low).

[5] Laura Peterson, *Divorce*, N.Y. Times, May 5, 1996, at 8.

[6] JBH, *The New Yorker*, Jun. 10, 1996, at 32.

[7] *Loving v. Virginia*, 388 U.S. 1, 11 (1967).

[8] *Zablocki v. Redhail*, 434 U.S. 374 (1978).

[9] *Loving v. Virginia*, 388 U.S. 1 (1967).

[10] American Bar Association, *Guide to Family Law* 5 (1996).

[11] Stephanie Coontz, *Taking Marriage Private*, N.Y. Times, Nov. 26, 2007, at A27 (www.nytimes.com/2007/11/26 /opinion/26coontz.html).

[12] Florida Marriage Preparation and Preservation Act (etd.fcla .edu/UF/UFE0015878/mayberry_j.pdf).

[13] For an example of an application for a confidential marriage in California, see www.co.marin.ca.us/depts/CC/Forms /Confidential_Marriage_License_Application.pdf.

[14] N.Y. Dom. Rel. § 11(4) (public.leginfo.state.ny.us/menugetf .cgi?COMMONQUERY=LAWS)(click DOM, then Article 3, then 11).

[15] Colorado Revised Statutes, § 14-2-109(1) (1993) (www .denvergov.org/TabId/383424/default.aspx).

[16] 48 U.S.C. § 1101(a)(35) (www.law.cornell.edu/uscode/8 /usc_sec_08_00001101----000-.html).

[17] Craig Smith, *A Love That Transcends Death Is Blessed by the State*, N.Y. Times, Feb. 19, 2004 (www.nytimes.com /2004/02/19/international/europe/19WIDO.html).

[18] *Baehr v. Lewin*, 74 Haw. 530, 852 P.2d 44 (1993).

[19] David Dunlap, *Fearing a Toehold for Gay Marriages, Conservatives Rush to Bar the Door*, N. Y. Times, Mar. 6, 1996, at A13. (www.nytimes.com/1996/03/06/us/fearing -a-toehold-for-gay-marriages-conservatives-rush-to-bar -thedoor.html?pagewanted=all&src=pm).

[20] 28 U.S.C. § 1738C *(www.law.cornell.edu/uscode /text/28/1738C)*.

[21] 1 U.S.C. § 7 (www.law.cornell.edu/uscode/text/1/7).

[22] United States Census Bureau, *Census Bureau Releases Estimates of Same-Sex Married Couples* (2011) (www.census .gov/newsroom/releases/archives/2010_census/cb11-cn181 .html).

[23] U.S. Const. Amend. XIV, § 1 (www.usconstitution.net/const .html).

[24] Matthew Coles, *Lawrence v. Texas and The Refinement of Substantive Due Process*, 16 Stanford Law and Policy Review 23, 30 (2005).

[25] *Lawrence v. Texas*, 539 U.S. 558, 577 (2003).

[26] *Lawrence v. Texas*, 539 U.S. at 562, 578.

[27] *Lawrence v. Texas*, 539 U.S. at 578.

[28] *Lawrence v. Texas*, 539 U.S. at 590.

[29] U.S. Const. Amend. XIV, § 1 (www.usconstitution.net/const .html).

[30] 440 Mass. 309, 798 N.E.2d 941 (Mass. 2003).

[31] 43 Cal. 4th 757, 183 P.3d 384, 76 Cal. Rptr.3d 683 (2008).

[32] 704 F. Supp. 2d 921 (N.D. Ca. 2010).

[33] 671 F.3d 1052 (9th Cir. 2012).

[34] 289 Conn. 135, 957 A.2d 407 (Conn. 2008).

[35] 763 N.W.2d 862 (Iowa 2009).

[36] *Chief Justice: Iowa Supreme Court Stronger After 2010 Ousters* (2012) (www.thonline.com/news/iowa-illinois-wisconsin /article_388029c7-80d9-5fdd-921a-7af8e02a2a93.html).

[37] www.coquilletribe.org.

[38] www.suquamish.nsn.us.

[39] To read the full dissent, see endnote 30.

[40] *Littleton v. Prange*, 9 S.W.3d 223 (Tex. App. 1999).

[41] *In re Estate of Gardiner*, 273 Kan. 191, 215, 42 P.3d 120, 137 (Kan. 2002).

[42] See, for example, *M.T. v. J.T.*, 140 N.J. Super 77, 355 A.2d 204 (N.J. Super. A.D. 1976).

[43] Louisiana Department of Justice, Office of the Attorney General, *Louisiana Laws on Community Property and Covenant Marriage* (no date) (www.caddoclerk.com /Covenant_Pamphlet.pdf); Louisiana Revised Statutes Annotated tit. 9, § 273.

[44] Laura A. Sanchez and James D. Wright, *Covenant Marriage: The Movement to Reclaim Tradition in America* 117 (2008).

[45] Texas is an exception. A couple in an informal marriage in Texas does not need to go through a divorce procedure if they have been separated for two years. The law will presume that they never had an informal marriage if they have been separated for this length of time. The presumption, however, is rebuttable. Tex. Fam. Code Ann. § 2.401(b) (law.onecle.com/texas/family/2.401.00.html).

[46] *Sorensen v. Sorensen*, 100 N.W. 930, 932 (Neb. 1904).

[47] *Collier v. City of Milford*, 537 A.2d 474, 478 (Conn. 1998).

[48] *John Crane, Inc. v. Puller*, 899 A.2d 879, 917 (Md. App. 2006).

[49] *United States Fidelity & Guarantee Co. v. Henderson*, 53 S.W.2d 811, 816 (Tex. Civ. App. 1932).

[50] 42 U.S.C § (h)(1)(B) (2011) (www.ssa.gov/OP_Home/ssact /title02/0216.htm). Similarly, a child can receive Social Security benefits through his or her parents if the parents "went through a marriage ceremony that would have been valid but for certain legal impediments." *Astrue v. Capato*, 132 S. Ct. 2021, 2028 (2012).

[51] Annotated Code of West Virginia, § 48-5-707 (a)(1). (www.legis.state.wv.us/WVCODE/ChapterEntire.cfm? chap=48&art=5&section=707#05).

[52] *Braschi v. Stahl*, 74 N.Y.2d 201, 543 N.E.2d 49, 544 N.Y.S.2d 784 (1989).

Annulment

CHAPTER OBJECTIVES

After completing this chapter, you should be able to:

- Define and distinguish annulment, divorce, and legal separation.
- Identify the kinds of annulment cases brought in the era of no-fault divorce.
- Know why the phrase "annulled marriage" is technically incorrect.
- State the effective date of an annulment.
- Identify the two categories of annulment grounds and list the grounds within each category.
- Know the distinctions between a voidable marriage and a void marriage.
- Identify who has standing to bring an annulment action.

- List the capacity and the intent/state-of-mind grounds for annulment.
- Understand the following capacity grounds for annulment: gender, prior existing marriage, consanguinity/affinity, nonage, and physical disability.
- Understand the following intent/state-of-mind grounds for annulment: sham marriage, mental disability, duress, and fraud.
- Know the effect of the last-in-time and the Enoch Arden presumptions.
- Explain how immigration officials treat green-card marriages.

- Distinguish civil and church annulment.
- Explain the conflict-of-laws rule in annulment cases.
- Describe the effect of a marriage-evasion statute.
- Explain the consequences of an annulment on the legitimacy of children, alimony and property division, child custody and child support, inheritance, workers' compensation, criminal bigamy, interspousal immunity, marital-communication privilege, and income tax status.

ANNULMENT, DIVORCE, AND LEGAL SEPARATION

annulment
A declaration by a court that a valid marriage never existed.

divorce
A declaration by a court that a validly entered marriage is terminated so that the parties are no longer married to each other. Also called *dissolution, marital dissolution,* and *divorce a vinculo matrimonii.*

legal separation
A declaration by a court that parties can live apart even though they are still married to each other. Also called judicial separation, limited divorce, *divorce a mensa et thoro,* and separation from bed and board.

no-fault divorce
A divorce that is granted without having to prove the marital wrongs that caused the break-up.

canon law
Church or ecclesiastical law.

ecclesiastical
Pertaining to the church.

In this chapter, we consider annulments, the first of the three major relationship changes we will examine in the book. See Exhibit 6-1. An **annulment** is a declaration by a court that a valid marriage never existed even though the parties may have obtained a marriage license, gone through a ceremony, lived together, and perhaps had children together over a period of many years. A **divorce**, on the other hand, is a declaration by a court that terminates a marriage that once validly existed. In a divorce, there is something to dissolve. An annulment is simply a judicial statement or declaration that a marital relationship never existed. A divorce is granted because of facts that occurred after the marriage was entered. With few exceptions, an annulment is granted because of facts in existence at the time the parties attempted to enter the marriage. A **legal separation** is a declaration by a court that the spouses can live separate and apart even though they remain married. The legal separation ends the "bed and board" relationship but not the marriage relationship. If the parties want to remarry, they must obtain an annulment or a divorce.

Not many annulments are granted in American courts today. This was not so years ago, when divorce was more difficult to obtain and annulment was a major way to end an unhappy marriage. In the current era of **no-fault divorce**, however, the option of divorce is readily available. Parties, therefore, are less likely to seek an annulment. When they do use this option, it is often for religious reasons. A spouse may want to end the marital relationship, but be opposed to divorce because divorce is not allowed by his or her religion. Another reason spouses might seek an annulment is to restore a benefit such as a pension or government benefit that ended when they entered a marriage that they now want annulled. These are among the themes we will explore in this chapter.

During client interviews, attorneys often need to provide basic information about this area of the law. Clients are sometimes confused about annulment, particularly the distinction between divorce and annulment. (Some Catholics are unclear about the distinction between civil annulment and church annulment.) Also, anyone conducting interviews or investigation needs to be alert to the facts that might trigger the availability of an annulment so that it can be presented to the client as an option along with the options of divorce and legal separation.

The law of annulment originated in the **canon law** of the **ecclesiastical** courts. For centuries in Europe (and later in the American colonies), divorce as we know it today was unavailable. The main way to end a dysfunctional marriage was to ask an ecclesiastical court of the church to declare that the marriage

EXHIBIT 6-1 Annulment, Divorce, and Legal Separation

Decree of Court	Definition	Also Called	Can Parties Now Marry?
Annulment	A declaration by a court that a valid marriage never existed.		Yes
Divorce	A declaration by a court that a validly entered marriage is terminated so that the parties are no longer married to each other.	• dissolution • marital dissolution • divorce a vinculo matrimonii	Yes
Legal Separation	A declaration by a court that parties can live apart even though they are still married to each other.	• judicial separation • limited divorce • divorce a mensa et thoro • separation from bed and board	No

was defective. The parties could remarry, not because the court divorced them, but because the court decreed that there never was a valid marriage. By the late nineteenth century, the exclusive jurisdiction of the ecclesiastical courts in this area ended. Laws were enacted allowing parties to obtain an annulment, legal separation, or divorce in the secular or civil courts of the country.

Not all states use the same terminology to describe court proceedings for an annulment. Here are the most common terms:

- action for annulment
- petition for annulment
- suit to annul
- libel for annulment
- action for a declaration of invalidity
- action for a judgment of nullity
- petition to issue a judgment of nullity
- action for a declaratory judgment that the marriage is invalid
- action to declare a marriage void
- action to declare the nullity of a void marriage
- action to affirm the validity of a marriage

Nullity means legally void. A **declaratory judgment** is a binding judgment that establishes (declares) rights or duties but does not order their enforcement.

It is technically incorrect to refer to an "annulled marriage." The word *marriage* means the legal union of two persons as spouses. To bring an action to "annul a marriage" means that you are seeking to invalidate something that never existed. It would be more logical to say that you are seeking to "annul an attempted marriage." (Some states used the phrases "supposed marriage," and "alleged marriage.") Because of habit and convenience, however, phrases such as "annulled marriage" are widely used throughout family law in spite of the slight lapse in logic this language entails. The same problem exists with the terms *spouse*, *husband*, and *wife*. These terms refer to persons in a legal marriage. In the context of annulment actions, some courts prefer the phrases **purported** spouse, purported husband, purported wife, and purported marriage. Purported means claimed or professed. Convenience, however, trumps logic and most courts do not use the qualifiers such as *purported*, *alleged*, and *supposed* before the words *marriage* and *spouse*. (We will adopt the convenience in this chapter.)

EFFECTIVE DATE OF THE ANNULMENT

Dates are important in annulment actions. In most states, the effective date of an annulment is the date the parties entered the marriage, not the date a court invalidates the marriage.

> *Paul and Karen are married on March 13, 2005. In 2008, Paul is killed in a work accident. Karen claims workers' compensation benefits as his surviving widow. Paul's parents, however, assert that the 2005 marriage was invalid and bring an annulment action to have it declared annulled. The marriage is annulled in 2009 and the parents now claim workers' compensation survivor benefits as the only surviving relatives of Paul.*

In this example, a 2005 marriage was declared invalid in 2009. In most states, the effective date of the invalidity would be 2005, not 2009. The invalidity "relates back" to the time when the parties tried to enter the marriage. The invalidity does not begin on the date the court declares the marriage to be invalid. Hence, Karen was not Paul's widow when he died in 2008. The logic of an annulment decree is that Paul never had a widow.

nullity
Legally void.

declaratory judgment
A binding judgment that establishes (declares) rights or duties but does not order their enforcement.

purported
Claimed or professed, often falsely.

This is dramatically different from divorce cases. If parties are married in 2005 and divorced in 2009, the effective date of the divorce is 2009, not 2005.

When, however, we examine the consequences of annulments later in the chapter, we will see that the courts do not always follow the logic of the relation-back rule.

THE VOID–VOIDABLE DISTINCTION
GROUNDS

To obtain an annulment, **grounds** (legally sufficient reasons) must be established. There are two categories of grounds for annulment: those that render the marriage **void** and those that render it **voidable**. (See Exhibit 6-2.) Although both grounds are serious, those that render a marriage void are the most serious because they offend a strong public policy. Before we examine each of these grounds in detail, we need to cover some important points about the void–voidable distinction. Even though some modern courts blur the distinction, it is still a factor in many court decisions.

NECESSITY OF A COURT DECISION

A **voidable marriage** requires a court decision to establish its invalidity. Voidable marriages are valid unless a court declares them to be invalid. A **void marriage** is invalid whether or not a court declares it invalid. (A void marriage is **void ab initio**, meaning that it is invalid from the beginning.) Something is void if it has no legal effect. If, however, something is voidable, it is valid unless it is canceled or invalidated. Hence a voidable marriage is valid for all intents and purposes unless someone is successful in asking a court to declare its invalidity. (This distinction can be critical, as we will see in the *Miller* opinion later in the chapter.)

Assume that two individuals have a voidable marriage, but that they die without anyone bringing an annulment action or challenging their marriage in any way. The practical effect of this inaction is that the entire world treats the marriage as if it is valid. In effect, there is no practical difference between a marriage that complies with all legal requirements and a voidable marriage that no one ever challenges. Of course, if a voidable marriage is successfully challenged in court, the marriage is declared invalid.

grounds
Reasons that are legally sufficient to obtain a particular remedy or result.

void
Of no legal effect; invalid whether or not a court declares it so.

voidable
Valid unless cancelled or invalidated.

voidable marriage
A marriage that is valid unless a court declares its invalidity.

void marriage
A marriage that is invalid even if no court ever declares its invalidity.

void ab initio
Invalid from the beginning, from the time something started.

EXHIBIT 6-2   Void or Voidable

Grounds That Render a Marriage Void
- Gender (for states that do not allow same-sex marriage)
- Prior existing marriage
- Consanguinity and affinity (improper relationship by blood or by marriage; too closely related)
- Sham marriage

Grounds That Render a Marriage Voidable
- Nonage (underage)
- Physical disability
- Mental disability
- Duress
- Fraud

© Cengage Learning 2013

Although there is no need for a court to declare void marriages to be invalid, courts often do so. The reason is that a party may want to use the courts to remove any uncertainty about the marriage (suppose, for example, that the other party disagrees that the marriage is void) and to have a public record of the invalidity.

ANNULMENT ACTION AFTER DEATH

Can a voidable marriage be declared invalid after the death of one of the spouses? No. A void marriage, however, is treated differently. It can be challenged in court and annulled after the death of one of the parties.

RATIFICATION

There can be a **ratification** of voidable marriages, but not of void marriages. Ratification is approval of something after it has occurred; the approval is manifested by agreement, by conduct, or by any inaction that can reasonably be interpreted as approval.

> *Bill and Gail are married in 2007. In 2008, Bill finds out that Gail lied to him about her age when she agreed to marry him. She was underage at the time but she led him to believe otherwise. They continue living together until 2010 when Bill brings an annulment against Gail on the ground of her being underage when they married.*

The annulment action will be dismissed. Paul continued to **cohabit** with Gail after he discovered in 2008 that she was underage in 2007. This conduct will constitute a ratification of the voidable marriage and will prevent Bill from being able to obtain the annulment. His continued cohabitation will be interpreted as an approval of the marriage despite the defect of age. This result will apply to all of the grounds discussed in this chapter that render the marriage voidable.

Suppose, however, that Bill discovered in 2008 that Gail was married to Fred when Bill married her in 2007 and that the marriage to Fred had never been dissolved. Does Bill's continued cohabitation after discovering the ground for the annulment constitute a ratification of the marriage, thereby preventing Bill from winning the annulment action in 2010? No. Bill can still bring the annulment action. The ground for the annulment (prior existing marriage) is a ground that renders the marriage void. You cannot ratify a void marriage.

CONFLICT OF LAWS

Later in the chapter, we will examine what happens when State #1 is asked to recognize a marriage that was entered in State #2 under the following circumstances:

- the marriage is valid in State #2
- the marriage would have been invalid if it had been entered in State #1

The answer to this conflict-of-law question will depend on whether State #1 considers the marriage void or voidable. In general, if it is voidable, State #1 will recognize the marriage, but not if it is void.

WHO CAN SUE?

The right to bring an action is called **standing**. Who has standing to bring an annulment action? A number of persons might want the opportunity to bring an action to annul a particular marriage. Possibilities include:

- The wrongdoer spouse. This is the spouse who knowingly did the act that constituted the ground for the annulment. Example: the spouse who commits fraud in order to convince the innocent spouse to enter the marriage.

ratification
Approval of something after it has occurred. Approval retroactively by agreement, conduct, or any inaction that can reasonably be interpreted as an approval. The verb is *ratify.*

cohabit
To live together in an intimate (usually sexual) relationship in the manner of a husband and wife. The noun is *cohabitation.*

standing
The right to bring a case and seek relief from a court.

guardian ad litem (GAL)
A special guardian (often, but not always, an attorney) appointed by the court to appear in court proceedings on behalf of a person who is a minor, is insane, or is otherwise incapacitated.

dirty hands
Wrongdoing or other inappropriate behavior that would make it unfair or inequitable to allow persons to assert a right or a defense they would normally have.

estopped
Prevented from asserting a right or a defense because it would be unfair or inequitable to allow the assertion. The noun is *estoppel*.

marriage by estoppel
A relationship that is recognized as a marriage because a party is prevented from asserting the invalidity of the marriage, even though grounds for its invalidity may exist.

impediment
A legal obstacle that prevents the formation of a valid marriage or other contract.

capacity
The legal power to do something such as enter a contract or a relationship. Also called *legal capacity*. (See glossary for an additional meaning.)

- The innocent spouse. This spouse did nothing that would give the other spouse grounds to annul the marriage.
- Parent or **guardian ad litem (GAL)** of the innocent spouse.

Substantial restrictions on standing are placed on the wrongdoer spouse who knowingly did the act that constituted the ground for annulment. This spouse has **dirty hands** and should not be allowed to "profit" from what he or she did by giving him or her standing to bring the annulment. In such cases, the wrongdoing party is prevented (**estopped**) from using an annulment action to get out of what might clearly be an invalid marriage. Suppose that the innocent spouse (who has standing) does not want an annulment. The marriage, therefore, is never invalidated. As we saw in Chapter 5, such a marriage is called a **marriage by estoppel**.

Of course, if a spouse cannot obtain an annulment, he or she can terminate the relationship through divorce (if the other spouse is still alive).

For some grounds, a parent or guardian ad litem may have independent standing to bring the annulment action even if the innocent spouse is either unwilling to sue or is incapable of doing so.

OVERVIEW OF GROUNDS FOR ANNULMENT

There are two main categories of grounds for annulment: capacity grounds and intent grounds. The grounds in both categories constitute **impediments**, preventing the formation of a valid marriage. First, we will examine those that relate to a party's **capacity** to marry. Capacity is the legal power to do something such as enter a contract or relationship. Then we will turn to the grounds that focus on whether a party who has the capacity to marry formed the requisite *intent* to marry. See Exhibit 6-3.

EXHIBIT 6-3   Grounds for Annulment

Capacity Grounds
- Gender
- Prior existing marriage
- Consanguinity and affinity (improper relationship by blood or by marriage; too closely related)
- Nonage (underage)
- Physical disability

Intent or State-of-Mind Grounds
- Sham marriage
- Mental disability
- Duress
- Fraud

© Cengage Learning 2013

ASSIGNMENT 6.1

List the grounds for annulment in your state. (See General Instructions for the State-Code Assignment in Appendix A.)

Later we will examine whether the violation of the technical or procedural requirements for entering a ceremonial marriage that we examined in Chapter 5 can be grounds for an annulment.

GROUNDS RELATING TO THE CAPACITY TO MARRY

GENDER

In most states, two persons of the same sex do not have the capacity to marry. See Chapter 5 for a discussion of the law governing same-sex marriage.

Of course, in a state where same-sex marriage is legal, all the other grounds for annulment apply. For example, a same-sex marriage can be annulled if one of the spouses was underage or had a prior existing marriage that was undissolved.

PRIOR EXISTING MARRIAGE (BIGAMY)

The first ground for an annulment that we will consider is *prior existing marriage* or **bigamy**. A person lacks the capacity to marry when he or she marries while still in a valid, undissolved marriage with someone else. If a person tries to live with more than one spouse simultaneously, it is **polygamy**. (*Polygyny* means having more than one *wife* at the same time; *polyandry* is having more than one *husband* at the same time.) In most states, the existence of a prior undissolved marriage renders the second marriage void. In only a few states is a bigamous marriage voidable.

In addition to being a ground for annulment, bigamy is a crime in most states. Hence, someone facing a civil action of annulment may also have to face a possible criminal **prosecution** for bigamy.

Several important **presumptions** need to be considered in annulment cases on the ground of prior existing marriage (bigamy). A presumption is an assumption or inference that a certain fact is true once another fact is established. Most presumptions are rebuttable, meaning that the other side can introduce evidence to try to **rebut** (attack or refute) the presumption. The two major **rebuttable presumptions** in this area of the law are the last-in-time marriage presumption and the Enoch Arden presumption.

Last-in-Time Marriage Presumption

Defendants in bigamy annulment cases sometimes claim that the first marriage was never valid or that the earlier marriage ended in divorce. Yet marriage records, particularly old ones, are sometimes difficult to obtain, and for common law marriages, there are no records. Consequently, proving the status of a prior marriage can sometimes be a monumental task. Was the marriage properly entered (recorded)? Was it dissolved? To assist parties in this difficult situation, the law has created the **last-in-time marriage presumption**, which provides that if more than one marriage is alleged to exist, the most recent marriage is presumed to be valid.

In Chapter 7, we will learn that a marriage is presumed to be valid unless someone claiming it is invalid proves its invalidity. Of course, this presumption does not help us in a case involving two marriages. It makes no sense to presume that both marriages are valid. Hence, in such cases, we apply the last-in-time presumption. The effect of this presumption is that the court will treat the first marriage as having been dissolved by death or divorce. Because the presumption is rebuttable, the party seeking to annul the second marriage can attempt to rebut the presumption by introducing evidence that the first marriage was not

bigamy
Marrying while still in a valid, undissolved marriage with someone else.

polygamy
The condition or practice of having more than one spouse at the same time.

prosecution
1. Bringing and processing criminal proceedings against someone. The words *prosecution* and *prosecute* can also refer to bringing and processing civil proceedings against someone, although the words are more commonly used in criminal proceedings.
2. The attorney representing the government in a criminal case. Also called the prosecutor.

presumption
An assumption or inference that a certain fact is true once another fact is established. The presumption is conclusive if a party is not allowed to introduce evidence to show that the assumption is false. The presumption is rebuttable if a party is allowed to introduce evidence to show that the assumption is false.

rebut
To attack, dispute, or refute.

rebuttable presumption
An assumption or inference of fact that a party will be allowed to try to disprove (rebut) but that will be treated as true if it is not disproved.

last-in-time marriage presumption
If more than one marriage is alleged to exist, the most recent marriage is presumed to be valid.

dissolved by death or divorce. Yet proving a negative is not always easy. It can be difficult to find evidence that a divorce has not occurred. You would have to go to every county where the spouse lived, check the records, and show that no record of divorce exists.

> *Frank seeks to annul his marriage to Diane because he believes that Diane was married to Ted at the time Frank married her and that the marriage to Ted was never dissolved. Diane does not want her marriage to Frank annulled and she asserts the last-in-time presumption. Under this presumption, the court will treat her marriage to Ted as having been dissolved and, therefore, her marriage to Frank (the most recent marriage) as valid. Frank, therefore, will lose his annulment action against Diane unless he can prove that the marriage to Ted was not dissolved.*

The value to Diane of the last-in-time presumption is that she does not have to prove that her marriage to Ted was dissolved; Frank has the burden of proving that it was not dissolved.

Enoch Arden Presumption

What happens if (a) spouse #1 disappears, (b) the left-behind spouse marries spouse #2, and then (c) spouse #1 reappears after the marriage to spouse #2?

> *Paul marries Cynthia. Cynthia disappears. Paul has not heard from her for fifteen years in spite of all his efforts to locate her. Paul then marries Mary in the honest belief that his first wife (Cynthia) is dead. Mary does not know anything about Cynthia. Suddenly Cynthia reappears, and Mary learns about the first marriage. Mary immediately brings an action against Paul to annul her marriage to him on the ground of a prior existing marriage (bigamy).*

Can the disappearance of a spouse be a defense to a civil annulment action on the ground of prior existing marriage (bigamy)? Can it be a defense to a criminal prosecution for bigamy? Not all states answer these questions in the same way. The answer depends on the availability and scope of the **Enoch Arden presumption**. Under this presumption, a spouse is presumed to be dead after being missing without explanation for a designated number of years (often 5 to 7 years) despite **due diligence** in attempting to locate him or her. (The name of the presumption comes from the narrative poem *Enoch Arden*, by Alfred Lord Tennyson, about a sailor who returned to his home years after being shipwrecked to discover that his wife had married again.)

Here are some of the differences among the states on the availability of the Enoch Arden presumption:

- In most states, Enoch Arden applies only as a defense to a criminal prosecution for bigamy. The presumption of death does not apply to annulment proceedings. In these states, the second marriage would be annulled because the first spouse is not presumed to be dead even if he or she never reappears.

- In some states, Enoch Arden applies to annulment proceedings as well as to criminal prosecutions. These states, however, treat the reappearance of the missing spouse in one of two ways: (1) the second marriage is valid and cannot be annulled even if the missing spouse reappears or (2) the second marriage can be annulled if the missing spouse reappears, so that the Enoch Arden presumption is effective as a defense in the annulment action only if the missing spouse stays missing. In the latter states, the second marriage is voidable, not void.

Enoch Arden presumption

A spouse is presumed to be dead after being missing without explanation for a designated number of years despite due diligence in attempting to locate him or her.

due diligence

Reasonable efforts to find and verify factual information needed to carry out an obligation, to avoid harming someone, or to make an important decision (e.g., to locate a parent).

SUMMARY OF GROUND FOR ANNULMENT: PRIOR EXISTING MARRIAGE

Definition: A marriage in which one or both parties lacked the capacity to marry because one or both already had a prior valid marriage that has not been dissolved by divorce, annulment, or the death of the first spouse.

Void or voidable: In most states, the establishment of this ground renders the second marriage void.

Who can sue: In most states, either party to the second marriage can bring the annulment action on this ground; both have standing.

Major defenses:

1. The first spouse is dead or presumed dead (Enoch Arden presumption).
2. The first marriage ended by divorce or annulment.
3. The plaintiff has "dirty hands" (available in a few states).

Is this annulment ground also a ground for divorce? Yes, in some states. It is called an *Enoch Arden divorce.*

© Cengage Learning 2013

Bigamy as a Crime

As indicated, bigamy is also a crime. (Occasionally, a state might bring the prosecution under other crime categories such as *criminal adultery* or *sexual abuse*.) In most states, *intent* is an element of the crime. When entering a second marriage, the spouse must know that the prior marriage had not been dissolved. Intent is not required in an annulment action on the ground of bigamy (prior existing marriage). The ground can exist even if a spouse innocently (but mistakenly) thought that his or her first spouse died or that the earlier marriage ended by a valid divorce.

The media is always interested in bigamy-related cases. Recently, a woman was prosecuted for applying for 27 marriage licenses over several years as part of an immigration scam to help foreign men obtain green cards. According to a city clerk, "these career brides earn $3,000 to $10,000 per fake marriage."[1] In another widely reported case, a wife initiated a bigamy prosecution after discovering on Facebook that her husband was still married to a woman in Italy.[2]

CONSANGUINITY AND AFFINITY LIMITATIONS

Next we examine the relationship ground for annulment. People may lack the capacity to marry because they are too closely related to each other. There are two ways that you can be related to someone: by **consanguinity** (blood) and by **affinity** (marriage). Here are examples of an attempted marriage of individuals related by consanguinity:

consanguinity
Relationship by blood.

affinity
Relationship by marriage rather than by blood.

- Father marries his daughter.
- Sister marries her brother.

Examples of an attempted marriage of individuals related by affinity would include:

- Man marries his son's former wife.
- Woman marries her stepfather.

Most of the prohibitions on who can marry are those based on consanguinity. The state has an interest in preventing genetic disorders that might occur in children of parents related by blood. An additional concern is the possibility of sexual exploitation of vulnerable family members when blood relatives marry, particularly when there is a significant disparity of age between the spouses. Only a few states prohibit marriages of persons related by affinity. Where affinity prohibitions still exist, they mainly cover marriage between stepparents and stepchildren because of the danger of sexual exploitation of children in such relationships.

half-blood
Having the same mother or father but not both.

full-blood
Having the same mother and father.

Not all consanguinity relationships are prohibited. Most states have statutes that indicate which relationships can be the basis of annulments. All states prohibit marriage within the immediate family such as brother and sister, father and daughter, and grandmother and grandson. Most states prohibit uncle–niece and aunt–nephew marriages. About half the states prohibit first-cousin marriages, but only a few prohibit second-cousin marriages. (The husband in a cousin–cousin marriage is sometimes referred to in the media as a *cusband*.) Prohibitions on **half-blood** marriages are usually treated the same as those on **full-blood** marriages. States differ on whether persons can marry their adopted sibling. Most states say that they can.

ASSIGNMENT 6.2

In the following list, you will find pairs of individuals. For each pair, check your state code and answer three questions: Can the individuals marry? If the marriage is prohibited, is it void or voidable? What code section gives you the answer? (See General Instructions for the State-Code Assignment in Appendix A.)

	Can They Marry?	Void or Voidable?	Code Section
a. Mother/son			
b. Father/daughter			
c. Brother/sister			
d. Grandparent/grandchild			
e. Uncle/niece or aunt/nephew			
f. First cousin/first cousin			
g. Second cousin/second cousin			
h. Half-brother/half-sister			
i. Father-in-law/daughter-in-law			
j. Mother-in-law/son-in-law			
k. Brother-in-law/sister-in-law			
l. Stepparent/stepchild			
m. Adoptive parent/adoptive child			

(If your state code does not provide a direct answer to any of the above questions, you may have to check court opinions. See General Instructions for the Court-Opinion Assignment in Appendix A.)

Notes on Consanguinity and Affinity

incest
Sexual relations between two people who are too closely related to each other as defined by law.

1. The Uniform Marriage and Divorce Act (§ 207) would prohibit all marriages between ancestors and descendants (e.g., father and daughter, grandmother and grandson); brother–sister marriages; and adopted brother–sister marriages. The act would permit first-cousin marriages and all affinity marriages.

2. The crime of **incest** consists of sexual relations between two people who are too closely related to each other as defined by law. In many states, the relationships that are incestuous under the criminal law are the same relationships that could lead to annulment if the parties married.

SUMMARY OF GROUND FOR ANNULMENT: CONSANGUINITY OR AFFINITY

Definition: A marriage by parties who lack the capacity to marry because their relationship by consanguinity (blood) or by affinity (marriage) is prohibited by law.

Void or voidable: In most states, the prohibited marriage is void.

Who can sue: Either party can be the plaintiff in the annulment action; both have standing.

Is this annulment ground also a ground for divorce? Yes, in most states.

© Cengage Learning 2013

NONAGE

In order to marry, a party must be a certain minimum age, e.g., 16 with parental or court consent and 18 without needing consent. A person marrying below the minimum age lacks the capacity to marry. The ground to annul a marriage in which one or both spouses was underage is called **nonage**. At one time, states imposed different age requirements for males and females. At common law, the minimum age to marry was 14 for males and 12 for females. This has been changed either by statute or by a court ruling that this kind of sex discrimination is unconstitutional. Within a state, the minimum age may differ depending upon whether:

nonage
Below the required minimum age to enter a relationship or perform a task. Minority.

- Parental or court consent exists.
- The female is already pregnant.
- A child has already been born out of wedlock.

Where parental consent is required, the consent of one parent is usually sufficient. In some states, a court may have the power to authorize a marriage of parties who are underage even if a parent has refused to consent to the marriage. In these states, the court will consider factors such as the maturity of the parties, their financial resources, and whether children (to be born or already born) would be illegitimate if the marriage were not authorized. Still another variation found in some states is that the courts have the authority to require that underage individuals go through premarital counseling as a condition of their being allowed to marry.

If an underage child marries, he or she can sue for annulment, as can the person he or she attempted to marry. A parent or guardian ad litem also has standing to seek the annulment in most states even if the minor does not want the annulment. There are, however, time limits. The annulment cannot be brought if the parties cohabit after the child reaches the statutory minimum age. Such conduct constitutes a *ratification* of the marriage.

States differ on whether the spouse who lied about his or her age can obtain an annulment on the ground of nonage. Because of this spouse's unclean hands, some states refuse to allow him or her to bring the annulment action. Other states allow it despite the lie.

SUMMARY OF GROUND FOR ANNULMENT: NONAGE

Definition: A marriage in which one or both parties lacked the capacity to marry because at the time of the marriage one or both were under the minimum age to marry.

Void or voidable: In most states, the marriage is voidable. In some states, however, a marriage of someone below the age of 7 is void.

Who can sue: Either party in most states. In some states, the spouse who lied about his or her age cannot sue for annulment on the ground of nonage. In many states, the parent or guardian ad litem of the underaged party also has standing.

Major defenses:

1. The parties were of the correct statutory age at the time of the marriage.

2. The underaged party affirmed or ratified the marriage by cohabitation after that party reached the statutory minimum age.

Is this annulment also a ground for divorce? Yes, in some states.

© Cengage Learning 2013

PHYSICAL DISABILITY

A person with certain physical disabilities lacks the capacity to marry. Examples include venereal disease, impotence (the most commonly cited in annulment statutes), epilepsy, and pulmonary tuberculosis in advanced stages.

Venereal Disease

States sometimes have a statutory requirement that parties contemplating marriage go through a medical examination as a condition of obtaining a marriage license. An important objective of this exam is to determine whether either party has a communicable venereal disease (VD). For a number of reasons, a spouse might marry despite having VD:

- The medical exam may have failed to detect the VD that was present.
- The parties falsified the results of the medical exam.
- The parties did not take the medical exam because they entered a common law marriage in a state where such marriages are allowed.

In a few states, marrying while suffering from a communicable VD is a ground for annulment, although in most states it is not. In some states, it is a crime knowingly to marry or have sexual intercourse with someone who has an infectious VD.

Impotence

Impotence is the inability to have sexual intercourse. In some states, it is called an incapacity to consummate the marriage. For males, it is often the inability to achieve or maintain an erection. An allegation of impotence can raise several issues:

- Inability to **copulate** that is incurable
- Inability to copulate that is curable
- **Sterility** (infertility)
- Refusal to have sexual intercourse

In most states, only the first situation, an incurable inability to copulate, is a ground for annulment. The standard for incurability is not the impossibility of a cure; rather, it is the present unlikelihood of a cure. The standard for copulation is the ability to perform the physical sex act naturally, without pain or harm to the other spouse. The "mere" fact that a spouse does not derive pleasure from the act is not what is meant by an inability to copulate. The *refusal* to copulate is not an inability to copulate, although the refusal is sometimes used as an indication of (i.e., as evidence of) the inability to copulate. In most states, it makes no difference whether the inability is due to physical (organic) causes or to psychogenic or emotional causes, nor does it matter that the person is impotent only with his or her spouse. If normal coitus is not possible with one's spouse, whatever the cause, the ground exists. There once was a rule called the doctrine of **triennial cohabitation** under which a man was presumed to be impotent if his wife remained a virgin after three years of cohabitating together. The doctrine no longer applies today.

It is a defense to an annulment action that the party seeking the annulment knew of the party's impotence (or other physical disability) at the time of the marriage and yet still went through with the marriage. Finally, time limits may exist for bringing the action on this ground. For example, a state may bar the action if it is not brought within a designated number of years (e.g., four or five years) after the marriage was entered.

---

impotence
The inability to engage in sexual intercourse. For males, it is often the inability to achieve or maintain an erection.

copulate
To engage in sexual intercourse.

sterility
Inability to have children; infertility.

triennial cohabitation
A man was presumed to be impotent if his wife remained a virgin after three years of cohabitating together.

Note on Testing for HIV

Some states require applicants for marriage to be given information about the human immunodeficiency virus (HIV) and acquired immunodeficiency syndrome (AIDS). West Virginia, for example, requires that "[e]very person who is empowered to issue a marriage license shall, at the time of issuance thereof, distribute to the applicants for the license, information concerning AIDS and inform them of the availability of HIV-related testing and counseling."[3] In other states, the applicant must sign a statement that he or she has been offered a list of sites in the state that offer HIV tests. At one time, Illinois went even further by requiring that every applicant be actually tested "to determine whether either of the parties to the proposed marriage has been exposed to human immunodeficiency virus (HIV) or any other identified causative agent of acquired immunodeficiency syndrome (AIDS)." During the first six months of the program, the number of marriage licenses issued in Illinois dropped by 22.5 percent, and the number of licenses issued to Illinois residents in surrounding states increased significantly.[4] Rather than bother with the test, many couples simply crossed state lines to obtain their marriage license. Consequently, Illinois abolished its program of mandatory testing. Today Illinois simply provides that county clerks "shall distribute free of charge, to all persons applying for a marriage license, a brochure prepared by the Department of Public Health concerning sexually transmitted diseases and inherited metabolic diseases."[5]

ASSIGNMENT 6.3

a. Should Illinois have abolished its program of mandatory testing for HIV?

b. Should Congress pass a federal law requiring every state to impose mandatory HIV testing? What problems would such a law solve and cause?

SUMMARY OF GROUND FOR ANNULMENT: PHYSICAL DISABILITY

Definition: A marriage in which one or both parties lacked the capacity to marry because one or both had a communicable venereal disease or an incurable inability to copulate without pain or harm to the other spouse.

Void or voidable: Voidable.

Who can sue: In most states, either spouse; both have standing. In some states, the nondisabled spouse who knew of the other's disability at the time of the marriage cannot sue.

Major defenses:

1. Neither party had a communicable venereal disease.

2. The impotence is curable.

3. The plaintiff waited too long to bring the annulment action on this ground.

Is this annulment ground also a ground for divorce? Yes, in some states.

GROUNDS RELATING TO THE INTENT TO MARRY

SHAM MARRIAGES

An essential element of a marriage contract is the intent to enter a marriage. Examine the following four cases in which couples went through all the marriage formalities (obtaining a license, having the blood test, etc.) and completed the marriage ceremony.

- Dennis and Janet enter a marriage solely to obtain permanent resident alien status for Dennis, who is not a U.S. citizen. Janet is a citizen. Dennis wants to use his marriage status to avoid deportation by immigration officials.

- After a great deal of laughing and boasting at a college party, Edna dares Stanley to marry her. He accepts the dare and they marry.
- Frank and Helen have an affair. Helen becomes pregnant. Neither wants the child to be born illegitimate. They never want to live together, but decide to be married solely for the purpose of having the child born legitimate. They agree that the child will live with Helen.
- Rachel and Ken have been dating for a number of months. They decide to get married "just to try it out." They feel this is a modern and rational way of determining whether they will want to stay together forever. Both fully understand that there will be "no hard feelings" if either of them wants to dissolve the marriage after six months.

All four of these couples go through the steps required to become married. To any reasonable outside observer of their outward actions, nothing unusual happened. They all intended to go through a marriage ceremony; they all intended to go through the outward appearances of entering a marriage contract. Subjectively, however, each couple had a hidden agenda.

According to traditional contract principles, if individuals give clear outward manifestations of mutual assent to enter a contract, the law will bind them to their contract, even though their unspoken motive was *not* to enter a binding contract. Many courts, however, apply a different principle to marriage contracts. The first three couples above engaged in totally **sham** marriages. The parties never intended to live together as husband and wife; they had a limited purpose of avoiding deportation, displaying braggadocio, or "giving a name" to a child. Many courts would declare such marriages to be void and would grant an annulment to either party. There is a minority of courts, however, that would conclude that a valid marriage exists whenever the formalities of marriage are followed regardless of the unspoken objectives or motives of the parties.

Assume that the first three couples cohabit for a period of time *after* they go through the marriage ceremony. Such cohabitation is strong evidence that they *did* intend to be married at the time of the ceremony and that they are now inventing reasons to get out of the marriage through an annulment.

What about the fourth case, in which the parties entered a *trial marriage*? The fact that the parties cohabited is evidence that they intended to be married at the time they entered the marriage contract. Most courts would find that this marriage is valid and deny an annulment to anyone who later claims that the parties never intended to assume the marital status. It cannot be said that they married in jest or that they married for a limited purpose. The fact that they did not promise to live together forever as husband and wife does not mean that they lacked the intent to be married at the time they entered the marriage.

sham

Pretended, counterfeit. Something false that purports to be genuine.

SUMMARY OF GROUND FOR ANNULMENT: SHAM MARRIAGE

Definition: A marriage in which one or both parties lacked the intent to marry in spite of the fact that they voluntarily went through all the formalities of a marriage.

Void or voidable: Void.

Who can sue: Either party; both have standing.

Major defense: The parties did have the intention to marry at the time they entered the marriage ceremony. A major item of evidence that this intention existed is that they cohabited after the ceremony. (*Note:* In some states, the annulment will be denied if the parties went through all the outward formalities of the marriage no matter what their unspoken objective was.)

Is this annulment ground also a ground for divorce? Usually not.

Sham Marriages and Immigration Law

A green card entitles an immigrant or **alien** to permanent resident status in the United States. One of the ways to obtain a green card is to enter a marriage in good faith with a U.S. citizen. Such a marriage is sometimes referred to as a **green-card marriage** or a spousal green card. The marriage, however, is a sham if the parties never intended to be married and were simply seeking legal entry into the country. The alien can be deported and the marriage annulled. To deter immigration-related marriage fraud, aliens deriving their immigrant status based on a marriage of less than two years are classified as *conditional* immigrants. To remove their conditional status, the immigrants must file an application with the U.S. Citizenship and Immigration Services during the 90-day period before their second-year anniversary of receiving conditional status. If the aliens cannot show that the marriage is a valid one, their conditional immigrant status may be terminated and they become deportable. There must be proof that the couple has maintained a valid marriage during the two-year period. The parties are interviewed separately and together by immigration officials. They are asked questions that a truly married couple would be expected to know about each other. For example, each spouse might be asked the following questions in separate interviews:

- What's the color of your spouse's toothbrush?
- Where do you keep the laundry hamper?
- Who cooks the meals? What did you eat the last time you had a meal together?
- What is your spouse's favorite music?
- What did the two of you do last New Year's eve?
- What did your spouse wear on your wedding day? Where did you go to celebrate?
- What is your spouse's birthday?
- How much do you pay for rent?
- What piece of jewelry means the most to you and to your spouse?

If the interviewer finds significant discrepancies in the answers given during the separate interviews, the application to remove their conditional status (and hence the green card itself) can be denied and the alien can face deportation.[6]

Marrying for Tuition

In some states, public universities have different tuition rates for in-state students and out-of-state students. In California, for example, it can take up to two years for out-of-state students to establish residency so that they qualify for the substantially lower in-state tuition fees. One of the requirements is that students be financially independent of their parents. Simply saying you are independent is not sufficient. Being married, however, does qualify as independence. Recently, a student from the Midwest attending a state university in California advertised on Facebook that she was looking for a husband. "An out-of-state student whom she did not know responded to her [Facebook] post, and they married in 2007, the summer before her junior year. She graduated in 2009 and estimated that the marriage had saved her $50,000. The couple has divorced."[7] Websites exist that help students enter such "marriages of convenience" (e.g., whypaytuition.com). Because the parties to such marriages never intended to marry (and rarely live together as husband and wife), the marriages could be annulled as shams.

alien
A person who was born outside the United States, is still a subject of a foreign nation, and has not been naturalized in the United States.

green-card marriage
A marriage of a foreigner with an American citizen that entitles the foreigner to permanent resident status in the United States.

ASSIGNMENT 6.4

a. Elaine is 20 years old, and Philip, a bachelor, is 75. Philip asks Elaine to marry him. Philip has terminal cancer and wants to die a married man. He and Elaine know that he probably has less than six months to live and that he will spend the rest of his life in a hospital bed. Under their arrangement, she does not have to continue as his wife after six months if he is still alive. They go through all the formal requirements to be married. On the day after the marriage ceremony, Elaine changes her mind and wants to end the marriage. Can she obtain an annulment? Philip does not want the marriage annulled. (See General Instructions for the Legal-Analysis Assignment in Appendix A.)

b. Draft a set of interrogatories from Philip to Elaine. Draft a separate set of interrogatories from Elaine to Philip. (See General Instructions for the Interrogatory Assignment in Appendix A.)

Multiple Purposes to Marry

In the *Miller* case, which we will now read, a party was alleged to have entered a common law marriage to avoid prosecution for a crime. Even if your state does not recognize common law marriages (see Chapter 5), the case is important because the issue would be the same if he entered a ceremonial marriage in order to avoid criminal prosecution. The case raises the question of what to do when someone has multiple purposes or intentions when entering a marriage. The case reminds us that motive to marry is not the same as intention to marry.

CASE

In the Interest of Melissa Miller
301 Pa. Super. 511, 448 A.2d 25 (1982)
Superior Court of Pennsylvania.

Background: *Edward Christoph is a 36-year-old English teacher who began a romantic relationship with one of his eighth-grade students, Melissa Miller (also called Missy). She was 14 years old at the time. Her mother had been having difficulty with her at home. Melissa would sneak out of the house through her bedroom window in the early morning hours and stay away for three or four hours. Her mother found letters to Melissa from Christoph that said, "You gave yourself fully," and "I love you." When the police began investigating Christoph for sexual involvement with a minor, he consulted an attorney who advised him how to enter a common law marriage. He then entered a common law marriage with Melissa. (At the time, common law marriages were allowed in Pennsylvania. Though the minimum age to enter a ceremonial marriage was 16, the age of consent to enter a common law marriage in the state was seven.) The mother asked the state to declare Melissa to be a dependent child because of her incorrigibility. The juvenile division of the lower court did so and ordered her placed in a foster home. Since Christoph's motive in marrying Melissa was to avoid criminal prosecution, the court also invalidated the* common law marriage. Melissa, as appellant, is now appealing this decision in the Superior Court of Pennsylvania. She does not want the marriage invalidated.

Decision on Appeal: *Reversed. The common law marriage was valid. Melissa should not have been declared a dependent child.*

OPINION OF THE COURT

Judge SPAETH delivered the opinion of the court. . . .

Mr. Christoph testified that his motive [in entering the common law marriage] was that appellant should "be my wife" and that his understanding, when he told her this, was that no criminal charges were going to be brought against him:

Q. What did you say to Melissa . . . on that occasion?
A. I said, "I marry you, Melissa." . . .
Q. And what did you intend when you said you married her?
A. I intended that she be my wife.
Q. And as your wife, what was your intention towards her? A. To take her home to live with me as my wife.
Q. Did you recognize any responsibility when you said

these words? A. Yes.

Q. What were the responsibilities that you recognized?

A. To take her, provide a home and all the necessities that you would normally provide for your wife.

Q. Mr. Christoph, at the time this alleged marriage is to have taken place between you and Missy, do you know—were you aware of the fact that the police were investigating you?

A. I had talked to the police at the time, yes.

Q. Were you afraid that charges would be filed against you by the police as a result of your involvement with Missy. A. No.

Q. You were not afraid of that? A. No.

Q. The crime, corrupting the moral[s] of minors, have you ever heard of that at the time you got married to Missy? A. Yes, I did.

Q. Did you have any concerns at the time this alleged marriage is to have taken place with you being charged by the police. A. No.

Q. Why not? A. Because when I talked to Detective Slupski he said . . . he was going to recommend to the D. A. that no charges be brought. . . .

It is true, as the lower court states in its opinion, that Mr. Christoph's sister, Virginia Byers, who was a witness to the marriage ceremony, testified that "one of Mr. Christoph's express motives in marrying Melissa Miller was to avoid criminal prosecution." . . . However, the sister also testified that another of Mr. Christoph's motives was that he loved appellant. . . . It seems to us that the fairest inference to be drawn from the evidence is that Mr. Christoph may have had at least two motives for marrying appellant—his love for her, and his desire to avoid criminal prosecution for his relationship with her. We find no support in the record for the lower court's assignment of priority to the second of these motives. . . .

Accepting the lower court's finding that Mr. Christoph married appellant to avoid criminal prosecution, still, we are unable to uphold its order. For contrary to the court's opinion, such a motive does not invalidate a common law marriage.

The controlling decision is *Estate of Gower,* 445 Pa. 554, 284 A.2d 742 (1971). In *Gower,* as here, the parties had by words in the present tense expressed their intent to marry one another. The lower court nevertheless held the marriage invalid because the appellant's motive in entering into the marriage was to avoid conscription for military service. Reversing, the Supreme Court held that "[t]he reason or motive underlying a decision to marry is not relevant to a finding of the *intention* to marry." Id. at 557, 284 A.2d at 744. (emphasis in original). Therefore, the appellant's motive to avoid conscription could not "render[ ] invalid his otherwise valid common law marriage." Id.

The record here establishes—and the lower court did not question—appellant's and Mr. Christoph's *intention* to marry. The fact—as the lower court found it to be—that Mr. Christoph's *motive* was to avoid prosecution could not render invalid their otherwise valid common law marriage. . . .

We have not overlooked the arguments of counsel for appellant's mother, urging that we re-examine the doctrine of common law marriage, and either abolish it or align the age of consent [for a common law marriage, 7] to that required for statutory marriage [16]. However, we have declined previous opportunities to abolish or modify the doctrine of common law marriage. . . . Past efforts in the Legislature to abolish common law marriage have failed. . . .

In conclusion, we wish to note that neither have we overlooked the anguish that this marriage has caused appellant's mother. We may hope that her fears are unfounded, as they may be, for the most devoted mother is sometimes mistaken about what is good for her child. But if we knew that the marriage would prove unhappy and short, that would not deflect us from our decision. Our responsibility is to interpret and apply the law. If a marriage is lawful, that is the end of our inquiry. For as judges, we are agents of the State, and whether a lawful marriage is happy or unhappy is none of the State's affair.

Reversed.

ASSIGNMENT 6.5

a. Why couldn't this marriage be annulled?

b. Assume that Edward Christoph files for divorce the day after the statute of limitations for corrupting the morals of a minor expires. If Melissa Miller then filed for an annulment, do you think Judge Spaeth would have reached a different result?

Statutory Rape

Matthew Koso was 20 years old when he started dating 12-year-old Chrystal in Nebraska. Their sexual relationship began when she was 13 years old. When she became pregnant, they traveled to neighboring Kansas where the minimum age for a girl to marry is 12 if her parents consent. They did consent. The minimum

statutory rape
Sexual intercourse with a person under a designated age (e.g., 16) even if the latter consents.

age to marry in their own state of Nebraska was 17. Annulment was not an issue because Matthew, Chrystal, and her parents did not want the marriage to end. Yet there was another legal problem. Matthew had sexual relations with a 13-year-old girl before and after the marriage. In Nebraska, it is **statutory rape** for a person over 18 to have sexual relations with someone under 15. This is what occurred between Matthew and Chrystal. When the couple returned to Nebraska, Matthew was convicted of a sex crime (called sexual assault in the first degree) and received a sentence of 18 to 30 months in prison. (The sentence could have been 50 years.) It was not a defense to the criminal charge that Chrystal consented to the sexual relations nor that they were now validly married. One editorial commented, "Prosecuting this case should send a warning to other adults who imagine they can turn sex crimes into romance by marrying their victims."[8]

MENTAL DISABILITY

A primary reason *mental disability* is a ground for annulment is that it may prevent people from marrying who are incapable of understanding the nature and responsibilities of the marriage relationship. Unfortunately, however, mental disability is very difficult to define. Various state statutes use different terms to describe this condition: insane, want of understanding, unsound mind, idiot, weak-minded, feeble-minded, mentally retarded, lack of mental capacity, imbecile, lunatic, incapable of consenting to a marriage, mentally ill, legally incompetent, mental defective, etc. One court provided the following definition:

> While there has been a hesitancy on the part of the courts to judicially define the phrase "unsound mind," it is established that such term has reference to the mental capacity of the parties at the very moment of inception of the marriage contract. Ordinarily, lack of mental capacity, which renders a party incapable of entering into a valid marriage contract, must be such that it deprives him of the ability to understand the objects of marriage, its ensuing duties and undertakings, its responsibilities and relationship. There is a general agreement of the authorities that the terms "unsound mind" and "lack of mental capacity" carry greater import than eccentricity or mere weakness of mind or dullness of intellect.[9]

Not all states would agree with every aspect of this definition of mental disability, although in general it is consistent with the definitions used by many courts.

All individuals are presumed to be sane (mentally competent) unless the contrary is proven. Suppose that someone was once committed to a mental institution and, upon release, seeks to be married. Surely, the fact of prior institutionalization does not prove that the person is *presently* incapable of understanding the marriage contract and the marriage relationship at the time he or she attempts to marry. Hence, prior institutionalization is not, in and of itself, sufficient to establish the mental-disability ground for annulment.

Assume that a person is mentally disabled but marries during a brief period of mental health before relapsing again to his or her prior state of mental disability. The marriage took place during what is called a **lucid interval**, and many states will validate such a marriage if there was cohabitation. Furthermore, some states will deny the annulment if the parties freely cohabited during a lucid interval at any time after the marriage was entered even if one or both parties were not lucid at the time of the marriage.

Suppose that a person is intoxicated or under the influence of drugs at the time the marriage contract is entered. In most states, this, too, would be a ground for annulment if the alcohol or drugs rendered the person incapable of understanding the marriage contract. Nevada law allows annulments for "want of understanding" that renders a party incapable of assenting to marriage.[10] Most of the cases interpreting this provision have involved persons who were intoxicated at the time of the marriage.

lucid interval
A period of time during which a mentally ill or insane person had the mental capacity to understand what he or she was doing before the mental illness or insanity returned.

SUMMARY OF GROUND FOR ANNULMENT: MENTAL DISABILITY

Definition: A marriage in which one or both parties lacked the intent to marry because one or both were unable to understand the marriage contract and the duties of marriage at the time they attempted to enter the marriage due to mental illness, the influence of alcohol, or the influence of drugs.

Void or voidable: Voidable in most states.

Who can sue: In some states, only the mentally ill person (or his or her parent or guardian ad litem) can bring the annulment action. In other states, only the mentally healthy person can sue. In many states, either can sue; both have standing.

Major defenses:
1. The person was never mentally disabled.
2. The marriage occurred during a lucid interval.
3. After the marriage began, there was a lucid interval during which the parties freely cohabited.

Is this annulment ground also a ground for divorce? Yes, in most states.

© Cengage Learning 2013

Notes on Mental Illness

1. Mental illness can be an issue in different kinds of civil and criminal cases. The definition of mental illness may not be the same in all of these cases. A state may have one standard of mental illness that will disable a person from being able to marry, another standard that will disable a person from being able to enter an ordinary business contract and handle his or her business affairs, another standard that will disable a person from being able to write a will, and still another standard to determine whether a person has the mental capacity to commit a crime.

2. **Insanity** is any mental illness that negates a person's civil or criminal responsibility or capacity. There are four major tests that courts have used in criminal cases: (1) The *M'Naghten* "right-wrong" test: "[A]t the time of the committing of the act, the party accused was laboring under such a defect of reason, from disease of the mind, as not to know the nature and quality of the act he was doing, or if he did know it, that he did not know he was doing what was wrong."[11] (2) The *Durham* "diseased mind" test: "[A]n accused is not criminally responsible if his unlawful act was the product of mental disease or mental defect."[12] (3) The Model Penal Code test: "A person is not responsible for criminal conduct if at the time of such conduct as a result of mental disease or defect he lacks substantial capacity either to appreciate the criminality (wrongfulness) of his conduct or to conform his conduct to the requirements of the law."[13] (4) The irresistible impulse test: an urge to commit an act induced by a mental disease so that the person is unable to resist the impulse to commit the act even if he or she knows that the act was wrong.[14]

insanity
Mental illness that negates a person's civil or criminal responsibility or capacity. Also called *lunacy.*

DURESS

Duress is the unlawful use of force or threats that overcome our will so that we do something we do not want to do. Anyone forced to consent to marry does not have the requisite intent to be married. There are four main ways to commit duress: (a) physical violence, (b) threats of physical violence, (c) **malicious** or groundless threats of criminal prosecution, or (d) malicious or groundless threats of civil litigation.

Applying physical force or threatening its use is clearly sufficient for this ground. If an individual is faced with a choice between a wedding and a funeral and chooses the wedding, the resulting marriage will be annulled as one induced by duress. The same is true if the choice is between bodily harm and marriage.

duress
The unlawful use of force or threats that overcome the will so that a person does something he or she does not want to do. Illegal coercion.

malicious
1. Pertaining to a wrongful act that is done intentionally and without just cause or excuse.
2. Pertaining to conduct that is certain or almost certain to cause harm.

Suppose, however, that the choice does not involve violence or the threat of violence. The most common example is as follows:

> *George is courting Linda. They have sexual relations several times. Linda announces that she is pregnant. Linda's father is furious at George and threatens to "turn him in" to the county district attorney to prosecute him for the crime of statutory rape (Linda is underage). Furthermore, Linda and her father will sue George in the county civil court for support of the child. On the other hand, no criminal prosecution will be brought and no civil action will be initiated if George agrees to marry Linda. George agrees, and the wedding promptly takes place. After the wedding, it becomes clear that Linda was not pregnant; everyone made an honest mistake. George then brings an action to annul the marriage on the ground of duress.*

Most courts would rule against George and deny him the annulment if he had a choice in deciding whether to enter the marriage despite the threat of criminal and civil litigation. The court might rule differently if Linda's father held a gun on George and threatened to shoot him if he did not marry Linda. Faced with a literal "shotgun wedding," George has a good annulment case.

Coercion is measured by a **subjective standard**. The test is whether the innocent party's will was actually overcome when he or she entered the marriage. The test is not whether a reasonable person's will would have been overcome. Reasonableness is an **objective standard**. The test is not objective; it is subjective.

In most states, marriages induced by duress are voidable rather than void, but only the innocent party will have standing to bring the annulment action on that ground. If, however, this innocent party voluntarily cohabited with the "guilty" party (i.e., the one who did the coercing) after the effects of the duress have worn off, then the annulment action will be denied on the theory that there has been a ratification of the marriage.

subjective standard
A standard by which something is measured by what a particular person actually knew, felt, or did.

objective standard
A standard by which something is measured by comparing (1) what a person actually knew, felt, or did with (2) what a reasonable person would have known, felt, or done under the same circumstances.

ASSIGNMENT 6.6

Do you think that any of the following marriages could be annulled on the ground of duress? (See General Instructions for the Legal-Analysis Assignment in Appendix A.)

a. Rita married Dan after Dan threatened to kill Rita's second cousin if she did not marry him. The only reason Rita married Dan was to save her cousin's life.

b. Tom married Edna after Tom's very domineering father ordered him to marry her. Tom had been in ill health lately. Tom married Edna solely because he has never been able to say no to his father.

c. Paula married Charles after Paula's mother threatened suicide if Paula would not marry him. Paula married Charles solely to prevent the suicide.

SUMMARY OF GROUND FOR ANNULMENT: DURESS

Definition: A marriage in which a party lacked the intent to marry because he or she was induced to enter the marriage by the unlawful use of force or threats that overcame his or her will.

Void or voidable: Voidable in most states.

Who can sue: The party who was coerced. In some states, his or her parent or guardian ad litem also has standing.

Major defenses:

1. There was no physical violence or threat of it.

2. The plaintiff did not believe the threat of violence and therefore was not coerced by it.

3. This is the wrong plaintiff (e.g., this plaintiff has "dirty hands" and lacks standing because this is the party who used duress).

4. The plaintiff voluntarily cohabited with the defendant after the effects of the duress had worn off (ratification).

Is this annulment ground also a ground for divorce?
Yes, in some states.

FRAUD

Fraud is an intentionally false statement of fact that is material, made to induce reliance by the plaintiff, and results in harm because of the reliance. A valid marriage requires an intent to marry, but the intent is compromised if the decision to marry has a foundation in fraud. A spouse-to-be intends one thing and gets another! Generally, for fraud to be a ground of annulment, the defendant must intentionally misrepresent or conceal a critically important fact and the person deceived must rely upon this fact in the decision to enter the marriage.

Not every false representation, however, will be sufficient to grant an annulment. As one court put it:

> [T]he fact that a brunette turned to a blond overnight, or that the beautiful teeth were discovered to be false, or the ruddy pink complexion gave way suddenly to pallor, or that a woman misstated her age or was not in perfect health, would lead no court to annul the marriage for fraud.[15]

What kind of false representation *is* ground for an annulment? Many courts require the representation to be **material** and essential. A representation is material if it pertains to something that was significant or important enough to influence the decision to enter the marriage. Even a blatant and serious lie would *not* be material if a person knew about the lie and decided to enter the marriage anyway. A representation is essential if it pertains to the heart or core of the marital relationship. (This is the **essentials test**.) Most courts say that the essentials are those marital duties that relate to having future sexual relations and having children. An example would be a man who misrepresents his intention to have children or who conceals his venereal disease. In general, misrepresentations about one's wealth ("I'm very well off"), health ("I am cancer-free"), character ("I never drink"), or affection ("I love you very much") would *not* be about the essentials.

It should be noted, however, that some states take a broader view of what is essential. Such states say that something is essential if it is *vital* to the marriage relationship, which can encompass matters other than sexual relations and having children. An example is a misrepresentation about one's religion. Lying about whether one is a practicing Catholic or observant Jew, for example, might be considered vital to the marriage and serious enough to warrant the annulment on the ground of fraud.

Can a man obtain an annulment on the ground of fraud if his wife lied about whether she became pregnant by him before the marriage? If she is pregnant by another man and falsely tells her husband that he is the father, many states would grant the annulment on the ground of fraud.

The state of mind of the deceiving party is critical. In most states, there must be an *intentional misrepresentation* of fact or an *intentional concealment* of fact. See the first two forms of communication in Exhibit 6-4 on the methods by which false facts are communicated. The third and fourth forms (innocent nondisclosure and innocent misrepresentation) will not be sufficient in most states.

fraud
An intentionally false statement of fact that is material, and made to induce reliance by the plaintiff, and that results in harm because of the reliance. Also called deceit, misrepresentation.

material
Important enough to influence the decision that was made.

essentials test
Did the matter go to the heart or essence of the marriage relationship?

EXHIBIT 6-4 Forms of Communication in Fraud Cases	
1. Just before their marriage, Joe tells Mary that he is anxious to have children with her. In fact, he intends to remain celibate after their marriage.	1. Joe's statement about children is an *intentional misrepresentation* of fact.
2. Joe says nothing about his planned celibacy because he knows that if he tells Mary, she will not marry him. He says nothing about children or celibacy, and the subject never comes up prior to their marriage.	2. Joe's silence is an *intentional concealment* of fact.
3. Joe does not tell Mary that he intended to remain celibate because he incorrectly assumed that Mary already knew.	3. Joe's silence is an *innocent* (or *good faith*) *nondisclosure* of fact.
4. Just before their marriage, Joe tells Mary that he is physically unable to have sexual intercourse and therefore he will have to stay celibate. To his surprise, Joe later finds out that he is not impotent.	4. Joe's statement is an *innocent* (or *good faith*) *misrepresentation* of fact.

Sometimes it is difficult to categorize a misrepresentation. For example:

One hour after Joe marries Mary, he gets on a bus and disappears forever. They never had sexual intercourse before or after marriage and never discussed the subject.

From Joe's conduct, we may be able to draw an *inference* that at the time he married Mary, he never intended to consummate the marriage. More evidence of misrepresentation, however, would be needed to determine whether the annulment can be granted on this ground.

In most states, marriages induced by fraud are voidable rather than void, but only the innocent party will have standing to bring the annulment action on that ground. If, however, this innocent party voluntarily cohabited with the "guilty" party (i.e., the one who committed the fraud), then the annulment action will be denied on the theory that there has been a ratification of the marriage.

SUMMARY OF GROUND FOR ANNULMENT: FRAUD

Definition: A marriage in which one of the parties lacked the intent to marry because of an intentional misrepresentation or intentional concealment of a fact that was material and essential to the marriage.

Void or voidable: Voidable in most states.

Who can sue: The innocent party. In some states, his or her parent or guardian ad litem also has standing.

Major defenses:

1. The fraud was not about an essential fact.

2. The fraud was not material; the plaintiff did not rely on the fraud in his or her decision to marry.

3. The fraud occurred after the marriage was entered (again, no reliance).

4. The plaintiff may have relied on the fraud, but he or she was unreasonable in doing so.

5. After the plaintiff discovered the fraud, he or she consummated the marriage or otherwise freely cohabited with the fraudulent party (ratification).

6. The misrepresentation or nondisclosure was innocent; it was made in good faith with no intention to deceive.

7. This plaintiff has no standing to bring the annulment action, since the plaintiff was the deceiver.

Is this annulment ground also a ground for divorce? Yes, in a few states.

© Cengage Learning 2013

I Take This Man for Richer Only: Who Wants to Marry a Multimillionaire?

At one time, Fox TV aired a program called *Who Wants to Marry a Multimillionaire?* in which a bachelor selected a bride from among fifty contestants he had never met. Immediately after his selection, marriage vows were exchanged before 23 million viewers. Apparently, however, the honeymoon of the instant bride and groom did not go well. Soon after the newlyweds returned, the bride asked a Nevada court for an annulment based on fraud. They had not consummated their relationship. The bride became disenchanted when she learned that a prior girlfriend had obtained a restraining order against him for **domestic violence (DV)**. His failure to disclose his "history of problems with prior girlfriends," she told the court, constituted fraud. This was not a particularly strong argument, however, because she knew that one of the show's main attractions was that she was willing to take her chances. If she did not have all the facts needed to make the marriage decision, she arguably was willfully ignorant.

Nevertheless, the court granted the annulment. As a condition of appearing on the show, the bachelor and all the contestants signed individual premarital agreements in which they agreed not to challenge any annulment action that might be filed in the future. In granting the annulment, however, the court did not base its decision on this agreement. Indeed, it is doubtful that such

domestic violence (DV)
Actual or threatened injury or abuse of one member of a family or household by another member.

agreements are enforceable. As a matter of public policy, courts do not want to encourage the dissolution of marriages by the device of an agreement. (See Chapter 4 on premarital agreements.) Why then was the annulment granted, particularly when the factual basis for fraud was relatively weak? The answer is not clear. First of all, the Nevada hearing was **uncontested**. The husband neither appeared nor was represented by counsel. Hence, there was no opposition to the petition to annul on the ground of fraud. Nor did anyone appeal. There was no written opinion in which the trial judge laid out his rationale for granting the annulment. Some have speculated that the judge may have been influenced by the negative public outcry over what had taken place. Of course, if the annulment had been denied, the parties would not have been forced to stay married. The option of divorce would have been readily available.

uncontested
Unchallenged; without opposition or dispute.

ASSIGNMENT 6.7

a. Do you think the annulment could have been granted on the ground that the marriage was a sham? (See the General Instructions for the Legal-Analysis Assignment in Appendix A.)

b. Later we will study no-fault divorce, in which marital fault is no longer relevant to the granting of divorce. Is there any reason why we should not have a system of no-fault annulment?

c. Is it relevant that the winning contestant agreed to pose for *Playboy* soon after the annulment was granted?

The Tort of Fraud

Occasionally, spouses try to sue each other for the **tort** of fraud. In one case, a husband's fraud suit against his wife alleged that she falsely told him that she loved him and was sexually attracted to him. He said he would not have married her if he had known this. The court, however, dismissed the action. In Chapter 17, we will see that some tort actions are allowed between spouses (e.g., a civil battery action). Torts based on the loss of love, however, are generally not allowed. They are called **heart-balm actions**. In the fraud suit, the court said, "[w]ords of love, passion and sexual desire are simply unsuited to the cumbersome strictures of common law fraud and deceit. The idea that a judge, or jury of 12 solid citizens, can arbitrate whether an individual's romantic declarations at a certain time are true or false, or made with intent to deceive, seems almost ridiculously wooden."[16]

tort
A civil wrong (other than a breach of contract) that causes injury or other loss for which our legal system deems it just to provide a remedy such as damages. Injury or loss can be to the person (a personal tort), to movable property (a personal property tort), or to land and anything attached to the land (a real property tort).

heart-balm action
An action based on the loss of love and relationships—a broken heart (e.g., breach of promise to marry, alienation of affections, and seduction).

VIOLATION OF TECHNICAL/PROCEDURAL REQUIREMENTS

In Chapter 5, we examined technical or procedural requirements for entering a ceremonial marriage. Examples include obtaining a marriage license and observing a waiting period. Suppose that such requirements for a ceremonial marriage have been violated. What consequences follow?

- Len and Helen want their good friend Fred (a dentist) to marry them. Fred signs up with an online ministry, which ordains 10,000 ministers a month. He becomes "ordained" simply by typing his name and address on the ministry's online form and by sending in a fee. He then marries Len and Helen. Later, they learn that Fred's ordination did not meet the state's criteria to be authorized to perform marriage ceremonies.

- Joe and Mary live in a state that requires a three-day waiting period between the date a marriage license is issued and the date of the ceremony. Because they wish to be married right away, they find a minister who marries them on the same day they obtained the license.

Are these couples validly married? In most cases, a marriage is valid even when there has been a failure to comply with one of the technical/procedural requirements discussed in Chapter 5 for a ceremonial marriage. In general, noncompliance with the requirements for a ceremonial marriage cannot later be used as a ground for annulment or divorce. The policy of the law is to recognize the validity of a marriage whenever possible. Violating these requirements is simply not serious enough for a court to declare that a marriage is invalid, particularly when the parties have lived together as husband and wife for a long time, raised a family, and amassed considerable property in the process. Courts conclude that the legislature did not intend to impose the penalty of invalidity for violation of such requirements.

Not all states, however, take this position. In a minority of states, compliance with the technical/procedural requirements of the statute is mandatory. Yet, even these states provide a way to avoid invalidating the marriage. If "there is a defect in the license, or a defect in the marrying official, but the parties consummate their marriage in the good faith belief that they have been lawfully joined in marriage, then the marriage is valid despite their statutory noncompliance."[17]

ASSIGNMENT 6.8

Assume that a statute in a state provides as follows:

§ 10 No marriage shall be invalid on account of want of authority in any person solemnizing the same if consummated with the full belief on the part of the persons so married, or either of them, that they were lawfully joined in marriage.

George and Linda read a newspaper article stating that five of seven ministers connected with the Triple Faith Church in their state had been fined for illegally performing marriage ceremonies. A week later they are married by Rev. Smith, who is in charge of Triple Faith Church but who has no authority to marry anyone. Can the validity of their marriage be called into question under § 10? (See General Instructions for the Legal-Analysis Assignment in Appendix A.)

CHURCH ANNULMENT

The Roman Catholic Church has its own separate system of annulment, which it calls a *declaration of nullity*. The church does not recognize divorce. Nor does it recognize the annulments discussed in this chapter that are granted by the civil courts. Having a civil annulment does not automatically lead to a church annulment. In the eyes of the church, the only way to terminate a marriage (other than by the death of one of the parties) is by seeking a petition of nullity in a church court applying canon law. The court can declare the marriage "null." Technically, the church does not dissolve the marriage. Rather, it makes a finding that a valid sacramental marriage was not created or entered on the wedding day. This will allow a Catholic to remarry in the church, to receive communion, and to participate in all the other sacraments. Full participation is denied to a Catholic who remarries without obtaining a church annulment—even if he or she obtained a civil annulment.

The main ground for a church annulment is *defective consent*. "The consent must be an act of the will, . . . free of coercion or grave external fear."[18] Defective consent is usually due to "lack of due discretion" or "lack of due competence." A primary focus of the church court is whether the parties entered the marriage through a free act of the will with the intention to accept the essential elements of marriage: permanence, fidelity, and conjugal love that is open to having children. Among the factors that can interfere with this intention are duress, fraud, conditions to one's consent, and psychological problems such as mental illness.[19]

To initiate a church annulment, the petitioner pays a processing fee (approximately $500) in order to have a formal hearing presided over by a tribunal judge. An advocate presents the case of the petitioner seeking the annulment. Also present is a *defender of the bond*, who monitors the proceeding to ensure that rights are protected and church law properly observed. The hierarchy in Rome has criticized American bishops for allowing too many church annulments. Over 30,000 annulments are granted each year in the 119 dioceses of the United States. This constitutes 70 percent of the annulments granted by the church worldwide.

CONFLICT OF LAWS

A **conflict of laws** exists when there is an inconsistency between the laws of different legal systems, such as two states or two countries. For example, two states could have different minimum ages to marry or different consanguinity requirements. (See also Chapter 5 where we examined conflict of laws on the issue of common law marriage.)

In annulment cases, the most common conflicts question arises when the parties are married in one state and then move to another state where one of the parties seeks an annulment. If these two states do not have the same annulment law, a **choice of law** must be made between (1) the law of the state where the parties were married (called the *state of celebration* and also *lex loci celebrationis*, *state of contract*, and *lex loci contractus*) and (2) the law of the state where the parties have a permanent home (called the state of **domicile** or the **domiciliary state**). A **domiciliary** is a person domiciled in a particular place. For example:

> *Jim and Jane marry in State X, where their marriage is valid. They then move to State Y. If they had married in State Y, their marriage would not have been valid. Jim sues Jane in State Y for an annulment. What annulment law does the court in State Y apply—the law of State X or the law of State Y?*

State X is the state of celebration or the state of contract (i.e., the state where the parties entered the marriage contract). State Y is the domiciliary state (i.e., the state where the parties are now domiciled). The state where the parties file the suit is called the **forum** state. (Forum also refers to the court or tribunal hearing the case.) In our example, State Y is both the domiciliary state and the forum state.

To place this problem in a concrete perspective, assume that Jim dies **intestate** (i.e., without a valid will). Assume further that he has children from a prior marriage that ended in divorce but no children with his second spouse, Jane. Under the intestacy laws of most states, his spouse and children receive designated portions of his estate. If there is no spouse, the children have more of an estate to share. Therefore, it is in the interest of the children to claim that Jane cannot be the surviving spouse of Jim because they were never validly married. The success of this claim may depend on which law applies—that of State X or State Y.

conflict of laws
An inconsistency between the laws of different legal systems such as two states or two countries.

choice of law
A selection of which law to apply when a court is being asked to apply the law of two states or two countries.

domicile
The place where a person has been physically present with the intent to make that place a permanent home (or with no intent to make any other place a permanent home); the place to which one intends to return when away. A residence, on the other hand, is simply the place where you are living at a particular time. A person can have more than one residence, but generally can have only one domicile.

domiciliary state
The state where one has a domicile.

domiciliary
One who is domiciled in a particular place.

forum
(1) A court. (2) The place where the parties are presently litigating their dispute. (3) A court or tribunal hearing a case.

intestate
(1) Pertaining to someone who dies without a valid will. (2) A person who dies without a valid will.

CONFLICT-OF-LAWS RULE IN ANNULMENT ACTIONS

In Chapter 5, we discussed the general conflict-of-laws rule on the validity of marriage:

Conflict of Laws and the Validity of a Marriage

The validity of a marriage is determined by the law of the state in which the marriage was entered or contracted. Another state will recognize that marriage unless to do so would violate a strong **public policy** of the state asked to recognize it.

public policy

The principles inherent in the customs, morals, and notions of justice that prevail in a state; the foundation of public laws; the principles that are naturally and inherently right and just.

Exhibit 6-5 states this same rule, using the language of the domiciliary state.

In most states, the violation of public policy depends on whether the state would consider the marriage to be void or voidable. In such states, it is against the strong public policy of the domiciliary state to recognize what it considers to be a void marriage (even if it is valid in the state of celebration). The domiciliary state, however, will recognize a voidable marriage (if it is valid in the state of celebration).

- *Void marriages.* The domiciliary state would refuse to recognize a marriage that is valid in the state of celebration if that marriage would have been void if the parties had tried to enter it in the domiciliary state. It is against the strong public policy of the domiciliary state to be asked to recognize what it considers to be a void marriage even though it is valid in the state of celebration.

- *Voidable marriages.* The domiciliary state *would* recognize a marriage that is valid in the state of celebration even if that marriage would have been voidable if the parties had tried to enter it in the domiciliary state. It is not against the strong public policy of the domiciliary state to be asked to recognize what it considers to be a voidable marriage if it was valid in the state of celebration.

Let's apply these rules to the Jim and Jane example. The state of celebration is State X where their marriage is valid. Let's assume that Jim and Jane are first cousins and that their marriage does not violate the consanguinity laws of State X. Their marriage is valid in State X. Now we must ask whether State Y (the domiciliary state) considers marriages between first cousins to be void or voidable:

- *Void.* If State Y considers marriages between first cousins to be void, then it will refuse to recognize it. In the annulment action of Jim against Jane, the annulment would be granted because State Y would apply its own annulment law, not that of State X. It is against the strong public policy of State Y to recognize a marriage that it considers void even if it is valid in the state of celebration.

- *Voidable.* If State Y considers marriages between first cousins to be voidable, then it will recognize it. In the annulment action of Jim against Jane, the annulment would be denied because State Y would apply the law of State X where the marriage is valid. It is not against the strong public policy of State Y to recognize a marriage that it considers voidable if it is valid in the state of celebration.

EXHIBIT 6-5 Conflict of Laws and the Validity of a Marriage

A domiciliary state will recognize as valid a marriage that was entered in another state if (a) the marriage was valid in the state where it was entered and (b) recognizing the marriage would not violate a strong public policy of the domiciliary state. If both conditions are met, the domiciliary marriage will treat the marriage as valid *even if* the marriage would not have been valid if it had been entered in the domiciliary state.

MARRIAGE EVASION STATUTES

Next we consider the conflicts problem that occurs when the parties travel to another state solely to evade the marriage law of their own state.

> *Bob and Mary are domiciled in State A. They cannot marry in State A because they are underage. After checking the law of neighboring states, they discover that they would not be underage in State B. They go to State B and are married. (State B is the state of celebration.) After the marriage, they return to State A (the domiciliary state). Later, Mary sues Bob in State A for an annulment. What annulment law does the court in State A apply—the law of the domiciliary state (A) or the law of the state of celebration (B)?*

In this example, Bob and Mary went to the state of celebration solely to evade the marriage law of the domiciliary state. Several states have enacted *marriage-evasion* statutes to cover this situation. In such states, the choice of law depends upon the presence or absence of an intent to evade. The statute might provide that the domiciliary state will refuse to recognize the marriage if the parties went to the state of celebration for the purpose of evading the marriage laws of the domiciliary state to which they later returned. This is what arguably occurred in the case of Bob and Mary. Hence, if the domiciliary state (A) has a marriage-evasion statute, it would refuse to recognize the marriage and would grant the annulment to Mary. If, however, Bob can prove that they did not go to State B to evade the marriage law of State A, then State A would apply the law of the state of celebration (B) and deny the annulment.

It is sometimes very difficult to prove whether the parties went to the other state with the intent to evade the marriage laws of their domiciliary state. It may depend on circumstantial evidence such as how long they remained in the state of celebration and whether they returned to their initial domiciliary state or established a domicile in another state altogether. The interviewing and investigation checklist below is designed to assist you in collecting evidence on intent:

☑ INTERVIEWING AND INVESTIGATION CHECKLIST

Factors Relevant to the Intent to Evade the Marriage Laws

Assume that the parties live in State A but were married in State B. (See also the Interviewing and Investigation on determining domicile in Chapter 7.)

LEGAL INTERVIEWING QUESTIONS

1. How long have the two of you lived in State A?
2. Why didn't you marry in State A?
3. When did you decide to go to State B?
4. Have you or D (Defendant) ever lived in State B?
5. Do you or D have relatives in State B? In State A?
6. Were you or D born in State B? In State A?
7. On what date did you and D go to State B?
8. Did you sell your home or move out of your apartment in State A?
9. When you left State A, did you intend to come back?
10. After you arrived in State B, when did you apply for a marriage license?
11. On what date were you married?
12. While you were in State B, where did you stay? Did you have all your clothes and furniture with you?
13. Who attended the wedding ceremony in State B?
14. Did you and D have sexual relations in State B?
15. Did you or D work or apply for work in State B?
16. How long did you and D stay in State B?
17. Did you and D vote or pay taxes in State B?
18. Did you and D open a checking account in any bank in State B?
19. Did you obtain a library card in State B?
20. What bills did you pay while in State B?
21. Where did you and D go after you left State B?

POSSIBLE INVESTIGATION TASKS

- Obtain copies of all records that tend to establish the kind of contact the parties had with State B (e.g., motel receipts, bank statements, rent receipts, employment records).
- Interview friends, relatives, and associates of the parties to determine what light they can shed on the intent of the parties in going to State B.

Thus far our main focus has been on marriages that are valid in the state of celebration but invalid and annullable in the domiciliary state if they had been contracted in the domiciliary state (see Exhibit 6-6). Suppose, however, that the marriage was invalid in the state of celebration. The parties then move to a new state where they establish a domicile. If they had been married in their new domicile state, their marriage would have been valid. An annulment action is brought in their new domicile state (see Exhibit 6-7).

EXHIBIT 6-6   Marriages Valid in State of Celebration

© Cengage Learning 2013

EXHIBIT 6-7   Marriages Invalid in State of Celebration

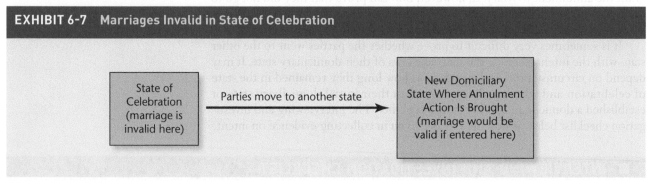

© Cengage Learning 2013

If a marriage is invalid where contracted (in the state of celebration), can it ever be recognized (considered valid) in any other state? Will a domiciliary state validate a marriage that is invalid according to the law of the state of celebration? Surprisingly, the answer is often yes. In some states, a domiciliary state will deny an annulment of a marriage that would have been valid if contracted in the domiciliary state but that is clearly invalid in the state where it was actually contracted. Such states take this position, in part because of the public policy (and indeed the presumption) favoring the validity of marriages.

CONSEQUENCES OF AN ANNULMENT DECREE

Many events usually occur between the time the parties enter an invalid marriage and the date of its annulment. What are the legal consequences of these events? In theory, an annulled marriage never existed. The old rule was that once a void or a voidable marriage was declared invalid, the declaration was **retroactive**; it related back to the time the parties attempted to enter the marriage. This rule, when strictly applied, resulted in some harsh consequences. Children born to parents before their marriage was annulled were, in effect, born out of wedlock and were **illegitimate children**. (They were referred to as "retroactive bastards.") Rigid application of the relation-back rule could also harshly impact support rights. Suppose that a woman lives with a man for 40 years before their marriage is annulled. She would not be entitled to support

retroactive
Applying to facts that arise before as well as after a particular event or date.

illegitimate child
Born to parents who are not married to each other and who never took the steps needed to legitimate the child. Also called nonmarital child, child of an informal relationship, child out of wedlock, child with no presumed father, bastard.

payments. A man has no duty to support someone who was never his wife! Clearly, these were unfair consequences, and all states have taken steps, often using the equity power of a court, to offset them. What follows is an overview of the present law in this area.

LEGITIMACY OF CHILDREN FROM AN ANNULLED MARRIAGE

Most states have passed statutes that declare the **legitimation** of children from an annulled marriage. Some of the statutes, however, are not absolute. For example, the statute might say that the children are legitimate only if one or both of the parents honestly believed that their marriage was valid when they entered it, or the statute might legitimate all the children born from an annulled marriage *except* when the annulment was granted on the ground of a prior existing marriage (bigamy).

CUSTODY AND CHILD SUPPORT

The courts handle child custody and child support in the same way in annulment cases and divorce cases. It makes no difference whether the parents have a valid marriage, an invalid marriage, or no marriage at all. Child-custody decisions are based on the best interests of the child, and child-support decisions are based on the support needs of the child within the framework of child-support guidelines. We will discuss child custody in Chapter 9 and child support in Chapter 10.

ALIMONY AND PROPERTY DIVISION

In some states, **alimony** cannot be awarded in annulment proceedings. In most states, however, statutes exist that allow alimony in such actions. This includes temporary alimony pending the final outcome of the action and permanent alimony following the annulment decree. It may be, however, that alimony will be denied to the "guilty" party (e.g., the party who committed the fraud, who used duress to pressure the other party to enter the marriage, or who committed other wrongful acts that created the ground for the annulment).

Another limitation on alimony in some states is that only defendants can receive it. By definition, the plaintiff seeking the annulment is saying that no marriage ever existed. A few courts say that it is inconsistent for the plaintiff to take this position and also to ask for alimony.

Similar problems exist with regard to the division of property that was accumulated during the marriage. Logically, if there was no marriage, there is no marital property to divide. Courts have devised various theories to provide a measure of fairness to the parties in annulment cases. For example, a court may refuse to apply the annulment retroactively so that property acquired during the marriage would be divided in a manner similar to property division upon divorce. Another form of relief is to allow a party to bring a suit on a theory of **implied-in-law contract** (also called *quasi contract*) to prevent **unjust enrichment**. Under this theory, the party may be able to obtain a return of goods acquired or the reasonable value of services provided during the relationship. Another theory that might allow marriage-like benefits such as a division of property acquired during the relationship is the putative-spouse doctrine. A **putative spouse** is a person who believes in good faith that he or she entered (and cohabited in) a valid marriage even though an impediment existed that rendered the marriage unlawful. An example of an impediment would be the existence of a prior existing marriage. For more on putative spouses, see Chapter 5. See also Chapter 4 where we discussed similar theories to obtain relief for parties who cohabited but never entered a valid marriage or never tried to enter one.

legitimation
1. The declaration that a child is legitimate. The verb is *legitimate*. 2. The steps taken to declare that a child is legitimate.

alimony
Money or other property paid in fulfillment of a duty to support one's spouse (or ex-spouse) after a legal separation, a divorce, or in some states, an annulment. Also called maintenance and spousal support.

implied-in-law contract
An obligation imposed by law to avoid unjust enrichment in the absence of an express or implied contract creating this obligation. Also called a quasi contract.

unjust enrichment
The receipt of a benefit in the form of goods or services from another when in fairness and equity the recipient should provide a return of the goods or compensation for the services even though there was no express or implied promise to do so. The amount the recipient should pay for services is called quantum meruit, the reasonable value of the services provided.

putative spouse
A person who believes in good faith that he or she entered (and cohabited in) a valid marriage even though an impediment made the marriage invalid. The marriage with such a spouse is called a putative marriage.

common law marriage

A marriage entered without license or traditional ceremony by persons who (a) agree to marry, (b) live together as husband and wife, and (c) hold themselves out as married. A marriage of two people who have not gone through a ceremonial marriage. Called "informal marriage" in Texas.

See also the discussion of **common law marriage** in Chapter 5. If a state recognizes common law marriages and the elements of such a marriage case be proven, a court might treat the annulled marriage as a common law marriage, which, upon its termination (divorce), can lead to alimony and property-division rights.

Where alimony is authorized in annulment actions, attorney fees might also be awarded. If so, the spouse able to pay, usually the husband, must pay the fees of the attorney for the other spouse in defending or initiating the annulment action.

PROBLEMS OF REVIVAL

Bob is validly married to Elaine. In 2008, they go through a valid divorce proceeding, which provides that Bob will pay Elaine alimony until she remarries. In 2010, Elaine marries Dan; Bob stops his alimony payments. In 2012, Elaine's marriage to Dan is annulled.

In this case, what is Bob's obligation to pay alimony to Elaine? Several possibilities exist:

- Option 1. Bob does not have to resume paying alimony. His obligation ceased forever when Elaine married Dan. The fact that the second marriage was annulled is irrelevant.

- Option 2. Bob does not have to resume paying alimony. Dan must start paying alimony in 2012 if the state authorizes alimony in annulment actions.

- Option 3. There is a **revival** of Bob's alimony obligation. Bob must resume paying alimony starting in 2012, the date of the annulment decree.

- Option 4. There is a revival of Bob's alimony obligation. Bob must resume paying alimony retroactive to when he stopped paying in 2010.

revival

Restoration of what was once inoperative or terminated.

Option 4 is the most logical. Because the technical effect of an annulment decree is to say that the marriage never existed, the decree should be retroactive to the date when Elaine and Dan entered the marriage that was later annulled. Although option 4 is the most logical of the four presented, it is arguably as unfair to Bob as option 1 is unfair to Elaine. Most states adopt options 2 or 3.

decedent

The person who has died; the deceased.

testate

(1) Pertaining to someone who dies with a valid will. (2) A person who dies with a valid will. Under this definition, also called the testator and, if female, the testatrix.

intestacy

The condition of dying without a valid will.

intestate succession

The transfer of a decedent's property to state-designated relatives of the decedent who dies without leaving a valid will. Also called descent and distribution or hereditary succession.

Uniform Probate Code

A law adopted by some states that covers (1) the probating of wills and (2) the distribution of the estate of persons who die without wills (intestate succession).

executor

A person designated in a will to carry out the terms of the will and handle related matters. If a female, this person is sometimes called an *executrix.*

trustee

The person or company holding legal title to property for the benefit of another.

conservator

A person appointed by the court to manage the affairs of persons who are not competent to do so on their own.

INHERITANCE

There are two main categories of **decedents**: those who die **testate** (leaving a valid will) and those who die intestate (without leaving a valid will). If a person dies testate, his or her estate is distributed according to the terms of the will. If a person dies intestate, his or her estate is distributed according to the laws of **intestacy**, which generally provide that a certain percentage of the estate goes to the surviving spouse, another percentage to children, etc. The transfer of property under these laws is called **intestate succession**.

Assume the marriage of a decedent has been annulled and that the decedent never remarried. What are the consequences if the decedent died intestate or if he or she died testate with a provision in the will to a "surviving spouse"?

- Intestate. A person who dies intestate does not have a surviving spouse if the marriage was annulled. An annulment (as well as a divorce) terminates mutual intestate rights of former spouses. Under the intestacy laws, all of the decedent's estate would go to other relatives such as children.

- Testate. The will of a person who dies testate does not have a surviving spouse if the marriage was annulled even if the will had a provision in it for a "surviving spouse." Under statutes such as the **Uniform Probate Code**, an annulment (or a divorce) automatically terminates or revokes provisions in a will for a surviving spouse unless the will specifically says otherwise. Furthermore, if before death the decedent had appointed his or her spouse as **executor**, **trustee**, or **conservator**, the annulment also automatically revokes these appointments.

WORKERS' COMPENSATION BENEFITS

Assume that a spouse is receiving **workers' compensation** benefits following the death of her husband, but that these benefits will cease when she remarries. If the second marriage is annulled, will the workers' compensation benefits be revived? Courts differ in answering this question. Some revive the benefits; some do not.

workers' compensation
A no-fault system of paying for medical care and providing limited wage benefits to a worker for an employment-related injury or illness regardless of who was at fault in causing the injury or illness.

CRIMINAL BIGAMY

Ed marries Diane. He leaves her without obtaining a divorce. He now marries Claire. This marriage to Claire is later annulled. He is charged with the crime of bigamy.

Can Ed use the defense that his marriage with Claire was annulled, and therefore, he was never married to Claire? Most of the cases that have answered this question have said that the subsequent annulment is *not* a defense to the bigamy charge.

INTERSPOUSAL IMMUNITY IN TORT ACTIONS

An **immunity** is a defense that prevents someone from being sued for what would otherwise be wrongful conduct. As we shall see in Chapter 17, spouses may have the benefit of an **interspousal immunity** that prevents certain kinds of tort litigation between spouses. The immunity does not cover property torts such as conversion and trespass. Spouses can still sue each other for property torts in most states. In some states, however, the immunity does cover personal torts such as the tort of assault.

Assume, for example, that George assaults his wife, Paulene, in a state where the interspousal immunity bars personal torts between spouses. She would not be able to sue him for the tort of assault in such states. She might be able to initiate a *criminal* action against him for the crime of assault or battery, but she could not bring a **civil** assault action against him.

Now assume that the marriage of George and Paulene is annulled. After the annulment, can Paulene sue George for an assault that occurred during the marriage? Because the annulment means that they were never validly married, the tort action for assault should, in theory, be allowed. Yet most courts would hold that the annulment does not wipe out the impact of the interspousal immunity for personal torts. Therefore, in such states, the assault action could not be brought; the immunity would bar the action despite the annulment.

There is no immunity, however, for torts committed *after* the parties go through an annulment or a divorce.

immunity
A defense that prevents someone from being sued for what would otherwise be wrongful conduct.

interspousal immunity
Spouses cannot sue each other for designated categories of torts. Also called *husband–wife immunity.*

civil
Pertaining to a private right or matter. Noncriminal; nonmilitary.

MARITAL COMMUNICATIONS PRIVILEGE

A **privilege** is a special legal benefit, right, exemption, or protection. Under the **marital-communications privilege**, a husband and a wife can refuse to disclose confidential communications between them during the marriage. The policy behind the privilege is to encourage open communication between spouses without fear that they might one day have to give court testimony about the communications. The privilege, however, does not apply to suits between the spouses themselves such as for divorce. The main value of the privilege is in third-party litigation. For example:

*Sam is married to Helen. Their marriage is annulled. A year later, Sam is sued by a neighbor who claims that Sam negligently damaged the neighbor's property. The alleged damage was inflicted while Sam was still married to Helen. At the trial, the neighbor calls (**subpoenas**) Helen as a witness and asks her to testify about what Sam told her concerning the incident while they were still living together.*

privilege
A special legal benefit, right, exemption, or protection. (See glossary for an additional definition.)

marital-communications privilege
A person can refuse to testify and can prevent his or her spouse or ex-spouse from testifying about any confidential communications made between them during the marriage. Also called *marital privilege* or *husband-wife privilege.*

subpoena
1. To command that someone appear at a certain time and place. 2. The command itself.

According to the marital-communications privilege, Helen can refuse to testify about what she and her husband told each other during the marriage. Their marriage, however, was annulled, so that in the eyes of the law they were never married. Does this change the rule on the privilege? Can Helen give this testimony? The answer is not clear; few cases have considered the issue. Of those that have, some have concluded that the annulment does not destroy the privilege, while others have reached the opposite conclusion.

INCOME TAX STATUS

A husband and wife can file a joint return so long as they were married during the taxable year. Suppose, however, that after 10 years of marriage and 10 years of filing joint returns, the marriage is annulled. Must the parties now file *amended* returns for each of those 10 years? Should the returns now be filed as separate returns rather than joint ones, again on the theory that the annulment meant the parties were never validly married? According to the Internal Revenue Service, you are considered unmarried for the whole year if you obtained a decree of annulment: "You must file amended returns [e.g., as a single taxpayer] for all tax years affected by the annulment not closed by the [three-year] period of limitations."[20]

ASSIGNMENT 6.9

How would the following two problems be resolved in your state? You may have to check both statutory law and case law. (See General Instructions for the State-Code Assignment and General Instructions for the Court-Opinion Assignment in Appendix A.)

a. Fred and Jill are married. Fred is killed in an automobile accident with a truck of the ABC Tire Company. Jill brings a wrongful death action against the ABC Tire Company. The attorney of ABC learns that Jill was married to someone else at the time she married Fred. The attorney claims that Jill cannot bring the wrongful death action, since she was never validly married to Fred.

b. Bob and Mary are married. Bob dies intestate. Mary claims Bob's estate (i.e., his property) pursuant to the state's intestate law. Bob's only other living relative, Fred, claims that he is entitled to Bob's estate. Fred argues that Mary is not entitled to any of Bob's property because the marriage between Bob and Mary was invalid and should be annulled.

ASSIGNMENT 6.10

Prepare a flowchart of annulment litigation in your state. (See General Instructions for the Flowchart Assignment in Appendix A.)

■ PARALEGAL ROLES

- For an overview of paralegal roles in family-law cases, see Exhibits 1-3 and 1-4 in Chapter 1.
- For all financial issues covered in Chapter 6, a paralegal may be asked to help collect documents and facts outlined in:
  - the checklist in Exhibit 3-1 of Chapter 3
  - the interrogatories in Appendix C

- The interviewing and investigation checklist in Chapter 5 also covers fact-finding roles of paralegals.
- Investigate facts that are relevant to the grounds for annulment.
- Draft pleadings for the annulment action.
- Provide referrals to religious annulments.

- Administrative Agency Roles. Although only courts can grant annulments, administrative agencies often play a large role in family-law practices that handle annulment cases. A major reason many people seek annulments is to obtain government benefits such as workers' compensation and Social Security and to avoid adverse decisions from the agencies such as the U.S. Citizenship and Immigration Services.
  - Obtain needed forms from administrative agencies (often available online).
  - Research administrative regulations of the agency (also often online).
  - Determine status of client's application for the benefit or other result sought at the agency.

■ CHECK THE CITE

The *Bonney* case involves the tax liability of a taxpayer who obtained an annulment of his marriage. On what ground did Theordore Bonney obtain the annulment? What tax deduction did he claim because of the fraud? How did the court rule on his claim? See *Bonney v. Commissioner of Internal Revenue*, 247 F.2d 237 (2d Cir. 1957). To read the opinion online: (1) Run a citation search ("247 F.2d 237") in the Legal Documents database of Google Scholar (scholar.google.com). (2) Run this search in the general search engines of Google or Bing: "247 F.2d 237."

■ PROJECT

In the Articles database of Google Scholar (scholar.google.com), enter the search: aa annulment (substitute the name of your state for "aa"). Give the citation of three articles that discuss the law of annulment in your state. Provide a short summary of what each article says about annulment in the state. For some articles, you may be given only the first page of the article. If so, base your summaries on what is provided. Avoid articles that do not clearly indicate on the first page of the article that it covers annulment in your state.

■ ETHICS IN A FAMILY LAW PRACTICE

You are a paralegal working at a law office that is representing Mary Smith in her annulment action against Paul Smith. The case is uncontested. Both parties want the annulment. After a state trial court grants the annulment, Paul Smith asks you to represent him as an independent paralegal in the petition he now wants to file for an annulment from the Catholic Church. Are there any ethical problems in your doing so?

■ WRITING SAMPLE

Draft a complaint for Elaine for her annulment action based on the facts in Assignment 6.4a. Assume she files an action for annulment, which Philip opposes. (See General Instructions for the Writing Sample in Appendix A. Also check the General Instructions for the Complaint-Drafting Assignment in Appendix A.)

SUMMARY

A divorce is a termination of a valid marriage. An annulment is a declaration that the parties were never validly married. A legal separation is a declaration by a court that parties can live separate and apart even though they are still married to each other. For convenience, we refer to an annulled marriage, although it would be more accurate to call it an alleged or purported marriage. The effective date of an annulment is the date the parties entered the marriage, not the date of the annulment decree. To obtain an annulment, a party must establish grounds and must have standing. Some grounds render a marriage void; others will render it voidable. A voidable marriage is valid unless it is cancelled or annulled by a court. A void marriage is invalid whether or not a court declares it so. Voidable marriages can be annulled after death; void marriages cannot. Voidable marriages can be ratified; void marriages cannot. If a party lacks standing, a marriage by estoppel may occur, which is a relationship that is recognized as a marriage because a party is prevented from asserting the invalidity of the marriage even though grounds for its invalidity may exist.

There are five grounds relating to the legal capacity to marry:

1. *Gender.* The state does not allow opposite-sex marriage.
2. *Prior existing marriage.* At the time of the marriage, a prior marriage had not been terminated.
3. *Consanguinity and affinity.* The parties married in violation of a prohibition against the marriage of certain categories of individuals who are too closely related to each other.
4. *Nonage.* A party was underage at the time of the marriage.
5. *Physical disability.* A party had a specified disease or was impotent at the time of the marriage.

There are four grounds relating to the intent to marry:

1. *Sham marriage.* The parties never intended to marry, i.e., to live together as husband and wife.
2. *Mental disability.* At the time of the marriage, a party was incapable of understanding the nature and duties of the marriage relationship.
3. *Duress.* A party was induced to enter the marriage by the unlawful use of force or threats that overcame his or her will.
4. *Fraud.* A party intentionally misrepresented or concealed a fact that was material and essential to the marriage.

Under the last-in-time marriage presumption, if more than one marriage is alleged to exist, the most recent marriage is presumed to be valid. Under the Enoch Arden presumption, a spouse is considered dead after being missing without explanation for a designated number of years despite due diligence in attempting to locate him or her. In most states, violations of the technical/procedural requirements for a ceremonial marriage are not grounds for annulment.

Under conflict-of-law principles, a marriage will be considered valid in a domiciliary state if (a) the marriage is valid according to the state where it was contracted and (b) recognizing the validity of the marriage would not violate a strong public policy of the domiciliary state. If both conditions are met, the domiciliary state will deny the annulment even though the marriage could have been annulled if it had been contracted in the domiciliary state. Generally, if a marriage would have been void had it been contracted in the domiciliary state, the latter state will not apply the law of the state of celebration, where the marriage is valid.

Some states have statutes that invalidate marriages contracted in other states solely to evade the domiciliary state's marriage laws. Some states will validate a marriage contracted in another state (even though the marriage is invalid in the state where it was contracted) so long as the marriage would have been valid if it had been contracted in the state where the parties are now domiciled. In effect, this state will deny the annulment even though the state of celebration would have granted it.

In most states, children born from an annulled marriage are considered legitimate. In an annulment proceeding, the court must award custody of the children and provide for their support. If the state does not allow alimony or property division in annulment cases, the court might use the theory of implied-in-law contract to prevent unjust enrichment. Other possible theories to consider are putative spouse and common law marriage.

If a divorced person's second marriage is annulled, states disagree on whether benefits and duties arising from the divorce in the first marriage are revived. Revival issues might also arise in cases that involve inheritance, workers' compensation, criminal bigamy, tort liability, marital-communications privilege, and income tax status.

KEY TERMS

annulment	bigamy	lucid interval
divorce	polygamy	insanity
legal separation	prosecution	duress
no-fault divorce	presumption	malicious
canon law	rebut	subjective standard
ecclesiastical	rebuttable presumption	objective standard
nullity	last-in-time marriage	fraud
declaratory judgment	presumption	material
purported	Enoch Arden presumption	essentials test
grounds	due diligence	domestic violence (DV)
void	consanguinity	uncontested
voidable	affinity	tort
voidable marriage	half-blood	heart-balm action
void marriage	full-blood	conflict of laws
void ab initio	incest	choice of law
ratification	nonage	domicile
cohabit	impotence	domiciliary state
standing	copulate	domiciliary
guardian ad litem (GAL)	sterility	forum
dirty hands	triennial cohabitation	intestate
estopped	sham	public policy
marriage by estoppel	alien	retroactive
impediment	green-card marriage	illegitimate child
capacity	statutory rape	legitimation

alimony
implied-in-law contract
unjust enrichment
putative spouse
common law marriage
revival
decedent

testate
intestacy
intestate succession
Uniform Probate Code
executor
trustee
conservator

workers' compensation
immunity
interspousal immunity
civil
privilege
marital-communications privilege
subpoena

REVIEW QUESTIONS

1. How do annulment, divorce, and legal separation differ?
2. Why are few annulments granted today?
3. Why is it important to understand annulment law despite the fact that few annulments are currently granted?
4. What is the historical origin of annulments?
5. What are some of the common terms for an annulment action?
6. Why is it technically incorrect to refer to an "annulled marriage"?
7. What is the effective date of an annulment?
8. What are the main grounds that render a marriage void?
9. What are the main grounds that render a marriage voidable?
10. What is the distinction between a voidable and a void marriage?
11. Can a marriage be annulled after the death of a spouse?
12. When can an annullable marriage be ratified?
13. What is standing?
14. What is a guardian ad litem?
15. What is a marriage by estoppel?
16. What are the capacity grounds for annulment?
17. What are the intent/state-of-mind grounds for annulment?
18. When can a same-sex marriage be annulled?
19. When can a prior existing marriage (bigamy) be the basis of an annulment?
20. What is the last-in-time presumption?
21. How does the Enoch Arden presumption affect annulments?
22. When can consanguinity and affinity be the basis of an annulment?
23. When can nonage be the basis of an annulment?
24. When can physical disabilities be the basis of an annulment?
25. When can sham marriage be the basis of an annulment?
26. How do immigration officials attempt to identify marriages that are not entered in good faith?
27. When can mental disability be the basis of an annulment?
28. What is a lucid interval?
29. When can duress be the basis of an annulment?
30. When can fraud be the basis of an annulment?
31. Can an annulment be granted on the grounds that the parties failed to comply with the technical/procedural requirements for a ceremonial marriage?
32. What is the main ground for an annulment in the Catholic Church?
33. What is meant by conflict of laws?
34. What is the general conflict-of-laws rule in marriage validity cases?
35. What is a marriage-evasion statute?
36. When will a domiciliary state recognize an out-of-state marriage if the marriage is valid in the state of celebration but would have been invalid if entered in the domiciliary state?
37. What effect does an annulment have on the legitimacy of children?
38. What effect does an annulment have on child custody and child support?
39. Can there be alimony and property division in an annulment action?
40. How can an implied-in-law contract provide a remedy in an annulment action?
41. When can the putative-spouse doctrine and common law marriage provide alternative remedies?
42. What is the problem of revival and how do different states handle it?
43. In what way can annulment affect intestate succession, workers' compensation, criminal bigamy, interspousal tort immunity, the marital-communications privilege, and income tax status?

HELPFUL WEBSITES

Annulment Overview

- www.nolo.com/legal-encyclopedia/annulment-vs-divorce-30234.html
- www.expertlaw.com/library/family_law/annulment.html
- www.womansdivorce.com/marriage-annulment.html
- marriage.about.com/cs/annulments/a/annulments.htm
- en.wikipedia.org/wiki/Annulment

Green-Card Marriage

- en.wikipedia.org/wiki/Green_card_marriage
- www.immihelp.com/greencard/familybasedimmigration/persons-in-us.html

Church Annulment

- www.newadvent.org/cathen/07695a.htm
- www.ewtn.com/expert/answers/annulment.htm
- en.wikipedia.org/wiki/Annulment_(Catholic_Church)

Google/Bing/Yahoo Searches

(on these search engines, run the following searches, substituting your state for "aa")

- annulment aa
- void marriage aa
- bigamy aa
- revival annulment aa
- Catholic annulment aa
- fraud annulment aa
- Enoch Arden annulment aa
- green card marriage aa

ENDNOTES

Note: All or most of the court opinions in these endnotes can be read online. To do so, go to Google Scholar (scholar.google.com), select "Legal documents," and in the search box, enter the cite (e.g., "104 N.W.2d 8") or name of the case (e.g., "Johnson v. Johnson") that is given in the endnote.

[1] Jennifer Leavitt-Wipf, *Marriage for a Green Card* (2008) (www.knowitallmall.com/od/familybased/a/marriagefraud.htm).

[2] John Wetenhall, *Alleged Bigamist's Defense: Never Married to First Wife* (Aug. 4, 2010) (abcnews.go.com/US/alleged-facebook-bigamists-defense-marriage-legal/story?id=11306824).

[3] West Virginia Code § 16-3C-2(g)(1) (1966) (www.wvfuneralboard.com/Portals/WVFuneralBoard/docs/Laws/163c.pdf).

[4] Bernard Turnock and Chester Kelly, *Mandatory Premarital Testing. . .*, 261 Journal of the American Medical Association 3415 (Jun. 15, 1989) (www.ncbi.nlm.nih.gov/pubmed/2635877).

[5] Illinois Compiled Statutes, 750 ILCS 5/204 (from Ch. 40, par. 204) (www.ilga.gov/legislation/ilcs/ilcs.asp).

[6] Nina Bernstein, *Do You Take This Immigrant?* N.Y. Times, June 13, 2010 at 31; James A. Jones, *The Immigration Marriage Fraud Amendments: Sham Marriages or Sham Legislation?* (1997) (www.law.fsu.edu/journals/lawreview/frames/243/jonefram.html) (8 U.S.C. §§ 1154, 1184, 1186a (1994)).

[7] Tess Townsend, *Get Married, Save Thousands on Tuition*, N.Y. Times, Feb. 6, 2011, at A27 (www.nytimes.com/2011/02/06/us/06bcmarriage.html).

[8] *What's the Matter With Kansas?*, editorial, N.Y. Times, Aug. 31, 2005, at A18.

[9] *Johnson v. Johnson*, 104 N.W.2d 8, 14 (N.D. 1960).

[10] Nevada Revised Statutes, § 125.330 (www.leg.state.nv.us/nrs/NRS-125.html#NRS125Sec330).

[11] *M'Naghten's Case*, 10 Clark & F. 200, 8 Eng. Rep. 718 (1843).

[12] *Durham v. United States*, 214 F.2d 862, 874–75 (D.C. Cir. 1954). See also *United States v. Brawner*, 471 F.2d 969 (D.C. Cir. 1972).

[13] Model Penal Code § 4.01. (law.fordham.edu/assets/Faculty/model_penal_code_selected_sections(1).pdf).

[14] Findlaw (criminal.findlaw.com/crimes/more-criminal-topics/insanity-defense/irresistible-impulse-test.html).

[15] Quoted in Philip Ryan & David Granfield, *Domestic Relations* 136 (1963).

[16] *Askew v. Askew*, 22 Cal. App. 4th 942, 959 (Cal. App. 4 Dist., 1994).

[17] John DeWitt Gregory et al., *Understanding Family Law* 38 (3d ed. 2005).

[18] *Catechism of the Catholic Church*, para. 1628 (2d ed. 1994) (www.vatican.va/archive/ENG0015/_INDEX.HTM).

[19] Rev. Michael Smith Foster, *How Is a Marriage Declared Null?* (www.bostoncatholic.org/Offices-And-Services/Office-Detail.aspx?id=11856&pid=1408).

[20] *Divorce or Separated Individuals*, 3, Publication 504 (Internal Revenue Service, 2009) (www.irs.gov/pub/irs-pdf/p504.pdf).

Divorce Grounds and Procedure

CHAPTER OUTLINE

CHAPTER OBJECTIVES

After completing this chapter, you should be able to:

- Know the three eras of divorce in our legal history.
- Distinguish between limited and absolute divorce.
- Explain why states added no-fault grounds for divorce.
- Describe the role of marital misconduct in a no-fault divorce.

- Describe the main no-fault grounds for divorce.
- Describe the main fault grounds for divorce and their defenses.
- Distinguish legal separation, separate maintenance, and divorce.

- Explain how domicile is determined.
- Know the meaning of full faith and credit.
- Explain what is meant by divisible divorce.
- Identify the three main kinds of jurisdiction.

- Know the kind of jurisdiction a court needs to dissolve a marriage and how it obtains this kind of jurisdiction.
- Know the kind of jurisdiction a court needs to order spousal support, child support, and property division and how it obtains this kind of jurisdiction.
- Explain when a party will be prevented from attacking the jurisdiction of a court that issued a divorce judgment.
- Distinguish between a direct and a collateral attack.

- Know when a state is a home state for purposes of child-custody jurisdiction.
- Know how venue is determined.
- Explain summary dissolution.
- State the requirement of procedural due process in divorce cases.
- Explain the options available for legal services in a divorce case.
- Describe the role of a guardian ad litem (GAL).
- Identify the components of a divorce complaint/petition.
- Know when a court will issue a default divorce.

- Explain what happens at a pretrial conference.
- Describe the main methods of discovery in divorce cases.
- List some of the major preliminary orders.
- Summarize what occurs in a divorce trial.
- Explain the main methods of alternative dispute resolution (ADR).
- Identify the major remedies available to enforce a divorce judgment.
- Describe divorce in the Jewish and Islamic traditions and know whether such traditions can be enforced in civil courts.

divorce

A declaration by a court that a validly entered marriage is terminated so that the parties are no longer married to each other. Also called dissolution, marital dissolution, *divorce a vinculo matrimonii* (divorce from the chains of marriage).

INTRODUCTION

Marriage can be dissolved in three ways: death of one of the spouses, annulment, or **divorce**. A divorce is a declaration by a court that a validly entered marriage (opposite-sex and same-sex) is terminated so that the parties are no longer married to each other. In this chapter, we cover the termination of a marriage. In separate chapters, we will examine in detail the topics of spousal support and property division (Chapter 8), child custody (Chapter 9), and child support (Chapter 10). In Chapter 5, we covered the termination of civil unions and domestic partnerships.

OVERVIEW

The history of divorce in the United States has gone through three main eras:

- The era of *restrictive divorce*, when it was very difficult to obtain a divorce because of the need to prove marital wrongdoing (fault). A dominant theme of divorce law was morality. Divorces were granted for specific wrongdoing (immorality) such as adultery, cruelty, and desertion.

collusive divorce

A divorce obtained in a proceeding in which the husband and wife agreed to lie to the court in order to facilitate the granting of the divorce.

grounds

Reasons that are legally sufficient to obtain a particular remedy or result.

no-fault divorce

A divorce that is granted without having to prove marital wrongs that caused the break-up.

- The era of *collusive divorce*, when a very large number of spouses lied to the court in order to make it appear that the fault **grounds** for divorce existed. Lying was one way to get around the often onerous, expensive, and debilitating task of proving whose fault caused the breakup. Lying was also common when parties wanted to bypass a procedural requirement for obtaining a divorce in their state.

- The era of *unilateral divorce*, when most divorces could be granted even if only one spouse wanted to terminate the marriage. Under a system of **no-fault divorce**, either party could precipitate the divorce without having to prove the marital wrongs that caused the break-up. The dominant theme of divorce law shifted from fault (who was in the wrong) to economics (how will the parties be supported and how should marital property be divided). It takes two people to create a marriage, but in the era of unilateral divorce, it can take only one of them to dissolve it by divorce.[1]

These are some of the themes we will be examining in this chapter.

HISTORICAL BACKGROUND

Under early English law, marriage law was within the province of the **ecclesiastical** courts of the Roman Catholic Church, which applied its own **canon law**. To understand church law in this area, we need to distinguish two kinds of divorce:

- **Limited divorce.** A declaration by a court that the spouses can live apart although they are still married to each other. Also called legal separation, judicial separation, separation from bed and board, and *divorce a mensa et thoro* (divorce from board and hearth).
- **Absolute divorce.** A declaration by a court that the marriage is terminated so that the parties can remarry. Also called complete divorce and *divorce a vinculo matrimonii* (divorce from the chains of marriage).

Canon law considered marriage to be a sacrament and an indissoluble bond. Hence, ecclesiastical courts were restricted to granting limited divorces; they could not grant an absolute divorce. They could, however, grant an annulment on the basis that a valid marriage never existed. Only an annulment would allow the parties to remarry.

One consequence of the Protestant Reformation in the sixteenth century was that the ecclesiastical courts began to lose their exclusive jurisdiction over divorce. As the secular courts took over, absolute divorce became possible so long as marital fault (e.g., adultery, cruelty, and desertion) could be established. In early American history, the New England colonies gave the legislature the power to grant an absolute divorce (called a legislative divorce), although such divorces were rarely granted. Eventually, this power was given to the courts, often the courts of equity.[2]

THE SHIFT FROM FAULT TO NO-FAULT DIVORCE

For many years, the main grounds for divorce were those based on fault, the premise being that a marriage should not be terminated unless there was evidence of serious wrongdoing by one of the spouses; in other words, blame had to be established. The fact that a couple could no longer get along was not enough of a reason to grant a divorce unless such wrongdoing existed. As one court commented in the mid-1950s:

> Testimony which proves merely an unhappy union, the parties being high strung temperamentally and unsuited to each other and neither being wholly innocent of the causes which resulted in the failure of their marriage, is insufficient to sustain a judgment.[3]

Many believed that stringent divorce laws would help prevent the failure of marriages. Even when serious misconduct was alleged, states often required **corroboration** (additional evidence) of the misconduct. In our early history, only the innocent party—the spouse who was not at fault in the breakdown of the marriage—could obtain a divorce. The innocent party could receive alimony, a favorable division of the marital property, and custody of the children. The guilty or at-fault party was punished on the issues of support, property division, and child custody. If a divorce was granted, it was common to deny the guilty spouse the right to remarry. In short, guilt, wrongdoing, and punishment were predominant themes of our divorce laws.

Fault-based divorce also encouraged widespread dishonesty. Over 90 percent of the divorces were **uncontested**, meaning that there was no dispute between the parties. The percentage of uncontested divorces was so high in large part because parties often flagrantly lied to the courts (committed **perjury**) about the facts of their case in order to quickly establish that fault existed or that they met the procedural requirements for a divorce. While such conduct was obviously illegal, the parties were seldom caught. Both sides wanted the divorce, so there was little incentive to reveal the truth. Judges were not unaware of what was going on; many simply looked the other way. The fault system also encouraged **migratory divorces**, where one of the parties would "migrate" or travel to

ecclesiastical
Pertaining to the church.

canon law
Church or ecclesiastical law.

corroboration
Additional evidence of a fact in dispute.

uncontested
Unchallenged; without opposition or dispute.

perjury
Making a false statement under oath concerning a material matter with the intent to provide false testimony. Also called false swearing.

migratory divorce
A divorce obtained in a state to which one or both of the spouses traveled before returning to their state of domicile.

another state solely to take advantage of its more lenient divorce laws before returning to his or her own state. Some of these states gained the reputation of being divorce mills. At one time, a favorite destination for a "quickie" divorce was Reno, Nevada, where someone could "take the cure" (as a Reno divorce was known) by meeting Nevada's minimal procedural requirements.[4]

contested

Challenged; opposed or disputed.

On those occasions when a divorce action was **contested**, court proceedings sometimes resembled a soap opera. A famous attorney, looking back over his long career, recalled the time when an indignant woman accused of infidelity broke down on the witness stand and screamed, "What you say isn't true. I've been faithful to my husband dozens of times."[5] In a similar vein, another attorney commented that for decades New York's divorce system was "built on a foundation of winks and falsehoods. If you wanted to split quickly, you and your spouse had to give one of the limited number of allowable reasons—including adultery, cruelty, imprisonment or abandonment—so there was a tendency to pick one out of a hat. Pregnant women have insisted they have not had sex in a year, one of the existing grounds; spouses claimed psychological cruelty for getting called fat; and people whose affairs have made [the society column] denied adultery. One legendary ploy involved listing the filing lawyer's secretary as the partner in adultery (which may even have been true in a few cases)."[6] In this environment, Elizabeth Gilbert, author of the international best seller *Eat, Pray, Love* had offered this caution in her book, "Here I pause to offer a prayer for my gentle reader: may you never, ever, have to get a divorce in New York."[7] Unfortunately, the trauma and chaos experienced by parties within the fault system of divorce were not unique to New York.

Reform was obviously needed. In 1969, California enacted the first no-fault divorce law in the country. Soon other states followed. Today no-fault grounds exist in every state. Some states have eliminated the word "divorce" and replaced it with the word **dissolution** as a symbolic gesture that a new day had arrived. The change from fault to no-fault dramatically increased the rate of divorce in the country. In the years between 1970 and 1996, the number of divorced people living in the country more than quadrupled, from 4.3 million to 18.3 million.[8] Estimates vary on the number of all current marriages that will eventually end in divorce. The range of estimates is between 40 and 50 percent. Many researchers believe that the more accurate estimate is 41 percent.[9]

dissolution

A divorce. A court's termination of a marriage for specified grounds. In a few states, however, a divorce is the result of a court proceeding in which one spouse establishes grounds against the other, whereas a dissolution is the result of a joint petition in which both spouses ask the court for the same relief pursuant to the separation agreement that they have negotiated.

CAUTIONARY NOTE

Not everyone, however, has been happy with the shift to no-fault divorce. There are social conservatives who regret that marriage is now so easy to dissolve. No-fault divorce has also removed an emotional outlet. Some clients want and need the opportunity to tell the world about the abuse they have received from their spouse. They become frustrated when they learn that they cannot do so in divorce court. In this sense, no-fault divorce prevents some spouses from attaining "emotional closure" through the divorce.[10] Finally, it has been argued that the end of fault grounds has placed some wives at a disadvantage. With divorce now so easy to obtain, a husband who wants to get out of the marriage does not have to bargain so hard on the issues of spousal support, child custody, and property division. If, however, the husband wants to stay in the marriage (and if he is the more powerful of the spouses), it may be that no-fault divorce can give the bargaining edge to the wife:

> In the United States, the availability of divorce has increased with unilateral divorce, which allows either member of the couple to dissolve the union. The change has been associated with lower rates of female suicide and domestic violence, and fewer wives murdered by their husbands. Unilateral divorce shifts the bargaining power to the person who is getting less out of the marriage and thus is most likely to leave. The partner getting more from the marriage has to work harder to keep the other person around, which can be good for the marriage and good for the couple. In other words, unilateral divorce benefits victims and potential victims.[11]

A RETURN TO FAULT?

In a few states (e.g., Louisiana), conservatives were able to reintroduce fault grounds into the law of divorce. In these states, parties wishing to marry can choose a conventional or standard marriage (which can be dissolved with no-fault grounds) and a **covenant marriage** (which requires a separation or fault grounds to dissolve). Not many states, however, allow covenant marriages, and few couples choose them in states that do allow them. See Chapter 5 for a discussion of covenant marriages.

THE ROLE OF MARITAL MISCONDUCT IN NO-FAULT DIVORCE

No-fault divorce does not always mean that marital fault has no role in divorce litigation. For some of the no-fault grounds (e.g., incompatibility and irreconcilable differences), it will be very difficult, if not impossible, to describe the facts that support the grounds without alleging who was at fault in creating those facts. Also, as we will see in later chapters, evidence of fault can be very important in child-custody disputes. Although a court's decisions on property division are generally unrelated to fault, there are some "economic faults" that can be considered, such as **dissipation**, which occurs when a spouse squanders marital assets just before or during the divorce litigation. According to the president of the American Academy of Matrimonial Lawyers, "No-fault does not mean that fault is irrelevant." On child-custody issues, it can be very important to introduce evidence that the opposing spouse has shown bad behavior in front of the children or that the spouse has an untreated substance abuse problem. Lying about money can also be key. "Once you catch them in one lie, nothing else they say is credible to the judge."[12]

Also, most states have retained the fault grounds for divorce along with the no-fault grounds. (See Exhibit 7-1). A party filing for divorce can choose which grounds to use. Most choose no-fault grounds. Some no-fault grounds, however, require the parties to have lived apart for designated periods of time, a requirement that most fault grounds do not have. A party might chose a fault ground to avoid this separation or waiting period.

A spouse might **plead** a no-fault ground and in the alternative plead a fault ground. This is done in the hope that the evidence of fault will lead to a more favorable ruling on other issues such as property division and child custody.

Finally, some states allow spouses to bring **tort** actions against each other in the divorce action. A tort is a civil wrong (other than a breach of contract) that causes injury or other loss for which our legal system deems it just to provide a remedy such as damages. By definition, a tort is wrongful conduct. Examples include the torts of fraud and intentional infliction of emotional distress. When, for example, Governor McGreevey of New Jersey and his wife divorced, one of his wife's claims was that he had committed the tort of fraud by tricking her into marrying a gay man who needed a wife to advance his political career. When a tort action such as this can be brought, it is not inconsistent for it to be brought at the same time that the parties are seeking a no-fault divorce. Not all tort actions, however, are allowed between spouses, as we will see when we discuss immunity and marital torts in Chapter 17.

covenant marriage
A form of ceremonial marriage (a) that is entered upon proof of premarital counseling and a promise to seek marital counseling when needed during the marriage, and (b) that is dissolved upon separation for a designated period or upon proof of marital fault. Also called high-test marriage.

dissipation
The improper reduction or waste of marital assets that should have been available for property division upon divorce.

plead
1. To file a pleading, a formal document that asserts or responds to claims or defenses.
2. To make a formal assertion or response.

tort
A civil wrong (other than a breach of contract) that causes injury or other loss for which our legal system deems it just to provide a remedy such as damages. Injury or loss can be to the person (a personal tort), to movable property (a personal property tort), or to land and anything attached to the land (a real property tort).

EXHIBIT 7-1 Grounds for Divorce

Major No-Fault Grounds for Divorce	Major Fault Grounds for Divorce
• Living apart	• Adultery
• Incompatibility	• Cruelty
• Irreconcilable differences	• Desertion

> ### ASSIGNMENT 7.1
>
> **a.** In your state code, find the statute that lists the grounds for divorce. Give the citation to this statute and list all the grounds for divorce provided therein. (See General Instructions for the State-Code Assignment in Appendix A.)
>
> **b.** For any three of the grounds of divorce in your state, draft a checklist of questions to help determine whether those grounds exist. (See General Instructions for the Checklist-Formulation Assignment in Appendix A.)

NO-FAULT GROUNDS FOR DIVORCE

As indicated in Exhibit 7-1, the three major no-fault grounds are living apart, incompatibility, and irreconcilable differences. In some states, the last two no-fault grounds require the spouses to live apart for a designated period of time.

LIVING APART

living apart

A no-fault ground for divorce that is established when spouses live separately for a designated period of consecutive time during which they intended to end the marriage.

Living apart (sometimes called *living separate and apart*) is a no-fault ground for divorce in many states. Parties do not have to prove that one of them was at fault in causing the separation. The statute authorizing this ground (or any other ground) must be carefully read; slight differences in wording in the statutes of different states may account for major differences in meaning. Most living-apart statutes require that the parties intend to end their marriage when they live separately for a designated period of consecutive time, as outlined below. Some states impose additional and more restrictive requirements. For example, the statute might specify that the living apart must be required by a court order or separation agreement.

APART The parties must be living apart, usually in different buildings. In some states, if they are living in separate parts of the same place ("under the same roof"), they are *not* living apart even if their sexual relationship has ended.

TIME In all states where living apart is a ground, the statute requires that the parties live apart for a designated period of time, ranging from six months to three years. A major purpose of the time limitation is to force the parties to think seriously about whether a reconciliation is possible.

CONSECUTIVENESS The separated time must be consecutive. Off-and-on separations do not qualify if one of the separations does not last the requisite length of time. This is true even if the total time spent apart from intermittent separations exceeds the required minimum. Furthermore, the qualifying period of separation must continue right up to the time one of the spouses brings the divorce action on the ground of living apart.

CONSENT Several states require that the period of separation be consensual or voluntary on the part of *both* spouses. Thus, if one spouse is drafted into the service or is hospitalized for an extended period of time, the separation is surely not by consent. Similarly, if one spouse wants to reconcile and the other does not, the former has not consented to the separation.

CAUSE Sometimes the *cause* of the separation may be relevant to its voluntariness. Suppose, for example, that Bob deserts his wife Linda and they live apart for a period in excess of that required by the statute. Arguably, the parties did not separate voluntarily; they separated as a result of the *fault* of Bob. Some states will deny the divorce on the ground of living apart because the separation was not voluntary. Others will deny the divorce on this ground only when the plaintiff seeking the divorce is the "guilty" party. Most states, however, will grant the divorce to either party on the basis that voluntariness and marital fault are irrelevant so long as there was a living apart for the requisite period of time.

☑ INTERVIEWING AND INVESTIGATION CHECKLIST

Divorce on the Ground of Living Apart

LEGAL INTERVIEWING QUESTIONS

1. How long have you lived apart?

2. On what date did you separate?

3. Since that date, what contact have you had with D (defendant)?

4. Have you ever asked D to live with you again? Has D ever asked you?

5. Have you had sexual relations with D since you separated?

6. Describe the circumstances of your separation with D.

7. When you separated, did you intend a permanent separation? If so, what indications of this did you give?

8. Did D intend a permanent separation? If so, what indications did D give?

9. What was the condition of your marriage at the time of separation?

10. Did you leave D? Did D leave you? Did you both leave at the same time by mutual agreement?

11. When the separation occurred, did either of you protest? Were you or D dissatisfied with the separation?

12. Since you separated, has either of you asked or suggested that the two of you get back together again? If so, what was the response of the other?

13. Has either of you obtained a legal separation or a judgment of separate maintenance? If so, when? Have you been living separate since that time? Have both of you abided by the terms of the legal separation or maintenance judgment?

14. Are you now living separate from D?

15. Since you separated, at what address have you lived? (Same question about D.)

16. Do you and D have a separation agreement? If so, when was it signed?

POSSIBLE INVESTIGATION TASKS

- Collect evidence that the parties have lived separate and apart (e.g., rent receipts from the apartments of the client and of D, copies of separate utility bills).

- Obtain witness statements from people aware of the separation.

ASSIGNMENT 7.2

Assume that a statute provides that one of the grounds for divorce is voluntary separation for a period of two consecutive years. This living-apart ground is the only one authorized in the state. Fred and Gail are married. On June 10, 2005, Fred moves out when they agree to separate. On May 15, 2007, when he learns that she is thinking about filing for divorce, he calls Gail and pleads with her to let him come back. She refuses. On July 25, 2007, she files for divorce on the ground of living apart. Could a divorce be granted on the ground of living apart? (See General Instructions for the Legal-Analysis Assignment in Appendix A.)

As we shall see, many states allow parties to seek a *legal separation*, which is a court authorization that the parties can live separate lives under specified terms (e.g., alimony, custody order) while still being married to each other. In some states, this legal separation can be *converted* into a divorce after a designated period of time. Similarly, a judgment of *separate maintenance* (spousal support), discussed later in the chapter, can often be converted into a divorce after this period of time.

SUMMARY OF GROUND FOR DIVORCE: LIVING APART

Definition: Living separately for a designated, consecutive period of time with the intent to end the marriage.

Who can sue: In most states, either party. In a few states, the party at fault (i.e., the party who wrongfully caused the separation) cannot bring the divorce action.

Major defenses:

1. The parties never separated.

2. The parties did not separate for the period designated in the statute.

3. The parties reconciled and cohabitated before the statutory period was over (i.e, the separations were not consecutive).

4. Living apart was a trial separation only; they did not intend to end the marriage.

5. The separation was not voluntary (this defense is available in only a few states).

6. The agreement to separate was obtained by fraud or duress.

7. The court lacks jurisdiction (discussed later in this chapter).

Is this also a ground for annulment? No.

Is this also a ground for legal separation? Yes, in many states.

Is this also a ground for separate maintenance? Yes, in many states.

© Cengage Learning 2013

INCOMPATIBILITY

incompatibility
A no-fault ground for divorce that is established when there is such discord between the husband and wife that it is impossible for them to live together in a normal marital relationship.

Some states list **incompatibility** as a ground for divorce. It consists of such rift or discord that it is impossible to live together in a normal marital relationship. "Petty quarrels" and "minor bickering" are usually not enough. For most of the states that have this ground, fault is not an issue; the plaintiff does not have to show that the defendant was at fault in causing the incompatibility, and the defendant cannot defend the action by introducing evidence that the plaintiff committed marital wrongs. There are a few states, however, that do require a showing of fault. In such states, incompatibility is not a no-fault ground.

Suppose that the plaintiff alleges that the parties are incompatible. Can the defendant defend by disagreeing? Do *both* husband and wife have to feel that it is impossible to live together? Assuming that the plaintiff is able to establish that more than "petty quarrels" are involved, most courts will grant the divorce to the plaintiff even though the defendant insists that they can still work it out. If, however, the court feels that the marriage is salvageable, some states will allow the judge to order the spouses into counseling or mediation. In many states, this problem is avoided by the additional requirement that the parties be separated (live apart) for a designated period of time (e.g., one year). When a separation of this duration has existed, courts are likely to accept the view of one party that the no-fault ground has been established despite what the other spouse thinks.

sham divorce
A divorce sought by parties who do not intend to stay divorced from each other once the divorce is granted.

If the court is convinced that the spouses are seeking a **sham divorce**, it can refuse to divorce them. Suppose, for example, the parties try to divorce at the end of the year in order to take advantage of a tax benefit and then remarry at the beginning of the next year. The complaint or petition stating that the parties are incompatible (or that there is an irretrievable breakdown in the marriage) would be fraudulent. (See the discussion below on collusion.)

When a no-fault ground asserted by one spouse is sufficient for a court to grant the divorce, it is referred to as a *unilateral no-fault ground*.

☑ INTERVIEWING AND INVESTIGATION CHECKLIST

Divorce on the Ground of Incompatibility

(This checklist is also relevant to the irreconcilable-differences ground, discussed next.)

LEGAL INTERVIEWING QUESTIONS

1. Are you and D (defendant) now living together? If not, how long have you been separated?

2. Have you ever sued D or been sued by D for separate maintenance or for a legal separation? If so, what was the result?

3. Describe your relationship with D at its worst.

4. How often did you argue? Were the arguments intense or bitter? Explain.

5. Did you or D ever call the police?

6. Did you or D receive medical attention as a result of your arguments or fights?

7. Did you or D have a drinking or drug problem?

8. How did D act toward the children? What is your relationship with them?

9. How would you describe your sexual relationship with D?

10. Has there been infidelity?

11. Do you feel that there is any possibility that you and D could reconcile your differences?

12. Do you think D feels that the two of you can solve the problems in the marriage?

13. Have you or D ever sought counseling or therapy of any kind? If so, describe the circumstances.

14. Are you now interested in any such help in order to try to save the marriage? Do you feel it would work? How do you think D feels about this?

POSSIBLE INVESTIGATION TASKS

- Obtain copy of legal separation judgment, separate maintenance judgment, police reports, and hospital records, if any.

ASSIGNMENT 7.3

One married partner says to the other, "I no longer love you." By definition, are they incompatible for purposes of this ground for divorce? (See General Instructions for the Legal-Analysis Assignment in Appendix A.)

SUMMARY OF GROUND FOR DIVORCE: INCOMPATIBILITY

Definition: The impossibility of two parties being able to continue to live together in a normal marital relationship.

Who can sue: Either party in most states.

Is this also a ground for annulment? No.

Is this also a ground for legal separation? Yes, in many states.

Is this also a ground for separate maintenance? Yes, in many states.

© Cengage Learning 2013

IRRECONCILABLE DIFFERENCES

The newest and most popular version of the no-fault ground for divorce in many states is **irreconcilable differences**. It consists of such discord between the husband and wife that there has been an irremediable breakdown of the marriage. The goal of the legislatures that have enacted this ground has been to focus on the central question of whether it makes any sense to continue the marriage. The statutes often have similar language and content. For example:

- Irretrievable breakdown of the marriage.
- Discord or conflict of personalities that destroys the legitimate ends of marriage and prevents any reasonable expectation of reconciliation.

irreconcilable differences
A no-fault ground for divorce that is established when there is such discord between the husband and wife that there has been an irremediable breakdown of the marriage.

- Breakdown of the marriage to such an extent that the legitimate objects of marriage have been destroyed and there remains no reasonable likelihood that the marriage can be preserved.

- Substantial reasons for not continuing the marriage.

- Insupportability, where discord or conflict of personalities destroys the legitimate ends of the marital relationship and prevents any reasonable expectation of reconciliation.

In some states, an additional requirement is that the parties be separated (live apart) for a designated period of time (e.g., a year).

What happens if the defendant denies that the breakdown of the marriage is irremediable and feels that marriage counseling would help? In most states, this is simply one item of evidence that the court must consider in deciding whether remediation is possible. It is likely, however, that if one party absolutely refuses to participate in any reconciliation efforts, the court will conclude that the breakdown of the marriage is total even if the other party expresses a conciliatory attitude.

If the court concludes that there is a reasonable possibility of reconciliation, its options may be limited to delaying the divorce proceedings—granting a **stay**—for a limited number of days (e.g., 30) to give the parties additional time to try to work out their difficulties.

If courts linger over the issue of the viability or survivability of a marriage, they run the risk of delving into the kind of fault analysis that no-fault divorce was designed to remove from the courtroom. One way to avoid this dilemma is for a court to treat the length of time the spouses have lived separately as the clearest indication of whether the marriage has died.

stay
The suspension of a judgment or proceeding.

✔ INTERVIEWING AND INVESTIGATION CHECKLIST

Divorce on the Ground of Irreconcilable Differences

(This checklist is also relevant to the incompatibility ground discussed earlier.)

LEGAL INTERVIEWING QUESTIONS

1. How long have you been married to defendant (D)? How many children do you have?

2. How does D get along with the children?

3. How often do you and D communicate meaningfully?

4. Does D insult you, ridicule your religion, your political views, or your family?

5. Does D do this in front of anyone? Who else knows that D does this? How do they know?

6. Have your friends, relatives, or associates told you that D has ridiculed or criticized you behind your back?

7. Do you think that D has ever tried to turn the children against you? If so, how do you know? What specifically have the children or others said or done to make you think so?

8. Does D drink or use drugs? If so, how much, how often, and how has it affected your marriage?

9. Has D ever hit you? If so, describe the circumstances. How often has D done this? Did the children see it? Has anyone else ever seen it?

10. Were there any other major events or scenes that were unpleasant for you? If so, describe them.

11. How would you describe your sexual relationship with D?

12. Have either of you ever accused the other of infidelity?

13. Does D stay away from home often? Does D ever not come home at night?

14. Have you had to call the police because of something D did?

15. Has D ever sued you, or have you ever sued D?

16. How often do you fight or argue with D?

17. Is D now living with you? If not, explain the circumstances of the separation.

18. Has D's behavior affected your physical health in any way? Have you had to see a doctor?

19. Have you seen or have you considered seeing a psychiatrist or some other mental-health professional?

20. Have you ever experienced any behavior like this before?

21. How was your physical and mental health before D started behaving this way?

22. Do you have any difficulty sleeping?

23. Do you have any difficulty doing your regular work because of D?

24. What is D's opinion of you as a spouse?

25. Do you think that you will ever be able to live in harmony with D? Explain why or why not.

26. Does D think the two of you will ever be able to get back together again? Explain why or why not.

POSSIBLE INVESTIGATION TASKS

- Obtain all of client's medical records, if any, from doctors, hospitals, etc., that have treated the client as a result of what D has done.

- If the children are old and mature enough, interview them to see how they viewed D's relationship with the client and, specifically, how D treated them.

- Obtain police records, if any, resulting from any fights or disturbances.

ASSIGNMENT 7.4

Dan and Helen were married in your state. Helen does not want to be married anymore. She loves Dan and enjoys being his wife, but simply wants to live alone indefinitely. Dan does not want a divorce. Can she obtain a divorce in your state? (See General Instructions for the State-Code Assignment and the Court-Opinion Assignment in Appendix A.)

SUMMARY OF GROUND FOR DIVORCE: IRRECONCILABLE DIFFERENCES

Definition: Such discord between the husband and wife that there has been an irremediable breakdown of the marriage.

Who can sue: Either party.

Is this also a ground for annulment? No.

Is this also a ground for legal separation? Yes, in many states.

Is this also a ground for separate maintenance? Yes, in many states.

© Cengage Learning 2013

FAULT GROUNDS FOR DIVORCE

The major fault grounds are adultery, cruelty, and desertion. Although they are less often used today, they remain in force. See the reasons discussed earlier on why a spouse might decide to seek a divorce on a fault ground (e.g., to avoid a waiting period).

ADULTERY

Adultery is voluntary sexual intercourse between a married person and someone to whom he or she is not married. There are some states that use a broader definition: voluntary intimate sexual relations between a spouse and someone other than his or her spouse, irrespective of the specific sexual acts performed, the marital status of the nonspouse, or the gender of the non-spouse. The person who has sexual relations with the defendant is called the **corespondent**.

Intercourse is not voluntary, of course, if the defendant is raped or if the defendant is insane at the time. Because direct evidence of adultery is seldom available, **circumstantial evidence** must be relied upon. Specifically, the plaintiff must prove that the defendant had the *opportunity* and the *inclination* to commit adultery.

Although rarely enforced, adultery is a crime in several states. In New York, for example, "A person is guilty of adultery [a class B misdemeanor]

adultery
1. Voluntary sexual intercourse between a married person and someone other than his or her spouse. 2. Voluntary intimate sexual relations between a spouse and someone other than his or her spouse, irrespective of the specific sexual acts performed, the marital status of the nonspouse, or the gender of the nonspouse.

corespondent
The person who allegedly had sexual relations with a defendant charged with adultery.

circumstantial evidence
Evidence of one fact from which another fact (not personally observed or known) can be inferred. Also called indirect evidence.

when he engages in sexual intercourse with another person at a time when he has a living spouse, or the other person has a living spouse."[13] Such statutes, however, are of questionable constitutionality after the U.S. Supreme Court held in *Lawrence v. Texas* that a state could not criminalize private, consensual, intimate same-sex conduct by adults.[14] Arguably, the same conclusion could apply to private, consensual adulterous conduct by adults. (See Chapter 5 for a discussion of *Lawrence*.)

CRUELTY

cruelty

The infliction of serious physical or mental suffering on another.

In most marriage ceremonies, the parties take each other "for better or worse." This concept was viewed quite literally early in our history, particularly when the woman was the one claiming to have received too much of the "worse." It was expected that a good deal of fighting, nagging, and mutual abuse would occur within a marriage. The concept of permitting marriage to be dissolved because of "mere" meanness or indignities was alien to our legal system for a long time. The change in the law came slowly. Eventually, when **cruelty** was allowed as a ground for divorce, the statute would often require that it be "extreme" or "inhuman" before the divorce could be granted. Furthermore, some states limited the ground to actual or threatened *physical* violence. (A 1956 Virginia court held that an attack by a husband in which he "grabbed her, threw her against the wall, and threatened her with a butcher knife" was not enough to amount to physical cruelty.[15]) Later, *mental anguish* came to be recognized as a form of cruelty, but there was often a requirement that the psychological cruelty result in an impairment of the plaintiff's health. There are states, however, that will accept a minimal health impairment (e.g., a loss of sleep). Only a few states will authorize a divorce on the ground of cruelty where the mental suffering does not produce physical symptoms.

---

domestic violence (DV)

Actual or threatened physical injury or abuse of one member of a family or household by another member.

stalking

1. Repeatedly following someone, often surreptitiously. 2. A course of conduct consisting of following or loitering around a person, who is thereby placed in reasonable fear of harm.

Some forms of cruelty can lead to criminal prosecution for the violation of laws against domestic violence and stalking. **Domestic violence (DV)** is actual or threatened physical injury or abuse by one member of a family or household on another member. **Stalking** is repeatedly following someone, often surreptitiously, or engaging in a course of conduct consisting of following or loitering around a person, who is thereby placed in reasonable fear of harm. We will examine this area of the law in Chapter 12.

DESERTION

desertion

The voluntary departure of one spouse from another (without justification or consent) with the intent not to return to resume cohabitation with the spouse. Also called abandonment.

Desertion (also called *abandonment*) occurs (1) when one spouse voluntarily leaves another, (2) for an uninterrupted period of time (e.g., two years), (3) with the intent not to return to resume cohabitation, and when (4) the separation occurred without the consent of the other spouse and (5) there was no justification or reasonable cause for the separation. An example would be a husband who goes to live with his mistress for several years after telling his wife that he no longer wanted to live with her.

constructive desertion

(1) A spouse's conduct that justifies the other spouse's departure from the home. (2) A spouse's rejection of a sincere offer of reconciliation from the spouse who left the home without justification.

It is also possible to commit desertion without leaving the home. **Constructive desertion** consists of either (1) engaging in conduct that justifies the other spouse's departure from the home (e.g., refusing all future sexual relations) or (2) rejecting a sincere offer of reconciliation from the other spouse who initially left the home without justification. In effect, the spouse who stayed home becomes the deserter! When constructive desertion has occurred, the spouse who left would be allowed to sue the other spouse for divorce on the ground of desertion.

OTHER GROUNDS

A number of other closely related and sometimes overlapping grounds exist in many states. Here is a partial list (some of which are also grounds for annulment):

- Bigamy
- Impotence
- Nonage
- Fraud
- Duress
- Incest
- Imprisonment for three consecutive years
- Conviction of a serious crime
- Insanity; mental incapacity for three years
- Habitual drunkenness
- Drug addiction
- Nonsupport
- Unexplained absence
- Neglect of duty
- Obtaining an out-of-state divorce that is invalid
- Venereal disease or AIDS
- Unchastity
- Pregnancy by someone else at the time of the marriage
- Treatment injurious to health
- Deviant sexual conduct
- Any other cause deemed by the court to be sufficient, if satisfied that the parties can no longer live together

In some states, a spouse's unexplained absence for a designated number of years (e.g., five) is a ground for divorce if there has been **due diligence** in the search for the missing spouse and a belief that he or she is dead. It is called an **Enoch Arden divorce**. As we saw in Chapter 6, the *Enoch Arden presumption* allowed a spouse to presume that the absent spouse was dead.

DEFENSES TO THE FAULT GROUNDS

The basic defenses to the fault grounds for divorce are defined as follows:

- **Collusion.** An agreement by spouses that one or both will lie to the court in order to help secure their divorce. The lie pertains to grounds for the divorce or to procedural requirements for obtaining the divorce (e.g., the spouses lie about violence in the marriage; the spouses lie about whether they are domiciled in the state).

- **Connivance.** A willingness or a consent by one spouse that a marital wrong be done by the other spouse (e.g., hiring someone to seduce one's spouse; knowing that one's spouse is inclined to commit a marital offense but doing nothing to prevent it).[16] The main difference between connivance and collusion is that connivance covers conduct that was actually committed, whereas collusion is an agreement to fabricate facts.

- **Condonation.** An express or implied forgiveness by the innocent spouse of the marital fault committed by the other spouse (e.g., a spouse continues to live with the other spouse for over a year after finding out that the latter had a weekend affair with an office worker on a business trip).

- **Recrimination.** A serious marital wrong committed by the spouse seeking the divorce even though this spouse is charging the other spouse with committing a serious marital wrong (e.g., bringing an action for divorce on the ground of adultery even though the plaintiff or petitioner has also committed adultery). If both spouses are "guilty," some courts will not allow either spouse to obtain the divorce. Other states will apply the doctrine of **comparative rectitude** and award the divorce to the spouse least at fault.

- **Provocation.** Inciting the conduct that constitutes the marital wrong by the other spouse.

due diligence
Reasonable efforts to find and verify factual information needed to carry out an obligation, to avoid harming someone, or to make an important decision, e.g., to locate a parent.

Enoch Arden divorce
A divorce granted on the ground that a spouse has disappeared for a designated number of years with no explanation.

comparative rectitude
A comparison of the wrongdoing of two spouses in causing the breakdown of the marriage so that the divorce can be given to the spouse least at fault.

Of course, because of the extensive use of no-fault grounds, these defenses to the fault grounds are seldom used or needed.

LEGAL SEPARATION

legal separation
A declaration by a court that parties can live apart even though they are still married to each other.

Two kinds of separation can exist when parties are having serious marital difficulties. Living apart from each other is an *informal separation* if it is not officially granted or approved by the courts. A **legal separation**, on the other hand, is a declaration or judgment by a court that two people can live apart—from bed and board—while still remaining husband and wife. A legal separation is also known as a:

- Judicial separation
- Limited divorce
- *Divorce a mensa et thoro* (divorce from bed and hearth)
- Separation from bed and board

Parties subject to a legal separation are not free to remarry. The marriage relationship remains until it is dissolved by the death of one of the parties, by annulment, or by an absolute divorce.

For religious or family reasons (e.g., concern over how the children would handle a divorce), the parties may not wish to end the marriage by obtaining a divorce. A divorce might result in the termination of medical care that is available through the other spouse's health policy at work. Some spouses might not be emotionally ready to accept the finality of a divorce. Yet they may need financial support. In such cases, legal separation is an option in many states. Spouses who separate but for whatever reason do not seek a divorce are sometimes referred to as the "un-divorced."

To obtain a legal separation, *grounds* must be established in the same manner as grounds must be established to obtain an absolute divorce. In fact, the grounds for legal separation are often very similar, if not identical, to the grounds for an absolute divorce (e.g., no-fault grounds such as incompatibility or irreconcilable differences and fault grounds such as adultery or cruelty).

When a court grants a legal separation, it may also be able to make rulings on spousal support, property division, child support, and child custody while the spouses are living apart. All of these decisions require special categories of jurisdiction. They are the same categories that a court must have when it grants a divorce. Hence, we will discuss them later in this chapter when we cover divorce procedure. To preview this discussion, a court needs *in rem jurisdiction* to order a legal separation or divorce and *personal jurisdiction* to order property division and spousal support. The details of jurisdiction needed for child custody and child support will be covered in Chapters 9 and 10.

separation agreement
A contract by married persons who have separated (or who are about to separate) that can cover support, custody, property division, and other terms of their separation and possible divorce.

We should distinguish a legal separation from a **separation agreement**. The latter is a private contract between a husband and wife who have separated (or who are about to separate) that can cover support, custody, property division, and other terms of their separation and possible divorce. The agreement may or may not become part of (i.e., be incorporated and merged in) the divorce judgment if one is later sought. Also, it is important that the words "separated" and "separation" be used carefully. Alone, these words mean simply a *physical* separation between the husband and wife. If, however, a court-sanctioned or court-ordered separation is involved, then the reference should be to a *legal separation* or to a *judicial separation*.

DOS
Date of separation.

Dates are important in separation cases, whether or not the parties obtain a formal judgment of legal separation. In most cases, the date of separation (**DOS**) helps determine whether property is classified as *marital property* or as *separate property*, as we will see in Chapter 8.

Once the parties are living apart, the property that each individually accumulates is considered *separate property*. In most states, separate property is not divided upon divorce. As we will see later, only marital property is subject to property division in such states.

ASSIGNMENT 7.5

Does your state have an action for a legal separation?

a. If so, what is the action called?

b. What is the citation of the statute authorizing this action?

d. What are the grounds in your state for a legal separation?

c. Are there any grounds for legal separation that are *not* grounds for divorce? (See General Instructions for the State-Code Assignment in Appendix A.)

d. Prepare a flowchart of the procedural steps that are necessary for a legal separation in your state. (See General Instructions for the Flowchart Assignment in Appendix A.)

After a legal separation judgment has been rendered, the fact that the parties reconcile and resume cohabitation does not mean that the judgment becomes inoperative. It remains effective until a court declares otherwise. Hence, a husband who is under an order to pay spousal support pursuant to a legal separation judgment must continue to pay alimony even though the parties have subsequently reconciled and are living together again. To be relieved of this obligation, a petition must be made to the court to change the judgment.

An important consequence of a separation in many states is its **conversion** feature. A legal separation can be converted into a divorce—an absolute divorce. In effect, the existence of the separation for a designated period of time can become a ground for a divorce. The Uniform Marriage and Divorce Act provides that "[n]o earlier than 6 months after entry of a judgment of legal separation, the court on motion of either party shall convert the judgment to a judgment of dissolution of marriage."[17]

conversion

Changing a legal separation into a divorce after the parties have lived apart for a designated period of time. The time they lived apart becomes a ground for divorce, called a conversion divorce or a convertible divorce. (See glossary for an additional meaning.)

SEPARATE MAINTENANCE

An action for **separate maintenance** (sometimes called separate support or alimony without divorce) is a proceeding brought by a spouse to secure support. The action is usually filed by wives, but an increasing number of husbands are seeking spousal support by this route. Like the legal separation judgment, a separate maintenance judgment does not alter the marital status of the parties; they remain married to each other while living separately.

The major ground for a separate maintenance judgment is the refusal of one spouse to support the other without just cause. In addition, most states provide that all of the grounds for divorce will also be grounds for separate maintenance. Furthermore, in a divorce action, if the court refuses to grant either party a divorce, it usually can still enter an order for separate maintenance.

If the plaintiff refuses a good faith offer by the defendant to reconcile, the plaintiff becomes a wrongdoer, which in some states may justify the defendant in refusing to provide support. If the separate maintenance action is still pending, the plaintiff will lose it. If a separate maintenance judgment has already been awarded, the defendant may be able to discontinue making payments under it.

The court determines the amount and form of a separate maintenance award in the same way that it makes the alimony determination in a divorce (see Chapter 8). If needed, the court can also make child-support and child-custody decisions in the separate maintenance action. In general, *property division* is not resolved by the court in a judgment of separate maintenance. If the parties cannot agree on how their marital property should be divided, they need to seek other avenues of relief, such as a divorce or legal separation.

When we discuss divorce procedure, we will cover the personal jurisdiction needed by a court to make an alimony order. The same kind of jurisdiction is needed when a court orders separate maintenance.

separate maintenance

Court-ordered spousal support while the parties are separated but still married. Also called separate support and alimony without divorce.

ASSIGNMENT 7.6

a. Does your state have an action for separate maintenance or its equivalent? If so, on what grounds will the action be granted? (See General Instructions for the State-Code Assignment in Appendix A.)

b. Prepare a flowchart of all the procedural steps required in a proceeding for separate maintenance or its equivalent.

(See General Instructions for the State-Code Assignment and for the Flowchart Assignment in Appendix A).

INTRODUCTION TO DIVORCE PROCEDURE

The overwhelming number of divorce cases are uncontested because the other side does not show up in court or does not dispute what the person filing for divorce is seeking. In many cases, the spouses have negotiated an agreement (on their own or through counsel) on the termination of the marital relationship, alimony, property division, child custody, and child support. In such cases, divorce procedure is often relatively simple.

In some states, short-term marriages with no children and no significant marital property can be dissolved under an accelerated or expedited procedure, often involving few or no trips to the court other than to file court documents such as a divorce complaint/petition and a statement of assets and debts. If, however, the bitterness of the past has not subsided and agreements have not been reached, the technicalities of procedure can occupy center stage in costly and complicated proceedings.

DOMICILE

To obtain a divorce, one or both parties must have a domicile in the state and be a resident of the state for a designated period of time. Unfortunately, the terms *domicile* and *residence* are sometimes confused. Some divorce statutes use the word *residence* even though the meaning intended is *domicile*. There are distinct differences between the two terms:

- **Residence.** The place where someone is living. A person can have many residences (e.g., a home in the city, plus a beach house, plus an apartment in another state or country).
- **Domicile.** The place (1) where a person has been physically present (2) with the intent to make that place a permanent home, or with no intent to make any other place a permanent home. It is the place to which one would intend to return when away. With rare exceptions, a person can have only one domicile.

A person with a residence is a **resident**; he or she resides there. A **nonresident** is someone who does not have a residence at a particular place. A **domiciliary** is someone who is domiciled in a particular place. A **nondomiciliary** is someone who is not domiciled in a particular place. For our purposes, the "place" under discussion is the state. Hence, when we refer to a nondomiciliary, we are referring to someone who does not have a domicile in a particular state.

It is important to be able to determine where a person's domicile is. Here are two specific reasons why:

- A court does not have divorce jurisdiction to dissolve a marriage unless one or both spouses are domiciled in the state where that court sits. (Later we will see that the jurisdiction to dissolve a marriage is called *in rem jurisdiction*.)
- Liability for the **estate tax** may depend upon the domicile of the decedent at the time of death.

resident
Someone who lives at a particular place.

nonresident
Someone who does not have a residence in a particular place.

domiciliary
One who is domiciled in a particular place.

nondomiciliary
One who is not domiciled in a particular place.

estate tax
A tax on money or other property that is transferred by someone who dies leaving a valid will (testate) or without such a will (intestate). There is a federal estate tax and some states impose a state estate tax.

Generally, children cannot acquire a domicile of their own until they reach the **age of majority** (e.g., 18 years of age) or become otherwise **emancipated**. In effect, a child acquires a domicile by **operation of law** rather than by choice. The law operates to impose a domicile on the child regardless of what the child may want (if the child is old enough to form any opinion at all). The domicile of the parents automatically becomes the domicile of the child. If the parents are separated, the child's domicile is that of the parent who has **legal custody**. An emancipated child and an adult can pick any domicile they want (**domicile by choice**) so long as they are physically present in a place and have the intention to make it their permanent home (or so long as they do not intend to make any other place a permanent home).

Intention can sometimes be very difficult to prove. Intent is a state of mind; the main way to determine a state of mind is by interpreting external acts. Verbal statements are not necessarily the best evidence of a person's state of mind. Suppose, for example, that Bill is domiciled in Connecticut and becomes violently ill during a visit to Maine. He knows that if he dies domiciled in Maine, his beneficiaries will pay a lower state estate tax than if he died domiciled in Connecticut. While lying in a Maine sick bed just before he dies, Bill openly says, "I hereby declare that I intend Maine to be my permanent home." This statement in itself fails to prove that Bill was domiciled in Maine at the time of his death. Other evidence may show that he made the statement simply to give the appearance of changing his domicile and that, if he had regained his health, he would have returned to Connecticut. If so, his domicile at death is Connecticut in spite of his declared intent; a court will conclude that he never actually intended to make Maine his permanent home, at least as of the time of his death.

age of majority
The age at which children reach legal adulthood, usually 18, entitling them to many civil rights, such as the right to manage their own affairs.

emancipated
Legally independent of one's parent or legal guardian. The noun is *emancipation*.

operation of law
The means by which legal consequences are imposed by law, regardless of (or even despite) the intent of the parties involved.

legal custody
The right to make the major child-rearing decisions on health, education, religion, discipline, and general welfare. Also called decision-making responsibility.

domicile by choice
A domicile selected by a person with the legal capacity to choose.

☑ INTERVIEWING AND INVESTIGATION CHECKLIST

How to Determine When a Person Has Established a Domicile

LEGAL INTERVIEWING QUESTIONS

1. When did you come to the state?
2. How often have you been in the state in the past? (Describe the details of your contacts with the state.)
3. Why did you come to the state?
4. Was your intention to stay there for a short period of time? A long period of time? Indefinitely? Forever?
5. While you were in the state, did you also have homes elsewhere in the state, and/or in another state, and/or in another country? If so, give details (addresses, how long you spent at each home, etc.).
6. In what state(s) do you own real property (land)? In what state(s) do you rent real property? For every property owned or rented, specify the location, dates of purchase/lease, length of time owned/leased, etc.
7. Where do you consider your permanent home to be?
8. Have you ever changed your permanent home in the past? (If so, give details.)
9. Where are you registered to vote? Where did you vote in the last election? In the election before that?
10. Where is your job or business?
11. In what state is your car registered?
12. What state issued your driver's license?
13. In what states do you have bank accounts?
14. In what states do you have club memberships?
15. In what state is your pet licensed?
16. In what state do you attend church or other house of worship?
17. If you have a will or trust, what address is listed for you in the will or trust?
18. Did you change your will or trust to mention your new state?
19. What is your address according to the credit card companies you use? Where are your statements sent?
20. Where do your relatives live?

POSSIBLE INVESTIGATION TASKS

- Interview persons with whom the client may have discussed the move to the state (e.g., relatives, neighbors, business associates).
- Obtain copies of records that would indicate the extent of contact with the state (e.g., state tax returns, bank statements, land ownership papers, leases, hotel receipts, voting records, library cards, and utility bills).

In the following situations, determine in what state the person was domiciled at the time of death. (See General Instructions for the Legal-Analysis Assignment in Appendix A.)

a. While living in Illinois, Fred hears about a high-paying job in Alaska. He decides to move to Alaska. He no longer wants to live in Illinois. He sells everything he owns in Illinois and rents an apartment in Alaska. There he discovers that jobs are not easy to find. He decides to leave if he cannot find a job in three months. If this happens, he arranges to move in with his sister in New Mexico. Before the three months are over, Fred dies jobless in Alaska.

b. Gloria moves to New York from Montana to attend New York University. Her husband lives in Montana. Gloria plans to rejoin her husband in Montana when she finishes school in six months. Two months before graduation, her husband decides to move to Oregon. Gloria is opposed to the move and tells him that she will not leave New York if he does not return to Montana. Her husband refuses to move back to Montana. One month before graduation, Gloria dies in New York.

FULL FAITH AND CREDIT

We live in a mobile society; individuals and families change their domiciles relatively often. This is particularly true of persons in families facing domestic difficulties.

Ted and Helen are married in Texas. After five years of marriage, Helen moves to California and files for divorce in a California court. The court grants the divorce and awards her $2,000 a month in alimony. A year later, Helen moves back to Texas and asks a Texas court to enforce the alimony order against Ted.

Texas is being asked to recognize and enforce a California judgment. Texas is the **forum state**, which is the state where the case is now being litigated. In the Texas litigation, the California divorce is considered a **foreign divorce**. *Foreign* means any state or country other than the forum state or country.

Is Texas required to recognize and enforce the California divorce judgment? This is a constitutional question. Under the U.S. Constitution, one state must give **full faith and credit (FFC)** to the legal decisions of another state. FFC is the obligation of one state to recognize and enforce the legal decisions of another state. The obligation is based on the U.S. Constitution, which provides that "Full Faith and Credit shall be given in each State to the public Acts, Records, and judicial Proceedings of every other State."[18]

Is Texas required to give FFC to the California judgment of divorce? The answer will depend on whether California had proper jurisdiction to render the divorce judgment. Furthermore, it is possible that the FFC obligation may apply to only part of the California judgment. To understand this conclusion, we need to cover what is called a *divisible divorce.*

Before we examine divisible divorce, it must be stressed that we are talking about divorces issued and enforced in the United States. Our courts are not required to give FFC to a divorce judgment granted in Mexico or in any other country. A state or federal court in the United States may decide to recognize a judgment from another country as a matter of deference and mutual respect (**comity**), but there is no FFC obligation to do so.

DIVISIBLE DIVORCE

A divorce judgment can consist of five major orders:

- dissolving the marriage
- awarding spousal support (alimony)

forum state
The state in which the case is now being litigated.

foreign divorce
A divorce obtained in another state or country. A divorce that was not obtained in the forum state where the parties are now in litigation.

full faith and credit (FFC)
The obligation of one state to recognize and enforce the legal decisions of another state. The obligation is based on the U.S. Constitution, which provides that "Full Faith and Credit shall be given in each State to the public Acts, Records, and judicial Proceedings of every other State." Article IV, § 1.

comity
A court's decision to give effect to the laws and judicial decisions of another state as a matter of deference and mutual respect even if no obligation exists to do so.

- dividing marital property (called a property division)
- awarding child support
- awarding child custody

In our Texas/California example involving Ted and Helen, the California issued two orders: It dissolved the marriage and awarded spousal support (alimony). When we want to know if a Texas court must give FFC to the California divorce judgment, we must ask: Which part of the California divorce judgment? Texas may be required to give FFC to only part of the California divorce judgment. If a divorce is enforceable only in part, it is a **divisible divorce**.

The enforceability of an order in a divorce judgment depends on whether the court had proper jurisdiction to issue that order. Because different orders require different kinds of jurisdiction, we must ask the following questions:

- What kind of jurisdiction does a court need to dissolve a marriage?
- What kind of jurisdiction does a court need to award spousal support (alimony)?
- What kind of jurisdiction does a court need to divide marital property (property division)?
- What kind of jurisdiction does a court need to award child support?
- What kind of jurisdiction does a court need to award child custody?

To answer these questions, we begin with a general introduction to jurisdiction.

JURISDICTION

There are two broad definitions of **jurisdiction**:

- Power definition. The power of a court to act in a particular case to resolve a legal dispute. We will be discussing three major kinds or categories of power jurisdiction: subject-matter jurisdiction, in rem jurisdiction, and personal jurisdiction.
- Geographic definition. The geographic area over which a particular court has authority or power. This definition of jurisdiction refers to a place on the map. A Nevada state court, for example, will often refer to its entire state as "this jurisdiction." Similarly, the U.S. Court of Appeals for the Tenth Circuit covers six states in the midwestern part of the country. When the Tenth Circuit refers to "this jurisdiction," it is referring to any one of these six states or to all six states collectively.

When we use the word *jurisdiction* in the remainder of the chapter, we will be referring to the power definition of jurisdiction. Our examination will focus on the following themes:

- Kinds of jurisdiction in a divorce case
- Who is attacking the divorce judgment

A divorce judgment might be challenged by attacking the jurisdiction of the court that rendered the divorce. The success of a jurisdictional attack on a divorce judgment depends on the kind of jurisdiction involved, the part of the divorce judgment being attacked, and the identity of the person bringing the attack. We now turn to an overview of these topics. Examples of their application will follow the overview.

KINDS OF JURISDICTION

As indicated, there are three major kinds of jurisdiction that relate to the power of a court: subject-matter jurisdiction, in rem jurisdiction, and personal jurisdiction.

divisible divorce

A divorce judgment or decree that is enforceable only in part. The part of a divorce decree that dissolves the marriage is enforceable (if the plaintiff was domiciled in the state), but the part of the divorce that ordered alimony, child support, or a property division is not enforceable (if the court did not have personal jurisdiction over the defendant).

jurisdiction

(1) The power of a court to act in a particular case to resolve a legal dispute. There are three major kinds of power jurisdiction: subject-matter jurisdiction, in rem jurisdiction, and personal jurisdiction. (2) The geographic area over which a particular court has authority or power.

Subject-matter jurisdiction

subject-matter jurisdiction
The court's power to resolve a particular type of legal dispute and to grant a particular type of relief.

    Subject-matter jurisdiction is required for all five orders that can be part of a divorce judgment. Subject-matter jurisdiction is a court's power to resolve a particular type of legal dispute and to grant a particular type of relief. A criminal law court, for example, would not have subject-matter jurisdiction to hear a divorce case. A divorce judgment rendered by a court without subject-matter jurisdiction over divorces is void. The divorce judgment is void in the state that granted it and in every other state. Such a judgment is not entitled to FFC. Therefore, another state is not required to enforce the divorce judgment.

    How does a court acquire subject-matter jurisdiction? The state constitution or a state statute determines the subject-matter jurisdiction of state courts.

    States differ on which courts are given subject-matter jurisdiction in family-law cases. In some states, divorce and other family-law cases are heard in a special division or section of the trial courts. Other states have established separate family-law or domestic-relations courts that have subject-matter jurisdiction in this area of the law. (See Exhibit 7-2.) In some states, even more specialized courts have been created, such as a *Fathering Court* to provide special attention and services to fathers who fall substantially behind in their child-support obligations.[19] Finally, some states give subject-matter jurisdiction to more than one kind of court, each of which has **concurrent jurisdiction** to hear some or all family-law cases.

concurrent jurisdiction
Subject-matter jurisdiction that resides in more than one kind of court in the same judicial system.

EXHIBIT 7-2

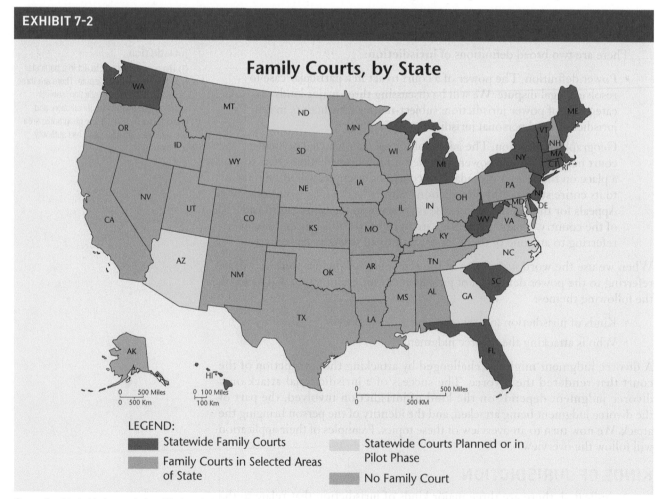

Family Courts, by State

LEGEND:
- Statewide Family Courts
- Family Courts in Selected Areas of State
- Statewide Courts Planned or in Pilot Phase
- No Family Court

Source: Reprinted with the permission of Barbara A. Babb, Director, Center for Families, Children and the Courts (CFCC) (law.ubalt.edu/cfcc); *United Family Court Connection* (Spring 2008) (law.ubalt.edu/downloads/law_downloads/UFC_Spring_2008.pdf).

Parties have no control over whether a particular court has subject-matter jurisdiction. They cannot **stipulate**, for example, that a court has this jurisdiction if in fact the laws indicated above do not specify that the court has it. This is different from *personal jurisdiction* discussed below. Consent between the parties can confer personal jurisdiction on a court.

The vast majority of family-law cases are heard in state courts. In the main, *federal* courts do not have subject-matter jurisdiction over such cases even if there is **diversity of citizenship** among the parties. When parties are citizens of different states, the federal courts have diversity jurisdiction, but under the **domestic-relations exception**, federal courts will not hear cases involving the granting of divorce, alimony, or child custody even if the parties are from different states. If the case does not involve granting or ending divorce, alimony, or child custody, the exception does not apply. For example, a federal court will hear some child-support enforcement cases in which a parent is prosecuted for willful nonpayment of child support if the parent does not live in the same state as the children. Such cases, however, are relatively rare.

In Rem Jurisdiction

In rem jurisdiction is required for a court to dissolve a marriage. In rem jurisdiction is a court's power over a particular **res**, which is a thing or status that is located within the territory over which the court has authority. An example of a thing is land or other property; an example of a status is a marriage.

How does a court acquire in rem jurisdiction in divorce cases? It is acquired by the domicile of the husband or the wife in the state. In divorce actions, the res is the marriage, which is "located" in any state where one or both spouses are domiciled. In rem jurisdiction gives a court the power to terminate the marriage. A court lacks in rem jurisdiction if it renders a divorce judgment when neither party is domiciled in that state. Such a judgment is not entitled to FFC. Therefore, another state is not required to enforce the divorce judgment. In rem jurisdiction, however, is *not* sufficient to give the court power to resolve support and property-division issues involving property in other states. Such issues require personal jurisdiction (see below).

A court also has in rem jurisdiction over any property (e.g., land) located in the state. This jurisdiction gives the court the power to issue rulings affecting that res in the divorce action. Courts, however, do not have in rem jurisdiction over property located in another state. If they want to make orders affecting such property, personal jurisdiction is needed.

In addition to proper jurisdiction, the other party (the nondomiciliary) must be given notice of the divorce proceeding and an opportunity to be heard. This is a basic requirement of due process of law. We will discuss this requirement later in the chapter.

Personal Jurisdiction

Personal jurisdiction is required for a court to order spousal support (alimony), property division, and child support. Personal jurisdiction (also called in personam jurisdiction) is a court's power over a person to determine his or her personal rights and duties. If a court makes any of these three orders without personal jurisdiction, the order can be attacked on jurisdictional grounds; it is not entitled to FFC. Personal jurisdiction is not required to dissolve the marriage; in rem jurisdiction is sufficient.

How does a court acquire personal jurisdiction in divorce cases? There are four ways:

- Personal **service of process** on the defendant when physically present in the state. The **process** documents (e.g., the complaint or petition and summons) are personally delivered (handed) to the defendant (or to the defendant's authorized representative) in the state. In most states, service

stipulate

To enter an agreement with an opposing party on a particular matter. The noun is *stipulation*.

diversity of citizenship

The disputing parties are citizens of different states and the amount in controversy exceeds $75,000. This diversity gives subject-matter jurisdiction to a federal trial court; that is, a U.S. District Court. It is called diversity jurisdiction.

domestic-relations exception

Federal courts do not have subject-matter jurisdiction over the granting of divorce, alimony, or child custody even if there is diversity of citizenship among the parties, which will usually give such jurisdiction to a federal court.

in rem jurisdiction

The court's power over a particular res, which is a thing (e.g., a car) or a status (e.g., a marriage) that is located within the territory over which the court has authority.

res

A thing (e.g., land) or a status (e.g., marriage). (See glossary for an additional meaning.)

personal jurisdiction

A court's power over a person to determine (adjudicate) his or her personal rights and duties. Also called *in personam jurisdiction*.

service of process

A formal delivery of notice to a defendant that a suit has been initiated to which he or she must respond. *Process* is the means used by the court to acquire or exercise its power or jurisdiction over a person.

process

The means (e.g., a summons, writ, or other court order) used by the court to acquire or exercise its power or jurisdiction over a person.

can be carried out by the sheriff or by any adult other than the plaintiff. Personal service gives the court personal jurisdiction over the defendant even if the defendant is a nonresident or a nondomiciliary who happens to be temporarily in the state. Under some circumstances, personal service can be made on residents by leaving the service documents with a competent adult at the defendant's usual place of residence.

- Consent. A defendant can agree to be subject to the personal jurisdiction of the court. This is usually done simply by appearing in court and defending the case. Note, however, that if the defendant is not domiciled in the state (is a nondomiciliary), he or she can appear solely to contest the court's jurisdiction without submitting to full personal jurisdiction. *Any* appearance by a domiciliary, however, constitutes consent to full personal jurisdiction over the defendant by the court.

- **Substituted service.** Under some circumstances, the state will allow service by mail or by publication in a newspaper. This method of conferring personal jurisdiction is called *constructive service*.

- **Long-arm statute.** If the defendant is a nonresident of the state, the long-arm statute allows substituted service to acquire personal jurisdiction if the defendant has sufficient purposeful contacts with the state. The personal jurisdiction acquired through the long-arm statute is called **long-arm jurisdiction**. The defendant must have sufficient **minimum contacts** with the state so that it is reasonable and fair to require the defendant to appear and be subjected to full personal jurisdiction in the state. What constitutes sufficient minimum contacts to meet this standard? Minimum contacts are those activities in or connected with a state by a nonresident that are substantial enough so that it can be said that the nonresident has invoked the benefits and protections of the state, thereby making it fair for the state to assert personal jurisdiction over the nonresident. Here are some of the factors that a court will consider in determining whether such contacts exist, no one of which is necessarily conclusive:

  - The defendant was domiciled in the state at one time before he or she left.
  - The defendant cohabited with his or her spouse in the state before the defendant left the state.
  - The defendant visits the state.
  - The defendant arranges for schooling for his or her children in the state, etc.

We will return to long-arm jurisdiction in Chapters 8 and 10 when we discuss the Uniform Interstate Family Support Act (UIFSA).

Of the five orders that can be part of a divorce judgment, the one we have not yet discussed is the child-custody order. We will cover such orders in Chapter 9 where we will see that one of the major bases of child-custody jurisdiction is the state that meets the requirements of being the *home state*.

Exhibit 7-3 summarizes our discussion thus far of subject-matter, in rem, and personal jurisdiction.

substituted service
An approved method of completing service of process other than by handing the process documents to the defendant (or to the defendant's authorized representative) in person (e.g., service by mail or by publication in a newspaper). Also called constructive service.

long-arm statute
A statute that allows a state to obtain personal jurisdiction over a nonresident defendant because of the latter's purposeful contact with the state.

long-arm jurisdiction
The personal jurisdiction that a state acquires over a nonresident defendant because of his or her purposeful contact with the state.

minimum contacts
Activities in or connected with a state by a nonresident that are substantial enough so that it can be said that the nonresident has invoked the benefits and protections of the state, thereby making it fair for the state to assert personal jurisdiction over the nonresident.

EXHIBIT 7-3 **Kinds of Divorce Jurisdiction**

Kind of Jurisdiction a Court Can Have	Definition	How This Kind of Jurisdiction Is Acquired	What the Court Can Do with This Kind of Jurisdiction	What Else Is Required?	Full Faith and Credit (FFC) Consequences
Subject-Matter Jurisdiction	The court's power to resolve a particular type of legal dispute and to grant a particular type of relief.	The state constitution or a state statute that gives the court the power to hear cases involving the subject matter of divorce.	The court can hear the divorce case, but it cannot issue any orders unless it also has the proper jurisdiction for the order. (See in rem jurisdiction and personal jurisdiction below. See also child-custody jurisdiction in Chapter 9.)	• The residency requirement for the state and for the county must be met (see discussion of venue later in the chapter). • The defendant must be given notice of the proceeding and an opportunity to be heard.	If a state court issues a divorce judgment but the court did not have subject-matter jurisdiction to grant divorces, other states do not have to enforce (i.e., do not have to give FFC to) the divorce judgment.
In Rem Jurisdiction	The court's power over a particular res. The res may be a thing (e.g., land) or a status (e.g., marriage) located within the territory over which the court has authority.	• One or both of the spouses are domiciled in the state. • Property (e.g., land) is located in the state.	• The court can dissolve the marriage. • The court can make orders that affect property that exists in the state (e.g., land owned in the state during the marriage). Note, however, that personal jurisdiction is needed over the defendant to make spousal-support, child-support, and property-division orders that do not affect property physically located in the state.		Other states must give FFC to the judgment that dissolves the marriage. If, however, a court issues a divorce judgment but neither spouse was domiciled in the state at the time, the judgment is not entitled to FFC.
Personal Jurisdiction	A court's power over a person to determine (adjudicate) his or her personal rights and duties.	• Service of process on the defendant in the state. • Consent to be subject to personal jurisdiction. • Substituted service. • Long-arm statute if there are sufficient purposeful contacts with the state (minimum required).	The court can issue orders for spousal support (alimony), child support, and property division.		Other states must give FFC to the judgment on spousal support (alimony), child support, and property division. Without personal jurisdiction, however, a judgment on spousal support, property division, or child support is not enforceable or entitled to FFC.

PERSON ATTACKING THE DIVORCE JUDGMENT

Thus far we have identified the categories of jurisdiction that exist and which of these categories are needed to challenge various parts of the divorce judgment. Jurisdiction, however, is not enough. The person seeking to attack or challenge the divorce judgment must be eligible to bring the attack. We need to discuss three categories of persons:

1. *The person who obtained the divorce judgment, who helped the other spouse obtain it, or who received benefits from the judgment.* Can this person bring a jurisdictional attack against the divorce judgment? Answer in most states: No. A person should not be allowed to attack a divorce judgment on jurisdictional grounds if that person was the spouse who obtained the judgment; that is, was the plaintiff or petitioner in the action that resulted in the judgment. This person will be **estopped** from denying the validity of the divorce judgment. The same result will occur if this person helped his or her spouse obtain the divorce judgment or received benefits because of the judgment. This rule of **equitable estoppel** prevents a person from attacking a divorce judgment even though the judgment may be clearly invalid. Note, however, that a few courts do not follow this rule and will allow persons to attack a divorce judgment they participated in obtaining or from which they obtained benefits.

2. *The person against whom the divorce judgment was obtained.* Whether the person against whom the divorce judgment was obtained can attack the judgment on jurisdictional grounds will depend on several factors:

   - *Both sides appeared.* Assume that the divorce judgment was granted after both sides appeared before the court and argued their positions. Can either side attack the divorce judgment on jurisdictional grounds? Answer: No. If the person now attacking the divorce judgment on jurisdictional grounds appeared as the defendant in the action that led to the divorce judgment in that divorce action, he or she will not be allowed to attack the judgment in a later proceeding. He or she should have raised the jurisdictional attack in the original divorce action.

   - *Ex parte proceeding.* In an **ex parte** proceeding only one side appears, usually the plaintiff or petitioner. Assume that the divorce was granted after only one side appeared before the court to argue its positions. It was an **ex parte divorce**. Can the *absent* party against whom the divorce was obtained attack the divorce judgment on jurisdictional grounds? Answer: Yes.

   - *Accepted the benefits.* Can a party against whom the divorce was obtained attack the divorce judgment on jurisdictional grounds if that party has accepted benefits from the divorce (e.g., alimony payments)? Answer in many states: No.

   - *Remarriage.* Can a party against whom the divorce was obtained attack the divorce judgment on jurisdictional grounds if that party has remarried and now wants to invalidate or annul the second marriage? Answer in many states: No. If the person against whom the divorce was obtained has remarried, he or she will not be allowed to claim that the second marriage is invalid because of jurisdictional defects in the divorce judgment on the first marriage. There are, however, some states that will allow the jurisdictional attack on the divorce judgment if the person making the attack did not know about the jurisdictional defect (e.g., no domicile) at the time.

3. *A person who was not a party to the divorce action.* Finally, we consider jurisdictional attacks against a divorce judgment brought by persons

---

estopped

Prevented from asserting a right or a defense because it would be unfair or inequitable to allow the assertion. The noun is *estoppel*.

equitable estoppel

The voluntary conduct of a person will preclude him or her from asserting rights against another who justifiably relied on the conduct and who would suffer damage or injury if the person is now allowed to repudiate the conduct. Also called *estoppel in pais*.

ex parte

With only one side present (usually the plaintiff or petitioner) when court action is requested.

ex parte divorce

A divorce rendered by a court when only one of the spouses participates or appears in court. Also called unilateral divorce.

who were not parties to the proceeding that granted the divorce judgment.

- *Second spouse*. After John divorces Mary, he marries Diane. Diane, of course, was not a party in the divorce action between John and Mary. Assume that Diane now wants to have her marriage to John annulled. She argues that when she married John, he was still married to Mary because the court that divorced John and Mary had no jurisdiction to award the divorce. Can a second spouse who was not a party to the prior divorce action challenge the validity of that divorce on jurisdictional grounds? Answer: No. The second spouse relied on the validity of the divorce when he or she entered the marriage and should not now be allowed to upset the validity of that marriage by challenging the validity of the divorce judgment.

- *Child of the parties*. Bill and Pat have one child, Greg. Bill and Pat obtain a divorce judgment. Years later, Greg wants to claim that the divorce of his parents was invalid because of jurisdictional defects in the proceeding that granted the divorce. Can a child of divorced parents challenge the validity of the divorce judgment on jurisdictional grounds? Answer: The child stands in the shoes of the parent. If the parent would have been prevented from attacking the divorce on jurisdictional grounds (see discussion above), the child will also be prevented from bringing such a challenge. If the parent would not be prevented, the child will not be prevented.

DIRECT ATTACK; COLLATERAL ATTACK

In the last example involving Greg and his parent's divorce judgment, Greg's challenge was not brought in the same proceeding that led to his parent's divorce judgment. There are two ways to challenge or attack a judgment: directly or collaterally. The difference depends on the proceeding in which the attack is made. A **direct attack** is a challenge or attack against the validity of a judgment raised in the same proceeding that rendered the judgment. A **collateral attack** is a challenge or attack against the validity of a judgment raised in a different proceeding from the one that rendered the judgment.

Assume, for example, that Mary goes to a state trial court to sue Ed for child support. She wins a judgment. Ed disagrees with the judgment. Let's look at two possibilities:

- Within the time period allowed to file an appeal, Ed appeals the judgment to the next highest court in the judicial system. This challenge brought immediately after the trial court rendered its judgment is a direct attack.

- Suppose, however, that the time for bringing a normal appeal has passed. In the same state or in a different state, Mary brings a separate suit against Ed to enforce the child-support judgment. In this new suit, Ed says the child-support judgment is invalid. This is a *collateral attack* against the judgment.

In general, an attack against a judgment is collateral when it is brought in a court proceeding that is outside the normal appeal process; it is direct when it is brought within the normal appeal process.

JURISDICTIONAL ANALYSIS: EXAMPLES

1. *Tom and Mary are married in Massachusetts, where both are domiciled. Mary moves to Ohio, which is now her state of domicile. Tom remains in Massachusetts. Mary obtains a divorce judgment from an Ohio state court. The judgment dissolves the marriage and awards Mary $500 a month in alimony. Tom was notified of the action by mail but did not appear. He was not served with process in Ohio. He has had no contacts with Ohio. Mary travels to Massachusetts and brings an action against Tom to enforce the alimony award of the Ohio court.*

direct attack

A challenge or attack against the validity of a judgment raised in the same proceeding that rendered the judgment (e.g., an appeal).

collateral attack

A challenge or attack against the validity of a judgment raised in a different proceeding from the one that rendered the judgment.

Jurisdictional Analysis

- The Ohio court had jurisdiction to dissolve the marriage because of Mary's domicile in Ohio. This part of the divorce judgment is entitled to full faith and credit (FFC) in Massachusetts (i.e., Massachusetts *must* recognize this aspect of the Ohio divorce judgment if the Massachusetts court determines that Mary was in fact domiciled in Ohio at the time of the divorce judgment).

- The Ohio court did not have jurisdiction to render an alimony award because it did not have personal jurisdiction over Tom. This part of the divorce judgment is not entitled to FFC in Massachusetts (i.e., the Massachusetts court does not have to enforce the Ohio alimony award).

2. *Ed and Sue are married in New York, where both are domiciled. Ed moves to Delaware, which is now his state of domicile. Sue remains in New York. Ed obtains a divorce judgment from a Delaware state court. The judgment dissolves the marriage but rules that Sue is not entitled to alimony from Ed. Sue was notified of the action by mail but did not appear. She was not served with process in Delaware. She has had no contacts with Delaware. In a New York state court, Sue brings an action seeking alimony from Ed. Ed argues that the Delaware ruling on alimony should be recognized and enforced in New York.*

Jurisdictional Analysis

- The Delaware court had jurisdiction to dissolve the marriage because of Ed's domicile in Delaware. This part of the divorce judgment is entitled to FFC in New York (i.e., New York *must* recognize this aspect of the Delaware divorce judgment if the New York court determines that Ed was in fact domiciled in Delaware at the time of the divorce judgment).

- The Delaware court did not have jurisdiction to decide whether Sue should be awarded alimony because it did not have personal jurisdiction over her. This part of the divorce judgment that said she should not be given alimony is not entitled to FFC credit in New York (i.e., New York court does not have to enforce the Delaware alimony decision).

3. *Bill and Pat are married in New Jersey, where both are domiciled. Bill travels to Michigan and files for divorce in a Michigan state court. Once the divorce is granted, he returns to New Jersey. Neither he nor Pat were ever domiciled in Michigan. Bill then marries Linda in New Jersey. Linda and Bill separate after having marital difficulties. Linda brings a support action (separate-maintenance action) against Bill in New Jersey. Bill's defense is that he is not married to Linda because the Michigan divorce is invalid due to the fact that neither he nor Pat was domiciled in Michigan when he obtained the Michigan divorce and hence the Michigan court did not have in rem jurisdiction to dissolve the marriage. Hence, he is still married to Pat and has no duty to support Linda.*

Jurisdictional Analysis

- Bill is raising a collateral attack against the divorce judgment. He is attacking the jurisdiction of the court to award the divorce because of the absence of domicile. He is raising this attack (via a defense to a separate-maintenance action) outside the appeal process for challenging a Michigan divorce judgment.

- Bill is the person who obtained the Michigan divorce judgment. In most states, he will be estopped from attacking the judgment on jurisdictional grounds. Even though he can prove that neither he nor Pat was domiciled in Michigan, he will not be allowed to do so. He relied on the divorce judgment and took the benefits of the divorce when he married Linda. He should not be allowed to attack the very thing he helped accomplish.

4. *Joe and Helen are married in Arizona, where both are domiciled. Helen goes to New Mexico and obtains a divorce judgment against Joe. Joe knows about the action but does not appear. Neither Joe nor Helen were ever domiciled in New Mexico. Joe marries Priscilla. When Helen dies, Joe claims part of her estate. His position is that he is her surviving husband because the New Mexico court had no jurisdiction to divorce them, since neither he nor Helen were ever domiciled there.*

Jurisdictional Analysis

- Joe was not the party who sought the New Mexico divorce. The divorce proceeding was ex parte. Normally, he would be allowed to attack the divorce judgment on the ground that no one was domiciled in New Mexico at the time of the divorce.

- But Joe relied upon the divorce and accepted its benefits by marrying Priscilla. It would be inconsistent to allow him to change his mind now, and it could be unfair to Priscilla. Hence, Joe will be estopped from attacking the divorce on jurisdictional grounds.

5. *Wayne and Olivia are married in Oregon, where both are domiciled. They have two children. Olivia decides she can no longer live with Wayne. She takes the children to Pennsylvania. Wayne stays in Oregon, although he visits the children about twice a year. During one of the visits, he cohabits with Olivia, but leaves after a week due to renewed marital difficulties. Olivia files for and is granted a divorce judgment in Pennsylvania. The judgment dissolves the marriage and awards Olivia the car that she and Wayne owned in Oregon, which Wayne still uses in Oregon. Wayne was never served with process in Pennsylvania. He was notified of the divorce action by mail but did not appear. Olivia also published a notice of the pending divorce action in a general circulation newspaper.*

Jurisdictional Analysis

- Pennsylvania had in rem jurisdiction because of Olivia's domicile in Pennsylvania. This part of the divorce judgment is entitled to FFC in every other state.

- The Pennsylvania court also awarded the Oregon car to Olivia. The vehicle is marital property; it was owned by both parties during the marriage. An award of marital property outside the state (a property division) requires personal jurisdiction. Did the Pennsylvania court have personal jurisdiction over Wayne, a nonresident of Pennsylvania? If Pennsylvania has a long-arm statute, it could acquire personal jurisdiction over a nonresident by substituted service if the nonresident has had sufficient purposeful contacts with Pennsylvania so that it is reasonable and fair to require the nonresident to appear and be subjected to full personal jurisdiction in the state. Wayne had such minimum contacts through his visits with the children in Pennsylvania and his cohabitation with Olivia in the state. Hence, Pennsylvania had personal jurisdiction (called long-arm jurisdiction) to order the property division and this order is entitled to FFC in every other state.

CUSTODY JURISDICTION

States differ on what is required for a court to have jurisdiction to make a decision on child custody. In some states, the court must have personal jurisdiction over both parents. Other states treat child custody as a status determination, which the court has jurisdiction to make if one parent and the child have a domicile in the state. A critical factor is the **home state** of the child. This is the state where the child has lived with a parent (or anyone acting as a parent) for at least six consecutive months immediately before the custody or support case begins in court or since birth if the child is less than six months old. We will examine custody jurisdiction in detail in Chapter 9.

VENUE

Venue means the place of the trial. Venue is different from subject-matter jurisdiction. The latter concerns the power of a court to hear a particular kind of case. Venue concerns the choice among several courts that have the power (jurisdiction) to hear the case. Every county in the state, for example, may contain a superior or county court with subject-matter jurisdiction to grant divorces. The choice of which superior or county court a party selects to file for divorce is called *choice of venue*. The state's statutory code will specify the requirements for the selection of venue. The requirements often relate to the residence (which may mean domicile) of the plaintiff or defendant. For example, the statute might specify that a divorce action can be filed in the county where the defendant spouse resides or in the county where either the plaintiff or the defendant has been a resident for three months preceding the commencement of the action. This residency requirement may be in addition to the requirement that the plaintiff be a resident of the state for a designated period of time (e.g., six months) immediately before filing the action.

SUMMARY DISSOLUTION

In some states, it is possible to obtain a divorce primarily through the mail without going through elaborate court procedures. Such a divorce is often referred to as a **summary dissolution** or a *simplified dissolution*. The requirements for taking advantage of this option are quite strict. In Illinois, for example, the

---

home state
The state where the child has lived with a parent (or anyone acting as a parent) for atleast six consecutive months immediately before the custody or support case begins in court or since birth if the child is less than six months old.

venue
The place of the trial. The proper county or geographical area in which a court with jurisdiction may hear a case. When more than one court has subject-matter jurisdiction to hear a particular kind of case, the selection of the court is called *choice of venue*.

summary dissolution
A divorce obtained in an expedited manner because of the brevity of the marriage, the minimal amount of marital property, and the lack of controversy between the husband and wife.

couple must be childless, be married for five years or less, have no interest in real property (other than a lease on a residence), waive any rights to spousal support, etc. In short, there must be very little need for courts, attorneys, and the protection of the legal system. The less conflict between parties over children, property, and support, the easier it is to obtain a divorce.

Unfortunately, however, even simple divorce cases can sometimes drag on for substantial periods of time because of crowded court calendars.

PRETRIAL MATTERS

NOTICE AND OPPORTUNITY TO BE HEARD

It is not enough that a court has proper jurisdiction to issue any of the five orders that often comprise a divorce judgment. Under the Due Process Clause of the U.S. Constitution, defendants have a **procedural due process** right to be given notice of divorce proceedings filed against them and an opportunity to be heard at the proceedings. The notice formally alerts defendants of this opportunity. Notice is achieved by service of process. As indicated earlier, a main method of completing service of process is by handing the process documents (e.g., the complaint/petition and summons) to the defendant in person.

In some cases, substituted service (e.g., U.S. mail and publication in a newspaper) can be used. The long-arm statute allows substituted service for nonresident defendants who cannot be served with process in the state if the minimum-contacts requirements of the statute can be met. In general, however, courts are reluctant to allow substituted or constructive service because of a suspicion that a plaintiff may not want the defendant to be found and thus may make little more than faint-hearted attempts to locate the defendant. Here is how one court described its conditions for allowing substituted service:

> [It is] incumbent upon a plaintiff in a divorce action to furnish the court with the following information before an order authorizing constructive notice is entered: (1) the time and place at which the parties last resided together as spouses; (2) the last time the parties were in contact with each other; (3) the name and address of the last employer of the defendant either during the time the parties resided together or at a later time if known to the plaintiff; (4) the names and addresses of those relatives known to be close to the defendant; and (5) any other information which could furnish a fruitful basis for further inquiry by one truly bent on learning the present whereabouts of the defendant. From such basic information, the plaintiff should then detail for the court the particular efforts which have been made in the effort to ascertain the defendant's present address.[20]

To be sure that the defendant has received notice of the proceedings, the plaintiff must file a **proof of service**, which is a sworn statement (or other evidence) that the requirements of in-person or substituted service of process on a party have been accomplished.

Courts are scrupulous in ensuring that the notice to the defendant is proper. In a recent case, a woman received a divorce judgment after her husband failed to respond to the divorce petition served on him. (See the discussion below on default divorce.) The court, however, vacated (voided) the judgment when it was later discovered that the notice she gave her husband of the divorce proceeding was defective. The divorce petition failed to indicate that she was pregnant. This should have been mentioned in the petition because (as we will see in Chapter 13 on paternity) a husband is presumed to be the father of a child born during the marriage and within a designated number of days after a divorce. When she became aware that she was pregnant, she should have amended her petition to indicate the pregnancy and served the amended petition on her husband.[21]

procedural due process
The constitutional requirement that the government provide fair procedures such as notice and an opportunity to be heard whenever the government seeks to deprive someone of life, liberty, or property.

proof of service
A sworn statement (or other evidence) that service of process on a party has been accomplished. Also called certificate of service and return of service.

REPRESENTATION

Parties to a divorce can be represented by counsel. If there is an imbalance of wealth at the outset of the divorce litigation, the court can issue an order requiring the more-well-off spouse to pay the attorney fees and court costs of the other spouse. **Indigent** parties are sometimes represented by legal aid societies or legal service offices that provide free legal services to individuals who cannot afford private counsel. With few exceptions, poor persons are not entitled to counsel at government expense. We will examine the limited exceptions in Chapter 10 when we cover child-support enforcement proceedings and in Chapter 13 when we cover paternity actions. As we will see, however, even in these limited areas of the law, a free government-paid attorney is not required in every child-support or paternity case.

More and more courts are providing different kinds of assistance to parties representing themselves (**pro se**) in uncomplicated divorce and other family-law cases. The assistance might consist of standard forms and instructions on court procedures provided by volunteer facilitators available in the courthouse or by online self-help centers. Occasionally, pro se parties seek the assistance of an attorney for discrete tasks rather than for full legal representation. See Chapter 2 for a discussion of the ethical issues involved in limited-scope representation (**unbundled legal services**) provided by attorneys. Chapter 2 also covers the legality of assistance provided by independent paralegals to pro se parties.

GUARDIAN AD LITEM (GAL)

If an individual in the litigation is a minor, is insane, or is otherwise incapacitated at the time of the divorce action, the court may appoint a guardian (called a **guardian ad litem (GAL)**) to protect his or her interests during the proceeding. Some GALs are attorneys who provide full representation of the individual being protected. Other GALs, however, have a narrower role of insuring that the best interests of the child are brought to the court's attention. They might, for example, prepare a home-study report on the living conditions of the child of a divorcing couple. In this role, courts can allow a nonattorney to be a GAL.

Courts often use **court appointed special advocates (CASAs)**. They are volunteers who act as fact-finders, interviewers, and investigators in cases involving child welfare. (Many paralegals have been appointed as CASA volunteers.) They do not represent the child, but they gather pertinent information on the child's welfare and report on these findings to the court. You can find CASA programs in your area by checking the main CASA website (www.nationalcasa.org).

PLEADINGS

Pleadings are the formal documents that contain claims or defenses of parties in litigation. Most states have what is called a *forms-driven practice*, which means that official standard forms have been prepared by the courts and must be used in divorce and other family-law cases. In such states, attorneys do not write (draft) many pleadings from scratch. Rather, the attorneys and their paralegals fill out and adapt the required standard forms.

The first pleading in a divorce case is called the **complaint** (or in some states, the **petition**). It states the claim or cause of action a party is seeking. The claim we are discussing here is a divorce. The party filing the complaint/petition is the plaintiff or **petitioner**; the opposing party is the defendant or **respondent**. See Exhibit 7-4 for an example of a divorce complaint/petition. (If both spouses have no significant disagreements between them, some states allow them to file a *joint petition* for the divorce.) The main parts of the complaint/petition are as follows:

- Caption. The **caption** consists of the heading or introductory part of a pleading or other document that identifies what it is (e.g., Petition for Dissolution or In the Matter of the Marriage of David Foley and Helen Foley), the names of the parties, the court involved, etc.

---

indigent

Poor; without means to afford something such as a private attorney or filing fees.

pro se

(on one's own behalf) Representing oneself; not being represented by an attorney. Also called *pro per (in propria persona)*.

unbundled legal services

Discrete task representation as opposed to providing services on all tasks needed by a client on a legal matter.

guardian ad litem (GAL)

A special guardian (often, but not always, an attorney) appointed by the court to appear in court proceedings on behalf of a person who is a minor, is insane, or is otherwise incapacitated.

court appointed special advocate (CASA)

A volunteer appointed by the court to undertake special assignments pertaining to children in the court system.

pleadings

Formal litigation documents (e.g., a complaint or petition, an answer) filed by parties that state or respond to claims or defenses of other parties.

complaint

A plaintiff's first pleading that states a claim against the defendant. Also called petition. (See glossary for an additional definition.)

petition

A complaint. (See glossary for an additional definition.)

petitioner

A party who files a petition or complaint. A plaintiff. (See glossary for an additional meaning.)

respondent

The party responding to a position or claim of another party; the defendant. (See glossary for an additional meaning.)

caption

The heading or introductory part of a pleading or other document that identifies what it is, the names of the parties, the court involved, etc.

EXHIBIT 7-4 Basic Structure of a Divorce Complaint/Petition

STATE OF _____

COUNTY OF _____

FAMILY COURT BRANCH

Mary Smith, Plaintiff

v.   Civil Action No. _____

Fred Smith, Defendant

COMPLAINT FOR ABSOLUTE DIVORCE

The plaintiff, through her attorney, alleges:

(1) The jurisdiction of this court is based upon section _____, title _____ of the State Code (2013).

(2) The plaintiff is fifty years old.

(3) The plaintiff is a resident of the State of _____, County of _____. She has resided here for five years immediately preceding the filing of this complaint.

(4) The parties were married on March 13, 1983, in the State of _____, County of _____.

(5) There are no children born of this marriage.

(6) The plaintiff and defendant lived and cohabitated together from the date of their marriage until February 2, 2012, at which time they both agreed to separate because of mutual incompatibility. This separation has continued voluntarily and without cohabitation for more than two years until the present time.

(7) Since the separation, the plaintiff has resided at _____, and the defendant has resided at _____.

(8) There is no reasonable likelihood of reconciliation.

WHEREFORE, the plaintiff PRAYS:

(1) For an absolute divorce.

(2) For alimony and a division of property.

(3) For restoration of her maiden name.

(4) For reasonable attorney's fees and costs.

(5) For such other relief as this Court may deem just and proper.

_____   _____

Linda Stout   Mary Smith, Plaintiff

Attorney for Plaintiff

234 Main St.

_____, _____ 07237

STATE of _____

COUNTY of _____

Mary Smith, being first duly sworn on oath according to law, deposes and says that she has read the foregoing complaint by her subscribed and that the matters stated therein are true to the best of her knowledge, information, and belief.

_____

Mary Smith

Subscribed and sworn to before me on this _____ day of _____, 2014

_____

Notary Public

My commission expires _____

Caption

Jurisdiction and Venue

Body

Prayer for Relief

Subscription

Verification

Notarization

© Cengage Learning 2013

- Jurisdiction and venue. The beginning of the complaint/petition contains a cite to the statute or constitutional provision giving the court subject-matter jurisdiction over divorces. It also states facts on why the venue of this court is appropriate, including how long the party has been

prayer
A formal request.

subscription
1. A signature. 2. The act of signing one's name.

verification
A formal declaration stating that a party has read the pleading and swears that it is true to the best of his or her knowledge.

notarize
To certify or attest to something, e.g., the authenticity of a signature.

template
A set of formulas used to perform a designated task.

summons
A court notice served on the defendant ordering him or her to appear and answer the allegations of the plaintiff.

in forma pauperis
As a poor person who is allowed to proceed without paying certain filing fees and other court costs.

answer
A party's pleading that responds to the petition or complaint of an opposing party. It is the first pleading of the defendant that responds to the plaintiff's claims.

affirmative defense
A defense raising facts or arguments that will defeat the opponent's claim even if the opponent's fact allegations in the claim are proven.

counterclaim
A claim by one side in a case (usually the defendant) that is filed in response to a claim asserted by an opponent (usually the plaintiff).

default judgment
A judgment against a party for failure to file a required pleading or otherwise respond to an opponent's claim.

prove-up
The presentation of evidence to support one's claims even if they are unopposed.

default divorce
A divorce that is granted because of the failure of a party to appear, plead, or otherwise defend the divorce action of the other party.

a resident of the state and county. Basic facts about the parties and the marriage are stated here or in the body of the pleading.

- Body. The body is the part of the pleading that contains the main allegations of the party.
- Prayer for relief. A **prayer** is a formal request. The prayer for relief asks the court for specific results, e.g., to dissolve the marriage and divide the marital property.
- Subscription. A **subscription** is a signature. Local law specifies who must subscribe (sign) the pleading, often the party and his or her attorney.
- Verification. The **verification** is a formal declaration stating that a party has read the pleading and swears that it is true to the best of his or her knowledge. The party thereby *verifies* the pleading.
- Notarization. To **notarize** means to certify or attest to something (e.g., the authenticity of a signature).

There are a number of assignments in this book that ask you to draft a complaint/petition. The general instructions for this assignment are found in Appendix A. Review these instructions now. They provide a good overview of the law governing this pleading.

High-volume offices that handle many of the same kinds of cases have their own forms for a complaint/petition and for other pleadings that they adapt for particular client cases. Many commercial companies also sell document assembly software with **templates** that provide the basic structure of the document that can be adapted. For example, see www.ProDoc.com and www.HotDocs.com.

The lawsuit begins when the plaintiff files the complaint/petition with the court (along with the appropriate filing fee). The court then issues a **summons**, which is a formal notice that informs the defendant a lawsuit has been filed and that orders the defendant to appear and answer the allegations of the plaintiff. A copy of the complaint and the summons are served on the defendant (see earlier discussion on notice). If the plaintiff is poor (indigent), he or she can apply to the court for a waiver of filing fees and related court costs in order to proceed **in forma pauperis** (as a poor person).

The response of the defendant is the **answer**, which is the pleading filed by the party who responds to the complaint/petition of an opposing party. For some claims, the defendant may want to file an **affirmative defense**, which raises facts or arguments that will defeat the opponent's claim even if the opponent's fact allegations are proven. In most states, the defendant can raise his or her own claim (called a **counterclaim**) against the plaintiff in the answer. Hence, when the plaintiff asks for a divorce in the complaint, the defendant's answer can also ask for a divorce in a counterclaim.

DEFAULT JUDGMENT; DEFAULT DIVORCE

The summons issued by the court and served on the defendant warns the defendant that if he or she does not respond within a designated number of days, a **default judgment** can be entered against him or her. (Such a judgment can be granted against a party for failure to file a required pleading or otherwise respond to an opponent's claim.) In divorce cases, a plaintiff who moves for (requests) a default judgment is still required to introduce evidence to establish his or her case. (This is done in what is often called a **prove-up** hearing.) Unlike other civil proceedings, the default judgment is not automatic in many family-law cases. A divorce granted in a default judgment is sometimes called a **default divorce**.

PRETRIAL CONFERENCES

Before the trial begins, the judge holds one or more **pretrial conferences** in order to narrow the issues, secure stipulations, establish parameters for discovery, make a final effort to settle the case without a trial, and cover other preliminary matters. See the discussion of preliminary orders below for a list of the kinds of orders that might be made in a preliminary conference. The decisions made at the conference become the blueprint for the case and are sometimes referred to as the *case management plan* or, collectively, as the *case management order.*

WAITING PERIOD

Some states have a compulsory *waiting period* or "cooling-off" period (e.g., 60 days) that usually begins to run from the time the divorce complaint/petition is filed. During this period of time, no further proceedings are held in the hope that tempers might calm down, producing an atmosphere of reconciliation.

DISCOVERY

Divorce cases can involve many facts, particularly when finances are in dispute: "Usually the parties have numerous assets and liabilities that need to be documented, discovered, and produced for review in order to settle or try cases."[22] (See the large list of relevant facts and documents outlined in the family history covered in Exhibit 3-1 in Chapter 3.) **Discovery** consists of methods or devices used by parties to force information from each other before trial to aid in trial preparation. For cases that involve substantial assets, discovery is "the most time-intensive and expensive phase of a family-law case."[23] One of the reasons for this is the broad scope of what is **discoverable**. The parties can use the discovery devices to obtain any facts that are relevant to the litigation so long as those facts are not protected by **privilege** such as the **attorney-client privilege** and the **doctor–patient privilege**. The major formal discovery devices are as follows:

- **Interrogatories.** A discovery device in which one party sends written questions to another party. Rogs, as they are called, cannot be sent to nonparties. For an example of a set of interrogatories, see Appendix C.
- **Deposition.** A discovery device in which one party questions another party (or questions the other party's witness), usually outside the courtroom, in the office of one of the attorneys. The person questioned is called the **deponent**. When someone is questioned, we say that he or she is being *deposed*. Most depositions are **transcribed** so that a word-for-word account of what took place is available to the parties. Some depositions are videotaped, particularly when the deponent is a child in a custody case. If a nonparty is being deposed, that person usually must be served with a **subpoena** to appear at the deposition. Parties and nonparties must be served with a **subpoena duces tecum** to require that they bring with them specific things such as documents.
- **Request for admissions (RFA).** A discovery device in which one party sends a request to another party that the latter agree that a certain fact or legal conclusion is true so that there will be no need to present proof or arguments about such matters during the trial.
- **Request for production (RFP).** A discovery device in which one party requests that another party provide access to documents or other tangible things (e.g., tax returns, credit card receipts, diaries, business records) for copying or inspection. The device also includes a request to enter the party's land.

pretrial conference
A meeting of the attorneys and the judge (or magistrate) before the trial to attempt to narrow the issues, secure stipulations, make a final effort to settle the case without a trial, and cover other preliminary matters. Also called a *trial management conference.*

discovery
Devices used by parties to force information from each other before trial to aid in trial preparation. (See glossary for an additional definition.).

discoverable
Pertaining to information or other materials an opponent can obtain through deposition, interrogatories, or other discovery device.

privilege
A special legal benefit, right, exemption, or protection. (See glossary for an additional meaning.)

attorney-client privilege
A client or a client's attorney can refuse to disclose any confidential (private) communication between them if the purpose of the communication was to facilitate the provision of legal services to the client.

doctor–patient privilege
A patient or a patient's doctor can refuse to disclose any confidential (private) communications between them that relate to the patient's medical care.

interrogatories
A discovery device in which one party sends written questions to another party.

deposition
A discovery device in which one party questions another party (or questions the other party's witness) usually outside the courtroom.

deponent
A person questioned in a deposition.

transcribed
Taken down in a word-for-word account.

subpoena
A command to appear at a certain time and place.

subpoena duces tecum
A command that a witness appear at a certain time and place and bring specified things such as documents or jewelry.

- **Independent Medical Examination (IME).** A discovery device in which a party obtains a court-ordered professional examination of a person whose physical or mental condition is in controversy. If paternity is at issue, for example, the court might order a man to undergo a blood-grouping or DNA test.

E-discovery

electronic data discovery (EDD)
The discovery of data found in e-mails, spreadsheets, databases, and other digital formats. Also called *e-discovery*.

Many records are created and maintained on computers and other digital devices. **Electronic data discovery (EDD)** (also called *e-discovery*) can be crucial in uncovering these records.

Today's American family is a digital family living in a digital ecosphere that can tell family stories and reveal family secrets better than any after-the-fact human recollection. The volume of a family's household data now rivals that of a small business. Simply put, family members do not just use some digital tools, they live digitally: e-mail, Facebook, Twitter, instant messaging, texting. Young people today were "born digital." . . . The family's financial records will be stored electronically. Banking, investments, retirement accounts, and profit-sharing plans will likely be managed electronically from the home computers. E-mails abound from the PTA, high school, and college networks, neighborhood associations, and sports teams. Employer-owned laptops brought home for work in the evenings also may contain these personal records.[24]

It is critically important during initial client interviews to find out what computers all family members have access to, what cell and other digital devices they have, what e-mail programs they use, what social networks they are on, and what other interactive websites they regularly use by uploading pictures and entering other data about themselves and their special interests. The client must be cautioned not to erase or alter any of this material; such tampering could lead to charges of destroying or altering evidence (**spoliation**). Computers outside the home, particularly those at business locations controlled by one or both spouses, also often contain data that will be relevant to property division and other divorce issues.

spoliation
Intentionally destroying, altering, or concealing evidence.

Limitations on Discovery

There are some limitations on the use of the discovery devices. For example, most states have restrictions on who can be deposed and on the number of questions one divorce party can ask of another in interrogatories. These restrictions may vary depending on the complexity of the case. The parties can always make requests to the court to have these restrictions lifted or waived based on the specific needs of a party.

Duty to Supplement Responses

Parties responding to discovery requests have a duty to supplement answers already given in depositions, interrogatories, and other discovery devices if the facts change or if further facts become known and the changed or new facts affect the accuracy or completeness of the facts given earlier to the other party. For example, if a spouse answered an interrogatory on the value of specific property and this value changes substantially after the interrogatory was answered, the responding spouse has a duty to provide the new value to the requesting spouse.

Discovery Abuse

privileged
Protected from disclosure; not discoverable.

If a party is abusing the discovery process by harassing the other side or is demanding information that is **privileged** or otherwise protected from disclosure by law, the responding party may bring a motion for a **protective order**. Upon motion by any party or by the person from whom discovery is sought, and for **good cause** shown, the court in which the action is pending may make any order that justice requires to protect a party or person from annoyance, embarrassment, oppression, or undue burden or expense.

Some feel that discovery abuse in divorce cases is all-too-common. According to one seasoned family-law attorney:

> In many cases, thousands of pages of documents exchange hands, and parties submit to a variety of mental health, financial, and other discovery examinations. Even nonparties whose lives somehow touch the litigants often are subject to deposition under compulsion of a subpoena and court orders. The universe of what is discoverable, the power to compel compliance with discovery demands, and the penalties for noncompliance all have been greatly enlarged. Practitioners and parties have benefited from the meaningful exchange of information necessary to resolve a case fairly. Yet, there is a trend toward excessive discovery, pushed in many cases by the defensive practice of law by attorneys who are far less concerned about what the discovery will reveal than they are about potential criticism from clients if they fail to obtain the information.[25]

INVENTORY OF ASSETS AND LIABILITIES

Discovery also includes information that the parties must exchange without being asked to do so (sometimes called *mandatory self-disclosure*). For example, at the beginning of the case, they must exchange and file with the court an *inventory of assets and liabilities* (also called *declaration of disclosure*, and *statement of* **net worth**). The inventory lists all the assets and debts that each spouse says are relevant to the support and property-division issues in the case. In some states they must also file a final inventory at the end of the case to reflect changes and updates since the last inventory.

If the data provided by a spouse in an inventory is unclear, incomplete, and deceptive, the other side can use the discovery devices outlined above to try to obtain a more accurate account of assets and liabilities. Suppose, for example, that the inventory says certain jewelry is separate (rather than marital) property because it was a gift from the spouse's parent. The interrogatories of the other spouse can seek details on the value of the jewelry, the date the spouse obtained it, the reason it was allegedly given as a gift, etc. A request for production could ask that the jewelry be turned over for purposes of inspection and independent evaluation by an appraiser.

A spouse's failure to be truthful in the inventory and during discovery can have severe consequences. In a widely publicized California case, a wife failed to tell her husband that her social group had won the lottery. The wife's share of the winnings was $1.3 million. Because of this fraud, the court ruled that the entire $1.3 million had to be given to her ex-husband.[26]

ASSIGNMENT 7.10

Pick any well-known married couple in the media. Assume that they are getting a divorce and that you work for the law firm that is representing the wife. You are asked to draft interrogatories meant to elicit as much relevant information as possible about the husband's personal and business finances. The information will be used in the firm's representation of the wife on alimony and property-division issues. Draft the interrogatories. You do not need to know actual information about the finances of the person questioned through the interrogatories. A major purpose of the interrogatories is to find out what you don't know. (See General Instructions for the Interrogatories Assignment in Appendix A.)

---

protective order

A court order directing a person to refrain from doing something such as harming or harassing another.

good cause

A legally sufficient ground or reason. Also called just cause, sufficient cause.

net worth

Total assets of a person or business less total liabilities.

PRELIMINARY ORDERS

Obtaining a divorce can be time-consuming even when the matter is uncontested. The court's calendar may be so crowded that it could take months to have the case heard. If the case is contested and some bitterness exists between the parties, the litigation can be protracted. Pending the outcome of the litigation (**pendente lite**), parties may ask the court (as part of what is called *motion practice*) to issue a number of *preliminary* orders (sometimes called temporary orders), which remain in effect only until final determinations are made later. A motion is made for the order, often accompanied by an **affidavit** that states what is being requested and why. (A **movant** is a person making a motion; an **affiant** is a person making an affidavit.) Unless the request is routine, the movant will also include citations to legal authority that supports the granting of the request. The preliminary orders can include the following:

- Granting temporary physical custody of the children to one of the parents, who will become the *custodial parent*, the parent with whom the child is living. (Often, temporary custody orders become permanent because of the reluctance of courts to disrupt the living environment of children.) A court can also grant temporary *legal* custody to one of the parents.

- Granting temporary child visitation to the *noncustodial parent (NCP)*—the parent who is not living with the child.

- Granting temporary exclusive occupancy of the marital home to one of the spouses (often the custodial parent).

- Granting temporary child support.

- Granting temporary spousal support (alimony).

- Granting temporary attorney's fees and related court costs. In divorce cases, spouses are responsible for paying their own fees and costs. If, however, one spouse does not have the resources to pay private counsel and the other spouse has substantial resources, the court might order the latter to pay the other's fees and costs.

- Enjoining one spouse from bothering or molesting the other spouse and children. (To **enjoin** something is to prohibit it through an **injunction**; an injunction is a court order requiring a person or organization to do or to refrain from doing a particular thing.)

- Enjoining a spouse from transferring any property if the transfer might make it unavailable for property division or for the support of the other spouse and children. We will discuss the consequences of **dissipation** (the improper reduction or waste of marital assets that should have been available for property division upon divorce) in the next chapter.

- Appointing a **receiver** to manage a spouse's property in order to prevent him or her from squandering the property or otherwise making it unavailable to meet the spouse's obligations.

- Issuing a **ne exeat**, which is a writ that forbids a person from leaving or from removing a child or property from the state, country, or jurisdiction of the court.

- Enjoining the parties from changing insurance policies.

- Ordering an inventory and appraisal of all family assets and debts.

- Granting one spouse control of a business operated by one or both spouses.

- Enjoining the defendant from obtaining a foreign divorce.

In some states, orders such as these are not necessary because they are automatically imposed. For example, a state might provide that once the divorce

---

pendente lite
Pending the [outcome of the] litigation.

affidavit
A written statement containing facts, claims, or other legal positions given under oath or affirmation.

movant
A person who is making a motion.

affiant
A person making an affidavit.

enjoin
To prohibit something through injunction.

injunction
A court order requiring a person or organization to do or to refrain from doing a particular thing.

dissipation
The improper reduction or waste of marital assets that should have been available for property division upon divorce.

receiver
A person appointed by the court to manage property in litigation or in the process of bankruptcy.

ne exeat
A writ that forbids a person from leaving or from removing a child or property from the state, country, or jurisdiction of the court.

action begins and service of process is made, the parties are automatically restrained from transferring marital property, canceling insurance that now benefits family members, and removing minor children from the state.

When a court issues a preliminary order, it usually does so after a full **adversary proceeding** where both parties are present to argue their respective positions on the proposed order. Some orders, however, are made in *ex parte proceedings* where only one party appears before the judge. Ex parte preliminary orders are often limited to emergency matters in which there is no time to have a full adversary proceeding or where a danger of domestic violence requires the court to act quickly. At a later date, the party against whom the ex parte order is issued will have the opportunity to contest the order before a judge in an adversarial proceeding.

Preliminary orders can also pertain to discovery that is underway or about to begin. The judge might issue an order limiting discovery to certain areas of inquiry in order to prevent harassment or undue burden on the responding party. Alternatively, if a party has been reluctant to respond to legitimate discovery requests, the judge can grant motions to compel discovery.

TRIAL

Some states do not permit jury trials in divorce cases. If there is no jury, the judge conducts a **bench trial** in which he or she decides the questions of fact (normally the responsibility of the jury) as well as the questions of law. If a jury trial is allowed, the jurors are selected through a procedure known as **voir dire**. During this procedure, the lawyers and/or judge ask questions of prospective jurors to assess their eligibility (e.g., the absence of **bias**) to sit on the jury.

A goal of the trial is to resolve all divorce issues in one proceeding. This would include the issues of dissolving the marriage, spousal support, property division, child support, and child custody. Sometimes, however, more than one proceeding is used. In a **bifurcated divorce**, the dissolution of the marriage is tried separately from other issues in the marriage such as the property division. Suppose, for example, that the parties have a bitter and complicated dispute over business assets and pension rights. Rather than waiting until these issues are resolved, the court may have the power to dissolve the marriage now in one proceeding and then resolve the economic issues in a separate proceeding later. A bifurcated divorce allows the parties to get on with their lives (e.g., to marry someone else) much sooner than would otherwise be possible.

The attorneys begin the trial by making *opening statements* outlining the evidence they intend to try to prove during the trial. The plaintiff's side will usually present its case first. The attorney will call the plaintiff's witnesses and directly examine them. The other side can cross-examine these witnesses. Physical evidence (e.g., documents) is introduced as exhibits. Some evidence may have to be *corroborated*, meaning that additional evidence must be introduced to support the position taken by the party. The plaintiff's side will "rest" its case after presenting all of its witnesses and evidence. The defendant's attorney then begins his or her case through direct examination of witnesses, introduction of exhibits, etc.

When a party has the burden of proving a fact, the standard of proof is usually a **preponderance of the evidence**: the fact finder must be able to say from the evidence introduced and found admissible that it is *more likely than not* that the facts have been established as alleged. Occasionally, however, the law requires a fact to meet a higher standard of proof (e.g., clear and convincing evidence). Who has the burden of proof? In general, the party asserting or alleging a fact has the burden of proof on that fact. For example, a spouse who claims that the other spouse has a hidden bank account and physically assaulted the children has the burden of proof on these facts.

adversary proceeding
A proceeding in which both sides appear and argue their positions when court action is requested.

bench trial
A nonjury trial.

voir dire
Jury selection.

bias
Prejudice for or against something or someone. A predisposition, inclination, or tendency to think or to act in a certain way. A danger of prejudgment.

bifurcated divorce
A case in which the dissolution of the marriage—the divorce itself—is tried separately from other issues in the marriage such as property division.

preponderance of the evidence
A standard of proof that is met when the evidence establishes that it is more likely than not that the facts are as alleged. Also called fair preponderance of evidence.

marital-communications privilege

A person can refuse to testify and can prevent his or her spouse or ex-spouse from testifying about any confidential communications made between them during the marriage. Also called marital privilege, husband-wife privilege.

The **marital-communications privilege** does not apply to the divorce action. The spouses are allowed to testify about what each said to the other when the testimony is relevant to issues such as support, property division, and child custody. Nor does the privilege apply to criminal proceedings in which one spouse is alleged to have committed a crime against the other or against the children. In the main, the privilege (which allows spouses to refuse to disclose their confidential communications during the marriage) is limited to cases in which a third party is suing one or both of the spouses and attempts to introduce into evidence what one spouse may have said to the other. When objected to, such evidence is inadmissible.

ALTERNATIVE DISPUTE RESOLUTION (ADR)

alternative dispute resolution (ADR)

A method or procedure for resolving a legal dispute without litigating the dispute in a court or administrative agency.

There are two main methods of resolving differences in a divorce case without expensive discovery and a full trial. The parties often use a combination of both methods. First, they engage in informal negotiation (on their own or through counsel) on property division, child custody, spousal support, child support, and other issues pertaining to the marriage. Second, they engage in **alternative dispute resolution (ADR)**. All states encourage the use of ADR. In Texas, for example, a party seeking a divorce is asked to sign a statement that he or she has been informed of the availability of ADR and will attempt in good faith to resolve the case through ADR. The issues resolved through informal negotiation and ADR are often formalized in a *separation agreement* (sometimes called a marital settlement agreement, agreed judgment, or stipulated judgment) that the parties then ask the court to approve. (We will cover separation agreements in Chapter 8.)

The major ADR programs in the country are arbitration, mediation, med-arb, private judging, neutral evaluation, and collaborative law.

ARBITRATION

arbitration

A method of alternative dispute resolution (ADR) in which the parties avoid litigation by submitting their dispute to a neutral third person (the arbitrator) who renders a decision resolving the dispute.

Arbitration is a method of ADR in which the parties avoid litigation by submitting their dispute to a neutral third person (the arbitrator) who renders a decision resolving the dispute. The arbitrator is usually a professional arbitrator hired through organizations such as the American Arbitration Association (www.adr.org). Arbitration is not used as extensively as mediation in family-law cases. In some states, the court can order the parties to arbitrate property-division issues involving relatively small property totals (e.g., under $50,000). A premarital agreement (see Chapter 4) may have a clause requiring arbitration of disputes. If the parties have already negotiated a separation agreement, it also might have an arbitration clause (see Chapter 8).

The parties can agree to binding or non-binding arbitration. If they choose binding arbitration, the arbitrator's decision is not appealable to a court or is subject to limited court appeal. In most states, however, decisions on child support and child custody *cannot* be subject to binding arbitration because there must be no limits on the court's duty to be the final word on whether children have been properly treated on support and custody matters. In non-binding arbitration, a party who is unhappy with an arbitrator's decision can appeal the decision in court but if the end result of the court appeal is the same as the arbitration decision (or is more favorable to the other spouse), some states will require the spouse who appealed to pay the attorney court fees and costs of the other spouse.

Spouses in arbitration appear before the arbitrator on their own or through their attorneys. Arbitrators do not have to be attorneys. The arbitration process can be informal and subject to agreement by the parties:

Each party has a right to be represented by an attorney, and the attorneys and the parties agree on the ground rules for the hearing, including, for example, the presentation of evidence, the scope of testimony, the scheduling of hearings, and the allocation of arbitration expenses. The benefits of arbitration are many. The process is confidential and private, and unless the parties agree otherwise, no record is kept of the proceedings. Both parties have some control over the process as they select by mutual agreement their decision maker, the location of the arbitration sessions, and the schedule. The parties determine by contract how evidence will be presented (by affidavit, live testimony, or via the telephone), what rules of court will apply, which issues will be decided, and whether the arbitrator's decision will be subject to judicial review or appeal. Finally, the arbitrator's decision, unless explicitly made subject to appellate review, is final and binding on the parties.[27]

MEDIATION

Mediation is a method of ADR in which the parties avoid litigation by submitting their dispute to a neutral third person (the mediator) who helps the parties resolve their dispute; he or she does not render a decision resolving it for them. The *Model Standards of Practice for Family and Divorce Mediation* defines mediation as "a process in which a mediator, an impartial third party, facilitates the resolution of family disputes by promoting the participants' voluntary agreement. The family mediator assists communication, encourages understanding and focuses the participants on their individual and common interests. The family mediator works with the participants to explore options, make decisions and reach their own agreements."[28] At the end of mediation, the mediator will draft a memorandum covering the agreements reached by the spouses. An attorney for one of the parties might then draft a formal agreement based on this memorandum.[29]

Mediation is the most commonly used ADR method in divorce cases. Although mediators do not render a decision resolving disputes for the parties, they may make suggestions or recommendations for a resolution. In general, if the spouses are unrepresented, mediation is not recommended for cases in which there is a substantial power imbalance between the spouses or where there has been a history of domestic violence (DV) between them. For mediation to work, there must be considerable give-and-take between the spouses as the mediator guides them toward mutual agreements. This is unlikely to work if one of the spouses cowers before the other or if one of them fears a continuation of prior violence.

In some states, mediation is mandatory; the parties are required to try to work out their differences before final action by a court. During the preliminary stages of the case, the judge might order the parties to attend mediation within the family-court services unit of the court itself. This is particularly true when the judge learns that the parties do not agree on custody and visitation issues.

For an example of a mediation conducted by an attorney, see Exhibit 7-5. Mediators, however, do not have to be attorneys. In fact, some paralegals have received special training and certification to be mediators in family-law cases. Allan Weltman is an example in Florida (www.divorce-bankruptcy.com). He believes that paralegals "who want rewarding work with a great deal of responsibility and self-direction should look into this area of endeavor."[30]

mediation
A method of alternative dispute resolution (ADR) in which the parties avoid litigation by submitting their dispute to a neutral third person (the mediator) who helps the parties resolve their dispute; he or she does not render a decision resolving it for them.

EXHIBIT 7-5   Example of Mediation

Revelations of a Family Law Mediator: What Goes on behind Closed Doors to Help Divorcing Couples Reach Agreement?
by Joshua Kadish

Over the past seven or eight years, I have mediated a substantial number of family-law cases. My office mates often inquire, "Just what happens behind those closed doors, anyway?" "What was the loud screaming about, followed by hysterical laughter and silence?" "How do you get these embattled couples to agree on anything if they hate each other so much?" I usually parry these questions with a crafty smile and a muttered, "I have my ways . . . " as I scuttle down the hallway.

EXHIBIT 7-5 *(continued)*

Bowing to pressure from various fronts, I have decided that the time has come to tell all. What follows is fiction, which I hope reveals the truth.

Fred and Wilma were a young couple in the process of divorcing. They had significant disagreement about custody of their two children, ages 11 and 6. Both had consulted with attorneys and, after receiving estimates of the cost of a custody battle, had followed their attorneys' recommendation to at least try mediation. Wilma had called me to set up an appointment, and at the appointed hour I ushered them into my office.

My office is somewhat different from many lawyers' offices. I do have a desk in one corner. Most of the office is given over to a sitting area consisting of a large, comfortable couch and two chairs grouped around a coffee table. I always let the couple enter my office first and seat themselves as they wish. Depending upon how they arrange themselves, I can get a preliminary idea of how hotly the battle is raging. Some couples will sit together on the couch. Most position themselves as far away from each other as possible. Fred and Wilma put a good deal of distance between themselves.

After we were settled, I spent a few minutes describing mediation to them. First, my job was to remain neutral and to help them reach agreements for themselves. My job was not to reach decisions for them. Second, what transpired in the mediation sessions was confidential and would not later be disclosed in a courtroom. Third, the process was voluntary and anyone was free to terminate the mediation at any time. Fourth, we would consider the interests of their children to be of paramount importance.

Without looking at either one of them, I then asked them to tell me about their current situation while I studiously looked down at my legal pad. I like to see who will start talking first. This gives me a clue about where the balance of power may lie in the relationship. I am always concerned about one party overpowering the other in mediation.

Fred started talking. Speaking angrily, he told me about their 10-year marriage, the two children and Wilma's affair and withdrawal from the marriage. He stated that although he worked hard, he spent more than an average amount of time caring for the children. He felt that in having an affair, Wilma had proved herself to be an unstable person and that he would be a preferable custodial parent. He pointed out that Wilma had worked during the course of the marriage and that parenting duties had been shared between them more or less equally.

During the course of his statement, Wilma had interrupted Fred to point out that although she had had an affair, it occurred after they had separated and that Fred had been emotionally distant and withdrawn from the marriage for a number of years. Her statement ignited a loud argument between them. I let them argue for a minute or two to get a sense of their style of arguing. This argument was a well-rehearsed one which they must have been through a hundred times. As each one spoke, I could see that neither party was listening but was marshaling arguments with which to respond, making sure that his or her position was well defended.

I interrupted the argument by stating that I suspected they had had this argument before. This brought a slightly sheepish smile to both faces. Humor is often useful in easing tension and getting people on another track. I then borrowed an idea from an excellent mediator, John Haynes, and asked each of them to take a few minutes to think about what was the absolute worst outcome they could imagine in mediation. By asking this question, I wanted to get them further off the track they had been racing down and to give them a few minutes to calm down. After a few minutes, I asked each to answer. Fred said he was afraid of losing everything, including his children. Wilma stated that she was afraid of the same thing.

I remarked that it was interesting that they were both afraid of exactly the same thing, specifically a loss of their children to the other party. I then asked whether it would be possible for them to agree that whatever the outcome of mediation was, it would not result in a complete loss of the children to the other person. They both indicated that they would agree to this.

From that point, the atmosphere eased considerably. Both Fred and Wilma had dramatically realized that each was concerned about exactly the same thing. When people realize that they have the same concerns, it makes them feel closer or at least less adversarial. Moreover, they had been able to reach their first agreement. They realized they had a common interest in not becoming estranged from their children and that they could agree this would not be a result of the mediation.

I then asked what the current situation was regarding the children. Fred stated that he had moved out and was living in a small apartment. He was seeing the children every other weekend. However, he emphasized that he was a very involved father and he wanted the children to spend at least half of their time with him on an alternating weekly basis. Wilma thought this would be bad for the children. She wanted them to be at home with her and see Fred every other weekend. She clearly wished to be the primary parent and felt that the children needed a mother's love. She was quite concerned about the children being in Fred's care for more than one overnight at a time. Fred interrupted her to state that he felt he was just as good a parent as she was. Wilma responded by telling an anecdote about Fred forgetting to feed the children lunch about three weeks ago.

Again, I interrupted. Taking a bit of a risk, I asked whether each parent thought the children loved and needed the other parent. Again, each parent responded affirmatively. My asking this question had the effect of derailing the disagreement and again bringing Fred and Wilma back to some common ground of understanding. Most parents will at least admit the children love and need the other parent.

The next task was to help Fred and Wilma learn to listen to each other and to start separating their positions from their interests. I asked them each if they thought they could state what the other person's position was regarding custody and visitation and the reasons for it. Fred thought he could, but when he tried, Wilma felt he was inaccurate. I then asked Wilma to tell him again what she was concerned about, which she did. Fred was then able to repeat Wilma's position back to her. We then reversed the process, and after a couple of tries, Wilma was able to state Fred's concerns back to him.

This is a simple technique known as "active listening" which I borrowed from the field of psychology. It is not too difficult to learn the rudiments, particularly when you are married to a clinical psychologist, as I am. The goal in active listening is to make each person feel understood. There is great power in helping each party feel his or her position is genuinely understood by the other person. In most marital disputes, as one party talks, the other party is not listening, but is preparing arguments to respond to the other. This results in long, well worked out and pointless disputes. Active listening slows the pace down and helps couples improve their communication; if you are assured that you will be listened to, you will be much more likely to be able to listen to another.

At this point Fred and Wilma understood not only each other's positions, but the interests and reasons behind the positions. Wilma was concerned about being separated from the children for too many overnight periods in a row. Fred was concerned about long periods of time going by without seeing the children. I pointed out that although their positions (alternating weekly versus every other weekend visitation) conflicted, their interests did not necessarily conflict. Perhaps it would be possible to work out a schedule where Fred saw the children frequently, but not for a long string of overnights. Perhaps every other weekend visitation with some shorter but frequent midweek visitations, plus frequent telephone contact would be acceptable.

I then hauled out a blank calendar. Using the calendar as the focus of discussion, we worked out a visitation schedule that seemed acceptable to both of them. During this discussion, I emphasized to them that they were fortunate to have the opportunity to experiment with different patterns of visitation because it is very difficult to sit in a room and decide what will and will not work in the long run. I suggested that they should commit to trying a certain pattern of visitation for perhaps two months and also commit to reviewing it and altering it as indicated by their needs and the children's.

By finally working out a schedule, I was trying to do several things. First, I was trying to show them that in some ways their interests could be meshed. Second, big problems can be broken down into small, manageable pieces. Rather than creating a visitation schedule which was engraved in stone and would last for the next 20 years, they could try something for two months. Finally, I had introduced the idea of experimentation and flexibility. They could adjust the situation based upon how they and the children actually reacted to the plan.

I ended the session by telling them I would write their agreement in memo form, which they could review with their attorneys. I then asked each of them to comment on the process of the session. Did either of them have any concerns about what had happened? What did they like about the session? What could we do differently next time when we moved to a discussion of financial issues? I try to make people feel that they are in control of the process. Fred and Wilma both stated that they were pleased with the session and surprised that they had been able to reach agreement. Fred asked how I had done it. "I have my ways . . . " I muttered as I ushered them to the door.

Source: Joshua Kadish. 52 *Oregon State Bar Bulletin* 27 (February/March 1992) (www.mediate.com/kadish).

MED-ARB

Med-arb is a method of ADR in which the parties first try mediation, and if it does not work, they try arbitration. Once it is clear that mediation will not be successful, the mediator switches roles and makes a decision as an arbitrator.

med-arb

A method of alternative dispute resolution (ADR) in which the parties first try mediation, and if it does not work, they try arbitration.

PRIVATE JUDGING

Private judging is a method of ADR consisting of arbitration or mediation in which the arbitrator or mediator is a retired judge. It is sometimes misleadingly referred to as *rent-a-judge*. The name is misleading because the retired judge has no more authority or power than any other arbitrator or mediator. Private judging is not a government proceeding.

private judging

A method of alternative dispute resolution (ADR) consisting of arbitration or mediation in which the arbitrator or mediator is a retired judge. Sometimes called *rent-a-judge*.

NEUTRAL EVALUATION

Neutral evaluation is a method of ADR in which both sides hire an experienced attorney or an expert in the area involved in the dispute who will listen to an abbreviated version of the evidence and arguments of each side and offer an evaluation in the hope that this will stimulate more serious settlement discussions. The process is sometimes called *case evaluation*.

neutral evaluation

A method of alternative dispute resolution (ADR) in which both sides hire an experienced attorney or an expert in the area involved in the dispute who will listen to an abbreviated version of the evidence and arguments of each side and offer an evaluation in the hope that this will stimulate more serious settlement discussions. Sometimes called *case evaluation*.

collaborative law
A method of practicing law in which the attorneys and parties seek to resolve their family-law differences without litigation. To encourage settlement, the attorneys refuse to continue representing the parties if litigation becomes necessary; the parties must find other attorneys if the case goes to trial. Collaborative law is a form of limited-scope representation and alternative dispute resolution (ADR).

interlocutory
Not final; interim.

judgment debtor
The person who loses and therefore must pay a money judgment.

judgment creditor
The person who wins and therefore has a right to collect a money judgment.

civil contempt
The refusal of a party to comply with a court order (usually issued for the benefit of another), which can lead to incarceration until the party complies with the order.

execution
A command or writ to a court officer (e.g., sheriff) to seize and sell the property of the losing litigant in order to satisfy the judgment debt. Also called *general execution* and *writ of execution*. (See glossary for additional definitions.)

COLLABORATIVE LAW

Collaborative law is a method of practicing law in which the attorneys and parties seek to resolve their family-law differences without litigation. To encourage settlement, primarily through mediation, the attorneys refuse to continue representing the parties if litigation becomes necessary; the parties must find other attorneys if the case goes to trial. Collaborative law is a form of limited-scope representation and ADR, both of which were discussed in Chapter 2 on ethics in a family-law practice.

DIVORCE JUDGMENT

An **interlocutory** judgment (or a *judgment nisi*) is one that will not become final until the passage of a specified period of time (e.g., 60 days). In many states, after the court has reached its decision to grant a divorce, an interlocutory judgment of divorce will be issued. During the period that this interim judgment is in force, the parties are still married.

A divorce judgment will also resolve the questions of alimony, child custody, child support, and property division. (All of this, of course, assumes that the court had proper jurisdiction to make these determinations as outlined earlier.) In addition, the judgment will often restore the woman's maiden name, if that is her wish, and determine what the surname of the children will be as part of the custody decision. We will have more to say about surnames in Chapters 9 and 12.

The divorce judgment can be set aside if the parties reconcile before the judgment becomes final. While a trial court's divorce judgment is being appealed, most states will not allow the parties to remarry. Appeals of trial court judgments are possible, but unless the case involves substantial property or bitterness over child custody, it is relatively rare for parties to appeal.

ENFORCEMENT OF DIVORCE JUDGMENT

Most of the controversy involving the enforcement of a divorce judgment has centered on enforcing support and custody orders, particularly across state lines. These topics will be examined at length in Chapters 8 and 9. What follows are some general observations on available enforcement options.

CIVIL CONTEMPT

A party who is ordered to pay a money judgment (e.g., an alimony order) is called the **judgment debtor**. The person in whose favor a money judgment is ordered is the **judgment creditor**. Judgment debtors who disobey such orders can be held in **civil contempt**, which can lead to jail time until they comply with the order. The remedy of jail through civil contempt is not used, however, if the judgment debtor does not have the present financial ability to pay. Inability to pay does not mean burdensome or inconvenient to pay. Using all resources currently available or those that could become available with reasonable effort, the judgment debtor must be able to comply with the payment order. Other remedies must be used to try to enforce the judgment if civil contempt cannot be used because the judgment debtor does not have the present financial ability to comply with the order.

States differ on whether civil contempt can be used to enforce property-division orders. The latter are more often enforced by execution, attachment, receivership, and constructive trust, which are discussed below.

EXECUTION

The **execution** of the judgment is a command or writ to a court officer (e.g., sheriff) to seize and sell the property of the losing litigant (the judgment debtor) in order to satisfy the judgment debt. For support orders payable in installments, execution is usually possible only if the orders are *final* and *nonmodifiable* by the court:

- In some states, each unpaid installment automatically becomes a final and nonmodifiable judgment of nonpayment to which execution will be available.
- In other states, each unpaid installment does not become a final and nonmodifiable judgment until the judgment creditor makes a specific application to the court for such a judgment and one is entered. Execution is available only after the judgment is so entered or docketed.

GARNISHMENT

When **garnishment** is used, the court authorizes the judgment creditor to reach money or other property of the judgment debtor that is in the hands of a third party such as the employer (who holds wages of the judgment debtor) or a bank (which holds deposits of the judgment debtor).

ATTACHMENT

Property of the judgment debtor is *attached* when the court authorizes its seizure to bring it under the control of the court so that it can be used to satisfy a judgment or be held as security for such satisfaction. The process is called **attachment**.

RECEIVERSHIP

The court can appoint a **receiver** over some or all the judgment debtor's property to prevent him or her from squandering it or otherwise making it unavailable to satisfy the judgment.

CONSTRUCTIVE TRUST

Assume that a judgment debtor conveys property to a "friendly" third party (e.g., the judgment debtor's mother) in an effort to make it appear that he or she no longer owns the property. To reach such property in order to make it available to satisfy the judgment debtor's debts, the court can impose a **constructive trust** on the property. This is a trust created by operation of law to prevent unjust enrichment by someone who has improperly obtained property through fraud, duress, abuse of confidence, or other wrongful conduct.

garnishment
A court proceeding by a creditor to force a third party in possession of the debtor's property (e.g., wages) to turn the property over to the creditor to satisfy a debt.

attachment
(1) A court authorization of the seizure of a person's property so that it can be used to satisfy a judgment against him or her.
(2) The seizure of such property as security for such a judgment.

receiver
A person appointed by the court to manage property in litigation or in the process of bankruptcy.

constructive trust
A trust created by operation of law to prevent unjust enrichment by someone who has improperly obtained property through fraud, duress, abuse of confidence, or other wrongful conduct.

ASSIGNMENT 7.11

Prepare a flowchart of the procedural steps that are necessary for a divorce in your state. Assume that the divorce you will be flowcharting is contested. (See General Instructions for the Flowchart Assignment in Appendix A.)

ASSIGNMENT 7.12

Interview a paralegal, attorney, or legal secretary who has been involved in divorce actions in your state. (See General Instructions for the Systems Assignment in Appendix A.) Questions to ask in the interview:

a. Approximately how many divorce cases have you worked on?

b. How many of them have been uncontested?

(continued)

c. Approximately how long does it take to process an uncomplicated, uncontested divorce?

d. Is there a difference between working on a divorce case and working on another kind of case in the law office? If so, what is the difference?

e. What are the major steps for processing a divorce action in this state? What documents have to be filed? What court appearances must be made? Etc.

f. What formbook, manual, or other legal treatise do you use, if any, that is helpful? Who is the publisher?

g. What websites are the most helpful?

h. Does your office have its own internal manual that covers any aspect of divorce practice?

i. In a divorce action, what is the division of labor among the attorney, the paralegal, and the legal secretary?

j. What computer software is used in divorce cases? What is its function and how useful is it? What would the office have to do if such software did not exist?

RELIGION AND DIVORCE PROCEDURE

Finally, we address two themes involving religion and divorce procedure. First, what divorce laws exist within the Jewish and Islamic traditions? Second, can these religious laws be enforceable in our civil courts?

RELIGIOUS DIVORCES

Jewish Divorce

> When a man hath taken a wife, and married her, and it come to pass that she find no favor in his eyes, because he hath found some uncleanliness in her: then let him write her a bill of divorcement, and give it in her hand, and send her out of his house. *Deuteronomy* 24:1 (King James)

get
A document that grants a Jewish divorce.

A Jewish couple seeking a religious divorce can go to a special court called a *Beth Din*, presided over by a rabbi. There the husband obtains a document called a **get** or bill of divorcement, which the husband hands to his wife. Fault does not have to be shown. In some Jewish traditions, the wife must consent to the divorce. In some Jewish communities in New York, a religious divorce is allowed only if a secular (i.e., civil) divorce or annulment is under way or has already been granted. If a Jewish man has a civil divorce but not a religious divorce, he can still be remarried by a rabbi. But a Jewish woman without a get—even if divorced in a civil court—is called an *agunah*, or abandoned wife, and cannot be remarried by a rabbi.[31] Agunah, Inc. is an organization of Orthodox Jewish women "chained to dead marriages" because their husbands refuse to grant them a Jewish divorce or get.[32] Some rabbis allege that increasing numbers of husbands try to withhold the get as a bargaining chip to obtain reduced support payments or more favorable custody rights. If the husband disappears, the wife's plight is even more desperate. Rabbi Shlomo Klein, based in Israel, travels the world in search of such husbands in order to pressure them into signing the divorce.[33]

shariah
Islamic law.

talak
"I divorce you." Words spoken by a husband to his wife in a Muslim divorce.

Islamic Divorce

Under **shariah** (Islamic law), a divorce is traditionally performed by a husband pronouncing the word **talak** (I divorce you) three times. The wife need not be present. One Islamic court recently ruled that sending her an e-mail announcing the talak is not sufficient, although the senior religious adviser in Malaysia has ruled that Muslim men can legally divorce their wives through text messages sent from their mobile phones ("I D4C U").[34] In some countries, the process is public. In Pakistan, for example, the husband must notify the chairman of an arbitration council that he has pronounced the talak. The council will then attempt to reconcile the parties. If this fails, the divorce becomes absolute 90 days after the husband pronounced the talak. In Egypt, the husband must pronounce the talak in the presence of two witnesses, who are usually officers of a special court.[35] If a wife wants a divorce, she must go to court and prove that her husband has mistreated her. Wives are not often successful. According to one person familiar with Islamic justice, if a husband slaps his wife "only once . . . , [she] has to forgive."[36] A recent change in Egyptian law allows a woman to obtain a divorce without proving mistreatment. She must, however, return her dowry and agree that there will be no alimony. In Iran, engaged couples negotiate a *mehrieh*, which is a single payment that the husband must pay the wife if he decides to divorce her. When the wife wants to get out of the marriage, she can waive part or all of the *mehrieh* as an incentive for the husband to divorce her.[37] Finally, under some interpretations of shariah, a woman can obtain a divorce if she can find a scholar of Islamic jurisprudence to confirm that she should be given a divorce.

RELIGIOUS TRADITIONS IN CIVIL COURT

What happens when parties ask a secular (civil) court to enforce a religious marriage or divorce? Of course, our courts cannot settle religious disputes, nor can they favor one religion over another. This would violate the First Amendment. There must be no impermissible entanglement in religious doctrine. Courts can, however, enforce contractual promises based on religious traditions if doing so involves applying neutral principles of law.

In a recent New Jersey divorce case involving an Islamic couple of Bangladeshi descent, the court ordered an ex-wife to return $12,500 to her ex-husband because of a dowry-like commitment that she agreed to under Islamic marriage law. When the parties entered an arranged marriage in Maryland, they both agreed to be united "under the law of Islam." Pursuant to Islamic custom, a sum of $12,500 was paid to the wife as an initial payment of "sadaq" or "mahr" by the husband or his family. The payment and retention of the sadaq is contingent upon neither party being at fault in precipitating a divorce. The husband alleged that the wife was at fault in the breakdown of the marriage, e.g., she refused to engage in marital relations and left the state on her own and relocated to another state. The court agreed that she was at fault and held that her commitment to return the sadaq was enforceable under basic contract law principles.[38]

Similarly, a New York court enforced an agreement entered into by a Jewish couple that they would appear before a designated Jewish tribunal. When the couple married, they signed a Ketubah, which said

> "[W]e, the bride and bridegroom . . . hereby agree to recognize the Beth Din of the Rabbinical Assembly and the Jewish Theological Seminary of America . . . as having authority to counsel us in the light of Jewish tradition . . . and to summon either party at the request of the other, in order to enable the party so requesting to live in accordance with the standards of the Jewish law of marriage throughout his or her lifetime. We authorize the Beth Din to impose such terms of compensation as it may see fit for failure to respond to its summons or to carry out its decision."

After the defendant (the ex-husband) obtained a divorce in a New York court, the plaintiff (the ex-wife) sought to have him summoned before the Beth Din. Her hope was that the Jewish court would order him to give her a get so that she could remarry in the Jewish tradition. He refused to appear before the Beth Din.

She then sued him in a New York court on the theory that he had violated his contractual commitment to appear before the Beth Din. The lower court dismissed her complaint on the basis that the Ketubah was a liturgical agreement that was entered as part of a religious ceremony and as such was unenforceable in a civil New York court. This decision was reversed by the New York Court of Appeals. The ex-husband's contractual agreement to appear before a Jewish body can be enforced. Doing so does not require the court to become involved in religious beliefs or disputes. The court said that "the relief sought by plaintiff in this action is simply to compel defendant to perform a secular obligation to which he contractually bound himself. In this regard, no doctrinal issue need be passed upon, no implementation of a religious duty is contemplated, and no interference with religious authority will result. Certainly nothing the Beth Din can do would in any way affect the civil divorce. To the extent that an enforceable promise can be found by the application of neutral principles of contract law, plaintiff will have demonstrated entitlement to the relief sought. Consideration of other substantive issues bearing upon plaintiff's entitlement to a religious divorce, however, is appropriately left to the forum the parties chose for resolving the matter."[39]

The dissenting justices on the Court of Appeals were adamant that the majority had made a serious mistake. "We are of the opinion," said the dissenters, "that to grant the relief plaintiff seeks in this action, even to the limited extent contemplated by the majority, would necessarily violate the constitutional prohibition against entanglement of our secular courts in matters of religious and ecclesiastical content."[40]

Some states are fearful that religious law, particularly sharia law, will be applied in civil courts. In 2010, for example, Oklahoma amended its constitution to provide that its courts "shall not consider . . . Sharia Law."[41]

■ PARALEGAL ROLES

- There is a great variety of roles that a paralegal can have in divorce litigation depending on the kind of practice where the paralegal works. For an overview of paralegal roles in family-law litigation (particularly during pretrial proceedings, discovery, alternative dispute resolution, trial, and post-trial enforcement of divorce judgments), see Exhibits 1-3 and 1-4 in Chapter 1.

- For all financial issues covered in Chapter 7, a paralegal may be asked to help collect documents and facts outlined in:
  - the checklist in Exhibit 3-1 of Chapter 3
  - the interrogatories in Appendix C

- The interviewing and investigation checklists in Chapter 7 also cover fact-finding roles of paralegals.

■ CHECK THE CITE

Welfare recipients seeking a divorce in Connecticut could not afford to pay court fees and the costs for service of process. What constitutional challenge did they raise to the requirement to pay these fees and costs? How did the U.S. Supreme Court rule on this challenge? Read *Boddie v. Connecticut*, 401 U.S. 371. (1971). To read this opinion online: (1) Run a citation search ("401 U.S. 371") in the Legal document database of Google Scholar (scholar.google.com). (2) Run a citation search ("401 U.S. 371") in Google, Bing, or Yahoo.

■ PROJECTS

(1) In Google, Bing, or Yahoo, run the following search: aa wiretapping evidence divorce (substitute the name of your state for aa in the search). Write an essay in which you explain whether one spouse can wiretap another spouse and use the evidence obtained in wiretapping in a divorce case against the spouse in your state. You must cite and quote from a minimum of five different sources that you find on the Internet. At least four of these sources should be statutes, court opinions, or other laws.

(2) List any five documents that could be filed in a divorce case in your state (e.g., petition, summons,

return of service). On the Internet, try to find two examples of each of the five documents you selected and give a brief summary of the function of each document. The examples can be blank or filled out. Begin your search by determining if your state courts have recommended or required standard forms.

(3) **a.** What are the names of the court(s) in your state that have the power (subject-matter jurisdiction) to grant a divorce? Give the cite to (and a brief quote from) the state constitution or state code that support your answer.

b. Attend a divorce hearing in one of these courts and answer the following questions concerning what you observe:

1. What court heard the case?

2. What was the name of the case?

3. Were both sides represented by counsel? What were the names of the attorneys?

4. Were both parties present?

5. What kind of evidence, if any, was introduced?

6. Use Google, Bing, or Yahoo to find information about the opposing attorneys (e.g., the name of the law firms where they work, their web addresses, and the kind of practices they have). Summarize what you find.

■ ETHICS IN A FAMILY LAW PRACTICE

You are a paralegal working at the law office of Smith & Smith. The office represents David Gerry in a divorce action against his wife, Lena Gerry. One of the disputes is how to divide business assets acquired during the marriage. In an effort to pressure Lena to divide the assets in his favor, David tells his attorney to request sole physical and legal custody of their two children even though David has no desire to raise the children. He knows, however, that Lena is terrified at the thought of losing sole custody herself. David wants his attorney to engage in extensive discovery (depositions, interrogatories, etc.) on the custody issue for the sole purpose of wearing Lena down in the hope that she will reduce her claims on the business assets. Any ethical problems?

■ WRITING SAMPLE

An impressive writing sample would be a well-drafted divorce complaint/petition. Draft one on behalf of either the husband or the wife. Make up the names and addresses of the parties. You can also make up other facts you need so long as they are consistent with the following facts: the parties have two minor children and both parties want sole legal and physical custody; each party wishes to receive spousal support from the other; they have a house that is jointly owned; they also have other substantial property. (See General Instructions for the Writing Sample in Appendix A.)

SUMMARY

A divorce is a declaration by a court that a validly entered marriage is terminated so that the parties are no longer married to each other. There have been three eras in the history of divorce: the eras of restrictive, collusive, and unilateral divorce. American divorce law is derived from the canon law of the Roman Catholic Church in early English history. Until the late 1960s, the main grounds for divorce were those based on fault. No-fault grounds were created primarily because of the dishonesty fostered by the fault system. Some individuals, however, say that no-fault places some women at a disadvantage. No-fault divorce does not mean that marital misconduct no longer has a role in divorce litigation. For example, marital fault that affects the children is relevant to child custody.

The major no-fault grounds are living apart, incompatibility, and irreconcilable differences. Living apart is established when spouses live separately for a designated period of consecutive time during which they intended to end the marriage. Incompatibility is established when there is such discord between the husband and wife that it is impossible for them to live together in a normal marital

relationship. Irreconcilable differences are established when there is such discord between the husband and wife that there has been an irremediable breakdown of the marriage. The major fault grounds are adultery (voluntary sexual relations between a married person and someone other than his or her spouse), cruelty (the infliction of serious physical or mental suffering on another), and desertion (the voluntary departure of one spouse from another, without justification or consent, with the intent not to return to resume cohabitation with the spouse). The major defenses to the fault grounds of divorce are collusion, connivance, condonation, recrimination, and provocation.

A legal separation is a declaration by a court that parties can live apart even though they are still married to each other. The court can also make orders for spousal support, child support, child custody, and property division. Separate maintenance is court-ordered spousal support while the parties are separated but still married. The court can also make orders for child support and child custody, but generally does resolve property-division issues.

Domicile is the place (1) where a person has been physically present (2) with the intent to make that place a permanent home, or with no intent to make any other place a permanent home. It is the place to which one would intend to return when away. With rare exceptions, a person can have only one domicile. Residence is the place where someone is living. A person can have many residences. Full faith and credit (FFC) is the obligation of one state to recognize and enforce the legal decisions of another state. A divorce judgment can dissolve a marriage, award spousal support, divide marital property, award child support, and award child custody. A divisible divorce is a divorce judgment or decree that is enforceable only in part.

Subject-matter jurisdiction is the court's power to resolve a particular type of dispute and to grant a particular type of relief. Some states have established special family-law courts or divisions to handle domestic relations cases. In rem jurisdiction is the court's power over a particular res, which is a thing or status that is located within the territory over which the court has authority. In rem jurisdiction is needed to dissolve a marriage and is acquired when one of the spouses is domiciled in the state. Personal jurisdiction is a court's power over a person to determine (adjudicate) his or her personal rights and duties. Personal jurisdiction is needed for a court to order spousal support, child support, and property division. It is acquired by personal service of process, consent, substituted service, or the long-arm statute. There are times when a party with a valid jurisdictional challenge to a divorce decree will be estopped from bringing the challenge. An example is the spouse who obtained the divorce judgment, helped the other spouse obtain it, or received benefits from the divorce judgment. A critical factor in a court's jurisdiction to award child custody is the home state of the child. The requirements for venue often relate to the residence (which may mean domicile) of the plaintiff or defendant (e.g., the state may provide that a divorce action can be filed in the county where the defendant spouse resides or in the county where either the plaintiff or the defendant has been a resident for three months preceding the commencement of the action).

Summary dissolution is a divorce obtained in an expedited manner because of the brevity of the marriage, the minimal amount of marital property, and the lack of controversy between the husband and wife. Procedural due process requires that defendants be given notice of divorce proceedings brought against them and an opportunity to be heard in those proceedings. Parties are responsible for the payment of their own attorney fees and court costs in divorce cases, although the court has the power to order the wealthy spouse to pay for the fees and costs of a needy spouse. Many divorce parties represent themselves, sometimes with the assistance of unbundled services from attorneys. A guardian ad litem (GAL) is a special guardian (often an attorney) appointed by the court to appear in court proceedings on behalf of a minor or an incompetent person.

The major pleading of the party seeking a divorce is the complaint/petition. Its main parts are the caption, statement of jurisdiction and venue, body, prayer for relief, subscription, and verification. A default divorce is granted because of the failure of a party to appear, plead, or otherwise defend the divorce action of the other party. A pretrial conference is a meeting of the attorneys and the judge (or magistrate) before the trial to attempt to narrow the issues, secure stipulations, make a final effort to settle the case without a trial, and cover other preliminary matters. The major formal discovery devices are interrogatories, deposition, request for admissions, requests for production, and independent medical examination. Another form of discovery is mandatory self-disclosure such as the inventory of assets and liabilities. Examples of preliminary orders a court can issue are temporary physical and legal child custody, temporary child support, and enjoining a party from transferring marital property. If a state does not allow juries in divorce cases, the judge decides all issues in a bench trial. Some divorces are bifurcated divorces in which the dissolution of the marriage—the divorce itself—is tried separately from other issues in the marriage, such as property division.

Alternative dispute resolution (ADR) is a method or procedure for resolving a legal dispute without litigating it in a court or administrative agency. The major vehicles for ADR are arbitration, mediation, med-arb, private judging, neutral evaluation, and collaborative law. An interlocutory judgment of divorce is a judgment that will not become final until the passage of a specified period of time (e.g., 60 days). The main options for enforcing a divorce judgment include civil contempt, execution, garnishment, attachment, receivership, and constructive trust. The Jewish and Islamic religions have their own systems (including special courts) to grant divorce within their traditions. Some civil courts will enforce agreements made within these religions so long as the court does not favor one religion over another, does not settle religious disputes, and applies neutral principles of law.

KEY TERMS

divorce	canon law	perjury
collusive divorce	limited divorce	migratory divorce
grounds	absolute divorce	contested
no-fault divorce	corroboration	dissolution
ecclesiastical	uncontested	covenant marriage

dissipation
plead
tort
living apart
incompatibility
sham divorce
irreconcilable differences
stay
adultery
corespondent
circumstantial evidence
cruelty
domestic violence (DV)
stalking
desertion
constructive desertion
due diligence
Enoch Arden divorce
collusion
connivance
condonation
recrimination
comparative rectitude
provocation
legal separation
separation agreement
DOS
conversion
separate maintenance
residence
domicile
resident
nonresident
domiciliary
nondomiciliary
estate tax
age of majority
emancipated
operation of law
legal custody
domicile by choice
forum state
foreign divorce
full faith and credit (FFC)
comity
divisible divorce
jurisdiction
subject-matter jurisdiction
concurrent jurisdiction
stipulate
diversity of citizenship
domestic-relations exception

in rem jurisdiction
res
personal jurisdiction
service of process
process
substituted service
long-arm statute
long-arm jurisdiction
minimum contacts
estopped
equitable estoppel
ex parte
ex parte divorce
direct attack
collateral attack
home state
venue
summary dissolution
procedural due process
proof of service
indigent
pro se
unbundled legal services
guardian ad litem (GAL)
court appointed special
    advocate (CASA)
pleadings
complaint
petition
petitioner
respondent
caption
prayer
subscription
verification
notarize
template
summons
in forma pauperis
answer
affirmative defense
counterclaim
default judgment
prove-up
default divorce
pretrial conference
discovery
discoverable
privilege
attorney-client privilege
doctor–patient privilege
interrogatories

deposition
deponent
transcribed
subpoena
subpoena duces tecum
request for admissions (FRA)
request for production (RFP)
independent medical
    examination (IME)
electronic data
    discovery (EDD)
spoliation
privileged
protective order
good cause
net worth
pendente lite
affidavit
movant
affiant
enjoin
injunction
dissipation
receiver
ne exeat
adversary proceeding
bench trial
voir dire
bias
bifurcated divorce
preponderance of the evidence
marital-communications privilege
alternative dispute resolution
    (ADR)
arbitration
mediation
med-arb
private judging
neutral evaluation
collaborative law
interlocutory
judgment debtor
judgment creditor
civil contempt
execution
garnishment
attachment
receiver
constructive trust
get
shariah
talak

REVIEW QUESTIONS

1. What is a divorce?
2. What are the main features of the three historical eras of divorce (restrictive, collusive, unilateral)?
3. How has American divorce law evolved from its origin in early English law?
4. What prompted the creation of no-fault grounds for divorce?

5. Why have some individuals criticized the no-fault divorce reforms?

6. What roles can marital misconduct play in no-fault divorce cases?

7. What are the main no-fault and fault grounds for divorce?

8. How is living apart established?

9. How is incompatibility established?

10. How are irreconcilable differences established?

11. How is adultery established?

12. How is cruelty established?

13. How is desertion established?

14. What are the major defenses to the fault grounds of divorce?

15. What is a legal separation and how does it differ from a divorce?

16. What is separate maintenance and how does it differ from legal separation and divorce?

17. How does residence differ from domicile?

18. How do children acquire a domicile?

19. What is full faith and credit?

20. What are the five major orders that can be part of a divorce judgment?

21. What is a divisible divorce?

22. What is the distinction between the power and the geographic definition of jurisdiction?

23. What is subject-matter jurisdiction and how is it established?

24. What is the domestic-relations exception?

25. What is in rem jurisdiction and how is it acquired?

26. What is personal jurisdiction and what are the four ways it can be established?

27. What is long-arm jurisdiction and how is it acquired?

28. What kind of jurisdiction is needed to dissolve a marriage?

29. What kind of jurisdiction is needed to order spousal support, child support, and property division?

30. When will a spouse with a valid jurisdictional challenge to a divorce judgment be estopped from bringing the challenge?

31. What is the distinction between a direct and a collateral attack against a judgment?

32. How does a court acquire jurisdiction to decide child custody?

33. How is venue determined?

34. What is a summary dissolution?

35. What is the procedural due process right of a party to notice and opportunity to be heard?

36. How are attorney fees and court costs paid in divorce cases?

37. When will a court appoint a guardian ad litem?

38. What are the main pleadings in a divorce case?

39. What are the components of a complaint/petition for divorce?

40. When can the court grant a default divorce?

41. What happens at a pretrial conference?

42. What is a waiting period?

43. What are the main formal discovery devices?

44. What is e-discovery?

45. How can a party respond to discovery abuse?

46. What is an inventory of assets and liabilities?

47. What are some of the main preliminary orders a court can issue?

48. What is a bench trial?

49. What is a bifurcated divorce?

50. How do the following ADR methods work: arbitration, mediation, med-arb, private judging, neutral evaluation, and collaborative law?

51. What is an interlocutory judgment?

52. How can the following options be used to enforce a divorce judgment: civil contempt, execution, garnishment, attachment, receivership, and constructive trust?

53. When will a civil court enforce an agreement within a religious tradition?

HELPFUL WEBSITES

Divorce Grounds

- patriot.net/~crouch/50states
- en.wikipedia.org/wiki/Grounds_for_divorce
- www.womansdivorce.com/state-divorce-resources.html
- www.americanbar.org/groups/family_law/resources /family_law_in_the_50_states.html

Divorce Procedure

- www.divorcelawinfo.com
- topics.law.cornell.edu/wex/table_divorce
- en.wikipedia.org/wiki/Divorce

Divorce Forms

- family.findlaw.com/divorce/divorce-forms /state-divorce-forms(1).html
- www.edivorcepapers.com

Divorce Mediation

- www.divorceinfo.com/mediation.htm
- www.professionalfamilymediators.org

Divorce Arbitration

- www.acresolution.org/divorce-arbitration.html
- www.equalityinmarriage.org/wdarb.html

Family Courts

- www.afccnet.org
- www.ncsc.org/Topics/Children-Families-and-Elders /Family-Courts/Resource-Guide.aspx

Pro Se Divorce

- www.selfrepresent.mo.gov/page.jsp?id=39815
- www.coconino.az.gov/uploadedFiles/Courts/legal _services/47.pdf
- www.texasbar.com (under "For the Public," click "Free Legal Information," then "Family Law")

Jewish Divorce

- en.wikipedia.org/wiki/Get_(divorce_document)
- www.chabad.org/library/article_cdo/aid/557897/ jewish/Divorce.htm

Muslim Divorce

- www.religioustolerance.org/mohd.htm
- en.wikipedia.org/wiki/Divorce_(Islamic)
- courtdecisionsandrulings.com/islamic-divorce-in -new-york-state.html

Google/Bing/Yahoo Searches

(on these search engines, run the following searches, substituting your state for "aa")

- divorce aa
- divorce grounds aa
- divorce fraud aa
- "separate maintenance" aa
- divorce jurisdiction aa
- divorce pleadings aa
- divorce "e-discovery" aa
- divorce mediation aa
- divorce enforcement aa
- no-fault divorce aa
- divorce adultery aa
- "legal separation" aa
- divorce domicile aa
- divorce "long-arm" aa
- divorce discovery aa
- divorce subpoena aa
- divorce arbitration aa
- divorce "pro se" aa

ENDNOTES

Note: All or most of the court opinions in these endnotes can be read online. To do so, go to Google Scholar (scholar .google.com), select "Legal documents," and in the search box, enter the cite (e.g., "124 A.2d 639") or name of the case (e.g., "Rankin v. Rankin") that is given in the endnote.

[1] Harry D. Krause & David D. Meyer, *Family Law in a Nutshell* 249 (5th ed. 2007).

[2] John DeWitt Gregory et al., *Understanding Family Law* 236 (3d ed. 2005).

[3] *Rankin v. Rankin*, 124 A.2d 639, 644 (Pa. 1956).

[4] Patricia Leigh Brown, *A Push to Preserve Reno's Landmarks As Divorce Capital*, N.Y. Times, Apr. 22, 2002, at A1.

[5] Erie Pace, *Louis Nizer, Lawyer to the Famous, Dies at 92*, N.Y. Times, Nov. 11, 1994, at A15.

[6] William Glaberson, *Change to Divorce Law Could Recall a TV Quiz Show: "To Tell the Truth,"* N.Y. Times, Jun. 16, 2010 (www.nytimes.com/2010/06/17/nyregion/17divorce.html).

[7] Elizabeth Gilbert, *Eat, Pray, Love*, 30 (Viking 2006).

[8] Arlene F. Saluter and Terry A. Lugaila, *Marital Status and Living Arrangements*, Current Population Reports (Mar. 1998) (www.census.gov/prod/3/98pubs/p20-496.pdf).

[9] DivorceRate (www.divorcerate.org); Americans for Divorce Reform (www.divorcereform.org); Dan Hurley, *Divorce*

Rate: It's Not as High as You Think, N.Y. Times, Apr. 19, 2005 (www.nytimes.com/2005/04/19/health/19divo.html).

[10] Brae Canlen, *No More Mrs. Nice Guy*, California Lawyer 51, 95 (Apr. 1994).

[11] Tyler Cowen, *Matrimony Has Its Benefits, and Divorce Has a Lot to Do with That*, N.Y. Times, Apr. 19, 2007, at C3 (www. nytimes.com/2007/04/19/business/19scene.html).

[12] Nadine Brozan, *Divorce Lawyers' New Friend: Social Networks*, N.Y. Times, May 13, 2011 (www.nytimes.com/2011/05/15 /fashion/weddings/divorce-lawyers-new-friend-social- networks.html?_r=1).

[13] Adultery is a class B misdemeanor, punishable by up to 90 days in jail or a $500 fine. New York Penal Code § 255.17 (public.leginfo.state.ny.us/menugetf .cgi?COMMONQUERY=LAWS)(Slick PEN and then Art. 255).

[14] *Lawrence v. Texas*, 539 U.S. 558 (2003).

[15] *DeMott v. DeMott*, 92 S.E.2d 342, 345 (Va. 1956).

[16] John DeWitt Gregory et al., *Understanding Family Law* 269 (2005).

[17] Uniform Marriage and Divorce Act, § 314(b) (www.uniformdivorce.com/UMDA.pdf).

[18] U.S. Const. art. IV, § 1.

[19] National Center for Fathering, www.fathers.com (Click "Programs & Events" and then "Fathering Court") (2007).

[20] *Bearstop v. Bearstop*, 377 A.2d 405, 408 (D.C. 1977).

[21] *In re Marriage of Hughes*, 116 P.3d 1042 (Wash. App. Div. 3 2005).

[22] Lindi Massey, *Discovery: Just What Are You Looking For?*, 9 Legal Assistant Today 128 (Jul./Aug. 1992).

[23] Donald Glenn, *Discovery*, 31 Family Advocate 8 (Spring 2009).

[24] William Hamilton and Wendy Akbar, *E-Discovery in the Age of Facebook, Twitter, & the Digital Family*, 33 Family Advocate 16 (Fall 2010).

[25] Samuel Schoonmaker, *Two Generations of Practitioners Assess the Evolution of Family Law*, 42 Family Law Quarterly 687, 690 (2008)

[26] In re Marriage of Rossi 90 Cal.App.4th 34, 108 Cal.Rptr.2d 270 (Cal. App. 2. Dist. 2001).

[27] Nancy Gordon, *This Judge Does Care About ADR*, 31 Family Advocate 12 (Fall 2008).

[28] Association of Family and Conciliation Courts, *Model Standards of Practice for Family and Divorce Mediation*, 1 (2000) (www.afccnet.org).

[29] Nancy Gordon, *This Judge . . .* supra note 27.

[30] Allan J. Weltman, *Family Mediation*, 28 Facts & Findings 27 (National Association of Legal Assistants, Nov. 2001).

[31] Lisa Green Markoff, *How Couples "Get" a Religious Divorce*, National Law Journal, Aug. 15, 1988, at 8.

[32] Rivka Haut, *Letter to the Editor*, N.Y. Times, Oct. 12, 1994, at A18. See also Agunah International (www.agunahinternational.com).

[33] John Donnelly, *Rabbi Is an Unorthodox Manhunter*, San Diego Union Tribune, Oct. 28, 1995, at A-22.

[34] Leela Jacinto, *"I D4C U" Declaring "I Divorce You" by Mail or Mobile Phone Is Easy for Muslim Men—Too Easy, Say Women*, ABCNEWS.com (Aug. 31, 2004) (groups.yahoo.com /group/mukto-mona/message/19291).

[35] *The Religious Effect of Religious Divorces*, 37 Modern Law Review 611-13 (1974). *Divorce (Islamic)* (en.wikipedia.org /wiki/Talaq_).

[36] Elaine Sciolino, *Britain Grapples with Role for Islamic Justice*, N.Y. Times, Nov. 19, 2008, at A1 (www .nytimes.com/2008/11/19/world/europe/19shariah .html?pagewanted=all).

[37] William Yong, *Iran's Divorce Rate Stirs Fears of Society in Crisis*, N.Y. Times, Dec. 6, 2010 (www.nytimes.com /2010/12/07/world/middleeast/07divorce.html).

[38] *Rahman v. Hossain*, 2010 WL 4075316 (N.J. Super. A.D. 2010).

[39] *Avitzur v. Avitzur*, 446 N.E.2d 136, 139 (N.Y., 1983).

[40] *Avitzur*, 446 N.E.2d at 139.

[41] Ok. Const. art. 7, § 1(C) (2010) (www.sos.ok.gov/documents /questions/755.pdf). The constitutionality of the Oklahoma law, however, is in serious doubt. See *Awad v. Ziriax*, 670 F.3d 1111 (10th Cir. 2012).

Spousal Support, Property Division, and the Separation Agreement

CHAPTER OUTLINE

CHAPTER OBJECTIVES

After completing this chapter, you should be able to:

- Know the main objectives of spouses entering a separation agreement.

- State when courts become involved in separation agreements.

- List the characteristics of an effective separation agreement.

- Identify the main checklists used in the preparation of a separation agreement.
- Explain how a separation agreement could violate public policy.
- State the duty of disclosure.
- Explain whether a court will force an ex-spouse to live with a bad bargain.
- List the main differences between alimony and property division.
- Explain the factors a court will use when deciding whether a clause in a separation agreement is alimony or property division.
- Distinguish the different kinds of alimony.
- Explain the criteria for awarding alimony.
- State when a court will modify an alimony award.

- Identify the main ways a payee can enforce an alimony obligation.
- State whether alimony and property-division debts are dischargeable in bankruptcy.
- Describe necessaries.
- Explain the tactic of spousal refusal.
- List the main steps in property division.
- Describe the different categories of property.
- List the main kinds of separate property.
- Explain the differences between common-law and community-property states.
- Explain transmutation.
- Explain the criteria for equitable distribution.

- Distinguish between marital and economic fault.
- Explain when appreciation is divisible.
- Know the effect of commingling.
- Explain how property division occurs for pensions, degrees/licenses, businesses, and goodwill.
- Describe how a court will treat debts, taxes, wills, insurance, and legal expenses.
- Know the effect of mutual mistake in a separation agreement.
- Explain the role of alternative dispute resolution (ADR).
- Understand the consequences of reconciliation on a separation agreement.

INTRODUCTION

It is sometimes said that marriage is about love and divorce is about money.[1] Chapter 8 begins our comprehensive study of two of the major money dimensions of divorce: spousal support (alimony) and property division. We will examine attempts by the parties to reach agreement on these matters in a separation agreement as well as how a court will force a resolution on the parties in the event that they cannot agree. In addition to alimony and property division, we will also cover other separation-agreement issues except for child custody (see Chapter 9) and child support (see Chapter 10).

SEPARATION AGREEMENTS AND LITIGATION

A **separation agreement** is a contract by married persons who have separated (or who are about to separate) that can cover support, custody, property division, and other terms of their separation and possible divorce. If the parties want a divorce based on the terms of the separation agreement, they must ask the divorce court to approve the terms. Most courts will approve them, although they are not required to do so. Between 80 and 90 percent of all divorces include some form of contractual agreement such as a separation agreement.[2] The separation agreement is an example of a **postnuptial agreement**, one made after the parties have been married. (See Exhibit 4-1 in Chapter 4 for a chart comparing the functions of separation agreements, premarital agreements, postnuptial agreements, and cohabitation agreements.)

Parties to a separation agreement have one of three possible objectives, at least initially. First, they may intend to dissolve the marriage through a divorce. Most spouses have this objective. Second, if they do not want a divorce, they may seek a **legal separation**, which defines their rights and duties while living apart but still married to each other (see Chapter 7). Third, they may simply want to remain separated without seeking a divorce or legal separation at

separation agreement

A contract by married persons who have separated (or who are about to separate) that can cover support, custody, property division, and other terms of their separation and possible divorce. Also called marital settlement agreement, agreed judgment, and stipulated judgment.

postnuptial agreement

A contract between married persons that covers financial and related matters between them. They may have no intention of separating. If they have this intention, the contract is commonly called a separation agreement.

legal separation

A declaration by a court that parties can live apart even though they are still married to each other. Also called judicial separation, limited divorce, *divorce a mensa et thoro*, and separation from bed and board.

the present time. Whatever the goal, spouses can use the separation agreement to specify how they propose to settle the questions of custody, support, property division, and all other major terms of their separation.

Separation agreements find their way into court in the following situations:

- The parties file for a divorce after negotiating the separation agreement; the court is asked to approve the terms of the agreement.

- One party sues the other for breach of contract (i.e., for violation of the separation agreement); the plaintiff in this suit wants the separation agreement enforced.

- After the divorce, one of the parties brings a suit to ask the court to modify the separation agreement (e.g., to reduce the amount of alimony).

- After the divorce, one of the parties brings a suit to set aside the separation agreement (e.g., because it was induced by fraud, or because of mutual mistake).

The law encourages parties to enter separation agreements. So long as certain basic public policies (to be discussed below) are not violated, the law gives a great deal of leeway to the parties to resolve their difficulties and, in effect, to decide what their relationship will be upon separation. The role of the attorney and paralegal is to assist the client in this goal.

A high priority of the family-law practitioner must always be to avoid litigation, which is often time-consuming, expensive, and emotionally draining for everyone involved. The marital breakdown of the parties was probably a most painful experience for the entire family. Litigation tends to remind the parties of old sores and to keep the bitterness alive. Although an effective separation agreement will not guarantee harmony between the spouses, it can help keep their disputes on a constructive level.

EFFECTIVE SEPARATION AGREEMENTS

An effective separation agreement is achieved through bargaining or negotiation. Initially, the spouses often do a good deal of bargaining on their own before they turn the task over to their attorneys. What is an effective separation agreement? Obviously, this will vary according to individual circumstances. Nevertheless, some general observations can be made about the characteristics of an effective separation agreement: It is comprehensive, fair, accurate, legal, and readable. (See Exhibit 8-1.)

EXHIBIT 8-1   Characteristics of an Effective Separation Agreement

1. *Comprehensive.* It covers all major matters. If a problem arises months or years later, the parties will not have to say, "We never thought of that when we drafted the agreement."

2. *Fair.* If the agreement is not fair to both sides, it may be unworkable, which will force the parties into expensive and potentially bitter litigation to interpret and enforce the agreement. Hence the worst kind of legal assistance a law office can provide is to "outsmart" the other side into "giving up" everything. Little is accomplished by winning the war but losing the peace: "You gain no advantage in depriving your ex-spouse of what he/she is entitled to. Remember, your ex-spouse has the ability to make your life miserable."[3]

3. *Accurate.* The agreement should accurately reflect the intentions of the parties. What they orally agreed to do in formal or informal bargaining sessions should be stated in the written agreement. No clause in the agreement should ever prompt one of the parties to exclaim, "That's not what we agreed to do when we talked about it!"

4. *Legal.* Certain things can and cannot be done in a separation agreement; the agreement must not attempt to do anything that is illegal.

5. *Readable.* The agreement should be written in language that the parties can understand without having to hire or rehire an attorney every time a question arises.

CHECKLISTS FOR THE PREPARATION OF A SEPARATION AGREEMENT

Before an intelligent separation agreement can be drafted, a great deal of information is needed. Chapter 3 (compiling a family history) covers many categories of questions that should provide needed background information. A major focus of the interrogatories in Appendix C will be on obtaining information from the opposing spouse that will be needed to negotiate and draft a separation agreement. In addition, here are some overview checklists of information and documents that the law office should collect at the outset of a case.

DATA NEEDED ON INDIVIDUALS

- Names and addresses of spouses and children (include phone numbers, e-mail address, all Internet addresses, e.g., Facebook page).
- Name and address of present attorney of the other spouse.
- Names and addresses of prior attorneys, if any, retained by either spouse at any time during (or in anticipation of) the marriage.
- Name and addresses of business associates (e.g., partners, senior employees) of each spouse.
- Name and addresses of major service providers (e.g., accountant, investment advisor, stockbroker, real estate agent) of each spouse.
- Names and addresses of individuals who might serve as character references (if needed on custody or credibility issues).
- Names and addresses of individuals trusted by both spouses (e.g., member of the clergy) who might serve as mediators.

FINANCIAL CHECKLISTS

- All prior agreements between spouses (e.g., premarital agreement, postnuptial agreements such as a loan between the spouses, drafts of separation agreements).
- All property held by the husband in his separate name.
- All property held by the wife in her separate name.
- All property held jointly; that is, in both names.
- All property the husband brought into the marriage and kept as his separate property.
- All property the wife brought into the marriage and kept as her separate property.
- All property the husband brought into the marriage that was jointly used during the marriage and/or whose upkeep/maintenance was jointly paid for during the marriage.
- All property the wife brought into the marriage that was jointly used during the marriage and/or whose upkeep/maintenance was jointly paid for during the marriage.
- All property received by one spouse alone (before or during the marriage) as a gift from a relative or from someone other than the other spouse.
- All property received by one spouse alone (before or during the marriage) from the will of a relative or of anyone else.
- All property received by one spouse alone (before or during the marriage) from a relative or from anyone else who died without leaving a valid will (**intestate succession**).
- All income earned or other property acquired by the husband after the DOS (date of the separation) but before the date of the final divorce.

intestate succession
The transfer of a decedent's property to state-designated relatives of the decedent who dies without leaving a valid will. Also called descent and distribution, hereditary succession.

- All income earned or other property acquired by the wife after the **DOS** (date of the separation) but before the date of the final divorce.
- All pending contracts for the purchase or sale of real property.
- All insurance policies currently in force.
- All insurance policies cancelled in the last five years.
- All debts currently **outstanding**, with an indication of who incurred each debt.
- The location of copies of all tax returns filed during the marriage and since the DOS.
- The location of copies of all wills, trusts, or other family **instruments**.
- The location of all **financial statements** prepared before the marriage, during the marriage, and after the DOS (e.g., statements filed with the government, a bank, or other institution).
- All income from any source earned by the husband.
- All income from any source earned by the wife.
- Projected future income of both parties (e.g., salary, dividends, interest, Social Security, pension rights, royalties, loans that will be repaid, future trust income, expected inheritance).
- All present and projected living expenses of the husband.
- All present and projected living expenses of the wife.
- All present and projected living expenses of the children.

CHECKLISTS FOR INDIVIDUAL CLAUSES IN THE SEPARATION AGREEMENT

1. *Spousal support (alimony):*
   - Waived by both spouses?
   - If included, who pays?
   - How much?
   - What is the method of payment?
   - What is the frequency of payment?
   - Does it terminate on the remarriage or the death of either spouse?
   - Does it fluctuate with income of **payor**?
   - Should the agreement include a no-modification clause stating that neither spouse will ask a court to modify the agreement once it is approved by the court?
   - What is the security for payment?
   - What are the methods of enforcement?
   - What are the tax consequences of spousal-support payments?
   - Any prior agreements about spousal support in a premarital agreement?

2. *Child support (see Chapter 10):*
   - Who pays?
   - How much (as per the state's mandatory child-support guidelines)?
   - Is amount modifiable?
   - What is the method of payment?
   - What is the frequency of payment?
   - What is the security for payment?
   - Does it terminate when a child reaches a certain age?
   - Does it terminate if the child is otherwise **emancipated**?

DOS
Date of separation.

outstanding
Unpaid; to be collected.

instrument
A formal written document that gives expression to or embodies a legal act or agreement (e.g., contract, will). (See glossary for an additional meaning.)

financial statement
A report covering the assets (e.g., income, investments) and debts of a person or business as of a particular date or over a designated period. A financial accounting or balance sheet.

payor
One who makes a payment of money or who is obligated to do so.

emancipated
Legally independent of one's parent or legal guardian. The noun is *emancipation.*

physical custody

The right of an adult to have a child reside with the adult. (See glossary for an additional meaning.)

legal custody

The right to make the major child-rearing decisions on health, education, religion, discipline, and general welfare.

noncustodial parent (NCP)

The parent who is not living with the child; the parent who does not have physical custody of the child.

custodial parent (CP)

The parent with whom the child is living; the parent with physical custody of the child.

- Day care expenses?
- Education expenses covering private schools, college, graduate school, etc.?
- What are the tax consequences of child-support payments?
- Are there any prior agreements about child support such as in a premarital agreement?

3. *Child custody (see Chapter 9):*
   - Custody options: Who has **physical custody** (sole or joint) and who has **legal custody** (sole or joint)?
   - What is the method of communicating/consulting on major child-rearing decisions such as health and education (if parties have joint legal custody)?
   - What are the visitation rights of **noncustodial parent (NCP)**?
   - What are the visitation rights of others (e.g., grandparents)?
   - Summer vacations and special holidays?
   - Transportation expenses?
   - Permissible removal of child from the state on a temporary or permanent basis?
   - Changing the last name of the child?
   - The child's participation in religious activity?
   - Any prior agreements about child custody in premarital agreement?

4. *Health expenses of **custodial parent (CP)** and children:*
   - Who pays? What is the method of payment?
   - What is the security for payment?
   - Medical?
   - Dental?
   - Drugs?
   - Special needs?
   - Expenses not covered by insurance?

5. *Insurance:*
   - Who pays? What is the method of payment?
   - What is the security for payment?
   - Can names of beneficiaries be changed?
   - Life insurance?
   - Health insurance?
   - Comprehensive vehicle insurance?
   - Disability insurance?
   - Homeowner's insurance?
   - Umbrella insurance?
   - Any prior agreements about insurance in premarital agreement, particularly life and medical insurance?

6. *Estate documents:*
   - Wills already in existence (individual or mutual): changes needed?
   - Family trust: changes needed?
   - Trust accounts for children?

7. *Debts still to be paid:*
   - Incurred by whom?
   - When incurred?
   - Why incurred?
   - Who pays?
   - **Hold-harmless** clause for party not obligated to pay debts?
   - Any prior agreements about debts in premarital agreement?

8. *Personal property:*
   - Who will own?
   - Cash?
   - Joint and separate bank accounts (savings, checking, certificates of deposit, etc.)?
   - Stocks, bonds, mutual funds, other kinds of securities?
   - Motor vehicles?
   - Works of art, jewelry, etc.?
   - Household furniture?
   - Business assets?
   - Rights to receive money in the future (e.g., retirement pay, stock options, royalties, rents, anticipated court judgment awards)?
   - Any prior agreements about personal property in premarital agreement?

9. *Real property:*
   - Who will own?
   - Residences?
   - Vacation home?
   - Business real estate?
   - Tax shelters?
   - Leases?
   - Any prior agreements about real property in premarital agreement?

10. *Income tax returns*
    - What returns will be filed after the separation but before the divorce?
    - Who will be responsible to pay deficiencies and penalties if the tax authorities audit the current year's tax return and the returns of prior years when the parties filed joint returns?
    - Hold-harmless clause on deficiencies and penalties?

11. *Attorney fees and court costs*
    - Each party pays own fees and costs?
    - One party pays the other's fees and costs (part or whole)?

12. *Separation agreement*
    - To be incorporated and merged into the divorce judgment?
    - To be incorporated but not merged into the divorce judgment?

13. *Conflict resolution for disagreements after separation agreement is **executed** (see Chapter 7)*
    - Arbitration?
    - Mediation?
    - Other method of **alternative dispute resolution (ADR)**?
    - How will a neutral third party be selected?
    - Payment of expenses for resolution process?

hold harmless

To assume any liability in a transaction and thereby relieving another from responsibility or loss arising out of the transaction. Also called save harmless.

executed

Performed or carried out according to its terms.

alternative dispute resolution (ADR)

A method or procedure for resolving a legal dispute without litigating the dispute in a court or administrative agency. ADR methods include mediation, arbitration, and Med-Arb.

14. *Reconciliation (what happens to the terms of the separation agreement if parties reconcile after the agreement is executed)*
    - What to do about the parts of the separation agreement that were already carried out before the reconciliation?
    - What to do about the parts of the separation agreement that were not carried out before the reconciliation?

PRELIMINARY CONSIDERATIONS

Before we begin our examination of alimony and property division, we need to consider some preliminary matters that pertain to the legality of separation agreements. To highlight some of the major issues we will consider, read the sample introductory clauses (Exhibit 8-2) that are sometimes found in separation agreements.

PUBLIC POLICY AND COLLUSION

The agreement in Exhibit 8-2 between Fred and Linda Jones is careful to point out that a separation has already occurred. Clause [4] says they have been living apart since June 1, 2014. When parties are still living together despite their decision to separate, the law operates on the assumption that there is still hope. Yet a separation agreement provides *benefits* to the parties in the form

---

EXHIBIT 8-2   Sample Introductory Clauses in a Separation Agreement

Separation Agreement

[1] THIS AGREEMENT is entered on this 21st day of September, 2014, by Fred Jones (referred to in this agreement as the Husband), residing at 465 East 8th Street, Braintree, MA, and by Linda Jones (referred to in this agreement as the Wife), residing at 8 Florida Street, Dorchester, MA.

Witnesseth:

[2] WHEREAS, the parties were married on June 22, 2000 in the state of Ohio, city of Blue Creek, and

[3] WHEREAS, two children were born of this marriage: Ava Jones (October 19, 2001) and Myles Jones (July 5, 2002), and

[4] WHEREAS, as a result of irreconcilable marital disputes, the parties have been voluntarily living apart since June 1, 2014, which both parties feel is in their own best interests and that of their children, and

[5] WHEREAS, both parties wish to enter this agreement for the purpose of settling all custody, support, and property rights between them, and any other matter pertaining to their marriage relationship, and

[6] WHEREAS, both parties acknowledge that they have received a full and accurate disclosure from each other of all assets (separate and marital) and debts that are relevant to spousal support, child support, child custody, property division, and all other matters pertinent to their separation and divorce (see Attachment "A" containing these financial disclosures), and

[7] WHEREAS, both parties acknowledge that they have had separate and independent legal advice from counsel of their own choosing on the advisability of entering this agreement, that they have not been coerced or pressured into entering the agreement, and that they voluntarily decide to enter it.

[8] NOW THEREFORE, in consideration of the promises and the mutual commitments contained in this agreement, the parties agree as follows:

[The full text of the agreement goes here in numbered paragraphs. See an example of an agreement at the end of this chapter.]

of money, freedom, etc. The very existence of such an agreement is viewed as an *inducement* to obtain a divorce unless the parties have already separated or are about to do so shortly. A separation agreement between two parties who are still living together and who intend to remain together indefinitely might be declared unenforceable. It would be the equivalent of one spouse saying to another, "If you leave me now, I'll give you $25,000." The agreement is invalid because it is **conducive to divorce**. This is against **public policy**. Although the reform of no-fault divorce has lessened a court's inclination to invalidate separation agreements that are conducive to divorce, the prohibition still exists in many states.

It is also illegal to agree to have a "private divorce." Suppose a husband and wife enter the following brief separation agreement:

> "We hereby declare that our marriage is over and that we will have nothing to do with each other henceforth. As we part, we ask nothing of each other, including support or property."

Assume further that this agreement is not shown to anyone. To permit parties to make such a contract would be to enable them to "divorce" themselves without the involvement of a court. At the time the parties attempted to enter this contract, it may have seemed fair and sensible. Suppose, however, that months or years later, one of them becomes destitute and sues the other for support or alimony. The defendant could not defend the action by raising the promise the parties made in the agreement not to ask for support from each other. Furthermore, if either later tries to marry someone else, he or she can be charged with a crime, **bigamy**.

Another category of illegal agreement between a husband and wife is **collusion**, which is an agreement to commit fraud. An example of a fraudulent agreement would be a plaintiff who falsely asserts that the defendant deserted her on a certain date and the defendant falsely admits to this or remains silent even though he knows that the assertion is false. Their *collusive* objective is usually to *facilitate* the granting of the divorce. Before no-fault divorce became part of our legal system (see Chapter 7), this kind of falsehood was common.

Below are several clauses sometimes found in separation agreements, with comments on how the courts have treated the issues of divorce facilitation and collusion raised by the clauses.

> "The wife agrees that she will file for a divorce against the husband within three months."
> "None of the terms of this separation agreement shall be effective unless and until either of the parties is granted a divorce."

The first clause is invalid; a party cannot promise to file for a divorce. The clause doesn't merely encourage divorce; it makes it close to inevitable. The second clause appears to be as bad as the first. Neither of the parties will obtain any of the benefits in the separation agreement unless one of them obtains a divorce. Arguably, this clause encourages one of the parties to file for divorce and the other party to refrain from contesting the divorce. Oddly, however, the courts have not interpreted the second clause in this way. It *is* legal to condition the entire separation agreement on the granting of a divorce.

> "In the event that the wife travels to another state to file for divorce, the husband agrees to go to that state, appear in the action, and participate therein."

Courts differ on the legality of this clause. The parties are clearly contemplating an out-of-state divorce, perhaps because they both realize that obtaining the divorce in their own state would be procedurally more difficult than obtaining it out of state. Such **migratory divorces** were once quite common. Is a clause conducive to divorce if it obligates the defendant to appear in the **foreign divorce** action? Some states think that it is and invalidate the agreement. Other states, however, uphold the clause.

---

conducive to divorce
Tending to encourage divorce.

public policy
The principles inherent in the customs, morals, and notions of justice that prevail in a state; the foundation of public laws; the principles that are naturally and inherently right and just.

bigamy
Marrying while still in a valid, undissolved marriage with someone else.

collusion
(1) An agreement to commit fraud.
(2) An agreement by spouses that one or both will lie to the court in order to help secure their divorce.

migratory divorce
A divorce obtained in a state to which one or both of the spouses traveled before returning to their state of domicile.

foreign divorce
A divorce obtained in another state or country. A divorce that was not obtained in the forum state where the parties are now in litigation. If, for example, you are domiciled in Florida and obtain a divorce in Ohio, you have a foreign divorce.

ASSIGNMENT 8.1

Do the following clauses improperly facilitate divorce or are they collusive? (See General Instructions for the Legal-Analysis Assignment in Appendix A.)

a. "In the event that the wife files a divorce action, the husband will pay in advance all expenses incurred by the wife in bringing said action."

b. "In the event that the wife files for a divorce, legal separation, or annulment, the husband agrees to cooperate fully in the wife's action."

CAPACITY TO CONTRACT

There was a time in our history when the very thought of a wife entering a contract with her husband was anathema. A married woman lacked the **capacity** to contract with her husband. **At common law**, the husband and wife were one, and "the one" was the husband. You cannot make a contract with yourself. This rule, of course, has been changed. A wife can enter a contract such as a separation agreement with her husband. (See the discussion in Chapter 4 on **postnuptial agreements**.)

Today the major question of capacity involves mental health. A separation agreement is invalid if either party lacked the capacity to understand the agreement and the consequences of signing it. The traditional test is that a person must understand the nature and consequences of his or her act at the time of entering the separation agreement. This understanding may not exist due to insanity, mental retardation, senility, temporary delirium due to an accident, intoxication, drug addiction, etc.

MUTUAL DISCLOSURE, FRAUD, AND DURESS

Clause [6] of the agreement in Exhibit 8-2 states that the parties have received a full and accurate disclosure of all assets and debts. Attachment "A" of the agreement contains this disclosure.

Spouses negotiating a separation agreement have a duty to make a full and accurate disclosure to each other of all the assets and debts that pertain to the marriage. They cannot treat each other at **arm's length** as two strangers in a business transaction can. This duty is based on the status of the parties as a married couple. Many states say that a husband and wife have a **fiduciary relationship** with each other, which requires fair dealing and openness. Their fiduciary duty does not end until the divorce is final. The failure to make a full and honest disclosure during negotiations for the separation agreement can be a violation of the fiduciary duty the parties owe each other. Serious nondisclosure or lying about assets can lead to the invalidation of part or all of the agreement on the ground of **fraud**. The latter is an intentionally false statement of fact that is **material**, made to induce reliance by the plaintiff, and results in harm because of the reliance. (Something is material if it is important enough to influence a decision.) An example of fraud is a spouse who intentionally fails to disclose or undervalues marital assets that should be part of the property division in the separation agreement.

Unfortunately, many spouses start hiding assets as soon as separation becomes a possibility. ("In a divorce, valuable items often mysteriously turn up 'missing.'"[4]) Unscrupulous spouses would probably agree with the advice a financial adviser gave to a husband who was about to start divorce proceedings: "You know what's the object in a divorce? . . . Pre-emptive retaliation. Here's what I want you to do. Clean out your bank account before she does it for you. Hide your assets."[5] Indeed, some spouses have kept assets and debts secret throughout the marriage. The task of uncovering this financial data can be daunting. The discovery devices discussed in

---

capacity

The legal power to do something such as enter a contract or a relationship. Also called legal capacity. (See glossary for an additional meaning.)

at common law

Law created by court opinions and legislatures during the early history of America, often before it was changed by later legislatures.

postnuptial agreement

A contract between married persons that covers financial and related matters between them. They may have no intention of separating. If they have this intention, the contract is commonly called a separation agreement.

arm's length

As strangers. Pertaining to how parties would treat each other if they were strangers looking out for their own self-interests with no confidential or other relationship between them that would cause one to expect the other to provide a special advantage or to act with fairness.

fiduciary relationship

The relationship that exists when one party (called the fiduciary) owes another loyalty, candor, and fair treatment. The fiduciary is required to act in the interest of and for the benefit of the other. Also called a confidential relationship.

fraud

An intentionally false statement of fact that is material, and is made to induce reliance by the plaintiff, and that results in harm because of the reliance. Also called deceit, misrepresentation

material

1. Important enough to influence the decision that was made. 2. Serious and substantial.

Chapter 7 are important tools in meeting this task. See also Appendix C for a set of interrogatories designed to uncover assets and debts.

In the excerpt from the Jones separation agreement in Exhibit 8-2, you will note that several times at the beginning of the agreement the parties mention that they are acting "voluntarily." (See clauses [4] and [7].) According to traditional contract principles, if a party enters a contract because of **duress**, it will not be enforced. Duress is the unlawful use of force or threats that overcome the will so that a person does something he or she does not want to do. Suppose that a wife is physically threatened if she does not sign the separation agreement. Clearly, the agreement would not be valid. The husband could not sue her for breaching it or attempt to enforce it in any other way.

Of course, simply because the separation agreement says that the parties enter it "voluntarily" does not necessarily mean that no duress existed. Either spouse could have been forced to say the agreement was signed "voluntarily." But to have the agreement say that it was "voluntarily" signed is at least *some* indication (however slight) that no duress existed. An **aggrieved** party, however, can still introduce evidence to the contrary. The same is true of clause [6] that says there has been full and accurate financial disclosure.

UNCONSCIONABILITY, OVERREACHING, AND LIVING WITH A BAD BARGAIN

Some courts say that an ex-spouse must live with a bad bargain so long as there was full financial disclosure and no fraud or duress. If, however, the terms of a separation agreement are so lopsided and intolerably unfair, it will be declared **unconscionable** and, therefore, unenforceable. A court can reach this result even if there was adequate financial disclosure and no fraud or duress. An example of unconscionability is a separation agreement in which the wife with limited job skills waives alimony and accepts a property division in which she receives $50,000 cash and her husband receives the remaining marital assets valued at $2.5 million. Even if the husband can demonstrate that there was no **overreaching** (taking advantage of another's vulnerability, especially by deception), the court might conclude that the agreement is unconscionable. Equally unacceptable is an agreement that is likely to result in one of the parties becoming a **public charge** because of the meagerness of the financial provisions for that party in the agreement despite the relative abundance of resources that went to the other party.

At one time, many courts presumed that a husband took unfair advantage of his wife unless he demonstrated otherwise. The women's movement has helped change this attitude. Courts no longer so blatantly protect women. Both sides will be forced to live with the agreement they signed if (1) there was full disclosure of assets and debts, (2) there was no fraud, duress, or overreaching, (3) the agreement is not unconscionable, (4) neither party is about to become a public charge, and (5) both parties had the opportunity to seek independent advice before they signed. If these conditions are met, most courts will presume that the agreement is valid and enforceable even if one of the parties later regrets signing it.

Ex-spouses who are stuck with a bad bargain sometimes turn against the attorney who represented them on the separation agreement. In a Connecticut case, for example, an ex-wife won a $1.5 million judgment against her attorney for **legal malpractice** in failing to do enough investigation of the value of her ex-husband's business before advising her to sign the separation agreement with him.[6]

Our focus thus far has been on the initial acceptability of the separation agreement to a court. Later we will discuss the separate issue of whether a court will *modify* an agreement that it approved at the time of the divorce.

duress
The unlawful use of force or threats that overcome the will so that a person does something he or she does not want to do. Illegal coercion.

aggrieved
Injured or wronged and thereby entitled to a remedy.

unconscionable
Shocking the conscience by heavily favoring one side due to the absence of meaningful choice and the highly unequal bargaining positions of the parties.

overreaching
Taking unfair advantage of another's naiveté or other vulnerability, especially by deceptive means.

public charge
An individual who is primarily dependent on the government for subsistence, as demonstrated by either the receipt of public cash assistance for income maintenance or by institutionalization for long-term care at government expense.

legal malpractice
The failure of an attorney to exercise the skills commonly applied by attorneys in the same area of practice under the same circumstances.

SEPARATE COUNSEL

The last WHEREAS clause [7] in the beginning of the Jones separation agreement in Exhibit 8-2 states that both Fred and Linda had the benefit of separate legal advice on the advantages and disadvantages of signing the agreement. This fact can be significant in a court's deliberation on whether to set the agreement aside on a ground such as duress. It is relatively difficult to challenge the validity of a separation agreement that was signed after both sides had the benefit of their own attorney—even though the spouse with most of the resources may have had to pay for both attorneys.

CONSIDERATION

consideration
Something of value that is exchanged between parties. It can be an act, a forbearance (not performing an act), a promise to perform an act, or a promise to refrain from performing an act.

Most contracts must be supported by **consideration** to be valid. (Consideration is something of value that is exchanged between the parties.) The separation agreement is a set of promises by the parties of what they will do. The exchange of these promises is the consideration for the separation agreement. A wife's promise to relinquish all claims she may have against her husband's estate when he dies is an example of her consideration to him. A husband's comparable release of claims in her estate or his promise to transfer to his wife full title to land he solely owns are examples of his consideration to her.

Perhaps the main consideration in the separation agreement is the separation itself. A husband and wife have the right to live with each other as husband and wife (i.e., the right of **cohabitation**). By reason of the separation agreement, the parties promise each other that they will never again claim this cohabitation right.

cohabitation
Living together in an intimate (usually sexual) relationship in the manner of a husband and wife.

ALIMONY PAYMENTS AND PROPERTY DIVISION: A SUMMARY OF CONSEQUENCES

alimony
Money or other property paid in fulfillment of a duty to support one's spouse (or ex-spouse) after a legal separation, a divorce, or in some states, an annulment. Also called maintenance, spousal support.

property division
The allocation and distribution of property between spouses (or ex-spouses) after a legal separation or divorce. Also called property settlement, property distribution.

We now begin our coverage of alimony and property division. **Alimony** is money or other property paid in fulfillment of a duty to support one's spouse after a legal separation or divorce. (Later, in Chapter 11 on taxation, we will see that the Internal Revenue Service uses a broader definition of alimony for income tax purposes.) Other terms used for alimony include *maintenance* and *spousal support*. **Property division** is the allocation and distribution of property between spouses (or ex-spouses) after a legal separation or divorce. Although alimony is still awarded in most states, its availability is in decline; the main way in which our legal system rearranges the financial lives of spouses upon divorce is through property division.

Exhibit 8-3 presents some major legal consequences of alimony and property division that we will be examining.

EXHIBIT 8-3 Alimony and Property Division Terms of a Separation Agreement	
Definitions	
Payor: One who makes a payment of money or who is obligated to do so.	Example: An ex-spouse who must pay alimony or child support is a payor.
Obligor: One who has a legal obligation to do something, usually to make a payment.	Example: An ex-spouse who must pay alimony or child support is an obligor.
Payee: One to whom money is paid or is to be paid.	Examples: An ex-spouse who receives alimony is a payee; a child who receives child support is a payee.
Obligee: One to whom a legal obligation is owed.	Examples: An ex-spouse who has a right to receive alimony is an obligee; a child who has a right to receive child support is an obligee.

Debtor: One who owes a debt.	Examples: An ex-spouse who must pay alimony is a debtor; an ex-spouse who must transfer property to the other ex-spouse as part of a property division is a debtor.
Transferor: The person who transfers an interest in property.	Example: The ex-spouse who gives his or her share of the marital home to the other spouse as part of the property division is a transferor.
Transferee: The person to whom an interest in property is transferred.	Example: The ex-spouse who will receive the other ex-spouse's share in the marital home as part of the property division is a transferee.
Interest: A legal share or right in something, which can often be sold or transferred.	Examples: A bank account that one owns or co-owns is an interest; a tenant's right to leased property is an interest.

Effect of Bankruptcy on Alimony and Property-Division Obligations

Alimony

- Domestic support obligations (DSO) such as alimony debts of the payor are *not* extinguished (discharged) by bankruptcy. After bankruptcy, the debtor (payor) who has an alimony obligation to the other spouse (the payee) continues to owe all arrears (unpaid or delinquent alimony debts) and must continue to pay all future alimony debts.

- Domestic support obligations (DSOs) are not dischargeable regardless of whether the debtor files for bankruptcy under chapter 7 or under chapter 13 of the bankruptcy code.

Property Division

- If the debtor files for bankruptcy under chapter 7 of the bankruptcy code, his or her property-division obligations cannot be discharged.

- If the debtor files for bankruptcy under chapter 13 of the bankruptcy code, his or her property-division obligations (which are not domestic support debts) *can* be discharged upon certifying that all outstanding alimony and child-support obligations have been met.

Effect of Remarriage on Alimony and Property-Division Obligations

Alimony

- If the person receiving alimony (the payee) remarries, the alimony payments cease (the payor no longer owes them) *unless* the separation agreement or a court specifically provides that the payments continue after the payee's remarriage.

- If the person paying alimony (the payor) remarries, the alimony payments to the first spouse must continue *unless* the separation agreement or a court provides that the payments cease or are reduced.

Property Division

- The remarriage of either the payor or the payee does not affect the terms of the property division. All remaining obligations under the property division must be fulfilled despite the remarriage of the payor or the payee.

Effect of Death on Alimony and Property-Division Obligations

Alimony

- If the payee dies, alimony payments cease.
- If the payor dies, alimony payments cease unless the separation agreement or a court provides that the payments continue.

Property Division

- The death of either the payor or the payee does not affect the terms of the property division. All remaining obligations under the property division must be fulfilled despite the death of the payor or the payee.

Effect of Cohabitation on Alimony and Property-Division Obligations

Alimony

- In some states, cohabitation by the payee either terminates the alimony or is some evidence that alimony is no longer needed.

- Cohabitation by the payor does not affect the payor's alimony obligation to the payee.

Property Division

- The cohabitation of either the payor or the payee does not affect the terms of the property division. All remaining obligations under the property division must be fulfilled despite the cohabitation of the payor or the payee.

(continued)

EXHIBIT 8-3 *(continued)*

Availability of Civil Contempt for Enforcement of Alimony and Property-Division Obligations

Alimony

- If an ex-spouse fails to pay alimony according to the terms of a separation agreement and falls into arrears, a court can use civil contempt to enforce payment if the separation agreement has been incorporated and merged into the divorce decree. To use the enforcement remedy of civil contempt, the debtor must have the ability to pay the support.

Property Division

- If an ex-spouse fails to transfer property according to the property-division terms of a separation agreement, states differ on whether a court can use civil contempt to enforce the transfer obligation. In many states, civil contempt can be used if the debtor has violated a court order to transfer the property, but not if the debtor's duty to transfer the property is based on the separation agreement alone.

The Court's Power to Modify Alimony or Property-Division Terms of the Separation Agreement

Alimony

- A court may have the power to increase alimony if there has been a substantial change of circumstances of a continuing nature that seriously affects the need of the payee for support.

- A court may have the power to decrease alimony if there has been a substantial change of circumstances of a continuing nature that seriously affects the ability of the payor to pay.

Property Division

- If either party later becomes dissatisfied with the terms of an otherwise valid property division, the court will rarely, if ever, modify those terms.

Federal Income Tax Treatment of Alimony and Property Division

Alimony

- Alimony payments are taxable income of the payee; the payments are included in the gross income of the payee, who must pay taxes on the alimony received.

- Alimony payments are deductible by the payor.

- Caution: a property division improperly disguised as alimony in order for the payor/transferor to take advantage of the alimony deduction will be thwarted by the recapture rule. (See Chapter 11.)

Property Division

- Transfers of property incident to a divorce are not reportable as income by the transferee or deductible by the transferor.

- The tax basis of the property in the hands of the transferee is the same as the transferor's tax basis. (See Chapter 11.)

DISTINGUISHING BETWEEN ALIMONY AND PROPERTY DIVISION

As you can see from Exhibit 8-3, it can make a great deal of difference whether a term of a separation agreement is classified as alimony or as property division. Unfortunately, it is not always easy to determine whether a term in a separation agreement is alimony or part of the property division. The classification hinges on the intent of the parties at the time they entered the separation agreement.

Assume, for example, that the agreement provides that one party will make a five-year annual payment of $50,000 to the other party. Is this alimony or property division? The parties may either be confused about the distinction or pay little attention to it. At a later date, however, when the parties realize the importance of the distinction (e.g., at tax time), they will probably make conflicting claims about what their intentions were. It is the court's job to turn the clock back to when they were negotiating the separation agreement and determine what their intent was at that time. The test is *not* what the payee actually uses the money or other property for. Proof that a payment was used for rent and groceries, for example, does not show that the payment was alimony. The test is the intent of the parties at the time of the agreement, *before the money or other property is used.*

When faced with the need to decide whether a transfer is alimony or property division, the court will consider a number of factors:

- Labels used in the agreement
- Contingencies
- Method of payment
- The nature of what is transferred

Usually, none of these factors is conclusive by itself. All of them must be considered. One of the factors may clearly indicate an intent that a term is alimony. If, however, the other factors clearly suggest that the term is part of the property division, the court may conclude that it is the latter. Unfortunately, the factors do not always point in the same direction.

LABELS USED IN THE AGREEMENT Often the separation agreement will explicitly label a provision as "alimony" or as a "property settlement" or "property division." These labels, however, do not always control. For example, suppose that an annual payment of $10,000 given to the wife is labeled "Property Division." If it is otherwise clear to the court that the parties intended this payment to be in the nature of support, the court will classify it as alimony in spite of the label. If, for example, it appears to the court that the wife clearly needs support but that the agreement fails to mention or provide support for her, the parties probably intended the "property division" to be her support, or the parties had this intent but wanted to disguise the alimony as property division.

CONTINGENCIES Terms that are **contingent** on the occurrences of certain events are often interpreted as alimony rather than as a property division (e.g., $10,000 a year to the wife until she finishes school or turns 60). The presence of such contingencies suggests an intent to provide support while needed rather than an intent to divide property.

METHOD OF PAYMENT A term may provide a single **lump-sum payment** (e.g., $10,000), **periodic payments** (e.g., $10,000 a year), or fluctuating payments (e.g., $10,000 a year to be increased or decreased depending upon earnings in a particular year). A lump-sum payment that is intended to be alimony is called **alimony in gross**. Lump-sum payments, however, usually suggest a property division. (Indeed, alimony in gross is often property division in disguise.) Periodic and fluctuating payments usually suggest alimony.

THE KIND OF PROPERTY TRANSFERRED A conveyance of property other than cash (e.g., a house, a one-half interest in a business) often suggests a property division. Cash alone, however, usually suggests alimony.

Again, these factors are only guides. All of the circumstances must be examined in order to determine the intent of the parties. It may be that a court will conclude that a transfer of a house was intended as alimony or support. The court might also conclude that a lump-sum payment was intended as alimony. Although a court will be inclined to rule otherwise in these examples, specific proof of intent will control.

ALIMONY

INTRODUCTION

At common law, the husband, as head of the household, had a legal duty to support his wife for life. This duty existed even after a divorce so long as the wife did not cause the breakup of the marriage. An ex-husband had a duty to provide alimony if his marital conduct caused the breakup. A wife did not have a duty to support her husband during or after marriage. After giving him her dowry, her duty was to provide her husband with services, not support.

contingent
Conditional; dependent on something that may or may not happen.

lump-sum payment
A single payment of an amount of money.

periodic payments
Payments to be made over a period of time as opposed to a single (lump sum) payment.

alimony in gross
Alimony in the form of a single (lump sum) payment.

Today, the support duty is mutual in the sense that it will be imposed on the party who has the resources for the benefit of the party in need. To impose the duty only on a man (the ex-husband) would amount to unconstitutional sex discrimination in violation of the Equal Protection Clause of the U.S. Constitution and in violation of comparable clauses in most state constitutions. In the case of *Orr v. Orr*, the U.S. Supreme Court held that a state law that allows alimony for women but not for men is unconstitutional.[7] In most divorces, it is the woman who is the recipient of support through a separation agreement and/or through a court order.[8] As more women become successful in their careers, however, the number of ex-wives paying alimony to their ex-husbands has increased. (Occasionally the media will use the nonlegal word "manimony" for support payments paid to an ex-husband by his more wealthy ex-wife.)

The mutual duty of spouses to support each other is based on the common law (later we will discuss the common law rule of *necessaries*) or on statutes such as the **family expense act**, which requires both spouses to provide for the basic support needs of each other and the rest of the family.

Once divorce occurs, there are a number of different kinds of alimony that are possible in most states. See Exhibit 8-4 for the kinds of alimony we will be discussing.

family expense act
A state statute that makes spouses jointly liable for the basic support needs of the family. Creditors that extend credit for such needs can reach the property of either spouse.

EXHIBIT 8-4 Kinds of Alimony

General Definition: Money or other property paid in fulfillment of a duty to support one's spouse (or ex-spouse) after a legal separation, a divorce, or in some states, an annulment. Also called maintenance, spousal support.

Category	Definition
Alimony in gross	Alimony in the form of a single (lump sum) payment. Also called lump-sum alimony.
Alimony pendente lite	See temporary alimony.
Bridge-the-gap alimony	See rehabilitative alimony.
Caregiver alimony	Alimony for an ex-spouse who cannot be self-supporting because of his or her need to care for a disabled child.
Durational alimony	See rehabilitative alimony.
Incapacity alimony	Alimony, usually long-term, for an ex-spouse unable to be self-supporting because of his or her severe physical or mental incapacity.
Lump-sum alimony	See alimony in gross.
Permanent alimony	Alimony that is awarded periodically (e.g., monthly) until a designated date or indefinitely (without a termination date). Also called traditional alimony.
Rehabilitative alimony	Support payments to an ex-spouse for a limited time to allow him or her to return to financial self-sufficiency through employment or job training. (Also called durational alimony, transitional alimony, and bridge-the-gap alimony.)
Reimbursement alimony	Alimony that repays an ex-spouse who worked or made other financial contributions during the marriage so that the other spouse could obtain training or otherwise enhance his or her future earning capacity. Also called restitutional alimony.
Restitutional alimony	See reimbursement alimony.
Temporary alimony	Alimony awarded on an interim basis before the court makes its final decision on alimony. Also called alimony pendente lite.
Traditional alimony	See permanent alimony.
Transitional alimony	See rehabilitative alimony.

Related Support Categories
Separate maintenance Court-ordered spousal support while the parties are separated but still married. (See Chapter 7.)
Palimony Support payments ordered after the end of a nonmarital relationship (a) if the party seeking support was induced to initiate or stay in the relationship by a promise of support or (b) if ordering support is otherwise equitable. (See Chapter 4.)

CRITERIA FOR AWARDING ALIMONY

In recent years, alimony has become disfavored, particularly *permanent alimony*, which is alimony awarded periodically (e.g., monthly) until a designated date or indefinitely (without a termination date). Statistics vary, but according to some estimates, only between 9 and 16 percent of divorce cases include alimony as part of a divorce settlement or court award.[9] The Internal Revenue Service reports that approximately $10 billion a year is declared on income tax returns. (Payees must pay taxes on the alimony they receive and payors can deduct the alimony they pay. The average annual amount deducted and paid is $17,300.)[10] The trend is to have short-term or no alimony in separation agreements and court awards unless:

(1) there is little marital property to divide,

(2) there is a significant disparity between the wealth of the parties,

(3) the more needy party's ability to earn a living after the separation is hampered by a lack of job skills, age, and/or by a need to care for children, and

(4) the marriage had lasted more than a year.

On financial matters other than child support, there is a "clean-break" mentality among most parties, attorneys, and judges. Alimony, particularly long-term alimony, prolongs the interaction—and probably the bitterness—between ex-spouses. As much as possible, a clean-break philosophy seeks to end the financial interdependency of the parties.

This was not always so. There was a time in our history when courts gave substantial alimony awards to wives, particularly when the husband tended to control the family finances and to place all property in his name alone. Today, large alimony awards are less common because reforms in the law of property division (considered later in the chapter) have placed women in a less vulnerable position. Indeed, many courts will not address the alimony question until after they have divided the marital property. This division will be critical to obtaining a realistic assessment of a spouse's need for support. An ex-spouse who has received millions in the property division is unlikely to need (or be granted) alimony.

Temporary alimony might be awarded while the parties are waiting for a final court decision on property division. Until the property-division decision is made, the court will not be able to assess the need for permanent alimony. Temporary alimony is also called *alimony pendente lite* (pending the outcome of the litigation or court case).

The modern view on court-ordered alimony is expressed in the **Uniform Marriage and Divorce Act (UMDA)**, which refers to alimony as *maintenance*:

> The maintenance order shall be in amounts and for periods of time the court deems just, without regard to marital misconduct, and after considering all relevant factors, including:
>
> (1) the financial resources of the party seeking maintenance, including marital property apportioned to him, his ability to meet his needs independently, and the extent to which a provision for support of a child living with the party includes a sum for that party as custodian;
>
> (2) the time necessary to acquire sufficient education or training to enable the party seeking maintenance to find appropriate employment;
>
> (3) the standard of living established during the marriage;
>
> (4) the duration of the marriage;
>
> (5) the age and the physical and emotional condition of the spouse seeking maintenance; and
>
> (6) the ability of the spouse from whom maintenance is sought to meet his needs while meeting those of the spouse seeking maintenance.[11]

Uniform Marriage and Divorce Act (UMDA)

A model statute on marriage and divorce proposed to the states for adoption.

Not all states agree with the position of UMDA that alimony should be awarded "without regard to marital misconduct," as we will see. Yet most states will consider the same kinds of factors listed in (1) to (6). A common catchall factor used in many states allows a court to consider anything else that the court deems "necessary to do equity and justice between the parties."

These standards for the award of alimony give judges considerable discretion on when to award alimony and on how much. Some complain that the standards are too broad. Judges "are on their own in deciding how to prioritize the various factors and how to translate them into dollar amounts, resulting in wildly inconsistent alimony awards. When asked how much alimony a lifelong homemaker married to a doctor deserved, judges in an Ohio survey estimated as little as $5,000 a year and as much as $175,000."[12]

One area of consistency among most states is that alimony should not last forever. The preference (in many states, the presumption) is for limited-term alimony. In some states, alimony cannot be granted for more than a specific number of years (e.g., three years) except in extreme cases. Hostility toward long-term alimony can be found in the observation sometimes heard from judges that a failed marriage should not be a ticket to a lifetime pension.

REHABILITATIVE ALIMONY

The most popular form of short-term alimony is called *rehabilitative alimony* (also called *durational alimony*, *transitional alimony*, or *bridge-the-gap alimony*.) It consists of support payments to an ex-spouse for a limited time to allow him or her to return to financial self-sufficiency through employment or job training. How long should this take? The answer, of course, depends on the payee's skills and health and on the state of the economy. (If the ex-spouse cannot return to self-sufficiency because of his or her severe physical or mental incapacity, the alimony provided is sometimes called *incapacity alimony*.) A minority of states take a broader view of rehabilitative alimony by pegging the standard for its award not to minimal self-sufficiency but to what would be needed to restore the ex-spouse to some measure of the standard of living enjoyed during the marriage.

The amount of rehabilitative alimony will also depend on whether the payee must spend time raising children. An ex-spouse raising school-age children will usually have considerably less time to transition back into the outside work world (or to obtain job training) than an ex-spouse without child-rearing duties. If a child is disabled, rehabilitative alimony for the caregiver is sometimes called *caregiver alimony*. Of course, all of these categories of alimony are separate from (and in addition to) the child support that must be paid for a child's needs.

REIMBURSEMENT ALIMONY

Reimbursement alimony (also called *restitutional alimony*) seeks to repay a spouse who worked (or made other financial contributions) during the marriage so that the other spouse could obtain training or otherwise enhance his or her future earning capacity. An example would be a wife who held a full-time job in order to help pay her husband's tuition in dental school. When the couple divorces, there may be no property to divide because of the length of the marriage and the sacrifices that both made to meet the expenses of dental school. The amount she contributed to his education could be returned to her upon divorce as reimbursement alimony payable in a lump sum or periodically over a designated period of time. Although called alimony, the funds or other property given to the payee are primarily designed to serve the cause of fairness and justice rather than to meet a specific support need.

Later we will discuss the separate issue of whether a degree or occupational license is marital property that can be divided upon divorce. Most states say no.

In such states, one way for the sacrificing ex-spouse to be compensated would be to give him or her reimbursement alimony.

OPPORTUNITY LOSS

In many marriages, the wife stays home to care for children and run the household. To do so, she may postpone her own education and entry (or reentry) into the work force. Consequently, she has lost opportunities she would have had to build her own financial identity. In many states, an "opportunity loss" will lead to an increased share of the property division, or, if there is little property to divide, to a larger alimony award. Additionally, an opportunity loss may further demonstrate her need for a generous award of rehabilitative alimony.

PAYOR'S ABILITY TO PAY

In addition to the payee's need for alimony, the ability of the payor to pay alimony must also be considered. All of the payor's earnings and other financial resources are considered in determining ability to pay. The test for calculating earnings is not the payor's actual earnings; it is his or her realistic *earning potential* now and in the future. A spouse cannot plead poverty that could be substantially eliminated by using available or obtainable employment skills. Nor can a spouse create self-imposed poverty by giving away or squandering assets. (This admonition against dissipating assets also applies to property division, as we will see when we study the case of *Gastineau v. Gastineau*.)

MARITAL FAULT

Note that the Uniform Marriage and Divorce Act says that alimony should be awarded "without regard to marital misconduct." Many courts follow this guideline, but some do not. There are courts that will decrease the amount of alimony to be paid to a spouse whose marital misconduct precipitated the divorce. More common are courts that will increase the amount of alimony to be paid by a spouse who has committed domestic violence or other marital fault if the wrongdoing has affected the victim's ability to be self-sufficient after the divorce: "In most cases, judges take fault into account only when the fault resulted in some tangible economic consequence—for example, if a husband's physical cruelty toward his wife rendered her unable to work, he might be required to pay greater alimony."[13]

The impact of fault also needs to be considered when one party seeks to *modify* an alimony award. We will consider modification shortly.

ASSIGNMENT 8.2

Answer the following questions after examining your state code. Also check state court opinions of your state if you cannot find an answer in the code. (See General Instructions for the State-Code and Court-Opinion Assignments in Appendix A.)

a. What standards will a court use in awarding alimony? For example, is marital fault relevant?

b. Are there any limitations on the form that alimony can take (e.g., periodic payments, lump sum, etc.)?

c. When alimony is awarded, is it always for an indefinite period? If not, under what circumstances can it be for a fixed period?

d. If the court denies the divorce to both parties, can alimony still be awarded?

> ## ASSIGNMENT 8.3
>
> **a.** Find an opinion decided within the last 10 years by a court in your state that awarded alimony to a woman. List all the considerations that the court used in making its alimony decision. Try to find an opinion in which the court mentioned a specific dollar amount as alimony. To find cases, go to Google Scholar (scholar.google.com) and enter the search (aa alimony) in "Legal documents," substituting the name of your state for aa.
>
> **b.** Repeat the assignment, except this time find an opinion in which the court awarded alimony to a man.
>
> **c.** Are the two opinions consistent with each other? Explain. (See also the General Instructions for the Court-Opinion Assignment in Appendix A.)

NEGOTIATING ALIMONY

During negotiations on a separation agreement, spouses often waive the right to receive spousal support (alimony) from each other after the divorce. They both know that the law does not favor long-term alimony for most marriages. They therefore are more likely to use property division as the main vehicle for settling their post-divorce financial lives.

premarital agreement
A contract by persons about to be married that can cover (1) financial and related matters once the marriage occurs and (2) spousal support, property division, and related matters in the event of death, separation, divorce, or annulment. Also called prenuptial agreement ("prenup"), antenuptial agreement.

Also, if the parties entered a valid **premarital agreement**, its terms may specify whether alimony is waived in the event of a divorce, or if it is not waived, how much alimony will be paid and who will pay it. (See Chapter 4.)

Let's assume that the parties will include alimony in their separation agreement. As we examine the options for doing so, keep in mind that no individual clause in the agreement can be fully understood in isolation. The negotiation process involves a large variety of factors. A party may agree to a clause not so much because that clause gives the party what he or she wants, but rather because the party decided to concede that clause in order to gain another clause (e.g., a wife may accept a lower alimony provision in exchange for the husband's agreement to give her sole physical and legal custody of their child). This is the nature of the bargaining process.

PERIODIC PAYMENTS OR LUMP SUM? In a few states, it is illegal for a husband and wife to agree to fulfill the support obligation through *alimony in gross*, which is alimony in the form of a single payment (a lump-sum). In most states, however, alimony in gross is allowed. For example, instead of an alimony payment of $1,000 a month for 10 years, the parties could agree that a single payment of $120,000 would satisfy the alimony obligation. Many variations of this arrangement are possible. For example, the $120,000 debt could be met by paying $50,000 when the divorce is granted and the remaining $70,000 in seven equal payments of $10,000 over the next seven months. From the perspective of the recipient, collectability is an important factor in deciding whether to seek a lump-sum alimony payment. A spouse may find it safer to take a lower lump-sum payment now rather than hassle with installment or periodic payments if there is any likelihood that the payor will fall behind in payments. It can be expensive and psychologically draining to have to go after a delinquent payor.

FIXED OR FLUCTUATING PERIODIC PAYMENTS? If periodic payments are agreed to, the most common method is a fixed dollar amount (e.g., $700 per month). A less common and more-difficult-to-enforce option is a fluctuating or flexible periodic payment. Under this method, the amount of the payment will fluctuate up or down depending upon the income of the ex-husband, ex-wife, or both. An alimony payment of 15 percent of the ex-husband's earnings (gross or net), for example, provides an automatic fluctuating standard. Another option is the gradual reduction of alimony payments over a designated period of time (e.g., alimony that decreases 10 percent every year).

MEDICAL AND DENTAL INSURANCE As part of spousal support (alimony), do the parties want to include the payee's medical and dental insurance costs? If not, do they want to include a clause in the separation agreement on how these costs are to be covered? We will cover medical care for children separately in Chapter 10 when we examine qualified medical child support orders (QMCSO).

LIFE INSURANCE Even though the duty of support usually ends at the death of the payor or of the payee, the parties might agree that the support payments will continue after the payor dies. If so, one way to do this is through a life insurance policy on the life of the payor. The beneficiary would be the payee—the other spouse. If a life insurance policy already exists, the parties may decide to include a clause in the separation agreement that requires the payor to continue paying the premiums, to increase the amount of the policy, to name the payee as the *irrevocable* beneficiary (meaning that the payor cannot change the beneficiary), etc. The agreement should also specify whether an existing policy remains in force if either side remarries. If no life insurance policy exists, the parties need to decide whether to take one out. Unfortunately, if a payor violates a clause requiring him or her to take out a life insurance policy, a court might take the position that it is powerless to enforce the clause if the state has a law that alimony must end upon the death of the payor or payee.

TERMINATION OF SUPPORT PAYMENTS The agreement should specify when alimony ends. After a designated number of months or years? After the payee becomes employed? After he or she remarries? Most payors want alimony to end if the payee remarries. Yet a clause to this effect might discourage the payee to remarry. Hence the payor might want to continue alimony after the payee's remarriage, but at a reduced amount. (If the second marriage is later annulled, states differ on whether the original alimony obligation of the first husband is *revived*. See Chapter 6.) Concerned about helping to support a live-in lover, some payors include a clause stating that alimony ends upon the payee's cohabitation with another adult. (We will discuss cohabitation more fully when we cover modification of alimony.)

The termination of future alimony payments does not affect **arrears** (i.e., unpaid back payments). All delinquent payments must be paid.

SECURITY When a payor fails to make a support payment, the payee can sue, but this is hardly a satisfactory remedy because of the delay and expense of litigation. The best way for a payee to avoid litigation is to be given *security* for the performance of the support obligation within the separation agreement itself. This security can be provided in a number of forms:

- **Escrow.** The payor deposits a sum of money with an escrow agent (e.g., a bank), with instructions to pay the payee a designated amount of money in the event that the payor falls behind in a payment.
- **Surety bond.** The payor gives the payee a surety bond. The payor pays premiums to the surety company. The surety company guarantees that if the payor fails to fulfill the alimony obligation, the company will meet the obligation up to the amount of the bond.

Here are two additional forms of security that do not depend upon a breach by the payor of the alimony obligation. They are simply methods of transferring all of the support payments to the payee.

- **Annuity.** The payor purchases an annuity contract that provides a fixed income payable periodically to the payee (**annuitant**) in the amount of the alimony obligation.
- **Trust.** The payor transfers property (e.g., cash) to a **trustee** (e.g., a bank) with instructions to pay a fixed income to the payee (the beneficiary) in the amount of the alimony obligation. This is called an **alimony trust.**

arrears
Payments that are due but have not been made. Also called arrearages.

escrow
Property (e.g., money, a deed) delivered to a neutral person (e.g., bank, escrow agent) to be held until a specified condition occurs, at which time the property is to be delivered to a designated person.

surety bond
A bond given as insurance to guarantee that a contract will be completed within the agreed-upon time. An obligation by a guarantor to pay X if Y fails to perform a duty that Y owes X. Also called a performance bond.

annuity
A fixed sum payable periodically for life or for a specific period of time.

annuitant
Recipient of an annuity.

trust
A device or arrangement by which its creator (the settlor or trustor) transfers property (the corpus) to a person (the trustee) who holds legal title for the benefit of another (the beneficiary or cestui que trust).

trustee
The person or company holding legal title to property for the benefit of another.

alimony trust
A trust to which a spouse or ex-spouse transfers funds that will be used to meet an alimony obligation.

MODIFICATION OF ALIMONY

Generally, a court has no power to alter the terms of a valid contract. A separation agreement is a contract. Can its terms be modified? Clearly, the parties to any contract can mutually agree to modify its terms. But can the court *force* a modification on the parties when only one party wants it? The answer may depend on which terms of the separation agreement are in question. *Property-division* terms, as indicated earlier, are rarely modifiable (see Exhibit 8-3). *Child-custody* and *child-support* terms, however, are almost always modifiable according to the court's perception of the best interests of the child (see Chapters 9 and 10 for special rules on modifying child-custody and child-support orders).

Can *alimony* (spousal support) terms be modified by a court? First, consider two extreme and relatively rare circumstances in which the court can modify alimony terms in most states:

- The separation agreement itself includes a provision allowing a court to modify its terms.
- The needy spouse becomes so destitute that he or she will become a public charge unless a modification is ordered.

If neither of these situations exists, can the court order a modification of the spousal-support terms of the separation agreement? This involves two separate questions: Does the court have the power to modify? And if so, when will it exercise this power?

Power to Modify

First of all, a court cannot modify alimony if the court does not have **personal jurisdiction** over the ex-spouse who is being asked to pay more or over the ex-spouse who is being asked to accept less than the original alimony award. A court does not need personal jurisdiction to dissolve a marriage (in rem jurisdiction is sufficient), but alimony orders (like child-support and property-division orders) require personal jurisdiction over the payor. In most states, if the court had jurisdiction over a party in the original proceeding that awarded the alimony, the court has **continuing jurisdiction** to revisit the award and modify it as needed. See Chapter 7 for a discussion of how a court obtains personal jurisdiction over a party.

In a few states, a court has no power to modify a spousal-support term unless the parties have agreed in the separation agreement to allow the court to do so. Most states, however, will allow their courts to modify a separation agreement even if it has a *no-modification clause* that expressly states that neither side will request modification. A number of theories have been advanced to support this view. Some states hold that the separation agreement is merely advisory to the court and that as a matter of public policy, the court cannot allow the question of support to be determined solely by the parties. The state as a whole has an interest in seeing to it that this sensitive question is properly resolved. What the parties have agreed upon will be a factor in the court's determination, but it will not be the controlling factor.

Other states advance the doctrine of merger. When a court accepts the terms of a separation agreement, the parties may ask the court to *incorporate* and *merge* the terms of the agreement into the divorce judgment. Incorporation occurs when the divorce judgment specifically refers to or mentions the alimony clauses in the separation agreement. Merger occurs when the separation agreement loses its separate identity once the divorce judgment is rendered. Upon **incorporation and merger**, the question is not whether the separation agreement can be modified, but whether the judgment can be modified. Courts are much less reluctant to modify their own judgments than they are to modify the private contracts of parties. Under the merger doctrine, the contract no

personal jurisdiction
A court's power over a person to determine (adjudicate) his or her personal rights and duties. Also called *in personam jurisdiction*.

continuing jurisdiction
A court's power (by retaining jurisdiction) to modify its orders after entering judgment.

incorporation and merger
The acceptance of the terms of one document (e.g., an agreement) and making the terms become part of another document (e.g., a court decree) so that the former document ceases to exist as a separate entity.

longer exists. Suppose, however, that a court incorporates but does *not* merge the separation agreement into the judgment. Here the court simply refers to the separation agreement in its decree and usually approves the alimony terms the parties negotiated. Because, however, there is no merger, the separation agreement remains as an independent contract, which can be the basis of a breach-of-contract suit.

Exercising the Power to Modify

Assuming the court has the power to modify alimony, when will the court use this power? The general rule is that a modification will be ordered only if the following conditions are met:

(1) there has been a substantial change of circumstances of a continuing nature and

(2) the ex-spouse is not using the change in circumstances as a pretext for avoiding the original alimony award.

Sometimes a court may also consider whether the change in circumstances was foreseeable when the original alimony award was made. If it was foreseeable, a court might deny the modification on the ground that the parties factored in the change (or should have factored it in) when they negotiated the original clause on alimony.

Unfortunately, however, courts are not always consistent in how they apply these factors in petitions for modification.

Tom and Mary enter a separation agreement that is incorporated and merged into a divorce judgment. Tom is required to pay Mary $750 a month alimony. Assume that a year later Tom asks the court for a decrease, and/or Mary asks for an increase.

Consider the following variations on these facts on why the modification is being sought. Assume that the payor in these examples is the ex-husband and the payee is the ex-wife:

1. *The ex-husband becomes sick and earns substantially less.* Most courts would modify the judgment to lessen the amount he must pay—at least during the period when his earning capacity is affected by the illness. If, however, the sickness was anticipated or foreseeable at the time the separation agreement was negotiated, a court may deny the modification on the ground that the parties should have factored the sickness into their calculations when they negotiated the agreement.

2. *The ex-husband is bankrupt.* Bankruptcy does not eliminate (discharge) past-due support debts. If, however, a payor is granted a bankruptcy, he may be able to go back to court and request a modification downward of future support payments on the ground that he is genuinely unable to pay the original amount.

3. *The ex-husband suddenly starts earning a great deal more.* The ex-wife will usually not be able to increase her alimony award simply because her ex-husband becomes more wealthy than he was at the time of the divorce judgment. The result might be different if she can show that the original alimony amount was inadequate due to his weaker earning capacity at that time.

4. *The ex-wife violates the terms of the separation agreement relating to the visitation rights of the ex-husband/father.* Most courts will not modify alimony for the sole reason that the payee interferes with the visitation rights of the payor. There are a few courts, however, that say that alimony payments and visitation rights *are* interdependent. If, for example, the ex-wife interferes with the father's visitation rights with the children, these courts might reduce her alimony, terminate her alimony,

or cancel any unpaid past alimony obligations due her (*arrears*). For such a result, however, the interference must be substantial.

5. *The ex-wife cohabits.* In many states, cohabitation by the payee can lead to a termination or other modification of alimony, particularly if the cohabitation is ongoing and open. (The statute authorizing this result is sometimes called the "live-in-lover" statute.) In some states, cohabitation creates a **rebuttable presumption** that the payee has a decreased need for alimony due to the new living arrangement. Of course, the main reason an ex-husband will petition the court for modification is his suspicion that his alimony payments are helping to support the new lover. Cohabitation means living together in an intimate (usually sexual) relationship in the manner of a husband and wife. A single act of sexual intercourse is usually not enough. To cohabit, the parties must be acting in the way that husbands and wives act such as by living together, having an ongoing sexual relationship, and sharing expenses.

6. *The ex-husband cohabits.* Cohabitation by the payor does not affect the payor's alimony obligation to the payee.

7. *The ex-husband wants to retire, change jobs, or go back to school.* When his income is reduced in this way, the courts will consider a downward modification of the alimony obligation if a number of conditions are met. First, the request for the reduction must be made in good faith and not be a mere strategy to avoid the original alimony award. A rich executive, for example, cannot "drop out" and become a poor farmer. Such an executive, however, may be able to take a lower paying job if this is required for his health. Second, the reduction, if awarded, must not leave the payee in dire financial straits. The court will balance the genuineness of the request for a reduction against the impact that it would have on the payee.

8. *The ex-wife wants to quit work.* A court will deny a request by a payee for increased alimony because the payee wants to quit work or retire.

9. *The ex-husband remarries.* In most states, if the payor remarries, the alimony payments to the first spouse must continue *unless* the separation agreement or a court provides that the payments cease or are reduced. A court might be inclined to a reduction if it is clear that the payor cannot meet the burden of supporting two families, particularly when there are children from the second marriage.

10. *The ex-wife remarries.* In most states, if the payee remarries, the alimony payments cease (the payor no longer owes them) *unless* the separation agreement or a court specifically provides that the payments continue after the payee's remarriage. Note, however, that if the ex-wife was allowed to receive lump-sum alimony (alimony in gross), her remarriage will not result in a court order to return any of the lump sum. Also, if the ex-wife was receiving *rehabilitation* alimony, she may be successful in arguing that the new marriage has not resulted in her self-sufficiency (rehabilitation) if the new husband has not increased her financial status.

11. *The ex-wife dies.* Alimony ends upon the death of the payee.

12. *The ex-husband dies.* Alimony ends upon the death of the payor *unless* the separation agreement provides for its continuance or the divorce judgment imposes the alimony obligation on the payor's estate. If an ex-wife is concerned about the end of alimony because of the death of her ex-husband, she can try to negotiate a clause in the separation agreement that would make her the beneficiary of a life insurance policy on his life or she can seek increased property division (payable in installments) in lieu of alimony.

rebuttable presumption
An assumption or inference of fact that a party will be allowed to try to disprove (rebut) but that will be treated as true if it is not disproved.

13. *The ex-wife undergoes a gender change.* In a recent Florida case, an ex-husband agreed in a separation agreement to pay his ex-wife $1,250 in alimony until she died or remarried. After the divorce judgment became final, the ex-wife changed her gender (and her name from Julia to Julio). The payor then asked a court to cancel the alimony obligation because of this change. The court denied the request, reasoning that under Florida law, sex-change surgery cannot legally change a person's birth gender. Therefore, technically the alimony payments to the **transsexual** were not being made to a man.[14]

14. *The ex-husband successfully challenges the basis of the alimony award.* In a recent divorce case involving a three-year marriage, the ex-wife was awarded $850 a month in alimony for life when she convinced the court that she was unable to work because of a car accident. When her ex-husband saw belly-dancing photos of her on an online blog, he went back to court and successfully argued that the alimony award should be cancelled.[15]

transsexual

(1) A person who has undergone a sex-change operation. (2) A person who wants to be considered by society as having a gender of the opposite sex.

ASSIGNMENT 8.4

Find authority (e.g., a statute or a court opinion) in your state for the court's power to modify an alimony award. When will such a modification be made? (See also General Instructions for the State-Code Assignment and the Court-Opinion Assignment in Appendix A.)

ASSIGNMENT 8.5

Karen and Jim obtain a divorce decree that awards Karen $500 a month in alimony "until she dies or remarries." A year after the divorce decree becomes final, Karen marries Paul. Jim stops the alimony payments. A year later, the marriage to Paul is annulled. Karen now wants Jim to resume paying her $500 a month alimony and to pay her $6,000 to cover the period when she was "married" to Paul ($500 x 12). What result? (See General Instructions for the Legal-Analysis Assignment in Appendix A.)

ENFORCING THE ALIMONY OBLIGATION

If the payor fails to fulfill his or her alimony obligation, the payee has a number of enforcement remedies that can be tried:

- *Execution.* An **execution** is a command or writ to a court officer (e.g., sheriff) to seize and sell the property of the delinquent party in order to satisfy the judgment debt. Here the judgment debt is the divorce judgment containing the order to pay alimony.

- *Garnishment.* **Garnishment** is a court proceeding by a creditor to force a third party in possession of the debtor's property to turn the property over to the creditor to satisfy a debt. The alimony payee is a creditor of the payor who is a debtor owing the alimony debt. An example of the debtor's property that could be garnished is the salary of the debtor. The third party would be the debtor's employer who normally pays the salary to the debtor but instead turns it over to the creditor because of the garnishment.

- *Fine.* The court could impose a fine for failure to obey a court order (the order to pay alimony).

- *Civil contempt.* **Civil contempt** is the refusal of a party to comply with a court order (usually issued for the benefit of another), which can lead

execution

A command or writ to a court officer (e.g., sheriff) to seize and sell the property of the losing litigant in order to satisfy the judgment debt. Also called general execution and writ of execution. (See glossary for an additional meaning.)

garnishment

A court proceeding by a creditor to force a third party in possession of the debtor's property (e.g., wages) to turn the property over to the creditor to satisfy a debt.

civil contempt

The refusal of a party to comply with a court order (usually issued for the benefit of another), which can lead to incarceration until the party complies with the order.

to incarceration until the party complies with the order. In general, civil contempt can be used to enforce an alimony obligation if the separation agreement containing the alimony clause has been incorporated and merged into the divorce judgment. (See the discussion earlier on incorporation and merger.) If the agreement has been incorporated and merged, then the failure to pay alimony is a violation of a court order for which civil contempt can result. If incorporation and merger has not occurred, the alimony order cannot be enforced by civil contempt.

Sometimes payors jailed for civil contempt protest that they are unable to pay and that, therefore, the foundation for civil-contempt incarceration does not exist. You cannot use imprisonment to pressure someone to pay a debt that the debtor is unable to pay. In a Pennsylvania case, an ex-husband (a practicing attorney) was jailed for 14 years for failing to produce $2.5 million that the court wanted to make available to pay the alimony award against him. He claimed that the money did not exist. After 14 years, however, when investigators could not locate the money, the court was finally convinced that the money did not exist and released him. Now impoverished, his license to practice law having been taken away, it made no sense to keep him locked up in order to pressure him to pay his alimony debt.[16] Fourteen years is believed to be the longest time anyone has ever been jailed for civil contempt.

- *Criminal contempt.* Civil contempt needs to be distinguished from **criminal contempt**. The purpose of the criminal contempt is to punish a party for repeated violation of a court order; the purpose of civil contempt is to enforce compliance with a court order. If a payor flagrantly and repeatedly violates a court order to pay alimony or to turn over property pursuant to a property-division order, the payor can be held in criminal contempt.
- *IV-D Agency.* In Chapter 10, we will learn how state child-support agencies, called **IV-D agencies**, can be used to collect child support. In most states, if the custodial parent is owed spousal support (alimony) and the child in the custodial parent's home is owed child support, the enforcement tools of the IV-D agency can be used to collect both delinquent spousal support and delinquent child support. We will cover those tools in Chapter 10.

When the delinquent spouse is in another state, the **Uniform Interstate Family Support Act (UIFSA)** allows the payee to use administrative and judicial tribunals to collect alimony. (We will discuss the UIFSA at length in Chapter 10 on child support.)

EFFECT OF BANKRUPTCY ON THE ALIMONY OBLIGATION

Bankruptcy will **discharge** (forgive) some debts so that the debtor can make a fresh start. There was a time when debtors with unpaid support and property-division debts filed for bankruptcy as a way to discharge these debts. If, for example, a separation agreement or divorce decree requires the payment of money or a share of a business as part of a property settlement, the debtor might try to avoid the requirement by declaring bankruptcy. Changes in the law have made this strategy no longer available, with very limited exceptions. Today, most debts that arise out of a separation or divorce are **nondischargeable**; they survive bankruptcy.

There are different categories of bankruptcy found in the chapters of the bankruptcy code. Our primary concern here are chapter 7 bankruptcy and chapter 13 bankruptcy. In a chapter 7 bankruptcy, the debtor is asking the court to liquidate (discharge) debts; in a chapter 13 bankruptcy, the debtor submits a plan for repaying his or her debts. Although some debts may be discharged in

---

criminal contempt

The refusal of a party to comply with a court order, which can result in incarceration or other punishment because of the repeated or aggravated nature of the refusal.

IV-D agency

A state agency that helps custodial parents enforce child-support obligations.

Uniform Interstate Family Support Act (UIFSA)

A state law on establishing and enforcing alimony and child-support obligations against someone who does not live in the same state as the person to whom the alimony and child support is owed.

discharge

Extinguish; forgive a debt so that it is no longer owed.

nondischargeable

Not eliminated or forgiven by bankruptcy.

a chapter 13 bankruptcy, the focus of chapter 13 is on repayment. Some debts, however, are nondischargeable under both chapter 7 and chapter 13:

- Domestic support obligations (DSO) such as alimony and child support are nondischargeable under all of the bankruptcy chapters.
- Property-division obligations are nondischargeable if the debtor obtains a bankruptcy under chapter 7.

Property-division obligations (which are not domestic support debts) are dischargeable if the debtor obtains a bankruptcy under chapter 13 of the bankruptcy code and certifies that he or she does not have any outstanding support obligations.

If a debtor ex-spouse seeks to discharge a property-division debt by filing for bankruptcy under chapter 13, the other ex-spouse can seek to challenge the discharge by arguing that the property division was in fact intended as support rather than as a division of marital assets and therefore is nondischargeable. (See the discussion above on the sometimes blurred distinction between alimony and property division.)

Although payors who have been granted bankruptcy may not be able to have their alimony debts discharged, they may be able to use the fact of bankruptcy as the basis of a request to the court to modify the original alimony by reducing it because of a genuine inability to pay the original amount.

NECESSARIES AND SPOUSAL REFUSAL

Before leaving the topic of alimony, we need to cover two related topics that pertain to spousal support within an ongoing marriage: necessaries and spousal refusal.

NECESSARIES

The rule on **necessaries** provides a seldom-used method for a wife (and child) to obtain support by going to merchants, making purchases of necessaries, and charging them to the credit of the nonsupporting husband/father. The latter must pay the bills, whether or not he knows about them or authorizes them so long as:

- They are in fact for necessaries, and
- The husband/father has not already provided them for the family

Here is how one court described the action for necessaries:

> The principle behind the suit for necessaries is that until the marriage relationship is severed, the husband is liable to his wife or his wife's creditors for her support and the support of his children. Although he cannot be charged with every expenditure that she may choose to make, the husband will be held responsible to the wife's creditors for all services and purchases found to have been necessary to support her in a style consistent with her habits and his means. The wife can maintain her action for necessaries even after the couple separates, as long as she did not cause the separation by her misconduct. Only termination of the marriage or a judicial or private financial settlement will relieve the husband of his liability for necessaries under most circumstances. Traditionally, the action for necessaries has included food, clothing, shelter, medical bills, and incidental living costs of various sorts. However, it has also been held to include necessary counsel fees that the wife may incur. Such fees have been allowed as 'necessaries' for purposes ranging from the wife's defense against criminal charges to costs incurred in connection with the marital dispute itself.[17]

Some hospitals have used the rule on necessaries to provide expensive medical care for a wife or child and then sued the husband/father for the cost of the care.

necessaries
The basic items needed by family members to maintain a standard of living, particularly food, shelter, and clothing. These items can be purchased and charged to the spouse who has failed to provide them.

The hospital may be required to sue the patient first for the cost of the care and then, if still unpaid, sue the other spouse on a necessaries theory.

Because merchants would have difficulty knowing whether a husband/father has already made provision for the necessaries of his family, few merchants are willing to extend credit without express authorization from the husband/father. Some states, however, have eliminated the requirement that there be evidence of a failure of the husband/father to provide necessaries before his credit can be charged.

Originally, the doctrine of necessaries applied against the husband only. At common law, a wife was not responsible for necessaries furnished to her child or husband. Today states have either extended the doctrine so that it now applies equally to both spouses, or they have abolished the doctrine altogether.

SPOUSAL REFUSAL

As senior citizens grow older, the need for long-term care increases, particularly after strokes and debilitating ailments such as Alzheimer's disease. The cost of such care is staggering. The poor can turn to Medicaid to pay most or all of this cost. To a large extent, others are on their own. Medicare covers hospitalization, doctor fees, and drug costs, but not the cost of nursing homes and similar long-term facilities. Private insurance can help, but its coverage is limited and few purchase it.

One desperate strategy of some spouses is to declare that they will no longer support their spouses so that the ailing spouse can become poor and thereby qualify for Medicaid. The practice is called **spousal refusal**. Without the option of spousal refusal, say attorneys for the elderly, "American health care is like a ghoulish lottery. Those who need doctors' care for illnesses like cancer or heart disease are covered by Medicare, the insurance program for the elderly, while those who need more custodial care for Alzheimer's or stroke must pay for it themselves or dispose of their assets to qualify for Medicaid."[18]

The strategy is not entirely successful. Eventually, the government can sue the healthy spouse for the Medicaid costs it covered. Yet some spouses still pursue the strategy: "Lawyers generally advise that even with the potential of being sued, spousal refusal makes sense because Medicaid pays less for nursing home care than private clients do."[19] Furthermore, the government is usually more amenable to lower negotiated settlements for the total amount owed than are nursing home providers.

Another desperate strategy is the so-called "Medicaid divorce." The parties end the marriage by divorce in the "hope" of sufficiently impoverishing the sick spouse so that the latter will qualify for Medicaid. The strategy assumes that the sick spouse will receive no alimony or assets in a property division. It is highly unlikely that a court would permit a divorce on such terms if the other spouse has the means to pay for the sick spouse's health care via alimony and property division.

PROPERTY DIVISION

Next we begin a more detailed look at property division, the allocation and distribution of property between spouses (or ex-spouses) after a legal separation or divorce. The five steps of property division are location, classification, valuation, tax-effecting, and distribution:

(1) locating all of the property of the spouses,

(2) classifying the property into what can and cannot be divided,

(3) determining the worth (valuation) of the property,

(4) tax-effecting each clause involving finances to determine the tax implications of the clause, and

(5) dividing the property according to the standard of division used in the state. In most states, the standard of division is equitable distribution.

See Exhibit 8-5

---

spousal refusal

A person's formal declaration that he or she will no longer support his or her ailing spouse so that the latter will qualify for Medicaid or other public benefits.

EXHIBIT 8-5 The Process of Property Division

Locating all the property	▶ Classifying what property is subject to division	▶ Determining the value of property	▶ Tax-effecting each clause to determine its tax implications	▶ Applying the governing principle in the state (usually equitable distribution) to divide the property

© Cengage Learning 2013

LOCATING PROPERTY TO DIVIDE AND FINANCIAL INFIDELITY

Before spouses can divide their property, they must know that the property exists. An early task of a family-law firm is to help a client locate this property, sometimes a difficult task. Studies have found that a large number of spouses are not truthful to each other about their finances—something that the media has called "financial infidelity." "In a recent survey, one in three Americans (31%) who have combined their finances admitted lying to their spouses about money, and another one-third of these adults said they'd been deceived." Although some of the deception involves minor purchases and petty cash, a significant number of spouses keep secret bank accounts and lie about their debt and earnings. According to the survey, "Financial infidelity may be the new normal."[20]

Elsewhere in the book, we discuss efforts to uncover assets that may have to be divided in a divorce and that may also be relevant to issues of alimony and child support. See, for example, the extensive checklists in Chapter 3 and the interrogatories in Appendix C. Here we cover the division of property that the parties have disclosed or uncovered.

SEPARATION AGREEMENT

In their separation agreement, spouses are generally free to divide property as they wish. For example,

- A wife can give some or all of her separate property (defined below) to her husband.
- A husband can give some or all of his separate property to his wife.
- A wife can give some or all of her share of the marital property (defined below) to her husband.
- A husband can give some or all of his share of the marital property to his wife.
- Husband and wife can split all categories of property in any percentages they want.

A court must approve the division negotiated by the parties, and often it does so, subject to the guideline on unconscionability discussed earlier. If the parties entered a valid premarital agreement, its terms may specify what property was brought into the marriage as separate property and how property acquired during the marriage should be divided in the event of a divorce (see Chapter 4).

When parties cannot agree on how to divide their property, the court will impose a division on them. Before we examine how a court will do so, we need to review some basic definitions and characteristics of different kinds of property. Paralegals are often asked to list and catalogue the property of spouses going through a divorce. The task requires a broad understanding of property.

REAL AND PERSONAL PROPERTY; TANGIBLE AND INTANGIBLE PROPERTY

There are many ways to categorize property. We begin with the two broadest categories: real property and personal property:

- **Real property.** Land and anything attached or affixed to the land. Also called real estate. Examples: residence, vacation home, fences, trees, building used in a business, etc.
- **Personal property.** Property other than land or other than things attached to the land. Also called *chattels*. Examples: cash, car, boat, stocks, bonds, furniture, jewelry, art objects, books, records, clothes, sports equipment, pets, business supplies (inventory), credits, **accounts receivable**, exclusive options to buy, insurance policies, etc.

Personal property can be further broken down into two subcategories:

- **Tangible.** Having a physical form; you can make contact with it by touch or by the other senses. Examples: cash, car. Also called corporeal personal property.
- **Intangible.** Not having a physical form even though evidence of intangible property may consist of something physical such as a written contract. Examples: copyright, goodwill of a business, share of stock. Intangible property consists primarily of a right to something. The right itself does not have a physical form. Also called incorporeal personal property.

Of course, all real property is tangible property.

GIFTS, BEQUESTS, DEVISES, AND INTESTATE SUCCESSION

Real and personal property can be acquired in a variety of ways:

- Property that was a **gift** to one spouse.
- Property that was a gift to both spouses.
- Property that was a **bequest** to one spouse.
- Property that was a bequest to both spouses.
- Property that was a **devise** to one spouse.
- Property that was a devise to both spouses.
- Property that one of the spouses receives by **intestate succession** (the acquisition of property by intestate succession is called **descent** and **inheritance**).
- Property that both spouses receive by intestate succession.
- Property purchased with funds from the salary or investments of one spouse.
- Property purchased with funds from the salaries or investments of both spouses.

TIME OF ACQUISITION

There are three major time periods in which property could be acquired: before the marriage, during the marriage, or after the separation:

- Before the marriage (either party brought the property into the marriage).
- During the marriage (either or both parties acquired it while married and still living together).

---

account receivable
A business debt that has not yet been collected.

gift
The voluntary delivery of something with the present intent to transfer title and control, for which no payment or consideration is made. The person making the gift is the *donor*. The person receiving it is the *donee*.

bequest
A gift of personal property in a will. (In some states, a bequest can be a gift of personal property or real property in a will.)

devise
A gift of real property in a will. (In some states, a devise can be a gift of real property or personal property in a will.) The person making the gift of property is the *devisor*. The person receiving it is the *devisee*.

intestate succession
The transfer of a decedent's property to state-designated relatives of the decedent who dies without leaving a valid will. Also called descent and distribution, hereditary succession.

descent
Acquiring property by inheritance rather than by will; acquiring property from a decedent who died intestate.

inheritance
Property received from someone who dies without leaving a valid will—by intestate succession. The state determines which relatives receive such property.

- After the DOS (date of separation) when the parties separated, before the DOF (date of filing) when the divorce petition was filed in court, or before the DOJ (date of judgment) when the divorce judgment became final.

When interviewing a client or conducting an investigation about assets, it can be important to place each acquisition within these different time periods.

SOLE OWNERSHIP AND CONCURRENT OWNERSHIP

There are different ways in which parties can hold title to property. Title-holders should be identified (as well as the reason why title is held in a certain way) even though title is rarely controlling on the question of who receives property upon divorce. Here are the major title options:

1. *Sole ownership: title in name of one spouse only.* The title to the property can be in the name of only one of the parties. There could be a number of reasons why this is so:
   - The sole owner may be the person who brought the property into the marriage.
   - The sole owner may have received the property during the marriage as a gift or as an inheritance (by intestate succession).
   - The sole owner may have purchased the property during the marriage with his or her separate funds (see discussion of separate property on the following page).
   - One spouse may have purchased the property with his or her own separate funds but placed the title to the property in the sole name of the other spouse (perhaps in an attempt to insulate the property from the claims of the creditors of the spouse who purchased the property).
   - The property may have been purchased with the funds of both spouses but they decided to place title in the name of only one of them.

2. *Concurrent ownership: title in the names of more than one person.* A **concurrent estate** is an estate that is owned by two or more persons at the same time. There are three kinds of concurrent estates: joint tenancy, tenancy by the entirety, and tenancy in common.
   - *Joint tenancy.* In a **joint tenancy**, each joint tenant (there can be more than two) owns an equal share and has an equal right to possess the entire property. They do not each own a piece of the property; each joint tenant owns it all. When one joint tenant dies, his or her interest passes to the surviving joint tenants by **right of survivorship**. The property automatically (i.e., by **operation of law**) goes to the surviving joint tenants. A joint tenancy is sometimes referred to as a joint tenancy with a right of survivorship—JTWROS.
     - If a joint tenant dies with a valid will, can the will give the deceased's interest to someone other than a surviving joint tenant? No.
     - If a joint tenant dies without a valid will, can someone other than a surviving joint tenant receive the deceased's interest by intestate succession? No.

     Only surviving joint tenants can receive the interest of a deceased joint tenant.
   - *Tenancy by the entirety.* A **tenancy by the entirety** is a joint tenancy held by a married couple and, in some states, by parties in a civil union or domestic partnership. The characteristics described above for a joint tenancy apply to a tenancy by the entirety (e.g., both

concurrent estate
An estate that is owned by two or more persons at the same time.

joint tenancy
Ownership of property by two or more persons (called joint tenants) in equal shares, equal rights to possess the whole property, and a right of survivorship. A joint tenancy is sometimes referred to as a joint tenancy with right of survivorship—JTWROS.

right of survivorship
When one owner dies, his or her share automatically goes to the other owners; it does not go through the estate of the deceased owner.

operation of law
The means by which legal consequences are imposed by law, regardless of (or even despite) the intent of the parties involved.

tenancy by the entirety
A joint tenancy held by a married couple and, in some states, by parties in a civil union or domestic partnership.

spouses own all of the property and upon the death of one spouse, the property goes to the other spouse by operation of law). In general, if the parties divorce, the tenancy by the entirety ends and, unless the separation agreement or the divorce judgment provides otherwise, the property becomes a tenancy in common (see below) with each spouse receiving an equal share of the property.

- *Tenancy in common.* A **tenancy in common (TIC)** is ownership of property by two or more persons in shares that may or may not be equal, each person having an equal right to possess the whole property but without the right of survivorship. When one tenant in common dies, the property goes to whomever the deceased designated by will or goes by intestate succession if the deceased tenant in common dies without a will. Hence, a major distinction between (1) a joint tenancy and a tenancy by the entirety and (2) a tenancy in common is that the property of a deceased tenant passes through the estate of that tenant (via will or intestacy) only in the case of a tenancy in common. In the other tenancies, the property passes immediately to the surviving tenant(s) by operation of law.

SEPARATE PROPERTY

Separate property is property acquired by one spouse before marriage and brought into the marriage or any property acquired during the marriage that is not marital or community property. States differ on whether separate property is divided upon divorce. Many states do not divide separate property between the ex-spouses, as we will see. Whether or not your state divides separate property, you need to know how to recognize it. There are at least 10 kinds of separate property:

Categories of Separate Property

- *Property that one spouse acquired before the marriage.* This is property that one spouse brought into the marriage. Example: Ted had a bank account containing $5,000 when he married Fran. The $5,000 (still in the same bank account of Ted) is the separate property of Ted.

- *Property one spouse acquired during the marriage by gift.* Example: A year after Sam married Mary, Sam's dad gave Sam a birthday gift of a gold watch. The watch is the separate property of Sam.

- *Property one spouse acquired during the marriage by will.* Example: A year after Rachel married Bill, Rachel's mother died; her will left a vacation home to Rachel. The vacation home is the separate property of Rachel.

- *Property one spouse acquired during the marriage by intestate succession.* Example: A year after Paul married George, Paul's aunt died. Paul is the only surviving relative of his aunt, who did not leave a will. When she died, her only asset was 1,000 shares of IBM stock. Under the intestate law of the state, the IBM shares go to Paul. They are his separate property.

- *Property that one spouse acquired during the marriage in exchange for separate property.* Example: Before Myles married Alice, he had a diamond watch. A week after the marriage, he sold the watch and used the money to buy a boat. The watch was the separate property of Myles. Because he used money from the sale of the watch to buy a boat, the boat is also his separate property.

- *Passive income earned from separate property during the marriage.* **Passive income** is income that is earned from money or other property without

tenancy in common (TIC)
Ownership of property by two or more persons (called tenants in common) in shares that may or may not be equal, each person having an equal right to possess the whole property but without a right of survivorship. Also called estate in common.

separate property
Property acquired by one spouse before marriage and brought into the marriage or any property acquired during the marriage that is not marital or community property.

passive income
Income that is earned from money or other property without direct involvement or active participation by the earner.

direct involvement or active participation by the earner. Example: John has a bank account that contains $12,000 that he brought into his marriage with Diane. During the marriage, the account has earned $500 in interest. The original bank account is John's separate property. The $500 interest is also separate property because it is passive income earned from separate property.

- *Passive appreciation of separate property during the marriage.* **Appreciation** is an increase in the value of property after it is acquired. **Passive appreciation** is an increase in the value of property that is due to inflation or market forces rather than to the active efforts of the owner. Example: Georgia inherits a vacation home from her father during her marriage to Todd. The property is located in another county. Because Georgia and Todd never intend to use the home, she sells it five months after receiving it. When her father died, the value of the house was $100,000. She sold it for $110,000. The vacation home is Georgia's separate property. Its appreciation of $10,000 is also her separate property if the appreciation was due solely to the state of the real estate market rather than to anyone's active efforts such as making repairs or remodeling.

- *Property that both spouses have agreed to designate as the separate property of one of the spouses.* Example: After Pat and Fran married, they bought a house together. The house is **marital property**, which is any property acquired by either or both spouses during the marriage that is not separate property. They enter a valid postnuptial agreement (see Exhibit 4-1 in Chapter 4) that the house will be the separate property of Fran. By mutual agreement, marital property has been transformed—transmuted—into separate property. (See *transmutation* below.)

- *The portion of an asset purchased with separate property if the asset was purchased with both separate property and marital property.* Example: During the marriage of Karen and Zeno they decide to buy a vacation condo for $50,000. To raise the money for the purchase, Karen uses $10,000 from an inheritance she received from her mother. They also use $40,000 in a joint account containing their salary deposits during the marriage. One-fifth of the vacation home ($10,000) is Karen's separate property. Four-fifths ($40,000) is marital property.

- *Property acquired by either spouse after the date of separation (DOS).* Example: Ursula and Alice separate on April 1, 2015. The final divorce judgment is December 1, 2015. The salary that each spouse earned after April 1, 2015, is his or her separate property. (Note, however, that some states disagree and say that the cutoff date is the date of filing for divorce or the date of the final judgment. Anything acquired before these dates is still marital property.)

appreciation
An increase in the value of property after it is acquired.

passive appreciation
An increase in the value of property that is due to inflation or market forces rather than to the active efforts of the owner.

marital property
Any property acquired by either spouse during the marriage that is not separate property.

ASSIGNMENT 8.6

Before Mary married Charles, she owned 100 shares of stock valued at $20 a share. During the marriage, the company in which the shares were owned executed a stock split. (In a stock split, each individual share is split into a larger number of shares without changing the total number of shareholders.) Her 100 shares turned into 200 shares valued at $30 a share. Was the 100 shares @ $20 a share separate or marital property? What about the 200 shares @ $30 a share? (See the General Instructions for the Legal-Analysis Assignment in Appendix A.)

INTRODUCTION TO COMMON LAW PROPERTY AND COMMUNITY PROPERTY

States fall into two categories: either common-law property states or community-property states. The community-property states are Arizona, California, Idaho, Louisiana, Nevada, New Mexico, Texas, Washington (and Wisconsin, whose law is similar to these eight states). Every other state is a common-law property state.

- **Community property:** Property in which each spouse has a 50 percent interest because it was acquired during the marriage other than by gift, will, or intestate succession (inheritance) to only one of the spouses.

- **Common law property:** Property acquired during the marriage in a state other than a community-property state. (Older definition: Property acquired during the marriage that is owned by the spouse who earned it or who has title to it.)

The law of community property is based on Spanish legal principles. Each spouse has a one-half interest in property acquired during the marriage. This half interest did not depend on who had title to the property or on whose income was used to purchase it. So long as the property was acquired during the marriage, it was community property and therefore subject to a one-half interest in each spouse. The exception was property that one spouse alone acquired by gift, will, or intestate succession (inheritance) during the marriage; such property was solely owned by the spouse receiving it.

The underlying principle of community property is that the efforts of both spouses contribute to the acquisition of property during the marriage. One spouse, for example, could not have gone to the office each day to work if the other spouse had not stayed home to take care of the household, which could include child rearing, home economics, and social outreach.

When property is acquired during the marriage in a community-property state, there is a presumption that it is community property. This presumption can be rebutted by showing that it was acquired by one spouse alone through gift, will, or intestate succession (inheritance), or that the parties had agreed to treat community property as separate property (see transmutation below).

quasi-community property
Personal property acquired during the marriage by the spouses when they lived in a non–community-property state before moving to a community-property state. If they had acquired it in a community-property state, it would have been community property.

If the spouses acquire personal property in a common-law property state and then move to a community-property state, the property would be classified as **quasi-community property** and treated as community property if that property would have been community property if it had been acquired in a community-property state. Quasi-community property is personal property acquired during marriage by the spouses when they lived in a non–community-property state before moving to a community-property state and which would have been community property if they had acquired it in a community-property state.

At one time, there were substantial differences between community property and common law property in three areas: the management of the property during the marriage, the disposition of the property upon death while the parties were still married, and the disposition of the property upon divorce. Many of these differences still exist in the first two areas (management and death). Our main concern in this chapter is the third area (divorce), where the differences have all but disappeared in most states, as we will see shortly.

Terminology

Terminology in this area of the law can sometimes be confusing when comparing common-law states and community-property states. The meaning of *separate property* is clear in both states. It is (a) property acquired by one spouse before marriage and brought into the marriage or (b) any property acquired during the marriage that is not marital or community property. What terminology should we use when referring to nonseparate property in both states?

The phrase *marital property* can refer to nonseparate property in both states. For purposes of discussion, however:

- we will use the phrase *marital property* to refer to nonseparate property in common-law property states
- we will use the phrase *community property* to refer to nonseparate property in community-property states, and
- we will use the phrase *marital/community property* to refer to nonseparate property in both states.

CUTOFF DATE

If a party acquires property after divorce, the property, of course, is not divided with the party's ex-spouse. Consider the following pre-divorce dates involving Irene and Jack:

- January 1, 2015: date of separation (DOS): Irene and Jack separate.
- February 20, 2015: date of filing (DOF): Irene files her divorce (dissolution) petition against Jack.
- March 20, 2015: date of judgment (DOJ). The divorce judgment of Irene and Jack becomes final.

Assume that Irene wins $25,000 in the instant lottery game on February 21, 2015, using her current salary to buy the ticket. Is the $25,000 the separate property of Irene or is it marital/community property that she must divide with Jack?

States answer the question in different ways. In some states, the cutoff date for determining separate property is the date of the final divorce judgment (DOJ). Salary and property acquired with one's salary prior to the DOJ is marital/community property. In other states, the cutoff date is the date of filing (DOF):

- Salary and property acquired with one's salary prior to the DOF is marital/community property.
- Salary and property acquired with one's salary after the DOF is separate property.

In still others, the cutoff date is the date of separation (DOS).

- Salary and property acquired with one's salary prior to the DOS is marital/community property.
- Salary and property acquired with one's salary after the DOS is separate property.

The answer to the $25,000 question, therefore, depends on which cutoff date is used in Irene and Jack's state. If they live in a DOS or a DOF state, the $25,000 is Irene's separate property. If they live in a DOJ state, it is marital/community property.

TRANSMUTATION

The categorizations of property within common-law states and within community-property states are not static. The parties can voluntarily agree to reclassify their property. The change is called **transmutation**:

- In a common-law property state, the parties can agree that specific separate property of one spouse will become marital property.
- In a community-property state, the parties can agree that specific separate property of one spouse will become community property.
- In a common-law property state, the parties can agree that specific marital property will become the separate property of one of the spouses.

transmutation

The voluntary change of separate property into marital property or vice versa (in a common-law state); the voluntary change of separate property into community property or vice versa (in a community-property state).

- In a community-law property state, the parties can agree that specific community property will become the separate property of one of the spouses.

The agreement is called a transmutation agreement. In some states, transmutation agreements must be in writing. The party seeking to establish that certain property is separate rather than marital/community property is called a **separatizer**.

It is not always easy to determine whether transmutation has occurred.

> *Jim and Diane own a vacation home as marital/community property. Both of their names are on the deed. They decide to change the deed so that only Diane has title. To accomplish this, Jim (the transferor)* **quitclaims** *the deed to Diane (the transferee) for $1. When the parties divorce five years later, the parties dispute whether the vacation home is marital/community property or is separate property.*

States disagree on how they handle title-transfer cases such as this when the parties do not specifically indicate whether they intend a transmutation. In some states, transferring the title of marital/community property automatically transmutes it into the separate property of the spouse receiving title. In other states, the transfer of title is merely a rebuttable presumption that the parties intended transmutation. The party who transferred title (the transferor) can try to prove that the transfer was for reasons other than transmutation. For example, the spouses may have been trying to insulate the property from the transferor's creditors. This evidence may convince a court that the mere change in title did not create separate property out of marital/community property.

Some transmutation disputes can be bitter. For example, when Frank and Jamie McCourt bought the Los Angeles Dodgers, they were living in Massachusetts, a common-law property state. California is a community-property state. Would the Dodgers become community property when they moved there? The parties signed six copies of a postnuptial agreement that attempted to clarify the transmutation intentions of the parties. The agreement declared the Dodgers to be the separate property of Frank and several homes around the world to be the separate property of Jamie. Unfortunately, several of the copies they signed contained a list stating that Frank's separate property did *not* include the Dodgers. Frank claimed that the list was an error that was later corrected on some of the copies. Jamie claimed that the corrections were made after the agreement was signed and notarized. She further asserted that she did not fully understand the agreement. Expensive litigation ensued on whether the Dodgers were community property. Ultimately, the parties sold the Dodgers and Frank agreed to give Jamie $135 million to settle the transmutation issue.

PROPERTY DIVISION IN COMMON-LAW STATES AND COMMUNITY-PROPERTY LAW STATES

We turn now to the question of how property is divided upon divorce in common-law states and in community-property states. Not all common-law property states have the same law of property division. The same is true of community-property states. Yet several major characteristics apply to both groupings of states. To understand the current law, we need to place it in the context of the prior law.

Common-Law Property States and Community-Property States: Prior Law

At one time, the predominant definition of common law property was property acquired during the marriage that is owned by the spouse who earned it or who has title to it. Under this definition, the spouse who owned particular property received it upon divorce. Ownership was determined by the name of the person on the title of the property or by the spouse who earned the money that was used to purchase it. Salaries, therefore, belonged to the spouse who

separatizer
The party seeking to prove that designated property (in whole or in part) is separate property rather than marital or community property.

quitclaim
A release or giving up of whatever claim or title you have in property. The party who quitclaims the property, turns over whatever he or she has, without guaranteeing anything.

earned it. These rules placed many stay-at-home spouses, usually the wife, at a disadvantage when it came time to divide property at divorce because the husband often controlled much of the family and business finances in his name alone. This inequity did not exist in community-property states where, in general, community property was divided equally upon divorce.

Common-Law Property States and Community-Property States: Current Law

As pointed out by the American Law Institute, the law has substantially changed in both common-law and community-property states:

> [The] sharp dichotomy between common law and community property traditions no longer prevails in the United States. All the common-law states now allow the divorce court to distribute the spouse's property between them on a basis other than common-law principles of ownership, under a doctrine known generally as "equitable distribution." Five of the eight community property states also instruct their divorce courts to divide the community property between the spouses "equitably" (rather than "equally"). Equitable distribution is therefore the dominant rule today, followed everywhere but in the three "equal division" community property states [of California, Louisiana, and New Mexico].[21]

Hence, in the vast majority of both common-law and community-property states, property division upon divorce is determined by **equitable distribution**, which is the just and fair, but not necessarily equal, division of property between spouses upon divorce. Although this is the general principle, not all equitable-distribution states define or apply equitable distribution in the same way.

Most states divide only marital/community property; the separate property of one spouse is not divided with the other spouse in these states. Phrased another way, most states divide only nonseparate property. In a few states, however, a court has discretion to reach a party's separate property where it determines that the division of the marital/community property alone would not be equitable or fair. States that allow a court to divide all property are sometimes called "all property" or "kitchen sink" states.

equitable distribution
The just and fair, but not necessarily equal, division of property between spouses upon divorce.

EQUITABLE DISTRIBUTION FACTORS

When applying equitable distribution, how does a court determine what is a "just and fair" division? Many factors are considered. Before examining these factors, it should be pointed out that many courts take the position that the division should be roughly proportionate to the contribution that each spouse made to the acquisition of the property. In some courts, however, there is a presumption that their contribution was equal and that therefore the division should be equal or approximately so.

Factors Considered in Equitable Distribution

- The length of the marriage.
- The contribution of each party in the acquisition, preservation, depreciation or appreciation of all assets, including the contribution of a party as homemaker.
- The contribution by one party to the education, training, or increased earning power of the other party.
- Any interruption in the educational opportunities or personal career of either party, particularly the one who stayed home to take care of the children.
- The income and property of both at the time the marriage was entered.
- The sources of income of both parties, including, but not limited to, retirement, insurance, or other benefits.
- Whether either party has been granted alimony or maintenance.

- The opportunity of each party for future acquisitions of capital assets and income, including the vocational skills and employability of each party.
- Whether either party will be serving as the custodian of dependent minor children.
- The need of the party with physical custody of the children to use the marital home.
- The desirability of keeping any asset (e.g., a business) intact.
- The expense of sale, transfer, or liquidation associated with a particular asset.
- Intentional dissipation of marital assets (see the discussion of dissipation below).
- The federal, state, and local tax ramifications associated with each asset to be divided regardless of whether the ramifications are immediate or certain (see the discussion of *tax-effecting* under the section headed "Taxes" below).
- The standard of living of the parties established during the marriage.
- The age and health of both parties.
- Any other factor that should be considered in order to achieve justice and fairness in the division.

Not all states use all of these factors. The divorce judge has considerable discretion because most states do not specify the weight or priority to give the factors to be considered.

As indicated in the factors, contribution does not simply mean who earned the money to purchase an asset; it encompasses the full range of homemaking services that made the earnings possible and the financial opportunities that the stay-at-home spouse gave up so that the other spouse could devote greater attention to training, investment, and earning. Furthermore, at a time when the law disfavors long-term alimony, many courts are inclined to use property division as the main vehicle for achieving economic justice for a spouse who is about to leave a long-term marriage with no (or minimal) independent resources or marketable skills.

MODIFICATION OF PROPERTY DIVISION

Earlier we saw that alimony awards can be modified under certain circumstances. The situation is different with property division. Courts will rarely, if ever, modify the property-division clause of a separation agreement that a divorce court has approved. See, however, the discussion below on the effect of mutual mistake.

Death or remarriage of either ex-spouse does not affect property-division obligations. They continue no matter who dies or remarries. For example, as part of a property division (having nothing to do with support), John agrees to pay Mary $50,000. After John has paid Mary $1,000 of this amount, he dies. Mary can make a claim against John's estate for $49,000. If Mary dies after John has paid the $1,000, her estate can require John to pay the remaining $49,000 to it for distribution according to Mary's will or according to the laws of intestate succession if she died without leaving a valid will. The same is true if either party remarries. Whatever is still owed under the property-division clauses of a separation agreement remain due and owing no matter who remarries.

MARITAL FAULT AND ECONOMIC FAULT

Marital Fault

In most states, marital fault—who caused the marriage to break up—is not a factor in the property division. Under the Uniform Marriage and Divorce Act, property is to be divided "without regard to marital misconduct" in causing the breakup of the marriage. (The same is true in the award of alimony or maintenance as we saw earlier.) There are a few states, however, that take a different view. These states are inclined to increase the share of the marital property given to the "innocent" spouse.

Economic Fault: Dissipation

Marital fault is different from economic fault. Marital fault is the blameworthiness of a party in causing the breakup of the marriage. Although most states do not consider marital fault in decisions on property division, they do consider economic fault as a factor. Economic fault is **dissipation**, the improper reduction or waste of marital assets that should have been available for property division upon divorce. For dissipation to exist, the marriage must be on the verge of a breakup or in serious relationship trouble at the time when a spouse improperly reduces or wastes a marital asset. To punish a spouse who has committed dissipation, a court might treat the dissipated funds as if they still existed when ordering the property division. This was the approach of the court in the *Gastineau* decision, which we will be reading.

The most extreme example of dissipation is property destruction. In a highly contentious New York divorce, a spouse blew up a multimillion dollar building to prevent his ex-wife from recovering her full share of its value in the property division. Reflecting on years of contentious cases, a veteran family-law attorney recently commented, "I've seen hundreds of thousands of dollars in property destroyed. People would rather break something than let the other party have it." In one of his cases, a spouse smashed an expensive collection of Dresden pottery. "It's soap-opera law."[22] Another attorney commented that "he has seen works of art and record collections slashed by angry spouses, a puppy put in the microwave and a cat in a washing machine. (The puppy died, the cat lived.)"[23]

Excessive spending can also constitute dissipation. In a recent case the wife "spent a fortune on jewelry and clothes before filing for divorce—only to have the judge notice the timing of her spree and dock her property settlement."[24]

Finally, spouses cannot avoid support or property-division obligations by voluntarily becoming poor. This was the major concern before the court in the *Gastineau* decision, to which we now turn.

dissipation
The improper reduction or waste of marital assets that should have been available for property division upon divorce.

CASE

Gastineau v. Gastineau
151 Misc. 2d 813, 573 N.Y.S.2d 819 (1991)
New York Supreme Court, Suffolk County

Background: *Marcus Gastineau was a professional football player for the New York Jets. His wife, Lisa, sued him for divorce and charged that he dissipated some of the marital assets. While the trial was in progress (i.e., pendente lite), the court ordered Marcus to make payments to Lisa to cover expenses. He fell $71,707 behind in these payments. The court then ordered the sequestration of his net severance pay of $83,000. (Sequestration is the removal or holding of assets until legal proceedings or legal claims are resolved.)*

Decision: *Marcus dissipated marital assets. In the equitable distribution of the marital assets, a court can treat dissipated assets as if they still exist. Marcus dissipated $484,437 in salary when he stopped playing football before his contract ended. When tax effected (i.e., when factoring in tax consequences of what he would have paid in taxes on this salary), the dissipated amount was $324,573.*

OPINION OF THE COURT:

Justice LEIS delivered the opinion of the court.

This action for divorce, equitable distribution and other ancillary relief was tried on February 25, 28, March 5, and

6, 1991. The Plaintiff, Lisa Gastineau, is represented by counsel. The Defendant, Marcus Gastineau appeared pro se. . . . The parties were married in December of 1979. This action was commenced in September 1986. Consequently, this is a marriage of short duration. The Plaintiff is thirty-one years old and the Defendant is thirty-four. The parties have one child, Brittany, born on 11/6/82.

Facts

The parties married just after Marc Gastineau had been drafted by the New York Jets to play professional football. The Plaintiff, at that time, was a sophomore at the University of Alabama. The Plaintiff never completed her college education, nor did she work during the course of the marriage.

In 1982, when Brittany was born, the parties purchased a house in Huntington, New York for $99,000. In addition to the purchase price, the Plaintiff and Defendant spent another $250,000 for landscaping and other renovations. This money came from the Defendant's earnings as a professional football player.

According to the uncontroverted testimony of the Plaintiff, in 1979 (the Defendant's first year in professional football) the

(continued)

CASE • **Gastineau v. Gastineau** (continued)

Defendant earned a salary of $55,000. In his second year, 1980, the Defendant's salary was approximately $75,000. In 1981 it was approximately $95,000 and in 1982 he earned approximately $250,000. The Defendant's tax returns (which were not available for the years 1979 through 1982) indicate that the Defendant earned $423,291 in 1983, $488,994 in 1984, $858,035 in 1985, $595,127 in 1986, $953,531 in 1987 and in 1988, his last year with the New York Jets, his contract salary was $775,000 plus $50,000 in bonuses. It must be noted that in most years the Defendant earned monies in excess of his contract salary as a result of promotions, advertisements and bonuses.

In 1985 the parties purchased a home in Scottsdale, Arizona, for $550,000. During the course of the parties' marriage Plaintiff and Defendant acquired many luxury items including a power boat, a BMW, a Corvette, a Rolls Royce, a Porsche, a Mercedes and two motorcycles. They continually had a housekeeper who not only cleaned the house but prepared the parties' meals. In addition, the parties frequently dined out at expensive restaurants. The Plaintiff testified that as a result of this lifestyle she has become accustomed to buying only the most expensive clothes and going to the best of restaurants.

In 1988 the Defendant began an illicit relationship with Brigitte Nielsen. When Ms. Nielsen was diagnosed as having cancer the Defendant testified that he could no longer concentrate on playing football. At that time the Defendant was under contract with the New York Jets at a salary of $775,000. He left professional football in October 1988 (breaking his contract) after the sixth game of the 1988 season. The Defendant went to Arizona and remained with Ms. Nielsen while she underwent treatment for cancer.

Regardless of whether the Defendant wanted to be with his girlfriend while she underwent treatment for cancer, he had a responsibility to support his wife and child. The Court cannot condone Mr. Gastineau's walking away from a lucrative football contract when the result is that his wife and child are deprived of adequate support.

According to the testimony adduced at trial, there are sixteen games per season in the NFL. Players are paid one-sixteenth of their contract salary at the end of each game. Based on the Defendant's salary for 1988 ($775,000), he received $48,437 per game. The Defendant played six games in the 1988 season and received approximately $290,622 plus $50,000 in bonuses. He was entitled to an additional $484,437 for the ten games remaining in the season. This Court finds that by walking away from his 1988–89 contract with the NFL the Defendant dissipated a marital asset in the amount of $484,437 (DRL § 236(B)(5)(d)(11)). [The Domestic Relations Law-DRL] provides as follows: "In determining an equitable disposition of property . . . , the court shall consider: . . . (11) the wasteful dissipation of assets by either spouse. . . ."]

Whether or not the Defendant would have been offered a contract by the New York Jets for the 1989/90 football season if he had not broken his 1988/89 contract is pure speculation. In professional football there are no guarantees. Variables such as age, how

an athlete plays, the ability of other players seeking to fill his position, as well as possible injuries sustained during the season, make it impossible to determine with certainty whether or not the Defendant would have been re-signed by the New York Jets had he finished the 1988/89 season. It must also be noted that there has been no testimony offered by the Plaintiff to establish that the Defendant would have been re-signed by the New York Jets for the 1989/90 season had he not broken his contract.

The speculative nature of the Defendant's future in professional football is highlighted by the fact that in 1989 he tried out for the San Diego Chargers, the LA Raiders and the Minnesota Vikings, without success. The New York Jets also refused to offer him a contract. In 1990 the Defendant did acquire a position with the British Colombia Lions in the Canadian Football League at a salary of $75,000. He was cut, however, less than half way through the season. The Defendant played five of the 18 scheduled games and was paid approximately $20,000. The Defendant's performance in the Canadian Football League lends credence to his claim that he no longer has the capacity to earn the monies that he once made as a professional football player. Under these circumstances the court is limited to considering the dissipation of a marital asset valued at $484,437, to wit: the remaining amount of money that the Defendant was eligible to collect pursuant to his 1988/89 contract.

While Defendant admits that he has name recognition, he claims that his name has a negative rather than a positive connotation. The Defendant testified that because of his antics on the field (such as his victory dance after sacking a quarterback), the fact that he crossed picket lines during the NFL player's strike and because he walked away from his professional football career, his name has no value for promotions or endorsements. There has been no evidence presented to the contrary by the Plaintiff.

The Defendant testified that his chances of obtaining employment with a professional football team are almost nil. Although he is presently attempting to obtain a position at a Jack LaLanne Health Spa he could not provide details as to the potential salary. The Defendant has also attempted to enter professional boxing. No testimony has been elicited by the Plaintiff, however, as to the Defendant's financial potential as a professional boxer. Since the Defendant left professional football he has not worked or earned any money (except for the $20,000 that he earned when he played football in Canada). According to the Defendant, Ms. Nielsen paid for all of the Defendant's expenses during the period of time that they lived together.

After the Defendant failed to appear for a number of court dates and also failed to comply with this Court's pendente lite order, the Court directed that the Defendant's NFL severance pay be sequestered pursuant to DRL § 243 and the Plaintiff be appointed receiver and sequestrator of said funds (which amounted to approximately $83,000 after deducting taxes).

According to Plaintiff the entire $83,000 (reflecting the Defendant's total net severance pay from the NFL) was spent by her as follows: Thirty-two thousand dollars ($32,000) was used to pay mortgage arrears on the Huntington house (which still has approximately $15,000 outstanding in arrears), $22,000 went to the Plaintiff's attorneys, $15,000 went to repay loans taken out by the Plaintiff to pay necessary expenses and the rest, approximately $14,000, went for landscaping, medical insurance, electricity, fuel oil, telephone bills, dental and doctor bills.

Primary Marital Assets

With all of the money that the Defendant earned throughout the course of his professional football career he has retained only three significant marital assets. (1) The Huntington house, which has been valued at approximately $429,000 and has an outstanding mortgage of $150,000. (2) A house located in the state of Arizona which was purchased for approximately $550,000 and has a $420,000 mortgage (which in all probability will be sold at foreclosure); (3) The Defendant's severance pay from the NFL of approximately $83,000.

It is clear that the Defendant has also dissipated a marital asset worth approximately $324,573 (to wit: $484,437 the Defendant was entitled to receive pursuant to his 1988/89 contract tax effected by 33%, reflecting approximate federal and state income tax). Although neither the Plaintiff nor the Defendant attempted to tax effect this dissipated marital asset, it is clear that the Defendant would not have actually received $484,437 had he finished the 1988/89 season. The Court therefore, on its own, has tax effected this amount by 33%, approximately what the defendant would have paid in federal and state taxes had he actually received the $484,437. . . .

Equitable Distribution

It is a guiding principle of equitable distribution that parties are entitled to receive equitable awards which are proportionate to their contributions, whether direct or indirect, to the marriage, *Ullah v. Ullah*, 555 N.Y.S.2d 834 (2nd Dep't 1990).

In this case, the Plaintiff testified that during the course of the marriage she supervised the renovations made on the Huntington house, traveled with the Defendant wherever he trained and, with the assistance of a full-time nanny, raised and cared for their child.

This is not a long-term marriage, and there has been minimal testimony elicited concerning the Plaintiff's direct or indirect contributions to the Defendant's acquisition of marital assets. Although it was the defendant's own athletic abilities and disciplined training which made it possible for him to obtain and retain his position as a professional football player, equity dictates, under the facts of this case, that the Plaintiff receive

one-third of the marital assets. The Defendant's decision to voluntarily terminate his contract with the New York Jets, depriving Plaintiff and the parties' child of the standard of living to which they had become accustomed, his failure to obtain meaningful employment thereafter and the indirect contributions made by the Plaintiff during the course of the marriage warrant an award to the Plaintiff of one third of the parties' marital assets. The Court is also mindful of the fact that during the years of the Defendant's greatest productivity, the Plaintiff enjoyed the fruits of Defendant's labors to the fullest (*Parlow v. Parlow*, 548 N.Y.S. 2d 373 (Sup. Ct. Westchester Co. 1989)), unlike the landmark *O'Brien* case (*O'Brien v. O'Brien*, 66 N.Y. 2d 576, 498 N.Y.S. 2d 743, 489 N.E. 2d 712 (1985)), where a newly licensed professional discarded his wife after she provided years of contributions to the attainment of his medical license.

There are only two marital assets to be considered in granting Plaintiff her one-third distributive award, (1) the Huntington house, and (2) the $324,573 dissipated marital asset. The Arizona house has no equity.

The Huntington house is valued at $429,000. It has a $150,000 mortgage with $15,000 owed in back mortgage payments. It thus has an equity of $264,000. One third of the equity would entitle the Plaintiff to $87,120. When one adds $107,109 (1/3 of the $324,573 tax effected marital asset which was dissipated), the Plaintiff would be entitled to $194,229. This would encompass Plaintiff's 1/3 distributive award of the parties' sole remaining marital asset (the Huntington house) and her 1/3 share of the marital asset dissipated by the Defendant. If one adds this $194,229 to the arrears owed by the Defendant on the pendente lite order ($71,707) Plaintiff could be awarded the total equity ($264,000) in the Huntington house in full satisfaction of her one-third distributive award of the parties' marital assets and still have approximately $1,936 remaining as a credit. The Court awards Plaintiff the Huntington house and grants her a Judgment for $1,936 for the remaining arrears owed to her.

Neither side has offered proof as to the present value of the Arizona house or the extent of arrears on mortgage payments (*Gluck v. Gluck*, 520 N.Y.S. 2d 581 (2nd Dep't 1987)). It would appear however, that there is no equity remaining in the Arizona house. The Court awards the Arizona house to the Defendant. The Court directs that each party take whatever steps are required to effect the transfer of the deed to the real property awarded to the other party so as to convey title to said property in said other's name alone.

ASSIGNMENT 8.7

Who was treated unfairly by the *Gastineau* case: Marcus? Lisa? Neither? Was her one-third share too high, too low, or just right? Have a debate in class on this question. (Note that this case did not cover child support. The court must make a separate decision on who pays child support and how much.)

APPRECIATION

Real or personal property can increase in value after it is acquired. It can be important to know if such appreciation has occurred, when it occurred, and why it occurred. Here are the main possibilities:

- The appreciation occurred before the marriage.
- The appreciation occurred during the marriage before the parties separated.
- The appreciation occurred after the parties separated; that is, after the DOS (date of separation).
- The appreciation was due to inflation or market forces rather than to the active efforts by the parties. Such appreciation, as we saw earlier, is called *passive appreciation.*
- The appreciation was due to the labor or investment activity (active efforts) of one or both spouses.

The appreciation of marital/community property is treated the same as the underlying property that appreciated regardless of why it appreciated. Suppose, for example, that a married couple used $100,000 of marital funds to buy stock during the marriage, which is worth $150,000 upon divorce. The stock has appreciated by $50,000. A court would decide how to divide the $50,000 the same way that it decides how to divide the $100,000. The entire value of the fund might be divided equally between the spouses or some other allocation to achieve an equitable distribution.

The appreciation of separate property is more complicated.

After six months of marriage, Alex and Greg decide to divorce. They do not have children. Before the marriage, Alex bought a painting for $2,000. Due to the fame of the artist, the painting is now worth $10,000. Before the marriage, Greg bought an antique car for $4,000. Due to the refinishing work that Greg did himself, the car is now worth $5,000.

The painting is Alex's separate property. The car is Greg's separate property. Upon divorce, most states would grant the painting to Alex and the car to Greg because each brought the asset into the marriage. But both assets appreciated during the marriage, the painting by $8,000 and the car by $1,000. Is the appreciation marital property that can be divided? Does Alex get to keep the entire $8,000 (in addition to the original value of $2,000) or should Greg be given a share of the $8,000 as marital property? Does Greg get to keep the entire $1,000 (in addition to the original value of $4,000) or should Alex be given a share of the $1,000 as marital property? States answer these questions in different ways.

- In some states, the owner of separate property keeps the appreciation. The appreciated value of the separate property does not have to be divided. In such states, neither Alex nor Greg would have to share the appreciation.
- In some states, the appreciation of separate property must be divided only if the appreciation was due to the active efforts of the owner of the separate property. *Passive appreciation* is not subject to property division. In the example, the appreciation of the painting was passive; it was due to market forces and inflation. Greg, therefore, does not have a claim for an equitable share of the $8,000 appreciation. The appreciation of the car, however, was due to the active labor of Greg. It, therefore, is subject to property division in these states.
- In some states, the appreciation of separate property must be divided regardless of whether the appreciation was active or passive.

COMMINGLING

Property division is further complicated when the parties mix or commingle assets in one account. For example:

Before Mary married Ted, she had her own $10,000 checking account. After the marriage, she and Ted opened a joint checking account into which Mary deposited the $10,000 she brought into the marriage. They both started depositing their paychecks into the joint account.

There has been a **commingling** (mixing together) of funds. The pre-marriage $10,000 (clearly separate property) has been deposited into the same account as the post-marriage paychecks of both spouses (clearly marital/community property). A court may treat all commingled property as marital/community property unless the party claiming part of the account as separate property can trace the existence of the separate property by producing adequate records or other evidence—an increasingly difficult task as time passes. If **tracing** does not establish what is separate property, the court will probably treat all the commingled property as marital/community property. The court will presume that the spouse who commingled his or her separate property intended a gift of the property to the marriage so that the property became marital/community property.

Earlier we discussed transmutation agreements in which spouses agree to convert separate property into marital/community property or vice versa. Commingling is some evidence of transmutation. In and of itself, however, commingling does not prove that the parties intended a transmutation.

A related problem exists when one spouse brings separate property into a marriage (e.g., car, jewelry) and the other spouse uses it extensively. A claim is sometimes asserted that a gift of the separate property was made to the other spouse during the marriage because of this extensive use, a claim that is often successful.

commingling
Mixing different kinds of funds or mixing funds from different sources.

tracing
Determining the ownership or characteristics of property from the time it came into existence.

PRACTICAL CONSIDERATIONS IN PROPERTY DIVISION

Once the decision is made on how to divide property, the next concern is to identify the most *practical* way to accomplish the division. Cash, of course, is easy to split (e.g., a 50/50 or 60/30 percent division of a bank account). Not so for the division of homes, vehicles, and businesses. They cannot be conveniently chopped up. Sometimes it is practical to sell an asset and divide the proceeds according to the allocation principle that applies. When this is not practical, other options are negotiated and/or ordered by the court:

- The wife will keep the house, and the husband will keep the car and his business.
- The wife will live in the house, but the husband will retain a designated amount of the equity in the house, which must be paid to him when the house is sold, which cannot occur until the children reach a designated age.
- The wife receives $250,000 as a lump-sum payment, and the husband receives all of the other property.

Sometimes such measures do not work because of the strained financial circumstances of the parties and a weak economy. Some ex-spouses have been forced to continue to live together after the divorce. In an article entitled *Alone Together in Tough Times*, the author said that "[w]ith the recession and the collapse of the housing market, more and more couples who have broken up are continuing to live under the same roof, according to judges and divorce lawyers. Some are waiting for housing prices to rebound; some are trying to get back on their feet financially."[25]

PENSIONS, DEGREES/LICENSES, BUSINESSES, AND GOODWILL

Four areas of possible contention involving property division are pensions, professional degrees (or occupational licenses), businesses, and goodwill. Until fairly recently, parties negotiating a separation agreement did *not* include these items in their bargaining. They were either considered too intangible or simply assumed to belong to one of the parties separately, usually the husband. Litigation and legislation, however, have forced drastic changes in these views. As a result, negotiations for a separation agreement now regularly take account of these items in one way or another. When the negotiations do not lead to agreement, the court will decide how these items will be handled in the divorce.

Pensions

PRIVATE PENSIONS Many workers are covered by one of the two kinds of private pension plans at work:

- **Defined-Benefit Plan (DB).** A pension plan that provides a set or defined pension benefit upon retirement, usually based on salary and years of employment.
- **Defined-Contribution Plan (DC).** A pension plan consisting of individual accounts for each worker (e.g., a 401(k) plan) whose retirement benefit depends on the amount in his or her account.

vested
Fixed so that it cannot be taken away by future events or conditions; accrued so that you now have a right to present or future possession or enjoyment.

Accumulated benefits in these plans are **vested** or nonvested. They are vested when they have been earned and cannot be taken away. Under some plans, pension benefits can be vested before retirement. This is usually true of the amounts that the employee pays into the plan. An example of a nonvested benefit might be funds that are lost (particularly the amounts contributed by the employer to the plan) if the employee quits before working a minimum number of years.

Upon divorce, pension benefits can be divided between spouses even though only one spouse worked at a job with pension benefits. Some courts refuse to divide nonvested pensions, calling them mere **expectancies**. Many courts, however, take a different view and divide both vested and nonvested pensions.

expectancy
The bare hope (but more than wishful thinking) of receiving a property interest.

coverture fraction
The portion of a pension earned during a marriage if part of the pension of a married worker was earned when the worker was not married.

If the worker began earning the pension before marriage, the amount of the pension earned during the marriage (called the **coverture fraction**) would have to be determined. In most states, only the pension benefits earned during the marriage is subject to property division.

In negotiations, the parties might agree on how to divide a pension. For example, the separation agreement might provide that each spouse will receive an agreed-upon percentage of every pension payout. Alternatively, one spouse might agree to relinquish all right to the other spouse's pension in exchange for a lump-sum cash payment or in exchange for some other benefit sought in the divorce. If they cannot agree, the court will decide what to do with the pension.

qualified domestic relations order (QDRO)
A court order that allows a nonworker to reach all or part of the pension or other retirement benefits of a worker or former worker in order to satisfy the worker's support or other marital obligation.

If the nonworker spouse is to receive a portion of a pension, the parties must obtain a court order to this effect and present it to the pension plan administrator where the worker has the pension. The order is called a **qualified domestic relations order (QDRO)**. It orders a company to divide the pension in a specified manner. Under a QDRO, a spouse, ex-spouse, or child can receive some or all of a worker's pension benefits. Any one of these individuals can become an **alternate payee** under the pension plan. In addition to being a way to divide a pension upon divorce, a QDRO can also be used to collect spousal-support (alimony) or child support (see Chapter 10 on child support).

The use of QDROs to divide pensions represents a dramatic change in the law. Before 1984, when QDROs were created, individuals other than the worker or employee could not have pension benefits paid directly to them. (To see examples of court orders that now make this possible, type "QDRO sample" in Google or any general search engine.) In Chapter 10, we will consider a similar device called a *qualified medical child support order*—QMCSO—that covers health insurance for children.

Before an employee's pension plan can be divided, its value must be determined. Value will depend on factors such as:

* Type of pension plan.
* Amount contributed to the plan by the worker and by the employer (a plan is *contributory* if the employee pays part of his or her salary into the plan; it is noncontributory if the funds in the plan come from the employer only).
* How benefits are determined (e.g., when they accrue or are vested).
* Age of employee.
* Employee's earliest retirement date.
* Employee's life expectancy.

The valuation process can be complex, often requiring the services of accounting specialists. Here, for example, is how a court described what steps would be needed to value the pension of a 55-year-old plaintiff who was still employed at the time of the divorce:

> Since . . . plaintiff was 55 years old at the time of the divorce and was not eligible to receive any pension benefits until at least age 59, the [following steps would be needed to value his pension]. . . . First, the lower court would have to ascertain the likelihood of a 55-year-old man dying before he becomes 59. If, for instance, five 55-year-old males out of each 100 die by the age of 59, the value of the pension benefits would have to be reduced by 5%. Second, the life expectancy of plaintiff at retirement age would have to be calculated. [Under statutory guidelines], a 59-year-old person has a life expectancy of 16.81 years. Third, the life expectancy of plaintiff would have to be multiplied by the yearly pension benefits the plan provides. Fourth, this figure must be reduced by the percentage of possibility that plaintiff would die before he is eligible for retirement. (In this example, we have used 5% for purposes of illustration only.) Fifth, this figure must be reduced to **present value**. This sum will constitute a reasonably ascertainable present value for the pension.[26]

Some law firms specialize in pension valuation and division. An attorney at one such firm claims that many attorneys are failing to provide competent representation in this area of practice. Flawed retirement-plan paperwork, he said, is a "ticking time bomb waiting to go off" in thousands of divorce cases across the country.[27]

PUBLIC PENSIONS Social security benefits, unlike private pensions, are not divisible marital property. A recipient of social security cannot agree to (or be forced to) transfer (**assign**) future benefits to another person. Divorced spouses, however, are entitled to collect social security benefits based upon the former spouse's earning record if the marriage lasted at least 10 years immediately before the divorce became final and the former spouse is entitled to or is receiving

alternate payee
A nonworker who is entitled to receive all or part of the pension or other retirement benefits of a current or former worker pursuant to a qualified domestic relations order (QDRO).

present value
The amount of money an individual would have to be given now in order to generate a certain amount of money within a designated period of time through prudent investment, usually at compound interest. Also called present cash value and present worth.

assign
To transfer rights or property to someone. The noun is *assignment*. The person who makes the transfer is called the *assignor*. The person who receives the transfer is called the *assignee* or the *assign*.

benefits. The divorced spouse seeking benefits through this route must be at least 62 years old.[28] This method of obtaining social security is quite different from receiving a share of the other spouse's benefits. The latter is not allowed.

Although social security is not divisible marital property, a recipient's income from social security can be considered when calculating the amount of alimony and child support that he or she is required to pay. In some states, courts consider a party's receipt of social security benefits when making an overall equitable distribution of marital property. Such states do not assume that these benefits do not exist. Critics claim that this approach results in an indirect division of social security benefits.

At one time, military pensions were also not divisible upon divorce. This was changed by the Uniformed Services Former Spouses' Protection Act (USFSPA).[29] Unlike social security benefits, military pensions can now be divided upon divorce.

At the state and local level, government employees are covered by over 2,600 retirement systems. Although many of these systems have only limited benefits for spouses and no provisions for divorced spouses, aggressive attorneys, with court orders in hand, are sometimes able to break through the maze in order to obtain a share of benefits for ex-spouses.

Degrees and Licenses

Bill and Pat are married in 2003 immediately after both graduated from high school. While Bill goes through college, medical school, and internship to become a doctor, Pat works full-time to support the two of them. On the day he obtains his license to practice medicine, they decide to divorce. During the long years of Bill's education, they have accumulated no property. Pat earns $25,000 a year at her job. Because she is fully capable of supporting herself, the court decides that she should receive no alimony. They have no children.

Many would consider it an outrage that Pat walks away from the marriage with nothing. In our example, she is not eligible for alimony, and there is no tangible property to divide. Bill walks away with a professional degree and a doctor's license ready to embark on a lucrative career.

Many spouses make substantial contributions to the other spouse's *enhanced earning capacity* in the form of a degree, a license, or, in some instances, a potentially profitable celebrity status. Courts have slowly come to the realization that the supporting spouse should be given a remedy in such situations. Yet the courts do not agree on what the remedy should be.

There are a number of different financial calculations that are relevant to what Pat contributed and expected out of her relationship with Bill in our example:

1. The amount Pat contributed to Bill's day-to-day living needs while he was in school, e.g., food, utilities, rent.

2. The amount Pat contributed to the payment of Bill's education expenses.

3. The amount Bill would have contributed to the marriage if he had worked during these years rather than going to school.

4. The increased earnings Pat might have had if she had taken a different job.

5. The increased earnings Pat would have had if she had continued her education rather than working to support Bill through his education.

6. The increased standard of living Pat would have enjoyed due to Bill's expected high earnings if they had stayed married.

7. The share of his increased earnings to which Pat would have been entitled if they had stayed married.

Most states will consider only items (1) and (2) in providing Pat with a remedy. As a matter of equity, she is entitled only to **restitution**—a return of what

restitution
An equitable remedy in which a person is restored to his or her original position prior to the loss or injury; restoring to the plaintiff the value of what he or she parted with.

she contributed while Bill was acquiring his degree and license. Such states do not consider a degree and license to be divisible property. They are personal to the holder. Under this view, it logically follows that she is not entitled to a share of his increased earnings as a result of the degree and license.

All of the above items (1–7) are taken into consideration in deciding the question of *spousal support.* Increased earnings as a result of the degree and license are taken into consideration because one of the factors in an alimony or maintenance judgment is the spouse's ability to pay. The problem, however, is that the wife may not be eligible for alimony because of her own employability. Nor can equity be done by giving the wife a generous share of tangible property if little or no such property has been accumulated due to the fact that the husband had high educational expenses and little or no income of his own. In such situations, a minimal remedy is a direct award for items (1) and (2) above, which amounts to little more than restitution. (As we saw earlier in Exhibit 8-4, the award is sometimes awkwardly referred to as reimbursement alimony or restitutional alimony even though its primary purpose is *not* to provide support.) A few states will deny even this remedy, taking the position that the wife, in effect, was making a gift of her money and other resources to the husband during his education.

There is another remedy that the sacrificing ex-spouse might be able to use in this situation to prevent **unjust enrichment**. He or she may be able to sue the now-educated or now-licensed ex-spouse on a theory of **implied-in-law contract** (also called quasi contract), which would seek to recover the value of the contributions made by the sacrificing ex-spouse toward the other's achievement of the degree or license.

There is, however, a small minority of states that are more sympathetic to the plight of spouses in Pat's situation. These states have ruled that the degree and license *do* constitute divisible marital property and that, therefore, more than restitution is needed. *Woodworth v. Woodworth* is an example of a case from such a state.

unjust enrichment

The receipt of a benefit in the form of goods or services from another when in fairness and equity the recipient should provide restitution for (a return of) the goods or compensation for the services even though there was no express or implied promise to do so. The amount the recipient should pay for services is called quantum meruit, the reasonable value of the services provided.

implied-in-law contract

An obligation imposed by law to avoid unjust enrichment in the absence of an express or implied contract creating this obligation. Also called *quasi contract.*

CASE

Woodworth v. Woodworth
126 Mich. App. 258, 337 N.W.2d 332 (1983)
Court of Appeals of Michigan

Background: *While Michael Woodworth went through law school in the 1970s, his wife, Ann, was a nursery school teacher. In their divorce action, she claimed that his law degree was a marital asset that should be divided. The trial court agreed. It valued the degree at $20,000 and ruled that he must pay her $2,000 per year for 10 years. The case is now on appeal before the Court of Appeals of Michigan. On appeal, Michael is the plaintiff and Ann is the defendant.*

Decision on Appeal: *A former husband's law degree, which was the end product of a concerted family effort, was marital property subject to distribution upon divorce. The case is remanded to the trial court to recalculate the value of the degree.*

OPINION OF THE COURT:

Judge BURNS delivered the opinion of the court.

On January 6, 1982, the parties' divorce was finalized. Both parties appeal as of right.

The parties were married on June 27, 1970, after plaintiff had graduated from Central Michigan University with a bachelor's degree in secondary education and defendant had graduated from Lansing Community College with an associate's degree. They then moved to Jonesville, where plaintiff worked as a teacher and coach for the high school and defendant worked as a nursery school teacher in Hillsdale. In the Fall of 1973, they sold their house, quit their jobs [defendant had already quit her job the year before after the parties' first child was born], and moved to Detroit, where plaintiff attended Wayne State Law School. Three years later, they moved to Lansing where plaintiff took and passed the bar exam and accepted a job as a research attorney with the Court of Appeals. Plaintiff is now a partner in a Lansing law firm.

For all intents and purposes, the marriage ended on August 25, 1980, when the parties separated. The [Earnings Chart] summarizes each party's earnings during the marriage.

(continued)

CASE • **Woodworth v. Woodworth** (continued)

Summary of Earnings during the Marriage

Year		Plaintiff		Defendant
1970	$ 2,591	Jonesville HS teacher/coach	$ 1,422	Nursery School Teach.
			$ 2,549	Grant Company (clerk)
1971	$ 7,989	Teacher	$ 4,236	Teacher
	$ 410	St. Anthony Ch. (instructor)	$ 280	St. Anthony Ch. (instructor)
1972	$ 9,691	Teacher	$ 2,525	Teacher
1973	$ 6,557	Teacher	$ 986	Bank Teller
1974	$ 2,483	Legal Aid (student lawyer)	$ 6,572	Bank Teller
1975	$ 2,588	Legal Aid (student lawyer)	$ 1,050	Bank Teller
			$ 8,191	Dept/Social Services (case worker)
1976	$ 6,342	Court of Appeals (attorney)	$10,276	Dept/Social Services (case worker)
1977	$12,493	Court of Appeals (attorney)	$ 1,586	Dept/Social Services (case worker)
	$ 5,595	Asst. Pros. Atty.		(defendant quit this job in January
				after the parties' third child was born)
1978	$21,085	Asst. Pros. Atty.	$—0—	
1979	$27,247	Asst. Pros. Atty.	$—0—	
1980	$ 2,057	Asst. Pros. Atty.	$—0—	
	$30,000	Private Practice		

The basic issue in this case is whether or not plaintiff's law degree is marital property subject to distribution. The trial court held that it was, valued it at $20,000, and awarded this amount to defendant in payments of $2,000 over ten years. Plaintiff contends that his law degree is not such a marital asset. We disagree.

The facts reveal that plaintiff's law degree was the end product of a concerted family effort. Both parties planned their family life around the effort to attain plaintiff's degree. Toward this end, the family divided the daily tasks encountered in living. While the law degree did not preempt all other facets of their lives, it did become the main focus and goal of their activities. Plaintiff left his job at Jonesville and the family relocated to Detroit so that plaintiff could attend law school. In Detroit, defendant sought and obtained full time employment to support the family.

We conclude, therefore, that plaintiff's law degree was the result of mutual sacrifice and effort by both plaintiff and defendant. While plaintiff studied and attended classes, defendant carried her share of the burden as well as sharing vicariously in the stress of the [law school] experience known as the "paper chase."

We believe that fairness dictates that the spouse who did not earn an advanced degree be compensated whenever the advanced degree is the product of such concerted family investment. The degree holder has expended great effort to obtain the degree not only for him or herself, but also to benefit the family as a whole. The other spouse has shared in this effort and contributed in other ways as well, not merely as a gift to the student spouse nor merely to share individually in the benefits but to help the marital unit as a whole. . . .

We are aware that numerous other cases have held that an advanced degree is not a marital asset and may be considered only (if at all) in determining alimony. However, we reject the [following four main] reasons given in these cases to support their conclusions.

[I]

The cases first contend that an advanced degree is simply not "property":

An educational degree, such as an M.B.A., is simply not encompassed by the broad views of the concept of "property." It does not have an exchange value or any objective transferable value on an open market. It is personal to the holder. It terminates on death of the holder and is not inheritable. It cannot be assigned, sold, transferred, conveyed, or pledged. An advanced degree is a cumulative product of many years of previous education, combined with diligence and hard work. It may not be acquired by the mere expenditure of money. It is simply an intellectual achievement that may potentially assist in the future acquisition of property. In our view, it has none of the attributes of property in the usual sense of that term. *Graham v. Graham*, 194 Colo. 432, 374 P.2d 75 (1978).

Yet whether or not an advanced degree can physically or metaphysically be defined as "property" is beside the point. Courts must instead focus on the most equitable solution to dissolving the marriage and dividing among the respective parties what they have.

> [T]he student spouse will walk away with a degree and the supporting spouse will depart with little more than the knowledge that he or she has substantially contributed toward the attainment of that degree. Comment, *The Interest of the Community in a Professional Education*, 10 Cal. West. L. Rev. 590 (1974).

In *DeLa Rosa v. DeLa Rosa*, 309 N.W.2d 758, (1981), the Minnesota Supreme Court added:

> [O]ne spouse has forgone the immediate enjoyment of earned income to enable the other to pursue an advanced education on a full time basis. Typically, this sacrifice is made with the expectation that the parties will enjoy a higher standard of living in the future.

Where, as in this case, the family goal of obtaining the law degree was the purpose of the substantial contribution and sacrifice, both the degree holder and his or her spouse are entitled to share in the fruits of the degree. The trial judge recognized as much:

> Here the plaintiff quit his job and entered law school. The defendant secured employment so plaintiff could become a professional with far greater earning capacity than he had, which would benefit him and their children. To permit this, upon divorce, to benefit only the party who secured the professional degree is unconscionable.

[II]

The next argument is that a marriage is not a commercial enterprise and that neither spouse's expectations are necessarily going to be met after the divorce:

> I do not believe that a spouse who works and contributes to the education of the other spouse during marriage normally does so in the expectation of compensation. *Sullivan v. Sullivan*, 184 Cal. Rptr. 801 (1982) (Kaufman, P. J., concurring).

Furthermore:

> They do not nor do they expect to pay each other for their respective contributions in any commercial sense. Rather, they work together, in both income and nonincome-producing ways, in their joint, mutual and individual interests. The termination of the marriage represents, if nothing else, the disappointment of expectations, financial and nonfinancial, which were hoped to be achieved by and during the continuation of the relationship. It does not, however, in our view, represent a commercial investment loss. Recompense for the disappointed expectations resulting from the failure of the marital entity to survive cannot, therefore, be made to the spouses on a strictly commercial basis

which, after the fact seeks to assign monetary values to the contributions consensually made by each of the spouses during the marriage. . . . If the plan fails by reason of the termination of the marriage, we do not regard the supporting spouse's consequent loss of expectation by itself as any more compensable or demanding of solicitude than the loss of expectations of any other spouse who, in the hope and anticipation of the endurance of the relationship in its commitments, has invested a portion of his or her life, youth, energy and labor in a failed marriage. *Mahoney v. Mahoney*, 182 N.J. Super. 612–614, 442 A.2d 1062 (1982).

We agree that a marriage is not intrinsically a commercial enterprise. Instead, it is a relationship sanctioned by law governed at its essence by fidelity and troth. Neither partner usually expects to be compensated for his or her efforts. But that consideration does not end the discussion. We are not presently concerned with how best to characterize a marriage while it endures. Instead, we are concerned with how best to distribute between the parties what they have once the marriage has for all intents and purposes dissolved. In other words:

> To allow a student spouse . . . to leave a marriage with all the benefits of additional education and a professional license without compensation to the spouse who bore much of the burdens incident to procuring these would be unfair. . . . *O'Brien v. O'Brien*, 452 N.Y.S.2d 801, 805 (1982).

Furthermore, we also agree that divorce courts cannot recompense expectations. However, we are not talking about an expectation here. Defendant is not asking us to compensate for a failed expectation that her husband would become a wealthy lawyer and subsequently support her for the rest of her life. Instead, she is merely seeking her share of the fruits of a degree which she helped him earn. We fail to see the difference between compensating her for a degree which she helped him earn and compensating her for a house in his name which her earnings helped him buy.

[III]

The third argument against including an advanced degree as marital property is that its valuation is too speculative. In *Lesman v. Lesman*, 452 N.Y.S. 2d 938-939 (1982), the Court stated:

> Gross inequities may result from predicating distribution awards [the term used in New York for property division] upon the speculative expectations of enhanced future earnings, since distributive awards, unlike maintenance, once fixed may not be modified to meet future realities. It is almost impossible to predict what amount of enhanced earnings, if any, will result from a professional education. The degree of financial success attained by those holding a professional degree varies greatly. Some, even, may earn less from their professional practices than they could

(continued)

have earned from nonprofessional work. Moreover, others, due to choice or factors beyond their control, may never practice their professions. . . .

Michigan has already recognized that:

> Interests which are contingent upon the happening of an event which may or may not occur are not distributable. The party seeking to include the interest in the marital estate bears the burdens of proving a reasonably ascertainable value; if the burden is not met, the interest should not be considered an asset subject to distribution. *Miller v. Miller*, 83 Mich. App. 672, 677, 269 N.W.2d 264 (1978).

> However, future earnings due to an advanced degree are not "too speculative." While a degree holder spouse might change professions, earn less than projected at trial, or even die, courts have proved adept at measuring future earnings in such contexts as personal injury, wrongful death, and workers' compensation actions. In fact, pain and suffering, professional goodwill and mental distress, within these general legal issues, have similar valuation "problems". . . . We, therefore, do not believe that the *Miller* contingency caveat applies to future earnings.

[IV]

The last argument is that these matters are best considered when awarding alimony rather than when distributing the property. . . . A trial judge is given wide discretion in awarding alimony. . . . However, alimony is basically for the other spouse's support. The considerations for whether or not a spouse is entitled to support are different than for dividing the marital property. *McLain v. McLain*, 108 Mich. App. 166, 310 N.W.2d 316 (1981), listed eleven factors that the trial judge is to consider in determining whether or not to award alimony. Some of these deal with the parties' financial condition and their ability to support themselves. If the spouse has already supported the other spouse through graduate school, he or she is quite possibly already presently capable of supporting him or herself. Furthermore, M.C.L.A. [Michigan Compiled Laws Annotated] § 552.13; M.S.A. [Michigan Statutes Annotated] § 25.93 gave the trial court discretion to end alimony if the spouse receiving it remarries. We do not believe that the trial judge should be allowed to deprive the spouse who does not have an advanced degree of the fruits of the marriage and award it all to the other spouse merely because he or she has remarried. Such a situation would necessarily cause that spouse to think twice about remarrying.

Having determined that the defendant is entitled to compensation in this case, we must next determine how she is to be compensated. Two basic methods have been proposed—[1] a percentage share of the present value of the future earnings attributable to the degree or [2] restitution.

[Some courts limit] the recovery to restitution for any money given to the student spouse to earn the degree. While this solution may be equitable in some circumstances, we do not believe that restitution is an adequate remedy in this case. Limiting the recovery to restitution "would provide [the supporting spouse] no realization of [his or] her expectation of economic benefit from the career for which the education laid the foundation." Pinnel, *Divorce After Professional School: Education and Future Earning Capacity May Be Marital Property*, 44 Mo. L. Rev. 329, 335 (1979). Clearly, in this case, the degree was a family investment, rather than a gift or a benefit to the degree holder alone. Treating the degree as such a gift would unjustly enrich the degree holder to the extent that the degree's value exceeds its cost. . . . We note that this case does not involve the situation where both parties simultaneously earned substantially similar advanced degrees during the marriage. In such a situation, equity suggests that the parties have already amply compensated each other.

The trial court in this case valued plaintiff's law degree at $20,000 and ruled that plaintiff must pay defendant $2,000 per year for ten years. We are unable to determine how this value was reached and therefore, remand to the trial court to permit that court to revalue the degree in light of the following factors:

- the length of the marriage after the degree was obtained,
- the sources and extent of financial support given plaintiff during his years in law school, and
- the overall division of the parties' marital property.

In determining the degree's present value, the trial court should estimate what the person holding the degree is likely to make in that particular job market and subtract from that what he or she would probably have earned without the degree. . . . The ultimate objective in a property distribution is to be fair. . . . Both parties may present new evidence on these matters and the degree's valuation.

One of the tragedies of this divorce, as in so many others, is that what used to be financially adequate is no longer enough. As the trial court aptly stated: "The tablecloths . . . will not cover both tables." We, therefore, note that the trial court has discretion to order that the payments be made on an installment basis. . . . If the trial court should order such a payment schedule, the trial court should also consider the possibility of insuring these payments by a life insurance policy on plaintiff's life benefitting defendant.

Plaintiff has also appealed the overall property division while defendant has cross-appealed from the alimony determination. If the trial court alters the value placed on plaintiff's law degree, the property division and alimony award must also be reassessed. We, therefore, refrain from addressing these issues at this time.

Pursuant to GCR [General Court Rules] 1963, 726.1, we order plaintiff to pay defendant reasonable attorney fees for this appeal. Costs to defendant.

Remanded with instructions to proceed in a manner consistent with this opinion. We do not retain jurisdiction.

ASSIGNMENT 8.9

a. Was *Woodworth v. Woodworth* correctly decided? Why or why not?

b. Frank and Elaine are married in your state. Both work at low-paying jobs at a fast-food restaurant. Elaine wishes to become a paralegal, and Frank would like to become an electrician. A local institute has a one-year paralegal training program and a nine-month electrician training program. Frank and Elaine decide that only one of them can go to school at a time. Frank volunteers to let Elaine go first, keeping his job at the restaurant to support them both while she is at the institute. A month before Elaine is scheduled to graduate, Frank has a serious accident at the restaurant. He will not recover fully from his injury or be able to go to school for at least five years. When Elaine is graduated, she obtains a good job as a paralegal. The parties seek a divorce a month after graduation. There are no children from the marriage, and no tangible property to divide. In the divorce proceeding, Frank tells the court that the only asset that can be divided is Elaine's paralegal certificate. He asks the court to award him a percentage of the earnings that Elaine will have during the next five years as a paralegal.

    i. How would *Woodworth v. Woodworth* apply to this case?

    ii. How would your state resolve the case of Elaine and Frank? (See General Instructions for the Court-Opinion Assignment in Appendix A.)

Dividing a Business

When a divorce occurs, one of the assets to be divided may be a business that was acquired during the marriage or was acquired before the marriage but developed or expanded during the marriage. The business could be a large corporation, a small sole proprietorship, a partnership, a law practice, a medical practice, etc. (Our focus here is a functioning business rather than a degree or license that will allow one to operate a business in the future.) In addition to plant and equipment, a number of intangible items must be valuated (e.g., patents, trademarks, employment agreements, copyrights, securities, and goodwill).

Many professional business appraisers are available for the task. Examples:

- Certified Public Accountant Accredited in Business Valuation (www.aicpa.org)
- Accredited Senior Appraiser (www.appraisers.org)
- Certified Valuation Analyst (www.nacva.com)
- Certified Business Appraiser (www.go-iba.org)

Because property can fluctuate in value, particularly securities, the parties need to agree on the date that will be used for purposes of valuation. The property to be divided will be valued as of the specific date (called the cutoff date) that they designate. Appraisers and other financial consultants will be asked to come up with valuations as of the cutoff date.

A great deal of documentation will be needed to perform the needed valuations. Here are some examples:

- Federal, state, and local tax returns for the last five years
- Annual and interim financial statements
- Bank statements
- Depreciation schedules
- Articles of incorporation and bylaws or partnership agreements, including amendments
- Minutes of meetings of shareholders and directors

- Buy/sell agreements of shareholders or partners, including amendments
- Loan applications
- W-2 statements (or the equivalent) for the highest-paid employees
- Leases
- Production schedules
- Inventory reports
- Management reports
- Billing records[30]

The fact that a business is a divisible part of the marital estate does not necessarily mean that upon divorce the business must be sold so that the proceeds can be physically divided. The separation agreement will probably try to accommodate the need to keep the business in operation. The agreement, for example, might provide that the husband will give the wife $150,000 in exchange for the release of any interest that the wife may have in his business—or vice versa if she is the one primarily responsible for the business. Similarly, a court may order such an exchange if the parties are not able to agree on dividing the business in their separation agreement.

Goodwill

One aspect of a business that is sometimes particularly difficult to evaluate is its **goodwill**, which is the reputation of a business that causes it to generate additional customers. It is the value of a business or practice that exceeds the value of the combined assets used in the business or practice. Because of goodwill, the company is expected to have earnings beyond what is considered normal for the type of business involved. Individuals providing services, such as accountants and lawyers, can also have goodwill:

> If you are a lawyer facing divorce, it is open season on your practice. . . . Like it or not, law practices and lawyer's goodwill are assets. That you can't sell your practice doesn't mean it has no value. And there are almost no legal limits on the methods an appraiser may use in assigning a value to a law practice. . . . One approach is called the *excess earnings method*. An appraiser looks at published surveys to find the average income for a lawyer of your experience and type of practice, then compares your earnings with the average. If your earnings are higher than the average, the increment is said to be attributable to goodwill. If your ability to attract clients and collect substantial fees from them brings you more income than you would earn working for an average salary, you have built real goodwill.[31]

If goodwill was developed during the marriage, the spouse who stayed at home may be deemed to have contributed to it (as well as to the rest of the business).

A distinction should be made between enterprise goodwill and personal goodwill. **Enterprise goodwill** is an asset of a business or practice that exists by virtue of its business location, existing arrangements with suppliers and employees, and anticipated future customer base but is not dependent on the continued presence of a particular individual in the business or practice. **Personal goodwill** is an asset of a business or practice that is dependent on the continued presence of a particular individual because the asset is attributed to that individual's personal skill, training, or reputation. In many states only enterprise goodwill is divisible property upon divorce because this is an asset that is marketable—it is part of what could be sold when the business or practice is sold. By definition, personal goodwill is not marketable. It has no exchange value; it cannot be sold. Therefore, personal goodwill is not divisible in these states. Other states, however, take a different position and allow both enterprise and personal goodwill to be divided upon divorce.

goodwill
The reputation of a business or professional practice that causes it to generate additional customers. The value of a business or practice that exceeds the value of the combined assets used in the business or practice.

enterprise goodwill
An asset of a business or practice that exists by virtue of its business location, existing arrangements with suppliers and employees, and anticipated future customer base but is not dependent on the continued presence of a particular individual in the business or practice.

personal goodwill
An asset of a business or practice that is dependent on the continued presence of a particular individual because the asset is attributed to that individual's personal skill, training, or reputation.

> ### ASSIGNMENT 8.10
>
> Does your state have any statutes on the division of (a) a pension, (b) a degree or license, (c) a business or profession, or (d) goodwill following a divorce? If so, briefly summarize some of their major terms. (See General Instructions for the State-Code Assignment in Appendix A.)

MISCELLANEOUS PROPERTY-DIVISION PROBLEMS

Sports Tickets

In a recent case calling for the wisdom of Solomon, a judge had to decide how to divide season tickets to basketball games of the New York Knicks. Both spouses were passionate fans. The option of giving them each one ticket to every game was unacceptable, since this would mean they would have to sit together: "This court will not compel them to team up once again at court-side."[32] The judge decided to give the husband both tickets to every even-numbered game and the wife both tickets to every odd-numbered game. Each spouse could then take someone else to the game and avoid having to face the other in the already emotionally charged environment of professional basketball games.

Pets

Pets are personal property (chattels) that are subject to property division. If the parties cannot agree on who gets the pet, the court must resolve the emotional battle. According to a veteran attorney, "Both parties will offer their version of why they are the best. They may have witnesses, neighbors who say, 'The father beat the dog,' or 'The mother kissed the dog.' I have heard the story of a case where both parties were in the courtroom, with the dog in the middle, to see which way it would go. They both whistled and called. The dog ran to the husband. It was not the deciding factor, but it was one of the factors" in the outcome.[33]

Tort Awards

What happens when one of the spouses receives damages from a tort case? For example, Harry wins $200,000 in a negligence case against a truck company for injuries he received in a collision with a driver of the company. A few months later, Harry and his wife Alice begin divorce proceedings. Is the $200,000 divisible property in the divorce? The answer may depend on what the $200,000 was for. Here are some of the main possibilities:

- Compensation for economic losses such as lost wages during the marriage, loss of earning capacity during the marriage, and medical bills that were paid during the marriage with marital funds. In most states, such compensation is marital or community property that is subject to property division upon divorce.

- Compensation for noneconomic losses such as pain and suffering. In most states, such compensation is the separate property of the spouse who won the tort case.

- Compensation for economic losses such as lost future wages and future medical expenses. In most states, such compensation is the separate property of the spouse who won the tort case.

States often assess the divisibility of workers'-compensation awards in the same way. They will determine what is separate and what is divisible based on an analysis of what the award covers.

Note, however, that separate property such as compensation received for pain and suffering might still be a source of alimony for the ex-spouse based on the criteria discussed earlier for alimony awards. An ex-spouse may not be entitled to a share or a division of certain funds, but the ex-spouse will be allowed to point to the existence of such funds as evidence of the other's ability to pay alimony (or child support).

Embryos

What happens to embryos that a married couple froze during the marriage for later implantation but never used as of the time of their divorce? How does a court resolve a disagreement between the divorcing spouses on what to do with the embryos? The dispute might center on whether they should be destroyed (often the ex-husband's wish) or kept in storage for later implantation by the ex-wife or by another woman to whom the embryos would be donated. Are the embryos "property" to be divided? Can one of the spouses allow another couple to "adopt" the embryos? In most states, embryos are considered property that can be disposed of by contract between the spouses and/or between the spouses and the company they hired to freeze and store the embryos. (Similarly, some courts have treated frozen sperm as property that can be disposed of by will and later used via artificial insemination to give birth to a child whose father was dead when the child was born—a posthumous birth.) In the case of embryos, the issue becomes considerably more complex in states that seek to give embryos the status of persons. We will examine the disposition of embryos upon divorce in Chapter 16 and the birth of posthumous children in Chapter 13.

OTHER MATTERS TO BE RESOLVED

Thus far in the chapter, we have covered two of the major components of separation agreements and divorces: alimony and property division. Before turning to child custody and support (in Chapters 9 and 10), we need to look at some other matters that are often part of the dissolution process: debts, taxes, wills, insurance, and legal expenses.

DEBTS

Debts, like assets, must be divided upon divorce. A great variety of debts may be outstanding (unpaid) when the parties divorce:

- Family debts incurred by the wife.
- Family debts incurred by the husband.
- Business debts incurred by the wife.
- Business debts incurred by the husband.
- Business or family debts incurred by both the husband and the wife so that there is **joint and several liability** on the debts, meaning that a creditor could sue the husband and wife *together* on the debt, or could sue *either* the husband or the wife for payment of the whole debt.
- Debts between the spouses (e.g., a loan made by one spouse to the other during the marriage).

The parties must decide who is going to pay what debts. One party may think that the other will pay a particular debt, but this should be spelled out in the separation agreement. Of course, if they cannot agree, the court will decide the issue for them. States differ on how they make this decision. In some states, all debts can be divided, no matter who incurred them. Other states distinguish between separate debts of one spouse (e.g., a debt brought into the

joint and several liability
Legally responsible together and individually. Each debtor is individually responsible for the entire debt; the plaintiff/creditor can choose to collect the full debt from one debtor or from all of them until the debt is satisfied.

marriage) and marital/community debts. In these states, separate debts are the responsibility of the spouse who incurred them. Marital/community debts are allocated according to factors such as the parties' relative ability to pay, the party who incurred the debt, and the party who was the main financial manager of the debt. In short, just as most states seek an equitable distribution of property, so also do most courts seek to achieve an equitable allocation of marital/community (nonseparate) debts.

Divorce often leads to massive financial upheaval for one or both spouses. The option of bankruptcy must be kept in mind throughout the negotiations for the separation agreement. A wife, for example, should not have the attitude that her husband's debts are "his problem." His bankruptcy will undoubtedly affect his ability to meet his support and property-division debts even though all support debts and most property-division debts are not discharged in bankruptcy. (See Exhibit 8-3 at the beginning of the chapter.)

Some future debts (those incurred after the separation) are imposed by the separation agreement and divorce judgment, e.g., child-support payments. These debts, of course, must be met by the party on whom they are imposed. As to other future debts after the divorce judgment, the normal expectation of the parties is that they will pay their own debts. A cautious party, however, will not only cancel all joint credit cards but also notify known large creditors that future debts will be the sole responsibility of the ex-spouse incurring the debts. Some separation agreements insert a clause in the agreement stating that each party promises not to attempt to use the credit of the other.

Finally, keep in mind that creditors are *not* bound by separation agreements or by court orders that allocate responsibility for paying debts between ex-spouses.

> *Paul and Karen are married. During the marriage, Paul buys a car on credit in his own name from Ford Motor Co. When they divorce, the balance owed on the car is $10,000. Because Karen was the primary user of the car throughout the marriage, the parties decide that the wife should pay the remaining $10,000 debt. This decision is stated in their separation agreement and approved by the court in the final divorce judgment.*

Ford can still sue Paul for the $10,000 debt if Karen fails to pay it. Parties do not have the right to switch debtors and force creditors to abide by the switch. The same is true if a court ordered Karen to pay the $10,000 as part of the divorce decree. Ford can still go after the party whose credit it relied on when extending credit — Paul. If Karen violates the separation agreement or divorce judgment by refusing to pay the debt, Paul can sue Karen. Such a suit, however, would not affect the contractual obligation that Paul has to Ford, which, of course, was not a party to the divorce judgment.

Another example:

> *The separation agreement of Jim and Alice gives their jointly owned Boston home to Alice. She must pay the remaining mortgage, which both she and Jim took out when they married. Jim quitclaims the Boston home to Alice so that his name is no longer on the title. A year after the divorce, Alice falls behind on her mortgage payments. Jim has remarried and has applied for a mortgage on a home in New York with his new wife. His application for the mortgage is denied because of the delinquent payments on the Boston home.*

The separation agreement obligated Alice to pay the mortgage on their Boston home. The agreement did not (and could not) remove Jim's name from the Boston mortgage. When the court approved their separation agreement, the court order did not (and could not) remove Jim's name from the Boston mortgage. Only if the Boston mortgage company was a party to the divorce case would a divorce court have the power to alter the company's contractual relationship with Jim, a named mortgagor.

TAXES

In Chapter 11, we will discuss the tax consequences of divorce. (They are summarized in Exhibit 8-3 above.) Our focus here is on the question of who pays the taxes and who will be able to take advantage of certain tax benefits. The following are the kinds of situations the parties need to anticipate:

- If the Internal Revenue Service (IRS) assesses a tax deficiency and penalty for a joint return filed in a year when the parties were still married, who pays the deficiency and penalty?
- If the parties file their last joint return in the current tax year, and then, many months later, the IRS assesses a tax deficiency and penalty on that last tax return, who pays this deficiency and penalty?

During a marriage, the couple's tax returns are often prepared by the husband with minimal involvement of the wife. This does not necessarily relieve her from liability for underpayments, errors, or fraud committed by her husband, although, as we will see in Chapter 11, a spouse might be able to obtain relief as an "innocent spouse." In the negotiations for the separation agreement, the wife might ask the husband to insert a clause that he will **indemnify** the wife against any tax deficiencies and penalties that may arise out of the joint returns filed in any year during their marriage. Under such a **hold-harmless** clause, he will have to pay the entire deficiency and penalty for which they both may be jointly and severally liable.

The parties must also agree on how tax refunds, if any, are to be divided. Such refunds are usually payable by government check to both of the parties. Two signatures may be required to cash such checks. Another concern is that the IRS might institute an audit years after a particular return is filed. It is a good idea to insert a clause in the separation agreement that both parties agree to cooperate with each other in responding to the issues raised during any possible audits in the future.

Every clause in the separation agreement involving financial matters can have immediate or long-term tax consequences. The separation agreement may specify a dollar amount to be transferred pursuant to a support clause or a property-division clause. If, however, all the tax factors have not been considered, the parties may later be surprised by the discrepancy between such stated dollar figures and the *real* amounts that they receive and pay out. To **tax effect** a clause in a separation agreement means to determine the tax consequences of that clause.

WILLS

The parties must consider a number of questions involving wills and estates:

- Do the spouses already have wills naming each other as beneficiary? If so, are these wills to be changed? In most states, a divorce automatically revokes gifts to a surviving spouse unless the will specifically says otherwise. Nevertheless, the parties may want to make this explicit in their separation agreement and also cover the contingency of death occurring after they sign the separation agreement but before the final divorce judgment.
- Have they named each other as **executor** of their estates? In most states, the divorce judgment will automatically revoke this appointment, but the revocation should be made explicit in the separation agreement.
- Is either spouse mentioned as a beneficiary in the will of a relative of the other spouse? If so, is this likely to be changed?

indemnify
To compensate another for any loss or expense incurred.

hold harmless
To assume any liability in a transaction and thereby relieve another from responsibility or loss arising out of the transaction. Also called save harmless.

tax effect
(1) To determine the tax consequences of something (verb). (2) The tax consequences of something (noun).

executor
A person designated in a will to carry out the terms of the will and handle related matters. If a female, this person is sometimes called an executrix.

ELECTIVE SHARE

In common-law property states, the death of a spouse gave the surviving spouse important rights in the estate of the deceased spouse, sometimes in spite of what the deceased spouse intended or provided for the surviving spouse in a will:

- **elective share**. The percentage of a deceased spouse's estate that the surviving spouse can choose (elect) to receive despite what the will of the deceased spouse provided for the surviving spouse. Also called statutory share, forced share.
- **dower.** The right of a widow to the lifetime use (called a *life estate*) of one-third of the land her deceased husband owned during the marriage.
- **curtesy.** The right of a husband to the lifetime use (life estate) of all the land his deceased wife owned during the marriage (if **issue** were born of the marriage).

Rights such as dower and curtesy have been abolished or substantially changed in most common-law property states, often replaced by laws establishing the right to an elective share. The separation agreement should make clear what happens to these rights upon divorce. The parties frequently insert a clause that each side **releases** all such rights in the other's property.

Note, however, that the rights of dower, curtesy, and elective share are not applicable in community-property states. The death of a spouse in a community-property state automatically gives the surviving spouse one-half of the community property. There is no need for the law to protect the survivor through devices such as dower and elective share.

INSURANCE

Several different kinds of insurance policies could be in effect at the time the parties draft the separation agreement in anticipation of a divorce:

- Life insurance
- Homeowner's insurance (covering fire and related damage to the home as well as liability claims by persons [e.g., mail carrier] injured on the premises)
- Hospitalization or other medical insurance
- Liability insurance (for business)
- Comprehensive vehicle insurance
- Disability insurance
- Umbrella insurance (covering designated amounts that exceed the limits of standard liability policies)

Detailed information should be obtained about each policy. How much are the premiums? Who has paid them in the past? Who are the beneficiaries? Can the beneficiaries be changed? If so, by whom?

As we have seen, one ex-spouse usually has no obligation to support the other ex-spouse or the children after the payor dies. The latter, however, may want to assume this obligation voluntarily. One way of accomplishing this is to take out a life insurance policy on the payor's life, with the beneficiaries being the ex-spouse and/or the children. If such a life insurance policy already exists, then the payor may agree to keep it effective (e.g., pay the premiums) after the separation. The payee, however, will not gain much protection from such an agreement if the payor can change the beneficiaries. Hence, as part of the bargaining process, the payee might ask that the designation of the beneficiaries be made **irrevocable**.

If the **custodial parent (CP)** is to remain in the home that the ex-spouses will continue to own jointly after the divorce, the separation agreement should

issue
A child and anyone else who has descended from a common ancestor. (See glossary for an additional meaning.)

release
To formally give up or relinquish (a claim or a right).

irrevocable
Not capable of being altered or revoked.

custodial parent (CP)
The parent with whom the child is living; the parent with physical custody of the child.

qualified medical child support order (QMCSO)

A court order to an employer to extend its group health insurance benefits to the child of one of its employees.

specify who is responsible for payment of homeowner's insurance. Health insurance is often critically important. To protect the children, a **qualified medical child support order (QMCSO)** can be sought. It is a court order that medical support or health benefits for the child of a parent must be included under a group health insurance plan at work. (See Chapter 10 for more on QMCSOs.)

LEGAL EXPENSES

One spouse is often ordered by the court to pay the attorney fees of the other in a divorce action. The parties may want to specify this in the separation agreement itself. They should consider not only the legal costs (attorney fees, filing fees, etc.) of a potential divorce but also the legal costs incurred in connection with the preparation of the separation agreement itself. Of course, if both have adequate resources of their own, the parties may agree (and the court will probably order) that they pay their own legal bills.

NONMOLESTATION

nonmolestation clause

A clause in an agreement that the parties will not disturb, annoy, or harass each other.

Most separation agreements contain a **nonmolestation clause**, in which both parties agree, in effect, to leave each other alone. Specifically, they will not try to live with the other person, interfere with each other's lifestyle, or bother each other in any way. This does not necessarily mean that they cannot have any future contact with each other. If, for example, one spouse has physical custody of the children, communication may be necessary in order to make or reschedule visitation arrangements.

MUTUAL MISTAKE

reformation

An equitable remedy to correct a writing so that it embodies the actual intent of the parties.

Mutual mistake is a commonly used theory to rescind a contract. If, for example, a seller and buyer are both mistaken on whether the violin being sold is as Stradivarius, the contract can be invalidated on the ground of mutual mistake. The principle also applies to separation agreements. Many states will allow a party to force a **reformation** of the separation agreement if the spouses operated under a substantial mutual mistake about something in existence at the time the agreement was negotiated. Reformation is an equitable remedy to correct a writing so that it embodies the actual intent of the parties. The party seeking to reform the agreement is asking for what is called a *do-over*. Here is how one court expressed the test for reformation:

> For a party to be entitled to reformation of a contract on the ground of mutual mistake, the mutual mistake must be material, i.e., it must involve a fundamental assumption of the contract. A party need not establish that the parties entered into the contract because of the mutual mistake, only that the "material mistake . . . vitally affects a fact or facts on the basis of which the parties contracted."[34]

For example, assume that the divorcing spouses negotiate the division of a specific number of shares that both believe are currently available from the husband's employer. Later, however, they find out that the number of available shares was substantially less than they both assumed to exist. On these facts, a court would probably hold that the property division could be reformed to reflect the actual number.

A recent New York reformation case involved the divorce of two prominent attorneys (Steven Simkin and Laura Blank) and the notorious Madoff Ponzi scheme. "The Simkin-Blank dispute riveted the state's matrimonial bar."[35] After a marriage of 33 years, Steven Simkin (a real-estate attorney) and Laura Blank (a labor attorney) obtained a divorce in 2006. In their separation agreement, they agreed to an approximately equal division of their marital property. They also agreed that the property would be valued as of September 1, 2004.

The largest asset to be divided was the account in Bernard Madoff Securities. It was valued at $5.4 million as of September 1, 2004. Blank received half of this amount in cash from Simkin to cover her share of the Madoff account, which Simkin would keep in his name.

Several years later, Simkin's account all but disappeared when Bernard Madoff was convicted of running a multi-billion dollar fraud, called "the world's largest Ponzi scheme" by the media. Simkin, therefore, had given Blank $2.7 million in cash to cover her share of an account that never existed. Simkin then sued Blank for a reformation of the property agreement based on mutual mistake. He argued that when they negotiated the property agreement, both he and Blank were under the mistaken impression that the Madoff account in fact existed. The widespread publicity to Simkin's suit dismayed some observers: "The decision could open the floodgates for people who want to challenge agreements after they go sour," said Peter Bienstock, a divorce lawyer not involved in the case. "Deals are done every single day based on assumptions about what things are worth. If the court allows this lawsuit to go forward, how can we be certain that deals will hold up?"[36] Eventually, however, the New York Court of Appeals denied Simkin's request for a reformation. The court said that only in exceptional situations should separation agreements be set aside for mutual mistake. The Madoff account existed at the time the parties negotiated the separation agreement. Simkin, in fact, withdrew some money from it to pay Blank. The mistake was as to the value of the account. This mistake is not a sufficient basis to warrant reformation. According to the court:

> This situation, however sympathetic, is . . . akin to a marital asset that unexpectedly loses value after dissolution of a marriage; the asset had value at the time of the settlement but the purported value did not remain consistent. Viewed from a different perspective, had the Madoff account or other asset retained by husband substantially increased in worth after the divorce, should wife be able to claim entitlement to a portion of the enhanced value? The answer is obviously no.[37]

ARBITRATION AND MEDIATION

Separation agreements often contain an **arbitration** clause, which provides that disputes arising in the future about the agreement will be arbitrated. Arbitration is a method of **alternative dispute resolution (ADR)** that seeks to resolve disputes without litigation. In arbitration, the parties hire an arbitrator, who will examine all the evidence and render a decision on the dispute. Normally, an arbitrator will be chosen from a professional organization, such as the American Arbitration Association (www.adr.org). A professional arbitrator, however, is not required. The parties can select a mutually trusted friend as the arbitrator. The agreement should specify who the arbitrator will be or how the arbitrator will be selected and who will pay the arbitration expenses.

Another ADR method is **mediation**. Unlike an arbitrator, a mediator does not make a decision. The mediator tries to guide the parties to reach a decision on their own in much the same manner as a labor mediator tries to assist union and management to reach a settlement. If mediation does not work, the parties either agree to submit the dispute to an arbitrator (in which case the two-step process is called **Med-Arb**) or they are forced to litigate the dispute in court. (For more on mediation and how it can be used elsewhere in the divorce process, see Exhibit 7-5 on alternative dispute resolution in Chapter 7 on divorce procedure.)

RECONCILIATION

What happens if the parties become reconciled to each other *after* they **execute** the separation agreement but before the divorce becomes final? They certainly have the power to cancel or rescind their contract so long

arbitration
A method of alternative dispute resolution (ADR) in which the parties avoid litigation by submitting their dispute to a neutral third person (the arbitrator) who renders a decision resolving the dispute.

alternative dispute resolution (ADR)
A method or procedure for resolving a legal dispute without litigating the dispute in a court or administrative agency. ADR methods include mediation, arbitration, and Med-Arb.

mediation
A method of alternative dispute resolution (ADR) in which the parties avoid litigation by submitting their dispute to a neutral third person (the mediator) who helps the parties resolve their dispute; he or she does not render a decision resolving it for them.

Med-Arb
A method of alternative dispute resolution (ADR) in which the parties first try mediation, and if it does not work, they try arbitration.

execute
To take needed steps to create a legal document. (See glossary for an additional meaning.)

as both do so voluntarily. If it is clear that they want to cancel, no problem exists. Legally, the separation agreement goes out of existence. The problem arises when the parties say nothing about the separation agreement after they reconcile and resume cohabitation. Sometime thereafter the parties separate again, and one of them tries to enforce the separation agreement, while the other argues that it no longer exists. Courts handle such cases in different ways:

- The reconciliation will cancel the alimony or spousal-support terms of the separation agreement, but will not cancel the property-division terms.
- The reconciliation will cancel the **executory** (unperformed) terms of the separation agreement, but will not cancel the terms that have already been performed.

executory
Unperformed as yet.

The case is somewhat more complicated if a divorce judgment exists that orders the parties to pay alimony or to divide the marital property. The parties cannot cancel a court judgment simply by reconciling and, in effect, ignoring the judgment. They must go back to court and petition for changes in the judgment that reflect their resumed relationship.

Reconciliation usually means the full and unconditional resumption of the marital relationship; occasional or casual contact will not suffice. The intent must be to abandon the separation agreement and to resume the marital relationship permanently.

☑ INTERVIEWING AND INVESTIGATION CHECKLIST

Have the Parties Reconciled?

LEGAL INTERVIEWING QUESTIONS

1. On what date did you both sign the separation agreement?

2. When did you stop living together?

3. Where did you both live when you were separated?

4. Was the separation bitter? Describe the circumstances of the separation.

5. After you signed the separation agreement, when did the two of you have your first contact? Describe the circumstances.

6. Have the two of you had sexual relations with each other since the separation agreement was signed? How often?

7. Did you ever discuss getting back together again? If so, describe the circumstances (e.g., who initiated the discussion, was there any reluctance)?

8. Did you move in together? If so, where? Did one of you give up a house or apartment in order to live together?

9. During this period, did the two of you abide by the terms of the separation agreement? If so, which parts or clauses? Which parts of the agreement did you ignore after you got together again?

10. Did you discuss what to do with the separation agreement?

11. Did the two of you assume that the separation agreement was no longer effective?

12. After you came together again, did either of you continue abiding by any of the terms of the separation agreement?

13. Did either of you give back whatever he or she received under the terms of the separation agreement?

14. When you resumed the relationship, did you feel that the reunion was going to be permanent? What do you think your spouse felt about it?

15. Did either of you attach any conditions to resuming the relationship?

16. What have the two of you done since you came together again to indicate that you both considered each other to be husband and wife (e.g., both sign joint tax returns, make joint purchases, spend considerable time together in public).

17. Do you have a reconciliation agreement? If so, what are its terms?

18. Have you separated again? If so, describe the circumstances of the most recent separation.

POSSIBLE INVESTIGATION TASKS

- Interview people who are well acquainted with the parties to find out what they know about the reconciliation.

- Obtain any documents executed after the separation agreement was signed that may indicate the extent to which the parties did things together during this time (e.g., rent receipts with both of their names on them, opening or continuing joint checking or savings accounts).

The reconciliation can be relatively spontaneous or it can be negotiated. If the latter, the parties may want to formalize the terms of their revived relationship in a written agreement. If they do so, the agreement is an example of a postnuptial agreement. (See Exhibit 4-1 in Chapter 4.)

ASSIGNMENT 8.11

Tom and Mary execute a separation agreement on February 17, 2008, in which they mutually release all rights (dower, curtesy, elective share, etc.) in each other's estate. They ceased living together on February 2, 2008. On March 13, 2008, Tom moves out of the city. On the next day, he makes a long distance call to Mary in which he says, "This is ridiculous. Why don't you come live with me? You know I still love you." Mary answers, "I guess you're right, but if we are going to live together again, I want you to come back here." Tom then says, "I'm sure we can work that out." They agree to meet the next week to discuss it further. Before they meet, Tom dies. Tom's will makes no provision for Mary. Mary now seeks an elective share of his estate, electing against his will. What result? At the time of Tom's death, he was still married to Mary. (See General Instructions for the Legal-Analysis Assignment in Appendix A.)

COMPUTER HELP

Computer companies have designed software to assist the law office in managing the large volume of data involved in the negotiation of a separation agreement. For example, Exhibit 8-6 presents a screen shot from software that enters data for the negotiation of property division. For more on the use of computers in a family-law practice, see Appendix B.

EXHIBIT 8-6 Software Used for Data Entry in a Property-Division Negotiation (Divorce of Lisa and Michael)

	Marital Equity Totals			Marital plus Separate Equity (Net Worth)	
Lisa's	Michael's		Lisa's	Michael's	
$86,263 (48.41%)	$91,928 (51.59%)		$86,263 (46.87%)	$97,782 (53.13%)	

	Who keeps? (for personal items)	Lisa % of Marital	Lisa Amount of Marital	Lisa Amount of Total	Michael % of Marital	Michael Amount of Marital	Michael Amount of Total
Securities and Real Estate:							
Joint Acct 23876		39	2,810	2,810	61	4,394	4,394
Stock fund 19-04		0	0	5,692	100	0	0
Personal Items:							
Lisa's Car	Lisa		7,200	7,200		0	0
Michael's car	Michael		0	0		11,300	11,300
Residences:							
Main home		50	75,785	75,785	50	75,786	75,786
IRAs and 401(k)s:							
Michael's IRA 72		0	0	0	100	6,140	6,302

DEBT:						
	Who will Pay This Debt?	Lisa Marital	Michael Marital	Lisa Separate	Michael Separate	
Debt:						
BigBank VISA	Lisa	5,224	0	0	0	

EXAMPLE OF A SEPARATION AGREEMENT

Exhibit 8-7 presents an example of a separation agreement with margin commentary on several of its major clauses.

EXHIBIT 8-7 Example of a Separation Agreement

(For some of the clauses, alternatives are presented to demonstrate additional drafting options for different facts.)

Separation Agreement

1. **Introduction.** Agreement between _____, residing at *[address] (Husband)*, and _____, residing at *[address] (Wife)*, dated _____ __, 20___, made in County of _____, State of _____.

2. **Date of Marriage.** _____ and _____ were married in the City of _____, State of _____ on _____ __, 20___.

3. **Children.** There are ___ children of the marriage: *[list names and birth dates of the children]*. They are the only issue of the marriage.

4. **Reason for Separation Agreement.** The parties are now living apart because of irreconcilable differences between them. They intend to continue living apart. It is the parties' intention to enter into and abide by this Agreement, which determines the financial, property, child custody, and visitation rights and obligations, and other rights and obligations, which arise out of their relationship.

5. **Parties Represented by Attorneys.** Each of the parties has retained counsel. Husband is represented by _____, with offices at _____, and Wife is represented by _____, with offices at _____. The parties have been advised of their legal rights and obligations as well as the terms and legal effect of this Agreement by their own counsel. Both parties agree that this Agreement is fair, equitable, just, and reasonable, and fully accept its terms and conditions.

   [Alternative clause 5]

   5. **Representation by Attorneys.** Wife was represented by _____, whose address is _____. Husband acknowledges that he was advised by Wife's attorney that he should seek independent counsel and that he has refused to do so, it being his belief that he can represent himself properly. Wife has been advised by her attorney of her legal rights and obligations as well as the terms and legal effect of this Agreement. Both parties agree that this Agreement is fair, equitable, just, and reasonable, and fully accept its terms and conditions.

6. **Parties May Live and Work As If They Were Single.** The parties will live separate and apart. Each will be free from the other's interference and control as if he or she were single and unmarried. Each may reside where he or she desires. Each may engage in any business, profession, or employment that he or she chooses.

7. **Separate Property of Each Party.** Each party owns the real and personal property that is now in his or her possession or is in his or her name alone, regardless of when acquired, free of any claim of the other. Such property shall be the separate property of each spouse. (A list of this separate property is attached to this agreement as Attachment #1.) However, any personal belongings or clothing of either party that is in the other's possession will be returned as quickly as possible.

   [Alternative clause 7]

   7. **Ownership of Real and Personal Property.** Each party owns the real and personal property that is now in his or her possession or in his or her name, regardless of when acquired, free of any claim of the other. However, any personal belongings or clothing of either party that is in the other's possession will be returned as quickly as possible. The parties presently lease premises is at *[address]*. The lease is in both of their names and they are jointly and severally responsible for the rent thereon. (A copy of the lease is attached to this agreement as Attachment #2.) Husband shall be solely responsible for, and shall hold Wife harmless from, all rent payments on the lease and, should the property be converted to condominium or cooperative ownership, shall have the sole right to exercise the option to purchase the property.

Margin commentary:

- *The early clauses of the agreement state its purpose and identify all family members involved.*

- *Clause 4 makes clear that the parties have already separated and intend to remain so. This helps counter an argument that the separation agreement is conducive to divorce.*

- *Clause 5 says that each party has his or her own counsel. It may be, however, that one party is paying the legal fees of the other party.*

- *Clause 6 on interference and control is a non-molestation clause.*

- *Clause 7 indicates the property that will not be divided. Note that the marital home is treated separately in clause 24. Clause 7 refers to an attachment to this agreement containing a list of the property that will not be divided. Other attachments are referred to elsewhere in the agreement.*

8. **Payment of and Liability for Debts.** The parties' debts are listed in Attachment #3. Husband will pay these debts. Debts incurred by either of the parties after the date of this Agreement will not be the other party's responsibility.

9. **Mutual Release of Claims.** The parties mutually release and discharge each other and each other's heirs, executors, administrators and assigns from any and all causes of action and claims that either now has against the other, by reason of their relationship as husband and wife or for any other reason, except for any cause of action or claim arising out of this Agreement or for an absolute divorce.

10. **Release of Rights in Each Other's Estates.** Neither party has any right to share in the estate of the other or to be appointed Executor or Administrator of the other's estate. This is a mutual waiver of each party's rights to elect to receive his or her statutory [elective] share of the other's estate.

11. **Execution of Additional Documents.** Each party will sign and deliver to the other any additional writing or document that is necessary to enforce or carry out the purposes of this Agreement.

12. **Custody of the Children.** Wife will have sole physical and sole legal custody of the parties' children during their minority, except as provided elsewhere in this Agreement.

13. **Right to Visit Children.** Husband may visit the parties' children subject to the conditions that follow.

    a. **Place of Visitation.** Visitation will take place away from Wife's residence.

    b. **Pick Up and Return of Children—Regular Meals During Visitation.** Husband will pick up the children at Wife's residence and will provide the children with regular meals during the visitation. Husband will return the children to Wife's residence upon the completion of visitation.

    c. **Limitation of Visitation.** Visitation is limited to weekends, commencing at _____ A.M. on Saturday and terminating at _____ P.M. on Sunday.

    d. **Each Child to Be Visited at the Same Time.** All rights of visitation, including vacation visitation rights, will be exercised with both children at the same time unless unusual circumstances (such as one child's illness or absence) intervene.

    e. **Summer and Vacation Visitation Rights.** In addition to other visitation rights, Husband has the right to visit with the children for _____ consecutive weeks during the children's summer vacation, provided Husband is also on vacation and provides continuous personal supervision of the children. Husband is not to exercise this right unless he gives Wife reasonable notice and provided it does not interfere with the children's other activities during this period.

    f. **Non-Interference with Children's Education and Religious Activities.** No visitation is permitted if it will interfere with the children's education or religious activities or adversely affect the children's health or general welfare.

    g. **Notification of Illness or Accident.** Each party will promptly notify the other of any illness, accident, or other incident affecting one or both of the children.

    h. **Notice of Intent Not to Visit.** Husband will notify Wife if he does not intend to exercise visitation rights or will be late for a visitation. The purpose of advance notification is to prevent disappointing the children.

    i. **Nothing to Estrange Children.** Neither party will do anything to estrange the children from the other party.

    j. **Names of Children.** The children are to continue to be known by their present given and family names even if either parent remarries.

    k. **Use of the Term Father or Mother.** The parties will not permit the children to call anyone "Father" or "Mother" other than the parties to this Agreement.

    l. **Right to Visit Confined Child or Children.** If a child is confined because of serious illness or injury, the party with whom the child is confined will allow the other to visit the child at reasonable times.

    m. **Neither Child to be Removed from the State.** Neither child will be taken outside of the State of _____ by either party without the other party's prior written consent.

• *Clause 10 gives up (releases) the right of election against the will.*

• *Clause 12 gives the Wife the right to make all major decisions on the raising of the children. Other clauses contain some restrictions: Clause 13m (moving out of state). Clauses 13g and 18 (right to notice and consultation on medical and dental treatment). Clause 19 (higher education costs).*

• *For additional and more comprehensive visitation schedules, see Exhibits 9-4 and 9-5 in Chapter 9.*

• *Clause 13i, as it pertains to children, is sometimes called the nonalienation-of-affections clause.*

(continued)

EXHIBIT 8-7 *(continued)*

14. **Support and Maintenance of Spouse—Fixed Sum.** Husband will pay Wife for her support and maintenance the sum of $ _____ each month, starting _____, 20___ and continuing on the _____ day of each month, thereafter.

[Alternative A for clause 14]

> 14. **Support and Maintenance of Spouse—Fixed Annual Amount Subject to Increase Based on Taxable Income.** Husband will pay Wife for her support and maintenance the sum of $ _____ per year in equal quarterly installments starting on _____ ___, 20 ___. If Husband's taxable income as shown on his federal income tax return exceeds $ _____ in any calendar year, then the payment to Wife for the next calendar year will be ___ percent of the taxable income instead of the sum originally provided. Husband will deliver to Wife a true and complete copy of his tax return for the prior calendar year on or before _____ each year.

[Alternative B for clause 14]

> 14. **Support and Maintenance of Spouse—Amount Determined by Gross Income— Establishment of Floors and Ceilings.** Husband will pay Wife for her support and maintenance the sum of $ _____ each year in monthly installments starting _____ ___ , 20 ___. Husband will pay Wife for additional support and maintenance a sum equal to ___ percent of his adjusted gross income as shown on his federal income tax return for the previous calendar year, no later than _____ of each year. In no event will the total yearly payment be less than $ _____ or more than $ _____ .

[Alternative C for clause 14]

> 14. **Support and Maintenance of Spouse—Lump Sum Paid Over Fixed Number of Years.** In full and final settlement of Husband's obligation to provide support and maintenance to Wife, Husband will pay Wife the sum of $ _____, in ____ equal annual installments, on the _____ day of __ in each year, starting _____ ___, 20 ___ and ending on _____ ___, 20 ___.

[Alternative D for clause 14]

> 14. **Support and Maintenance of Spouse—Three Fixed Payments Over First Three Years.** Husband shall pay Wife the sum of $ _____ for her support and maintenance. The said $ _____ shall be paid in three equal annual installments of $ _____ each on the _____ day of _____ in each year commencing with _____ ___, 20 ___. Upon the payment of the last of such installments, Husband shall have no further obligation to support Wife. Should Husband or Wife die before the last of the aforesaid installments has been made, payment thereof shall cease. Wife shall have no claim upon Husband's estate for any unpaid installments if Husband dies before Wife. If Wife dies before Husband, Wife's executors, administrators, or heirs shall have no claim upon Husband for any unpaid installments. Should Wife remarry before the last of the aforesaid installments has been made, payment thereof shall cease and Wife shall have no claim upon Husband for the unpaid installments.

[Alternative E for clause 14]

> 14. **Support and Maintenance of Spouse—Increasing Fixed Installments Over Five Years.** Husband shall pay Wife the following sums for her support and maintenance: (a) The sum of $ _____ in the first calendar year in which this agreement is in force; (b) the sum of $ _____ in the second calendar year; (c) the sum of $ _____ in the third calendar year; and (d) the sum of $ _____ annually in each of the fourth and fifth calendar years. Each payment shall be made on the _____ day of _____ in each year commencing with _____, 20 ___. It is the parties' intention that the payment made in the first calendar year shall not exceed the average of the payments made in the second and third calendar years by more than $15,000 and that the payment made in the second calendar year shall not exceed the payment made in the

Marginal notes (right column):

- *Clause 14 provides for permanent alimony (with a reduction provided for in clause 15). Permanent alimony is relatively rare. See Alternatives A-E for clause 14.*

- *Alternative A for clause 14 also provides for permanent alimony but with fluctuating payments based on the Husband's taxable income.*

- *Lump-sum alimony payable in installments may trigger tax rules on improper attempts to disguise a property division or child support as alimony in order for the payor to deduct the alimony payments. See Chapter 11 for a discussion of the recapture rule.*

- *Alternative E for clause 14 seeks to avoid front loading that will trigger the recapture rule discussed in Chapter 11. The aim of Alternative E is to preserve the payor's deduction for alimony payments.*

third calendar year by more than $15,000. If either or both of these conditions are not met, an adjustment shall be made in the third calendar year by reducing the payment then due accordingly. Upon the payment of the last of such installments, Husband shall have no further obligation to support Wife. Should Husband or Wife die before the last of the aforesaid installments has been made, payment thereof shall cease. Wife shall have no claim upon Husband's estate for any unpaid installments if Husband dies before Wife. If Wife dies before Husband, Wife's executors, administrators, or heirs shall have no claim upon Husband for any unpaid installments. Should Wife remarry before the last of the aforesaid installments has been made, payment thereof shall cease and Wife shall have no claim upon Husband for the unpaid installments.

15. **Reduction of Spouse's Support and Maintenance Payments.** The amount to be paid for Wife's support and maintenance has been set at $ _____ annually because Wife is not presently employed and has no income or assets other than those described in this Agreement. Should Wife become employed at an annual salary in excess of $ _____ or receive annual income in excess of $ _____, Husband's obligation to pay support and maintenance will be reduced by ___ percent of Wife's excess annual income.

16. **Termination of Support and Maintenance Payments.** Payments for Wife's support and maintenance will terminate upon the occurrence of any of the following events:

    a. **Death.** The death of either party.

    b. **Remarriage.** Wife's remarriage even if such marriage is annulled or otherwise terminated.

    c. **Meretricious Relationship.** The establishment by Wife of a relationship with a third party in which they hold themselves out to be married (even if they are not) or in which they maintain a single abode and openly and notoriously live together in the manner of a husband and wife (even if they are not married).

17. **Child Support.** Husband will pay to Wife in addition to the payments provided for Wife's support and maintenance, the sum of $ _____ annually, per child, for the support and maintenance of each child of the marriage. The payments are to be made in equal monthly installments on the _____ day of each month, starting _____ __, 20___. Wife agrees that so long as Husband makes the foregoing payments on a timely basis, he will be entitled to the income tax exemption for dependents for each of the children.

    [Alternative clause 17]

    17. **Child Support and Release of Tax Exemption.** Husband will pay to Wife, in addition to the payments provided for Wife's support and maintenance, the sum of $ _____ annually, per child, for the support and maintenance of each child of the marriage. The payments are to be made in equal installments on the _____ __ day of each month, starting _____, 20___. Wife hereby releases to Husband all rights that Wife has in fact and in law to claim the parties' minor children as dependents for federal and local income tax purposes. In furtherance of Husband's right to claim the parties' minor children as dependents for federal and local income tax purposes, Wife will execute and acknowledge a release of Wife's right thereto so that the children may be claimed by Husband as dependents. Such release shall be made on Internal Revenue Service Form 8332 or such other form that complies with the applicable sections of the Internal Revenue Code then in effect and any regulations adopted in furtherance thereof. Husband may demand delivery of any such release at any time in or following the taxable year to which such release applies, provided all payments due from Husband to Wife pursuant to this Agreement and any additions or amendments thereto or pursuant to any other agreements between the parties, regardless of when executed, are current. If any such payments are in arrears, Wife shall not be obligated to deliver such release to Husband until all such payments have been made and Husband's obligations to Wife are current.

18. **Children's Medical and Dental Expenses.** The payments by Husband to Wife for the children's support and maintenance do not include the cost of the children's medical and dental care. These are Husband's obligations and Wife will cause all bills from physicians, dentists, and other health care professionals and facilities to be sent to Husband. Wife will notify and consult with Husband

- *Clause 16b seeks to prevent a revival of alimony if the wife's second marriage is annulled or otherwise terminated. For more on revival, see Chapter 6.*

- *As we will see in Chapter 10, all states have mandatory guidelines on the minimum amount of child support that parents must provide. Parents can agree to provide support above the minimum, but not below the minimum.*

- *See clause 12 above on sole legal custody, which includes the right to make final decisions on medical and dental treatment.*

(continued)

EXHIBIT 8-7 *(continued)*

before either child enters into elective medical or dental treatment, such as plastic surgery or orthodontic treatment.

[Alternative clause 18]

18. **Special Medical and Dental Needs of Children.** The payments by Husband to Wife for the children's support and maintenance includes medical and dental expenses of $ _____ per year for each child. If the expenses of either child's medical and dental care that is not reimbursed by insurance exceeds that sum in any year, Husband will pay the excess either directly to the person or facility providing the care or to Wife upon proper proof of payment of the expense by her. Wife will notify and consult with Husband before either child enters into elective medical or dental treatment regardless of the cost of such treatment.

19. **Costs of Children's Education.** The payments by Husband to Wife for the children's support do not include tuition payments to private schools or to colleges, universities, professional schools, or trade schools. Tuition payments of this nature will be made by Husband, provided Wife consults with Husband before a child enrolls or is enrolled in an educational institution and the parties mutually agree upon the advisability of the child's attendance at such institution.

20. **Termination of Child Support.** Payments for the support of any child of the marriage will terminate upon the occurrence of any of the following events:

    a. **Reaching Majority.** The child reaches the age of _____ years, provided the child is not in full-time attendance in a college, graduate school, or professional or trade school.

    b. **Completion of Education.** The child completes his or her college education, including graduate or professional school, or completes his or her trade school course.

    c. **Marriage.** The child marries, even though the marriage is later annulled or terminated.

    d. **Permanent Residence.** The child establishes a permanent residence away from Wife's residence, provided the residence was not established to attend school or because of active military service.

    e. **Death.** The child or Husband dies.

    f. **Full-Time Employment.** The child obtains full-time employment, provided such employment is not engaged in only during school vacations or summer recesses. If the full-time employment terminates before the child reaches the age of _____ years, child support payments will resume.

21. **Method of Payment of Support and Maintenance.** All payments of support and maintenance for the spouse and children of the marriage will be by cash, money order, bank check, or certified check. When payment is made by mail, the envelope containing the payment will be posted at least ____ days prior to the date on which the payment is due, addressed to Wife at the address given above or such other address as she may advise Husband of, in writing, from time to time.

22. **Adequacy of Support and Maintenance Payments.** Wife acknowledges that the support and maintenance payments provided for her and those provided for the children are adequate and in keeping with the living standards maintained by the parties immediately prior to the date of this Agreement.

23. **Reduction of Support and Maintenance Payments Because of Changes in Internal Revenue Code.** Wife acknowledges that the payments Husband is to make for Wife's support and maintenance are based on the assumption that they will be included in Wife's taxable income and will be deductible for income tax purposes by Husband. If, because of changes in the federal income tax laws, all or any part of the aforesaid payments is no longer deductible by Husband, the parties will attempt to adjust the payments on a fair and equitable basis. If the parties are unable to agree upon an adjustment, the controversy shall be determined by arbitration before the American Arbitration Association in accordance with its rules then obtaining.

24. **Transfer of Marital Residence to Wife.** The parties presently own as tenants by the entirety the real property at *[insert street address]*, Town of _____, State of _____. Husband will convey his interest in the property to Wife by quitclaim deed simultaneously with the execution of this Agreement. In addition, Husband will transfer to Wife the fixtures, furnishings, and personal property listed in Attachment #4.

• *See Chapter 14 on emancipation, which allows a child to live independent of his or her parent or guardian.*

• *Arbitration is one of the methods of alternative dispute resolution (ADR).*

[Alternative clause 24]

24. **Disposition of Marital Residence.** The parties presently own as tenants by the entirety the real property at *[insert street address]*, Town of _____, State of _____. Wife will have the exclusive use and occupancy of these premises until the occurrence of any of the following events:

    a. **Vacating Premises.** Wife leaves the premises and sets up a permanent abode elsewhere.

    b. **Remarriage.** Wife remarries even though the subsequent marriage is annulled or terminated.

    c. **Meretricious Relationship.** Wife establishes a relationship with a third party in which they hold themselves out to be married (even if they are not) or in which they maintain a single abode and openly and notoriously live together in the manner of a husband and wife (even if they are not married).

    d. **Emancipation of Children.** All the children of the marriage are emancipated.

    Husband will not institute any action for partition of the premises or any other litigation that would or could terminate Wife's occupancy. Upon termination of Wife's occupancy in accordance with the provisions of this Clause, the parties will sell the premises upon the best terms possible. The proceeds of the sale will be distributed in the following order:

    (1) Payment of the expenses and costs of the sale, including attorney fees and broker's commissions;

    (2) Repayment to Husband for carrying charges (including principal and interest), taxes, insurance, and repairs during Wife's occupancy;

    (3) $ _____ to Husband as a repayment of his contribution to the parties' equity in the property;

    (4) The balance divided equally between the parties.

- *See Chapter 14 on emancipation—living independent of one's parent or guardian.*

25. **Maintenance of Life Insurance.** Attachment #5 lists the life insurance policies Husband will maintain in full force and effect insuring his life. Husband will maintain Wife as beneficiary of these policies so long as he is obligated to make support and maintenance payment to Wife. The children of the marriage will be maintained as contingent beneficiaries, or prime beneficiaries if Wife is removed as prime beneficiary, of the policies with equal interest so long as Husband is obligated to make payments for any of the children's support. Husband will have possession of the policies and will deliver to Wife proof of timely payment of all premiums when made. Husband represents that he has not pledged, hypothecated, or encumbered any of the policies and will do nothing to impair their full value.

26. **Income Tax Returns.** The parties will sign and file joint federal, state, and local income tax returns for the year in which this agreement is executed. Any tax due will be paid by Husband and any refund will be Husband's sole property. Husband agrees to hold Wife harmless from any losses suffered as a result of additional assessments of tax, fines, or penalties arising out of audits of any income tax return signed jointly by both parties at any time.

- *Clause 26 protects the wife by a hold-harmless clause.*

27. **Right to Sue for Divorce—Incorporation of Separation Agreement in Divorce Decree.** Neither party will be precluded from obtaining a divorce. If a divorce action is brought by either party, this Agreement may be offered into evidence and may be incorporated in any decree or judgment, but this Agreement will survive and will not be merged into such decree or judgment.

- *Under clause 27, the parties wish the separation agreement to be incorporated but not merged into the divorce judgment. The parties want the agreement to survive as a separate contract.*

28. **Modification of Agreement—Effect of Waiver.** This Agreement or any part of it cannot be amended or modified except by an agreement in writing, executed with the same formality as this Agreement. Any waiver by either party of a breach of any provision of this Agreement will not prevent that party from enforcing the provision thereafter. The failure of either party to insist upon the strict performance by the other party will not be construed as a future waiver or relinquishment of any such term or provision.

29. **Illegality or Invalidity of Part of Agreement.** If any provision of this Agreement is held to be illegal or invalid, such holding will not affect the other provisions, all of which will continue in full force and effect.

- *Clause 29 is a severability clause. It states that if one clause is illegal or invalid, the other clauses will not be affected.*

30. **Governing Law.** This Agreement will be governed and interpreted in accordance with the laws of the State of _____.

(continued)

EXHIBIT 8-7   *(continued)*

31. **Entire Understanding.** This Agreement constitutes the parties' entire understanding. They acknowledge that there have not been and are not now any representations, warranties, covenants, or understandings other than those expressly provided in this Agreement. This Agreement is binding upon the parties' heirs, assigns, executors, and administrators.

32. **Filing of Agreement with Public Official.** This Agreement or a Memorandum of this Agreement may be filed by either party with the Clerk of _____, County of _____, State of _____.

    IN WITNESS WHEREOF, the parties have set their hands and seals this _____ day of _____, 20___.

    _____ Wife

    _____ Husband

[Acknowledgment]

Attachments (not included here)
Attachment #1. List of personal and real property that is the separate property of each spouse (see clause 7).
Attachment #2. Copy of lease (see alternative clause 7).
Attachment #3. List of debts (see clause 8).
Attachment #4. List of fixtures, furnishings, and personal property in marital residence they own as tenants by the entirety (see clause 24).
Attachment #5. List of life insurance policies to be kept in force (see clause 25).

Reprinted from Vincent DiLorenzo and Clifford Ennico, *Basic Legal Transactions*, § 43:32. Separation Agreement (West Group, November 2010) with permission of Thomson Reuters.

ASSIGNMENT 8.12

Two members of the class will role-play in front of the rest of the class a negotiation session involving a husband and wife who want to enter a separation agreement. They have two children, ages two and three. The role-players can make up the facts as they go along, e.g., names of the parties, addresses, kinds of assets involved. Use the checklist at the beginning of this chapter as an overview of the topics to be negotiated. In the negotiation session, the role-players should not act hostile toward each other. They should be courteous but anxious to protect their own rights. Finally, they should not leave any matters unresolved—everything should result in some form of agreement through the process of bargaining and negotiation. After the negotiators have concluded the negotiation, the rest of the class can ask questions of the negotiators. The questions should ask for clarification on what has been negotiated and should ask the negotiators to negotiate topics that they have not yet covered.

Each member of the class (including the two role-players) will draft a separation agreement that is based on the facts negotiated in the role-playing session. The agreement should conform to the standards for an effective separation agreement outlined in Exhibit 8-1. (See General Instructions for the Agreement-Drafting Assignment in Appendix A.)

■ PARALEGAL ROLES

- For an overview of paralegal roles in family-law cases, see Exhibits 1-3 and 1-4 in Chapter 1.
- For all financial issues covered in Chapter 8, a paralegal may be asked to help collect documents and facts outlined in:
  - the checklist in Exhibit 3-1 of Chapter 3
  - the interrogatories in Appendix C

- The interviewing and investigation checklist in Chapter 8 also covers fact-finding roles of paralegals.
- Paralegals often have important roles in the separation-agreement phase of a divorce case. According to one paralegal:

  The identification and evaluation of a marital estate is often more complex than one might think. One of my favorite things to do is review documentation provided by our client and received through discovery. I do the following:

- Prepare a detailed chart of the parties' assets and debts.
- Note any challenges such as claims that certain assets or debts are premarital or the non-marital property of one party.
- Note any disagreement in the valuation of certain marital assets such as real property, collections, and antiques.
- Determine the marital portion of investment and retirement accounts that the parties owned prior to the marriage.
- Identify any deficiencies in documentation needed to present evidence at trial.[38]

- Other Duties
  - Compile factual data to support client's need for rehabilitative alimony.
  - Compile factual data to support client's petition for a modification of alimony.
  - Identify lists of appraisers for the valuation of marital/community property.
  - Collect documents and relevant data needed by the appraisers for their valuation.
  - Maintain and update the property list.
  - Categorize property into separate property and marital/community property.
  - Categorize debts as separate or marital/community.
  - Organize documents and fact sheets to be used by attorney in negotiating the separation agreement.
  - Prepare draft of the separation agreement.

■ CHECK THE CITE

Under the separation agreement of Joseph and Ida Richardson, Joseph was obligated to pay alimony (maintenance) to Ida. When Ida hired someone to murder Joseph, he filed a motion in court to terminate his alimony obligation. Why did the court deny his motion? See *Richardson v. Richardson*, 218 S.W.3d 426 (Mo. 2007). To read the opinion online: (1) Run this

search in Google's general search engine: "Richardson v. Richardson" "No. SC 87641." (2) Run a citation search ("218 S.W.3d 426") in the Legal documents database of Google Scholar (scholar.google.com).

■ PROJECT

Parties contemplating or undergoing divorce might hire a large variety of experts and professionals (in addition to the attorneys who represent them). In Google, Bing, or Yahoo, run the following search: aa expert divorce (substitute the name of your state for aa in the search, e.g., Georgia expert divorce). Identify as many different kinds of such experts and professionals (other than attorneys) as you can. Give an example of each category of professional or expert, his or her Internet address, the services offered in divorce cases, and, if available, the cost for his or her services.

■ ETHICS IN A FAMILY LAW PRACTICE

You are a paralegal working at the law office of James & James. The law firm represents the husband in a divorce action. One of the largest assets in the marriage is the husband's pension. The wife's attorney, however, fails to inquire into the pension because this attorney mistakenly believes that pensions are not divisible as marital property. Since the wife's attorney does not mention it, the James attorney is silent about the pension. Consequently, the final divorce decree does not divide the pension. Any ethical problems?

■ WRITING SAMPLE

Draft a separation agreement. You can make up the names of the divorcing parties and the facts of their marriage so long as the facts meet the following general guidelines: it was a long-term marriage; the ex-wife will need alimony; there are two small children (the ex-wife will have sole legal and physical custody with visitation rights to the ex-husband); both parties brought some separate property into the marriage; the parties acquired a house together (which has a mortgage); etc. Fill in the facts to cover the specifics. Use the checklists at the beginning of the chapter as a guide for other matters that should be covered in the clauses of the separation agreement. (See General Instructions for the Writing Sample in Appendix A.)

SUMMARY

A separation agreement is a contract by married persons who have separated (or who are about to separate) that can cover support, custody, property division, and other terms of their separation and divorce. A major goal of the law office is to prepare an effective separation agreement that will avoid litigation. The first step is the

collection of extensive information, particularly financial information pertaining to everyone involved. Elaborate checklists can be helpful in this effort. Spouses must have the legal capacity to enter a separation agreement. A court can refuse to enforce an unconscionable agreement or one that is the product of overreaching, but if there has been adequate financial disclosure, adequate opportunity to consult with independent advisers, no fraud, and no duress, the parties will have to live with the bargain they made so long as neither party is about to become a public charge.

Alimony is money or other property paid in fulfillment of a duty to support one's spouse (or ex-spouse) after a legal separation, a divorce, or in some states, an annulment. Property division is the allocation and distribution of property between spouses (or ex-spouses) after a legal separation or divorce. The law office needs to be aware of the alimony and property-division issues in a number of areas (e.g., the effect of bankruptcy, the effect of remarriage and death, the effect of cohabitation, the availability of enforcement by contempt, the power of the court to modify terms, and federal tax treatment). Unfortunately alimony and property division are not always easy to distinguish. The distinction is based on the intent of the parties as evidenced by the labels they used, whether they used contingencies, the method of payment, and the kind of property transferred.

Alimony is disfavored. The trend is to have short-term or no alimony in separation agreements and court awards unless (1) there is little property to divide, (2) there is a significant disparity between the wealth of the parties, (3) the more needy party's ability to earn a living after the separation is hampered by a lack of job skills, age, and/or by a need to care for children, and (4) the marriage had lasted more than a year. When alimony is awarded, the primary factors courts consider are the financial resources of the parties, the time needed to become self-sufficient, the length of the marriage, the age and physical condition of the payee, and the responsibility to care for others, particularly young children. States differ on whether marital fault is a factor in the award of alimony.

Rehabilitative alimony is support payments to an ex-spouse for a limited time to allow him or her to return to financial self-sufficiency through employment or job training. Reimbursement alimony repays a spouse who worked or made other financial contributions during the marriage so that the other spouse could obtain training or otherwise enhance his or her future earning capacity.

In most states, courts have the power to modify an alimony award. They will do so, for example, if the payor becomes ill and is earning substantially less than when the award was made. An example of when they will not do so is when the payor seeks to retire or change to a lower paying job primarily as a strategy to avoid the original alimony award.

Methods of enforcing an alimony award include execution, garnishment, fines, civil contempt (if incorporation and merger has occurred), criminal contempt, and the enforcement tools of IV-D agencies (if the custodial parent owed alimony is living with a child who is owed child support). Support debts cannot be discharged in bankruptcy. It might be possible to discharge a property-division debt in a chapter 13 bankruptcy. Necessaries provides a seldom-used method for spouse (and child) to obtain support by going to merchants, making purchases of necessaries, and charging them to the credit of the other spouse/parent.

The five stages of property division are locating assets, classifying them, determining their value, tax-effecting them, and distributing them between the spouses. There are many different ways to classify property: real property, personal property, tangible property, intangible property, property received as a gift (or as a bequest, as a devise, or by intestate succession), solely owned property, concurrently owned property, separate property, marital property, common-law property, community property, quasi-community property, transmuted property, appreciated property, commingled property, etc. In most states, the governing law of property division is equitable distribution based on factors such as the length of the marriage and the contribution each made to the acquisition of the property. In most states, marital fault (who caused the breakup of the marriage) is not relevant to property division, but economic fault (dissipation) is. Special problems can exist in the division of a pension, license, business, and goodwill. In most states, only marital/community property is divided. In some states, however, separate property can be divided as well.

Other matters that should be covered in separation agreements are debts, taxes, wills, insurance, legal expenses, nonmolestation, and alternative dispute resolution (arbitration, mediation, and Med-Arb). Parties sometimes try to rescind or modify the separation agreement because of mutual mistake. If the parties reconcile, some states will cancel the executory terms of the separation agreement. If the divorce judgment contained court orders, the reconciled parties may have to return to court to have the orders adjusted or cancelled.

KEY TERMS

separation agreement
postnuptial agreement
legal separation
intestate succession
DOS
outstanding
instrument
financial statement

payor
emancipated
physical custody
legal custody
noncustodial parent (NCP)
custodial parent (CP)
hold harmless
executed

alternative dispute resolution (ADR)
conducive to divorce
public policy
bigamy
collusion
migratory divorce
foreign divorce

capacity
at common law
postnuptial agreement
arm's length
fiduciary relationship
fraud
material
duress
aggrieved
unconscionable
overreaching
public charge
legal malpractice
consideration
cohabitation
alimony
property division
obligor
payee
obligee
debtor
transferor
transferee
interest
contingent
lump-sum payment
periodic payments
alimony in gross
family expense act
alimony pendente lite
bridge-the-gap alimony
caregiver alimony
durational alimony
incapacity alimony
lump-sum alimony
permanent alimony
rehabilitative alimony
reimbursement alimony
restitutional alimony
temporary alimony
traditional alimony
transitional alimony
separate maintenance
palimony
Uniform Marriage and Divorce Act
   (UMDA)
premarital agreement

arrears
escrow
surety bond
annuity
annuitant
trust
trustee
alimony trust
personal jurisdiction
continuing jurisdiction
incorporation and merger
rebuttable presumption
transsexual
execution
garnishment
civil contempt
criminal contempt
IV-D agency
Uniform Interstate Family
   Support Act (UIFSA)
discharge
nondischargeable
necessaries
spousal refusal
real property
personal property
account receivable
tangible
intangible
gift
bequest
devise
intestate succession
descent
inheritance
concurrent estate
joint tenancy
right of survivorship
operation of law
tenancy by the entirety
tenancy in common
separate property
passive income
appreciation
passive appreciation
marital property
community property

common-law property
quasi-community property
transmutation
separatizer
quitclaim
equitable distribution
dissipation
commingling
tracing
defined-benefit plan (DB)
defined-contribution plan (DC)
vested
expectancy
coverture fraction
qualified domestic relations order
   (QDRO)
alternate payee
present value
assign
restitution
unjust enrichment
implied-in-law contract
goodwill
enterprise goodwill
personal goodwill
joint and several liability
indemnify
hold harmless
tax effect
executor
elective share
dower
curtesy
issue
release
irrevocable
custodial parent (CP)
qualified medical child support order
   (QMCSO)
nonmolestation clause
reformation
arbitration
alternative dispute resolution (ADR)
mediation
Med-Arb
execute
executory

REVIEW QUESTIONS

1. What is a separation agreement?

2. What are the three objectives parties can have in a separation agreement?

3. What are some of the main ways that separation agreements are the basis of litigation in court?

4. What are the characteristics of an effective separation agreement?

5. What financial checklists are needed to prepare for the drafting of a separation agreement?

6. What other checklists can be helpful?

7. When is a separation agreement conducive to divorce?

8. What financial disclosure obligation does each spouse have when divorcing?

9. What is fraud and duress and how do they affect the separation agreement?

10. When is an agreement unconscionable?

11. What is the consideration for a separation agreement?

12. What is the effect of bankruptcy, remarriage, death, or cohabitation on alimony and property-division obligations?

13. When can civil contempt be used to enforce alimony and property-division obligations?

14. When can a court modify alimony and property-division obligations?

15. What are the tax implications of alimony and property-division payments?

16. How will a court distinguish between alimony and property-division obligations?

17. What different kinds of alimony exist?

18. What criteria will a court use when deciding if alimony should be awarded?

19. How does a court determine the amount of rehabilitative alimony to be awarded?

20. When will a court award reimbursement alimony?

21. What is the role of marital fault in the award of alimony?

22. What are some of the main options spouses should consider when including alimony in their separation agreement?

23. When does a court have power to alter alimony?

24. When will a court exercise this power?

25. How can an alimony obligation be enforced?

26. What are necessaries?

27. What is spousal refusal and Medicaid divorce?

28. What are the five steps in the process of property division?

29. What is financial infidelity?

30. What is the distinction between real and personal property?

31. What is the distinction between tangible and intangible property?

32. What are the different ways that real and personal property can be acquired?

33. What three time periods should be identified for every property that is acquired?

34. What is the distinction between sole ownership and concurrent ownership?

35. What are the main concurrent estates?

36. What are the 10 categories of separate property?

37. What is the distinction between community property and common law property?

38. What are the main cutoff dates used by states in determining when separate property is acquired?

39. What is a transmutation agreement?

40. How is property divided today in most common-law property states and in most community-property states?

41. What factors are considered in equitable distribution?

42. How does economic fault (dissipation) affect property division?

43. How is appreciation divided?

44. What is commingling and how does it affect property division?

45. How are private pensions divided?

46. How are public pensions handled upon divorce?

47. How have the courts handled degrees and licenses upon divorce?

48. How is a business divided upon divorce?

49. What categories of goodwill can and cannot be divided?

50. How are tort awards divided?

51. How are debts divided?

52. What are the ways in which tax law can affect a divorcing couple?

53. What happens to wills upon divorce?

54. What happens to an elective share upon divorce?

55. What insurance options should divorcing parties consider?

56. How are legal expenses paid?

57. What is a nonmolestation clause?

58. How does mutual mistake affect a separation agreement?

59. What role can alternative dispute resolution play in disputes after a separation agreement is entered?

60. How does reconciliation affect a separation agreement?

HELPFUL WEBSITES

Fifty State Summaries of Divorce Law
- www.divorcemag.com/articles

Alimony/Spousal Support Factors (ABA Chart)
- www.americanbar.org/groups/family_law/resources /family_law_in_the_50_states.html

Property Division (ABA Chart)

- www.americanbar.org/groups/family_law/resources/family_law_in_the_50_states.html

What Can and Cannot Be Discharged in Bankruptcy

- www.okbar.org/public/brochures/bankruptcy.htm

Institute for Divorce Financial Analysts

- www.institutedfa.com

Association of Divorce Financial Planners (ADFP)

- www.divorceandfinance.org

Asset Search

- www.assetsearchblog.com

Online-Income and Tax Calculator

- www.familylawsoftware.com/calc/budget.htm

Online-Property-Division Calculator

- www.familylawsoftware.com/calc/property_division.htm

Online-Alimony Buyout Calculator

- www.familylawsoftware.com/calc/lump_sum.htm

Sample Separation Agreements or Forms

- www.flcourts.org/gen_public/family/forms_rules/902f3.pdf
- family.findlaw.com/divorce/divorce-forms/le22_3_1.html
- www.rosen.com/divorce/divorceforms/sample-separation-agreement
- www.hampshireprobate.com/Divorce%20Info/SeparAgreewchildren.pdf
- www.3stepagreement.com/sampleagreement.shtml
- www.docstoc.com/docs/598704/Marital-Separation-and-Property-Settlement-Agreement

Google/Bing/Yahoo Searches

(on these search engines, run the following searches, substituting your state for "aa")

- "separation agreement" aa
- "postnuptial agreement" aa
- alimony aa
- palimony aa
- UIFSA aa
- QDRO aa
- pension divorce aa
- divorce mediation aa
- "marital agreement" divorce aa
- divorce adultery aa
- "property division" aa
- alimony trust aa
- "community property" divorce aa
- "common law property" divorce aa
- QMCSO aa
- divorce arbitration aa

ENDNOTES

Note: All or most of the court opinions in these endnotes can be read online. To do so, go to Google Scholar (scholar.google.com), select "Legal documents," and in the search box, enter the cite (e.g., "646 A.2d 195") or name of the case (e.g., "*Grayson v. Wofsey*") that is given in the endnote.

[1] See, for example, Financial Advantage, *Dollars of Divorce* (www.dollarsofdivorce.com).

[2] John DeWitt Gregory et al., *Understanding Family Law* 97 (3d ed. 2005).

[3] Mississippi State Bar, Family Law Section, *Consumers Guide to Divorce* 4 (1990).

[4] Liesl Schillinger, *Playing Fair at Divorce, Cheating on the Other Stuff*, N.Y. Times, Dec. 23, 2007 (www.nytimes.com/2007/12/23/fashion/23books.html).

[5] Richard Shweder, *Reader, I Divorced Her*, N.Y. Times Book Review, Apr. 4, 1999 at 9 (a review of John Taylor, *The Story of One Marriage*) (www.nytimes.com/1999/04/04/books/reader-i-divorced-her.html?src=pm).

[6] *Grayson v. Wofsey . . .*, 646 A.2d 195 (Conn. 1994).

[7] *Orr v. Orr*, 440 U.S. 268 (1979).

[8] Jennifer Levitz, *The New Art of Alimony*, The Wall Street Journal, Oct. 31, 2009 (online.wsj.com/article/SB10001424052748703399204574505700448957522.html).

[9] Robert Oliphant & Nancy Ver Steegh, *Family Law* 235 (3d ed. 2010); Harry D. Krause & David D. Meyer, *Family Law in a Nutshell* 296 (5th ed. 2007).

[10] Alexandra Harwin, *Ending the Alimony Guessing Game*, N.Y. Times, Jul. 4, 2011, at A17 (www.nytimes.com/2011/07/04/opinion/04harwin.html). Ry Rivard, *State Supreme Court Names Alimony Committee*, Charleston Daily Mail (Nov. 1, 2011) (www.dailymail.com/News/201110310164).

[11] Uniform Marriage and Divorce Act, § 308(b) (www.law.cornell.edu/uniform/vol9.html#mardv).

[12] Alexandra Harwin, supra note 10.

[13] Joanna Grossman, *Punishing Adultery in Virginia*, FindLaw (Dec. 16, 2003) (writ.news.findlaw.com/grossman/20031216.html).

[14] *Sex Change Does Not Void Alimony Pact*, Los Angeles Times (Mar. 29, 2007) (articles.latimes.com/2007/mar/29/nation/na-alimony29).

[15] Tina Moore, *Staten Island belly-dancing wife who lost alimony claim*, NYDailyNews.com (Apr. 17, 2011) (articles.nydailynews.com/2011-04-17 /local/29461319_1_belly-dancing-belly-dancing-legal-fees).

[16] Mari Schaefer, *Judge frees Pa. inmate who served record term for delinquent alimony amount*, Pittsburg Post-Gazette (Jul. 11, 2009) (www.post-gazette.com/pg/09192/983301-454.stm).

[17] *Phillips, Nizer . . . v. Rosenstiel*, 490 F.2d 509, 517 (2d Cir. 1973).

[18] Anemona Hartocollis, *Full Wallets, but Using Health Care for Poor*, N.Y. Times, Dec. 10, 2010 (www.nytimes .com/2010/12/12/nyregion/12medicaid.html).

[19] Ibid.

[20] Jenna Goudreau, *Is Your Partner Cheating on You Financially? 31% Admit Money Deception*, Forbes (Jan. 13, 2011). Jennifer Schultz, *Financial Infidelity*, N.Y. Times, Feb. 26, 2011, at B5.

[21] American Law Institute, *Principles of the Law of Family Dissolution*, 8 Duke Journal of Gender Law & Policy 1, 20 (2001).

[22] Mickey Rapkin, *Where There's Gay Marriage Comes . . . The Rise of Gay Divorce*, Details (Oct. 2011).

[23] Anemona Hartocollis, *Real Estate and Rubble: When Marriages Go Awry*, N.Y. Times, Jul. 12, 2006 (www .nytimes.com/2006/07/12/nyregion/12divorce. html?ref=anemonahartocollis).

[24] Liesl Schillinger, *Playing Fair at Divorce, Cheating on the Other Stuff*, N.Y. Times, Dec. 23, 2007. (www .nytimes.com/2007/12/23/fashion/23books.html).

[25] Associated Press, *Alone Together in Tough Times*, Los Angeles Times (Dec. 4, 2008) (articles.latimes.com/2008 /dec/04/business/fi-divorce4).

[26] *Boyd v. Boyd*, 323 N.W.2d 553, 555 (Mich. App. 1982).

[27] Lynn Asinof, *Divorcing? Attend to the Nest Egg*, Wall Street Journal, Nov. 13, 2000, at C1.

[28] Social Security Online (www.ssa.gov/gethelp1.htm) (www .benefits.gov/benefits/benefit-details/4388).

[29] 10 U.S.C § 1408 (www.law.cornell.edu/uscode/text /10/1408).

[30] List adapted from Business Valuation Research, Inc., of Seattle, Washington.

[31] Jan Gabrielson and Stuart Walzer, *Surviving Your Own Divorce*, California Lawyer 76 (Jun. 1987) (emphasis added).

[32] Salvatore Arena, *Couple Must Be Sports in Ducat Split*, Daily News (Feb. 6, 1998).

[33] Alexandra Zissu, *After the Breakup, Here Comes the Joint-Custody Pet*, N.Y. Times, Aug. 24, 1999, at B1, B4

[34] *True v. True*, 882 N.Y.S.2d 261, 264 (N.Y.A.D. 2 Dept., 2009).

[35] Peter Lattman, *Madoff Victim Seeks Divorce Do-Over*, N.Y. Times, May 31, 2011, at B1 (dealbook.nytimes.com/2011/05/30 /madoff-victim-seeks-do-over-in-divorce-deal).

[36] Ibid.

[37] *Simkin v. Blank*, 968 N.E.2d 459, 464 (N.Y. 2012).

[38] Lori Froistad, *My Specialty: Divorce Law*, 27 Paralegal Today 60 (Apr./Jun. 2010) (www.paralegaltoday.com/issue _archive/toc/toc_aj10.htm).

Child Custody

CHAPTER OUTLINE

CHAPTER OBJECTIVES

After completing this chapter, you should be able to:

- Know how child-custody disputes were handled in our early history.

- Identify the major kinds of custody.

- List the major considerations of parents when negotiating the custody terms of a separation agreement.

- Describe possible roles for a BIA, a GAL, a CASA, and a PC in child-custody cases.

- Know the main factors a court will consider when resolving a custody dispute between two biological parents.

- Know why legal preferences are disfavored.

- State the nexus test on lifestyle and morality in custody decisions.

- List the major components of an effective visitation schedule.

- Know how a court will resolve a challenge by a noncustodial parent against a move by the custodial parent out of the area.

- List the major enforcement remedies for violation of custody orders.

- Know how a court will resolve a custody dispute between a biological parent and a psychological parent.

- Understand when a court can modify its own custody order.

- Know how a court obtains jurisdiction to modify the custody order of another state.

- Identify when a court can refuse to use the custody jurisdiction that it has.

- Understand how international custody disputes are resolved.

INTRODUCTION

> Then the king said, "Bring me a sword." So they brought a sword for the king. He then gave an order: "Cut the living child in two and give half to one and half to the other." 1 *Kings* 3:24–25 (NIV)

Researchers estimate that 40 percent of children have experienced or will experience the divorce of their parents.[1] In most divorce cases, however, there is little or no dispute over who should have custody of the children. The parties often negotiate a mutually acceptable arrangement. When the parents agree on custody and visitation, they simply ask a court to approve the arrangement they devise. In the vast majority of cases, the court does so.

When there is a dispute, however, the process can be intense. In a recent case, the judge ordered parents to exchange each other's usernames and passwords for Facebook and dating sites such as eHarmony and Match.com when one of the parents suspected that there were compromising pictures and other data on the sites that were relevant to the custody dispute in the divorce. Judges, forced into the role of King Solomon, say that child custody is one of the most painful issues they face. "We are asked to play God, a role we are neither trained nor prepared for," lamented a family-law judge. Sometimes the bitterness between parents in what are called high-conflict custody battles can be extraordinary. In a Michigan case, the child tragically died in the midst of his parents' marital difficulties. This did not stop the rancor. The divorcing parents could not agree on who should control the disposition of their 13-year-old son's body. In a decision "reminiscent of Solomon," the judge ruled that if they could not agree on who should bury their son, he would order the body cremated and each given "half the ashes."[2] While not all cases are this rancorous, it does demonstrate the level of hostility that is possible. In this chapter, we will explore the spectrum of child-custody cases, from those in which the parties are in agreement to those in which their disagreement is little short of open warfare.

In our early history, child-custody disputes were rare because the wishes of the father were almost always followed. Children were considered to be his property. If he wanted custody upon divorce, the courts gave it to him. A radical change occurred in the early nineteenth century, when almost all courts began awarding custody based on a determination of the **best interests of the child**.[3] The new standard, however, was controversial, because courts often concluded—aided by some presumptions about child rearing—that it would be in the best interests of a child that the mother be awarded custody. Critics argued that a father-dominated system had been replaced by a mother-dominated one. Yet the best-interests-of-the child standard remains dominant today when the custody dispute is between biological parents. These are among the themes we will be exploring in this chapter.

best interests of the child
A standard used by a court to decide what would best serve a child's welfare when the court must make custody, visitation, adoption, guardianship, and change-of-name decisions.

KINDS OF CUSTODY

Custody has two general meanings: (1) the *right* to the care and control of a person or thing and (2) the *actual* care and control that someone has over a person or thing. When, for example, we say that someone has custody of a car, we mean either that this person has the right to care for and control the car (whether or not the car is in the person's possession), or we simply mean that the person is actually caring for and controlling the car (whether or not the person has the right to such care and control).

custody
(1) The right to the care and control of a person or thing. (2) The actual care and control that someone has over a person or thing.

When discussing **child custody**, our focus is primarily on the right of an adult to the care and control of a child. We need to distinguish between physical custody and legal custody:

- **Physical custody** (sometimes called *residential custody* or *custodial responsibility*) is the right of an adult to have a child reside with the adult. When a court grants a parent physical custody, that parent is given the right to have the child live with him or her. The parent with physical custody is called the **custodial parent (CP)** (or the *residential parent*). The other parent is the **noncustodial parent (NCP)**. Although the child lives with the CP, the NCP has **visitation**, which is the right to have access to a child who resides with another.

- **Legal custody** (sometimes called *decision-making responsibility*) is the right to make the major child-rearing decisions on health, education, religion, discipline, and general welfare.

If only one parent is granted both kinds of custody, he or she has *sole physical custody* and *sole legal custody*. Such phrases are more accurate than the phrase "sole custody." If you are told that a parent has sole custody, you need to determine whether this includes physical *and* legal custody.

If *both* parents are granted physical and legal custody, they have **joint physical custody** (also called shared physical custody) and **joint legal custody** (also called shared legal custody). These phrases are more accurate than the phrases "joint custody" or "shared parenting." If you are told that parents have joint custody or that they share the task of parenting, you need to determine whether this includes both physical and legal custody. Joint physical custody means that the child spends alternating, but not necessarily equal, periods of time in the homes of the mother and father. Joint legal custody means that the mother and father must agree on the major child-rearing decisions such as where the child will go to school or whether he or she will have a medical operation.

> *Under the terms of a separation agreement that was approved by the divorce court, 10-year-old Mary Teller lives year-round with Grace Teller, her mother. Mary's father, Peter Teller, lives in a different state, a hundred miles away. Grace and Peter, ex-spouses, regularly talk on the phone about all the major decisions in Helen's life. No decision is made unless both agree.*

In this example, Grace and Peter have joint legal custody, and Grace has sole physical custody.

Coparenting is shared responsibility by two adults to raise a child, regardless of the marital status or sexual orientation of the adults. Often coparenting consists of both joint physical custody and joint legal custody.

When parents have more than one child, courts try to place all the children with the same parent in order to encourage sibling bonding. If this is not possible, the custody arrangement in which siblings are placed with different parents or guardians is called **split custody**. Occasionally, parents with joint physical custody alternate living in the home with the child. In this custody arrangement, called *bird nesting* or *nesting*, the child stays in the same house; the parents rotate in and out of the house separately on alternating dates.

States do not always use the same terminology for custody. In a few states, for example, the word *conservatorship* is used in place of *custody*. The person with primary responsibility for raising the child is called the *managing conservator*. Some states prefer the phrase "parenting plan" or "coparenting plan" to the phrase "custody arrangement." And some states prefer the phrase "parenting time" to the word "visitation" when the "visiting" parent is not the custodial parent.

---

child custody

The right of an adult to the care and control of a child.

physical custody

(1) The right of an adult to have a child reside with the adult. Also called residential custody, custodial responsibility. (2) Where the child is actually living.

custodial parent (CP)

The parent with whom the child is living; the parent with physical custody of the child.

noncustodial parent (NCP)

The parent who is not living with the child; the parent who does not have physical custody of the child. Also called nonresidential parent.

visitation

(1) The right to have access to a child who resides with another. Some states prefer the phrase "parenting time" when the person "visiting" the child is the noncustodial parent. (2) Actual time spent by a noncustodial parent with his or her child.

legal custody

The right to make the major child-rearing decisions on health, education, religion, discipline, and general welfare. Also called decision-making responsibility.

joint physical custody

The right of both parents to have the child reside with both for alternating (but not necessarily equal) periods of time. Also called shared physical custody.

joint legal custody

The right of both parents to make child-rearing decisions on health, education, religion, discipline, and general welfare. Also called shared legal custody.

coparenting

Shared responsibility by two adults to raise a child, regardless of the marital status or sexual orientation of the adults.

split custody

A custody arrangement in which siblings are in the physical custody of different parents or guardians.

Finally, it should be pointed out that these categories of custody can be somewhat fluid in practice in spite of what was originally agreed upon by the parents or imposed by a court. Suppose, for example, that a mother and father have joint physical and joint legal custody but that the father's involvement with the children gradually decreases. After a while, the mother may find herself making all the child-rearing decisions on her own and living with the child full-time. In another example, circumstances may force a father's visitation to become much more extensive than originally contemplated or authorized. He might take over the roles of sole physical and sole legal custodian when the mother becomes ill. Such rearranging may occur without formal changes in the custody clauses of the original separation agreement. Unless child support becomes an issue, the courts may never become aware of these informal adjustments.

We turn now to the custody decision itself—both when the parties are able to reach agreement in their separation agreement, and when the custody decision is forced upon them because of their inability to agree.

SEPARATION AGREEMENT

Before we examine how courts resolve custody disputes, we need to look at attempts by divorcing parents to work out a mutually agreeable custody arrangement.

REACHING A MUTUALLY ACCEPTABLE CUSTODY DECISION

In attempting to negotiate the custody clauses of a separation agreement, the parties have many factors to consider:

- The kind of custody they want.
- The age and health of the child.
- The age and health of the parents. Which parent is physically and mentally more able to care for the child on a day-to-day basis?
- The parent with whom the child has spent the most time up to now. With whom are the emotional attachments the strongest?
- Which parent must work full-time?
- The availability of backup assistance (e.g., from grandparents or close friends who can help in emergencies).
- The availability of day-care facilities.
- Details on the visitation schedule of the noncustodial parent (NCP).
- Can the child be moved out of the area?
- How will decisions be made on the child's medical care, schooling, religion, discipline, and other general welfare matters? Must one parent consult the other on such matters? Is joint consent needed? Is such consent practical?
- Can the child's surname be changed if the mother remarries?
- Who would receive custody if both parents died?
- If disputes arise between the parents concerning custody, how are they going to be resolved? Arbitration? Mediation?
- Do the parties specifically agree to encourage the child to love both parents?

Unfortunately, parents do not always have the welfare of the child in mind when negotiating the custody term of the separation agreement. For example, a father's request for joint custody may be no more than a bargaining chip to pressure the mother to agree to a property settlement that favors the father. If she agrees to the property settlement he wants, he may no longer challenge the sole custody she wants.

JOINT PHYSICAL CUSTODY AND JOINT LEGAL CUSTODY

The most common custody arrangement worked out by the parties is sole physical custody and sole legal custody with the mother and visitation for the father.

Parents do not often use joint physical custody because of the disruptive impact on a child of constantly changing households. Joint physical custody might work if the child is very young, the parents live close to each other, and the parents are relatively well-to-do. In most cases, however, joint physical custody is not practical. Also, if either of the parties applies for public assistance, joint physical custody might raise questions about eligibility. For example, under the federal program **Temporary Assistance for Needy Families (TANF)**, benefits may depend in part on having an eligible child in the home. A parent may have difficulty meeting this requirement if the child spends long alternating periods with the other parent.

Joint *legal* custody, on the other hand, is more common. In approximately 20 percent of separations and divorces, the parents have joint legal custody, with one parent having sole physical custody.[4] Some states use a **presumption** that joint legal custody is in the best interests of the child and should be ordered unless the facts of the case demonstrate that this arrangement would not work. Advocates of joint custody claim that it is psychologically the healthiest alternative for the child. It arguably produces less hostility between parents, less hostility between child and individual parent, less confusion in values for the child, less sexual stereotyping of parental roles (one parent "works," the other raises the children), less manipulation of the child by one or both parents, less manipulation of one or both parents by the child, etc. Joint custody arrangements also dramatically increase the likelihood that child support will be consistently paid.

Critics, however, argue that the decision on joint custody should be approached with great caution because it will work only in exceptional circumstances. The parents have just separated. In this environment, it is often doubtful that they will be able to cooperate in the manner called for by a joint legal custody arrangement. A study of 700 divorce cases in Massachusetts concluded that couples with joint legal custody are more than twice as likely to reopen lawsuits over child-care arrangements than couples where only one parent had custody. In addition, it is by no means clear that a child is more likely to be better off when living under a joint custody arrangement. Recent studies have found no significant difference in a child's development under joint custody and under more traditional sole custody arrangements.[5]

The following questions cover factors that are relevant to a decision on whether joint legal custody will work. Answers to any one of the questions might tip the scale either way on whether joint legal custody is feasible.

- Is each parent fit and mentally stable?
- Do both parents agree to joint legal custody, or is one or both hesitant or opposed?
- Have the parents demonstrated that they are able to communicate at least to the extent necessary to reach shared decisions in the child's best interests?
- Is joint custody in accord with the child's wishes (if mature enough to state a preference), or does the child have strong opposition to such an arrangement?

COURT GUIDELINES FOR PARENTS

In **contested** custody cases, many courts require the parties to attend parenting classes. (Some states mandate such classes for all divorcing parties with children even if they have reached agreement on the custody issues.)

Temporary Assistance for Needy Families (TANF)
The federal-state welfare system (42 U.S.C. § 601) that replaced Aid to Families with Dependent Children (AFDC). Unlike AFDC, benefits under TANF are limited to five years.

presumption
An assumption or inference that a certain fact is true once another fact is established.

contested
Challenged; opposed or disputed.

For example, a county family-law court might require attendance at a four-hour seminar on how parents can help their children cope with separation and visitation. Using video and role-playing, the seminar emphasizes the emotional harm that fighting parents can continue to inflict on their children.

Most courts have guidelines they distribute to the parties on the effect of divorce on children, how to make coparenting work after divorce, and how to resolve disputes that arise under an approved custody arrangement. Sometimes these guidelines are made part of the court's custody decree. For an example of parental guidelines, see Exhibit 9-1, which is written on the assumption that the mother is awarded custody.

EXHIBIT 9-1   Court Guidelines for Parents

Relation toward Children

Although the court does have the power to dissolve the bonds of matrimony, the court does not have the power to dissolve the bonds that exist between you as parents and your children. Both of you, therefore, are to continue your responsibility to emotionally support your children. You are to cooperate in the duty and right of each other to love those children. By love, the court means the training, the education, the disciplining and motivation of those children. Cooperation means to present the other party to the children with an attitude of respect either for the mother or for the father. Neither of you should in any way downplay, belittle, or criticize the other in the presence of those children because you may emotionally damage your children and foster a hatred for the demeaned parent. It is of utmost importance you both recognize your children's right to love both parents without fear of being disloyal to either one of you.

In support of this admonition, the courts have drafted written guidelines on your future conduct relating to the best interest of your children. I sincerely urge that you preserve them, periodically read them, and always be guided by them.

Guidelines for Separated Parents

As you know, your children are usually the losers when their parents separate. They are deprived of full-time, proper guidance that two parents can give—guidance and direction essential to their moral and spiritual growth.

It is highly desirable that you abstain from making unkind remarks about each other. Recognize that such remarks are not about a former spouse but are about a parent of your children. Such comments reflect adversely upon the children.

It is urged that both parties cooperate to the end that mutual decisions concerning the interest of the children can be made objectively. Parents should remember that the mother who has custody should urge the children to find time to be with the father and encourage them to realize that their father has affection for them and contributes to their support. The father should recognize that his plans for visitation must be adjusted from time to time in order to accommodate the planned activities of the child. Visitation should be a pleasant experience rather than a duty. Cooperation in giving notice and promptness in maintaining hours of visitation are important to avoid ruffled feelings.

Although there is probably some bitterness between you, it should not be inflicted upon your children. In every child's mind there must and should be an image of two good parents. Your future conduct with your children will be helpful to them if you will follow these suggestions.

I. *Do Not's*

a. Do not poison your child's mind against either the mother or father by discussing their shortcomings.
b. Do not use your visitation as an excuse to continue the arguments with your spouse.
c. Do not visit your children if you have been drinking.

II. *Do's*

a. Be discreet when you expose your children to anyone with whom you may be emotionally involved.
b. Visit your children only at reasonable hours.
c. Notify your spouse as soon as possible if you are unable to keep your visitation. It's unfair to keep your children waiting—and worse to disappoint them by not coming at all.
d. Make your visitation as pleasant as possible for your children by not questioning them regarding the activities of your spouse and by not making extravagant promises which you know you cannot or will not keep.
e. Minimize the amount of time the children are in the care of strangers and relatives.
f. Always work for the spiritual well-being, health, happiness and safety of your children.

III. *General*

a. The parent with whom the children live must prepare them both physically and mentally for the visitation. The children should be available at the time mutually agreed upon.

b. If one parent has plans for the children that conflict with the visitation and these plans are in the best interests of the children, be adults and work out the problem together.

c. Arrangements should be made through visitation to provide the mother with some time "away" from the family. She needs the time for relaxation and recreation. Upon her return, she will be refreshed and better prepared to resume her role as mother and head of the household. Therefore, provide for extended periods of visitation such as weekends and vacations.

Bill of Rights for Children in a Divorce Action

1. The right to be treated as important human beings, with unique feelings, ideas, and desires and not as a source of argument between parents.

2. The right to a continuing relationship with both parents and the freedom to receive love from and express love for both.

3. The right to express love and affection for each parent without having to stifle that love because of fear of disapproval by the other parent.

4. The right to know that their parents' decision to divorce is not their responsibility and that they will live with one parent and will visit the other parent.

5. The right to continuing care and guidance from both parents.

6. The right to honest answers to questions about the changing family relationships.

7. The right to know and appreciate what is good in each parent without one parent degrading the other.

8. The right to have a relaxed, secure relationship with both parents without being placed in a position to manipulate one parent against the other.

9. The right to have the custodial parent not undermine visitation by suggesting tempting alternatives or by threatening to withhold visitation as a punishment for the children's wrongdoing.

10. The right to be able to experience regular and consistent visitation and the right to know the reason for a cancelled visit.

Source: Dane County Family Court, Madison, Wisconsin. See also www.countyofdane.com/familycourtcounseling/child_rights.aspx.

CONTESTED CUSTODY

Parties who are able to agree on custody and visitation submit their plan to the court in writing, usually in the separation agreement. The court will approve the plan if it determines that the plan is in the best interests of the child. If, however, the parties cannot agree or if the court determines that what they agreed to is not in the best interests of the child, a custody decision will be imposed on them by the court.

Often, the first step is for the court to force the parents into **mediation** where they will try to reach agreement on a workable custody plan they both can support. (Mediation is a form of **alternative dispute resolution [ADR]** that seeks the resolution of legal disputes without litigation.) In mandatory mediation, the mediator is a private citizen or a government employee, often in the family services division of the court, who meets with the parents to try to help them reach an agreement. The mediator does not force a decision on them. Although mediators may ultimately recommend a custody/visitation arrangement to the court, the primary objective of mediation is to pressure the parents to reach their own agreement, which they can take before the judge for approval. For an example of a mediation session, see Exhibit 7-5 in Chapter 7.

Throughout the divorce process, the mother and father are represented by their own attorneys. In addition, most states have the power to appoint *separate* counsel for the child who will act independently of the attorneys for the parents. If the child is mature enough to express his or her rational wants, the child's attorney will perform traditional advocacy functions on behalf of the child. For children who do not have this level of maturity, the court may have the power to appoint what is called a **best interests attorney (BIA)**. This is an attorney who provides legal representation for a child to protect the child's best interests without being bound by the child's directives or objectives.[6] The court may also

mediation

A method of alternative dispute resolution (ADR) in which the parties avoid litigation by submitting their dispute to a neutral third person (the mediator) who helps the parties resolve their dispute; he or she does not render a decision resolving it for them.

alternative dispute resolution (ADR)

A method or procedure for resolving a legal dispute without litigating the dispute in a court or administrative agency. ADR methods include mediation, arbitration, and Med-Arb.

best interests attorney (BIA)

An attorney who provides legal representation for a child to protect the child's best interests without being bound by the child's directives or objectives.

guardian ad litem (GAL)

A special guardian (often, but not always, an attorney) appointed by the court to appear in court proceedings on behalf of a person who is a minor, is insane, or is otherwise incapacitated.

court appointed special advocate (CASA)

A volunteer appointed by the court to undertake special assignments pertaining to children in the court system.

parenting coordinator (PC)

A professional who assists parents in resolving custody disputes that arise under a parenting plan.

attorney-client privilege

A client or a client's attorney can refuse to disclose any confidential (private) communication between them if the purpose of the communication was to facilitate the provision of legal services to the client.

have the power to appoint a **guardian ad litem (GAL)**. A GAL is an individual appointed to appear in court on behalf of a minor. The GAL can be asked by the court to serve different functions, for example, investigate the home environment of the child, and mediate or resolve custody disputes between the parties that arise after the divorce. Often the GAL is an attorney, although in some states, it can be a nonattorney such as a social worker.

Finally, as we saw in Chapter 2, many courts can appoint a **court appointed special advocate (CASA)**. A CASA is a volunteer who undertakes special tasks such as investigating the home environment of the child. A CASA does not have to be an attorney. Many paralegals volunteer for this role.

In some custody cases, the parties use the services of a **parenting coordinator (PC)** to assist them in resolving custody disputes that arise under the parenting plan. Parent coordinating is another method of alternative dispute resolution (ADR). Here is how the Association of Family and Conciliation Courts describes the role:

> Parenting coordination is a child-focused alternative dispute resolution process in which a mental health or legal professional with mediation training and experience assists high conflict parents to implement their parenting plan by facilitating the resolution of their disputes in a timely manner, educating parents about children's needs, and with prior approval of the parties and/or the court, making decisions within the scope of the court order or appointment contract.[7]

As valuable as such individuals can be in child-custody cases, it is important to understand their limitations. For example, the **attorney-client privilege** does not apply to nonattorneys who are acting in coordinator or investigative roles unless special legislation exists that extends the privilege to them. An employee (e.g., paralegal) of an attorney representing a party *is* protected by the privilege but usually these other individuals are not. Hence, they can be subpoenaed to give testimony on what they heard the child or one of the parents say.

PARENT VS. PARENT

The ultimate decider on custody is the court. The court must approve the custody agreement worked out by the parents or the court must make the decision for them if they are not able to agree. How does the court make this decision?

First, we consider the custody decision when the dispute is between the two *biological parents* who cannot agree on custody. The standard used by the court, as we have seen, is the best interests of the child. We will examine this standard through the following themes:

- Court discretion
- Parenting plan
- Stability
- Attitude on visitation
- Availability
- Emotional ties
- Parental alienation syndrome
- Career choice
- Wealth
- Legal preferences
- Morality and lifestyle
- Domestic violence
- Religion
- Race
- Wishes of the child
- Expert witnesses

COURT DISCRETION

Trial judges are given great discretion in making the custody decision, so much so that critics claim that custody decisions are often unpredictable and sometimes arbitrary. Unlike determining child support (see Chapter 10), there are no formulas the court can use to reach the custody decision. The standard is very broad: the best interests of the child. Inevitably, the judge's personal views and philosophy of life help shape his or her concept of what is in the best interests of a child (e.g., views on the traditional family, alternative lifestyles, working women, child discipline). Of course, a judge would never admit that he or she is following his or her own personal views and philosophy; judges are supposed to be guided by "the law" and not by their individual biases. In reality, however, they are guided by both.

PARENTING PLAN

The starting point in the process is the submission to the court of the proposed **parenting plan** of each parent. See Exhibit 9-2. Of course, if the two plans differ, each parent will have to litigate the differences by presenting evidence showing that his or her plan is in the best interests of the child.

STABILITY

By far one of the most important considerations is stability. Courts are inclined to award custody to the parent who will cause the least amount of disruption to the disintegrating life of the child. The loss of a household with two functioning parents can be a shattering experience for children. They will need as much stability as possible in their living arrangement, schooling, religious practice, access to relatives and friends, and participation in activities of their cultural heritage. The court will scrutinize the parenting plan of each parent to assess how the plan proposes to maintain maximum stability and continuity in these areas.

ATTITUDE ON VISITATION

Attorneys often advise clients seeking sole custody to tell the court that visitation by the noncustodial parent (NCP) is important and they will fully cooperate with the NCP to make visitation work. Judges, for example, like to hear mothers say that they want their children to stay in contact with their father and want to isolate the children from the marital problems as much as possible. Of course, if there has been domestic violence in the home, a parent would be understandably reluctant to endorse significant visitation by a parent with a history of abuse. Nevertheless, the attorney is likely to tell the client that courts are inclined to grant visitation rights even to parents who have been abusive. Hence, the attorney is likely to advise the client to try to express at least some support for restricted visitation such as supervised visitation (see discussion of domestic violence below). Of course, if the domestic violence has been substantial, the client is unlikely to be able to express such a sentiment.

parenting plan
A plan for separated parents that states (1) where and with whom the children will live (physical custody); (2) who will make child-rearing decisions on schooling, discipline, religion, health, and general welfare (legal custody); (3) what the visitation schedule for the noncustodial parent will be; and (4) related matters such as what method the parents will use to resolve future child-rearing disagreements between them.

EXHIBIT 9-2 **Components of a Parenting Plan**

(1) where and with whom the children will live (physical custody);

(2) who will make child-rearing decisions on schooling, discipline, religion, health, and general welfare (legal custody);

(3) if the child has special needs (e.g., illness, learning disability), how these needs will be met;

(4) what the visitation schedule of the noncustodial parent (NCP) will be;

(5) how the parties will communicate with each other on custody matters such as rescheduling visits;

(6) who will pay what expenses related to the components of the custody arrangement; and

(7) related matters such as the method of resolving child-rearing disagreements between the parents.

AVAILABILITY

Which parent will be available to spend the time that is required to respond to the day-to-day needs of the child? There is a danger that the child will feel abandoned and responsible for the divorce. To offset this danger, it is important that at least one of the parents is available to provide reassurance and comfort. To gauge availability, the court will want to know which parent in the past:

- Took the child to doctor's appointments
- Met with teachers
- Took the child to church, synagogue, or mosque
- Helped with homework
- Attended school plays with the child
- Involved the child in athletic activities
- Arranged and attended birthday parties
- Arranged for baby-sitters when needed
- Changed diapers
- Took care of the child's bathing, grooming, and dressing needs
- Purchased, cleaned, and cared for the child's clothes
- Administered discipline and taught manners
- Stayed up with the sick child during the night
- Taught elementary reading, writing, and arithmetic skills

These activities are sometimes referred to as *indicia of parenthood*—indications that the adult is actively involved in the nurturing and care of a child.

An office representing a parent seeking custody should make sure that he or she is able to answer questions such as the following during a **deposition** or on the witness stand during the trial:

- What is the name of the child's pediatrician?
- When was the last time the child saw the pediatrician and for what reason?
- What is the name of the child's dentist?
- When was the last time the child saw the dentist and for what reason?
- Does the child have nightmares? If so, about what?
- What television programs do you watch with the child?
- What is the name of one of the child's main teachers? What does this teacher think are the child's strengths and weaknesses as a student?
- In what subject has the child received the best grade and the worst grade?
- What are the names of some of the child's friends at school?
- What are the names of some of the child's friends at home?

deposition
A discovery device in which one party questions another party (or questions the other party's witness), usually outside the courtroom.

A parent may not be able to answer all of these questions from direct knowledge because he or she is at work most of the day. Yet a responsible parent would be interested enough in the child to find out answers to such questions by talking with the other parent and with the child. There is no law that requires a parent to know the answers to these questions, but being able to answer as many as possible bolsters the parenting plan proposed by a parent.

Immediately after the separation, it is common for one of the parents to have temporary custody. Upon filing for divorce, the court will formally order a temporary-custody arrangement (with visitation rights) pending the final court proceeding, which may take place months later. During this interval, the court will inquire into the amount and kind of contact each parent had with the child. Again, the above list of questions becomes important, particularly with respect to the parent who moved out. How much time has this parent spent with the child? Have letters and gifts been sent? What about visits, telephone calls, Skype calls, and e-mail messages? To what extent has this parent gone out of his or her way to be with the child?

EMOTIONAL TIES

Closely related to time availability is the emotional relationship that has already developed between a parent and child and the future prospects for this development. Which parent has been sensitive or insensitive to the psychological crisis that the child has experienced and will probably continue to experience because of the divorce? Of particular importance is the extent to which one parent has tried and succeeded in fostering the child's love for the *other* parent. Often, a qualification to become a custodial parent is the ability and inclination to cooperate in arranging visitations by the other parent. Hence, a major issue will be which parent can separate his or her own needs and lingering bitterness from the need of the child to maintain emotional ties with both parents.

A number of other factors are relevant to the emotional needs of the child:

- *Education.* The level of a parent's education may be some indication of the parent's ability to cope with difficult emotional needs of a child.
- *Psychological health.* Has the parent been in therapy for any reason? Has it been helpful? What is the parent's attitude about seeking such help? Positive? Realistic? Does the parent think that the *other* parent is the only one who needs help?
- *Work history.* How stable has the parent been in his or her work history?
- *Parenting norms.* What are the parent's views on discipline, TV watching, computer games, texting, studying, religious activities, cleaning the child's room, etc.?
- *Siblings.* How do siblings get along in the home?
- *General home and neighborhood environment.* Cramped apartment conditions? Residential area? Easy accessibility to school, friends, and recreational facilities?

Also, does the parent seeking sole custody plan to move from the area? If so, into what kind of environment? How will the proposed move affect the other parent's ability to visit the child? Depending upon the circumstances of the case, a court might award custody to a parent on condition that he or she *not* move out of a designated area without the consent of the other parent. We will return to the issue of parental relocations when we cover modification of custody orders.

CASE

Schutz v. Schutz
581 So. 2d 1290 (1991)
Supreme Court of Florida

Background: *Following a divorce, custody of the children was given to the mother, Laurel Schutz (the petitioner). When the trial court became concerned that the children had negative feelings about their father, Richard Schutz (the respondent), it ordered Laurel to do everything in her power to create in the minds of the children a loving feeling toward their father. Laurel objected that this interfered with her First Amendment free speech rights and appealed. The case is now on appeal before the Supreme Court of Florida.*

Decision on Appeal: *Judgment affirmed. The state (as parens patriae) has an interest in protecting children and was properly pursuing this interest by encouraging meaningful contact between the children and their father.*

OPINION OF THE COURT

Justice KOGAN delivered the opinion of the court. . . .

[T]he petitioner contends [that the order] requires her to affirmatively express feelings and beliefs which she does not

(continued)

CASE • Schutz v. Schutz (continued)

have in violation of her first amendment right of free expression. . . . A final judgment dissolving the six-year marriage of petitioner, Laurel Schutz (mother) and respondent, Richard R. Schutz (father) was entered by the trial court on November 13, 1978. Although custody of the parties' minor children was originally granted to the father, the final judgment was later modified in 1979. Under the modified judgment, the mother was awarded sole custody of the children, and the father was both granted visitation rights and ordered to pay child support.

As noted by the trial court, the ongoing "acrimony and animosity between the adult parties" is clear from the record. The trial court found that in February 1981 the mother moved with the children from Miami to Georgia without notifying the father. After moving, the mother advised the father of their new address and phone number. Although the father and children corresponded after the move, he found an empty house on the three occasions when he traveled to Georgia to visit the children. The father was not notified that after only seven months in Georgia the mother and children had returned to Miami. Four years later in 1985, upon discovering the children's whereabouts, the father visited the children only to find that they "hated, despised, and feared" him due to his failure to support or visit them. After this visit, numerous motions concerning visitation, custody and support were filed by the parties.

After a final hearing on the motions, the trial court found that "the cause of the blind, brainwashed, bigoted belligerence of the children toward the father grew from the soil nurtured, watered and tilled by the mother." The court further found that "the mother breached every duty she owed as the custodial parent to the noncustodial parent of instilling love, respect and feeling in the children for their father." The trial court's findings are supported by substantial competent evidence.

Based on these findings, the trial court ordered the mother "to do everything in her power to create in the minds of [the children] a loving, caring feeling toward the father . . . [and] to convince the children that it is the mother's desire that they see their father and love their father." The court further ordered that breach of the obligation imposed "either in words, actions, demeanor, implication or otherwise" would result in the "severest penalties . . . , including contempt, imprisonment, loss of residential custody or any combination thereof.". . .

We begin our analysis by noting our agreement with the district courts of appeal that have found a custodial parent has an affirmative obligation to encourage and nurture the relationship between the child and the noncustodial parent. See *Gardner v. Gardner,* 494 So. 2d 500, 502 (Fla. 4th DCA 1986); *In re Adoption of Braithwaite,* 409 So. 2d 1178, 1180 (Fla. 5th DCA 1982). This duty is owed to both the noncustodial parent and the child. This obligation may be met by encouraging the child to interact with the noncustodial parent, taking good faith measures to ensure that the child visit and otherwise have frequent and continuing contact with the noncustodial parent and refraining from doing anything likely to undermine the relationship naturally fostered by such interaction.

Consistent with this obligation, we read the challenged portion of the order at issue to require nothing more of the mother than a good faith effort to take those measures necessary to restore and promote the frequent and continuing positive interaction (e.g., visitation, phone calls, letters) between the children and their father and to refrain from doing or saying anything likely to defeat that end. There is no requirement that petitioner express opinions that she does not hold, a practice disallowed by the first amendment. *Coca-Cola Co. v. Department of Citrus,* 406 So. 2d 1079, 1087 (Fla. 1981) ("the state may never force one to adopt or express a particular opinion"); *West Virginia State Board of Education v. Barnette,* 319 U.S. 624, 642 (1943) (state cannot "prescribe . . . matters of opinion or force citizens to confess by word or act their faith therein").

[The] order may be sustained against a first amendment challenge if "it furthers an important or substantial governmental interest . . . and if the incidental restriction on alleged First Amendment freedoms is no greater than is essential to the furtherance of that interest." *United States v. O'Brien,* 391 U.S. 367, 377 (1968). Accordingly, we must balance the mother's right of free expression against the state's parens patriae interest in assuring the wellbeing of the parties' minor children. However, as with all matters involving custody of minor children, the interests of the father and of the children, which here happen to parallel those of the state, must also factor into the equation.

In this case, the court, acting on behalf of the state as parens patriae, sought to resolve the dispute between the parties in accordance with the best interests of their children by attempting to restore a meaningful relationship between the children and their father by assuring them unhampered, frequent and continuing contact with him. . . . In resolving the matter, the court also properly considered the father's constitutionally protected "inherent right" to a meaningful relationship with his children. . . .

There is no question that the state's interest in restoring a meaningful relationship between the parties' children and their father, thereby promoting the best interests of the children, is at the very least substantial. Likewise, any restriction placed on the mother's freedom of expression is essential to the furtherance of the state's interests because affirmative measures taken by the mother to encourage meaningful interaction between the children and their father would be for naught if she were allowed to contradict those measures by word or deed. . . .

Accordingly, construing the order as we do, we find no abuse of discretion by the trial court, nor impermissible burden on the petitioner's first amendment rights. . . . [T]he result reached is approved.

It is so ordered.

a. Would the court have reached the same result if the mother was ordered to tell the children every day "Your father is a good man"?

b. Keeping in mind that the mother continues to be bitter about the father, give five examples of things she could say about the father to the children that would promote positive feelings about him without constituting opinions that she does not hold.

c. Would the mother violate the order if she refused to ever mention the father in the presence of the children?

d. What are the father's options if, a year after this case, he concludes that the children "still hate me"?

PARENTAL ALIENATION SYNDROME

In some custody disputes, one of the parents (often the father) argues that he does not have a good relationship with his children because the mother has turned the children against him. A controversial name for this situation is the **parental alienation syndrome (PAS)**. It asserts that the children have been brainwashed by one parent to hate the other parent. Some women's groups have been highly critical of PAS. They claim that it is a mere theory that has not been scientifically tested. Most courts agree. These courts will allow a parent to introduce specific evidence that the other parent has persistently portrayed him/her in a negative light in the eyes of the children, but not allow the alleged victimized parent to assert that the child is suffering from a disorder called PAS. A more serious challenge against the use of PAS is that abusive parents have tried to use PAS as a defense against the domestic violence they have allegedly committed. The following caution about PAS has been issued by the National Council of Juvenile and Family Court Judges:

> The discredited "diagnosis" of PAS (or an allegation of "parental alienation"), quite apart from its scientific invalidity, inappropriately asks the court to assume that the child's behaviors and attitudes toward the parent who claims to be "alienated" have no grounding in reality. It also diverts attention away from the behaviors of the abusive parent, who may have directly influenced the child's responses by acting in violent, disrespectful, intimidating, humiliating, or discrediting ways toward the child or the other parent. The task for the court is to distinguish between situations in which the child is critical of one parent because they have been inappropriately manipulated by the other . . . , and situations in which the child has his or her own legitimate grounds for criticism or fear of a parent, which will likely be the case when that parent has perpetrated domestic violence.[8]

parental alienation syndrome (PAS)

A disorder characterized by a child's obsessive and unjustified denigration of a parent that results both from the child's persistent attacks on the parent and from manipulation (brainwashing) by the other parent of the child's attitude toward the targeted parent.

CAREER CHOICE

Courts are sensitive to the need of many women to work outside the home after divorce. In a custody dispute, such women should not be penalized simply because their job commitments require them to use housekeepers, nannies, or daycare facilities. A court will be impressed by a father who commits to being a stay-at-home dad, but this would not automatically lead to a custody ruling in his favor against a working mother. The parenting plans of both parents would have to be carefully scrutinized by the court to determine what custody arrangement would be in the best interests of the child. It may be that the balance could tip in favor of the working mother so long as her career choice does not adversely affect the child.

WEALTH

After a divorce, both parents have an equal obligation to provide child support. In a custody dispute, a wealthy parent is not preferred over a less well-to-do parent if the child support each parent must provide is adequate to care for the child. Although the relative wealth of the parents is a factor that the courts will consider in the custody decision, it should not be the determinative factor.

LEGAL PREFERENCES

At one time, custody decisions favored one gender (usually the mother) over the other. Today, however, courts use gender-neutral standards in the custody decision, although some critics argue that mothers are still preferred.

The old rule was stated in the form of a presumption. A mother was presumed to be better suited to raising her young children (under five years of age) and should be awarded custody unless she is unfit. This **tender-years presumption** was justified on the basis of biological dependence, socialization patterns, and tradition: "There is but a twilight zone between a mother's love and the atmosphere of heaven, and all things being equal, no child should be deprived of that maternal influence."[9] A very strong case had to be made against the mother to overcome the tender years presumption, primarily by proving that she was unfit.

Most states have abolished the tender-years presumption. Fathers successfully argued that this gender-based presumption was an unconstitutional violation of the equal protection of the law. Male anger and frustration over the presumption were main reasons for the growth of the men's rights movement. As a result, more fathers are granted sole physical custody. "Single dads now account for 8 percent of American households with children, up from 6.3 percent in 2000 and 1.1 percent in 1950."[10] One in six custodial parents (CPs) today are fathers.[11] Not all of them became CPs because of decisions in disputed custody cases. Many "Mr. Moms" are widowers or assumed the CP role when mothers abandoned the child or voluntarily agreed with the father that he should be the CP. Yet a significant number of fathers are CPs because of custody decisions made after the tender-years presumption was abolished.

The cases in which fathers tend to be successful in custody cases are those in which they are seeking custody of an older male child. At one time, courts established a presumption that it was in the best interests of an older boy to be with his father. This gender-based presumption, however, is as constitutionally suspect as the tender-years presumption. No court today would openly acknowledge that it is using a pro-father presumption when the custody of an older male is in dispute.

Although the number of father CPs has increased, mothers are still granted custody in the large majority of cases. A number of factors account for this. Perhaps the primary reason is the fact that many fathers simply do not ask for custody. Becoming a full-time, at-home parent does not fit into the life plan of large numbers of men, particularly if it means significant interference with their occupations. Arguably, another major reason is that fathers are still handicapped by the tender-years presumption in spite of its formal abolition. Many older judges now sitting on the bench grew up with full-time moms at home. Some experts feel it is difficult for these judges to accept the notion of giving sole custody to working fathers. But new judges are on the way. It "will take a generation of judges who are brought up by, or married to career women" before there is more sympathy for granting custody to working parents—particularly fathers.[12]

In place of the tender-years presumption, a few courts have substituted a **primary-caregiver presumption**, by which the court presumes that custody should go to the parent who has thus far been the primary person who has taken care of the child's daily needs unless this parent is unfit. The major caregiver

---

tender-years presumption
In general, mothers are better suited to raise their young children (usually under five years of age) and should be awarded custody of such children unless the mothers are unfit. Also called maternal preference.

primary-caregiver presumption
Custody should be granted to the parent who thus far has taken care of most of the daily needs of the child unless this parent is unfit.

tasks include making meals, bathing, grooming, dressing, cleaning, disciplining, tending to medical needs, and arranging the child's social, religious, educational, and cultural life. Fathers often claim that the primary-caregiver presumption means that the mother continues to receive sole custody in most cases, because she is usually the one who stays home to care for the child. Even when both the mother and the father work outside the home, the mother is more likely to be awarded custody as the primary caregiver. Hence, critics argue that this presumption is simply the tender-years presumption in disguise. In most states, therefore, primary caregiving is not a presumption; it is simply one of the factors a court will consider in determining what is in the best interests of the child.

A less controversial presumption is that brothers and sisters are best kept together with the same parent whenever possible. (In effect, this was a presumption that split custody should be avoided.) Older children are often treated differently. Most courts say that the preference of older, more mature children as to their own custody should be given great, though not necessarily controlling, weight.

The modern trend, however, is to avoid all presumptions and simply to apply the gender-neutral standard of best interests of the child with all of the factors being considered.

MORALITY AND LIFESTYLE: THE NEXUS TEST

Just as marital fault or misconduct should not control whether a court will grant a divorce (see Chapter 7), it should not determine who receives custody—unless the fault affects the child. This is the *nexus test*. There must be a causal relationship—a nexus—between the parent's conduct or lifestyle and the child's well-being.

Smoking, for example, is considered a poor lifestyle choice. Yet a parent who smokes would not be automatically disqualified from obtaining custody. Suppose, however, that the parent's child has asthma. In such a case, a court would be concerned about the health effects of secondhand smoke on the child. This would be a nexus between lifestyle and child welfare that a court would consider. If, after all factors are considered, a court grants physical custody to a smoker, the court is likely to impose a condition that the parent not smoke in the presence of the child, especially in vehicles.

Similarly, a court would want to know if a parent's new romantic partner has had, or is likely to have, a negative effect on a child. According to one court:

> A judge should not base his decision upon [a] disapproval of the morals or other personal characteristics of a parent that do not harm the child. . . . We do not mean to suggest that a person's associational or even sexual conduct may not be relevant in deciding a custody dispute where there is compelling evidence that such conduct has a significant bearing upon the welfare of the children objectively defined.[13]

Assume that Bill and Mary are married with one child, Alice. After Mary and Bill separate, Mary and Alice move into an apartment where Mary begins living with her boyfriend. In the divorce proceeding, Bill argues that he should have sole physical custody because Mary is living in "illicit cohabitation" with her boyfriend. This argument will lose unless Bill can show that Mary's relationship with her boyfriend is having a detrimental effect on Alice. An example would be evidence that Alice is becoming emotionally upset because of the boyfriend's presence in the home and that this is negatively affecting her schoolwork. If, however, the relationship is not affecting Alice, the presence of the boyfriend will not be relevant to the determination of custody despite Bill's plea that his daughter should not be exposed to the "sin and immorality" of Mary's conduct.

Some judges take a different position when the parent seeking custody has a homosexual partner in the home. For example, in a 2002 concurring opinion of the Alabama Supreme Court, the chief justice said that "[h]omosexual conduct by its very nature is immoral, and its consequences are inherently destructive to the natural order of society. Any person who engages in such conduct is presumptively unfit to have custody of minor children under the established laws of this State."[14]

This view, however, is a minority view. Most judges apply the same nexus test in homosexual and heterosexual cases. A court will want to know if the couple is discreet in the expression of their mutual affection. If sexuality is flaunted, whether heterosexual or homosexual, a court is likely to conclude that a child will be adversely affected. Courts have granted custody to a gay or lesbian parent when all of the factors point to a healthy home environment for the child and there is no evidence that the homosexuality will have an adverse impact on the child. At one time, there was fear that a parent's homosexuality would cause the child to be homosexual. There are studies rejecting this conclusion, particularly because a child's sexual preference is developed during its infancy and very early years, which is often well before the homosexual parent seeks custody. It must be acknowledged, however, that a gay or lesbian parent has a substantial uphill battle in gaining custody or in keeping custody if the homosexuality is revealed only after the parent has been awarded custody. Homosexual parents have been most successful in winning custody when the heterosexual parent is either no longer available or is demonstrably unfit. In such cases, the homosexual parent wins by default unless his or her conduct is so offensive that the court will grant custody to neither biological parent.

The landmark case of *Lawrence v. Texas*, which we discussed in Chapter 5, is not directly relevant to custody disputes involving gay or lesbian parents. *Lawrence* held that it is unconstitutional to criminalize private same-sex conduct between consenting adults.[15] This is a very different issue from whether it is in the best interests of a child to be in the custody of a homosexual parent.

DOMESTIC VIOLENCE

domestic violence (DV)
Actual or threatened injury or abuse of one member of a family or household by another member.

Domestic violence (DV) is actual or threatened injury or abuse of one member of a family or household by another member. The most common examples are abuse against a spouse (spousal abuse) and abuse against a child (child abuse).

Spousal Abuse

Most courts take the position that a parent who commits spousal abuse is not necessarily an unfit parent. The court will want to know what effect the abuse has had on the child. Evidence of spousal abuse could be damaging if it was consistently committed in front of the child or if the anger and violence seriously disturbed the child's ability to function normally. It is possible, however, for the offending parent to show that the abuse was isolated and has not affected the home environment of the child. It may also help if this parent can show that he or she is seeking psychological counseling for anger control.

In some cases, both spouses charge each other with spousal abuse. One of the spouses, for example, may assert that he or she was simply acting in self-defense to the other's violent attack. The court may have to determine who was the primary aggressor and who was the primary victim. In general, a court will lean toward granting custody to the primary victim.

Child Abuse

child abuse
Serious physical, emotional, or sexual mistreatment of a child that is not the result of accident or of circumstances beyond the control of the parent or guardian.

If the domestic violence is directed at the child, the abuser will have great difficulty obtaining custody. **Child abuse** is serious physical, emotional, or sexual mistreatment of a child that is not the result of accident or of circumstances beyond the control of the parent or guardian. A court is obviously unlikely to grant custody to a parent who has a history of child abuse. We will see this hesitancy when we study the *Allen* case. Furthermore, the visitation rights of a violent parent are likely to be substantially restricted, such as by limiting the parent to supervised visitation, which we will examine shortly.

The "Terror Weapon"

> *"I had to face the fact that for one year [during the exercise of unsupervised visitation rights by the father], I sent my child off to her rapist."*[16]

> *"For many parents engaged in seriously contested child-custody disputes, false allegations of child abuse have become an effective weapon for achieving an advantage in court."*[17]

In alarming numbers, parents are being accused of sexually abusing their children, usually during visitation. The issue can also arise during an initial custody proceeding where one parent claims that the other committed sex abuse during the marriage, and hence should not be granted custody, or should not be granted visitation rights in unsupervised settings.

The level of bitterness generated by this accusation is incredibly high. It is the equivalent of a declaration of total war between the parties. One attorney calls accusations of such abuse "the new terror weapon in child-custody cases."[18] The chances of reaching a settlement or of mediating the custody dispute— or anything else that is contested—often vanish the moment the accusation is made. Protracted and costly litigation is all but inevitable.

Nor does litigation always resolve the matter. Assume that a mother with sole custody is turned down when she asks a court to terminate the father's right to visit the child because of an allegation of serious child abuse. The court finds the evidence of abuse to be insufficient and orders a continuation of visitation. Unable to accept this result, the mother goes underground out of desperation and a total loss of faith in the legal system. She flees with the child, or she turns the child over to sympathetic third parties who agree to keep the child hidden from the authorities. The child might be moved from one "safe house" to another to avoid detection. This underground network consists of a core of dedicated women who at one time were in a similar predicament, or who are former child-abuse victims themselves.

If the mother remains behind, she is hauled back into court. If she refuses to obey an order to produce the child, she faces an array of possible sanctions, including imprisonment for **civil contempt**, **criminal contempt**, or even prosecution for criminal kidnapping. Unfortunately, the media have an excessive interest in cases of this kind. Once reporters and cameras become involved, a circus atmosphere tends to develop.

Attorneys can find themselves in delicate situations. The first question they face is whether to take the case of an alleged child abuser—usually the father. Many attorneys need to believe in the father's innocence before agreeing to defend him. According to a prominent matrimonial attorney, "I have a higher duty to make sure some wacko doesn't get custody of his child." Before proceeding, therefore, the attorney might ask the prospective client to:

- Take a lie detector test.
- Take the **Minnesota Multiphasic Personality Inventory Test (MMPI)**, which may help reveal whether someone has a propensity to lie and is the kind of person who statistically is likely to be a child abuser.
- Be evaluated by a knowledgeable psychologist or psychiatrist.

civil contempt

The refusal of a party to comply with a court order (usually issued for the benefit of another), which can lead to punishment (including incarceration) until the party complies with the order.

criminal contempt

The refusal of a party to comply with a court order, which can lead to punishment (including incarceration) because of the repeated or aggravated nature of the refusal.

Minnesota Multiphasic Personality Inventory Test (MMPI)

A psychological test designed to assess personality characteristics.

Some attorneys have even insisted that the father undergo hypnosis as a further aid in trying to assess the truth of the allegation.

Attorneys representing the mother face similar concerns. Is she telling the truth? Is she exaggerating, knowingly or otherwise? Is she trying to seek some other strategic advantage from the father (e.g., more financial support, custody blackmail)? What advice should the attorney give her when she first reveals the charge of sexual abuse, particularly when the evidence of abuse is not overwhelming? Should she be advised to go public with the charge? As indicated, the consequences of doing so—and of not doing so—can be enormous. Bitter litigation is almost assured. What if the attorney talks her out of going public with the charge in order to settle the case through negotiation, "and a month or two later something terrible happens"? Faced, therefore, with a need to know if the accusation is true, the attorney may ask *her* to take a polygraph test or an MMPI, or to undergo an independent evaluation by a psychologist or psychiatrist.

Other attorneys disagree with this approach. They do not think that clients should be subject to such mistrust by their own attorneys. They fail to see much value in some of the devices used to assess the truth. Typical comments from such attorneys are that professionals "trained in sexual abuse are wrong very often"; "Frankly, I trust my horse sense more than I trust psychiatrists"; and "There is no research that says the polygraph or MMPI is of any use."[19]

Of course, attorneys for both sides will have to interview the child. This can be a very delicate task. There is a danger of emotional damage every time the child is forced to focus on the events in question. Even though children are generally truthful, many are susceptible to suggestion and manipulation. Very often the charge is made that the child has been "brainwashed" into believing that abuse did or did not occur. Clearly, the child needs protection. A separate attorney is usually appointed by the court to represent the child in the litigation. Guidelines may exist in the state on who can interview the child and in what setting. Trained child counselors are commonly used. Using special anatomically correct dolls, the counselor will ask the child to describe what happened. These interviews are usually videotaped. When the time comes for a court hearing, the judge will often interview the child outside the courtroom (e.g., in the judge's chambers) without either parent being present.

ASSIGNMENT 9.2

Diane and George are the parents of Mary. When the child is two years old, the parents divorce. The decree awards Diane sole physical and sole legal custody with visitation rights to George (on alternating weekends). Diane suspects that George is sexually abusing Mary during the visits. Answer the following questions for your state. (See General Instructions for the State-Code Assignment and General Instructions for the Court-Opinion Assignment in Appendix A.)

a. What options does Diane have?

b. Under what circumstances can the child be interviewed about the alleged molestation? Are there any restrictions on such interviews?

c. Can Diane be jailed for contempt of court if she refuses to obey an order to disclose Mary's location following a court decision that there was no sexual abuse by George? If so, for how long? Indefinitely?

CASE

Allen v. Farrow
197 A.D.2d 327, 611 N.Y.S.2d 859 (1994)
Supreme Court, Appellate Division, New York

Background: *Woody Allen is an internationally famous director and actor. His custody case generated widespread publicity. When it was over, Allen commented, "I was on the cover of every magazine, and magazines all over the world. I couldn't believe the amount of interest." (Frank Rich, "The Age of Mediathon," N.Y. Times, Sept. 29, 2000, at A58.) His opponent in the case was Mia Farrow, an actress who starred in thirteen of his movies. Allen had a romantic relationship with Farrow. She was formerly married to singer Frank Sinatra and conductor André Previn. (With Previn she had six children, three biological and three adopted. One of the adopted children was Soon-Yi Previn.) Farrow and Allen never married, but they had a child together, Satchel Farrow, and Allen adopted two of Farrow's other children, Moses Amadeus Farrow and Dylan O'Sullivan Farrow. The relationship between Allen and Farrow fell apart when Allen began a romantic relationship with Soon-Yi when she was nineteen or twenty-one years old. (There is some doubt about her date of birth in Korea.) At the time the affair began, Allen was fifty-seven years old. Farrow discovered the relationship after finding sexually explicit pictures that Allen took of Soon-Yi. Farrow also accused Allen of sexually abusing Dylan. (He was never criminally prosecuted for this charge.) A drawn-out, well-financed, and highly publicized custody trial ensued. Allen (the petitioner) went to court asking for custody of Satchel, Moses, and Dylan or for better visitation than Farrow was allowing him. He objected to supervised visitation. The trial court denied his request. Farrow (the respondent) was granted custody and counsel fees. Allen's visitation with the three children was severely limited: (1) He was granted supervised visitation with Satchel for two hours, three times a week. (2) Visitation with Dylan was to be "conducted in a therapeutic context" until the therapist recommends to the court that other visitation is appropriate. (3) Moses, now fifteen years old, refused to see Allen and the court refused to force him to do so. Allen has now appealed to the Supreme Court, Appellate Division.*

Decision on Appeal: *The decision of the trial court in Farrow's favor on custody, visitation, and counsel fees is affirmed.*

OPINION OF THE COURT

Justice ROSS delivered the opinion of the court. . . .

The petitioner and the respondent have brought themselves to this unhappy juncture primarily as a result of two recent events. These are, Mr. Allen's affair with Soon-Yi Previn and the alleged sexual abuse of Dylan O'Sullivan Farrow by Mr. Allen. While the parties had difficulties which grew during Ms. Farrow's pregnancy with Satchel, it was the discovery of the relationship between Mr. Allen and Ms. Previn that intensified Ms. Farrow's concerns about Mr. Allen's behavior toward Dylan, and resulted

in the retention of counsel by both parties. While various aspects of this matter remain unclear, it is evident that each party assigns the blame for the current state of affairs to the other.

The parties' respective arguments are very clear. The petitioner maintains that he was forced to commence this proceeding in order to preserve his parental rights to the three infant children, because the respondent commenced and continues to engage in a campaign to alienate him from his children and to ultimately defeat his legal rights to them. The petitioner contends, inter alia, that the respondent seeks to accomplish her goals primarily through manipulation of the children's perceptions of him. He wishes to obtain custody, ostensibly to counteract the detrimental psychological effects the respondent's actions have had on his children, and to provide them with a more stable atmosphere in which to develop. Mr. Allen specifically denies the allegations that he sexually abused Dylan and characterizes them as part of Ms. Farrow's extreme overreaction to his admitted relationship with Ms. [Soon-Yi] Previn.

The respondent maintains that the petitioner has shown no genuine parental interest in, nor any regard for, the children's welfare and that any interest he has shown has been inappropriate and even harmful. Respondent cites the fact that the petitioner has commenced and maintained an intimate sexual relationship with her daughter Soon-Yi Previn, which he has refused to curtail, despite the obvious ill effects it has had on all of the children and the especially profound effect it has had on Moses. It is also contended that petitioner has, at best, an inappropriately intense interest in, and at worst, an abusive relationship with, the parties' daughter Dylan. Further, the respondent maintains that petitioner's contact with the parties' biological son, Satchel, is harmful to the child in that petitioner represents an emotional threat and has on at least one occasion threatened physical harm. Respondent contends that the petitioner's only motive in commencing this proceeding was to retaliate against the allegations of child sexual abuse made against him by Ms. Farrow.

Certain salient facts concerning both Mr. Allen's and Ms. Farrow's relationships to their children and to each other are not disputed. Review of these facts in an objective manner and the conclusions that flow from them, demonstrate that the determination of the [trial] court as to both custody and visitation is amply supported by the record before this Court.

From the inception of Mr. Allen's relationship with Ms. Farrow in 1980, until a few months after the adoption of Dylan O'Sullivan Farrow on June 11, 1985, Mr. Allen wanted nothing to do with Ms. Farrow's children. Although Mr. Allen and Ms. Farrow attempted for approximately six months to have a child of their own, Mr. Allen did so apparently only after Ms. Farrow promised to assume full responsibility for the child. Following the adoption, however, Mr. Allen became interested in

(continued)

CASE • Allen v. Farrow (continued)

developing a relationship with the newly adopted Dylan. While previously he rarely spent time in the respondent's apartment, after the adoption of Dylan he went to the respondent's Manhattan apartment more often, visited Ms. Farrow's Connecticut home and even accompanied the Farrow family on vacations to Europe. Allen also developed a relationship with Moses Farrow, who had been adopted by the respondent in 1980 and was seven years old at the time of Dylan's adoption. However, Allen remained distant from Farrow's other six children.

In 1986 Ms. Farrow expressed a desire to adopt another child. Mr. Allen, while not enthusiastic at the prospect of the adoption of Dylan in 1985, was much more amenable to the idea in 1986. Before the adoption could be completed Ms. Farrow became pregnant with the parties' son Satchel. While the petitioner testified that he was happy at the idea of becoming a father, the record supports the finding that Mr. Allen showed little or no interest in the pregnancy. It is not disputed that Ms. Farrow began to withdraw from Mr. Allen during the pregnancy and that afterwards she did not wish Satchel to become attached to Mr. Allen.

According to Mr. Allen, Ms. Farrow became inordinately attached to the newborn Satchel to the exclusion of the other children. He viewed this as especially harmful to Dylan and began spending more time with her, ostensibly to make up for the lack of attention shown her by Ms. Farrow after the birth of Satchel. Mr. Allen maintains that his interest in and affection for Dylan always has been paternal in nature and never sexual. The various psychiatric experts who testified or otherwise provided reports did not conclude that Allen's behavior toward Dylan prior to August of 1992 was explicitly sexual in nature. However, the clear consensus was that his interest in Dylan was abnormally intense in that he made inordinate demands on her time and focused on her to the exclusion of Satchel and Moses even when they were present.

The record demonstrates that Ms. Farrow expressed concern to Allen about his relationship with Dylan, and that Allen expressed his concern to Ms. Farrow about her relationship with Satchel. In 1990 both Dylan and Satchel were evaluated by clinical psychologists. Dr. Coates began treatment of Satchel in 1990. In April of 1991 Dylan was referred to Dr. Schultz, a clinical psychologist specializing in the treatment of young children with serious emotional problems.

In 1990 at about the same time that the parties were growing distant from each other and expressing their concerns about the other's relationship with their youngest children, Mr. Allen began acknowledging Farrow's daughter Soon-Yi Previn. Previously he treated Ms. Previn in the same way he treated Ms. Farrow's other children from her prior marriage, rarely even speaking to them. In September of 1991 Ms. Previn began to attend Drew College in New Jersey. In December 1991 two events coincided. Mr. Allen's adoptions of Dylan and Moses were finalized and Mr. Allen began his sexual relationship with their sister Soon-Yi Previn.

In January of 1992, Mr. Allen took the photographs of Ms. Previn, which were discovered on the mantelpiece in his apartment by Ms. Farrow and were introduced into evidence at the [trial court] proceeding. Mr. Allen in his trial testimony stated that he took the photos at Ms. Previn's suggestion and that he considered them erotic and not pornographic. We have viewed the photographs and do not share Mr. Allen's characterization of them. We find the fact that Mr. Allen took them at a time when he was formally assuming a legal responsibility for two of Ms. Previn's siblings to be totally unacceptable. The distinction Mr. Allen makes between Ms. Farrow's [older adopted children] and Dylan, Satchel and Moses is lost on this court. The children themselves do not draw the same distinction that Mr. Allen does. This is sadly demonstrated by the profound effect his relationship with Ms. Previn has had on the entire family.

Allen's testimony that the photographs of Ms. Previn ". . . were taken, as I said before, between two consenting adults wanting to do this . . ." demonstrates a chosen ignorance of his and Ms. Previn's relationships to Ms. Farrow, his three children and Ms. Previn's other siblings. His continuation of the relationship, viewed in the best possible light, shows a distinct absence of judgment. It demonstrates to this court Mr. Allen's tendency to place inappropriate emphasis on his own wants and needs and to minimize and even ignore those of his children. At the very minimum, it demonstrates an absence of any parenting skills.

We recognize Mr. Allen's acknowledgment of the pain his relationship with Ms. Previn has caused the family. We also note his testimony that he tried to insulate the rest of the family from the "dispute" that resulted, and tried to "de-escalate the situation" by attempting to "placate" Ms. Farrow. It is true that Ms. Farrow's failure to conceal her feelings from the rest of the family and the acting out of her feelings of betrayal and anger toward Mr. Allen enhanced the effect of the situation on the rest of her family. We note though that the reasons for her behavior, however prolonged and extreme, are clearly visible in the record. On the other hand the record contains no acceptable explanation for Allen's commencement of the sexual relationship with Ms. Previn at the time he was adopting Moses . . ., or for the continuation of that relationship at the time he was supposedly experiencing the joys of fatherhood.

While the petitioner's testimony regarding his attempts to de-escalate the dispute and to insulate the family from it displays a measure of concern for his three children, it is clear that he should have realized the inevitable consequences of his actions well before his relationship with Ms. Previn became intimate. Allen's various inconsistent statements to Farrow of his intentions regarding Ms. Previn and his attempt to have Dr. Schultz explain the relationship to Dylan in such a manner as to exonerate himself from any wrong doing, make it difficult for this court to find that his expressed concern for the welfare of the family is genuine.

As we noted above, Mr. Allen maintains that Ms. Farrow's allegations concerning the sexual abuse of Dylan were fabricated by Ms. Farrow both as a result of her rage over his relationship with Ms. Previn and as part of her continued plan to alienate him from his children. However, our review of the record militates against a finding that Ms. Farrow fabricated the allegations without any basis. . . . [There is evidence to] suggest that the abuse did occur. While the evidence in support of the allegations remains inconclusive, it is clear that the investigation of the charges in and of itself could not have left Dylan unaffected.

Any determination of issues of child custody or visitation must serve the best interests of the child and that which will best promote the child's welfare (*Domestic Relations Law* § 70; *Eschbach v. Eschbach,* 56 N.Y.2d 167, 171). . . . It was noted by the [trial] court that the psychiatric experts agreed that Mr. Allen may be able to fulfill a positive role in Dylan's therapy. We note specifically the opinion of Dr. Brodzinsky, the impartial expert called by both parties, who concluded that contact with Mr. Allen is necessary to Dylan's future development, but that initially any such visitation should be conducted in a therapeutic context. The [trial] court structured that visitation accordingly and provided that a further review of Allen's visitation with Dylan would be considered after an evaluation of Dylan's progress.

Although the investigation of the abuse allegations have not resulted in a conclusive finding, all of the evidence received at trial supports the determination as to custody and visitation with respect to this child. There would be no beneficial purpose served in disturbing the custody arrangement. Moreover, even if the abuse did not occur, it is evident that there are issues concerning Mr. Allen's inappropriately intense relationship with this child that can be resolved only in a therapeutic setting. At the very least, the process of investigation itself has left the relationship between Mr. Allen and Dylan severely damaged. The consensus is that both Mr. Allen and Ms. Farrow need to be involved in the recovery process. The provision for further review of the visitation arrangement embodied in the trial court's decision adequately protects the petitioner's rights and interests at this time.

With respect to Satchel, the [trial] court denied the petitioner's request for unsupervised visitation. While the court stated that it was not concerned for Satchel's physical safety, it was concerned by Mr. Allen's "demonstrated inability to understand the impact that his words and deeds have upon the emotional well-being of the children." We agree. The record supports the conclusion that Mr. Allen may, if unsupervised, influence Satchel inappropriately, and disregard the impact exposure to Mr. Allen's relationship with Satchel's sister, Ms. Previn, would have on the child. His failure to understand the effect of such exposure upon Satchel as well as upon his other children is evidenced by his statement on direct examination in which he stated:

If you ask me personally, I would say the children, the children adore Soon-Yi, they adore me, they would be

delighted, if you asked me this personally, I would say they would be delighted and have fun with us, being taken places with us. But, I don't want to give you my amateur opinion on that. That's how I feel. And I know it counts for very little.

The record indicates that Ms. Previn when not at college spends most of her time with Mr. Allen. Contact between Ms. Previn and her siblings in the context of the relationship with Mr. Allen would be virtually unavoidable even if Mr. Allen chose to insulate his children from the relationship. Expert medical testimony indicated that it would be harmful for Ms. Previn not to be reintegrated into the family. However, the inquiry here concerns the best interests of Dylan, Moses and Satchel. Their best interests would clearly be served by contact with their sister Soon-Yi, personally and not in Mr. Allen's presence. Seeing both Ms. Previn and Mr. Allen together in the unsupervised context envisioned by Mr. Allen would, at this early stage, certainly be detrimental to the best interests of the children. It has been held that the desires of the child are to be considered, but that it must be kept in mind that those desires can be manipulated (*Friederwitzer v. Friederwitzer,* 55 N.Y.2d 89, 94). In considering the custody and visitation decision concerning Moses, who is now a teenager, we cannot ignore his expressed desires. The record shows that he had a beneficial relationship with the petitioner prior to the events of December 1991. However, that relationship has been gravely damaged. While Moses' feelings were certainly affected by his mother's obvious pain and anger, we concluded that it would not be in Moses' best interests to be compelled to see Mr. Allen, if he does not wish to.

Therefore, we hold that in view of the totality of the circumstances, the best interests of these children would be served by remaining together in the custody of Ms. Farrow, with the parties abiding by the visitation schedule established by the trial court.

With respect to the award of counsel fees we note that the record demonstrates that Mr. Allen's resources far outpace those of Ms. Farrow. Additionally, we note the relative lack of merit of Mr. Allen's position in commencing this proceeding for custody. It became apparent, during oral argument, that there was serious doubt that Mr. Allen truly desired custody. It has been held that "in exercising its discretionary power to award counsel fees, a court should review the financial circumstances of both parties together with all the other circumstances of the case, which may include the relative merit of the parties' positions" (*DeCabrera v. Cabrera-Rosete,* 70 N.Y.2d 879, 881). We find no abuse of discretion in the court's award of counsel fees in this case.

Accordingly, the judgment [below] . . . , which, inter alia, denied the petitioner Woody Allen's request for custody of Moses Amadeus Farrow, Dylan O'Sullivan Farrow, and Satchel Farrow, set forth the terms of visitation between the petitioner and his children and awarded Ms. Farrow counsel fees, is affirmed in all respects, without costs.

(continued)

CASE • Allen v. Farrow (continued)

CARRO, Justice (dissenting in part).

I agree with the majority's conclusions, except for the affirmance of the order of visitation with respect to Mr. Allen's son Satchel, which I find unduly restrictive.

There is strong evidence in the record from neutral observers that Mr. Allen and Satchel basically have a warm and loving father-son relationship, but that their relationship is in jeopardy, in large measure because Mr. Allen is being estranged and alienated from his son by the current custody and visitation arrangement. Frances Greenberg and Virginia Lehman, two independent social workers employed to oversee visitation with Satchel, testified how "Mr. Allen would welcome Satchel by hugging him, telling him how much he loved him, and how much he missed him." Also described by both supervisors "was a kind of sequence that Mr. Allen might say, I love you as much as the river, and Satchel would say something to the effect that I love you as much as New York City . . . then Mr. Allen might say, I love you as much as the stars, and Satchel would say, I love you as much as the universe." Sadly, there was also testimony from those witnesses that Satchel had told Mr. Allen: "I like you, but I am not supposed to love you;" that when Mr. Allen asked Satchel if he would send him a postcard from a planned trip to California with Ms. Farrow, Satchel said "I can't [because] Mommy won't let me;" and on one occasion when Satchel indicated that he wanted to stay with Mr. Allen longer than the allotted two-hour visit, "Satchel did say he could not stay longer, that his mother had told him that two hours was sufficient." Perhaps most distressing, Satchel "indicated to Mr. Allen that he was seeing a doctor that was going to help him not to see Mr. Allen anymore, and he indicated that he was supposed to be seeing this doctor perhaps eight or ten times, at the end of which he would no longer have to see Mr. Allen."

In contrast to what apparently is being expressed by Ms. Farrow about Mr. Allen to Satchel, Mr. Allen has been reported to say only positive things to Satchel about Ms. Farrow, and conveys only loving regards to Moses and Dylan through Satchel. Thus I find little evidence in the record to support the majority's conclusion that "Mr. Allen may, if unsupervised, influence Satchel inappropriately, and disregard the impact exposure to Mr. Allen's relationship with Satchel's sister, Ms. Previn, would have on the child."

The majority's quotation of Mr. Allen's testimony with respect to Soon-Yi in support of its conclusion respecting visitation should be viewed in the context of Dr. David Brodzinsky's testimony. Dr. Brodzinsky is an expert in adoption with considerable experience in court-related evaluations of custody and visitation disputes. . . . It was his clinical judgment that Mr. Allen had more awareness of the consequences of his actions than he was able to articulate in the adversarial process, and he was optimistic about Mr. Allen's ability to accept his share of responsibility for what had taken place in light of his love for his children, his capacity for perspective taking and empathy, and his motivation and openness toward the ongoing therapeutic process. In addition, Dr. Susan Coates, Satchel's therapist until December 1992, and the only expert to testify about Satchel's mental health, stated that Mr. Allen's parental relationship with Satchel was essential to Satchel's healthy development. . . .

I do not believe that Mr. Allen's visitation with Satchel for a mere two hours, three times a week, under supervision, is reasonable and meaningful under the circumstances, or that exceptional circumstances are presented that warrant such significant restriction on visitation with Satchel. Mr. Allen and Satchel clearly need substantial quality time together to nurture and renew their bonds and to foster a warm and loving father-son relationship. Obviously this cannot occur overnight; but more significantly, it is almost inconceivable that it will occur even over an extended period of time if visitation is limited to three two-hour periods per week under the supervision of strangers, as ordered by the trial court and affirmed by the majority. Accordingly I would modify the judgment appealed from to provide that Mr. Allen shall have unsupervised visitation with Satchel for four hours, three times weekly, plus alternate Saturdays and Sundays for the entire day, plus alternate holidays to be agreed upon by the parties.

ASSIGNMENT 9.3

a. Was Allen denied custody because of his immoral behavior?

b. (i) For Allen, prepare a list of factual allegations that support his position that he should be given custody rather than Farrow. (ii) For Farrow, prepare a list of factual allegations that support her position that she should be given custody rather than Allen. (iii) In class, be prepared to be called upon to debate who should have custody. Provide separate answers, as needed, for each child: Satchel, Dylan, and Moses.

c. Is it relevant that Allen married Soon-Yi soon after the case?

d. What responsibility, if any, did the court assign to the behavior of Mia Farrow? Did she help cause Allen's deterioration with the children? Does the parental alienation syndrome (PAS) apply?

e. If Allen is correct that Farrow has poisoned his relationship with the children, wouldn't keeping him away from them reward her efforts?

f. The court said Allen agreed to have a biological child "apparently only after Ms. Farrow promised to assume full responsibility for the child." If Farrow did make this promise, what legal effect do you think it would have? For example, would it affect Allen's duty of child support? (See Chapter 10.)

g. The dissent says that in the "clinical judgment" of Dr. Brodzinsky, an adoption expert, "Allen had more awareness of the consequences of his actions than he was able to articulate in the adversarial process." What do you think Brodzinsky meant? Is a courtroom the best place to resolve disputed custody cases? Is there an alternative?

RELIGION

Twenty-seven percent of married people live in religiously mixed marriages.[19a] Most do so in harmony, but when divorce occurs, the religion of minor children can become part of the custody dispute in the divorce. Under the U.S. Constitution, a court cannot resolve this dispute by favoring one religion over another or by preferring organized religion over less orthodox forms of religious beliefs. To do so could amount to an unconstitutional "establishment" of religion. The state must remain neutral. The parenting plans of the parties will state how they propose to handle religion in the life of the child. In the court's response to these plans,

- the focus of the court must be to determine what effect, if any, the practice of religion in the parenting plan is likely to have on the child;

- courts are not as concerned about the religious *beliefs* that one parent will inculcate in the child as they are about the religious *conduct* that the parent will be asking the child to engage in;

- the focus of the court cannot be on whether one religion or religious practice is preferable or correct (1) according to the judge's personal standards, (2) according to the standards of the majority in the community, or (3) according to "respectable" minorities in the community.

The court will want to know what religion, if any, the child has practiced to date. Continuity is highly desirable. Also, will the practice of a particular religion tend to take the child away from other activities? For example, will the child be asked to spend long hours in door-to-door selling of religious literature and hence be unable to attend regular school? If so, the court will be reluctant to award custody to the parent who would require this of the child.

Courts sometimes have to walk a thin line between protecting a child and keeping out of religious disputes. In one case, for example, the mother was an observant orthodox Jew and the father was a fundamentalist Christian who believed that anyone who did not accept Jesus was destined for hell. During the marriage, the parents had agreed to raise the children in the Jewish tradition, including allowing their son, Ariel, to grow payes (side curls). In the divorce, the mother was granted sole physical custody but both parents were given joint legal custody. The mother asked the court to limit the exposure of the children to their father's religion. The court appointed a guardian ad litem (GAL) to help the parents resolve future inter-religious conflicts and issued the following order:

RESTRICTIONS UPON RELIGIOUS EXPOSURE: Each parent shall be entitled to share his/her religious beliefs with the children with restrictions as follows: neither may indoctrinate the children in a manner which substantially promotes their . . . alienation from either parent or their rejection of either parent. The [father] shall not take the children to his church (whether to church services or Sunday School or church educational programs); nor engage them in prayer or bible study if it promotes rejection rather than acceptance, of their mother or their own Jewish self-identity. The [father] shall not share his religious beliefs with the children if those beliefs cause the children significant emotional distress or worry about their mother or about themselves. Thus, for example, [the father] may have pictures of Jesus Christ hanging on the walls of his residence, . . . [but he] may not take the children to religious services where they receive the message that adults or children who do not accept Jesus Christ as their lord and savior are destined to burn in hell. By way of further example, [he] may not shave off [their son's] payes. This provision shall not be construed so as to prevent [the father] from having the children with him at events involving family traditions at Christmas and Easter. In the event that there is a disagreement between the parents as to whether one or more of the children could be exposed to the religious belief(s) of [the father] without substantial negative impact upon their emotional health, the parents shall engage the services of Michael Goldberg, Ph.D., to act as G.A.L./investigator/evaluator on such issues and disputes. The fee of Dr. Goldberg shall be shared equally by the parties. In the event that Dr. Goldberg is unable to serve in this capacity, then the parties shall agree upon an alternate child psychologist, or an alternate shall be selected by the Court. . . .[20]

ASSIGNMENT 9.4

When Helen married John, she converted from Catholicism to his religion, Judaism. Neither Helen nor John, however, was a very religious person. To a moderate extent, their two children were raised in the Jewish faith. The couple divorced when the children were aged four and five. Because of John's job, he could not spend much time with the children. Hence, he agreed that Helen receive sole physical and sole legal custody. But he asked the court to order Helen to continue raising the children in the Jewish faith.

a. Under what circumstances do you think a court can grant this request, so that, in effect, John will be granted *spiritual custody* of the children even though physical custody and legal custody (in all matters except religion) will be granted to Helen? (See General instructions for the Legal-Analysis Assignment in Appendix A.)

b. Suppose that Helen returns to her original religion and starts taking the children to Catholic services. What options does John have in your state? (See General Instructions for the State-Code Assignment and the Court-Opinion Assignment in Appendix A.)

RACE

A child's ethnic and cultural heritage is important. Suppose, for example, that a child has been raised in a Mexican American community. If possible, a court will want to grant custody to the parent who will help the child maintain his or her contacts with this community. Race, however, cannot be the *sole* factor that determines custody. Assume that a divorced white parent asks a court for custody because the other parent has married a black person. A court's grant of custody for this reason would be an unconstitutional denial of the equal protection of the law.[21] Race cannot be the sole factor in a custody decision.

WISHES OF THE CHILD

Older children are almost always asked where they would want to live. Greater caution, however, is needed when the child-custody dispute centers on young children. If asking such children about their preferences became commonplace, there would be an incentive for both parents to pressure the child to choose one side or the other. If, however, the court is convinced that the child is mature enough to state a rational preference and that doing so would not harm the child, evidence of such a preference will be admissible. The judge might decide to speak to the child outside the formal courtroom (with the attorneys but not the parents present), or the judge might allow a professional (e.g., child psychologist, social worker) to interview the child at home.

EXPERT WITNESSES

Psychologists, psychiatrists, social workers, and other experts can be called as expert witnesses by either parent to testify on the home environment, the child's emotional development, the mental stability of the parents, the suitability of various parenting plans, etc. Experts can be asked to conduct investigations, make recommendations, give second opinions, and act as mediators.

Care is needed when experts are used in a custody case. Overreliance on experts can cause problems. It would be an error, for example, for a court to rule that a parent should not have visitation rights until a psychiatrist or other professional concludes that such visitation would be beneficial. It is for the court to decide when custody and visitation is proper. Experts can give their opinions to the judge, who will make the decision on what is in the best interests of the child. The decision cannot be delegated to a professional.

Either parent, or the guardian ad litem for the child, can make a motion that the court order a custody evaluation by an expert. See the example of a custody-evaluation report by such an expert in Exhibit 9-3.

EXHIBIT 9-3   Example of a Custody Evaluation by an Expert

Psychiatric Custody Evaluation

Honorable James K. O'Brien
Supreme Court of New York
New York County
60 Centre Street
New York, New York 10007

Re: Johnson v. Johnson
Docket No. M-3784-06

Dear Judge O'Brien:

This report is submitted in compliance with your court order dated June 9, 2006, requesting that I conduct an evaluation of the Johnson family in order to provide the court with information that would be useful to it in deciding which of the Johnson parents should have custody of their children Tara, Elaine, and Charles.

My findings and recommendations are based on interviews conducted as itemized below:

July 6, 2006—Mrs. Carol Johnson and Mr. Frank Johnson, seen jointly	2 hours
July 7, 2006—Mr. Frank Johnson	1 hour
July 11, 2006—Mrs. Carol Johnson	1 hour
July 13, 2006—Tara Johnson	1½ hours
July 14, 2006—Mr. Frank Johnson	1 hour
July 20, 2006—Mrs. Carol Johnson	1 hour
July 21, 2006—Charles Johnson	¾ hour

(continued)

EXHIBIT 9-3 *(continued)*

Elaine Johnson	¾ hour
July 22, 2006—Tara Johnson	½ hour
Mrs. Carol Johnson and Tara Johnson, seen jointly	½ hour
July 24, 2006—Mrs. Carol Johnson	1 hour
July 27, 2006—Mrs. Carol Johnson and Mr. Frank Johnson, seen jointly	1 hour
Aug. 3, 2006—Elaine Johnson	¾ hour
Aug. 4, 2006—Tara Johnson	¼ hour
Mr. Frank Johnson and Tara Johnson, seen jointly	½ hour
Aug. 10, 2006—Tara Johnson	
Mr. Frank Johnson and Mrs. Carol Johnson, seen jointly	¾ hour
Aug. 11, 2006—Tara Johnson	
Elaine Johnson	
Charles Johnson	
Mrs. Carol Johnson and Mr. Frank Johnson, seen jointly	¾ hour
Aug. 14, 2006—Tara Johnson	
Elaine Johnson	
Charles Johnson	
Mrs. Carol Johnson and Mr. Frank Johnson, seen jointly	1 hour
Total Time	16 hours

In addition, on August 16, 2006, Mr. and Mrs. Johnson were seen together for the purpose of my presenting these findings and recommendations to them. This interview lasted two hours, bringing to 18 the total number of hours spent with the Johnson family in association with this evaluation.

Mr. Frank Johnson, an airline pilot, is 43 years old. His first wife died soon after the delivery of Tara, who is now 16 years of age. He married Mrs. Carol Johnson when Tara was 2 years old. Mrs. Johnson, a housewife, who was formerly an elementary school teacher, is now 40. Her first marriage ended in divorce. A child of this relationship died soon after birth. There are two children of the Johnson marriage: Elaine, 11 and Charles, 7. Mrs. Johnson adopted her stepdaughter Tara in July 2005. In October 2005, Mr. Johnson initiated divorce proceedings because he felt that his wife no longer respected him and that she was a poor mother for the children, especially his daughter Tara. However, Mr. and Mrs. Johnson are still occupying the same domicile.

Both parents are requesting custody of all three children. It is this examiner's recommendation that Mr. Frank Johnson be granted custody of Tara and that Mrs. Carol Johnson be granted custody of Elaine and Charles. The observations that have led me to these conclusions will be divided into four categories:

1. Mr. Frank Johnson's assets as a parent,
2. Mr. Frank Johnson's liabilities as a parent,
3. Mrs. Carol Johnson's assets as a parent, and
4. Mrs. Carol Johnson's liabilities as a parent.

Following these four presentations I will comment further on the way in which my observations brought about the aforementioned recommendations. Although much information was obtained in the course of the evaluation, only those items specifically pertinent to the custody consideration will be included in this report.

1. Mr. Frank Johnson's Assets as a Parent

Mr. Frank Johnson is Tara's biological father. The special psychological tie that this engenders is not enjoyed by Mrs. Carol Johnson and Tara. It is not the genetic bond per se that is crucial here; rather, it is the psychological attachment that such a bond elicits. Mr. Johnson had already started to develop a psychological tie with Tara while his first wife was pregnant with her. He was actually present at her birth and assumed an active role in her rearing—almost from birth because of the illness and early death of his first wife. This situation prevailed until the time of his marriage to Mrs. Johnson when Tara was 2 years of age. Although Mrs. Johnson has been Tara's primary caretaker since then, Mr. Johnson's early involvement with Tara during these crucial years of her development contributes to a very strong psychological tie between them that has continued up to the present time.

My observations have convinced me, and both parents agree, that at this time, Tara has a closer relationship with her father than her mother. Her relationship with Mrs. Johnson at this time is characteristically a difficult one in that there are frequent battles and power struggles. Although Tara is not completely free of such involvement with her father, such hostile interaction is far less common. In my interviews with Mr. Johnson and Tara, I found her to be far more friendly with him than I observed her to be with Mrs. Johnson in my joint interviews with them.

In every interview, both alone and in joint sessions with various members of the family, Tara openly and unswervingly stated that she wished to live with her father: "I want to live with my father. I am closer to him." "When I was younger, my mother did more things; but since I'm older, my father does more things." "My father listens to what I say; my mother doesn't."

Mr. Johnson and Tara both utilize a similar method of communication. Neither feels a strong need to give confirmation of examples to general statements that they make, and they are therefore comfortable with one another. Mrs. Johnson, on the other hand, is much more specific in her communications and this is a source of difficulty, not only in her relationship with Tara, but in her relationship with her husband as well.

All five family members agree that Mr. Johnson spends significant time with Charles, involved in typical father-son activities (sports, games, etc.). It is also apparent that Charles has a strong masculine identification and this arose, in part, from his modeling himself after his father.

2. Mr. Frank Johnson's Liabilities as a Parent

Mr. Johnson states that he would not have involved himself in the custody evaluation conducted by this examiner if he had to contribute to its financing. Accordingly, Mrs. Johnson assumed the total financial obligation for this evaluation. I conclude from this that with regard to this particular criterion for comparing the parents, Mr. Johnson's position is less strong than Mrs. Johnson's.

On many occasions Mr. Johnson made general comments about his superiority over his wife with regard to parental capacity. For example, "She's a very poor mother," "She neglects the children," and "If you had all the information you would see that I'm a better parent." However, it was extremely difficult to elicit from Mr. Johnson specific examples of incidents that would substantiate these statements. I not only considered this to be a manifestation of Mr. Johnson's problem in accurately communicating, but also considered it to be a deficiency in his position. One cannot be convinced of the strength of such statements if no examples can be provided to substantiate them.

In the hope that I might get more specific information from Mr. Johnson I asked him, on at least three occasions, to write a list of specifics that might help corroborate some of his allegations. He came to three subsequent interviews without having written anything in response to my invitation. I consider such failure to reflect a compromise in his motivation for gaining custody of the three children. When he did finally submit such a list it was far less comprehensive than that which was submitted by Mrs. Johnson and in addition, the issues raised had far less significance, e.g., "She's late once in a while," "She's sometimes forgetful," and "She doesn't like playing baseball with Charles."

(continued)

EXHIBIT 9-3 *(continued)*

Although I described Mr. Johnson's communication problem as a factor supporting his gaining custody of Tara, I would consider it a liability with regard to his gaining custody of Elaine and Charles. Tara (possibly on a genetic basis) communicates in a similar way and so, as mentioned, is comfortable with her father when they communicate. Elaine and Charles, however, appear to be identifying with their mother with regard to communication accuracy. Accordingly, intensive exposure to Mr. Johnson might compromise what I consider a healthier communicative pattern.

Mr. Johnson's profession as an airline pilot has not enabled him to have predictable hours. Not only is his schedule variable, but there are times when he is required to work on an emergency basis. All three children agree that Mrs. Johnson is more predictably present. Mr. Johnson's irregular schedule is not a significant problem for Tara who, at 16, is fairly independent and would not suffer significantly from her father's schedule. The younger children, however, are still in need of predictability of parental presence and Mr. Johnson has not demonstrated his capacity to provide such predictability. In my final interview with Mr. Johnson he stated that he would change his work pattern to be available to his children during non-school hours. Mrs. Johnson was very dubious that this could be arranged because his job does not allow such flexibility. Both parents agreed, however, that it had not occurred in the past and that such predictability was not taking place at the time of this evaluation.

Both Charles and Elaine stated that they wanted to live with their mother and not live with their father. Charles stated, "I want to be with my mother. I'd be alone when my father goes to work." Elaine stated, "I want to live with my mother. I'm closer to my mother. I'm not as close to my father."

In a session in which I was discussing his future plans with Mr. Johnson, he stated that he was considering moving to California because he could earn more money there by supplementing his income with certain business ventures that he had been invited to participate in. He stated also that he would still move even if he were only to be granted custody of Tara. Although I appreciate that a higher income could provide Mr. Johnson's children with greater financial flexibility, I believe that the disadvantages of such a move would far outweigh its advantages from their point of view. Specifically, the extra advantages they might enjoy from such a move would be more than offset by the even greater absence of their father who, his liabilities notwithstanding, is still an important figure for them.

In an interview in which I discussed with Mr. Johnson how he would react to the various custodial decisions, he was far more upset about the prospect of losing Tara than he was about the possibility of losing Charles and Elaine. In fact, he appeared to be accepting of the fact that Elaine would go to her mother. Although somewhat distressed about the possibility of Charles' living with his mother, he did not show the same degree of distress as his wife over the prospect of losing the younger two children.

3. Mrs. Carol Johnson's Assets as a Parent

Mrs. Carol Johnson was far more committed to the custody evaluation than her husband. As mentioned, she was willing to make the financial sacrifices involved in the evaluation. I consider this to be a factor reflecting greater motivation than her husband for gaining custody of the children. Mrs. Johnson is more available to the children during non-school hours than her husband and this is one element in her favor regarding gaining custody, especially of the younger children. Mrs. Johnson is a more accurate and clearer communicator than her husband and this is an asset. As mentioned, the younger children do not seem to have been affected by their father's communication difficulty. Having them live with him might result in their acquiring this maladaptive trait.

During her pregnancy with Elaine, Mrs. Johnson suffered with toxemia and associated high blood pressure and convulsions. Most physicians generally discourage women with this disorder from becoming pregnant again because it is genuinely life endangering. However, Mrs. Johnson did wish to have a third child, primarily because her husband, she states, was so desirous of having a son. Her pregnancy with Charles was complicated by the exacerbation of a preexisting asthmatic condition from which she states that she almost died. A less maternal woman would not have become pregnant again.

Elaine stated on many occasions, and in every interview, both alone and with other family members, that she wished to live with her mother: "I'm closer to my mother," "She's home more than my father," "They call my father to do things at work all the time," and "My mother has more feelings for me than my father."

Charles also, both in individual session and in joint interviews, emphatically stated that he wished to live with his mother: "I want to stay with my mother because she doesn't work as much as my father." "If you get sick the father might not know what to do, but the mother does." "My mother knows how to take care of me." "She doesn't work that much." "She reads me books more than my father."

On one occasion Mr. Johnson stated: "Carol is closer to Elaine than I am. They are similar. They're both sore losers. Both get emotional if they don't have their way." Mrs. Carol Johnson agrees that she and her daughter Elaine have these traits, but not to the degree described by her husband. Although there are certainly negative elements regarding the reasons why Mr. Johnson sees Elaine to be closer to his wife, this statement is an admission of his recognition of this preference of Elaine for her mother. The situation is analogous to Mr. Johnson's involvement with Tara. They are closer to one another, yet maladaptive and undesirable factors are contributing to the closeness.

<u>4. Mrs. Carol Johnson's Liabilities as a Parent</u>

Tara is not Mrs. Johnson's biological daughter. Although she has raised Tara from her infancy, as if she were her own biological child, and although she has adopted her, Mrs. Johnson is at a certain disadvantage regarding the development of a strong psychological parent-child tie. As mentioned, I believe that a biological relationship increases the strength of the psychological bond. Accordingly, Mrs. Johnson is at a disadvantage when compared to Mr. Johnson regarding this aspect of the custody consideration.

Mrs. Johnson and Tara have a poor relationship at this point. In my interviews with Mrs. Johnson and Tara I found the latter to view her mother scornfully and to be openly resentful of her authority. On one occasion Tara said: "She has a lot of nerve telling me what to do." Were this an isolated statement, it would probably not have much significance. However, all agreed that it epitomized her general attitude toward her mother. Although some of the scornful attitude Tara exhibits toward her mother can be viewed as age-appropriate, I believe the extent goes beyond what is to be expected for teenagers.

Mrs. Johnson cannot provide Charles with the same kind of father model and father-type involvement that her husband can. Although she claims an interest in sports and a greater degree of facility than the average woman, it is still clear that her husband has been far more involved in this type of activity with his son than has Mrs. Johnson.

Mr. Johnson accuses Mrs. Johnson of being excessively punitive and too strong a disciplinarian. Mrs. Johnson claims that her husband is too lax with the

(continued)

EXHIBIT 9-3 *(continued)*

children and does not implement proper disciplinary measures. I believe that it is most likely that Mrs. Johnson is a little too punitive and that Mr. Johnson is a little too lenient. However, neither parent exhibits these difficulties to a degree that would be significantly injurious to the children, nor would I consider this to be a factor compromising either of their capacities as parents. It is probable, however, that these differences are playing a role in Tara's antagonism to her mother and her gravitating toward her father.

In every interview, both individual and joint, Tara openly stated that she wished to live with her father. "I would be very unhappy if the judge made me go with my mother." "He can't make me live with my mother. I'd run away to my father if he did."

Conclusions and Recommendations

Weighing the above factors as best I can, I believe that the evidence is strongly in favor of Mr. Johnson being given custody of Tara. I believe, also, that the above evidence strongly supports the conclusion that Elaine should be given to Mrs. Johnson. Although there are certain arguments supporting Mr. Johnson's gaining custody of Charles, I believe that these are greatly outweighed by arguments in favor of Mrs. Johnson's gaining custody. Were the court to conclude that Tara would be better off living with Mrs. Johnson, I believe that there would be a continuation of the present hostilities, and this could be disruptive to the healthy psychological development of the younger children if they were exposed to such hostile interactions over a long period. I believe that if Mr. Johnson were to be granted custody of Elaine and Charles it is most likely that they would suffer psychological damage. All things considered, I believe he is the less preferable parent for the young children and, if they had to live with him, they would suffer emotional deprivations that could contribute to the development of psychiatric disorders.

Reprinted with the permission of Richard A. Gardner. *Family Evaluation in Child Custody Litigation*, 318–25 (1982).

RAPE-CONCEIVED CHILDREN

Over 25,000 rape-related pregnancies occur every year. Statistics vary on the number of these pregnancies that are ended by abortion. One study said 50 percent; another concluded 26 percent. What is clear is that a substantial number of women raise their children conceived by rape. Most do so alone because the rapists have no interest in the children they fathered. This is not so, however, in all cases. Some rapists seek the custody and visitation rights of a father. Remarkably, most states do not have laws that deny them this right. Only a few states allow the termination of a father's parental rights solely due to the fact that his child was the result of his act of rape. One woman exclaimed, "I was raped . . . and the rapist has been taking me to court for 5 years for the right to see his son."

"Under most states' laws, a man who fathers a child through rape has the same legal rights to custody and visitation in regard to that child as does any other father of a child due to the absence of any laws restricting or terminating such rights; as a result, many raped women face significant consequences following their decisions to raise the children they conceived through rape. They may be forced to share custody privileges of their children with their rapists, to ensure their rapists' access to their children, to foster their rapists' relationships with their children, and, in some cases, to make joint decisions about their children's welfare."[21a]

To compound the problem, some women feel pressured into not cooperating with the state in the prosecution of the father for rape in the hope that the father will simply go away and never seek access to the child or that he will voluntarily relinquish his parental rights.

VISITATION (PARENTING TIME)
INTRODUCTION

Courts want to preserve as much of the child's relationship with both parents as possible. Hence, visitation (or to use the preferred modern term, **parenting time**) is almost always granted to the noncustodial parent (NCP) even if it must be exercised in the presence of third-party strangers (see the discussion of *supervised visitation* below).

parenting time
Visitation.

Whenever possible, the court will favor frequent and regular visitation by the NCP (e.g., every other weekend, alternating holidays, substantial summer vacation time). When the custody battle is between two relatively fit parents, the court is even more inclined to grant greater visitation rights to the loser.

NEGOTIATING VISITATION

Negotiating a mutually acceptable custody and visitation plan is not always easy: "For many family-law practitioners, the seemingly endless wrangling over days and even hours is one of the most time-consuming but least rewarding parts of custody practice."[22] In the negotiation, the parties need to work out a number of important details:

- When can the visitation occur by the noncustodial parent (NCP)? Alternating weekends? School vacations? Holidays? Which ones? How much advance notice is needed if additional time is desired?
- At what time is the child to be picked up and returned?
- Can the NCP take the child on long trips? Is the consent of the custodial parent (CP) needed?
- Can the CP move out of the area even though this makes visitation more burdensome and costly? Should a clause be inserted in the separation agreement that the permission of the NCP is needed before the child can be moved more than a specified number of miles away?
- Who pays the transportation costs, if any, when the child visits the NCP?
- When the NCP decides not to visit at a given time, must he or she notify the CP in advance, or attempt to?
- Do any third parties have visitation rights (e.g., grandparents)?
- If disputes arise between parents on visitation, how are they resolved? Arbitration? Mediation? Who pays for arbitration or mediation services?
- Will nonvisitation be a violation of the separation agreement or is visitation at the sole discretion of the NCP?
- What happens if one of the parties violates the agreement on visitation?

There are two major choices in selecting visitation times. The parties can simply state in their separation agreement that visitation will be at "reasonable" times to be mutually agreed upon by the parties in the future, with adequate advance notice to be given by the NCP when he or she wants visitation. Such flexibility, however, often turns out to be unworkable, particularly since many divorcing parents have ongoing difficulty communicating with each other. The alternative is a visitation schedule that spells out precise times for child–NCP interaction. For an example, see Exhibit 9-4.

EXHIBIT 9-4 Sample Visitation Schedule

(assumes the mother has sole physical and sole legal custody)

I. Father.

Father shall have the children with him at the following times:

A. Regular Visitation:

1. On alternate weekends from 7 p.m. Friday to 7 p.m. Sunday, commencing Friday, January 16, 2015.
2. The entire month of July, 2015, and the entire month of August, 2016, and alternating July and August in subsequent years.

B. Holidays and Special Days:

1. Lincoln's Birthday, 2015, from 7 p.m. the day before said holiday to 7 p.m. the day of said holiday, and thereafter on alternate years.
2. Washington's Birthday, 2015, from 7 p.m. the day before said holiday to 7 p.m. the day of said holiday, and thereafter on alternate years.
3. Memorial Day, 2015, from 7 p.m. the day before said holiday to 7 p.m. the day of said holiday, and thereafter on alternate years.
4. Independence Day, 2015, from 7 p.m. the day before said holiday to 7 p.m. the day of said holiday, and thereafter on alternate years.
5. Labor Day, 2015, from 7 p.m. the day before said holiday to 7 p.m. the day of said holiday, and thereafter on alternate years.
6. Columbus Day, 2015, from 7 p.m. the day before said holiday to 7 p.m. the day of said holiday, and thereafter on alternate years.
7. Veterans Day, 2015, from 7 p.m. the day before said holiday to 7 p.m. the day of said holiday, and thereafter on alternate years.
8. Thanksgiving Day, 2015, from 7 p.m. the day before said holiday to 7 p.m. the day of said holiday, and thereafter on alternate years.
9. Christmas, 2015, the first week of the Christmas school vacation, commencing 7 p.m. the last day of school before the vacation and ending at 11 a.m. Christmas Day to 5 p.m. New Year's Day, and thereafter on alternate years.
10. Christmas Day, 2015, the second week of Christmas school vacation, commencing 11 a.m. Christmas Day to 5 p.m. New Year's Day, and thereafter on alternate years.
11. The entire Easter school vacation in the year 2015, including Easter Sunday, commencing 7 p.m. the last day of school before the vacation and ending at 7 p.m. the day before school resumes, and thereafter during the Easter vacation on alternate years.
12. On the children's birthdays in the year 2015, and thereafter on alternate years.
13. Every Father's Day.
14. Every Father's birthday.
15. Religious Holidays (where applicable):
    a. Good Friday of 2015, from noon to 6 p.m. of said day, and thereafter on alternate years, or
    b. The first day of the Jewish Holidays of Yom Kippur, Rosh Hashanah, and Passover during 2015, commencing at 5 p.m. on the eve of each such day and terminating at 7 p.m. on such day, and thereafter on alternate years.

II. Mother.

1. Mother shall have the children with her on the holidays and special days listed in Clause I-B in the years alternate to the years in which Father has the children with him pursuant to Clause I-B.
2. Mother shall also have the children on every Mother's Day and on every Mother's birthday.

> *[Editor's Note: A common variation would be to split the holidays between Father and Mother and have them switch halves in alternate years. Another suggested addition if the children are young is Halloween in alternating years.]*

III. Priorities:

1. The rights of Mother under Clause II shall override the regular visitation rights of Father set forth in Clause I-A, in the event of conflict between Clause I-A and Clause II.
2. Father shall not be limited in his right to take the children out of the city during the period set forth in Clause I-A2, even though Mother shall thereby be deprived of the right she would otherwise have under Clause II to have the children with her during said period.
3. In the event of conflict between Clause I-B and Clause II, the rights of Father under Clause I-B shall override the rights of Mother under Clause II.

> *[Note: The significance of Clause III cannot be overrated. A key function of any drafter is to avoid disputes over meaning and intention. A provision establishing a hierarchy of clauses will help meet this goal.]*

VISITATION SOFTWARE

Computer programs exist to help parties plan and understand timesharing schedules. This can be particularly helpful in cases where the family has more than one child. Joint custody options in such cases can be complex. Computer programs can generate color-coded calendar graphics to help the parties visualize what is involved. For an example of software that assists parents in devising a parenting plan, see Exhibit 9-5.

EXHIBIT 9-5   Example of Visitation Software for a Parenting Plan

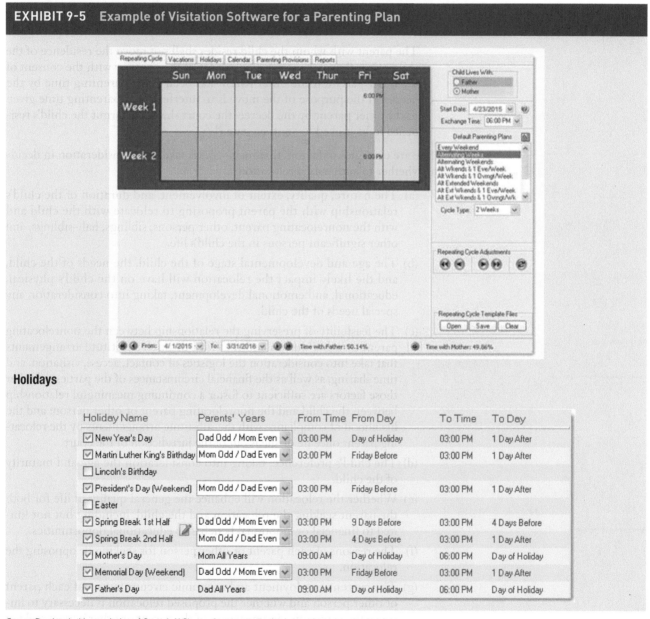

Holidays

Holiday Name	Parents' Years	From Time	From Day	To Time	To Day
☑ New Year's Day	Dad Odd / Mom Even	03:00 PM	Day of Holiday	03:00 PM	1 Day After
☑ Martin Luther King's Birthday	Mom Odd / Dad Even	03:00 PM	Friday Before	03:00 PM	1 Day After
☐ Lincoln's Birthday					
☑ President's Day (Weekend)	Mom Odd / Dad Even	03:00 PM	Friday Before	03:00 PM	1 Day After
☐ Easter					
☑ Spring Break 1st Half	Dad Odd / Mom Even	03:00 PM	9 Days Before	03:00 PM	4 Days Before
☑ Spring Break 2nd Half	Mom Odd / Dad Even	03:00 PM	4 Days Before	03:00 PM	1 Day After
☑ Mother's Day	Mom All Years	09:00 AM	Day of Holiday	06:00 PM	Day of Holiday
☑ Memorial Day (Weekend)	Dad Odd / Mom Even	03:00 PM	Friday Before	03:00 PM	1 Day After
☑ Father's Day	Dad All Years	09:00 AM	Day of Holiday	06:00 PM	Day of Holiday

Source: Reprinted with permission of Custody X Change (www.custodyxchange.com).

ASSIGNMENT 9.5

Richard and Helen Dowd have been married for six years. They are both financial consultants who work out of their home. They have one child, Kevin, aged four years. Recently, they decided to separate. Draft the clauses of their separation agreement that would provide joint physical custody and joint legal custody. Assume that both want to be active in raising Kevin. (See General Instructions for the Agreement-Drafting Assignment in Appendix A.)

RELOCATION: THE MOVE-AWAY CASE

Relocation cases "present some of the knottiest and most disturbing problems that courts are called upon to resolve."[23] A CP, like all citizens, has a fundamental right under the U.S. Constitution to travel (and to relocate) to another part of the state or to another state altogether. This right, however, is not absolute. When balanced against the best interests of the child, a court can refuse to allow the custodial parent to move significant distances with the child (e.g., over 50 miles) if the move substantially interferes with the visitation rights of the NCP. A common feature of statutes on this problem in many states is the restriction on relocation (called a move-away case). For example:

> The parent with whom the child resides shall not move the residence of the child to another state except upon order of the court or with the consent of the other parent, if the other parent has been given parenting time by the decree. If the purpose of the move is to interfere with parenting time given to the other parent by the decree, the court shall not permit the child's residence to be moved to another state.[24]

Here are examples of factors that many courts take into consideration in deciding whether to authorize a relocation:

(a) The nature, quality, extent of involvement, and duration of the child's relationship with the parent proposing to relocate with the child and with the nonrelocating parent, other persons, siblings, half-siblings, and other significant persons in the child's life.

(b) The age and developmental stage of the child, the needs of the child, and the likely impact the relocation will have on the child's physical, educational, and emotional development, taking into consideration any special needs of the child.

(c) The feasibility of preserving the relationship between the nonrelocating parent or other person and the child through substitute arrangements that take into consideration the logistics of contact, access, visitation, and time sharing, as well as the financial circumstances of the parties; whether those factors are sufficient to foster a continuing meaningful relationship between the child and the nonrelocating parent or other person; and the likelihood of compliance with the substitute arrangements by the relocating parent once he or she is out of the jurisdiction of the court.

(d) The child's preference, taking into consideration the age and maturity of the child.

(e) Whether the relocation will enhance the general quality of life for both the parent seeking the relocation and the child, including but not limited to financial or emotional benefits or educational opportunities.

(f) The reasons of each parent or other person for seeking or opposing the relocation.

(g) The current employment and economic circumstances of each parent or other person and whether the proposed relocation is necessary to improve the economic circumstances of the parent or other person seeking relocation of the child.

(h) Whether the relocation is sought in good faith.

(i) The extent to which the objecting parent has fulfilled his or her financial obligations to the parent or other person seeking relocation, including child support, spousal support, and marital property and marital debt obligations.

(j) The career and other opportunities available to the objecting parent if the relocation occurs.

(k) Any other factors affecting the best interests of the child.[25]

In extreme cases, the court might order the custodial parent to post a bond to secure compliance with the visitation rights of the noncustodial parent.

VIRTUAL VISITATION

Courts are willing to accommodate the realities of modern living in order to preserve a child's contact with both parents. In one state, the court approved the CP's relocation out of state but gave the NCP the right to two virtual visits a week via Skype (an Internet calling service that uses video) so that the NCP could interact with his children by reading them bedtime stories. When a judge allows virtual visitation (also called *e-visitation*), limitations are usually imposed, such as when the visits can occur and how long they can last. Also, virtual visitation is not a replacement for traditional visits. When a NCP is allowed Skype or webcam visits, he or she is usually also allowed face-to-face visits.

THIRD-PARTY VISITATION AND THE *TROXEL* CASE

Another issue that is occasionally litigated is whether *third parties* can have visitation rights (e.g., grandparents, former stepparents) over the objection of the biological parents. The issue has profound implications for the relationship between the family and the state. If a state is allowed to force a parent to allow third parties to visit the parent's children, the question arises as to how far the state can go in overruling parental decisions. What is the boundary line between what parents think is good for their children and what the state thinks is good for them?

The U.S. Supreme Court was concerned about this boundary line when it faced the issue of third-party visitation in the case of *Troxel v. Granville*.[26] In this important case, the Court reinforced the "fundamental right of parents to make decisions concerning the care, custody, and control of their children." Specifically, the Court ruled that visitation by third parties must not substantially interfere with the primary right of fit biological parents to raise their children.

The *Troxel* case arose in the state of Washington, which had a statute that allowed "[a]ny person" "at any time" to petition the court for visitation, which could be granted if the court felt it would be in the best interests of child. The statute gave no special consideration or weight to the opinion of the parents on whether third-party visitation should be allowed. When a parent opposed such visitation, for example, the statute did not say that the third party had to overcome a presumption that the parent's opposition was valid. The statute gave no such presumption of validity to the parent's views.

This statute was called "breathtakingly broad" and declared unconstitutional in violation of the Due Process Clause. Tommie Granville and Brad Troxel were the unmarried parents of Isabelle and Natalie Troxel. After the parents separated, the girls lived with Tommie. Brad lived with his parents, Jenifer and Gary Troxel, the girls' paternal grandparents. Brad regularly brought his daughters to his parents' home for weekend visits. When Brad committed suicide, the grandparents continued to see the girls on a regular basis. Tommie, however, informed the Troxels that she wished to limit their visitation with her daughters to one short visit per month. The grandparents used the Washington State statute to petition the court for two weekends of overnight visitation per month and two weeks each summer. Over Tommie's objection, the court granted them one weekend per month, one week during the summer, and four hours on both of the grandparents' birthdays. Tommie's appeal eventually reached the U.S. Supreme Court.

The U.S. Supreme Court began its analysis by acknowledging the changing reality of family life in America:

> The demographic changes of the past century make it difficult to speak of an average American family. The composition of families varies greatly from household to household. While many children may have two married parents and grandparents who visit regularly, many other children are raised in single-parent

households. In 1996, children living with only one parent accounted for 28 percent of all children under age 18 in the United States. U.S. Dept. of Commerce, Bureau of Census, Current Population Reports, *1997 Population Profile* of the United States 27 (1998). [In 2010 it was over 34 percent.] Understandably, in these single-parent households, persons outside the nuclear family are called upon with increasing frequency to assist in the everyday tasks of child rearing. In many cases, grandparents play an important role. For example, in 1998, approximately 4 million children—or 5.6 percent of all children under age 18—lived in the household of their grandparents. U.S. Dept. of Commerce, Bureau of Census, Current Population Reports, *Marital Status and Living Arrangements: March 1998* (Update), p. i (1998).[27]

The Court specified, however, that if a fit parent is present in the home, his or her right to raise a child is entitled to constitutional protection. The Fourteenth Amendment to the U.S. Constitution provides that no state shall "deprive any person of life, liberty or property, without due process of law."[28] This clause gives parents the fundamental right to make decisions concerning the care, custody, and control of their children:

> The Fourteenth Amendment provides that no State shall "deprive any person of life, liberty, or property, without due process of law." We have long recognized that the Amendment's Due Process Clause . . . "guarantees more than fair process." *Washington v. Glucksberg*, 521 U.S. 702, 719 (1997). The Clause also includes a substantive component that "provides heightened protection against government interference with certain fundamental rights and liberty interests." Id., at 720. . . . The liberty interest at issue in this case—the interest of parents in the care, custody, and control of their children—is perhaps the oldest of the fundamental liberty interests recognized by this court. More than 75 years ago, in *Meyer v. Nebraska*, 262 U.S. 390, 399 (1923), we held that the "liberty" protected by the Due Process Clause includes the right of parents to "establish a home and bring up children" and "to control the education of their own." Two years later, in *Pierce v. Society of Sisters*, 268 U.S. 510, 534–535 (1925), we again held that the "liberty of parents and guardians" includes the right "to direct the upbringing and education of children under their control."[29]

There was no indication in this case that Tommie was an unfit parent. When fit parents make a decision in raising their child, they are entitled to a presumption that the decision is in the child's best interests. The presumption means that the parent's decision controls unless someone proves that the decision is not in the best interests of the child. It is not enough to show that someone else's decision is a good idea.

Tommie was not given the benefit of this presumption. Her opposition to the grandparents' request was given no "special weight." The judge simply disagreed with her on whether more extensive visitation with the paternal grandparents was in the best interests of the children. This troubled the U.S. Supreme Court:

> [S]o long as a parent adequately cares for his or her children (i.e., is fit), there will normally be no reason for the State to inject itself into the private realm of the family to further question the ability of that parent to make the best decisions concerning the rearing of that parent's children. . . . [T]he Due Process Clause does not permit a State to infringe on the fundamental right of parents to make childrearing decisions simply because a state judge believes a "better" decision could be made.[30]

Although the Court ruled that a fit parent must be given the presumption of correctness, the Court did not clarify what kind of evidence would overcome this presumption. The Court left this question for another day. Therefore, we do not know the precise scope of the constitutional right of parents to raise their children, but we do know that the Court will take a dim view of any effort by the state to interfere with the child-rearing decisions of a fit parent.

SUPERVISED VISITATION

Supervised visitation by the NCP occurs in the presence of a third party, someone other than the CP. Occasionally, a CP will ask the court to deny all visitation rights to the NCP because of a fear that the child might be taken out of the state or country or might be physically or emotionally harmed by unrestricted visitation. As indicated, courts are reluctant to deny all visitation rights to a parent. If the court is convinced that unrestricted visitation would not be in the best interests of the child, supervised visitation is a possible alternative. When used, the CP usually takes the child to a facility that is equipped to monitor visitation in a safe environment. The facility might be a government agency or, more commonly, a private nonprofit group (e.g., a unit of the YWCA) that charges a fee for its services. After the CP drops off the child and leaves, the NCP has a visit of several hours (as designated by the court order) in rooms available in the facility. The CP then returns to pick up the child. Supervised visitation can also occur in less formal settings such as at the home of a relative that both parents trust. It is more common, however, for supervised visitation to occur at a facility that is professionally organized to offer such visitation.

supervised visitation
Visitation of a child while another adult is present (other than the custodial parent).

COHABITATION

In most cases, **cohabitation** by the NCP should not affect the NCP's visitation rights. If, however, the court determines that exposing a younger child to the NCP's romantic partner will (or has) unduly upset the child, the court might place restrictions on visitation, such as not allowing overnight visits with the NCP.

cohabitation
Living together in an intimate (usually sexual) relationship in the manner of a husband and wife. A de facto husband and wife relationship. The verb is cohabit. Although a married couple cohabits, the word *cohabitation* is more often used in reference to unmarried couples.

ASSIGNMENT 9.6

Flora Smith and Harry Smith have one child, 10-year-old Mary Smith. Flora and Harry are separated. Flora wants supervised visitation of Mary by Harry Smith because he often misses child-support payments and has a girlfriend who is an alcoholic. Flora is afraid that if Harry takes Mary to his home, she will be exposed to drinking. How should the court rule? (See General Instructions for the Legal-Analysis Assignment in Appendix A.)

SHARED CUSTODY AND COPARENTING

Courts have held that a parent can voluntarily enter an agreement with a nonparent that allows the nonparent some measure of custody of the parent's child. Such agreements are called *shared-custody agreements*. In most states, the agreement can be between two opposite-sex adults or two same-sex adults. The arrangement is also referred to as *coparenting*, the shared responsibility by two adults to raise a child, regardless of the marital status or sexual orientation of the adults.

These arrangements do not violate the parent's *Troxel* rights because the parent voluntarily agrees to share custody with the nonparent. A court will enforce the agreement if the court concludes that the agreement is in the best interests of the child. In a recent case involving a suit for visitation rights by a former lesbian partner of a woman who gave birth to a child by in vitro fertilization while the women were living together, the court said that

> [A] parent may voluntarily share with a nonparent the care, custody, and control of his or her child through a valid shared-custody agreement. The essence of such an agreement is the purposeful relinquishment of some portion of the parent's right to exclusive custody of the child. A shared-custody agreement recognizes the general principle that a parent can grant custody rights to a nonparent and will be bound by the agreement. A valid shared-custody agreement is reviewed by the . . . court and is an enforceable

contract subject only to the court's determinations that the custodian is "a proper person to assume the care, training, and education of the child" and that the shared-legal-custody arrangement is in the best interests of the child.[31]

The court went further and said that a parent could enter an enforceable agreement to relinquish his or her *full* custody to a third party.

In Chapter 10, we will consider the question of when a parent and a nonparent in a shared-custody arrangement can be ordered to pay child support.

ENFORCING THE RIGHT TO VISITATION

When a CP interferes with the visitation rights of a NCP, a number of remedies are possible:

ne exeat
A writ that forbids a person from leaving or from removing a child or property from the state, country, or jurisdiction of the court.

- The court could issue a **ne exeat**, which is a writ that orders the CP not to remove the child from the area.
- The court could order an increase of the visitation rights of the NCP.
- The court could order that custody be given to the NCP.
- The CP could be held in civil contempt.
- The CP could be held in criminal contempt.
- The CP could be ordered to place a designated amount of money in escrow or in a bond that can be reached by the NCP if the CP continues to interfere with visitation.
- Custodial interference is a crime in some states.[32]
- The interference could be a step in the direction of terminating the parental rights of the CP (see Chapter 15).
- A few states allow a NCP to bring a tort action for interference with parental rights or tortious interference with custody (see Chapter 17).

Some of these remedies (e.g., civil contempt, criminal contempt, escrow/bond, criminal prosecution, termination of parental rights, and tort) may also be available to the CP against the NCP if the latter seriously interferes with the parental/custodial rights of the CP.

It is never permissible for a parent to terminate child-support payments in retaliation for the other parent's violation of visitation or other custody rights. In Chapter 10, we will discuss remedies against the NCP for failure to pay child support. It is rare that a court will terminate the visitation rights of the NCP for not paying child support.

BIOLOGICAL PARENT VS. PSYCHOLOGICAL PARENT

Thus far, our main focus has been a custody dispute between two biological parents. Suppose, however, that the dispute is between one biological parent and a third party such as one of the following:

- Grandparent
- Other relative
- Former opposite-sex lover/stepparent (who never adopted the child)
- Former same-sex lover/stepparent (who never adopted the child)
- Foster parent (initially assigned to the child by **foster care**)
- Neighbor
- Friend

foster care
A child welfare service that provides shelter and substitute family care when a child's own family cannot provide this care.

Assume that the other biological parent is out of the picture because he or she has died, has disappeared, or does not care. The third party is usually someone with whom the child has established close emotional ties. Frequently, the child has lived with the third party for a substantial period of time. This may have occurred for a number of reasons:

- The biological parent was ill, out of state, out of work, in prison, etc.
- The biological parent was in school for substantial periods of time.
- The state asked the third party to care for the child temporarily as a foster parent (see Chapter 14).
- The child could not stay at home because of marital difficulties between the biological parents.
- The biological parent once considered giving the child up for adoption.

A third party who has formed such ties with a child is often referred to as a **psychological parent**. This is an adult who, in a substantial and continuing way, has provided for the physical and emotional needs of a child. The adult can be a biological parent, but most often the term refers to someone other than a biological or adoptive parent. Another term sometimes used is **fictive kin**, a person who is not related by birth or marriage but who has an emotionally significant and family-like relationship with another. An example is a close family friend who is called aunt or uncle by the children. A court might refer to a psychological parent or fictive kin as being **in loco parentis**, which means standing in the place of a parent by assuming some or all parental responsibilities without being a biological or adoptive parent.

In a custody dispute between a biological parent and a psychological parent (or fictive kin), the determining test in most states is whether the biological parent is **unfit**. The test is *not* the best interests of the child. Except in extraordinary circumstances, if the biological parent is fit, he or she is awarded custody.

Unfit means demonstrating abuse or neglect that is substantially detrimental to a child. As we will see in Chapter 14, **child neglect** is the failure of a parent or other caregiver to provide the basic needs of a child, including physical needs (e.g., food and shelter), emotional needs, medical needs, and educational needs; *child abuse* is serious physical, emotional, or sexual mistreatment of a child that is not the result of accident or of circumstances beyond the control of the parent or guardian.

As we saw in the *Troxel* case, a fit custodial parent has a constitutional (due process) right to raise his or her children. When the custodial parent is a biological parent, the question is not whether the biological parent or the psychological parent can provide the best home for the child. The question is whether the biological parent is unfit. Although a child may suffer some disruption if his or her relationship with the psychological parent is severed, this does not necessarily overcome the biological parent's overriding right to raise the child. The law is very reluctant to take children away from their natural parents because of a determination that someone else could do a better job raising them.

In practice, however, some courts tend to blur the distinction between the fitness of a biological parent and the comparative benefits that can be offered by a psychological parent. A court that emphasizes the rights of a biological parent might still undertake a comparison between the benefits to the child living with the biological parent and the benefits of living with the psychological parent. When the benefits to be derived from the latter are overwhelming, the court might be more inclined to find unfitness in the biological parent and to conclude that giving custody to the biological parent would be detrimental to the child. The interpretation of the evidence can be very subjective. Often, there are enough data to support any conclusion the court wants to reach. A person's mistakes in raising children can be viewed either as an inability to be a competent parent or as an inevitable component of the nearly impossible job of parenting in today's society.

psychological parent
An adult who, in a substantial and continuing way, has provided for the physical and emotional needs of a child. The adult can be a biological parent, but most often the term refers to someone other than a biological or adoptive parent.

fictive kin
A person who is not related by birth or marriage but who has an emotionally significant and family-like relationship with another.

in loco parentis
Standing in the place of a parent by assuming some or all parental responsibilities without being a biological or adoptive parent.

unfit
Demonstrating abuse or neglect that is substantially detrimental to a child.

child neglect
The failure of a parent or other caregiver to provide the basic needs of a child, including physical needs (e.g., food and shelter), emotional needs, medical needs, and educational needs.

CHANGING THE CHILD'S SURNAME

Once the court decides who receives custody, the custodial parent (CP) might request that the surname of the child be changed. For example, a mother might ask that the child's surname be changed to her maiden name or to the surname of her new husband. This change-of-name request might also be made at a later time in a separate proceeding. Assume that the child has always had the surname of the noncustodial parent (NCP). The court must determine whether a surname change is in the best interests of the child. The following excerpt from a court opinion explains the factors that most courts consider in applying this standard:

> We first note that neither parent has a superior right to determine the initial surname their child shall bear. . . . However, once a surname has been selected for the child, be it the maternal, paternal, or some combination of the child's parents' surnames, a change in the child's surname should be granted only when the change promotes the child's best interests. In determining the child's best interests, the trial court may consider, but its consideration is not limited to, the following factors: the child's preference; . . . the effect of the change of the child's surname on the preservation and the development of the child's relationship with each parent; the length of time the child has borne a given name; the degree of community respect associated with the present and the proposed surname; and the difficulties, harassment or embarrassment that the child may experience from bearing the present or the proposed surname.[33]

The court stressed what when the NCP objects to the change, the evidence that the change is in the best interests of the child should be "clear and compelling."

A court's approval of a change in the surname of a child does not alter the parent–child relationship that the child has with both natural parents. Unless there has been an adoption or termination of parental rights (see Chapter 15), a surname change has no effect on a parent's rights and responsibilities.

MODIFICATION BY THE STATE THAT ISSUED THE ORDER

In this section, we consider the modification of a custody order by the *same* state that issued the order. Assume that the court has jurisdiction to issue and modify custody orders. (We will focus on jurisdiction in the next section when we examine child snatching and special interstate problems.) Although our discussion will focus on the two biological parents, the same principles apply no matter who was given custody by the original order.

Two reasons justify a court in modifying its own custody order:

- There has been a substantial change in circumstances since the original order or
- Relevant facts were not made available to the court at the time of its original order.

In either situation, new facts are now before the court. The question becomes whether it is in the best interests of the child for the court to change its mind and award custody to the other parent. Given the disruption of such a change, the answer is *no* unless the new facts *substantially* alter the court's perception of the child's welfare. For example:

- The CP has been neglecting or abusing the child.
- The CP has moved from the area, contrary to the court's order, thus making visitation by the NCP extremely difficult or impossible.
- The CP has adopted an unorthodox lifestyle that has negatively affected the child's physical or mental health.

Given the potential for disruption in a child's life, the standard a parent must meet to obtain a change in custody is generally higher than the standard needed to obtain an initial custody order. To justify modification, it is not enough that the CP has experienced hard times such as sickness or loss of a part-time job since the initial order. Nor is it enough to show that mistakes have been made in raising the children. To justify a modification, the adverse circumstances or mistakes must be (1) ongoing, (2) relatively permanent, (3) serious, and (4) detrimental to the child. In some states, courts will not hear a request for modification within at least two years after the initial custody order unless the child has been abandoned or faces serious endangerment. (No such time limits apply, however, for requests to modify a visitation order.) For an argument by a NCP on why custody should be changed, see the affidavit in support of a motion to modify custody in Exhibit 9-6.

EXHIBIT 9-6   Affidavit in Support of a Motion to Modify a Custody Decree

AFFIDAVIT IN SUPPORT
STATE OF _____
COUNTY OF _____
John Davis v. Mary Davis
CV-2347-FC-2011
February 10, 2013

John Davis, being duly sworn, deposes and says:

1. This affidavit is submitted in support of an application for reconsideration of the decision of the court made in this action on March 13, 2010, insofar as custody of my children is concerned.

2. Custody of the children has been awarded to my ex-wife, Mary Davis. I did not contest her claim in the divorce. When I reported this to the children, they became extremely upset. My son told me that he did not want to live with his mother and that he felt it was unfair for a boy of his age to be forced to live with a parent contrary to his desires. My daughter had a similar reaction.

3. I love my children very much. A history of prior proceedings between my wife and myself indicates that she had been awarded custody of the children under a Family Court order on March 13, 2010. At that time, she lived with the children in our house in Peekskill. I paid support, as directed, for the children and my wife, and for the upkeep of the house. About two years ago my wife ousted my son from the house and sent him to live with me. At that time, I occupied a small apartment in Peekskill so that I could be near the children. I would see them quite often and would take them to school on many mornings. When my son came to me, I made room for him and we lived together until my daughter came to live with us about a year ago. We made room for her. My wife made no objections to the children living with me and made no attempts to get them to come back to her. While we all lived in my small apartment, my wife continued to live in the Peekskill house all by herself. I continued paying the upkeep on the house, although my wife permitted it to fall into a state of deteriorating disrepair. I contributed to her support.

4. I took care of my children as best I could. They were grown and attended school most of the day. In the evening we enjoyed a family life. We were together on the weekends. There were many weekends when their mother would not attempt to spend any time with them. My son stayed away from the Peekskill house. My daughter visited there with her mother on occasion. I know that on many occasions my wife stayed away from the Peekskill house for days at a time.

5. I have devoted my non-working hours to my children. I altered my schedule so that I would see them off to school each morning when I was not away from the City. If I was to be away, I would arrange adult supervision. I worked with my children on their homework and on anything else where they sought my participation. We shopped together and played together. My children were encouraged to maintain their friendships and to bring their friends to our home. Because of cramped quarters, my children would often visit with their friends and I encouraged them to maintain relationships with companions of their respective ages. I shared their problems and their joys. I tried to set responsible examples for them. My son had demonstrated to me that he is growing into a responsible young man who aspires to attend Massachusetts Institute of Technology. I am proud of his seriousness and of his healthy outlook in times like this. I have tried to maintain a closely knit family between my children and myself so that they should know the advantages of love, companionship, and security. I know that they did not find any such relationship at their mother's bosom.

6. My children have revealed to me that they were wrong in not having made a definite choice during the interview with the court on the matter of their preference of a home. I understand that they will still love their mother and I have not attempted to sway them from that plateau. They told me that they wanted the court to decide the problem for them and that they had hoped that they could be the force which could solve the rift between plaintiff and myself. They were unaware that at the time of the interview, my wife's prayer for divorce had already been granted. My son told me that he indicated to the court that he preferred to live with me although he did not state, unequivocally, that he did not desire to live with his mother.

(continued)

EXHIBIT 9-6 *(continued)*

7. I gather from my children's reaction and from what they have told me that they misunderstood what was required of them during their interview with the court. Had I not seen the effect of the custody decision on my children and had they not indicated their grief over it, I would sit back and abide by the will of the court.

8. I seriously question my wife's fitness as our children's custodian. She voluntarily relinquished their custody, as aforesaid. Under adverse living conditions (cramped quarters), my children have thrived and demonstrated a progression toward adulthood. I believe that my wife's having been competitive instead of being cooperative with the children operated to compromise their welfare. I believe that using the children as a pawn has lost our children's respect. I feel that my pleasures must be subservient to the welfare of my children. They deserve as real a home as can be possible under the circumstances. They are entitled to eat a meal in peace and one which shows concern in its preparation. I believe that the children deserve some security in the knowledge that they have the genuine care and love of a parent. I believe that they cannot get this from their mother.

9. WHEREFORE, I respectfully pray that this application be granted and that upon reconsideration I be awarded custody of my children.

[Signature]

_____

Source: Reprinted from Joseph Marino, West's McKinney's Forms, Matrimonial and Family Law Form 20:152 (West 2011) with permission of Thomson Reuters.

ASSIGNMENT 9.7

Do you think the court should reconsider the custody order as requested in Exhibit 9-6? What further facts, if any, would you like to have? (See General Instructions for the Investigation-Strategy Assignment in Appendix A.)

INTERSTATE MODIFICATION

INTRODUCTION

We have been discussing the modification of a child-custody order by the state that issued the order. The court's jurisdiction or power to modify its own order is rarely in doubt because all of the parties and the child are usually still in the state. Suppose, however, that a party tries to have the order modified by *another* state. Interstate modification of custody orders presents more serious problems.

> *Dan and Ellen are divorced in New York, where they live. Ellen receives sole physical custody and sole legal custody of their child. Dan moves to Delaware. During a visit of the child in Delaware, Dan petitions a Delaware court for a modification of the New York custody order. Ellen does not appear in the Delaware proceeding. Dan tells the Delaware court a horror story about the child's life with Ellen in New York. The Delaware court modifies the New York order on the basis of changed circumstances, awarding full custody to Dan.*

Or worse:

> *Dan and Ellen's child is playing in the yard of a New York school. Dan takes the child from the yard and goes to Delaware without telling Ellen. Dan petitions a Delaware court for a modification of the New York custody order. If he loses, he tries again in Florida. If he loses, he tries again in another state until he finds a court that will grant him custody.*

forum

(1) A court. (2) The place where the parties are presently litigating their dispute. (3) A court or tribunal hearing a case.

forum shopping

When more than one court has subject-matter jurisdiction over a claim, choosing the court that is most likely to issue a favorable ruling.

The latter situation involves what has been commonly called *child snatching.* The parent "grabs" the child and then "shops" for a favorable **forum** (court) in which to relitigate the custody issue. For years, the problem of **forum shopping** reached epidemic proportions.

Before Reforms Were Implemented

Before the law was reformed, courts were caught in a dilemma. They did not want to close their doors to children in need of custody changes; yet, their availability encouraged child snatching and forum shopping. Custody orders were always modifiable on the basis of changed circumstances that affected the welfare of the child. Under the traditional rule, if an order is not final, it is not entitled to **full faith and credit (FFC)** by another state (i.e., another state is not required to abide by it). Hence, other states were free to reexamine the case to determine whether new circumstances warranted a modification. To maintain flexibility, states required very little to trigger their jurisdiction to hear a modification case (e.g., the domicile or mere presence of the child in the state along with one of the parents). The result was chaos: scandalous child snatching and unseemly forum shopping.

Reforms to End the Chaos

To solve the problem, uniformity in the law of custody jurisdiction among the states was required. To try to achieve this uniformity, three major legislative efforts occurred:

- In 1968, many states adopted the *Uniform Child Custody Jurisdiction Act* (UCCJA) proposed by the National Conference of Commissioners on Uniform State Laws (NCCUSL). Unfortunately, all states did not adopt the UCCJA. Furthermore, some states adopted their own version of the UCCJA, which meant that the "uniform" act was not uniform throughout the country.

- In 1980, Congress passed the *Parental Kidnapping Prevention Act* (PKPA) because of its concern that the UCCJA was not going to solve the problem of child snatching and the relitigation of custody disputes. The PKPA specified when the custody decrees of one state had to be accepted in (i.e., had to be given full faith and credit by) every other state.[34] Although the word "kidnapping" is used in the title of the PKPA, the act covers any custody decree that someone tries to modify in another state, not just cases involving child snatching.

- In 1997, the most important step toward uniformity occurred when the NCCUSL revised the UCCJA in order to conform it to the PKPA. The revision is called the *Uniform Child Custody Jurisdiction and Enforcement Act* (UCCJEA).[35]

We need to examine how the UCCJEA and the PKPA work together.

UNIFORM CHILD CUSTODY JURISDICTION AND ENFORCEMENT ACT

The **Uniform Child Custody Jurisdiction and Enforcement Act (UCCJEA)** is designed to avoid jurisdictional competition and conflict among state courts that can arise when parents shift children from state to state in search of a favorable custody decision. Two important questions are covered in the UCCJEA:

- When does a court in the state have the power or jurisdiction to make the *initial* decision on child custody?
- When can a court modify a custody order of another state?

Jurisdiction to Make the Initial Child Custody Decision

Under the UCCJEA, mere physical presence of the child in the state is *not* sufficient to give the state jurisdiction to enter an initial custody order. Nor is

full faith and credit (FFC)
The obligation of one state to recognize and enforce the legal decisions of another state. The obligation is based on the U.S. Constitution, which provides that "Full Faith and Credit shall be given in each State to the public Acts, Records, and judicial Proceedings of every other State." Article IV, § 1.

Uniform Child Custody Jurisdiction and Enforcement Act (UCCJEA)
A model state statute on the enforcement of custody and visitation orders across state lines.

the mere physical presence of one of the parents sufficient. There are four major foundations for custody jurisdiction under the UCCJEA:

- Home state custody jurisdiction
- Significant connection/substantial evidence (sc/se) custody jurisdiction
- Temporary emergency custody jurisdiction
- Last resort custody jurisdiction

home state
The state where the child has lived with a parent (or anyone acting as a parent) for at least six consecutive months immediately before the court proceedings began, or since birth if the child is less than six months old.

Home state custody jurisdiction is the most important and has ultimate priority. It is based on where the child has lived for the last six months with a parent (or anyone acting as a parent) before the court proceedings began. For a summary of the four categories of child-custody jurisdiction under the UCCJEA, see Exhibit 9-7.

EXHIBIT 9-7 Jurisdiction to Make an Initial Custody Decision under the Uniform Child Custody Jurisdiction and Enforcement Act (UCCJEA)

General Rule: A state must have one of the following four kinds of custody jurisdiction to be able to make an initial custody order: (1) home state, (2) significant connection/substantial evidence (sc/se), (3) temporary emergency, or (4) last resort jurisdiction if no other state has or wants jurisdiction over the case.

Kind of Custody Jurisdiction	When Does a State Have This Kind of Custody Jurisdiction?	Notes
Home State Custody Jurisdiction	A state has home state custody jurisdiction if one of two conditions exist: • This state is the home state of the child. A home state is the state in which the child has lived with a parent (or anyone acting as a parent) for at least six consecutive months immediately before the court proceedings began. If the child is less than six months old, the home state is the state where the child has lived since birth. (Temporary absences count as part of the six months or as part of the time since birth.) OR • This state *was* the home state of the child within six months before the court proceedings began and the child is now absent from the state, but a parent continues to live in this state.	• If the state that made the initial custody order had home state custody jurisdiction, that state will have continuing jurisdiction to make future custody determinations for the child so long as at least one parent continues to live in the state. • A state with home state custody jurisdiction has priority over a state with sc/se custody jurisdiction.
SC/SE Custody Jurisdiction	A state has sc/se custody jurisdiction if three conditions exist: • No other state is the home state of the child (or if another state is the home state, it has declined to exercise the custody jurisdiction that it has). AND • The child and at least one parent have a *significant connection (sc)* with this state other than mere presence in this state. AND • There is *substantial evidence (se)* in this state concerning the child's care, protection, training, and personal relationships.	• A state with sc/se custody jurisdiction cannot enter a custody decision if another state has home state jurisdiction unless the home state declines to act.

| Temporary Emergency Custody Jurisdiction | A state has temporary emergency custody jurisdiction if two conditions exist:
• The child is present in the state.
AND
• The child has been abandoned or there is an emergency requiring protection of the child because the child, a sibling, or a parent is being mistreated or abused or threatened with mistreatment or abuse (domestic violence). | • Temporary emergency custody jurisdiction can be exercised by a state that does not have home state or sc/se jurisdiction.
• The need to protect the child takes precedence because of the emergency.
• But the custody order made by a court with temporary emergency jurisdiction can remain in effect only until a state with home state or sc/se jurisdiction intervenes.
• Hence temporary emergency jurisdiction has a lower priority than home state jurisdiction and sc/se jurisdiction. |
| Last Resort Custody Jurisdiction | A state has last resort jurisdiction if one of two conditions exist:
• No other state has home state jurisdiction or sc/se jurisdiction.
OR
• Every state that has jurisdiction has declined to exercise it. | |

© Cengage Learning 2013

ASSIGNMENT 9.8

a. Fred and Jane were married in Iowa on 1/1/1999. On 3/13/2000 in Iowa, they had a child, Bob. From the first day of their marriage, however, they had been having marital difficulties. On 7/4/2000, Fred moved to California. Bob continued to live with his mother in Iowa. By mutual agreement, Fred occasionally takes the child to California for visits. This occurs several times without incident.

After a scheduled one-day visit on 11/5/2000, however, Fred decides not to return the child.

He keeps Bob until 11/2/2001, when Fred changes his mind and returns Bob to Jane in Iowa.

Fred then joins the Army on 11/10/2001.

When he is discharged on 10/1/2003, he returns to California.

If an action for custody had been filed on the following dates, which state (Iowa or California) would have home state jurisdiction under the UCCJEA to render a custody decision?

1. 4/4/2000
2. 11/6/2000
3. 1/1/2001
4. 11/1/2001
5. 10/6/2003

(See General Instructions for the Legal-Analysis Assignment in Appendix A.)

b. Assume Fred is convinced that he is the better parent because of what he believes to be a pattern of neglect in Jane's care of Bob. What facts would you investigate in order to support or discredit Fred's position? Include questions that you would ask Fred. See General Instructions for the Investigation-Strategy Assignment in Appendix A.

Forum non Conveniens

You will note that Exhibit 9-7 refers to courts that decline to use the custody jurisdiction that they have. Assume that a court has jurisdiction to make the initial custody decision because it is the home state or because it

forum non conveniens
The discretionary power of a court to decline the exercise of its jurisdiction when it would be more convenient and the ends of justice would be better served if the action were tried in another court.

is the state with sc/se. Nevertheless, this court may decline to exercise this jurisdiction because it determines that it is an *inconvenient forum*. This determination is based on **forum non conveniens**, which is the discretionary power of a court to decline the exercise of its jurisdiction when it would be more convenient and the ends of justice would be better served if the action were tried in another court.

How does a state decide whether it is an inconvenient forum? There is no rigid formula. It will consider a number of factors. Let's look at an example:

> *Sid and Fran have lived in Tennessee since their marriage there in 2006. On 1/10/09, Fran gives birth to their child, Jim. On 2/10/10, Sid takes Jim to live with his mother in Oregon because of marital difficulties with Fran. On 12/10/10, Sid files for divorce in Oregon. In the divorce action, he asks the Oregon court to be awarded full custody of Jim. A month later (1/10/11), Fran files an action in Tennessee asking that she be granted full custody.*

Oregon is Jim's home state. He has been with a parent (Sid) in Oregon for at least six consecutive months (from 2/10/10 to 12/10/10) immediately before the court action was filed in which Sid made the initial custody request. Under the UCCJEA, Oregon has jurisdiction to issue a custody order. Under the rule of forum non conveniens, however, Oregon can decline to exercise this jurisdiction if another state (e.g., Tennessee) would be a more convenient forum to litigate the custody dispute.

Here are some of the factors an Oregon court will consider in determining whether Tennessee is a more convenient forum for the parties to litigate the custody matter:

- *Domestic violence.* If domestic violence has been committed or threatened in Tennessee (e.g., Sid alleges that Fran was physically abusive to Jim in Tennessee), an Oregon court might decide that Tennessee is in the best position to resolve the allegation of child abuse and protect the parties. If so, Tennessee would be the most convenient state to make the custody decision.

- *Length of time the child has been outside the state.* Jim was in Tennessee from 1/10/09 to 2/10/10 (thirteen months). He has been in Oregon from 2/10/10 to 12/10/10 (eight months). An Oregon court could conclude that this disparity of time bolsters the argument for letting Tennessee decide the custody issue.

- *Relative financial circumstances of the parties.* If litigating the custody case in Oregon would impose extreme financial burdens on the party in Tennessee (Fran) and if the party in Oregon (Sid) would have the financial resources to litigate in Tennessee, then an Oregon court might decide that Tennessee is the most convenient forum to make the custody decision.

- *Nature and location of the evidence.* If the important evidence needed to resolve the custody matter is in Tennessee, then an Oregon court might decide that Tennessee would be the most convenient forum to make the custody decision.

The decision is discretionary with Oregon. In our example, we have assumed that Oregon has home state custody jurisdiction and has the right to exercise it. The UCCJEA encourages, but does not require, such a state to relinquish its jurisdiction if it decides that another state would be a more convenient state to render the custody decision.

Jurisdiction to Modify a Custody Order of Another State

Thus far our primary focus has been the jurisdiction of a state to make an *initial* custody order under the UCCJEA. When does a court have jurisdiction to decide the custody question for the first time? We now turn to the question of when a state has jurisdiction to *modify* a custody order of another state.

The underlying principle on jurisdiction in modification cases is as follows:

> Once a court has made an initial custody order under the UCCJEA because it has home state jurisdiction or sc/se jurisdiction, that court has **exclusive, continuing jurisdiction (ECJ)** over the case. *Continuing* means that the case is kept open; *exclusive* means that no other court has authority to act in the case unless the initial state declines to use its ECJ because another state is a more convenient forum.

For example, if Florida was the home state or the state with sc/se and made the initial custody decision, then Florida has ECJ. North Carolina cannot modify Florida's custody order so long as Florida continues to have ECJ unless Florida declines to use its ECJ because it determines that North Carolina would be a more convenient forum.

It is possible, however, for a state to lose its ECJ. This would allow another state to become the home state (or to become the state with sc/se) and thereby modify the initial state's custody order. An example of an initial state that loses its ECJ would be when both parents and the child no longer reside in the initial state.

Suppose, for example, that Connecticut issues an initial custody order and has ECJ. The dissatisfied parent then takes the child to Maine. Can a Maine court modify the Connecticut order? Not if one of the parents remains in Connecticut. The dissatisfied parent would have to go back to Connecticut to ask the Connecticut court to modify its order or to rule that Maine is a more convenient forum.

An exception exists when there is an emergency, but only on a temporary basis. A state court with temporary emergency custody jurisdiction (see Exhibit 9-7) can modify the custody decision of any other court if the child is present in the state and has been abandoned or if there is an emergency requiring protection of the child because the child, a sibling, or a parent is being mistreated or abused or threatened with mistreatment or abuse (domestic violence). In our Maine/Connecticut example, if the Maine court concluded that it had temporary emergency jurisdiction because of abandonment or violence in Maine, the Maine court could issue a custody order that would have the effect of modifying a Connecticut order. (A Maine court, for example, might issue a **protective order** or **restraining order** to keep a violent parent away from the child until a further hearing can be held.) As indicated in Exhibit 9-7, however, temporary emergency jurisdiction is *temporary*. A court with home state or sc/se jurisdiction—Connecticut in our example—can step in and change (modify) the temporary emergency custody order of a Maine court.

When a parent has **dirty hands**, a court might decline to exercise its jurisdiction. Dirty hands means wrongdoing or other inappropriate behavior that would make it unfair or inequitable to allow persons to assert a right or a defense they would normally have. Suppose, for example, that a parent engages in blatant forum shopping by moving a child from state to state for the sole purpose of trying to find a friendly court. In the unlikely event that this parent eventually finds a court that has jurisdiction under the UCCJEA, this court can decline to take the case because of the parent's dirty hands. But the court will make such a decision only if it determines that the refusal to take the case would not harm the child.

exclusive, continuing jurisdiction (ECJ)
The authority of a court, obtained by compliance with the Uniform Child Custody Jurisdiction and Enforcement Act (UCCJEA), to make all initial *and modifying* custody decisions in a case to the exclusion of courts in any other state.

protective order
A court order directing a person to refrain from doing something such as harming or harassing another. Also called order of protection.

restraining order
A form of injunction, initially issued ex parte (with only one side present), to restrain the defendant from doing a threatened act. Also called order of protection, personal protection order (PPO), protection from abuse.

dirty hands
Wrongdoing or other inappropriate behavior that would make it unfair or inequitable to allow persons to assert a right or a defense they would normally have. A person without dirty hands is said to have *clean hands*.

ASSIGNMENT 9.9

a. Ted and Ursula Jackson have one child, Sam. Sam was born on 4/13/10 in New York, where Ted, Ursula, and Sam have lived since the beginning of 2010. Upon discovering that Ted is having an affair with an office worker, Ursula takes Sam to Florida on 5/1/10, where her parents live. Ted continues to live in New York.

　1. On 5/1/10, could Ted go to a court in New York to obtain an initial custody order?

　2. Could Ursula obtain an initial custody order in Florida on 5/1/10?

b. Assume that Ted obtains a valid initial custody order in New York on 5/1/10. On 7/1/10 Ursula goes to a Florida court to seek a modification of the New York order. Under what circumstances, if any, will the Florida Court modify the New York order? (See General Instructions for the Legal-Analysis Assignment in Appendix A.)

Parental Kidnapping Prevention Act (PKPA)

A federal statute that requires a state to enforce (give full faith and credit to) child-custody orders of other states (28 U.S.C. § 1738A).

PARENTAL KIDNAPPING PREVENTION ACT

Thus far we have been talking about *state* laws on child-custody jurisdiction. There is also a *federal* statute designed to combat child snatching and forum shopping: the **Parental Kidnapping Prevention Act (PKPA)**. This statute covers all interstate child-custody disputes, not just those that involve child snatching or kidnapping. The PKPA requires states to give full faith and credit (FFC) to the custody decree of the state that issued the initial decree if this state had jurisdiction to do so (with priority given to the state with home-state jurisdiction). Another state "shall not modify" it. An exception exists if an emergency requires intervention because of abandonment, abuse, or neglect.

The PKPA also made available to the states the *Federal Parent Locator Service*, which will help to locate an absent parent or child. As we will see in Chapter 10, this service was initially created as a tool for collecting child support. The PKPA also makes the service available in child-custody cases where there is a need to locate a parent or child in order to enforce a child-custody order.

CHILDREN ABROAD

As we have seen, parental kidnapping within the United States can lead to complex jurisdictional problems. These problems multiply when the child is taken out of the country. The most difficult and frustrating reality for most parents whose children have been abducted abroad is that U.S. laws and court orders are not usually recognized in foreign countries and therefore are not directly enforceable abroad. A custody order in the United States can be meaningless abroad.[36]

When a child who is a U.S. citizen is abducted abroad, the U.S. State Department can work with U.S. embassies and consulates abroad to assist the child and left-behind parent. The first step is to open an International Parental Child Abduction Case with the Department of State's Office of Children's Issues (OCI). The concerned parent should also contact local police, file a missing person report, and request that the child's name be entered into the National Crime Information Center (NCIC) computer database of the Federal Bureau of Investigation.[37]

THE HAGUE CONVENTION The Hague Convention on the Civil Aspects of International Child Abduction (Hague Abduction Convention) is a treaty that seeks to deter international child abduction. It applies when the following three conditions are met:

　1. The child was "habitually resident" (it was the child's home for a significant amount of time) in one Convention country, and was wrongfully removed to or retained in another Convention country (taken or retained in violation of the aggrieved parent's custody rights).

2. The wrongful removal or retention occurred between two Convention countries that have a treaty relationship on or after the date the treaty came into force between the two countries (the dates are different for every country).

3. The child is under the age of 16.

Convention countries have agreed that a child who was living in one Convention country, and who has been removed to or retained in another Convention country in violation of the aggrieved parent's custodial rights, shall be promptly returned. Once the child has been returned, the custody dispute can then be resolved, if necessary, in the courts of that jurisdiction. The Hague Convention does not address who should have custody of the child; it addresses where the custody case should be heard. Each country that is party to the Convention has designated a central authority (a specific government office) to carry out specialized duties related to the Convention. Central authorities communicate with each other and assist parents in filing applications for return of or access to their children under the Convention. The central authority for the United States is the Department of State's Office of Children's Issues (OCI).

If the abducting parent does not voluntarily agree to return the child, the aggrieved parent may need to hire legal counsel in the foreign county to seek the return of the child pursuant to the Hague Convention. The U.S. Department of State's OCI does not provide representation, but it can provide information and coordination assistance. If the foreign country is not a Convention country, the process is similar except that the foreign country is not obligated to follow the procedures in the Convention.

EMBRYOS

An **embryo** is an egg that has been fertilized by a sperm and is in the early stage of development; it has undergone one or more divisions. The embryo is the product of conception to about the eighth week of pregnancy. Child custody and adoption laws do not apply to embryos or sperm that are frozen for possible future use in attempting conception. Most states consider frozen embryos and sperm to be property that can be used or destroyed by contractual arrangements between the adults involved and the companies that do the freezing. As we will see in Chapter 16, however, the issue becomes more complex when a state attempts to define embryos as persons.

When a child is born using modern reproductive technologies such as in vitro fertilization, child-custody disputes can arise among the multiple parties involved in the child's conception and birth. We will also discuss such disputes in Chapter 16.

embryo

An egg that has been fertilized by a sperm and is in the early stage of development; it has undergone one or more divisions. The product of conception to about the eighth week of pregnancy.

■ PARALEGAL ROLES

- For an overview of paralegal roles in family-law cases, see Exhibits 1-3 and 1-4 in Chapter 1.
- For all financial issues covered in Chapter 9, a paralegal may be asked to help collect documents and facts outlined in:
  - the checklist in Exhibit 3-1 of Chapter 3
  - the interrogatories in Appendix C
- Interview the client and conduct an investigation into the facts that support parental involvement in the child's life to date in order

to bolster the positions taken in the parent's parenting plan.

- Comment by a paralegal on a child-custody case: "In cases where child-custody is an issue, be it the initial dissolution case or a modification of decree, the client provides me with names of potential witnesses to testify in their behalf. I contact each person and determine if they should be interviewed. As in a recent case, sometimes all witnesses live hours away, requiring me to travel and spend a few days interviewing. In these cases, it is a juggling [act] trying to schedule everyone."[38]

- Miscellaneous duties:
  - Help prepare client for deposition on custody issues.
  - Research potential expert witnesses for home evaluations.
  - Draft the visitation schedule that has been negotiated by the parties.
  - Interview individuals concerning the home, school, and social environment of the child.
  - Draft affidavits for modification of custody orders.
  - Inform (and remind) client of attendance at court-mandated parenting session for divorcing parents.
  - Conduct investigation to collect evidence to demonstrate (or disprove) the nexus between a parent's lifestyle/morality and the welfare of the child.
  - Prepare timeline of parent–child interactions since birth.
  - In interstate custody cases, prepare timeline of presence in both states of the child and the two parents in order to establish a state's jurisdiction to make the initial custody order and to modify an earlier order.
  - Act as liaison between of the office and the guardian ad litem (GAL), parenting coordinator (PC), and court appointed special advocate (CASA).
  - Research community resources to support client's child-rearing responsibilities, particularly if the child has special needs.
  - Compile a health record of client to demonstrate his or her suitability as a parent.
  - Compile a health record of child.
  - Obtain police and other law-enforcement reports if domestic violence has occurred.
  - Obtain school records of child.
  - Provide referrals to resources of the State Department in international custody cases.

■ CHECK THE CITE

A father has legal custody of his son. During the marriage, the boy was raised in the Russian Orthodox Church, which the mother still attends. At the time of the divorce, the father converted to Judaism and now wants to have his son circumcised. The mother has asked the court for an order preventing the circumcision or for an order granting her legal custody. Which parent has the right to make the decision on whether to circumcise a child? Explain how the court resolved the conflict. Read *In re Marriage of Boldt*, 344 Or. 1, 176 P.3d 388 (Or. 2008). To read this opinion

online: (1) Run a citation search ("176 P.3d 388") in the Legal documents database of Google Scholar (scholar.google.com). (2) Run this search in Google's general search engine: "In re Marriage of Boldt" circumcision.

■ PROJECT

In Google, Bing, or Yahoo, run the following search: aa "parenting coordinator" (substitute the name of your state for aa in the search). Write a short essay in which you (a) describe the benefits and potential difficulties of hiring a parenting coordinator. You must cite and quote from a minimum of five different sources that you find on the Internet. (b) Find three different parenting coordinator services on the Internet. They can be from any state. How do the three services differ? In what ways are they the same? Compare what they offer, their experience, what they claim their strengths to be, their costs, etc.

■ ETHICS IN A FAMILY LAW PRACTICE

You are a paralegal working at the law office of Harris and Harris, which represents William Norton in a custody dispute with his wife, Irene Norton. Irene is represented by Davis & Davis. Your supervisor asks you to prepare interrogatories to be sent to Irene about her employment. You are not sure whether to include questions about her pension plan. Before you write any pension questions, you call Irene and ask her if she has a pension plan at her work. She is very cooperative, telling you that she does not have a pension. You then go back to drafting the interrogatories. Any ethical problems?

■ WRITING SAMPLE

George Smith and Alice O'Toole have one child, six-year old Thomas. When George and Alice divorced, Alice was granted sole legal and sole physical custody of Thomas with visitation rights to George. The parties have always disagreed about how to raise their child. The disagreements continue after the divorce. Assume that George's attorney is going to draft a motion to modify the custody order so that George receives sole legal and sole physical custody. Alice's attorney will file an opposing motion. George's attorney asks George to write an affidavit that the attorney will file with the motion to modify. George's affidavit will state the facts that George believes justify the modification. Alice's attorney asks Alice to write an affidavit containing her version of the facts and opposing the modification of the custody order. Write both affidavits, one for George and one for Alice. (See Exhibit 9-6 for an example of a client affidavit.) You can make up the facts that are the basis of their custody dispute. Each affidavit should have a strong factual basis to support its position. (See General Instructions for the Writing Sample in Appendix A.)

SUMMARY

Physical custody is the right of an adult (the custodial parent) to have a child reside with that adult. Legal custody is the right to make the major child-rearing decisions on health, education, religion, discipline, and general welfare. Both kinds of custody can be sole or joint. In negotiating custody and visitation clauses of a separation agreement, many factors need to be considered, such as the age and health of the parents and child, the emotional attachments of the child, the work schedules of the parents, etc. If negotiations fail and the parties cannot agree, litigation is necessary. This can be a stressful experience, not only for the parents but also for the person caught in the middle—the child. Courts often require divorcing parents to participate in short training programs to help relieve this stress.

When custody is contested, participants can include (in addition to parents, child, and judge) the attorneys for the parents, a best interests attorney (BIA), a guardian ad litem (GAL), a court appointed special advocate (CASA), and a parenting coordinator (PC). A custody dispute between the biological parents is resolved by a judge's considerable discretion in determining what is in the best interests of the child as reflected in the proposed parenting plans. The factors a judge will consider include stability in the child's life, availability to respond to the child's day-to-day needs, emotional ties that have already developed, amenability to visitation by the other parent, etc. At one time, courts applied guidelines such as the presumption that a child of tender years is better off with his or her mother. Today most courts reject gender-based presumptions, although fathers continue to complain that the mother is still given an undue preference. The moral values and lifestyles of the parent seeking custody are generally not considered by the court unless, under the nexus test, they affect the welfare of the child. Domestic violence that affects the child's welfare is also a factor. If the parents practice different religions, the court cannot prefer one religion over another, but can consider any effect the practice of a particular religion will have on the child. To the extent possible, the court will try to maintain continuity in the child's cultural development. The custody decision cannot be based solely on race. If the child is old enough to express a preference, it will be considered. Often the court will also consider the testimony of expert witnesses.

The court will generally favor liberal visitation rights for the noncustodial parent. Supervised visitation might be ordered if the court feels it is necessary because of violence or other concerns. Occasionally, such rights will be granted to individuals other than biological parents (e.g., grandparents), if doing so does not interfere with the constitutional right of a fit custodial parent to make child-rearing decisions. When a custodial parent wants to move out of the area, the court will balance how the move will affect the noncustodial parent's visitation rights and the best interests of the child. Enforcement remedies can include ne exeat, civil and criminal contempt, and changes in the custody and visitation orders.

When the custody battle is between a biological parent and a nonparent (often called a psychological parent), the biological parent usually wins unless he or she can be shown to be unfit. If the parents disagree on whether the child's surname should be changed, the court will resolve the issue on the basis of whether the change is in the best interests of the child.

Occasionally, it is in the best interests of the child for a court to modify an earlier custody decision because of changed circumstances. Frantic parents will sometimes engage in child snatching and forum shopping in order to find a court that will make a modification order. To cut down on this practice, two important laws have been enacted: the state Uniform Child Custody Jurisdiction and Enforcement Act and the federal Parental Kidnapping Prevention Act. The primary tool used by these statutes to cut down on forum shopping is to give priority to the child's home state among possible competing states that could be asked to issue or modify a custody decision. When the child has been taken to a foreign country, the aid of the Department of State and the Hague Convention on Child Abduction can be sought.

KEY TERMS

best interests of the child
custody
child custody
physical custody
custodial parent (CP)
noncustodial parent (NCP)
visitation
legal custody
joint physical custody
joint legal custody
coparenting
split custody

Temporary Assistance for Needy
    Families (TANF)
presumption
contested
mediation
alternative dispute resolution (ADR)
best interests attorney (BIA)
guardian ad litem (GAL)
court appointed special advocate
    (CASA)
parenting coordinator (PC)
attorney-client privilege

parenting plan
deposition
parental alienation syndrome (PAS)
tender-years presumption
primary-caregiver presumption
domestic violence (DV)
child abuse
civil contempt
criminal contempt
Minnesota Multiphasic Personality
    Inventory Test (MMPI)
parenting time

supervised visitation
cohabitation
ne exeat
foster care
psychological parent
fictive kin
in loco parentis
unfit

child neglect
forum
forum shopping
full faith and credit (FFC)
Uniform Child Custody
    Jurisdiction and Enforcement
    Act (UCCJEA)
home state

forum non conveniens
exclusive, continuing jurisdiction (ECJ)
protective order
restraining order
dirty hands
Parental Kidnapping Prevention
    Act (PKPA)
embryo

REVIEW QUESTIONS

1. What is meant by custody, physical custody, legal custody, sole physical custody, sole legal custody, joint physical custody, joint legal custody, and split custody?
2. What are some of the decisions parents must make when negotiating the child-custody clauses of their separation agreement?
3. When is joint legal custody likely to be effective?
4. What are some of the major guidelines that courts often present to divorcing parents to lessen the stress of divorce on children?
5. How is mediation often used in contested custody cases?
6. What are the roles of a best interests attorney (BIA), a guardian ad litem (GAL), a court appointed special advocate (CASA), and a parenting coordinator (PC)?
7. What factors do courts consider when determining the best interests of the child in a custody dispute between the two biological parents?
8. What are the components of a parenting plan?
9. How does a parent's attitude on visitation affect the court's decision on whether to allow that parent to become the custodial parent?
10. What are indicia of parenthood?
11. What is parental alienation syndrome and why is it disfavored?
12. What is the tender-years presumption and how is it used in custody decisions today?
13. What is the primary-caregiver presumption and how is it used in custody decisions today?
14. What is the nexus test in regard to the morality and lifestyle of a parent seeking custody?
15. How does domestic violence affect a court's decision on custody?
16. What is the dilemma faced by attorneys asked to represent parents accused of child sexual abuse?
17. What is the role of religion in the custody decision?
18. What is the role of race in the custody decision?
19. What roles do expert witnesses play in custody disputes?
20. What details should parents work out when negotiating the visitation clauses of the separation agreement?
21. When will a court grant a request by the custodial parent to move away from the area?
22. What is virtual visitation?
23. What is the holding in the *Troxel* case?
24. When will a court require supervised visitation?
25. What is a shared-custody agreement?
26. What remedies are available to enforce a visitation order?
27. How does a court resolve a custody dispute between a biological parent and a psychological parent?
28. When can a divorced parent change the surname of a child?
29. Under what circumstances can a court modify its own custody order?
30. What are child snatching and forum shopping?
31. What are the possible bases of jurisdiction under the Uniform Child Custody Jurisdiction and Enforcement Act?
32. When will a court refuse to exercise the custody jurisdiction that it has?
33. When does a court have jurisdiction to modify the custody order of another state?
34. What is the effect of the Parental Kidnapping Prevention Act?
35. What is the Hague Convention on the Civil Aspects of International Child Abduction?
36. Are embryos subject to the laws of child custody?

HELPFUL WEBSITES

Child Custody Legal Research
- www.familylaw.org/custodyresearch.htm

Child Custody Jurisdiction
- www.familylaw.org/uccja.htm

Shared Parenting: A Guide for Parents Living Apart

- www.mass.gov/courts/courtsandjudges/courts /probateandfamilycourt/afccsharedparenting.pdf

Parental Guide to Making Child-Focused Parenting Time Decisions

- www.mncourts.gov/documents/0/Public/Court _Information_Office/PARENTING_TIME _PAMPHLET.pdf

A Judicial Guide to Child Safety in Child Custody Cases

- www.ncjfcj.org/images/stories/dept/fvd/pdf /judicial%20guide.pdf

Child Custody Evaluations

- law.ubalt.edu/downloads/law_downloads/April2009 _ChildCustodyEvalauations_FINAL.pdf

Association of Family and Conciliation Courts

- www.afccnet.org

FBI Wanted List: Parental Kidnappings

- www.fbi.gov/wanted/parent

Grandparents' Rights

- www.grandparentsrights.org
- www.grandparentsforchildren.org

Stepparents

- www.stepfamilies.info

Supervised Visitation Network

- www.svnetwork.net

Court Appointed Special Advocates (CASA)

- www.casaforchildren.org

Winning Child Custody

- www.winchildcustody.com

Child Custody and Visitation Software

- JointParents.com
- ParentingTime.net
- www.kidmate.com
- www.kidshare.com
- CustodyPlanner.com

Father's Rights

- www.dadsdivorce.com

Abuse-Excuse (unfounded claims of child abuse)

- www.abuse-excuse.com

A Family Resource Guide on International Parental Kidnapping

- www.ncjrs.gov/pdffiles1/ojjdp/215476.pdf

Google/Bing/Yahoo Searches

(on these search engines, run the following searches, substituting your state for "aa")

- "child custody" aa
- joint custody divorce aa
- visitation divorce aa
- mediation "child custody" aa
- CASA child neglect aa
- "parenting plan" aa
- UCCJEA aa
- gay lesbian child custody aa
- PKPA custody aa
- international "child custody"
- "parenting coordinator" aa
- sole custody divorce aa
- coparenting aa
- "supervised visitation" aa
- guardian ad litem "child custody" aa
- "best interests of the child" aa
- "parental alienation syndrome" aa
- "primary caregiver" custody aa
- "tender years" "child custody" aa
- contempt "child custody" aa
- "child abuse" "child custody" aa

ENDNOTES

Note: All or most of the court opinions in these endnotes can be read online. To do so, go to Google Scholar (scholar .google.com), select "Legal documents," and in the search box, enter the cite (e.g., "404 A.2d 88") or name of the case (e.g., "Berman v. Allen") that is given in the endnote.

[1] Robert Oliphant and Nancy Ver Steegh, *Family Law* 103 (3d ed. 2010).

[2] UPI, A *"Solomon Ruling—Half Son's Ashes,"* Sydney Morning Herald (July 23, 1978); Chicago Daily Law Bulletin, July 21, 1978, at 1; Harry Krause et al., *Family Law* 628 (4th ed. 1998).

[3] Carl Schneider and Margaret Brinig, *An Invitation to Family Law* 62 (1996).

[4] Scott Coltrane and Randall Collins, *Sociology of Marriage and the Family* 530 (2001).

[5] Mary Ann Lamanna and Agnes Riedmann, *Marriages and Families* 481 (2000).

[6] National Conference of Commissioners on Uniform State Laws, *Uniform Representation of Children in Abuse, Neglect, and Custody Cases* (2006) (apps.americanbar.org /legalservices/probono/nccusl_act_rep_children.pdf) (www .law.upenn.edu/bll/archives/ulc/rarccda/2007_final.pdf).

[7] The AFCC Task Force on Parental Coordination, *Guidelines for Parental Coordination* 2 (May 2005) (www.afccnet.org).

[8] National Council of Juvenile and Family Court Judges, *A Judicial Guide to Child Safety in Child Custody Cases* 13 (2008) (www.ncjfcj.org/images/stories/dept/fvd/pdf /judicial%20guide.pdf).

[9] *Tuter v. Tuter*, 120 S.W.2d 203, 205 (Mo. App. 1938).

[10] Joel Stonington and Frank Bass, *Single-Dad Courtroom Wins Show Greater Embrace of New Families*, Bloomberg News (July 25, 2011) (mobile.bloomberg.com/news/2011-07-25 /single-dad-courtroom-victories-show-greater-u-s-embrace -of-new-families).

[11] Timothy Grall, *Custodial Mothers and Fathers and Their Child Support: 2009* (Current Population Reports, Dec. 2011) (www.census.gov/prod/2011pubs/p60-240.pdf).

[12] Jan Hoffman, *Divorced Fathers Make Gains in Battles to Increase Rights*, N.Y. Times, Apr. 26, 1995, at A11 (www .nytimes.com/1995/04/26/nyregion/divorced-fathers -make-gains-in-battles-to-increase-rights.html).

[13] *In re Marriage of Wellman*, 164 Cal. Rptr. 148, 151–52 (Cal. App. 1980).

[14] *Ex parte H.H.*, 830 So. 2d 21, 38 (Ala., 2002).

[15] *Lawrence v. Texas*, 539 U.S. 558 (2003).

[16] M. Szegedy-Maszak, *Who's to Judge*, N.Y. Times Magazine, May 21, 1989, at 28. (www.nytimes.com/1989/05/21 /magazine/who-s-to-judge.html).

[17] Cory Gordon, *False Allegations of Abuse in Child Custody Disputes*, 2 Minnesota Family Law Journal 225 (1985).

[18] Catherine Paquette, *Handling Sexual Abuse Allegations in Child Custody Cases*, 25 New England Law Review 1415, 1419, n. 32 (1991) citing *Abuse: The New Weapon*, National Law Journal, July 17, 1989, at 20, col. 1.

[19] Margaret Fisk, *Abuse: The New Weapon in Divorces*, National Law Journal, July 17, 1989, at 20.

[19a] Pew Forum on Religion & Public Life, *U.S. Religious Landscape Survey*, 34 (2007) (religions.pewforum.org/pdf /report-religious-landscape-study-chapter-2.pdf).

[20] *Kendall v. Kendall*, 687 N.E.2d 1228, 1231 (Mass. 1997).

[21] *Palmore v. Sidoni*, 466 U.S. 429 (1984).

[21a] Shauna R. Prewitt, *Giving Birth to a "Rapist's Child,"* 98 Georgetown Law Journal 827, 829, 831 (2010) (georgetownlawjournal.org/files/pdf/98-3/Prewitt.PDF).

[22] James E. Manhood, *Kidmate Simplifies Custody Scheduling for Lawyers, Clients*, 16 Matrimonial Strategist 5 (Aug. 1998).

[23] *Tropea v. Tropea*, 665 N.E.2d 145, 148 (N.Y. 1996).

[24] Minnesota Statutes Annotated § 518.175(3)(a) (www .revisor.mn.gov/statutes/?id=518.175&year=2010&key word_type=all&keyword=518.175).

[25] Based on Florida Statutes, § 61.13001 (www.lrcvaw.org/laws /flrelocation.pdf).

[26] *Troxel v. Granville*, 530 U.S. 57 (2000).

[27] Id. at 64.

[28] U.S. Const. amend. XIV, § 1.

[29] *Troxel*, 530 U.S. at 65.

[30] Id at 68.

[31] *In re Mullen*, 953 N.E.2d 302, 305-06 (Ohio 2011). Although the court affirmed the validity of shared-custody agreements, it denied the petitioner's request for visitation rights because of insufficient evidence that such an agreement had been entered.

[32] For example, see Revised Code of Washington, § 9A.40.060, Custodial Interference in the First Degree (apps.leg .wa.gov/rcw/default.aspx?cite=9A.40.060).

[33] *In re Saxton*, 309 N.W.2d 298, 301 (Minn. 1981).

[34] 28 U.S.C. § 1738A (www.law.cornell.edu/uscode/28/1738A .html).

[35] Uniform Law Commission (uniform laws on family law), (www.nccusl.org/Acts.aspx?category=ULC_Family).

[36] U.S. Department of State, Office of Children's Issues, *International Parental Abduction* 3 (1997)

[37] Federal Bureau of Investigation, National Crime Information Center, (www.fas.org/irp/agency/doj/fbi/is/ncic.htm).

[38] Cathy Lenihan, *Role of the Family Law Paralegal*, 10 Oregon Legal Assistant Association Newsletter 7 (Aug. 1987).

Child Support

CHAPTER OUTLINE

CHAPTER OBJECTIVES

After completing this chapter, you should be able to:

- Understand the impact of federal law on child support.

- Know when persons other than parents can be liable for child support.

- State when child support might continue after the age of majority.

- List the major issues divorcing parents should cover in the child-support clauses of their separation agreement.

- Explain how a state determines the amount of child support that is due.

- Know when income will be imputed for purposes of determining a child-support obligation.

- Identify the main kinds of assistance provided by an IV-D agency.

- List the main methods of enforcing a child-support obligation.

- Explain when an attorney must be provided for an indigent obligor.

- Distinguish between obtaining jurisdiction over a resident and

a nonresident parent for the establishment and enforcement of a child-support order.

- Explain how a support order can be enforced against a nonresident obligor.

- Understand when a state will modify its child-support order.

- Know when an out-of-state support order can be modified.

- Know whether a state can refuse to grant a marriage license to someone until he or she pays past-due child support.

INTRODUCTION

Family law, as we have seen, is primarily governed by state law. The law of child support, however, is a major exception. Although child support is still a function of state and local government, federal law has substantially influenced the field. In the 1970s, Congress began passing laws designed to increase the collection of child support and thereby decrease the cost of **public assistance** (welfare), which is funded in large measure by federal money. When parents fail to pay child support, the last resort is often public assistance. Congress said to the states that their receipt of federal money was conditioned on their passing strong laws on the establishment and enforcement of child support. One of the most significant laws requires employers to withhold child-support payments from the paychecks of delinquent parents, usually **noncustodial parents (NCP)** who do not have physical custody of their children. The result of such laws has been a dramatic increase in the collection of child support and a decline in the number of **custodial parents (CPs)** receiving public assistance. Between 1993 and 2007, the number of CPs receiving **Temporary Assistance for Needy Families (TANF)**, the main public assistance program, declined from 22 percent to 4.3 percent.[1]

Unfortunately, however, collection is still a huge problem. Approximately 38 percent of child support is not paid. This amounts to over $13 billion a year. (See Exhibit 10-1.) Delinquent parents (often fathers) have devised elaborate methods of avoiding their support duty.

> [M]any "deadbeat dads" opt to work in the underground economy to shield their earnings from child support enforcement efforts. To avoid attempts to garnish their wages or otherwise enforce the support obligation, "deadbeats" quit their jobs, jump from job to job, become self-employed, work under the table, or engage in illegal activity.[2]

Often, delinquent parents move out of state in order to avoid payment. The total amount of **arrearages** (uncollected payments that are due) of all prior years is over $110 billion. The average amount of annual child support received by a CP is $5,160, or $430 a month. Over 28 percent of all CPs have incomes below the poverty level. Many CPs (27 percent) contact a government office for help in collecting child support. As we will see, a CP does not have to be on public assistance to receive government help in collecting child support.

public assistance

Welfare or other forms of financial help from the government to the poor.

noncustodial parent (NCP)

The parent who is not living with the child; the parent who does not have physical custody of the child. Also called nonresidential parent.

custodial parent (CP)

The parent with whom the child is living; the parent with physical custody of the child. Also called residential parent.

Temporary Assistance for Needy Families (TANF)

The federal-state welfare system (42 U.S.C. § 601) that replaced Aid to Families with Dependent Children (AFDC). Unlike AFDC, benefits under TANF are limited to five years.

arrearages

Payments that are due but have not been made. Also called arrears.

EXHIBIT 10-1 **Comparison of Child Support Received by Custodial Mothers and Custodial Fathers**

Custodial Mothers Entitled to Child Support	Custodial Fathers Entitled to Child Support
Number of Custodial Mothers Entitled to Receive Child Support: 11,358,000	**Number of Custodial Fathers Entitled to Receive Child Support:** 2,387,000
Annual Amount of Child Support to Which Custodial Mothers Are Entitled: $29.8 billion	**Annual Amount of Child Support to Which Custodial Fathers Are Entitled:** $4.3 billion
Amount Custodial Mothers Actually Received: $18.6 billion	**Amount Custodial Fathers Actually Received:** $2.8 billion
Full Payment	**Full Payment**
• Number of custodial mothers who received the full amount of child support they were owed: 2,615,000	• Number of custodial fathers who received the full amount of child support they were owed: 371,000
• Percentage of custodial mothers who received the full amount of child support they were owed: 42 percent	• Percentage of custodial fathers who received the full amount of child support they were owed: 34 percent
No Payment	**No Payment**
• Number of custodial mothers receiving no child support they were owed: 1,298,000	• Number of custodial fathers receiving no child support they were owed: 213,000

Source: U.S. Census Bureau, The 2011 Statistical Abstract, *Table 566 Child Support: Award and Recipiency Status of Custodial Parent: 2007* (www.census.gov/compendia/statab/2011/tables/11s0566.pdf); U.S. Census Bureau, *Custodial Mothers and Fathers and Their Child Support: 2007* (Current Population Reports) (November 2009). (www.census.gov/prod/2009pubs/p60-237.pdf) (www.acf.hhs.gov/programs/cse/pubs/2011/reports/preliminary_report_fy2010).

WHO MUST PAY?

PARENTS

The traditional rule was that only the father had the legal duty to support his children. Today each parent has an equal duty of support regardless of who has **physical custody** (the right to decide where the child resides) or who has **legal custody** (the right to make the major child-rearing decisions on health, education, religion, discipline, and general welfare). A parent who does not have physical or legal custody has the same duty of support as the parent with both physical and legal custody. The duty is not dependent on the existence of a marriage, on the sexual orientation of the parents, or on who caused the divorce. With limited exceptions, the duty is based on parentage.

The parent who must pay child support is the **obligor**; the parent who is entitled to receive child support on behalf of the child is the **obligee**. The obligor who pays (or who is obligated to pay) is also called the **payor**. The obligee to whom this payment is made (or to whom it must be paid) is also called the **payee**.

ADOPTIVE PARENTS

Once a child is adopted, the adoptive parent has the same child-support duty as any other parent. This reality became painfully clear to a woman in Tennessee who had adopted a young boy from Russia. When she could no longer handle the boy's disruptive behavior and possible mental illness, she bought him a one-way ticket back to Russia and put him on a plane alone, with a note saying that she was returning him because of all the trouble he was causing. As we will see in Chapter 17, this is not the way to undo an adoption. The event became a world media story. The adoptive parent is facing numerous legal problems as a result of what she did. One of those problems is child support. An American court has ordered her to pay $150,000 in child support to the foster home in Russia where the boy was placed.[2a]

GRANDPARENTS

Grandparents do not have a duty to support their grandchildren. A state, however, may create an exception for an unmarried, underage grandchild who gives birth to a child. The statute might require the grandparents to support such a grandchild if the mother was living with the grandparents at the time of the birth of the grandchild.

STEPPARENTS

The general rule is that a **stepparent** (someone who has married the natural or adoptive parent of a child) does not have a duty to support a stepchild. Adoption of the child by the stepparent does require the stepparent (now the adoptive parent) to support the child. As we will see in Chapter 15, the adoption may be a traditional adoption or an **equitable adoption** in which the adult intended to adopt the child and acted as the child's parent, but never went through the formal adoption procedures. If the adoptive parent later divorces the natural parent, the adoptive parent's duty to support the child continues after the divorce.

Under some circumstances, a court might impose a duty of child support on a stepparent even without adoption. The duty could be based on a special statute in the state imposing the support duty on the stepparent. In the absence of such a statute, a court might impose the duty because the stepparent is **in loco parentis**, meaning that the stepparent has taken the place of a biological parent and has voluntarily assumed some or all parental responsibilities, including the provision of support. Where in loco parentis applies, the support duty of the stepparent exists only while the stepparent is married to the natural parent.

---

physical custody

(1) The right of an adult to have a child reside with the adult. Also called residential custody, custodial responsibility. (2) Where the child is actually living.

legal custody

The right to make the major child-rearing decisions on health, education, religion, discipline, and general welfare. Also called decision-making responsibility.

obligor

One who has a legal obligation to do something, usually to make a payment.

obligee

One to whom a legal obligation is owed.

payor

One who makes a payment of money or who is obligated to do so.

payee

One to whom money is paid or is to be paid.

stepparent

A person who marries the natural mother or father of a child, but who is not one of the child's natural or adoptive parents.

equitable adoption

A child will be considered the adopted child of a person who intended to adopt the child and acted as the child's parent but failed to go through the formal adoption procedures. Also called adoption by estoppel, de facto adoption, virtual adoption.

in loco parentis

Standing in the place of a parent by assuming some or all parental responsibilities without being a biological or adoptive parent.

equitable estoppel

The voluntary conduct of a person will preclude him or her from asserting rights against another who justifiably relied on the conduct and who would suffer damage or injury if the person is now allowed to repudiate the conduct. Also called estoppel in pais.

estopped

Prevented from asserting a right or a defense because it would be unfair or inequitable to allow the assertion. The noun is *estoppel*.

In most states, when the relationship terminates, so does the support duty, unless **equitable estoppel** applies.

Under equitable estoppel, the voluntary conduct of a person will preclude him or her from asserting rights against another who justifiably relied on the conduct and who would suffer damage or injury if the person were now allowed to repudiate the conduct. For example, a stepparent would be **estopped** from denying a duty to support a child when the stepparent has been voluntarily supporting the child, has allowed the child to be assimilated into the family, has induced the child (and the biological parent) to rely on the stepparent's emotional and financial support, and has encouraged the child to believe that the stepparent is a biological parent. One possible hardship suffered by children as a result of their reliance on such a stepparent is the fact that they were discouraged from trying to locate the other biological parent. The children did not seek support from the other biological parent because of the stepparent's assumption of the parental role. Hence, the children have suffered financial hardship because of their reliance on the stepparent. When such hardship exists, a court might prevent (*estop*) the stepparent from denying a duty to continue the support, even after stepparent divorces or otherwise ends his or her relationship with the mother or father.

COPARENTS

coparenting

Shared responsibility by two adults to raise a child, regardless of the marital status or sexual orientation of the adults.

Coparenting is a general term that simply means shared responsibility by two adults to raise a child, regardless of the marital status or sexual orientation of the adults. The two adults can be married, single, of the opposite sex, of the same sex, transgender, etc. Assume, for example, that a lesbian couple wants to have a child that the two women will raise together. Using a sperm donor, one of the women becomes pregnant by artificial insemination (see section titled "SPERM DONORS"). Upon birth, the women give the child a surname that is a hyphenated combination of the names of both women. For two years, they care for the child and pay the expenses of upbringing. They let everyone know that the child is "theirs." When the women separate, the child stays with the woman who gave birth to the child. On these facts, some courts could hold that both women have an equal duty of child support even though one of the women (the one who left) is not biologically related to (and never adopted) the child.

Several theories could account for this result.

- *Statute*. The state may have a statute that gives rights and duties to adults who take a child into their home and hold the child out to the world as their natural child even though the adult is not biologically related to the child.

- *Breach of promise*. When one adult agrees to conceive a child upon the express or implied promise of the other adult to support that child, a court may enforce this contractual promise.

- *In loco parentis*. Both women assumed the full responsibilities of parents.

- *Equitable estoppel*. The birth mother relied on the departing mother in their joint plan to bring a child into the world and to raise it together. The reliance would cause hardship on the child if the departing woman is now able to walk away from the plan and leave the support burden on the birth mother alone.

presumed parent

A person who, under the Uniform Parentage Act, is presumed to be the natural parent of a child if the person receives the child into his or her home and openly holds out the child as his or her natural child. The presumed parent does not have to be biologically related to the child.

Under the Uniform Parentage Act (UPA), a person can be a **presumed parent** without being biologically related to the child and without being married to the biological parent. The key criteria is receiving the child into the home and holding the child out as one's natural child. "Nevertheless, a presumed parent is not just a casual friend of the other parent, or even a long-term boyfriend or girlfriend, but someone who has entered into a familial relationship with the child: someone who has demonstrated an abiding commitment to the child and the child's well-being, regardless of his or her relationship with the child's other parent."[2b]

SPERM DONORS

A sperm donor is a male who provides his sperm to a woman so that she can have a child. The woman might be (1) the wife of another man, (2) a lesbian in a same-sex relationship, or a (3) a single person wishing to become a mother. Most women obtain donated sperm through a **sperm bank**, which is a facility that collects and stores human sperm from donors who will usually be anonymous to the women who use the sperm to become pregnant by **artificial insemination (AI)**.

If the woman is married and her spouse consents to the artificial insemination (performed under the supervision of a licensed physician), the sperm donor has no custody rights or support duties for the child even if the donor and the mother agreed otherwise. If the woman is unmarried, the same general rule applies (the donor has no rights or duties), but an agreement or a bonding relationship might change this result. A court might give the donor custody rights (e.g., visitation) and require him to pay child support if he entered an agreement with the mother to provide such support or if he establishes a bonding relationship with the child such as by visiting the child, regularly sending presents to the child, and the like.

Suppose, however, that a man has sexual intercourse with a woman solely to impregnate her, making no promise and having no expectation of assuming parental duties. Does he have a duty of child support? Yes. Only sperm donors via artificial insemination can avoid the duty. This is so even if the man and the woman agree (prior to or after their intercourse) that he will not be involved in the raising of the child and will not owe child support. In this situation, the father must support the child. (See the *Straub* case below.)

> **sperm bank**
> A facility that collects and stores human sperm from donors who will usually be anonymous to any woman who uses the sperm to become pregnant by artificial insemination. Also called cryobank.

> **artificial insemination (AI)**
> Inserting sperm into the uterus by a method other than sexual intercourse.

ASSIGNMENT 10.1

Under what circumstances, if any, will a sperm donor be required to pay child support in your state? (See the General Instructions for the State-Code Assignment and the Court Opinion Assignment in Appendix A.)

FOR HOW LONG?

With few exceptions, a parent's duty of child support ends when the child reaches the **age of majority** (usually 18) or becomes **emancipated**. If an unemancipated child is still in school, the support duty may be extended (see the section titled "College"). Similarly, a parent can be required to support a disabled child after the age of majority (see the section titled "Disability"). In most states, the death of the parent ends his or her duty of child support, although most states can require a parent to maintain a life insurance policy with the child as the beneficiary so that a measure of support continues after the parent's death.

> **age of majority**
> The age at which children reach legal adulthood, usually 18, entitling them to many civil rights such as the right to manage their own affairs.

> **emancipated**
> Legally independent of one's parent or legal guardian. The noun is *emancipation*.

EMANCIPATION

Emancipation means being legally independent of one's parent or legal guardian. Children can be emancipated before the age of majority if certain events take place that clearly indicate they are living independently with the consent of their parents or legal guardians. Such events include marriage and entering military service. We will examine emancipation in greater depth in Chapter 14.

COLLEGE

A good deal of litigation has centered on the issue of educational expenses, particularly higher education. Does a divorced parent have a duty to send his or her child to college? Arguments *against* imposing this duty are as follows:

- A parent's support duty is limited to providing a child with necessities (e.g., food, shelter, clothing). A large percentage of Americans do not attend college. College, therefore, is a luxury, not a necessity.

- A parent's support duty terminates when the child reaches the age of majority (e.g., 18). Children in college will be over the age of majority during some or most of their college years.

- Children of parents who are still married have no right to force their parents to send them to college. Why should children of divorced parents have the right to be sent to college?

Some states, however, have rejected these arguments and have required the divorced parent to pay for a college education if the parent has the ability to pay and the child has the capacity to go to college. Several arguments support this position:

- In today's society, college is not a luxury. A college degree, at least the first one, is a necessity.

- A parent's duty to provide child support does not terminate in all cases when the child reaches majority. For example, a physically or mentally disabled child may have to be supported indefinitely. Some courts take the position that the support duty continues so long as the child's need for support continues (i.e., so long as the child remains dependent). This includes the period when the child is in college.

- It is true that married parents have no obligation to send their children to college. But there is a strong likelihood they will do so if they have the means and their children have the ability. When the court requires a divorced parent to send his or her children to college, the same tests are applied: ability to pay and capacity to learn. Thus, the court, in effect, is simply trying to equalize the position of children of divorced parents with that of children of married parents.

Whether or not a state says that college expenses are part of child support, divorcing parents often agree on their own to cover the expenses of college. Their separation agreement reflects this decision.

DISABILITY

In most states, the duty of support extends beyond the age of majority if the child becomes physically or mentally disabled before that age. The duty continues during the disability. Suppose, however, that the disability arises during adulthood—*after* the child reaches the age of majority. An example is an adult child incapacitated in an automobile accident. Only a few states would impose the duty in such cases.

SUPPORT BEFORE BIRTH?

After a child is born, the father becomes jointly responsible with the mother for all pregnancy-related costs associated with the birth. The father's liability is determined by his acknowledgement of paternity or by the paternity tests that we will discuss in Chapter 13. Such tests are administered after the child is born. Suppose, however, that fatherhood could be established by safe paternity tests *during* the pregnancy. Should the father become liable for his share of pregnancy costs before the child is born? No state requires such payments, but the emerging availability of safe prenatal paternity tests have encouraged some advocates to argue for a change in the law. One advocate would call the required payments *preglimony*.[2c]

SEPARATION AGREEMENT

Only three out of four custodial parents (CPs) have an agreement or a court order requiring noncustodial parents (NCPs) to pay child support. The reasons CPs do not have formal agreements are outlined in Exhibit 10-2.

We need to examine some of the major considerations faced by parents that *do* want a formal support agreement, usually in their **separation agreement**. When they are negotiating the child-support clauses of such agreements, they need to consider a wide range of factors:

- *State guidelines.* Each state has **child-support guidelines** on the amount of child support that must be paid. The guidelines set the minimum. The parents must decide whether they want to exceed the minimum. If they have the resources to meet the minimum, they cannot agree to a child-support amount that is *lower* than what the guidelines mandate. When the separation agreement eventually comes before the court for approval, the child-support clauses will be rejected if they fall below the minimum specified by the guidelines, which we will consider in detail later. Parents cannot bargain away the basic need of their children for support as reflected in the child-support guidelines.

- *Standard of living.* What standard of living was the child accustomed to during the marriage? Do the parents have the financial resources to maintain this standard of living?

- *Payment dates.* On what day is each child-support payment to be made?

- *Kinds of payments.* Most child support is paid in cash on a periodic basis. The parties, however, can decide to use other assets as child support, such as the marital home, stocks or other securities, and motor vehicles.

separation agreement
A contract by married persons who have separated (or who are about to separate) that can cover support, custody, property division, and other terms of their separation and possible divorce. Also called marital settlement agreement.

child-support guidelines
State-mandated rules for calculating the amount of child support owed by adults obligated to pay such support (obligors).

EXHIBIT 10-2	**Reasons Custodial Parents Say They Do Not Have Formal Child Support Agreements**

Other parent provides what he or she can — 34.4
Did not feel need to make legal — 32.1
Other parent could not afford to pay — 29.2
Did not want other parent to pay — 21.1
Child stays with other parent part of the time — 17.7
Could not locate other parent — 16.8
Did not want to have contact with other parent — 16.7
Other reasons — 13.1
Did not legally establish paternity — 8.4
Child was too old — 0.3

Source: U.S. Census Bureau, *Current Population Survey* (April 2010).

(The tax consequences of such payments are covered below and in Chapter 11.)

- *Frequency of payments.* How many payments are to be made? Will they be monthly payments covering everyday expenses and separate payments covering large, emergency expenses (e.g., hospitalization)?

- *Insurance.* Will insurance be taken out or maintained if already in existence? What kind? Medical insurance? Who will be covered? How will premiums be paid? (Later we will see that the obligor may be required to provide medical insurance for the child.) Life insurance? Will the child be the beneficiary of a life insurance policy on the life of the obligor? If so, for how much, who pays the premiums, and can the beneficiaries be changed by the obligor? Does the payment of premiums (and hence the insurance coverage) end when the child reaches the age of majority (usually 18)?

- *Escalation clause.* Will there be an **escalation clause** under which payments will be increased or decreased based on a factor over which the parties do not have complete control such as the Consumer Price Index? Do the child-support payments fluctuate with the income of either of the parents? Do the support payments fluctuate with the income of the child (e.g., summer jobs, inheritance)?

- *Termination of payments.* When do the child-support payments end? When the child reaches a certain age (e.g., the age of majority), marries, or moves out of the house? The separation agreement should specify the intention of the parents, although the law may require continuation of support payments despite their intention.

- *Education expenses.* What education costs will be covered? Private grade school? Tutors? College? Graduate school? Will education-related expenses (e.g., transportation, books) be covered? If tuition is to be paid, does the obligor send tuition money directly to the school or to the custodial parent?

- *Reductions.* Will the amount of child support be reduced for every day the child spends overnight visiting the NCP (or a relative of the NCP)? Will there be a reduction if the child is away at boarding school?

- *Security for nonpayment.* Will there be security for the child-support payments (e.g., a **trust** account, an **escrow** account that can be used in the event of nonpayment)?

- *Death of obligor.* When the obligor dies, is his or her estate obligated to continue child-support payments? If so, must the obligor's will so state?

- *Disputes.* How will the parents resolve disputes concerning child support? Will they use arbitration or mediation?

- *Taxes.* Child and spousal support have the following tax consequences:
  - Child support is not deductible by the obligor who pays child support.
  - The obligee who receives child support does not pay taxes on what is received.
  - Alimony is deductible by the obligor.
  - Alimony recipients must pay taxes on alimony that is received.

During the negotiations on the separation agreement, the obligor may try to convince the other parent to agree to lower child-support payments in exchange for a higher alimony payment in order to take advantage of the alimony deduction. In Chapter 11, we will examine when such an agreement will work and what offsetting benefits the recipient might be offered.

escalation clause
A provision in a contract or other document that provides for an increase or decrease in the amount to be paid based upon a factor over which the parties do not have complete control.

trust
A device or arrangement by which its creator (the settlor or trustor) transfers property (the corpus) to a person (the trustee) who holds legal title for the benefit of another (the beneficiary or cestui que trust).

escrow
Property (e.g., money, a deed) delivered to a neutral person (e.g., bank, escrow agent) to be held until a specified condition occurs, at which time the property is to be delivered to a designated person.

As indicated, parents cannot agree to support a child at an amount lower than the minimum required by state guidelines. Also, many states do not allow parents to agree that child support will be paid as a one-time payment (a **lump-sum payment**). Attempts to remove a parent's *continuing* obligation of support are void in such states. The case of *Straub v. B.M.T.* presents an even more extreme example of what parents cannot attempt to accomplish through agreement.

lump-sum payment

A single payment of an amount of money to fulfill what would otherwise be a continuing obligation.

CASE

Straub v. B.M.T., by Next Friend, Francine Todd
645 N.E.2d 597 (1994)
Supreme Court of Indiana

Background: *Edward Straub and Francine Todd are having an affair. Straub impregnates Todd after she agrees not to hold him financially responsible for children born from the union (a hold-harmless agreement). But three years after the birth of a child (referred to as B.M.T. by the court), Todd sued Straub for child support. The trial court ordered him to pay $130 per week. Straub appealed. The state court of appeals affirmed. The case is now on appeal before the Supreme Court of Indiana.*

Decision on Appeal: *Affirmed. The agreement to relieve a father of financial responsibility is void as a matter of public policy.*

OPINION OF THE COURT

Justice SHEPARD delivered the opinion of the court.

I. Summary of Facts ...

[In] 1986 Francine Todd and Edward Straub engaged in a romantic relationship and sexual relations. In December of that year, Todd informed Straub of her desire to have a child. Straub was a divorcé with five children from a previous marriage, and he expressed resistance to fathering another child. Todd threatened to end the relationship, however, unless he agreed to impregnate her.

Straub handwrote the following statement and told Todd he would attempt to impregnate her if she signed it.

> To whom it may concern. I Francine Todd in sound mind & fore thought have decided not to marry, but would like to have a baby of my own. To support financially & emotionally. I have approached several men who will not be held responsible financially or emotionally, who's [sic] names will be kept secret for life. Signed Francine E. Todd Dec. 15 1986

Todd signed the statement, and the couple thereafter began having unprotected intercourse. Todd became pregnant in March 1987 and gave birth [to B.M.T.] that November. The birth certificate did not list anyone as the father. [Straub and Todd continued their relationship, but Straub did not establish a relationship with the child.]

On January 7, 1991, Todd filed a petition asking the trial court to declare Straub the father of the child and require him to pay child support and certain medical expenses. . . . The trial court found Straub to be the father of the child and ordered him to pay support in the sum of $130 per week, arrearages of $20 per week and certain medical expenses. . . .

Straub raises three issues, but the essence of all three may be stated as follows: whether a parent may contract away his or her rights and obligations to a child and/or the child's right to support through a preconception contract for fertilization. . . .

II. Some Agreements Concerning Children Are Void

Three rudimentary elements must be present before an agreement may be considered a contract: offer, acceptance of the offer and consideration. . . . If these components are present, a legal obligation results from the bargaining of the parties as found in their language or by implication from other circumstances, as affected by the rules of law. See, e.g., U.C.C. § 1-201(3).

There are instances, however, in which an agreement is not an enforceable contract despite proper formation. Where a properly formed agreement contravenes the public policy of Indiana, for instance, courts have traditionally said it is void and unenforceable. . . . Leading commentators frame the principle somewhat differently, saying that in such circumstances there is no contract, because such an agreement produces no legal obligation upon the part of the promisor. . . .

In any event, certain agreements are prohibited outright by statute and thus void. . . [such as contingent fee agreements in criminal cases. This court demonstrated the public policy of protecting the welfare of children by adopting the Indiana Child Support Guidelines. The purpose of the Guidelines is threefold: establishing as state policy an adequate standard of support for children; making awards more equitable by ensuring a more consistent treatment of people in similar circumstances; and improving the efficiency of courts by promoting settlements.]

In keeping with this public policy, Indiana courts have from time to time voided agreements reached by parents. Agreements which yield up a support opportunity for a child have been especially suspect. We have treated custodial parents who receive child support as trustees of the payments for the use and the benefit of the child. *Stonehill v. Stonehill* (1896), 45 N.E. 600, 601 ("The person to whom money for support of a child is ordered paid by the court, receives it as a trustee, and can only expend the same for the benefit of the child."); . . . Neither parent

(continued)

CASE • Straub v. B.M.T., by Next Friend, Francine Todd (continued)

has the right to contract away these support benefits. The right to the support lies exclusively with the child. Any agreement purporting to contract away these rights is directly contrary to this State's public policy of protecting the welfare of children, as it narrows the basis for support to one parent. . . .

[In addition,] consideration for this agreement, received by Straub, was sexual intercourse with Todd. Using sexual intercourse as consideration is itself against public policy. *Glasgo v. Glasgo*, (1980), Ind. App., 410 N.E.2d 1325, 1331. . . .

For these reasons, we hold the Todd agreement to be void and unenforceable. We affirm the trial court.

DeBRULER, Justice, dissenting.

I agree with the majority that one cannot contract away the right of a child to financial support from one of her parents. . . . [To make certain that B.M.T. receives adequate support, the contract should be treated as an assumption by Todd of Straub's obligation of support. Todd agreed to hold Straub harmless for his support obligation to B.M.T. Straub's support obligation to B.M.T. cannot be enforced against him unless Todd herself is without the means to pay that obligation.] If a person promises to pay the father's share of child support then, if that person is able, he or she should pay.

ASSIGNMENT 10.2

a. Who is correct? The majority opinion or the dissent? Is the majority opinion anti-woman?

b. In the discussion of the *Marvin v. Marvin* case in Chapter 4 on cohabitation agreements, we learned that sexual intercourse cannot be a valid consideration for an enforceable contract. Was this rule also applied in the *Straub* case?

c. George and Helen are not married but are living together. George impregnates Helen. He asks her to have an abortion. She refuses. When the child is born, can she force George to support it? Would it make any difference if Helen became pregnant after lying to George about using contraceptives? (See General Instructions for the Legal-Analysis Agreement in Appendix A.)

HOW MUCH?

When a CP seeks help from a court, there are two main kinds of child support that can be asked for: temporary and permanent. If the parents are married and are in the process of seeking a divorce, the CP might ask a court for an award of temporary child support **pendente lite** while the case is being resolved in court. At the conclusion of the case, the court will decide on permanent child support.

When a court determines the amount of child support that must be paid, it will consider a number of factors, the most important of which are the child-support guidelines for determining child support.

CHILD SUPPORT GUIDELINES

Every state has adopted child-support guidelines for the determination of child support by its courts. The guidelines use a formula to determine an amount of child support based on variables such as a parent's income and the number of children to be supported. The guidelines also list circumstances that will allow a court to deviate from the amount set by the formula. The resulting amount establishes a **rebuttable presumption** on what should be awarded. The amount must be accepted as the minimum amount due unless the court provides written findings on why this amount should not be used. Courts may deviate from the guidelines only upon making a specific finding that application of the guidelines would be unjust or inappropriate. Factors that might cause a court to change the amount set by the guidelines include medical costs, private school costs, high parental income, the existence of other families that the parents must support, and the amount of time the child spends with each parent.

pendente lite
Pending the [outcome of the] litigation.

rebuttable presumption
An assumption or inference of fact that a party will be allowed to try to disprove (rebut) but that will be treated as true if it is not disproved.

The federal law that establishes this rule provides as follows:

There shall be a rebuttable presumption . . . that the amount of the award which would result from the application of such guidelines is the correct amount of child support to be awarded. A written finding or specific finding on the record that the application of the guidelines would be unjust or inappropriate in a particular case, as determined under criteria established by the State, shall be sufficient to rebut the presumption in that case.[3]

The starting point in using the guidelines is the identification of a parent's income. Income has a broad definition and includes any form of periodic payment that a parent can receive, such as wages and salaries, self-employment income, commissions, bonuses, dividends, workers' compensation payments, disability payments, Social Security benefits, earned interest, pension payments, annuities, lottery winnings, and alimony income.

The guidelines are not the same in every state, although they are substantially similar. Most states base their calculations on either the *income-shares model* or the *percentage-of-income model.*

• Income-Shares Model

The income-shares model is used in the majority of states. Child support under this model is calculated as a *share* of each parent's income that would have been spent on the children if the parents and children were living in the same household. In an intact household, the income of both parents is generally pooled and spent for the benefit of all household members, including any children. The first step under this model is to calculate the net income (defined by the state) of each parent for child-support purposes. For example, assume that the mother has net income of $2,000 a month and the father has net income of $6,000 a month. The combined income available for child support is $8,000. The mother's income is 25 percent of this total; the father's is 75 percent. These percentages will determine how much of the child's support needs each parent will pay. The next step is to consult a state-mandated chart that identifies the amount of support that must be paid based on the number of children needing support. Assume, for example, that the chart says that parents with a combined net income of $8,000 must pay $1,600 a month for one child. The mother would be required to pay 25 percent of this amount ($400) and the father would be required to pay 75 percent ($1,200). If the chart says that they must pay $2,400 if they had two children, the mother's share would be 25 percent ($600) and the father's share would be 75 percent ($1,800).

• Percentage-of-Income Model

Calculations under the percentage-of-income model are less complex. The noncustodial parent (NCP) pays a percentage of his or her income. The income of the custodial parent (CP) is not considered. Once the NCP's state-defined net income is calculated, a state chart sets the percentage of that income that must be paid for child support. For example, child support for one child might be 24 percent if the net income is between $951 and $1,000 a month. The percentage increases if there are more children to be supported. There are two variations on the percentage: the flat percentage model (the percentage of income for child support stays constant for all income levels) and the varying percentage model (the percentage of income for child support varies according to level of income).

If a state does not use the income-shares model or the percentage-of-income model, it will use one of several alternatives, such as the *Melson-Delaware model,* which first identifies an amount needed for the parent's own basic needs and then designates a portion of the parent's remaining income for the child. There may also be variations among states using the same model. For a list of the states and the models they use, see Exhibit 10-3.

EXHIBIT 10-3   Child Support Guidelines Used by the States

States Using Income Shares Model		States Using Percentage-of-Income Model	States Using Melson Model
Alabama	New Jersey	Alaska	Delaware
Arizona	New Mexico	Arkansas	Hawaii
California	New York	Georgia	Montana
Colorado	North Carolina	Illinois	
Connecticut	Ohio	Massachusetts	
Florida	Oklahoma	Minnesota	
Idaho	Oregon	Mississippi	
Indiana	Pennsylvania	Nevada	
Iowa	Rhode Island	North Dakota	
Kansas	South Carolina	Tennessee	
Kentucky	South Dakota	Texas	
Louisiana	Utah	Wisconsin	
Maine	Vermont	Also:	
Maryland	Virginia	District of Columbia	
Michigan	Washington		
Missouri	West Virginia		
Nebraska	Wyoming		
New Hampshire			
Also:			
Guam			
U.S. Virgin Islands			

© Cengage Learning 2013

Whatever model a state uses, adjustments can be made when the parties have joint physical custody of the child, when a child has special medical or child-care needs, or when there is extensive visitation with the NCP. There may also be separate guidelines when the combined incomes of the parents exceed a high amount, such as $100,000. (See the three-pony rule on page 434.)

The calculation of child support under the guidelines is relatively mechanical. A number of commercial software companies sell computer programs that can be used to determine the amount of child support that is due under the guidelines used by a particular state. Several states have placed calculation worksheets on their Internet site. This allows a custodial parent, an NCP, and others to enter their own financial data to determine the amount of child support that would be required. In Exhibit 10-4, there are examples of online worksheets from the Web.

ASSIGNMENT 10.3

Answer the following questions by checking your state code and opinions of courts in your state. (See General Instructions for the State-Code Assignment and General Instructions for the Court-Opinion Assignment in Appendix A.)

a. How does a court determine the amount of child support in your state? Describe the main features of whatever guidelines exist and explain how they are used.

b. Make up a fact situation involving two parents (John Smith and Mary Smith) and one infant child (Billy Smith). Your facts should include the income and resources available to each parent. Now determine how much each parent would owe in child support in your state. Use any available online calculators or worksheets.

c. Under what circumstances, if any, does an NCP have an obligation to pay for his or her child's college education in your state?

d. Under what circumstances, if any, will your state make adjustments to what an NCP must pay if the NCP has additional children with a new spouse?

EXHIBIT 10-4 Examples of Online Worksheets to Calculate Child Support

Income Shares Online Worksheet (Maryland)

Circuit Court for _____ City or County ▸ Case No. _____

vs.

Name _____ State ___ Zip Code ___ Area Code ___ Telephone ___

Name _____

Street Address _____ Apt # ___

Street Address _____ Apt # ___

City ___ State ___ Zip Code ___ Area Code ___ Telephone ___

City ___ State ___ Zip Code ___ Area Code ___ Telephone ___

CHILD SUPPORT GUIDELINES WORKSHEET A
(Primary Physical Custody to One Parent)
(DOM REL 34)

Name of Child _____ Date of Birth ___

Name of Child _____ Date of Birth ___

Name of Child _____ Date of Birth ___

Name of Child _____ Date of Birth ___

Name of Child _____ Date of Birth ___

Name of Child _____ Date of Birth ___

	Mother	Father	Combined
1. MONTHLY ACTUAL INCOME (Before taxes)(Code, Family Law Article, §12-201(b))	$	$	
a. Minus pre-existing child support payment actually paid	-	-	
b. Minus alimony actually paid	-	-	
c. Plus / minus alimony awarded in this case	+/-	+/-	
2. MONTHLY ADJUSTED ACTUAL INCOME	$	$	$
3. PERCENTAGE SHARE OF INCOME (Divide each parent's income on Line 2 by the combined income on Line 2)	%	%	
4. BASIC CHILD SUPPORT OBLIGATION (Apply Line 2 Combined Income to Child Support Schedule)			$
a. Work-Related Child Care Expenses (Code, FL § 12-204(g))			+
b. Health Insurance Expenses (Code, FL § 12-204(h)(1))			+
c. Extraordinary Medical Expenses (Code, FL § 12-204 (h)(2))			+
d. Additional Expenses (Code, FL § 12-104(i))			+
5. TOTAL CHILD SUPPORT OBLIGATION (Add lines 4, 4a, 4b, 4c and 4d)			$
6. EACH PARENT'S CHILD SUPPORT OBLIGATION (Multiply Line 5 by Line 3 for each parent)	$	$	
7. TOTAL DIRECT PAY BY EACH PARENT (Add the expenses shown on lines 4a, 4b, 4c and 4d paid by each parent)	$	$	
8. RECOMMENDED CHILD SUPPORT AMOUNT (Subtract line 7 from line 6 for each parent)	$	$	
9. RECOMMENDED CHILD SUPPORT ORDER (Bring down amount from line 8 for the non-custodial parent only. If this is a negative number, see Comment (2) below.)	$		

Comments or special adjustments, such as: (1) any adjustment for certain third party benefits paid to or for the child of an obligor who is disabled, retired, or receiving benefits as a result of a compensable claim (see Code, Family Law Article, § 12-204(f)) or (2) that there is a negative dollar amount on line 9, which indicates a recommended child support order directing the custodial parent to reimburse the non-custodial parent this amount for "direct pay" expenses):

PREPARED BY: _____ Date: _____

Source: Maryland Department of Human Resources (www.dhr.state.md.us/csea/download/work_a.pdf).

Percentage-of-Income Online Worksheet (Illinois)

To establish a child support order in Illinois, the amount of child support considered for the order depends on the non-custodial parent's net income and the number of children for which he or she is responsible. The chart below represents the minimum of what may be ordered according to the Illinois Statutory Guidelines (750 ILCS 5/505 Sec. 505).

Statutory Guidelines of Child Support

Number of Children	Percent of Non-Custodial Parent's Net Income
1	20%
2	28%
3	32%
4	40%
5	45%
6 or more	50%

The guidelines in the chart are applied to each case unless the court makes a finding that the amount determined in the guidelines would be inappropriate after considering the best interests of the child. Relevant factors for deviations may include but are not limited to:

- The financial resources and needs of the child(ren);
- The financial resources and needs of the custodial parent;
- Standard of living the child(ren) would have enjoyed had the marriage not been dissolved, the separation not occurred, or if the parties had married;
- The physical and emotional condition of the child(ren) and their educational needs; and
- The financial resources and needs of the non-custodial parent.

To calculate a minimum child support order, fill in the blanks below and add or multiply as appropriate:

1. **Non-Custodial Parent's Income**

   Gross Income from Employer _____

   Other Income _____ +

   Total Income _____ =

2. **Deductions from Gross Income**

   Federal Income Tax Withholding _____

   State Income Tax Withholding _____ +

   FICA _____ +

   Mandatory Retirement Deduction _____ +

   Union Dues _____ +

   Health/Hospitalization Insurance Premiums _____ +

   Prior Support Orders Actually Paid _____ +

   Total Deductions _____ =

3. **Net Income** _____

   (Total #1 (Gross Income) MINUS Total #2 (Deductions)

4. **Guidelines Percentage for number of children** _____ ×

   (20%, 28%, 32%, 40%, 45%, 50%)

5. **Amount of child support that will be due** _____ =

   (#3 multiplied by #4)

Source: Illinois Child Support Services (www.childsupportillinois.com/general/calculating.html; www.childsupportillinois.com/assets/hfsweb016.pdf) (www.childsupportillinois.com/general/calculating.html; www.childsupportillinois.com/assets/hfsweb016.pdf).

THREE-PONY RULE

For high-income parents, the strict application of the guidelines in some states can occasionally lead to large awards of child support. A state might take a share-the-wealth attitude and allow the child to share in the good fortune of the prosperous parent by ordering a high child-support award. Most states, however, do not want to order child support beyond the reasonable needs of the child. According to one court,

> While to some degree children have a right to share in each parent's standard of living, child support must be set in an amount which is reasonably and rationally related to the realistic needs of the children. This is sometimes referred to as the "Three Pony Rule." That is, no child, no matter how wealthy the parents, needs to be provided more than three ponies.[4]

three-pony rule
(No child needs more than three ponies.) Child support for children of parents with very high incomes should be adjusted so that payments do not go beyond what is reasonably and rationally related to the realistic needs of the child.

The **three-pony rule** has come to mean that child support for children of parents with high incomes should be adjusted so that payments do not go beyond what is reasonably and rationally related to the realistic needs of the child. Once child-support payments exceed this level, the payments begin to look like alimony because the money is far beyond what can be spent to meet the needs of the child.

States have different methods of making this adjustment for high-income parents. For example, a state may use separate guidelines if the combined incomes of the parents exceed a certain amount, such as $100,000 a year or over $4,000 a month. Alternatively, a state may provide that if the combined parents' monthly gross income exceeds the highest level specified in the schedule, the court has discretion to set the amount in accordance with the best interest of the child and the circumstances of each parent.

Of course, an NCP can always agree to provide a high level of child support, which, if not paid, can be the basis of a breach of contract suit to enforce the agreement. Our focus here has been on child-support payments that are ordered by a court. The parties can always enter enforceable agreements for higher amounts.

SECOND FAMILY

Many states will take into consideration the fact that the NCP has a second family to support. It could affect the amount of support the NCP owes to the first family. We will discuss second families later in the chapter when we cover modifications of child-support orders.

IMPUTED INCOME

imputed income
Income that will be assumed to be available regardless of whether it is actually available.

fraudulent transfer
A transfer of an asset for little or no payment or consideration that is made to avoid an obligation to a creditor.

When parents improperly reduce their income capacity, a court can treat the amount of the reduction as if it is income that was actually earned. This **imputed income** will be used in the calculation of the income that is available to pay child support. The two major ways that NCPs improperly reduce their assets are fraudulent transfers and refusal to work at capacity. A **fraudulent transfer** is a transfer of an asset for little or no payment or consideration that is made to avoid an obligation to a creditor. An example is an NCP who places all of his salary in the bank account of his brother. An example of a refusal to work at capacity is a parent who is voluntarily unemployed or voluntarily underemployed. An example of the latter is a skilled NCP who voluntarily leaves a high-paying job to take a minimum-wage job. A court can *impute* to the NCP the salary transferred to the brother's account and can impute to the NCP the salary he or she is capable of earning. For an unskilled NCP who refuses to do any work, a court can impute the equivalent of the minimum wage.

CASE

Goldberger v. Goldberger
96 Md. App. 313, 624 A.2d 1328 (1993)
Court of Special Appeals of Maryland

Background: *The Circuit Court awarded Esther Goldberger a divorce from Aron Goldberger and custody of their six children: Chana Frumit, Mamele, Meir, Chaim Tzvi, Eliezer, and Yaacov. The court also ordered Aron to pay $4,066 per month in child support for the six children. It found that he had impoverished himself voluntarily and that his potential income was $60,000 per year. The court based this figure on the amount of money others had contributed to his litigation expenses. The case is now on appeal before the Court of Special Appeals of Maryland. Aron is the appellant and Esther is the appellee.*

Decision on Appeal: *Affirmed in part; reversed in part. The trial court correctly concluded that Aron voluntarily impoverished himself but failed to properly calculate the amount he should pay for child support.*

OPINION OF THE COURT

Judge LEVITZ delivered the opinion of the court.

The odyssey of the young children of Aron and Esther Goldberger has led them from Lakewood, New Jersey, to Israel, to Belgium and England, and finally to Baltimore, Maryland. These children have been the subject of the attention of various courts including: The High Court of Justice, Family Division, London, England; the Ecclesiastical Court of the Chief Rabbi of London (Beth Din); and, finally, the Circuit Court for Baltimore City. [Eight judges of the Circuit Court (nearly 30% of the Bench) have been involved in the case to date.]

Prior to the trial of this matter before the Circuit Court, the parties and their children had been examined and evaluated by ten physicians or psychologists. When the trial began, Esther and Aron Goldberger were fighting only about the custody of their children and related matters of support and visitation. Allegations of sexual child abuse, kidnapping, insanity and unfitness were made by one or the other of the parents. Other extended family members were brought into the conflict and took an active part in it. Since both parties are devout Orthodox Jews, noted Rabbis in this country and in Europe and Israel were consulted by the parties for advice, guidance and support. . . .

[T]he evidence revealed that appellant was 32 years old and healthy, with many years of higher education. It was undisputed that appellant had earned no actual income, as he had never worked at any income-producing vocation. Appellant planned his life to be a permanent Torah/Talmudic student. He was a student before he was married and before any of his children were born. Appellant testified that he studies "for the sake of studying, which is a positive commandment to study the Torah for the sake of studying it." Further, appellant testified that it was his intention to continue his life of study forever: ". . . I should continue to study

the rest of my life, to always be in studying. . . ." Throughout his life appellant has been supported by others, first, his parents, thereafter, his father-in-law, and most recently, friends in the Orthodox community. Nevertheless, appellant fathered six children whom he has refused to support, arguing that he has no means to support and never will have the means to provide support.

A life devoted to study is viewed by many in the Orthodox community as a true luxury that very few can enjoy. [Even Teveya, the fictional lead character of *Fiddler on the Roof,* recognizes that a life of study is a luxury when he sings, *"If I were a rich man. . . . Wouldn't have to work hard. . . . I'd discuss the Holy books with the learned men seven hours every day; that would be the sweetest thing of all."*] Unfortunately for the appellant's children, permanent Torah/Talmudic students must depend on the charity of others to provide the necessities of life. Those who support a Torah student have no legal obligation to continue such support in either duration or amount.

Nevertheless, through a network of family and Orthodox communities in Europe and the United States, approximately $180,000 had been contributed to appellant over a three-year period to enable him to pursue his custody claim. Approximately $3,000 of that sum was once used to purge appellant of contempt for failing to pay child support.

Based on these facts, the court determined (1) that appellant had voluntarily impoverished himself, and (2) that his potential income was equivalent to the money that had been contributed by others to his cause. It therefore regarded his income, for purposes of paying child support as $60,000 per year and ordered that he pay $4,066 per month for the support of his six children. Appellant challenges both the finding of voluntary impoverishment and the calculation of potential income.

The obligation of parents to support their minor children has been consistently upheld by the Court of Appeals of Maryland. In *Carroll County v. Edelman,* 577 A.2d 14, 23 (1990), the court stated,

> Parenthood is both a biological and a legal status. By nature and by law, it confers rights and imposes duties. One of the most basic of these is the obligation of the parent to support the child until the law determines that he is able to care for himself. . . .

The legislature of Maryland has made it a crime for parents to fail to support their minor children. Md. Code Ann., Fam. Law § 10–203 (1991). . . . [T]here can be no question that appellant has a legal obligation to financially support his children until they reach the age of legal majority. The more difficult question is how to calculate the proper amount of that support. Fortunately, that question has been answered by the

(continued)

CASE • Goldberger v. Goldberger (continued)

Legislature of Maryland. Md. Code Ann., Fam. Law § 12-202(a)(1) (1991) states,

> "[I]n any proceeding to establish or modify child support, whether pendente lite or permanent, the court shall use the child support guidelines set forth in this subtitle."

In order to use the guidelines as required by § 12–202(a)(1), it is necessary to calculate the income of the parents. "Income" is defined in § 12–201(b) of the Family Law Article as: (1) actual income of a parent, if the parent is employed to full capacity; or (2) potential income of a parent, if the parent is voluntarily impoverished.

The legislature's purpose in including potential income was to implement state and federal policy of requiring adequate support by precluding parents from avoiding their obligation by deliberately not earning what they could earn. While the Code does not define the term "voluntarily impoverished," in *John O. v. Jane O.,* 90 Md. App. 406, 601 A.2d 149 (1992), we had occasion to address the meaning of that term. We noted that neither the Legislature nor the courts in existing case law had defined what "voluntarily impoverished" meant. We noted that no clear definition was found in any Maryland resource materials. Accordingly, we looked to the dictionary definitions of the words "voluntarily" and "impoverished." We noted that "voluntarily" means "done by design or intention; proceeding from the free and unrestrained will of the person; produced in or by act of choice. . . ." "Impoverished" means "to make poor, reduce to poverty or to deprive. . . of resources, etc.". . .

The issue of voluntary impoverishment most often arises in the context of a parent who reduces his or her level of income to avoid paying support by quitting, retiring or changing jobs. The intent of the parent in those cases is often important in determining whether there has been voluntary impoverishment. Was the job changed for the purpose of avoiding the support obligation and, therefore, voluntary, or was it for reasons beyond the control of the parent, and thus involuntary?. . . A parent who chooses a life of poverty before having children and makes a deliberate choice not to alter that status after having children is. . ."voluntarily impoverished." Whether the voluntary impoverishment is for the purpose of avoiding child support or because the parent simply has chosen a frugal lifestyle for another reason, doesn't affect that parent's obligation to the child. Although the parent can choose to live in poverty, that parent cannot obligate the child to go without the necessities of life. A parent who brings a child into this world must support that child, if he has or reasonably could obtain, the means to do so. The law requires that parent to alter his or her previously chosen lifestyle if necessary to enable the parent to meet his or her support obligation.

Accordingly, we now hold that, for purposes of the child support guidelines, a parent shall be considered "voluntarily impoverished" whenever the parent has made the free and conscious choice, not compelled by factors beyond his or her control, to render himself or herself without adequate resources. To determine whether a parent has freely been made poor or deprived of resources the trial court should look to the factors enunciated in *John O. v. Jane O.,* 90 Md. App. 406, at 422:

1. his or her current physical condition;
2. his or her respective level of education;
3. the timing of any change in employment or financial circumstances relative to the divorce proceedings;
4. the relationship of the parties prior to the divorce proceedings;
5. his or her efforts to find and retain employment;
6. his or her efforts to secure retraining if that is needed;
7. whether he or she has ever withheld support;
8. his or her past work history;
9. the area in which the parties live and the status of the job market there; and
10. any other considerations presented by either party.

Based on a review of the evidence before the circuit court, there was no error in finding that appellant was "voluntarily impoverished."

Once a court determines that a parent is voluntarily impoverished, the court must then determine the amount of potential income to attribute to that parent in order to calculate the support dictated by the guidelines. Some of the factors the court should consider in determining the amount of potential income include:

1. age;
2. mental and physical condition;
3. assets;
4. educational background, special training or skills;
5. prior earnings;
6. efforts to find and retain employment;
7. the status of the job market in the area where the parent lives;
8. actual income from any source;
9. any other factor bearing on the parent's ability to obtain funds for child support.

After the court determines the amount of potential income to attribute to the parent, the court should calculate the amount of support by using the standardized worksheet authorized in Family Law § 12–203(a) and the schedule listed in Family Law § 12–204(e) [dhr.maryland.gov/csea/worksheet.php]. Once the guideline support figure is determined, the court must then determine whether the presumptive correctness of the guideline support figure has been overcome by evidence that application of the guidelines would be unjust or inappropriate. Md. Code Ann., Fam. Law § 12–202(a)(2) (1991).

Unfortunately, the court below erred in determining that appellant's potential income was $60,000 per year, based solely on his ability to raise funds to support and carry on this litigation. Although the court may consider the ability of appellant to persuade others to provide him with funds to pay child support in the future, the court cannot assume this will occur merely because appellant has been able to convince others to support this litigation up until now. The court needs to hear testimony and make findings regarding the factors relating to potential income previously enunciated. No such findings were made in this case. After calculating the guidelines using appellant's realistic potential income, the court must decide whether the presumptive correctness of the guidelines has been overcome. Accordingly, this matter must be remanded to the trial court for such determinations. . . .

We vacate the court's child support order and remand the matter to the trial court to recalculate the appellant's child support obligation in light of this opinion. Judgment affirmed in part.

ASSIGNMENT 10.4

a. Did the court violate Aron Goldberger's First Amendment right to freedom of religion by forcing him to pay child support?

b. Assume you work for the law firm that represents Esther Goldberger. To determine how much child support Aron should pay, what facts would you investigate as a result of the *Goldberger* opinion? (See General Instructions for the Investigation-Strategy Assignment in Appendix A.)

ENFORCEMENT OF CHILD SUPPORT ORDERS

When Congress concluded that the efforts of state governments to collect child support were inadequate, it enacted federal legislation that created national standards of enforcement. If states wanted federal dollars, they had to enact state enforcement laws that complied with these standards. The centerpiece of federal legislation was title IV-D of the Social Security Act.[5]

IV-D AGENCY

Title IV-D of the Social Security Act encouraged the creation of a new child-support enforcement agency and new enforcement tools that could be used in every state. Each state now has this agency, consisting of a central state office and units throughout the state, usually within each county. States use different names for the agency, such as Child Support Enforcement Division or Office of Recovery Services. They are collectively known as **IV-D agencies** because they were proposed in title IV-D of the Social Security Act. To find the IV-D agencies in your state (and the rules governing the agency), see Appendix D. You can also run this search on Google, Bing, or Yahoo: "IV-D" aa "child support" (in place of aa, type the name of your state).

The services provided by an IV-D agency are substantial. The agency can

IV-D agency
A state agency that helps custodial parents enforce child-support obligations.

- Help to locate absent parents
- Help to establish paternity
- Help to establish a child-support order
- Help to establish a medical-support order
- Help to modify a support order
- Arrange for the withholding of the obligor's wages
- Intercept federal and state tax refunds to make them available for support
- Arrange for the withholding of the obligor's passive income
- Help collect child support if the obligor is in another state (using the agency's Interstate Central Registry)

In addition to these enforcement remedies, the IV-D agencies can be quite persistent in going after the NCP through automatic billing, telephone reminders, delinquency notices, etc. When an IV-D agency collects child support from an obligor, the agency can deposit the funds directly into the bank account of the obligee through electronic funds transfer (EFT).

The caseload of IV-D agencies is 17.5 million children. Any custodial parent (obligee) with a child under eighteen is eligible for the services of an IV-D agency. A custodial parent does not have to be receiving public assistance through a program such as Temporary Assistance for Needy Families (TANF). Those not receiving public assistance, however, may be charged a nominal fee for the services of the IV-D agency. Obligees on public assistance must cooperate with the IV-D agency to establish paternity and collect child support. If, however, obligees can show "good cause," they are relieved of this requirement of cooperation. An example of good cause is a mother who faces a serious threat of physical violence from the father if she cooperates with the IV-D agency's efforts to collect child support from him.

Obligees who are on public assistance must **assign** (transfer) their support rights to the state IV-D agency or county welfare agency that collects support from obligors. The assignment means that the obligee gives the agency the right to keep any support money that it collects from the obligor up to the amount it has given the obligee in public assistance. This money is used to offset the TANF money the obligee has received. If an obligee fails to cooperate in assigning these rights, his or her share of the TANF benefits can be terminated, and the TANF benefits of the children can be sent to some other responsible adult who will agree to make them available for the children.

There is a federal agency that coordinates, evaluates, and assists state IV-D agencies. It is the U.S. Office of Child Support Enforcement (OCSE) within the U.S. Department of Health and Human Services.[6] (See Exhibit 1-14 in Chapter 1.)

assign

To transfer rights or property to someone. The noun is *assignment*. The person who makes the transfer is called the assignor. The person who receives the transfer is called the assignee or the assign.

ASSIGNMENT 10.5

(1) What is the name and website of the IV-D agency in your state?

(2) Summarize the kinds of assistance the IV-D agency provides for custodial parents.

(3) Is the IV-D agency's application for assistance online? If so, what is the website of the application? (See the General Instructions for the State-Code Assignment in Appendix A.)

LOCATING MISSING PARENTS

First things first: the NCP must be located. A very large number of NCPs disappear, or try to do so. It can sometimes be a challenge to find such NCPs in order to obtain a child-support order, and to enforce one. One of the services provided by an IV-D agency is its **State Parent Locator Service (SPLS)**, which helps locate parents through sources such as:

- records on birth, marriage, death, and other **vital statistics**
- state tax files
- real property records
- personal property records (when titles to such property are filed)
- occupational and professional license records
- business filings
- employment security records

State Parent Locator Service (SPLS)

A state government program that helps locate parents for purposes of child-support enforcement.

vital statistics

Data on major events such as births, deaths, marriages, divorces, and abortions, often kept current by the government for public health and other civic purposes.

- public assistance (welfare) records
- motor vehicle records
- law enforcement records
- records of public utilities and cable television companies
- credit bureau records
- information held by financial institutions, including asset and liability data

The SPLS obtains assistance from the **Federal Parent Locator Service (FPLS)** within the U.S. Office of Child Support Enforcement. The FPLS has access to the vast databases of the federal government (e.g., Social Security numbers, data on veterans and current members of the military, IRS records, and FBI data), which it makes available to the state agencies. A unique part of the FPLS is the **National Directory of New Hires (NDNH)**, which, as we will see, collects data on newly hired employees throughout the country. One-third of all child-support cases involve parents living in different states. The NDNH is a major tool to locate such parents because of its extensive data on employment, unemployment insurance, and quarterly wages.

To begin the search for an NCP, the IV-D agency will ask the custodial parent to provide the following leads to the NCP:

- Social Security number (check old state and federal tax returns, hospital records, police records, bank accounts, insurance policies, credit cards, loan applications, pay slips, union records, etc.)
- Last known residential address
- Current or recent employer's name and address
- Prior employer names and addresses
- Place of birth
- Names and addresses of relatives and friends
- Local clubs and organizations to which the NCP once belonged
- Local banks, public utilities, and other creditors the NCP may have had or now has

SPLS will use the leads provided by the custodial parent to try to locate the NCP. If the NCP has moved to another state, the IV-D agency in that state can be asked to provide comparable search services. The success of the SPLS and the FPLS in finding NCPs has in large measure been due to the centralization and computerization of data on parents and children involved in child-support cases. The computer databases of state and federal child-support agencies are linked in order to facilitate matches between child-support orders and obligors.

These agencies, however, must be careful about the locator information they release, particularly in cases where domestic violence against a spouse or child is a reasonable possibility. Without safeguards, for example, a husband might be able to use available locator services to find a wife or child who is in hiding because of his abuse. In a system containing millions of records, this is a distinct possibility. To try to prevent it from happening, a "flag" called a **family violence indicator (FVI)** is placed on the name of a person who has been abused or threatened with abuse. The FVI goes on the victim's name in the state and federal case registries that are part of the vast network of databases in the enforcement system. The victim might have a **restraining order** (also called a personal protection order [PPO]) in effect against the abuser, or might simply have told the IV-D agency of the danger of family violence. This leads to the placement of a flag on her name and that of her children. States are prohibited from releasing information on the whereabouts of a "flagged" parent or child to someone who has committed or threatened domestic violence. Furthermore, the address of a victim is shielded or otherwise blocked out in the maze of online paperwork

Federal Parent Locator Service (FPLS)

A program of the U.S. Office of Child Support Enforcement that uses data in federal databases to locate parents for purposes of child-support enforcement. Requests for information from the FPLS go through a State Parent Locator Service (SPLS).

National Directory of New Hires (NDNH)

A national database of wage and employment information used to assist state child-support agencies in locating noncustodial parents in order to establish paternity and enforce child-support obligations.

family violence indicator (FVI)

A designation placed on a participant in a child-support case indicating that he or she may be a victim of domestic violence so that access to information about the participant is restricted.

restraining order

A form of injunction, initially issued ex parte (with only one side present), to restrain the defendant from doing a threatened act. Also called order of protection, personal protection order (PPO), protection from abuse (if personal violence is threatened).

that will eventually be exchanged in the enforcement of a child-support order. Access to locator information such as addresses is highly restricted once a victim is flagged with an FVI.

ASSIGNMENT 10.6

Run the following search in a search engine: State Parent Locator Service aa (with aa replaced with the name of your state). How does the State Parent Locator Service of the IV-D agency in your state operate? Describe how the service functions. (See General Instructions for the State-Code Assignment in Appendix A.)

NEW HIRE REPORTING

Employers are required to report information about all newly hired employees to a *State Directory of New Hires (SDNH)* shortly after the hire date. (In many states, it is 20 days.) The "New Hire" report from the employer must provide the employee's name, address, and Social Security number as listed on his or her W-4 form. The SDNH will then match these data against its child-support records to locate delinquent parents so that income-withholding orders/notices can be issued. To help locate parents in other states, the SDNH submits its data to the *National Directory of New Hires (NDNH)*, which is a national database that is part of the Federal Parent Locator Service (FPLS). To help locate parents who have moved across state lines, the NDNH compiles data on new hires from every state and federal agency and also unemployment-compensation data from every state. The NDNH is an important locator tool because of the large percentage of child-support cases that involve NCPs who do not live in the same state as their children.

The scope of the data collected in the NDNH is vast:

> The National Directory of New Hires is a database that contains personal and financial data on nearly every working American, as well as those receiving unemployment compensation. Contrary to its name, the National Directory of New Hires includes more than just information on new employees. It is a database that includes information on (1) all newly hired employees, compiled from state reports (and reports from federal employers), (2) the quarterly wage reports of existing employees (in Unemployment Compensation-covered employment), and (3) unemployment compensation claims. The National Directory of New Hires was originally established to help states locate noncustodial parents living in a different state so that child support payments could be withheld from that parent's paycheck. Since its enactment in 1996, the National Directory of New Hires has been extended to several additional programs and agencies to verify program eligibility, prevent or end fraud, collect overpayments, or assure that program benefits are correct.[7]

The new hire program has been quite successful. In the first two years of its operation, over 2.8 million delinquent parents were uncovered. There have been side benefits as well. Citizens collecting unemployment compensation should not be working full-time. Yet the new hire program has found thousands who have been fraudulently collecting unemployment benefits while employed. In 1998, for example, Pennsylvania identified 4,289 overpayments in unemployment with a dollar value of $2.3 million. Among the new hires, the government has also found numerous individuals who are in default on their student loans. Their names have been shared with the U.S. Department of Education, which has initiated successful loan collection efforts. Clearly, the benefits of the new hire program have extended beyond improved child-support collection.

PATERNITY

Where needed, the IV-D agency will help a mother obtain a court order establishing paternity or an acknowledgement of paternity by the father. (We will cover paternity in depth in Chapter 13.) Every state has expedited paternity procedures, including standard forms in maternity wards on which unwed fathers are encouraged—voluntarily—to acknowledge paternity immediately after birth. (See Exhibit 13-6 in Chapter 13 for an example of such a form.) In 2010, 1.7 million paternities were established or acknowledged, of which 1.1 million were in-hospital or other paternity acknowledgments.[8]

ENFORCEMENT OPTIONS

The most dramatic modern development in the law of child support has been a substantial increase in the number of remedies that are available to enforce the duty of child support. For a summary of the remedies we will examine, see Exhibit 10-5.

EXHIBIT 10-5   Remedies to Enforce the Duty of Child Support

Name of Remedy	Description
Civil and criminal contempt	Civil contempt is the refusal of a party to comply with a court order (e.g., to pay support), which can lead to punishment (including incarceration) until the party complies with the order. Criminal contempt is the refusal of a party to comply with a court order (e.g., to pay support), which can lead to punishment (including incarceration) because of the repeated or aggravated nature of the refusal.
Criminal nonsupport	The willful, repeated, or aggravated failure to pay support for a person that the defendant is obligated to support from available resources.
Execution	A command or writ to a court officer (e.g., sheriff) to seize and sell the property of the losing litigant in order to satisfy the judgment debt such as delinquent child support.
Income withholding	The process whereby an employer is required to deduct some of an employee's income, which will be used to meet the child-support obligations of the employee.
Garnishment	A court proceeding by a creditor to force a third party in possession of the debtor's property (e.g., wages) to turn the property over to the creditor to satisfy a debt such as delinquent child support.
License and registration denial, delay, or revocation	Delinquent obligors can have their applications for an occupational license, driver's license, or vehicle registration denied or delayed (or have their current licenses or registrations revoked) for nonpayment of child support.
Passport denial, revocation, or restriction	Delinquent obligors can have their application for a passport denied or have their current passport revoked or restricted for nonpayment of child support.
Tax refund offset	Delinquent obligors can have their tax refunds intercepted so that they can be used to pay child support.
IRS Full Collection	The IRS will attempt to collect the full amount of delinquent child support in the same manner as the IRS collects a tax debt.
Unemployment compensation and workers' compensation intercept	Delinquent obligors can have their unemployment-compensation and workers'-compensation benefits intercepted so that they can be used to pay child support.
Qualified domestic relations order (QDRO)	A court order that allows a nonworker to reach all or part of the pension or other retirement benefits of a worker or former worker in order to satisfy the worker's child support or other marital obligation.
Qualified medical child support order (QMCSO)	A court order to an employer to extend its group health insurance benefits to the child of one of its workers even if the child does not live with the worker.
Credit bureau referral (credit clouding)	Notification of a creditor or a credit bureau that an obligor/debtor is delinquent on certain debts such as child support.
Financial institution data match (FIDM) (freeze and seize)	Identification and seizure of funds that a delinquent obligor has in financial institutions so that they can be used for child support.
Lien	A security, encumbrance, or claim on property that remains until a debt is paid. Prevents the sale of an obligor's assets by imposing a lien on cars, boats, and other property that must be registered.
Post security	Requiring a delinquent obligor post a bond or other guarantee to cover child support.
Wheel boot; wanted posters	Placing a wheel boot on a delinquent obligor's car. Placing the image of delinquent obligors on wanted posters.

contempt

Conduct that defies or disrespects the authority of a court or legislative body. When the court is defied or disrespected, it is called *contempt of court*.

civil contempt

The refusal of a party to comply with a court order (usually issued for the benefit of another), which can lead to punishment (including incarceration) until the party complies with the order.

criminal contempt

The refusal of a party to comply with a court order, which can lead to punishment (including incarceration) because of the repeated or aggravated nature of the refusal.

Civil Contempt

Contempt is conduct that defies or disrespects the authority of a court or legislative body. The conduct is called *contempt of court* if a court is defied or disrespected. There are two kinds of contempt, civil and criminal, both of which can lead to the jailing of the offender. **Civil contempt** is the refusal of a party to comply with a court order (usually issued for the benefit of another), which can lead to punishment (including incarceration) until the party complies with the order. **Criminal contempt** is the refusal of a party to comply with a court order resulting in punishment (including incarceration) because of the repeated or aggravated nature of the refusal. The purpose of a civil contempt proceeding is to compel future compliance with the court order, whereas the purpose of a criminal contempt proceeding is to punish the offender because of the repeated or aggravated nature of the conduct.

When civil contempt occurs in child-support cases, the nonpaying obligor can be jailed until he or she agrees to comply with the court order. Suppose, however, that the offender has no resources and thus cannot comply. In effect, such a person would be imprisoned because of his or her poverty. This is unconstitutional. Before ordering imprisonment, a court must determine that the offender has the *present ability* to pay the child-support debt (from current or available resources) but simply refuses to do so. Such an individual is in control of how long the sentence will be. In effect, the keys to jail are in his or her own pocket. As one court recently said,

> There is no constitutional impediment to imposition of contempt sanctions on a parent for violation of a judicial child support order when the parent's financial inability to comply with the order is the result of the parent's willful failure to seek and accept available employment that is commensurate with his or her skills and ability.[9]

In addition to jailing the obligor, most courts have the power to order the less drastic sanction of imposing a fine when the obligor is found to be in civil contempt. Also, an alternative to incarceration is **house arrest**, which confines the obligor to his or her home except for approved travel such as for employment.

Obligors faced with imprisonment for civil or criminal contempt can hire a private attorney to represent them. On whether they are entitled to a free attorney at government expense, see Attorney Representation on page 448.

house arrest

The confinement of an accused or convicted person to his or her home except for approved travel such as for employment. If an electronic device (e.g., a bracelet) is attached to the body to monitor the arrest, it is called Electronic House Arrest (EHA).

ASSIGNMENT 10.7

What steps must be taken in your state to use a civil contempt proceeding to enforce a child-support order? (See General Instruction for the Flowchart Assignment in Appendix A.)

---

criminal nonsupport

The willful, repeated, or aggravated failure to pay support for a person that the defendant is obligated to support from available resources.

Criminal Nonsupport

In most states, **criminal nonsupport** is the willful, repeated, or aggravated failure to pay support for a person that the defendant is obligated to support from available resources. It is a *state* crime for which the obligor can be prosecuted. (This failure is separate from criminal contempt of court mentioned earlier, which is the failure to obey a specific court order.) The criminal-nonsupport statute might provide that the crime is committed if there is an intentional failure to pay spousal or child support for a designated number of consecutive days (e.g., 120). The punishment can consist of jail, imprisonment, or a fine.

Except for relatively wealthy offenders, locking someone up is seldom an effective method of enforcing child support. Most obligors are wage earners, and once they are jailed, their primary source of income obviously dries up.

One way out of this dilemma is for the judge to agree to suspend the imposition of the jail sentence on condition that the obligor fulfill the support obligation, including the payment of arrearages. The obligor would be placed on **probation** under this condition.

probation

Living in the community (in lieu of institutionalization) so long as there is compliance with court-imposed conditions. (See glossary for an additional meaning.)

ASSIGNMENT 10.8

a. Is it a crime in your state to fail to pay child support? If so, quote the essential elements of the crime. (See General Instructions for the State-Code Assignment in Appendix A.)

b. Prepare a list of questions that you would ask and facts that you would investigate in order to help determine whether this crime was committed. (See General Instructions for the Investigation-Strategy Assignment in Appendix A.)

c. What steps must be taken in your state to prosecute someone for committing this crime? (See General Instructions for the Flowchart Assignment in Appendix A.)

If a nonpayment case involves more than one state, a *federal* crime may have been committed under the **Deadbeat Parents Punishment Act (DPPA)**. A sentence of between six months and two years can be imposed when the obligor repeatedly fails to pay child support for a child living in another state, or who crosses state lines in order to avoid paying child support.[10] To be prosecuted under the DPPA, the obligor must be financially able to pay the child support that is due. Federal prosecutors in the United States Attorney's Office, however, are reluctant to bring a case until civil and criminal remedies at the *state* level have been tried. Furthermore, federal prosecutors will give priority to cases (1) where there is a pattern of moving from state to state to avoid payment, (2) where there is a pattern of deception such as the use of a false name or a false Social Security number, (3) where there is failure to make support payments after being held in contempt of court, and (4) where failure to make support payments is connected to another federal offense, such as bankruptcy fraud.

The creation of federal crimes in this area by Congress has been criticized as inappropriately "federalizing" family law. For example, the former chief justice of the U.S. Supreme Court, William H. Rehnquist, complained that Congress was enacting too many federal laws to cover conduct that should be the exclusive domain of the state criminal justice system. One of the examples he cites is the DPPA.

Deadbeat Parents Punishment Act (DPPA)

A federal statute that makes it a crime for a parent to repeatedly fail to pay child support for a child living in another state or to cross state lines to avoid paying child support. 18 U.S.C. § 228.

Execution

Once an obligor fails to pay a judgment ordering child support, the sheriff can be ordered to seize the personal property or real property of the obligor in the state. This is called an **execution** or a *writ of execution*. The initial effect of execution is to create a **lien**, which is a claim on property that remains until a debt is paid. The property that is seized can be sold by the sheriff. The proceeds from this execution sale (also called a *forced sale*) are used to pay the judgment and the expenses of the execution. Not all property of the obligor, however, is subject to execution in every state. Certain property (e.g., clothes and cars) may be exempt from execution.

execution

(1) A command or writ to a court officer (e.g., sheriff) to seize and sell the property of the losing litigant in order to satisfy the judgment debt. Also called general execution and writ of execution. (2) Carrying out or performing some act to its completion (e.g., the process of carrying into effect the decisions in a judgment). (See glossary for additional meanings.)

lien

A security, encumbrance, or claim on property that remains until a debt is paid.

Income Withholding

One of the most successful enforcement programs is **income withholding**, which is a mandatory, automatic deduction by an employer from the paycheck (or other income) of an employee who falls behind in child-support payments.

income withholding

The process whereby an employer is required to deduct some of an employee's income, which will be used to meet the child-support obligations of the employee. (In some states the deductions can also be used to meet spousal support obligations.)

Nearly 70 percent of all child support is collected by employers through this method (over $21 billion a year). An income-withholding order/notice is sent to employers in any state where the obligor works. In addition to wages, employers can withhold commissions and retirement payments. Each pay period, the employer deducts a specified amount and sends it to the IV-D agency, to the court, or, in some cases, directly to the custodial parent. The process begins when the IV-D agency sends the employer an order/notice to withhold income for child support. (See Exhibit 10-6.)

EXHIBIT 10-6   Child Support Order/Notice to Employer of Obligor for Income Withholding

ORDER/NOTICE TO WITHHOLD INCOME FOR CHILD SUPPORT

State _____

Co./City/Dist. of _____

Tribunal/Case Number _____

Employer's/Withholder's Name _____

Employee/Obligor's Name _____

Names of Children and Dates of Birth _____

_____

Employee/Obligor's Social Security Number _____

Employee/Obligor's Case Identifier _____

Custodial Parent's Name _____

[ ] If checked, you are required to enroll the child(ren) identified above in any health insurance coverage available to the employee/obligor through his/her employment.

ORDER INFORMATION: **This Order/Notice is based on the support order from [State]** _____. **You are required by law to deduct these amounts from the employee's/obligor's income until further notice.**

$ _____ Per _____ current child support

$ _____ Per _____ past-due child support

$ _____ Per _____ current medical support

$ _____ Per _____ past-due medical support

$ _____ Per _____ spousal support

for a total of $ _____ Per _____ to be forwarded to the payee below.

REMITTANCE INFORMATION: When remitting payment, provide the pay date/date of withholding and the case identifier. If remitting payment by EFT/EDI, call _____ before first submission. Use this FIPS code: _____ : Bank routing code: _____ Bank account number: _____.

Make check payable to _____

                      Payee and Case Identifier

Send check to: _____

Source: Adapted from Order/Notice, Office of Child Support Enforcement (www.acf.hhs.gov/programs/cse/pol/AT/2001/at-01-07a.htm).

The order/notice can also include a requirement that the employer enroll the employee's children in health insurance coverage made available to its employees. There is a space on the order that says, "If checked, you are required to enroll the child(ren) identified above in any health insurance coverage available to the employee/obligor through his/her employment." The employer cannot deny coverage for children simply because they may no longer live with the employee. (See also the discussion on page 447 on the qualified medical child support order, or QMCSO, a method of accomplishing the same objective of health coverage for children.)

Employers must comply with all the requirements listed in the order/notice. They can be fined or otherwise sanctioned for failure to withhold income or for failure to include children in the company health insurance plan. Most states allow employers to charge an employee an administrative fee for processing the withholding, but they cannot fire or discipline the employee because of withholding.

If the employee quits or is terminated by the employer, the employer must send the IV-D agency or court a notice giving the date of termination, the employee's last known home address, and the new employer's address, if known. A form to provide this notice of termination is found on the reverse side of the original order/notice to withhold income for child support received by the employer.

Garnishment

Income withholding is similar to **garnishment**, which is a court proceeding by a creditor to force a third party (e.g., a bank or employer) in possession of the debtor's property (e.g., bank account, wages) to turn the property over to the creditor to satisfy a debt. Garnishment, however, is usually less effective than income withholding because of the more cumbersome procedures for instituting garnishment and the restrictions that may exist on how long it can be in effect.

garnishment
A court proceeding by a creditor to force a third party in possession of the debtor's property (e.g., wages) to turn the property over to the creditor to satisfy a debt.

License and Registration Denial, Delay, or Revocation

To engage in certain occupations, a person must obtain a license from the state. Examples include plumber, hairdresser, real estate broker, accountant, electrician, teacher, doctor, and attorney. Many states will deny an initial application for a license, deny an application for a renewal of a license, or revoke the license of a parent who is delinquent in making child-support payments. In Illinois, for example, the license statute that applies to attorneys provides as follows:

No person shall be granted a license or renewal authorized by this Act who is more than 30 days delinquent in complying with a child support order. . . .[11]

Many states will also revoke or suspend a delinquent obligor's driver's license or vehicle registration. The state will send him or her an "intent to revoke" letter. If the child-support debt is not satisfied, an investigator locates the car or other vehicle, removes the license plate, and leaves a bright orange decal on the driver's side window explaining the seizure and the steps to take through the IV-D agency to have the license plate restored.

Courts have rejected claims that these penalties violate the constitutional rights of obligors. Before the penalties are imposed, the obligor is notified of the penalty, given an opportunity for a hearing, and given the right to avoid the penalty by signing a payment agreement or otherwise satisfying the IV-D agency or the court that payment will be made. These procedures satisfy the due-process rights of the obligor.

Passport Denial, Revocation, or Restriction

Individuals who owe over $2,500 in child support can have their passport application denied. In addition, the U.S. Secretary of State, the federal official in charge of the Passport Office, can take action to revoke or restrict a passport previously issued to those who have this amount of child-support debt. Every year, the U.S. Department of State receives over 4 million requests to block the passports of delinquent obligors.[12]

Federal Tax Refund Offset Program

Delinquent child support can be collected out of tax refunds that obligors would otherwise receive. This occurs under the Federal Tax Refund Offset Program. Each year IV-D agencies submit to the Internal Revenue Service (IRS) the names, social security numbers, and amounts of past-due child support owed by parents. The IRS then determines whether these individuals are scheduled to receive tax refunds on their returns. If so, the IRS sends them an offset notification that informs them of the proposed offset and gives them an opportunity to pay the past-due amount or to contest the amount with the IV-D agency.

In addition, a program exists to intercept and offset tax refunds due on state returns. In 2011, $2.3 billion was collected from federal tax intercepts and $204 million was collected from state tax intercepts.

IRS Full Collection

In addition to tax refund intercepts, the IRS can do an IRS Full Collection in which the full power of the IRS is used to collect all of the obligor's delinquent child-support debt. In this collection effort, the IRS acts in the same manner as it would when collecting a tax debt. The amounts collected are then turned over to the obligee through the IV-D agency. IRS Full Collection can be used after the other major enforcement efforts have been tried without success.

Unemployment Compensation and Workers' Compensation Intercept

The unemployment-compensation benefits of the obligor can be intercepted to meet child-support obligations. This method of withholding enables the IV-D agency to collect at least some support from an unemployed obligor. Nothing is left to chance. Computers at the unemployment-compensation agency and at the IV-D agency communicate with each other to identify delinquent parents who have applied for or who are eligible for unemployment compensation. An investigator from the IV-D agency will then contact the surprised obligor. It may even be possible to intercept benefits across state lines pursuant to reciprocal agreements among cooperating states. In 2010, over $2 billion was collected from the unemployment-compensation intercept program. In most states, a similar intercept program can reach an obligor's workers'-compensation benefits.

Qualified Domestic Relations Order (QDRO)

qualified domestic relations order (QDRO)

A court order that allows a nonworker to reach all or part of the pension or other retirement benefits of a worker or former worker in order to satisfy the worker's support or other marital obligation.

Often an obligor will have a pension or other retirement benefits through an employer. A special court order, called a **qualified domestic relations order (QDRO)**, allows a person other than the obligor to reach some or all of these benefits in order to meet a support obligation of the obligor, such as child support. The child becomes an *alternate payee* under these plans. This person cannot receive benefits under the plan that the obligor would not have been able to receive. For example, if the obligor is not entitled to a lump-sum payment, the child as alternate payee is also subject to this limitation.

Qualified Medical Child Support Order (QMCSO)

Many children of NCPs have no health insurance. Assume that such a parent is working for a company that has a group health plan. But the parent either refuses to add the child to the plan, or the insurance company tells the parent that the child is ineligible because he or she does not live with the parent, does not live in the insurer's service area, is not claimed as a dependent on the parent's tax return, or was born to unmarried parents. In 1993, Congress passed a law that made it illegal for employers and their insurance companies to use such reasons to deny coverage to children. A court order can now be obtained to require coverage. It is called the **qualified medical child support order (QMCSO)**. The child becomes an *alternate recipient* under the health plan. The employer can deduct the cost of adding the child to the plan from the parent's pay. As we saw in Exhibit 10-6, the child-support order/notice to an employer of an obligor has a space, which, when checked, requires the employer to add named children of the obligor to the health insurance plan of the employer.

qualified medical child support order (QMCSO)
A court order to an employer to extend its group health insurance benefits to the child of one of its workers even if the child does not live with the worker.

Credit Bureau Referral (Credit Clouding)

An obligor can be warned that a credit bureau (e.g., Experian, TransUnion, Equifax) will be notified of a delinquency in making child-support payments unless the delinquency is eliminated by payment or unless satisfactory arrangements are made to pay the debt. Once the computers of a credit bureau have information on such payment problems, a "cloud" on the obligor's credit rating is created. **Credit clouding** notifies potential creditors that the obligor may be a bad credit risk. This method of pressuring compliance with child-support obligations is particularly effective with self-employed obligors, who often do not have regular wages that can be subjected to income withholding or garnishment. Many states now routinely report child-support debts to credit bureaus.

credit clouding
Notifying a creditor or credit bureau that a debtor is delinquent on certain debts such as child support.

Financial Institution Data Match (FIDM)("Freeze and Seize")

State IV-D agencies can attach and take ("freeze and seize") the accounts of delinquent obligors in financial institutions and use the funds for child support. The accounts can include savings, checking, time deposit, and money market accounts at large banks, credit unions, and money-market mutual funds. The IV-D agency issues a lien on the account. A lien, as we saw earlier, is a security, encumbrance, or claim on property that remains until a debt is paid. The lien impedes the debtor's ability to transfer the property. The debtor must satisfy the lien before the property may be sold or transferred. A **levy** is an actual collection or seizure of the property. Liens and levies are governed by state law. Some states, for example, require a minimum dollar amount of child-support debt in arrears before a lien can be imposed.

levy
The collection or seizure of property by a public official to satisfy a judgment. (See glossary for an additional meaning.)

Liens

Liens can be placed on property of the obligor that must be registered, such as cars and boats. The effect of the lien is to inhibit the sale of the property by the obligor. No one would want to buy it unless the liens were removed, and they can be removed only by paying the debt that caused the lien to be imposed. In some states, the obligee does not have to go to court to obtain the lien. An administrative agency can impose the lien. Such liens are called administrative liens.

Post Security

In some cases, the delinquent obligor can be required to post security in the form of a bond or other guarantee (including cash) that will cover future support obligations. This security will be held by the IV-D agency and used if the obligor falls behind in child-support payments.

Wheel Boot; Wanted Posters

In some states, a delinquent obligor's car can be immobilized by clamping a wheel boot on it until he or she pays past-due child support. Also, the threat of **prosecution** has encouraged some delinquent obligors to come forward. States can post "wanted lists" (e.g., the Ten Most Wanted Parents, the Deadbeat of the Month) containing the pictures of individuals who have been convicted of criminal nonsupport or for whom arrest warrants have been issued because of the amount of child support owed. (To find such lists, run the search *deadbeats wanted list* on Google, Bing, or Yahoo.) Several states have launched highly publicized **amnesty** programs (see Exhibit 10-7).

ATTORNEY REPRESENTATION

Because of the extensive assistance provided by the IV-D agency in collecting child support, most obligees do not need to hire private attorneys. Such attorneys are available for hire, but except in high-income cases, they are rarely used.

The IV-D agency, of course, does not assist NCP obligors except to remind them of their duty to pay support and to work out payment options where appropriate. Obligors often need legal help when faced with severe sanctions such as loss of occupational license, seizure of bank accounts, and imprisonment. The extensive amount of self-help information on the Internet for obligees and obligors may not be enough. When obligors cannot afford private counsel (i.e., when they are **indigent**), is the state required to provide free representation for them? The answer, in part, depends on what the obligor is being charged with.

CRIMINAL CONTEMPT AND CRIMINAL NONSUPPORT CASES

If the obligor is charged with criminal contempt (or the crime of criminal nonsupport), the Sixth Amendment of the U.S. Constitution grants an indigent criminal defendant the right to counsel. In most serious criminal cases, the state will provide free counsel if the defendant cannot afford his or her own attorney.

prosecution
1. Bringing and processing criminal proceedings against someone. The words prosecution and prosecute can also refer to bringing and processing *civil* proceedings against someone, although the words are more commonly used in criminal proceedings.
2. The attorney representing the government in a criminal case. Also called the prosecutor.

amnesty
Forgiveness; a pardon issued by the state.

indigent
Poor; without means to afford something such as a private attorney or filing fees.

CIVIL CONTEMPT

As indicated earlier, the purpose of criminal contempt is to punish the obligor, whereas the purpose of civil contempt to force the obligor to comply with an order. Imprisonment for criminal contempt can be ordered because of the affront that the defendant has shown the system. This affront must be punished. Imprisonment for civil contempt, on the other hand, is mainly an enforcement tool to pressure the obligor to pay support. Because of the punishment component that is part of criminal contempt, but not of civil contempt, obligors charged with civil contempt are entitled to fewer procedural rights than obligors charged with criminal contempt. For example, the appointment of counsel is required in cases of criminal contempt. What about in civil contempt cases?

The Sixth Amendment does not apply to civil cases. Hence, the question is whether the Due Process of Law clause of the Fourteenth Amendment requires the appointment of counsel in a civil contempt case. On this question, the U.S. Supreme Court has held that obligors charged with civil contempt are not entitled to free counsel (1) if the custodial parent (obligee) is not represented by counsel and (2) if the state has fair procedures that allow a noncustodial parent (obligor) to prove that he or she is unable to pay the child support. These procedures include an opportunity to contest the claim of child support; the use of a relatively straightforward method (e.g., a form) that allows the obligor to state his or her financial information; and adequate notice to the obligor that imprisonment for civil contempt will be not be imposed if the obligor is unable to pay the support alleged to be due. If, however, the obligee has counsel and the case is relatively complex, the state may have a duty to provide free counsel to an indigent obligor faced with civil contempt.[13]

DOMESTIC VIOLENCE

As indicated earlier, violence against custodial parents is an ongoing concern. Some NCPs, particularly fathers, do not react kindly to requests that they meet their child-support obligations. Occasionally, they may physically assault the CP or threaten to do so. The police may be called in, although some critics have complained that the police do not take so-called domestic disputes seriously. Usually, the woman can go to the local prosecutor or district attorney to obtain a restraining order, which warns the NCP that he will be arrested and jailed unless he stays away from the children and the custodial parent. Initially, the order is usually issued by the court with only one party present in the court (**ex parte**). At a later time, the target of the order is allowed to contest its validity in court. (For more on domestic violence, see Chapter 12.)

ex parte
With only one side present (usually the plaintiff or petitioner) when court action is requested.

JURISDICTION

As we learned in Chapter 7, a divorce judgment can accomplish the following five objectives:

(1) dissolve the marriage
(2) award spousal support
(3) divide marital property
(4) award child support
(5) award child custody

For all five, a court needs **subject-matter jurisdiction**, which is the court's power to resolve a particular type of legal dispute and to grant a particular type of relief. In addition, a court order for each of the five objectives requires another kind of jurisdiction. (See Exhibit 7-3 in Chapter 7.) Our focus here is on the kind of jurisdiction needed for an order of child support in the **forum** state where the CP is seeking child support from the NCP.

To order a NCP to pay child support, the court needs **personal jurisdiction** over him or her. Such jurisdiction gives the court power to determine someone's

subject-matter jurisdiction
The court's power to resolve a particular type of legal dispute and to grant a particular type of relief.

forum
(1) A court. (2) The place where the parties are presently litigating their dispute. (3) A court or tribunal hearing a case.

personal jurisdiction
A court's power over a person to determine (adjudicate) his or her personal rights and duties. Also called in personam jurisdiction.

full faith and credit (FFC)

The obligation of one state to recognize and enforce the legal decisions of another state. The obligation is based on the U.S. Constitution, which provides that "Full Faith and Credit shall be given in each State to the public Acts, Records, and judicial Proceedings of every other State." Article IV, § 1.

service of process

A formal delivery of notice to a defendant that a suit has been initiated to which he or she must respond. *Process* is the means used by the court to acquire or exercise its power or jurisdiction over a person.

personal service

Handing the service-of-process documents to the person who is the target of the service.

substituted service

An approved method of completing service of process other than by handing the process documents to the defendant (or to the defendant's authorized representative) in person (e.g., service by mail or by publication in a newspaper). Also called constructive service.

Uniform Interstate Family Support Act (UIFSA)

A state law on establishing and enforcing alimony and child-support obligations against someone who does not live in the same state as the person to whom the alimony and child support is owed.

personal rights and duties. If a court makes an order of child support against someone over whom it does not have personal jurisdiction, a court in another state does not have to enforce it (i.e., the support order is not entitled to **full faith and credit [FFC]**).

JURISDICTION OVER A RESIDENT PARENT

How does a court acquire personal jurisdiction over a NCP? There are two main categories of NCPs: those who are resident in the state where the custodial parent is seeking child support and those who are nonresidents of this state. First we will examine the resident NCP.

The first step in acquiring personal jurisdiction over a resident parent is **service of process**, which is the formal delivery of notice to a defendant that a suit has been initiated to which he or she must respond. The defendant is also given a copy of the petition/complaint. If the defendant can be found, **personal service** consists of handing the service-of-process documents to the defendant in person. If the resident defendant cannot be found in the state, **substituted service** is often allowed, such as service by U.S. mail or by publication in a newspaper.

JURISDICTION OVER A NONRESIDENT PARENT

A more serious problem is collecting child support from a *nonresident* parent. Approximately 34 percent of child-support cases are brought by CPs against nonresident NCPs. The major concerns in collecting child support from nonresidents are jurisdiction and convenience. How does the forum state (where the CP and child live) obtain personal jurisdiction over a person who does not live in the forum state? How can a CP overcome the inconvenience (and often total impracticality) of traveling to the state where the NCP lives (assuming the NCP can be found) and bringing a support action in that state?

A related problem is the proliferation of child-support orders. Assume that after state A issues a child-support order, the NCP moves to state B and asks for a new or a modified order based on changed circumstances. Before the law was changed, state B did not have to give full faith and credit (FFC) to the child-support order of state A because child-support orders were not final judgments and only final judgments were entitled to FFC.

To help solve the problem of obtaining personal jurisdiction over nonresident NCPs, Congress required every state to enact the **Uniform Interstate Family Support Act (UIFSA)**. To help solve the problem of proliferating child-support orders, Congress passed the *Full Faith and Credit for Child Support Orders Act* (*FFCCSOA*). We will examine UIFSA here and FFCCSOA later, under the topic of modification.

Under the UIFSA, there are eight ways a forum state can acquire personal jurisdiction over a nonresident defendant NCP. See Exhibit 10-8.

EXHIBIT 10-8 Obtaining Personal Jurisdiction over a Nonresident under the Uniform Interstate Family Support Act (UIFSA)

Eight Possible Reasons a Forum State Can Assert Personal Jurisdiction over a Nonresident Under the UIFSA

1. *Presence.* The nonresident happens to be in the forum state and is personally served while there.

2. *Consent.* The nonresident submits (i.e., consents) to the jurisdiction of the forum state
   (a) by entering a general appearance, and thereby litigates the merits of the case, or
   (b) by filing a responsive pleading such as an answer that has the effect of waiving

any objection to the assertion of personal jurisdiction over the nonresident filer of the responsive pleading.

3. *Former residence in state with child.* The nonresident once resided with the child in the forum state.

4. *Former residence in state plus expenses or support.* The nonresident once resided in the forum state and paid prenatal expenses or support for the child.

5. *Causing the child to reside in the state.* The child resides in the forum state as a result of the acts or directives of the nonresident.

6. *Possible conception in the state.* The nonresident engaged in sexual intercourse in the forum state and the child may have been conceived by that act of intercourse.

7. *Asserting parentage in the state.* The nonresident asserted parentage in the forum state, such as through the putative father registry (see Chapter 13).

8. *Catch-all alternative.* Any other basis consistent with the constitution of the forum state and the U.S. Constitution for the exercise of personal jurisdiction.

Source: 9 Uniform Laws Annotated pt. 1, § 201 (Supp. 1996).

Presence and Consent

The first two UIFSA reasons in Exhibit 10-8 pose little difficulty. It is easy for a court to acquire personal jurisdiction over a nonresident defendant who is served with process in the forum state, who enters a **general appearance** and thereby litigates the merits of the case, or who shows up and files an answer or other **responsive pleading**.

A general appearance occurs when a person goes to court as a party without restrictions and thereby submits to the full jurisdiction of the court. A **pleading** is a formal litigation document (e.g., complaint, petition, answer) filed by a party that states or responds to claims or defenses of other parties. A responsive pleading is a pleading that replies to a prior pleading of an opponent.

Long-Arm Jurisdiction: Minimum Contacts

Reasons 3 to 7 in Exhibit 10-8 are based on the nonresident's **minimum contacts** with the state. The U.S. Supreme Court has said that it is not fair for a court to assert personal jurisdiction over a nonresident unless that nonresident has had (or currently has) enough activities in or connections with the state. Such contacts are called *minimum contacts.*

The list of minimum contacts in 3 to 7 of Exhibit 10-8 includes residing in the forum state with the child at one time, residing in the forum state at one time and covering prenatal expenses or support for the child in the state (even if the nonresident never lived with the child in the state), causing the child to reside in the state, engaging in sexual intercourse in the state that may have led to the conception of the child, and using the laws of the state to assert parentage of the child.

Because these contacts (3–7) with the state are considered sufficiently *purposeful*, it is fair and reasonable for a court in that state to resolve (i.e., to **adjudicate**) disputes arising out of those contacts. An example of such a dispute is whether the nonresident is the child's father and, therefore, should pay child support. The personal jurisdiction that a state acquires over a nonresident defendant because of his or her purposeful contact with that state is called **long-arm jurisdiction**. A statute authorizing it is called a **long-arm statute**. The state extends its "arm" of power across state lines to assert personal jurisdiction over someone who in fairness should answer to the authority of the court because of his or her sufficiently purposeful contacts with that state.

general appearance
Coming to court as a party without restrictions and thereby submitting to the full jurisdiction of the court.

responsive pleading
A pleading that replies to a prior pleading of an opponent.

pleadings
Formal litigation documents (e.g., a complaint or petition, an answer) filed by parties that state or respond to claims or defenses of other parties.

minimum contacts
Activities in or connected with a state by a nonresident that are substantial enough so that it can be said that the nonresident has invoked the benefits and protections of the state, thereby making it fair for the state to assert personal jurisdiction over the nonresident.

adjudicate
To decide by judicial process; to judge.

long-arm jurisdiction
The personal jurisdiction that a state acquires over a nonresident defendant because of his or her purposeful contact with the state.

long-arm statute
A statute that allows a state to obtain personal jurisdiction over a nonresident defendant because of the latter's purposeful contact with the state.

The long-arm jurisdiction provisions of the UIFSA can also be used in the enforcement of *spousal* support orders against obligor spouses who live in another state. (See Chapter 8.)

Enforcing a Support Order against a Nonresident

interstate central registry

An office in each state that receives and responds to cases involving interstate child-support enforcement.

Within the IV-D agency in every state is an **interstate central registry** that handles the enforcement of child support across state lines. Let's examine two case examples:

> *CASE I. Ted and Wilma live in New York, where they were married. While on a two-week vacation in Maine, they conceive their only child, Mary. Upon returning to New York, they decide to separate. Wilma and Mary then move to Maine. Except for the two-week vacation, Ted has never been to Maine. Before Wilma leaves, he tells her that if she moves to Maine, he will have nothing to do with her or Mary. She goes anyway, and Ted carries out his threat of having no contact with either. He never pays child support. After establishing domicile in Maine, Wilma obtains a divorce and a child-support order from a Maine court. Ted is never served in Maine and does not appear in Wilma's divorce action. He knows about the case because Wilma has mailed him all the divorce pleadings, to which he never responds.*

domicile

The place where a person has been physically present with the intent to make that place a permanent home (or with no intent to make any other place a permanent home); the place to which one intends to return when away. A residence, on the other hand, is simply the place where you are living at a particular time. A person can have more than one residence, but generally can have only one domicile.

Wilma's **domicile** in Maine gave the Maine court **in rem jurisdiction** to dissolve the marriage. With this jurisdiction, the court's judgment dissolving the marriage is entitled to full faith and credit (FFC) in every other state so long as Ted was given notice of the proceeding and an opportunity to appear if he so chose. Personal jurisdiction over the nonresident (Ted) is not needed to dissolve the marriage. (See Exhibit 7-3 in Chapter 7.)

Personal jurisdiction, however, *is* needed to for a court to be able to make an order of child support. Did the Maine court have personal jurisdiction over Ted? Yes. Under one of the long-arm methods of the UIFSA, Maine had personal jurisdiction over Ted to make the child-support order because Ted's act of sexual intercourse in Maine leading to conception was a sufficiently purposeful contact with the state of Maine to give it personal jurisdiction over him.

in rem jurisdiction

The court's power over a particular *res*, which is a thing (e.g., a car) or a status (e.g., a marriage) that is located within the territory over which the court has authority.

Once personal jurisdiction is acquired over a nonresident in this way, issues such as paternity and child support can be resolved. Under the UIFSA, special rules exist in conducting the proceeding against the nonresident. For example, the Maine court can accept testimony from witnesses in New York by telephone, video, or other electronic means. Also, assuming Ted continues to refuse to come to Maine, a Maine court can ask a New York court to force Ted to submit to discovery *in New York* on issues such as his financial resources.

Next we examine how to enforce a child-support order against a nonresident. It is not enough simply to have the order in hand. Assume that Wilma has obtained a valid Maine child-support order under the long-arm statute. How does she enforce it if the nonresident (Ted) refuses to obey it; that is, if he doesn't pay? She has two main choices:

- First, she can take the expensive and cumbersome (but traditional) step of traveling to New York in order to ask a New York court to enforce her Maine order. Such travel, however, is impractical for most CPs. The same is true of hiring a New York attorney.

- Second, the UIFSA allows her to use a special registration procedure to enforce the Maine order in New York. Without traveling to New York, she can use the Maine IV-D agency to help her send the Maine order to the appropriate tribunal in New York for the purpose of registering the order. Once registered in New York, her order can then be enforced in the same manner as a New York order can be enforced against a New York resident with the help of a New York IV-D agency. Thus, the UIFSA registration procedure allows a Maine resident (Wilma) to obtain and enforce a Maine support order against a New York resident (Ted) even if Wilma never travels to New York and Ted never travels to Maine. From Wilma's perspective, what would normally be a two-state lawsuit has become a one-state lawsuit. This efficiency was one of the main reasons the UIFSA was enacted.

In our example, Maine is the **initiating state**—the state in which a support case is filed in order to forward it to another state. New York is the **responding state**—the state to which the case was forwarded for enforcement. A responding state can enforce, but cannot modify, an order registered from an initiating state.

Suppose, however, that Maine *cannot* obtain personal jurisdiction over Ted under the long-arm provisions of the UIFSA. Let's change some of the facts of our example:

> *CASE II. Ted and Wilma live in New York, where they were married and where their only child, Mary, was conceived and born. They decide to separate. Wilma and Mary move to Maine. Ted has never been to Maine. Before Wilma leaves, he tells her that if she moves to Maine, he will have nothing to do with her or Mary. She goes anyway, and Ted carries out his threat of having no contact with either. He never pays child support. After establishing domicile in Maine, Wilma obtains a divorce and a child-support order from a Maine court. Ted is never served in Maine and does not appear in Wilma's divorce action. He knows about the case because Mary has mailed him all the divorce pleadings, to which he never responds.*

Case II raises two questions under the UIFSA:

- Can Wilma obtain and enforce a *Maine* child-support order against a New York resident (who is a nonresident of Maine) without traveling to New York?

- Can Wilma obtain and enforce a *New York* child-support order against a New York resident (who is a nonresident of Maine) without traveling to New York?

The answer to the first question is *no*. The answer to the second question is *yes*.

MAINE CHILD SUPPORT ORDER The major fact difference between Case I and Case II is that Mary was not conceived in Maine. Reread the seven ways for a state to obtain personal jurisdiction over a nonresident under the UIFSA (Exhibit 10-8). *None* of them applies to Ted in Case II. He was not personally served in Maine, he never consented to Maine jurisdiction, he never lived in Maine with his child, he never sent child support to Maine, he never arranged for his daughter to live in Maine, he never had sexual intercourse in Maine, and he never asserted his parentage in Maine. Therefore, in Case II, a Maine court could not obtain personal jurisdiction over Ted by the long-arm method, and Wilma cannot use the efficient and inexpensive registration process in New York.

In Exhibit 10-8, there is the eighth method—the catch-all alternative—of acquiring personal jurisdiction under the UIFSA. Perhaps parties will be able to think of additional ways of acquiring personal jurisdiction (i.e., in addition to 1–7) that will be constitutionally acceptable, but it is unlikely that they would be sufficient to reach someone like Ted in Case II, who has close to zero contact with Maine.

In Case II, the Maine court's dissolution of the marriage is valid and enforceable because Wilma's domicile in Maine gave the court in rem jurisdiction to dissolve the marriage. The Maine court also issued a child-support order against Ted. This order, however, is not enforceable; it is not entitled to full faith and credit because it was issued against a defendant over whom the court did not have personal jurisdiction. This is an example of **divisible divorce**, which we studied in Chapter 7; only part of the divorce judgment is enforceable.

---

initiating state
The state in which a support case is filed in order to forward it to another state (called the responding state) for enforcement proceedings under the UIFSA.

responding state
The state to which a support case is forwarded for enforcement proceedings under the UIFSA. The case was forwarded by the initiating state.

divisible divorce
A divorce judgment or decree that is enforceable only in part. The part of a divorce decree that dissolves the marriage is enforceable (if the court had in rem jurisdiction because the plaintiff was domiciled in the state), but the part of the divorce that ordered alimony, child support, or a property division is not enforceable (if the court did not have personal jurisdiction over the defendant).

NEW YORK CHILD SUPPORT ORDER If Wilma wants child support from Ted in Case II, she will need a child-support order *from a New York court*. Obtaining a support order from a Maine court and registering it in New York for enforcement will not work because Maine cannot obtain personal jurisdiction over Ted. But a New York court can obtain personal jurisdiction over Ted with relative ease because he is a resident of New York. (See the discussion earlier about acquiring personal jurisdiction over a resident.)

To obtain a New York support order in Case II, does Wilma have to travel to New York and hire a New York attorney? Fortunately, under the UIFSA, she does not have to do either. Another efficient and inexpensive process is available to her. Here are the steps involved:

- Wilma files a petition for child support in Maine.
- A Maine IV-D agency helps her forward the petition to New York.
- New York obtains personal jurisdiction over Ted (e.g., by service of process in person or by substituted service).
- New York conducts an administrative or judicial proceeding on issues such as paternity and child support.
- The New York court orders Ted to pay child support.
- A New York IV-D agency uses its collection powers to force Ted to pay this support obligation.

In Case II, Maine again is the initiating state and New York is the responding state. Everything is handled on Wilma's behalf by the IV-D agency in Maine and the IV-D agency in New York. At no time is Wilma required to appear in New York. Her testimony can be received in New York by telephone, video, or other electronic means.

Note the procedural difference between Case I and Case II:

- Case I: A *Maine* support order is enforced against a New York resident in New York by the registration process.
- Case II: A *New York* support order is enforced against a New York resident in New York.

The difference is based on which state could obtain personal jurisdiction over Ted.

If Wilma does not want the IV-D agency to act on her behalf in Maine or New York, she can hire a private attorney to represent her. The role of the IV-D agency would then be to assist any attorney she decides to hire.

MODIFICATION OF CHILD SUPPORT ORDERS

After a court makes a child-support order, the parties can go back to court at a later time and argue that the amount of child support is too high (according to the obligor/NCP) or too low (according to the obligee/CP). In this section, we consider how courts resolve requests for modification of child-support orders.

CHANGED CIRCUMSTANCES

The standard rule is that a child-support order can be modified on the basis of a substantial change of circumstances that has arisen since the court granted the order. The changed circumstances must be serious enough to warrant the conclusion that the original award has become inequitable. For example:

- The child's welfare will be jeopardized if the child-support award is not increased due to an unexpected illness of the child, which requires costly medical care.
- The child has acquired independent resources or moved out on his or her own, and therefore, child support should be ended or decreased.

Under federal law, states are allowed to permit parties to request a review of a child-support order every three years (or such shorter cycle as a state deems appropriate) to make sure that the order complies with the child-support guidelines and to add cost-of-living adjustments as needed.[14]

Frequently, the custodial parent claims that child support should be increased because the NCP's ability to pay has increased since the time of the original order (e.g., by obtaining a better-paying job). This is a ground to increase child support only when it is clear that the original decree was inadequate to meet the needs of the child. At the time of the original decree, a lesser amount may have been awarded because of an inability to pay more *at that time*. Hence, a later modification upward is simply a way for the court to correct an initially inadequate award. Since many initial awards *are* inadequate, courts are inclined to grant the modification.

What happens when the NCP seeks a modification downward because he or she can no longer afford the amount originally awarded? If the circumstances that caused this change are beyond the control of the parent (e.g., a long illness), a court will be sympathetic. Suppose, however, that the change is voluntary. For example:

> At the time of a 2013 child-support order, Dan was a 50-year-old sales manager earning $120,000 a year. The order required him to pay his ex-wife $3,000 a month in child support. In 2015, Dan decides to go to evening law school. He quits his job as a sales manager and takes a part-time job as an investigator earning $10,000 a year. He then petitions the court to modify his child-support payments to $250 a month.

In many courts, Dan's petition would be denied because he has not lost the *capacity* to earn enough to pay the original support order. The test is earning capacity, not actual earnings. Self-imposed poverty is not a ground to reduce child support in such courts. Other courts are not this dogmatic. They will grant the modification petition if:

- The child will not be seriously harmed and
- The petitioner is acting in good faith.

The court will want to know whether a legitimate change of career or change of lifestyle is involved. Is it the kind of change that the party would probably have made if the marriage had not ended? If so, the court will be inclined to grant a modification downward, so long as the child is not seriously harmed thereby. On the other hand, is the parent acting out of *bad faith* or malice (e.g., to avoid paying child support or to make life more miserable for the custodial parent)? If so, the modification request will be denied.

ASSIGNMENT 10.9

Harry is fired from his job because of unsatisfactory performance. As a result, he is living on unemployment insurance. He no longer has enough money to pay child support. Will a court grant him a modification? (See the General Instructions for the Legal-Analysis Assignment in Appendix A.)

TWENTY-PERCENT RULE

Assume that a party is able to convince a court that the child-support order should be increased or decreased. The next question is: by how much? In some states, there is a 20 percent floor. After the guidelines are applied to the new financial facts, a court in these states will apply a presumption that the amount should *not* be made unless the result would be an increase or decrease of more than 20 percent of the amount originally ordered by the court. Special circumstances might overcome the presumption, but the court does not want to encourage the parties to keep coming back to court every time the financial facts of the parties change.

SECOND FAMILY

Another area of controversy concerns the NCP's responsibility of supporting others. Should the amount of child support be less because this parent has since taken on the responsibility of supporting a second family? Suppose there is a remarriage with someone who already has children and/or the parent and new spouse have additional children of their own. The old view was that the parent's primary responsibility was to the first family. No adjustment would be made because the parent has voluntarily taken on additional support obligations. Many courts, however, no longer take this hard line. Although they will not permit the parent to leave the first family destitute, they will take into consideration the fact that a second family has substantially affected the parent's ability to support the first. Given this reality, an appropriate adjustment might be made. It must be emphasized, however, that not all courts are this accommodating. Some continue to adhere to the old view.

FRAUD

Finally, suppose that a man asks a court to modify or cancel a child-support order because he is not the child's biological father. The mother lied to him and he believed her. Years later, scientific tests prove that he is not the biological father.

States handle this situation in different ways. In some states, the man is relieved of his obligation to pay child support; he can disestablish paternity. In other states, however, he must continue paying child support because continuation is in the best interests of the child, which is the paramount consideration. As one court said, "Where a father challenges a paternity judgment, courts have pointed to the special needs of children that must be protected, noting that consideration of what is in a child's best interests will often weigh more heavily than the genetic link between parent and child."[14a] A court might allow a finding of paternity to be challenged within a reasonable time after the finding is made, but not if years pass during which the man has held himself out to be the child's father, and a relationship has developed between him and the child. Unless there is clear and convincing evidence that reopening a paternity judgment will serve the best interests of the child, a man will not be allowed to avoid paying child support by offering genetic proof that he is not the biological father.

ARREARAGES

Note that we have been discussing the modification of *future* child-support payments. What about arrearages? Can a court modify a delinquent obligation? There was a time when courts were sympathetic to requests by delinquent obligors to forgive past-due debts, particularly when the court was convinced that future obligations would be met. Congress changed this in 1986 when the Bradley Amendment banned retroactive modification of child-support arrearages in most cases.[15]

CHILD SUPPORT OR PROPERTY DIVISION?

We saw in Chapter 8 that separation agreements sometimes fail to distinguish between property division terms (which in general are not modifiable by a court) and support terms (which are). For example, suppose that the parties agree to give to the "wife the exclusive use of the marital home until the youngest child reaches the age of twenty-one." Is this a division of property or a child-support term? If it is the former, then the husband cannot modify it on the basis of changed circumstances (e.g., the wife's re-marriage). If it is a child-support term, then a modification is possible. Most courts would interpret the above clause to mean that the parties intended it as a child-support term because it is tied to a period of time when the child would most likely need support. Yet a court *could* rule the other way. Need-less litigation often results from poor drafting. (For a discussion of when the Internal Revenue Service will treat a payment as child support *for tax purposes*, see Chapter 11.)

ASSIGNMENT 10.10

a. What standards apply to a request to modify child-support payments in your state? (See General Instructions for the State-Code Assignment in Appendix A.)

b. Sara pays her ex-husband, Harry, $800 a month in child support under a 2010 court order that granted sole physical and legal custody to Harry but gave liberal visitation rights to Sara. Due to continuing bitterness, Harry refuses to allow Sara to see their child. Sara then petitions the court to reduce her child-support payments. How would her request for a modification be handled in your state? (See General Instructions for the Court-Opinion Assignment in Appendix A.)

c. Reread the facts involving Dan in the chapter, the 50-year-old former sales manager who wants to go to law school. How would this request for a modification be handled in your state? (See General Instructions for the Court-Opinion Assignment in Appendix A.)

MODIFYING OUT-OF-STATE ORDERS

Parents dissatisfied with a support order in one state might try to modify it up or down in another state. In such an environment, one judge commented that child-support orders can "proliferate like mushrooms."[16] The UIFSA tries to prevent this.

Once a court issues a valid support order under the UIFSA, that court has **continuing, exclusive jurisdiction (CEJ)** over the case. (CEJ under the UIFSA is very similar to exclusive, continuing jurisdiction—ECJ—which we examined in child-custody cases in Chapter 9.) CEJ under the UIFSA means that no other state can modify the order. A state retains its CEJ so long as the CP, the NCP, or the child continues to reside in the state. If they all leave the state, the court loses its CEJ, and another state can acquire CEJ over the case. (Another way for a court to lose its CEJ is if all the parties agree that another state can have CEJ to modify the order.)

If, in spite of these rules, the parties have generated competing support orders from courts that have jurisdiction or if the parties seek simultaneous support orders in different states, the UIFSA gives preference to the order issued in the **home state**. This is the state in which a child has lived with a parent (or a person acting as a parent) for at least six consecutive months immediately before the court proceedings began. If the child is less than six months old, the home state is the state in which the child has lived since birth with the parent. Periods of temporary absence are counted as part of the six months or the time since birth. To further prevent proliferating child-support orders, Congress passed the **Full Faith and Credit for Child Support Orders Act (FFCCSOA)**, which requires states to enforce (i.e., give full faith and credit to) and not modify valid child-support orders of other states except in limited circumstances.[17] (As we saw in Chapter 9, the home state is also the basis of determining child-custody jurisdiction in interstate cases.)

continuing, exclusive jurisdiction (CEJ)
The authority of a court, obtained by compliance with the Uniform Interstate Family Act (UIFA), to make all initial and modifying support decisions in a case to the exclusion of courts in any other state.

home state
The state where the child has lived with a parent (or anyone acting as a parent) for at least six consecutive months immediately before the court proceedings began or since birth if the child is less than six months old.

Full Faith and Credit for Child Support Orders Act (FFCCSOA)
A federal statute governing when states must give full faith and credit to each other's child-support orders.

IMPROPER ENFORCEMENT

There are limits to what a state can do to enforce a child-support order. For example, a state cannot imprison parents for failure to pay child support when they do not have the financial resources or capability to make such payments. Some states have tried to enforce support obligations through their marriage license statutes. One state refused to issue marriage licenses to individuals who had failed to support their children in the custody of someone else. As we saw in Chapter 5 on marriage formation, however, the U.S. Supreme Court has held that this method of child-support enforcement is invalid because it is an unconstitutional interference with the fundamental right to marry.[18]

Although the failure to pay child support cannot be used to interfere with the right to marry, can such failure be used to interfere with the right to procreate? Can the state say to a "deadbeat dad," stop having more children until you pay for the ones you already have? The U.S. Supreme Court has not yet answered this question. In 2001, however, the Supreme Court of Wisconsin answered it in the affirmative. The Wisconsin court held that a father who intentionally refused to pay child support can be required to avoid having another child until he makes sufficient efforts to support his existing children.[19]

In the Wisconsin case, David Oakley was convicted of intentionally failing to support the nine children he fathered with four different women, even though nothing prevented him from obtaining gainful employment. He could have been sent to prison for eight years. Instead, the court released him on probation under the condition that he avoid fathering another child until he complied with his support obligation to the nine he had already fathered. He faced eight years in prison if he violated this condition. Oakley argued that the condition violated his fundamental right to procreate. The court acknowledged "the fundamental liberty interest of a citizen to choose whether or not to procreate."[20] Yet the court said that this interest had not been violated. Oakley was a convicted felon, and therefore, he was subject to more restrictions than ordinary citizens. Furthermore, the condition was reasonably related to his rehabilitation. To avoid eight years of prison (where he would face a total ban on his right to procreate), he merely had to make the efforts required by law to support his current children. The condition simply required him to avoid creating another victim of willful nonsupport.

The vote of the Wisconsin justices upholding the probation condition was 4–3. The dissenters were concerned that the right to have children was based on a parent's financial resources. One dissenter said that the condition "is basically a compulsory, state-sponsored, court-enforced financial test for future parenthood."[21] Another dissenter commented that the condition creates a strong incentive for Oakley to demand an abortion from any woman he impregnates in the future. An attorney for the American Civil Liberties Union called the decision "a dangerous precedent" in the area of reproductive rights.[22] The case received widespread publicity. Some of the news accounts thought it relevant to point out that the four justices in the majority were male and that the three dissenters were female.

NECESSARIES

necessaries
The basic items needed by family members to maintain a standard of living, particularly food, shelter, and clothing. These items can be purchased and charged to the spouse who has failed to provide them.

A seldom-used method for a wife and child to obtain support is to go to merchants, make purchases of **necessaries**, and charge them to the credit of the nonsupporting husband/father. For a discussion of this remedy, see Chapter 8.

BANKRUPTCY

As we saw in Chapter 8, child-support payments are not discharged (eliminated) in bankruptcy. Obligors who successfully obtain a Chapter 7 or a Chapter 13 bankruptcy must still pay past-due child support and future child support. Of course, obligors who are bankrupt have substantially less income and assets as a result of the financial plight that led them into bankruptcy. Although bankruptcy cannot discharge past-due child-support debts, the obligor's altered financial circumstances may be grounds for the obligor to go back to court and request a downward modification based on current ability to pay.

■ PARALEGAL ROLES

- For an overview of paralegal roles in family-law cases, see Exhibits 1-3 and 1-4 in Chapter 1.
- For all financial issues related to child support covered in Chapter 10, a paralegal may be asked to help collect documents and facts outlined in:
  - the checklist in Exhibit 3-1 of Chapter 3
  - the interrogatories in Appendix C
- Because of the availability of legal and administrative help from IV-D agencies, most custodial parent/obligees do not hire attorneys to obtain or enforce child-support orders. The exception is the high-income case in which the custodial parent/obligee is seeking an unusually large amount of child support. Noncustodial parent/obligors, however, are more likely to need legal help defending themselves against the large array of enforcement remedies that can be brought against them, including imprisonment. When attorneys are used for either parent, duties of their paralegals can include the following:
  - Refer the custodial parent/obligee to the local IV-D agency for assistance.
  - Assist the custodial parent/obligee to collect documents (e.g., pay stubs) that will help locate the noncustodial parent/obligor.
  - Compile a detailed financial statement on both parents that will be relevant to the amount of child support that will likely be ordered.
  - Using worksheets and online calculators, apply the child-support guidelines to determine the amount of child support that a court is likely to order.
  - Compile documents for the attorney who will be negotiating the terms of a separation agreement between the parents (including the child-support terms).
  - Help the noncustodial parent/obligor compile documentation of proof of payments of child support to date and current arrearages.
- Collect evidence to help a nonparent (stepparent, coparent, or sperm donor) prove the extent of his or her involvement or noninvolvement in the rearing of the child.
- Many IV-D agencies employ paralegals in assisting custodial parents to establish paternity, obtain child-custody orders, and enforce such orders. The duties of a child-support paralegal in such an agency might include the following:
  - Assist an attorney or administrative supervisor in child-support enforcement.
  - Conduct extensive interviews of custodial parents on issues of paternity and child-support eligibility.
  - Compose correspondence in response to inquiries where considerable knowledge of child-support policy, procedures, and guidelines is required.
  - Attend meetings in the supervisor's absence or on the supervisor's behalf.
  - Contact attorneys and judicial personnel in the compilation of information.
  - Provide clerical and administrative support.

■ CHECK THE CITE

Lois May Mills is the mother of a child born out of wedlock. She sued the alleged father to establish his paternity so that child support could be ordered. What statute-of-limitations argument did the alleged father raise in response to the suit against him? What constitutional arguments did Lois May Mills make to the alleged father's defense of the statute of limitations? How did the court rule? See *Mills v. Habluetzel*, 456 U.S. 91 (1982). To read this opinion online, run a citation search ("456 U.S. 91") in the Legal Documents database of Google Scholar (scholar.google.com).

■ PROJECT

In Google, Bing, or Yahoo, run the following search: aa military veteran "child support" (substitute the name of your state for aa in the search). Write a short essay in which you explain how a custodial parent/obligee can collect child support from a current or former member of the military. You must cite and quote from a minimum of 10 different federal or state sources that you find on the Internet. At least five of these sources should be statutes, court opinions, or other laws.

■ ETHICS IN A FAMILY LAW PRACTICE

You are a paralegal working at the law office of Helen Farrell, Esq. Claire Richardson asks Farrell to represent her in a child-support case. The court ordered the father of their child to pay $1,000 a month in child support. He is currently $25,000 in arrears. Farrell agrees to take the case. Her fee will be 40 percent of whatever amount of the arrears she collects. In addition, she will receive 10 percent of every future monthly child-support payment. Any ethical problems?

■ WRITING SAMPLE

Sam and Jill Adams were married and had two children in your state. Two years ago, Jill obtained a divorce from Sam in which the court gave Jill sole physical custody and sole legal custody. Sam was ordered to pay Jill $1,200 a month in child support. A month after this order, Sam moved to Canada. He has paid no child support. Jill has come to the law firm where you work as a paralegal. Your supervisor has asked you to prepare a memo in which you outline what steps Jill can take to obtain and then enforce a child-support order. She cannot afford to hire a Canadian attorney, nor can she afford to go to Canada. (See General Instructions for the Writing Sample in Appendix A.)

SUMMARY

Child support is heavily influenced by federal law. Vast amounts of child-support debts are not paid. The primary criterion for paying child support is parentage; both parents have an equal obligation to support their children. A grandparent, stepparent, coparent, or sperm donor does not have a duty of support unless a statute says otherwise, unless the individual agrees to provide such support, or unless the doctrines of in loco parentis or equitable estoppel apply. With some exceptions, the duty of support ends upon the age of majority or emancipation. States differ on whether a parent has an obligation to pay for a child's college education. In most states, the duty to support a child extends beyond the age of majority if the child is physically or mentally disabled. When parents are negotiating the child-support terms of their separation agreement, they must consider a number of factors such as child-support guidelines, standard of living, payment dates, kinds and frequency of payments, insurance and tax considerations. Parents cannot agree that one of the parents will not owe child support, nor can they agree to an amount of child support that will fall below the minimum required in the state.

The amount of child support is determined primarily by the child-support guidelines of each state. The guidelines set the presumptively correct amount of support that is due. Factors that might cause a court to change the amount set by the guidelines include medical costs, private school costs, high parental income, the existence of other families that the parents must support, and the amount of time the child spends with each parent. Most states use calculations based on either the income-shares model or the percentage-of-income model. Under the three-pony rule, child support for children of parents with very high incomes should be adjusted so that payments do not go beyond what is reasonably and rationally related to the realistic needs of the child. When parents improperly reduce their income capacity, a court can treat the amount of the reduction as if it is income that was actually earned—as imputed income.

All obligees in the state can use the services of an IV-D agency to establish child-support orders and to enforce child support. (The services are not limited to recipients of public assistance.) The assistance includes helping to locate the noncustodial parent and to establish paternity. Obligees on public assistance must assign their right of child support to the IV-D agency or county welfare agency. Major tools of the IV-D agency for use in locating missing noncustodial parents are the State Parent Locator Service (SPLS), the Federal Parent Locator Service (FPLS), and the National Directory of New Hires (NDNH). To protect abused custodial parents, a family violence indicator (FVI) can prevent the release of identifying information to unauthorized persons.

Enforcement remedies include civil and criminal contempt; criminal nonsupport (including the Deadbeat Parents Punishment Act); execution; income withholding; garnishment; license and registration denial, delay, or revocation; passport denial, delay, or revocation; tax refund offset; IRS Full Collection; unemployment compensation and workers' compensation intercept; qualified domestic relations order (QDRO); qualified medical child support order (QMCSO); credit bureau referral (credit clouding); financial institution data match (FIDM); and liens, posting security, wheel boots, and wanted posters. Indigent, delinquent obligors are not entitled to free attorney representation when charged with civil contempt if the obligee is unrepresented and the state provides procedural protections such as an opportunity to be heard and clear notice that imprisonment will not be ordered if the obligor cannot pay.

To issue a child-support order, a court needs subject-matter jurisdiction over child-support cases and personal jurisdiction over the obligor. Without such jurisdiction, the order is not entitled to full faith and credit (FFC). Personal jurisdiction over a resident obligor can be obtained by service of process. The long-arm statute can be used to obtain personal jurisdiction over nonresidents if they have sufficient minimum contacts with the forum state. A registration procedure can then be used to enforce the order in the state where the nonresident resides. The state that used the long-arm statute to obtain personal jurisdiction and issue the order is called the initiating state. The state where the defendant resides is called the responding state. The initiating state sends its order to the responding state, which registers the order and enforces it against the defendant. If a custodial parent cannot use the long-arm statute to obtain personal jurisdiction over a nonresident defendant, the IV-D agency can assist the custodial parent in obtaining and enforcing a support order in the defendant's state.

A child-support order can be modified on the basis of a substantial change of circumstances that has arisen since the court granted the order, rendering the order inequitable. No modification will be ordered if a parent voluntarily reduces his or her income-earning capacity in order to avoid paying support, nor will there be a modification if it results in harm to the child. In some states, after the guidelines are applied to the new financial facts, a court will apply a presumption that the amount should not be changed unless the result would be an increase or decrease of more than 20 percent of the amount originally ordered by the court. If the obligor takes on a new family, many courts will take this into consideration when deciding whether to modify the child-support order downward so long as the first family is not left destitute thereby. Courts differ on whether a man can modify a child-support order that was issued against him by proving that he is not the biological father of the child.

In most cases, the Bradley Amendment forbids retroactive modification of arrearages. The Uniform Interstate Family Support Act (UIFSA) and the Full Faith and Credit for Child Support Orders Act (FFCCSOA) seek to prevent a state from modifying an out-of-state child-support order by giving priority to the state that initially made the order. This state has continuing exclusive jurisdiction (CEJ), which all other states must respect, so long as the custodial parent, the noncustodial parent, or the child continues to reside in the state.

A state cannot refuse to give a marriage license to a person who has failed to pay child support for children in the custody of someone else. This interferes with the fundamental right to marry. If the obligor obtains a bankruptcy, his or her child-support debts are not discharged.

KEY TERMS

public assistance
noncustodial parent (NCP)
custodial parent (CP)
Temporary Assistance for Needy
    Families (TANF)
arrearages
physical custody
legal custody
obligor
obligee
payor
payee
stepparent
equitable adoption
in loco parentis
equitable estoppel
estopped
coparenting
presumed parent
sperm bank
artificial insemination (AI)
age of majority
emancipated
separation agreement
child-support guidelines

escalation clause
trust
escrow
lump-sum payment
pendente lite
rebuttable presumption
three-pony rule
imputed income
fraudulent transfer
IV-D agency
assign
State Parent Locator Service (SPLS)
vital statistics
Federal Parent Locator Service (FPLS)
National Directory of New Hires (NDNH)
family violence indicator (FVI)
restraining order
contempt
civil contempt
criminal contempt
house arrest
criminal nonsupport
probation
Deadbeat Parents Punishment Act (DPPA)
execution

lien
income withholding
garnishment
qualified domestic relations order
    (QDRO)
qualified medical child support order
    (QMCSO)
credit clouding
levy
prosecution
amnesty
indigent
ex parte
subject-matter jurisdiction
forum
personal jurisdiction
full faith and credit (FFC)
service of process
personal service
substituted service
Uniform Interstate Family Support
    Act (UIFSA)
general appearance
responsive pleading
pleadings

minimum contacts
adjudicate
long-arm jurisdiction
long-arm statute
interstate central registry

domicile
in rem jurisdiction
initiating state
responding state
divisible divorce

continuing, exclusive jurisdiction (CEJ)
home state
Full Faith and Credit for Child Support
    Orders Act (FFCCSOA)
necessaries

REVIEW QUESTIONS

1. Why did Congress write laws on child support and how do they influence state child-support laws?

2. What are some of the ways in which noncustodial parents (NCPs) avoid paying child support?

3. What is an obligor/payor and an obligee/payee?

4. Under what circumstances is a duty of child support owed by a grandparent, stepparent, coparent, or sperm donor?

5. What is a presumed parent?

6. When does the duty of support end?

7. When do some states require a parent to pay college expenses of a child over the age of majority?

8. What factors must parents take into consideration when negotiating the child-support clauses of their separation agreement?

9. What is the role of child-support guidelines in determining the amount of child support?

10. What kinds of parental income does a court consider in determining child support?

11. When can a court deviate from the presumptively correct amount of support set by the guidelines?

12. What is the difference between the income-shares model and the percentage-of-income model?

13. What is the three-pony rule?

14. When will a court impute income to an obligor?

15. What is the role of an IV-D agency?

16. What is meant by assigning support rights to the government and when does it occur?

17. How do the following entities function in locating noncustodial parents: State Parent Locator Service (SPLS), the Federal Parent Locator Service (FPLS), and the National Directory of New Hires (NDNH)?

18. What is a family violence indicator (FVI) and how is it used?

19. What is the scope of data contained in the National Directory of New Hires?

20. How do civil and criminal contempt differ?

21. When is the crime of criminal nonsupport committed?

22. What is the Deadbeat Parents Punishment Act?

23. What happens when an execution occurs?

24. How does income withholding work and how does it differ from garnishment?

25. How can the license and registration process be used in the collection of child support?

26. How can the passport process be used in the collection of child support?

27. What is the tax offset program and how does it differ from IRS Full Collection?

28. What is unemployment compensation and workers' compensation intercept?

29. What is a QDRO and a QMCSO?

30. How do credit clouding and FIDM work?

31. What is a lien?

32. What is meant by posting security?

33. How does amnesty work?

34. When does the state have to provide a free attorney to indigent obligors who are in arrears?

35. What kinds of jurisdiction does a court need to issue a child-support order?

36. How does a state acquire personal jurisdiction over a resident obligor?

37. What is the Uniform Interstate Family Support Act (UIFSA)?

38. What is long-arm jurisdiction and what are the ways in which it can be acquired?

39. What is an interstate central registry?

40. How does registration allow enforcement of a child-support order against a nonresident?

41. If the state of the obligor cannot obtain personal jurisdiction over the nonresident, how can the obligee obtain and enforce a child-support order against the obligor in the obligor's state without traveling to that state?

42. When will a court modify a child-support order?

43. What is the twenty-percent rule?

44. Will a court modify a child-support order because the obligor has remarried and must now support a new family?

45. How do courts respond to proof that a man is not the biological father of a child after a finding of paternity has been made?

46. What is the effect of the Bradley Amendment?

47. How do the UIFSA and the FFCCSOA seek to prevent a state from modifying an out-of-state child-support order?

48. Can a state refuse to give a marriage license to a person who has failed to pay child support for children in the custody of someone else?

49. What are necessaries?

50. What is the effect of bankruptcy on child-support debts?

HELPFUL WEBSITES

Handbook on Child Support Enforcement

- publications.usa.gov/USAPubs.php?PubID=5001
- www.acf.hhs.gov/programs/cse/pubs/2005/handbook_on_cse.pdf

Child Support Guidelines: Fifty States

- www.supportguidelines.com
- www.supportguidelines.com/links.html
- www.supportguidelines.com/famlawsections.html

IV-D agencies and Child Support Enforcement

- www.acf.hhs.gov/programs/cse/extinf.html

QDRO: Qualified Domestic Relations Orders

- www.dol.gov/ebsa/faqs/faq_qdro.html
- www.qdrodesk.com/sampleqdro.pdf

QMCSO: Qualified Medical Child Support Orders

- www.dol.gov/ebsa/publications/qmcso.html

Child Support and the Courts

- www.acf.hhs.gov/programs/cse/courts/child_support_and_the_judiciary.html
- www.childsupportandthecourt.org

National Council of Juvenile and Family Court Judges, *A Practice Guide: Making Child Support Orders Realistic and Enforceable*

- www.ncjfcj.org (type child support in the search box)

Fathering Courts

- www.ncsc.org/Topics/Problem-Solving-Courts/Fathering-Courts/Resource-Guide.aspx
- www.fathers.com/documents/fatheringcourt/Fathering_Court_Booklet_Final.pdf

Child Support Collection Statistics

- www.census.gov/hhes/www/childsupport/childsupport.html
- www.census.gov/prod/2011pubs/p60-240.pdf

Interstate Child Support

- www.acf.hhs.gov/programs/cse/pol/IM/2006/im-06-02a.pdf

UIFSA Procedural Guidelines Handbook

- www.acf.hhs.gov/programs/cse/fct/uifsahb.htm

Fathers' Rights, Child Support, Custody

- ancpr.com

International Child Support

- www.acf.hhs.gov/programs/cse/international

Child Support and the Military

- www.acf.hhs.gov/programs/cse/newhire/employer/publication/military_quick_guide.htm#1

Google/Bing/Yahoo Searches

(on these search engines, run the following searches, substituting your state for "aa")

- "child support" aa
- UIFSA aa
- stepparent "child support" aa
- estoppel "child support" aa
- emancipation "child support" aa
- contempt "child support" aa
- crime "child support" aa
- disability "child support" aa
- garnishment "child support" aa
- international "child support" aa
- interstate "child support" aa
- IV-D "child support" aa
- "home state" "child support" aa
- "paternity fraud" "child support" aa
- "child support" enforcement aa
- coparenting "child support" aa
- "fathers rights" "child support" aa
- "child support" arrears aa
- "child support" guidelines aa
- domestic violence "child support" aa
- "parenting plan" "child support" aa
- "income withholding" "child support" aa
- jurisdiction "child support" aa
- "long arm" "child support" aa
- UIFSA "child support" aa
- FFCCSOA aa
- "initiating state" "child support" aa

ENDNOTES

Note: All or most of the court opinions in these endnotes can be read online. To do so, go to Google Scholar (scholar .google.com), select "Legal documents," and in the search box, enter the cite (e.g., "131 S. Ct. 2507") or name of the case (e.g., "Turner v. Rogers") that is given in the endnote.

[1] U.S. Census Bureau, Custodial Mothers and Fathers and Their Child Support: 2007 (Current Population Reports) (Nov. 2009). (www.census.gov/prod/2009pubs/p60 -237.pdf).

[2] *Turner v. Rogers*, 564 U.S. __, ___, 131 S. Ct. 2507, 2526 (2011) (Thomas dissent).

[2a] Kirit Radia, *Adopted Boy Rejected by U.S. Mom Adjusts in Foster Care*, ABC News (Apr. 13, 2012).

[2b] *E.C. v. J.V.*, 202 Cal. App. 4th 1076, 1085 (3d Dist. 2012).

[2c] Shari Motro, *Responsibility Begins at Conception*, N.Y. Times, July 7, 2012, at A15 (www.nytimes.com/2012/07/07 /opinion/time-for-pregnancy-support-alimony.html).

[3] 42 U.S.C. § 667(b)(2) (www.law.cornell.edu/uscode/ text/42/667).

[4] *Downing v. Downing*, 45 S.W.3d 449, 456 (Ky. App., 2001).

[5] 42 U.S.C. §§ 651-65. (www.law.cornell.edu/uscode/html /uscode42/usc_sup_01_42_10_7_20_IV_30_D.html).

[6] www.acf.hhs.gov/programs/cse.

[7] Carmen Solomon-Fears, *The National Directory of New Hires*, iii (Congressional Research Service 2011).

[8] Child Support Enforcement *FY 2010 Preliminary Report* (May 2011) (www.acf.hhs.gov/programs/cse/pubs/2011/reports /preliminary_report_fy2010).

[9] *Moss v. Superior Court*, 950 P.2d 59 (Calif. 1998).

[10] 18 U.S.C. § 228 (codes.lp.findlaw.com/uscode/18/I/11A/228).

[11] 705 Illinois Compiled Statutes Annotated § 205/1 (www.ilga .gov/legislation/ilcs/fulltext.asp?DocName=070502050K1).

[12] Rebecca Hamil, *Western Hemisphere Travel Initiative*, 28 Child Support Report 6 (Office of Child Support Enforcement, Aug. 2006) (www.acf.hhs.gov/programs/cse/pubs/2006 /csr/csr0608.pdf).

[13] *Turner v. Rogers*, 564 U.S. __, 131 S. Ct. 2507 (2011).

[14] 42 U.S.C.. § 666(a)(10) (www.law.cornell.edu/uscode/42 /usc_sec_42_00000666----000-.html).

[14a] *In re Paternity of Cheryl*, 746 N.E.2d 488, 495 (Mass. 2001).

[15] 42 U.S.C. § 666(a)(9) (www.law.cornell.edu/uscode/42 /usc_sec_42_00000666----000-.html).

[16] Thomas J. Devine, *From the Bench*, 24 Vermont Bar Journal & Law Digest 10 (Mar. 1998).

[17] 28 U.S.C. § 1738B (www.law.cornell.edu/uscode/uscode28 /usc_sec_28_00001738---B000-.html).

[18] *Zablocki v. Redhail*, 434 U.S. 374 (1978).

[19] *State v. Oakley*, 629 N.W.2d 200 (Wisc. 2001).

[20] 629 N.W.2d at 207.

[21] 629 N.W.2d at 221.

[22] Tamar Lewin, *Father Owing Child Support Loses a Right to Procreate*, N.Y. Times, Jul. 12, 2001, at A14.

Tax Consequences of Separation and Divorce

CHAPTER OUTLINE

THE ROLE OF TAX LAW IN THE BARGAINING PROCESS

ALIMONY
  Deductible Alimony: The Seven Tests

The Recapture Rule: Front Loading Payments to Disguise Property Division as Alimony

PROPERTY DIVISION
  Tax Consequences of a Property Division

Incident to a Divorce

LEGAL AND RELATED FEES IN OBTAINING A DIVORCE

INNOCENT SPOUSE RELIEF

CHAPTER OBJECTIVES

After completing this chapter, you should be able to:

- Know what is meant by "tax effecting" a clause in a separation agreement.

- State the tax consequences of alimony, child support, and property division.

- Understand how parties bargain some of the terms of their divorce based on tax considerations.

- State how the payment and receipt of alimony are reported on the 1040 return.

- List and explain the seven tests for deductible alimony.

- Explain the recapture rule.

- Describe when the IRS will treat a reduction of "alimony" as child support.

- Explain when a property division is a nontaxable event.

- State the basis of property in the hands of the ex-spouse transferee as part of a property division.

- Know which legal and related fees paid obtaining a divorce are deductible.

- State the innocent-spouse rule.

THE ROLE OF TAX LAW IN THE BARGAINING PROCESS

tax-effect

(1) To determine the tax consequences of something (verb). (2) The tax consequences of something (noun).

Tax law should play a major role in the representation of divorce clients. The **tax-effect** of every clause in a separation agreement must be determined. The phrase *tax-effect* is also used as a verb. If, for example, you are asked to tax effect a clause in a proposed separation agreement, you are being asked to determine what, if anything, is deductible and what, if anything, is taxable if the clause is agreed to by the parties. Tax effects often become part of (or should become part of) the bargaining process between the soon-to-be ex-spouses.

We will be examining the three major financial components of separation and divorce: alimony, child support, and property division. Exhibit 11-1 summarizes the tax law governing each.

Because alimony is deductible but child-support and property-division payments are not, attempts are sometimes made to disguise child-support or property-division payments as alimony. Why would alimony recipients agree to the disguise in view of the fact that they would have to pay taxes on the alimony received? A woman might want the highest reportable income possible in order to qualify for credit later when she applies for a car loan or a house mortgage. In the bargaining process, recipients may be given some other benefit in the separation agreement (e.g., sole legal custody of the children) in exchange for cooperation in disguising child-support or property-division payments as alimony. The effort, however, may not work. A major theme of this chapter is determining when the Internal Revenue Service (IRS) will challenge the disguise and deny the alimony deduction to the payor/transferor.[1]

ALIMONY

Alimony payments are:

- Reported as taxable income on line 11 of page 1 of the recipient's 1040 federal tax return and

gross income

The total amount received or earned before deductions.

- Deducted from **gross income** on line 31a of page 1 of the payor's 1040 return.

adjusted gross income (AGI)

The total income from all of a person's taxable sources less specifically allowed deductions.

Once the payor's alimony and other specified deductions are made, the result will be the payor's **adjusted gross income (AGI)**. Because the deduction comes through the determination of AGI on page 1 of the 1040, there is no need to itemize deductions in Schedule B in order to take advantage of the deduction.

EXHIBIT 11-1   Tax Consequences of Separation and Divorce

Alimony	Child Support	Property Division
• The person who pays alimony (the payor) can deduct alimony payments. • The person who receives alimony (the recipient or payee) must report it as income and pay taxes on it.	• The person who pays child support (the payor) cannot deduct child-support payments. • The person who receives child-support payments (the recipient or payee) on behalf of a child does not report it as income and does not pay taxes on it.	• The person who transfers cash or other property (the transferor) as part of a property division cannot deduct what is transferred. • The person who receives cash or other property (the transferee) as part of a property division does not report it as income and does not pay taxes on it. • The basis of the property in the hands of the transferee is the same as the transferor's basis.

EXHIBIT 11-2 Federal Income Tax Form 1040

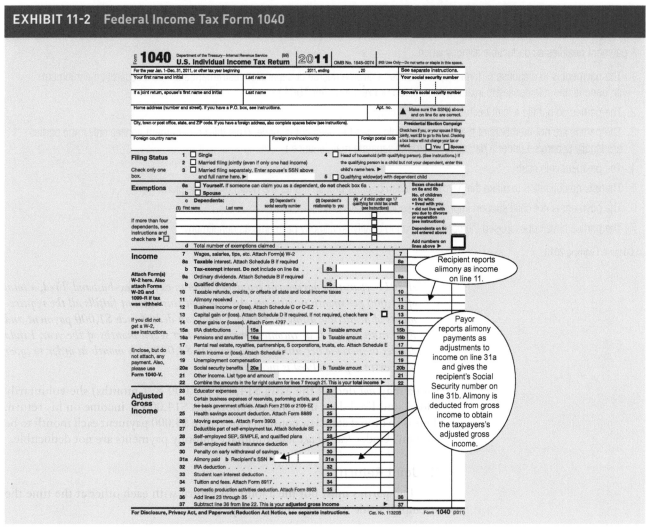

Source: Internal Revenue Service (www.irs.gov/pub/irs-pdf/f1040.pdf).

Note that line 31b in Exhibit 11-2 requires the payor to give the Social Security number of the recipient. Failure to do so can result in a $50 penalty and a disallowance of the deduction. Providing this information will make it easier for the IRS to check its own records to make sure that the recipient is reporting as income what the payor is deducting as alimony.

DEDUCTIBLE ALIMONY: THE SEVEN TESTS

When does a payment qualify as alimony for tax purposes? When it meets the seven requirements for alimony listed in Exhibit 11-3.

Divorce or Separation Instrument

As indicated in Exhibit 11-3, the payment must be to a spouse or former spouse pursuant to and required by a divorce decree or by a separation **instrument** such as a separation agreement that was entered or executed after 1984. The decree does not have to be final. A payment ordered by an **interlocutory** (not final) decree or a decree **pendente lite** (while awaiting the court's final decree) can also qualify.

If a spouse makes an *additional* payment beyond what is required by the divorce or separation agreement, the additional payment is considered a voluntary payment and is not alimony for tax purposes.

instrument
A formal written document that gives expression to or embodies a legal act or agreement (e.g., contract, will). (See glossary for an additional meaning.)

interlocutory
Not final; interim.

pendente lite
Pending the [outcome of the] litigation.

EXHIBIT 11-3 Requirements for Deductible Alimony

A payment qualifies as deductible alimony when:

1. The payment is to a spouse or former spouse under a divorce decree or separation instrument such as a separation agreement. (In general, the rule applies to instruments entered or executed after 1984.)
2. The parties do not file a joint tax return with each other.
3. The parties are not members of the same household when the payment is made. (This third requirement applies only if the parties are legally separated under a decree of divorce or separate maintenance.)
4. The payment is in cash.
5. There is no obligation to make the payment (in cash or other property) after the death of the recipient.
6. The payment is not child support improperly disguised as alimony.
7. The parties have not exercised the option of treating qualifying alimony payments as nonalimony.

© Cengage Learning 2013

A 2011 separation agreement requires Linda to pay her ex-husband, Fred, a total of $1,000 per month in alimony. Assume that this amount fulfills all the requirements of deductible alimony. Hence, Linda can deduct each $1,000 payment and Fred must report it as income. During the last seven months of the year, Linda decides to increase her alimony payments to $3,000 each month in order to cover some extra expenses Fred is incurring.

Linda may *not* deduct the extra $14,000 ($2,000 × 7 months) she voluntarily added, and Fred does not have to report this $14,000 as income on his return. This is so even if state law considers the entire $3,000 payment each month to be alimony. Under *federal tax* law, voluntary alimony payments are not deductible.

No Joint Return

The parties must not file a joint tax return with each other at the time the attempt is made to deduct the alimony.

Parties Are Not Members of the Same Household

If the parties have been separated under a decree of divorce or separate maintenance, they must not be members of the same household when the alimony payment is made. Living in separate rooms or otherwise physically separating themselves is not enough if they are still living in the same home or apartment.

There is, however, a one-month grace period. If one of the parties is planning to move and in fact does move within one month after the date of the payment, the payment *is* deductible, even though the individuals were living together when the payment was made.

Jack and Tara live at 100 Elm Street. They are divorced on January 1, 2010. Jack moves out of the Elm Street house on February 15, 2010. Under the divorce decree, Jack is obligated to pay Tara $500 a month in alimony on the first of each month. He makes his first payment on January 1, 2010.

The January 1, 2010, payment is *not* deductible. The parties have a divorce decree, but they must not be living in the same household at the time of the alimony payment under the divorce. Jack and Tara were both living at 100 Elm Street—the same household—at the time of that payment. The one-month grace period does not apply because Jack did not move out within a month of this payment. If he had left earlier (e.g., January 29, 2010), the payment *would* have been deductible. Of course, the February 1, 2010, payment and all payments after February 15, 2010 (when they opened separate households) are deductible if the other requirements for deductible alimony are met.

There is an exception to the same-household rule. If the parties are not legally separated under a decree of divorce or separate maintenance, but make a payment pursuant to a separation agreement, support decree, or other court order, the payment may qualify as alimony even if the parties are members of the same household when the payment is made.

Payment in Cash

Only *cash* payments can qualify as deductible alimony. The preferred way to transfer cash is by check or money order so that there is an adequate record of the transfer.

> *Under the terms of a separation agreement and divorce decree of Bob and Mary, Bob:*
>
> * *Gives Mary, his ex-wife, a car*
> * *Paints Mary's house*
> * *Lets Mary use his mother's vacation house*
> * *Gives Mary stocks, bonds, and an annuity contract*
> * *Gives Mary free accounting advice*

The value of these items cannot be deducted as alimony because they are not in cash. This is so even if the agreement or decree labels each item "alimony."

Can cash payments made by the payor *to a third party* be deducted as alimony?

> *Under the terms of a separation agreement and divorce decree of Bob and Mary, Bob:*
>
> * *Sends $1,000 to Mary's landlord to pay her rent*
> * *Sends $800 to Mary's college to cover part of her tuition*
> * *Sends $750 to Mary's bank to pay the mortgage on the vacation home she owns*

Can Bob deduct any of these payments as alimony, and does Mary have to report them as income? The answer is yes if the cash payment to the third party is required by the divorce decree or by the separation agreement and meets all other requirements for deductible alimony. The payments to the third parties that meet this test are treated as having been received by Mary.

Suppose that the third party is an insurance company.

> *Under the terms of a separation agreement and divorce decree of Bob and Mary, Bob pays an annual premium of $1,700 on a life insurance policy on his life, with Mary as the beneficiary.*

Can he deduct these premiums as alimony? The answer is yes, but only if:

* The payor (Bob) is obligated to make these premium payments by the divorce decree or separation agreement and
* The beneficiary (Mary) *owns* the policy so that the payor cannot change the beneficiary.

No Payment after Death of Recipient

If the payor is obligated (under the divorce decree or separation agreement) to make payments after the death of the recipient, none of the payments made after *or before* the death of the recipient qualifies as alimony. Here, the IRS is trying to catch a blatant and improper attempt to disguise **property division** as alimony in order to take advantage of a deduction.

property division

The allocation and distribution of property between spouses (or ex-spouses) after a legal separation or divorce. Also called property settlement or property distribution.

> *Under the terms of a separation agreement, Bob agrees to pay Mary $10,000 a year "in alimony" for 15 years. If Mary dies within the 15 years, Bob must make the remaining annual payments to Mary's estate. In the twelfth year of the agreement, after Bob has paid Mary $120,000 (12 years × $10,000), Mary dies. For the next three years, Bob makes the remaining annual payments, totaling $30,000 (3 years × $10,000), to Mary's estate.*

All of the payments made by Bob—the entire $150,000 covering the periods before and after Mary's death—will be disallowed as alimony. It makes no difference that the separation agreement called the payments "alimony." It makes no difference that the payments were used for day-to-day support. To qualify as deductible alimony, one of the tests is that the payor must have no liability for "alimony" payments after the death of the recipient.

In general, debts continue in effect after the death of either party. If, for example, I pay you $3,500 to buy your car and you die before delivering the car to me, it is clear that your obligation to give me the car survives your death. Your estate would have to give me the car. The same is true of a property-division debt. Assume that Bob is obligated under a property-division agreement to transfer a house to Mary, his ex-wife. If Bob dies before making this transfer, his estate can be forced to complete the transfer to Mary. Property-division debts survive the death of either party. (See Exhibit 8-3 in Chapter 8.) Alimony is different. It is rare for a "real" alimony debt to continue after the death of the recipient. Once the recipient dies, he or she does not need alimony! Whenever the payor must make payments beyond the death of the recipient, the payments are really part of a property division.

Let's look at another example:

> At the time of their separation, Mary had a separate career in which she earned a high salary and Bob owned a successful trucking business valued at $400,000. He started this business when he married Mary. Bob and Mary agreed that she should have a substantial share of the trucking business as part of the property division that they negotiate. But Bob does not want to sell the business in order to give Mary her share. In the negotiations, Mary asks for $150,000 as her share of the business, payable immediately. Bob agrees that $150,000 is a fair amount, but he doesn't have the money to give her. He counters by offering her $200,000 payable over 10 years in $20,000 annual payments to be labeled as "alimony" in their separation agreement. If Mary dies within the 10 years, Bob will make the annual payments to Mary's estate. The extra $50,000 is added to offset the fact that Mary will have to wait in order to receive all her money and will have to pay income tax on whatever Bob declares as deductible alimony.

Again, this arrangement will not work. There are ways to disguise property division as alimony, but this is not one of them. The $200,000 can never be deductible alimony because the parties planned to continue the payments after the death of the recipient.

Payment Is Not Child Support Improperly Disguised As Alimony

Child support is neither deductible by the payor nor includible in the income of the recipient. The divorce decree or separation agreement might specifically designate or fix a payment (or part of a payment) as child support.

> Under the terms of a divorce decree, Jane must pay Harry $2,000 a month, of which $1,600 is designated for the support of their child in the sole physical custody of Harry.

The $1,600 has been fixed as child support. Therefore it is not deductible by Jane nor includible in the income of Harry. This remains true even if the amount so designated varies from time to time.

Occasionally, the parties may try to disguise child support as alimony in order to take advantage of the deductibility of alimony for the payor. The payor wants all of the payments to be deductible but knows that child-support payments are not deductible. To get around this hurdle, the payor calls all the payments alimony but states that the payments will be reduced if the ex-spouse dies while the children are still minors. To the IRS, those after-death payments are child support in disguise.

Deductibility will be lost if either of two tests applies:

- Contingency test. The payment is reduced upon the happening of a **contingency** relating to the child. A contingency is simply an event that may or may not occur.

- Clear-association test. The payment is reduced at a time that is clearly associated with a contingency relating to the child. A contingency relates to a child when the contingency depends on something involving the child.

For a summary of the tests, see Exhibit 11-4.

contingency
An event that may or may not occur.

EXAMPLE OF A REDUCTION UPON A CONTINGENCY RELATING TO A CHILD

Under the terms of a separation agreement, Bill will pay Grace "alimony" of $2,000 a month, which will be reduced to $800 a month when their child marries.

There is a contingency in this example that will trigger a reduction of $2,000 to $800. The contingency relates to the child of Bill and Grace—when the child marries. The parties are trying to disguise child support of $1,200 a month as alimony. They are reducing $2,000 to $800 at a time when the child would probably no longer need support. Under these facts, the IRS will allow the payor to deduct only $800 of each $2,000 payment. Other contingencies that will lead to a similar result include the child becoming employed, reaching a specified income level, leaving the household, leaving school, reaching a specified age, or dying (see Exhibit 11-4).

EXHIBIT 11-4   Reduction of "Alimony" Treated As Child Support

Reduction upon a Contingency Relating to the Child

A reduction in a payment will be treated as child support (regardless of how it is labeled by the parties) if the reduction will occur upon the happening of a contingency relating to a child such as:

- the child becomes employed
- the child reaches a specified income level
- the child leaves the household
- the child marries
- the child leaves school
- the child reaches a specified age
- the child dies

Reduction at a Time Clearly Associated with a Contingency Relating to the Child

There are two circumstances in which the IRS will presume that a reduction in a payment is so closely associated with a contingency involving a child that the amount of the reduction will be treated as child support (regardless of how it is labeled by the parties). The two presumptions depend on how many children are involved in the reduction:

- *One child.* The reduction will be presumed to be child support if the reduction is to occur not more than 6 months before or after the date the child will reach the age of majority in the state (usually 18).

- *More than one child.* The reduction will be presumed to be child support if the reduction is to occur on two or more occasions not more than one year before or after a different child reaches a certain age from 18 to 24. (This certain age must be the same for each child, but need not be a whole number of years.)

Source: Internal Revenue Service, *Publication 504* (www.irs.gov/publications/p504/ar02.html#en_US_2010_publink1000175928).

EXAMPLE OF A REDUCTION AT A TIME CLEARLY ASSOCIATED WITH A CONTINGENCY RELATING TO A CHILD Occasionally, the parties will try to be creative in disguising child support by triggering a reduction in payment at designated times that may or may not explicitly mention a child. To combat such creativity, the IRS uses the presumptions listed in Exhibit 11-4.

> *Leo and Elaine have one child, Fred. They live in a state where the age of majority is 18. Fred was born on March 13, 1992. Leo and Elaine are divorced on January 12, 2010. Under the terms of the divorce decree, Elaine receives sole physical custody of Fred, and Leo must pay Elaine $2,200 a month in "alimony" until July 13, 2010, when the monthly payments will be reduced by $1,000 to $1,200.*

Note that the child is not specifically mentioned in relation to the time of the reduction. Yet on these facts, the IRS will presume that the amount of the reduction ($1,000) is child support. Fred reaches the age of majority on March 13, 2010, when he turns 18. The reduction occurs on July 13, 2010, four months afterward. Because this reduction occurs not more than six months after the child reaches the age of majority, the presumption of child support applies. The IRS will presume that the amount of the reduction ($1,000) is child support. Only $1,200, therefore, is deductible alimony. This conclusion applies even if there is another clause in the agreement that specifies another amount (e.g., $500 a month) as child support for Fred. The $500 will be treated as child support for tax purposes, but $1,000 of the "alimony" will still be treated as child support because of the timing of the reduction within six months of the age of majority.

Now let's change the timing of the reduction:

> *Same facts as above example involving Leo, Elaine, and Fred except that the reduction from $2,200 to $1,200 is to occur on March 13, 2011.*

On these facts, the presumption that the amount of the reduction is child support does not apply. The reduction occurs one year after Fred reaches the age of majority, which of course is more than six months. The entire $2,200, therefore, is deductible alimony.

When the presumption applies, the parties can overcome it by showing that the reduction is not dependent (contingent) on the child. An example might be a local rule that calls for a reduction based on the duration of the marriage rather than on the circumstances of a child.

Parties Have Not Exercised Nonalimony Option

Assume that all of the first six tests for determining alimony (see Exhibit 11-3) are met by the parties. As a result, the payor can deduct the payments and the recipient must include them in income. Suppose, however, that the parties do *not* want the payments to be deductible/includible. It may be, for example, that the tax brackets of the parties are such that neither would benefit significantly more than the other by having the alimony tax rules apply. They can decide to treat otherwise qualifying alimony payments as *nonalimony*. This can be done by including a provision in the separation agreement that the payments will *not* be deductible to the payor and will not be included in the income of the recipient.

THE RECAPTURE RULE: FRONT LOADING PAYMENTS TO DISGUISE PROPERTY DIVISION AS ALIMONY

Child support is not the only financial matter that the parties may try to disguise as alimony. Like child support, a property division is nondeductible. Hence, parties may try to disguise property division as alimony. When property division is paid in installments, a common tactic of a party who wants to try to disguise property-division payments as alimony is to make substantial payments shortly after the divorce or separation (i.e., to **front load** the payments).

front load

Make substantial "alimony" payments shortly after the separation or divorce in an attempt to disguise nondeductible property division as deductible alimony.

Jim runs a cleaning business, which he developed during his marriage to Pat. When they divorce in 2009, the value of the business is $234,000. During their negotiations for the separation agreement, they both agree that each should receive a one-half share ($117,000) of the business, which Jim wants to continue to run after the divorce. They are clearly thinking about a property division. Of course, any payments pursuant to a property division are not deductible. Jim suggests a different route: He will pay Pat the following amounts of "alimony" during the first three years of their separation:

Year	Amount Paid
2009	$50,000
2010	$45,000
2011	$22,000

In return, Pat will give Jim a release of her interest in the business.

When "alimony" payments decrease or terminate (generally during the first three years after a divorce or separation agreement is in place), a **recapture** may be needed. Recapture is a recalculation of a tax liability in order to remove a deduction (or other tax benefit) to which the taxpayer was not entitled. Here the recalculation would be needed to take back an alimony deduction created by front loading payments that are, in fact, part of a nondeductible property division.

Every three-year reduction (or termination) of "alimony" payments, however, does not trigger the need for a recapture. The general rule is that a recapture is required only in the third year after a taxpayer starts making "alimony" payments under a divorce decree or separation agreement if one of the following conditions is met:

- the "alimony" paid in the third year decreases by more than $15,000 from the second year or
- the "alimony" paid in the second and third years decreases significantly from the alimony paid in the first year.

In the cleaning-business example involving Jim and Pat, the "alimony" payment in the third year was $23,000 less than the "alimony" payment made in the second year ($45,000 − $22,000 = $23,000). This is a decrease of more than $15,000. Therefore, the recapture rule applies. Both Jim and Pat must use an IRS worksheet to determine the amount of the "alimony" deduction that must be recaptured in the third year.

How is the recapture accomplished? As we have seen, a proper alimony payment gives a deduction to the payor and requires the recipient to pay taxes on the alimony received. Both results must be undone if the recapture rule applies. The payor now owes the IRS whatever amount the deduction provided. The recipient can now get back from the IRS (via a deduction) whatever taxes were paid on the mislabeled alimony.

recapture
The recalculation of a tax liability in order to remove a deduction (or other tax benefit) to which the taxpayer was not entitled. An example is an alimony deduction created by front loading payments that are part of a nondeductible property division.

PROPERTY DIVISION

In this section, our focus will be the division of marital property between spouses. Before discussing the tax consequences of such a property division, we need to review some basic terminology.

Tom buys a house in 2002 for $60,000. He spends $10,000 to add a new room. In 2011, he sells the house to a stranger for $100,000.

- ***Transferor*** *The person who transfers an interest in property. Tom is the transferor. An **interest** is a legal share or right in something, which can often be sold or transferred. Here the interest is the ownership of the house.*

- ***Transferee*** *The person to whom an interest in property is transferred. The stranger is the transferee.*

- *Appreciation* An increase in value of property after it is acquired. Tom's house appreciated by $40,000 (from $60,000 to $100,000). He has made a profit, called a gain. The gain, however is not $40,000. See the definition for adjusted basis *below*.

- *Depreciation* A decrease in value of property after it is acquired. If the highest price Tom could have obtained for his house had been $55,000, the house would have depreciated by $5,000.

- *Realize* To receive an actual benefit or to suffer an actual loss from something as opposed to a mere potential (paper) benefit or loss. Income, gain, or loss is usually realized when it is received. Suppose that Tom has an offer to buy his house for $90,000, but he decides not to sell at the present time. He has not realized any income. He has a "paper" gain only, a mere potential gain. He does not have to pay taxes on a gain until he has realized a gain, such as by selling the house.

- *Fair Market Value* The price that could be obtained in an open market between a willing buyer and a willing seller dealing at **arm's** length, *neither being under any compulsion to buy or sell and both having reasonable knowledge of or access to the relevant facts. A transaction is at **arm's length** if the parties treat each other as strangers looking out for their own self-interests with no confidential or other relationship between them that would cause one to expect the other to provide a special advantage or to act with fairness. A sale between a parent and a child will usually not be at fair market value, since the fact that they are related will probably affect the price paid. It is possible for a happily married husband and wife to sell things to each other at fair market value, but the likelihood is that they will not. In our example, Tom sold his house for $100,000 to a stranger. There is no indication that the buyer or seller was pressured into the transaction or that either had any special relationship with each other that might have affected the price or the terms of the deal. The price paid, therefore, was the fair market value.*

- *Basis* The initial capital investment, usually the cost of acquiring the property (also called cost basis). Tom's basis in his house is $60,000.

- *Adjusted Basis* The basis of the property after adjustments and deductions are made. The basis is either adjusted upward (increased) by the amount of **capital improvements** (i.e., structural improvements on the property) or adjusted downward (e.g., for a casualty loss due to a tornado). Tom added a room to his house—a structural improvement. His basis ($60,000) is increased by the amount of the capital expenditure ($10,000), giving him an adjusted basis of $70,000.

When Tom sold his house for $100,000, he *realized* income. To determine whether he realized a gain or profit, we need to compare this figure with his adjusted basis. The amount of gain for tax purposes is determined as follows:

SALE PRICE − ADJUSTED BASIS = TAXABLE GAIN
$100,000 $70,000 $30,000

Tom must declare this gain of $30,000 on his tax return. Of course, if the sale price had been *less* than the adjusted basis, he would have realized a loss. If, for example, he had sold the house for $65,000, his loss would have been $5,000 ($70,000 − $65,000).

TAX CONSEQUENCES OF A PROPERTY DIVISION

The general rule on the tax treatment of property divisions is as follows:

Transfers of property because of a divorce (i.e., incident to a divorce) are not reportable as income by the transferee, nor are they deductible by the transferor. The basis of the property in the hands of the transferee is the same as the transferor's basis, which is his adjusted basis.

A property division can be in cash or in noncash. To illustrate:

Cash property division: Ex-wife receives a lump sum of $50,000 (or five yearly payments of $10,000) in exchange for the release of any rights she may have in property acquired during the marriage.

Noncash property division: Ex-wife receives the marital home, and ex-husband receives stocks and the family business. They both release any rights they may have in property acquired during the marriage.

Cash property divisions rarely pose difficulties unless the parties are trying to disguise property division as alimony in order to take advantage of the deductibility of alimony. We already discussed the circumstances under which such attempts will be unsuccessful. A true property division in cash is a nontaxable event; nothing is deducted and nothing is included in the income of either party. The IRS will assume that what was exchanged was of equal value.

Suppose, however, that property other than cash is transferred in a property division and that the noncash property so transferred has *appreciated* in value since the time it was acquired.

In 1995, Tom inherits a cottage from his aunt with a fair market value of $60,000. In 1996, he spends $10,000 to add a room to the cottage. In 2001, Tom marries Tara. They divorce in 2011. As part of their property division, Tom transfers the cottage to Tara. Its fair market value in 2011 is $100,000.

The adjusted basis of the house in 2011 is $70,000 (the inheritance value of $60,000 plus the capital improvement of $10,000). If Tom had transferred the house to a stranger for $100,000, he would have realized a gain of $30,000 ($100,000 less his adjusted basis of $70,000). The picture is dramatically different, however, when property is transferred to a spouse because of (i.e., incident to) a divorce.

When *appreciated* property is transferred as part of a property division in a divorce, there is no gain or loss realized. In the example of Tara and Tom, the transferor (Tom) does not realize a gain, even though he transferred a $100,000 house with an adjusted basis of $70,000 to the transferee (Tara).

What is the transferee's basis in appreciated property that is transferred as part of a property division? The transferee's basis is the same as the adjusted basis of the transferor at the time of the transfer.[2] Hence, Tara's basis in the house when she receives it is $70,000, which was Tom's adjusted basis when he transferred it to her as part of the divorce settlement.

Assume that a week after Tara receives the cottage, she sells it to a stranger for $105,000. On these facts, she would realize a gain of $35,000 because her basis in the cottage is $70,000, which was its adjusted basis when she received it from Tom.

$$\text{SALE PRICE} - \text{ADJUSTED BASIS} = \text{TAXABLE GAIN}$$
$$\$105,000 \qquad \$70,000 \qquad \$35,000$$

Needless to say, it is essential that a spouse know the adjusted basis of the property in the hands of the other spouse before accepting that property as part of a property division. It can be meaningless, for example, to be told that property is "worth $150,000" on the market unless you are also told what the adjusted basis of that property is. Furthermore, the law office representing the transferee must insist that the transferor turn over records that will allow the transferee to determine the adjusted basis of the property. This could include a copy of the original purchase contract and all contractor bills or statements that will prove what capital improvements were made to the property. Without such records, the transferee will not be able to tell the IRS, perhaps years later, what the adjusted basis of the property is.

INCIDENT TO A DIVORCE

To take advantage of the basis rule we have been discussing, the property division must be **incident to divorce**. A property transfer is incident to a divorce when:

incident to divorce
(a) Occurring within one year after the date a marriage ends or (b) relating to the ending of a marriage because it occurs within six years after a marriage ends pursuant to a divorce decree or separation agreement.

- the transfer occurs within one year after the marriage ends *or*
- the transfer is related to the ending of the marriage.

A property transfer is related to the ending of the marriage when:

- the transfer occurs within six years after the marriage ends *and*
- the transfer is made under the divorce or separation instrument.

LEGAL AND RELATED FEES IN OBTAINING A DIVORCE

Obtaining a divorce can be expensive. In addition to attorney fees, one or both parties may have to hire an accountant, actuary, and appraiser. Only two types of such fees are deductible:

- Fees paid for tax advice in connection with a divorce
- Fees paid to obtain alimony

Other fees are not deductible. For example, you cannot deduct legal fees paid to negotiate the property division. Also, when legal fees are deductible, they must be your own legal fees. An ex-husband, for example, cannot deduct legal fees he is required to pay for his ex-wife's attorney even if the fees are for tax or alimony advice for her.

Bills from professionals received by a taxpayer should include a breakdown showing the amount charged for each service performed.

Examples:

For legal representation in divorce case	$9,000
For tax advice in connection with the divorce	$ 800
Total bill	$9,800

Only $800 is deductible.

For legal representation in divorce case	$6,500
For legal representation in obtaining alimony	$1,200
Total bill	$7,700

Only $1,200 is deductible.

To deduct fees for these services, the taxpayer must itemize deductions in the year claimed. They go on Schedule A of the 1040 return under Miscellaneous Deductions.

Fees paid to appraisers, actuaries, and accountants can also be deducted but only to the extent of their services in determining how much tax is owed or in helping to obtain alimony.

INNOCENT SPOUSE RELIEF

What happens when the IRS determines that taxes, interest, and penalties are due on prior joint returns of spouses who have just divorced? Who pays? Frequently, one of the spouses simply signed the return prepared by the other spouse with little knowledge of the sources of income reported on the return—or that should have been reported on the return. Although the less-involved spouse can be the husband or the wife, the following discussion will assume it is the homemaker/wife because this is the most common occurrence.

When the IRS audits the return, the ex-wife says, "I was not involved in his business; I just signed what he told me to sign; I never kept any of the records. I have no idea how to come up with records or anything involved with the return." The general rule, however, is that the signers of a joint return are jointly *and individually* responsible for taxes, interest, and penalties due on the return. (It is called **joint and several liability**.) The IRS has the right to collect all of taxes, interest, and penalties from either spouse even if:

- the spouses are now divorced
- the separation agreement specifies that only the ex-husband must pay
- the divorce decree orders only the ex-husband to pay

The IRS could still demand payment from the wife. This, of course, could create a substantial hardship if the husband is unwilling or unable to pay due to obstinacy, disappearance, or financial setbacks.

The IRS never signed the separation agreement and was not a party to the divorce litigation. Hence, the IRS is not bound by the separation agreement or divorce decree. The ex-husband is bound by them. If the ex-wife is forced to pay the IRS, she can sue the ex-husband for violating the separation agreement or court order, but she cannot escape the rule of joint and several liability with the IRS. There is, however, a possible way out for her if she qualifies for an exception to this rule.

The exception is called **innocent spouse relief.** The ex-spouse claiming this relief must prove that at the time she signed the return she did not know and had no reason to know that her husband had understated the taxes that were due. The IRS will decide whether, under all the facts and circumstances of the case, it would be unfair to hold her responsible for the understatement of tax due on the return.

In 2010 there were 50,149 applications for innocent-spouse relief. Of this number, 7,683 were granted in full; 6,383 were partially granted.[3]

joint and several liability
Legally responsible together and individually. Each debtor is individually responsible for the entire debt; the plaintiff/creditor can choose to collect the full debt from one debtor or from all of them until the debt is satisfied.

innocent-spouse relief
A former spouse will not be liable for taxes, interest, and penalties owed on prior joint returns if (a) he or she did not know or have reason to know that the other spouse understated the taxes due and (b) it would be unfair to hold the innocent spouse responsible for the understatement of tax on the return.

ASSIGNMENT 11.1

John and Carol are divorced on September 1, 2011. Their separation agreement requires John to pay Carol $500 a month for her support until she dies. Use the guidelines of this chapter to answer the following questions, which present a number of variations in the case of John and Carol. (See General Instructions for the Legal-Analysis Assignment in Appendix A.)

a. Carol has an automobile accident. To help her with medical bills, John sends her a check for $900 with the following note: "Here's my monthly $500 payment plus an extra $400 alimony to help you with your medical bills." Can John deduct the entire $900 as alimony?

b. A year after the divorce, Carol has trouble paying her state income tax bill of $1,200. John wants to give her a gift of $1,200 in addition to his regular $500 monthly alimony. He sends $1,200 to the state tax department on her behalf. Can John deduct the $1,200 as alimony?

c. A September 1, 2011, divorce decree awards Carol $1,500 a month in alimony, effective immediately and payable on the first of each month. John makes a payment on September 1, 2011, and on October 1, 2011. When John made these two payments, he lived in the basement of their home, which has a separate entrance. He moves into his own apartment in another town on October 25, 2011. Which of the following 2011 payments, if any, are deductible: $1,500 (on September 1) and $1,500 (on October 1)?

(continued)

ASSIGNMENT 11.1 *(continued)*

d. Under the terms of a separation agreement, John must make annual alimony payments to Carol of $30,000, ending on the earlier of the expiration of 15 years or the death of Carol. If she lives for 15 years, he would have paid her $450,000 ($30,000 × 15). The agreement also provides that if Carol dies before the end of the 15 years, John must pay Carol's estate the difference between the total amount he would have paid her if she lived the 15 years and the amount actually paid. Carol dies after the tenth year, after John had paid her $300,000 ($30,000 × 10). John now pays her estate $150,000 ($450,000 − $300,000). How much of the $300,000 paid before her death is deductible alimony? How much of the $150,000 lump sum is deductible alimony?

ASSIGNMENT 11.2

a. Under the terms of a separation agreement, John will pay Carol $200 a month in child support for their teenage child, Nancy, and $900 a month as alimony. If Nancy marries, however, the $900 alimony payment will be reduced to $400 a month. What is deductible?

b. Greg was born on July 31, 1990. He is the only child of Bill and Karen. Under the terms of their separation agreement, which becomes effective on December 5, 2005, Bill is to have custody of Greg, and Karen is to pay him $4,000 a month in alimony. The agreement specifies that "none of the alimony is to be used for child support." On April 15, 2008, the alimony payment is to be reduced to $2,200 a month. What will be deductible in 2008?

ASSIGNMENT 11.3

Millie pays Paul the following amounts of alimony under the terms of her 1987 divorce decree:

Year	Amount
1987	$25,000
1988	$ 4,000
1989	$ 4,000

Does any alimony have to be captured? Why or why not?

ASSIGNMENT 11.4

Under a 2009 separation agreement and divorce decree, Helen transfers a building (which is her separate property) to her ex-husband, Ken, in exchange for his release of any rights he has in other property that Helen acquired during the marriage. The transfer is made on the day of the divorce. Helen had bought the building in 1986 for $1,000,000. In 2007, she made $200,000 worth of capital improvements in the building. Its fair market value on the date she transfers it to Ken is $1,500,000. A week later, however, the market crashes, and Ken is forced to sell the building for $800,000. What are the tax consequences of these transactions?

■ PARALEGAL ROLES

- For an overview of paralegal roles in family-law cases, see Exhibits 1-3 and 1-4 in Chapter 1.

- For many of the financial issues related to taxation and divorce covered in Chapter 11, a paralegal may be asked to help collect documents and facts outlined in:
  - the checklist in Exhibit 3-1 of Chapter 3
  - the interrogatories in Appendix C

- Miscellaneous duties:
  - Enter due dates on tickler system for final income tax returns and estate tax returns.
  - Assist the attorney negotiating the separation agreement by collecting all documentation needed to argue the tax effect of proposed terms.
  - Use tax software to prepare reports on the tax effects of various negotiating positions the attorney will present.
  - Obtain needed tax return forms (state income, federal income, and estate).
  - Assist client in gathering needed data and support documentation for the tax returns.
  - Locate candidates for appraisers, accountants, and other professionals needed for the preparation of the returns.
  - Act as liaison with and monitor professionals hired by the firm.
  - Prepare a preliminary draft of the estate tax returns.
  - Secure client signature on the returns.

■ CHECK THE CITE

James Guth formed a church (Universal Life Church) and named himself pastor for perceived tax advantages. He named his wife, Arlys Guth, treasurer of the church's bank account. They both signed the joint tax returns that were filed. The IRS later determined that deductions made on the returns for charitable purposes were improper. Why did the IRS assert that Arlys Guth was liable for the deficiencies that resulted from these deductions? Why was she successful in asserting the defense of innocent spouse? See *Guth v. C.I.R.*, 897 F.2d 441 (9th Cir. 1990). To read the opinion online, run a name search ("Guth v. C.I.R.") in the Legal Documents database of Google Scholar (scholar.google.com).

■ PROJECT

In Google, Bing, or Yahoo, run the following search: "dependency exemption" tax divorce. Write a short essay in which you explain how a divorced couple can determine who is entitled to the dependency exemption on the tax returns filed after the divorce. You must cite and quote from a minimum of 10 different sources that you find on the Internet. At least four of these sources should be statutes, court opinions, regulations or other laws.

■ ETHICS IN A FAMILY LAW PRACTICE

You are a paralegal working at a law office that is representing David Harrison, a wealthy landowner whom everyone knows because of his exposure in the media. He is challenging the IRS's rejection of his claim of the deductibility of over $2 million in alimony. You work on this case because your supervising attorney is the main tax attorney at the firm. One day after a long day at work, your spouse asks you if you have had a bad day. You respond, "The Harrison case is driving me crazy; there is a good chance he may lose his $2 million deduction." Any ethical problems?

■ WRITING SAMPLE

Select one of the fact situations in Assignment 11.1, 11.2, 11.3, or 11.4 and prepare a legal memo in which you discuss the federal law that applies to the facts. (If you use 11.1 or 11.2, you can do the memo on one of its subparts.) You must cite and quote from a minimum of five different sources that you find on the Internet. All of the sources must be federal statutes, federal court opinions, federal regulations, or other federal laws. (See General Instructions for the Writing Sample in Appendix A.)

SUMMARY

Tax consequences should be a part of the negotiation process in a separation and divorce. The parties must know the tax effect of every financial component involved. Alimony is deductible by the payor and taxable for the payee. Child-support payments and property divisions are neither deductible nor taxable.

Alimony is deductible if it is paid to a spouse or former spouse under a divorce decree or separation instrument; if the parties do not file a joint tax return with each other; if they are not members of the same household when the payment is made; if the payment is in cash; if there is no obligation to make the payment after the death of the recipient; if the payment is not improperly disguised as alimony; and if the parties have not exercised the option of treating qualifying alimony payments as nonalimony.

The deductibility of alimony can be lost if a payment is to be reduced upon the occurrence of a contingency relating to a child, or is reduced at a time that is clearly associated with a contingency relating to a child. If substantial payments are made within three years after a divorce or separation, the IRS will suspect that the parties are trying to disguise nondeductible, property-division payments as deductible alimony payments. Such excessive front loading may result in a recalculation of taxes paid in the third year in order to recapture improper deductions for alimony.

In a property division incident to a divorce, property is transferred from one ex-spouse to the other. The property can be cash (e.g., $50,000) or noncash (e.g., a house). When there is a transfer of cash, none of it is deducted by the transferor, and none of it is included in the income of the transferee. When there is a transfer of noncash property that has appreciated in value, the transferor cannot deduct anything, the transferee does not include anything in income, the transferor does not pay taxes on the amount of the appreciation, and the basis of the property in the hands of the ex-spouse transferee is the adjusted basis that the property had in the hands of the transferor.

A fee paid to your own attorney, accountant, or other professional is deductible if paid to obtain tax advice in connection with a divorce or if paid to help you obtain alimony that is included in gross income. Under the innocent-spouse rule, a former spouse will not be liable for taxes and penalties owed on prior joint returns if he or she can prove that at the time he or she signed the return, he or she did not know and had no reason to know that the other spouse understated the tax due and if the IRS concludes that it would be unfair to hold this spouse responsible for the understatement of tax on the return.

KEY TERMS

tax effect	front load	fair market value
gross income	recapture	arm's length
adjusted gross income (AGI)	transferor	basis
instrument	interest	adjusted basis
interlocutory	transferee	capital improvement
pendente lite	appreciation	incident to divorce
property division	depreciation	joint and several liability
contingency	realize	innocent spouse relief

REVIEW QUESTIONS

1. What is meant by tax effecting a clause in a separation agreement?

2. What are the tax consequences of alimony payments, child-support payments, and property division?

3. In what ways does taxation enter the bargaining process for a separation agreement?

4. Where is the payment and receipt of alimony entered on the 1040 return?

5. What are the seven tests for deductible alimony?

6. What is the one-month grace period on living in the same household?

7. When can cash payments made to a third person be deductible alimony?

8. When does a reduction in "alimony" payments constitute nondeductible child support?

9. What is front loading?

10. What is the recapture rule?

11. When is gain or loss realized?

12. What is the fair market value of something?

13. How is the adjusted basis of property determined?

14. What are the tax consequences of a property division in cash?

15. What are the tax consequences of a property division of appreciated property?

16. When is a property transfer incident to a divorce?

17. What legal and related fees in obtaining a divorce are deductible?

18. When will an innocent spouse be given relief on past-due taxes, interest, and penalties on joint tax returns?

HELPFUL WEBSITES

DivorceInfo: Taxes in Divorce
- www.divorceinfo.com/taxes.htm

Tax Resources on the Web
- taxtopics.net/topic4.htm#div

Internal Revenue Service: Divorce and Separation
- www.irs.gov/publications/p17/ch02.html

Internal Revenue Service: Alimony
- www.irs.gov/taxtopics/tc452.html
- www.irs.gov/publications/p17/ch18.html

Internal Revenue Service: Innocent Spouse Relief
- www.irs.gov/publications/p971/ar02.html
- www.irs.gov/pub/irs-pdf/p971.pdf
- www.irs.gov/individuals/content/0,,id=130302,00.html

Internal Revenue Service: Injured Spouse Allocation
- www.irs.gov/pub/irs-pdf/f8379.pdf

Miscellaneous Tax Sites for Divorce and Separation
- www.hrblock.com/taxes/tax_tips/tax_planning/divorce.html
- www.divorcenet.com/states/nationwide/legal_fees_what_is_deductible
- www.divorcenet.com/states/nationwide/the_seven_alimony_rules

Google/Bing/Yahoo Searches
(on these search engines, run the following searches, substituting your state for "aa")
- tax divorce aa
- alimony tax aa
- "front loading" alimony aa
- estoppel "child support" aa
- "incident to divorce" aa
- "child support" taxation aa
- "property division" tax aa
- recapture tax divorce aa
- divorce tax penalty aa
- "innocent spouse" divorce tax aa

ENDNOTES

[1] Internal Revenue Service, *Publication 504* (2014).

[2] The rule was otherwise before 1984, when gain was recognized if appreciated property was transferred because of a divorce. This was the ruling of *United States v. Davis*, 370 U.S. 65 (1962). Transferors complained bitterly. They could not claim a deduction (since the property division was not alimony), and they had to pay taxes on paper gains due to the appreciation. Congress changed the law in 1984 so that gains and losses were no longer recognized in property divisions due to a divorce. The change negated the ruling of *United States v. Davis*.

[3] Charles Delafuente, *Some Advice for Wary Spouses: Consider Filing a Separate Return*, N.Y. Times, Feb. 13, 2011, at BU11 (www.nytimes.com/2011/02/13/business/yourtaxes/13spouse.html).

12 The Legal Rights of Women

CHAPTER OUTLINE

CHAPTER OBJECTIVES

After completing this chapter, you should be able to:

- Know the disabilities faced by married women at common law.

- Explain what disabilities no longer exist under current law.

- State the impact of the married women's property acts.

- Understand dower and curtesy and their substitute, elective share.

- Explain how a person can change a surname.

- List the prohibitions on discrimination against women in obtaining credit.

- Understand when a job requirement is a bona fide

occupational qualification (BFOQ).

- Explain when wage discrimination is illegal.

- Know what kinds of questions are illegal in a job interview.

- Explain pregnancy, breast milk expression, family leave, and medical leave rights of a female employee.

- Distinguish between the two categories of sexual harassment.

- Explain why Paula Jones lost her claim of sexual harassment against Governor Bill Clinton.

- Describe how sex discrimination laws are enforced.

- State the right of individuals to contraceptives.

- Know when a person can be sterilized.

- State the abortion rights of a woman.

- List the major categories of domestic violence and the available remedies to respond to it.

- Explain the battered woman syndrome.

- State whether marital rape is a crime.

- Explain ways in which sensitivity can be shown to victims of domestic violence.

U.S. Supreme Court (1872):

Man is, or should be, woman's protector and defender. The natural and proper timidity and delicacy which belongs to the female sex evidently unfits it for many of the occupations of civil life. The constitution of the family organization, which is founded in the divine ordinance, as well as in the nature of things, indicates the domestic sphere as that which properly belongs to the domain and function of womanhood. . . . The paramount destiny and mission of woman are to fulfill the noble and benign offices of wife and mother. This is the law of the Creator. *Bradwell v. Illinois*, 83 U.S. (16 Wall.) 130, 141, 21 L. Ed. 442 (1872).

———————

U.S. Supreme Court (1975):

No longer is the female destined solely for the home and the rearing of the family, and only the male for the marketplace, and the world of ideas. *Stanton v. Stanton*, 421 U.S. 7, 14 (1975).

THE STATUS OF WOMEN AT COMMON LAW

Today a married woman would consider it condescending to be told that she has the right to:

- Make her own will
- Own her own property
- Make a contract in her own name
- Be a juror
- Vote
- Sue someone (and be sued)
- Execute a deed
- Keep her own earnings

There was a time in our history, however, when a married woman could engage in none of these activities, at least not without the consent of her husband. When a woman married, "the common law took the view that she forfeited her legal existence and became the property of her husband, and her services and earnings belonged to him."[1] A married woman was a **feme covert**, a covered woman—covered by the identity of her husband. The legal status of a married woman was called **coverture**, whereby her civil existence for many purposes merged with (was covered up by) that of her husband. For example, she could not bring a suit against a third party unless her husband agreed to join in the suit as a party. Upon marriage, she could not own personal property. Any personal property that she acquired automatically became her husband's property. If she committed a crime in the presence of her husband, the law assumed that he forced her to commit it. If she worked outside the home, her husband was entitled to her earnings. To a large degree, a married woman was the property of her husband. In short, **at common law**, the husband and wife were considered one person, and the one person was the husband. This was the essence of the **unity of person** or spousal-unity rule.

An *un*married woman at common law was not as restricted; she could own property and enter into contracts in her own name. But she could not vote or serve on juries, and her inheritance rights were limited.[2]

Today, a married woman has her own legal identity: "In today's society, regardless of what individual couples believe and practice, the law does not recognize the husband as the 'one public voice' or as the automatic head

feme covert
(A covered woman) A married woman.

coverture
The legal status of a married woman whereby her civil existence for many purposes merged with (was covered up by) that of her husband.

at common law
During a time in our early history when law was created by court opinions and legislatures, often before it was changed by later legislatures.

unity of person
The now-rejected view that the legal identity of a wife was subsumed into the legal identity of the husband. Also called doctrine of oneness, spousal-unity rule.

of household with supreme authority over his nonresponsible feme covert. A married woman now has her own separate legal identity."[3] Consequently, family law has gone through what is called *degenderization*, a gradual shifting away from a system that defines family roles and most property rights on the basis of gender.

CONTRACTS AND CONVEYANCES

Women now have the power to enter all forms of **contracts** and **conveyances** in their own names, independent of their husbands. If, however, both spouses own property together, the wife normally must have the consent of her husband—and vice versa—to convey the property to someone else.

Contracts *between* the spouses in an ongoing marriage are also possible. Such agreements are often referred to as **postnuptial agreements**. (For examples of such agreements, see Exhibit 4-1 in Chapter 4.) There are, however, some restrictions on what spouses can do in a postnuptial agreement. For example, they cannot contract away their obligation to support each other (although this is possible in a separation agreement, as we saw in Chapter 8).

Courts tend to be very suspicious of conveyances of property between husband and wife. Suppose, for example, that a husband transfers all his property into his wife's name (for which she pays nothing), so that when he is sued by his creditors, he technically does not own any assets from which they can satisfy their claims. Because the transfer was made with little or no **consideration** and was made to avoid an obligation to a creditor, it is a **fraudulent transfer** and, if challenged, would be invalidated by a court.

Nonfraudulent transactions between spouses can also cause difficulty when a spouse uses his or her separate funds to buy property that he or she then places in the sole name of the other spouse:

- A husband buys a cottage with his separate funds and places the title to the cottage in his wife's name. (Assume that this is not a fraudulent transfer; he is not trying to defraud his creditors.)
- The wife buys stock with her separate funds and places the title to the stock in her husband's name. (Again, assume no intent to defraud her creditors.)

Many courts presume that when husbands or wives use their own money to buy property that they put into the names of the other spouse, they are making a **gift** of the property to the other spouse unless it is clear that they had a different intention. There are some courts, however, that treat the two examples differently. In the first, they presume the husband was making a gift to his wife, but in the second, they presume that the wife intended the husband to hold the property in **trust** for her. Arguably, however, treating husbands and wives differently in this regard is unconstitutional as a violation of equal protection.

MARRIED WOMEN'S PROPERTY ACTS

Most states have enacted **married women's property acts**, which remove disabilities married women suffered at common law. Under the terms of such statutes, married women are given the right to enter contracts, own and dispose of their property, and be parties to litigation (suing and being sued) independent of their husbands. Without such laws, a married woman would not have a separate legal existence. The effect of the married women's property acts was to abolish the unity of person.

---

contract

A legally enforceable agreement. The elements of most contracts are offer, acceptance, and consideration. Some contracts must be in writing.

conveyance

The transfer of an interest in property. The verb is *convey*.

postnuptial agreement

A contract between married persons that covers financial and related matters. The spouses may have no intention of separating. If they have this intention, the contract is commonly called a separation agreement.

consideration

Something of value that is exchanged between parties. It can be an act, a forbearance (not performing an act), a promise to perform an act, or a promise to refrain from performing an act.

fraudulent transfer

A transfer of an asset for little or no payment or consideration that is made to avoid an obligation to a creditor.

gift

The voluntary delivery of something with the present intent to transfer title and control, for which no payment or consideration is made. The person making the gift is the *donor*. The person receiving it is the *donee*.

trust

A device or arrangement by which its creator (the settlor or trustor) transfers property (the corpus) to a person (the trustee) who holds legal title for the benefit of another (the beneficiary or cestui que trust).

married women's property acts

Statutes removing all or most of a woman's legal disabilities on matters such as entering contracts, disposing of her property, and being a party to litigation independent of her husband.

EQUITABLE DISTRIBUTION

In Chapter 8, we examined the law of **property division** upon divorce in common-law states and in community-property states. We saw that changes in the law have resulted in a substantial leveling of the field in establishing the property rights of husbands and wives upon divorce. In both kinds of states, most courts use varying versions of **equitable distribution**—the just and fair, but not necessarily equal, division of property between spouses upon divorce.

DOWER, CURTESY, AND ELECTIVE SHARE

At common law, when a husband died, the surviving wife was given the protection of **dower**, which was the right of a surviving wife to the lifetime use of one-third of all the land her deceased husband owned during the marriage. (The right to use property during one's life is called a **life estate**.) The practical impact of dower was that the husband could not sell his property to others unless his wife waived her dower rights. Buyers were unlikely to want to buy property encumbered by the dower rights of the seller's wife.

If the wife died first, the husband's comparable right at common law was called **curtesy**—his right to a life estate in all the land his wife owned during the marriage (with the added proviso that his right was contingent on a child having been born to the couple).

Today most states have abolished dower and curtesy. In its place they give the surviving spouse an **elective share** in all of the property the deceased spouse owned at death. The elective share is also called a *forced share* because the surviving spouse can elect to take it in place of, *and in spite of,* what the will of the deceased spouse says the surviving spouse should receive.

- If the surviving spouse does *not* choose the elective share, he or she receives whatever is provided for him or her in the will of the deceased spouse.

- If the surviving spouse *does* choose the elective share, he or she usually receives the equivalent of an **intestate** share of the deceased spouse's assets. Intestacy means dying without a valid will. When someone dies intestate, designated relatives receive designated shares of the deceased's assets. When a surviving spouse chooses an elective share, the deceased's will is ignored. Indeed, the deceased is treated as if he or she had died intestate. Whatever share is given to the surviving spouse of a deceased intestate spouse is given to the surviving spouse who chooses the elective share. (In one state, for example, the elective share is $50,000 or one-third of the net estate of the deceased spouse, whichever is greater.)

Unfortunately, relics of the old law still exist on the books of many states. New Jersey, for example, did not repeal the following outrageous law until 2011:

> If a wife after being ravished, consent to the ravisher, she shall be disabled and forever barred from having her . . . dower, unless her husband is voluntarily reconciled to her and permits her to dwell with him, in which case she shall be restored to her . . . dower.[4]

ASSIGNMENT 12.1

If a surviving spouse in your state is not satisfied with the property left for him or her in the deceased spouse's will, what are the options of the surviving spouse? Can he or she elect against the will? If so, what does the election provide? (See General Instructions for the State-Code Assignment in Appendix A.)

---

property division

The allocation and distribution of property between spouses (or ex-spouses) after a legal separation or divorce. Also called property settlement, property distribution.

equitable distribution

The just and fair, but not necessarily equal, division of property between spouses upon divorce.

dower

The right of a widow to the lifetime use (called a life estate) of one-third of the land her deceased husband owned during the marriage. (Owned means *fee simple*, the most complete form of ownership possible.) For dower to exist, some states imposed the requirement that she die leaving issue capable of inheriting the estate.

life estate

An interest in property whose duration is limited to the life of an individual. An ownership of property that lasts as long as a designated person is alive. Also called estate for life, life tenancy.

curtesy

The right of a husband to the lifetime use (called a life estate) of all the land his deceased wife owned during the marriage (if issue were born of the marriage).

elective share

The percentage of a deceased spouse's estate that the surviving spouse can choose (elect) to receive despite what the will of the deceased spouse provided for the surviving spouse. Also called right of election, statutory share, forced share.

intestate

(1) Pertaining to someone who dies without a valid will. (2) A person who dies without a valid will.

Dower and curtesy were legal doctrines used in common-law states. In community-property states (see Chapter 8), there was no need for such doctrines because each spouse owned 50 percent of all marital (community) property by virtue of the marriage.

SURNAME CHANGE

In most states, there are two main ways that persons can legally change their surname: the *usage* method (often called the common law method) and the *statutory* method. The usage method simply involves using a new surname. The new name becomes one's legal name without going through any court or agency procedure. The main requirement is that the use of the name must be

* exclusive (only one new name will be used),
* consistent (the new name will be used for all purposes), and
* nonfraudulent (the new name is not used to avoid creditors or to help commit some other illegal act).

The statutory method is a formal *change-of-name* procedure involving several steps (e.g., filing a petition to change one's name in the appropriate state court, stating the reasons for the change, paying a fee to the court, and publishing a notice of the court proceeding in a local newspaper). The procedure is usually not complicated so long as the court is convinced that the name change will not mislead anyone who may need to contact the individual (e.g., police officials, a former spouse, creditors). The main reason many persons use the statutory method is to have an official acknowledgement that the change has been made, an important step in the age of identity theft. Once the name is changed, it is the responsibility of the individual to notify insurance companies, motor vehicle departments, banks, etc., of the change.

Many women change their surnames to those of their husbands at the time of marriage or use a hybrid or combination name consisting of her maiden name and his surname. The change occurs by the usage method. By custom, they simply start using the new names. No formal procedures are necessary. Because name changes upon marriage are relatively common, women upon marriage rarely, if ever, use the statutory method.

In some states, grooms are treated differently. If a man wishes to change his surname upon marriage, these states require him to use a version of the statutory method. Because brides do not have this requirement, the different treatment is subject to challenge as a denial of the equal protection of the law.

Brides who keep their maiden names are likely to be older, career women. About 23 percent of women kept their maiden names in the 1990s; the percentage fell to about 18 percent in the 2000s.[5] Women who take their husbands' names do so for one of two reasons:

* The law of the state gives them a choice of keeping their maiden names or taking their husbands' names, and they choose the latter.
* The law of the state gives them a choice that they do not know about; they use their husbands' names simply because that is the custom.

At one time, the law of some states *required* a woman to use her husband's name. Such laws either have been repealed or struck down as a violation of equal protection because husbands were not required to take the names of their wives.

In states where same-sex marriage is legal, the couple has the same name-change rights as an opposite-sex couple. In most states that recognize domestic partnerships, a domestic partner can change his or her name to that of the other partner, or use a hyphenated name.

Upon divorce, all courts will grant a woman's request that she be allowed to resume her maiden name or to use another name. Suppose, however, that she asks the divorce court to change the name of the children of the marriage. She may want them to have her new name or to take the name of the man she will marry when the divorce is final. Courts will not automatically grant such a request. They will want to be sure that the change would not harm the relationship between the child and the noncustodial father and that the change would be in the best interests of the child.

ASSIGNMENT 12.2

Prepare a flowchart of all the steps that an individual must go through to change his or her name in your state through the appropriate statutory procedure. (See General Instructions for the Flowchart Assignment in Appendix A.)

CREDIT

The federal Equal Credit Opportunity Act prohibits discrimination on the basis of sex or marital status in a credit application.[6] Creditors such as banks, finance companies, and department stores that violate the prohibition can be liable for damages, attorney fees, and court costs.

- When you apply for credit, a creditor:
  1. Must not discourage you from applying or reject your application because of your marital status.
  2. Must not consider your sex.
  3. Must not impose different terms or conditions (e.g., higher interest rate or fees) based on your sex or marital status.
  4. Must not discount income because of your sex or marital status (e.g., a creditor cannot count a man's salary at 100 percent and a woman's at 75 percent; a creditor may not assume a woman of childbearing age will stop working to raise children).
  5. Must not ask if you are widowed or divorced.
  6. Must not ask about your marital status if you are applying for a separate, unsecured account. However, the creditor (a) may ask about your marital status if you live in a community-property state or (b) may ask about your marital status in every state if you are applying for a joint account or for an account secured by property.
  7. Must not request information about your spouse except (a) when your spouse is applying with you, (b) when your spouse will be allowed to use the account, (c) when you are relying on your spouse's income or on alimony or child-support income from a former spouse, or (d) when you live in a community-property state.
  8. Must not ask about your plans for having or raising children (the creditor, however, can ask about expenses related to your dependents).
  9. Must not ask if you receive alimony, child-support, or separate-maintenance payments unless you will be relying on these payments to obtain credit. If you are not relying on these payments to obtain credit, the creditor can ask if you receive these payments but must tell you that you do not have to provide this information. A creditor can ask if you are required to *make* alimony, child-support, or separate-maintenance payments.
  10. Must not refuse your request that alimony, child-support, or separate-maintenance payments be considered. A creditor may ask you to prove you have received this income consistently.

cosigner
A person who signs a document along with the main signer, usually to agree to pay the debt created by the document in the event that the main signer fails to pay it.

- You also have the right to:
  1. Have credit in your birth name (Mary Smith), your first and your spouse's last name (Mary Jones), or your first name and a combined last name (Mary Smith-Jones).
  2. Obtain credit without a **cosigner** if you meet the creditor's standards.
  3. Have a cosigner other than your spouse if you legitimately need a cosigner.
  4. Keep your own accounts with the creditor after you change your name, change your marital status, reach a certain age, or retire, unless the creditor has evidence that you are not willing or able to pay.
- If you suspect discrimination, you should:
  1. Complain to the creditor; make it known that you are aware of your rights under the law.
  2. Report violations to the appropriate government agency. If you are denied credit, the creditor must give you the name and address of the agency to contact.
  3. Check with your state attorney general to see if the creditor violated state equal credit opportunity laws and, if so, whether the state will prosecute the creditor.
  4. Bring a case in federal district court.[7]

The Federal Trade Commission adds this note of caution to women:

> A good credit history—a record of your bill payments—often is necessary to get credit. This [requirement] can hurt many married, separated, divorced, and widowed women. Typically, there are two reasons women don't have credit histories in their own names: either they lost their credit histories when they married and changed their names, or creditors reported accounts shared by married couples in the husband's name only. If you're married, separated, divorced, or widowed, contact your local credit reporting companies to make sure all relevant bill payment information is in a file under your own name. Your credit report includes information on where you live, how you pay your bills, and whether you've been sued, arrested or filed for bankruptcy. National credit reporting companies sell the information in your report to creditors, insurers, employers, and other businesses that, in turn, use it to evaluate your applications for credit, insurance, employment, or renting a home. The Fair Credit Reporting Act (FCRA) requires each of the three nationwide credit reporting companies—Equifax, Experian, and TransUnion—to give you a free copy of your credit report, at your request, once every twelve months. Use the Internet (annualcreditreport.com) to request your free reports. Also, contact the Federal Trade Commission for assistance (1-877-FTC-HELP; www.ftc.gov).[8]

EMPLOYMENT

BONA FIDE OCCUPATIONAL QUALIFICATION (BFOQ)

There are many laws that in theory have eliminated job discrimination against women. For example, the Equal Protection Clause in the Fourteenth Amendment of the U.S. Constitution provides that:

> No State shall . . . deny to any person within its jurisdiction the equal protection of the laws.

If a state passes a law that treats women differently from men, it will be invalidated unless the different treatment is substantially related to serve an important state interest. (See Exhibit 1-2 in Chapter 1, in which gender is listed as a **quasi-suspect class** calling for **intermediate scrutiny**.) Also, Title VII of the 1964 Civil Rights Act provides that:

> It shall be an unlawful employment practice for an employer . . . to fail or refuse to hire or to discharge any individual, or otherwise to discriminate against any individual with respect to his compensation, terms, conditions, or privileges of employment, because of such individual's . . . sex. . . . [9]

This does not mean that all gender discrimination in employment is illegal. Job-related gender discrimination is permitted if gender is a **bona fide occupational qualification (BFOQ)**, meaning that the gender discrimination is reasonably necessary to the normal operation of a particular business or enterprise. For different treatment (discrimination) of the sexes to be a BFOQ, the essence of the business would have to be undermined if the discrimination could not be used.

Examples:

- It is a BFOQ for an advertising agency to hire only males to model for men's clothes.
- It is a BFOQ for a theater to hire only men to play fathers, sons, and uncles in a play.
- It is a BFOQ for a state prison to exclude women from being guards in all-male prisons where a significant number of the inmates are convicted sex offenders. It is reasonable to anticipate that some of the inmates would attack the female guards, creating a security problem. In this instance, discrimination based on sex (i.e., requiring that guards be male) in an all-male prison is a BFOQ because gender is related to the job of maintaining security.[10]
- It is not a BFOQ for a company to hire only women as bookkeepers because the boss wants to work with women. Gender has no relationship to being a bookkeeper.
- It is not a BFOQ for an airline to hire only female flight attendants even though market research shows that most passengers prefer female flight attendants. Gender has no relationship to performing the job of a flight attendant.
- It is not a BFOQ for a battery manufacturer to discourage women (but not men) from working in jobs that expose them to lead. The exposure has the potential of harming the reproductive process of both women and men. The gender of the worker is not related to the worker's ability to perform the job of making batteries.[11] (See also the discussion of pregnancy on page 491.)

Even if an agency or court ultimately determines that a woman has failed to prove wrongful job discrimination, it is illegal for an employer to retaliate against an employee who files a charge of employment discrimination.

INTERVIEW QUESTIONS

There are certain questions that a job interviewer must not ask at the risk of committing unlawful sex discrimination. Questions about marital status or family life are often based on the assumption that female employees are not as work-oriented as male employees and will be less available and less productive than male employees. Such questions can violate federal or state employment discrimination laws.

quasi-suspect class
A class based on gender or on a child's legitimacy.

intermediate scrutiny
The government's action must be substantially related to serve an important state interest. Also called heightened scrutiny, elevated scrutiny.

bona fide occupational qualification (BFOQ)
An employment qualification based on gender, religion, or other characteristic that is reasonably necessary for the normal operation of a particular business and hence is not an illegal requirement under federal employment discrimination laws.

Examples of Potentially Illegal Questions

- *Are you married?* A woman is not required to disclose her marital status. After a person is hired, however, marital status will be relevant for insurance and tax matters.
- *What is your maiden name?* A woman is not required to disclose her marital status. It is not related to legitimate job requirements.
- *Do you have any children? Do you plan to have any children?* An employer cannot ask about children unless the applicant brings up the topic of children.
- *What kinds of childcare arrangements do you have?*
- *Are you Miss or Mrs.?* Questions should not be asked about marital status.
- *What is the name of your spouse? Does your spouse work? What does your spouse do for a living?* This is another indirect way of asking about marital status.
- *How tall are you? How much do you weigh?* Such questions cannot be asked unless height and weight are necessary job requirements.

Examples of Questions That Can Be Asked

- *What are your career objectives?*
- *Can you make a long-term commitment (e.g., five years) to the employer?*
- *Would you be available to work overtime?*
- *Is there anything that you know of that could cause regular absences from work?*
- *Do you have any restrictions that would prevent you from traveling?*
- *Do you have any relatives who work for this company?* This information may be needed because of the company's **nepotism** policy.

nepotism
Favoritism shown to relatives. A rule against nepotism is called an antinepotism rule.

COMPENSATION

In 2009, the median earnings for full-time, year-round working women were 78.2 percent of men's earnings—$35,549 compared with $45,485.[12] "Women have higher graduation rates than men at all academic levels and by 2019 they are projected to account for 60 percent of all American undergraduates. In 2009, they accounted for more than half of all people employed in management and professional occupations. But at all levels of education, women still earn only 75 percent of what men earn."[13] (See Exhibit 12-1.)

Wage discrimination on the basis of sex can be a violation of Title VII of the 1964 Civil Rights Act discussed earlier. One of the "unlawful employment practice[s]" under Title VII is to discriminate on a matter of compensation because of a person's sex. In addition, the Equal Pay Act of 1963 (EPA) prohibits discrimination on the basis of sex in the payment of wages or benefits, where men and women perform work of similar skill, effort, and responsibility for the same employer under similar working conditions.[14] Under the EPA:

- Employers may not reduce wages of either sex to equalize pay between men and women.
- Employers may not pay a different wage to a person who works in the same job before or after an employee of the opposite sex.

There can, however, be pay differences based on seniority or merit.

Most of the pay-discrimination litigation centers on whether the compensation policy of a business or organization is gender neutral and whether wage disparities are due to legitimate business reasons such as the education, training, or experience requirements of a particular job.

EXHIBIT 12-1 Pay Disparity between Men and Women

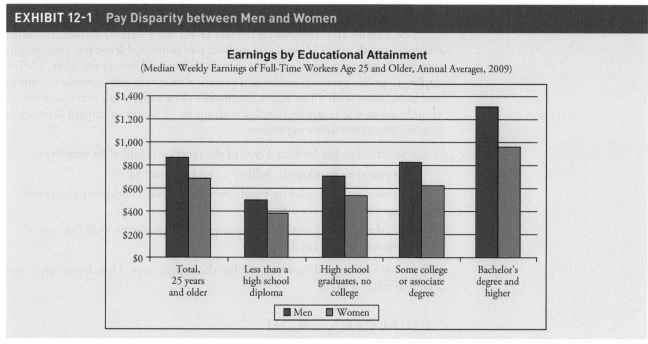

Earnings by Educational Attainment
(Median Weekly Earnings of Full-Time Workers Age 25 and Older, Annual Averages, 2009)

Source: White House Council on Women and Girls, Women in America 32 (March 2011) (www.whitehouse.gov/sites/default/files/rss_viewer/Women_in_America.pdf).

PREGNANCY

An employer cannot:

- Refuse to hire a woman because of her pregnancy-related condition so long as she is able to perform the major functions necessary for the job.
- Terminate a female worker because of pregnancy.
- Force a woman to go on leave at an arbitrary point during pregnancy if she is still able to work.
- Penalize a woman in reinstatement rights, including credit for previous service, accrued retirement benefits, and accumulated seniority.

If a woman is temporarily unable to perform her job due to a medical condition related to pregnancy or childbirth, the employer must treat her the same as any other temporarily disabled employee (e.g., an employee recovering from heart surgery). For example, the employer may have to provide modified tasks, alternative assignments, disability leave, or unpaid leave. These rights are mandated by the Pregnancy Discrimination Act, which is part of Title VII of the Civil Rights Act.[15]

EXPRESSING BREAST MILK

The federal Fair Labor Standards Act requires employers to provide reasonable break time for an employee to express (remove) breast milk for her nursing child for one year after the child's birth, each time the employee needs to express the milk. Employers are also required to provide a place, other than a bathroom, that is shielded from view and free from intrusion from coworkers and the public, which may be used by an employee to express breast milk. Some states have break-time laws that provide more extensive rights for the mother, such as requiring breastfeeding accommodation beyond one year of the baby's birth.[16]

FAMILY AND MEDICAL LEAVE

The Family and Medical Leave Act (FMLA), a federal statute, provides employees with up to 12 weeks of unpaid, job-protected leave per year. It also requires that their group health benefits be maintained during the leave. FMLA applies to public agencies, public and private elementary and secondary schools, and companies with 50 or more employees. The employers must provide an eligible employee (male or female) with up to 12 weeks of unpaid leave each year for any of the following reasons:

* to attend to the birth and care of the newborn child of an employee;
* to attend to an adopted child or a child in foster care;
* to care for an immediate family member (spouse, child, or parent) with a serious health condition; or
* to take medical leave when the employee is unable to work because of a serious health condition.[16a]

A few states offer paid family leave for these purposes. This, however, is not required under FMLA.

SEXUAL HARASSMENT

sexual harassment
Unwanted and offensive sexual advances, contact, comments, or other interaction.

Sexual harassment is unwanted and offensive sexual advances, contact, comments, or other interaction. On the job, two categories of sexual harassment constitute an unlawful employment practice under Title VII of the Civil Rights Act:

Quid pro quo sexual harassment: Submission to or rejection of unwelcome sexual conduct used as a basis for employment decisions on promotion or other job-related benefits.

Hostile environment sexual harassment: Pervasive unwelcome sexual conduct or sex-based ridicule that unreasonably interferes with an individual's job performance or that creates an intimidating, hostile, or offensive working environment, even if no tangible or economic consequences result.

An example of quid pro quo sexual harassment is a worker who is fired for refusing to become sexually intimate with a supervisor. An example of hostile environment sexual harassment is an office or other workplace that is pervaded by people telling dirty jokes, displaying obscene pictures, making graphic comments about the bodies of other persons, touching themselves sexually in the presence of others, persistently asking for dates, etc. This can be sexual harassment even if the person offended by such conduct is not being asked to engage in such behavior or is not being denied an employment benefit for refusing to do so.

Harassment does not have to be of a sexual nature; it can include offensive remarks about a person's sex. For example, it is illegal to harass a woman by making offensive comments about women in general. Both victim and the harasser can be either a woman or a man, and the victim and harasser can be the same sex. The harasser can be the victim's supervisor; a supervisor in another area; a co-worker; or someone who is not an employee of the employer, such as a client or customer.[17]

An employer must actively combat sexual harassment by:

* Establishing a written policy against sexual harassment and distributing it throughout the office.
* Investigating all accusations of sexual harassment promptly.
* Establishing appropriate sanctions for employees who commit sexual harassment.

- Informing employees of their right to raise a charge of sexual harassment under Title VII.

- Informing employees how to assert a complaint of sexual harassment under Title VII.

It is not a defense for an employer to say that it did not know that one of its employees engaged in sexual harassment of another employee or that the harassment took place in spite of a company policy forbidding it. If the employer *should have known of the harassing conduct*, the employer must take immediate and appropriate corrective action, which usually entails more than merely telling all employees not to engage in sexual harassment.

SEXUAL HARASSMENT AND THE GOVERNOR

In 1991, Paula Corbin Jones was a low-level employee of the State of Arkansas. While attending a conference in a Little Rock hotel, Governor Bill Clinton invited her to his hotel room after he thought she displayed "that come-hither look" because of the suggestive way she acted and dressed. The encounter in the suite led to an allegation that he committed sexual harassment. After he became President Clinton, she brought an action against him for sexual harassment and other wrongs. According to plaintiff Jones:

> [U]pon arriving at the suite and announcing herself, the Governor shook her hand, invited her in, and closed the door. She states that a few minutes of small talk ensued, which included the Governor asking her about her job and him mentioning that Dave Harrington, plaintiff's ultimate superior . . . and a Clinton appointee, was his "good friend." Plaintiff states that the Governor then "unexpectedly reached over to [her], took her hand, and pulled her toward him, so that their bodies were close to each other." She states she removed her hand from his and retreated several feet, but that the Governor approached her again and, while saying, "I love the way your hair flows down your back" and "I love your curves," put his hand on her leg, started sliding it toward her pelvic area, and bent down to attempt to kiss her on the neck, all without her consent. Plaintiff states that she exclaimed, "What are you doing?," told the Governor that she was "not that kind of girl," and "escaped" from the Governor's reach "by walking away from him." She states she was extremely upset and confused and, not knowing what to do, attempted to distract the Governor by chatting about his wife. Plaintiff states that she sat down at the end of the sofa nearest the door, but that the Governor approached the sofa where she had taken a seat and, as he sat down, "lowered his trousers" [and requested oral sex]. She states that she was "horrified" by this and that she "jumped up from the couch" and told the Governor that she had to go, saying something to the effect that she had to get back to the registration desk. Plaintiff states that the Governor, [while fondling himself] said, "Well, I don't want to make you do anything you don't want to do," and then pulled up his pants and said, "If you get in trouble for leaving work, have Dave call me immediately and I'll take care of it." She states that as she left the room (the door of which was not locked), the Governor "detained" her momentarily, "looked sternly" at her, and said, "You are smart. Let's keep this between ourselves."

In her suit, Jones alleged both kinds of sexual harassment: quid pro quo and hostile environment, asserting that "[t]here are few more outrageous acts than a criminal sexual assault followed by unwanted exposure, coupled with a demand for oral sex by the most powerful man in the state against a very young, low-level employee."[18]

The trial judge, Susan Webber Wright, disagreed. She dismissed the action by granting the president's motion for a summary judgment. "While the Court will certainly agree that plaintiff's allegations describe offensive conduct, the . . . conduct as alleged by plaintiff describes a mere sexual proposition or encounter, albeit an odious one, that was relatively brief in duration, did not involve any coercion or threats of reprisal, and was abandoned as soon as plaintiff made clear that the advance was not welcome." There was no proof that Governor Clinton's conduct affected any tangible aspects of Jones's compensation, terms, conditions, or privileges of employment. Hence there was no quid pro quo harassment. "Moreover, notwithstanding the offensive nature of the Governor's alleged conduct, plaintiff admits that she never missed a day of work following the alleged incident . . . , she continued to go on a daily basis to the Governor's Office to deliver items and never asked to be relieved of that duty, she never filed a formal complaint or told her supervisors of the incident . . . , she never consulted a psychiatrist, psychologist, or incurred medical bills as a result of the alleged incident, and she acknowledges that her two subsequent contacts with the Governor involved comments made "in a light vein" and nonsexual contact that was done in a "friendly fashion." . . . Plaintiff certainly has not shown under the totality of the circumstances that the alleged incident in the hotel and her additional encounters with . . . the Governor were so severe or pervasive that it created an abusive working environment."[19]

While this court victory was welcomed by President Clinton, his troubles were far from over. Before Judge Wright rendered her decision, the president gave a deposition in the case that gained worldwide notoriety and eventually was a major factor in his impeachment, only the second time in history that a president of the United States has been impeached. During the deposition, the president answered "none" when asked whether there were any female employees of the federal government with whom he had had sexual relations. In particular, he denied having such relations with Monica Lewinsky, a White House intern. A special prosecutor and almost all Republicans in Congress charged that his answers were intentionally false. They believed that lying in a deposition was one of the "high crimes and misdemeanors" that should lead to his removal from office. Ultimately, the Senate as a whole disagreed when it failed to convict the president by the required two-thirds vote. (The vote on this count was 55 [not guilty] and 45 [guilty]. All the senators voting guilty were Republicans.) By acquitting the president, the Senate was saying either that it did not believe the president lied, or that even if he did, the lie and the other charges were not serious enough to remove him from office.

As indicated, the president also won the sexual harassment case when the trial court judge, Susan Wright, eventually ruled that his conduct did not constitute sexual harassment (or the tort of intentional infliction of emotional distress, called outrage in Arkansas). In a stinging rebuke, however, Judge Wright ruled that he had lied during his deposition and held him in civil contempt. One of the consequences of the lie was that the Jones legal team had to spend extra time preparing its case. Hence, the judge ordered the president to pay a fine of $90,000 for reasonable legal fees covering this time. The fee request included an hourly rate for the work of two paralegals on the Jones legal team. In the meantime, Jones was set to appeal Judge Wright's ruling that the president did not commit sexual harassment. The president, however, did not relish the prospect of fighting the appeal, particularly since the appeal would have taken place before the impeachment proceeding in Congress was concluded. Hence, the president decided that the safest legal and political strategy was to settle the case in order to prevent the appeal from going forward. He agreed to pay Jones $850,000 in exchange for her decision to drop her appeal of Judge Wright's ruling against her on the sexual harassment and tort claims.

ENFORCEMENT

Critics claim that the laws outlawing sex discrimination in employment have been inadequately enforced. The law of discrimination can be complex and confusing. Bringing a discrimination case is often time-consuming and expensive.

The **Equal Employment Opportunity Commission (EEOC)** is a federal agency with the primary responsibility of enforcing Title VII of the Civil Rights Act. A charge of employment discrimination (see Exhibit 12-2) can be made to the EEOC in its offices throughout the country. In 2011, 99,947 work-place discrimination complaints were filed with the EEOC; 28.5 percent of them alleged sex discrimination.[20]

Equal Employment Opportunity Commission (EEOC)

The federal agency that enforces federal laws against employment discrimination (www.eeoc.gov).

EXHIBIT 12-2 EEOC Intake Questionnaire (excerpts)

U.S. EQUAL EMPLOYMENT OPPORTUNITY COMMISSION
INTAKE QUESTIONNAIRE

Please immediately complete this entire form and return it to the U.S. Equal Employment Opportunity Commission ("EEOC"). **REMEMBER**, a charge of employment discrimination must be filed within the time limits imposed by law, within 180 days or in some places within 300 days of the alleged discrimination. When we receive this form, we will review it to determine EEOC coverage. **Answer all questions completely, and attach additional pages if needed to complete your responses. If you do not know the answer to a question, answer by stating "not known." If a question is not applicable, write "N/A." (PLEASE PRINT)**

1. Personal Information

Last Name: _____ First Name: _____ MI: _____

....

2. I believe that I was discriminated against by the following organization(s): (Check those that apply)

☐ Employer   ☐ Union   ☐ Employment Agency   ☐ Other (Please Specify) _____

....

4. What is the reason (basis) for your claim of employment discrimination?

FOR EXAMPLE, if you feel that you were treated worse than someone else because of race, you should check the box next to Race. If you feel you were treated worse for several reasons, such as your sex, religion and national origin, you should check all that apply. If you complained about discrimination, participated in someone else's complaint, or filed a charge of discrimination, and a negative action was threatened or taken, you should check the box next to Retaliation.

☐ Race   ☐ Sex   ☐ Age   ☐ Disability   ☐ National Origin   ☐ Religion   ☐ Retaliation   ☐ Pregnancy   ☐ Color (typically a difference in skin shade within the same race)   ☐ Genetic Information; circle which type(s) of genetic information is involved: i. genetic testing   ii. family medical history   iii. genetic services (genetic services means counseling, education or testing)

....

8. Describe who was in the same or similar situation as you and how they were treated. For example, who else applied for the same job you did, who else had the same attendance record, or who else had the same performance? Provide the race, sex, age, national origin, religion, or disability of these individuals, if known, and if it relates to your claim of discrimination. For example, if your complaint alleges race discrimination, provide the race of each person; if it alleges sex discrimination, provide the sex of each person; and so on. Use additional sheets if needed.

Of the persons in the same or similar situation as you, who was treated *better* than you?

| Full Name | Race, Sex, Age, National Origin, Religion or Disability | Job Title | Description of Treatment |

A. _____

....

Of the persons in the same or similar situation as you, who was treated *worse* than you?

| Full Name | Race, Sex, Age, National Origin, Religion or Disability | Job Title | Description of Treatment |

A. _____

....

13. Are there any witnesses to the alleged discriminatory incidents? If yes, please identify them below and tell us what they will say. (Please attach additional pages if needed to complete your response)

| Full Name | Job Title | Address & Phone Number | What do you believe this person will tell us? |

A. _____

....

Please check one of the boxes below to tell us what you would like us to do with the information you are providing on this questionnaire. If you would like to file a charge of job discrimination, you must do so either within 180 days from the day you knew about the discrimination, or within 300 days from the day you knew about the discrimination if the employer is located in a place where a state or local government agency enforces laws similar to the EEOC's laws. **If you do not file a charge of discrimination within the time limits, you will lose your rights.** If you would like more information before filing a charge or you have concerns about EEOC's notifying the employer, union, or employment agency about your charge, you may wish to check Box 1. If you want to file a charge, you should check Box 2.

BOX 1 ☐ I want to talk to an EEOC employee before deciding whether to file a charge. I understand that by checking this box, I have not filed a charge with the EEOC. **I also understand that I could lose my rights if I do not file a charge in time.**

BOX 2 ☐ I want to file a charge of discrimination, and I authorize the EEOC to look into the discrimination I described above. I understand that **the EEOC must give the employer, union, or employment agency that I accuse of discrimination information about the charge, including my name.** I also understand that the EEOC can only accept charges of job discrimination based on race, color, religion, sex, national origin, disability, age, genetic information, or retaliation for opposing discrimination.

Source: Equal Employment Opportunity Commission (www.eeoc.gov/form/upload/Uniform-Intake-Questionnaire.pdf).

Fair Employment Practices Agencies (FEPAs) and Dual Filing

fair employment practices agency (FEPA)
A state or local government agency that enforces state or local employment discrimination laws, often in coordination with the Equal Employment Opportunity Commission (EEOC), which enforces federal employment discrimination laws.

Many states, counties, cities, and towns have their own laws prohibiting discrimination, as well as agencies responsible for enforcing those laws. These state and local agencies are called **fair employment practices agencies (FEPAs)**. The laws enforced by these agencies are often similar to those enforced by EEOC. In some cases, however, the FEPAs enforce laws that offer greater protection to workers, such as protection from discrimination because of sexual orientation. There also may be different deadlines for filing a charge, different standards for determining whether someone is protected by these laws, and different types of relief available to victims of discrimination.

Victims can file discrimination charges with either the EEOC or with a FEPA. When an individual initially files with a FEPA that has a work-sharing agreement with the EEOC, and when the allegation is covered by a law enforced by the EEOC, the FEPA will dual file the charge with EEOC. This means that EEOC will receive a copy of the charge, but the FEPA will usually retain the charge for processing. If the charge is initially filed with EEOC and the charge is also covered by state or local law, EEOC will dual file the charge with the state or local FEPA. This means that the FEPA will receive a copy of the charge, but EEOC will retain the charge for processing.

SEXUALITY AND REPRODUCTIVE RIGHTS

Topics relevant to a discussion of sexuality and reproductive rights include:

- Contraception
- Sterilization
- Abortion
- New routes to motherhood
- Same-sex relationships

The first three topics are discussed below. New routes to motherhood, such as surrogate motherhood, in vitro fertilization, and similar themes, are examined in Chapter 16. Legal problems involving same-sex relationships are covered in Chapter 5 on marriage and Chapter 15 on adoption.

CONTRACEPTION

fundamental right
A right that (a) is specifically guaranteed in the U.S. Constitution, (b) is implicit in the concept of ordered liberty, or (c) is deeply rooted in the nation's history and tradition.

right to privacy
A constitutional right to make personal decisions without undue government interference on matters such as marriage, procreation, family relationships, child rearing and education, contraception, and abortion. The right is implied in specific provisions of the constitution such as the Due Process Clause of the Fourteenth Amendment. Also called right to personal autonomy.

strict scrutiny
The government's action must be narrowly tailored to serve a compelling state interest.

compelling state interest
An interest that is of the highest order; an interest that has a clear justification in the necessities of national or community life.

Married and unmarried individuals cannot be denied access to contraceptives. The decision on whether to procreate is a **fundamental right**, part of the individual's constitutional **right to privacy**: "If the right of privacy means anything, it is the right of the *individual,* married or single, to be free from unwarranted governmental intrusion into matters so fundamentally affecting a person as the decision whether to bear or beget a child."[21] Restrictions on fundamental rights are valid only if they pass the test of **strict scrutiny**: The restriction must be narrowly tailored to serve a **compelling state interest**. (See Exhibits 1-1 and 1-2 in Chapter 1.) The U.S. Supreme Court has held that a law banning contraceptives to adults serves no compelling state interest, and therefore is unconstitutional.

STERILIZATION

Some states have laws that authorize the forced sterilization of persons who are legally considered mentally retarded or insane. Over 60 years ago, the U.S. Supreme Court decided that a state could legally sterilize a person it termed "feeble-minded." The woman in question was an institutionalized 18-year-old who was the daughter of a feeble-minded woman in the same institution; the 18-year-old had already had a baby that was feeble-minded. In an infamous passage, Justice Oliver Wendell Holmes in *Buck v. Bell* said, "Three generations of imbeciles are enough."[22] States that allow forced sterilization have strict requirements for its use. California law, for example, allows the procedure when a guardian (called a conservator) petitions the court and the court finds beyond a reasonable doubt that the person named in the petition is incapable of giving consent to sterilization; is fertile and capable of procreation; is likely to engage in sexual activity leading to pregnancy; and is either permanently incapable of caring for a child (even with appropriate training and reasonable assistance) or would face a substantial medical risk if she became pregnant or gave birth to a child. Sterilization will be ordered only if all less-invasive contraceptive measures are unworkable.[23]

ABORTION

An **abortion** is an induced termination of a pregnancy in order to destroy an **embryo** or **fetus**. A **therapeutic abortion** is an abortion undertaken in order to safeguard the mother's life or health. An **elective abortion** is an abortion performed at the request of the woman for nonmedical reasons.

In the early 1970s, abortion was a crime in every state. It was permitted only when the health of the woman necessitated it (usually to preserve her life) or under special circumstances (e.g., when the pregnancy was caused by rape or incest).

Roe v. Wade

In 1973, the law was dramatically changed by the landmark case of *Roe v. Wade*,[24] in which the U.S. Supreme Court held that a pregnant woman's right to privacy included the fundamental right to terminate her pregnancy. A woman's decision to terminate her pregnancy is a "liberty" protected against state interference by the Due Process Clause of the Fourteenth Amendment, which provides that no state shall "deprive any person of life, liberty, or property, without due process of law."[25] Under the test of strict scrutiny, this fundamental right could not be restricted unless the restriction was narrowly tailored to serve a compelling state interest. The ruling in *Roe* was later modified by the 1992 case of *Planned Parenthood of Southeastern Pennsylvania v. Casey*. Before examining *Casey*, however, we need to look at the *Roe* decision.

In *Roe v. Wade*, the Court did not hold that the right to have an abortion was absolute. The extent of the right depended on the stage of a woman's pregnancy:

1. For the stage prior to approximately the end of the first trimester (the first three months), the abortion decision and its effectuation must be left to the medical judgment of the pregnant woman's attending physician.

2. For the stage subsequent to approximately the end of the first trimester, the state, in promoting its interests in the health of the mother, may, if it chooses, regulate the abortion procedure in ways that are reasonably related to maternal health.

3. For the stage subsequent to viability, the state in promoting its interest in the potentiality of human life may, if it chooses, regulate, and even proscribe, abortion except where it is necessary, in appropriate medical judgment, for the preservation of the life or health of the mother.

A major theme of *Roe* was that the state should not be regulating abortions until viability unless the regulations were clearly necessary to protect the health of the mother. **Viable** means able to live indefinitely outside the womb by natural or artificial support systems. If the regulations are not necessary to protect the health of the mother, the state could not prohibit a woman from obtaining an abortion during the first trimester when a fetus is not viable.

abortion
An induced termination of a pregnancy in order to destroy an embryo or a fetus.

embryo
An egg that has been fertilized by a sperm in the early stage of development; it has undergone one or more divisions. The product of conception to about the eighth week of pregnancy.

fetus
A developing organism (unborn offspring) from the eighth week after conception until birth.

therapeutic abortion
An abortion undertaken in order to safeguard the mother's life or health. Also called induced abortion.

elective abortion
An abortion that is performed at the request of the woman for nonmedical reasons.

viable
Able to live indefinitely outside the womb by natural or artificial support systems.

Different considerations applied during the next 12 weeks, or the second trimester. Between the end of the first trimester and the beginning of the child's viability (a child is usually considered viable after about six months), the state could regulate medical procedures to make sure that abortions are performed safely but could not prohibit abortions altogether. Once the child is viable—during the third trimester—abortions could be prohibited unless they were necessary to preserve the life or health of the mother.

The court later reinforced *Roe* by holding that a wife may have an abortion without the consent of her husband.

After *Roe* was decided, the court approved some limits on abortion. For example, if a poor woman wanted an abortion for nonhealth reasons (i.e., a nontherapeutic abortion), the state was *not required* to pay for it, although a number of states decided to set aside funds to pay for such abortions. Also, abortions could be prohibited if not performed by licensed physicians. If a pregnant minor is living with and dependent on her parents, it is permissible for a state to require the parents to be notified of the child's desire to have an abortion. If the parents refuse to consent to the abortion, the minor can be denied the abortion so long as she has the opportunity to go to court to try to convince a judge (in what is called a "bypass proceeding" or a "judicial bypass") that she is a mature minor and that therefore parental notice and consent are not needed in her particular case.

ASSIGNMENT 12.3

In Chapter 9 on child custody, we examined the U.S. Supreme Court case of *Troxel v. Granville* on the fundamental right of parents to make decisions concerning the care, custody, and control of their children. The *Troxel* Court held that court-ordered visitation by a nonparent (e.g., a grandparent) must not substantially interfere with the primary right of fit biological parents to raise their children. Is the authorization of a bypass proceeding for a pregnant minor consistent with the fundamental right of fit parents to raise their children, including the right to refuse to allow their daughter to have an abortion? (See the General Instructions for the Legal-Analysis Assignment in Appendix A.)

Planned Parenthood of Southeastern Pennsylvania v. Casey

Approximately 1.5 million abortions are performed each year. It is one of the most common medical procedures performed in America. The Supreme Court has acknowledged that abortion continued to be "the most politically divisive domestic legal issue of our time."[26] Some activists argued for a constitutional amendment that would return us to the pre-*Roe* days when states could outlaw abortion. Others hoped that the appointment of conservatives to the Supreme Court by Republican presidents would lead to an overruling of *Roe* by the Court itself. It has not happened. Indeed, the essential holding of *Roe* was reaffirmed in the important 1992 opinion of *Planned Parenthood of Southeastern Pennsylvania v. Casey*.[27] The *Casey* case laid out three principles:

1. Before viability, a woman has a right to choose to terminate her pregnancy; this liberty right is guaranteed by the Due Process Clause of the Fourteenth Amendment.

2. A law that imposes an *undue burden* on a woman's decision before viability is unconstitutional. An undue burden exists when the purpose or effect of the state's regulation is to place a *substantial obstacle* in the path of a woman seeking an abortion of a nonviable fetus.

3. After viability, the state, in promoting its interest in the potentiality of human life, may, if it chooses, regulate, and even prohibit, abortions except where an abortion is medically necessary to preserve the life or health of the mother.

Under *Casey*, the key test continues to be viability. In *Roe*, the Court used a trimester analysis as a guide in the determination of viability. In *Casey*, the Court decided to reject this analysis as too rigid. In the future, the question of when a child is able to survive outside the womb will be determined by the facts of medicine and science rather than by rigid assumptions of what is possible during the trimesters of pregnancy.

Before viability, a state cannot place an "undue burden" on the right of a woman to seek an abortion. The state can pass laws designed to encourage women to choose childbirth over abortion and laws designed to further her health or safety so long as these laws do not place a "substantial obstacle" in the path of her decision to abort a nonviable fetus: "Regulations which do no more than create a structural mechanism by which the State, or the parent or guardian of a minor, may express profound respect for the life of the unborn are permitted, if they are not a substantial obstacle to the woman's exercise of the right to choose."

Using the undue-burden test, the Court in *Casey* reached the following conclusions about specific laws that were challenged in the case:

- It is *not* an undue burden on the right to abortion for a state to require (except in a medical emergency) that at least 24 hours before performing an abortion a physician give a woman information about the nature of the procedure, the health risks of abortion and of childbirth, the probable gestational age of her unborn child, available medical assistance for childbirth, methods of obtaining child support from the father, and a list of agencies that provide adoption and other services as alternatives to abortion. Providing this information is not a substantial obstacle because the information allows women to give informed consent to whatever decision they make.

- It *is* an undue burden on the right to abortion for a state to require a signed statement from the woman that she has notified her spouse that she is about to undergo an abortion. This is a substantial obstacle because many women may not seek an abortion due to a fear of psychological and physical abuse from their husband if they tell him about their plan to have an abortion. Furthermore, a woman does not need her husband's consent to undergo an abortion. He does not have a veto. Therefore, notifying him about the planned abortion is not necessary.

The *Casey* case did not resolve the abortion controversy. Many states have enacted restrictions that the U.S. Supreme Court may one day have to decide are or are not "undue burdens" on a woman's right to abortion. The restrictions include mandatory waiting periods and counseling sessions (called needlessly onerous by critics); requiring a woman to view an ultrasound of the fetus; prohibitions on abortion coverage in insurance policies; and "safety" rules on facilities that perform abortions, such as the width of hallways. Other efforts to undermine the *Roe* and *Casey* decisions include proposed laws that grant legal rights to embryos and that define a fetus as a person. Mississippi almost passed a law that defined "person" to "include every human being from the moment of fertilization, cloning, or the functional equivalent thereof." (See the related discussion of fetal homicide on page 500.)

Partial-Birth Abortion

Partial-birth abortion is a late-term abortion in which the fetus is destroyed after it is partially extruded from the womb. Doctors use different terms for the procedure such as dilation and extraction (D & X) or intact dilation and evacuation (intact D & E).

partial-birth abortion
An abortion in which the fetus is destroyed after it is partially extruded from the womb.

In 2000, the U.S. Supreme Court held that a state's ban on partial-birth abortion was unconstitutional. One of the dissenting justices said that the opinion allowing partial-birth abortion will become as infamous as the Court's *Dred Scott* decision (protecting the rights of slave owners) and the *Korematsu* decision (allowing the internment of Japanese Americans during World War II).[28] Three years later, Congress passed the Partial-Birth Abortion Ban Act, which prohibited abortions that involve partial delivery of a living fetus in late-term pregnancies. This time, the Court allowed the ban when it was challenged. The Partial-Birth Abortion Ban Act states that "[a]ny physician who, in or affecting interstate or foreign commerce, knowingly performs a partial-birth abortion and thereby kills a human fetus shall be fined under this title or imprisoned not more than 2 years, or both. This subsection does not apply to a partial-birth abortion that is necessary to save the life of a mother whose life is endangered by a physical disorder, physical illness, or physical injury, including a life-endangering physical condition caused by or arising from the pregnancy itself."[29]

The act defines partial-birth abortion as "an abortion in which the person performing the abortion (A) deliberately and intentionally vaginally delivers a living fetus until, in the case of a head-first presentation, the entire fetal head is outside the body of the mother, or, in the case of breech presentation, any part of the fetal trunk past the navel is outside the body of the mother, for the purpose of performing an overt act that the person knows will kill the partially delivered living fetus; and (B) performs the overt act, other than completion of delivery, that kills the partially delivered living fetus."

The law was upheld by a divided U.S. Supreme Court in *Gonzales v. Carhart*.[30] The Court held that safe alternatives to the banned procedure are available to the woman, the act was not too vague, and most importantly, the act did not place a substantial obstacle in the path of a woman's decision to abort a nonviable fetus and hence did not violate the undue-burden test of *Casey*.

FETAL HOMICIDE

criminal homicide
Causing the death of a person without justification or excuse.

murder
Killing a person (1) with the intent to kill, (2) with the intent to cause grievous bodily harm, (3) with reckless disregard for human life, or (4) while committing a designated felony.

manslaughter
The unlawful killing of a person that does not constitute murder.

feticide
The unlawful killing of a fetus.

Criminal homicide is causing the death of a person without justification or excuse. The two major categories of criminal homicide are **murder** and **manslaughter**. When does a fetus become a person so that it can become the victim of a criminal homicide? In most states, the baby must be *born alive* for this to occur, usually meaning that the baby must have an independent circulation; in other words, it must be breathing. In a few states, however, the killing of a fetus without the consent of the mother is murder. In New York, for example, homicide includes the death of an "unborn child" of a woman "pregnant for more than twenty-four weeks under circumstances constituting murder."[31]

It is also a crime to unlawfully terminate life before birth. The crime is called **feticide**, the unlawful killing of a fetus. In Georgia, for example, an unborn child is defined as "a member of the species homo sapiens at any stage of development who is carried in the womb." *Feticide by vehicle* in Georgia is committed if someone causes the death of an unborn child by any injury to the mother of such child that would be *homicide by vehicle* if it resulted in the death of the mother.[32] Similarly, an Indiana statute provides that a "person who knowingly or intentionally terminates a human pregnancy with an intention other than to produce a live birth or to remove a dead fetus commits feticide, a Class B felony. This section does not apply to an abortion."[33]

At the federal level, the Unborn Victims of Violence Act treats an unborn child as a victim by making it a federal crime to injure or kill a "child" "who is in utero" during the commission of one of over sixty specified federal crimes. The law defines "child in utero" as "a member of the species Homo sapiens, at any stage of development, who is carried in the womb."[34] Although the act contains an exception for abortion and does not say that a fetus is a child or a person, critics charged that it is a step in the direction of granting that status to a fetus. An editorial in the *New York Times*, for example, said that the law is an attack on abortion rights masquerading as law enforcement: "This equivalence between a fetus in its earliest stages and a child sets a dangerous legal precedent."[35]

These laws on criminal liability are different from the *civil* liability of a defendant for killing a fetus. It is possible for a defendant to escape criminal liability for killing a fetus but still face civil liability. We will consider civil liability in Chapter 17 when we discuss prenatal torts.

VIOLENCE AGAINST WOMEN

Domestic violence (DV) is actual or threatened injury or abuse by one member of a family or household on another member. DV can be committed against a spouse, children, and same-sex partners, and in some states, against a dating partner. There are four major patterns of DV:

domestic violence (DV)
Actual or threatened injury or abuse by one member of a family or household on another member.

- *Coercive-control violence.* Classic battering. The abuser (often male) uses force as a tactic in a larger escalating pattern aimed at intimidating and controlling the victim. Physical violence and sexual abuse are often accompanied by threats, psychological and emotional abuse, isolation of the victim, manipulation of children, and exercise of economic control.

- *Violent resistance or self-defense.* The victim (usually female) uses violence to protect herself against a perpetrator who is using force as a part of a larger pattern of coercive control.

- *Conflict-instigated violence.* An unresolved disagreement spirals into a violent incident, but the violence is not part of a larger pattern of coercive control. It may be initiated by either the male or female partner, although female victims are more likely to suffer injury than are men. If the first violent incident occurs in response to the separation of the parties (and there is no history of coercive controlling behavior), the violence is sometimes called *separation-instigated violence.*

- *Violence caused by mental illness.* Violence resulting from abusers who suffer from severe mental illness such as psychosis and paranoia.[36]

The statistics on domestic violence in America are staggering:

- One in four women has been the victim of severe physical violence by an intimate partner (one in seven men have experienced severe physical violence by an intimate partner).

- Over 1 million women a year are raped.

- One in five women has been raped in her lifetime (1 in 71 men have been raped in their lifetime).

- One in six women has been the victim of **stalking** in her lifetime (1 in 19 men have been stalked in their lifetime).

stalking
1. Repeatedly following someone, often surreptitiously. 2. A course of conduct consisting of following or loitering around a person, who is thereby placed in reasonable fear of harm.

- Thirty percent of Americans say they know a woman who has been physically abused by her husband or boyfriend.

- About one in five female high school students reports being physically and/or sexually abused by a dating partner.

- On average, more than three women (and one man) are murdered by their intimate partners every day.

- About half of all female victims of intimate violence report an injury of some type, and about 20 percent of them seek medical assistance.

- Fifty percent of men who frequently assaulted their wives also frequently abused their children.

- The health-related costs of intimate partner violence exceed $5.8 billion a year.[37]

As alarming as these statistics are, the numbers above are considered low estimates because the crimes involved are among the most unreported in the country. For example, the National Crime Victimization Survey reports that between 2004 and 2008, police were not notified of half of all incidents of rape.[38] Only one out of every 100 perpetrators of domestic violence is arrested.

There are, however, some positive trends. For example, although spouse-on-spouse violence continues to be alarmingly high, the rate of such violence has fallen by more than 30 percent over the last three decades "largely because individuals no longer feel forced to stay in a bad marriage."[39]

At one time in our history, wives were considered the property of their husbands. This reality encouraged the use of violence against wives. Indeed, there was religious and legal approval for a husband's use of force against his wife. Around 1475, for example, Friar Cherubino of Siena compiled the following *Rules of Marriage*:

> When you see your wife commit an offense, don't rush at her with insults and violent blows. . . . Scold her sharply, bully and terrify her. And if this still doesn't work . . . take up a stick and beat her soundly, for it is better to punish the body and correct the soul than to damage the soul and spare the body. . . . Then readily beat her, not in rage but out of charity and concern for her soul, so that the beating will redound to your merit and her good.[40]

Wife beating was acceptable and indeed was considered a duty of the husband. Society even condoned a particular weapon for the deed: a "rod not thicker than his thumb," a guideline that came to be called the rule of thumb.[41] Some authorities, however, say that the rule of thumb is more legend than fact.[42]

Eventually, of course, laws were passed outlawing wife beating. Yet the crime continues to be committed at an alarming rate today. As indicated, women frequently do not report such violence, particularly when they are still living with their abusers. Furthermore, when a woman does report the incident to the authorities, she often is not taken seriously. Many complain that the police handle violence in a "domestic quarrel" differently, that is, less seriously, from an assault on the street between strangers. Women's groups have campaigned for a change in the attitude and policies of courts, legislatures, and law enforcement agencies. (See the section on mandatory arrest and mandatory prosecution below.) In addition, they have fought for the creation of shelters to which battered women can flee.

If a woman is persistent and desperate enough, her main civil remedy is to go to court to ask for an **injunction**. This remedy seeks to stop the abuse against the plaintiff and/or her children. Depending on the state, the injunction is called a *restraining order*, an *order of protection*, or a *protection from abuse* (*PFA*) *order*. The order might also be called a **stay-away order** or *no-contact order*, which forbids the defendant from being in a designated area (e.g., within 200 feet of the alleged domestic-violence victim), or from contacting the person except for approved reasons.

For purposes of obtaining the order, abuse is often defined as attempting to cause bodily injury; intentionally, knowingly, or recklessly causing bodily injury; or by threat of force placing another person in fear of imminent serious physical harm. The first step in obtaining the order is often the filing of an application for a temporary injunction based on actual or threatened abuse. The petitioner files the application **ex parte**, meaning that only one party is before the court. A judge (or sometimes a clerk) can issue the temporary injunction. The injunction or order is served on the defendant, who is ordered to stay away from or to refrain from contacting the petitioner. A date is set for a hearing at which both sides can address the question of whether the injunction should be made permanent, which usually means being in effect for a year or more. The woman is urged

injunction
A court order requiring a person or organization to do or to refrain from doing a particular thing.

restraining order
A form of injunction, initially issued ex parte (with only one side present), to restrain the defendant from doing a threatened act. Also called order of protection, personal protection order (PPO), protection from abuse (PFA).

stay-away order
A court order forbidding a person from being in a designated area (e.g., within 200 feet of an alleged domestic-violence victim of the defendant) or from contacting the person except for designated purposes. Also called no-contact order.

ex parte
With only one side present (usually the plaintiff or petitioner) when court action is requested.

to carry the temporary or permanent injunction with her at all times so that she can show it to the police in the event that the defendant violates its terms.

In addition to the civil remedy of an injunction, a woman can ask the state to prosecute the defendant for a crime (e.g., assault, aggravated assault, battery, aggravated battery, reckless conduct, disorderly conduct, harassment). Some states have special crimes that specifically cover violence committed by one family member against another, such as unlawful spouse-against-spouse violence.

A major attempt to address the problem at the national level occurred when Congress passed the Violence Against Women Act (VAWA). The Act (1) created an Office on Violence Against Women (OVW) in the U.S. Department of Justice to provide grants and support services to domestic-violence prevention programs throughout the country; (2) made it a federal crime to cross state lines with the intent to injure or harass a former or current spouse or intimate partner (opposite-sex or same-sex); (3) required states to give **full faith and credit** to the protection orders of other states; and (4) established a federal civil rights **cause of action** for victims of violence motivated by "animus" toward the victim's gender. The U.S. Supreme Court, however, struck down the cause-of-action part of the VAWA as an unconstitutional exercise of the Commerce Clause of the U.S. Constitution.[43] The Court held that gender violence did not have a substantial enough effect on interstate commerce to justify the regulation of such violence through the VAWA. The Court also expressed its concern about imposing additional federal laws in this area of family relations. The Court, however, left intact the other portions of the VAWA.

Another attempt by Congress to regulate gender-related violence was its passage of the Freedom of Access to Clinic Entrances Act (FACE), which gives a cause of action to anyone who is the victim of assault or other attack while seeking "reproductive health services," such as an abortion.[44] In view of the Court's rejection of the cause-of-action provision of VAWA, however, it is unclear whether FACE will eventually be held to be an unconstitutional intrusion by Congress on the right of the states to regulate family law.

Later, in Chapter 17, we will examine whether a spouse who is the victim of domestic violence can bring a traditional personal injury *tort* action (e.g., assault, battery, false imprisonment, and intentional infliction of emotional distress) against the other spouse in a state court.

MANDATORY ARREST; MANDATORY PROSECUTION

By some estimates, a large majority of domestic-violence cases are dismissed because of the refusal of the victims to cooperate with the prosecution.[45] Victims often fear further violence from their batterers if they cooperate. Some states have responded by passing *mandatory-arrest* laws that require the police to make an arrest if **probable cause** exists that a crime has been committed, regardless of the wishes of the victim. The law might prohibit the police from asking the victim whether an arrest should be made. Under such a law, victims are not asked if they wish to press charges. The policy of mandatory arrest is controversial.

> Opponents of mandatory arrest argue that: (1) because domestic violence is a crime of passion, arrest is unlikely to deter crime; (2) arrest before all the facts are known leads to the arrest of innocent people; (3) mandatory arrest often punishes the alleged victim as well as the suspect since a bread-winner may lose his job after being arrested, or the arrest may cause the suspect to retaliate further against the victim upon release; and (4) fear of these adverse consequences may lead victims to refuse to call police for help out of fear that arrest will be the result.[46]

full faith and credit (FFC)
The obligation of one state to recognize and enforce the legal decisions of another state. The obligation is based on the U.S. Constitution, which provides that "Full Faith and Credit shall be given in each State to the public Acts, Records, and judicial Proceedings of every other State." Article IV, § 1.

cause of action
1. A legally acceptable reason for bringing a suit. A rule that constitutes a legal theory for bringing a suit. 2. The facts that give a person a right to judicial relief. When you state a cause of action, you list the facts that give you a right to judicial relief against the wrongdoer.

probable cause
1. A reasonable belief that a specific crime has been committed and that the accused committed the crime. 2. A reasonable belief that good grounds exist to bring civil proceedings against someone.

Furthermore, if a fight occurs, the police may have no way of sorting out who did what to whom, and end up arresting both parties. Dual arrests increased significantly in many mandatory-arrest states. Batterers have been known to sound convincing when they tell a police officer that they were just defending themselves.

Yet some states have gone even further and have instituted mandatory prosecution, called a *no-drop policy*. The district attorney or prosecutor is not allowed to drop the charges. Government attorneys are required to bring criminal charges against batterers even if the victim refuses to cooperate.

RIGHT OF CONFRONTATION

When victims refuse to cooperate, they often refuse to answer further questions from the police and fail to show up for court proceedings against the alleged batterer. They may even say that it was all a mistake and that there was no violence. This poses serious problems of proof for prosecutors. How can they convict someone for what the victim now says did not happen? A further problem for prosecutors is the **Confrontation Clause** of the U.S. Constitution, which gives a criminal defendant the right to confront and cross-examine an accusing witness.[47] A victim who refuses to show up cannot be confronted and cross-examined. Therefore the defendant goes free. Suppose, however, that *other* evidence is available? Often, the police have a recording of the 911 phone call that the victim made to the police in the middle of or just after the violent acts occurred. Can the statement on the recording be used against the defendant? Would the use of this statement violate the defendant's right of confrontation when the maker of the statement—the alleged victim—refuses to appear or say anything in court? The answer depends on how we characterize the statement.

- If it is a *testimonial* statement, the Confrontation Clause is violated by its use when the maker of the statement is not available for cross-examination.
- If it is a *nontestimonial* statement, the Confrontation Clause is not violated by its use when the maker of the statement is not available for cross-examination.

The distinction between testimonial and nontestimonial depends on the purpose and circumstances of the statement. Here is how the U.S. Supreme Court explained the difference:

> Statements are nontestimonial when made in the course of police interrogation under circumstances objectively indicating that the primary purpose of the interrogation is to enable police assistance to meet an ongoing emergency. They are testimonial when the circumstances objectively indicate that there is no such ongoing emergency, and that the primary purpose of the interrogation is to establish or prove past events potentially relevant to later criminal prosecution.[48]

Under these definitions, a panicked 911 call to the police would be considered nontestimonial if the caller is reaching out to the police for help in a crisis. The caller's statement can be introduced in court against the defendant even though the caller refuses to give testimony in court about what happened. On the other hand, if the police arrive after the emergency is over and take a written statement from the victim about what happened, the statement would be considered testimonial, and therefore, could not be used in court against the defendant unless the defendant had the right to cross-examine the maker of the statement.

PRIMARY AGGRESSOR LAW

As indicated, mandatory-arrest laws sometimes lead to the arrest of both parties. One way to avoid dual arrests when there are allegations of mutual violence is to require the police to determine who was the *primary* aggressor and to

Confrontation Clause
A clause in the U.S. Constitution stating that a criminal defendant has a right to confront an accusing witness face-to-face and to cross-examine him or her. U.S. Const. amend. VI.

arrest only that person. Some states have laws to this effect based on the Model Code on Domestic and Family Violence of the National Council of Juvenile and Family Court Judges. Under the model code:

> If a law enforcement officer receives complaints of domestic or family violence from two or more opposing persons, the officer shall evaluate each complaint separately to determine who was the primary aggressor. If the officer determines that one person was the primary physical aggressor, the officer need not arrest the other person believed to have committed domestic or family violence. In determining whether a person is the primary aggressor the officer shall consider:
>
> **(a)** Prior complaints of domestic or family violence;
>
> **(b)** The relative severity of the injuries inflicted on each person;
>
> **(c)** The likelihood of future injury to each person; and
>
> **(d)** Whether one of the persons acted in self-defense.[49]

BATTERED WOMAN SYNDROME

Some women have taken the extreme step of killing the husband or other intimate partner who has been abusing them. Does the killing constitute the crime of murder or manslaughter? In part, the answer depends on when the killing occurs. Compare the predicament of the women in the following two situations. Assume that both women had been physically abused by their husband or boyfriend for years:

- Carol is being physically attacked by her husband, who is coming at her with a knife. As he approaches, Carol shoots him.
- Hours after being beaten by her boyfriend, Helen takes a gun to his bedroom and shoots him while he is asleep.

It is highly unlikely that Carol has committed a crime. She is protected by the traditional defense of **self-defense**. Citizens can use *deadly* force that they reasonably believe is necessary to protect themselves from **imminent** death or serious bodily injury.

What about Helen? Unless she can prove temporary insanity, she must establish the elements of self-defense to avoid conviction. But she apparently was not in *imminent* danger at the time she shot her boyfriend. Arguably, for example, she could have left the home while he was sleeping if she felt that he might kill or maim her once he awoke. Women in Helen's situation have been prosecuted for crimes such as manslaughter and murder.

In these prosecutions, a novel argument that is often raised by the woman is the battered wife syndrome or, more broadly, the **battered woman syndrome**. She claims that she acted out of a *psychological helplessness or paralysis*. A variety of circumstances combined to block all apparent avenues of escape: financial dependence, loneliness, guilt, shame, and fear of reprisal from her husband or boyfriend.[50] From this state of "learned helplessness," she kills him. This argument is not an independent defense; it is an argument designed to bolster the self-defense argument. More accurately, it is an attempt to broaden the definition of *imminent danger* in self-defense. To a woman subjected to the psychological terror and paralysis of long-term abuse, the danger from her husband or boyfriend is real and close at hand. At any moment, his behavior might trigger a flashback in her mind to an earlier beating, causing her to honestly believe that she is in immediate danger.

Prosecutors are not sympathetic to the battered-woman-syndrome argument. They say it is too easy to exaggerate the extent of the abuse and the extent to which the abuse resulted in such a state of paralysis that the woman felt her only way to protect herself in the immediate short term was to kill her husband. Some courts, however, are at least willing to listen to testimony on the syndrome. This has been very helpful for the defendant because when jurors

self-defense
The use of reasonable force to prevent harmful or offensive contact to one's person when there is an imminent danger of such contact.

imminent
Near at hand; coming soon; about to happen; immediate.

battered woman syndrome
A woman's psychological helplessness or paralysis because of conditions such as financial dependence, loneliness, guilt, shame, and fear of reprisal from her husband or boyfriend who has repeatedly subjected her to physical, sexual, or emotional abuse in the past.

voluntary manslaughter

The intentional, unlawful killing of someone but with extenuating circumstances such as provocation. Murder reduced to manslaughter because of the absence of malice or premeditation.

hear this testimony, they are often reluctant to return guilty verdicts despite the absence of clear facts needed to show self-defense. Prosecutors are aware of this reluctance, and therefore many are more inclined to bring charges on lesser crimes such as **voluntary manslaughter** and, in some instances, not to bring any charges. Therefore, although prosecutors may deride the battered woman syndrome as an "abuse excuse," raising the syndrome can still be an important part of the strategy of the attorney representing the woman.

ASSIGNMENT 12.4

For the following questions, see General Instructions for the State-Code Assignment in Appendix A.

a. In your state, if a woman is threatened with violence, what remedies does she have?

b. When, if ever, can an injunction or protective order be issued when the defendant is not present in court (i.e., ex parte)?

c. Without justification, a husband stabs his wife, but does not kill her. What are the possible crimes he can be charged with in your state?

ASSIGNMENT 12.5

a. Do you think that a court encourages killing when it allows evidence of the battered woman syndrome to be introduced in trials of women who kill their spouses or boyfriends? Explain why or why not.

b. Do you think it is possible for a battered *man* syndrome to exist? Explain why or why not.

MARITAL RAPE

The common law rule was that a husband cannot rape his wife. The "husband cannot be guilty of rape committed by himself upon his lawful wife, for by their mutual matrimonial consent and contract, the wife hath given up herself in this kind unto her husband which she cannot retract."[51] This view is still the law in some states. Most states, however, allow prosecution if the couple is living apart and a petition has been filed for divorce or separate maintenance. The reluctance of courts and legislatures to allow the criminal law of rape to apply to married couples is in part based on a fear that a wife will lie about whether she consented to sexual intercourse. As we will see in the case of *Warren v. State*, however, this fear is largely unfounded.

CASE

Warren v. State
255 Ga. 151, 336 S.E.2d 221 (1985)
Supreme Court of Georgia

Background: *Daniel Steven Warren was indicted for rape and sodomy of his wife while they were still living together. He moved to dismiss the indictment on the ground that a husband cannot be convicted of committing these crimes against his wife. The motion was denied. He then appealed to the Supreme Court of Georgia, where he is the appellant.*

Decision on Appeal: *Denial of motion to dismiss is affirmed. The rape statute in the state does not contain a marital exception.*

OPINION OF THE COURT:

Justice Smith delivered the opinion of the court.

"When a woman says I do, does she give up her right to say I won't?" This question does not pose the real question, because rape and aggravated sodomy are not sexual acts of an ardent husband performed upon an initially apathetic wife, they are acts of violence that are accompanied with physical and mental abuse and often leave the victim with physical and

(continued)

CASE • Warren v. State (continued)

psychological damage that is almost always long lasting. Thus we find the more appropriate question:

When a woman says "I do" in Georgia does she give up her right to State protection from the violent acts of rape and aggravated sodomy performed by her husband[?] The answer is no. We affirm. . . .

The appellant asserts that there exists within the rape statute an implicit marital exclusion that makes it legally impossible for a husband to be guilty of raping his wife. Until the late 1970's there was no real examination of this apparently widely held belief. Within the last few years several jurisdictions have been faced with similar issues and they have decided that under certain circumstances a husband can be held criminally liable for raping his wife.

What is behind the theory and belief that a husband could not be guilty of raping his wife? There are various explanations for the rule and all of them flow from the common law attitude toward women, the status of women and marriage.

Perhaps the most often used basis for the marital rape exemption is the view set out by Lord Hale in 1 Hale P.C. 629. It is known as Lord Hale's contractual theory. The statement attributed to Lord Hale used to support the theory is: "but a husband cannot be guilty of a rape committed by himself upon his lawful wife, for by their mutual matrimonial consent and contract the wife hath given up herself in this kind unto her husband which she cannot retract."

There is some thought that the foundation of his theory might well have been the subsequent marriage doctrine of English law, wherein the perpetrator could, by marrying his victim, avoid rape charges. It was thus argued as a corollary, rape within the marital relationship would result in the same immunity. Another theory stemming from medieval times is that of a wife being the husband's chattel or property. Since a married woman was part of her husband's property, nothing more than a chattel, rape was nothing more than a man making use of his own property. A third theory is the unity in marriage or unity of person theory that held the very being or legal existence of a woman was suspended during marriage, or at least was incorporated and consolidated into that of her husband. In view of the fact that there was only one legal being, the husband, he could not be convicted of raping himself.

These three theories have been used to support the marital rape exemption. Others have tried to fill the chasm between these three theories with justifications for continuing the exemption in the face of changes in the recognition of women, their status, and the status of marriage. Some of the justifications include: Prevention of fabricated charges; Preventing wives from using rape charges for revenge; Preventing state intervention into marriage so that possible reconciliation will not be thwarted. A closer examination of the theories and justifications indicates that they are no longer valid, if they ever had any validity.

Hale's implied consent theory was created at a time when marriages were irrevocable and when all wives promised to "love, honor, and obey" and all husbands promised to "love, cherish, and protect until death do us part." Wives were subservient to their husbands, her identity was merged into his, her property became his property, and she took his name for her own.

There have been dramatic changes in women's rights and the status of women and marriage. Today our State Constitution provides that, "no person shall be deprived of life, *liberty,* or property except by due process," and "protection to *person* and property is the paramount duty of government and shall be impartial and complete. No person shall be denied the equal protection of the laws." Our state Constitution also provides that each spouse has a right to retain his or her own property. Our statutory laws provide that, "[t]he rights of citizens include, *without limitation,* the following: (1) The right of *personal security,* [and] (2) The right of personal liberty. . . ." (Emphasis supplied.) OCGA § 1–2–6. Women in Georgia "are entitled to the privilege of the elective franchise and have the right to hold any civil office or perform any civil function as fully and completely as do male citizens." OCGA § 1–2–7. Couples who contemplate marriage today may choose either spouse's surname or a combination of both names for their married surname. No longer is a wife's domicile presumed to be that of her husband, and no longer is the husband head of the family with the wife subject to him. Marriages are revocable without fault by either party; either party, not just the husband, can be required to pay alimony upon divorce; and both parties have a joint and several duty to provide for the maintenance, protection, and education of their children. Couples may write antenuptial agreements in which they are able to decide, prior to marriage, future settlements; and our legislature has recognized that there can be violence in modern family life and it has enacted special laws to protect family members who live in the same household from one another's violent acts. . . .

One would be hard pressed to argue that a husband can rape his wife because she is his chattel. Even in the darkest days of slavery when slaves were also considered chattel, rape was defined as "the carnal knowledge of a female whether free or slave, forcibly and against her will." Georgia Code, § 4248 (1863). Both the chattel and unity of identity rationales have been cast aside. "Nowhere in the common law world—[or] in any modern society—is a woman regarded as chattel or demeaned—by denial of a separate legal identity and the dignity associated with recognition as a whole human being." *Trammel v. United States*, 445 U.S. 40, 52 (1980).

We find that none of the theories have any validity. The justifications likewise are without efficacy. There is no other crime we can think of in which all of the victims are denied protection simply because someone might fabricate a charge; there is no evidence that wives have flooded the district attorneys with revenge filled trumped-up charges, and once a marital relationship is at the point where a husband rapes his wife, state intervention is needed for the wife's protection. . . .

Judgment affirmed.

PRO BONO ASSISTANCE

pro bono
Concerning or involving legal services that are provided for the public good (pro bono publico) without fee or compensation. Sometimes also applied to services given at a reduced rate. Shortened to pro bono.

A law office becomes involved in domestic-violence cases in a number of ways. In a divorce case, for example, there may have been violence or a threat of violence during the marriage. A criminal case could have begun when the police were called because of violence committed in the home. Attorneys and paralegals may be involved in a **pro bono** project in which they give free legal services to victims of domestic violence. (For a dramatic description of one paralegal's participation in such a pro bono program, see Exhibit 12-3.)

EXHIBIT 12-3   A Paralegal's Experience with Domestic-Violence Cases

Protection from Abuse Program
by Laurie R. Mansell Reich, RP, Senior Paralegal
Equitable Resources, Inc.

I can still clearly remember my first day as a pro bono volunteer with the Protection From Abuse Program (PFA) in Allegheny County, PA (www.pcadv.org/Resources/PFA_Brochure.pdf). I entered the PFA area of the City-County Building clutching a binder of sample forms, sweating profusely from nervousness and feeling very scared.

The PFA area is an austere section just off the elevators on the eighth floor that has been partitioned off and "decorated" with old, well-worn government-issue tables and chairs. There is one desk, and that is reserved for a volunteer. A sheriff's deputy sits on a plastic chair by the pay phone in case trouble breaks out between petitioners, which does happen. And did I mention that the building has no air conditioning and an overzealous heating system?

I had received my required one hour of training (from whence came the binder of forms) from the PFA coordinator of the Pittsburgh Paralegal Association. For some six years, the Association has participated in the PFA program, which is run by Allegheny County in conjunction with Neighborhood Legal Services and the women's shelters in the area.

I decided to volunteer one Monday a month. We were told at training that Monday is the worst day, especially following a three-day holiday weekend or a weekend sporting event. PFA assistance is available from 9:00 to 11:00 a.m. each day, Monday through Friday. If a PFA is needed over the weekend or in the evening, the petitioner must go to night court and obtain an emergency PFA until the program's office opens on Monday—thus the Monday crowd.

When I first arrived, I thought, how bad could this be? Well, on my first day, there were 50 petitioners. The PFA program had one paid advocate and three or four volunteer advocates who are trained counselors. These volunteer advocates show up, unpaid, day in and day out. And then, there was me. I leave you to count the odds.

The stories the women tell are chilling. One woman's boyfriend held her by the neck from a third story apartment building. Another woman had gasoline poured down her throat and suffered permanent physical damage. One woman's fingernails were ripped off, and she could not even hold a pen. Sometimes these women are harassed at work or by telephone with as many as 30 or 40 calls during the night. Often their lives are threatened. Many are raising four or five children on $500 a month. I cannot tell you how fortunate and how humble I felt each time I left the PFA office.

In Pennsylvania, abuse is considered to have occurred if there is a family or sexual relationship between the parties and the abuse is imminent. So it is important first to establish that a family or sexual relationship exists. For example, a roommate cannot apply for a PFA against another roommate if there is no sexual relationship. If the defendant is a minor, the matter is referred to juvenile court. If the plaintiff is a juvenile, a parent or guardian must complete the paperwork on his or her behalf.

It is important to make sure that the abuse was very recent, usually within the last few days. Otherwise, the judge will dismiss the allegation as not meeting the imminence test (The threatened abuse must be imminent, meaning about to happen, close at hand, or immediate.) If the abuse did not happen recently, the plaintiff would have to show a good reason for the delay in applying for the PFA, such as being hospitalized or perhaps having to flee the area.

I can remember bumbling my way through that first day, trying desperately to help and worrying that I would get something wrong and ruin someone's chances of getting his or her PFA. I think I spent more time frantically searching through my reference binder and asking questions of other staff than I did helping the clients.

Even now after two years of PFA volunteering, I have never stopped being nervous. It is a big responsibility to help someone to fill out a complaint that will be read by a judge. These people desperately need help. Most of the petitioners are women, but a few men come in. Usually the men are there petitioning for a PFA at the same time their wives or girlfriends are petitioning for a PFA against them. It is very important to note that it is considered a conflict of interest for us to assist them both with their complaints, no matter how dispassionate we may feel or act.

It is also crucial to point out that at no time do we give legal advice even though we are asked for such advice. I explain to the people that I am not an attorney and refer them to Neighborhood Legal Services. . . . For this reason, when I became the Pittsburgh Paralegal Association's PFA coordinator, I made nametags for paralegal volunteers with the Association's name on top and the first name of the paralegal below. This gave a clear message as to who we are. For safety's sake, we put only first names on the nametags so volunteers could not be contacted outside of the program.

The petitioners who come for help go through a full day of paperwork and hearings before they obtain a temporary PFA, assuming they get a sympathetic judge. The temporary PFA is good for ten days, at which time a hearing of both parties is held to determine whether a permanent PFA, good for one year, should be issued. The volunteer's role is to help an applicant obtain a temporary PFA.

Many of the women come in exhausted. They have been up all night and have their children with them. Recently, I brought in coloring books and crayons so the children could have something to do for the two hours that the parent is filling out paperwork.

And the paperwork (five to six forms) is daunting, I can assure you. Some petitioners are illiterate. We are encouraged to have petitioners complete the paperwork themselves, mainly because there just are not enough volunteers to go around. If we do end up writing the actual description of the incident, we have to initial our description and have the petitioner read and initial it as well. This is to ensure that the petitioner will not tell the judge that he or she was unaware of what we wrote. The petitioner must initial the description to show he or she has read the description and agrees that it is accurate.

The experience gave me a whole new perspective on life and the use of my paralegal skills. Often when I would finish working with these women, they would have tears in their eyes as they thanked me for my help. They gratefully acknowledged that they could never have completed the forms without help. I listen to them carefully and try to help; they appreciate that.

Although the training session is essential, going and doing (i.e., on-the-job experience) are the best lessons. I encourage all paralegals to become involved in pro bono activity. You will never find a better or more rewarding way to use your skills. As few as two hours a month (if your employer is a concern, the time is easily made up) is not too much to ask—particularly considering the satisfaction you receive in return.

Reprinted with permission of Laurie Mansell Reich.

CLIENT SENSITIVITY

When working with a victim of domestic violence, special sensitivity is required. The following guidelines in handling such cases assume that the victim is a woman and the perpetrator or batterer is a man, although similar guidelines apply if the roles are reversed or if the violence is being committed within a same-sex relationship.

- *Focus on immediate safety needs.* The client may be in immediate danger. The batterer, for example, may be following or stalking the client. Ask the client if she is safe at the present moment. Are the children safe? If danger exists, suggest to the client that she consider calling the police or the emergency 911 phone number from your office. Ask if the batterer knows where the client is. Does she have any relatives where she can safely stay? Is the client interested in staying at a woman's shelter for the night? In short, before exploring the niceties of the law and legal procedures with the client, focus on any immediate safety concerns.

- *Take the client seriously.* If the client says there is danger, believe it. Too often society does not take domestic violence seriously. The police, for example, may feel that nothing more than a "lover's quarrel" is taking place. Their attitude might be "just go back and work things out." Many victims of domestic violence have been subjected to this attitude. They should not find it in a law office.

- *Know the community resources for battered women.* Run this search in Google or other search engine: domestic violence resources aa (with aa being the name of your city, county, or state). Someone in the city or county has probably already compiled a list of resources for domestic-violence victims such as counseling, hotline numbers, overnight shelters, battered women's support groups, hospitals, emergency financial assistance from public welfare agencies, and information on obtaining a restraining order or a protective order. To find such a list, run the Internet search listed above. Also make inquiries about such a list at the police department, district attorney office, the mayor's office, a local public library, Catholic Charities, the Salvation Army, the YWCA, and any special offices or task forces on women's issues. You need to know where victims can turn for social, psychological, financial, and security assistance. In the unlikely event that this list does not exist where you live, start compiling your own.

- *Avoid being judgmental.* You may not approve of some of the client's decisions. You may think she has helped cause her own predicament. You may be shocked if you learn that the client has regularly returned to the batterer after repeated incidents of violence over a long period of time. This is not the time to judge the morality or wisdom of the client's life choices. This is not the time for a lecture or sermon.

- *Understand the client's point of view.* The client may feel afraid, ashamed, confused, angry, or even guilty about the violence that has occurred. When you speak to her, she may be exhausted from being up all night on the run from her abuser, trying to protect herself and her children. She may be in physical pain. The crisis brought on by violence may be overwhelming. It is extremely important that you exhibit concern and understanding. The client may not be capable at the moment of grasping technical legal concepts. She needs information, but perhaps most of all, she needs a sympathetic ear.

- *Leave the critical decisions to the client.* It is the client's life that is on the line. Every decision she makes, including contacting the police, has the potential of escalating the violence when the batterer finds out what she has done. Let the client make the decisions. Provide options and information on the pros and cons of each option. Help the client think through the safety and other consequences of each step.

- *Alert the client to the danger of false security.* A restraining order or a protective order is a court document that orders the batterer to stay away from the victim and authorizes the police to arrest the batterer if he violates its terms. But these orders are not self-executing. Many batterers are not intimidated by them. In fact, such an order may provoke the batterer to further violence. Hence clients should not feel 100 percent safe simply because they have the court order. They should carry it with them at all times but not have a false sense of security about it. Clients still need to take active steps to protect themselves such as locating safe places to stay. In a crisis, a 911 call will probably be much more effective than showing the batterer another copy of the order.

- *Do not leave phone messages that will alert the batterer.* If the batterer does not know that the victim is seeking legal help, he may become enraged when he finds out. Ask the client if it is safe to call her at home and leave a message. When you leave a message, it may not be wise to indicate that you are calling from a law office. It may also be unsafe to leave a phone number. If the batterer hears the message, he may call the number and find out you were calling from a law office. Arrange with the client ahead of time how to reach you so that you do not have to leave too much identifying information in a phone message. Alternatively, ask the client if she has a relative or close friend with whom messages can be left safely.

- *Help the client develop a safety plan.* When the client leaves the office, she should have identified the locations and situations that are likely to lead to further violence. Help the client prepare a safety plan that will address these potential sources of further violence. The plan should outline how the client will try to avoid further violence (e.g., where to stay away from, what to avoid saying if/when she sees the batterer again) and what she will do if the violence recurs (e.g., what emergency phone numbers to call, where to take the children). Although every eventuality cannot be predicted, a safety plan should be able to cover the major vulnerabilities in the client's life and give her some direction on how to respond to them.

■ PARALEGAL ROLES

- For an overview of paralegal roles in family-law cases, see Exhibits 1-3 and 1-4 in Chapter 1.
- For many of the financial issues related to women and the law covered in Chapter 12, a paralegal may be asked to help collect documents and facts outlined in:
  - the checklist in Exhibit 3-1 of Chapter 3
  - the interrogatories in Appendix C
- Miscellaneous duties
  - Investigate facts of alleged employment discrimination.
  - Help client answer questionnaire of the Equal Employment Opportunity Commission for purposes of filing a discrimination complaint.
  - Help draft a petition for filing a discrimination complaint before the local Fair Employment Practices Agency.
  - Help client identify the assets of the client's deceased spouse in order to calculate the amount that would be received upon exercising the right to an elective share.
  - Help client prepare needed documents for the statutory change-of-name procedures.
  - Help identify emergency resources (e.g., shelters) for battered women.
  - Help the client fill out a petition for a restraining order or order of protection.
- For paralegal tasks in pro bono domestic-violence cases, see Exhibit 12-3.

■ CHECK THE CITE

A class action is a lawsuit in which one or more members of a class sue (or are sued) as representative parties on behalf of everyone in the class, all of whom do not have to be joined in the lawsuit. Over 1.5 million current and former female employees of Wal-Mart sought a class action in which they asserted that the discretion exercised by Wal-Mart's local supervisors over pay and promotion matters violates Title VII by discriminating against women. Why did the U.S. Supreme Court refuse to allow the class action to be brought? See *Wal-Mart Stores, Inc. v. Dukes*, __ U.S.__, 131 S. Ct. 2541 (2011). To read the opinion online: (1) Run a citation search ("131 S. Ct. 2541") in the Legal Documents database of Google Scholar (scholar.google.com). (2) Run a case name search ("Wal-Mart Stores, Inc. v. Dukes") in the search engine of Google, Bing, or Yahoo.

■ PROJECT

In Google, Bing, or Yahoo, run the following search: aa discrimination complaint (substitute the name of your state for aa in the search). Write a report in which you explain the options available to a woman in your state who alleges sex discrimination in employment. You must cite and quote from a minimum of 10 different sources that you find on the Internet. At least four of these sources should be statutes, court opinions, or other laws.

■ ETHICS IN A FAMILY LAW PRACTICE

You are a paralegal who works in the office of Linda Williams, who is defending Richard Summer against a charge of raping his girlfriend. Linda asks you to do some paralegal work on the case. You have never told anyone that you were a victim of date rape 10 years ago. The date rape was never reported. Any ethical problems?

■ WRITING SAMPLE

On the Internet, find a petition for a restraining order, order of protection, or whatever the order is called in your state. Make up a fact situation in which a woman alleges violence by her husband. Prepare the petition. (See General Instructions for the Writing Sample in Appendix A.)

SUMMARY

Historically, a married woman had very few rights independent of her husband. Today her situation is very different. For example, largely due to the married women's property acts, her right to own and dispose of property and to enter contracts is now equal to that of her husband. There are some restrictions on contracts and conveyances between spouses (e.g., they cannot enter a contract to deny each other spousal support, and they cannot transfer property to each other in order to defraud creditors). However, these restrictions apply equally to husbands and wives.

When a husband dies, his wife has a right of dower in his property. The corresponding right of the husband is curtesy. Both have been replaced by the elective share. A wife is not required to take her husband's surname upon marriage (though many do so by custom), nor, of course, is she required to keep it upon divorce if she used it when married.

An applicant for credit cannot be discriminated against on the basis of sex or marital status. Sex discrimination in employment is illegal unless sex is a bona fide occupational qualification (BFOQ). Wage discrimination on the basis of sex can be a violation of Title VII of the 1964 Civil Rights Act. Salaries cannot be determined on the basis of gender. The Equal Pay Act (EPA) prohibits discrimination on the basis of sex in the payment of wages or benefits, where men and women perform work of similar skill, effort, and responsibility for the same employer under similar working conditions. Pregnant women cannot be discriminated against on the job because of their pregnancy. Additional employment rights are provided by the Family and Medical Leave Act (FMLA).

The two categories of sexual harassment are quid pro quo harassment and hostile environment harassment. Employers must do more than forbid such harassment; they must actively combat it. Laws on sexual harassment are enforced by the federal Equal Employment Opportunity Commission and by state fair employment practices agencies.

In the area of sexuality and reproductive rights, adults cannot be denied access to contraceptives. Forced sterilization can be legal for someone who is mentally retarded or insane. A state cannot place undue burdens on a woman's right to an abortion before viability. A state can encourage women to choose childbirth over abortion so long as these laws do not present a "substantial obstacle" in the path of her decision to abort a nonviable fetus. Feticide is a crime, but the crime does not apply to legal abortions. The Unborn Victims of Violence Act makes it a federal crime to injure or kill a "child" "who is in utero" during the commission of a specified federal crime.

Domestic violence (DV) is actual or threatened injury or abuse by one member of a family or household on another member. DV against women is a major national problem. Among the remedies women can use when they are victims of DV are restraining orders, which are initially obtained ex parte. The Violence Against Women Act (VAWA) has provisions that seek to strengthen laws against domestic violence. The Free Access to Clinic Entrances Act (FACE) gives a cause of action to anyone who is the victim of assault or other attack while seeking "reproductive health services," such as an abortion. Mandatory arrest and mandatory prosecution require the arrest and prosecution of alleged batterers even if the victim refuses to cooperate. The Confrontation Clause prohibits the use of testimonial statements made by an alleged victim, who now refuses to cooperate in the case against the alleged batterer. To avoid arresting both parties involved in domestic violence, the law may require the arrest of the primary aggressor only. Some women have taken the drastic step of killing their abusers. In such cases, the defense of the battered woman syndrome is sometimes raised within the context of self-defense. Marital rape is not a crime in every state, although most states allow prosecution if the parties are separated and a petition has been filed for divorce or separate maintenance.

Important guidelines when assisting victims of domestic violence include focusing on immediate safety needs, knowing the community resources for battered women, avoiding a judgmental attitude, understanding the client's point of view, taking the client seriously, leaving critical decisions to the client, alerting the client to the danger of false security, and helping the client develop a safety plan.

KEY TERMS

feme covert	fraudulent transfer	curtesy
coverture	gift	elective share
at common law	trust	intestate
unity of person	married women's property acts	cosigner
contract	property division	quasi-suspect class
conveyance	equitable distribution	intermediate scrutiny
postnuptial agreement	dower	bona fide occupational qualification (BFOQ)
consideration	life estate	nepotism

sexual harassment
quid pro quo sexual harassment
hostile environment sexual harassment
Equal Employment Opportunity
    Commission (EEOC)
fair employment practices agency (FEPA)
fundamental right
right to privacy
strict scrutiny
compelling state interest
abortion
embryo

fetus
therapeutic abortion
elective abortion
viable
partial-birth abortion
criminal homicide
murder
manslaughter
feticide
domestic violence (DV)
stalking
injunction

restraining order
stay-away order
ex parte
full faith and credit (FFC)
cause of action
probable cause
Confrontation Clause
self-defense
imminent
battered woman syndrome
voluntary manslaughter
pro bono

REVIEW QUESTIONS

1. What rights were denied to married women at common law?

2. What is meant by coverture?

3. Describe the effect of the unity of person.

4. What restrictions apply to contracts between spouses?

5. What is a fraudulent transfer?

6. What are the possible legal consequences of a spouse using his or her separate funds to buy property that is placed in the sole name of the other spouse?

7. What was accomplished by the married women's property acts?

8. What is equitable distribution?

9. What is the relationship among dower, curtesy, and elective share?

10. What are the two ways a surname can be changed?

11. What rights did the Equal Credit Opportunity Act give to women?

12. What is a BFOQ?

13. What are some examples of illegal job interview questions asked of women?

14. What does the Equal Pay Act provide?

15. What rights do pregnant women have on the job?

16. Can a mother express breast milk on the job?

17. What rights is an employee given under the Family and Medical Leave Act (FMLA)?

18. How do the two kinds of sexual harassment differ?

19. What duties do employers have concerning sexual harassment?

20. How did Governor Clinton win the claim of sexual harassment against him?

21. How are laws on sexual harassment enforced?

22. What contraceptive rights do adults have?

23. When can a person be sterilized?

24. What abortion rights were established by *Roe v. Wade*?

25. What abortion rights were established by *Planned Parenthood of Southeastern Pennsylvania v. Casey*?

26. What is the Partial-Birth Abortion Ban Act and is it constitutional?

27. What is feticide?

28. What does the Unborn Victims of Violence Act provide?

29. What is domestic violence?

30. What remedies does a woman have when she is a victim of domestic violence?

31. How does a victim of domestic violence obtain a restraining order or order of protection?

32. How does the Violence Against Women Act (VAWA) try to protect women who are victims of violence?

33. What does the Free Access to Clinic Entrances Act (FACE) provide?

34. What are mandatory arrest and mandatory prosecution?

35. When does the Confrontation Clause prevent the state from using the statement of an alleged victim who now refuses to cooperate in the case against the alleged batterer?

36. What is the primary aggressor law?

37. What is the battered woman syndrome and how is it used in court?

38. What are some of the major guidelines for assisting victims of domestic violence?

HELPFUL WEBSITES

Women's Rights

- www.catalaw.com/cattopics/Women.shtml
- wbl.worldbank.org/genderlibrary/elibrary.aspx?libid=17
- www.whitehouse.gov/sites/default/files/rss_viewer/Women_in_America.pdf
- www.aclu.org/womens-rights
- en.wikipedia.org/wiki/Women's_rights
- www.now.org

Women's Legal History

- wlh.law.stanford.edu

Employment Discrimination

- www.eeoc.gov/facts/qanda.html
- www.law.cornell.edu/wex/employment_discrimination
- www.hg.org/employment-discrimination-law.html
- www.bls.gov/regions/womensearnings.htm

Equal Employment Opportunity Commission

- www.eeoc.gov

Abortion

- www.guttmacher.org/statecenter/spibs/spib_OAL.pdf
- en.wikipedia.org/wiki/Abortion_law
- www.ncsl.org/issues-research/health/abortion-laws.aspx
- www.law.duke.edu/voices/stenberg

Domestic Violence

- www.probono.net/dv/oppsguide
- www.ncdbw.org

Institute for Women's Policy Research

- www.iwpr.org/press-room

Progress of the World's Women 2011-2012: In Pursuit of Justice

- progress.unwomen.org/pdfs/EN-Report-Progress.pdf

Google/Bing/Yahoo Searches

(on these search engines, run the following searches, substituting your state for "aa")

- coverture aa
- dower aa
- BFOQ aa
- pregnancy law aa
- "family leave" aa
- abortion law aa
- marital rape aa
- "married women's property" aa
- women "common law" aa
- "employment discrimination" aa
- EEOC discrimination aa
- "sexual harassment" aa
- "domestic violence" aa
- "battered woman syndrome" aa

ENDNOTES

Note: All or most of the court opinions in these endnotes can be read online. To do so, go to Google Scholar (scholar.google.com), select "Legal documents," and in the search box, enter the cite (e.g., "867 N.E.2d 903") or name of the case (e.g., "State v. Donkers") that is given in the endnote.

[1] Robert Oliphant and Nancy Ver Steegh, *Family Law* 239 (3d ed. 2010).

[2] Homer Clark, *The Law of Domestic Relations in the United States* § 8.1, p. 498 (Practitioner's ed. 2d ed. 1987).

[3] *State v. Donkers,* 867 N.E.2d 903, 939 (Ohio Court of Appeals, 2007).

[4] N.J.S.A. § 3A:37-3 (www.njleg.state.nj.us/2010/Bills/S3000/2665_I1.HTM).

[5] Sue Shellenbarger, *The Name Change Dilemma,* The Wall Street Journal (May 8, 2011) (blogs.wsj.com/juggle/2011/05/08/the-name-change-dilemma).

[6] Or on the basis of race, color, religion, national origin, or age. 15 U.S.C. § 1691 (www.law.cornell.edu/uscode/15/1691.shtml).

[7] Federal Trade Commission, *Equal Credit Opportunity* (Mar. 1998) (www.ftc.gov/bcp/edu/pubs/consumer/credit/cre15.shtm).

[8] Federal Trade Commission, Facts for Consumers (May 2009) (www.ftc.gov/bcp/edu/pubs/consumer/credit/cre15.shtm).

[9] 42 U.S.C. § 2000e-2(a)(1) (1974) (www.law.cornell.edu/uscode/42/usc_sec_42_00002000---e002-.html).

[10] *Dothard v. Rawlinson,* 433 U.S. 321 (1977).

[11] *International Union, United Auto., Aerospace and Agr. Implement Workers of America, UAW v. Johnson Controls, Inc.,* 499 U.S. 187 (1991).

[12] U.S. Census Bureau, *Men's and Women's Earnings . . .* (Sept. 2010) (www.census.gov/prod/2010pubs/acsbr09-3.pdf).

[13] Sheryl Stolberg, *White House Issues Report on Women in America*, N.Y. Times, Mar. 1, 2011 (thecaucus .blogs.nytimes.com/2011/03/01/white-house-issues -report-on-women-in-america).

[14] 29 U.S.C. § 206(d) (www.eeoc.gov/laws/statutes/epa.cfm).

[15] 42 U.S.C. § 2000e(k) (www.eeoc.gov/facts/fs-preg.html) (www.eeoc.gov/laws/statutes/pregnancy.cfm).

[16] United States Department of Labor, *Break Time for Nursing Mothers* (www.dol.gov/whd/nursingmothers).

[16a] Family and Medical Leave Act (www.dol.gov/whd/fmla /#.UI3EDcU818E).

[17] U.S. Equal Employment Opportunity Commission, *Sexual Harassment* (www.eeoc.gov/laws/types/sexual_harassment .cfm) (www.eeoc.gov/facts/fs-sex.html).

[18] *Jones v. Clinton*, 990 F. Supp. 657, 663–64, 677 (E.D. Ark 1998).

[19] Id. at 675, 677–78.

[20] U.S. Equal Employment Opportunity Commission, *Charge Statistics FY 1997 Through FY 2011* (www.eeoc.gov/eeoc /statistics/enforcement/charges.cfm).

[21] *Eisenstadt v. Baird*, 405 U.S. 438, 453 (1972).

[22] *Buck v. Bell*, 274 U.S. 200, 207 (1927).

[23] West's Annotated California Probate Code § 1958 (law .onecle.com/california/probate/1958.html).

[24] 410 U.S. 113 (1973).

[25] U.S. Const. amend. XIV (www.law.cornell.edu/constitution /amendmentxiv).

[26] *Webster v. Reproductive Health Services*, 492 U.S. 490, 559 (1989) (Blackmun).

[27] 505 U.S. 833 (1992).

[28] *Stenbert v. Carhart*, 530 U.S. 914, 953 (2000) (Scalia dissenting).

[29] 18 U.S.C. § 1531 (www.law.cornell.edu/uscode/18/usc _sec_18_00001531----000-.html).

[30] 550 U.S. 124 (2007).

[31] New York Penal Law § 125.00 (ypdcrime.com/penal.law /article125.htm).

[32] Georgia Code Annotated, § 40-6-393.1 (www.lexisnexis .com/hottopics/gacode).

[33] Indiana Code, § 35-42-1-6 (www.in.gov/legislative/ic/code /title35/ar42/ch1.html).

[34] 18 U.S.C. § 1841 (www.law.cornell.edu/uscode/usc _sec_18_00001841----000-.html).

[35] Editorial, *A Misleading Fetal Violence Law*, N.Y. Times, Mar. 29, 2004 (www.nytimes.com/2004/03/29/opinion /a-misleading-fetal-violence-law.html).

[36] Nancy Ver Steegh and Clare Dalton, *Report from the Wingspread Conference on Domestic Violence and Family Courts*, 46 Family Court Review, 454, 458 (Jul. 2008).

[37] Domestic Violence Resource Center, *Domestic Violence Statistics* (www.dvrc-or.org/domestic/violence/resources /C61). *The National Intimate Partner and Sexual Violence Survey* (www.cdc.gov/violenceprevention/NISVS/index .html).

[38] White House Council on Women and Girls, Women in America, 53 (Mar. 2011) (www.whitehouse.gov/sites /default/files/rss_viewer/Women_in_America.pdf).

[39] Stephanie Coontz, *Marriage: Saying I Don't*, Los Angeles Times (Jan. 19, 2012) (articles.latimes.com/2012 /jan/19/opinion/la-oe-coontz-marriage-20120119).

[40] Quoted in T. Davidson, *Conjugal Crime* 99 (1978). See also The Language of Violence (cyber.law.harvard.edu/vaw00 /History.html).

[41] United States Commission on Civil Rights, *Under the Rule of Thumb: Battered Women and the Administration of Justice* 2 (Jan. 1982) (www.law.umaryland.edu/marshall/usccr /documents/cr12w8410.pdf).

[42] Ansgar Kelly, *Rule of Thumb and the Folklaw of the Husband's Stick*, 44 Journal of Legal Education 341 (Sept. 1994). See also dynamic.uoregon.edu/~jjf/essays/ruleofthumb .html.

[43] *United States v. Morrison*, 529 U.S. 598, 120 S. Ct. 1740, 146 L. Ed. 2d 658 (2000).

[44] Freedom of Access to Clinic Entrances, 18 U.S.C. § 248 (www.law.cornell.edu/uscode/18/usc_sec_18_00000248--- -000-.html).

[45] Michael Rips and Amy Lester, *When Words Bear Witness*, N.Y. Times, Mar. 20, 2006 (www.nytimes.com /2006/03/20/opinion/20rips.html).

[46] Paul Clark, *Mandatory Arrest for Misdemeanor Domestic Violence: Is Alaska's Arrest Statute Constitutional?*, 27 Alaska Law Review 151 (2010).

[47] U.S. Const. amend. VI (caselaw.lp.findlaw.com/data /constitution/amendment06).

[48] *Davis v. Washington*, 547 U.S. 813, 822 126 S. Ct. 2266, 2273-74, 165 L. Ed. 2d 224 (2006).

[49] National Council of Juvenile and Family Court Judges, *Family Violence: A Model State Code*, § 205(a)(1994) (www .ncjfcj.org/sites/default/files/modecode_fin_printable.pdf).

[50] Michael Buda and Theresa Butler, *The Battered Wife Syndrome*, 23 Journal of Family Law 359 (1984–85).

[51] M. Hale, *The History of the Pleas of the Crown* 629 (1736).

CHAPTER OUTLINE

CHAPTER OBJECTIVES

After completing this chapter, you should be able to:

- Explain the evolving terminology of illegitimacy and nonmarital children.

- State the position of the Uniform Parentage Act on the distinction between marital and nonmarital children.

- Know the test used by the U.S. Supreme Court to determine whether a classification of nonmarital children violates equal protection of the laws.

- State the rights of nonmarital children in the areas of inheritance, wills, child support, wrongful death, workers' compensation, Social Security, and immigration.

- Explain the different kinds of artificial insemination and the paternity consequences of each.

- Describe medical and legal issues that arise in the operation of sperm banks.

- Identify the different ways that a child can be legitimated.

- List the major reasons it is important to determine the paternity of a child.

- Know the kinds of questions commonly found on a paternity questionnaire.

- State the standard of proof needed to determine paternity.

- Explain why it can be important to know whether a child had his or her own attorney in a paternity action.

- Know the kind of jurisdiction a court needs to make a paternity determination and how it can obtain that jurisdiction.

- Explain Lord Mansfield's rule.

- Explain the presumption of legitimacy and how it can be overcome.

- Explain the presumption of paternity and how it can be overcome.

- Understand how a court might resolve conflicting presumptions of paternity.

- Explain how blood-group and DNA testing are used in determining paternity.

- Explain the legal consequences of signing a voluntary recognition of parentage (ROP).

- Know whether a person has standing to assert his paternity of a child born to a woman married to another man.

- Explain paternity by estoppel.

ILLEGITIMACY

INTRODUCTION

A **legitimate child** is a child born to parents who are married to each other. (Later we will see that another way for a child to be considered legitimate is through a process called legitimation.) Legitimacy is determined at birth, not at conception. A child conceived by an unmarried couple is legitimate if the parents are married at the time of the birth. An **illegitimate child** is one born to parents who were not married at the time of birth and who never took the steps needed to legitimate the child. In 2009, there were 4,130,665 births in the United States; 41 percent of the births were to unmarried women.[1] This large number has contributed to the decline in the stigma that society attaches to children of unmarried parents.

At one time, however, the stigma was culturally and legally severe. The former legal term for a child born out of wedlock was **bastard**. His or her status was referred to as **bastardy**. We no longer use this terminology today. The predominant term is **nonmarital child**, although the term *illegitimate child* is still used. Other terms include child of an informal relationship, child out of wedlock, and child with no presumed father.

At common law, the illegitimate child was **filius nullius**, the child of nobody. The central legal disability imposed by this status was that the child born out of wedlock had no right to inherit from either parent. In addition, the child was prohibited from entering certain occupations and, except by decree of some **ecclesiastical** (church) courts, had no right to be supported by the father. Fortunately, the pronounced discrimination that existed for centuries between the legitimate and the illegitimate child is eroding. States that have adopted the **Uniform Parentage Act (UPA)** have abolished the distinction between legitimate and illegitimate children. ("A child born to parents who are not married to each other has the same rights under the law as a child born to parents who are married to each other."[2]) States that have not adopted the UPA have laws to the same effect. This change in the law has been due largely to decisions of the U.S. Supreme Court, which we will be examining in this chapter. In 1972, the Court summarized the change:

> The status of illegitimacy has expressed through the ages society's condemnation of irresponsible liaisons beyond the bonds of marriage. But visiting this condemnation on the head of an infant is illogical and unjust. Moreover, imposing disabilities on the illegitimate child is contrary to the basic concept of our system that legal burdens should bear some relationship to individual responsibility or wrongdoing. Obviously, no child is responsible for his birth and penalizing the illegitimate child is an ineffectual—as well as an unjust—way of deterring the parent. Courts are powerless to prevent the social opprobrium suffered by these hapless children, but the Equal Protection Clause does enable us to strike down discriminatory laws relating to status of birth where . . . the classification is justified by no legitimate state interest, compelling or otherwise.[3]

Not all discriminatory laws against nonmarital children, however, have been eliminated. As we will see, some of the laws have been upheld.

NONMARITAL CHILDREN AS A QUASI-SUSPECT CLASS

In Chapter 1, we saw that when the law treats one group differently from another group, it is setting up a class or a **classification**. We need to ask when such a classification is a violation of **equal protection of law (EPL)**. There are different kinds of classifications. A class based on a child's legitimacy is an example of what is called a **quasi-suspect class**. (See Exhibit 1-2 in Chapter 1.)

---

legitimate child
A child born to parents who are married to each other.

illegitimate child
A child born to parents who are not married to each other and who never took the steps needed to legitimate the child. Also called nonmarital child, child of an informal relationship, child out of wedlock, child with no presumed father, bastard.

bastard
A child born to parents who are not married to each other and who never legitimated the child. Also called illegitimate child, nonmarital child, child of an informal relationship, child out of wedlock, child with no presumed father.

bastardy
Pertaining to a child born to unmarried parents who never legitimated the child. Also called illegitimacy.

nonmarital child
A child born to parents who are not married to each other and who have not legitimated the child. Also called illegitimate child, child of an informal relationship, child out of wedlock, child with no presumed father, bastard.

filius nullius
"The son [or child] of no one." The status of an illegitimate child at common law.

ecclesiastical
Pertaining to the church.

Uniform Parentage Act (UPA)
A model statute that has been adopted by most states on how paternity or parenthood is determined.

classification
(1) A group the government treats differently from another group in that the government discriminates for or against that group. (2) The government's different treatment of one group over another. (See glossary for an additional meaning.)

equal protection of law (EPL)
The constitutional requirement that the government treat one group or class the same as it treats another group or class in like circumstances. Shortened to equal protection.

quasi-suspect class
A class based on gender or on a child's legitimacy.

intermediate scrutiny
The government's action must be substantially related to serve an important state interest. Also called heightened scrutiny, elevated scrutiny.

intestate
(1) Pertaining to someone who dies without a valid will. (2) A person who dies without a valid will.

paternity
The biological fatherhood of a child.

testate
(1) Pertaining to someone who dies with a valid will. (2) A person who dies with a valid will. Under this definition, also called the testator and, if female, the testatrix.

wrongful death
A death caused by a tort or other wrong.

Assume, for example, that a state passes a law that treats marital and nonmarital children differently by giving different inheritance rights to each. The test used by the courts to determine whether this different treatment of a quasi-suspect class violates EPL is the **intermediate scrutiny** test. Under this test, the classification will be declared unconstitutional unless it can be shown that the classification is substantially related to the achievement of an important state interest. In this chapter, we will examine some of the laws on nonmarital children that courts have held to be unconstitutional. The main test used by the courts in reaching this conclusion is the intermediate scrutiny test.

INHERITANCE

Assume that a parent dies **intestate** (without leaving a valid will). The estate of the deceased then passes by inheritance rather than by will. It is a denial of equal protection to allow a marital child to inherit from an intestate mother or father but to say that a nonmarital child can inherit from an intestate mother but not from an intestate father.[4]

All inheritance discrimination, however, is not unconstitutional. For example, assume that a nonmarital child waits until after his or her father dies before asserting that a parent-child relationship exists. Some states would not allow such a child to inherit, insisting that **paternity** (i.e., biological fatherhood) must be determined by a court *before* death as a condition of inheriting from an intestate parent. (No such requirement exists for a marital child seeking to inherit from his or her intestate parent.) The pre-death requirement for nonmarital children is considered reasonable and is substantially related to the important public purpose of preventing false or fraudulent inheritance claims against the estate of an alleged father who is now deceased.

Not all states insist that a nonmarital child obtain a court finding of paternity before the death of the alleged father. In some states, it is sufficient if, before death, the alleged father publicly acknowledged the child as his, supported the child, or otherwise clearly indicated that he was the child's father.

INTERPRETATION OF A WILL

Assume that the father of a nonmarital child dies **testate** (leaving a valid will) and that a clause in the will gives property "to my children" or "to my heirs." If the father has marital and nonmarital children living when he dies, the question sometimes arises as to whether he intended "children" or "heirs" to include his nonmarital children. This is not a constitutional question; it is simply a question of intent. To resolve this question, the court must look at all of the circumstances (e.g., how much contact the nonmarital child had with the father at the time the father wrote the will and at the time he died). A significant number of cases exist in which the court concluded that the nonmarital child was *not* included in the meaning of "children" or "heirs."

SUPPORT

Today both parents have an equal obligation to support their children, both marital and nonmarital. A testate father can decide to leave his nonmarital children out of his will, but he cannot refuse to support them during his lifetime (see Chapter 10).

WRONGFUL DEATH

When a parent dies due to the wrongful act of another, marital and nonmarital children have an equal right to bring **wrongful death** actions against defendants who have caused the death of the parent.

Suppose, however, that it is the child who dies. Mothers and fathers of marital children have an equal right to sue for the wrongful death of children born from their marriage. If the child is nonmarital, the mother can sue for its wrongful death. Can the father? Many courts are concerned about absent fathers who suddenly appear when there is the prospect of collecting tort damages due to the death of their nonmarital child. Hence states may impose restrictions on a father's right to sue. The U.S. Supreme Court upheld a Georgia statute that denied the right of a father to sue for the wrongful death of his nonmarital child unless he had legitimated the child before its death.[5]

WORKERS' COMPENSATION

When a parent dies from an injury on the job, the **workers' compensation** laws of the state permit the children of the deceased to recover benefits. If the state gives a preference to marital children over nonmarital children in claiming these benefits, the state is unconstitutionally denying equal protection of the law to the nonmarital children.[6]

SOCIAL SECURITY

It would be unconstitutional if social security **survivors benefits** (also called survivorship benefits) were denied to a child solely because that child is nonmarital. Yet it is permissible to impose greater procedural burdens on non-marital children than on marital children in applying for such benefits. Suppose, for example, that a child applies for survivorship benefits following the death of his or her parent. To be eligible, the child must have been "dependent" on the deceased parent. A nonmarital child can be forced to *prove* that he or she was dependent on the parent, whereas no such requirement will be imposed on a marital child—the law will *presume* that the marital child was dependent on the parent without requiring specific proof of it. The difference in treatment is considered reasonable because nonmarital children are generally less likely to be dependent on their parent than marital children.[7]

Other cases on survivors benefits have also come before the courts. After the death of Karen Capato's husband in Florida, she gave birth to twins. They were conceived through in vitro fertilization (IVF) using her husband's sperm shortly after he died. (See discussion of artificial insemination on the following page and IVF in Chapter 16. Children born after the death of a parent are called *posthumous children*.) When she applied for social security survivors benefits for the twins as survivors of a wage earner (their father), her application was denied. The U.S. Supreme Court upheld the denial. Under social security rules, children can qualify for survivors benefits if they are entitled to inherit from their parent under state law. In Florida, a child *born* after the death of the father can inherit from him, but a child *conceived* after his death cannot. Florida's inheritance law requires conception to occur before he died. The Caputo twins were conceived after their father's death through IVF and hence were not entitled to inherit from him. Under social security rules, this inability to inherit disqualified them from receiving survivors benefits.[7a] Not all states have the same law as Florida. In other states, children conceived after the death of their father can inherit from him. In such states, they would be entitled to social security survivors benefits.

IMMIGRATION

Immigration law allows nonmarital children born abroad to become U.S. citizens when one of the parents is a U.S. citizen. The requirements for citizenship, however, differ depending on whether the citizen parent is the mother or father. If the citizen parent is the father, he must take affirmative steps in order for his child to acquire citizenship (i.e., initiate legitimation, declare paternity under oath, or obtain a court order of paternity). If, however, the citizen parent is the mother, such steps are not required. The U.S. Supreme Court has held that this discrimination does not violate equal protection

workers' compensation
A no-fault system of paying for medical care and providing limited wage benefits to a worker for an employment-related injury or illness regardless of who was at fault in causing the injury or illness.

survivors benefits
A form of life insurance from Social Security in which widows, children, and other designated survivors can receive monthly payments and other benefits upon the death of a worker. Also called survivorship benefits.

of law. The government has an important interest (1) in ensuring that the child is biologically related to the U.S. citizen and (2) that there has been an opportunity for a meaningful relationship between the parent and child during the child's minority. It is significantly easier to verify the parentage of a mother (she is present at the birth!) and to verify her connecting relationship with the child than it is to verify a father's parentage and connecting relationship. In some cases, for example, the father may not be aware that conception or birth has occurred until many years later. Even if the father is present at birth, his presence is not proof of his parentage nor does it prove that he developed a connecting relationship with the child. Therefore the different citizenship requirements for mothers and fathers are justifiable.[8]

ASSIGNMENT 13.1

Explain whether you think the following feminist critique of the immigration decision on foreign-born children of fathers is correct: "Making parenthood a biological fact for women but legally optional for men promotes men's control over women and children, allowing men to take or leave fatherhood at their whim. It lets men decide whether their country has obligations to their progeny. And it defines women as mothers—alone, unless men choose to acknowledge the existence of children they jointly created." Catherine MacKinnon, *Can Fatherhood Be Optional?* N.Y. Times, June 17, 2001 (www.nytimes.com/2001/06/17/opinion/17MACK.html).

ARTIFICIAL INSEMINATION (AI)

HUSBAND AND WIFE USING AI

Assume that a woman is fertile but cannot conceive a child with her partner through sexual intercourse. His sperm may have poor motility, he may carry a genetically transmissible disease, or he may be sterile. In such cases, the couple might try **artificial insemination (AI)**. A physician injects sperm into the woman's vagina during a time that she is ovulating.

There are three main kinds of AI that married couples consider:

- AI with the semen of the husband (AIH)
- AI with the semen of a third-party donor (AID)
- AI in which the semen of the husband is mixed (confused) with that of a third-party donor (AIC)

artificial insemination (AI)
Inserting sperm into the uterus by a method other than sexual intercourse.

The advantage in AIH is that the physician may be able to use "better" or concentrated sperm of the husband than would be achieved through sexual intercourse. One of the psychological advantages of AIC is the knowledge that the child *might* have been fathered by the husband.

In cases where the donor is the mother's husband (AIH), the child is legitimate, and the husband has full parental rights and responsibilities. At one time, there was some doubt about the legitimacy of a child born through AID or AIC. Today there is no longer any doubt in cases where the husband has consented to an AID or AIC procedure. Under § 5 of the Uniform Parentage Act:

> If, under the supervision of a licensed physician and with the consent of her husband, a wife is inseminated artificially with semen donated by a man not her husband, the husband is treated in law as if he were the natural father of a child thereby conceived. The husband's consent must be in writing and signed by him and his wife.... The donor of semen ... is treated in law as if he were not the natural father of a child thereby conceived.[9]

Most states have adopted this statute or one similar to it. See Exhibit 13-1 for an example of a consent form used for AI.

EXHIBIT 13-1 **Consent for Artificial Insemination (AI)**

SECTION I – TO BE COMPLETED BY BIRTH MOTHER AND BIRTH MOTHER'S HUSBAND/CIVIL UNION PARTNER

We, _____ *(birth mother)* and _____
(birth mother's husband or civil union partner), the undersigned are each 18 years or older.

We understand that according to New Jersey law that if, under the supervision of a licensed physician and with the consent of her husband, a wife is inseminated artificially with semen donated by a man not her husband, the husband is treated in law as if he were the natural father of a child thereby conceived. Pursuant to the Civil Union Act, N.J.S.A. 37:1-28, et seq., civil union partners are entitled to the same legal presumption.

Our signatures below indicate that we have read and understood the above information and that we consent to the performance of artificial insemination with semen donated by a man who is not an individual listed above. We acknowledge that our relationship, rights and obligations to any child born as a result of artificial insemination herein consented to shall be the same to all legal intents and purposes as if the child had been naturally and legitimately conceived by us as husband and wife.

We understand that if a child is born who may have been the result of the artificial insemination consented to herein, the licensed physician is required by law to file a copy of this consent with the Department of Health. Pursuant to N.J.S.A. 9:17-44(a), this document is a confidential record and is not available for public inspection. This document may be subject to inspection upon an order of the court.

Name of Birth Mother *(Print)*			Name of Birth Mother's Husband or Civil Union Partner *(Print)*		
(First)	*(Middle)*	*(Last)*	*(First)*	*(Middle)*	*(Last)*
Signature of Birth Mother			Signature of Birth Mother's Husband or Civil Union Partner		
Date			Date		

SECTION II – TO BE COMPLETED BY PHYSICIAN

Name of Physician *(Print)*			License Number	
(First)	*(Middle)*	*(Last)*		
Practice Name			Telephone Number	
Mailing Address (Street)		City, State, Zip Code		

On, _____, a child/children was born to _____. On the following dates, I certify that artificial insemination was performed in accordance with the above-consent:

(List dates of insemination within one year prior to child/children's birth.)

and that the individuals named above appeared before me and signed this form.

Signature of Licensed Physician Named Above	Date

Source: New Jersey Department of Health and Senior Services, Vital Statistics and Registration (www.state.nj.us/health/forms/reg-64.dot).

OTHERS USING AI

A single woman or a lesbian couple might also consider AI, using sperm that has been purchased anonymously from a commercial **sperm bank** or that has been donated by a known male. If both women want to conceive, they might decide to use the same sperm donor so that there is a biological link between each child. A same-sex male couple that wants a biological child would have to use the services of a surrogate mother. We will study surrogacy arrangements in Chapter 16.

sperm bank

A facility that collects and stores human sperm from donors who will usually be anonymous to the woman who uses the sperm to become pregnant by artificial insemination. Also called cryobank.

SPERM DONORS

When a husband is involved in AI (through AID or AIC), the sperm donor has no rights or duties with respect to the child born with his sperm. The sperm donor, for example, does not have to pay child support. The rights and duties of a sperm donor are not always as clear, however, when AI is used by a lesbian couple or a single heterosexual woman. Not many cases on such insemination have been litigated. The few that do exist say that a donor of semen to someone other than his wife has no parental rights or duties to a child conceived through AI unless the donor and the woman have entered into a written contract to the contrary or unless the donor has established a bonding relationship with the child. (See Chapter 10 for a discussion of child support and sperm donors.)

AI cases need to be distinguished from cases of one-night stands (or more extended affairs) involving traditional sexual intercourse. The father of a child conceived through the traditional method has the full duties of a father, including the duty to pay child support. It is not a defense for the man to say that he never intended to have or support a child.

Sperm banks (also called cryobanks) are facilities that collect and store human sperm. The donors of the sperm will usually be anonymous to the women who will later use the sperm to try to become pregnant by AI. Sperm banks have become big business. Ads for donors often appear in college newspapers and on the Internet. Because sperm is frequently sold to the banks, it is more accurate to say that the men are sperm vendors than sperm donors. Sellers can earn up to $100 per donation. (Buyers of sperm pay sperm banks between $200 and $600 per vial.) Sperm banks often encourage repeat donations from males with specific characteristics (e.g., college educated, athletic, and no family history of heart disease). Popular donor males have said that the income they received from the sperm banks helped pay for their college education. Some of these males have fathered multiple children.

The system has worked well, but it has not been without controversy. One sperm bank tried to recruit Nobel Prize winners as sperm donors. Not many came forward. Critics ridiculed the bank as elitist genetic engineering. It is no longer in existence. In 1992, a Virginia fertility doctor was arrested after it was discovered that he was using his own sperm to impregnate his patients through AI. Prosecutors said that he may have fathered up to 75 children. In 1991, in what the media called the "scrambled eggs" case, a white woman gave birth to a black child after the sperm bank accidentally injected her with the sperm of a black man. And in 2000, a trial court ordered a sperm bank to reveal the identity of "donor 276" when it became clear that the child born with his sperm had a genetic disease. There was no allegation in the case that the donor had lied about his medical condition when he agreed to donate. Nor was there an allegation that the donee (the mother) was not given sufficient information about the risks of AI. Doctors simply wanted more information about the father to help them in their diagnosis and treatment of the child. The court agreed and ordered the disclosure of the identity of donor 276.

ACCIDENTAL INCEST

Accurate statistics on the number of children born through sperm donation do not exist. Estimates vary from 30,000 to 60,000 babies a year. (For information on egg donation, see Chapter 14.) As the numbers of babies from anonymously donated semen increase, *accidental incest* becomes a concern. When the babies grow up, two of them who are unaware of their biological relationship might become sexually intimate. If they produce children, there is a risk of genetic diseases caused by inbreeding. Even if the danger of incest is small, some health officials are worried about what is called genetic bewilderment—stress resulting from confusion about the identity of one's biological parents. Some European countries have passed laws banning the anonymous donation of genetic material, a controversial decision because of the steep decline in sperm donations that result from such laws. Less controversial are laws that limit the number of children that one donor can father.

There is no official way for the vast majority of these children to find each other and learn of their potential **consanguinity** (relationship by blood). The Internet offers some options. For example, the Donor Sibling Registry helps persons conceived as a result of sperm, egg, or embryo donation to find others with

consanguinity
Relationship by blood.

whom they have genetic ties.[10] A sperm donor participates by voluntarily giving the registry his donor ID number. Users of sperm banks generally know the ID number of their donor and hence can use the number to search the registry for others who used a male with the same number. The registry claims to have helped connect over 9,000 half-siblings and/or donors with each other. In one case, the mothers of 21 children of the same father have established an ongoing network of contact: "These children are all 3 and under, and their families—four lesbian couples, three heterosexual couples and six single mothers—have formed their own Listserv, where photographs of the children (all blond, with a strong familial resemblance) are posted, and daily e-mail messages are exchanged about birthdays, toilet training and the like."[11]

LEGITIMATION

Legitimation confers the status of legitimacy on a nonmarital child. Legitimation is not the same as paternity. A paternity proceeding determines the identity of the father; legitimation confers the status of legitimacy on a child who is or who might be a nonmarital child.

States have different methods by which nonmarital children can be legitimated:

- *Acknowledgment.* The father publicly recognizes or acknowledges the nonmarital child as his. States differ on how the acknowledgment takes place. In some states, it must be in writing and witnessed. (For a form acknowledging parentage that is used in many maternity wards, see Exhibit 13-6 at the end of the chapter.) In some states, a written acknowledgment of paternity is not required if the man's activities strongly indicate that he is the father of the child (e.g., the father treats the child the same as the children who were born legitimate).

- *Marriage.* If the mother and father of the nonmarital child marry, the child is often automatically legitimated.

- *Combination of acknowledgment and marriage.* Some states require marriage of the parents and some form of acknowledgment by the father.

- *Legitimation proceeding.* A few states have special proceedings by which nonmarital children can be legitimated.

- *Paternity proceedings.* In a few states, a finding of paternity also legitimates the child.

- *Legitimation by birth.* In some states, all children are legitimate whether or not their parents were married at the time of birth.

Children of annulled marriages are considered legitimate according to special statutes, even though technically the parents were not validly married at the time the children were born. As we saw in Chapter 6, however, some of the statutes are not absolute. For example, the statute might say that the children are legitimate only if one or both of the parents honestly believed that their marriage was valid when they entered it, or the statute might legitimize all the children born from an annulled marriage except when the annulment was granted on the ground of a prior existing marriage (bigamy).

legitimation

1. The declaration that a child is legitimate. The verb is *legitimize*. 2. The steps taken to declare that a child is legitimate.

ASSIGNMENT 13.2

In what way(s) can an illegitimate child be legitimated in your state? (See General Instructions for the State-Code Assignment in Appendix A.)

PATERNITY

INTRODUCTION

Determining paternity of a nonmarital child can affect many different areas of a child's life. Examples include:

- the availability of child support
- the right to inherit from one's father
- Social Security survivors benefits as the child of a deceased father
- insurance claims upon the death of the father
- citizenship status as a foreign-born child of a father who is a U.S. citizen
- the right to share in damages for the wrongful death of a father
- the child custody and visitation rights of the father
- the identification of paternal grandparents and siblings

For most children, the most important of these consequences is child support. A major method by which a father is forced to support his nonmarital child is through a paternity proceeding. Other names for this proceeding include a **filiation** action, a suit to determine parentage, or, in our early history, a bastardy proceeding. Once fatherhood is determined, the support obligation is imposed. Paternity proceedings are often instigated by the state to try to recover some of the welfare or public assistance money paid to custodial parents. These parents are required to cooperate in instituting paternity proceedings. The program has been very successful. In 2010, 1.7 million paternities were established or acknowledged with the help of state child-support agencies (IV-D agencies) that exist in every state. This is triple the number obtained in 1992.[12]

The starting point in establishing paternity is to obtain detailed facts from the mother. The questionnaire in Exhibit 13-2 has this objective.

PATERNITY PROCEEDINGS

A **putative father** is the man believed to be the biological father of a child but who has not yet been medically or legally declared to be the father. Paternity is determined by a court in what is called a paternity proceeding. In most states, paternity must be established by a **preponderance of the evidence**—the evidence must show that it is more likely than not that the putative father is in fact the father. Some states, however, require a higher standard of proof: **clear and convincing evidence**. The **statute of limitations** in most states is 18 years so that the paternity action against the alleged father can be brought at any time before the child reaches the age of majority. In some states, however, there is no statute of limitations. In these states, the paternity action can be brought against the putative father at any time. (Exhibit 13-3 shows an example of a paternity petition.)

REPRESENTATION

In paternity actions, the mother and alleged father can be represented by their own attorneys. In some paternity actions, the child may have his or her separate attorney, often appointed by the court. It can sometimes be important to determine whether the child had separate representation.

> *Mary, the mother of Sam, brings a paternity proceeding against Kevin, alleging that he is the father of Sam. The court finds that Kevin is not the father of Sam. Ten years later Sam brings his own action against Kevin for support, alleging that he is the son of Kevin.*

Is Sam's support action 10 years later barred by the defense of **res judicata**? That is, was the fatherhood issue already resolved in the paternity proceeding so that it cannot be relitigated? States differ in their answer to this question. Some states will not allow the relitigation. Other states will allow it if Kevin was not a formal party in the first case and if he did not have his own separate representation.

---

filiation

1. A judicial determination of paternity. 2. The relation of child to a particular parent.

putative father

The man believed to be the biological father of a child but who has not yet been medically or legally declared to be the father. Also called alleged father, reputed father.

preponderance of the evidence

A standard of proof that is met when the evidence establishes that it is more likely than not that the facts are as alleged. Also called fair preponderance of evidence.

clear and convincing evidence

A standard of proof that is met when the evidence demonstrates that the existence of a disputed fact is much more probable than its nonexistence. This standard is stronger than preponderance of the evidence but not as strong as beyond a reasonable doubt.

statute of limitations

A law stating that civil or criminal actions are barred if not brought within a specified period of time. The action is time-barred.

res judicata

A defense raised to prevent the same parties from retrying a claim that has already been resolved in a prior case or to prevent the litigation of a claim arising out of the same transaction involved in the first case that could have been raised in the first case but was not.

EXHIBIT 13-2 Paternity Questionnaire

PATERNITY QUESTIONNAIRE
Page 1 of 4

A **separate** paternity questionnaire must be completed **for each child** that paternity must be established for.

Child's Name: _____ _____ _____ _____
First   Middle   Last   Suffix

SECTION I: (Complete and then follow the instructions listed after question #5.)

1. Is there a court order establishing the noncustodial parent's parentage of child?   [ ] Yes   [ ] No
2. Is the noncustodial parent willing to agree to a court order of parentage?   [ ] Yes   [ ] No
3. When your child was born, did you and the noncustodial parent sign a Declaration of Paternity?   [ ] Yes   [ ] No
   If yes, in what County and State (attach a copy):
4. Were you married to and living with the noncustodial parent when you became pregnant?   [ ] Yes   [ ] No

INSTRUCTIONS: If you answered "NO" to **all** of the above questions, continue with Section II now and complete Sections II through X.

If you answered "YES" to questions 1 or 3, sign and date below. You do not need to complete Sections II through X. If you answered "YES" to question 4, you do not need to complete Sections II through X, UNLESS your husband was impotent or sterile at the time you became pregnant.

I declare under penalty of perjury under the laws of the State of California that the foregoing is true and correct.

_____   _____
Signature   Date

(Complete the remaining sections of this questionnaire only if all your answers in Section I were "No")

SECTION II: ABOUT THE CHILD AND YOUR PREGNANCY

Important Note: If this child is not yet born, write down in the following space the date you expect this child to be born: _____ Now, skip down to Item Number 4 in this Section.

Expected due date ___ / ___ / ___
                              MM   DD   CCYY

1. This child's birth date is: ___ / ___ / ___   2. This pregnancy was full term: [ ] Yes   [ ] No
                                          MM   DD   CCYY
3. The City and State in which this child was born are:
4. The City and State where you became pregnant:
5. The date you believe you became pregnant: _____ _____ _____
                                                                          Month   Day (if known)   Year
6. Doctor's name and address for this pregnancy are:

SECTION III: ABOUT THE CHILD'S MOTHER

1. Name: _____ _____ _____ _____
              First   Middle   Last   Suffix

2. Address: _____ _____ _____
                    Street   Unit #
   _____ _____ _____
   City   State   Zip Code

3. Social Security Number: ___ – ___ – ___   4. Date of birth: ___ / ___ / ___
                                                                                            MM   DD   CCYY

SECTION IV: ABOUT THE CHILD'S FATHER

1. His name is: _____ _____ _____ _____
                       First   Middle   Last   Suffix

2. The other names he uses are:

3. His last known address is: _____ _____ _____
                                              Street   Unit #
   _____ _____ _____
   City   State   Zip Code

4. His Social Security Number is: ___–___–___   5. His date of birth is: ___ / ___ / ___
                                                                                                                    MM   DD   CCYY

6. His height is: _____ feet _____ inches   7. His weight is: _____ lbs.

8. His hair color is: 9. His eye color is:

10. His ethnic origin is: ( ) African American   ( ) American Indian/Alaskan Native   ( ) Cambodian   ( ) Caucasian
    ( ) Chinese   ( ) Filipino   ( ) Guamanian   ( ) Hawaiian   ( ) Hispanic   ( ) Japanese   ( ) Korean   ( ) Laotian
    ( ) Other Asian   ( ) Pacific Islander   ( ) Samoan   ( ) Vietnamese   ( ) Other:

11. The name of his last known employer is:

12. Address of his last known employer is: _____ _____ _____
                                                                  Street
    _____ _____ _____
    City   State   Zip Code

SECTION V: ABOUT PRIOR COURT ORDERS

1. A court has already entered an order establishing the father of the child: [ ] Yes   [ ] No   If "yes," provide the following information:
2. The name of the court is:
3. The date the court order was entered is: ___ / ___ / ___   4. The court case number is:
                                                                          MM   DD   CCYY
5. The name of the father in the court order is: _____ _____ _____ _____
                                                                        First   Middle   Last   Suffix

SECTION VI: ABOUT MY RELATIONSHIP WITH THE FATHER

1. [ ] Yes   [ ] No   I was married to the father when I became pregnant with the child. If "yes," state the date and place of marriage:
                                    Date: ___ / ___ / ___   Place: _____ _____
                                                  MM   DD   CCYY   City   State

2. [ ] Yes   [ ] No   I was married to, but not living with, the father when I became pregnant with the child. If "yes," state the date you separated
                                    from the father (MM/DD/CCYY):

3. [ ] Yes   [ ] No   I was married to the father when the child was born.

4. [ ] Yes   [ ] No   I was married to, but not living with, the father when the child was born. If "yes," state the date you separated from the father
                                    (MM/DD/CCYY):

5. [ ] Yes   [ ] No   I have never been married to the father.

6. [ ] Yes   [ ] No   I have never been married to the father, but I have lived with him. If "yes," state all the time periods you lived with him:
                                    From: ___ / ___ / ___   to: ___ / ___ / ___
                                    From: ___ / ___ / ___   to: ___ / ___ / ___

7. [ ] Yes   [ ] No   I first had sexual intercourse with the father on (MM/DD/CCYY):
8. [ ] Yes   [ ] No   The place where I first had sexual intercourse with the father was: _____ _____
                                                                                                                                      City   State
9. [ ] Yes   [ ] No   I have had sexual intercourse with the father the following number of times:
10. [ ] Yes   [ ] No   The last time I had sexual intercourse with the father was on (MM/DD/CCYY):
11. [ ] Yes   [ ] No   The last place I had sexual intercourse with the father was: _____ _____
                                                                                                                          City   State
12. [ ] Yes   [ ] No   The father and I used birth control. If "yes," the methods we used were:

(continued)

EXHIBIT 13-2 *(continued)*

SECTION VII: ABOUT MY RELATIONSHIPS WITH OTHER MEN

1. [ ] Yes [ ] No   I had sexual intercourse with someone other than the father of the child within 30 days before I believe I became pregnant. If "yes," please state the name and address of each person:

2. [ ] Yes [ ] No   I had sexual intercourse with someone other than the father of the child within 30 days after I believe I became pregnant. If "yes," please state the name and address of each person:

3. [ ] Yes [ ] No   I was married to someone other than the father when the child was born. If "yes," the person I was married to was:

4. [ ] Yes [ ] No   I was married to someone other than the father when I became pregnant with the child. If "yes," the person I was married to was:

5. [ ] Yes [ ] No   I was married when I became pregnant with the child.

6. [ ] Yes [ ] No   I was married when the child was born.

SECTION VIII: ABOUT POSSIBLE WITNESSES WHO CAN SUPPORT MY CLAIM

1. [ ] Yes [ ] No   There were other people present when I told the father I was pregnant with the child. If "yes," their names and addresses are:

2. [ ] Yes [ ] No   There were other people present when I told the father I had given birth to the child. If "yes," their names and addresses are:

3. [ ] Yes [ ] No   There were other people present when I first showed the child to the father. If "yes," their names and addresses are:

4. [ ] Yes [ ] No   The father admitted to other people that he was the child's father. If "yes," state their names and addresses:

5. [ ] Yes [ ] No   When I had sexual intercourse with the father, there were other people present or nearby. If "yes," state their names and addresses:

6. [ ] Yes [ ] No   Other people have seen the father with me and/or the child. If "yes," state their names and addresses:

7. [ ] Yes [ ] No   The father's parent's, or other family members, have spent time with the child. If "yes," state their names and addresses:

SECTION IX: ABOUT THE FATHER'S RELATIONSHIP WITH THE CHILD

1. [ ] Yes [ ] No   The father was present when this child was born.

2. [ ] Yes [ ] No   The father visited me and this child at the hospital after the child's birth.

3. [ ] Yes [ ] No   The father has seen the child. If "yes," state what he said or did:

4. [ ] Yes [ ] No   The father has provided food, clothing, gifts and/or other financial support for the child.

5. [ ] Yes [ ] No   The father lived with this child. If "yes," state the time periods he lived with the child:
From: ___/___/___ to: ___/___/___
From: ___/___/___ to: ___/___/___

6. [ ] Yes [ ] No   The father had his picture taken with the child. If "yes," please provide copies.

SECTION X: ADDITIONAL FACTS WHICH SUPPORT MY CLAIM

1. [ ] Yes [ ] No   The father is listed on the child's birth certificate. If "no," state the name, if any, of the person listed as the child's father:

Why do you believe this person is not the child's real father?

2. [ ] Yes [ ] No   I heard the father admit that he is the natural father of this child.

3. [ ] Yes [ ] No   The father signed an acknowledgment of paternity. If "yes," please provide a copy of the acknowledgment.

4. [ ] Yes [ ] No   I have letters from the father which talk about this child. If "yes," please provide copies.

5. [ ] Yes [ ] No   The father offered to pay for me to get an abortion, or offered to pay for my medical expenses.

6. [ ] Yes [ ] No   The father, or his insurance company, did in fact pay for some or all of my medical expenses.

7. [ ] Yes [ ] No [ ] Don't know   The father has claimed this child on his tax returns.

8. [ ] Yes [ ] No   The child looks like the father. If "yes," describe how the child looks like him:

9. [ ] Yes [ ] No   There are more facts not mentioned above which support my claim. They are:

I have made all of the above responses as best as I can remember. I understand that I made these responses under penalty of perjury under the laws of the State of California.

_____   _____
Signature   Date

Source: State of California Health and Welfare, Department of Employment and Human Services, Contra Costa County (www.co.contra-costa.ca.us/depart/famsupp/pdf/paternity.pdf).

EXHIBIT 13-3 **Paternity Petition**

FAMILY COURT OF
COUNTY OF
....

In the Matter of a Paternity Proceeding
_____ Petitioner,

—against—

_____ Respondent,

Docket No.
PATERNITY PETITION
(Parent)

TO THE FAMILY COURT:

The undersigned Petitioner respectfully shows that:

1. Petitioner resides at _____.

2. Petitioner had sexual intercourse with the above named Respondent on several occasions covering a period of time beginning on or about the _____ day of _____, 20 _____, and ending on or about the _____ day of _____, 20 _____, and as a result thereof (Petitioner) became pregnant.

3. *(a) (Petitioner) gave birth to a (male) (female) child out of wedlock on the _____ day of _____, 20 _____, at _____

   *(b) (Petitioner) is now pregnant with a child who is likely to be born out of wedlock.

4. (Respondent) who resides at _____ is the father of the child.

5. (Respondent) (has acknowledged) (acknowledges) paternity of the child (in writing) (and) (by furnishing support).

6. No previous application has been made to any court or judge for the relief sought herein (except _____.)

WHEREFORE, Petitioner prays that this Court issue a summons or warrant requiring the Respondent to show cause why the Court should not enter a declaration of paternity, an order of support, and such other and further relief as may be appropriate under the circumstances.

_____
Petitioner

Dated: _____, 20 _____.
*Alternative allegations.

© Cengage Learning 2013

A related question is whether the mother can enter a settlement with the putative father under which she agrees to drop the paternity proceeding in exchange for the defendant's agreement to pay a certain amount for the support of the child and for the mother's expenses in giving birth to the child. In some states, it is illegal to enter into such an agreement. In states where this type of settlement is permitted, the child must have separate representation and/or the settlement must be approved by the court.

PERSONAL JURISDICTION OVER PUTATIVE FATHER

The paternity proceeding requires **personal jurisdiction** over the putative father (see Chapter 7). This generally means that service of process must be made on the defendant in person within the **forum** state (i.e., the state where the paternity proceeding is brought). If the defendant is not a resident of the forum state, **long-arm jurisdiction** over him may be obtainable on the ground that he engaged in sexual intercourse in the state, which may have led to the conception of the child. (Long-arm jurisdiction is the name for personal jurisdiction acquired under the state's long-arm statute.) For other ways to obtain long-arm jurisdiction, see Exhibit 10-8 on the Uniform Interstate Family Support Act (UIFSA) in Chapter 10.

LORD MANSFIELD'S RULE

In a paternity proceeding, it is understandable that a husband would want to raise the defense of **nonaccess**, which is the absence of opportunities for sexual intercourse with the mother around the time of conception. In most states, he is allowed to raise this defense. There was a time, however, when he was not allowed to do so.

personal jurisdiction
A court's power over a person to determine (adjudicate) his or her personal rights and duties. Also called in personam jurisdiction.

forum
(1) A court. (2) The place where the parties are presently litigating their dispute. (3) A court or tribunal hearing a case.

long-arm jurisdiction
The personal jurisdiction that a state acquires over a nonresident defendant because of his or her purposeful contact with the state.

nonaccess
Evidence of the absence of opportunities for sexual intercourse with the mother of a child around the time the child was conceived.

Lord Mansfield's rule
The testimony of either spouse is inadmissible on the question of whether the husband had access to the wife at the time of conception if such evidence would tend to bastardize (i.e., declare illegitimate) the child.

Under **Lord Mansfield's rule**, the testimony of either spouse was inadmissible on the question of whether the husband had access to the wife at the time of conception if such evidence would tend to bastardize (i.e., declare illegitimate) the child. Hence, under this rule, if a defendant had not had sexual intercourse with his wife in years, he could not give testimony or introduce other evidence to this effect if it would tend to bastardize the mother's recently born child. In most states today, Lord Mansfield's rule has been abolished so that the defense of nonaccess can be used.

PRESUMPTION OF LEGITIMACY

presumption of legitimacy
A child born to a married woman is presumed to be legitimate unless conclusively proven otherwise.

Another major evidentiary rule is the **presumption of legitimacy**: a child born to a married woman is presumed to be legitimate unless conclusively proven otherwise. This presumption has been called "one of the strongest and most persuasive known to the law."[13] If the defendant is the husband of the mother and denies paternity, he must introduce very strong evidence that he is not the father, e.g., blood or DNA test results or evidence that he is physically incapable of fathering a child because of impotence or sterility. (Lord Mansfield's rule, where it applied, prevented the husband or wife from introducing evidence of nonaccess to rebut the presumption.)

The modern version of the presumption of legitimacy is found in the Uniform Parentage Act. In states that have adopted this act, a man is presumed to be the natural father of a child (and will be referred to as the *presumed father*) if he and the child's natural mother are married to each other and the child is born during the marriage, or within 300 days after the marriage is terminated.[14]

PRESUMPTION OF PATERNITY

The focus of legitimacy is whether a child is a marital child (legitimate) or a nonmarital child (illegitimate). As most of the major discrimination against nonmarital children has been eliminated, the law governing legitimacy has become much less important than the law governing paternity. The focus of paternity is the biological fatherhood of a child. When paternity is in doubt, the major way to prove the identity of the genetic or biological father is by using the scientific tests that have been discovered, such as DNA testing. Before we examine these tests, we need to examine the starting point in many cases—the **presumption of paternity**. Very often, a statute will define when the presumption exits. For example, the statute may say that a man will be presumed to be the natural father of a child if:

presumption of paternity
A man is presumed to be the father of a child (until proven otherwise) if he is married to the mother at the time of conception or birth, he marries the mother after the birth, he formally acknowledges paternity, he allows his name on the birth certificate, he receives the child into his home and holds the child out as his own, or he is obligated to pay child support.

- he is married to the mother at the time of the child's conception or birth or within 300 days after the marriage is terminated by death, divorce, or annulment;

- he acknowledges paternity (without objection from the mother) in a writing that is filed with a government body such as the clerk of the family court;

- he consents to have his name on the child's birth certificate as the father;

- he receives the child into his home and holds the child out to the world as his own;

- he is obligated to support the child by agreement or court order.

In most cases, a presumption of paternity can be rebutted by acceptable evidence such as by the results of paternity tests. As we will see later, however, in the discussion of paternity by estoppel, there are circumstances in which a party will not be allowed to rebut the presumption.

CONFLICTING PRESUMPTIONS OF PATERNITY

Sometimes a conflict of presumptions can occur. Example:

Carol is the daughter of Lena and Frank. When Carol was born, Lena and Frank were married, although they separated and divorced shortly thereafter. When Carol was six months old, Lena and Ted began living together. They never married. For six years, Ted has supported Carol in his home and told everyone that Carol is his child.

In many states, both Frank and Ted are presumed to be the father of Carol, Frank because he was married to the mother at the time of the birth, and Ted because he took the child into his home and held it out as his child. States handle this conflict of presumptions differently. Some states will give priority to the presumption based on marriage and declare that Frank is presumed to be the father. Other states, however, use policy considerations to resolve the conflict. For example, a court may use the best-interests standard. The concern of the court will be the best interests of the child in deciding which man should be presumed to be the father.

EVIDENCE OF PATERNITY

We turn now to an examination of the kind of evidence that can be considered by a court in paternity cases. In most of these cases, an unmarried man is trying to prove that he is not the father, or a married man (the presumed father) is trying to overcome the presumption that he is. In our early history, courts had few tools to help them decide whether a man had fathered a particular child: "Indeed, in former times, the most scientific method conceivable was to hold the child up before the jury for its consideration of whether it bore a physical resemblance to the putative father. Things have changed."[15]

Blood-Grouping Tests

The discovery of human blood groups and types has been of great assistance in paternity cases because they:

- Can be determined at birth or shortly thereafter
- Remain constant throughout an individual's life
- Are inherited

It is also possible for blood tests to determine paternity during pregnancy, although such tests are not often performed.

Here is what the U.S. Supreme Court has said about the operation and effectiveness of blood group tests:

> If the blood groups and types of the mother and child are known, the possible and *impossible* blood groups and types of the true father can be determined under the rules of inheritance. For example, a group AB child cannot have a group O parent, but can have a group A, B, or AB parent. Similarly, a child cannot be type M unless one or both parents are type M, and the factor rh' cannot appear in the blood of a child unless present in the blood of one or both parents. Since millions of men belong to the possible groups and types, a blood grouping test cannot conclusively establish paternity. However, it can demonstrate *nonpaternity*, such as where the alleged father belongs to group O and the child is group AB. It is a negative rather than an affirmative test with the potential to scientifically exclude the paternity of a falsely accused putative father. The ability of blood grouping tests to exonerate innocent putative fathers was confirmed by a 1976 report developed jointly by the American Bar Association and the American Medical Association. . . . The joint report recommended the use of seven blood test "systems" [ABO, Rh, MNS, Kell, Duffy, Kidd, and HLA] when investigating questions of paternity. These systems were found to be reasonable in cost and to provide a 91% cumulative probability of negating paternity for erroneously accused Negro men and 93% for white men. The effectiveness of the seven systems attests the probative value of blood test evidence in paternity cases.[16]

DNA Testing

The effectiveness of paternity testing continues to increase significantly. Although traditional blood tests work on the principle of exclusion, **DNA testing** has the potential to go beyond exclusion to positive identification of the biological father.[17] Genes are the hereditary units that determine the particular characteristics

DNA testing

Genetic testing on deoxyribonucleic acid removed from cells.

of living organisms. The hereditary units consist of a DNA sequence. (DNA stands for deoxyribonucleic acid.) Hence, genetic testing for paternity is referred to as DNA testing. The success of the test is due to the fact that the configuration of DNA is different in virtually all individuals except in identical twins. DNA, the "blueprint of life," determines each person's unique genetic individuality. The chances that two unrelated persons will have the same DNA fingerprint are as low as one in 30 billion. Although some authorities assert that this calculation of odds is exaggerated, there is almost universal agreement that DNA evidence is highly reliable.

To begin the test, the most common procedure is to remove DNA from cells obtained in a blood sample of a mother, child, and possible father. An alternative to drawing blood is to use a "buccal swab." To obtain cells by this method (most often used on small children), a cotton swab is rubbed on the inside of a person's cheeks. See Exhibit 13-4 for a description of how DNA identity testing works and Exhibit 13-5 for a sample test report. The results will often state that:

- The tested man is not the biological father of the child, or
- The probability is greater than 99.9 percent that the tested man is the biological father of the child in comparison to the general population of men of the same race.

EXHIBIT 13-4   How DNA Identity Testing Works

Testing Technical Information

A sample is collected from the mother, child and alleged father for DNA parentage testing. Single parent testing (the child and the alleged father only) may also be performed. The genetic material itself is directly examined in DNA parentage testing.

What Are Genes?

The human body consists of trillions of cells. Most of these cells have a nucleus or center. The nucleus contains genes, the fundamental units of our heredity. These genes are grouped into separate bundles called chromosomes. We have forty-six chromosomes inside every cell in our body. Twenty-three of these chromosomes came from the biological mother and twenty-three came from the biological father. Chromosomes are named by a letter "D" followed by a number [i.e., chromosome #1 is named D1; and chromosome #2 is named D2, etc.]. Genes are named by the number of the chromosome they inhabit. A DNA Parentage Testing report identifies the genes that were analyzed during the process of testing. When the test results refer to D2S44, you know that the gene analyzed was on chromosome #2 at locus 44.

The Chemistry of Genes

Twenty-six letters of the alphabet are the basic units of our English language. Words and sentences are formed from these 26 letters. Genes on the other hand are formed from only 4 chemicals, or bases. These bases are named: (1) adenine, (2) cytosine, (3) guanine, and (4) thymine. Like the letters of the alphabet that form sentences, these 4 bases form long gene fragments called deoxyribonucleic acid—DNA. We can measure the length of the gene fragments by the number of bases they have. When you see the gene fragment on your DNA Parentage Test report, if it is 2.34 kilobases, that means the gene fragment consists of 2,340 bases [kilobase = 1,000 bases].

All children have a biological mother and a biological father. For each gene in the child, there is one genetic variant size that came from the father and one genetic variant size that came from the mother. A DNA Parentage Test determines and examines the genetic variant sizes (i.e. allele sizes) found in the mother, the child and the alleged father.

In the sample report shown, the upper gene fragment in the child (3.76-kb size) matches the upper gene fragment size of the mother. The child received the lower gene fragment (1.46-kb size) from his/her biological father.

The alleged father #1 has gene fragment sizes different from those found in the child. Therefore, the alleged father #1 cannot be the child's biological father. The alleged father #2 has the same gene size fragment as that found in the child (i.e., 1.46 kb). He could be the child's biological father. The probability that he is the child's biological father depends on the frequency with which this gene fragment is found in the male population. The fewer men who have this gene fragment size, the greater probability that the tested man is the biological father of the child.

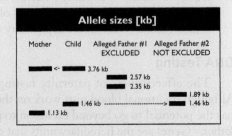

This process is repeated several times and each time a different gene is analyzed. The accuracy of the DNA test results depends on the extent of the DNA testing process. With sufficient testing, DNA technology provides an extremely powerful method of discriminating between fathers and non-fathers.

Source: Genetica, DNA Laboratories, Inc., 8740 Montgomery Road, Cincinnati, OH 45236, www.genetica.com, identity@genetica.com, 800-433-6848.

EXHIBIT 13-5   Sample DNA Test Result

the GENETICA DNA Test™

No. 79746 897	MOTHER		CHILD		ALLEGED FATHER	
Patient Name	XXXX XXXXX		YYYY XXXXX		ZZZZ ZZZZZ	
Date of Birth	January 1, 1979		January 1, 2011		January 1, 1975	
Race	Caucasian				Caucasian	
Date Collected	May 16, 2011		May 16, 2011		May 16, 2011	
Test Number	79746-1		79746-2		79746-3	
Genetic Systems Tested	**Allele**		**Allele**		**Allele**	
TPOX 2p23-2pter PI 1.25	7	9		9	8	9
D2S1338 2q35-37.1 PI 2.64	14	16	17	16	17	20
D3S1358 3p PI 4.21	15	16	15	18	17	18
FGA 4q28 PI 3.24	19	20		20		20
D5S818 5q21-31 PI 3.11	11	12	11	12	11	12
CSF1PO 5q33.3-34 PI 1.79	10	11	10	13	11	13
D7S820 7q PI 2.18	9	10	9	11	10	11
D8S1179 8 PI 5.69	12	14	12		12	
THO1 11p15.5 PI 1.45	9		9	6.3	8	6.3
vWA 12p12-pter PI 3.77	16	18	17	18	17	19
D13S317 13q22-31 PI 7.04	10	12	10		10	13
D16S539 16q24-qter PI 1.47	11		11		11	12
D18S51 18q21.3 PI 2.89	11	12	13	12	13	14
D19S433 19q12-13.1 PI 3.17	13.2	15		15	16	15
D21S11 21q11.2-q21 PI 5.21	29	31	28	31	28	30

Interpretation: Combined Parentage Index **8,393,003**   Probability of Parentage **99.9999%**
The alleged father, ZZZZ ZZZZZ, cannot be excluded as the biological father of the child named YYYY XXXXX. Based on testing results obtained from analyses of 15 different DNA probes, the probability of paternity is 99.9999%. This probability of paternity is calculated by comparing to an untested, unrelated man of the North American Caucasian population (assumes prior probability equals .50). This DNA Parentage Test excluded greater than 99.99% of the male population from the possibility of being the biological father of the tested child.

COURT/ADMIN Case No.:   Report Date **May 17, 2011**

Source: Genetica, DNA Laboratories, Inc., 8740 Montgomery Road, Cincinnati, OH 45236, www.genetica.com, identity@genetica.com, 800-433-6848.

indigent
Poor; without means to afford something such as a private attorney or filing fees.

civil contempt
The refusal of a party to comply with a court order (usually issued for the benefit of another), which can lead to punishment (including incarceration) until the party complies with the order.

One consequence of the effectiveness of these tests is that most disputed paternity cases today are resolved on the basis of the tests rather than by a court trial. Testing, however, can be expensive. If the putative father is **indigent**, the state must pay for the tests. If he refuses to undergo the tests, many states will either force him to be tested or allow the trial court to take his refusal into consideration in making the paternity decision. The strong implication of such a refusal is that he has something to hide.

Many states provide state-appointed counsel for an indigent putative father in these proceedings. As we saw in Chapter 10, if the state is charging a putative father with **civil contempt** for failure to pay child support (in which disputed paternity may have to be resolved), the state is not required to provide him with a free attorney if the mother is unrepresented and the state provides procedural protections such as an opportunity to be heard and clear notice that he can avoid imprisonment if he is unable to pay child support.

ASSIGNMENT 13.3

Prepare a flowchart of all the procedural steps taken in your state to resolve contested paternity. (See General Instructions for the Flowchart Assignment Appendix A.)

In every state, maternity wards have forms on which fathers and mothers are asked to sign a voluntary recognition of parentage (ROP). (See Exhibit 13-6 for an example of a ROP that can be used in hospitals or elsewhere.) Before signing, the parties are told that parents have a duty to support their children and that the signed form is the legal equivalent of a court order determining parentage. Months or years later, a man who has signed the form will have a difficult time establishing that he is not the father. (See also the putative father registry in Exhibit 15-5 of Chapter 15, containing a form that is used if an unwed father wants to acknowledge the possibility of paternity so that he will be notified if someone in the future petitions to adopt his child.)

EXHIBIT 13-6   Voluntary Recognition of Parentage (ROP)

Each state has its own form for voluntary acknowledgement or recognition of parentage, usually signed in the hospital upon the birth of a child. Here are excerpts from the form of one state:

Child

FIRST NAME	MIDDLE NAME	LAST NAME	SUFFIX (Jr., Sr., I, II, etc.)
BIRTH DATE (mm/dd/yy)	BIRTH PLACE (city/state)		

Do you want to change your child's last name? ☐ Yes ☐ No   CHILD'S LAST NAME
If yes, write the new last name in the box to the right.
If no, write the current last name in the box to the right.

Mother

FIRST NAME	MIDDLE NAME	LAST NAME	BIRTH DATE (mm/dd/yy)
MAILING ADDRESS		BIRTH PLACE (city/state/country)	
CITY	STATE	ZIP CODE	SOCIAL SECURITY NUMBER

Were you married to a man other than the biological father when this child was conceived or born? ☐ Yes ☐ No
If yes, the husband/ex-husband must also file a Husband's Non-paternity Statement (Form DHS-3159C)
within one year of this child's birth to put the name of the biological father on this child's birth record.

Father

FIRST NAME	MIDDLE NAME	LAST NAME	BIRTH DATE (mm/dd/yy)
MAILING ADDRESS		BIRTH PLACE (city/state/country)	
CITY	STATE	ZIP CODE	SOCIAL SECURITY NUMBER

I have read the instructions and I understand the "Parent's statement," "Waiver of rights" and "Custody and parenting time information" sections of this form. I have examined this form and, to the best of my knowledge and belief, I declare that it is a true and correct statement of every important point.

Mother's signature x _____   Father's signature x _____

Parent's statement:

Under oath, I state that:

- I have been told about the Recognition of Parentage (ROP) form and understand my rights and responsibilities created and waived by signing this form.

- I have a copy of *Being a Legal Father: Parentage Information for Mothers and Fathers.* I read the booklet or had someone else read it to me.

- I have received additional oral notice about my rights, responsibilities and alternatives to signing this form.

- I understand that either of us may choose not to acknowledge paternity. As alternatives to signing the ROP, either of us could ask the court to decide on paternity or we could acknowledge paternity later.

- I acknowledge that we are the biological parents of the child named in this ROP.

- I understand that this ROP does not give custody or parenting time to the legal father. However, this ROP gives the father the right to ask the court for custody or parenting time.

- I understand that either of us can take legal action to establish paternity instead of signing the ROP and that either of us may apply for paternity establishment services at our local child support office.

- I understand that either of us can choose to have genetic testing done before we sign the ROP.

- I accept responsibility to provide financial support for my child. I understand that a court can order financial support that can include payments for basic support, medical support, and child-care support starting from my child's birth until a court order for support ends.

- I understand that both parents have the right to all notices of any adoption proceedings.

- I understand that this is a legal document. If we are both age 18 or older when we sign this form, this ROP is the same as a court order determining the legal relationship between a father and child.

- I understand that if either of us is under age 18 when we sign this form, this ROP is only a presumption of paternity. It is not final. I understand that this ROP will be the same as a court order determining the legal relationship between a father and child six months after the youngest of us turns 18. If I want to stop this ROP from becoming a legal document, I understand that I must take legal action before the six months ends.

- I understand that either of us can cancel this ROP by stating in writing that, "I am revoking the ROP." I understand that I must sign the revocation in front of a notary public and that I must file the revocation with the Office of the State Registrar within 60 days after I complete this ROP form. If I have not filed a revocation within 60 days and still want to cancel this ROP, I understand that I will need to take legal action to request a change to any of the information in this ROP.

- I understand that this ROP will not be considered valid if the mother of the child was married to another man at the time this child was conceived or born unless this ROP is filed in conjunction with a Husband's Non-paternity Statement.

- To the best of my knowledge, the information on this form is true.

- I am signing this form voluntarily. No one forced me to sign this ROP.

Source: Minnesota Department of Human Services, *Voluntary Recognition of Parentage* (edocs.dhs.state.mn.us/lfserver/Public/DHS-3159-ENG).

THIRD PARTIES SEEKING TO PROVE PATERNITY

In most cases, the presumed father will be trying to overcome the presumption that he is the biological father by using DNA testing and other evidence. Suppose, however, that a *third party* wants to prove that he is the biological father.

> *Todd and Ellen are married. Ellen gives birth to Mildred while having an affair with a neighbor. Todd is the presumed father because the child was born during his marriage with Ellen. The neighbor now wants to go to court to prove that he is in fact the biological father so that he can have custody or visitation rights. Todd objects because he wants to raise Mildred as his own.*

States differ on whether a third party such as the neighbor would have **standing** to prove to a court that he is in fact the biological father of the child. Some states will give him standing but may impose a time limit within which he must bring the suit to establish his paternity (e.g., within two years after the birth of the child). Other states would deny him standing.

standing

The right to bring a case and seek relief from a court.

In a 1989 case, the U.S. Supreme Court held that it is constitutional for a state to favor a husband (the presumed father) over a biological father and deny standing to the latter.[18] In this case, the plaintiff, Michael, sought to establish paternity of a child born to a woman who was married to (and still cohabitating with) another man, Gerald. Despite the fact that blood tests indicated a 98.07 percent probability that Michael was the father and the fact that Michael had established a relationship with the child, the court upheld the rights of the husband (Gerald) as the presumed father and denied Michael any rights. Under California's version of the presumption of legitimacy, only the husband and wife could rebut the presumption and neither wanted to do so in this case even though both knew that the husband was not the father. Hence it is constitutional for a state to deny the right of a biological father to prove that he is the father if the mother of the child was married to someone else when the child was born. A judge in another state commented that "interlopers" like Michael should not be allowed to "use their own adulterous behavior as a license to invade and disrupt the matrimonial circle."[19]

Not all states, however, go as far as California in their law on standing in paternity actions. There are states that will give third parties standing to prove their paternity if certain restrictions are met, such as the requirement that the suit be brought within two years after the child is born.

PATERNITY BY ESTOPPEL

equitable estoppel
The voluntary conduct of a person will preclude him or her from asserting rights against another who justifiably relied on the conduct and who would suffer damage or injury if the person is now allowed to repudiate the conduct. Also called estoppel in pais.

paternity by estoppel
Paternity that is established when a court does not allow the presumption of paternity to be rebutted even though there is no biological relationship between the presumed (putative) father and the child.

Suppose that a mother denies that her husband is the father of her child but that under the presumption of paternity, he is the presumed (putative) father. In some cases, **equitable estoppel** will prevent her from asserting this denial even if paternity tests prove that she is right. In equitable estoppel, the voluntary conduct of a person will preclude him or her from asserting rights against another who justifiably relied on the conduct and who would suffer damage or injury if the person is now allowed to repudiate the conduct. When equitable estoppel prevents a mother from denying paternity, the result is called **paternity by estoppel**. The court does not allow the presumption of paternity to be rebutted even though there is no biological relationship between the presumed (putative) father and the child. We will now examine the *Pettinato* case, in which the mother's conduct equitably estopped her from denying the paternity of her husband even though tests proved that he was not the biological father of her child.

CASE

Pettinato v. Pettinato
582 A.2d 909 (1990)
Supreme Court of Rhode Island

Background: *Gregory Pettinato sued Susanne Pettinato for divorce and custody of their son Gregory, Jr. During the litigation, she denied that he was the father. The Family Court granted the divorce and gave custody to the father. The case is now on appeal brought by Susanne before the Supreme Court of Rhode Island.*

Decision on Appeal: *Affirmed. Susanne is estopped from denying Gregory's paternity.*

OPINION OF THE COURT

Justice Shea delivered the opinion of the court. . . .

Although many of the facts were disputed, it appears that a relationship developed between Gregory and Susanne in the fall of 1984. The parties disagreed about the date when they began

sexual relations. However, it is undisputed that the parties were engaging in sexual relations by February 1985. Susanne testified that she did not engage in sexual relations with Gregory between February 14, 1985, and April 7, 1985. During that period she traveled to Florida for two weeks. Moreover, Susanne testified, she did not speak with Gregory until after November 1985 when she returned to Rhode Island from her second trip to Florida.

Susanne gave birth to Gregory, Jr., on January 5, 1986. Despite the parties' discrepancies regarding events leading to the child's birth, Gregory was named as the child's father on the birth certificate filed on January 13, 1986.

Susanne testified that she told Gregory while in the hospital after giving birth that Gregory, Jr., was the child of the man she had stayed with while in Florida. Gregory disputed this testimony. He testified that Susanne telephoned him in April 1985, informed him of her pregnancy, and stated that he, Gregory, was the father. Gregory first became aware of Susanne's denial of his paternity at the time of this divorce action when she filed her answers to interrogatories.

The evidence established that the parties had a fairly nomadic existence after the birth of Gregory, Jr. For approximately one month after the child's birth, Susanne and the child lived at her parents' home. Gregory was forbidden by her parents to visit Susanne or Gregory, Jr., although the parties would arrange to meet at a friend's house without the knowledge of Susanne's parents. Thereafter, Susanne and the child shared a rented apartment with a friend for approximately three months before moving into an apartment with Gregory.

Gregory, Susanne, and Gregory, Jr., lived in an apartment from May 1986 until October 1986. All three then moved into Gregory's parents' home in October 1986. Gregory and Susanne married on December 21, 1986. Gregory testified that he married Susanne because he "thought it would be the proper thing to do to make a family and be on our own together and bring up our child." The parties remained at his parents' home until Susanne moved out on April 26, 1987. Susanne initially left Gregory, Jr., with Gregory and his parents. Susanne testified, however, that the Cranston police retrieved Gregory, Jr., the next day and brought the child to her at a friend's home. . . .

Over the objections of Gregory, the court heard testimony from Marjorie Kimball, a medical technologist at the Rhode Island Blood Center. Kimball testified that she performed genetic blood testing on Gregory, Susanne, and Gregory, Jr. As a result of this genetic blood testing, Kimball concluded that it was not possible for Gregory to be the biological father of Gregory, Jr.

The trial justice issued an interlocutory decision pending entry of final judgment on October 11, 1988. He granted the petition of Gregory for an absolute divorce and awarded Gregory permanent custody of Gregory, Jr., subject to all reasonable rights of visitation for Susanne. In his decision the trial justice based the award on the care given Gregory, Jr., by Gregory, the length of time Gregory, Jr., spent with Gregory, and the bonding that had occurred between Gregory, Jr., and Gregory. . . .

On appeal Susanne argues that the trial justice improperly overlooked and/or misconceived the expert testimony regarding the genetic blood testing that excluded Gregory as the biological father of Gregory, Jr. Susanne contends that as the natural parent of Gregory, Jr., she is entitled to custody of the child absent a showing of unfitness. . . .

In this case we consider for the first time the rights of parents whose legal presumption of paternity is later challenged during a divorce proceeding. It is undisputed that Gregory is the presumptive natural father of Gregory, Jr. . . . § 15–8–3 Presumption of paternity:

    (a) A man is to be the natural father of a child if: . . .
        (3) After the child's birth, he and the child's natural mother have married, or attempted to marry, each

other by a marriage solemnized in apparent compliance with law, although the attempted marriage could be declared invalid, and: (i) He has acknowledged his paternity of the child in writing filed with the clerk of the [F]amily [C]ourt; or (ii) With his consent, he is named as the child's father on the child's birth certificate; or, (iii) He is obligated to support the child under a written voluntary promise or by court order; (4) He acknowledges his paternity of the child in a writing filed with the clerk of the [F]amily [C]ourt, who shall promptly inform the mother of the filing of the acknowledgement, and she does not dispute the acknowledgement, within a reasonable time after being informed thereof, in a writing filed with the clerk of the [F]amily [C]ourt. If another man is presumed under this section to be the child's father, acknowledgement may be effected only with the written consent of the presumed father or after the presumption has been rebutted.

    (b) A presumption under this section may be rebutted in an appropriate action only by clear and convincing evidence. If two (2) or more presumptions arise which conflict with each other, the presumption which on its facts is founded on the weightier considerations of policy and logic controls. The presumption is rebutted by a court decree establishing paternity of the child by another man.

Susanne admits that Gregory has met the requirements of § 15–8–3(a)(3)(ii). The parties married after Gregory, Jr.'s birth, and with his consent Gregory was named as the child's father on the birth certificate. Nevertheless, Susanne contends, the results of the genetic blood testing that excluded Gregory as the biological father provide the "clear and convincing" evidence required by § 15–8–3(b) to rebut the presumption of Gregory's paternity.

We are concerned about the situation before the court wherein a mother can tell a man that he is the father of her child, marry him and live together as a family, and then illegitimize the child during a divorce proceeding by attacking the legal presumption of paternity that she helped to bring about. The situation before us is a matter of first impression in this state. After reviewing the conclusions arrived at by other states that have considered this issue, we have reached the conclusion that Susanne may not defeat Gregory's legal presumption of paternity.

We are of the opinion that a mother should be equitably estopped from using the genetic blood testing permitted by § 15–8–11 to disestablish a child's paternity in connection with a routine divorce proceeding. The underlying rationale of the equitable estoppel doctrine is that "under certain circumstances, a person might be estopped from challenging paternity where that person has by his or her conduct accepted a given person as father of the child." *John M. v. Paula T.*, 524 Pa. 306, 318, 571 A.2d 1380, 1386 (1990). Where the equitable-estoppel

(continued)

CASE • Pettinato v. Pettinato (continued)

doctrine is operative, evidence of genetic blood tests is considered irrelevant in a divorce proceeding wherein the basic issue is the termination of the marriage bond—not the paternity of a child. "[T]he law will not permit a person in these situations to challenge the status which he or she has previously accepted [or created]." Id.

The circumstances of the case before us, in our opinion, compel the application of the equitable estoppel doctrine. Gregory has represented himself to be and has been accepted as Gregory, Jr.'s natural father. He married Susanne, believing her representation that the child was his child. He married her with the intention that the couple would raise their child in a family unit. Gregory consented to being named as the father on Gregory, Jr.'s birth certificate. The three lived together and represented themselves to the community as a family. Susanne never questioned Gregory's paternity until after he commenced divorce proceedings that followed her leaving him. At the time

he filed for divorce, Susanne had become pregnant again but not by Gregory.

Taken together, this court's adherence to the statutory presumption of paternity in § 15–8–3(a)(3)(ii) and the court's application of the equitable-estoppel doctrine lead to the same point: the genetic blood test results offered into evidence were not relevant because legal paternity had been established and biological paternity was not at issue. *Scott v. Mershon*, 394 Pa. Super. 411, 417–418, 576 A.2d 67, 71 (1990). Therefore, the genetic blood test results disestablishing Gregory's paternity should not have been admitted. We reject Susanne's contention that the trial justice overlooked and/or misconceived the expert testimony regarding genetic blood testing. That testimony should have been excluded as irrelevant on Gregory's objection to its admission. . . .

For these reasons the defendant's appeal is denied and dismissed, the judgment appealed from is affirmed, and the papers of the case are remanded to the Family Court.

ASSIGNMENT 13.4

a. What is the difference between legal paternity and biological paternity? Why was the distinction important in *Pettinato*?

b. Assume that the paternity issue is not raised in the divorce case and that Susanne is granted custody of the son. Years later, Gregory refuses to pay child support. In a support action against him, he wants to introduce evidence of the genetic blood tests that prove he is not the father. Can he introduce this evidence?

c. In Chapter 9 on child custody, we discussed at length the U.S. Supreme Court case of *Troxel v. Granville*, which said that a fit parent has a fundamental constitutional right to raise his or her child against the wishes of a grandparent or other nonparent. Was Susanne Pettinato's fundamental constitutional right as a parent violated in *Pettinato v. Pettinato*? Phrased another way, is *Pettinato v. Pettinato* consistent with *Troxel v. Granville*?

■ PARALEGAL ROLES

- For an overview of paralegal roles in family-law cases, see Exhibits 1-3 and 1-4 in Chapter 1.

- For many of the financial issues related to paternity covered in Chapter 13, a paralegal may be asked to help collect documents and facts outlined in:
  - the checklist in Exhibit 3-1 of Chapter 3
  - the interrogatories in Appendix C

- Miscellaneous duties
  - Do fact research on the sperm bank used by or being considered for use by the client.
  - Assist the client in obtaining and filling out the paternity questionnaire for the

child-support agency (the IV-D) agency and court.

- Explain the various paternity test options used in the state.

- Investigate the chain of custody for the specimen used by the lab to assess paternity (e.g., who received it, when, and who handled it after the testing).

- Prepare a preliminary draft of the paternity petition.

- Draft documents needed for a legitimation proceeding.

- Assist the client in filing for Social Security survivors benefits.
- Investigate facts that tend to show that the father did or did not take the child into his home and let the world know that it was his.
- Obtain birth certificates, hospital records, and other relevant documents.

■ CHECK THE CITE

Walter Little denies that he is the father of Kenyatta. He asked the court to order a blood test in order to prove his claim. At the time, Walter was incarcerated and could not afford the cost of the blood test. He therefore asked the state to pay for the test. How did the U.S. Supreme Court rule on his request and what reasons did the Court give for its decision? Read *Little v. Streater*, 452 U.S. 1 (1981). To read the opinion online: (1) Go to the FindLaw site (www.findlaw.com/casecode/supreme.html). In the box before "U.S.," type 452. In the box after "U.S.," type 1. (2) Run a citation search ("452 US 1") in the Legal Documents database of Google Scholar (scholar.google.com).

■ PROJECT

Using Google, Bing, or Yahoo, locate the sites for three different sperm banks. (Some of the sites may offer services in addition to sperm availability.) Select banks that have information on their sites that describe government laws and regulations that the bank must follow. Describe these laws and regulations as explained by the sites. Do not simply copy what the sites say. Prepare a report in which you compare what the different sites say about the relevant laws and regulations. Indicate which sites are more comprehensive in describing the laws and regulations. After you have completed the description, select any of the laws or regulations mentioned on one of the sites. Find that law or regulation on the Internet. Give the citation, the Internet address where you found

it, and a quote from any sentence in the law or regulation itself.

■ ETHICS IN A FAMILY LAW PRACTICE

You are a paralegal working at the law office of James Adams, Esq. On November 10, 2010, Adams is assigned by the court to represent John Edwinson against whom a paternity petition has been filed. There is a hearing scheduled for March 13, 2011. Edwinson is not a cooperative client. He frequently misses appointments at the law firm office. Frustrated, Adams sends Edwinson a short letter on March 1, 2011, that says, "Due to your noncooperation, I am withdrawing from the case as your representative effective immediately." Any ethical problems?

■ WRITING SAMPLE

The writing sample for this chapter will be a brief of a recent opinion of a state court in your state on paternity. The paternity opinion must involve a dispute over who is the father of a particular child. Use the search guidelines below in order to find such an opinion. The brief should cover the name of the case, citation, facts, issues, holding, and reasoning. To find the opinion:

- In Google, Bing, or Yahoo, run the following search: aa paternity (substitute the name of your state for aa in the search).
- In Google Scholar (scholar.google.com) enter the search aa paternity in the Articles database and then in the Legal Documents database (substitute the name of your state for aa in each search).

Your instructor will let you know of any special instructions on preparing the brief. For additional guidance, run the search "how to brief a case" in Google, Bing, or Yahoo. (See General Instructions for the Writing Sample in Appendix A.)

SUMMARY

An illegitimate (nonmarital) child is one born to parents who were not married at the time of birth. At one time, an illegitimate child had very few rights. This situation has changed, although the discrimination between marital and nonmarital children has not been entirely eliminated. Nonmarital children are a quasi-suspect class; discrimination against them is measured by the intermediate scrutiny test. A nonmarital child can fully inherit from his or her father if the father dies intestate. Some states insist, however, that paternity be established before the intestate parent dies. If the parent

dies testate, leaving property "to my children" or "to my heirs," the answer to the question of whether nonmarital children were included in these phrases depends on the intent of the parent.

Legitimate and nonmarital children have the same right to be supported, to bring wrongful-death actions because of the death of a parent, and to receive workers' compensation benefits if the parent dies on the job. If the nonmarital child dies a wrongful death, a state can require the father to have legitimated the child before death in order to sue for his child's wrongful death. To obtain social security survivors benefits, a nonmarital child must prove that he or she was dependent on a deceased father, whereas the law presumes the dependence of a marital child. Survivors benefits can be given to a child born after the death of his father through artificial insemination. Children can qualify for survivors benefits if they are entitled to inherit from their father under state law. The government can impose different requirements for citizenship of a nonmarital child born abroad to a citizen mother as opposed to a citizen father.

In most states, when a child is born through artificial insemination (AI) with the semen of a man other than the husband, the husband has a duty to support the child, and the child is considered legitimate if the husband consented to the insemination. A donor of semen to someone other than his wife has no parental rights or duties to a child conceived through AI unless the donor and the woman have entered into a written contract to the contrary or the donor has established a bonding relationship with the child. Although sperm banks are commonly used, health concerns exist and the anonymity of donors can raise potential problems of inbreeding among the resulting children.

Legitimation can occur in a number of ways: acknowledgment of paternity, marriage of the mother and father, legitimation proceeding, paternity proceeding, etc. In some states, all children are legitimate regardless of whether the mother and father ever married.

A major function of a paternity proceeding is to establish a father's duty of support. For this purpose, the court must have personal jurisdiction over him. The child should be joined as a party in the proceeding to ensure that the judgment will be binding on the child. If the defendant is married to the mother, he may face a number of evidentiary obstacles at the trial (e.g., the presumption of paternity). Occasionally, more than one man may be presumed to be the father of the child.

Traditional blood-group testing can help establish the nonpaternity, though not the paternity, of a particular defendant. More modern scientific techniques such as DNA testing can establish a high probability of paternity. Another way that paternity can be established is by the father completing a voluntary recognition of parentage (ROP).

Some states deny standing to a man who wants to prove that he is the father of a child born to a woman married to another man. A state can subordinate his rights as a biological father to the rights of the husband as the presumed father even if the husband is not the biological father. Some states, however, will give the biological father standing to prove his paternity.

Equitable estoppel can prevent a person from denying the paternity of a particular person. Paternity by estoppel is paternity that is established when a court does not allow the presumption of paternity to be rebutted even though there is no biological relationship between the presumed (putative) father and the child.

KEY TERMS

legitimate child	testate	personal jurisdiction
illegitimate child	wrongful death	forum
bastard	workers' compensation	long-arm jurisdiction
bastardy	survivors benefits	nonaccess
nonmarital child	artificial insemination (AI)	Lord Mansfield's Rule
filius nullius	sperm bank	presumption of legitimacy
ecclesiastical	consanguinity	presumption of paternity
Uniform Parentage Act (UPA)	legitimation	DNA testing
classification	filiation	indigent
equal protection of law	putative father	civil contempt
quasi-suspect class	preponderance of the evidence	standing
intermediate scrutiny	clear and convincing evidence	equitable estoppel
intestate	statute of limitations	paternity by estoppel
paternity	res judicata	

REVIEW QUESTIONS

1. What is an illegitimate (nonmarital) child?

2. What was the status of nonmarital children at common law?

3. What does the Uniform Parentage Act say about the distinction between marital and nonmarital children?

4. What is the intermediate scrutiny test for a classification based on legitimacy?

5. What distinctions, if any, exist between marital and nonmarital children on inheritance rights, suing for wrongful death, workers' compensation, social-security survivors benefits, and immigration?

6. What will-interpretation problem might exist upon the death of the father of a nonmarital child?

7. Who has the duty of child support for a nonmarital child?

8. Can a child born after the death of his or her biological parent receive social security survivors benefits?

9. What are the rights of a husband who consents to the artificial insemination of his wife with his semen or that of another man?

10. What are the obligations of anonymous semen donors?

11. What health problems are posed by sperm banks?

12. In what ways can legitimation of a nonmarital child occur?

13. What are the benefits of establishing paternity?

14. What is the standard of proof in a paternity action?

15. What is the statute of limitations for bringing a paternity action against an alleged father?

16. What are the possible consequences of a child not having his or her own attorney in a paternity action?

17. What kind of jurisdiction is needed over a putative father?

18. What is Lord Mansfield's rule?

19. What is the presumption of legitimacy and when does it arise?

20. What is the presumption of paternity and when does it arise?

21. When could there be conflicting presumptions of paternity and how will a court resolve the conflict?

22. How can blood-grouping and DNA tests be used in paternity cases?

23. What is a voluntary recognition of parentage (ROP)?

24. Can a state prevent a man from proving that he is the biological father of the child given birth to by a woman still married to another man?

25. What are equitable estoppel and paternity by estoppel?

HELPFUL WEBSITES

Paternity

- www.hg.org/paternity-law.html
- en.wikipedia.org/wiki/Paternity_(law)
- members.peak.org/~jedwards/paternity.html
- www.oag.state.tx.us/ag_publications/txts/paternity.shtml

Uniform Parentage Act

- apps.leg.wa.gov/rcw/default.aspx?cite=26.26
- www.aals.org/profdev/family/sampson.pdf

Paternity Establishment: State Use of Genetic Testing

- oig.hhs.gov/oei/reports/oei-06-98-00054.pdf

Establishing Paternity

- www.acf.hhs.gov/programs/cse/courts/benchcards /establishing_paternity.html

Donor Sibling Registry

- www.donorsiblingregistry.com

Father Knows Best, But Which Father

- digitalcommons.lmu.edu/cgi/viewcontent .cgi?article=1696&context=llr

Paternity Fraud

- www.paternityfraud.com

Paternity Forms

- www.uslegalforms.com/paternity

Gay and Lesbian Parents

- www.therainbowbabies.com

Google/Bing/Yahoo Searches

(on these search engines, run the following searches, substituting your state for "aa")

- paternity aa
- bastardy aa
- paternity fraud aa
- sperm bank aa
- "Lord Mansfield's Rule" aa
- genetic test paternity aa
- DNA paternity law aa
- "paternity by estoppel" aa
- "illegitimate child" aa
- "Uniform Parentage Act" aa
- paternity forms aa
- legitimation child aa
- "presumed father" aa
- "presumption of legitimacy" aa
- "presumption of paternity" aa
- gay lesbian paternity aa

ENDNOTES

Note: All or most of the court opinions in these endnotes can be read online. To do so, go to Google Scholar (scholar .google.com), select "Legal documents," and in the search box, enter the cite (e.g., "406 U.S. 164") or name of the case (e.g., "Weber v. Aetna Casualty & Surety Co") that is given in the endnote.

[1] Centers for Disease Control and Prevention, National Vital Statistics System, *Key Birth Statistics* (www.cdc.gov/nchs /births.htm) (2011).

[2] Uniform Parentage Act, § 202 (www.law.upenn.edu/bll /archives/ulc/upa/final2002.htm).

[3] *Weber v. Aetna Casualty & Surety Co.*, 406 U.S. 164, 175 (1972).

[4] *Trimble v. Gordon*, 430 U.S. 762 (1977).

[5] *Parham v. Hughes*, 441 U.S. 347 (1979).

[6] *Weber v. Aetna Casualty & Surety Co.*, supra note 3.

[7] *Mathews v. Lucas*, 427 U.S. 495 (1976).

[7a] *Astrue v. Capato*, ___ U.S. ___, 132 S. Ct. 2021 (2012).

[8] *Nguyen v. Immigration and Naturalization Service*, 533 U.S. 53 (2001). See also *Flores-Villar*, 130 S. Ct. 2428 (2010), affirming *U.S. v. Flores-Villar*, 536 F.3d 990 (9th Cir. 2008).

[9] For a state that has adopted the Uniform Parentage Act, see Minnesota Statutes, § 257.56 (1987) (www.revisor .mn.gov/statutes/?id=257.56). States can always make changes in uniform laws. Minnesota, for example, uses the phrase "biological father" rather than "natural father" in the statute quoted in the text.

[10] www.donorsiblingregistry.com.

[11] Jennifer Egan, *Wanted: A Few Good Sperm*, N.Y. Times Magazine (Mar. 19, 2006) (www.nytimes .com/2006/03/19/magazine/319dad.html?pagewanted=all).

[12] Office of Child Support Enforcement, *Child Support Enforcement FY 2010 Preliminary Report* (May 2011) (www.acf.hhs.gov/programs/cse/pubs/2011/reports /preliminary_report_fy2010).

[13] *In re Findlay*, 170 N.E. 471, 472 (N.Y. 1930).

[14] *Uniform Parentage Act*, § 204 (www.law.upenn.edu/bll /archives/ulc/upa/final2002.htm).

[15] *J.A.S. v. Bushelman*, 342 S.W.3d 850, 861 (Ky., 2011).

[16] *Little v. Streater*, 452 U.S. 1, 8 (1981).

[17] Note, *Implications of DNA Testing on Posthumous Paternity Determination*, 35 Boston College Law Review 747, 798 (1994).

[18] *Michael H. v. Gerald D.*, 491 U.S. 110 (1989).

[19] *J.A.S. v. Bushelman*, 342 S.W.3d 850, 866 (Ky., 2011)(dissent).

The Legal Status of Children

CHAPTER OBJECTIVES

After completing this chapter, you should be able to:

- Know in what sense minority is a disability.

- Explain emancipation and how a minor achieves it.

- List the contracts that a minor can and cannot disaffirm.

- State when, if ever, a parent has the right to keep a child's real and personal property (including earnings).

- State how a minor acquires a domicile.

- State when a child can write a will and what duties a guardian

- has when the parent of a minor dies and when a minor inherits property.

- Explain the requirement of compulsory education, when corporal punishment is allowed in school, and what constitutional rights students have.

- State the meaning of child maltreatment, child neglect, child abuse, dependency, and abandonment.

- Know when a parent's substance abuse can constitute child maltreatment.

- Explain the meaning of parens patriae.

- List the effects of the Child Abuse Prevention and Treatment Act (CAPTA).

- Understand mandatory reporting.

- Distinguish between the jurisdictional and dispositional stages of court proceedings on child maltreatment.

- Define juvenile delinquency and status offenses, and state how they are treated in the courts.

age of majority
The age at which children reach legal adulthood, usually 18, entitling them to many civil rights such as the right to manage their own affairs.

minor
A person under age of legal adulthood, often 18. One who has not reached the age of majority. Also called infant.

minority
The status of being under age of legal adulthood—under the age of majority.

disability
Not having the legal capacity to perform a certain task such as entering a contract.

emancipated
Legally independent of one's parent or legal guardian. The noun is *emancipation*.

operation of law
The means by which legal consequences are imposed by law, regardless of (or even despite) the intent of the parties involved.

public assistance
Welfare or other forms of financial help from the government to the poor.

AGE OF MAJORITY AND EMANCIPATION

In most states and for most purposes, an adult is an individual who is 18 years of age or older. When children reach the **age of majority**, they are entitled to many civil rights such as the right to manage their own affairs. A **minor** (also called an *infant*) is anyone under 18. **Minority** is the status of being under the age of legal adulthood—under the age of majority. Because minority prevents a person from being able to perform certain tasks legally, minority is an example of a **disability**.

Reaching the age of majority is one of the ways that a child is **emancipated**. Emancipation means being legally independent of parents or legal guardians. In most states, there are two ways that a child can be emancipated: (1) by **operation of law** and (2) by special court procedure.

OPERATION OF LAW

Emancipation can occur by operation of law. If a legal consequence results by operation of law, the consequence happens automatically once a designated event occurs. No special court procedure is required. The events that trigger this kind of emancipation include reaching the age of majority, entering a marriage, joining the military, abandonment of the child by the parent, and an explicit agreement between parent and child that the child can live independently.

COURT PROCEDURE

In the absence of one of these events that trigger emancipation by operation of law, a child can petition a court for an order or declaration of emancipation. The child must be a minimum age (16 in many states) before making such a petition. In addition, most states require the applicant to prove that he or she is financially self-sufficient. This requirement is particularly important in cases where a parent might be pressuring or forcing the child to seek emancipation. Because one of the consequences of emancipation is that the parents are no longer obligated to support the child, some parents might be tempted to precipitate emancipation in order to avoid their support obligation. A court will not be interested in allowing an impoverished minor to be emancipated from relatively well-to-do parents when there is a good likelihood that the child will end up on **public assistance**.

EMANCIPATION AND MINIMUM AGE REQUIREMENTS

As indicated, emancipation ends the parent's duty of child support. Also, emancipated children are no longer obligated to provide services to the parent (e.g., doing household chores), and are now able to

- make their own health decisions,
- live where they wish (see domicile below),
- work without needing parental consent,
- keep their own earnings,
- sue and be sued in their own names, etc.

Emancipation, however, does not necessarily mean that the child can do anything that all other adults can do. The law imposes some age requirements that must be met whether or not emancipation has occurred. For example, a 17-year-old emancipated person must wait until he or she is 18 to vote and 21 to purchase alcoholic beverages in most states.

ASSIGNMENT 14.1

a. Rich, age 16, becomes emancipated by operation of law when he marries Mary. Rich's parents stop supporting him on the date of his marriage. Six months after the marriage, Mary obtains a decree annulling the marriage on the ground of duress. Are Rich's parents now obligated to resume supporting him? If so, as of what date? (See the General Instructions for the Legal-Analysis Assignment in Appendix A.)

b. Draft a flowchart of the procedural steps involved in petitioning a court for an order or declaration of emancipation in your state. (See General Instructions for the Flowchart Assignment in Appendix A.)

CONTRACTS

A **contract** is a legally enforceable agreement. Minors, however, have an important defense (called the defense of **infancy**) that they can raise if a merchant tries to sue the minor for breach of contract. Minors have the right to **disaffirm** and, in effect, to walk away from most of the contracts they enter. Why are they given this right? The objective of the law is to protect young people from their immaturity. Merchants are on notice that if they deal with minors, they do so at their own risk. For this reason, many merchants refuse to enter contracts with minors (particularly involving expensive goods or services) unless a parent or other financially responsible adult agrees to become a **cosigner** on the contract.

Contracts that a minor can disaffirm are **voidable**, meaning that they can be canceled or invalidated by choice—in this case, by the choice of the minor. A voidable contract, however, is valid and enforceable unless and until it is canceled.

> *Tom is 15 years of age. He goes to ABC Micro Co. and purchases an expensive computer. The sales contract calls for a small down payment (which Tom pays) with the remainder to be paid in installments—on credit. Six months later, Tom changes his mind about the computer and decides to take it back to the dealer. The computer is still in good working order.*

If Tom were an adult, he would be bound by his contract. Once an adult and a merchant enter a contract, they both are bound by it. Neither party can rescind or cancel a contract simply because of a change of mind. Store policy or a special consumer law might allow a change of mind by the customer within a certain number of days of purchase, but these are exceptions to the standard contract rule of no undoing of the contract so long as the customer received what the sale called for.

In our example, however, Tom is a minor. Most states give minors the right to disaffirm such contracts if they do so while they are still minors or within a reasonable time (e.g., several months) after they reach the age of majority. In Tom's case, this would mean that he is not bound by the contract to buy the computer. He can return it and perhaps even force the company to refund whatever money he already paid on it. In some states, however, the merchant can keep all or part of the purchase price paid thus far to cover depreciation resulting from the minor's use of the item. Could Tom refuse to return the computer? States differ in their answers to this question. Some states allow a minor to keep the goods after disaffirming, while other states require a return of what remains of the goods.

Not all contracts by minors can be disaffirmed. Here are examples of contracts that minors cannot disaffirm in many states:

- Contracts the minor entered fraudulently by lying about his or her age (note, however, that some states *will* allow minors to disaffirm such contracts)

- Contracts by minors in the sports and entertainment industry (some states only)

contract
A legally enforceable agreement. The elements of most contracts are offer, acceptance, and consideration. Some contracts must be in writing.

infancy
1. Minority. 2. The defense of being a minor, which allows the minor to disaffirm a voidable contract.

disaffirm
To repudiate or cancel. To exercise a right to repudiate and refuse to perform one's own contract.

cosigner
A person who signs a document along with the main signer, usually to agree to pay the debt created by the document in the event that the main signer fails to pay it.

voidable
Valid unless canceled or invalidated.

- Contracts by minors with banks and other lending institutions (some states only)
- Contracts by minors for the purchase of necessaries (discussed below)
- Contracts for minors made by their guardians
- Contracts made by guardians on behalf of minors under the Uniform Transfers to Minors Act (UTMA) (discussed below)

In some states, if minors commit fraud to induce the merchant to enter a contract (e.g., lie about their age), the wrongdoing will prevent them from being able to disaffirm. They will be **estopped** from asserting the defense. Other courts, however, argue that the policy of protecting minors from their own immaturity is so strong that even their own fraud will not destroy their right to disaffirm.

Special statutes have been passed in many states to limit the minor's right to disaffirm, particularly with respect to certain kinds of contracts. In several states, for example, some employment contracts, such as sports and show-business contracts, are binding on minors. Similarly, contracts with banks and other lending institutions cannot be disaffirmed in many states. Finally, when a minor makes a contract with a merchant for **necessaries** such as food or clothing, the contract can rarely be fully disaffirmed. (Necessaries are the basic items needed by family members to maintain a standard of living, particularly food, shelter, and clothing.) If minors disaffirm a contract for necessaries, they may still be liable for the reasonable value of the goods or services provided but not necessarily for the full amount of the purchase price the minor initially agreed to pay. (As we saw in Chapter 10, however, the merchant can charge the minor's parent for the necessaries.)

When a **guardian** has been appointed over a minor and the guardian enters a contract on behalf of that minor, the contract generally cannot be disaffirmed by the minor. A guardian is someone who has legal authority to care for the person or property of another. A guardian who acts on behalf of the child in court is sometimes called a **guardian ad litem (GAL)**. If a GAL negotiates a settlement contract to end the court case on behalf of the minor, which the court finds is fair, the minor cannot later disaffirm the settlement.

Most states have enacted the **Uniform Transfers to Minors Act (UTMA)**. Under this statute, gifts of certain kinds of property (e.g., securities) can be made to minors through guardians (called **custodians**) of the property. The custodian can sell the property on behalf of the minor. Contracts made by the custodian for this purpose cannot be disaffirmed by the minor.

Suppose that a minor has become emancipated before reaching the age of majority (e.g., by marrying). Does this end the child's power to disaffirm? There is no absolute answer to this question. A minor so emancipated may be denied the power to disaffirm in some states, while in others, it will not affect the power.

Finally, an unemancipated pregnant minor has the capacity to consent to an adoption so long as her consent was not obtained with fraud or duress. In Chapter 15, we will consider when a woman can revoke her consent to the adoption.

---

estopped

Prevented from asserting a right or a defense because it would be unfair or inequitable to allow the assertion. The noun is *estoppel*.

necessaries

The basic items needed by family members to maintain a standard of living, particularly food, shelter, and clothing.

guardian

A person who has legal authority to care for the person or property of another. Also called custodian.

guardian ad litem (GAL)

A special guardian (often, but not always, an attorney) appointed by the court to appear in court proceedings on behalf of a person who is a minor, is insane, or is otherwise incapacitated.

Uniform Transfers to Minors Act (UTMA)

A statute adopted by many states that allows transfers of property to minors and allows custodians to manage the property.

custodian

A person or institution in charge of something. A caretaker. Also called guardian.

ASSIGNMENT 14.2

George is a wealthy 13-year-old who owns an expensive painting. He signs a contract to exchange the painting for a valuable horse owned by Helen, an equally wealthy 12-year-old. Both George and Helen are represented by their separate attorneys during the negotiations on the contract. Once the contract is signed and the items are exchanged, what rights do George and Helen have? Can they disaffirm? Assume that there are no problems with the quality and condition of the painting and the horse. (See General Instructions for the Legal-Analysis Assignment in Appendix A.)

PROPERTY AND EARNINGS

Minors can own **real property** and most **personal property** in their own names. The parents of a minor do not own and cannot dispose of the minor's property. Earnings (which are personal property) are an exception. A minor does *not* have a right to keep his or her own earnings. The parent with the duty to support the child has a right to keep the child's earnings. Because a mother and father are both obligated to support their child, they are equally entitled to the child's earnings. In most states, if a child is employed, the employer must pay wages directly to the child unless one of the parents instructs the employer to pay the parent. Once a child has been emancipated (e.g., by express agreement with the parents, by marriage, or by abandonment by the parents), the parents are no longer entitled to the child's earnings. A state may have special laws governing the pay of actors who are minors (e.g., a requirement that the parents deposit a designated percentage of the actor's earnings in a trust for the minor).

real property
Land and anything attached or affixed to the land, such as buildings, fences, and trees. Also called real estate.

personal property
Property other than land or other than things attached to the land. Also called chattels.

DOMICILE

The **domicile** of a minor is the domicile of the parents—even if the minor lives in a different state from the parents. For example, if five-year-old Greg has lived for three years with his grandmother in Massachusetts while his parents are working at an extended job in New York, his domicile is New York. With parental consent, however, a minor can acquire his or her own separate domicile. Similarly, if a minor who has not yet reached the age of majority is emancipated, most states give that individual the power to acquire his or her own domicile.

domicile
The place where a person has been physically present with the intent to make that place a permanent home (or with no intent to make any other place a permanent home); the place to which one intends to return when away. A residence, on the other hand, is simply the place where you are living at a particular time. A person can have more than one residence, but generally can have only one domicile.

ESTATES

Everyone, including a minor, has an **estate**. It consists of everything that one owns and owes (assets and liabilities), particularly at the time of death. The word *estate* also means the legal entity created upon a person's death consisting of all of the person's assets and liabilities. The estate, for example, must pay taxes and can be sued.

One of the major estate **instruments** is the **will**, which specifies how the **decedent** wishes to dispose of his or her property upon death. States have specified a minimum age for a person to have the legal capacity to dispose of his or her property in a will. Some states have different minimum ages for the disposition of personal property (e.g., clothes, cash) and of real property (e.g., land). In a few states, the emancipation of the minor by his or her marriage will enable the minor to make a valid will before reaching the minimum age.

If both parents die, the court will appoint a guardian over the person and/or estate of the minor. This person might be called a general guardian, a guardian of the estate, or a GAL. If the guardian is not an attorney and legal services are required, the guardian will hire an attorney on behalf of the minor. It is a guardian's duty to:

- Manage the minor's assets
- Collect assets due the minor
- Sell, lease, or mortgage the minor's assets (with the approval of the court)
- Invest the minor's assets
- Pay the minor's debts from the minor's assets
- Support the minor from the minor's assets
- Represent (or obtain representation for) the minor in court when needed

estate
All of the assets and liabilities of a decedent upon his or her death. (See glossary for additional meanings.)

instrument
A formal written document that gives expression to or embodies a legal act or agreement (e.g., contract, will). (See glossary for an additional meaning.)

will
An instrument (legal document) that specifies the disposition of one's property (and related instructions) upon death.

decedent
The person who has died; the deceased.

For such services, the minor must pay the guardian a fee, which might be a percentage of the minor's estate.

Even when parents are alive, most states give minors the right to inherit property in their own names (e.g., a gift of stock or of land from a deceased uncle). Again, a guardian would probably be appointed by the court to manage the property. The most likely candidate to be such a guardian would be a parent of the minor. Title to the inherited property would remain in the name of the minor. Finally, minors can receive gifts in their own names that take effect during their lives (**inter vivos gift**). For example, see the discussion earlier on Uniform Transfers to Minors Act (UTMA) under the topic of contracts.

inter vivos gift
A gift that takes effect when the donor is living.

EDUCATION

COMPULSORY EDUCATION

All states have compulsory-education laws for children of designated ages, usually between 5 and 17. The education does not have to take place in a public school if an alternative private school (or home-schooling instruction) meets minimum educational standards. The liberty interest in the Due Process Clause of the U.S. Constitution includes the **fundamental right** of fit parents to raise their children, including the control of their education. (See Exhibit 1-1 in Chapter 1 on the Due Process Clause). Violating compulsory-attendance laws can lead to criminal charges against the parents and juvenile court proceedings against the child for **truancy**. The latter is the willful and unjustified failure to attend school by one who is required to attend. The state may have special categories of truants, such as a *habitual truant*—a student with four or more such absences.

fundamental right
A right that (a) is specifically guaranteed in the U.S. Constitution, (b) is implicit in the concept of ordered liberty, or (c) is deeply rooted in the nation's history and tradition.

truancy
The willful and unjustified failure to attend school by one who is required to attend.

CORPORAL PUNISHMENT

Children at home can be subjected to **corporal punishment** by their parents so long as the punishment does not constitute abuse (see discussion of child abuse on page 548). Teachers are **in loco parentis**, which means that they stand in the place of parents and can assume some of the supervisory rights of the parents. As such, teachers can also impose corporal punishment on children if reasonably necessary for proper education and discipline. (In the 2005–2006 school year, the U.S. Department of Education estimated that 223,190 children were subjected to corporal punishment.[1]) Reasonable punishment at school is not cruel and unusual punishment under the U.S. Constitution, is not a crime, and is not a **tort** such as battery even if the punishment is carried out against the wishes of the parents. In some states, however, statutes exist that prohibit corporal punishment of students by teachers or school officials. The statute might prohibit teachers from hitting students except in self-defense or to protect others. New York State, for example, has specific regulations on when physical force can be used by teachers:

corporal punishment
Punishment inflicted on the physical body.

in loco parentis
Standing in the place of a parent by assuming some or all parental responsibilities without being a biological or adoptive parent.

tort
A civil wrong (other than a breach of contract) that causes injury or other loss for which our legal system deems it just to provide a remedy such as damages.

- To protect oneself from physical injury;
- To protect another pupil or teacher or any other person from physical injury;
- To protect the property of the school or of others;
- To restrain or remove a pupil whose behavior is interfering with the orderly exercise and performance of school district functions, powers, or duties, if that pupil has refused to comply with a request to refrain from further disruptive acts, provided that alternative procedures and methods not involving the use of physical force cannot reasonably be employed.[2]

CONSTITUTIONAL RIGHTS

Students have constitutional rights. For example, a school violates the First Amendment right of free speech when it prohibits students from wearing black armbands in school to protest the Vietnam war if this activity does not substantially disrupt school activities:

> It can hardly be argued that either students or teachers shed their constitutional rights to freedom of speech or expression at the schoolhouse gate.... School officials do not possess absolute authority over their students. Students in school as well as out of school are "persons" under our Constitution. They are possessed of fundamental rights which the State must respect, just as they themselves must respect their obligations to the State. In our system, students may not be regarded as closed-circuit recipients of only that which the State chooses to communicate. They may not be confined to the expression of those sentiments that are officially approved.[3]

Although wearing protest armbands was held not to disrupt school activities in a substantial way, the U.S. Supreme Court took a different view when drugs were involved. In 2007, the Court held that a school could punish a student for refusing to take down a banner ("Bong Hits 4 Jesus") that school officials concluded promoted illegal drug use at a school-supervised event.[4]

Students also have a Fourth Amendment right not to be subjected to unreasonable search and seizure. The right, however, differs for adults and students:

- *Adults*: The search is allowed if there is **probable cause** to believe that an offense has been committed. For the search to be constitutional, there must be at least a fair probability or a substantial chance of discovering evidence of criminal activity by the adult.
- *Students*: The search is allowed if there is reasonable suspicion of illicit activity by the student. For the search to be constitutional, there must be at least a moderate chance of finding evidence of wrongdoing by the student.

probable cause
A reasonable belief that a specific crime has been committed and that the accused committed the crime. (See glossary for an additional meaning.)

The standard is broader for students than it is for adults (thus allowing for more searches to be valid) because of the age of the students and the school environment of the search. It is still possible, however, to violate a student's Fourth Amendment right. In a recent case, the U.S. Supreme Court held that it was unconstitutional for school officials to strip search a 13-year-old girl to try to find prescription and over-the-counter drugs. There was an insufficient basis to suspect that the drugs presented a danger or that they were concealed in her underwear.[5] School officials can conduct a search of a student's locker, school bag, or body, but only if there is reasonable suspicion and at least a moderate chance of finding evidence of wrongdoing. Schools also have the right to implement reasonable policies that deter illegal activities. For example, it is constitutional for a school to require all students who participate in competitive extracurricular activities to submit to random urinalysis drug testing. This is a reasonable means for deterring drug use.[6]

SUSPENSION AND EXPULSION

A student cannot be expelled or given a long-term suspension from school without being accorded certain procedural rights under the U.S. Constitution. For example:

- The right to receive written notice of the charges against him or her.
- The right to a hearing on the charges to determine whether they are valid.

- The right to an impartial hearing officer. (The latter cannot be directly involved in the matter. For example, the teacher who brought the charges against the student cannot be the hearing officer.)
- The right to be represented by counsel at the hearing.
- The right to present evidence and to confront the accuser at the hearing.

If the student is faced with a less severe punishment, such as a short-term suspension, all of these procedural rights are not provided. The student has a right to know the basis of the charges and the right to respond to them, but not necessarily to a hearing with legal representation.

CHILD ABUSE AND NEGLECT

INTRODUCTION

Early in our history, children were considered the property of their parents. In colonial Massachusetts, a law based on the *Book of Deuteronomy* said that if a child "disobeyed his father's voice, he could be put to death."[7] In nineteenth-century America, courts often refused to "interfere in the domestic government of families" by punishing a parent for correcting his child, however severe or unmerited the punishment, unless it produced permanent injury or was inflicted from malicious motives.[8]

Today, the situation is drastically different. A large network of law enforcement and social service agencies exist to respond to children at risk. Unfortunately, however, child abuse and neglect continue to be a major problem in our society.

DEFINITIONS

Child Maltreatment

States use different terms to cover harm caused to children by parents or caregivers. All of the terms fall under the general category of **child maltreatment**, which is an act or failure to act by a parent or caretaker that intentionally or carelessly results in physical or emotional harm to a child or that presents an imminent risk of such harm to a child. Researchers prefer the term "child maltreatment," although all of the harms covered by this term may have different labels in the statutes of different states. The harms may be called:

- abuse
- child abuse
- child abuse and neglect

Sometimes the term **child abuse** is defined as serious physical, emotional, or sexual mistreatment of a child that is not the result of accident or of circumstances beyond the control of the parent or guardian. In general, **child neglect** is the failure of a parent or other caregiver to provide the basic needs of a child, including physical needs (e.g., food and shelter), emotional needs, medical needs, and educational needs. Child neglect may be caused by poverty, unorthodox cultural or religious practices, or a lack of parenting skills. **Dependency** is the condition of a child who has been placed in the custody of the state because the child has been abused, neglected, or abandoned. **Abandonment** is a major example of child maltreatment. It consists of relinquishing parental responsibilities by voluntarily leaving a child or ending communication with a child for a specific period or indefinitely without arranging for alternative care and supervision while away.

Exhibit 14-1 gives a further breakdown of categories of maltreatment.

---

child maltreatment
An act or failure to act by a parent or caretaker that intentionally or carelessly results in physical or emotional harm to a child or that presents an imminent risk of such harm to a child.

child abuse
Serious physical, emotional, or sexual mistreatment of a child that is not the result of accident or circumstances beyond the control of the parent or guardian.

child neglect
The failure of a parent or other caregiver to provide the basic needs of a child, including physical needs (e.g., food and shelter), emotional needs, medical needs, and educational needs.

dependency
(1) The condition of a child who has been placed in the custody of the state because the child has been abused, neglected, or abandoned. (2) Pertaining to a child who lacks basic care through no fault of the parent or guardian.

abandonment
Voluntarily leaving a child or ending communication with a child for a specific period or indefinitely without arranging for alternative care and supervision while away. Conduct that constitutes a relinquishing of one's parental responsibilities.

EXHIBIT 14-1   Examples of Child Maltreatment

Sexual Abuse
Intrusion sex without force
Intrusion sex involving use of force
Child's prostitution or involvement in pornography
  with intrusion
Molestation with genital contact
Exposure/Voyeurism
Providing sexually explicit materials.
Child's involvement in pornography without intrusion
Failure to supervise child's voluntary sexual activity
Attempted/threatened sexual abuse with physical contact
Other/unknown sexual abuse

Physical Abuse
Shake, throw, purposefully drop
Hit with hand
Hit with object
Push, grab, drag, pull
Punch, kick
Other physical abuse

Emotional Abuse
Close confinement: tying/binding
Close confinement: other
Verbal assaults and emotional abuse
Threats of sexual abuse (without contact)
Threats of other maltreatment
Terrorizing the child
Administering unprescribed substances
Other/unknown abuse

Other Maltreatment
Lack of preventive health care
General neglect—other/unspecified neglect allegations
Custody/child support problems
Behavior control/family conflict issues
Parent problem
General maltreatment—unspecified/other

Physical Neglect
Refusal to allow or provide needed care for diagnosed condition
  or impairment
Unwarranted delay or failure to seek needed care
Refusal of custody/abandonment
Other refusal of custody
Illegal transfers of custody
Other or unspecified custody-related maltreatment —
  unstable custody arrangements
Inadequate supervision
Inadequate nutrition
Inadequate personal hygiene
Inadequate clothing
Inadequate shelter
Other/unspecified disregard of child's physical needs and
  physical safety

Educational Neglect
Permitted chronic truancy
Other truancy
Failure to register or enroll
Other refusal to allow or provide needed attention to diagnosed
  educational need

Emotional Neglect
Inadequate nurturance/affection
Domestic violence
Knowingly permitting drug/alcohol abuse
Knowingly permitting other maladaptive behavior
Refusal to allow or provide needed care for diagnosed emotional
  or behavioral impairment/problem
Failure to seek needed care for emotional or behavioral
  impairment/problem
Overprotectiveness
Inadequate structure
Inappropriately advanced expectations
Exposure to maladaptive behaviors and environments
Other inattention to development/emotional needs

Other
Involuntary neglect
Chemically dependent newborns

Source: Typology for Classifying Maltreatment, Table 6, Fourth National Incidence Study of Child Abuse and Neglect: Design and Methods Study (NIS-4), 19 (U.S. Department of Health and Human Services 2010) (www.nis4.org/DOCS/Nis4Design_Method_Summary.pdf).

Statistics

For statistics on the scope of child maltreatment, see Exhibit 14-2. Note that these statistics are limited to cases that are reported and investigated. The numbers would be considerably higher if unreported cases were added.

A recent study of the perpetrators of child maltreatment concluded that:

- 81.2 percent are parents; 6.1 percent are other relatives of the victim.
- 45.2 percent are men and 53.6 percent are women.
- 36.3 percent are between the ages of 20 and 29; 84.2 percent are between the ages of 20 and 49.
- 84.2 percent of the parent perpetrators are the biological parent of the victim.[9]

EXHIBIT 14-2   Statistics on Child Maltreatment (number of cases reported and investigated)

Item	2000		2005[1]		2007[1]		2008[5]	
	Number	Percent	Number	Percent	Number	Percent	Number	Percent
TYPES OF SUBSTANTIATED MALTREATMENT[2]								
Victims, total	**864,837**	**116.5**	**900,642**	**113.1**	**760,863**	**114.0**	**773,792**	**115.0**
Neglect	517,118	59.8	566,277	62.9	533,995	70.2	549,399	71.0
Physical abuse	167,713	19.4	149,328	16.6	122,383	16.1	125,971	16.3
Sexual abuse	87,770	10.2	83,786	G.3	71,115	9.3	71,162	9.2
Emotional maltreatment	66,965	7.7	63,438	7.0	55,223	7.3	55,236	7.1
Medical neglect	25,498	3.0	17,653	2.0	16,279	2.1	16,783	2.2
Other and unknown	146,184	16.9	137,946	15.3	68,054	8.9	71,237	9.2
SEX OF VICTIM[3,4]								
Victims, total	**864,837**	**100.0**	**882,23S**	**100.0**	**758,587**	**100.0**	**770,868**	**100.0**
Male	413,744	47.8	426,019	48.3	366,587	48.3	373,889	48.5
Female	446,230	51.6	456,220	51.7	392,000	51.7	396,979	51.5
AGE OF VICTIM[3,4]								
Victims, total	**864,837**	**100.0**	**881,058**	**100.0**	**755,164**	**100.0**	**770,907**	**100.0**
1 year and younger	133,094	15.4	154,399	17.3	144,257	19.1	150,866	19.5
2 to 5 years old	205,790	23.8	222,387	24.7	190,206	25.2	194,342	25.2
6 to 9 years old	212,186	24.5	193,089	21.4	166,853	22.1	168,055	21.8
10 to 13 years old	176,071	20.4	171,776	19.0	135,416	17.9	135,338	17.6
14 to 17 years old	126,207	14.6	138,934	15.4	118,021	15.6	121,164	15.8
18 years old and over	992	0.1	473	0.1	411	0.1	642	0.1

[1] Data have been revised. [2] A child may be a victim of more than one maltreatment. Therefore, the total for this item adds up to more than 100 percent. [3] The increase in unknown age, sex, and race in 2005 is due to some states reporting summary data without breakdown of corresponding fields. [4] Unknown data not shown. [5] Data have been updated since the release of the annual report.

Source: U.S. Census Bureau, Statistical Abstract of the United States (2011) (www.census.gov/compendia/statab/2011/tables/11s0339.pdf).

There are substantially more perpetrators in cohabitating families than in families where the parents are married:

- The rate of harm of children living with two married biological parents is 6.8 per 1,000 children.
- The rate of harm of children living with a parent who had an unmarried partner in the house was 57.2 per 1,000 children.[10]

Substance Abuse

Substance abuse can lead to child maltreatment. Here are some examples:

- Prenatal exposure of a child to harm due to the mother's use of an illegal drug or other substance.
- Manufacture of methamphetamine in the presence of a child.
- Selling, distributing, or giving illegal drugs or alcohol to a child.
- Using a controlled substance that impairs the caregiver's ability to adequately care for the child.[11]

Safe-Haven Law

Some mothers are so overwhelmed by their personal problems (often involving drug addiction) that they cannot provide care for their babies. They are afraid, however, of seeking help for the child because of a concern that they might be prosecuted for criminal child neglect or some other crime. In extreme cases, **infanticide** has occurred as mothers throw babies into dumpsters. To encourage women in such straits to come forward, some states have enacted **safe-haven laws**, which allow the mother to leave the child at designated locations such as a hospital or doctor's office. The woman can do this anonymously or by disclosing information about herself and the child to the place where the child is brought. She will not be prosecuted for abandonment so long as there is no evidence that the child has been abused. States have different requirements for these laws, such as the maximum age of the child that can be left.

PARENS PATRIAE

Parens patriae is the state's role in protecting children and others under a disability. The state, as parent of the country, exerts its authority to enact laws that protect its vulnerable citizens. An example is the compulsory-education laws we examined earlier. Another major example of the parens patriae power of the state is its law on child abuse. Parents have a fundamental constitutional right to raise their children, but the state can override that right when necessary to protect children.

Every state has an agency for **child protective services** designed to investigate child abuse and neglect, offer assistance to families of children at risk, and administer foster care or other placement programs. At the federal level, Congress enacted the **Child Abuse Prevention and Treatment Act (CAPTA)** to help fund state programs for the identification, prevention, and treatment of child abuse and neglect. CAPTA has also had an important role in defining and collecting data on child abuse and neglect.

As a condition for receiving federal funds under CAPTA, the states must agree that "in every case involving a victim of child abuse or neglect which results in a judicial proceeding, a guardian ad litem, who . . . may be an attorney or a **court appointed special advocate [CASA]** . . . (or both), shall be appointed to represent the child in such proceedings."[12] A paralegal can be a CASA. For more on CASAs, see Paralegal Roles at the end of the chapter.

MANDATORY REPORTING

Every state has a **mandatory reporting** law. Under this law, designated individuals such as teachers, doctors, nurses, social workers, day care workers, and counselors are classified as "mandatory reporters" who are required to report suspected child abuse or neglect to the police, child protective services, or other child welfare authorities. For example, one state requires a mandated reporter to file a report when he or she "has knowledge of or observes a child whom the mandated reporter knows or reasonably suspects has been the victim of child abuse or neglect." For the purposes of this requirement, "reasonable suspicion" means that "it is objectively reasonable for a person to entertain a suspicion, based upon facts that could cause a reasonable person in a like position, drawing, when appropriate, on his or her training and experience, to suspect child abuse or neglect."[13]

In most states, if a report turns out to be false, the person making the report is granted **immunity** from civil liability so long as the report was made in **good faith**.

Some states have established a *central registry* that contains the names of persons involved in cases of suspected child abuse if there is credible evidence of the abuse. The registry is available to child-care employers so that they can do a background search of prospective employees.

infanticide
The unlawful killing of a newborn.

safe-haven law
A law that protects a woman from prosecution if she abandons a baby at designated locations such as a hospital or doctor's office where it can receive immediate medical care.

parens patriae
Parent of the country, referring to the state's role in protecting children and those under disability.

child protective services
A state agency that investigates child neglect and abuse, offers assistance to families of children at risk, and administers foster care or other placement programs.

Child Abuse Prevention and Treatment Act (CAPTA)
A federal statute that helps fund state programs for the identification, prevention, and treatment of child abuse and neglect (42 U.S.C. § 5101).

court appointed special advocate (CASA)
A volunteer appointed by the court to undertake special assignments pertaining to children in the court system.

mandatory reporting
Required communication of designated information to a public authority, such as informing the police or child protective services of suspected child abuse or neglect.

immunity
A defense that prevents someone from being sued for what would otherwise be wrongful conduct.

good faith
The absence of wrongful intent or desire to take inappropriate advantage of someone. Also called bona fides.

JURISDICTIONAL STAGE AND DISPOSITIONAL STAGE

Child maltreatment can result in three major categories of court cases:

- *Criminal case.* The alleged perpetrator of child maltreatment is charged with a crime (e.g., child endangerment or sexual assault), and the case proceeds through the criminal courts.
- *Tort case.* The victim, or a representative of the victim, may be able to sue the perpetrator in a civil action for damages such as a tort suit for battery.
- *Family or juvenile court case.* The most common judicial consequence of child maltreatment is intervention by the state to take steps to protect the child from further harm. This occurs primarily in family or juvenile court.

When the third option is taken by the state, a two-stage procedure usually occurs:

- *Jurisdictional stage.* The court determines if it has **subject-matter jurisdiction** by deciding whether the facts of the case come within the definition of abuse, neglect, or dependency used in the state as established by statute and court opinion.
- *Dispositional stage.* If the court has jurisdiction, it must decide what to do—what disposition to make. The court's judgment is sometimes called a *dispositional* order. A number of options are possible. Examples:
  - Leave the child with the current parent or other caregiver under the supervision of child protective services or a child welfare agency and require counseling or other conditions designed to prevent future maltreatment.
  - Place the child in **foster care** or in an institution.
  - Begin proceedings to terminate the parental rights of the parent so that the child can be adopted (see Chapter 15).

The normal procedure is for the parent or caregiver to be given notice of the alleged child maltreatment and an opportunity to be heard before the state takes any action. **Summary seizure,** however, is allowed if the child is in danger of serious **imminent** harm. In summary seizure, the state takes possession of the child without notice to the parent and without a prior hearing. Shortly after the child is removed, the parents are notified and given the right to contest the removal in court.

subject-matter jurisdiction
The court's power to resolve a particular type of legal dispute and to grant a particular type of relief.

foster care
A child welfare service that provides shelter and substitute family care when a child's own family cannot provide this care.

summary seizure
Taking possession of a person or property without notice or prior hearing.

imminent
Near at hand; coming soon; about to happen; immediate.

ASSIGNMENT 14.3

a. Prepare a checklist of questions you can use to help determine whether a child has been neglected or abused. (See General Instructions for the Checklist-Formulation Assignment in Appendix A.)

b. Draft a flowchart of the procedural steps that are necessary in your state to determine whether a child has been neglected or abused. (See General Instructions for the Flowchart Assignment in Appendix A.)

DELINQUENCY

At common law:

- A minor below the age of seven was incapable of committing a crime. This was a **conclusive presumption**, meaning that evidence that such a child was in fact capable of committing a crime (and intended to commit it) was inadmissible.

conclusive presumption
An assumption or inference of fact that a party will not be allowed to try to disprove.

- A minor between the ages of 7 and 14 could be guilty of a crime if the prosecutor could show that the minor was mature enough to have formed the criminal intent necessary for the particular crime. For example, the crime of theft requires the intent to deprive someone permanently of his or her property. A **rebuttable presumption** existed that a minor between seven and fourteen could *not* possess the requisite criminal intent. This meant that the court would assume the absence of this intent unless the prosecutor affirmatively proved otherwise.

- A minor over fourteen was treated and tried the same as adults.

rebuttable presumption
An assumption or inference of fact that a party will be allowed to try to disprove (rebut) but that will be treated as true if it is not disproved.

In the early part of the twentieth century, a trend developed to remove the stigma of criminality from the misconduct of minors. Juvenile courts were created in which judges meted out large dosages of counseling and social services to **juvenile delinquents**—young people under a designated age (e.g., 16) whose conduct would constitute a crime if committed by an adult. Although a juvenile court judgment could be severe (e.g., institutionalization), the goal was less to punish than to encourage responsible behavior and rehabilitation.

If, however, a minor commits a particularly heinous act such as killing a parent, the state may have the authority to prosecute the minor in the regular criminal courts for adults.

juvenile delinquent
A young person under a designated age whose conduct would constitute a crime if committed by an adult. Sometimes called PINS (Person In Need of Supervision), MINS (Minor In Need of Supervision), or CHIPS (Child In Need of Protection and Services).

Juvenile or family courts also handle what were called **status offenses**—disruptive behavior by a young person under a designated age (e.g., 16) that would not be considered illegal by an adult. Examples of such offenses include habitual truancy from school and incorrigibility at home. A juvenile delinquent or minor who commits a status offense was sometimes categorized as a PINS (Person In Need of Supervision), MINS (Minor In Need of Supervision), or CHIPS (Child In Need of Protection and Services).

Juvenile and family courts often go through the same two-stage process mentioned earlier for child neglect and abuse cases: a *jurisdictional stage* to determine whether the court has jurisdiction and a *dispositional stage* during which the court would design an appropriate judgment (disposition) that emphasized rehabilitation where appropriate. The court could order counseling, institutionalization in a juvenile facility, probation under the supervision of a youth counselor, and foster home placement.

status offense
Disruptive behavior by a young person under a designated age that would not be considered illegal by an adult (e.g., leaving home without permission, habitual truancy). The state might refer to a status offender (or a juvenile delinquent) as a PINS (Person In Need of Supervision), MINS (Minor In Need of Supervision), or CHIPS (Child In Need of Protection and Services).

ASSIGNMENT 14.4

a. What is a juvenile delinquent in your state? (See General Instructions for the State-Code Assignment in Appendix A.)

b. Draft a flowchart of the procedural steps required in your state to process a juvenile delinquency case. (See General Instructions for the Flowchart Assignment in Appendix A.)

■ PARALEGAL ROLES

- For an overview of paralegal roles in family-law cases, see Exhibits 1-3 and 1-4 in Chapter 1.

- For many of the financial issues related to child neglect and dependency covered in Chapter 14, a paralegal may be asked to help collect documents and facts outlined in:
  - the checklist in Exhibit 3-1 of Chapter 3
  - the interrogatories in Appendix C

- Court Appointed Special Advocate (CASA). A CASA is a court appointed special advocate, a volunteer appointed by the court to undertake special assignments pertaining to children in the court system. Paralegals can become CASA volunteers for children in abuse and neglect cases, particularly children in the foster care system. CASAs are not substitutes for attorneys, social workers, or other child welfare personnel. The CASA's role is to be an independent voice for the child, assisting the judge to better understand the needs of the child. A CASA's tasks can include:

- Conducting an independent investigation of the child's home environment.
- Acting as a facilitator to achieve resolution of problems pertaining to a child's difficulties.
- Appearing at all hearings to advocate for the child's best interests and providing testimony when necessary.
- Making recommendations for specific, appropriate services for the child and the child's family, and advocating for necessary services.
- Monitoring implementation of case plans and court orders, checking to see that court-ordered services are provided in a timely manner.
- Administrative Agency Roles of Family Law Paralegals
  - Research resources for the dispositional hearing.
  - Obtain needed forms from child protective services and other child welfare agencies (often available online).
  - Research administrative regulations of the agencies.
  - Determine status of client's application for services from the agencies.
  - Monitor the service provided by the agencies.
  - Assist client in the school suspension or revocation hearing.
- Miscellaneous tasks
  - Interview client on the facts of the alleged child abuse, neglect, or abandonment.
  - Investigate facts of the alleged child abuse, neglect, or abandonment.
  - Assist client in designing alternative plans for the dispositional hearing on the child.

CHECK THE CITE

Four-year-old Joshua DeShaney became comatose and then profoundly retarded after being beaten on the head by his father. Although the Winnebago County Department of Social Services responded to complaints of child abuse and took steps to protect Joshua, it did not remove him from the custody of his father. Joshua's mother then sued the social workers and local officials. What was her theory of recovery? What specific rights did she claim they violated by refusing to remove Joshua? How did the U.S. Supreme Court resolve the case and what were the reasons for its decision? Read *DeShaney v. Winnebago County Department of Social Services*, 489 U.S. 189 (1989).

To read this opinion online, (1) go to Google Scholar (scholar.google.com) and enter the search "489 U.S. 189" in the Legal documents database; (2) Go to the FindLaw site (www.findlaw.com/casecode/supreme.html). In the box before "U.S.," type 489. In the box after "U.S.," type 189.

PROJECT

In Google, Bing, or Yahoo, run the following search: aa children "mandatory reporting" (substitute the name of your state for aa in the search). Write a short essay in which you explain the mandatory reporting laws in your state. Cover the topics of who must report, when they must report, to whom they must report, the consequences of failing to report, and what happens if the report turns out to have been in error. You must cite and quote from a minimum of eight different sources that you find on the Internet. At least four of these sources should be statutes, court opinions, or other laws. The cites from the laws must quote the relevant language of the laws. Do not, however, simply copy long sections of the laws. Quote the essential language in the laws and summarize the rest.

ETHICS IN A FAMILY LAW PRACTICE

You are a paralegal working at the law office of Daniel Britton, Esq. At a Halloween party, you begin talking to a 16-year-old guest. The guest tells you he is having troubles at home. You tell him about applying for emancipation and explain how it is accomplished. You also give him your business card. Any ethical problems?

WRITING SAMPLE

In 2010, Torry Hansen, an unmarried nurse in Tennessee, became so frustrated over the behavior of the boy she had adopted in Russia that she put him on a plane back to Russia. Traveling alone, the boy carried a note from Hansen saying that she could no longer handle the boy's mental problems and violent behavior. Your supervisor has asked you to write a memo in which you explain what child maltreatment laws would apply if this case had arisen in your state. You can find out more facts on the case by running this search in Google, Bing, or Yahoo: Russian adoption return child Tennessee Hansen. The memo should cite specific laws of your state that would apply. Quote from these laws and explain how they might apply. Do not explain the law of adoption in your state. Your supervisor does not want to know what adoption law applied to the case. The supervisor wants coverage of child abuse, child neglect, or other child maltreatment laws. To find the laws, run this search: child abuse neglect abandonment aa (substitute the name of your state for aa in the search). (See the General Instructions for the Writing Sample in Appendix A.)

SUMMARY

The age of majority is 18 in most states, but a state may impose different age requirements for performing different activities. Emancipation before the age of majority can make a minor eligible for some of these activities. Emancipation is legal independence from one's parents or legal guardians. It is obtained by operation of law (e.g., when the child reaches the age of majority or marries) or by a special court procedure.

A number of special laws apply to minors. For example, they have the right to disaffirm certain contracts they have entered. Some states, however, will not allow disaffirmance of sports or entertainment contracts, or if the minors lied about their age. Minors can own real and personal property in their own names, but unless they have been emancipated, their parents have a right to keep their earnings. Also, minors cannot acquire their own domicile without parental consent. States have a minimum age for the making of a will. Some states allow an emancipated minor to make a will if he or she has not reached the minimum age. If the parents of a minor die, the court will appoint a guardian to oversee his or her affairs. Most states give minors the right to inherit property in their own names.

School is compulsory until a designated age. Teachers stand in the place of parents (in loco parentis) and, as such, can impose reasonable corporal punishment. Students have First Amendment free speech rights and Fourth Amendment search and seizure rights while in school. The exercise of these rights, however, must not be unduly disruptive of school discipline. Students are entitled to procedural rights (e.g., a hearing) if the school wants to expel or suspend them long term.

Child maltreatment is an act or failure to act by a parent or caretaker that intentionally or carelessly results in physical or emotional harm to a child or that presents an imminent risk of such harm to a child. Child abuse is serious physical, emotional, or sexual mistreatment that is not the result of accident or circumstances beyond the control of the parent or guardian. Child neglect is the failure of a parent or other caregiver to provide the basic needs of a child, including physical needs, emotional needs, medical needs, and educational needs. Dependency is the condition of a child who has been placed in the custody of the state because the child has been abused, neglected, or abandoned. Abandonment is voluntarily leaving a child or ending communication with a child for a specific period or indefinitely without arranging for alternative care and supervision while away. Substance abuse can constitute child maltreatment such as prenatal exposure of the child to the mother's use of illegal drugs. A safe-haven law protects a woman from prosecution if she abandons a baby at designated locations such as a hospital or doctor's office where it can receive immediate medical care. The state's right to intervene in order to protect children is its parens patriae power. The Child Abuse Prevention and Treatment Act (CAPTA) funds state programs for the identification, prevention, and treatment of child abuse and neglect. CAPTA has helped define and collect data on child abuse and neglect. States have mandatory reporting laws that require certain individuals to report suspected child maltreatment to the police or child protective services.

Child maltreatment can result in a criminal case, a tort case, or a family/juvenile court case. If the latter, the jurisdictional stage determines whether the child fits within the state's definition of abuse, neglect, or other maltreatment. At the dispositional state, the court decides what order will best suit the rehabilitation needs of the child.

At common law, there was a conclusive presumption that a child below the age of seven could not commit a crime and a rebuttable presumption that a child between seven and fourteen cannot commit a crime. Minors over fourteen were treated as adults. Today, misconduct by children is often handled as juvenile delinquency and status offenses in juvenile or family courts where the emphasis is on rehabilitation.

KEY TERMS

age of majority	guardian	truancy
minor	guardian ad litem (GAL)	corporal punishment
minority	Uniform Transfers to Minors	in loco parentis
disability	Act (UTMA)	tort
emancipated	custodian	probable cause
operation of law	real property	child maltreatment
public assistance	personal property	child abuse
contract	domicile	child neglect
infancy	estate	dependency
disaffirm	instrument	abandonment
cosigner	will	infanticide
voidable	decedent	safe-haven law
estopped	inter vivos gift	parens patriae
necessaries	fundamental right	child protective services

Child Abuse Prevention and Treatment
   Act (CAPTA)
court appointed special advocate (CASA)
mandatory reporting
immunity

good faith
subject-matter jurisdiction
foster care
summary seizure
imminent

conclusive presumption
rebuttable presumption
juvenile delinquent
status offense

REVIEW QUESTIONS

1. What is the age of majority?
2. What is emancipation?
3. How is emancipation obtained by operation of law?
4. What is the court procedure that can result in emancipation?
5. When can minors disaffirm their contracts?
6. What is the Uniform Transfers to Minors Act (UTMA)?
7. What property can minors own in their own name?
8. What is the domicile of a minor?
9. What is an estate?
10. When can a minor make a will?
11. What happens if the parent of a minor dies?
12. What are the duties of the guardian of a minor?
13. Can minors inherit property in their own names if their parents are still living?
14. Can minors receive inter vivos gifts in their own names?
15. What constitutional right do parents have over the education of their children?
16. What is meant by in loco parentis?
17. When can corporal punishment be used on a child?
18. What First Amendment speech rights and Fourth Amendment search and seizure rights do students have in school?
19. How does the Fourth Amendment right of an adult differ from that of a student?
20. What procedural rights do students have when the school wants to expel them or suspend them long term?
21. What is child maltreatment?
22. Distinguish between child abuse and child neglect.
23. What is dependency and abandonment?
24. When can substance abuse constitute child maltreatment?
25. What is a safe-haven law?
26. What is parens patriae?
27. What is the Child Abuse Prevention and Treatment Act (CAPTA)?
28. How does mandatory reporting protect children?
29. What are the three major categories of court cases involving child maltreatment?
30. What is the distinction between the jurisdictional stage and the dispositional stage?
31. What are some of the options of a court at the dispositional stage if it finds that child maltreatment has occurred?
32. How did the common law treat crimes committed by children?
33. What is juvenile delinquency and what are status offenses?

HELPFUL WEBSITES

Emancipation
- www.law.cornell.edu/wex/table_emancipation
- en.wikipedia.org/wiki/Emancipation_of_minors

Contracts by Minors
- en.wikipedia.org/wiki/Capacity_(law)
- voices.yahoo.com/disafirrming-contracts -minors-266758.html

Corporal Punishment
- en.wikipedia.org/wiki/Corporal_punishment
- www.aacap.org/cs/root/policy_statements/corporal _punishment_in_schools

Child Welfare Information Gateway
- www.childwelfare.gov

Child Abuse Prevention Network
- child.cornell.edu

Child Abuse and Neglect Overview
- www.childwelfare.gov/can/statistics
- family-law.lawyers.com/child-abuse-and-neglect

Reporting Child Abuse and Neglect
- www.childwelfare.gov/responding/reporting.cfm

Abuse, Neglect, Adoption, and Foster Care Research

- www.acf.hhs.gov/programs/opre/abuse_neglect/natl_incid
- www.acf.hhs.gov/programs/opre/project/abuseProjects.jsp

Representation of Children at Child Abuse and Neglect Proceedings

- www.childwelfare.gov/systemwide/laws_policies/statutes/represent.cfm

Online Resources for State Child Welfare Law and Policy

- www.childwelfare.gov/systemwide/laws_policies/statutes/resources.pdf

Child Trends Databank

- www.childtrendsdatabank.org

Mandatory Reporting

- www.childwelfare.gov/systemwide/laws_policies/statutes/manda.cfm
- www.childwelfarepolicy.org/maps/single?id=160

Google/Bing/Yahoo Searches

(on these search engines, run the following searches, substituting your state for "aa")

- "age of majority" aa
- emancipation minor aa
- school discipline hearing aa
- "corporal punishment" aa
- "child abuse" aa
- safe-haven law baby aa
- child abandonment aa
- "juvenile delinquency" aa
- child crimes prosecution aa
- minor disaffirm contract aa
- child earnings parent emancipated aa
- school expulsion hearing aa
- student constitution rights aa
- "child neglect" aa
- "parens patriae" aa
- "mandatory reporting" aa
- "status offense" aa

ENDNOTES

Note: All or most of the court opinions in these endnotes can be read online. To do so, go to Google Scholar (scholar.google.com), select "Legal documents," and in the search box, enter the cite (e.g., "393 U.S. 503") or name of the case (e.g., Tinker v. Des Moines Independent Community School District") that is given in the endnote.

[1] Dan Frosch, *A Trip to These Principals May Mean a Paddling*, N.Y. Times, Mar. 30, 2011 at A15 (query.nytimes.com/gst/fullpage.html?res=9A05EFDB1430F933A05750C0A9679D8B63).

[2] *New York Code, Rules and Regulations* (NYCRR) § 100.2(l)(3)(i) (government.westlaw.com/linkedslice/default.asp?SP=nycrr-1000)(title 8).

[3] *Tinker v. Des Moines Independent Community School District*, 393 U.S. 503, 506 (1969).

[4] *Morse v. Frederick*, 551 U.S. 393 (2007).

[5] *Safford Unified School Dist. No. 1 v. Redding*, 557 U.S. 364 (2009).

[6] *Board of Ed. of Independent School Dist. No. 92 of Pottawatomie Cty v. Earls*, 536 U.S. 822 (2002).

[7] Walter Weyrauch et al., *Family Law* 949 (1994).

[8] *State v. Jones*, 95 N.C. 588, 1886 WL 1152, at 1 (1886).

[9] U.S. Department of Health & Human Services, Children's Bureau, *Child Maltreatment 2010* x (2010) (www.acf.hhs.gov/programs/cb/pubs/cm10/cm10.pdf).

[10] Sabrina Taverise, *More Unwed Parents Live Together, Report Finds*, N.Y. Times, Aug. 16, 2011 (www.nytimes.com/2011/08/17/us/17cohabitation.html).

[11] U.S. Department of Health and Human Services, *What Is Child Abuse and Neglect?* (2008) (www.childwelfare.gov/pubs/factsheets/whatiscan.cfm).

[12] 42 U.S.C. § 5106a(b)(2)(B)(xiii) (www.acf.hhs.gov/programs/cb/laws_policies/cblaws/capta).

[13] California Penal Code § 11166 (www.leginfo.ca.gov/cgi-bin/displaycode?section=pen&group=11001-12000&file=11164-11174.3).

CHAPTER OUTLINE

CHAPTER OBJECTIVES

After completing this chapter, you should be able to:

- Know the definition and effect of adoption.

- Distinguish between a traditional adoption and a second-parent adoption.

- Distinguish between a public-agency adoption and a licensed private-agency adoption.

- Describe a tribal adoption and an intercountry adoption.

- List the persons who can be involved in bringing about an independent adoption.

- Know when an adoption becomes a black-market adoption.

- Explain when a court will approve the adoption of an adult.

- List the criteria that a court will use when deciding whether an adoption is in the best interests of the child.

- Explain the effect of the Multiethnic Placement Act (MEPA).

- Describe the difficulties faced by gays and lesbians when they want to adopt.

- List the procedures involved in an adoption.

- Explain the notice and consent rights of an unmarried father of a child whom others want to adopt.

- State when consent can be revoked.

- Understand the grounds for a termination of parental rights.

- Identify the major procedural issues in a proceeding to terminate parental rights.

- Describe the roles of a guardian ad litem (GAL) and a court appointed special advocate

- (CASA) when child abuse or neglect is alleged in court.

- Explain the effect of the Adoption and Safe Families Act (ASFA).

- Explain why it is legally impossible for children to "divorce" their parents.

- Explain the challenges that can be brought against an adoption decree.

- Describe the function of a putative father registry.

- Explain the effect of the Interstate Compact on the Placement of Children (ICPC).

- List the consequences of an adoption.

- Distinguish between a confidential adoption and an open adoption.

INTRODUCTION

TERMINOLOGY

Adoption is the legal process by which one person (the **adoptive parent**) becomes the parent of another person (the adoptee). For most adoptions, two steps are required: the prior parent–child relationship ends by a termination of parental rights and a new parent–child relationship is created. The two steps may occur in two separate court proceedings or both might occur in the same proceeding.

Adoption establishes a permanent, legal parent–child relationship between the child and a person who is not the biological parent of the child. In many states, an adoption leads to the reissuance of the child's birth certificate, listing the adoptive parent as the "mother" or "father" of the child. The relationship is permanent in that only a court can end the relationship by terminating the parental rights of the adoptive parent. Even the divorce or death of the adoptive parent does not end the relationship. Assume, for example, that Tom marries Linda and then adopts her son, Dave, by a previous marriage. If Tom subsequently divorces Linda (or if his marriage to her ends by annulment), he does not cease to be Dave's parent. His obligation to support Dave, for example, continues after the divorce or annulment. Similarly, when Tom dies, Dave can inherit from Tom as if he were a biological child of Tom. In this sense, the parent–child relationship continues even after the death of the adoptive parent.

At the outset, we need to define and distinguish some important terms that relate to the law of adoption:

- **Custody** (1) The right to the care and control of something, either a person or a thing. (2) The actual care and control that someone has over a person or thing.
- **Legal custody** (in reference to children) The right to make the major child-rearing decisions on health, education, religion, discipline, and general welfare.
- **Ward** A person (e.g., minor) placed by the court under the care or protection of a guardian.
- **Guardian** A person who has legal authority to care for the person or property of another. Also called custodian.
- **Guardian ad litem (GAL)** A special guardian (often, but not always, an attorney) appointed by the court to appear in court proceedings on behalf of a person who is a minor, is insane, or is otherwise incapacitated.
- **Paternity** The biological fatherhood of a child.
- **Foster care** A child welfare service that provides shelter and substitute family care when a child's own family cannot provide this care. Foster care is designed to last for a temporary period during which adoption is neither desirable nor possible, or during the period when adoption is under consideration. The temporary home is called a foster home, which can be an individual family or a group home.
- **Stepparent** A person who marries the biological mother or father of a child, but who is not one of the child's biological parents. For example, assume that Ted and Mary marry each other. It is the second marriage for both. Ted has a son, Bill, from his first marriage. Mary has a daughter, Alice, from her first marriage. Ted is the biological father of Bill and the stepfather of Alice. Mary is the biological mother of Alice and the stepmother of Bill.

adoption
The legal process by which one person (the adoptive parent) becomes the parent of another person (the adoptee).

adoptive parent
A person who adopts another person.

SECOND-PARENT ADOPTION

As indicated, one of the steps in the adoption process is the termination of the prior parent–child relationship. Suppose, however, that the prospective adoptive parent is the spouse or romantic partner of the biological parent. Examples:

- Georgia is a widow with one child. When Georgia remarries, her new husband, John, wishes to adopt her child.
- Ted is a single father in a romantic relationship with Ursula. Ursula wishes to adopt Ted's child.
- Helen becomes a single parent through artificial insemination from an anonymous donor. Helen's romantic partner, Paula, wishes to adopt Helen's child.

In each of these examples, the child has a biological parent. This parent does not want to give up his or her parental rights in order to allow a new spouse or romantic partner to adopt the child. Yet the traditional rule is that an adoption terminates all prior parent–child relationships. States handle this predicament in one of three ways:

- The state makes an exception for stepparent adoptions. If a stepparent adopts the child, the parental rights of the biological parent are not terminated. Some states, however, apply this rule only if the stepparent marries the biological parent.
- The state allows all **second-parent adoptions**. This is an adoption of a child by an unmarried partner (or cohabitant) of a biological parent who does not give up (relinquish) his or her own parental rights when the adoption occurs.
- The state follows the traditional rule and will not allow the adoption without terminating the parental rights of the biological parent.

Where the third option applies, biological parents, of course, are rarely, if ever, willing to allow their child to be adopted. This is particularly difficult for homosexual couples in which the new romantic partner would like to adopt the child.

STATISTICS

Exhibit 15-1 presents some of the major statistics that pertain to this area of family law.

second-parent adoption
The adoption of a child by an unmarried partner (or cohabitant) of a biological parent who does not give up (relinquish) his or her own parental rights when the adoption occurs.

EXHIBIT 15-1 Adoption Statistics

- **Total numbers**
  - Number of children who have been adopted: 1.5 million (some estimates, however, range from 2 million to 5 million)
  - Percentage of all children who have been adopted: over 2%
  - Number of children adopted per year: approximately 136,000
  - Increase in number of annual adoptions between 1900 and 2008: 16%
  - Percentage of Americans who know someone who has been adopted: 58%
- **Adoptions by source (2008)**
  - Adoptions that occurred through public child welfare agencies: 41% (55,303)
  - Intercountry adoptions: 13% (17,416)
  - Other types of adoption (private agency, tribal, facilitated, independent, and stepparent): 46% (63,094)
- **Categories of adoptive parents**
  - Married couples: 66%
  - Unmarried couples: 2%
  - Single females: 30%
  - Single males: 2%
  - Adoptive parents who knew the adoptees prior to the adoption: 33%
  - Adoptive parents who were relatives of the adoptees: 24%
- **Categories of adoptees**
  - 37% were in foster care
  - 67% were White, non-Hispanic
  - 17% were Black, non-Hispanic
  - 5% were Hispanic
  - 8% were transracial (child and adoptive parents are of different races)
- **Ages of the adoptees**
  - Under 1 year: 2%
  - 1–5 years: 46%
  - 6–10 years: 37%
  - 11–15 years: 13%
  - 16–18 years: 2%
- **Couples seeking to adopt**
  - For every actual adoption, there are approximately 5 to 6 couples seeking to adopt
  - Over 1 million couples compete for 30,000 healthy white infants each year (adoption agencies sometimes refer to such children born in this country as DWIs—domestic White infants)
- **Waiting time to adopt**
  - Healthy infant: 1 to 7 years
  - International: 6 to 18 months
- **Percentage of unmarried women who place their babies for adoption**
  - 1998: under 2%
  - Before 1973 (the year abortion was legalized): 9%
- **Women who place their babies for adoption**
  - White women: 19% (from 1965 to 1972)
  - White women: 1.7% (from 1989 to 1995)
  - Black women: under 1% (a number that has remained constant)
  - Latina women: under 2% (a number that has remained constant)

(continued)

EXHIBIT 15-1   *(continued)*

- **Birth parents and adoptive parents**
  - Traditional adoption. Percentage in which there is some contact between birth parent and adoptive parent before the adoption: 95%
  - Traditional adoption. Percentage in which they meet before the adoption: 69%
  - Open adoption. Percentage in which there is ongoing contact (including with the child) after the adoption: 55%
  - Mediated adoption. Percentage in which an adoption agency facilitates periodic exchanges of picture and letters, but not direct contact, after the adoption: 40%
- **Cost of adoption to adoptive parent(s)**
  - Cost range of many adoptions of American infants (domestic adoptions): $20,000 – $40,000
  - Cost range of adopting children in foster care: $0 – $2,500
  - Private domestic adoptions that cost between $5,000 and $10,000: 13%
  - Private domestic adoptions that cost more than $20,000: 12%
  - International adoptions that cost between $5,000 and $10,000: 5%
  - International adoptions that cost more than $20,000: 49%
  - International adoptions that cost more than $35,000: 4%
- **Some specific adoption expenses**
  - Attorney fees: $2,500 – $12,000
  - Maternity home care during third trimester and postdelivery: $6,000
  - Prenatal and hospital care (normal delivery): $6,000
  - Prenatal and hospital care (caesarean section): $9,000
  - Prenatal and hospital care (major complications): $100,000
  - Home study and post-placement evaluation visits: $1,000 – $3,000
  - Other costs (travel, phone, insurance): $2,000 – $6,000
  - Additional costs of international adoption: $7,000 – $10,000
- **Financial assistance**
  - Federal tax credit in 2011 for qualified adoption expenses: up to $13,360 (the amount of the credit, however, phases out for high-income taxpayers)
  - Some special needs children adopted from foster care are eligible to receive federal or state adoption assistance
- **Number of adopted adults who search for their biological parents: 2% to 4%**
- **Children in foster care**
  - Total number (2009): 423,773
  - Total number (2000): 544,000
  - Median age of children in foster care: 9.7
  - Percentage of foster children in homes of non-relatives: 48%
  - Percentage of foster children in homes of relatives (called kinship care): 26%
  - Total number of children needing adoptive parent(s): 115,000 (photos available at adoptuskids.org)
  - Number of these children who are African-American: 33,000
  - Number of children older than 12 needing adoptive parent(s): 30,000
  - Number of children in foster care adopted by a single adoptive parent: 34%
  - Average (mean) time in foster care: 33 months
  - Total number of children adopted from foster care annually: 55,000

Sources: U.S. Department of Health and Human Services, Administration for Children and Families, *The AFCARS Report* (2010) (www.acf.hhs.gov/programs/cb/stats_research /afcars/tar/report17.htm). U.S. Department of Health and Human Services, Child Welfare Information Gateway, *How Many Children Were Adopted in 2007 and 2008?* (2011). U.S. Department of Health and Human Services, Office of the Assistant Secretary for Planning and Evaluation, *Adoption USA: A Chartbook Based on the 2007 National Survey of Adoptive Parents* (2009) (www.childwelfare.gov/systemwide/statistics/adoption.cfm#gen). Evan B. Donaldson Adoption Institute, *Research: Adoption Facts* (www.adoptioninstitute .org/research/adoptionfacts.php).

CATEGORIES OF ADOPTION

The three major categories of adoptions are public-agency, licensed private-agency, and independent adoption. Ultimately, they all require a home study to determine the suitability of the adoptive parents and a court decision allowing the adoption. The three major categories differ primarily on how the adoptive parents and child are brought together:

- *Public-agency adoption.* An adoption that occurs directly through a public agency or through a private agency under contract with a public agency. The public agency usually has legal and physical custody of the child in the foster-care system, often due to abuse or neglect. Among the most difficult to place are special needs children such as those over eight years of age, sibling groups, and children with disabilities. Online adoption exchanges provide photo listings with pictures and brief descriptions of children in the foster-care system who need adoptive parents.

- *Licensed private-agency adoption.* An adoption that occurs through a private agency licensed by the state. It is often a nonprofit agency that has a religious focus. If the state allows the agency to be for-profit, it is more likely to be nonsectarian (and more expensive). Women who wish to give their children up for adoption often use licensed private agencies.

- *Independent adoption.* Also called *private adoption, direct-placement adoption, private-placement adoption*, and *facilitated adoption*. An **independent adoption** is one that is arranged by the birth parents and the adoptive parents without the involvement of a public agency but often with the assistance of a facilitator or intermediary who brings them together.

Independent Adoption

A large network of service providers is available to facilitate independent adoptions. The central service provider is the facilitator or intermediary who helps bring the biological parent (birth mother) and the adoptive parents together for a fee. The facilitator acts on behalf of a birth parent or on behalf of a prospective adoptive parent. The facilitator can be an attorney, a doctor, a member of the clergy, a relative, or an unregulated service agency with a large Internet presence. Some states, however, limit the placement of children to licensed agencies and thereby prohibit the use of facilitators and intermediaries. Other states allow their use but impose restrictions such as the amount of the fee they can charge.

Also available for hire are photographers and web designers to help childless couples design their own websites as part of their search for pregnant mothers thinking about adoption. Several insurance companies sell adoption cancellation insurance to recover expenses if a birth mother changes her mind. Other available resources include numerous support groups, adoptive parent groups, and adoption exchanges that operate out of living rooms and office buildings. (An adoption exchange is an organization that seeks adoptive parents for foster care or special needs children.) In states where ads are legal, you can find ads directed at young, unmarried pregnant women ("Loving couple wishes to adopt your child"). The ads are placed on the Internet, in newspapers, and on bulletin boards where young women congregate.

The independent-adoption process can be arduous. Here is an example:

> *When Ralph and Nancy Smith discovered that they were infertile, they decided to adopt. Several visits to adoption agencies, however, were discouraging. One agency had a long waiting list of couples seeking to adopt healthy, white infants; the agency was not taking any new applications at the present time. Another agency accepted their application, but warned that the process might take up to five years, with no guarantee that a child would eventually become available. Nationally, hundreds of*

independent adoption
An adoption that is arranged by the birth parents and the adoptive parents without the involvement of a public agency but often with the assistance of a facilitator or intermediary. Also called private adoption, direct-placement adoption, private-placement adoption, and facilitated adoption.

thousands of couples are waiting to adopt a relatively small number of healthy, white infants. The small number of available children is due to the widespread use of abortion and the declining social stigma attached to the single-parent motherhood.

Acting on the advice of a friend, the Smiths then tried the alternative of an independent adoption. They placed personal ads on the Internet and in newspapers seeking to contact an unwed pregnant woman willing to relinquish her child for adoption. They created their own web page containing photographs and video clips of their home life in order to give a birth mother an idea of what life would be like for her child if she chose the Smiths as adoptive parents. They also sent their résumé and letters of inquiry to doctors, members of the clergy, and attorneys specializing in independent adoptions. In some cities, the Yellow Pages had listings for attorneys with this specialty. Their efforts were finally successful when an attorney led them to Diane Kline, a 17-year-old pregnant girl. The Smiths prepared a scrapbook on their life, which Diane reviewed along with their web page. She then interviewed the Smiths and decided to allow them to adopt her child. The Smiths paid the attorney's fees, Diane's medical bills, the cost of her psychological counseling, travel expenses, and living expenses related to the delivery of the baby. Eventually, Diane signed a consent form relinquishing her rights in the baby and agreeing to the adoption by the Smiths, who formally applied to the court for the adoption. A private agency investigated the case and made a home-study report to the court, which then issued an order authorizing the adoption.

In this example, the biological mother had personal contact with the adoptive parents. This occurs with increasing frequency, particularly in independent adoptions. When, however, anonymity of the biological parents is desired, it can easily be accomplished.

Tribal and Intercountry Adoptions

There are two major special-category adoptions:

- A *tribal adoption* occurs within the American Indian community. States are required to place American Indian children in adoptive homes that reflect Indian culture. Tribal courts can request exclusive jurisdiction to make the adoption decision, which, under tribal law, does not always require the termination of the parental rights of the birth parents.

- An *intercountry adoption* (also called an *international adoption*) is the adoption of a child who is a citizen of one country by persons who are citizens of a different country. Intercountry adoptions are finalized abroad or in the United States, depending on the laws of the country where the child resides. If the adoption is granted (finalized) abroad, it is often refinalized in the United States as a U.S. adoption in order to ensure compliance with the law of the state where the child will live and to obtain a U.S. birth certificate. The United States is a member of the Hague Adoption Convention, which regulates adoptions between member nations.[1] A major concern of the convention is to combat baby trafficking in which mothers in foreign countries are pressured into giving their children to orphanages, which then charge large fees to potential adoptive parents in the United States and other wealthy countries.

ADOPTION ABUSE

In the Smith example, the money paid by the adoptive parents covered medical, legal, and related expenses. A person may pay expenses that are naturally and reasonably connected with the adoption, so long as no cash or other consideration is given to induce someone to participate in the adoption. The law assumes that this is what occurs when there is a payment beyond reasonable expenses. Such payments turn the transaction into a **black-market adoption**, also called baby-buying. Assume, for example, that Diane had hesitated about going through with

black-market adoption

An illegal adoption that involves a payment beyond reasonable expenses in order to facilitate the adoption.

the adoption and the Smiths had offered her $20,000 above expenses. This would constitute baby-buying. An adoption becomes baby-buying when a payment to a birth parent, to an attorney, or to anyone else is for finding or placing a child rather than for reasonable expenses. At the extreme end of this illegal practice are *baby brokers* who financially entice women to give up their children and then charge adoptive parents a large fee for arranging the adoption. Black-market adoptions can involve payments of up to $50,000. (The separate but related problems of payments for surrogate motherhood will be considered in the next chapter.)

It is difficult to know how many independent adoptions turn into black-market adoptions because the participants have an interest in keeping quiet about the illegal payment. Although a fee for finding a baby or for placing a child for adoption is illegal, it is not always easy to distinguish such fees from the legitimate payment of reasonable fees connected with the cost of adoption services. To discourage illegal payments, most states require the adoptive parent to file with the court a list of all expenditures pertaining to the adoption. This, however, has not stopped black-market adoptions from occurring. Some argue that the only way to do so is to eliminate independent adoptions so that all adoptions will be more adequately supervised by traditional public and private agencies. Only a few states have taken this route.

Other abuses can also occur:

- In Los Angeles, the police recently arrested a woman for promising her unborn child to seven couples seeking to adopt. She was charged with adoption fraud.

- A woman was charged with child abandonment when she tried to place her son for adoption with someone she met on eBay, the Internet auction site.

- A New York City attorney was convicted in the battery death of a six-year-old girl who had been placed in his care so that he might arrange an independent adoption. The attorney kept the child—and then abused her—when the prospective adoptive parents failed to pay his fee for the adoption.

- A facilitator used her Internet service to collect thousands of dollars from two separate adoptive couples, one in the United States and one in England. Neither couple knew the other existed. In the midst of the chaos, the biological mother changed her mind about wanting to go through with the adoption.

Such stories always lead to calls for additional regulation. Proponents of independent adoptions, however, view these cases as aberrations and maintain that the vast majority of independent adoptions are legal and are adequately supervised.

ASSIGNMENT 15.2

Answer the following questions based on your state code. (See General Instructions for the State-Code Assignment in Appendix A.)

a. Are independent or private adoptions allowed in your state? If so, how do they differ from agency adoptions? In what ways does the state try to prevent baby-buying?

b. Is it a crime to "buy" a baby? If so, how is this crime committed?

WHO MAY BE ADOPTED?

In most cases, the person adopted (the adoptee) is a child, usually an infant. Yet in many states it is possible for one adult to adopt another adult. The most common reason for this practice is that the adoptive parent wants to give the adopted adult rights of inheritance from the adoptive parent. In effect, the latter is naming an heir. In ancient Greece and Rome, perpetuating the family line by designating an heir was the main purpose of adoption.

In addition to creating inheritance rights, a major reason that courts approve adult/adult adoptions is to provide long-term or perpetual care to a disabled adult adoptee.

Another use of adult/adult adoption is to try to create a family so that a rent-controlled apartment can be transferred to a family member. If, for example, an adult tenant has a rent-controlled apartment (one that the landlord cannot rent at market rates), the tenant may not be able to transfer the apartment to another person unless that person is a member of the tenant's immediate family. To create such a member, the tenant might try to adopt another adult, e.g., an intimate companion. This strategy, however, is often challenged by landlords who are eager to convert rent-controlled apartments into market-rate apartments. Although the legality of this use of adoption is not clear, there are courts that have said that it is legal.[2] States that approve it are likely to say that adoption to confer the economic benefit of an apartment is similar to an adoption to confer the economic benefit of inheritance. Similarly, a recent case permitted a disabled grandfather to adopt his adult grandson to allow the grandson to qualify for financial aid available to children of disabled veterans.[3]

In 2012, a wealthy defendant in a wrongful-death case adopted his girlfriend in an alleged strategy to shield some of his assets in the event that he is found liable in the wrongful-death case. The judge who granted the adoption did not know that the defendant was about to be sued for wrongful death at the time the adoption was approved. The adoption was then challenged on the ground that adoption cannot be used to shield assets from potential creditors.

Can a homosexual adult adopt his or her intimate partner? This question is separate from the issue of whether homosexuals can adopt children, which we will consider later in the chapter. Here our focus is on whether a homosexual person can adopt his or her homosexual partner. Most adoption statutes appear to be broad enough to allow it, but not many courts have had occasion to consider the issue. Those that have are split. Delaware allowed it as a way to "formalize the close emotional relationship" of the two men involved.[4] Hence adult/adult adoption could be used in Delaware (a state where same-sex couples could not marry) as a way to create inheritance, hospital visitation, and other family rights to persons denied the right to marry. In effect, adoption law is used to bypass the law against same-sex marriage, at least as it relates to some of the rights enjoyed by married couples. New York, however, took the opposite position. The "sexual intimacy" between such individuals "is utterly repugnant to the relationship between child and parent in our society, and . . . a patently incongruous application of our adoptive laws."[5] After New York reached this result, however, the state legalized same-sex marriage. It is unclear whether the state will continue to oppose adoption by one homosexual person of another.

When adult adoptions are allowed, they differ from adoptions of minors in that adult/adult adoptions do not require a home study, and the consent of the biological parents of the adult adoptee is not required. The biological parents may have to be given notice of the adoption, but they cannot veto it.

WHO MAY ADOPT?

The petitioners (i.e., the persons seeking to become the adoptive parents) will be granted the adoption if it is in **best interests of the child**. Such a broad standard gives the judge considerable discretion. In many states, there is a presumption or a preference that the adoptive parent(s) should be a relative of the child. Although such **kinship adoptions** are desirable, other factors may lead a court to conclude that it would be in the best interests of the child to be placed with nonrelated adoptive parent(s).

We turn now to an overview of the factors considered in most adoptions.

best interests of the child
A standard used by a court to decide what would best serve a child's welfare when the court must make custody, visitation, adoption, guardianship, and change-of-name decisions.

kinship adoption
An adoption in which the adoptive parent is related to the adoptee.

FACTORS CONSIDERED

To apply the best-interests standard, the judge will consider the following factors, no one of which is usually controlling:

1. Age
2. Marital status
3. Health
4. Race
5. Religion
6. Wishes of the child
7. Economic status
8. Home environment and morality

1. *Age of petitioner.* Most states require the petitioner to be an adult. The preference is for someone who is not unusually older than the child. A court would be reluctant, for example, to allow a 75-year-old to adopt an infant, unless special circumstances warranted it.

2. *Marital status of petitioner.* Single persons are allowed to adopt, although the preference is for someone who is married. His or her spouse is usually required to join the petition.

3. *Health of petitioner.* Adoptive parents are not expected to be physically and emotionally perfect. If a particular disability will not seriously interfere with the raising of the child, it will not by itself bar the adoption.

4. *Race.* Race can be a factor in the adoption decision of a court, but it cannot be the sole factor or the determining factor in the decision. Racial *matching* (placing children with adoptive parents of the same race as the child) cannot be required. **Transracial adoptions** have been controversial. In 1972, the National Association of Black Social Workers expressed strong opposition to such adoptions. The problem, however, is that there are not enough same-race adoptive parents available. The net effect is to lengthen the time children must wait to be adopted, a reality referred to as *foster-care drift*. In an attempt to remedy the problem, Congress passed a statute on "interethnic adoption," the **Multiethnic Placement Act (MEPA)**. It prohibits the delay or denial of adoptions on account of race:

   > A person or government that is involved in adoption or foster care placements may not (A) deny to any individual the opportunity to become an adoptive or a foster parent, on the basis of the race, color, or national origin of the individual, or of the child, involved; or (B) delay or deny the placement of a child for adoption or into foster care, on the basis of the race, color, or national origin of the adoptive or foster parent, or the child, involved.[6]

   American Indians, however, are treated differently. Congress has determined that "an alarmingly high percentage of Indian families are broken up by the removal, often unwarranted, of their children from them by nontribal public and private agencies and that an alarmingly high percentage of such children are placed in non-Indian foster and adoptive homes and institutions."[7] Consequently, the adoption of American Indian children by non-Indians today is relatively rare. As indicated earlier, tribal courts can request exclusive jurisdiction to make the adoption decisions involving American Indian children.

5. *Religion.* When possible or practicable, the religion of the adoptive parents should be the same as the religion of the biological parents. Interfaith adoptions, though allowed, are generally not encouraged.

6. *Wishes of the child.* The court will consider the opinion of the prospective adoptee if he or she is old enough to communicate a preference.

7. *Economic status.* The adoptive parents must have the financial means (on their own or with available assistance from other sources) to care

transracial adoption
An adoption of a child whose race is different from the race of the adoptive parents. Also called interracial adoption.

Multiethnic Placement Act (MEPA)
A federal statute that forbids delay or denial of adoption on the basis of race, color, or national origin.

for the child. The court will examine their current financial status and prospects for the future in light of the child's support needs.

8. *Home environment and morality.* The goal is for the child to be brought up in a wholesome, loving home where values are important and where the child will be nurtured to his or her potential. Illegal or conspicuously unorthodox lifestyles are frowned upon and may lead to a denial of the adoption petition.

GAYS AND LESBIANS

Earlier we saw that states differ on whether to allow the adoption of a homosexual adult by another homosexual adult. Here we focus on a homosexual person's adoption of a minor. (See Exhibit 15-2.)

A gay or lesbian person who petitions for adoption could fall into one of several categories. He or she might:

- Live alone and hence seek to become the sole parent.
- Live with a same-sex partner who is a biological parent of the child. The same-sex partner would be seeking a second-parent adoption.
- Live with a same-sex partner who is not a biological parent of the child, so that both would petition the court for a **joint adoption**, which is an adoption by two adults who both seek to become adoptive parents of a child.

joint adoption

An adoption by two adults (usually married) who both seek to become adoptive parents of a child.

Most states allow single adults of any sexual orientation to adopt children. The law in New York is typical of this position:

Applicants shall not be rejected solely on the basis of homosexuality. A decision to accept or reject when homosexuality is at issue shall be made on the basis of individual factors as explored and found in the adoption study process as it relates to the best interests of adoptive children.[8]

This policy decision on who should be allowed to adopt is supported by a 2004 resolution of the American Psychological Association that "[t]here is no scientific basis for concluding that lesbian mothers or gay fathers are unfit parents on the basis of their sexual orientation" and that "results of research suggest that lesbian and gay parents are as likely as heterosexual parents to provide supportive and healthy environments for their children."[9]

The number of states that explicitly ban adoption by gays and lesbians is steadily decreasing. One of the last states with such a ban was Florida, whose statute provided that "No person eligible to adopt under this statute may adopt if that person is a homosexual." This statute was held to violate the equal protection clause of the Florida Constitution.[10] Other bans have been subjected to similar state and federal constitutional challenges.

EXHIBIT 15-2   Adoption: Gays and Lesbians

- Over 65,000 adopted children live in homes headed by non-heterosexual individuals or couples
- Over 14,000 foster children live in homes headed by non-heterosexual individuals or couples
- Over 50% of gay and lesbian parents adopt children from the foster care and child welfare system
- Over 60% of gay and lesbian parents adopt children of a race different from their own (transracial adoptions)
- Over 10% of gay and lesbian parents adopt children who are six years of age or older (generally, a difficult age for a child to be adopted)
- 21,740 same-sex couples adopted children in 2009 (6,477 did so in 2000)
- Over 2,000,000 gays, lesbians, or bisexuals are interested in adopting

Sources: Evan B. Donalson Adoption Institute, *Expanding Resources for Children III* (2011) (www.adoptioninstitute.org/research/2011_10_expanding_resources_bestpractices .php). Gary Gates, et al, *Adoption and Foster Care by Gay and Lesbian Parents in the United States* (Williams Institute & Urban Institute, March 2007) (www.urban.org/uploaded PDF/411437_adoption_foster_care.pdf).

Although few outright bans remain on the books, the agencies and judges interpreting the law can use their extensive discretion to disfavor prospective adoptive parents who are gay or lesbian. Critics charge that such discrimination exists to a very large extent. Furthermore, about half the states do not allow second-parent adoptions. In these states, the biological parent would have to give up his or her parental rights in order to let his or her partner adopt the child they are raising together. The state might make an exception when a stepparent wants to adopt the child, but only if the stepparent marries the biological parent. States that allow second-parent adoptions (or stepparent adoptions) would allow the gay or lesbian partner of a biological parent to adopt without terminating the existing partner's parental rights.[11]

If adoption is denied, an alternative route to obtaining parental rights can be found in the rules on *equitable estoppel* and *in loco parentis*. See Chapter 10, in which we discussed how these rules can give parental status to individuals (straight or homosexual) who have already established a bonding relationship with the child.

ASSIGNMENT 15.3

To answer the following questions, check your state code and court opinions. (See General Instructions for the State-Code Assignment and the Court-Opinion Assignment in Appendix A.)

a. In your state, who is eligible to adopt children? Who is not eligible?

b. What standards exist to guide a judge's decision in your state on whether to approve a particular adoption?

c. Mary Jones is a Baptist. She wants to place her one-year-old child for adoption. Mr. and Mrs. Johnson want to adopt the child and file the appropriate petition to do so in your state. The Johnsons are Jewish. Mary Jones consents to the adoption. What effect, if any, will the religious differences between Mary Jones and the Johnsons have on the adoption? Assume that Mary has no objection to the child's being raised in the Jewish faith.

d. Same facts as in part (c) above except that the Johnsons are professed atheists. Mary Jones does not care.

e. Under what circumstances can a homosexual adopt a minor in your state?

f. Under what circumstances can a single person—an adult who lives alone—adopt a minor in your state?

ASSIGNMENT 15.4

Both Paul and Helen Smith are deaf and mute. They wish to adopt the infant daughter of Helen's best friend, a widow who just died. Prepare an investigation strategy to collect evidence relevant to whether the adoption should be permitted. (See General Instructions for the Investigation-Strategy Assignment in Appendix A.)

ADOPTION PROCEDURE

It is not easy to adopt a child. Elaborate procedures have been created to protect the interests of the child, the biological parents, and the adoptive parents. When the most sought-after babies (i.e., healthy, DWIs—domestic white infants) are in short supply, the temptation to "buy" a baby on the black market is heightened. One way to try to control this is by increasing procedural safeguards in the process. Fewer safeguards, however, are usually needed in stepparent adoptions of children who will continue to live with a biological parent. In stepparent adoptions, courts may have discretion to use an **expedited procedure** such as waiving (or doing a shortened version of) the home study. Some states, however, will not streamline the process in this way unless the biological parent has been married to the stepparent for at least a year.

expedited procedure
An accelerated procedure achieved by bypassing some of the procedural steps that are normally required.

subject-matter jurisdiction
The court's power to resolve a particular type of legal dispute and to grant a particular type of relief.

venue
The place of the trial. The proper county or geographical area in which a court with jurisdiction may hear a case.

petition
A formal request that the court take some action.

JURISDICTION AND VENUE

Subject-matter jurisdiction refers to the power of the court to hear a particular kind of case and to grant a particular kind of relief. Not every court in a state has subject-matter jurisdiction to issue adoption decrees. The state constitution or a state statute will designate one or perhaps two courts that have authority to hear adoption cases (e.g., the state family court, probate court, surrogate court, or juvenile court). There are also specifications for selecting the **venue** or place of the trial, which become important when more than one county or district has subject-matter jurisdiction over adoptions in the state. The selection is referred to as the *choice of venue*. It will often depend on the residence of one or more of the participants, usually the biological parents, the adoptive parents, or the child.

PETITION

States differ on the form and content of the adoption **petition** filed by the adoptive parents to begin the adoption proceeding. The petition will contain such data as the names of the petitioners; the petitioners' ages; whether the petitioners are married and, if so, whether they are living together; the name, age, and religion of the child, etc. Not all states require that the biological parents be named in the petition itself. (For an example of the format of a petition, see Exhibit 15-3.)

EXHIBIT 15-3 Adoption Petition

ADOPTION OF_____
(Name after adoption)
CASE NO._____

PETITION FOR ADOPTION OF MINOR
[R.C. 3107.05]

The undersigned petitions to adopt_____

a minor, and to change the name of the minor to_____.

The petitioner states the following:　　**PETITIONER**

Full Name:_____ Age_____

Full Name:_____ Age_____

Place of Residence:_____
Street Address

City or Village or Township if unincorporated area　　County

Post Office　　State　　Zip Code　　Duration of residence

Marital Status:_____ Date and Place of Marriage:_____

Relationship of Minor to Petitioner:_____

The petitioner has facilities and resources suitable to provide for the nurture and care of the minor and it is the desire of the petitioner to establish the relationship of parent and child with the minor.

MINOR TO BE ADOPTED

Birth Name:_____ Date of Birth:_____

Place of Birth:_____ Property and Value:_____

☐　The minor is living in the home of the petitioner, and was placed therein for adoption on the _____ day of _____, _____ by _____

☐　The minor is not living in the home of the petitioner, and resides at_____

☐　The minor will be an adopted person as defined in R.C. 3107.39;
☐　The minor will be an adopted person as defined in R.C. 3107.45;

A certified copy of the birth certificate of the minor is filed with this petition or is not available due to the following:
_____

A Preliminary Estimate Accounting (Form 18.9), if required, is filed with this petition.

Source: Hamilton Probate Court, Ohio (www.probatect.org/services/adoption.htm)(Individual Forms; 18.0).

In some states, once the adoption petition is filed, the child is placed with the prospective adoptive parents on a probation basis to assess how well the child adjusts to the new home. Of course, if the child is already living with the prospective parents (e.g., a foster parent or a stepparent who wants to adopt the child), the court will already have access to the data on adjustment.

ASSIGNMENT 15.5

a. What must a petition for adoption contain in your state? Must it name the biological parents? (See General Instructions for the State-Code Assignment in Appendix A.)

b. Draft an adoption petition. Assume that you are seeking to adopt the one-year-old baby of a friend, a woman who has recently been hospitalized. This friend has no other relatives. The biological father of the child is no longer alive. You can make up facts you need to draft the petition. (See General Instructions for the Complaint-Drafting Assignment in Appendix A.)

NOTICE

Procedural due process of law requires that both biological parents be given *notice* of the petition to adopt the child by the prospective adoptive parents. (Later, when we study the *Baby Richard* and *Baby Jessica* cases, we will see examples of the critical importance of this requirement.) The preferred method of providing notice is to personally serve the biological parents with **process** within the state where the adoption petition is brought. If this is not possible, the court may allow **substituted service** (e.g., by registered mail or publication in a newspaper).

There was a time when the father of a nonmarital (illegitimate) child was not entitled to notice of the adoption proceeding; only the mother of such a child was given notice. This has changed, however, due to decisions of the U.S. Supreme Court. Petitioners for the adoption are now required to use **due diligence** to locate and identify the father in order to give him notice. Although the full scope of the rights of the father of a nonmarital child has not yet been fully defined by the courts, it is clear that he can no longer be ignored in the adoption process. As we shall see, however, there is a difference between a parent's right to notice of the adoption proceeding and a parent's right to prevent the adoption by refusing to consent to it.

CONSENT

Consent of Biological Parents

Adoption occurs in two ways: with or without the consent of the biological parents. When consent is necessary, the state's statute will usually specify the requirements of consent:

- whether the consent must be notarized and witnessed
- when a formal relinquishment of parental rights (**surrender**) must be filed in court (when a parent seeks the assistance of an agency for the adoption of her child, the agency asks her to sign a surrender of parental rights to the agency)
- whether special steps must be taken if the birth mother is a minor (e.g., appointment of counsel or guardian ad litem for her)
- whether the formalities for consent differ for agency adoptions as opposed to independent adoptions
- whether consent can be given before the birth of the child (most states say that that only *post*-birth consent is valid)
- whether the consent form must mention the names of the parties seeking to adopt the child

procedural due process
The constitutional requirement that the government provide fair procedures such as notice and an opportunity to be heard whenever the government seeks to deprive someone of life, liberty, or property.

process
The means (e.g., a summons, writ, or other court order) used by the court to acquire or exercise its power or jurisdiction over a person.

substituted service
An approved method of completing service of process other than by handing the process documents to the defendant (or to the defendant's authorized representative) in person (e.g., service by mail or by publication in a newspaper). Also called constructive service.

due diligence
Reasonable efforts to find and verify factual information needed to carry out an obligation, to avoid harming someone, or to make an important decision (e.g., to locate a parent).

surrender
A voluntary relinquishment of rights.

opportunity interest
The right of a father to develop a relationship
with his child.

indicia of parenthood
Conduct that indicates or evidences a parental
relationship with a child.

Women who change their minds about giving up their babies often claim that they were coerced or unduly pressured into consenting. In one case, the woman alleged that she was pressured to choose the adoptive parents while she was in labor and to sign the adoption papers while she was under the influence of the sedative Demerol. In light of such problems, most states say that the consent is not valid if it is obtained prior to the birth of the child. The state may not allow the consent to be sought until at least 72 hours after birth.

Both biological parents must consent to the adoption unless the parental rights of one or both of them have been formally terminated (see discussion of termination on the following page) or unless one of the parents, mainly the father, has failed to take adequate steps to protect his paternal rights. All fathers have what is called an **opportunity interest**, which is a constitutional right to develop a relationship with his child. This includes fathers of nonmarital (illegitimate) children. Of course, fathers cannot pursue this interest if their parental rights are terminated through an adoption. Hence, a father has the right to stop the adoption by withholding his consent, but only if he has shown sufficient **indicia of parenthood**. Such indicia (indications or evidence) can include establishing his paternity, living with the child, supporting the child, or otherwise maintaining close contacts with the child. Such a father will be given the same rights as the mother. He *will* be allowed to veto the proposed adoption. A father who fails to demonstrate sufficient indicia of parenthood has, in effect, abandoned his opportunity interest and cannot prevent the adoption. The standard used by the courts is "biology plus." The biological relationship between father and child is not sufficient to allow him to veto the adoption. To have this right there must be *biology plus* indicia of parenthood.

Suppose, however, that a father fails to demonstrate sufficient indicia of parenthood (biology plus) because he never knew that he was a father (e.g., the birth mother lied about whether the baby was born alive). We will cover this issue later in the chapter when we discuss the *Baby Richard* case, the *Baby Jessica* case, and putative father registries.

Consent of Others

If the biological parents have already relinquished or surrendered their parental rights to an agency, then the consent of the agency to the adoption will be required.

If the prospective adoptive parent is married, the consent of his or her spouse is often required even if this spouse is not also adopting the child. In most states, the child to be adopted—the adoptee—must consent to the adoption if he or she has reached a specified age (e.g., 12 or 14) unless the court determines that it would not be in the child's best interests to ask the child.

If the child is in foster care, the consent of foster parents is not required when the child is eventually adopted by someone else. Foster parents cannot prevent the adoption from occurring. This does not mean that the foster parents can be ignored entirely. When an agency attempts to remove the child from the foster home, many states give the foster parents the right to object to the removal and to present their arguments against the removal. Although foster parents may be given a right to be heard on the removal, they cannot veto the adoption of the child.

ASSIGNMENT 15.6

In Assignment 15.5, part (b), you drafted an adoption petition based primarily on facts that you invented yourself. Using those facts, draft a consent form (to be signed by the mother) that complies with the statutory requirements for consent in your state.

Revocation of Consent

A biological parent can change her mind and revoke her consent to the adoption. Most states allow the birth mother to revoke her consent at any time before the birth of the child. As indicated, a state may not allow consent to be sought until a designated time after birth (e.g., 72 hours) and may give her a designated time after birth (e.g., 10 days) during which she can revoke her consent.

INVOLUNTARY TERMINATION OF PARENTAL RIGHTS

Grounds for Termination

A **termination of parental rights (TPR)** is a judicial declaration that ends the legal relationship between parent and child when this is in the best interests of the child. The parent no longer has any right to participate in decisions affecting the welfare of the child and no longer has any duties toward the child. TPR can be voluntary or involuntary.

- It is voluntary when the biological parent wants to end the parent-child relationship in order to allow someone to adopt the child. For an agency adoption, the biological parent executes a document called a *surrender* (relinquishment of parental rights), releasing parental rights to the agency. In a private or independent adoption, the biological parent's written consent to the adoption is filed in court as part of the adoption papers.
- It is involuntary when the termination is forced on the parent because of being ruled **unfit**.

The grounds for involuntary termination of parental rights vary among the states, although a central theme of these grounds is the unfitness of the biological parent(s). These grounds are summarized in the following overview found in the statutes of many states:

> In addition to any other proceeding provided by law, the relationship of parent and child may be terminated by a court order issued in connection with an adoption proceeding under this Act on any ground provided by other law for termination of the relationship, and in any event on the ground (1) that the minor has been abandoned by the parent, (2) that by reason of the misconduct, faults, or habits of the parent or the repeated and continuous neglect or refusal of the parent, the minor is without proper parental care and control, or subsistence, education, or other care or control necessary for his physical, mental, or emotional health or morals, or, by reason of physical or mental incapacity the parent is unable to provide necessary parental care for the minor, and the court finds that the conditions and causes of the behavior, neglect, or incapacity are irremediable or will not be remedied by the parent, and that by reason thereof the minor is suffering or probably will suffer serious physical, mental, moral, or emotional harm, or (3) that in the case of a parent not having custody of a minor, his consent is being unreasonably withheld contrary to the best interests of the minor.[12]

A parent is unfit when he or she demonstrates abuse or neglect that is substantially detrimental to a child. Unfitness is demonstrated by conduct such as **abandonment**, extreme cruelty, chronic abuse and neglect, conviction of certain crimes, willful neglect, or substantial incapacity to provide care. Some states may list unfitness as one of several grounds for involuntary TPR rather than as a catchall to cover all the grounds. A statute might also refer to children who are *dependent* or in a state of **dependency**, which can mean children who are abused, neglected, or abandoned, or children lacking basic care through no fault of their parent or guardian. A consequence of involuntary TPR is that the consent of the parent is not needed for the child to be adopted.

termination of parental rights (TPR)
A judicial declaration that ends the legal relationship between parent and child when this is in the best interests of the child. The parent no longer has any right to participate in decisions affecting the welfare of the child and no longer has any duties toward the child.

unfit
Demonstrating abuse or neglect that is substantially detrimental to a child.

abandonment
Voluntarily leaving a child or ending communication with a child for a specific period or indefinitely without arranging for alternative care and supervision while away. Conduct that constitutes a relinquishing of one's parental responsibilities.

dependency
(1) The condition of a child who has been placed in the custody of the state because the child has been abused, neglected, or abandoned. (2) Pertaining to a child who lacks basic care through no fault of the parent or guardian.

Because parents have a fundamental right under the U.S. Constitution to raise their children, parental rights cannot be involuntarily terminated simply because someone else is more stable and has more resources than biological parents. A showing of unfitness (or a comparable ground) is key to a forced severance of parental rights. The standard is not the best interests of the child. It may be in the best interests of the child to be placed with a wealthy family. However, only after a biological parent is found to be unfit because of abuse or neglect in failing to provide for a child's basic needs will a court determine if it is in the best interests of the child to be adopted by someone else. As one court put it:

> The inability of parents to provide the basic necessities of life for their children is certainly not in the child's best interest. However, even though it may be in a child's best interest to live with a family of comfortable means rather than a poorer family, this standard may not justify the state's intervention into a family relationship absent a finding of parental unfitness.[13]

As demonstrated in the checklist in Exhibit 15-4, many factors are relevant to the question of whether a parent is unfit. A court will consider all of these factors in combination; no one factor is usually determinative.

EXHIBIT 15-4   Factors Relevant to Determining Parental Unfitness

Questions to Ask a Client Charged with Unfitness

- How old are you now?
- With whom is your child living?
- Is the person who is caring for the child your relative, a friend, or a stranger?
- How did the child get there?
- How long has the child been there?
- When is the last time you saw the child?
- How often do you see your child per month?
- How many times do you speak to your child on the phone per month?
- How often do you write to or e-mail your child?
- Did you ever say to anyone that you did not want your child or that you wanted your child to find a home with someone else? If so, explain.
- Did you ever say to anyone that you wanted your child to live with someone else temporarily until you got back on your feet again? If so, explain.
- Have you ever placed your child with a public or private adoption agency? Have you ever discussed adoption with anyone? If so, explain.
- Have you ever been charged with neglecting, abandoning, or failing to support your child? If so, explain.
- Has your child ever been taken from you for any period of time? If so, explain.
- Have you ever been found by a court to be mentally ill?
- How much have you contributed to the support of your child while you were not living with the child?
- Did you give the child any presents? If so, what were they and when did you give them?
- While your child was not with you, did you ever speak to the child's teachers or doctors? If so, explain how often you did so and the circumstances involved.
- Were you on public assistance while the child was not living with you? If so, what did you tell the public assistance workers about the child?
- How well is the child being treated now?
- Could anyone claim that the child lived under immoral or unhealthy circumstances while away from you and that you knew of these circumstances?
- Has the child ever been charged with juvenile delinquency? Has the child ever been declared a Person in Need of Supervision (PINS), Minor in Need of Supervision (MINS), or Child in Need of Protection and Services (CHIPS)?

Investigation Tasks

- Find and interview relatives, friends, and strangers who may have information on whether the client visited or otherwise contacted the child.

- Find and interview anyone with whom the client may have discussed the reasons for leaving the child with someone else.

- Prepare an inventory of all the money and other property given by the client for the support of the child while the child was living with someone else.

- Collect receipts (e.g., canceled check stubs) for all funds given by the client for such support.

- Locate all relevant court records, if any (e.g., custody order in divorce proceeding, neglect or juvenile delinquency petitions and orders).

- Interview employees of state agencies that have been involved with the child. Determine how responsive the client has been to the efforts of the agency to help the child and the client.

- Prepare a parenting plan on how the client will be able to care for the basic needs of the child if parental rights are not terminated.

© Cengage Learning 2013

Procedural Issues in Terminating Parental Rights

To take the drastic step of ordering an involuntary termination of parental rights, there must be **clear and convincing evidence** that the parent is unfit. This is a higher standard of proof than **preponderance of the evidence**, which is commonly used in civil cases.

The parent can be represented by counsel at the termination proceeding. Some states provide state-appointed counsel if the parent cannot afford to pay one. The U.S. Supreme Court, however, has ruled that states are not required to provide free counsel to **indigent** defendants in every termination case. A court must decide on a case-by-case basis whether an indigent parent needs free counsel because of the complexity of the case.[14]

Although an appointed attorney is not required in every indigent case, a guardian ad litem (GAL) must be appointed to represent the child's best interests whenever child abuse or neglect is alleged in a court case.[15] The GAL can be an attorney or a **court appointed special advocate (CASA)**, who can be a nonattorney. (For a list of the duties of a CASA, see Paralegal Roles at the end of Chapter 14.) If the CASA is a nonattorney and the child needs legal advice, an attorney must provide this advice.

A parent who loses in the trial court and wishes to appeal the termination of parental rights must be given a free transcript if he or she cannot afford the cost of the transcript, which can amount to several thousand dollars.

If parental rights are terminated and there are adoptive parents available, a separate adoption procedure will take place or the adoption will be finalized in the same proceedings that led to the termination of parental rights.

clear and convincing evidence
A standard of proof that is met when the evidence demonstrates that the existence of a disputed fact is much more probable than its nonexistence. This standard is stronger than preponderance of the evidence but not as strong as beyond a reasonable doubt.

preponderance of the evidence
A standard of proof that is met when the evidence establishes that it is more likely than not that the facts are as alleged. Also called fair preponderance of evidence.

indigent
Poor; without means to afford something such as a private attorney or filing fees.

court appointed special advocate (CASA)
A volunteer appointed by the court to undertake special assignments pertaining to children in the court system.

ASSIGNMENT 15.7

a. When will parental rights be terminated in your state? What are the grounds? What standard of proof must be met? Clear and convincing evidence? (See the General Instructions for the State-Code Assignment in Appendix A.)

b. Mary is the mother of two children. She is convicted of murdering her husband, their father. What facts do you think need to be investigated in order to determine whether Mary's parental rights should be terminated? (See General Instructions for the Investigation-Strategy Assignment in Appendix A.)

c. Prepare a flowchart of all the procedural steps necessary to terminate parental rights in your state. (See General Instructions for the Flowchart Assignment in Appendix A.)

Adoption and Safe Families Act (ASFA)

A great many children spend substantial time in foster care. Critics have argued that the foster-care system is overly concerned with the rights of the biological parent from whom the child will be taken. While waiting to determine whether reunion with biological parents is possible, many children languish for years in multiple foster homes. In 1997, Congress passed the **Adoption and Safe Families Act (ASFA)**.[16] This law had the effect of speeding up adoptions of children in foster care by forcing states to hold regularly scheduled hearings on whether reunion with the biological parents is feasible and safe and, if not, whether termination of parental rights is warranted. States must seek termination of parental rights if a child has been in foster care for 15 of the last 22 months unless special circumstances exist to warrant otherwise.

STANDING: CAN CHILDREN DIVORCE THEIR PARENTS?

It is, of course, impossible to divorce someone to whom you are not married. The concept of parental divorce was created by the media in cases such as that of *Gregory K. v. Rachel K.* in which an 11-year-old **unemancipated** child asked a Florida Court to terminate the rights of his biological mother so that his foster parents could adopt him. Because he was the party who initiated the action, the media described him as a child who wanted to "divorce" his parents. The trial court allowed him to bring the action, terminated the parental rights of his mother, and granted the adoption.

The decision sparked considerable controversy. Some hailed it as the beginning of a major child's rights movement, comparing Gregory to the black woman who began the civil rights movement by refusing to give up her seat on the bus. "Gregory is the Rosa Parks of the youth rights movement," according to the chairperson of the National Child Rights Alliance.[17] Others were deeply disturbed by the decision. They thought it would open a floodgate of litigation brought by disgruntled children against their parents. A presidential candidate lamented that "kids would be suing their parents for being told to do their homework or take out the trash."[18]

On appeal, however, the Florida Court of Appeals ruled it was an error for the trial court to allow Gregory to initiate the termination action. A minor suffers the disability of **nonage** and hence does not have **standing** to ask a court to terminate the rights of his or her biological parents. Yet the court agreed that the parental rights of Gregory's mother should be terminated. When Gregory filed his petition, his foster parent simultaneously brought his own petition to terminate the rights of Gregory's biological mother on the ground that she had abandoned him. Foster parents *do* have standing in Florida to bring such petitions, and in this case, the adult's termination petition had merit. Hence, although Gregory eventually obtained the result he wanted (termination of parental rights plus adoption), the court, in effect, shut the door to comparable actions initiated by children in the future: "Courts historically have recognized that unemancipated minors do not have the legal capacity to initiate legal proceedings in their own names."[19]

INTERLOCUTORY DECREE

In many states, an adoption decree does not become final immediately. An **interlocutory** (temporary) decree of adoption is first issued, which becomes final after a set period of time. If the child is not already living with the adoptive parents, he or she can be placed with them during the interlocutory period to assess the child's adjustment to the new home environment. After this period, the decree can be made final.

CHALLENGES TO THE ADOPTION DECREE

Because it would be disruptive for the child to be moved from place to place as legal battles continue to rage among any combination of adoptive parents, biological parents, and agencies, there are time limits within which challenges

---

Adoption and Safe Families Act (ASFA)
A federal statute that requires states to take specific placement action on behalf of children in foster care, such as terminating parental rights in order to facilitate adoption after a designated period of time trying to reunite the child with its biological parents.

unemancipated
Legally dependent on one's parent or legal guardian.

nonage
Below the required minimum age to enter a relationship or perform a task. Minority.

standing
The right to bring a case and seek relief from a court.

interlocutory
Not final; interim.

to the adoption decree must be brought (e.g., two years). A major ground for an **abrogation of adoption** (which annuls the adoption) is that the adoption decree was obtained by duress, fraud, or undue influence and abrogation would be in the best interests of the child.

If the court denies the petition for abrogation, an action for *wrongful adoption* is possible if the adoption agency or intermediary acted wrongfully in the adoption process. Wrongful adoption will be covered in Chapter 17.

abrogation of adoption
A cancellation or nullification of a decree of adoption.

ASSIGNMENT 15.8

Draft a flowchart of all the procedural steps involved in an adoption proceeding in your state. (See General Instructions for the Flowchart Assignment in Appendix A.)

"JOURNALISTIC TERRORISM"

We turn now to one of the more dramatic cases in the history of family law, the Illinois case of Baby Richard: *In re Petition of Doe*. Before the glare of cameras and national media, a four-year-old boy was taken from his adoptive parents and turned over to his natural father, Otakar Kirchner, whom the boy had never met. One newspaper account said the biological father "took physical custody of the sobbing child as he frantically reached for his adoptive mother in front of the house where the boy had lived since he was four days old."[20] The public's reaction was intense. Newspapers, newscasts, and talk shows gave the story extensive coverage. The case was called "nightmarish," "monstrous," "absolutely horrible," and "state sanctioned child abuse." The governor of Illinois said that Baby Richard was being "brutally, tragically torn away from the only parents he has ever known." The opinion in the case (*In re Petition of Doe*) was written by Justice Heiple. When it was published, he was denounced. One columnist, Bob Greene, was particularly critical. Justice Heiple took the highly unusual step of responding to this criticism in the supplemental opinion he wrote denying a rehearing of the case. He referred to the criticism as "journalistic terrorism." As we study *In re Petition of Doe*, you need to decide for yourself to what extent the case demonstrates a collapse of the legal system.

CASE

In re Petition of Doe & Doe to Adopt Baby Boy Janikova
159 Ill. 2d 347, 638 N.E.2d 181 (1994)
Supreme Court of Illinois

Background: *Daniella Janikova and Otakar Kirchner were not married when their son, Baby Boy Janikova, was born. The media called him Baby Richard. Otakar was out of the country at the time. Four days after the birth, Daniella consented to have the baby adopted by John and Jane Doe. Daniella did not tell Otakar about the adoption by the Does. In fact, she told him the baby was born dead. Fifty-seven days after the boy's birth, Otakar learned the truth. Within two weeks, he challenged the legality of the adoption on the ground that he did not consent to it. Lengthy litigation and media attention followed. The trial court found that Otakar was unfit because he did not show sufficient interest in the child during the first thirty days of the child's life, and therefore his consent to the adoption was not required. On appeal*

before the appellate court, Justice Rizzi affirmed, ruling that the adoption was in the best interests of the child. The case is now on appeal before the Supreme Court of Illinois. (During the litigation, Daniella married Otakar and, therefore, now joins him in seeking to revoke the adoption to which she initially consented.)

Decision on Appeal: *Reversed. Justice Heiple of the Supreme Court held that the adoption was invalid because it violated the rights of the natural father. The use of the best-interests-of-the-child standard by Justice Rizzi in the appellate court "grossly misstated the law." When this decision was rendered, Baby Richard was four years old and had lived with John and Jane Doe for three years.*

(continued)

CASE • In re Petition of Doe & Doe to Adopt Baby Boy Janikova (continued)

OPINION OF THE COURT:

Justice HEIPLE delivered the opinion of the court. . . .

Otakar and Daniella began living together in the fall of 1989, and Daniella became pregnant in June of 1990. For the first eight months of her pregnancy, Otakar provided for all of her expenses.

In late January 1991, Otakar went to his native Czechoslovakia to attend to his gravely ill grandmother for two weeks. During this time, Daniella received a phone call from Otakar's aunt saying that Otakar had resumed a former romantic relationship with another woman.

Because of this unsettling news, Daniella left their shared apartment, refused to talk with Otakar on his return, and gave birth to the child at a different hospital than where they had originally planned. She gave her consent to the adoption of the child by [John and Jane Doe], telling them and their attorney that she knew who the father was but would not furnish his name. Daniella and her uncle warded off Otakar's persistent inquiries about the child by telling him that the child had died shortly after birth.

Otakar found out that the child was alive and had been placed for adoption 57 days after the child was born. He then began the instant proceedings by filing an appearance contesting the Does' adoption of his son. . . . [T]he trial court ruled that Otakar was an unfit parent under section 1 of the Adoption Act (750 ILCS 50/1 [West 1992]) because he had not shown a reasonable degree of interest in the child within the first 30 days of his life. Therefore, the father's consent was unnecessary under section 8 of the Act (750 ILCS 50/8 [West 1992]).

The finding that the father had not shown a reasonable degree of interest in the child is not supported by the evidence. In fact, he made various attempts to locate the child, all of which were either frustrated or blocked by the actions of the mother. Further, the mother was aided by the attorney for the adoptive parents, who failed to make any effort to ascertain the name or address of the father despite the fact that the mother indicated she knew who he was. Under the circumstances, the father had no opportunity to discharge any familial duty.

In the opinion below, the appellate court, wholly missing the threshold issue in this case, dwelt on the best interests of the child. Since, however, the father's parental interest was improperly terminated, there was no occasion to reach the factor of the child's best interests. That point should never have been reached and need never have been discussed.

Unfortunately, over three years have elapsed since the birth of the baby who is the subject of these proceedings. To the extent that it is relevant to assign fault in this case, the fault here lies initially with the mother, who fraudulently tried to deprive the father of his rights, and secondly, with the adoptive parents and their attorney, who proceeded with the adoption when they knew that a real father was out there who had been denied knowledge of his baby's existence. When the father entered his appearance in the adoption proceedings 57 days after the baby's birth and demanded his rights as a father, the petitioners should have relinquished the baby at that time. It was their decision to prolong this litigation through a lengthy, and ultimately fruitless, appeal.

The adoption laws of Illinois are neither complex nor difficult of application. Those laws intentionally place the burden of proof on the adoptive parents in establishing both the relinquishment and/or unfitness of the natural parents and, coincidentally, the fitness and the right to adopt of the adoptive parents. In addition, Illinois law requires a good-faith effort to notify the natural parents of the adoption proceedings. These laws are designed to protect natural parents in their preemptive rights to their own children wholly apart from any consideration of the so-called best interests of the child. If it were otherwise, few parents would be secure in the custody of their own children. If best interests of the child were a sufficient qualification to determine child custody, anyone with superior income, intelligence, education, etc., might challenge and deprive the parents of their right to their own children. The law is otherwise and was not complied with in this case.

Accordingly, we reverse.

SUPPLEMENTAL OPINION UPON DENIAL OF REHEARING

Justice HEIPLE, writing in support of the denial of rehearing:

On Thursday, June 16, 1994, this court reversed a decision by a divided appellate court which had affirmed certain adoption proceedings in the circuit court of Cook County. Our reversal was the result of the failure of the courts below to correctly apply Illinois law in terminating the natural father's parental rights. This cause is now before the court on petitions for rehearing filed by the adoptive parents and the guardian ad litem for the child. The following is offered in support of today's order denying rehearing.

I have been a judge for over 23 years. In that time, I have seldom before worked on a case that involved the spread of so much misinformation, nor one which dealt with as straightforward an application of law to fact.

[A] . . . conspiracy was undertaken to deny the natural father any knowledge of his son's existence. It began when the biological mother, 8 1/2 months pregnant, was misinformed that the father, her fiancé, had left her for another woman. She left their shared home and, at the encouragement of a social worker, agreed to give up her child. The social worker called her personal attorney, who contacted the adoptive mother (that attorney's friend and employee). At the behest of the adoptive parents and their attorney, the mother gave birth at a different hospital than she and the father had planned to avoid the father's intervention; the mother surrendered the baby to strangers four days after his birth; and then falsely told the father that the child had died. All of this occurred in the space of less than three weeks.

The father did not believe the mother, and he immediately began an intensive and persistent search and inquiry to learn the truth and locate the child. On the 57th day following the child's birth, the father learned of his son's existence and of the pending adoption. On that day, he hired a lawyer and contested the adoption of his son by strangers. One may reasonably ask, What more could he have done? What more should he have done? The answer is that he did all that he could and should do.

The . . . adoptive parents should have relinquished the baby at that time. That is to say, on the 57th day. Instead of that, however, they were able to procure an entirely erroneous ruling from a trial judge that allowed the adoption to go forward. The father's only remedy at that stage was a legal appeal which he took. He is not the cause of the delay in this case. It was the adoptive parents' decision to prolong this litigation through a long and ultimately fruitless appeal. Now, the view has been expressed that the passage of time warrants their retention of the child; that it would not be fair to the child to return him to his natural parents, now married to each other, after the adoptive parents have delayed justice past the child's third birthday.

For a fuller and more detailed account of the father's efforts and the underlying facts, one may refer to the dissenting opinion authored by Justice Tully in the appellate court decision rendered below. (254 Ill. App. 3d 405, 418, 627 N.E.2d 648 (Tully, P. J., dissenting).) As noted by Justice Tully, Justice Rizzi, writing the majority opinion for himself and Justice Cerda, "patently distorted and slanted the facts on a number of important points." I would further add that Justice Rizzi grossly misstated the law.

If, as stated by Justice Rizzi, the best interests of the child is to be the determining factor in child custody cases (254 Ill. App. 3d at 412), persons seeking babies to adopt might profitably frequent grocery stores and snatch babies from carts when the parent is looking the other way. Then, if custody proceedings can be delayed long enough, they can assert that they have a nicer home, a superior education, a better job or whatever, and that the best interests of the child are with the baby snatchers. Children of parents living in public housing or other conditions deemed less than affluent and children with single parents might be considered particularly fair game. The law, thankfully, is otherwise.

In 1972, the United States Supreme Court, in the case of *Stanley v. Illinois* (1972), 405 U.S. 645 ruled that unmarried fathers cannot be treated differently than unmarried mothers or married parents when determining their rights to the custody of their children. The courts of Illinois are bound by that decision. Subsequently, in 1990, a unanimous Illinois Supreme Court pointed out that when ruling on parental unfitness, a court is not to consider the child's best interests, since the child's welfare is not relevant in judging the fitness of the natural parent; that only after the parent is found by clear and convincing evidence to be unfit does the court proceed to consider the child's best interest and whether that interest would be served if the child were adopted by the petitioners. *In re Adoption of Syck* (1990), 138 Ill. 2d 255, 276–78, 562 N.E.2d 174.

Under Illinois law, a parent may be divested of his parental rights either voluntarily (e.g., consenting to an adoption (see Ill. Rev. Stat. 1991, ch. 40, par. 1513)) or involuntarily (e.g., finding of abuse, abandonment, neglect or lack of sufficient interest (see Ill. Rev. Stat. 1991, ch. 40, par. 1510)). . . . [T]he adoption laws of Illinois are neither complex nor difficult of application. These laws intentionally place the burden of proof on the adoptive parents.

In addition, Illinois law requires a good-faith effort to notify the natural father of the adoption proceedings. (Ill. Rev. Stat. 1991, ch. 40, par. 1509.) We call this due process of law. In the case at hand, both the adoptive parents and their attorney knew that a real father existed whose name was known to the mother but who refused to disclose it. Under these circumstances, the adoptive parents proceeded at their peril.

The best interest of the child standard is not to be denigrated. It is real. However, it is not triggered until it has been validly determined that the child is available for adoption. And, a child is not available for adoption until the rights of his natural parents have been properly terminated. Any judge, lawyer, or guardian ad litem who has even the most cursory familiarity with adoption laws knows that. Justice Rizzi, if he is to be taken at face value, does not know that.

Columnist Bob Greene apparently does not care. Rather, columnist Greene has used this unfortunate controversy to stimulate readership and generate a series of syndicated newspaper columns in the Chicago Tribune and other papers that are both false and misleading. In so doing, he has wrongfully cried "fire" in a crowded theatre, and has needlessly alarmed other adoptive parents into ill-founded concerns that their own adoption proceedings may be in jeopardy. In support of his position, Greene has stirred up contempt against the Supreme Court as an institution, concluding one of his columns by referring to all of the Justices with the curse, "Damn them all." Chicago Tribune, June 19, 1994, page 1.

Greene's implicit objective is to secure justice for a child. With that ethical and moral imperative, of course, no one could disagree. Greene, however, elevates himself above the facts, above the law, and above the Supreme Court of Illinois. He arrogates to himself the right to decide the case.

In support of his objective, Greene brings to bear the tools of the demagogue, namely, incomplete information, falsity, half-truths, character assassination and spurious argumentation. He has conducted a steady assault on my abilities as a judge, headlining one of his columns "The Sloppiness of Justice Heiple." Another was entitled "Supreme Injustice for a Little Boy." He has shown my picture in his columns with bylines reading, respectively, "Justice Heiple: Ruling takes boy from home," and "James D. Heiple: No justice for a child."

Make no mistake about it. These are acts of journalistic terrorism. These columns are designed to discredit me as a judge and the Supreme Court as a dispenser of justice by stirring up disrespect and hatred among the general population.

Lest we forget the place from which he comes, let us remind ourselves that Greene is a journalist with a product to sell. He writes columns for a living. His income is dependent on writing and selling his columns to newspapers. He cannot secure either sales or earnings by writing on subjects that lack impact or drama. So, he must seek out subjects that are capable of generating wide public interest. An adoption case involving two sets of parents contesting for the custody of a three-year-old boy is a ready-made subject for this type of journalist. So far, so good.

(continued)

CASE • In re Petition of Doe & Doe to Adopt Baby Boy Janikova (continued)

The trouble with Greene's treatment of the subject, however, is that his columns have been biased, false and misleading. They have also been destructive to the cause of justice both in this case and in the wider perspective. Part of Greene's fury may be attributable to the fact that he staked out his views on this case in a published column that appeared on August 22, 1993. (Chicago Tribune, August 22, 1993, page 1.) Subsequently, on June 16, 1994, the Supreme Court had the audacity to base its decision on the law rather than on his newspaper column. So much for his self-possessed moralizing.

That Greene has succeeded to a limited degree cannot be denied. I have, indeed, received several pieces of hate mail with such epithets as idiot, jerk, etc. The Governor, in a crass political move, announced his attempt to intervene in the case. And the General Assembly, without meaningful debate of consideration, rushed into law a constitutionally infirm statute with the goal of changing the Supreme Court's decision.

Both the Governor and the members of the General Assembly who supported this bill might be well advised to return to the classroom and take up Civics 101. The Governor, for his part, has no understanding of this case and no interest either public or private in its outcome. The legislature is not given the authority to decide private disputes between litigants. Neither does it sit as a super court to review unpopular decisions of the Supreme Court. We have three branches of government in this land. They are designated as the legislative, the executive and the judicial. Legislative adjudication of private disputes went by the wayside generations ago. Moreover, this case cannot be decided by public clamor generated by an irresponsible journalist. Neither can it be decided by its popularity or lack thereof. This case can only be decided by a court of law. That is a judicial function pure and simple. For the Supreme Court to surrender to this assault would be to surrender

its independence, its integrity and its reason for being. In so doing, neither justice to the litigants nor the public interest would be served. Under the circumstances, this case looms even larger than the child or the two sets of contesting parents.

Many law suits are painful matters. This case is no exception. Capital cases, for instance, demand the forfeiture of the life of the defendant. Damage suits take money away from some people and give it to others. No one ever claimed that both sides walk away from a law suit with smiles on their faces. No member of this court ever entertained any thought that the decision it rendered in this case would be easy to accept by the losing litigants. Such an event would be incredible.

As for the child, age three, it is to be expected that there would be an initial shock, even a longing for a time in the absence of the persons whom he had viewed as parents. This trauma will be overcome, however, as it is every day across this land by children who suddenly find their parents separated by divorce or loss to them through death. It will not be an insurmountable trauma for a three-year-old child to be returned, at last, to his natural parents who want to raise him as their own. It will work itself out in the fullness of time. As for the adoptive parents, they will have to live with their pain and the knowledge that they wrongfully deprived a father of his child past the child's third birthday. They and their lawyer brought it on themselves.

This much is clear. Adoptive parents who comply with the law may feel secure in their adoptions. Natural parents may feel secure in their right to raise their own children. If there is a tragedy in this case, as has been suggested, then that tragedy is the wrongful breakup of a natural family and the keeping of a child by strangers without right. We must remember that the purpose of an adoption is to provide a home for a child, not a child for a home.

ASSIGNMENT 15.9

a. Someone obviously made a major blunder in this case. From infancy, Baby Richard lived with one set of adults. Years later he is forced to live with other adults. Who does Justice Heiple say is to blame? Why? Which of the following cast of characters do *you* think is to blame and why: the biological mother, her attorney, the relatives of the biological mother, her social worker, the biological father, his attorney, the adoptive parents, their attorney, Baby Richard's guardian ad litem, the trial court (which granted the adoption), the appellate court (which said it was in the best interests of the child that he go with the Does), or the Supreme Court of Illinois (which gave the child to his biological father)?

b. What do you think of the quality of the legal representation given to the Does by their attorney?

c. In Chapter 9 we learned that custody decisions are based on the best interests of the child. Did this case say that the best interests of the child are irrelevant?

d. What do you think could have been done to avoid what occurred in this case?

e. Is it relevant that Daniella married Otakar and therefore agreed with him that the adoption should be set aside?

f. Do you think it was wise for Justice Heiple to attack Bob Greene as a journalistic terrorist?

g. Justice Heiple said, "It will not be an insurmountable trauma for a three-year old child to be returned, at last, to his natural parents who want to raise him as their own." Do you agree? If Justice Heiple thought the trauma *would be* insurmountable, would he have ruled differently? Recall that he said the best interests of the child were irrelevant in this case.

h. Rich and Paula Davis are the biological parents of John. Following a divorce, Rich is granted custody of John. Rich illegally takes John to another state, where his girlfriend adopts him. During the adoption proceeding, Rich falsely tells the court that John's mother, Paula, is dead. Paula, therefore, never receives notice of the adoption proceeding. Years later, Paula learns about the adoption for the first time. Can she still challenge the adoption? How would this case be decided in Illinois in view of *In re Petition of Doe*?

BABY JESSICA

The *Baby Jessica* case is another highly publicized example of a biological father successfully challenging an adoption on the basis of the biological mother's lies. Cara Clausen gave birth to Baby Jessica in Iowa. Within days of the birth, she put her up for adoption to Jan and Roberta DeBoer, who took her to Michigan. In the adoption proceedings, Cara lied about who the biological father was. Three weeks later she had a change of heart and told the biological father, Dan Schmidt, what had happened. He then sought to get Baby Jessica back from the adoptive parents. He argued that he never consented to the adoption and was never found to be unfit. After two and a half years of litigation, the Iowa and Michigan courts nullified the adoption and ordered Baby Jessica returned.[21] The federal courts refused to change this result. In *DeBoer v. Schmidt*, the U.S. Supreme Court said, "Neither Iowa law, Michigan law, nor federal law authorizes unrelated persons to retain custody of a child whose natural parents have not been found to be unfit simply because they may be better able to provide for her future and her education. . . . '[C]ourts are not free to take children from parents simply by deciding another home appears more advantageous.'"[22]

PUTATIVE FATHER REGISTRY

How do we protect the rights of an unmarried father who does not become aware of the adoption of his child until it is too late to intervene? How can we prevent heart-rending scenes of children being forced from their adoptive parents and returned to their biological father—sometimes years after their placement with the adoptive parents? The father needs notice of the proposed adoption so that he has time to intervene. Yet he cannot be given notice if the mother lies about who the father is or where he can be found.

At one time, Florida had a law providing that if a mother (seeking to allow her child to be adopted) said she did not know the identity or whereabouts of the father, she had to publish a notice in the newspaper that

> "must contain a physical description, including, but not limited to, age, race, hair and eye color, and approximate height and weight of the minor's mother and of any person the mother reasonably believes may be the father; the minor's date of birth; and any date and city, including the county and state in which the city is located, in which conception may have occurred."[23]

This method of giving notice to fathers was widely criticized. To avoid the humiliation of publishing her sexual history, a young woman may be more likely to abort or abandon her baby than go through with an adoption procedure that has this publication requirement. In 2003, a Florida court ruled that the law was an unconstitutional invasion of privacy. Eventually, the Florida legislature repealed what the media called the "Scarlet Letter" adoption law.[24]

Today the most common method used by states (including Florida) to try to protect the rights of an unmarried father is to establish a **putative father registry**. A **putative father** is the alleged or reputed father of a child. He will be given notice of the proposed adoption of his child (which would include the proposed termination of his parental rights) if he registers with the putative father registry within a specific time frame. By registering, he announces his intent to assert his rights and responsibilities as a parent. The failure to register may preclude his right to notice of the adoption proceedings. For an example of a putative father registry, see Exhibit 15-5.

putative father registry

A government office where the father of a child can register so that he can be notified of a proposed adoption of the child.

putative father

The man believed to be the biological father of a child but who has not yet been medically or legally declared to be the father. Also called alleged father, reputed father.

EXHIBIT 15-5 Putative Father Registry

USE A SEPARATE FORM FOR EACH CHILD.   PRINT OR TYPE ALL INFORMATION.

My name is: _____
first   middle   last

My current address is: _____
street number, name, apartment number, P.O. box

_____
city   state   zip code

My date of birth is: _____
month, day, year

My social security number is: _____

I hereby indicate the possibility of paternity of the child described below without acknowledging paternity.

The name of the mother of the child is: _____
first   middle   last

The mother's social security number is: (if known) _____

The mother's address is: _____
street number, name, apartment number, P.O. box

_____
city   state   zip code

The child's name is: (if known) _____
first   middle   last

The child (**select one**)   (   ) was born on _____ sex of child _____
month, day, year   male or female

OR   _____
city   state

(   ) is estimated to be born in _____
month   year

As detailed above, I hereby register on the Putative Father Registry as provided by law. I do so to indicate the possibility of my paternity of the child, but I understand I am not formally acknowledging paternity of this child.

Signature of Registrant: _____   *Date Signed:* _____

Source: Georgia Department of Community Health, Putative Father Registry Registration Form (health.state.ga.us/programs/vitalrecords/fatherregprint.asp).

The registry is by no means a perfect solution. It can work well when the man knows about the registry and knows he has impregnated an unmarried woman. Difficulties arise when the woman with whom he is intimate does not tell him she is pregnant or falsely tells him that she had an abortion. Realistically, the only way he can protect his rights is to register every time he has sexual relations with an unmarried woman. Some states are unsympathetic to the man who says, "I didn't know." A Utah statute, for example, provides that "[a]n unmarried biological father, by virtue of the fact that he has engaged in a sexual relationship with a woman . . . is considered to be on notice that a pregnancy and an adoption proceeding regarding that child may occur . . . and has a duty to protect his own rights and interests."[25] The burden, therefore, is on the man to find out whether he is about to become or has become a father and, if so, to take steps to protect his rights such as by helping to arrange prenatal and delivery care, paying child support, petitioning a court for an order of paternity, or making sure his name is on the birth certificate. If in doubt, register! Whether this approach violates the constitutional rights of the father is unclear. This is an area of the law in which we can expect continued litigation.

A few states allow defrauded fathers to bring a tort action for **tortious interference with parental relationships** against mothers and others who conceal the whereabouts of an infant in order to deprive a father of his right to object to an adoption of his child. We will consider this tort in Chapter 17.

tortious interference with parental relationships
Fraud in concealing the whereabouts of a child or otherwise wrongfully interfering with a parent's relationship with his or her child.

INTERSTATE COMPACT ON THE PLACEMENT OF CHILDREN

The **Interstate Compact on the Placement of Children (ICPC)** governs adoptions of a child born or living in one state (called the *sending state*) who will be adopted by someone in another state (called the *receiving state*). The ICPC does not cover all interstate adoptions. It applies mainly to so-called *stranger adoptions*, those undertaken by individuals other than relatives, guardians, or stepparents. (An adoption by a relative of a birth parent is a *kinship adoption*.)

Interstate Compact on the Placement of Children (ICPC)
A statute that governs adoption of a child born or living in one state who will be adopted by someone in another state.

To coordinate the adoption, an ICPC office is established in each state. When a court approves the adoption, the ICPC office in the sending state gives written notice to the ICPC office in the receiving state of the proposed adoption. The notice provides identifying information about the child, the child's parents or guardians, and the person, agency, or institution with whom the child is to be placed. Also included are a statement of reasons for the proposed placement and "evidence of the authority pursuant to which the placement is proposed to be made." The ICPC office in the receiving state reviews this information. If approved, it submits to the ICPC office in the sending state a written notice that "the proposed placement does not appear to be contrary to the interests of the child."[26] The parties are then given permission to bring the child across state lines so that the placement can occur. A violation of these ICPC requirements can result in a voiding of the adoption.

CONSEQUENCES OF ADOPTION

Once the adoption becomes final, the adopted child and the adoptive parents have the rights and obligations toward each other that biological parents and children have toward each other. In most respects, an adopted child is treated the same as a biological child.

- *Surname.* Adoptees can be given the surname of their adoptive parents.
- *Birth certificate.* The birth certificate of the adoptee can be changed to reflect the surname of the adoptive parent.
- *Earnings and services.* An adoptive parent has a right to the services and earnings of an adoptee.

- *Support.* An adoptive parent must provide child support for the adoptee. This duty continues even if the adoptive parent divorces the biological parent or their marriage is annulled after the adoption.
- *Workers' compensation.* Adoptees are entitled to workers' compensation benefits in the event that an adoptive parent suffers an on-the-job injury.
- *Priority over biological grandparents.* An adoptive parent has priority over biological grandparents when the adoptive parent objects to their visitation.

intestacy

The condition of dying without a valid will.

intestate

(1) A person who dies without a valid will. (2) Pertaining to someone who dies without a valid will.

intestate share

A designated portion of the estate of a person who dies intestate (i.e., without a valid will) to which a specific relative of the deceased is entitled according to state law.

Special rules sometimes exist in the area of **intestacy**—dying without a valid will. The standard rule is that if someone dies **intestate** (without a valid will), state law specifies which relatives of the deceased inherit an **intestate share**, which is a designated portion of the estate of the deceased. Can an adoptee receive an intestate share? The answer may depend on who died. If the deceased is the adoptive parent, the adoptee receives the same intestate share as a biological child of the deceased. Suppose, however, that a relative of the adoptive parent dies intestate.

Mary is the biological mother of Kevin. After her paternal rights are terminated, Paul adopts Kevin. Paul's brother, Bill, dies intestate. Can Kevin inherit from Bill?

States differ in their answer to this question. Some states will *not* allow an adoptee to inherit from a relative of his or her adoptive parent if the relative dies intestate. Other states, however, do not impose this restriction on adoptees.

Suppose that the biological parent of the adoptee dies intestate. In our example, Mary is the biological parent of Kevin. What happens if Mary dies intestate? In most states adoptees cannot inherit from a biological parent whose parental rights have been terminated. The termination of parental rights also terminates intestate inheritance rights. There are a few states, however, that take a different view and allow adoptees like Kevin to inherit from a biological parent in Mary's situation.

testate

(1) Pertaining to someone who dies with a valid will. (2) A person who dies with a valid will. Under this definition, also called the testator and, if female, the testatrix.

testamentary

Pertaining to a will.

Thus far we have limited our discussion to intestacy. The law is dramatically different when the deceased dies **testate**—leaving a valid will. There are no restrictions on persons to whom gifts can be made in a will. **Testamentary** gifts (i.e., gifts in a will) can be made to anyone. Hence Kevin's uncle Bill and Kevin's biological mother (Mary) in our examples can leave Kevin a gift in their wills in the same manner as his adoptive parents can.

Occasionally, problems of interpretation arise over language in wills. Suppose, for example, an adoptive parent dies with a will leaving property to "my heirs" or to "my children" or to "my issue," without mentioning any individuals by name. Is an adoptee included within such language? Most (but not all) courts are inclined to conclude that the intention of the deceased adoptive parent was to include adopted children as well as biological children within the designation of "heirs," "children," or "issue."

Can a biological parent be granted visitation rights even though this parent's parental rights were terminated in an adoption? In general, the answer is no. There are cases, however, in which a court has enforced an agreement between the biological parent and the adoptive parent to allow visitation by the biological parent and the visits were held to be in the best interests of the child. Such cases are rare. A fit adoptive parent has the primary right to raise the child including the decision on who should be allowed to visit the child.

Finally, as we saw in Chapter 6 on annulment of marriages, states differ on whether a person can marry his or her adopted sibling. Most states say that they can. In these states, such a marriage is not a ground for an annulment.

CONFIDENTIALITY

In recent years, there has been great controversy over whether adopted children have a right to discover the identity of their biological parents. In a traditional adoption, the answer has been no, with limited exceptions. Once the adoption becomes final, the record is sealed. The data within it are confidential. There are, however, limited exceptions to this traditional rule. If **good cause** can be shown, access to part of the adoption records may be allowed. For example, an adopted child may need medical or genetic information on its biological parents to help treat diseases that might be hereditary. Similarly, the adopted child may need some information about the identity of his or her biological parents to avoid unknowingly marrying a biological brother or sister. Access to such information, however, is the exception. It is rare that *identifying* information is released. (Identifying facts are facts that would assist the recipient in determining who the biological parent is.) The norm is *nonidentifying* information consisting of social or medical facts that would not allow positive identification of any person who was a party to the adoption. The need for information must be great. Many courts have held that it is not enough for the adopted child to prove that he or she is experiencing emotional distress due to not knowing the identity of his or her biological parents.

Although many states continue to follow this narrow approach on confidentiality, there is a trend in the other direction. Some states have broadened the categories of nonidentifying information they will release without compromising anonymity. In one recent case, for example, an adult adoptee was allowed to discover information on the race of the birth parents, the general health of the adoptee at the time of the adoption, the reasons assigned for the adoption, and the length of time the adoptee was in the custody of her adoptive parents prior to the adoption. A few states (e.g., Kansas and Alaska) have created a system of complete openness. Adult adoptees, without restriction, can see their adoption records or original birth certificate. Reform in most other states has not been this radical.

Some states have created a **reunion registry**, which contains identifying information about adoptees and biological parents. There are two kinds of registries: passive and active.

- A *passive registry* (also called a *mutual consent registry*) requires both the adoptee and the biological parent to register their consent to release identifying information. When both have registered and a match is made, a registry employee tells both to let them know how to contact each other.

- An *active registry* does not require the adoptee and the biological parent to register their consent to release information. Once one of them registers, a registry employee will contact the other to determine his or her wishes for the release of information.

Contact vetoes are used in some states. A contact veto is a denial of consent to have contact between the adoptee and the biological parent, although permission for the release of identifying information might be given. In a few states, the release of information also requires the consent of the adoptive parents. Biological fathers can use the registry, but most states condition such use on the fathers' acknowledgment of paternity.

Some independent or private adoptions give the participants the option of maintaining limited contact between the biological parent and the child after the adoption. These are called **open adoptions**, involving an exchange of identifying information or face-to-face meetings with the child, usually after the biological parent has selected the adoptive parent(s). If there is no direct face-to-face contact but there is a periodic exchange of pictures and letters facilitated by an agency, the adoption is sometimes called a *mediated adoption*.

Some believe that open or mediated adoptions should be discouraged. Young women "are finding it harder to get on with their lives. . . . " "They start living for the photos that the adoptive parents send them every month." Adoptive parents sometimes "find themselves not only raising a new baby but providing counseling

good cause
A legally sufficient ground or reason. Also called just cause, sufficient cause.

reunion registry
A central adoption file that could be used to release identifying information about, and allow contact between, adult adoptees and biological parents.

contact veto
A denial of consent to have contact between the adoptee and the biological parent, although permission for the release of identifying information might be given.

open adoption
An adoption in which the biological parent maintains certain kinds of initial and/or ongoing contact with the adoptee, whose adoptive parent(s) may have been selected by the biological parent. The contact might consist of letters or visits.

for the birth mother who often finds it difficult to break her bond with the child."[27] Not many adoptive parents, therefore, pursue open adoptions.

A number of adoptees are using the Internet to try to locate biological parents and other relatives regardless of whether their own adoption was traditional (confidential). One woman, for example, set up a Facebook page seeking help among her Facebook "friends" in her search for what she called her "first" family. In two days, she was in touch with her birth mother, and in six weeks, she was in contact with her biological father.[28] Also, DNA testing companies are available to try to provide links to blood relatives. For a fee, an adoptee can send in a swab of her cheek and receive back e-mail addresses of relatives. "Some DNA testing companies have been stepping up their efforts to reach out to this community over the past several years, posting advertisements on adoption message boards and testimonials on their websites."[29] The Internet "is changing nearly every chapter of adoption. It can now start with postings by couples looking for birth mothers who want to place children, and end years later with birth mothers looking to reunite with children they've placed. A process that once relied on gatekeepers and official procedures can now be largely circumvented with a computer, Wi-Fi and some luck."[30]

EQUITABLE ADOPTION

Assume that John Smith agrees with Mary Jones to adopt Mary's child, Bill, but fails to carry out the agreement. Such agreements are occasionally put in writing but more often are simply oral understandings between parties who know each other very well. Assume further that John takes custody of Bill, treats him as a member of his family, but never goes through formal adoption procedures as he had promised. John then dies intestate (i.e., without leaving a valid will). Technically, Bill cannot inherit from John because the adoption never took place. This argument might be used by John's biological children to prevent an unadopted child—in this case, Bill—from sharing in the estate.

Many feel that it would be unfair to deny the child inheritance benefits simply because the deceased failed to abide by the agreement to adopt. To avoid the unfairness, some courts apply the doctrine of **equitable adoption**. Under this doctrine, a child will be considered the adopted child of a person who intended to adopt the child and acted as the child's parent but failed to go through the formal adoption procedures. The doctrine does not create a full parent–child relationship in the traditional sense. Its effect is limited to avoiding unfairness or injustice by allowing the child to claim specific benefits such as the intestate share of an adoptee. Other benefits are also possible. For example, a court might allow the child to bring a **wrongful death** action as a surviving child of the deceased. The doctrine is also called *adoption by estoppel*. Persons are **estopped** (i.e., prevented) from denying that such a child has been adopted. Suppose, for example, that the biological children do not want the unadopted child to share in the estate of their deceased intestate father. If the doctrine applies, the biological children would be estopped from taking this position.

Because it is relatively easy (and tempting) for someone to claim that a deceased person agreed to an adoption that never took place, a court may require that the agreement to adopt be proven by *clear and convincing evidence* rather than by the lower standard of preponderance of the evidence.

Some courts will grant inheritance rights *even if there was no initial agreement to adopt*. If clear evidence exists that the deceased treated the child as his or her own in every way, a court might rule that a contract to adopt was *implied*. When the deceased dies intestate, equitable-adoption status will be accorded to the child so that he or she will have full inheritance rights from the deceased.

equitable adoption
A child will be considered the adopted child of a person who intended to adopt the child and acted as the child's parent but failed to go through the formal adoption procedures. Also called adoption by estoppel, de facto adoption, virtual adoption.

wrongful death
A death caused by a tort or other wrong.

estopped
Prevented from asserting a right or a defense because it would be unfair or inequitable to allow the assertion. The noun is *estoppel*.

ASSIGNMENT 15.10

Contact a paralegal, an attorney, or a legal secretary in your state who has worked on adoption cases in the past. Obtain answers to the following questions. (See General Instructions for the Systems Assignment in Appendix A.)

a. How many adoption cases have you worked on?

b. How many of them have been uncontested?

c. Approximately how long does it take to process an uncomplicated, uncontested adoption?

d. Is there a difference between working on an adoption case and working on another kind of case in the law office? If so, what is the difference?

e. What are the major steps for processing an adoption in this state? What documents must be filed? What court appearances must be made? Etc.

f. What formbook or other treatise do you use, if any, that is helpful? What software? What Internet sites?

g. Does your office have its own internal manual that covers any aspect of adoption practice?

h. In an adoption case, what is the division of labor among the attorney, the paralegal, and the legal secretary?

EMBRYO "ADOPTION?"

An **embryo** is an egg that has been fertilized by a sperm and is in the early stage of development. Couples having difficulty conceiving will sometimes freeze their embryos for later implantation. In Chapter 16, we will cover the legal controversy that can exist when a couple divorces and cannot agree on what to do with unused frozen embryos. Can these embryos be adopted? Probably not. Embryos can be *donated* as property to other couples (or to individual women), but no state requires persons to go through the adoption process described in this chapter before allowing others to use (implant) the embryos. This is true even in Louisiana where embryos are categorized as "juridical persons," as we will see in Chapter 16. Private agencies exist to help persons donate embryos in a process that has similarities to adoption, e.g., the agency will do a home study and provide the prospective donors with background information on the prospective recipients (donees) so that the donors would know what kind of home in which the baby from the embryo (if one is born) will live. (Children born from such agencies were invited to the White House by President George W. Bush. They wore t-shirts that said "Former Embryos.") These embryo adoption steps, however, are voluntary. There are no adoption laws that require them.

embryo
An egg that has been fertilized by a sperm and is in the early stage of development; it has undergone one or more divisions. The product of conception to about the eighth week of pregnancy.

WRONGFUL ADOPTION

For a discussion of the tort of **wrongful adoption**, covering the failure to disclose relevant information to the adoptive parents, see Chapter 17.

wrongful adoption
An action seeking damages for carelessly stating (or failing to disclose) to prospective adoptive parents available facts on the health or other condition of the adoptee that would be relevant to the decision on whether to adopt.

■ PARALEGAL ROLES

- For an overview of paralegal roles in family-law cases, see Exhibits 1-3 and 1-4 in Chapter 1.
- For many of the financial issues related to adoption covered in Chapter 15, a paralegal may

be asked to help collect documents and facts outlined in:

- the checklist in Exhibit 3-1 of Chapter 3
- the interrogatories in Appendix C

- A veteran paralegal who has many years of experience working on adoption cases made the following comment about the challenges in this area of law:

  In adoption law, the most challenging aspect of working with families is the anxiety and other emotions involved with wondering whether the adoption will fall through. Another challenge are deadlines that are the equivalent to a "race to the courthouse" since petitions often need to be filed the same day they are signed. Adoption laws change regularly, and keeping up with the changes can be a challenge. . . . My most memorable case was a maternal grandparent adoption. The birth mother was 100 percent sure she was going to place the child until she was asked to sign the consent for adoption. The birth mother was crying and shaking and saying she just wanted to try to parent her child. [Six months later, she signed.] It then took me about two years to secure the birth father's signature on the consent because he was always out of the country. [Perseverance paid off.] The greatest joy of my job is making families' dreams come true.[31]

- Miscellaneous tasks

  - Help prospective adoptive parents prepare a portfolio and website that will attract birth mothers seeking to place their children for adoption.

  - Help a birth mother locate prospective adoptive parents for her child.

  - Obtain certified copies of marriage records of the prospective adoptive parents and divorce decrees, if any.

  - Screen prospective adoptive parents for a mother seeking to place her child for adoption (e.g., do criminal-background checks).

  - Research federal and state adoption laws.

  - Conduct due diligence in locating an absent father.

  - Draft petitions and related pleadings needed for an adoption.

  - Arrange for a home study of the prospective adoptive parents.

  - Prepare consent or surrender document in which the birth mother relinquishes her parental rights.

  - Investigate the extent to which a parent seeking to prevent an adoption has demonstrated indicia of parenthood.

  - Coordinate an out-of-state adoption under the Interstate Compact on the Placement of Children (ICPC).

- Draft agreement for an open adoption.

- Document payments made for the medical and related expenses of the birth mother.

- Document communication between the birth mother and the prospective adoptive parents.

- Accompany client to court to provide needed support.

- Assist adoptive parents in obtaining a new birth certificate or in verifying that one has been issued.

- Assist an adult adoptee to obtain identifying and nonidentifying information about his or her natural parent(s).

■ CHECK THE CITE

Terry Helms is a nonattorney GAL (guardian ad litem) appointed to represent two children in a termination-of-parental-rights proceeding against their father. Terry was later replaced by another nonattorney GAL, Karen Moorefield. The children were also represented by an attorney. When the father's parental rights were terminated, the GAL was not present in the courtroom. The attorney for the father objected, arguing that the GAL should have been present. How did the court rule on this objection and what did the court say was the proper relationship between the nonattorney GAL and the children's attorney? Read *In the Matter of J.H.K. and J.D.K.*, 365 N.C. 171, 711 S.E.2d 118 (N.C. 2011) To read the opinion online: (1) Go to the court site of the Supreme Court of North Carolina. (www.nccourts.org/courts/appellate/supreme). Click "Court Opinions," and then "2011." Scroll down to *In re J.H.K. and J.D.K.* (2) Run a citation search ("711 S.E.2d 118") in the Legal documents database of Google Scholar (scholar.google.com).

■ PROJECT

In Google, Bing, or Yahoo, run the following search: aa "open adoption" (substitute the name of your state for aa in the search). Write a short essay in which you describe the extent to which open adoption is allowed in your state. Cover the different circumstances that will allow contact among a birth mother, the adoptee, and the prospective adoptive parents after the adoption. You must cite and quote from a minimum of eight different sources that you find on the Internet. At least four of these sources should be statutes, court opinions, or other laws.

■ ETHICS IN A FAMILY LAW PRACTICE

a. You are a paralegal working at the law office of Daniel Johnson, Esq. The office takes adoption cases. While working on one of these cases, you learn that Mr. Johnson told a birth mother that she can have a job as receptionist at the law firm if she agrees to give up her baby for adoption to one of the firm's clients. You are asked to interview the birth mother for this job. During the interview, you learn that she is clearly not qualified for the job and that the only reason she is giving up her baby for adoption is that she needs the job. You do not say anything to anyone about her suitability for the job or her hesitancy about going through with the adoption. Any ethical problems?

b. You are a paralegal working at the law offices of Karen Smith, Esq. Smith represents Helen Owens, a birth mother who wants to place her child for adoption. Smith asks you to interview Rachael Davis, a prospective adoptive parent. You do so. When it becomes clear that Davis is a good candidate for the adoption, Smith explains the adoption process to Davis. Any ethical problems?

■ WRITING SAMPLE

Alice Thompson is 15 years old and pregnant. A neighbor, Helen Foley, wishes to adopt Alice's child. Alice agrees. On January tenth of this year, Alice signs a consent form that relinquishes her parental rights to her baby. The baby is born the following March. Helen Foley is represented by the law firm where you work as a paralegal. Your supervisor asks you to write a memorandum of law in which you examine the issue of whether the prebirth consent is valid in your state. To locate the governing law, run this search in Google, Bing, or Yahoo: aa consent adoption prebirth consent (substitute the name of your state for aa in the search). Your memo must cite and quote from a minimum of eight different sources that you find on the Internet. At least four of these sources should be statutes, court opinions, or other laws. (See General Instructions for the Writing Sample in Appendix A.)

SUMMARY

Adoption is the legal process by which one person (the adoptive parent) becomes the parent of another person (the adoptee). The prior parent's parental rights are terminated. An exception exists for stepparent adoptions and for second-parent adoptions in some states. The three main kinds adoptions are public-agency adoption, licensed private-agency adoption, and independent adoption. Special categories include tribal adoption and intercountry adoption. An independent adoption is an adoption that is arranged by the birth parents and the adoptive parents without the involvement of a public agency but often with the assistance of a facilitator or intermediary. Among the possible available facilitators or intermediaries are attorneys, doctors, clergy members, unregulated service agencies, photographers, and web designers. A black-market adoption is an illegal adoption in which there is a payment to a biological parent beyond reasonable expenses in order to facilitate the adoption.

Most adoptees are infants. It is also possible to adopt an adult. This is usually done for inheritance purposes. States differ on whether a homosexual adult can adopt another homosexual adult. In deciding whether an adoption of a minor is in the best interests of the child, judges have considerable discretion. Courts often presume that kinship adoptions are best for the child. The factors considered by a court include the petitioner's age, marital status, health, religion, economic status, home environment, and morality. Race can be considered, but it cannot be the sole or determining factor in the court's decision. Adoptions cannot be delayed or denied because of race. If the child is old enough, his or her preference will usually be considered. Most states allow gays and lesbians to adopt minors, but discrimination against homosexuals still exists among individuals who exercise discretion in adoption decisions.

An adoption must follow strict procedures. The court must have subject-matter jurisdiction. Proper venue must be selected. The petition must contain the required information. The biological parents must be notified of the proceeding and must consent to the adoption unless their parental rights have been terminated or, in the case of the father of a nonmarital (illegitimate) child, there has been an insufficient indicia of parenthood. A parent without such indicia can lose his opportunity interest. Consent is also required of the agency if parental rights were initially surrendered to the agency. If the prospective adoptive parent is married, the consent of his or her spouse is often required even if this spouse is not also adopting the child. If old enough, a court can ask for the consent of the adoptee if the request would be in the best interests of the child. Foster parents must be notified of a proposed adoption, but they do not have the right of consent. Consent can be revoked in many states when given before birth and for a designated number of days after birth.

A termination of parental rights (TPR) is a judicial declaration that ends the legal relationship between parent and child when this is in the best interests of the child. The TPR can be voluntary because of the biological parent's consent, or involuntary if the parent is found to be unfit. The grounds must be proved by clear and convincing evidence. Some states provide free counsel for defendants, but such counsel is not constitutionally requited except in relatively complex cases. A guardian ad litem (GAL) must be appointed to represent the child in every court case that involves child abuse or neglect. The GAL can be an attorney or a nonattorney court appointed special advocate (CASA). The Adoption and Safe Families Act (ASFA) requires states to take specific placement action on behalf of children in foster care such as terminating parental rights in order to facilitate adoption after a designated period of time trying to re-unite the child with its biological parents.

A child does not have standing to petition a court to terminate the parental rights of his or her parent. In many states, an adoption decree does not become final immediately. An interlocutory decree of adoption is first issued, during which the child can be placed with the prospective adoptive parents.

A major ground for an abrogation of adoption (which annuls the adoption) is that the adoption decree was obtained by duress, fraud, or undue influence and abrogation would be in the best interests of the child. Fathers of nonmarital (illegitimate) children must register with a putative father registry if they want the right to be notified of a proposed adoption so that they can assert their objection. The Interstate Compact on the Placement of Children facilitates interstate adoptions.

Once the adoption becomes final, the adopted child is treated the same as a biological child with respect to inheritance rights, support rights, etc. In a traditional adoption, the records are sealed; matters such as the identity of the biological parents are kept confidential except in relatively rare circumstances. Some states have created active or passive reunion registries that can be the basis of the release of identifying information about adoptees and biological parents. In an open adoption, there may be varying degrees of contact between a biological parent and the child after the adoption becomes final.

An equitable adoption occurs when a person dies before fulfilling a contract to adopt a child and when unfairness can be avoided only by treating the child as having been adopted for purposes of inheritance. Frozen embryos can be donated, but not adopted in the legal sense of adoption. The failure of an adoption agency to give available information about the health of the prospective adoptee might constitute the tort of wrongful adoption.

KEY TERMS

adoption	petition	putative-father registry
adoptive parent	procedural due process	putative father
custody	process	tortious interference with parental
legal custody	substituted service	relationships
ward	due diligence	Interstate Compact on the Placement
guardian	surrender	of Children (ICPC)
guardian ad litem (GAL)	opportunity interest	intestacy
paternity	indicia of parenthood	intestate
foster care	termination of parental rights (TPR)	intestate share
stepparent	unfit	testate
second-parent adoption	abandonment	testamentary
independent adoption	dependency	good cause
black-market adoption	clear and convincing evidence	reunion registry
best interests of the child	preponderance of the evidence	contact veto
kinship adoption	indigent	open adoption
transracial adoptions	court appointed special advocate (CASA)	equitable adoption
Multiethnic Placement Act	Adoption and Safe Families Act (ASFA)	wrongful death
(MEPA)	unemancipated	estopped
joint adoption	nonage	embryo
expedited procedure	standing	wrongful adoption
subject-matter jurisdiction	interlocutory	
venue	abrogation of adoption	

REVIEW QUESTIONS

1. What is an adoption?

2. What is a second-parent adoption?

3. Approximately how many children are adopted every year?

4. What are a public-agency adoption, a licensed private-agency adoption, an independent adoption, a tribal adoption, and an intercountry adoption?

5. What are the roles of the various service providers who provide assistance in independent adoptions?

6. How does a prospective adoptive parent go about finding a birth mother interested in placing her child for adoption?

7. When does an adoption become a black-market adoption?

8. For what reasons do persons sometimes adopt adults?

9. Can a homosexual adult adopt his or her homosexual partner?

10. How do adult/adult adoptions differ from adoptions of minors?

11. What standard does a judge use in deciding whether to allow an adoption?

12. What is a kinship adoption?

13. What factors will a court consider in deciding whether an adoption is in the best interests of the child?

14. How does the Multiethnic Placement Act (MEPA) affect the adoption of children in foster care?

15. Can gays and lesbians adopt minors?

16. What court procedures govern adoption?

17. What due diligence requirement exists in reference to fathers of nonmarital (illegitimate) children?

18. What rules govern obtaining consent of the birth mother?

19. When does the father of a nonmarital (illegitimate) child lose his right to consent to an adoption?

20. What is a parent's opportunity interest and when is it lost?

21. What are the consent rights or duties, if any, of the agency, the spouse of a prospective adoptive parent, the adoptee, and the foster parents?

22. When can a biological parent revoke her consent to an adoption?

23. What are the grounds for an involuntary termination of parental rights (TPR)?

24. What is the standard of proof for an involuntary TPR?

25. Is an indigent defendant in an involuntary TPR case entitled to appointed counsel?

26. Does a guardian ad litem have to be an attorney?

27. What is the purpose of the Adoption and Safe Families Act (ASFA)?

28. Can a child divorce his or her parents through a TPR proceeding?

29. What is an interlocutory decree of adoption?

30. What grounds can be alleged to challenge an adoption decree?

31. When will a court abrogate an adoption?

32. What is the function of a putative father registry?

33. What is the Interstate Compact on the Placement of Children?

34. What are the intestate and testate consequences of an adoption?

35. What is the rule of confidentiality in a traditional adoption?

36. What is the distinction between an active and a passive reunion registry?

37. What is an open adoption?

38. When will an equitable adoption be ordered?

39. Can an embryo be adopted?

40. What is an action for wrongful adoption?

HELPFUL WEBSITES

Adoption Law

- www.childwelfare.gov/adoption/laws/state
- law.capital.edu/adoption
- www.law.cornell.edu/wex/table_adoption
- www.law.cornell.edu/topics/Table_Emancipation.htm

National Adoption Statistics

- www.adoptioninstitute.org/ressta.html
- www.acf.hhs.gov/programs/cb/stats_research

National Adoption Clearinghouse

- www.adoption.org/adopt/national-adoption-clearinghouse.php
- www.adoption.org/adopt/national-adoption-information-clearinghouse.php

Adoption Options

- www.childwelfare.gov/pubs/f_adoptoption.cfm

Major Federal Legislation on Adoption and Child Welfare

- www.childwelfare.gov/pubs/otherpubs/majorfedlegis.cfm

Child Welfare Information Gateway

- encyclopedia.adoption.com/entry/Child-Welfare-Information-Gateway/238/1.html

State Child Welfare Agencies

- www.childwelfare.gov/pubs/reslist/rl_dsp_website.cfm?rs_ID=16&rate_chno=AZ-0004E

Child Welfare Policy Manual

- www.acf.hhs.gov/programs/cb/laws_policies/index.htm

Adoption Forms

- www.formsworkflow.com/FindLegalForms.aspx?q=adoption&s=

State Adoption Photolisting Services

- www.childwelfare.gov/pubs/reslist/rl_dsp_website
  .cfm?typeID=82&rate_chno=AZ-0005E

Evan B. Donaldson Adoption Institute

- www.adoptioninstitute.org

American Academy of Adoption Attorneys

- adoptionattorneys.org

Legal Center for Foster Care and Education

- www.americanbar.org/groups/child_law/projects
  _initiatives/education.html

Search for Birth Parents

- www.adoption.com/topics/search
- www.donorsiblingregistry.com
- www.omnitrace.com

National Directory of Putative Father Registries

- adoption.about.com/cs/adoptionrights/a
  /putative_list.htm

Rights of Unmarried Fathers

- www.childwelfare.gov/systemwide/laws_policies
  /statutes/putative.pdf

National Embryo Adoption Center

- www.embryodonation.org

Google/Bing/Yahoo Searches

(on these search engines, run the following searches, substituting your state for "aa")

- adoption aa
- paternity adoption aa
- "black-market" adoption aa
- "independent adoption" aa
- transracial adoption aa
- unfit adoption aa
- ASFA adoption aa
- "open adoption" aa
- "mediated adoption" aa
- ICPC adoption aa
- "adoptive parent" aa
- "foster care" adoption aa
- "second parent" adoption aa
- kinship adoption aa
- "opportunity interest" child aa
- CASA adoption aa
- "putative father registry" aa
- gay lesbian adoption aa
- "termination of parental rights" aa

ENDNOTES

Note: All or most of the court opinions in these endnotes can be read online. To do so, go to Google Scholar (scholar .google.com), select "Legal documents," and in the search box, enter the cite (e.g., "503 N.Y.S.2d 752") or name of the case (e.g., "*333 East 53rd St. Assocs. v. Mann*") that is given in the endnote.

1 U.S. Department of State, *Understanding the Hague Convention* (adoption.state.gov/hague_convention/overview.php).

2 *333 East 53rd St. Assocs. v. Mann,* 503 N.Y.S.2d 752 (N.Y. App. Div. 1986).

3 *In re Adoption of Holland,* 965 So. 2d 1213 (Fla. App. 2007).

4 *In re Adoption of Swanson,* 623 A.2d 1095, 1096 (Del. 1993).

5 *In the Matter of the Adoption of Robert Paul P.,* 63 N.Y.2d 233, 236, (N.Y. 1984).

6 42 U.S.C. § 1996b (www.law.cornell.edu/uscode
  /text/42/1996b).

7 25 U.S.C. § 1901 (www.law.cornell.edu/uscode/text/25
  /chapter-21).

8 New York State Compilation of Codes, Rules & Regulations, 18 NYCRR 421.16 (h)(2) (www.dos.ny.gov/info/nycrr .html) (government.westlaw.com/linkedslice/default .asp?SP=nycrr-1000).

9 American Psychological Association, *Sexual Orientation, Parents, and Children* (2004) (www.apa.org)(type the title of this report in the search box).

10 *Florida Dept. of Children and Families v. Adoption of X.X.G.,* 45 So. 3d 79 (Fla. App. 3 Dist., 2010).

11 Abby Bushlow, *Information Packet: Gay and Lesbian Second- Parent Adoptions* (National Resource Center for Foster Care and Permanency Planning, May 2002).

12 See, for example, North Dakota Century Code Annotated, § 14-15-19 (2007) (www.legis.nd.gov/cencode/t14c15.pdf). See also Uniform Adoption Act (1971) (www.law.cornell .edu/uniform/vol9.html#adopt).

13 *In re Kristina L.,* 520 A.2d 574, 581 (R.I., 1987).

14 *Lassiter v. Department of Soc. Servs.,* 452 U.S. 18 (1981).

15 Child Welfare Information Gateway, *Representation of Children in Child Abuse and Neglect Proceedings* (2011) (www.childwelfare.gov/systemwide/laws_policies/statutes /represent.pdf).

16 42 U.S.C. § 671 (1997) (www.law.cornell.edu/uscode/42 /usc_sec_42_00000671----000-.html).

17 Mark Hansen, *Boy Wants "Divorce" from Parents,* 78 American Bar Association Journal 24 (Jul. 1992).

18 Mark Hansen, *Boy Wins "Divorce" from Mom,* 78 American Bar Association Journal 16 (Dec. 1992).

19 *Kingsley v. Kingsley,* 623 So. 2d 780, 783 (Fla. Dist. Ct. App. 1993).

20 *Unnecessary Cruelty*, San Diego Union-Tribune, May 4, 1995, at B12.

21 *In re Baby Girl Clausen*, 502 N.W.2d 649 (Mich. 1993).

22 *DeBoer v. Schmidt*, 509 U.S. 1301, 1302 (1993).

23 2001 Florida Session Law Service, Ch. 2001–3 (H.B. 141) (West Group).

24 *G.P. v. State*, 842 So.2d 1059 (Fla. Dist. Ct. App. 2003).

25 Utah Statutes § 78B–6-110 (2008) (le.utah.gov/~code /TITLE78B/htm/78B06_011000.htm).

26 icpc.aphsa.org.

27 Council of State Governments, *Adoption*, State Government News, Sept. 1989, at 31.

28 Belinda Luscombe, *Adoption 2.0: Finding Mom on Facebook*, Time Magazine (Aug. 21, 2010) (www.time.com/time /magazine/article/0,9171,2008885,00.html).

29 Rachel Swarns, *With DNA Testing, Suddenly They Are Family*, N.Y. Times, Jan. 23, 2012.

30 Lisa Belkin, *I Found My Mom Through Facebook*, N.Y. Times, June 24, 2011.

31 Danielle Stewart, *Adoption Law*, 25 Legal Assistant Today 88 (2007).

16 The New Science of Motherhood

CHAPTER OUTLINE

CHAPTER OBJECTIVES

After completing this chapter, you should be able to:

- Define infertility and state its main causes.

- Define assisted reproductive technology (ART).

- Explain the process of in vitro fertilization (IVF).

- List the primary sources of eggs used in IVF.

- Understand the function of cryopreservation.

- Explain how a court will resolve a dispute on the disposition of unused frozen embryos upon divorce.

- Explain the consequences of defining an embryo as a person.

- Distinguish between posthumous birth and posthumous conception or fertilization.

- Understand the ethical and legal controversy surrounding stem-cell research.

- Understand the role of a surrogate mother.

- Define intended parent.

- Distinguish between traditional and gestational surrogacy.

- Explain the controversy involving Baby M.

- List the policy reasons for and against allowing surrogacy arrangements.

- Explain the relationship between surrogacy and the following areas of law: adoption, paternity, child custody, and contracts.

- List the major restrictions different states place on surrogacy.

- List the factors a court will consider when deciding who the legal mother is when a surrogate refuses to give the child to the intended parent(s).

INTRODUCTION

A major area of family law in which legal principles have failed to keep pace with technological and scientific advances is the law governing parent identity. Courts have traditionally been a forum for establishing paternity. Only recently have courts had to struggle with the issue of establishing maternity and of deciding whether it is possible for a child to have more than one mother. As one court commented:

> [The] technological fragmentation of the procreative process . . . has engendered a bewildering variety of possibilities which are not easily reconciled with our traditional definitions of "mother," "father," and "parent."[1]

In this chapter, we will examine some of these "bewildering" aspects of family creation in the twenty-first century.

INFERTILITY AND ITS TREATMENT

INFERTILITY

Infertility is the inability to conceive a child. A working definition of the term within the medical community is the failure of a couple to conceive in over a year in spite of having sexual relations without contraceptives. Either or both partners can be the source of the infertility. The approximate causal percentages are as follows:

- Infertility cases due solely to the male: 33 percent
- Infertility cases due solely to the female: 33 percent
- Infertility cases due to both male and female: 33 percent[2]

Male infertility is due to low sperm count, poor semen motility, impaired delivery of sperm, and the effects of sexually transmitted diseases. Female infertility is due to blocked fallopian tubes, dysfunctional ovaries, hormonal imbalance, and the effects of sexually transmitted diseases.

One in eight couples in the United States today need some form of medical help to create their families. Of the approximately 62 million women of reproductive age in the most recent study, about 1.2 million, or 2 percent, have had an infertility-related medical appointment within the previous year and an additional 10 percent received infertility services at some time in their lives. (Infertility services include medical tests to diagnose infertility, medical advice and treatments to help a woman become pregnant, and services other than routine prenatal care to prevent miscarriage.)[3] Every year, approximately $3 billion is spent on infertility services.[4]

A major fertility treatment for producing a child without sexual intercourse is called **assisted reproductive technology (ART)**. ART helps a woman become pregnant by procedures such as surgically removing eggs from a woman's ovaries, combining them with sperm in a laboratory, and returning the result to the woman's body or donating them to another woman. These steps, occurring over a period of approximately two weeks, constitute an ART cycle. There are several categories of ART:

- nondonor eggs: the woman uses her own eggs in the ART cycle
- donor eggs: the woman uses eggs from (donated by) another woman in the ART cycle
- fresh embryos: the embryos (see definition in Exhibit 16-1) used in the ART cycle were newly fertilized eggs
- frozen embryos: the embryos used in the ART cycle were previously fertilized, frozen, and then thawed

infertility
The inability to conceive a child. The failure of a couple to conceive in over a year in spite of having sexual relations without contraceptives.

assisted reproductive technology (ART)
Fertility treatment to help a woman become pregnant by procedures such as surgically removing eggs from a woman's ovaries, combining the eggs with sperm in a laboratory, and returning the fertilized eggs to the woman's body or donating them to another woman.

A federal law (the Fertility Clinic Success Rate and Certification Act) requires clinics performing ART to report their success rate to the Centers for Disease Control and Prevention.[5] Exhibit 16-2 presents a breakdown of the ART cycles that occurred in 2009.

Worldwide, more than three million babies have been born through ART since 1978, when the first child, Louise Brown, was born in England using the in vitro fertilization method (section titled "In Vitro Fertilization (IVF)) of ART. This is an area in which the science of motherhood, called by some the "ovarian Olympics" on a high-tech treadmill,[6] is moving much faster than the law. Increasingly, courts are faced with legal issues for which there are no precedents.

EXHIBIT 16-1   Terminology: The Biology of Reproduction

conception   Fertilization; the union of a sperm and an ovum; the formation of a viable zygote by the union of a sperm and an ovum.

egg   An unfertilized female reproductive cell; also called an *ovum* or *oocyte.*

embryo   An egg that has been fertilized by a sperm and is in the early stage of development; it has undergone one or more divisions. The product of conception to about the eighth week of pregnancy. Called a preembryo before being implanted in the uterus.

fallopian tube   The passageway for the eggs from the ovary to the uterus. Normal fertilization takes place in this tube. Also called *uterine tube* or *oviduct.*

fertilization   Conception; the initial union of a sperm and an egg (ovum) that becomes an embryo. Penetration of an egg by a sperm.

fetus   A developing organism—the unborn offspring—from the eighth week after conception until birth.

gamete   A reproductive cell, either a sperm or an egg. A reproductive cell with a specified number of chromosomes. A mature sperm or egg that is capable of fusing with the gamete of the opposite sex to produce a fertilized egg.

gene   A hereditary unit (on a chromosome) that has a specific hereditary function determined by a DNA sequence.

genetic   Pertaining to genes.

genetic parent   A mother or father who is biologically related to a child.

gestation   Pregnancy; the period of development in the uterus from conception to birth.

gestational carrier   (also called a *gestational surrogate*). A woman who gestates, or carries, an embryo that was formed from the egg of another woman. The gestational carrier usually has a contractual obligation to give the infant to its intended parents.

gonad   A gland that produces gametes. Gonads include an ovary or a testis.

oocyte   The female reproductive cell. An *egg.*

ovum   An egg; a female reproductive cell. (Plural, *ova.*)

ovary   One of the two female sex or reproductive glands that produce eggs; female sex cells.

ovulation   The release of a mature egg from the ovary.

ovum   A female gamete or reproductive cell.

pregnancy   The period of development of the fetus from conception to birth.

preembryo   (pre-embryo) A fertilized egg up to 14 days old, before it becomes implanted in the uterus. The "period of development from the end of the process of fertilization until the appearance of a single primitive streak, a period that lasts approximately fourteen days."[7] (Also called a *prezygote.*) Note, however, that the terms *embryo* and *preembryo* are often used interchangeably.

procreate   To reproduce, to bring forth offspring.

semen   Sperm and other secretions expelled through the male reproductive tract.

sperm   The male gamete or reproductive cell. A mature male germ cell.

uterus   A hollow, pear-shaped organ that holds a fertilized ovum during pregnancy.

viable   Able to live indefinitely outside the womb by natural or artificial support systems.

zygote   A fertilized egg. A cell formed by the union of a male sex cell and a female sex cell.

EXHIBIT 16-2   ART Cycle Success Rate (2009)

- Number of ART cycles performed in the United States: 146,244 (as reported by 441 of the 484 clinics in the country)

- Average age of the women using ART cycles: 36

- Number of infants born from these cycles: 60,190 (10 years ago the number was 30,629)

- Percentage of ART cycles that used fresh (not frozen) nondonor eggs or embryos: 70 percent

- Percentage of ART cycles that used eggs or embryos donated by another woman: 12 percent

- Percentage of ART cycles that used frozen nondonor embryos: 18 percent

- Percentage of ART pregnancies resulting in multiple births (twins or higher) from fresh (not frozen) nondonor eggs or embryos: approximately 32 percent

- Number of pregnancies from ART cycles that ended in miscarriage, stillbirth, induced abortion, or maternal death: 6,837

Source: Centers for Disease Control and Prevention, *2009 Assisted Reproductive Technology Report* (November 2011) (www.cdc.gov/art/ART2009/PDF/ART_2009_Full.pdf).

IN VITRO FERTILIZATION (IVF)

The most commonly performed ART (70 percent) is **in vitro fertilization (IVF)**, sometimes referred to as fertilization "in a glass," meaning in a petri dish (which the media often mischaracterizes as conception "in a test tube"). IVF consists of the surgical removal of a woman's eggs from her ovaries, their fertilization with a man's sperm in a petri dish in a laboratory, and the transfer of the resulting embryos (or preembryos) into the uterus through the cervix. The cost of each IVF cycle can be between $10,000 and $15,000. Because more than one IVF cycle is often needed, the estimated average cost per live birth is between $66,000 and $114,000.[8]

Here is how a recent court opinion described the IVF procedure:

> IVF involves injecting the woman with fertility drugs in order to stimulate production of eggs which can be surgically retrieved or harvested. After the eggs are removed, they are combined in a petri dish with sperm produced by the man, on the same day as the egg removal, in an effort to fertilize the eggs. If fertilization between any of the eggs and sperm occurs, preembryos are formed that are held in a petri dish for one or two days until a decision can be made as to which preembryos will be used immediately and which will be frozen and stored by the clinic for later use.[9]

In most IVF procedures, the fertilized egg is implanted in the uterus of the woman from whom the egg was taken. (If they are transferred to the uterus of *another* woman, a *surrogacy* arrangement is involved, as we will see later.)

Suppose that a woman's eggs are not usable. Assume that she is able to carry a child, but not with her own egg. One of her options is to be implanted with the egg of someone else—an *egg donor*—with whom the sperm of her husband (or of another male) is joined via IVF. Just as high-quality sperm donors are in demand (see Chapter 13 on paternity), so too there is competition for egg donors who meet certain criteria. Ads are placed in college newspapers that urge female students to "donate eggs to pay for college." More dramatically, the following ad in Exhibit 16-3 was placed in several Ivy League college newspapers such as those at Harvard and Yale. The ad was eventually given national publicity and generated hundreds of responses from women claiming to meet the requisite qualifications. Soon thereafter another ad appeared that sought a "Caucasian"

in vitro fertilization (IVF)
The surgical removal of a woman's eggs from the ovaries, the fertilization of the eggs with sperm (in the laboratory), and the transfer of the resulting embryos (or preembryos) into the uterus through the cervix. An ART method.

EXHIBIT 16-3   Egg Donor for Cash

EGG DONOR NEEDED
Large Financial Incentive:
$50,000
Intelligent, Athletic Egg Donor Needed
for Loving Family
You must be at least 5'10"
Have a 1400 SAT score
Free Medical Screening
All Expenses Paid

© Cengage Learning 2013

with "proven college-level athletic ability." The price for the right woman was $100,000. A more typical fee for an egg donor would be in the range of $2,000 to $5,000. To obtain a sense of the "market" for this service, run this search in Google or other search engine, "egg donor wanted" (see, for example, elitedonors.com). Egg donation typically requires daily hormone injections and minor surgery to remove the eggs, the entire process taking about 60 hours.

It should be noted, however, that the risks of egg donation have not been adequately studied: "Although the consensus among most reproductive endocrinologists is that extraction is safe, five deaths have been reported in Britain." Moreover, "[e]thicists and some women's health advocates worry that lucrative payments are enticing young women with credit-card debt and steep tuition bills to sell eggs without seriously evaluating the risks."[10]

Although it is legal for a woman to donate her eggs to help another woman have a baby and to be paid a substantial fee for this service, the situation is different if the eggs are going to be used for research. Many states either ban paying women for eggs or place significant limitations on what they can be paid when the recipients of the eggs are going to use them for research. As a matter of ethics and public policy, our society is uncomfortable about encouraging potentially unsavory experimentation in this sensitive area of human existence.

OTHER ART METHODS

In addition to IVF, other major ART methods include:

- *Gamete intrafallopian transfer (GIFT):* using a fiber-optic instrument called a laparoscope to guide the transfer of unfertilized eggs and sperm (gametes) into the woman's fallopian tubes through small incisions in her abdomen.

- *Zygote intrafallopian transfer (ZIFT):* fertilizing a woman's eggs in the laboratory and then using a laparoscope to guide the transfer of the fertilized eggs (zygotes) into her fallopian tubes (combining IVF and GIFT).

- *Embryo transplant:* placing a fertile woman's embryo into the uterus through the cervix. Also called *embryo transfer, ovum transfer,* or *ovum transplant.*

artificial insemination (AI)
Inserting sperm into the uterus by a method other than sexual intercourse.

first impression
Concerning an issue being addressed by a court for the first time.

Artificial insemination (AI) is not an ART method. AI occurs by inserting sperm into the uterus by a method other than sexual intercourse. ART methods consist of fertility treatments in which both sperm and eggs are handled in the laboratory. In AI, only the sperm is handled (see Chapter 13).

The new science of motherhood has generated many legal issues of **first impression**—those that the courts have had to face for the first time. Among the areas of controversy have been the status of frozen embryos in a divorce, the ethical propriety of stem-cell research, and the legality of surrogacy contracts.

THE STATUS OF FROZEN EMBRYOS

Some embryos resulting from IVF are not immediately implanted into the uterus. Through **cryopreservation**, embryos can be frozen for transfer or implantation at a later time. Over 400,000 frozen embryos (or preembryos) are in storage throughout the country:

- Being stored for family building: 88 percent
- Being stored for "adoption" by another woman: 2.3 percent
- Being stored for research: under 3 percent
- Being stored for other reasons (e.g., lost contact with the person who hired the storage service): 6.7 percent

It is not known how long the embryos remain viable in storage.[11] Estimates range from 10 to 15 years. Storage costs are about $400 a year.

DISPUTES OVER DISPOSITION OF EMBRYOS

Suppose that a husband and wife file for divorce *before* all their frozen embryos are used. Who receives "custody" of the embryos? Who "owns" them? Are they subject to **property division** along with everything else the parties acquired during the marriage?

The problem arises when the divorcing parties disagree about what should be done with the embryos. Suppose that the husband wants them destroyed because he does not want to become the father of a child with his soon-to-be ex-wife, but she wants them kept alive so that they can be implanted in her at a later time. Can he be forced to become a father against his will? In a different context, a man cannot force a woman whom he has impregnated to have an abortion in order to avoid being the father of a child he does not want. Is the situation different here? Can he force a laboratory to destroy a frozen embryo that the woman wants to preserve?

The first major case to address this issue arose in Tennessee: *Davis v. Davis*.[12] Junior Lewis Davis sought a divorce from his wife, Mary Sue Davis. The parties were able to agree on all the terms of dissolution except one. Who was to have custody of seven frozen preembryos stored in a Knoxville fertility clinic that had attempted to assist the Davises in achieving a much-wanted pregnancy during a happier period of their relationship? Mary did not want to use the frozen embryos herself but wanted to donate them to a childless couple. Junior was adamantly opposed to such donation; he wanted the preembryos destroyed. When the Davises enrolled in the IVF program at the Knoxville clinic, the agreement they signed did not specify what disposition should be made of any unused preembryos in the cryopreservation facility. Nor were there any Tennessee statutes on what to do in this situation.

The Tennessee court resolved the dispute by writing guidelines on what to do when parties cannot agree:

- The party wishing to avoid procreation should ordinarily prevail, assuming the other party has a reasonable possibility of achieving parenthood by means other than the use of the frozen preembryos in question.

- If no other reasonable alternatives exist, the argument in favor of using the preembryos to achieve pregnancy should be considered.

- If, however, the party seeking control of the preembryos intends merely to donate them to another couple, the objecting party has the greater interest and should prevail.

Using these guidelines in the *Davis* case, Junior Lewis Davis prevailed, because Mary Sue Davis did not want to use the preembryos herself. The preembryos were discarded.

---

cryopreservation

The storage of cells or whole tissues at sub-zero temperatures for later thawing and use. For example, freezing embryos from an ART cycle for potential use (transfer or implantation) at a later time.

property division

The allocation and distribution of property between spouses (or ex-spouses) after a legal separation or divorce. Also called property settlement, property distribution.

A much different result would have been reached if the *Davis* case had arisen in Louisiana. A statute in Louisiana specifies that a "human embryo" is a fertilized "human" ovum "with certain rights granted by law." The principles laid out in the Louisiana statute are as follows:

- A viable in vitro fertilized human ovum is a juridical person which shall not be intentionally destroyed.

- If the IVF patients renounce their parental rights for in utero implantation, then the in vitro fertilized human ovum shall be available for adoptive implantation in accordance with written procedures of the facility where it is housed or stored.

- The in vitro fertilization patients may renounce their parental rights in favor of another married couple if the other couple is willing and able to receive the in vitro fertilized ovum.

- No compensation shall be paid or received by either couple to renounce parental rights.

- Disputes between parties should be resolved in the "best interest" of the in vitro fertilized ovum.[13]

Hence, in the dispute between Mary Sue Davis (who wanted to keep the embryos alive for adoption) and Junior Lewis Davis (who wanted them destroyed), Mary Sue would have won if the case had been brought in Louisiana. It could hardly be said that the "best interest" of the embryos would be to destroy them.

As a result of the difficulties that arose in the *Davis* case, IVF contracts that couples sign with fertility clinics today almost always specify what should happen to unused frozen embryos or preembryos. (Florida, for example, *requires* couples to execute a written agreement on how "eggs, sperm, or preembryos" are to be disposed of in the event of death, divorce, or other unforeseen event.[14] Courts are generally inclined to enforce such an agreement unless they are faced with a statute as stringent as Louisiana's.

In a New York case several years after *Davis* case, the parties underwent several unsuccessful attempts to have a child through IVF at a cost in excess of $75,000. The agreement they signed said, "In the event that we no longer wish to initiate a pregnancy or are unable to make a decision" on the disposition of their frozen preembryos, they should be donated to the IVF clinic for research purposes and then disposed of by the clinic. After the parties divorced, the ex-wife wanted the preembryos implanted in her, claiming that it would be her only chance for genetic motherhood. The ex-husband, however, objected and asked the court to enforce the agreement so that the IVF clinic would dispose of them. The court ruled that the agreement was binding and should be enforced. The clinic kept the preembryos.[15]

Although most states (other than Louisiana) would follow this position, there are limitations. In a Massachusetts case, for example, the court said that it would not enforce an agreement on the disposition of frozen preembryos if it has the effect of forcing one of the parties to become a parent against his or her will. The ex-wife in the case wanted to use the preembryos for implantation. The ex-husband objected. The court ruled in his favor even though the agreement they signed appeared to favor the option she now wanted. The court said that it

> "would not enforce an agreement that would compel one donor to become a parent against his or her will. As a matter of public policy, we conclude that forced procreation is not an area amenable to judicial enforcement. . . . We would not order either a husband or a wife to do what is necessary to conceive a child or to prevent conception, any more than we would order either party to do what is necessary to make the other happy."[16]

THE OCTOMOM AND THE SCRAMBLED EGGS CASE

Considerable disagreement exists over whether the science of motherhood is sufficiently regulated. Widespread media attention given to problems in the fertility industry suggests that more regulation is needed. Examples:

- A single mother of six children gave birth to eight additional children (octuplets) after undergoing IVF. Her doctor was disciplined for implanting an excessive number of embryos in his patient, referred to as "octomom" in the media after the eight babies were born.

- In the famous "scrambled eggs" case, a white woman at a fertility clinic gave birth to unrelated twins, one white and one black. The clinic made a serious error. It was unclear whether a black couple's fertilized egg was mistakenly implanted in the white woman (along with her own fertilized egg), or whether the black man's sperm had been used to fertilize the white woman's egg. The twins were not genetically related. Fortunately, the couples amicably agreed that each twin would go home with its biological parents.

Publicity about fertility mix-ups has given rise to increased concern. One woman, worried about the procedures used by private clinics that store and handle eggs and embryos, said, "What if they put them on the wrong shelf?"[17]

POSTHUMOUS REPRODUCTION

The most common example of a child born after the death of one or both of its parents (posthumous birth) is a pregnant woman whose husband (or other male partner) dies before the birth of their child. But can a child be *conceived* after the death of one or both or their genetic parents? There can be posthumous birth. Can there be posthumous fertilization or reproduction? Yes.

- Sperm can be removed from a recently deceased man and either frozen for later IVF or immediately inserted into the uterus of a woman. The requests for such sperm has come from wives, girlfriends, and parents of the deceased: "In fact, retrieving sperm from the dead is now so common that the American Society of Reproductive Medicine has developed a protocol, 'Posthumous Reproduction,' for dealing with it. And one bioethicist, Timothy Murphy, has coined a term for this new kind of father: the sperminator."[18]

- A woman can freeze her own egg for later fertilization. If this woman dies before the egg is fertilized and before the embryo is implanted in a surrogate, the resulting baby would be born after the death of its genetic mother. If the man who provided the sperm dies before fertilization and before implantation in the surrogate, the resulting baby would be born after the death of both genetic parents.

A major issue that can arise in situations such as these is whether the child born after the death of its genetic parent can inherit from that parent. The few cases that have addressed the issue have said that the child can inherit but only if there is sufficient proof that the deceased expressed a desire or intent to be a parent before death.

STEM-CELL RESEARCH

The human embryo contains *stem cells* that can grow into (i.e., differentiate into) other cells that make up the heart, brain, kidney, and other organs. In a laboratory, stem cells can be removed from the embryo and grown into *cell lines* that multiply indefinitely. These laboratory-grown cells have the potential of being used to repair or replace damaged tissue or organs and to treat or cure numerous diseases such as Alzheimer's. To remove stem cells for this purpose, however, the embryo must be destroyed. Opponents argue that the human embryo is the earliest stage of human life and, therefore, must be protected. Some church leaders and pro-life activists believe it is morally wrong to destroy embryos because life begins at fertilization. In their view, the embryos should be donated to women who wish to use them in order to have children.

Scientists have two main sources of embryos from which they can extract stem cells:

- Embryos produced for in vitro fertilization (IVF) procedures but that are scheduled for destruction because the couples no longer need or want them.
- Embryos produced for the sole purpose of scientific research rather than for use in IVF procedures.

Conservatives oppose the destruction of both categories of embryos. They consider the latter particularly heinous since the embryos that are destroyed are not surplus embryos. Rather, they are created from donated eggs and sperm for the express purpose of medical experimentation. Others, however, take the position that embryos not needed for IVF and already scheduled for destruction should be available for research.

There is widespread legal, ethical, and policy disagreement over what stem-cell research can be undertaken. The Dickey-Wicker Amendment prohibits federal funding for "research in which a human embryo or embryos are destroyed."[19] Different presidents have issued conflicting guidelines on the meaning of this prohibition and ongoing litigation has kept the issue unresolved. While the debate continues at the federal level, some states have spent state government money and some private individuals have spent private money on embryo research, but advocates of expansive stem-cell research say that major breakthroughs will not occur until substantial federal funding is made available.

Stem cells are not limited to embryos. Adult stem cells can be found in blood, skeletal muscle, skin, and elsewhere. These cells can be extracted without destroying anything. Yet adult stem cells are more difficult than embryonic stem cells to grow in the laboratory. Also, embryonic stem cells are considered more versatile and promising for medical research.

ASSIGNMENT 16.2

Do you think that there should be restrictions on stem-cell research? Should there be limitations imposed on public or private funding of such research?

SURROGACY

INTRODUCTION

Surrogacy is the status or act of being a substitute for another. For our purposes, surrogacy is the carrying and delivering of a child for another. The person performing this motherhood service is called the **surrogate mother**, or the surrogate. She becomes pregnant, usually by artificial insemination (AI) or in vitro fertilization (IVF) with the semen of a man who is not her husband, with the understanding that she will surrender her legal rights to the baby upon birth. The surrender leads to a **termination of parental rights (TPR)** of the surrogate mother. It is also possible for a surrogate to become pregnant through sexual intercourse, called natural insemination (NI). For example, in Genesis, Abram's then-barren wife, Sarai, told him to sleep with her slave, Hagar. ("The Lord has kept me from having children. Why don't you sleep with my slave girl? Perhaps I can build a family through her."[20]). In the vast majority of cases, however, pregnancy occurs through AI or IVF.

A person seeking to raise a child born with the services of a surrogate mother is called the **intended parent**. An intended parent is a person who wants to raise a child as its legal parent and who enters an agreement with a surrogate mother to bear and deliver the child. The person hiring the surrogate mother may or may not be genetically (biologically) related to the child. Intended parents using the services of a surrogate mother can include:

- A wife who is infertile because she cannot produce her own eggs. The semen of her husband fertilizes an egg provided by a surrogate mother who carries and delivers the baby.

- A wife who is infertile because she does not have a functioning uterus, but she can produce healthy eggs. The semen of her husband fertilizes his wife's egg. A surrogate mother carries and delivers the baby.

- An unmarried man who wants to raise a child on his own. He fertilizes an egg provided by a surrogate mother who carries and delivers the baby.

- Two gay men who want to raise a child together. One of them fertilizes an egg provided by a surrogate mother who carries and delivers the baby.

There are two main kinds of surrogacy: traditional and gestational.

- **Traditional surrogacy:** A woman (using her own egg) becomes pregnant for someone else. The woman agrees (1) to become impregnated (usually by artificial insemination) using her own egg and the sperm of the intended father or of another man, and (2) to relinquish her parental rights upon the birth of the child. Under traditional surrogacy, the surrogate is genetically or biologically related to the child because she uses her own egg.

- **Gestational surrogacy:** A woman (not using her own egg) becomes pregnant for someone else. The woman agrees (1) to have an embryo produced by the egg and sperm of the intended parents (or of other donors) implanted (by IVF) into her uterus and (2) to relinquish her parental rights upon the birth of the child. Under gestational surrogacy, the surrogate is not genetically or biologically related to the child because she does not use her own egg.

Of course, under either method of surrogacy, the man who contributes the semen is genetically or biologically related to the child.

We do not have accurate statistics on the number of births that occur through the use of a surrogate. Between 2004 and 2008, the estimate of the number of babies born through surrogacy arrangements is 5,238.[21] This number is incomplete, however, because it mainly covers gestational surrogacy; we do not have good data on traditional surrogacy.

surrogacy

1. The carrying and delivering of a child for another. 2. The status or act of being a substitute for another.

surrogate mother

A woman who becomes pregnant (usually by artificial insemination or in vitro fertilization) with the semen of a man who is not her husband, with the understanding that she will surrender her legal rights to the baby upon its birth.

termination of parental rights (TPR)

A judicial declaration that ends the legal relationship between parent and child when this is in the best interests of the child. The parent no longer has any right to participate in decisions affecting the welfare of the child and no longer has any duties toward the child.

intended parent

A person who wants to raise a child as its legal parent and who enters an agreement with a surrogate mother to bear and deliver the child. The person hiring the surrogate mother may or may not be genetically (biologically) related to the child.

traditional surrogacy

The carrying and delivering of a child for another in which the woman uses her own egg and is therefore genetically related to the child.

gestational surrogacy

The carrying and delivering of a child for another in which the woman does not use her own egg and is therefore not genetically related to the child.

SURROGACY CONTRACTS

Surrogacy comes into existence by agreement. An unpregnant woman enters a contract to become pregnant, to give birth to a child, and then to relinquish all parental rights to the couple (usually a husband and wife), who will then adopt the child. The couple agrees to pay her medical and related expenses. In addition, some surrogates are paid a fee, often between $12,000 and $25,000. When a fee is to be paid, critics of surrogacy contracts deride the arrangement as a "womb for hire." The total cost to the intended parents who hire the surrogate is between $40,000 and $120,000.[22]

Unfortunately, surrogacy contracts do not always operate as planned. Suppose, for example, that the surrogate mother changes her mind and refuses to relinquish the child upon birth? What law applies? Different states answer this question differently. In some states, surrogacy contracts are illegal. In New York, for example, "[s]urrogate parenting contracts are hereby declared contrary to the public policy of this state, and are void and unenforceable."[23] In such states, it is against public policy to give birth to a child with the sole purpose of surrendering it for adoption. Most states also object to the payment of an adoption fee other than to cover the reasonable expenses involved, as we saw in Chapter 15 on adoption.

Of course, the media is ever ready to sensationalize anything that goes awry or that is unusual about the world of surrogacy. In Kansas, for example, extensive coverage was given to a woman who became the surrogate for her daughter who was born without a uterus. The daughter's eggs were fertilized with the sperm of the daughter's husband in the laboratory before being implanted in the daughter's mother. She gave birth to twins. Although some praised the sacrifice of a woman who would give birth to her own grandchildren, some ethicists were concerned, one commenting that it was a bad idea "that could create problems for the children."[24]

The frantic search for egg donors and surrogates has given rise to the phrase "Google baby," referring to donors and surrogates located online through search engines such as Google. A number of fertility agencies have lined up women in India who become surrogates at substantially less cost than what would have to be spent in the United States: "Logistically, this involves freezing multiple donor embryos and shipping them to a surrogacy center [such as the one] in Anand, India, packaged in liquid nitrogen."[25] When surrogacy is performed abroad for Americans, the media calls it "reproductive outsourcing."

The report in Exhibit 16-4 provides an overview of how the courts and legislatures have attempted to respond to this new area of the law. The report also highlights the major legal issues that have not yet been definitively resolved.

EXHIBIT 16-4   Policy and Legal Issues in Surrogacy

I. The Baby M Case

In March 1987, the nation's attention focused on a breach-of-contract battle underway in New Jersey. The contract in question was between Elizabeth and William Stern and Mary Beth Whitehead (now Mary Beth Whitehead-Gould). The Sterns had contracted with Ms. Whitehead in 1985 to act as a surrogate mother. Under the terms of the contract, Ms. Whitehead was to be artificially inseminated with Mr. Stern's sperm, become pregnant, give birth to a baby, turn it over to the Sterns, and cooperate in the termination of her parental rights. Mrs. Stern would then adopt the baby. Upon the birth of the baby (known as Baby M) Ms. Whitehead reconsidered and refused to relinquish her parental rights. The Sterns then sued in an attempt to hold Ms. Whitehead to the terms of the contract.

On March 31, 1987, a New Jersey trial court upheld the contract, granted permanent custody to the Sterns, permitted Mrs. Stern to adopt the child, and denied any rights to Ms. Whitehead. On February 3, 1988, the New Jersey Supreme Court approved only the custody portion of the lower court's decision, ruling that surrogate parenting contracts fall under the New Jersey "baby-selling" statutes and are therefore illegal.[26] In spite of the illegality of the contract, the court ruled that it would be in the best interests of Baby M to be in the custody of her biological father and his wife.

The publicity surrounding this case led to a flurry of activity in legislative bodies around the country as pro- and anti-surrogacy groups attempted to sway policymaking bodies to one side or the other.

II. Definitions

Although the term surrogate parenting has become widely used since the Baby M case, it can refer to more than one method of achieving parenthood. In addition, the parties involved in a surrogacy contract may not necessarily be limited to a married couple contracting with a single woman. The parties could involve a married surrogate mother, a single father, or same-sex couples. However, for ease of discussion, the terms "married couple," "husband," and "wife" will be used, keeping in mind that a broader definition may apply to these words.

A. Methods

Four general methods of surrogate parenting are recognized. These methods are:

1. *Artificial Insemination by Husband (AIH).* The AIH method is an arrangement in which the surrogate, a woman other than the wife of the sperm donor, is artificially inseminated with the sperm of the husband of a married couple.

2. *In Vitro Fertilization (IVF).* In vitro fertilization is a process by which a sperm and an egg are joined in a laboratory and the fertilized egg is implanted in the surrogate.

3. *Artificial Insemination by Donor (AID).* The AID method is a technique in which the surrogate is artificially inseminated with the sperm of a third-party donor—someone other than the male who has hired the surrogate. Such sperm is typically a specimen obtained from a sperm bank.

4. *Natural Insemination (NI).* The NI consists of sexual intercourse between the surrogate and the husband of a married couple.

Of the four methods, AIH is the most common. It is often substantially less expensive than IVF. The remaining discussion will assume that AIH is the method chosen in the surrogate agreement.

B. Agreements

Here is an example of a typical surrogate agreement:

- Harry and Mary are a married couple who hire the surrogacy services of Linda.

- Linda will be artificially inseminated with Harry's sperm, carry the child to term, and surrender her parental rights to Harry, the biological father, upon the birth of the child.

- Once Harry has full parental rights to the child, his wife Mary (technically the child's stepmother) begins adoption proceedings.

- Harry and Mary agree to pay all of Linda's medical and other necessary expenses (e.g., maternity clothes).

Brokers are often used in surrogacy contracts to bring the parties together and to coordinate the arrangement. The broker is usually an attorney or a private agency that receives a fee (e.g., $20,000) for this service. In some agreements, the surrogate mother is also paid a fee (e.g., $15,000). Her fee cannot be paid in exchange for her agreement to give up her parental rights. This would be blatant baby-selling. Fees beyond reasonable expenses also turn the transaction into illegal baby selling. Many surrogacy agreements are between family members or friends and do not involve the payment of a separate fee to the surrogate mother. If such a fee is paid, the arrangement is a *commercial surrogacy agreement*; if a fee is not paid, it is a *noncommercial surrogacy agreement*.

III. Reasons for Choosing Surrogate Parenting Agreements

According to a study of surrogacy in Wisconsin, the demand for surrogate mothers stems primarily from female infertility. The National Center for Health Statistics estimates that 10 to 15 percent of all married couples are infertile (defined as partners who are sexually active, not using contraception, and unable to conceive in over a year). These statistics do not include the surgically sterile. The Wisconsin study also cites evidence that suggests that the number of infertile women is on the rise due to the use of intrauterine birth control devices, greater incidence of sexually transmitted diseases, previous abortions, and the postponement of childbearing to establish careers. Studies indicate that women who delay having children have a greater risk of being infertile, bearing children with birth defects, and/or bearing children who are physically impaired. The most common treatments for female infertility are drugs and surgery. Until recently, when these treatments failed, adoption of an unrelated child was the only alternative available.

Couples who want children but cannot conceive usually consider adoption. The Wisconsin study noted that, despite a marked increase in the number of live births to single women, fewer unrelated individuals are adopted. Adoption experts believe that the increasing willingness of single mothers to keep their children is a significant factor in limiting the number of infants available for adoption. The stigma once attached to single mothers has diminished. Peers and relatives often encourage single mothers to keep their babies. Medical personnel and social workers are less likely to encourage women to give babies up for adoption.

(continued)

EXHIBIT 16-4 *(continued)*

Laws have changed in recent years to allow single mothers more time to make or revoke their consent to allow adoption. Consequently, couples often cite long waiting periods and other obstacles to adoption (such as the age limit placed on prospective parents) as reasons for seeking surrogate mothers.[27]

Not all couples who contract with a surrogate have failed at adoption. Some couples would rather be childless than adopt an unrelated child and, therefore, use traditional surrogacy. For such families, a genetic link to their child is of primary importance. For example, in the New Jersey Baby M case, William Stern lost most of his family in Adolf Hitler's holocaust and wanted a child biologically linked to him. Newspaper interviews of intended fathers confirm the importance some of them place on a biological link when seeking surrogates. One father favored a surrogate birth because "that child will be biologically half-mine" while another father stated, "[W]e believe strongly in heredity."

IV. Major Arguments for and against Surrogate Parenting

A review of the literature on surrogate parenting reveals several common policy positions on each side of this issue.

A. Supporting Arguments

Due to the decreasing number of babies available for adoption and the advancement of technology in the area of human reproduction, couples who desperately want children will continue to seek out surrogate mothers. Even though the vast majority of surrogacy agreements are completed without controversy, there is a need for additional protection for the intended parents, the surrogate mother, and the resulting child. Proposed regulation should include:

- Limitations on the fees charged by brokers, who should be better regulated to ensure competency, honesty, and legitimacy in the surrogacy process.
- Proper examination of both the intended parents and the surrogate mother to ensure:
    1. That the couple is emotionally and financially ready to bear the responsibility of parenthood.
    2. That the couple is truly in need of this service, such as when the wife is unable to carry a child to term.
    3. That the woman who will bear the child is emotionally, physically, and psychologically able to carry the child and to give up her rights to the child at birth.

By and large, these safeguards do not exist. Instead of banning surrogacy, however, greater efforts should be made to enact the safeguards into law.

B. Opposing Arguments

Those people who advocate a ban on surrogacy contracts argue that:

- Children will be psychologically damaged when they discover that they were "bought."
- Surrogate parenting arrangements are in violation of the Thirteenth Amendment of the U.S. Constitution, which applies to slavery and can be interpreted to forbid the buying and selling of people.
- Surrogate parenting will become another form of economic exploitation of rich people over poor. As exemplified by the Baby M case, the intended parents will almost always have an economic and educational advantage over the surrogate mother. Many surrogate mothers are unemployed or on some form of public assistance. Few have more than a high school diploma. Thus, surrogate parenting arrangements will serve to create a class of "womb-sellers."
- There are plenty of nonwhite babies, older children, and special needs children available for adoption. Surrogacy is not needed.
- Women will be forced (by the terms of the surrogacy agreement) to abort fetuses upon demand if the intended parents conclude that the child might be born with a defect or the women will be contractually obligated to become pregnant again in the case of a miscarriage.

V. Issues in State Law

Traditional legal rules governing parents and children do not always fit the facts of surrogacy arrangements. When disputes arise in a surrogacy case, courts may struggle to try to fit the traditional rules into the facts of the case. Four areas of state law that have raised concerns are (1) adoption, (2) paternity, (3) child custody, and (4) contract law. These concerns have been largely responsible for the decision of some states to ban surrogacy contracts.

A. Adoption Laws

Two aspects of many state adoption laws (compensation and pre-birth consent) may restrict or prevent surrogate parenting agreements.

Some states prohibit the payment of compensation for an adoption. Other states limit the adoption expenses that can be paid for in the adoption agreement. The major concern of these payment restrictions is the prevention of baby-selling. Adoption is also part of the surrogacy process. The child that results from surrogacy is adopted by at least one of the intended parents. Proponents of surrogacy agreements point out that modern anti-baby-selling laws predate surrogate parenting and were designed to protect unwed mothers. Under a surrogacy agreement, however, the intended father is also the biological father. It cannot be said that he is buying his own child. Also, proponents argue that surrogates have voluntarily agreed to surrender the child. They are not doing so under pregnancy-related stress. Finally, the fees to the surrogate mother are paid primarily to replace lost work time or for pain and suffering she must endure.

Most states prohibit a mother from granting consent to adoption before a child's birth or for a designated period of time after birth. Waiting periods range up to as much as 20 days (Pennsylvania). A mother's consent to surrender a newborn for adoption is not valid in Nevada until at least 72 hours after birth. However, as with baby-selling laws, consent laws were designed to protect unwed mothers. The decisions facing an unwed mother are not like those facing the surrogate mother who has voluntarily chosen to bear children for another couple.

B. Paternity Laws

Paternity laws may also affect surrogate arrangements. If the surrogate mother is married, her husband is presumed to be the father of the child in states that retain the common law rule that the husband of a woman who gives birth to a child during the marriage is presumed to be the father. Courts in some of these states will not admit evidence to the contrary. A majority of states, however, allow a rebuttal to the presumption of paternity, even though they place a strict burden of proof on anyone challenging the presumption.

Supporters of surrogacy argue that paternity laws were designed to protect the child, particularly the rights to inheritance, and were not drafted in anticipation of surrogate parenting arrangements. Rights and duties outlined in surrogate agreements fall on the natural father and would secure the child's rights.

C. Child-Custody Issues

The traditional basis for custody decisions is a determination of the *best interests of the child.* The standards for judging the suitability of prospective adoptive parents include marital and family status, mental and physical health, income and other assets, history of child abuse or neglect, and other relevant facts. In the case of Baby M, custody of the child was awarded to the Sterns because the court felt it was in the best interests of the child.

A spokesperson for the National Committee for Adoption objects to surrogate contracts because they are not required to take into account the best interests of the child. Unlike normal adoption proceedings, no one screens intended parents in surrogacy arrangements. Currently, surrogacy agreements require nothing more than the financial ability to hire a lawyer and pay the surrogate mother.

Supporters of surrogate agreements argue that the agreements are inherently in the best interests of the child because the intended parents have given much thought to their actions and have decided that they truly want a child. Adoption proceedings, on the other hand, were devised to provide a permanent home for a child who otherwise would not have one. In a surrogate agreement, the child's home is provided by contract.

D. Contract Law

Current law in most states does not address the issue of the surrogate's liability or of acceptable remedies if there is a breach of the surrogacy agreement. Nor does current law adequately address the responsibilities of the intended parents.

Surrogacy agreements impose a number of duties on one or both of the intended parents. The duties include the payment of expenses and fees and the assumption of responsibility for the child at birth. If the surrogate mother performs as agreed, does she have recourse if the other party refuses to pay all or part of the expenses and fees? What happens if the intended parents refuse to take the child? Can the surrogate mother sue the natural father for child support?

Some of these issues are already facing state courts. For example, in Texas, a 24-year-old surrogate mother died of heart failure in her eighth month of pregnancy; in Washington, D.C., a baby born through a surrogate agreement was diagnosed as having acquired immune deficiency syndrome (AIDS). Now, neither the surrogate mother nor the contracting parents want the baby with AIDS. These issues were not previously addressed in the contracts.

Enforcement of a surrogate mother's duties is even more difficult. She agrees to be inseminated, bear a child, and surrender all parental rights. She is also to refrain from sexual intercourse during the insemination period and to refrain from activities that may harm the fetus. If medical clauses are included in the agreement, what recourse do the intended parents have if the surrogate refuses to follow them? If she refuses the insemination, are any expenses refunded to the intended parents? If the surrogate chooses to have an abortion in the first trimester, which is legally her right, can the intended parents sue for expenses? Can they sue for damages if the surrogate decides to keep the child? Questions such as these have yet to receive clear answers from courts and legislatures.

(continued)

EXHIBIT 16-4 *(continued)*

VI. State Regulation

As indicated, states differ on how to handle surrogacy contracts:

- Some states are silent on the subject. No statutes exist and no cases have yet been litigated in the courts.

- Some states have outright bans on all commercial and noncommercial surrogacy agreements.

- Some states prohibit commercial surrogacy contracts but allow noncommercial ones.

- Some states prohibit separate fees to the surrogate beyond the expenses involved.

- Some states prohibit fees to a broker or intermediary.

- Some states allow surrogacy contracts, but closely regulate the process, including medical and psychological screening, home studies, the payment of fees, time periods within which the surrogate can change her mind, the identification of the legal parents, etc.

The National Conference of Commissioners on Uniform State Laws has drafted a Uniform Status of Children of Assisted Conception Act (later revised by the Uniform Parentage Act). The uniform act provides two alternatives for consideration by state legislatures: one to regulate surrogate agreements (Alternative A), and the other to ban the agreements (Alternative B).

Alternative A would allow surrogate contracts and provides a regulatory framework for their creation and enforcement. A court hearing would be held at which both parties would be required to submit medical evidence to prove that the would-be mother cannot bear her own child and that the surrogate mother is mentally and physically fit to bear the child. The proposal also would allow the surrogate mother to withdraw from the agreement up to 180 days into her pregnancy.

Alternative B, however, simply bans all surrogate agreements. It does not make any distinction between commercial and noncommercial agreements; all such contracts are void.

Source: Adapted from Dina Bennett, *Surrogate Parenting* (Background Paper 88-2 prepared for the Legislative Counsel Bureau of Nevada [1988]) (www.leg.state.nv.us/Division /Research/Publications/Bkground/BP88-02.pdf).

ASSIGNMENT 16.3

a. Should surrogacy contracts be banned? If not, what kind of regulation is needed? Do you favor the regulation in Alternative A of the Uniform Status of Children of Assisted Conception Act? Why?

b. Do you approve of an advertisement such as the following, placed in the classified section of the newspaper along with ads for accountants and truck drivers:

> CASH AVAILABLE NOW. Married or single women needed as surrogate mothers for couples unable to have children. Conception to be by artificial insemination. We pay well! Contact the Infertility Clinic today.

WHO IS THE LEGAL MOTHER?

When a surrogacy agreement comes apart, it is often because the surrogate mother changes her mind about turning over the baby to the person(s) who sought her services. The court must then decide who receives custody of the child based on a decision of who is the legal mother. There are three factors courts will consider in making this decision:

- *Genetics.* Who is biologically related to the child?
- *Gestation.* Who carried the child to its date of birth?
- *Intent.* Who intended to be the permanent parent of the child?

We begin our examination of these factors with the case of *Johnson v. Calvert.*

CASE

Johnson v. Calvert
5 Cal. 4th 84, 851 P.2d 776, 19 Cal. Rptr. 2d 494 (1993)
Supreme Court of California

Background: *This is a case of gestational surrogacy in which the sperm and egg of a couple are combined in vitro (IVF) in a laboratory and the resulting embryo is then implanted in a surrogate mother who carries the child to term. The surrogate mother gives birth to a child with whom she has no genetic relationship.*

Anna Johnson, a licensed vocational nurse, agreed to become a gestational surrogate. An embryo created by the sperm and egg of Mark and Crispina Calvert was implanted in Johnson. The agreement, however, fell apart while Johnson was still pregnant. Crispina Calvert and Anna Johnson filed separate actions to be declared the mother of the child who was eventually born. (Anna named the child Matthew; the Calverts named him Christopher.) The cases were consolidated. The trial court ruled that Mark and Crispina were the child's "genetic, biological and natural" father and mother. It called Anna a "genetic stranger" to the child. The court of Appeal affirmed. The case is now on appeal before the Supreme Court of California.

Decision on Appeal: *Judgment affirmed. In a gestational surrogacy contract, the natural mother of the child is the woman whose intent was to raise the child as her own. Only Crispina had this intent.*

OPINION OF THE COURT

Justice PANELLI delivered the opinion of the court.

In this case we address several of the legal questions raised by recent advances in reproductive technology. When, pursuant to a surrogacy agreement, a zygote formed of the gametes of a husband and wife is implanted in the uterus of another woman, who carries the resulting fetus to term and gives birth to a child not genetically related to her, who is the child's "natural mother" under California law?. . . And is such an agreement barred by any public policy of this state? We conclude that the husband and wife are the child's natural parents, and that this result does not offend . . . public policy.

Mark and Crispina Calvert are a married couple who desired to have a child. Crispina was forced to undergo a hysterectomy in 1984. Her ovaries remained capable of producing eggs, however, and the couple eventually considered surrogacy. In 1989 Anna Johnson heard about Crispina's plight from a coworker and offered to serve as a surrogate for the Calverts.

On January 15, 1990, Mark, Crispina, and Anna signed a contract providing that an embryo created by the sperm of Mark and the egg of Crispina would be implanted in Anna and the child born would be taken into Mark and Crispina's home "as their child." Anna agreed she would relinquish "all parental rights" to the child in favor of Mark and Crispina. In return, Mark and Crispina would pay Anna $10,000 in a series of installments, the last to be paid six weeks after the child's birth. Mark and Crispina were also to pay for a $200,000 life insurance policy on Anna's life. The zygote was implanted on January 19, 1990. Less than a month later, an ultrasound test confirmed Anna was pregnant.

Unfortunately, relations deteriorated between the two sides. Mark learned that Anna had not disclosed she had suffered several stillbirths and miscarriages. Anna felt Mark and Crispina did not do enough to obtain the required insurance policy. She also felt abandoned during an onset of premature labor in June. In July 1990, Anna sent Mark and Crispina a letter demanding the balance of the payments due her or else she would refuse to give up the child. The following month, Mark and Crispina responded with a lawsuit, seeking a declaration they were the legal parents of the unborn child. Anna filed her own action to be declared the mother of the child, and the two cases were eventually consolidated. . . .

The child was born on September 19, 1990, and blood samples were obtained from both Anna and the child for analysis. The blood test results excluded Anna as the genetic mother. The parties agreed to a court order providing that the child would remain with Mark and Crispina on a temporary basis with visits by Anna.

At trial in October 1990, the parties stipulated that Mark and Crispina were the child's genetic parents. After hearing evidence and arguments, the trial court ruled that Mark and Crispina were the child's "genetic, biological and natural" father and mother, that Anna had no "parental" rights to the child, and that the surrogacy contract was legal and enforceable against Anna's claims. The court also terminated the order allowing visitation. Anna appealed from the trial court's judgment. The Court of Appeal for the Fourth District, Division Three, affirmed. We granted review. . . .

[In California, there are two kinds of evidence that can be used to establish the existence of a parent-child relationship: evidence on who gave birth to the child, and genetic evidence derived from blood testing. Our statutes do not say what a court must do when the two kinds of evidence lead to conflicting results. There is] . . . undisputed evidence that Anna, not Crispina, gave birth to the child and that Crispina, not Anna, is genetically related to him. Both women thus have adduced evidence of a mother and child relationship. . . . Yet for any child California law recognizes only one natural mother, despite advances in reproductive technology rendering a different outcome biologically possible. . . .

[We decline to accept the contention of the American Civil Liberties Union (ACLU) that we should find the child has two mothers. Even though rising divorce rates have made multiple parent arrangements common in our society, we see no compelling reason to recognize such a situation here. The Calverts are the genetic and intending parents of their son and have provided him, by all accounts, with a stable, intact, and nurturing home. To recognize parental rights in a third party—Anna—with whom the Calvert family has had little contact since shortly after the child's birth would diminish Crispina's role as mother.]

Because two women each have presented acceptable proof of maternity, we do not believe this case can be decided without enquiring into the parties' intentions as manifested in the surrogacy agreement. Mark and Crispina are a couple who desired to have a child of their own genetic stock but are physically unable to do so without the help of reproductive technology. They affirmatively intended the birth of the child, and took the steps necessary to effect in vitro fertilization. But for their acted-on intention, the child would not exist. Anna agreed to facilitate the procreation of Mark's and Crispina's child. The parties' aim was to bring Mark's and Crispina's child into the world, not for Mark and Crispina to donate a zygote to Anna. Crispina from the outset intended to be the child's mother. Although the gestative function Anna performed was necessary to bring about the child's birth, it is safe to say that Anna would not have been given the opportunity to gestate or deliver the child had she, prior to implantation of the zygote, manifested her own intent to be the child's mother. No reason appears why Anna's later change of heart should vitiate the determination that Crispina is the child's natural mother.

We conclude that although [California law] recognizes both genetic consanguinity and giving birth as means of establishing a mother and child relationship, when the two means do not coincide in one woman, she who intended to procreate the child—that is, she who intended to bring about the birth of a child that she intended to raise as her own—is the natural mother under California law. . . .

Anna urges that surrogacy contracts violate several social policies. Relying on her contention that she is the child's legal, natural mother, she cites the public policy embodied in Penal Code section 273, prohibiting the payment for consent to adoptions of a child. She argues further that the policies underlying the adoption laws of this state are violated by the surrogacy contract because it in effect constitutes a prebirth waiver of her parental rights.

We disagree. Gestational surrogacy differs in crucial respects from adoption and so is not subject to the adoption statutes. The parties voluntarily agreed to participate in in vitro fertilization and related medical procedures before the child was conceived; at the time when Anna entered into the contract, therefore, she was not vulnerable to financial inducements to part with her own expected offspring. As discussed above, Anna was not the genetic mother of the child. The payments to Anna under the contract were meant to compensate her for her services in gestating the fetus and undergoing labor, rather than for giving up "parental" rights to the child. Payments were due both during the pregnancy and after the child's birth. We are, accordingly, unpersuaded that the contract used in this case violates the public policies embodied in . . . the adoption statutes. . . .

It has been suggested that gestational surrogacy may run afoul of prohibitions on involuntary servitude. (See U.S. Const.,

Amend. XIII.) Involuntary servitude has been recognized in cases of criminal punishment for refusal to work. (*Pollack v. Williams* (1944) 322 U.S. 4, 18; see, generally, 7 Witkin, *Summary of Cal. Law* (9th ed. 1988) Constitutional Law, §§ 411–414, pp. 591–596.) We see no potential for that evil in the contract at issue here, and extrinsic evidence of coercion or duress is utterly lacking. We note that although at one point the contract purports to give Mark and Crispina the sole right to determine whether to abort the pregnancy, at another point it acknowledges: "All parties understand that a pregnant woman has the absolute right to abort or not abort any fetus she is carrying. Any promise to the contrary is unenforceable." We therefore need not determine the validity of a surrogacy contract purporting to deprive the gestator of her freedom to terminate the pregnancy.

Finally, Anna and some commentators have expressed concern that surrogacy contracts tend to exploit or dehumanize women, especially women of lower economic status. Anna's objections center around the psychological harm she asserts may result from the gestator's relinquishing the child to whom she has given birth. Some have also cautioned that the practice of surrogacy may encourage society to view children as commodities, subject to trade at their parents' will.

We are all too aware that the proper forum for resolution of this issue is the Legislature, where empirical data, largely lacking from this record, can be studied and rules of general applicability developed. However, in light of our responsibility to decide this case, we have considered as best we can its possible consequences.

We are unpersuaded that gestational surrogacy arrangements are so likely to cause the untoward results Anna cites as to demand their invalidation on public policy grounds. Although common sense suggests that women of lesser means serve as surrogate mothers more often than do wealthy women, there has been no proof that surrogacy contracts exploit poor women to any greater degree than economic necessity in general exploits them by inducing them to accept lower-paid or otherwise undesirable employment. We are likewise unpersuaded by the claim that surrogacy will foster the attitude that children are mere commodities; no evidence is offered to support it. The limited data available seem to reflect an absence of significant adverse effects of surrogacy on all participants.

The argument that a woman cannot knowingly and intelligently agree to gestate and deliver a baby for intending parents carries overtones of the reasoning that for centuries prevented women from attaining equal economic rights and professional status under the law. To resurrect this view is both to foreclose a personal and economic choice on the part of the surrogate mother, and to deny intending parents what may be their only means of procreating a child of their own genetic stock. Certainly in the present case it cannot seriously be argued that Anna, a licensed vocational nurse who had done well in school and who had previously borne a child, lacked the intellectual wherewithal or life experience necessary to make an informed decision to enter into the surrogacy contract. . . .

The judgment of the Court of Appeal is affirmed.

ASSIGNMENT 16.4

a. Isn't it true that the child in the *Johnson* case has three parents, two of whom are mothers? Why couldn't there be a three-parent solution to this case?

b. Do you think a gestational mother can bond with her child prenatally? If so, would this be relevant to Anna Johnson's claim to be declared the natural or legal mother?

c. Do you think that a gestational mother makes a substantial or significant contribution to the birth of a child? If so, why not determine who the legal/natural parent is on the basis of whether it would be in the best interests of the child to be with the gestational mother or with the intended genetic mother? Since both have serious claims, why shouldn't the test be: Who would make the better parent?

d. Assume that Anna Johnson was genetically related to the baby because she used her own egg but that all of the other facts in the case are the same. Who would the legal mother be?

Belsito

Not all courts agree with the intent test used in the *Johnson* case. Similar facts arose in the Ohio case of *Belsito v. Clark*.[28] An embryo from the sperm and ovum of a husband and wife was transferred to a gestational mother (referred to in the opinion as the "surrogate host"). The wife asked the hospital to list her as the mother on the birth certificate. The hospital refused, telling her that the woman who gave birth to the child must be listed as the mother on the birth certificate. Furthermore, since the father was not married to the birth mother, the child would be considered illegitimate. The husband and wife then asked a court to declare them the genetic and natural parents of the child so that they could both be listed on the birth certificate as the natural parents of a legitimate child. (The birth mother was the wife's sister, who was not being compensated for carrying the child. Although the birth mother was related to the child as an aunt, she was not a "genetic provider.") The *Belsito* court was faced with the same questions as the *Johnson* court: Who is the mother of the child? The woman who provided the genetic link via the egg or the woman who gave birth? Although the *Belsito* court and the *Johnson* court both concluded that the woman who provided the genetic link is the legal mother, the *Belsito* court refused to use the intent test to reach its conclusion. The following excerpt from *Belsito v. Clark* explains the court's reasoning:

> In *Johnson v. Calvert* (1993), 851 P.2d 776, the facts are very similar to this case, with a married couple supplying the egg and sperm and a surrogate agreeing to carry and deliver the child. . . . The court in *Johnson* looked for the intent to procreate and to raise the child, in order to identify the natural mother. Since the genetic mother in *Johnson* intended to procreate, she was the natural parent. The *Johnson* Court discarded both genetics and birth as the primary means of identifying the natural maternal parent, and replaced both with a test that involves intent of the parties. . . .

> [We do not find the *Johnson* case] to be persuasive. . . . Intent can be difficult to prove. Even when the parties have a written agreement, disagreements as to intent can arise. In addition, in certain fact patterns when intent is clear, the *Johnson* test of intent to procreate and raise the child may bring about unacceptable results. As an example, who is the natural parent if both a nongenetic-providing surrogate and the female genetic provider agree that they both intend to procreate and raise the child? It is apparent that the *Johnson* test presents problems when applied. . . .

[In addition, it] has long been recognized that, as a matter of public policy, the state will not enforce or encourage private agreements or contracts to give up parental rights. . . . See *Matter of Baby M.* (1988), 109 N.J. 396, 537 A.2d 1227. . . . Through the intent to procreate, the *Johnson* case allows the nongenetic carrier/surrogate to be designated as the natural mother. The possibility of recognition as a parent means that a potential right is implicit in any agreement or contract to act as gestational surrogate. A surrogate who chooses not to be the natural parent forfeits her right to be considered the natural and legal parent. Because a fee is often involved in a surrogacy service, that assent amounts to selling a parental right, and is in contradiction to the public policy against private contracts to surrender parental rights.

[The intent test also conflicts with] the underlying public policy of adoption law. Adoption laws of Ohio have long required that a relinquishing natural mother be given an unpressured opportunity before a disinterested magistrate to surrender her parental rights. R.C. 3107.08. Considering the substantial rights involved, the possible financial pressures, and the value our society places on procreation, the need for such procedures is evident.

In addition to protecting the interest of the mother, adoption law has attempted to protect the interest of the child. By agreement or otherwise, the natural mother is not free to surrender her child to whomever she wishes. Through the use of its **parens patriae** powers, the state closely supervises the process, and ultimately selects or approves of the new parents. . . . The underlying public policy is to provide for the best interest of the child: to ensure that the abandoned child is not given to persons who will abuse or neglect the child, but will be placed in a home with caring and competent parents. . . .

The *Johnson* court's formulation of the intent-to-procreate test does not . . . provide a means to review and ensure the suitability of the gestational surrogate or her spouse as parents. In addition, because it is based on private agreement or intent that has not been sanctioned by a court proceeding, it raises the question of future legal challenges, and thus undermines the stability of the child-parent relationship. The *Johnson* intent formulation ignores those concerns and relies on the whims of private intent and agreement. It is, in effect, a private adoption process that is readily subject to all the defects and pressures of such a process. . . .

[T]here is abundant precedent for using the genetics test for identifying a natural parent. For the best interest of the child and society, there are strong arguments to recognize the genetic parent as the natural parent. The genetic parent can guide the child from experience through the strengths and weaknesses of a common ancestry of genetic traits. Because that test has served so well, it should remain the primary test for determining the natural parent, or parents, in nongenetic-providing surrogacy cases. . . . When dealing with a nongenetic-providing surrogate, such a rule minimizes or avoids the question of the surrogate selling her right to be determined the natural parent. . . . In addition, given the relative certainty of DNA blood testing, such a foundation or test for parental identity would be simpler to apply and more certain in results than a *Johnson*-type intent test. . . .

In conclusion, under Ohio law, when a child is delivered by a gestational surrogate who has been impregnated through the process of in vitro fertilization, the natural parents of the child shall be identified by a determination as to which individuals have provided the genetic imprint for that child. If the individuals who have been identified as the genetic parents have not relinquished or waived their rights to assume the legal status of natural parents, they shall be considered the natural and legal parents of that child.[29]

parens patriae
Parent of the country, referring to the state's role in protecting children and those under disability.

ASSIGNMENT 16.5

a. Which court is correct? The *Johnson* Court or the *Belsito* Court? Why?

b. Mary and Beverly are a lesbian couple. Each wants to give birth to and to raise a child together. Mary becomes pregnant and gives birth to a child whose genetic parents are an anonymous sperm donor and Beverly, who provided the egg that was implanted in Mary by IVF. Who should be declared the legal mother?

■ PARALEGAL ROLES

- For an overview of paralegal roles in family-law cases, see Exhibits 1-3 and 1-4 in Chapter 1.

- For many of the financial issues related to surrogacy covered in Chapter 16, a paralegal may be asked to help collect documents and facts outlined in:
  - the checklist in Exhibit 3-1 of Chapter 3
  - the interrogatories in Appendix C

- Miscellaneous duties
  - Help the client compile resources on assisted reproductive technology (ART), particularly in vitro fertilization (IVF).
  - Assist the attorney-intermediary in locating an egg donor or surrogate mother and in coordinating the transaction.
  - Help collect evidence of the parties' intentions when they froze the embryos that they did not use.
  - Obtain copies of agreements signed by egg donor, sperm donor, surrogate, and others involved in the fertility procedure.
  - Prepare a draft of the agreements that the attorney-intermediary will ask his/her clients to sign.
  - Research statutory and case law on surrogacy in the state.
  - Prepare adoption pleadings for the non-genetic parent who will be adopting the child given birth by the surrogate mother.

■ CHECK THE CITE

Gina is a surrogate mother who gives birth to a child pursuant to an agreement with Andrea and Peter, the biological parents. The court described the issue in the case as follows: "The novel issue presented in this surrogacy matter is whether or not a court may issue a pre-birth order directing a delivering physician to list the man and woman who provided the embryo carried by a third party as legal parents on a child's birth certificate."

How did the court resolve the issue and what was its reasoning? Read *A.H.W. v. G.H.B.*, 339 N.J. Super. 495, 772 A.2d 948 (N.J. Super. Ch., 2000). To read the opinion online, run a citation search ("772 A.2d 948") in the Legal documents database of Google Scholar (scholar.google.com). (Note that in New Jersey, a surrogate mother is a person who uses her own egg as opposed to a surrogate who is not genetically related to the child.)

■ PROJECT

In Google, Bing, or Yahoo, run the following search: aa surrogate mother (substitute the name of your state for aa in the search). Write a short essay in which you describe the law governing surrogacy in your state. Cover what is legal and what is illegal. Explain the regulations governing this area of fertility. You must cite and quote from a minimum of eight different sources that you find on the Internet. At least four of these sources should be statutes, court opinions, or other laws. (If your state bans all surrogacy agreements, do this project on a neighboring state that does not ban them.)

■ ETHICS IN A FAMILY LAW PRACTICE

You are a paralegal working at the law office of Franklin & Franklin. One of the clients at the office is a biotechnology company. When you learn that the company is about to announce the discovery of a new fertility drug, you buy 1,000 shares of its stock. Any ethical problems?

■ WRITING SAMPLE

You work for a law office where one of the clients is a married couple who have asked a woman to be the surrogate mother of their child. The surrogate will be a gestational mother, using an embryo from the egg and sperm of the married couple. The surrogate mother is the first cousin of the wife. Prepare a draft of the surrogacy agreement that the married couple and the surrogate will be asked to sign. (See General Instructions for the Writing Sample in Appendix A.)

SUMMARY

Infertility is the inability to conceive a child, and more specifically, the failure of a couple to conceive in over a year in spite of having sexual relations without contraceptives. A major method of treatment for infertility is assisted reproductive technology (ART), in which eggs are removed from a woman's ovaries and combined with sperm in the laboratory to help a woman become pregnant. Fertility clinics performing ART must report their success rate to the Centers for Disease Control and Prevention. A major ART is in vitro fertilization (IVF), which involves surgically removing a woman's eggs from the ovaries, fertilizing the eggs with sperm (in the laboratory), and transferring the resulting embryos (or preembryos) into the uterus through the cervix. Some women undergoing IVF use an egg donor. Many states either ban egg donation for research or place significant limitations on such use. Other ART methods include gamete intrafallopian transfer (GIFT), zygote intrafallopian transfer (ZIFT), and embryo transplant.

Using cryopreservation, embryos from an ART cycle can be frozen for potential use at a later time. States do not agree on what to do with unused frozen embryos after a couple divorces or separates. Louisiana will not allow the embryos to be destroyed. Other states will try to abide by the contract the couple signed regarding what to do with the frozen embryos. If there is no such contract, Tennessee gives preference to the party who wants to avoid procreation unless the other party does not have a reasonable chance of procreating without the frozen embryos. Massachusetts is reluctant to enforce any agreement that has the effect of compelling someone to be a parent against his or her will. Posthumous reproduction is the conception of a child after the death

of one or both of its genetic parents. A child born after the death of its genetic parent can inherit from that parent if there is sufficient proof that the deceased expressed a desire or intent to be a parent before the death.

Stem cells in human embryos hold great promise for medical research. The country is divided, however, on the ethical and legal propriety of destroying embryos in order to extract such cells. The Dickey-Wicker Amendment prohibits federal funding for "research in which a human embryo or embryos are destroyed." State and private funding may provide alternative resources for research prohibited by the amendment.

Under a surrogacy contract, a pregnant woman enters a contract to become pregnant, to give birth to a child, and then to relinquish all parental rights to the couple who hired her services. Brokers are often used to bring the parties together and to coordinate the arrangement. If the surrogate supplies the egg, she is genetically related to the child; she is the genetic mother. This is called traditional surrogacy. If the surrogate carries an embryo that was formed from the egg of another woman, the surrogate is not genetically related to the child. This is called gestational surrogacy. States have different laws on surrogacy contracts. Some states ban them; other states permit them, but regulate how they are created and enforced.

Courts must sometimes determine who is the legal mother of a child when the surrogate mother refuses to give the child to the intended parents. Some courts say that the legal mother is the woman who had the intent to procreate and to raise the child even if she has no genetic link to the child. Other courts say that the legal mother is the woman who has the genetic link to the child.

KEY TERMS

infertility	cryopreservation	intended parent
assisted reproductive technology (ART)	property division	traditional surrogacy
in vitro fertilization (IVF)	surrogacy	gestational surrogacy
artificial insemination (AI)	surrogate mother	parens patriae
first impression	termination of parental rights (TPR)	

REVIEW QUESTIONS

1. What is infertility? What are the major causes of infertility, and how many people suffer from it?

2. What is assisted reproductive technology (ART)?

3. What are some of the major ART methods?

4. What does the Fertility Clinic Success Rate and Certification Act require?

5. What is in vitro fertilization (IVF)?

6. What is an egg donor?

7. What risks does an egg donor face?

8. Can eggs be donated for purposes of research?

9. What is cryopreservation?

10. How do different states resolve a dispute between a divorcing couple on what to do with unused frozen embryos (or preembryos)?

11. In what ways can a child be born after the death of one or both of the child's genetic parents?

12. When can a posthumously conceived child inherit from his or her deceased parent?

13. What are the two main sources of embryos from which stem cells can be extracted?

14. What is the controversy over stem-cell research?

15. What does the Dickey-Wicker Amendment provide?

16. What is a surrogate mother?

17. What does a surrogate agreement or contract contain?

18. What is the distinction between a genetic mother and a gestational mother?

19. What is the distinction between traditional and gestational surrogacy?

20. Who is an intended parent?

21. What was the controversy involving Baby M, and how was it resolved?

22. What is the role of a broker in a surrogacy contract?

23. What are the policy reasons for and against surrogacy agreements?

24. What is the relationship between surrogacy and adoption law?

25. What is the relationship between surrogacy and paternity law?

26. What is the relationship between surrogacy and child-custody law?

27. What is the relationship between surrogacy and contract law?

28. How have different states regulated surrogacy agreements?

29. How do different states determine who is the legal mother when the surrogate mother refuses to give the child to the intended parents?

HELPFUL WEBSITES

Fertility Law and Ethics

- www.fertilitytoday.org/fertility_law_ethics.html
- www.ihr.com/infertility/articles/legal_rights.html
- www.ivf-infertility.com/ivf/standard/regulations.php

American Fertility Association

- www.theafa.org

National Infertility Association

- www.resolve.org

Surrogacy

- www.creatingfamilies.com
- www.selectsurrogate.com/surrogacy-laws-by-state.html
- www.creatingfamilies.com/home/surrogacy_law.aspx
- www.surrogacy-surrogate-mother.com /surrogacy-statistics.html
- www.councilforresponsiblegenetics.org /pagedocuments/kaevej0a1m.pdf

Gestational Surrogacy Agreement

- www.allaboutsurrogacy.com/sample_contracts /GScontract2.htm

Traditional Surrogacy Agreement

- www.allaboutsurrogacy.com/sample_contracts /contracts.htm

Women's Health

- www.womenshealth.gov

National Embryo Adoption Center

- www.embryodonation.org

Google/Bing/Yahoo Searches

(on these search engines, run the following searches, substituting your state for "aa")

- infertility aa
- paternity adoption aa
- cryopreservation baby
- "surrogate mother" aa
- "natural mother" aa
- "assisted reproductive technology" aa
- "in vitro fertilization" aa
- surrogacy aa
- "legal mother" aa
- "intended parent" aa

ENDNOTES

Note: All or most of the court opinions in these endnotes can be read online. To do so, go to Google Scholar (scholar .google.com), select "Legal documents," and in the search box, enter the cite (e.g., "173 S.W.3d 714") or name of the case (e.g., "In re C.K.G.") that is given in the endnote.

[1] *In re C.K.G.*, 173 S.W.3d 714, 721 (Tenn. 2005).

[2] Mayo Clinic, *Infertility Causes* (www.mayoclinic.com/health /infertility/DS00310/DSECTION=causes).

[3] Centers for Disease Control and Prevention, *2002 National Survey of Family Growth* (www.cdc.gov/art/ART2008/faq .htm#1).

[4] Magdalina Gugucheva, *Surrogacy in America 26* (Council for Responsible Genetics, 2010) (www .councilforresponsiblegenetics.org/pagedocuments /kaevej0a1m.pdf).

[5] 42 U.S.C. § 263a-1 (wwwn.cdc.gov/dls/art/fcsrca.aspx) (www.cdc.gov/art).

[6] Sheryl Gay Stolberg, *For the Infertile, a High-Tech Treadmill* N.Y. Times, Dec. 14, 1997 (www.nytimes.com /1997/12/14/us/for-the-infertile-a-high-tech-treadmill .html).

[7] Howard Jones, *And Just What Is a Pre-Embryo?*, 52 Fertility & Sterility 189, 190 (1989).

[8] Glen Cohen and Daniel Chen, *Trading-Off Reproductive Technology and Adoption*, 95 Minnesota Law Review 485, 486 (2010).

[9] *A.Z. v. B.Z.*, 725 N.E.2d 1051, 1053 (Mass. 2000).

[10] Roni Rabin, *As Demand for Donor Eggs Soars, High Prices Stir Ethical Concerns*, N.Y. Times, May 15, 2007 (www.nytimes .com/2007/05/15/health/15cons.html).

[11] *How Many Frozen Human Embryos Are Available for Research?* (Society for Assisted Reproductive Technology and Rand, 2003) (www.rand.org/pubs/research_briefs/RB9038/index1.html).

[12] 842 S.W.2d 588 (Tenn. 1992).

[13] Louisiana Statutes Annotated §§ 9-129 to 9-131 (2008).

[14] Florida Statutes Annotated § 742.17 (1993).

[15] *Kass v. Kass*, 91 N.Y.2d 554, 696 N.E.2d 174, 673 N.Y.S.2d 350 (1998).

[16] *A.Z. v. B.Z.*, 725 N.E.2d 1051, 1057-58 (Mass. 2000).

[17] Sarah Hall, *Whites Have Black Twins in In-Vitro Mix-Up*, N.Y. Times, Jul. 9, 2002 (www.nytimes.com/2002/07/09 /world/whites-have-black-twins-in-in-vitro-mix-up.html).

[18] Lori Andrews, *The Sperminator*, N.Y. Times, Mar. 28, 1999 (www3.sympatico.ca/cogito/Gr11/sperminator.html).

[19] Balanced Budget Downpayment Act, Pub. L. No. 104-99, § 128, 110 Stat. 26, 34 (1996).

[20] *Genesis* 16:1–2 (NIV).

[21] Magdalina Gugucheva, *Surrogacy in America 7* (Council for Responsible Genetics, 2010) (www .councilforresponsiblegenetics.org/pagedocuments /kaevej0a1m.pdf).

[22] Id at 26.

[23] N.Y. Domestic Relations Law § 122 (codes.lp.findlaw.com /nycode/DOM/8/122).

[24] Gina Kolata, *When Grandmother Is the Mother, Until Birth*, N.Y. Times, Aug. 5, 1991.

[25] Ginia Bellafante, *Google Baby: Surrogate Pregnancy Becomes Global*, N.Y. Times, Jun. 15, 2010 (www.nytimes .com/2010/06/16/arts/television/16google.html).

[26] *In the Matter of Baby M*, 109 N.J. 396, 537 A.2d 1227 (1988).

[27] Richard Roe, *Childbearing by Contract 4* (Wisconsin Legislative Bureau, Mar. 1988).

[28] 644 N.E.2d 760 (Ohio C.P. 1994).

[29] Id. at 764–67.

Torts and Family Law

CHAPTER OUTLINE

CHAPTER OBJECTIVES

After completing this chapter, you should be able to:

- State the relationship between marital torts and no-fault divorce.

- Define intrafamily tort.

- List the two major intrafamily tort immunities.

- Explain why the legal system has historically disfavored intrafamily torts.

- List the major categories of harm and the categories of torts that can cause that harm.

- List the different ways that states treat spouse-against-spouse torts for property damage or interference and for personal harm.

- List the different ways that states treat torts brought by children against their parents for property damage or interference and for personal harm.

- State the rules on immunity in torts among family members other than among spouses and children.

- Explain the nature of sexual torts between spouses.

- Know why some states do not want marital torts to be brought in a divorce action.

- Explain when prenatal torts can be brought.

- Define wrongful life, birth, and pregnancy.

- Understand why suits for wrongful life are disfavored.

- Explain when an action for wrongful adoption can be brought.

- Describe the different kinds of consortium and when suits for

- their interference or loss can be brought.

- Understand the objective of an action for loss of services.

- Define heart-balm actions and list the major ones that have existed.

- Distinguish between vicarious liability and independent liability.

- Explain the extent of vicarious liability of parents for the torts of their child.

- Explain the family-purpose doctrine.

- Distinguish between negligent supervision and negligent entrustment.

- List examples of intrafamily crimes.

tort

A civil wrong (other than a breach of contract) that causes injury or other loss for which our legal system deems it just to provide a remedy such as damages. Injury or loss can be to the person (a personal tort), to movable property (a personal property tort), or to land and anything attached to the land (a real property tort).

no-fault divorce

A divorce that is granted without having to prove marital wrongs that caused the break-up.

intrafamily tort

A tort committed by one family member against another.

marital tort

A tort that one spouse commits against another. Also called domestic tort.

immunity

A defense that prevents someone from being sued for what would otherwise be wrongful conduct.

liability insurance

Insurance in which the insurer agrees to pay damages that an insured is obligated to pay to a third person because of a legal liability that the insured owes the third person for committing a tort or other wrong covered by the insurance policy.

at common law

During a time in our early history when law was created by court opinions and legislatures, often before it was changed by later legislatures.

INTRODUCTION

A **tort** is a civil wrong (other than a breach of contract) that causes injury or other loss for which our legal system deems it just to provide a remedy such as damages. Injury or loss can be to the person (a personal tort), to movable property (a personal property tort), or to land and anything attached to the land (a real property tort).

Tort law is becoming increasingly important in the practice of family law. In North Carolina, for example, a litigation attorney estimates that over 200 cases a year are filed for *alienation of affections,* a tort we will examine in this chapter. The typical alienation case involves an ex-wife who sues "the other woman" for enticing her husband into having an affair, thereby destroying (alienating) his affections for the wife. In a recent case, the jury returned a verdict of $9 million against the husband's mistress.[1]

Also, more and more courts are allowing spouses to sue each other for torts committed during the marriage. Some states allow tort claims to be brought in the divorce action. In a world of **no-fault divorce**, this has the effect of reintroducing concepts of fault and blame, which are central to the resolution of most tort claims.

There are two main categories of tort cases that we need to consider: those in which spouses or other family members bring tort actions against each other (intrafamily torts) and those in which one or both spouses sue someone else for a tort that has seriously harmed the family.

INTRAFAMILY TORTS AND IMMUNITY

An **intrafamily tort** is a tort committed by one family member against another. A major category of intrafamily tort is the **marital tort**, which is a tort that one spouse commits against another. Some intrafamily torts, however, cannot be brought; an **immunity** exists for such torts. An immunity is a defense that prevents someone from being sued for what would otherwise be wrongful conduct. In this area of family law, the main kinds of immunity are:

- *Interspousal immunity.* Under this immunity, a spouse cannot sue his or her spouse for designated torts.
- *Parental immunity.* Under this immunity, children and parents cannot sue each other for designated torts.

Historically, courts have been reluctant to allow family members to sue each other for certain torts. This reluctance is based on several factors. First was the theory that family harmony would be threatened if members knew that they could sue each other in tort. Second, if the family carries a policy of **liability insurance**, there is a fear that family members will fraudulently try to collect under the policy by fabricating tort actions against each other. When the insurance company pays the tort claim, the payment might go into the same house where both plaintiff and defendant live, thereby allowing both to benefit by the payment. (Note, however, that insurance policies often have a *family exclusion clause* that denies liability coverage among family members living in the same household.) Third, **at common law**, husbands and wives could not sue each other because a husband and wife were considered to be one person, and that one person was the husband. Therefore, to allow a suit between spouses would theoretically amount to one person suing himself and any damages from the suit would be paid and received by the same person—the husband.

In modern times, many, but not all, of the immunities have been abolished. To understand current law, we need to distinguish between (1) personal injury and (2) property damage or property interference. We also need to know what kind of tort caused the injury, damage, or interference.

- *Personal injury.* The main personal injury that can be committed is to one's body. The tort causing this injury (1) can be an **intentional tort** (e.g., **battery**, such as by intentionally knocking someone to the ground in an argument) or (2) it can be the tort of **negligence** (e.g., carelessly colliding with someone).

- *Property damage or interference.* The damage or interference can be to a person's **real property** or one's **personal property**. The tort causing this damage or interference can be (1) an intentional tort (e.g., **conversion**, such as by taking someone's money without permission) or (2) the tort of negligence (e.g., losing someone's money by carelessly investing it).

There is considerable diversity among the states as to when an immunity will bar a suit for these different kinds of torts. The existence of an immunity will depend on:

- the kind of harm the family member caused
- the kind of tort that caused the harm
- who the victim of the tort is and
- if a child is involved, whether the child is **emancipated** or **unemancipated.**

See Exhibit 17-1.

intentional tort
A tort in which a person either desired to bring about the result or knew with substantial certainty that the result would follow from what the person did or failed to do.

battery
An unpermitted and intentional physical contact with a person that is harmful or offensive.

negligence
The failure to use reasonable care that an ordinary prudent person would have used in a similar situation, resulting in injury or other loss.

real property
Land and anything attached or affixed to the land, such as buildings, fences, and trees. Also called real estate.

personal property
Property other than land or other than things attached to the land. Also called chattels.

conversion
An intentional interference with another's personal property, consisting of an exercise of dominion over it. (See glossary for an additional meaning.)

emancipated
Legally independent of one's parent or legal guardian. The noun is *emancipation.*

unemancipated
Legally dependent on one's parent or legal guardian.

EXHIBIT 17-1 Intrafamily Torts and Immunities

SPOUSE AGAINST SPOUSE

A. Property Damage or Interference

- In most states, spouses can sue each other for intentional torts and for negligence covering damage or substantial interference with the other spouse's personal property or real property. Intrafamily immunity has been abolished for all torts causing property damage or interference in these states.

B. Personal Injury

- In some states, spouses can sue each other for personal injury caused by intentional torts or by negligence. Intrafamily immunity has been abolished for all torts causing personal injury in these states. (The most common torts for personal injury are those growing out of domestic violence such as battery and intentional infliction of emotional distress.)

- In some states, spouses cannot sue each other for personal injury caused by intentional torts or by negligence.

- In some states, spouses can sue each other for personal injury caused by intentional torts but not if the injury was caused by negligence.

- In some states, if the tort is covered by liability insurance, spouses can sue each other for personal injury caused by intentional torts or by negligence.

CHILD AGAINST PARENT(S)

A. Property Damage or Interference

- In all states, a child can sue his or her parent for intentional torts and for negligence covering damage or substantial interference with the child's personal property or real property. Intrafamily immunity has been abolished for all such property torts in all states. This is so whether the child is unemancipated or emancipated.

(continued)

EXHIBIT 17-1 *(continued)*

B. Personal Injury

- In some states, an unemancipated child can sue a parent for personal injury caused by intentional torts or by negligence except if the tort arises out of the parent's exercise of discipline over the child. (Parents have a privilege to exercise discipline in raising their children, which includes the use of nonexcessive corporal punishment.)
- In many states, an unemancipated child cannot sue a parent for personal injury caused by intentional torts or by negligence.
- In some states, an unemancipated child can sue a parent for personal injury caused by intentional torts but not if the injury was caused by negligence.
- In all states, an emancipated child can sue a parent for personal injury caused by intentional torts or by negligence.

OTHER RELATED PERSONS

Property Damage or Interference and Personal Injury

No intrafamily immunity exists for other related persons. Brothers and sisters, aunts and uncles, grandparents and grandchildren, and other relatives can sue each other for intentional torts and for negligence that cause property damage or interference or personal injury. The restrictions imposed on spouse suits and child suits do not apply to tort actions involving other relatives.

© Cengage Learning 2013

ASSIGNMENT 17.1

A husband in your state intentionally kills his wife and son. Can the estate of the wife bring a tort action against him for wrongful death? Can the estate of the son bring a tort action for wrongful death against his father? (See General Instructions for the State-Code Assignment and General Instructions for the Court-Opinion Assignment in Appendix A.)

SEXUAL TORTS

In every state, unmarried persons can sue each other for negligence in transmitting a venereal disease by carelessly failing to disclose the disease to his or her sexual partner or for fraud if false statements of fact were made (e.g., "I am clean") to induce a partner to engage in sexual relations. Can spouses sue each other for the same torts? Yes, if their state allows suits for personal injury between spouses—if the interspousal immunity does not apply (see Exhibit 17-1). In such states, one spouse, for example, can sue another for failing to disclose the presence of a venereal disease, which was passed on to the victimized spouse. According to the *Restatement (Second) of Torts*, "A husband or wife who fraudulently conceals from the other a physical condition that makes cohabitation dangerous to the health of the other spouse is subject to liability to the other spouse for the harm suffered as a result."[2] Similarly, where marital rape is illegal (see Chapter 12), the spouse-rapist can be sued for the torts of battery or **intentional infliction of emotional distress**.

intentional infliction of emotional distress
Intentionally causing severe emotional distress by extreme or outrageous conduct.

TORT CLAIMS BROUGHT WITHIN A DIVORCE ACTION

Spouses who commit torts against each other often end up in a divorce. When a state allows one soon-to-be ex-spouse to bring a tort action against another, can the tort action be brought in the divorce action or must the tort be brought in a separate action? Not all states answer this question in the same way. Some states are against allowing torts to be asserted in the divorce action because most marital torts are based on marital fault and introducing evidence of such fault is inconsistent with the reason no-fault divorce was created. Other states, however, take the view that it would be a waste of time and a needless expense to require two separate suits, one for the divorce and another for the tort.

In the following case, *Hakkila v. Hakkila*, a wife was allowed to bring a tort action in a divorce case. The tort was intentional infliction of emotional distress (also called the tort of *outrage*). Yet the extreme reluctance of the court to rule for the wife demonstrates the great disfavor that many courts have about allowing tort actions between spouses, even when they are about to end their marriage in divorce.

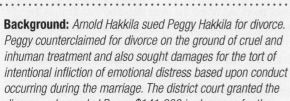

CASE

Hakkila v. Hakkila
112 N.M. 172, 812 P.2d 1320 (1991)
Court of Appeals of New Mexico

Background: *Arnold Hakkila sued Peggy Hakkila for divorce. Peggy counterclaimed for divorce on the ground of cruel and inhuman treatment and also sought damages for the tort of intentional infliction of emotional distress based upon conduct occurring during the marriage. The district court granted the divorce and awarded Peggy $141,000 in damages for the tort. The case is now on appeal before the Court of Appeals of New Mexico.*

Decision on Appeal: *Reversed. Although the tort action between the spouses will be allowed, the husband's insults and outbursts during the ten-year marriage were insufficiently outrageous to establish liability for intentional infliction of emotional distress.*

OPINION OF THE COURT

Justice HARTZ delivered the opinion of the court. . . .

Husband and wife were married on October 29, 1975. Each had been married before. They permanently separated in February 1985. Husband filed his petition for dissolution of marriage the following month. Husband, who holds a Ph.D. in chemistry, had been employed at Los Alamos National Laboratory throughout the marriage. Wife, a high school graduate with credit hours toward a baccalaureate degree in chemistry and a vocational degree as a chemical technician, had been employed at the laboratory as a secretary for seven years and as a chemical technician for about seven and one-half years. She voluntarily terminated her employment in December 1979.

The district court found that "[wife's] emotional and mental health, especially since the parties' separation, has been shown to have been characterized by acute depression and one psychotic episode." The district court's findings noted conflicting testimony concerning wife's past and current mental condition. The district court summarized one psychologist's testimony as diagnosing wife "as subject to a borderline personality disorder pre-dating the parties' marriage," and summarized another's as diagnosing her as "an intellectualizing personality in the early years of her marriage and as suffering from acute depression since approximately 1981." Apparently all the experts agreed that wife was temporarily emotionally disabled at the time of the hearing.

Finding No. 22 summarized husband's intentional misconduct: The manner in which [husband] treated [wife] during the marriage and which resulted in her disability and impairment is as follows. [Husband] on occasions throughout the marriage and continuing until the separation[:] **a.** assaulted and battered [wife,] **b.** insulted [wife] in the presence of guests, friends, relatives, and foreign dignitaries, **c.** screamed at [wife] at home and in the presence of others, **d.** on one occasion locked [wife] out of the residence overnight in the dead of winter while she had nothing on but a robe, **e.** made repeated demeaning remarks regarding [wife's] sexuality, **f.** continuously stated to [wife] that she was crazy, insane, and incompetent, **g.** refused to allow [wife] to pursue schooling and hobbies, **h.** refused to participate in normal marital relationship with [wife] which ultimately resulted in only having sexual relations with [wife] on four occasions in the last three years of the marriage, **i.** blamed his sexual inadequacies upon [wife]. Finding No. 26 stated: [Husband's] acts in intentionally inflicting severe emotional distress upon [wife] was so outrageous in character and so extreme in degree as to be beyond all possible bounds of decency and were atrocious and utterly intolerable. . . . With respect to each of the matters listed by the district court in Finding No. 22, the record shows:

a. There was evidence of several incidents of assault and battery. In late 1984 when wife was pushing her finger in husband's chest, he grabbed her wrist and twisted it severely. In 1981 during an argument in their home husband grabbed wife and threw her face down across the room, into a pot full of dirt. In 1978 when wife was putting groceries in the camper, husband slammed part of the camper shell down on her head and the trunk lid on her hands. In 1976 and "sometimes thereafter" during consensual sexual intercourse husband would use excessive force in attempting to stimulate wife with his hands.

b. The one incident in which husband insulted wife in the presence of others was at a friend's Christmas party. At about 11:00 p.m. wife approached husband, who was "weaving back and forth with his hands in his pockets,"

(continued)

CASE • Hakkila v. Hakkila (continued)

and suggested that they go home. Husband began screaming, "You f_____ bitch, leave me alone." Wife excused herself and walked home alone.

c. Wife also testified that when she and husband were home alone he would go into rages and scream at her. There was no evidence of his screaming at her in the presence of others except for the incident described in "b."

d. The locking-out incident occurred after husband returned from a trip. Wife had been at a friend's home where she had eaten dinner and had some wine. During an argument that had ensued when he returned, she grabbed his shirt and popped all the buttons off. She went downstairs and stepped outside. He closed and locked the door. She went across the street to a home of neighbors, who let her in. He then threw his clothes into a camper and drove off for the night. When he returned the next morning, they made up and made love.

e. On several occasions husband told wife that "you prefer women to men." He did not use the word "lesbian." He testified that he meant only that wife preferred the company of other women to his company. She did not testify that his remarks had sexual connotations.

f. Throughout the marriage husband made remarks such as, "You're just plain sick, you're just stupid, you're just insane."

g. With respect to the finding that husband "refused to allow [wife] to pursue schooling and hobbies," husband's brief-in-chief contends that no evidence supports the finding. Wife's answer brief does not respond to the contention, so we will not consider that finding as support for the judgment.

h., i. With respect to the final two items in the finding, husband acknowledges that their sexual relationship atrophied and that wife testified that (1) it was his decision not to engage in sexual relations more frequently, and (2) he blamed her for their poor sexual relationship.

Should We Recognize the Tort of Intentional Infliction of Emotional Distress in the Marital Context?

Husband argues that as a matter of public policy one spouse should have no cause of action against the other spouse for intentional infliction of emotional distress. . . . We reject, at least for the time being, husband's suggestion. Nevertheless, the policy grounds opposing recognition of the tort in this context counsel caution in permitting lawsuits of this nature. . . .

The tort (also known as the tort of "outrage") is described in *Restatement (Second) of Torts* Section 46 (1965) (the *Restatement*): Outrageous Conduct Causing Severe Emotional Distress. (1) One who by extreme and outrageous conduct intentionally or recklessly causes severe emotional distress

to another is subject to liability for such emotional distress, and if bodily harm to the other results from it, for such bodily harm. . . .

Wife contends that we must recognize the tort when committed by one spouse against the other because New Mexico has abandoned immunity for interspousal torts. . . . Yet the abolition of immunity does not mean that the existence of the marriage must be ignored in determining the scope of liability. After explaining the reasons for abolition of interspousal immunity, the commentary to *Restatement* Section 895F points out: The intimacy of the family relationship may . . . involve some relaxation in the application of the concept of reasonable care, particularly in the confines of the home. Thus, if one spouse in undressing leaves shoes out where the other stumbles over them in the dark, or if one spouse spills coffee on the other while they are both still sleepy, this may well be treated as not negligence. Id., comment h. The comment refers to Section 895G comment k, which explains that despite abolition of parental immunity: The intimacies of family life also involve intended physical contacts that would be actionable between strangers but may be commonplace and expected within the family. Family romping, even roughhouse play and momentary flares of temper not producing serious hurt, may be normal in many households, to the point that the privilege arising from consent becomes analogous.

Thus, the family relationship can be an important consideration in analyzing intrafamilial torts, both negligent and intentional. Despite the abolition of interspousal immunity, we must still evaluate wife's claims in light of the marital context in which they arose. . . .

Conduct intentionally or recklessly causing emotional distress to one's spouse is prevalent in our society. This is unfortunate but perhaps not surprising, given the length and intensity of the marital relationship. Yet even when the conduct of feuding spouses is not particularly unusual, high emotions can readily cause an offended spouse to view the other's misconduct as "extreme and outrageous." Thus, if the tort of outrage is construed loosely or broadly, claims of outrage may be tacked on in typical marital disputes, taxing judicial resources.

In addition, a spouse's most distressing conduct is likely to be privileged. Partners who are pledged to live together for a lifetime have a right to criticize each other's behavior. Cf. Cole, *Intentional Infliction of Emotional Distress Among Family Members,* 61 Denver U.L. Rev. 553, 574 (1984) ("Because the family's functioning depends on open and free communication, even negative give and take is necessary."). Even though one may question the utility of such comments, spouses are also free to express negative opinions of one another. "You look awful" or even "I don't love you" can be very wounding, but these statements cannot justify liability. See *Restatement* § 46 illustration 13 (you look "like a hippopotamus").

Not only should intramarital activity ordinarily not be the basis for tort liability, it should also be protected against disclosure in tort litigation. Although the spouse who raises a claim of outrage has no right to complain of the exposure of matters relevant to the claim, courts must be sensitive to the privacy interests of the defending spouse. Any litigation of a claim is certain to require exposure of the intimacies of married life. This feature of the tort distinguishes it from intramarital torts already recognized in New Mexico. For example, a suit by one spouse against another arising out of an automobile accident poses no such risk. Nor does one ordinarily think of exposure of an incident of battery as implicating legitimate privacy interests. In contrast, in this case the judge found that it was extreme and outrageous conduct for husband to refuse sexual relations with wife. Should we really use this tort as a basis for inquiry into a matter of such intimacy? Cf. *Thompson v. Chapman,* 93 N.M. 356, 600 P.2d 302 (Ct. App. 1979) (actions for alienation of affections engender more harm than good). In determining the scope of the tort of outrage in the marital context, it is necessary to consider the privacy interests of the accused spouse.

Moreover, largely because so much interspousal communication is privileged (not in the evidentiary sense, but in the sense that it cannot be the basis for liability), a reliable determination of causation is difficult if not impossible when outrage is alleged in this context. The connection between the outrageousness of the conduct of one spouse and the severe emotional distress of the other will likely be obscure. Although the victim spouse may well be suffering severe emotional distress, was it caused by the outrageousness of the conduct or by the implied (and privileged) message of antipathy? What could be more devastating to one's spouse than to say, "I don't love you any more"—a statement that could not form the basis for a cause of action? Rejection alone can create severe emotional distress. Suicides by jilted lovers are legion. Every adult knows individuals who have sunk into disabling depression when a spouse seeks divorce. As a result, litigation of an interspousal claim of outrage could easily degenerate into a battle of self-proclaimed experts performing psychological autopsies to "discover" whether the cause of the emotional distress was some particular despicable conduct or simply rejection by a loved one. Of course, no such problem arises in the context of previously recognized intramarital torts. If one spouse commits battery on another or causes an accident by driving negligently, the injuries to the other spouse can readily be tied to the tortious conduct. . . .

A cautious approach to the tort of intramarital outrage also finds support in the public policy of New Mexico to avoid inquiry into what went wrong in a marriage. New Mexico was the first state to provide for no-fault divorce on the ground of incompatibility. See NMSA 1978, § 40–4–1(A). New Mexico apportions community property without regard to fault, and grants alimony without consideration of punishment to either spouse.

In addition, although the tort has not been formally abolished, our courts have expressed dissatisfaction with the tort of alienation of affection, which has features similar to the tort of outrage in the marital context. . . .

Consequently, in determining when the tort of outrage should be recognized in the marital setting, the threshold of outrageousness should be set high enough—or the circumstances in which the tort is recognized should be described precisely enough, e.g., child snatching—that the social good from recognizing the tort will not be outweighed by unseemly and invasive litigation of meritless claims. . . .

Thus far, however, New Mexico has not witnessed an onslaught of claims of outrage by one spouse against the other. There is no need at this time to adopt husband's recommendation that all such claims be barred.

We now move to the specifics of the case before us. The merits of wife's claim can be disposed of summarily. Husband's insults and outbursts fail to meet the legal standard of outrageousness. See, e.g., *Sanders v. Lutz,* 109 N.M. 193, 196, 784 P.2d 12, 15 (1989) (to recover, must show conduct was "'beyond all possible bounds of decency . . . and utterly intolerable'"). He was privileged to refrain from intercourse. There was no evidence that the other conduct caused severe emotional distress, as opposed to transient pain or discomfort. See *Restatement* § 46. . . .

Indeed, this case illustrates the risk of opening the door too wide to claims of this nature. Despite the claim's lack of merit, husband was subjected to a six-day trial, to say nothing of discovery and other preparation, surveying the rights and wrongs of a ten-year marriage. Motions for summary judgment should be viewed sympathetically in similar cases. If the potential harms from this kind of litigation are too frequently realized, it may be necessary to reconsider husband's suggestion that the tort of outrage be denied in the interspousal context.

We reverse the decision in favor of wife on her claim of intentional infliction of emotional distress.

ASSIGNMENT 17.2

If you were the judge, how would you have decided *Hakkila v. Hakkila*? Does the court suggest that the *husband* was a victim? Do you think he was?

PRENATAL TORTS

prenatal tort
A tort committed against a fetus.

It is possible to commit a tort against a fetus—a **prenatal tort**.

Mary is pregnant. While on the freeway one day, Tom negligently drives his car into Mary's car. The impact causes a head injury to the unborn child that Mary is carrying.

Mary, of course, can sue for her own injuries and for damage to her car caused by the defendant's negligence. Also, if the child is later born alive, an action can be brought on its behalf to cover the head injury. Suppose, however, the prenatal injury results in the death of the child. In such cases, many states will allow a **wrongful-death** action to be brought, but only if the child was **viable** at the time of death. (*Viable* means able to live indefinitely outside the womb by natural or artificial support systems.) A few states, however, will allow a wrongful-death action in stillborn cases even if the child was not viable at the time of death.

Suppose that a fertility clinic carelessly destroys embryos that a couple had cryopreserved for future implantation. Wrongful death? Most states would say no, because the embryo is not a person or a viable fetus. The couple can recover damages for the loss of the embryo (e.g., medical expenses in creating the embryo) but not the more extensive damages that are usually associated with wrongful-death actions.

wrongful death
A death caused by a tort or other wrong.

viable
Able to live indefinitely outside the womb by natural or artificial support systems.

WRONGFUL LIFE, BIRTH, AND PREGNANCY

Doctors and pharmaceutical companies have been sued for negligence that results in the birth of an unwanted child. When the child is born deformed or otherwise impaired, two categories of suits have been attempted:

Wrongful life: An action by or on behalf of an unwanted child who is impaired; the child seeks its own damages in this action.

Wrongful birth: An action by the parents of an unwanted child who is impaired; the parents seek their own damages in this action.

Suppose, for example, a woman contracts German measles early in her pregnancy. Her doctor negligently advises her that the disease will not affect the health of the child. In fact, the child is born with severe defects caused by the disease. If the woman had known the risks, she would have had an abortion. Can an action for wrongful life or wrongful birth be brought in such a case?

A small number of states would allow suits for *wrongful life* to cover the child's damages. The vast majority of states, however, do not. Courts are very reluctant to recognize a right *not* to be born. Several reasons account for this result. First, there is the enormous difficulty of calculating damages. According to a New Jersey court, it is literally impossible to measure the difference in value between life in an impaired condition and the "utter void of nonexistence."[3] Second, some courts feel that allowing the suit might encourage unwanted children to sue for being born to a poverty-stricken family or to parents with criminal records. Finally, anti-abortion activists have argued that no one should be allowed to sue for missing the opportunity to have been aborted.

In 2001, the highest court in France (the Cour de Cassation) ruled for the first time that damages for wrongful life could be awarded to a severely handicapped child. The ruling created an uproar and led to a national debate over the implication of the ruling. The head of gynecology at a Paris hospital said, "This is the first time that doctors have been condemned for not having killed." A leading legislator in the country told the press, "This sends a message to handicapped people that their life is worth less than their death."[4] Soon after the court's ruling, France's national legislature passed a statute that barred future

wrongful life
An action by or on behalf of an unwanted impaired child for negligence that precluded an informed parental decision to avoid the child's conception or birth. The child seeks its own damages.

wrongful birth
An action by parents of an unwanted impaired child for negligence in failing to warn them of the risks that the child would be born with birth defects. The parents seek their own damages.

suits that asserted the right not to be born. The new law states that "nobody can claim to have been harmed simply by being born."[5]

Wrongful-birth cases, on the other hand, have been more successful. Here the parents sue for their own damages to cover their emotional distress and the cost of prenatal care and delivery. Courts disagree on whether other categories of damages (e.g., extra caretaking expenses due to the impairment) can be obtained in a wrongful-birth action.

Finally, we examine negligence that leads to the birth of an unwanted *healthy* child:

> **Wrongful pregnancy:** An action by the parents of an unplanned child who is healthy; the parents seek their own damages in this action.

Cases of wrongful pregnancy (also called wrongful conception) are allowed in most states. The most common example is a suit against a doctor for negligently performing a vasectomy or against a pharmaceutical company for producing defective birth control pills. Damages are limited to the expenses of prenatal care and delivery; they rarely extend to the costs of raising a healthy child. Furthermore, the unwanted healthy child is usually not allowed to bring the same kind of action in his or her own right.

wrongful pregnancy

An action by parents of an unplanned healthy child for a wrong related to pregnancy such as negligent performance of a vasectomy. The parents seek their own damages. Also called wrongful conception.

ASSIGNMENT 17.3

A pregnant woman in your state has a genetic disease that could lead to the birth of a child with disabilities. Her doctor negligently fails to diagnose this disease and inform the woman. The child is born deformed with this disease. If she had known of the disease, she would have aborted the pregnancy. Who can bring an action in your state against the doctor for negligence and for what damages? (See General Instructions for the Court-Opinion Assignment in Appendix A.)

WRONGFUL ADOPTION

Suppose that an adoption agency misrepresents the physical or mental health of a child or misrepresents the medical history of the child's birth family.

Alice and Stan Patterson want to adopt a child. They go to the Riverside Adoption Agency (RAA), which introduces them to Irene, an infant available for adoption. The Pattersons adopt Irene. Before the adoption, RAA told the Pattersons that Irene did not have any genetic disorders. This turned out to be false. RAA knew that Irene had phenylketonuria (PKU) (a disorder that affects how the body processes protein), but it did not inform the Pattersons of this. After Irene has been living with the Pattersons for a while, they discover that she has severe medical and psychological problems.

Can the Pattersons sue RAA for damages covering the increased cost of child rearing? The period for challenging the adoption itself may have passed. Furthermore, the adoptive parents may have bonded with the child and do not want to "send the child back" even if it were possible to annul or abrogate the adoption. In such cases, some states have allowed the adoptive parents to sue, particularly when they made clear to the agency that they did not want to adopt a problem child. Their argument is that information about the child's health was **material**. They would not have adopted the child if they had been presented with all the facts. Of course, prospective adoptive parents cannot expect a guarantee that the child will be perfect. But they are entitled to available information that might indicate a significant likelihood of future medical or psychological problems. The careless failure to provide such information may constitute the

material

(1) Important enough to influence the decision that was made. (2) Serious and substantial.

wrongful adoption

An action seeking damages for carelessly stating (or failing to disclose) to prospective adoptive parents available facts on the health or other condition of the adoptee that would be relevant to the decision on whether to adopt.

consortium

A right to the benefits that are naturally expected in a particular family relationship.

spousal consortium

The right of one spouse to the relational benefits naturally expected from the other spouse. The benefits include companionship, love, affection, sexual relations, and services (e.g., cooking, making repairs around the house).

loss of consortium

Interference with the companionship, love, affection, sexual relations, and services that a person naturally expects to receive from his or her spouse.

tort of **wrongful adoption**. In an action for this tort, the adoptive parents sue the adoption agency for carelessly stating or failing to disclose available facts on the health or other condition of the child (the adoptee) that would have been relevant to their decision of whether to adopt.

CONSORTIUM, SERVICES, AND EARNINGS
LOSS OF CONSORTIUM (SPOUSAL CONSORTIUM)

Consortium is a right to the benefits that are naturally expected in a particular family relationship. **Spousal consortium** is the right of one spouse to the relational benefits that are naturally expected from the other spouse. The benefits include companionship, love, affection, sexual relations, and services (e.g., cooking, making repairs around the house). An interference with these benefits can lead to the recovery of damages. The interference is called **loss of consortium**, although a more accurate term would be *loss of spousal consortium*. At one time, only the husband could recover for loss of consortium. In every state, this view has been changed by statute or has been ruled unconstitutional as a denial of the equal protection of the law. Either spouse can now recover for loss of consortium. Here is an overview of how the loss is claimed:

- *Rich and Ann are married.*
- *Paul, a stranger, injures Ann by negligently hitting her with his car.*
- *Ann sues Paul for negligence. She receives damages to cover her medical bills, lost wages, and pain and suffering.*
- *Rich then brings a separate claim against Paul for his loss of consortium. He receives damages to compensate him for whatever loss or impairment he can prove to the relationship he had with Ann before the accident—to the love, affection, sexual relations, and services that she gave him as his wife before the accident.*

To receive damages for loss of consortium, the loss or interference with the consortium must be wrongful. It is wrongful if the injury to the other spouse was wrongful. If Ann loses her negligence suit against Paul, Rich will not be able to prevail on his consortium claim. To recover for loss of consortium, there must be an underlying successfully litigated tort.

Recovery for loss of consortium is limited to individuals in a marriage, a domestic partnership, or a civil union. Most states deny recovery for individuals who do not fit into these categories.

- *Jim and Rachel are engaged to be married. The defendant negligently incapacitates Rachel the day before the wedding. Rachel sues the defendant to recover for her injuries.*
- *Mary and John have lived together for 40 years. They have never married and do not live in a state that recognizes common law marriage. The defendant negligently incapacitates John, who sues the defendant to recover for his injuries.*
- *George and Bob are homosexuals who have lived together as a couple for 10 years. They have not married and they are not domestic partners. Nor have they entered a civil union. The defendant negligently incapacitates Bob, who sues the defendant to recover for his injuries.*

Most states would deny Jim, Mary, and George the right to sue for loss of consortium. This may seem unfair, particularly to a couple who is hours away from being married. The law, however, must draw a line somewhere. A court would have a difficult time distinguishing between Jim and Rachel (a day away from their wedding) and an engaged couple whose wedding is one or two years away. What about someone whose wedding was six months or six weeks away? The practical problem of drawing the line has led courts to limit the action for loss of consortium to married individuals, domestic partners, and individuals in a civil union.

PARENTAL CONSORTIUM AND FILIAL CONSORTIUM

In addition to spousal consortium, two other kinds of consortium exist: parental and filial consortium. In general, however, courts are not as willing to award damages for interferences with these categories of consortium.

- **Parental consortium.** The right of a child to the normal companionship and affection of a parent.
- **Filial consortium.** The right of a parent to the normal companionship and affection of a child.
  - *Bill is the father of Sam.*
  - *Case 1: Bill is negligently injured by Alice. Bill sues Alice to recover for his injuries.*
  - *Case 2: Sam is negligently injured by Mary. Sam sues Mary to recover for his injuries.*

In Case 1, Sam also suffered a loss, a loss of parental consortium, when his father was injured. Yet, most states do *not* allow suits for damage to parental consortium. Suppose, however, that the parent (Bill) dies from Alice's negligence. In an action for wrongful death, relatives of Bill (such as his son Sam) are able to recover financial losses due to Bill's death. In a few states, children can also recover for the loss of companionship and affection (parental consortium) they had with their deceased parent. Most states, however, will *not* allow a suit for loss of parental consortium when the injured parent is still alive.

In Case 2, Bill also suffered a loss, a loss of filial consortium, when his son was injured. As we will see in the next section, parents can sue someone who interferes with their right to receive the services of their children, such as doing household chores. States differ, however, on a parent's right to recover for interference with (loss of) filial consortium—the companionship and affection the parent has with a child. Many states deny such recovery. There are, however, a number of states that take a different position and allow recovery for interference with filial consortium.

parental consortium
The right of a child to the normal companionship and affection of a parent.

filial consortium
The right of a parent to the normal companionship and affection of a child.

LOSS OF SERVICES; LOSS OF EARNINGS

A parent has the right to the services of his or her unemancipated child. This would include tasks such as cutting the grass and running errands for the household.

> *Mary is the 12-year-old child of Victor and Helen. The defendant negligently injures Mary in a car accident. In a negligence action against the defendant, Mary can recover damages for her injuries.*

Victor and Helen can also recover damages from the defendant for causing a **loss of services** by Mary to them. A loss of services is an interference with the right of a parent to the services of his or her unemancipated child. For example, she probably helps around the house. The parents can recover for any interference with such services that is wrongfully caused.

Parents are also entitled to the earnings of their unemancipated children, such as from part-time jobs. If the defendant's negligence against the child interferes with the earning capacity of the child, the parents can recover for this loss.

loss of services
Interference with the right of a parent to the services of his or her unemancipated child, such as doing household chores.

HEART-BALM ACTIONS

At common law, there were a number of tort causes of actions that were designed to salve a broken heart. They were called **heart-balm actions**.

- alienation of affections
- criminal conversation

heart-balm action
An action based on the loss of love and relationships—on a broken heart (e.g., breach of promise to marry, alienation of affections, and seduction).

- enticement of a spouse
- abduction or enticement of a child
- seduction

As we saw in Chapter 5, heart-balm actions also included breach of promise to marry. Today, many states have abolished these causes of action because of changing mores, difficulties of proof, and the danger of fabricating claims. A statute that abolishes heart-balm actions is called a **heart-balm statute**. Not all states have such statutes, and some of the causes of action (particularly alienation of affections) are still used. A state that keeps the cause of action might restrict it, such as by limiting or not allowing damages to be collected by a successful plaintiff.

heart-balm statute
A statute that abolishes heart-balm actions.

ALIENATION OF AFFECTIONS

Alienation of affections consists of causing a diminishment of the marital relationship or interfering with the consortium rights that a plaintiff has with his or her spouse.

alienation of affections
The tort of causing a diminishment of the marital relationship or interfering with the consortium rights that a plaintiff has with his or her spouse.

Elements

1. The defendant intended to diminish the marital relationship (love, companionship, and comfort) between the plaintiff and the latter's spouse.
2. Affirmative conduct by the defendant.
3. Affections between the plaintiff and spouse were in fact alienated.
4. The defendant caused the alienation (but for the defendant, the alienation would not have occurred; or, the defendant was a substantial factor in producing the alienation).

As indicated earlier, the most common alienation case brought by a spouse asserts that the other spouse's affections were diminished (alienated) when the defendant engineered an affair with the spouse.

CRIMINAL CONVERSATION

Criminal conversation exists when the defendant has sexual relations with the plaintiff's spouse.

criminal conversation
The tort that occurs when the defendant has sexual relations with the plaintiff's spouse.

Element

The defendant had sexual relations with the plaintiff's spouse (the latter commits adultery).

ENTICEMENT OF A SPOUSE

Enticement of a spouse exists when the defendant encourages the plaintiff's spouse to leave or to stay away from the plaintiff.

enticement of a spouse
A tort in which the defendant encourages the plaintiff's spouse to leave or to stay away from the plaintiff.

Elements

1. The defendant intended to diminish the marital relationship between the plaintiff and the latter's spouse.
2. The defendant engaged in affirmative conduct either:
   a. to entice or encourage the spouse to leave the plaintiff's home, or
   b. to harbor the spouse and encourage the latter to stay away from the plaintiff's home.
3. The plaintiff's spouse left home or stayed away.

4. The defendant caused the plaintiff to leave home or to stay away (but for what defendant did, the plaintiff would not have left home or stayed away; or, the defendant was a substantial factor in the spouse's leaving or staying away).

ABDUCTION OR ENTICEMENT OF A CHILD (TORTIOUS INTERFERENCE WITH CUSTODY; TORTIOUS INTERFERENCE WITH PARENTAL RELATIONSHIPS)

Abduction or enticement of a child consists of serious interference with a parent's custody of his or her child.

Elements

1. The defendant intended to interfere with the parent's custody of the child.

2. Affirmative conduct by the defendant:

    a. to abduct or force the child from the parent's custody,

    b. to entice or encourage the child to leave the parent, or

    c. to harbor the child and encourage the latter to stay away from the parent's custody.

3. The child left the custody of the parent or stayed away.

4. The defendant caused the child to leave or to stay away (but for what the defendant did, the child would not have left or stayed away; or, the defendant was a substantial factor in the child's leaving or staying away).

This tort is sometimes called tortious interference with custody and tortious interference with parental relationships.

Under the *Restatement (Second) of Torts*, "One who, with knowledge that the parent does not consent, abducts or otherwise compels or induces a minor child to leave a parent legally entitled to its custody or not to return to the parent after it has . . . left him, is subject to liability to the parent." One parent, however, cannot sue another for this tort if both parents are entitled to custody of the child: "When the parents are by law jointly entitled to the custody and earnings of the child, no action can be brought against one of the parents who abducts or induces the child to leave the other. When by law only one parent is entitled to the custody and earnings of the child, only that parent can maintain [the action]. One parent may be liable to the other parent for the abduction of his own child if by judicial decree the sole custody of the child has been awarded to the other parent."[6]

Of course, third parties can also be liable for this tort. In a recent Virginia case, an unwed father of an infant was able to sue an adoption attorney for tortious interference with parental rights. The attorney counseled the mother of the child to lie on adoption papers about whether she knew the address of the baby's father. The father was thereby kept in the dark about the adoption proceedings and was forced to initiate extensive custody proceedings to stop the adoption. The father then sued the attorney for tortious interference with parental rights. In allowing the suit, the court listed the following elements of the tort:

(1) the complaining parent has a right to establish or maintain a parental or custodial relationship with his/her minor child; (2) a party outside of the relationship between the complaining parent and his/her child intentionally interfered with the complaining parent's parental or custodial relationship with his/her child by removing or detaining the child from returning to the complaining parent, without that parent's consent, or by otherwise preventing the complaining parent from exercising his/her parental

abduction or enticement of a child
A tort involving serious interference with a parent's custody of his or her child. Also called tortious interference with custody, tortious interference with parental relationships.

or custodial rights; (3) the outside party's intentional interference caused harm to the complaining parent's parental or custodial relationship with his/her child; and (4) damages resulted from such interference.[7]

SEDUCTION

Seduction occurs when the defendant engages in sexual relations with the plaintiff's minor daughter by force or with the consent of the daughter.

Element

The defendant had sex with the plaintiff's minor daughter by force or with the consent of the daughter.

Heart-balm statutes have abolished the parent's action for this tort, but the state might allow the daughter to sue for fraud or misrepresentation if the seducer made false statements of fact (e.g., "I love you") in order to entice her to bed. Of course, a state that allows such a suit would also have to allow a man to sue a woman for fraud if she seduces him by false statements of fact.

VICARIOUS LIABILITY AND INDEPENDENT LIABILITY

VICARIOUS LIABILITY

Vicarious liability is liability that is imposed on a person because of the conduct of another, based solely on the status of the relationship between the two. The person liable is not the person whose conduct led to the liability. For example, if a trucker negligently hits a pedestrian while making a delivery, the trucker's boss, the *employer*, is liable. The liability is vicarious, because it is based on the status of the trucker as an employee of the boss. The employer is liable because of what someone else—the employee—has done.

The person injured could *also* sue the trucker, the employee who is directly responsible for the injury. We are all personally liable for our own torts even if someone else is vicariously liable. Often, however, the one directly responsible has minimal resources out of which to satisfy a judgment. The person who is vicariously liable is usually the **deep pocket**, who does have such resources.

Family members are rarely employees of each other. Hence, vicarious liability does not exist for the vast majority of torts committed by family members against someone outside the family. For example:

> *Mary is the 10-year-old daughter of Diane. Mary throws a brick through the window of Jim's hardware store.*

Jim must sue *Mary* for the damage done to the store. Her parents are *not* vicariously liable for the tort of their daughter. There are, however, two exceptions to the general rule of no vicarious liability among family members: parental-liability laws and the family-purpose doctrine.

Parental-Liability Laws

Most states have passed **parental-liability laws** (also called *parental-responsibility laws*) that make parents vicariously liable for the torts of their children, but only up to a relatively modest amount (e.g., $1,000).

Family-Purpose Doctrine

The second exception is the **family-purpose doctrine**, according to which the owner of a car (or person controlling the use of a car) is liable for the negligence committed by a family member using the car for a family purpose.

Not all states have the doctrine, and those that have it do not all agree on its elements. A state may not need the doctrine if it has adequate requirements for automobile-liability insurance so that pedestrians and other cars on the road are protected no matter who is driving the family car or for what purpose.

Elements of Family-Purpose Doctrine

1. Defendant must own the car, have an ownership interest in it (e.g., co-owner), or control the use of the car.
2. Defendant must make the car available for family use rather than for the defendant's business (in some states, the defendant must make it available for general family use rather than for a particular occasion only).
3. The driver must be a member of the defendant's immediate household.
4. The driver must be using the car for a family purpose at the time of the accident.
5. The driver must have had the defendant's express or implied consent to be using the car at the time of the accident.

The defendant does not have to be the traditional head of the household and does not have to be in the car at the time of the accident. Again, individual states, by case law or by statute, may impose different elements to the doctrine or may reject it entirely.

INDEPENDENT LIABILITY

Sometimes parents are *independently* liable for the torts of their children because of what the parents themselves have done or failed to do. Two major examples of such liability are negligent supervision and negligent entrustment:

- **Negligent supervision.** Carelessly monitoring or supervising an incompetent person who thereby poses an unreasonable risk of harm to others.
- **Negligent entrustment.** Carelessly allowing the use of a vehicle, tool, or other object by someone whose use poses an unreasonable risk of harm to others.

Assume that a father is aware of the fact that his young son plays with matches in the alley by their home. If the father fails to use reasonable care to control this habit of his son, the father could be liable for the fire damage the son causes to a neighbor's house in the alley. When parents act unreasonably in failing to use available opportunities to control their children, the parents are *independently* liable for negligence in a suit brought by the person injured by the child. The liability is called *negligent supervision.* Defendants, however, might have a difficult problem of proof when alleging negligent supervision. Parents often assert that they were unaware of the child's bad habit or that they did everything reasonably possible to control it. If either of these positions is accurate, there is no negligent supervision.

Another example of independent (not vicarious) parental liability is *negligent entrustment.* An example would be allowing a 10-year-old to drive a tractor or a truck on a public highway, resulting in a collision with another vehicle.

INTRAFAMILY CRIMES

As we saw in earlier chapters, there are crimes that spouses can commit within the family relationship. Examples include incest and bigamy. The epidemic of domestic violence can lead to prosecutions for various crimes, including, in many states, marital rape. We also discussed crimes that parents can commit against their children, such as criminal nonsupport and sexual abuse. There is no immunity for such crimes.

At one time, most states included adultery, fornication, and sodomy as crimes, although the constitutionality of criminalizing such conduct between adults is in doubt as a result of *Lawrence v. Texas*, the decision of the of U.S. Supreme Court on private consensual sexual behavior by same-sex adults (see Chapter 5).

Spouses can also be prosecuted for crimes against each other's separate property. For example, a husband is guilty of larceny if he uses his wife's password without her permission and withdraws money from her solely owned account containing only her separate property.

■ PARALEGAL ROLES

- For an overview of paralegal roles in family-law cases, see Exhibits 1-3 and 1-4 in Chapter 1. Many of the roles listed in these exhibits pertain to litigation, which are at the core of tort cases.

- For many of the financial issues related to the calculation and enforcement of damages for the torts covered in this chapter, a paralegal may be asked to help collect documents and facts outlined in:
  - the checklist in Exhibit 3-1 of Chapter 3
  - the interrogatories in Appendix C

■ CHECK THE CITE

Kentucky has abolished the tort of alienation of affections based on adultery. Yet an ex-husband was allowed to bring a tort action against a priest who had an affair with his ex-wife during marriage counseling sessions, which led to the divorce of the couple. What was the tort the ex-husband brought and was adultery alone sufficient to establish that tort? Read *Osborne v. Payne*, 31 S.W.3d 911 (Ky. 2000). To read the opinion online: (1) Run a citation search ("31 S.W.3d 911") in the Legal Documents database of Google Scholar (scholar.google.com). (2) Run a case name search ("Osborne v. Payne") in a general search engine such as Google, Bing, or Yahoo.

■ PROJECT

In Google, Bing, or Yahoo, run the following search: aa tort immunity family (substitute the name of your state for aa in the search). Write an essay in which you explain the extent of intrafamily tort immunity in your state. Cover torts for property and personal harm caused by one spouse against another, by a parent against a child, and between other relatives. You must cite and quote from a minimum of eight different sources that you find on the Internet. At least four of these sources should be statutes, court opinions, or other laws.

■ ETHICS IN A FAMILY LAW PRACTICE

You are a paralegal working at the law office of Francis Reardon, Esq. Reardon represents David Richardson, who is suing his ex-wife, Mary Richardson, to attempt to stop Mary from aborting the child conceived months before the divorce. You are an ardent abortion rights advocate. Any ethical problems?

■ WRITING SAMPLE

Prepare a torts complaint that would be acceptable in a trial court in your state. You can make up the facts of the complaint so long as it covers the following basic fact outline: The alleged tort was committed by one spouse against the other while living apart but still married. The tort should grow out of incidents of domestic violence alleged by the spouse bringing the suit. The tort can seek damages for personal harm or for property loss or both. (See General Instructions for the Writing Sample in Appendix A.)

SUMMARY

A tort is a civil wrong (other than a breach of contract) that causes injury or other loss for which our legal system deems it just to provide a remedy such as damages. An intrafamily tort is a tort committed by one family member against another. An interspousal immunity bars certain torts between spouses; a parental immunity bars certain torts between parents and children. Courts traditionally have been reluctant to allow suits for intrafamily torts for several reasons, such as an unseemly intrusion into family harmony and the danger of fraud among the family members involved in the tort. Intrafamily torts can cause personal injury or property damage/interference. The two categories of torts that can cause these harms are intentional torts and negligence. The existence of an immunity depends on the kind of harm the family member caused; the kind of tort that caused the harm; who the victim of the tort is; and, if a child is involved, whether the child is emancipated.

Spouses can sue each other for any tort that causes property damage or interference. In general, this is also true of torts that cause personal injury, although some states maintain some or all of the immunity for such torts. Children can sue their parents for any tort that causes property damage or interference. In general, there are more restrictions on parent–child suits for torts that cause personal injury, particularly if the parent was disciplining the child. There is no immunity for suits between other family members. If the interspousal immunity does not apply, one spouse can sue the other for transmitting venereal disease. States differ on whether a marital tort claim can be brought in the divorce action.

A prenatal tort is a tort against a fetus. The tort can be brought if the child is born alive. If it is stillborn, many states will allow a wrongful-death action if the unborn child was viable. If a defendant such as a doctor makes a negligent mistake that results in the birth of an impaired child, the parents can bring a wrongful-birth action. If the child is born healthy, the parents may be able to bring an action for wrongful pregnancy or for wrongful conception, but the damages are limited. The courts, however, usually do not allow an impaired child to bring his or her own separate wrongful-life action. The failure of an adoption agency to give prospective adoptive parents available information about the health or other condition of the prospective adoptee may constitute the tort of wrongful adoption.

Loss of consortium covers injury to the companionship, love, affection, sexual relationship, and services that one spouse provides another. States differ on whether parents and children can sue for tortious interference with parental or filial consortium. Loss of services covers an interference with the right of parents to the services of their unemancipated child. Other family torts include the heart-balm actions for alienation of affections, criminal conversation, enticement of a spouse, abduction or enticement of a child (tortious interference with custody), and seduction. Many states have passed heart-balm statutes that abolish these actions.

Vicarious liability exists when one person is liable for someone else's wrongful conduct. Vicarious liability does not exist among family members, with two major exceptions. First, some states have parental-liability laws that impose limited vicarious liability on parents for the torts committed by their children. (Negligent supervision and negligent entrustment can make a parent independently liable for the torts of his or her children.) Second, under the family-purpose doctrine, the owner of a car can be liable for a tort committed by a family member driving the car for a family purpose. An intrafamily crime is a crime that one family member commits against another for which the former can be prosecuted.

KEY TERMS

tort	intentional infliction of emotional	loss of services
no-fault divorce	distress	heart-balm action
intrafamily tort	prenatal tort	heart-balm statute
marital tort	wrongful death	alienation of affections
immunity	viable	criminal conversation
liability insurance	wrongful life	enticement of a spouse
at common law	wrongful birth	abduction or enticement of a child
intentional tort	wrongful pregnancy	seduction
battery	material	vicarious liability
negligence	wrongful adoption	deep pocket
real property	consortium	parental-liability law
personal property	spousal consortium	family-purpose doctrine
conversion	loss of consortium	negligent supervision
emancipated	parental consortium	negligent entrustment
unemancipated	filial consortium	

REVIEW QUESTIONS

1. What is a tort?
2. In what way are marital tort actions inconsistent with no-fault divorce?
3. What is an intrafamily tort and what is a marital tort?
4. What is an immunity?

5. What are the two major intrafamily tort immunities?

6. Historically, why has the law been reluctant to allow suits for intrafamily torts?

7. What are the two main categories of harm that can be the subject of an intrafamily tort, and what are the two main categories of torts that can cause this harm?

8. What is the distinction between an emancipated and an unemancipated child?

9. When can one spouse bring a tort action against another for torts that cause property damage or interference?

10. When can one spouse bring a tort action against another for torts that cause personal injury?

11. When can a child bring a tort action against a parent for torts that cause property damage or interference?

12. When can a child bring a tort action against a parent for torts that cause personal injury?

13. What sexual torts can spouses bring against each other?

14. Why are some states against allowing marital torts to be brought in a divorce action?

15. What is a prenatal tort and when can it be brought?

16. What is an action for wrongful life and when can it be brought?

17. What is an action for wrongful birth and when can it be brought?

18. What is an action for wrongful pregnancy and when can it be brought?

19. What is an action for wrongful adoption and when can it be brought?

20. What is an action of loss of consortium and when can it be brought?

21. When can an action be brought for interference with parental consortium and filial consortium?

22. What is loss of services and when can a suit for the loss be brought?

23. What are the main heart-balm actions?

24. What is a heart-balm statute?

25. What is the distinction between vicarious liability and independent liability?

26. When are parents vicariously liable for the torts of their children?

27. When are parents independently liable for the torts of their children?

28. What intrafamily crimes can be prosecuted?

HELPFUL WEBSITES

Marital Torts

- www.ncdsv.org/images/MaritalTortActionsFamily Law.pdf
- www.smartdivorce.com/articles/torts.shtml
- www.noteboom.com/library/Divorce_Torts.pdf
- www.gourvitz.com/domestic_torts.asp

Domestic Violence, Domestic Torts, and Divorce

- www.nesl.edu/lawrev/vol31/vol31-2/DALTON.htm

Interspousal Tort Claims (Texas)

- www.divorcesource.com/research/edj/torts/98jul80 .shtml

Loss of Consortium

- en.wikipedia.org/wiki/Loss_of_consortium
- www.injuryinfo.com/blog/loss-of-consortium/

Prenatal Injury

- scholar.valpo.edu/cgi/viewcontent.cgi?article=1645& context=vulr
- scholarship.law.duke.edu/cgi/viewcontent.cgi?article =1081&context=faculty_scholarship

Wrongful Life

- en.wikipedia.org/wiki/Wrongful_life
- www.genomicslawreport.com/index.php/2009/09/22 /the-wrongful-life-debate

Wrongful Birth

- en.wikipedia.org/wiki/Wrongful_birth

Wrongful Adoption

- www.adoptionagency.com/agencies/wrongful -adoption-and-agency-liability.html

Heart-Balm Actions

- lawprofessors.typepad.com/tortsprof/2007/11/the -complete-en.html
- www.illinoisdivorce.com/family_law_articles/tort _basics.php

Parental Liability

- www.enotes.com/family-law-reference/parent -liability-child-s-act
- www.mwl-law.com/CM/Resources/PARENTAL%20 RESPONSIBILITY%20CHART%20(00033309).pdf

Google/Bing/Yahoo Searches

(on these search engines, run the following searches, substituting your state for "aa")

- family tort aa
- divorce tort aa
- tort immunity family aa
- domestic violence tort aa
- "wrongful life" aa
- "marital tort" aa
- "no fault" divorce tort aa
- emancipation family tort aa
- intrafamily tort aa
- "wrongful birth" aa
- "wrongful adoption" aa
- "heart balm" tort aa
- "spousal consortium" tort aa
- "vicarious liability" tort aa
- tortious interference parent aa
- "wrongful pregnancy" aa
- "prenatal tort" aa
- "loss of consortium" aa
- "filial consortium" aa
- "loss of consortium" aa

ENDNOTES

Note: All or most of the court opinions in these endnotes can be read online. To do so, go to Google Scholar (scholar.google.com), select "Legal documents," and in the search box, enter the cite (e.g., "404 A.2d 8") or name of the case (e.g., "Berman v. Allen") that is given in the endnote.

[1] Alics Gomstyn, *Wife's $9M Message to Mistresses: "Lay Off,"* ABC Good Morning America (Mar. 23, 2010).

[2] § 554.

[3] *Berman v. Allen*, 404 A.2d 8, 12 (N.J. 1979).

[4] Marlise Simons, *French Uproar over Right to Death for Unborn*, N.Y. Times, Oct. 19, 2001, at A3.

[5] "France Rejects Right Not to Be Born," BBC News (Jan. 10, 2002).

[6] *Restatement (Second) of Torts*, § 700, Comment c (1977).

[7] *Wyatt v. McDermott*, 725 S.E.2d 555, 562 (Va, 2012).

APPENDIX A

General Instructions for the Assignments and Projects in the Book

OUTLINE

INTRODUCTION

Throughout the chapters of this book, there are 13 major kinds of skill assignments and projects:

- State-Code Assignment
- Legal-Analysis Assignment

- Complaint-Drafting Assignment
- Agreement-Drafting Assignment
- Court-Opinion Assignment
- Checklist-Formulation Assignment
- Investigation-Strategy Assignment
- Interview Assignment
- Interrogatory Assignment
- Flowchart Assignment
- Systems Assignment
- Projects
- Writing Samples

On the pages where these assignments and projects are found, you will be given *specific instructions*. In addition, a set of *general instructions* is available for each of the 13 categories of assignments and projects. These general instructions are provided here in Appendix A. Throughout the chapters of the book, you are referred to Appendix A for *general instructions* for most of the assignments.

THE CARTWHEEL

Several of the assignments, particularly the state-code and court-opinion assignments, ask you to check basic law books such as the statutory code (containing the full text of the statutes of the legislature) and to use search engines to locate family-law materials on the Internet. The **CARTWHEEL** will help you find items in these sources. The CARTWHEEL is an index technique. Its objective can be simply stated: to help you develop the habit of phrasing every word involved in the client's problem *in multiple different ways!* When you go to the index of a law book, you naturally begin looking up the words and phrases that you think should lead you to the relevant material in the book. The same is true when you type key words into search engines. If you do not find anything on point, two conclusions are possible:

CARTWHEEL
A research technique designed to help you think of a large variety of words and phrases to check in indexes, tables of contents, and online search engines.

- There is nothing on point in the law book or on the Internet.
- You checked the wrong words in the index or in the search boxes.

Too often we make the mistake of thinking that the first conclusion is accurate. Nine times out of ten, the second conclusion is more accurate. The solution is to be able to phrase a word in as many different ways and in as many different contexts as possible—hence the CARTWHEEL. See Exhibit A-1.

Assume, for example, that one of the major words in the client's case or in the assignment is the word *wedding*. Place this word in the center of the CARTWHEEL. It will be the first word that will be CARTWHEEL-ed. Look up the word *wedding* in the index of whatever law book you are checking. Type the word in the search box of whatever search engine you are using. If you are not successful with this word, it may be (1) because the word is not in the index, (2) because the page or section references after the word in the index do not lead you to relevant material in the body of the book, or (3) because the sites the search engine led you to are equally unproductive.

The next step is to think of as many different phrasings and contexts of the word *wedding* as possible. This is where the 18 steps of the CARTWHEEL can be useful. If you applied the steps of the CARTWHEEL to the word *wedding*, here are some of the words and phrases that should come to mind:

1. *Broader words:* celebration, ceremony, rite, ritual, formality, festivity.
2. *Narrower words:* civil wedding, church wedding, golden wedding, proxy wedding, sham wedding, shotgun marriage.
3. *Synonyms:* marriage ceremony, nuptial.
4. *Antonyms:* alienation, annulment, divorce, separation, legal separation, judicial separation.

EXHIBIT A-1 The CARTWHEEL: Creating Search Terms

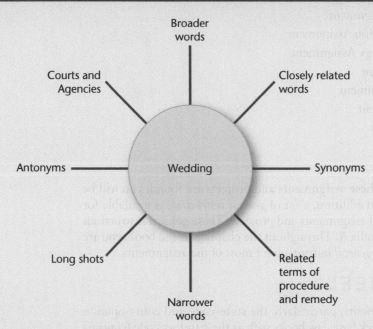

1. Identify all the *major words* from the facts of the client's problem or of the assignment (e.g., wedding). One at a time, place each word or small set of words in the center of the CARTWHEEL.

2. In the index, look up (or type in) all of these words.

3. Identify the *broader categories* of the major words.

4. In the index, look up (or type in) all of these broader words.

5. Identify the *narrower* categories of the major words.

6. In the index, look up (or type in) all of these narrower words.

7. Identify all *synonyms* of the major words.

8. In the index, look up (or type in) all of these synonyms.

9. Identify all of the *antonyms* of the major words.

10. In the index, look up (or type in) all of these antonyms.

11. Identify all words that are *closely related* to the major words.

12. In the index, look up (or type in) all of these closely related words.

13. Identify all terms of *procedure* and *remedy* related to the major words.

14. In the index, look up (or type in) all of these procedural and remedial terms.

15. Identify all *courts* and *agencies,* if any, that might have some connection to the major words.

16. In the index, look up (or type in) all of these courts and agencies.

17. Identify all *long shots*.

18. In the index, look up (or type in) all of these long shots.

Note: The above categories are not mutually exclusive.

© Cengage Learning 2013

5. *Closely related words:* matrimony, marital, conjugal, domestic, husband, wife, bride, license, anniversary, custom, children, blood test, premarital, spouse, relationship, family, home, consummation, cohabitation, sexual relations, betrothal, minister, wedlock, path, contract, community property, name change, domicile, residence.

6. *Procedural and remedial terms:* action, suit, statute of limitations, petition, complaint, discovery, defense, jurisdiction, court, superior court, county court.

7. *Courts and agencies:* Superior Court, Family Court, Juvenile Court, Office of Child Support Enforcement, Bureau of Vital Statistics, County Clerk, Department of Social Services, License Bureau, Secretary of State, Justice of the Peace.

8. *Long shots:* dowry, common law, single, blood relationship, fraud, religion, illegitimate, remarriage, antenuptial, alimony, bigamy, pregnancy, gifts, chastity, impotence, incest, virginity, support, custody, consent, paternity, property division, separate maintenance, etc.

If the CARTWHEEL can generate this many words and phrases from a starting point of just one word (wedding), potentially hundreds more can be generated when you subject all of the important words from the client's case or assignment to the CARTWHEEL. Do you check them all in the index volume of every law book or type them all in search engines? No. You cannot spend your entire legal career working on one case or one assignment! Common sense will tell you when you are on the right track and when you are needlessly duplicating your efforts. You may get lucky and find what you are after in a few minutes. For important tasks in any line of work (or play), however, being comprehensive is usually time-consuming.

The categories in the CARTWHEEL will overlap; they are not mutually exclusive. Also, it is not significant whether you place a word in one category or another as long as the word comes to your mind. The CARTWHEEL is, in effect, a *word association game* that should become second nature to you with practice. Perhaps some of the word selections in the wedding example seem a bit far-fetched. You will not know for sure, however, whether a word will be fruitful until you try it. Be imaginative, and take some risks.

A legal thesaurus or a general thesaurus can often be helpful in generating word alternatives when using the CARTWHEEL technique. See, for example, West's *Legal Thesaurus/Dictionary* or *Roget's International Thesaurus*.

UNE A-1 ▼

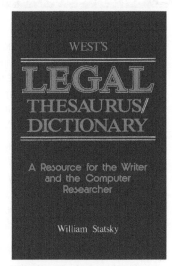

William Statsky, *West's Legal Thesaurus /Dictionary*. © 1985 Delmar Learning, Inc. Reproduced by permission. www.cengage .com/permissions

---

ASSIGNMENT A.1

Cartwheel the following words:

a. cruelty

b. support

c. paternity

STATE-CODE ASSIGNMENT

A great deal of family law consists of statutory law written by your state legislature. This law will be found within the state statutory code. (See Exhibit 1-6 in Chapter 1 for an example.) It is important that you become acquainted with the family-law sections of your statutory code. Many of the assignments in this book ask you to examine this code on a particular family-law topic.

✓ GENERAL INSTRUCTIONS FOR THE STATE-CODE ASSIGNMENT

1. The first step is to make sure you know the name and location of the statutory code for your state. Some states have more than one code—usually from different publishers.

2. Be sure you are using the latest edition of the state code.

3. See Appendix D for leads to the online site to your state code that can be used without cost. The following sites provide links to the online state codes of every state:

- www.law.cornell.edu/statutes.html
- www.findlaw.com/casecode
- www.whpgs.org/f.htm
- law.justia.com

In addition:

- Go to the home page of your state government (www.aa.gov) (insert your state's abbreviation or full name in place of aa). On this page, look for links to the legislature of your state. You will be told what statutes are available.

- In Google, Bing, or Yahoo, do a legislature search (aa legislature) (insert your state's abbreviation or full name in place of aa). This search should lead you to your state legislature.

Online statutory codes have search boxes. The CARTWHEEL will help you identify search terms to type in these boxes.

(continued)

✔ GENERAL INSTRUCTIONS FOR THE STATE-CODE ASSIGNMENT *(continued)*

4. For statutory codes on the shelves of a law library, use the CARTWHEEL to help you use the various indexes in the code. (There is often a general index at the end of the code volumes as well as smaller indexes after each volume or set of volumes covering the same topic area.) The CARTWHEEL will help you identify search terms for the search engines you use.

5. Statutes can change. There may be new sections added, revised language, or repeals. When you use the online version of the code (particularly at the site of the state legislature), these changes are usually already incorporated into the site. If you are using the hard copy of the code in the library, you need to look for changes by:

- Checking the pocket part, if any, of every volume you use
- Checking replacement volumes, if any
- Checking supplement volumes or pamphlets, if any
- Shepardizing the statute. To Shepardize something means to use the volumes of *Shepard's Citations* to obtain specific information about a document. When you Shepardize a statute, you go to the set of *Shepard's Citations* covering your state code and examine all of the references provided on your statute (e.g., amendments, repeals, opinions interpreting the statute). Find the citation of your statute in black bold print within each *Shepard's* pamphlet and bound volume. The references, if any, will be found in columns immediately beneath the citation of your statute.

6. You can also find statutes on fee-based online services such as Westlaw, Lexis Nexis, and Loislaw. If you have access to these services, go to the database that contains the statutes of your state legislature and formulate a "query," which is simply a question. The CARTWHEEL can help you decide what words or phrases to use in your query.

7. Give a complete citation for every statute that you think covers the assignment. (A citation is a reference to any material printed on paper or stored in a computer database. It is the "address" where you can locate and read the material.) Citation formats usually include:

- The title or chapter number of the statute
- The abbreviated name of the code

- The section number of the statute
- The date of the code

8. When you quote from a statute, use quotation marks around the language you are quoting.

9. If the assignment asks you to apply the statute to the facts of a problem in the assignment, follow the General Instructions for the Legal-Analysis Assignment below on applying elements.

10. When you need help in understanding a statute, use the following approaches:

- See if there are definition statutes that define some of the words in the statute you are examining. (If such definition statutes exist, they will usually precede the statute you are examining at the beginning of the cluster of statutes on that topic.)
- Examine opinions that have interpreted the statute. You can obtain leads to these opinions, if any exist, by checking the Notes to Decisions, which are summaries of opinions. They are found immediately after the text of the statute in annotated editions of the code. (Annotated simply means organized by subject matter with research references such as Notes to Decisions or other commentary.) You can also find opinions interpreting the statute by Shepardizing the statute.

11. If you cannot find what you are looking for in the statutory code, proceed as follows:

- Repeat step 4. Frequently, the difficulty lies in the failure to use indexes and search engines creatively. Do the CARTWHEEL again to try to come up with more words and phrases to check in the indexes and to type in the search boxes.
- Check the court rules of your state courts to determine whether they treat the topic you are pursuing.
- Check the constitution of your state to determine whether it treats the topic you are pursuing.
- Find out if any court opinions have been written by your state courts on the topic you are pursuing. For techniques to find court opinions, see the General Instructions for the Court-Opinion Assignment below. See also the instruction on Notes to Decisions above.

ASSIGNMENT A.2

a. What is the name of the statutory code of your state? (If more than one exists, list each one.)

b. Who publishes it?

c. How is it updated? By pocket parts? By supplemental pamphlets? Both?

d. Give the address of Internet sites that give the full text of the statutes in your state.

e. In this question, you will locate the same statute (i) in the hard copy of the code volumes in a law library and (ii) on the Internet. Go to your code in a law library and pick any statute on divorce or on any other area of family law. Quote the first line of the statute you select. Give the citation of the quote in the code. Now go on the Internet and find the same statute. Quote the first line. Give the citation of the quote on the Internet. If you cannot find the same code statute on the Internet, pick a different code statute.

LEGAL-ANALYSIS ASSIGNMENT

Before we examine the general instructions for the legal-analysis assignment, here is a brief introductory refresher on legal reasoning, or **legal analysis**. The process of legal analysis can be diagrammed as follows:

legal analysis
The application of one or more rules to the facts of a client's case in order to answer a legal question that will help (1) avoid a legal dispute, (2) resolve a legal dispute that has arisen, or (3) prevent a legal dispute from becoming worse.

Let's look at a simple example.

Facts: George and Helen are married. One day, after a big argument, George walks out of the house and says, "Good-bye. Find someone else to take care of you." As he walks out, he resolves to stay away forever.

Rule: One spouse abandons another by leaving without any intention of returning.

Application of rule to facts: When George walked out of the house resolving to stay away forever, he left "without any intention of returning." This is abandonment.

Most legal analysis, however, is not this simple. This can be due to a number of factors, including the following:

- A word or phrase in the rule is ambiguous.
- You need more facts than you are given.

AMBIGUITY IN THE RULE

Facts: George and Helen are married. One day, after a big argument, George walks out of the apartment and says, "Good-bye. Find someone else to take care of you." As he walks out, he resolves to stay away forever. He moves downstairs to a vacant, never-used room in the same building that he and his wife jointly own. The room has its own exit to the street.

Rule: One spouse abandons another by leaving without any intention of returning.

In this example, there is ambiguity in the rule. What does "leaving" mean? At least two interpretations are possible:

- Moving out of the entire dwelling.
- Moving out of the part of the dwelling in which both spouses normally live together.

Which is the correct definition of "leaving"? The difference in the definitions is critical. Depending on which definition is adopted, a different result is reached:

- According to the first definition, George did not abandon Helen because he did not move out of the entire dwelling.
- According to the second definition, George did abandon Helen, since he moved out of the rooms where they both normally lived. Under this definition, he can commit abandonment without moving out of the entire building.

Your task in legal analysis is to be sensitive to such ambiguity in the rules that you are trying to apply to facts. Do not accept language at face value. Look at every word in the rule you are applying and ask yourself: What is the definition of this word? Is more than one definition possible?

When you are using legal analysis in an interoffice memorandum or in a school examination, one of the biggest mistakes you can make is to hit the reader over the head with one conclusion. Do not overlook ambiguity. When it exists, find it and write about it. Good legal analysis articulates both sides of the controversy. If you personally favor one side over the other, you may state your opinion, but only after you have placed yourself in the shoes of both sides and presented the best argument for each.

Once you have identified ambiguity in the rule, how do you *resolve* the ambiguity? You do legal research. For example, you find out whether any courts have interpreted the ambiguous words/phrases. Are there court opinions that have defined the word *leaving* in our rule? If so, you need to find the opinions containing the definition. (For purposes of the legal-analysis assignments in this book, however, you will not do further legal research of this kind unless the instructions in the assignment, or your instructor, tell you otherwise.)

THE NEED FOR MORE FACTS

In the process of trying to connect rules to facts, you may sometimes feel that you need more facts to assess whether the rule applies. If so, state what additional facts you would like to have and *state why they may be helpful to your analysis.*

In the example involving George and Helen, suppose we are told that George said to Helen, "Good-bye. Find someone else to take care of you," but we are not told whether he walked out. In your analysis, you would have to point out that the facts do not state what George did immediately after he made this statement to Helen. You need additional facts. You need to know whether he left the building or any part of the building after he made the statement. The rule refers to "leaving," and you do not know whether or how he left.

Also, if the facts do not clearly show that George left with the intent of never returning, you would need additional facts to help resolve the intent issue. For example:

- Did he take all of his clothes with him?
- Did he speak to anyone else after he left about what he was doing?
- How far away did he go when he left?
- Did he change his address officially (e.g., at the post office)?
- Did he open any new bank accounts or change old ones?
- Did he call Helen or otherwise contact her after he left? If so, how long after he left, how often, and about what?

State why you need these additional facts. For example, if George took all of his clothes with him when he left, this fact would be evidence that his departure was permanent (i.e., he had no intention of returning when he left). This should be stated as such in your legal analysis.

ANALYSIS OF ELEMENTS

One of the most important skills of legal analysis is the ability to break down any rule into its **elements**:

Element

1. A *portion* of a rule that can be conveniently discussed separately from the other elements and

2. A *precondition* to the applicability of the entire rule (if one of the elements of the rule does not apply, the entire rule does not apply).

To a very large extent, legal analysis proceeds by element analysis, as we shall see. In addition, we use element analysis as an aid in performing other tasks. For example:

- When drafting a petition or complaint, the drafter often tries to allege enough facts to establish each element of the **cause of action**.

- When a trial judge gives instructions (the charge) to a jury, he or she must cover all of the elements of the cause of action and of the defenses. When counsel submits proposed instructions to the judge, the elements must likewise be covered.

- When an attorney is conducting a deposition, he or she will frequently organize the questions around the elements of the causes of action and defenses in the case.

- The organization of a memorandum of law will often follow the list of elements of the rules being discussed.

A major characteristic of *sloppy* legal analysis is that it does not clearly take the reader through the elements of a rule. Good analysis discusses every element, with an emphasis on the element(s) in contention. No element is passed over.

Suppose you are analyzing the following rule found in a statute:

§ 25–403 A pharmacist must not sell prescription drugs to a minor.

Note that the rule is not broken down into elements. As with most rules, you must identify the elements on your own:

Elements of § 25–403

1. Pharmacist
2. Must not sell
3. Prescription drugs
4. To a minor

No violation exists unless all four elements of this statute are established. If a pharmacist sells simple aspirin (a nonprescription drug), he or she is not liable under the statute. The third element cannot be established. Hence no violation, because one of the elements (preconditions) cannot be met.

For a number of reasons, rules such as statutes and regulations can be difficult to break into elements. For example, the rule may be long or may contain:

- Lists
- Alternatives
- Exceptions or provisos

Nevertheless, the same process is used. You must take the time to dissect the rule into its component elements. Examine the following rule and its elements:

§ 5 While representing a client in connection with contemplated or pending litigation, a lawyer shall not advance or guarantee financial assistance to his

element
A portion of a rule that is a precondition to the applicability of the entire rule.

cause of action
1. A legally acceptable reason for bringing a suit. A rule that constitutes a legal theory for bringing a suit. 2. The facts that give a person a right to judicial relief. When you state a cause of action, you list the facts that give you a right to judicial relief against the wrongdoer.

client, except that a lawyer may advance or guarantee court costs, expenses of investigation, expenses of medical examination, and costs of obtaining and presenting evidence provided the client remains ultimately liable for such costs or expenses.

Section 5 can be broken down into three elements:

Elements of § 5

1. A lawyer
2. Representing a client in connection with contemplated litigation or in connection with pending litigation
3. Shall not advance financial assistance to his client or guarantee financial assistance to his client, except that the following is proper:

   a. lawyer advances or guarantees court costs provided the client remains ultimately liable for these costs, or
   b. lawyer advances or guarantees expenses of investigation provided the client remains ultimately liable for these expenses, or
   c. lawyer advances or guarantees expenses of medical examination provided the client remains ultimately liable for these expenses, or
   d. lawyer advances or guarantees costs of obtaining and presenting evidence provided the client remains ultimately liable for these costs.

When an element is stated in the alternative, list all the alternatives within the same element. Alternatives related to one element should be kept within the phrasing of that element. The same is true of exception or proviso clauses. State them within the relevant element when they are intimately related to the applicability of that element. In our § 5 example, the most complicated element is the third (3). It contains lists, alternatives, an exception, and a proviso. But they all relate to the same point—the propriety of financial assistance. None of the subdivisions of the third element should be stated as a separate element.

Sometimes you must do some unraveling of a rule in order to identify its elements. This certainly had to be done with the third element of § 5. Do not be afraid to pick the rule apart in order to cluster its thoughts around unified themes that should stand alone as elements. Diagram the rule for yourself as you examine it.

If more than one rule is involved in a statute, regulation, constitutional provision, charter, ordinance, etc., treat one rule at a time. Every rule should have its own elements, and, when appropriate, each element should be subdivided into its separate components, as in the third element of § 5.

Once you have broken the rule into its elements, you have the structure of the analysis in front of you. Each element becomes a separate section of your analysis. You discuss one element at a time, concentrating on those that pose the greatest difficulties.

ASSIGNMENT A.3

Break the following rules into their elements:

a. **§ 800.** The parties can by mutual agreement elect to terminate their separation agreement.

b. **§ 52.** A court of this State shall not exercise its jurisdiction under this Act if at the time of filing the petition a proceeding concerning the custody of the child was pending in a court of another state exercising jurisdiction substantially in conformity with this Act, unless the proceeding is stayed by the court of the other state because this State is a more appropriate forum or for other reasons.

> **c. § 10.2.** With respect to a child who has no presumed father under Section 4, an action may be brought by the child, the mother or personal representative of the child, the appropriate state agency, the personal representative or a parent of the mother if the mother has died, a man alleged or alleging himself to be the father, or the personal representative or a parent of the alleged father if the alleged father has died or is a minor.
>
> **d. § 107(b).** When the mental or physical condition (including the blood group) of a party, or a person in the custody or under the legal control of a party, is in controversy, the court in which the action is pending may order the party to submit to a physical or mental examination by a physician or to produce for examination the person in his custody or legal control. The order may be made only on motion for good cause shown and upon the notice to the person to be examined and to all parties and shall specify time, place, manner, conditions, and scope of the examination and the person or persons by whom it is to be made.

PHRASING ISSUES

To do legal analysis, you must identify the **legal issue**. To fail to identify the issue would be like trying to steer a ship without a rudder or to drive a car without the steering wheel: your legal analysis would drift aimlessly.

A legal issue has two components:

- A brief quote from the element of the rule in contention
- Several of the important facts relevant to that contention

In formal legal analysis, both components should be present in your statement of the legal issue.

Every element of a rule is potentially the basis of a separate issue. A rule with five elements, for example, could lead to five separate issues, each structured around whether one of the elements applies. In practice, however, it is rare for every element to lead to a separate issue. This is because every element of a rule will probably not be an **element in contention**. To have such an element, you must be able to make a reasonable prediction that the parties to the dispute will probably disagree on whether the element applies. If it is clear that both parties will agree on the applicability or nonapplicability of a particular element, it would be a waste of time to construct an issue around that element and to spend time analyzing it.

At the time you write your memorandum, you may not know for certain what the other side will eventually say about the applicability of a rule. You must do your best to anticipate what your opponent *might* argue about the rule and any element within it.

There are two main kinds of disagreements that the parties can have about an element:

1. *Disagreement about definitions.* If you anticipate that the other side will disagree over the definition of an element, you should draft an issue around that element. We saw an example of this earlier when we asked whether "leaving" in the abandonment rule meant moving out of the entire dwelling or moving out of that part of the dwelling in which both spouses normally live together.

2. *Disagreement about the facts.* If you anticipate that the other side will disagree over whether the facts fit within an element, you should draft an issue around that element. In a child-custody case, for example, each parent may present numerous conflicting facts on whether it would be in the "best interests" of the child to be placed with one parent or the other. An issue clearly exists on the element of "best

legal issue
A question of law; a question of what the law is, or what the law means, or how the law applies to a set of facts. Also called *issue of law.* If the dispute is over the existence or nonexistence of the alleged facts, it is referred to as a *question of fact,* a *factual issue,* or an *issue of fact.*

element in contention
The element or portion of a rule about which the parties cannot agree. The disagreement may be over the definition of the element, whether the facts fit within the element, or both.

interests." Sometimes fact gaps will interfere with your ability to identify issues. (See the earlier discussion on the need for more facts.) If, for example, a tax deduction can be taken for alimony payments, but we are not told in the problem whether the alimony was in fact paid by the ex-husband, we have a fact gap. We will not know whether there is an alimony-tax issue until we close this gap by finding out.

Let's return to the pharmacy example:

§ 25–403 A pharmacist must not sell prescription drugs to a minor.

Suppose that Fred Jones owns a drugstore and is a licensed pharmacist. One day he sells tetracycline to Phil, a 19-year-old male. Has Fred violated § 25–403? Step one in answering this question is to break § 25–403 into its elements:

Elements of § 25–403

1. Pharmacist
2. Must not sell
3. Prescription drugs
4. To a minor

These elements become a checklist from which we begin to explore the presence of legal issues.

Elements 1 and 2 are not realistic candidates for legal issues. There is no reasonable doubt over whether Fred is a pharmacist and over whether he engaged in selling. The facts clearly tell us that he is a pharmacist who did make a sale.

What about element 3? Should it become the basis of a legal issue? Did Fred sell a "prescription drug"? Is tetracycline such a drug? There is a *factual* gap that hinders our ability to answer the question. The facts do not tell us whether tetracycline is sold over the counter or whether Phil purchased it by prescription. Further interviewing or investigation is needed on this factual question. This is a "next step" that should be listed at the end of the memo.

Element 4 also poses some ambiguity. Who is a minor? Is a 19-year-old a minor? It is not clear. This ambiguity should prompt the preliminary draft of a legal issue:

Is a 19-year-old a "minor" within the meaning of § 25–403?

An alternate (more formal) phrasing of the issue would be as follows:

When a pharmacist sells tetracycline to a 19-year-old, has the pharmacist violated § 25–403, which prohibits sales of "prescription drugs" to "a minor"?

ASSIGNMENT A.4

In each of the following situations, you are given a fact situation plus a rule in the form of a statute. Phrase the legal issue involved in each situation.

a. *Facts:* Len is divorced from Mary, who is now deceased. His 20-year-old son, Sam, has just graduated from Benton College. Len paid all of Sam's expenses at Benton. Sam has been accepted by the Benton dental school. Len can afford to pay Sam's dental school expenses but refuses to do so. Sam says that his father is obligated to pay these expenses.

Statute: § 49(g). Child support shall include payment of college expenses if the child has the ability to attend and the parent has the ability to pay.

b. *Facts:* Jane and her two children by a former marriage receive public assistance. Jane's friend Jack, who is a traveling salesman, stays at Jane's apartment during his monthly business trips. This allows him to stay in town five to ten days at a time. He does not give Jane any money while he is with her.

Statute: § 11351. Whenever an unrelated adult male resides with a family applying for or receiving public assistance, he shall be required to make a financial contribution to the family which shall not be less than it would cost him to provide himself with an independent living arrangement.

INTEROFFICE MEMORANDUM

One format in which you present your legal analysis to your supervisor is the **interoffice memorandum**. Exhibit A-2 presents an example.

interoffice memorandum
A written report addressed to someone in the office where you work, usually a supervisor. If the report explains how the law applies to a given set of facts, it is a memorandum of law.

EXHIBIT A-2 Interoffice Memorandum

INTEROFFICE MEMORANDUM

TO:	Mary Adams
FROM:	George Wilson
DATE:	March 26, 2011
NAME OF CASE:	Hagerty v. Hagerty
OFFICE FILE NO.:	11-49
COURT DOCKET NO.:	B-408-11
RE:	"Serious marital discord" and the refusal to seek alcoholism treatment under § 402(b)

Statement of Assignment
You have asked me to determine whether our client, Linda Hagerty, can prevent her husband from dissolving the marriage on the ground of "irretrievable breakdown" under § 402(b).

Issue
Is there "serious marital discord" constituting an "irretrievable breakdown" of a marriage under § 402(b) when one party believes that the marriage can be saved if the other party seeks treatment for alcoholism, which the latter refuses to seek?

Facts
Paul Hagerty has filed for dissolution of the marriage on the ground of "irretrievable breakdown of the marriage." Linda and Paul Hagerty have been married for four years. They have two children. Paul has a serious drinking problem according to our client. While intoxicated, he breaks furniture and is abusive to the children and his wife. She has repeatedly asked him to seek rehabilitation treatment through AA or some other counseling service. Two months ago she told him that he must leave unless he seeks treatment. He did leave but has refused treatment. She now insists that he return and undergo treatment. He has filed for a dissolution of the marriage on the ground of an "irretrievable breakdown of the marriage." He feels that their marriage is hopeless. Our client wants to defend the action and prevent the dissolution.

Analysis
Section 402(b) provides as follows:

A court may make a finding that there has been an irretrievable breakdown of the marriage relationship if the finding is supported by evidence of serious marital discord adversely affecting the attitude of the parties toward the marriage.

(continued)

Two elements must be present before a court will declare the existence of an "irretrievable breakdown of the marriage":

> (1) serious marital discord;

> (2) adversely affecting the attitude of the parties toward the marriage.

Section 402(b) has been in existence for less than a year. No case law exists defining the terms of § 402(b), and no other statutes exist providing these definitions.

(1) Serious Marital Discord

Two definitions of the phrase "serious marital discord" are possible. Mr. Hagerty will argue that such "discord" exists if either party to the marriage feels that there is no likelihood of reconciliation. Our client, on the other hand, should argue that both parties must agree that reconciliation is unlikely, or at least that evidence of marital collapse must exist in addition to the views of only one of the spouses. Under Mr. Hagerty's definition, there is "serious marital discord" because one party (himself in this case) feels that there is no likelihood of reconciliation. Our client feels that a reconciliation is likely if her husband will seek treatment for his alcoholism. Our client can argue that "marital discord" was meant to refer to the opinions of *two* people — the partners to the marriage. The agreement of both sides on the likelihood of reconciliation is critical to a determination of whether the marriage can survive. The lack of such a likelihood in the minds of *both* spouses amounts to an "irretrievable breakdown."

But our client is convinced that the marriage is retrievable. A court should not rule otherwise when one of the parties takes this position. In her view, Mr. Hagerty is sick and is in no position to judge whether a reconciliation is possible. His refusal to seek help for the treatable illness or sickness of alcoholism should disqualify him from making meaningful assessments as to whether the marriage can survive. The legislature could not have intended that a marriage would end simply at the whim of one of the parties, particularly when the party who wants out is too ill to make a considered judgment on the likelihood of reconciliation.

She can further argue that § 402(b) does not state that either party can obtain a dissolution of the marriage simply because one of the spouses says he or she wants it. The statute calls for "evidence" of "serious marital discord." There must be a showing of irretrievability. This must mean that a court is required to look at the underlying evidence of whether there is hope. A mere statement by one of the parties that there is no hope is not enough "evidence." More is required. The court should examine Mr. Hagerty's condition and listen to whatever expert witnesses she may be able to call. She will want an opportunity to prove through such witnesses that hope does exist because of treatment. This opportunity is destroyed if the court accepts Mr. Hagerty's statement at face value that the marriage cannot be saved. Section 402(b) calls for a more thorough probe by a court.

Mr. Hagerty, on the other hand, will argue that our client is using the wrong definition of "serious marital discord" for purposes of establishing an "irretrievable breakdown." If either side feels that there is no likelihood of reconciliation, a court should find evidence of "serious marital discord" for purposes of establishing an "irretrievable breakdown." Otherwise, one of the parties could force a dead marriage to continue out of stubbornness, unreasonableness, or malice. The legislature could not have intended such a result.

Mr. Hagerty will argue that our client told him to leave and to enter treatment. We can probably assume from the facts that Mr. Hagerty does not want to enter treatment or that he thinks treatment will not be effective. In either event, Mrs. Hagerty has laid down a condition that Mr. Hagerty says cannot be met. He will argue that to force him into treatment would be as unproductive as to force him to continue his marriage.

He will further try to argue that our client's actions demonstrate that even she feels that "serious marital discord" exists. She threw him out, and she insisted on an unacceptable condition. She may say that she thinks the marriage is salvageable, but her actions point to the opposite conclusion.

(2) Adversely Affecting the Attitude of the Parties toward the Marriage

It is unlikely that this element will be in contention. Both parties will probably agree that the difficulties have adversely affected their views of the marriage. The phrase "adversely affecting" is not defined in the statute or in any court opinions. An "attitude" that has been "adversely" affected means no more than negative feelings toward something — the marriage. Even Mrs. Hagerty cannot deny that she has negative feelings about the marriage as a result of the controversy surrounding alcoholism. She may not think the marriage is hopeless, but her feelings are certainly negative, as evidenced by the fact that she told him to leave the house.

It might be significant to note that the second element refers to "parties" — in the plural. The statute does not say "attitude of one of the parties." This point might bolster Mrs. Hagerty's argument on the first element that the legislature intended both parties to feel that reconciliation was not possible.

Conclusion

The only element in contention will be the first. I think that Mr. Hagerty has the stronger argument. If Mr. Hagerty feels that the treatment for his alcoholism will not help the marriage and if he refuses to undergo this treatment, it is difficult to avoid the conclusion that the parties to the marriage cannot be reconciled. The main argument favoring our client is that the legislature may not have intended a marriage to be terminated this easily.

NEXT STEPS

There are two things that I have not yet done on this case. Let me know if you want me to do either of them:

(1) I have not yet checked the legislative history of §402(b) to determine whether it will provide any guidance on the meaning of § 402(b).

(2) I have not yet checked the statutes of other states to see if they have the same language as our § 402(b). If such statutes exist, then I would check opinions interpreting these statutes as potential persuasive authority for our case.

ASSIGNMENT A.5

Bill and Pat were married in State A on March 13, 1983, where they continue to live. They have one child, Brenda, age 15. Since 2000, Bill and Pat have been having marital difficulties. Bill is a traveling salesman who spends a good deal of time away from State A. From 2001 to 2004, he did not see his family at all. He returned on February 4, 2005. He and Pat attended marital counseling sessions for about three months. By the summer of 2005, problems again arose. Bill left home. On the day he left, he said to Pat, "If you can straighten yourself out, I'll consider coming back." He packed all of his clothes and books but left behind the high school trophy he received for swimming. Although the departure was bitter, both sides agreed to maintain their joint checking account. Bill made deposits in the account. Pat wrote checks on the account to cover household expenses.

In September of 2005, Bill contacted a real estate broker in State B about renting an apartment for six months in that state. The broker suggested tax advantages of buying a condominium in State B as opposed to renting. Bill was persuaded. He had been in State B only once or twice for his job, but wanted to explore the possibility of more extensive business opportunities there. On October 1, 2005, the broker called to inform Bill of a good condominium prospect in State B. On October 5, 2005, Bill was killed in an automobile accident on a highway in State B while on the way to examine the condominium for the first time.

State B wants Bill's estate to pay a state inheritance tax on the theory that at the time of death, Bill was domiciled in State B. The representative of Bill's estate disagrees and claims that Bill was domiciled in State A at the time of death. In State B, the following statute exists, which is the basis of State B's claim:

§ 14. Inheritance taxes are owed by persons who die domiciled in this state, which exists when the decedent had a physical presence in the state with the intent of making the state a permanent home.

Prepare an interoffice memorandum of law on the question of State B's right to inheritance taxes. Do not do any legal research on the problem. Do the memo solely on the basis of the information provided above.

The office file number is 05-421. There is no court docket number because no court action has yet been initiated. The Tax Department of State B has taken the position that inheritance taxes are due under § 14. The law office where you work has been retained by the representative of Bill's estate, which does not want to pay the inheritance tax to State B. Because the inheritance tax rate for State A is lower than for State B, it would be to the advantage of the estate to obtain a ruling that at the time of death, Bill was domiciled in State A.

For purposes of this assignment, you can assume the following definitions apply:

- *Physical presence:* actually being in a place

- *Intent of making the state a permanent home:* the desire to live in the state indefinitely; the place to which one intends to return when away (a person can have only one permanent home)

☑ GENERAL INSTRUCTIONS FOR THE LEGAL-ANALYSIS ASSIGNMENT

1. The starting point in the legal-analysis assignment is a set of facts in the assignment. It is to this set of facts that you must apply the rule or rules.

2. How do you find the rule or rules to apply to the facts?

   - By examining the text of the chapter immediately preceding the assignment, or

   - By examining the state code of your state—if you are told to do so in the assignment.

3. Carefully examine each word/phrase in the rule being applied. Break the rule into its elements, and concentrate on those elements in contention.

4. Define each important word/phrase in each element.

5. Determine whether more than one definition exists for each important word/phrase.

6. If more than one definition is possible, state each definition and show what effect the different definitions would have on the result of the analysis. How would each side use the definition that is favorable to itself?

7. State the legal issue(s).

8. Carefully examine each of the facts given to you in the assignment.

9. Note any differences between the fact situation given in the assignment and comparable fact situations discussed in the text of the chapter immediately preceding the assignment. Assess whether such fact differences are significant.

10. If you determine that you need more facts to provide the analysis, state what facts you need and why you would like to have the additional facts. Specifically,

how will the additional facts assist in completing the analysis?

11. Analyze the facts from the perspective of both sides. Do not be dogmatic in your analysis. Whenever possible, show how the facts might be interpreted differently by both sides.

12. If requested by your instructor, give your answers in the format of an interoffice memorandum of law, as presented in Exhibit A-2.

13. Do not do any legal research on the assignment unless you are specifically instructed to do so.

COMPLAINT-DRAFTING ASSIGNMENT

Court litigation begins when one party files a petition or complaint against another party. This is the pleading that must state a cause of action such as negligence, breach of contract, or divorce on the ground of irretrievable breakdown. See Exhibit 7-4 for a sample divorce petition/complaint.

Before you begin drafting the complaint (or any document) from scratch, find out if someone has already prepared a standard form that you can use. These are available in a number of places. To locate forms on the Internet, run these searches on Google, Bing, or Yahoo:

- family law forms divorce aa
- family law forms agreement aa

In place of aa, type the name of your state. See also the links to forms for your state in Appendix D and in the Helpful Websites section at the end of Chapters 4, 7, 8, and 15 in this book. In the law library, standard forms can be found in formbooks, manuals, practice texts, some statutory codes, and some court rules. Many legal stationery stores print and sell them. Most are written by private attorneys. Occasionally, however, a standard form will be written by the legislature or by the court as the suggested or required format to be used.

Many law offices have "forms files" (often on the computer) that contain forms used in prior cases that might be adaptable for the case of a current client. The forms file may also contain commercial forms purchased by the office. As the forms file grows, it becomes a regular source of standard forms.

Considerable care must be exercised in the use of standard forms. They can be very deceptive in that they appear to require little more than a filling in of blanks. Intelligent use of the forms, however, usually requires much more. The guidelines in the following list should be kept in mind.

HOW TO AVOID ABUSING A STANDARD FORM

1. The cardinal rule is to *adapt* the form to the particulars of the client's case on which you are working.

2. Do not be afraid of changing the preprinted language of the form if you have a good reason for doing so. Whenever you make such a change, bring it to the attention of your supervisor for approval.

3. Never use a standard form unless and until you have satisfied yourself that you know the meaning of every word and phrase on it, especially **boilerplate**. The great temptation of most form users is to ignore what they do not understand because the form has been used so often in the past with no apparent difficulty. Do not give in to this temptation. Find out what everything means by:

- Asking your supervisor
- Asking more experienced paralegals or other knowledgeable people

boilerplate
Standard or often-used language that is commonly found in the same kind of document. Standard verbiage.

- Doing other legal research
- Using a legal dictionary

4. Once you have found a form that appears useful, look around for another form that covers the same topic. Analyze the different forms available. Which one is preferable? Why? Always be on the lookout for a better form.

5. Do not leave any blank spaces on the form. If a question does not apply to your case, write NA (not applicable) in the space for that question.

6. If the form was written for another state, be sure it can be adapted and is adapted to the law of your state. Very often, out-of-state forms are unadaptable.

7. Often you will be told to go to an old case file to find a document in that file that might be used as a model for a similar document you need to draft for a current case. Many offices have collected older forms (and commercially bought forms) in a *forms file* stored on their computers. This file is a valuable source of standard forms. All of the above cautions apply equally to the adaptation of such forms.

✔ GENERAL INSTRUCTIONS FOR THE COMPLAINT-DRAFTING ASSIGNMENT

1. Your objective is to draft a complaint (called a petition in some states) that would be acceptable to a trial court in your state. For an example of the general structure of many divorce complaints, which you need to adapt to the law of your state, see Exhibit 7-4 in Chapter 7.

2. Go to your state statutory code and read everything you can about complaints in general and about complaints involving divorce and other family-law matters in particular. To help you find material in the statutory code, use the CARTWHEEL.

3. Go to the court rules of the courts of your state and read everything you can about complaints in general and about complaints involving divorce and other family-law matters in particular. To help you find material in the court rules, use the CARTWHEEL.

4. Find out if your state has any standard-form complaints written by the court or other official entity. Your state code or court rules will tell you if such forms exist and whether they are optional or required. Caution must be exercised in using standard forms. See How to Avoid Abusing a Standard Form.

5. Many states have practice manuals, formbooks, or other practice materials written by attorneys. These materials often contain standard-form complaints that may be helpful. See How to Avoid Abusing a Standard Form.

6. In the complaint-drafting assignments, you will often need additional facts in order to write the complaint (e.g., the names of the parties, the parties' addresses, the docket number of the case, some of the basic facts that prompted the plaintiff to file the complaint). You can make up the facts that you need so long as your facts are consistent with the limited facts that are provided in the assignment.

7. The heading or introductory part of the complaint is called the *caption*. Normally, it contains:

- The name of the court
- The parties' names and their litigation status (plaintiff, defendant, etc.)
- The docket number assigned by the court
- The title of the pleading (Complaint for . . .)

8. Each paragraph is usually numbered separately. The content of each paragraph should be limited to a single allegation or to a small number of allegations that are closely related.

9. The *commencement* goes after the caption. Find out what your state requires in the commencement of a complaint (see instructions 1–5). Some states require a citation to the statute that gives the court its subject-matter jurisdiction (its power to hear this kind of case) and to the statute on the court's venue. These statutes require a statement of basic facts that covers the residence of the plaintiff, the existence of a marriage, etc.

10. The *body* of the complaint contains a statement of the plaintiff's cause of action. In a divorce action, for example, this would consist of the facts constituting the grounds for the divorce.

11. The cause of action should be stated briefly and concisely. Avoid long recitations of the facts.

12. You cannot draft a complaint unless you know every component or element of the cause of action. For a divorce on the ground of living apart, for example, there must be a voluntary living apart for a designated period of time, and the time apart must be consecutive. In most states, there

should be allegations of fact in the complaint that cover each of these elements of the ground.

13. With the exception of the citation to the statutes on subject matter jurisdiction and venue referred to in instruction 9, you do not give citations to statutes, court rules, or opinions in the complaint. Limit yourself to the statement of facts—the essential facts.

14. If you are not sure of a fact, you can state it "on information and belief."

15. If the plaintiff has more than one cause of action or theory of recovery, you should state all of them. Each should be

stated separately and numbered I, II, III, etc. Each separate theory or cause of action is called a *count*.

16. The *prayer* for relief should contain everything the plaintiff is asking the court to do.

17. The court may require the *subscription* (signature) of the party filing the complaint plus the subscription of that party's attorney.

18. The *verification* is a formal declaration that a party has read the pleading and swears that it is true to the best of his or her knowledge. The party thereby verifies the pleading.

AGREEMENT-DRAFTING ASSIGNMENT

Some of the assignments in this book ask you to draft an agreement (e.g., prenuptial agreement, cohabitation agreement, separation agreement, custody agreement).

☑ GENERAL INSTRUCTIONS FOR THE AGREEMENT-DRAFTING ASSIGNMENT

1. You will need additional facts in order to draft the agreement (e.g., you may need the names of the parties, their addresses, the property they own, how they own it, other economic facts). You can make up these facts unless the assignment tells you to obtain them otherwise (e.g., by interviewing a fellow student).

2. It is often useful to obtain copies of similar agreements that were written in the past for other clients and/or to obtain copies of model agreements available online, in formbooks, manuals, practice books, etc. Such material may provide effective starting points for your own drafting. Proceed with caution, however. See How to Avoid Abusing a Standard Form. The complaint-drafting instructions give you suggestions on finding forms online.

3. It is critical that you know the law of the area covered by the agreement. What can and cannot be accomplished by the agreement? What legal pitfalls must be avoided? Research in the area of the law, therefore, is an essential precondition of drafting.

4. For purposes of the agreement-drafting assignments in this book, however, you do not have to do any legal research unless your instructor tells you otherwise. You will find all the law you need by reading the chapter text immediately preceding the drafting assignment you are doing.

5. When tax considerations are relevant, take them into account in drafting the agreement. For the basics of taxation, see Chapter 11.

6. Know what the client wants to accomplish by the agreement. Know the specific client objectives. (If you do not know what they are, see instruction 1 on obtaining facts

for the agreement.) It is too general, for example, to say that the client wants to divide the property of the spouses in an equitable manner. A more *specific* and acceptable example of an objective would be to have the other spouse use the vacation home for 10 years or until she remarries, whichever occurs earlier. Have all the specific objectives in mind when you draft. Each clause in the agreement should relate to one or more of the objectives. Your drafting guide is your statement of objectives.

7. At the beginning of the agreement, label the kind of agreement that it is (e.g., *Separation Agreement*). Also at the beginning, state the names and addresses of the parties entering the agreement.

8. Number each paragraph consecutively (1, 2, 3, etc.). Limit the subject matter of each paragraph to a single topic or to closely related topics. Be as narrow as possible in selecting the topic of a paragraph. For example, in a separation agreement dealing with the disposition of the property that the spouses accumulated during the marriage, each paragraph should cover a separate category of property. Similarly, there should be separately numbered paragraphs covering custody of the children, visitation rights, alimony, etc.

9. A mistake made by many drafters is to assume that everyone will be using the same definition of words. *Major words* should always be defined. A major word is any important word that could have more than one meaning. The word "property," for example, has several meanings (e.g., real property, personal property, property in one's possession now, property to be received in the future). What meaning

(continued)

☑ **GENERAL INSTRUCTIONS FOR THE AGREEMENT-DRAFTING ASSIGNMENT** *(continued)*

did the parties intend for the word *property*? Such words should be carefully defined in the agreement.

10. One sign of an effective agreement is fairness. Avoid trying to take unfair advantage of the other side in drafting the agreement. The result may be an unworkable agree-

ment leading to delay, animosity, and litigation expense. The cooperation of both sides is necessary to make the agreement work. An important incentive to such cooperation is a feeling by both parties that the agreement is fair.

COURT-OPINION ASSIGNMENT

You need to know how to locate court opinions on family-law topics for two reasons:

- To help you find opinions that have interpreted statutes on family-law topics.
- To help you find the **common law.** A considerable amount of family law is part of the common law, which is judge-made law in the absence of controlling statutory law or other higher law. If the legislature passes a statute that covers a controversy in litigation, the statute controls even if there is also common law that covers the controversy. Suppose, however, there are no statutes governing the dispute. In such a case, the court may be free to create new law to resolve the litigation. If it does so, the new law becomes part of the common law.

common law

Judge-made law in the absence of controlling statutory law or other higher law. (See glossary for additional meanings.)

☑ **GENERAL INSTRUCTIONS FOR THE COURT-OPINION ASSIGNMENT**

1. To find court opinions (and other laws) written by your state online (without cost), see Appendix D and the following sites:

   - www.findlaw.com/casecode
   - www.lexisone.com
   - findacase.com
   - law.justia.com
   - www.plol.org
   - www.law.stanford.edu/library/research
   - www.ll.georgetown.edu/guides/freelowcost.cfm
   - www.law.cornell.edu/states/listing.html
   - openjurist.org

   In addition:

   - Go to the home page of your state government (www.aa.gov) (insert your state's abbreviation or full name in place of aa). On this page, look for links to the courts of your state. You will be told what opinions are available.
   - In Google, Bing, or Yahoo, do a court search (aa courts) (insert your state's abbreviation or full name in place of aa). This search should lead you to your state courts.

2. Once you find a court site, look for links on the site to its opinions. Then use the CARTWHEEL technique to help you choose words or phrases to use in the search box for the opinions. The same is true if you are using any of the major fee-based search services such as Westlaw, LexisNexis, and LoisLaw.

3. To find court opinions written by your state in a traditional law library, use these leads:

   - Notes to Decisions found within most annotated statutory codes
   - The state digest or the regional digest covering opinions of your state, or the American Digest System
   - *American Law Reports (A.L.R.)*
   - Footnote references in formbooks, hornbooks, manuals, legal encyclopedias, legal periodical literature, etc.
   - *Words and Phrases* (a multi-volume legal dictionary)

   We will briefly review each of these resources.

4. You may not be familiar with all the legal resources mentioned above. If so, do not wait for a course in legal

research before starting to learn how to use them. Start *now* by asking questions. Ask librarians, fellow students, teachers, practicing attorneys, and paralegals, etc. Above all, browse through these resources on your own as often as you can. With practice and determination, you will soon be able to obtain materials from them.

5. *Notes to Decisions.* To know how to use Notes to Decisions, you must first know how to use an annotated statutory code. (Review the General Instructions for the State-Code Assignment.) The notes contain summaries of opinions that have interpreted statutes. Therefore, in order to find these notes, you must first find a statute that covers the topic under examination. If opinions exist interpreting this statute, they will be summarized in the Notes to Decisions following the statute. Be sure to check for more recent notes in the pocket parts of the code.

6. *Digests.* Digests are volumes containing thousands of small paragraph summaries of court opinions. A digest is, in effect, a massive index to court opinions and consequently is often called a "case finder." There are three kinds of digests—all of which contain the same basic material and format:

- State Digest. Most states have their own digest (i.e., volumes of small paragraph summaries of all the opinions written by courts in a particular state).

- Regional Digest. There are a number of regional digests covering the opinions written by the state courts of several neighboring states.

- American Digest System. This is the most comprehensive digest of all, covering the opinions of almost every court in the country.

The main index in each of these digests is in separate volumes called the *Descriptive Word Index.* To use these indexes effectively, use the CARTWHEEL.

7. *American Law Reports* (A.L.R.). These volumes contain the full text of selected court opinions plus extensive research material on issues in the opinions. (For an example, see Exhibit 1-13 in Chapter 1.) The material in A.L.R. is called an *annotation.* The annotations often include a state-by-state breakdown of the legal issues treated in the annotation. Hence, when you find an annotation on a family-law topic, you can look for court opinions from your state on that topic. (The citations to these opinions are arranged alphabetically at the beginning of each annotation.) There are eight units of the *American Law Reports* volumes: A.L.R., A.L.R.2d, A.L.R.3d, A.L.R.4th, A.L.R.5th, A.L.R.6th, A.L.R. Fed., and A.L.R. Fed. 2d. The main index to these volumes is called the *Index to Annotations.* The CARTWHEEL will help you use this index.

8. Footnote references in other books. Often the footnotes are the most valuable part of formbooks, hornbooks, manuals, legal encyclopedias, and legal periodical literature. (For examples of these volumes, see Exhibits 1-9, 1-10, 1-11, and 1-12 in Chapter 1.) These footnotes usually give citations to court opinions on the topics being discussed in the body of the text. In a set of books that has extensive footnotes, such as either of the major legal encyclopedias (*Corpus Juris Secundum* and *American Jurisprudence 2d*), the references to court opinions in the footnotes may be organized alphabetically by state, which will make it easier for you to determine if opinions of your state are provided.

9. *Words and Phrases.* This is a multivolume set of books containing thousands of definitions of legal terms. The definitions are quotations from court opinions. Try to find definitions of words from court opinions of your state on the family-law topic under examination.

ASSIGNMENT A.6

Answer the following questions by going to the nearest large law library to which you have access.

a. Give the name of every reporter in the library that will contain the full text of court opinions written by state courts of your state. Who publishes each reporter? What courts are covered in each?

b. Give the name of every digest that will provide small paragraph summaries of the court opinions of your state.

c. Go to one of the digests you mentioned in part (b) above. Use the index features of this digest to locate a key topic and number for *any* five family-law subjects. (Select five different family-law subject areas.) What are the key topics and numbers? Give the cite of the first opinion summarized under each key topic and number you selected.

CHECKLIST-FORMULATION ASSIGNMENT

It is important that you learn how to write checklists that could become part of a manual. Every rule that you are told about or that you read about can be "translated" into a checklist. Checklist formulation should eventually become second nature to you. The sooner you start thinking about and creating lists of dos, don'ts, tasks, etc., the better.

Suppose that you have before you the following statute of your state:

§ 1742 No marriage shall be solemnized without a license issued by the county clerk of any county of this state not more than thirty days prior to the date of the solemnization of the marriage.

One way to handle this statute is to create a checklist of questions that you would ask a client in order to determine whether the statute has been complied with or violated. Some of the questions would be:

1. Did you have a marriage license?
2. Where did you get the license? Did you obtain it from a county clerk in this state?
3. On what date did you obtain the license?
4. On what date did you go through the marriage ceremony ("solemnization")? (You want to determine if there were more than 30 days between the date the county issued the license and the date of the ceremony.)

These are some of the questions that must be asked as part of a large number of questions concerning the validity of a particular marriage. If you were creating a manual, the above four questions in your checklist for § 1742 could go under the manual topic of "Marriage Formation" or "Marriage License." Most laws can be translated into checklists in this way.

☑ GENERAL INSTRUCTIONS FOR THE CHECKLIST-FORMULATION ASSIGNMENT

1. The starting point in all the checklist-formulation assignments will be a rule. The rule usually will be found within a statute or a court opinion to which you will be referred.

2. Your objective is to make a list of questions that you would ask yourself, a client, or a witness for the purpose of determining whether the rule might apply.

3. Make sure you understand the rule. Closely analyze it. Make inquiries about what you do not understand in the rule. Consult a legal dictionary. Read closely related rules in order to see the rule you are examining in context. Read the rule again.

4. Break the rule down into elements, as discussed earlier.

5. For each element of the rule, design a question or a series of questions.

6. Every time the rule says that something must be done or that something must not be done, create a question or a series of questions designed to determine whether it was done.

7. Every time the rule imposes a precondition (i.e., *if* such and such occurs, *then* . . .), create a question or a series of questions designed to determine whether the precondition occurred.

8. Be alert to the word *and* in a rule. It usually refers to additional requirements. Create questions designed to determine whether all the additional requirements were met.

9. Be alert to the word *or* in a rule. It usually refers to alternative requirements. Create questions designed to determine if *both* alternatives were met.

10. If you have been diligent in creating checklists, you will be taking major steps toward the creation of your own manual. Even if you do not create manuals, checklist creation is still valuable as a practical way of thinking about any law. (For other components of such a manual, see the General Instructions for the Systems Assignment below.)

FACT-GATHERING ASSIGNMENTS

The next three categories of assignments cover various facets of fact-gathering in family law. A cardinal principle in this process is the necessity of obtaining relevant factual detail. This is achieved through a technique called **fact particularization**. Once you identify the facts collected in the case thus far, you assume that these facts are woefully incomplete. For example, they fail to give more than one version of what happened. Then you identify a large number of basic *who, what, where, how, when,* and *why* questions that, if answered, will provide as complete a picture of what happened as is possible at this particular time.

Suppose you are working on a child-custody case. To particularize this case, you ask a series of questions centered on the following interrelated and overlapping clusters: participant details, place details, time details, incident details, and verification details.

1. *Participant details.* Who is involved in the case? Obtain the names of children, parents, grandparents, other relatives, neighbors, government agency workers connected with the case, friends of the children and of the parents, teachers and ministers who know the family, employers of the parents, medical personnel who have treated the children, witnesses to specific events, etc. What does each participant know about current and past family living conditions? How do you know? What have the participants said? What is the age and the educational background of each participant? etc.

2. *Place details.* Where do the children live? Where else have they lived? Where do they go for school, religious services, recreational activities, medical care, cultural events, etc.? For each place, give the address, how far away from home it is, how the children get there, what costs are involved, who pays them, what happens there, what the feelings of the children are about the place, why they think so, what they have said about it, what other participants think about the place, etc.

3. *Time details.* In an average day, how much time do the children spend on their normal activities? When did any of the important events occur (e.g., abuse)? How long did it last? Has it occurred more than once in the past? When?

4. *Incident details.* What happened? What events are relevant to the well-being of the children and the fitness of the parents to be guardians? Explain ordinary and extraordinary occurrences in their day-to-day lives.

5. *Verification details.* Every fact you have obtained has a source (e.g., the client, a record). Assume that you wanted to obtain an additional source to verify the original source of every important fact. Where would you go? Whom would you ask? What additional records would you try to obtain? How would you try to obtain them? Assess the believability of each source, etc.

These categories of questions are interrelated. You will be simultaneously probing for details on people, incidents, dates, etc. There may be considerable overlap in your questions. This is not significant so long as you achieve comprehensiveness in factual detail (i.e., so long as you achieve factual particularity). Also, the above list of questions is just the tip of the iceberg. Scores and scores of additional questions of the same kind must be pursued. Given the complexity of human events and of human relationships, a great deal of factual detail is needed before you are able to achieve factual comprehensiveness. The objective of fact particularization is to get you into the habit of going beneath the surface in order to look at people and events from a variety of perspectives. Nothing is taken at face value.

fact particularization (FP)
A fact-gathering technique to generate a large list of factual questions (who, what, where, how, when, and why) that will help you obtain a specific and comprehensive picture of all available facts that are relevant to a legal issue.

INVESTIGATION-STRATEGY ASSIGNMENT

In many cases, an enormous number of facts must be gathered and verified. To keep from becoming overwhelmed, a plan of action must be developed. The investigation-strategy assignment is designed to help you construct such a plan in order to give the investigation some direction.

☑ GENERAL INSTRUCTIONS FOR THE INVESTIGATION-STRATEGY ASSIGNMENT

1. The starting point in this assignment is a set of facts you are given in the assignment. Assume you have entered the case after these facts have been collected by someone else.

2. Assume further that these facts are inadequate because *many* more facts are needed. Review the material on *fact particularization* discussed earlier.

3. Closely examine the facts you have. Are they arranged chronologically? If not, rearrange them chronologically so that the facts tell a story with a beginning, middle, and end. Of course, there will be many gaps in the story. Your task will be to identify these gaps and to raise the questions that the investigator would need to ask to try to fill or close the gaps. These questions will become the investigator's strategy or plan for further investigation.

4. The focus of the questions will be on what you *do not* know about the facts you have.

5. Isolate the facts you have into small clusters of facts (e.g., the child is unhappy, the husband left the house in a rage). For each small set of facts that you identify or isolate in this way, make a *large* list of questions that fall into two interrelated categories:

   - Questions designed to obtain additional facts that will help you compile a much more detailed picture of what happened. To aid you in this list, ask the basic who, what, where, how, when, and why questions about every fact. (See the material on fact particularization.)

   - Questions designed to obtain facts that will help substantiate (or prove) the facts that you already have. There is no rigid formula to follow in making these lists of

questions. The goal is a comprehensive list of questions that, if answered, would provide a comprehensive picture of what happened.

6. Consider structuring questions to elicit details on participants, places, times, and incidents.

7. Be particularly scrupulous about dates. Ask questions about the dates that you have and also about the dates that are missing.

8. In your questions on participants, try to identify a diversity of *versions.* Make a list of every person who is involved or who could be involved in the facts. Assume that each person potentially has a different version of a critical incident or series of incidents. Structure questions that will elicit these different versions.

9. Preceding most of the assignments will be a discussion of some legal principles or rules of law governing family-law topics. Include questions on the elements of any relevant rules of law. (On breaking rules into their elements, see the earlier discussion; see also General Instructions for the Checklist-Formulation Assignment.)

10. The list of questions in this assignment does not have to be written in any particular order. Select any format that is readable.

11. In some of the chapters, you will find lists of interviewing questions and investigation tasks. If these lists are relevant to the area of the assignment, expand on them. Use the lists as points of departure for further fact particularization.

INTERVIEW ASSIGNMENT

The interview assignment relies on some of the skills covered earlier, especially fact particularization and checklist formulation.

☑ GENERAL INSTRUCTIONS FOR THE INTERVIEW ASSIGNMENT

1. In this assignment, you are asked to interview another person (e.g., a fellow student, someone at home).

2. Review the material on *fact particularization.* One of your objectives is to obtain substantial factual specificity. As the

interviewer, you should strive for a comprehensive picture of the people and events involved in the assignment.

3. In some of the chapters, you will find lists of interviewing questions. If the lists are relevant to the area of the assignment,

expand on them. Use the lists as points of departure for further fact particularization.

4. After you complete the interview, prepare a report from your notes. For the heading of your report, see Exhibit A-2, Interoffice Memorandum. (If you are interviewing a new client, label your report "Intake Memorandum.") Indicate who wrote the report or memo (you), who will receive it (your instructor or supervisor), the name of the person interviewed (the interviewee), the date of the interview, and the date you turned in the report or memo. The first paragraph should state the assignment (e.g., "You have asked me to interview [*name of the interviewee*] in order to [*state the purpose of the interview assignment*]).

5. In preparation for your interview, identify every rule of law that might be relevant to the fact situation (see the discussion in the text preceding the interview assignment). Break down each rule into its elements. Be sure to ask questions that are relevant to the applicability of every element. (See also the General Instructions for the Checklist-Formulation Assignment.)

6. Try to arrange the facts in your intake memorandum in roughly chronological order so that the facts unfold as a story with a beginning, middle, and end.

7. *Instructions to Interviewee:* Tell the person you are interviewing (the interviewee) that he or she can make up the facts in answer to your questions. so long as the facts are reasonably consistent with the facts initially provided.

8. Your instructor may decide to role-play the interview in front of the class. If so, the class may be asked to comment on how the interview was conducted (e.g., did the interview follow the assignment, was there adequate fact particularization, did the interview ramble, was the interviewee placed at ease, how could the interview have been improved?).

INTERROGATORY ASSIGNMENT

The purpose of **interrogatories** is to obtain factual information about the other party's case in order to prepare for trial. See Appendix C for an example of comprehensive interrogatories.

interrogatories

("rogs") A discovery device in which one party sends written questions to another party. (Discovery consists of devices used by parties to force information from each other before trial to aid in trial preparation. Examples of such devices include interrogatories and depositions.)

☑ GENERAL INSTRUCTIONS FOR THE INTERROGATORY ASSIGNMENT

1. Your objective in writing the questions (i.e., the interrogatories) is to obtain as much information as possible from the other side in order to assist you in preparing a case. See the material on *fact particularization.* The material on preparing investigation strategies should also be helpful in drafting interrogatories.

2. The interrogatories you draft should be acceptable in your state, which means that you should know whatever restrictions exist in statutes and in court rules of your state on the scope and format of interrogatories in family-law cases. For example, is there a limited number of questions that can be sent? (The example of the interrogatories in Appendix C assumes that there is no limit on the number of questions that can be asked.)

3. The scope of questions you can ask is usually quite broad. The test is whether the question is reasonably calculated to lead to evidence that will be admissible in court. This is a much broader standard than whether the answer itself would constitute admissible evidence.

4. Avoid questions that improperly seek **privileged** information. For example:

a. Questions that violate the privilege against self-incrimination (e.g., "Did you burn your house on purpose?").

b. Questions that violate the attorney–client privilege (e.g., "What did you tell your attorney about the child?").

c. Questions that violate the doctor–patient privilege (e.g., "What did you tell your doctor about the pain?").

d. Questions that violate the husband–wife privilege (e.g., "What did you tell your wife about the pain?"). This privilege does not apply when spouses are suing each other.

e. Questions that violate the attorney **work-product rule** (e.g., "Can I see the letter your attorney wrote you about the claim?").

5. In most states, it is permissible to ask a question that would involve the application of law to fact—sometimes called "contention interrogatories." Examples:

• "Do you contend that Mr._____ had no intent to marry you at the time of the wedding ceremony?"

• "Is it your position that Ms. _____ took the child out of the state in order to avoid complying with the custody decree?"

(continued)

If you ask such a question, be sure to follow it with a series of detailed questions that seek the factual reasons for the possible answers that could be given.

6 Be careful about the verb tense used in questions. Present tense (e.g., "is") is used to determine facts that are still current. Past tense (e.g., "was") is used to determine events that are over. If a question relates to past and present tense, break the question down into several questions.

7. It can be useful to try to find sample interrogatories online, in manuals, formbooks, and other practice materials. (See Appendix C.) Such interrogatories, of course, would have to be adapted to the particular needs of the client's case on which you are currently working. On the dangers of using such forms, see How to Avoid Abusing a Standard Form.

8. In a law office, it can be useful to go to the closed case file of another case that contains interrogatories in order to try to adapt them. Again, the use of such materials is only a point of departure. Great care must be used in determining what, if anything, can be borrowed from other interrogatories.

9. Before you draft your interrogatories, know the case (on which you are working) inside out. Read all pleadings filed to date (e.g., petition/complaint, answer, correspondences in the file, intake memorandum, etc.). Many ideas for questions will come from this knowledge. For purposes of the assignments in this book, however, you will not have access to such data, since the assignments will be based on hypothetical cases.

10. Litigation involves causes of action and defenses. Each of these causes of action and defenses can be broken down into elements. Each of these elements should become the basis of a checklist. Ask interrogatory questions that seek facts that could potentially be used to support each of the elements. (See also the General Instructions for the Checklist-Formulation Assignment.)

11. Consider phrasing your questions in such a way that the "story" of the facts unfolds chronologically.

12. Be constantly concerned about dates, full names, addresses, exact amounts, etc.

13. Ask what witnesses the other side intends to rely on to support its version of the facts at the trial. Ask for the names and addresses of such witnesses.

14. Ask what documentation, physical things, or exhibits the other side will rely on to support its version of the facts. You may want to ask that such items be sent along with the answers to the interrogatories or that such items be brought to a later deposition. (When you ask that a witness appear and bring specified items, you serve a **subpoena duces decum** on the witness.)

15. Avoid questions that call for simple "yes" or "no" answers unless you immediately follow up such questions with other questions that ask for details.

16. Include a definition section at the beginning of the interrogatories to avoid confusion and undue repetition in the later questions. This section will define words and phrases you intend to use in more than one question. For example: "A 'medical practitioner' as used in these interrogatories is meant to include any medical doctor, osteopathic physician, podiatrist, doctor of chiropractic, naturopathic physician, nurse, or other person who performs any form of healing art."

17. Phrase the questions so that the person answering will have to indicate whether he or she is talking from first-hand knowledge or second-hand knowledge (hearsay).

18. As to each fact, ask questions calculated to elicit the respondent's ability to comment on the fact (e.g., how far away was he or she, does he or she wear glasses, how long has he or she known the party, in what capacity?).

19. Avoid complicated and difficult-to-read questions. Be direct and concise.

privileged
Protected from disclosure; not discoverable.

work-product rule
Notes, working papers, memoranda, or similar things prepared by or for an attorney in anticipation of litigation are not discoverable by an opponent, absent a showing of substantial need. They are protected by privilege. Also called attorney work product.

subpoena duces tecum
A command that a witness appear at a certain time and place and bring specified things such as documents or jewelry.

FLOWCHART ASSIGNMENT

A flowchart is a step-by-step account of how something is done (e.g., a divorce or a particular kind of administrative proceeding such as a workers' compensation claim). A number of assignments in this book ask you to prepare a flowchart on the legal process under discussion.

☑ GENERAL INSTRUCTIONS FOR THE FLOWCHART ASSIGNMENT

1. Design the flowchart based upon the law of your state. The chart will give an overview of how something is done in your state (e.g., how to adopt a child, how to change your name).

2. The two primary sources of information for the flowchart are your state statutory code and the court rules for the courts in your state. See General Instructions for the State-Code Assignment. See also the CARTWHEEL technique for using the index of statutory codes, court rules, or any reference materials on the shelf or online.

3. You may be able to obtain information for the flowchart from manuals, formbooks, and other practice material online or in bound volumes on the shelf. It is recommended, however, that you try to obtain the information directly from the statutory code and the court rules. The practice materials may be out of date. Furthermore, to use practice materials intelligently, you must know how to check the accuracy and timeliness of such materials by going to the primary sources, namely, the statutory code and the court rules (and occasionally the constitution).

4. The flowchart must be chronological, moving from the first step of the process to the last step.

5. The structure and graphics that present the steps in the flowchart can be varied:

   - Use a series of boxes (one step per box) with all the boxes connected by arrows to show the progression of the process.
   - Use a list of brief, numbered paragraphs with each paragraph stating one step.
   - Use an outline with the major headings being the key phrases of the process (e.g., agency contact, pretrial, conference etc.).

   Use your imagination in designing the sequence of events outlined in the flowchart. To see examples of flowcharts, run this search in the images page of Google, Bing, or Yahoo: flowchart examples law.

6. The information in the chart should pertain to **procedural law** rather than **substantive law**. Procedural law consists of the technical steps for bringing or defending actions in litigation before a court or an administrative agency. An example would be the number of days within which a party can request an extension of time to file an answer after the complaint has been filed. Substantive law consists of rights and obligations other than purely procedural matters. An example would be the right to a divorce on the ground of irreconcilable differences.

7. For each item of information in the flowchart, state your source (e.g., the citation to the statute or court rule that provided you with the procedural information you used in the flowchart).

8. Statutory codes and court rules may have sections that deal with litigation in general. Such sections are often listed in the index and table of contents of the codes and court rules under broad topics such as "Civil Procedure," "Actions," "Court Procedures," "Courts," etc. You should check these sections to see what, if anything, they say about the topic of your flowchart.

9. In addition, your state statutory code and court rules may have special sections that cover the procedural steps that are unique to the topic of your flowchart. Check these as well.

10. If you are flowcharting litigation of any kind, numerous steps are often involved at the pretrial, trial, appeal, and enforcement stages. These steps need to be incorporated into your flowchart. Here are some examples of questions you should ask yourself about most litigation. The answers to such questions must be outlined in your flowchart if they are relevant to whatever you are flowcharting.

    - What agency, if any, has jurisdiction over the case?
    - What is the application process at the agency?
    - What court(s) have jurisdiction?
    - How is service of process made?
    - How is venue determined?
    - Do you need to use any special format for the petition/complaint?
    - How is the petition/complaint served and filed?
    - Do you need to use any special format for the answer?
    - How is the answer served and filed?
    - Are there special rules for raising counterclaims?
    - Are there any special motions that can be made (e.g., motion to dismiss)?
    - What rules govern pretrial discovery: depositions, interrogatories, requests for production (RFP) of documents and things, requests for admissions (RFA), and court-ordered examinations (physical and mental)?
    - What sanctions can be imposed for violation of the pretrial discovery rules?
    - What preliminary orders can be requested, and how must the request be made?
    - What rules govern the issuing of the final judgment?
    - How many days does a party have to appeal?
    - What court has jurisdiction to hear the appeal?
    - How can a judgment be enforced?

    The above list is not exhaustive. If there are other steps or more detailed steps that apply to the process you are flowcharting for your state, include them.

procedural law
The rules that govern the mechanics of resolving a dispute in court or in an administrative agency (e.g., a rule on the time by which a party must respond to a complaint).

substantive law
Nonprocedural laws that define or govern rights and duties.

SYSTEMS ASSIGNMENT

A system is a method of organizing people and resources to accomplish a task. Skill is required in designing and implementing an effective system. A good way to start learning the necessary skills is to identify and describe a system (or lack of a system) in the work lives of others. The systems assignment is designed to help you make such a start.

☑ GENERAL INSTRUCTIONS FOR THE SYSTEMS ASSIGNMENT

1. Your goal is to interview practicing attorneys, paralegals, law office administrators, and/or legal secretaries who handle family-law cases in order to identify their system for providing legal services on a certain kind of case.

2. You are seeking the following kinds of information about the system for handling the kind of case involved in this assignment:

   - Who does what on the case? What does the attorney do? The paralegal? The secretary?

   - In what sequence is it all done?

   - How long does the process take from beginning to end? Does the time involved differ from case to case? If so, what are the main factors causing the differences?

   - What equipment is used (e.g., fax machines, computers)?

   - What computer software, if any, is used (e.g., word processing, spreadsheet)?

   - What Internet sites, if any, are sometimes useful?

   - What standard forms are used?

   - Are any manuals particularly helpful? If so, were they written by the office or by someone else?

   - Has the office changed its system for handling this kind of case? If so, what were the changes and why were they made?

   - Does anyone have any problems with how the present system now works? If so, what are they and what recommended improvements are contemplated?

3. If possible, try to interview someone from another firm that handles the same kind of case so that you can compare the systems used.

4. How do you find practicing attorneys, paralegals, legal administrators, and secretaries in the field of family law?

   - You may have fellow classmates who are secretaries or paralegals.

   - Check with your paralegal association.

   - Check with the local association of legal secretaries or legal administrators.

   - Ask your instructor for leads.

5. Another person who would have valuable information for this assignment is the law office manager or legal administrator of a larger firm.

6. Everyone is busy, and this is certainly true of people working in a law office. You must not give the impression that you are going to take up a lot of the time of the people you interview. Have a checklist of questions ready. Be prepared. Guard against giving the impression that you are not sure what you want.

7. People you interview should never reveal any information about any particular clients in their offices, including the identity of the clients. This information is confidential. You are seeking generic information on systems for handling categories of cases. If by mistake you learn information about particular clients, be sure that you keep it confidential.

CHAPTER PROJECTS

☑ GENERAL INSTRUCTIONS FOR THE CHAPTER PROJECTS

1. The goal of the chapter project is to use the Internet to undertake research on a specific topic.

2. Be scrupulous about citing your sources. A major problem in research papers is that the writers are using material on the Internet without citing the sources of the materials. This is plagiarism.

3. When you find comprehensive discussions on the Internet that are relevant to the chapter project, it is tempting to highlight the material, copy it, and drop it into your answer. Avoid this temptation. Lifting large segments of text is rarely adequate, even if you cite the material to avoid the charge of plagiarism. It is easy to spot this cut-and-paste method

of "writing." You need to organize your own answer. The outline of your presentation should be your own. Be selective in what you use.

4. The citation to an Internet page should contain:

- the name of the person or organization authoring or sponsoring the site
- the name of the site (in italics)
- the full Internet address

Examples:

National Federation of Paralegal Associations, *What Is a Paralegal?*, www.paralegals.org

Peter W. Martin, *Introduction to Basic Legal Citation*, www.law.cornell.edu/citation

5. Many individual attorneys, law firms, and associations have summaries of the law on their web pages. These summaries are a major marketing tool to attract the public to their services. Be cautious about these summaries. They may contain errors and outdated material. You need to check multiple sources for everything that you use. The best sources to use are government sites containing primary authority such as statutes, court opinions, and agency regulations.

WRITING SAMPLES

For every course you take, you should have a file or portfolio of writing samples that can be used in a job search. A family-law course presents a number of opportunities to prepare such samples. Prospective employers are often impressed by well-drafted documents, particularly from job applicants who have not had prior legal experience.

☑ GENERAL INSTRUCTIONS FOR THE WRITING SAMPLE

1. The writing sample needs to be of the highest professional quality. It should be a document that you can present to a prospective employer.

2. Before a writing sample is ready for use in a job search, it needs to go through several drafts. It is rare for a sample to be ready after it is completed the first time. Hence, consider the writing sample you prepare for this course to be a first draft. It needs to be evaluated and rewritten based on the feedback you are given on how it can be improved. There probably will not be enough time in this course for you to do more than one draft. After the course is over, you need to seek further feedback from instructors, attorneys, and experienced paralegals.

3. Most of the writing samples will be on the law of your state. Follow the general guideline in the instructions on finding this law. See also Appendix D for additional leads to the law of your state.

4. Avoid plagiarism. Give a citation for any material that you use.

5. You need to know the citation system used in your state. See the following leads to citation formats in every state:

- www.law.cornell.edu/citation
- www.alwd.org/publications/pdf/CM2_Appendix1.pdf

If there are no special citation rules in your state, follow either of the following citation manuals:

- *The Bluebook: A Uniform System of Citation* (www .legalbluebook.com)
- *ALWD Citation Manual* (www.alwd.org/publications.html)

6. Avoid the cut-and-paste method of "writing." It is tempting to highlight large amounts of material on the Internet, copy it, and drop it into your paper. This is not writing. It is note-collecting dressed up as writing. An experienced reader (e.g., someone interviewing you for a job) can easily spot work that is pieced together from multiple sources rather than carefully thought through, outlined, and written.

7. Perfection in grammar and spelling is essential. One grammatical or spelling error is often enough to cause a prospective employer to reject a job candidate.

APPENDIX B

Computer Generated Reports:
The Divorce of Margaret and Nelson Paris

As we saw in Chapters 8 and 9, computer programs can be very helpful in the negotiation of custody and other issues in a divorce settlement. Here we present a sample set of reports generated for such negotiation.

The reports in the following exhibits present the facts in the divorce of Margaret Paris and Nelson Paris. The couple has one child, Justine. Their major asset is a residence (242 Westerly Pl.).

EXHIBIT B-1   One-Page Summary of the Financial Data

One-Page Summary

Annual totals for Margaret Paris or Nelson Paris.

Total Income	Margaret	Nelson
Wages and Salary	$54,838	$24,000
Child Support Received	0	0
Alimony Received	12,000	0
All Other Income	28,000	28,000
TOTAL INCOME	94,838	52,000

Total Expenses		
Child Support Paid	0	0
Alimony Paid	0	12,000
All Other Expenses	89,623	16,205
TOTAL EXPENSES	89,623	28,205

Liquidations		
Liquidations	6,000	0

Taxes		
Federal Income Tax	13,390	8,077
State Income Tax	4,814	2,701
Other Taxes	4,195	1,836
TOTAL TAXES	22,399	12,614

After-Tax Cash	Margaret	Nelson
AFTER-TAX CASH	−17,184	11,181

Property		
Marital Property	168,858	220,196
Separate Property	16,110	−431
TOTAL PROPERTY	$184,968	$219,765

Miscellaneous		
Number of Dependents	1	0
Filing Status	Single	Single
Alimony Paid, % of Gross Income	0	23
Child Support Paid, % of Gross Income	0	0
Combined Pmts, % of Gross Income	0	23

Reprinted with permission of Family Law Software, Inc.

EXHIBIT B-2   Projected After-Tax Cash Report for 20 Years

Projected After-Tax Cash Report

Projected After-Tax Cash for Margaret Paris or Nelson Paris for 20 years.

	Margaret	Nelson		Margaret	Nelson
2005	($ 17,184)	$ 11,181	2015	($ 16,676)	$ 32,083
2006	$ 636	$ 11,655	2016	($ 18,712)	$ 33,215
2007	$ 3,202	$ 16,905	2017	($ 20,849)	$ 34,409
2008	$ 2,076	$ 17,551	2018	($ 23,104)	$ 35,618
2009	$ 885	$ 18,214	2019	($ 26,566)	$ 36,890
2010	($ 7,742)	$ 26,868	2020	($ 30,417)	$ 38,189
2011	($ 9,542)	$ 27,201	2021	($ 34,553)	$ 39,635
2012	($ 11,182)	$ 28,856	2022	($ 39,137)	$ 41,048
2013	($ 12,917)	$ 29,888	2023	($ 44,167)	$ 42,504
2014	($ 14,747)	$ 30,950	2024	($ 49,658)	$ 44,005

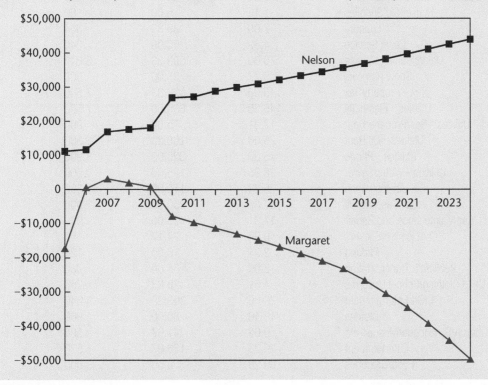

Reprinted with permission of Family Law Software, Inc.

EXHIBIT B-3 Budget Report for Margaret

Budget Report for 2005

Budget Report for Margaret for 2005

This report shows Margaret Paris's income, taxes, expenses, alimony, and child support.

	Weekly	Monthly	Annual
Income			
Wages	$1,054.58	$4,569.83	$54,838
Total Wage and Non-Wage Income	$1,054.58	$4,569.83	$54,838
Business Income			
Paris Plumbing Supply	$538.46	$2,333.33	$28,000
Total Business Income	$538.46	$2,333.33	$28,000
Support Received			
Alimony Received	$230.77	$1,000.00	$12,000
Total Support Received	$230.77	$1,000.00	$12,000
TOTAL INCOME	**$1,823.81**	**$7,903.17**	**$94,838**
Mortgage Payments			
242 Westerly Pl	$386.08	$1,673.00	$20,076
Total Mortgage Payments	$386.08	$1,673.00	$20,076
Living Expenses			
Union Dues	$19.23	$83.33	$1,000
Cable TV	13.15	57.00	684
Dry Cleaning	12.00	52.00	624
Furniture & Appliance repair/Replacement	3.92	17.00	204
Homeowners' Insurance	27.69	120.00	1,440
Household Maintenance/Repair	7.92	34.33	412
Household Supplies	1.15	5.00	60
Laundry	7.00	30.33	364
Lawn Service	4.62	20.00	240
Maid/cleaning Service	70.00	303.33	3,640
Snow Removal	5.77	25.00	300
Tax - Property Tax	145.00	628.33	7,540
Utilities - Electricity	145.38	630.00	7,560
Utilities - Gas/Propane Heat	17.31	75.00	900
Utilities - Oil Heat	25.00	108.33	1,300
Utilities - Phone	75.00	325.00	3,900
Utilities - Water/Sewer	28.85	125.00	1,500
Car Insurance	25.38	110.00	1,320
Car Gasoline/Oil	57.69	250.00	3,000
Car Maintenance and Repair	17.31	75.00	900
Car License/Stickers	0.96	4.17	50
Parking	2.31	10.00	120
Public/alt. Transportation	15.00	65.00	780
Child Clothing/School Uniforms	4.81	20.83	250
Child Entertainment	70.00	303.33	3,640
Clothes	18.46	80.00	960
Church/Synagogue/Mosque etc	9.62	41.67	500
Entertainment	29.23	126.67	1,520
Food/Groceries	69.23	300.00	3,600

Gifts	10.00	43.33	520
Hair	30.00	130.00	1,560
Internet Access	15.00	65.00	780
Misc Other	3.85	16.67	200
Pets	9.62	41.67	500
Restaurants	55.00	238.33	2,860
Therapist/Counselor	27.69	120.00	1,440
Toiletries/Grooming/Drug Store	5.77	25.00	300
Vacations	96.15	416.67	5,000
Health Insurance	110.00	476.67	5,720
Dental Exp	6.92	30.00	360
Optical Exp	4.62	20.00	240
Total Living Expenses	**$1,303.62**	**$5,649.00**	**$67,788**
Payments on Debt			
Sallie Mae Loan	$10.17	$44.08	$529
Citibank Visa	10.96	47.50	570
American Express Platinum	2.08	9.00	108
Student Loan	10.62	46.00	552
Total Payments on Debt	**$33.83**	**$146.58**	**$1,759**
TOTAL EXPENSES	**$1,723.52**	**$7,468.58**	**$89,623**
Taxes			
Federal Taxes	$257.50	$1,115.83	$13,390
FICA & Medicare	$80.67	$349.58	$4,195
State Taxes	$92.58	$401.17	$4,814
TOTAL TAXES	**$430.75**	**$1,866.58**	**$22,399**
Total Income	**$1,823.81**	**$7,903.17**	**$94,838**
Minus Total Expenses	**(1,723.52)**	**(7,468.58)**	**(89,623)**
Minus Total Taxes	**(430.75)**	**(1,866.58)**	**(22,399)**
AFTER-TAX CASH	**$(330.46)**	**$(1,432.00)**	**$(17,184)**

Reprinted with permission of Family Law Software, Inc.

EXHIBIT B-4 Division of Marital Property

Division of Marital Property

Property division report for Margaret Paris and Nelson Paris.

	Margaret Amount	Pct	Nelson Amount	Pct	Total Amount	
Residence Equity						
242 Westerly Pl	$135,250		$182,250		$317,500	1
Total Residence Equity	$135,250	43%	$182,250	57%	$317,500	
Investments						
Total Investments	$0	0%	$0	0%	$0	
Businesses						
Paris Plumbing Supply	$40,000		$40,000		$80,000	2
Total Businesses	$40,000	50%	$40,000	50%	$80,000	

(*Continued*)

EXHIBIT B-4 (Continued)

Personal Items					
Car	$2,000		$0		$2,000 ₃
Sofa	$1,750		$0		$1,750 ₄
Oil Painting	$3,000		$0		$3,000 ₅
Sculpture	$0		$3,500		$3,500 ₆
Desk	$0		$1,750		$1,750 ₇
Total Personal Items	$6,750	56%	$5,250	44%	$12,000
Subtotal Non-Retirement	**$182,000**	**44%**	**$227,500**	**56%**	**$409,500**
Defined Benefit Pensions					
Federated Pension Plan	$14,515		$14,515		$29,030 ₈
Total Pensions	$14,515	50%	$14,515	50%	$29,030
Subtotal Retirement	**$14,515**	**50%**	**$14,515**	**50%**	**$29,030**
Total Assets	**$196,515**	**45%**	**$242,015**	**55%**	**$438,530**
Debts					
Insurance Policies	$0		($1,593)		($1,593) ₉
Bathroom Renovations	$0		($5,500)		($5,500) ₁₀
Sallie Mae Loan	($8,696)		($8,696)		($17,392) ₁₁
Citibank Visa	($4,717)		$4,717		$0 ₁₂
American Express Platinum	($1,749)		$1,749		$0 ₁₃
Student Loan	($12,495)		($12,495)		($24,990) ₁₄
Total Debt	($27,657)	56%	($21,818)	44%	($49,475)
Total Debts	**($27,657)**	**56%**	**($21,819)**	**44%**	**($49,476)**
Total Property	**$168,858**	**43%**	**$220,196**	**57%**	**$389,054**

Note: "Total Amount" column may not add due to rounding.

Reprinted with permission of Family Law Software, Inc.

EXHIBIT B-5   Projected Net Worth for 20 Years

Projected Net Worth Report

Projected Net Worth for Margaret Paris or Nelson Paris for 20 years.

	Margaret	Nelson		Margaret	Nelson
2005	$ 164,830	$ 226,639	2015	$ 108,842	$ 464,292
2006	$ 154,224	$ 221,932	2016	$ 91,352	$ 497,464
2007	$ 160,308	$ 241,244	2017	$ 71,312	$ 531,415
2008	$ 165,189	$ 261,149	2018	$ 48,522	$ 566,078
2009	$ 168,784	$ 281,645	2019	$ 21,674	$ 601,421
2010	$ 163,638	$ 310,707	2020	($ 9,736)	$ 637,350
2011	$ 156,554	$ 339,775	2021	($ 46,223)	$ 673,784
2012	$ 147,665	$ 369,656	2022	($ 88,336)	$ 710,587
2013	$ 136,842	$ 400,371	2023	($ 136,704)	$ 747,624
2014	$ 123,950	$ 431,909	2024	($ 192,028)	$ 784,697

Reprinted with permission of Family Law Software, Inc.

EXHIBIT B-6 Key Entries and Assumptions

Key Entries and Assumptions

This report presents the key assumptions behind the income and asset projections for Margaret Paris and Nelson Paris.

Key Rates

1. Inflation.. 3.1 %
2. After-tax rate of return on Accumulated Savings (reinvested income)......................... 3.0 %
3. Cost of borrowing (%) for net deficits.. 8.0 %

Plan Start Date

1. The start year for plan is 2005.

Taxes

1. Federal taxes are calculated on a detailed basis using the tax laws for each year, including Earned Income Credit, Alternative Minimum tax, and phase-outs currently enacted.
2. Taxes for Margaret Paris

    Federal and state filing status for 2005.. Single

    Filing status for subsequent years... Single

    State taxes are estimated based on an abbreviated version of the New York State tax form.
3. Taxes for Nelson Paris

    Federal and state filing status for 2005.. Single

    Filing status for subsequent years... Single

    State taxes are estimated based on an abbreviated version of the New York State tax form.

Assumptions Relating to Children

	Custody	Tax Exemption
1. Justine......................................	Margaret	Margaret

Assumptions Relating to Child Support

1. No child support is entered.

Assumptions Relating to Alimony

1. Nelson paying alimony through 2009.. $1,000 per month

Residence Assumptions - 242 Westerly Pl

1. Market Value.. $700,000
2. Rate of appreciation of residence... With Inflation
3. This residence will be sold in 2006.
4. There is a first mortgage with a current mortgage balance of $335,000.
5. This mortgage will be paid by Margaret.
6. There is a second mortgage with a current mortgage balance of $47,500.
7. This mortgage will be paid by Margaret.

Assumptions Relating to Wages

	Margaret	Nelson
1. Wage amount and period...............................	$54,838/year	$2,000/month
2. Rate of increase of wages.............................	With Inflation	With Inflation
3. Retirement age..	65	65

Assumptions Relating to Cash & Investments

1. Chase [Checking]: The current market value is $4,000.
2. Chemical [Checking]: The current market value is $12,500.
3. Bank of America [Money market]: The current market value is $2,000.
4. Investment # 4: The current market value is $0.

Assumptions Relating to Defined Benefit Pensions

1. Federated Pension Plan.

    The plan is owned by Margaret Paris.

    The monthly benefit specified by the plan administrator is $1,231.

(Continued)

EXHIBIT B-6 *(Continued)*

This assumes the employee works until the cut-off date and begins receiving payments at age 65.
The discount rate is 4.64%.
We are using mortality table GAR-94.

Assumptions Relating to Debts

1. Insurance Policies. The current balance is $1,593. The current rate is 0.00%.
   No monthly payment has been entered.
2. Bathroom Renovations. The current balance is $5,500. The current rate is 3.00%.
   The monthly payment is $75.00.
3. Sallie Mae Loan. The current balance is $17,392. The current rate is 4.50%.
   The monthly payment is $88.00.
4. Citibank Visa. The current balance is $9,433. The current rate is 18.00%.
   The monthly payment is $95.00.
5. American Express Platinum. The current balance is $3,498. The current rate is 0.00%.
   The monthly payment is $18.00.
6. Student Loan. The current balance is $24,989. The current rate is 4.50%.
   The monthly payment is $92.00.

Reprinted with permission of Family Law Software, Inc.

EXHIBIT B-7 "What-If" Alimony and Child Support

"What-If" Alimony and Child Support

After-tax cash projections for Margaret Paris and Nelson Paris, for alimony paid by Nelson to Margaret.

What-If	Amount ($/mo.)	Through (year)
Alimony:	500	2009
Child Support:	1,000	2023

Results:

Year	Annual After-Tax Cash (*)		
	Margaret	Nelson	Combined
2005	−8,901	3,055	−5,846
2006	−10,468	3,317	−7,151
2007	−12,986	3,616	−9,370
2008	−15,346	3,911	−11,435
2009	−17,878	4,210	−13,668
2010	−24,202	8,392	−15,810
2011	−27,705	8,171	−19,534
2012	−31,276	9,255	−22,021
2013	−35,178	9,700	−25,478
2014	−39,434	10,156	−29,278
2015	−44,076	10,664	−33,412
2016	−49,137	11,154	−37,983
2017	−54,644	11,686	−42,958
2018	−60,645	12,214	−48,431
2019	−67,181	12,784	−54,397
2020	−74,282	13,360	−60,922
2021	−81,927	14,060	−67,867
2022	−90,300	14,706	−75,594
2023	−99,423	15,372	−84,051
2024	−121,335	28,059	−93,276

(*) The After-Tax Cash calculation excludes down payments, refinancings, and income from sales of residences.

Reprinted with permission of Family Law Software, Inc.

EXHIBIT B-8 Alimony After Tax

Alimony After-Tax

The total alimony payments are $60,000.
The total after-tax cost of the alimony to the payer is $45,428.
The total net benefit of the alimony to the recipient, after paying taxes, is $42,352.

There is a net tax *loss* of $3,076 due to the alimony payments.

Analysis:

The chart below shows the net tax savings to alimony.

Numbers in parentheses are negative — that is, net tax losses.

Net Tax Savings Due to alimony

Year	(a) Nelson's Tax Reduction Due to Alimony	(b) Margaret's Tax Increase Due to Alimony	(c) Net Tax Change Due to Alimony (a) - (b)
2005	$3,000	$3,488	($488)
2006	$2,968	$3,550	($582)
2007	$2,915	$3,620	($705)
2008	$2,867	$3,520	($653)
2009	$2,822	$3,470	($648)
Total tax svgs/pmts:	$14,572	$17,648	($3,076)
Total payments made:	$60,000	$60,000	
Cost/Inc after taxes:	$45,428	$42,352	

Explanation or Analysis:

When alimony is paid, the payer gets a tax deduction and the recipient pays tax on the alimony income.

The tax deduction is a benefit to the payer (Nelson). We calculate Nelson's tax with the alimony deduction. Then we calculate Nelson's tax as if there were no alimony payment. The difference is Nelson's tax benefit due to the alimony payment.

Note that we do not simply apply a marginal tax rate to the alimony amount. We do a complete tax calculation. This counts the impact of the alimony deduction on exemption phase-outs, itemized deduction phase-outs, the Alternative Minimum Tax, etc., and therefore it is the most accurate way to calculate the tax benefit.

We then do a similar set of calculations for Margaret, to find the extra tax that Margaret is paying due to the alimony income.

We then subtract Margaret's tax cost from Nelson's tax benefit, to get the net tax benefit.

Typically, the payer is in a higher tax bracket than the recipient. This means that the payer's tax savings is more than the recipient's tax cost. So there is a net tax benefit.

In this case, Margaret, after alimony payments, is in a higher tax bracket than Nelson, so there is actually a net tax loss due to alimony payments.

EXHIBIT B-9 After-Tax Income on Sale of 242 Westerly Pl

After-Tax Income on Sale of 242 Westerly Pl

This report details the income, tax, and after-tax income on the sale of 242 Westerly Pl.

I. Calculating Income on Sale of 242 Westerly Pl:

1. Current Value of 242 Westerly Pl.....................................	$700,000
2. Times: Appreciation of 3.100% per year for 1 Year..........	1.031
3. Equals: Sale Price of 242 Westerly Pl	$700,000
4. Less: First Mortgage Balance on Sale Date	$338,484
5. Less: Second Mortgage Balance on Sale Date.................	$50,530
6. Less: Expense of Sale..	$33,000
7. Equals: Equity After Mortgages and Expenses	$277,986
8. Percent of Equity to Margaret..	43.00%
9. Percent of Equity to Nelson	57.00%
10. Income on Sale, for Margaret (line 7 * line 8)	$119,534
11. Income on Sale, for Nelson (line 7* line 9)......................	$158,452

II. Estimating Tax Payable on Sale of 242 Westerly Pl.

	Margaret	Nelson
1. Sale Price of 242 Westerly Pl.......................................	$301,000	$399,000
2. Less: Expense of Sale...	$14,190	$18,810
3. Equals: Amount Realized..	$286,810	$380,190
4. Less: Adjusted Basis...	$0	$520,000
5. Equals: Potentially Taxable Gain....................................	$0	$147,000
6. Less: Exclusion Amount	$250,000	$250,000
7. Equals: Taxable Gain...	$0	$0
8. Federal Tax Payable (additional tax vs. home not sold) (*)......	$0	$0
9. Estimated State Tax Payable (addt'l vs. home not sold)	$0	$0

III. Estimating After-Tax Income on Sale of 242 Westerly Pl.

	Margaret	Nelson
1. Income on Sale (from Sections 1.10 and 1.11 above)......	$119,534	$ 158,452
2. Less: Estimated Incremental Tax (from Sec II.8 & 9 above)......	$0	$0
3. Equals: Estimated After-Tax Income on Sale	$119,534	$158,452

(*) Taxes may increase because of the loss of the mortgage deduction as well as gain on sale.

Reprinted with permission of Family Law Software, Inc.

EXHIBIT B-10 Pension Valuation Report

Pension Valuation Report

This valuation is for the plan: Federated Pension Plan.

This report values the plan as of the evaluation date, which is: 01/01/2004.

Based on the information entered (see below), the value of the pension as of the evaluation date is:

$37,589, using the RP-2000 mortality tables and a gender-specific approach.

As of 01/01/2004, 74.17% of this pension is so-called 'marital property.'

The "marital amount" is typically the amount the judge will divide. (The rest stays with the employee.)

Using a gender-specfic approach, the marital amount of the pension plan is $27,880 (that is, 74.17% of $37,589).

Using a gender-specific approach, if the judge divides the pension 50/50, for example, then $13,940.00 (half of $27,880) would be awarded to each spouse.

These comments about marital property apply in most states, even community property states.

Value of Pension at Retirement:

The value of the pension is $210,394 (gender-specific approach) as of regular retirement age.

This is typically more than the value as of the evaluation date because, like money in a bank account, a pension's value increases over time.

Knowing the value at earliest retirement age tends to be most useful if the worker is near retirement, or is likely to reach retirement with this company.

If the non-worker spouse is considering taking a share of the payout, as opposed to a cash buyout today, this number helps both spouses see what that payout might be.

This report is based on the following data entered:

Key Dates:

09/01/1975	Employee's birth date.
08/26/1990	Date the employee was married.
4,876	Number of days from marriage to separation.
1/1/1986	Date the employee started in the plan.
01/01/2004	Date the employment stopped being 'marital.' (This is usually the separation date).
01/01/2004	Date to evaluate the plan. (This should be the date on the pension benefits administrator's statement).
65	Employee's regular retirement age.
62	Employee's earliest retirement age.
NO	Is the employee already retired?

The Plan:

$1,231	Monthly benefit, provided by plan administrator, at "as if" retirement date.
1.0%	Cost of living adjustment (COLA) percent
4.64%	Interest rate (also known as the "discount rate").

Calculation Options Selected:

The pension benefit and marital portion are calculated "as if" the employee works until the cut-off date.

"Cut-off" means the date after which the plan is no longer marital. This is typically the separation date.

The pension's value is calculated assuming the employee retired or will retire on the regular retirement date.

The employee is a female.

EXHIBIT B-11 Tax Calculation

Tax Calculation

Taxes for Margaret Paris in 2005 are $22,399, and taxes for Nelson Paris are $12,614.

Margaret	Nelson	
Single	Single	Filing Status in 2005
2	1	Number of exemptions
Income:		
54,838	24,000	Wages and salary.
0	0	Taxable interest income.
0	0	Taxable dividend income.
12,000	0	Alimony income.
28,000	28,000	Business and farm income.
0	0	Capital gain taxable.
0	0	Other gains and losses.
0	0	Taxable IRA and pension income.
0	0	Rent, royalty, partnership, S corporation.
0	0	Social Security taxable.
0	0	Other income.
94,838	52,000	Taxable Gross Income.
Adjustments:		
0	0	IRA deduction.
0	0	Moving expenses.
1,978	1,978	Deduction of 1/2 of self-employment tax.
0	0	Part of health insurance for self-employed people.
0	12,000	Alimony paid.
0	0	Interest on education loans.
0	0	Other deductions.
1,978	13,978	Total adjustments.
92,860	38,022	Adjusted Gross Income ("AGI") = gross income − total adjustments.
Itemized Deductions:		
795	0	Deductible medical expenditures.
6,093	2,701	State income taxes.
0	0	Local income taxes.
7,540	0	Property taxes.
20,076	0	Mortgage interest.
500	300	Charitable contributions.
1,000	324	Miscellaneous, subject to 2% AGI threshold.
0	0	Miscellaneous, after 2% AGI threshold.
0	0	Miscellaneous, not subject to 2% AGI threshold.
35,004	3,001	Itemized deductions before phase-out.
35,004	3,001	Itemized deductions after phase-out.
5,000	5,000	Compare: standard deduction.
Exemptions:		
6,400	3,200	Deduction for exemptions before phase-out.
6,400	3,200	Deduction for exemptions after phase-out.
Tax Before Credits and Other Taxes:		
51,456	29,822	Taxable Income = AGI − greater of itemized or standard deductions − exemptions.
9,534	4,121	Tax before credits and other taxes (from tax table or formula).

Non-refundable Credits:

0	0	Child care credit.
0	0	Hope education credit.
0	0	Lifetime learning credit.
0	0	Child credit, alter phase-out, non-refundable portion.
0	0	Total Non-refundable Credits (reduce tax, but not below zero).

Refundable Credits:

100	0	Child credit, after phase-out, refundable portion.
0	0	Earned income credit.
100	0	Total Refundable Credits (can reduce tax below zero and generate a payment from the IRS).

Other Taxes on Form 1040:

0	0	Tax on retirement plan premature distribution.
0	0	Alternative minimum tax.
0	0	Lump-sum distribution 5- or 10- year averaging.
3,956	3,956	Self-employment tax.

Total Federal Income Tax:

		= tax before credits and other taxes
		− total nonrefundable credits (down to zero)
		− total refundable credits
		+ other taxes on Form 1040
13,390	8,077	Total Federal Income Tax.

Taxes Not on Form 1040:

3,400	1,488	FICA Taxes.
795	348	Medicare Taxes.
4,814	2,701	State Income Tax (NY: 10.5% of income).

Total Taxes:

22,399	12,614	Total Taxes.

Reprinted with permission of Family Law Software, Inc. (www.familylawsoftware.com).

Appendix C

Interrogatories on Financial Assets

INTRODUCTION

Gaining access to all the personal and financial information needed to negotiate a separation agreement or to prepare for trial is not always easy. In fact, one of the major reasons separation agreements are later challenged is that one of the parties was not given a complete inventory of the other spouse's financial assets before signing. In Chapter 7, we examined discovery devices that are designed to help an office obtain this kind of information. One of these devices is interrogatories, which can be particularly effective when seeking financial assets. Interrogatories are a discovery device in which one party sends written questions to another party in order to prepare for trial. Here we will explore interrogatories directed at a spouse's finances. In some states, there are limits on the number of interrogatories one party can send another. For the interrogatories given on the next page, we will assume that there are no such limits.

Carefully examining these interrogatories will increase your understanding of the potential complexity of someone's financial affairs. As you read the questions, make note of the categories of financial data sought and the comprehensiveness of the questions in these categories. A paralegal must pursue the same kind of information with the same comprehensiveness when given interviewing and investigative tasks designed to help the office identify the financial assets of a client's spouse.

DOCUMENT HUNT

Uncovering financial assets is primarily a document hunt. Here is a list of the documents that our interrogatories will be seeking:

- Medical reports
- Physician letters
- Canceled rent checks
- Lease or rental agreements
- Real estate closing statements
- Deeds
- Real estate appraisals
- Real estate mortgages
- Real estate tax bills
- Contracts to buy real estate
- Contracts to sell real estate
- Pay stubs
- W-2 forms
- Employment contracts
- Car lease agreements
- Deferred compensation agreements
- Account statements for deferred compensation
- Federal income tax returns
- State tax returns
- Local tax returns
- Gift tax returns
- 1099 tax forms for miscellaneous income
- Partnership agreements
- Partnership tax returns
- Articles of incorporation
- Corporate tax returns
- Bank account statements
- Appraisals of livestock
- Appraisals of jewelry
- Appraisals of other collectibles

- Royalty statements
- Securities account statements
- Trust instruments
- Trustee accounting reports

- Pension account statements
- Credit card statements
- Financial statements
- Loan applications

Some of these documents only indirectly relate to someone's financial worth. Knowing a person's medical history, for example, is some evidence of whether health problems interfere with an ability to earn income.

INTERROGATORIES

I. General Matters
II. Residences
III. Other Real Property
IV. Income and Employment
V. Self-Employment
VI. Personal Assets
VII. Securities, Inheritance, and Gifts
VIII. Trusts
IX. Insurance
X. Liabilities
XI. Assets Acquired before the Marriage
XII. Assets Acquired during the Marriage
XIII. Assets Acquired after the Separation
XIV. Miscellaneous

These interrogatories must be answered by the defendant under oath. All answers should be supplemented after they are submitted if the defendant becomes aware of any new or changed facts that would alter any of the answers previously provided.

I. GENERAL MATTERS

1. State your full name, age, residence and post office address, home telephone number, Social Security number, business addresses, business phone numbers, personal and business e-mail addresses, and all personal and business Internet sites (including but not limited to blogs and social-network sites such as LinkedIn and Facebook).

2. Provide
   (a) The names, dates of birth, and current addresses of all children born or adopted during the marriage.
   (b) State whether any of the children have been emancipated.
   (c) Who has physical and legal custody of each minor child?
   (d) Does any minor child need medical or mental health care? If so, explain the details. What kind of treatment is needed? What are the names and addresses of medical care providers who have provided treatment or whose treatment will be needed? State the cost (past and projected) of such treatments and the anticipated length of the treatment needed. (Attach copies of reports or letters of medical care providers.)

3. (a) What is your own state of health at the present time?
   (b) What medical care needs do you currently have, if any?

4. (a) Describe your employment skills.
   (b) Do you have or have you ever had a license to practice any occupation? If so, describe each license, the dates received, and the name of the agency that granted the license.
   (c) What is your educational background? List the schools you attended and the years of attendance. List your degrees, certificates, or other indicia of completion.
   (d) For each school you attended, who paid the education expenses? If others provided gifts or loans for all or some of the expenses, state the names and addresses of the persons who provided this aid, the amounts provided, and the circumstances of such assistance.
   (e) While you attended schools or other training, did your spouse provide financial support for your education and living expenses? If so, describe the support provided in detail, including specific dollar amounts involved.
   (f) Was your spouse working at any time you were obtaining your own education? If so, where did the spouse work, how much did your spouse earn, and how were the earnings used during your relationship?

5. Do you have any disabilities that have limited or that now limit your ability to perform your gainful work? If the answer is yes, attach medical reports on each disability and provide the following details:
   (a) A description of each disability and how it affected your work.
   (b) The medical care you received for each disability, including the names of doctors and other medical care providers, and the names of hospitals, clinics, and other facilities where you received treatment.
   (c) The dates of the treatment.
   (d) The expenses incurred for the treatment.
   (e) The cost of the treatment.
   (f) The resources used to pay for the treatment, including your own funds, insurance proceeds, employer contribution, and any other third-party assistance.

II. RESIDENCES

6. What is your primary residence? How long have you lived there?

7. For 10 years prior moving into your current primary residence, where did you reside and for what periods of time?

8. Do you currently live with your spouse? If not, do other persons live with you on a temporary or permanent basis? If so, what are their names and ages and their relationship to you?

9. Do you currently rent your primary residence? If so, what are the terms, including amount of rent, term of the rental or lease, and the name and address of the owner or other entity to whom payments are made? (Attach a copy of the lease and copies of canceled rent checks or other record of payment for the last twelve [12] months.)

10. What is the source of funds used to make rental payments? Give the name and address of anyone who assists you in making these payments. State the relationship between you and any such persons.

11. Do you own your present primary residence? If so, state:
    (a) The percentage of the residence that you own.
    (b) Does your spouse have an ownership interest in the residence? If so, what is the interest?
    (c) Who else has an ownership interest and in what percentages?

(d) When did you acquire your interest?

(e) What was the tax basis of the residence on the date of purchase?

(f) What is the name of the seller(s)?

(g) How much did you pay for your interest?

(h) Where did you obtain the funds for this payment?

(i) Where did your spouse obtain the funds to purchase his or her interest?

(j) What was the amount of the original mortgage on the residence?

(k) Who is the mortgagee?

(l) What was the amount of the mortgage on the date you and your spouse separated?

(m) How much is currently owed on the mortgage?

(n) What was the market value of the residence on the date of separation?

(n) For property tax purposes, what is the assessed value of the residence according to the county or other level of government? (Attach a copy of the government's notice on this value.)

(o) What is the current market value of the residence?

(p) What was the adjusted tax basis of the residence on the date of separation?

(q) What is the current adjusted tax basis?

(r) Are there any other mortgages, liens, or other encumbrances on the residence? If so, for how much? State the details of when they were acquired and from whom, as well as the source of funds used to make payments toward each.

(s) List all annual, quarterly, monthly, and other recurring operating expenses for the residence, including taxes, mortgage payments, insurance, utilities, repairs, and maintenance.

(t) What major expenses for capital improvements have been paid since the residence was purchased? For each improvement, state the nature of the improvement, the cost, the person or company performing the improvement, the source of the funds to pay the expense, and whether any balance remains for the expense.

(u) What major capital improvements are now needed? For each need, state the estimated cost.

(v) Attach copies of closing statements, deeds, appraisals, mortgages, contractor statements, and the most recent bills for property taxes.

12. Is your present primary residence your marital residence? If not, answer questions 11(a) to 11(v) for your marital residence.

13. Since the date of the separation, what has been the source of funds used to pay all mortgages and other costs for the residences referred to in the questions above? Indicate who made these payments.

14. Since the date of the separation, what has been the source of funds used to pay property taxes on all of the residences referred to in the questions above? Indicate who made these payments.

III. OTHER REAL PROPERTY

15. Do you have an ownership, possessory, or other interest in any real property other than indicated above? If so, for each such interest, provide the following information:

(a) Address of the property.

(b) The nature of your interest.

(c) When you acquired your interest.

(d) The date you acquired the interest.

(e) The person or entity from whom you obtained the interest.

(f) The names and addresses of other persons or entities who also have an interest in the property.

(g) The manner in which you acquired the interest. If by purchase, state the price or other consideration paid.

(h) The reason you acquired the interest.

(i) The amount you owed on the interest on the date of separation from your spouse.

(j) The amount currently owed.

(k) The involvement, if any, of your spouse in acquiring the interest.

(l) The market values of the property on the date you acquired it, on the date of separation, and currently.

(m) The assessed value of the property for property tax purposes.

(n) The recurring operating expenses for the property, including property taxes, insurance, and utilities.

(o) The source of funds used to pay these operating expenses.

(p) The income generated by the property including but not limited to rental income.

(q) Attach copies of the closing statements, deeds, and appraisals for each property covered in question 15.

16. Did you buy, sell, or otherwise transfer real property during the marriage and before the separation? If so, answer questions (a) to (q) of question 15 for each such property.

17. Did you buy, sell or otherwise transfer real property after the separation? If so, answer questions (a) to (q) of question 15 for each such property.

IV. INCOME AND EMPLOYMENT

18. For the last 10 years, state the names, street addresses, telephone numbers, e-mail addresses, and Internet addresses of your prior employers, with dates of each employment, positions held, salary, other compensation, and reasons for ending each employment.

19. What is the name, street address, e-mail address, and Internet address of your current employer?
    (a) How long have you been employed there?
    (b) Describe the kind of work you do.
    (c) How are your earnings determined? Include all forms of compensation, including salary, commissions, bonuses, and other remuneration.
    (d) Attach copies of pay stubs, W-2 forms, and other records you have received that demonstrate your answers to (c) for the past twelve (12) months.

20. Describe the employee benefits provided to you and/or to your family or dependents (indicating for each benefit the amount contributed by your employer and the amount contributed by you) in the following categories:
    (a) Health insurance for current employees
    (b) Health insurance for retirees
    (c) Life insurance
    (d) Disability insurance
    (e) Health and wellness programs
    (f) Child care subsidy
    (g) Pension, profit sharing, annuities, or retirement programs
    (h) Car or other vehicle allowance
    (i) Thrift savings plan
    (j) Stock options
    (k) Other benefits or perquisites

21. What deferred compensation in the form of cash, securities, or other assets are you currently entitled to (or might you be entitled to upon the happening of conditions) from any employment during the marriage?
    (a) State the details of such entitlement, including the person, company, or other entity that has or may have the duty of paying the deferred compensation and the amounts or value of the potential compensation involved.
    (b) Attach copies of contracts or other documents stating or indicating your entitlement to the deferred compensation.

22. For your current employment, list all the deductions from your gross earnings every pay period.

23. Do you have a written contract of employment or are you an at-will employee?
    (a) If the former, state the terms of the contract, including compensation, other benefits, and when the contract terminates.
    (b) If you currently have more than one written contract, answer this question for each.
    (c) Attach copies of all employment contracts.

24. In the last five years, have you had written contracts of employment other than those mentioned in question 23?
    (a) If so, for each state the terms of the contract, including compensation, other benefits, and when the contract terminates.
    (b) Attach copies of such contracts.

25. For any year during the marriage for which you earned income or other compensation, did you fail to file federal, state, or local income tax returns? If so, for what years and for what reason(s) were the returns not filed?

26. Attach copies of the federal, state, and local income tax returns that you filed in the last seven years.

27. Name each bank or other financial institution into which you deposit any salary or other compensation from your employment or other work endeavors. Include the account number(s) at each institution.

28. Do you expect to obtain a raise next year due to a promotion, union contract, regular incremental increase, performance review, or otherwise? Answer this question even if you do not know the exact amount of any such increase.

29. Have you ever received any government benefits such as unemployment compensation, workers' compensation, Social Security, etc.? If so, describe each including the dates received, amounts, etc.

30. Do you have any sources of income or economic benefits not covered in the above interrogatories? If so, describe each, including the nature of the income or benefit, amounts, sources, etc.

V. SELF-EMPLOYMENT

31. Are you self-employed? If so, describe the nature of your work.

32. State whether you are a sole proprietor, have an ownership interest in a partnership, work for or in a corporation in which you own any stock, or work for or in any other type of venture or entity in which you have an ownership interest.
    (a) Provide details on your ownership interest in said proprietorship, partnership, corporation, venture, or other entity, including the market value of your ownership interest and the source of funds you used to acquire the interest.

(b) If others also have an ownership interest, state their names, the nature of their interest, and their relationship to you.

33. Have you ever sold any part of your ownership interests mentioned in 32(a)? If so, state what was sold, the names of the buyers, the dates of the sales, and the price or other consideration you received.

34. State the name and address of the following:
    (a) All accountants consulted during the last five years.
    (b) All attorneys consulted during the past five years.
    (c) Your stockbroker(s) during the past five years.
    (d) Your investment advisor(s) during the past five years.

VI. PERSONAL ASSETS

35. Give the name and address of every bank or other financial institution in which you wholly or partially own or once owned within the last five years any account offered by the bank or institution. Attach copies of the account statements for each account for the last six (6) months.

36. For each account listed in question 35, state the name and address of each co-owner.

37. For each account listed in question 35, state the current balance and, where applicable, the balance on the date of separation.

38. Within twelve (12) months prior to the date of separation, state the withdrawals you made from the accounts mentioned in your answer to question 35 and the purposes for such withdrawals.

39. Do you own or have access to the contents of a safe deposit box? If so, where is the box located? Itemize the contents of the box and itemize the withdrawals you have made from the box in the last three years.

40. Do you own or have a partial interest in cars, boats, or any other kind of vehicle? If so, describe each vehicle, when you obtained your interest, the purchase price, the amounts still owed, and the present location of said vehicles.

41. Do you own any jewelry that was purchased or that has a present value of $100 or more? If so, itemize each such piece of jewelry, indicating the circumstances of its purchase, its value, and its present location.

42. Itemize any personal property not mentioned in your answers to questions 35–41 (including but not limited to furnishings and collectibles) that has a value of over $300 that you own or in which you have an ownership interest.

43. Do you have a right to receive royalty income? If so, describe the source of your right and the amounts you have received from such royalties in the last three years.

44. Have you been a plaintiff in a lawsuit in any court in the last 10 years? If so, state the cause(s) of action asserted in the suit, the court(s) involved, the damages or other relief you sought, the outcome of the proceedings, and the names of the attorney(s) who represented you.

45. If any suit mentioned in question 44 is still pending, answer all parts of the question except for the outcome.

46. At any time during the marriage, did you receive any prize or gambling awards of over $100 in cash or value? If so, for each such prize or award, describe what you received, the date received, and the payor.

VII. SECURITIES, INHERITANCE, AND GIFTS

47. Do you currently own any securities not covered in previous interrogatories?
(a) If so, for each security (as defined below), describe the security and your interest in it, the date of acquisition, the price paid, the source of the funds used to make the payment, the present value of the security, and the income currently derived from the security. Definition of security: A financial instrument that is evidence of a debt interest (e.g., a bond), an ownership/equity interest (e.g., a stock), or other specially defined rights (e.g., a futures contract).
(b) Attach monthly statements on each security for the past five years.

48. In the last three years, have you sold, transferred, or exchanged any securities as defined in question 47? If so, for each sale, transfer, or exchange, state the nature of the transaction, the transaction date, and the price or other consideration received.

49. Does any person, institution, or organization owe you money or other assets, whether informally or as evidenced by instruments such as promissory notes, mortgages, accounts receivables, or other securities? If so, for each such debt, state its nature, amounts or values owed (whether principal, interest, or otherwise), and the terms of anticipated payment.

50. Did you receive any money or other asset by inheritance (will or intestate):
(a) during the marriage?
(b) before the marriage?
(c) after the date of separation?
(d) If so, for each inheritance listed in questions a through c, state what you received, the source, the date received, and what you did with what you received.

51. State (or estimate) the present market value of all noncash assets referred to in question 50.

52. For each gift you have made in the last five years in cash or other property in excess of $300, state the nature of the gift, the name and address of the recipient, the reason for the gift, and the date of the gift.

VIII. TRUSTS

53. Have you created a trust of any kind?
(a) If so, for each trust, state the names of the beneficiaries, the names of the trustees, the amount in the trust (the corpus), and the major terms of the trust.
(b) Attach a copy of each trust instrument.

54. Are any of the following the beneficiary of a trust: you, a member of your family, or any business or other entity in which you have an interest?
(a) If so, for each trust, state the names of the beneficiaries, the names of the trustees, the amount in the trust (the corpus), and the major terms of the trust.
(b) Attach a copy of each trust instrument and the most recent report or accounting statement received on the status of each trust.

IX. INSURANCE

55. What insurance policies do you have?
(a) For each policy, state the kind of insurance, the name of the insurance company, the policy number, and, if applicable, the face amount of the policy, the premium, and the name of beneficiaries. Include life, disability, annuity, health, property, and any other kind of insurance.

(b) On which of these policies do you have the right to change the beneficiaries?

56. Have you ever assigned any insurance policy? If so, provide the date, the name of the assignee(s), and the circumstances of each assignment.

57. Have you made a claim against an insurance policy in the last five years? If so, for each claim, state the date of the claim; the insurance company involved; and the action taken on your claim, including the monies you received on each claim.

X. LIABILITIES

58. List of all credit card balances on any card for which you have full or shared responsibility. For each card, state:
   (a) The name in which the card is listed and the names of all persons entitled to use the card.
   (b) The total amount currently due.
   (c) The total amount due on the date of the separation.
   (d) Attach copies of all credit card statements for the past twelve (12) months.

59. List any outstanding obligations, including mortgages, conditional sales contracts, contract obligations, promissory notes, or government agency loans not included in your answers to any previous interrogatory, stating for each:
   (a) The nature of the obligation.
   (b) The date(s) the obligation was incurred or renewed.
   (c) The names of each person responsible for payments in addition to yourself and the relationship of each person to you.
   (d) The name and address of each creditor and the creditor's relationship to you.
   (e) A description of any security or collateral given for the obligation.
   (f) The amount currently owed on the obligation.
   (g) The amount owed on the obligation on the date of separation.
   (h) The source(s) of the funds used to make payments on the obligation.

60. List all judgments outstanding against you or your spouse not included in your answer to a previous interrogatory, and for each state:
   (a) The names of the parties and their respective attorneys.
   (b) The courts in which the judgments were entered.
   (c) The amount of the judgment.
   (d) Attach a copy of the judgment.

61. List all pending suits against you or your spouse not included in your answer to a previous interrogatory, and for each, state:
   (a) The names of the parties and their respective attorneys.
   (b) The court in which the suit is pending.
   (c) The amount of the damages or other relief sought.
   (d) Attach a copy of the complaint.

62. List any lien or security interest not disclosed in a previous interrogatory to which any of your property or assets can be reached for payment. For each, state:
   (a) The name and address of the person or entity holding the lien or security interest.
   (b) The amount owed.

XI. ASSETS ACQUIRED BEFORE THE MARRIAGE

63. List the amount of cash not disclosed in prior interrogatories that you amassed before the marriage and that you brought into the marriage. For these amounts, state:
    (a) How it was obtained.
    (b) Where it was kept or deposited.
    (c) The extent to which your spouse had access to and could use it.
    (d) For what purposes all or part of it was spent.
    (e) The amount remaining on the date of separation.
    (f) The amount currently remaining.

64. List each asset valued over $300 not disclosed in prior interrogatories that you acquired before the marriage and that you brought into the marriage. For each asset, state:
    (a) The nature of the asset.
    (b) The source of the asset.
    (c) The funds used to acquire the asset.
    (d) The asset's market value on the date of the marriage.
    (e) The asset's market value on the date of the separation.
    (f) Your efforts that helped cause any appreciation.
    (g) Your spouse's efforts that helped cause any appreciation.

XII. ASSETS ACQUIRED DURING THE MARRIAGE

65. Explain the understanding of, and practice between, you and your spouse on the following matters:
    (a) Where monies earned by you would be deposited, whether your spouse had access to and could use the monies, and the extent to which your spouse did use any of them.
    (b) Where monies earned by your spouse would be deposited, whether you had access to and could use the monies, and the extent to which you did use any of them.

66. List each asset valued over $300 not disclosed in prior interrogatories that you, your spouse, or both acquired during the marriage. For each asset, state:
    (a) The nature of the asset.
    (b) The source of the asset.
    (c) The funds used to acquire the asset.
    (d) The asset's market value on the date of acquisition.
    (e) The asset's market value on the date of the separation.
    (f) The asset's current value.
    (g) Your efforts that helped cause any appreciation.
    (h) Your spouse's efforts that helped cause any appreciation.

67. List any gifts over the value of $300 received during the marriage by you, by your spouse, or by both of you not covered in prior interrogatories. For each gift, state:
    (a) The nature of the gift.
    (b) The amount or value of the gift on the date of receipt.
    (c) The source of the gift.
    (d) To whom the gift was given.
    (e) The gift's amount or market value on the date of the separation.
    (f) The current amount or market value of the gift.
    (g) Your efforts that helped cause any increase or appreciation.
    (h) Your spouse's efforts that helped cause any increase or appreciation.

68. List any inheritance over the value of $300 received during the marriage by you, by your spouse, or by both of you not covered in prior interrogatories. For each gift, state:
    (a) The nature of the inheritance.
    (b) The amount or value of the inheritance on the date of receipt.
    (c) The source of the inheritance.
    (d) To whom the inheritance was given.
    (e) Inheritance's amount or market value on the date of the separation.
    (f) Inheritance's current amount or market value.
    (g) Your efforts that helped cause any increase or appreciation.
    (h) Your spouse's efforts that helped cause any increase or appreciation.

XIII. ASSETS ACQUIRED AFTER THE SEPARATION

69. List the amount of cash not disclosed in prior interrogatories that you amassed after the date of separation. For this amount, state:
    (a) How it was obtained.
    (b) The extent to which your spouse had access to and could use it.
    (c) For what purposes all or part of it was spent.
    (d) The amount currently remaining.

70. List each asset valued over $300 not disclosed in prior interrogatories that you acquired after the date of separation. For each asset, state:
    (a) The nature of the asset.
    (b) The source of the asset.
    (c) The funds used to acquire the asset.
    (d) Asset's current market value.
    (e) Your efforts that helped cause any appreciation.
    (f) Your spouse's efforts that helped cause any appreciation.

XIV. MISCELLANEOUS

71. If you have prepared a financial statement of your assets and liabilities, either individually or for any business in which you have an interest within the past five years, state:
    (a) The dates of all such statements.
    (b) The name and address of the person, firm, company, partnership, corporation, or entity for whom they were prepared.
    (c) The name and address of all persons who worked on the preparation of such statements.
    (d) Attach copies of all such financial statements.

72. State whether you have made application for loan(s) with any individual, lending institutions, or other entity during the past five years. If so, state for each:
    (a) The name and address of the individual, lending institution, or other entity.
    (b) The date of the application.
    (c) The amount of the loan request.
    (d) Whether your application was approved or denied and in what amount.
    (e) Attach a copy of all such loan applications.

73. State what counsel fees you have paid or agreed to pay for services rendered in connection with the separation of the parties and the names of the attorney(s) to whom such fees have been paid or are owed.

Family Law in Your State

ALABAMA FAMILY LAW

Alabama Family Code/Domestic Relations Code
- law.onecle.com/alabama/marital-and-domestic-relations/index.html
- law.onecle.com/alabama
- alisondb.legislature.state.al.us/acas/CodeofAlabama/1975/coatoc.htm

Alabama Marriage Law (formation)
- www.law.cornell.edu/wex/table_marriage
- usmarriagelaws.com/search/united_states/index.shtml
- marriage.about.com/cs/marriagelicenses/p/alabama.htm

Alabama Common Law Marriage
- www.law.cornell.edu/wex/table_marriage
- www.buddybuddy.com/common.html
- www.unmarried.org/common-law-marriage-fact-sheet.html

Alabama Same-Sex Marriage, Domestic Partnership, Civil Union, Defense of Marriage Status (Baby-DOMA)
- Ala. Code § 30-1-19
- www.ncsl.org/issues-research/human-services/civil-unions-and-domestic-partnership-statutes.aspx

Alabama Divorce Law
- Ala. Code § 30-2-1
- www.hg.org/divorce-law-alabama.html
- www.alabamalegalhelp.org/issues/families-and-children/divorce
- www.divorcelawinfo.com/states/AL/alabama.htm

Alabama Legal Separation Law
- Ala. Code § 30-2-40
- www.hg.org/divorce-law-alabama.html#7

Alabama Property Division Law
- www.divorcelawinfo.com/states/AL/alabama.htm

Alabama Child Custody Law
- Ala. Code § 30-3-160
- www.alabamalegalhelp.org/issues/families-and-children/custody

Alabama Relocation of Child
- Ala. Code § 30-3-163

Alabama Guardian Ad Litem and Attorney for Child
- Ala. Code §§ 26-14-11, 12-15-304
- www.childwelfare.gov/systemwide/laws_policies/statutes/represent.pdf#Page=9&view=Fit

Alabama Child Support Law
- www.alacourt.gov/ChildSupportInfo.aspx
- www.alabamalegalhelp.org/issues/families-and-children/child-support

Alabama Paternity Law
- www.alabamalegalhelp.org/issues/families-and-children/paternity
- www.uslegalforms.com/paternity

Alabama Adoption Law
- Ala. Code, § 26-10A-1
- www.alabamalegalhelp.org/issues/families-and-children/adoption
- laws.adoption.com/statutes/alabama-adoption-laws.html

Alabama Termination of Parental Rights
- Ala. Code § 12-15-319
- www.law.cornell.edu/wex/table_emancipation
- www.childwelfare.gov/systemwide/laws_policies/statutes/groundtermin.cfm

Alabama Putative Father Registry
- Ala. Code, § 26-10C-1
- dhr.alabama.gov/services/Adoption/How_to_register.aspx
- adoption.about.com/od/adoptionrights/p/alabamafather.htm

Alabama Emancipation Law
- Ala. Code. § 26-13-1
- www.law.cornell.edu/wex/table_emancipation
- www.youthrights.net/index.php?title=Alabama_Emancipation_Law

Alabama Age of Majority
- Ala. Code § 26-1-1

Alabama Child Protection/Protective Services
- Ala. Code, § 26-14-3
- dhr.alabama.gov/services/Child_Protective_Services/Child_Protective_Services.aspx

Alabama Child Welfare Agencies
- dhr.alabama.gov

Alabama Juvenile Law
- www.ncjj.org/State/Alabama.aspx
- www.alabamalegalhelp.org/issues/families-and-children/juveniles

Alabama Domestic Violence
- law.onecle.com/alabama/marital-and-domestic-relations/index.html
- www.alabamalegalhelp.org/issues/families-and-children/domestic-violence

Alabama Surrogacy Law
- Ala. Code §§ 26-10A-34
- www.selectsurrogate.com/surrogacy-laws-by-state.html

Alabama Grandparent Rights
- Ala. Code §§ 30-3-4.1

Alabama Annulment Law
- www.hg.org/divorce-law-alabama.html

Alabama Family Law Forms

- eforms.alacourt.gov
- family.findlaw.com/divorce/divorce-forms-by-state.html
- www.uslegalforms.com/divorce/alabama-divorce-forms .htm?auslf=woman
- www.uslegalforms.com/rominger/divorce.htm
- www.edivorcepapers.com/alabama

Alabama Vital Records (Birth, Marriage, Divorce, Death)

- publicrecords.onlinesearches.com/Alabama.htm
- www.cdc.gov/nchs/w2w/alabama.htm
- www.cdc.gov/nchs/w2w.htm

Alabama Self-Help Services in Family Law Cases

- www.alabamalegalhelp.org
- www.courtreference.com/Alabama-Courts-Self-Help.htm

Alabama State Legal Research

- judicial.alabama.gov/library/collection.cfm
- www.ll.georgetown.edu/states/alabama.cfm
- www.loc.gov/law/help/guide/states/us-al.php

Alabama Court Rules

- judicial.alabama.gov/library/rules_of_court.cfm
- www.llrx.com/courtrules-gen/state-Alabama.html

ALASKA FAMILY LAW

Alaska Family Code/Domestic Relations Code

- www.touchngo.com/lglcntr/akstats/Statutes/Title25/Chapter24.htm
- www.law.cornell.edu/wex/table_family
- w3.legis.state.ak.us

Alaska Marriage Law (formation)

- codes.lp.findlaw.com/akstatutes/25/25.05.
- www.touchngo.com/lglcntr/akstats/Statutes/Title25 /Chapter05.htm
- www.usmarriagelaws.com/search/united_states/alaska /marriage_licenses
- marriage.about.com/cs/marriagelicenses/p/alaska.htm

Alaska Common Law Marriage

- www.law.cornell.edu/wex/table_marriage
- www.buddybuddy.com/common.html
- www.unmarried.org/common-law-marriage-fact-sheet.html

Alaska Same-Sex Marriage, Domestic Partnership, Civil Union, Defense of Marriage Status (Baby-DOMA)

- www.akclu.org/LGBT/AK-Domestic-Partnership-Benefits.pdf
- www.touchngo.com/lglcntr/akstats/Statutes/Title25/Chapter05.htm

Alaska Divorce Law

- courts.alaska.gov/shcstart.htm
- www.courts.alaska.gov/civ2.htm#90.1
- www.hg.org/divorce-law-alaska.html
- www.divorcelawinfo.com/states/alaska/alaska.htm
- www.alaskalawhelp.org/AK/index.cfm (click Family and Life Planning)

Alaska Discovery and Disclosure in Divorce

- www.courts.alaska.gov/civ.htm#26.1

Alaska Legal Separation Law

- Alaska Stat. § 25.24.410
- www.hg.org/divorce-law-alaska.html#7

Alaska Alimony/Spousal Support/Maintenance Law

- Alaska Stat. § 25.24.160

Alaska Property Division Law

- Alaska Stat. § 25.24.160
- courts.alaska.gov/selfhelp.htm
- www.hg.org/divorce-law-alaska.html

Alaska Child Custody Law

- Alaska Stat. § 25.20.090
- courts.alaska.gov/selfhelp.htm
- www.divorcelawinfo.com/states/alaska/alaska.htm

- www.hg.org/divorce-law-alaska.html
- www.alaskalawhelp.org/AK/index.cfm (click Family and Life Planning)

Alaska Guardian Ad Litem and Attorney for Child

- Alaska Stat. § 47.10.050
- www.courts.alaska.gov/del.htm#15
- www.courts.alaska.gov/del.htm#16
- www.alaskalawhelp.org/AK/index.cfm (click Family and Life Planning)

Alaska Child Support Law

- www.csed.state.ak.us
- www.courts.alaska.gov/civ2.htm#90.3
- www.courts.alaska.gov/support.htm
- www.alaskalawhelp.org/AK/index.cfm (click Family and Life Planning)

Alaska Paternity Law

- Alaska Stats. § 25.27.040
- courts.alaska.gov/selfhelp.htm
- www.csed.state.ak.us/FAQ/FAQ_Paternity.asp
- www.uslegalforms.com/paternity

Alaska Adoption Law

- Alaska Stat. Ann. §§ 25.23.010 et seq.
- courts.alaska.gov/shcadop.htm
- laws.adoption.com/statutes/alaska-laws,5.html
- www.alaskalawhelp.org/AK/index.cfm (click Family and Life Planning)

Alaska Termination of Parental Rights

- Alaska Stat. § 47.10.088
- www.law.cornell.edu/wex/table_emancipation

Alaska Putative Fathers

- Alaska Stats. §§ 18.50.165; 25.20.055
- www.ncsl.org/documents/cyf/putative_father_registries.pdf

Alaska Emancipation Law

- Alaska Stat. Ann. § 09.55.590
- www.youthrights.net/index.php?title=Alaska_Emancipation_Law

Alaska Age of Majority

- Alaska Stat. Ann. § 25.20.010

Alaska Child in Need of Aid Rules

- www.courts.alaska.gov/cina.htm

Alaska Child Welfare Agencies

- www.hss.state.ak.us/ocs

Alaska Juvenile Law

- www.courts.alaska.gov/del.htm
- www.ncjj.org/State/Alaska.aspx
- www.alaskalawhelp.org/AK/index.cfm (click Family and Life Planning)

Alaska Domestic Violence Law

- courts.alaska.gov/shcdv.htm
- www.andvsa.org

Alaska Surrogacy Law

- www.selectsurrogate.com/surrogacy-laws-by-state.html

Alaska Grandparent Rights

- www.courts.alaska.gov/shcgrandparent.htm
- www.alaskalawhelp.org/AK/index.cfm (click Family and Life Planning)

Alaska Annulment Law

- Alaska Stat. Ann. § 25.05.051
- www.touchngo.com/lglcntr/akstats/Statutes/Title25/Chapter05.htm
- www.hg.org/divorce-law-alaska.html
- www.womansdivorce.com/alaska.html

Alaska Family Law Forms

- www.courts.alaska.gov/aklegal.htm#forms
- www.edivorcepapers.com

- www.courts.alaska.gov/support.htm
- family.findlaw.com/divorce/divorce-forms-by-state.html
- www.uslegalforms.com/rominger/divorce.htm

Alaska Vital Records (Birth, Marriage, Divorce, Death)

- publicrecords.onlinesearches.com/Alaska.htm
- www.cdc.gov/nchs/w2w/alaska.htm
- www.cdc.gov/nchs/w2w.htm

Alaska Self-Help Services in Family Law Cases

- www.alaskalawhelp.org/AK/index.cfm
- courts.alaska.gov/selfhelp.htm

Alaska State Legal Research

- www.courts.alaska.gov/aklegal.htm
- www.loc.gov/law/help/guide/states/us-ak.php
- www.ll.georgetown.edu/states/alaska.cfm
- www.loc.gov/law/help/guide/states/us-ak.php
- www.romingerlegal.com/state/alaska.html

Alaska Court Rules

- www.courts.alaska.gov/rules.htm
- www.courts.alaska.gov/civ2.htm#90.1
- www.courts.alaska.gov/civ2.htm#90.3
- www.courts.alaska.gov/civ.htm#26.1
- www.llrx.com/courtrules-gen/state-Alaska.html

ARIZONA FAMILY LAW

Arizona Family Code/Domestic Relations Code

- www.azleg.gov/ArizonaRevisedStatutes.asp?Title=25
- www.law.cornell.edu/wex/table_family
- www.azleg.gov

Arizona Marriage Law (formation)

- marriage.about.com/cs/marriagelicenses/p/arizona.htm
- www.usmarriagelaws.com/search/united_states/arizona/marriage_licenses
- www.law.cornell.edu/wex/table_marriage

Arizona Common Law Marriage

- topics.law.cornell.edu/wex/table_marriage
- www.buddybuddy.com/common.html

Arizona Covenant Marriage

- Ariz. Rev. Stat. § 25-901
- www.supreme.state.az.us/dr/pdf/covenant.pdf
- www.azlawhelp.org/articles_info.cfm?mc=1&sc=3&articleid=4

Arizona Same-Sex Marriage, Domestic Partnership, Civil Union, Defense of Marriage Status (Baby-DOMA)

- Ariz. Rev. Stat. § 25-101
- phoenix.about.com/od/gay/qt/domesticpartner.htm
- www.lambdalegal.org/publications/nationwide-status-same-sex-relationships

Arizona Divorce Law

- www.divorcelawinfo.com/states/az/arizona.htm
- www.hg.org/divorce-law-arizona.html
- www.azlawhelp.org/documents/SelfServiceDivorceGuide.pdf
- www.azlawhelp.org/documents/azlawhelp_Divorce.pdf

Arizona Legal Separation

- Ariz. Rev. Stat. § 25-313
- www.hg.org/divorce-law-arizona.html#8

Arizona Property Division Law

- Ariz. Rev. Stat. § 25-318
- www.hg.org/divorce-law-arizona.html

Arizona Child Custody Law

- Ariz. Rev. Stat. § 25-403
- www.hg.org/divorce-law-arizona.html
- www.azlawhelp.org/articles_info.cfm?mc=1&sc=1&articleid=68

Arizona Guardian Ad Litem and Attorney for Child

- Ariz. Rev. Stat. §§ 8-523, 8-524
- Ariz. Rev. Stat. §§ 8-221; 25-321
- www.childwelfare.gov/systemwide/laws_policies/statutes/represent.pdf

Arizona Child Support Law

- www.azdes.gov/main.aspx?menu=24&ID=2652
- www.azlawhelp.org/articles_info.cfm?mc=1&sc=2&articleid=53
- www.supportguidelines.com/links.html

Arizona Paternity Law

- Ariz. Rev. Stat. § 25-812
- www.azlawhelp.org/viewquestions.cfm?mc=1&sc=10
- www.acf.hhs.gov/programs/cse/pubs/2002/reports/essentials/c8.html
- www.uslegalforms.com/paternity/arizona-paternity-forms.htm

Arizona Adoption Law

- Ariz. Rev. Stat. §§ 8-101 et seq.
- www.azleg.gov/ArizonaRevisedStatutes.asp?Title=8
- laws.adoption.com/statutes/arizona-adoption-laws.html
- www.formsworkflow.com/FindLegalForms.aspx?q=adoption&s=

Arizona Termination of Parental Rights

- Ariz. Rev. Stat. § 8-534
- www.law.cornell.edu/wex/table_emancipation

- www.childwelfare.gov/systemwide/laws_policies/statutes
  /groundtermin.cfm

Arizona Putative Father Registry
- Ariz. Rev. Stat. § 8-106.01
- laws.adoption.com/statutes/arizona-laws,5.html
- www.courts.state.nh.us/probate/registrylist.pdf

Arizona Emancipation Law
- Ariz. Rev. Stat. § 12-2451
- www.youthrights.net/index.php?title=Arizona_Emancipation_Law

Arizona Age of Majority
- Ariz. Rev. Stat. § 8-201(3)

Arizona Child Protection/Protective Services
- Ariz. Rev. Stat. § 8-800
- www.azdes.gov/dcyf/cps

Arizona Child Welfare Agencies
- www.azdes.gov/main.aspx?menu=46&id=2338

Arizona Juvenile Law
- Ariz. Rev. Stat. §§ 8-201 et seq.
- azcourts.gov/PublicServices/JuvenileLaw.aspx
- www.ncjj.org/State/Arizona.aspx

Arizona Domestic Violence Law
- www.azcadv.org
- www.azcourts.gov/domesticviolencelaw
  /DomesticViolenceInformation.aspx

Arizona Surrogacy Law
- Ariz. Rev. Stat. § 25-218; *Soos v. Sup. Ct,* 897 P.2d 1356 (Ariz. App.1994)
- www.selectsurrogate.com/surrogacy-laws-by-state.html#AZ

Arizona Grandparent Rights
- Ariz. Rev. Stat. § 25-409

Arizona Annulment Law
- Ariz. Rev. Stat. §§ 25-101, 25-302
- www.hg.org/divorce-law-arizona.html
- law.findlaw.com/state-laws/annulment-and-prohibited-marriage
  /arizona

Arizona Family Law Forms
- www.azcourts.gov/selfservicecenter/SelfServiceForms.aspx
- www.uslegalforms.com/paternity/arizona-paternity-forms.htm
- www.uslegalforms.com/rominger/divorce.htm
- family.findlaw.com/divorce/divorce-forms-by-state.html#AZ

Arizona Vital Records (Birth, Marriage, Divorce, Death)
- www.cdc.gov/nchs/w2w.htm
- publicrecords.onlinesearches.com/Arizona.htm

Arizona Self-Help Services in Family Law Cases
- www.azcourts.gov/selfservicecenter/SelfServiceForms.aspx
- www.azlawhelp.org/documents/SelfServiceDivorceGuide.pdf
- www.law.arizona.edu/Library/Research/Guides/familylaw
  /default.cfm

Arizona State Legal Research
- www.ll.georgetown.edu/states/arizona.cfm
- www.loc.gov/law/help/guide/states/us-az.php

Arizona Court Rules
- www.azcourts.gov/rules/Home.aspx
- www.llrx.com/courtrules-gen/state-Arizona.html
- government.westlaw.com/linkedslice/default
  .asp?SP=AZR-1000

ARKANSAS FAMILY LAW

Arkansas Family Code/Domestic Relations Code
- www.lexisnexis.com/hottopics/arcode/Default.asp
- www.law.cornell.edu/wex/table_family

Arkansas Premarital Agreement Law
- Ark. Code Ann. § 9-11-406

Arkansas Marriage Law (formation)
- statutes.laws.com/arkansas/title-9/subtitle-2/chapter-11
- www.usmarriagelaws.com/search/united_states/arkansas
  /marriage_licenses
- www.law.cornell.edu/wex/table_marriage

Arkansas Common Law Marriage
- topics.law.cornell.edu/wex/table_marriage
- www.buddybuddy.com/common.html

Arkansas Covenant Marriage
- Ark. Code Ann. §§ 9-11-803, 9-12-423
- littlerock.about.com/b/2005/02/14/covenant-marriage.htm
- www.marriagedebate.com/ml_marriage/cat02-ml02.php

Arkansas Same-Sex Marriage, Domestic Partnership, Civil Union, Defense of Marriage Status (Baby-DOMA)
- en.wikipedia.org/wiki/LGBT_rights_in_Arkansas
- www.lambdalegal.org/publications/nationwide-status-same-sex
  -relationships

- www.ncsl.org/issues-research/human-services/civil-unions-and
  -domestic-partnership-statutes.aspx

Arkansas Divorce Law
- Ark. Code Ann. § 9-12-301
- www.divorcelawinfo.com/states/ark/arkansas.htm
- www.hg.org/divorce-law-arkansas.html

Arkansas Legal Separation Law
- Ark. Code Ann. § 9-11-808
- www.hg.org/divorce-law-arkansas.html

Arkansas Alimony/Spousal Support Law
- Ark. Code Ann. § 9-12-312

Arkansas Property Division Law
- Ark. Code Ann. § 9-12-315
- www.hg.org/divorce-law-arkansas.html

Arkansas Child Custody Law
- Ark. Code Ann. §§ 9-13-101, 9-19-201
- www.hg.org/divorce-law-arkansas.html

Arkansas Guardian Ad Litem and Attorney for Child
- Ark. Code Ann. § 9-27-316
- www.childwelfare.gov/systemwide/laws_policies/statutes
  /represent.pdf

Arkansas Child Support Law

- www.dfa.arkansas.gov/offices/childSupport/Pages/default.aspx
- courts.arkansas.gov/aoc/acs_guidelines.cfm
- www.supportguidelines.com/links.html
- www.acf.hhs.gov/programs/cse/extinf.html

Arkansas Paternity Law

- www.dfa.arkansas.gov/offices/childSupport/custodialParty/Pages/paternity.aspx
- secure.uslegalforms.com/cgi-bin/forms/query.pl?S-C-AR-B-paternity
- www.acf.hhs.gov/programs/cse/pubs/2002/reports/essentials/c8.html

Arkansas Legal Definition of Father

- Ark. Code Ann. § 20-18-701
- www.childwelfare.gov/systemwide/laws_policies/statutes/putative.pdf

Arkansas Adoption Law

- Ark. Code Ann. §§ 9-9-206 et seq.
- laws.adoption.com/statutes/arkansas-adoption-laws.html

Arkansas Termination of Parental Rights

- Ark. Code Ann. § 9-27-341
- www.law.cornell.edu/wex/table_emancipation
- www.childwelfare.gov/systemwide/laws_policies/statutes/groundtermin.cfm

Arkansas Putative Father Registry

- comp.uark.edu/~ksampson/putative_father_registry.html
- laws.adoption.com/statutes/arkansas-laws,5.html
- www.courts.state.nh.us/probate/registrylist.pdf

Arkansas Emancipation Law

- Ark. Code Ann. § 9-27-362
- www.law.cornell.edu/topics/Table_Emancipation
- www.youthrights.net/index.php?title=Arkansas_Emancipation_Law

Arkansas Age of Majority

- law.findlaw.com/state-laws/minors-and-the-law/arkansas
- www.law.cornell.edu/topics/Table_Emancipation

Arkansas Child Protection/Protective Services

- humanservices.arkansas.gov/dcfs/Pages/default.aspx

Arkansas Child Welfare Agencies

- humanservices.arkansas.gov/Pages/default.aspx

Arkansas Juvenile Law

- www.ncjj.org/State/Arkansas.aspx
- arkansascoalitionforjuvenilejustice.arkansas.gov

Arkansas Domestic Violence Law

- Ark. Code Ann. § 9-15-103
- www.arlegalservices.org/orderofprotection

Arkansas Surrogacy Law

- Ark. Code Ann. § 9-10-201
- www.selectsurrogate.com/surrogacy-laws-by-state.html

Arkansas Grandparent Rights

- Ark. Code Ann. § 9-13-101

Arkansas Annulment Law

- Ark. Code Ann. § 9-11-105

Arkansas Family Law Forms

- courts.arkansas.gov/aoc/forms.cfm
- www.arlegalservices.org/interactiveforms
- www.uslegalforms.com/rominger/divorce.htm

Arkansas Vital Records (Birth, Marriage, Divorce, Death)

- www.cdc.gov/nchs/w2w.htm
- publicrecords.onlinesearches.com/Arkansas.htm

Arkansas Self-Help Services in Family Law Cases

- www.arlegalservices.org/interactiveforms
- www.arlegalservices.org/divorcepacket
- www.lawhelp.org/leaving_lawhelp.cfm/state/AR

Arkansas State Legal Research

- courts.arkansas.gov/library/index.cfm
- www.ll.georgetown.edu/states/arkansas.cfm
- www.loc.gov/law/help/guide/states/us-ar.php
- www.findlaw.com/11stategov/ar/index.html

Arkansas Court Rules

- courts.arkansas.gov/rules/index.cfm
- www.llrx.com/courtrules-gen/state-Arkansas.html

CALIFORNIA FAMILY LAW

California Family Code/Domestic Relations Code

- www.leginfo.ca.gov/cgi-bin/calawquery?codesection=fam&codebody=&hits=20
- www.leginfo.ca.gov/calaw.html
- www.law.cornell.edu/wex/table_family
- www.leginfo.ca.gov/cgi-bin/calawquery?codesection=fam

California Marriage Law (formation)

- Cal. Family Code §§ 300 et seq.
- www.cdph.ca.gov/certlic/birthdeathmar/pages/marriagelicenseinformation.aspx
- www.usmarriagelaws.com/search/united_states/california/marriage_licenses
- www.law.cornell.edu/wex/table_marriage

California Common Law Marriage

- topics.law.cornell.edu/wex/table_marriage
- www.buddybuddy.com/common.html

California Same-Sex Marriage, Domestic Partnership, Civil Union, Defense of Marriage Status (Baby-DOMA)

- en.wikipedia.org/wiki/Same-sex_marriage_in_California
- www.lambdalegal.org/publications/nationwide-status-same-sex-relationships
- www.ncsl.org/issues-research/human-services/civil-unions-and-domestic-partnership-statutes.aspx

California Divorce Law

- Cal. Family Code § 2310
- www.divorcelawinfo.com/states/ca/california.htm
- www.courts.ca.gov/selfhelp-divorce.htm
- www.hg.org/divorce-law-california.html

California Legal Separation Law

- Cal. Family Code § 2310
- www.courts.ca.gov/selfhelp-divorce.htm

California Alimony/Spousal Support Law

- www.courts.ca.gov/1038.htm
- www.courts.ca.gov/9050.htm

California Community Property Division Law

- www.courts.ca.gov/1039.htm
- www.hg.org/divorce-law-california.html

California Child Custody Law

- Cal. Family Code § 3048
- www.courts.ca.gov/selfhelp-custody.htm

California Guardian Ad Litem and Attorney for Child

- www.childwelfare.gov/systemwide/laws_policies/statutes
  /represent.pdf

California Child Support Law

- Cal. Family Code §§ 4050 et seq.
- www.childsup.ca.gov/Default.aspx
- www.supportguidelines.com/links.html
- www.acf.hhs.gov/programs/cse/extinf.html

California Paternity Law

- www.courts.ca.gov/selfhelp-parentage.htm
- www.childsup.ca.gov/Resources/EstablishPaternity
  /FileaDeclarationofPaternity.aspx
- www.acf.hhs.gov/programs/cse/pubs/2002/reports/essentials
  /c8.html

California Legal Definition of Father

- Cal. Family Code §§ 7601, 7611
- www.childwelfare.gov/systemwide/laws_policies/statutes
  /putative.pdf

California Adoption Law

- Cal. Family Code §§ 8502 et seq.
- laws.adoption.com/statutes/california-adoption-laws.html

California Termination of Parental Rights

- Cal. Welf. & Inst. Code § 366.26
- www.law.cornell.edu/wex/table_emancipation
- www.childwelfare.gov/systemwide/laws_policies/statutes
  /groundtermin.cfm

California Putative Father Registry

- laws.adoption.com/statutes/california-laws,5.html

California Emancipation Law

- Cal. Family Code § 7820
- www.youthrights.net/index.php?title=California_Emancipation_Law
- www.law.cornell.edu/topics/Table_Emancipation

California Age of Majority

- Cal. Family Code § 6500
- law.findlaw.com/state-laws/minors-and-the-law/california
- www.law.cornell.edu/topics/Table_Emancipation

California Child Protection/Protective Services

- www.dss.cahwnet.gov/cdssweb/pg93.htm

California Child Welfare Agencies

- www.childsworld.ca.gov

California Juvenile Law

- www.courts.ca.gov/selfhelp-delinquency.htm
- www.cdcr.ca.gov/juvenile_justice/index.html
- www.ncjj.org/State/California.aspx

California Domestic Violence Law

- Cal. Family Code §§ 6211 et seq.
- www.courts.ca.gov/selfhelp-domesticviolence.htm

California Surrogacy Law

- Cal. Family Code §§ 7600 et seq.
- www.selectsurrogate.com/surrogacy-laws-by-state.html

California Grandparent Rights

- Cal. Family Code § 3047

California Annulment Law

- Cal. Family Code § 2210

California Family Law Forms

- www.courts.ca.gov/forms.htm
- www.uslegalforms.com/rominger/divorce.htm

California Vital Records (Birth, Marriage, Divorce, Death)

- publicrecords.onlinesearches.com/California.htm
- www.cdc.gov/nchs/w2w.htm

California Self-Help Services in Family Law Cases

- www.courts.ca.gov/formsrules.htm

California State Legal Research

- www.ll.georgetown.edu/states/california.cfm
- www.loc.gov/law/help/guide/states/us-ca.php
- california.lp.findlaw.com/index.html

California Court Rules

- www.courts.ca.gov/rules.htm
- www.courts.ca.gov/formsrules.htm
- www.llrx.com/courtrules-gen/state-California.html

COLORADO FAMILY LAW

Colorado Family Code/Domestic Relations Code

- www.lexisnexis.com/hottopics/colorado
- www.law.cornell.edu/wex/table_family

Colorado Marriage Law (formation)

- Colo. Rev. Stat. Ann. § 14-2-104
- www.usmarriagelaws.com/search/united_states/colorado
  /marriage_licenses
- www.colorado.gov/colorado-how-do-i/living-here-get-married
  .html
- www.law.cornell.edu/wex/table_marriage

Colorado Common Law Marriage

- Colo. Rev. Stat. Ann. § 14-2-109.5
- topics.law.cornell.edu/wex/table_marriage
- www.buddybuddy.com/common.html

Colorado Same-Sex Marriage, Domestic Partnership, Civil Union, Defense of Marriage Status (Baby-DOMA)

- en.wikipedia.org/wiki/Recognition_of_same-sex_unions_in
  _Colorado
- www.lambdalegal.org/publications/nationwide-status-same-sex
  -relationships

- www.ncsl.org/issues-research/human-services/civil-unions-and
  -domestic-partnership-statutes.aspx

Colorado Divorce/Dissolution Law

- Colo. Rev. Stat. Ann. § 14-10-101
- www.divorcelawinfo.com/states/co/colorado.htm
- www.hg.org/divorce-law-colorado.html

Colorado Legal Separation Law

- Colo. Rev. Stat. Ann. § 14-10-106

Colorado Property Division Law

- Colo. Rev. Stat. § 14-10-113
- www.hg.org/divorce-law-colorado.html

Colorado Child Custody Law

- Colo. Rev. Stat. Ann. § 14-10-124
- www.womenslaw.org/laws_state_type.php?id=111&state_code=CO

Colorado Guardian Ad Litem and Attorney for Child

- Colo. Rev. Stat. § 19-1-111
- www.childwelfare.gov/systemwide/laws_policies/statutes
  /represent.pdf

Colorado Child Support Law

- Colo. Rev. Stat. §§ 14-10-115
- childsupport.state.co.us/siteuser/do/vfs/Frag?file=
  /cm:home.jsp
- www.supportguidelines.com/links.html
- www.acf.hhs.gov/programs/cse/extinf.html

Colorado Paternity Law

- www.courts.state.co.us/Forms/Forms_List.cfm?Form_Type
  _ID=81
- www.acf.hhs.gov/programs/cse/pubs/2002/reports/essentials
  /c8.html

Colorado Legal Definition of Father

- Colo. Rev. Stat. § 19-4-105
- www.childwelfare.gov/systemwide/laws_policies/statutes
  /putative.pdf

Colorado Adoption Law

- Colo. Rev. Stat. § 19-4-203
- laws.adoption.com/statutes/colorado-adoption-laws.html

Colorado Termination of Parental Rights

- Colo. Rev. Stat. § 9-5-105
- www.law.cornell.edu/wex/table_emancipation
- www.childwelfare.gov/systemwide/laws_policies/statutes
  /groundtermin.cfm

Colorado Putative Father Registry

- laws.adoption.com/statutes/colorado-laws,5.html
- www.courts.state.nh.us/probate/registrylist.pdf

Colorado Emancipation Law

- www.law.cornell.edu/topics/Table_Emancipation
- www.youthrights.net/index.php?title=Colorado_Emancipation_Law

Colorado Age of Majority

- law.findlaw.com/state-laws/minors-and-the-law/colorado
- www.law.cornell.edu/topics/Table_Emancipation

Colorado Child Protection/Protective Services

- www.colorado.gov/cs/Satellite/CDHS-ChildYouthFam
  /CBON/1251588267351

Colorado Child Welfare Agencies

- www.colorado.gov/cs/Satellite/CDHS-ChildYouthFam
  /CBON/1251586904497

Colorado Juvenile Law

- cdpsweb.state.co.us/cccjj
- www.ncjj.org/State/Colorado.aspx

Colorado Domestic Violence Law

- Colo. Rev. Stat. § 18-6-800.3
- www.womenslaw.org/laws_state.php?state_code=CO

Colorado Grandparent Rights

- Colo. Rev. Stat. §§ 19-1-117

Colorado Annulment Law

- Colo. Rev. Stat. Ann. § 14-2-110

Colorado Family Law Forms

- www.courts.state.co.us/Forms/Index.cfm
- www.courts.state.co.us/Forms/Forms_List.cfm?Form_Type_ID=81
- www.uslegalforms.com/rominger/divorce.htm

Colorado Vital Records (Birth, Marriage, Divorce, Death)

- publicrecords.onlinesearches.com/Colorado.htm
- www.cdc.gov/nchs/w2w.htm

Colorado State Legal Research

- www.ll.georgetown.edu/states/colorado.cfm
- www.loc.gov/law/help/guide/states/us-co.php
- www.law.cornell.edu/states/colorado.html

Colorado Court Rules

- www.coloradosupremecourt.com/regulation/rules.htm
- www.llrx.com/courtrules-gen/state-Colorado.html

CONNECTICUT FAMILY LAW

Connecticut Family Code/Domestic Relations Code

- www.jud.state.ct.us/lawlib/statutes.htm
- www.law.cornell.edu/wex/table_family

Connecticut Premarital Agreement

- www.jud.ct.gov/lawlib/law/parentalkidnapping.htm

Connecticut Marriage Law (formation)

- www.jud.ct.gov/lawlib/law/marriage.htm
- www.ct.gov/dph/cwp/view.asp?a=3132&q=390672
- www.usmarriagelaws.com/search/united_states/connecticut
  /marriage_licenses
- www.law.cornell.edu/wex/table_marriage

Connecticut Common Law Marriage

- topics.law.cornell.edu/wex/table_marriage
- www.buddybuddy.com/common.html

Connecticut Same-Sex Marriage, Domestic Partnership, Civil Union, Defense of Marriage Status (Baby-DOMA)

- www.jud.ct.gov/lawlib/law/civilunion.htm
- en.wikipedia.org/wiki/Same-sex_marriage_in_Connecticut
- www.lambdalegal.org/publications/nationwide-status-same-sex
  -relationships
- www.ncsl.org/issues-research/human-services/civil-unions-and
  -domestic-partnership-statutes.aspx

Connecticut Cohabitation Law

- www.jud.ct.gov/lawlib/law/cohabitation.htm

Connecticut Divorce Law

- Conn. Gen. Stats. § 46b-40
- www.jud.ct.gov/lawlib/law/divorce.htm
- www.divorcelawinfo.com/states/ct/connecticut.htm
- ctlawhelp.org/self-help-guides/family/divorce
- www.hg.org/divorce-law-connecticut.html

Connecticut Legal Separation Law

- Conn. Gen. Stats. § 46b-40
- www.jud.ct.gov/lawlib/law/separation.htm

Connecticut Alimony Law

- Conn. Gen. Stats. § 46b-1
- www.jud.ct.gov/lawlib/law/alimony.htm

Connecticut Property Division Law

- Conn. Gen. Stats. § 46b-81

Connecticut Child Custody Law

- Conn. Gen. Stats. §§ 46b-56 et seq.
- www.jud.ct.gov/lawlib/law/custody.htm
- ctlawhelp.org/self-help-guides/family/child-custody
- www.hg.org/divorce-law-connecticut.html

Connecticut Parental Kidnapping Law

- www.jud.ct.gov/lawlib/law/parentalkidnapping.htm

Connecticut Relocation of Child

- Conn. Gen. Stats. § 46b-56d
- www.jud.ct.gov/lawlib/law/partrelocation.htm

Connecticut Guardian Ad Litem and Attorney for Child

- www.jud.ct.gov/lawlib/law/guardianship.htm
- www.childwelfare.gov/systemwide/laws_policies/statutes
  /represent.pdf

Connecticut Child Support Law

- www.jud.ct.gov/lawlib/law/childsupport.htm
- www.ct.gov/dss/site/default.asp
- www.ct.gov/dss/cwp/view.asp?a=2353-&Q=305184
- www.acf.hhs.gov/programs/cse/extinf.html

Connecticut Paternity Law

- www.jud.ct.gov/lawlib/law/paternity.htm
- www.acf.hhs.gov/programs/cse/pubs/2002/reports/essentials/c8.html

Connecticut Legal Definition of Father

- Conn. Gen Stat. § 45a-604
- www.childwelfare.gov/systemwide/laws_policies/statutes
  /putative.pdf

Connecticut Adoption Law

- Conn. Gen Stat. § 45a-707
- www.jud.ct.gov/lawlib/law/adoption.htm
- laws.adoption.com/statutes/connecticut-adoption-laws.html

Connecticut Termination of Parental Rights

- Conn. Gen Stat. § 45a-717
- www.law.cornell.edu/wex/table_emancipation
- www.childwelfare.gov/systemwide/laws_policies/statutes
  /groundtermin.cfm

Connecticut Putative Father Registry

- laws.adoption.com/statutes/connecticut-laws,5.html
- www.courts.state.nh.us/probate/registrylist.pdf

Connecticut Termination of Parental Rights Law

- Conn. Gen Stat. § 45a-715
- www.jud.ct.gov/lawlib/law/tpr.htm
- www.law.cornell.edu/wex/table_emancipation
- www.childwelfare.gov/systemwide/laws_policies/statutes
  /groundtermin.cfm

Connecticut Emancipation Law

- www.jud.ct.gov/lawlib/law/emancipation.htm
- www.jud.ct.gov/lawlib/law/minors.htm
- www.law.cornell.edu/topics/Table_Emancipation
- www.youthrights.net/index.php?title=Connecticut
  _Emancipation_Law

Connecticut Child Protection/Protective Services

- www.ct.gov/ocpd/cwp/view.asp?a=4117&Q=481642&ocpdNav=|

Connecticut Child Welfare Agencies

- www.ct.gov/dcf/site/default.asp

Connecticut Juvenile Law

- www.jud.ct.gov/lawlib/law/minors.htm
- www.ct.gov/opm/cwp/view.asp?A=2974&Q=383628
- www.ncjj.org/State/Connecticut.aspx

Connecticut Domestic Violence Law

- www.jud.ct.gov/lawlib/Law/domesticviolence.htm

Connecticut Surrogacy Law

- *Doe v. Doe*, 710 A.2d 1297 (Conn. 1998)
- www.selectsurrogate.com/surrogacy-laws-by-state.html

Connecticut Grandparent Rights

- Conn. Gen. Stats. § 46b-59
- www.jud.ct.gov/lawlib/law/grandparent.htm

Connecticut Annulment Law

- Conn. Gen. Stats. § 46b-40
- www.jud.ct.gov/lawlib/law/annulment.htm

Connecticut Domestic Tort Law

- www.jud.ct.gov/lawlib/law/domestic_torts.htm

Connecticut Parental Liability for Acts of Minors

- www.jud.ct.gov/lawlib/law/domestic_torts.htm

Connecticut Family Law Forms

- www.jud.ct.gov/webforms/#FAMILY2
- www.jud.ct.gov/webforms
- www.uslegalforms.com/rominger/divorce.htm

Connecticut Vital Records (Birth, Marriage, Divorce, Death)

- www.cdc.gov/nchs/w2w.htm
- publicrecords.onlinesearches.com/Connecticut.htm

Connecticut Self-Help Services in Family Law Cases

- www.jud.ct.gov/selfhelp.htm
- www.slsct.org

Connecticut Family Law Legal Research

- www.jud.ct.gov/lawlib/law
- www.jud.ct.gov/lawlib/law/famdiscovery.htm

Connecticut State Legal Research (general)

- www.jud.state.ct.us/lawlib
- www.ll.georgetown.edu/states/connecticut.cfm
- www.loc.gov/law/help/guide/states/us-ct.php

Connecticut Family Support Magistrate Decisions
- www.jud.state.ct.us/lawlib/fsm.htm

Connecticut Court Rules
- www.jud.ct.gov/PB.htm
- www.llrx.com/courtrules-gen/state-Connecticut.html

DELAWARE FAMILY LAW

Delaware Family Code/Domestic Relations Code
- delcode.delaware.gov/title13/c015/index.shtml
- delcode.delaware.gov
- www.law.cornell.edu/wex/table_family

Delaware Marriage Law (formation)
- www.usmarriagelaws.com/search/united_states/delaware/marriage_licenses
- delcode.delaware.gov/title13/c001/sc01/index.shtml
- www.law.cornell.edu/wex/table_marriage

Delaware Common Law Marriage
- topics.law.cornell.edu/wex/table_marriage
- www.buddybuddy.com/common.html

Delaware Same-Sex Marriage, Domestic Partnership, Civil Union, Defense of Marriage Status (Baby-DOMA)
- en.wikipedia.org/wiki/LGBT_rights_in_Delaware
- www.lambdalegal.org/publications/nationwide-status-same-sex-relationships
- www.ncsl.org/issues-research/human-services/civil-unions-and-domestic-partnership-statutes.aspx

Delaware Divorce Law
- 13 Del. Code §§ 1501 et seq.
- courts.delaware.gov/Help/Divorce/index.stm
- www.divorcelawinfo.com/states/de/delaware.htm
- www.delcobar.org/index.php/self-helplegal-information

Delaware Alimony/Spousal Support Law
- 13 Del. Code § 1512

Delaware Property Division Law
- 13 Del. Code § 1513

Delaware Child Custody Law
- 13 Del. Code § 1920
- courts.delaware.gov/Help/Custody/index.stm
- courts.delaware.gov/Help/ParentVisitation/index.stm
- www.delcobar.org/index.php/self-helplegal-information

Delaware Guardian Ad Litem and Attorney for Child
- 29 Del. Code § 9007A, 31 Del. Code §§ 3605 et seq.
- www.childwelfare.gov/systemwide/laws_policies/statutes/represent.pdf

Delaware Child Support Law
- www.dhss.delaware.gov/dcse/index.html
- www.supportguidelines.com/links.html
- www.acf.hhs.gov/programs/cse/extinf.html

Delaware Paternity Law
- www.dhss.delaware.gov/dcse/estpat.html
- www.acf.hhs.gov/programs/cse/pubs/2002/reports/essentials/c8.html

Delaware Legal Definition of Father
- 13 Del. Code § 8-102
- laws.adoption.com/statutes/delaware-laws,5.html

- www.childwelfare.gov/systemwide/laws_policies/statutes/putative.pdf

Delaware Adoption Law
- courts.delaware.gov/Help/Adoption/index.stm
- laws.adoption.com/statutes/delaware-adoption-laws.html

Delaware Termination of Parental Rights
- 13 Del. Code § 1103
- courts.delaware.gov/Help/TPR/index.stm
- www.law.cornell.edu/wex/table_emancipation
- www.childwelfare.gov/systemwide/laws_policies/statutes/groundtermin.cfm

Delaware Putative Father Registry
- 13 Del. Code § 8-402
- laws.adoption.com/statutes/delaware-laws,5.html
- www.courts.state.nh.us/probate/registrylist.pdf

Delaware Emancipation Law
- www.law.cornell.edu/topics/Table_Emancipation
- www.youthrights.net/index.php?title=Delaware_Emancipation_Law

Delaware Age of Majority
- delcode.delaware.gov/title1/c007/index.shtml
- www.law.cornell.edu/topics/Table_Emancipation

Delaware Child Protection/Protective Services
- kids.delaware.gov/fs/fs_cai.shtml

Delaware Child Welfare Agencies
- kids.delaware.gov

Delaware Juvenile Law
- cjc.delaware.gov/juvjustice/index.shtml
- www.ncjj.org/State/Delaware.aspx

Delaware Domestic Violence Law
- 11 Del. Code § 3906
- www.dcadv.org/legal-remedies

Delaware Grandparent Rights
- 13 Del. Code § 2410
- courts.delaware.gov/Help/GrandparentVisitation/index.stm

Delaware Annulment Law
- 13 Del. Code §§ 1506 et seq.
- delcode.delaware.gov/title13/c001/sc01/index.shtml

Delaware Family Law Forms
- courts.state.de.us/forms
- www.uslegalforms.com/rominger/divorce.htm

Delaware Vital Records (Birth, Marriage, Divorce, Death)
- www.cdc.gov/nchs/w2w.htm
- publicrecords.onlinesearches.com/Delaware.htm

Delaware Self-Help Services in Family Law Cases
- courts.delaware.gov/Help
- www.delcobar.org/index.php/self-helplegal-information

Delaware State Legal Research

- www.ll.georgetown.edu/states/delaware.cfm
- www.loc.gov/law/help/guide/states/us-de.php
- www.findlaw.com/11stategov/de/index.html

Delaware Court Rules

- courts.state.de.us/Rules
- www.llrx.com/courtrules-gen/state-Delaware.html

DISTRICT OF COLUMBIA FAMILY LAW

District of Columbia Family Code/Domestic Relations Code

- government.westlaw.com/linkedslice/default
  .asp?SP=DCC-1000
- www.law.cornell.edu/wex/table_family

District of Columbia Marriage Law (formation)

- www.dccourts.gov/internet/public/aud_marriage/marriage.jsf
- www.dccourts.gov/internet/public/aud_divorce/main.jsf
- www.law.cornell.edu/wex/table_marriage

District of Columbia Common Law Marriage

- *U.S. Fidelity v. Britton*, 269 F.2d 249 (C.A.D.C. 1959).
- topics.law.cornell.edu/wex/table_marriage
- www.buddybuddy.com/common.html

District of Columbia Same-Sex Marriage, Domestic Partnership, Civil Union, Defense of Marriage Status (Baby-DOMA)

- en.wikipedia.org/wiki/Same-sex_marriage_in_the_District_of
  _Columbia
- www.lambdalegal.org/publications/nationwide-status-same-sex
  -relationships
- www.ncsl.org/issues-research/human-services/civil-unions-and
  -domestic-partnership-statutes.aspx

District of Columbia Divorce Law

- DC Code § 16-904
- www.dccourts.gov/internet/public/aud_divorce/main.jsf
- www.divorcelawinfo.com/DC/flc.htm
- www.lawhelp.org/dc (click Family Law)

District of Columbia Legal Separation Law

- DC Code § 16-904

District of Columbia Alimony/Spousal Support Law

- DC Code § 16-913
- www.lawhelp.org/dc (click Family Law)

District of Columbia Property Division Law

- DC Code § 16-910

District of Columbia Child Custody Law

- DC Code § 16-914
- www.lawhelp.org/dc (click Family Law)

District of Columbia Guardian Ad Litem and Attorney for Child

- DC Code § 16-2304
- www.childwelfare.gov/systemwide/laws_policies/statutes
  /represent.pdf

District of Columbia Child Support Law

- DC Code § 16-916.01
- csgc.oag.dc.gov/application/main/intro.aspx
- www.acf.hhs.gov/programs/cse/extinf.html

District of Columbia Paternity Law

- DC Code § 16-909
- www.acf.hhs.gov/programs/cse/pubs/2002/reports/essentials/c8.html

District of Columbia Adoption Law

- law.findlaw.com/state-laws/adoption/district-of-columbia

District of Columbia Termination of Parental Rights

- DC Code § 16-2353
- www.law.cornell.edu/wex/table_emancipation
- www.childwelfare.gov/systemwide/laws_policies/statutes
  /groundtermin.cfm

District of Columbia Putative Father Registry

- library.adoption.com/articles/district-of-columbia-presumed
  -putative-father-laws.html
- www.courts.state.nh.us/probate/registrylist.pdf

District of Columbia Emancipation Law

- www.law.cornell.edu/topics/Table_Emancipation

District of Columbia Age of Majority

- minors.uslegal.com/age-of-majority/district-of-columbia-age
  -of-majority-law
- www.law.cornell.edu/topics/Table_Emancipation

District of Columbia Child Protection/Protective Services

- www.dcrcc.org/resources/category/child_protection_services
  _district_of_columbia/C68

District of Columbia Child Welfare Agencies

- cfsa.dc.gov/DC/CFSA

District of Columbia Juvenile Law

- DC Code § 16-2301
- www.dccourts.gov/internet/superior/org_social/main.jsf
- www.ncjj.org/State/Washington-DC.aspx

District of Columbia Domestic Violence Law

- DC Code §§ 16-1001 et seq.
- www.lawhelp.org/dc (click Family Law)
- www.dccourts.gov/internet/superior/org_dvu/main.jsf

District of Columbia Surrogacy Law

- DC Code §16-401
- www.selectsurrogate.com/surrogacy-laws-by-state.html

District of Columbia Annulment Law

- DC Code §§ 16-903, 16-904
- www.lawhelp.org/dc (click Family Law)

District of Columbia Family Law Forms

- www.dccourts.gov/internet/formlocator.jsf
- www.dcbar.org/for_the_public/legal_information/family/family
  _court_forms/index.cfm
- www.uslegalforms.com/rominger/divorce.htm

District of Columbia Vital Records (Birth, Marriage, Divorce, Death)

- www.cdc.gov/nchs/w2w.htm
- publicrecords.onlinesearches.com/Districtofcolumbia.htm

District of Columbia Self-Help Services in Family Law Cases

- www.dccourts.gov/internet/public/aud_family/selfhelp.jsf
- www.dccourts.gov/internet/public/aud_family/main.jsf
- www.lawhelp.org/dc (click Family Law)

District of Columbia State Legal Research

- www.ll.georgetown.edu/states/dc.cfm

- www.loc.gov/law/help/guide/states/us-dc.php

District of Columbia Court Rules

- www.dccourts.gov/internet/superior/dcscrules.jsf
- www.llrx.com/courtrules-gen/state-District-of-Columbia.html

FLORIDA FAMILY LAW

Florida Family Code/Domestic Relations Code

- www.leg.state.fl.us/Statutes (click Domestic Relations)
- www.law.cornell.edu/wex/table_family

Florida Marriage Law (formation)

- usmarriagelaws.com/search/united_states/florida/index.shtml
- www.law.cornell.edu/wex/table_marriage

Florida Common Law Marriage

- Fla. Stat. § 741.211
- topics.law.cornell.edu/wex/table_marriage
- www.buddybuddy.com/common.html

Florida Same-Sex Marriage, Domestic Partnership, Civil Union, Defense of Marriage Status (Baby-DOMA)

- Fla. Stat. §741.212
- en.wikipedia.org/wiki/Recognition_of_same-sex_unions_in_Florida
- www.lambdalegal.org/publications/nationwide-status-same-sex-relationships
- www.ncsl.org/issues-research/human-services/civil-unions-and-domestic-partnership-statutes.aspx

Florida Divorce Law

- Fla. Stat. § 61.052
- www.floridalawhelp.org/FL/index.cfm (click Family Law)
- www.divorcelawinfo.com/states/fla/florida.htm
- www.hg.org/divorce-law-florida.html

Florida Alimony/Spousal Support Law

- Fla. Stat. § 61.08
- www.hg.org/divorce-law-florida.html

Florida Legal Separation Law

- Fla. Stat. § 61.031

Florida Property Division Law

- Fla. Stat. § 61.075

Florida Child Custody Law

- Fla. Stat. §§ 61.13, 61.514
- www.floridalawhelp.org/FL/index.cfm (click Family Law)
- www.hg.org/divorce-law-florida.html

Florida Guardian Ad Litem and Attorney for Child

- Fla. Stat. § 39.822
- www.childwelfare.gov/systemwide/laws_policies/statutes/represent.pdf

Florida Child Support Law

- Fla. Stat. § 61.13
- dor.myflorida.com/dor/childsupport
- dor.myflorida.com/dor/childsupport/guidelines.html
- www.acf.hhs.gov/programs/cse/extinf.html

Florida Paternity Law

- dor.myflorida.com/dor/childsupport/paternity.html

- www.acf.hhs.gov/programs/cse/pubs/2002/reports/essentials/c8.html
- www.floridalawhelp.org/FL/index.cfm (click Family Law)

Florida Adoption Law

- www.floridalawhelp.org/FL/index.cfm (click Family Law)
- laws.adoption.com/statutes/florida-adoption-laws.html
- law.findlaw.com/state-laws/adoption/florida

Florida Termination of Parental Rights

- Fla. Stat. § 39.806
- www.law.cornell.edu/wex/table_emancipation
- www.childwelfare.gov/systemwide/laws_policies/statutes/groundtermin.cfm
- www.floridalawhelp.org/FL/index.cfm (click Family Law)

Florida Putative Father Registry

- www.doh.state.fl.us/planning_eval/vital_statistics/Putative.htm
- laws.adoption.com/statutes/florida-laws,5.html
- www.courts.state.nh.us/probate/registrylist.pdf

Florida Emancipation Law

- www.law.cornell.edu/topics/Table_Emancipation
- www.youthrights.net/index.php?title=Florida_Emancipation_Law

Florida Age of Majority

- Fla. Stat. § 743.07
- www.supportcollectors.com/resources_florida.php#majority
- www.law.Cornell.edu/topics/Table_Emancipation

Florida Child Protection/Protective Services

- www.dcf.state.fl.us

Florida Child Welfare Agencies

- www.dcf.state.fl.us/index.shtml

Florida Juvenile Law

- www.djj.state.fl.us
- www.ncjj.org/State/Florida.aspx
- www.floridalawhelp.org/FL/index.cfm (click Family Law)

Florida Domestic Violence Law

- Fla. Stat. § 741.28
- www.floridalawhelp.org/FL/index.cfm (click Family Law)

Florida Grandparent Rights

- Fla. Stat. § 39.509

Florida Annulment Law

- *Sack v. Sack*, 184 So. 2d 434 (Fla. App. 1966)
- www.hg.org/divorce-law-Florida.html

Florida Family Law Forms

- www.flcourts.org/gen_public/family/forms_rules/index.shtml
- www.uslegalforms.com/rominger/divorce.htm

Florida Vital Records (Birth, Marriage, Divorce, Death)
- www.cdc.gov/nchs/w2w.htm
- publicrecords.onlinesearches.com/Florida.htm

Florida Self-Help Services in Family Law Cases
- www.flcourts.org/gen_public/family/self_help/map.shtml
- www.floridalawhelp.org/FL/index.cfm (click Family Law)

Florida State Legal Research
- library.ucf.edu/govdocs/legal/florida.php
- www.ll.georgetown.edu/states/florida.cfm
- www.loc.gov/law/help/guide/states/us-fl.php

Florida Court Rules
- www.floridasupremecourt.org/decisions/barrules.shtml
- www.llrx.com/courtrules-gen/state-Florida.html

GEORGIA FAMILY LAW

Georgia Family Code/Domestic Relations Code
- www.lexisnexis.com/hottopics/gacode/default.asp
- www.law.cornell.edu/wex/table_family

Georgia Marriage Law (formation)
- www.usmarriagelaws.com/search/united_states/georgia/marriage_licenses
- marriage.about.com/cs/marriagelicenses/p/georgia.htm
- www.law.cornell.edu/wex/table_marriage

Georgia Common Law Marriage
- Ga. Code Ann., § 19-3-1.1
- topics.law.cornell.edu/wex/table_marriage
- www.buddybuddy.com/common.html

Georgia Same-Sex Marriage, Domestic Partnership, Civil Union, Defense of Marriage Status (Baby-DOMA)
- en.wikipedia.org/wiki/LGBT_rights_in_Georgia
- www.lambdalegal.org/publications/nationwide-status-same-sex-relationships
- www.ncsl.org/issues-research/human-services/civil-unions-and-domestic-partnership-statutes.aspx

Georgia Divorce Law
- Ga. Ann. Code § 19-5-3
- www.legalaid-ga.org/GA/index.cfm (click Family Law)
- www.divorcelawinfo.com/states/ga/georgia.htm
- www.hg.org/divorce-law-Georgia.html

Georgia Legal Separation Law
- www.hg.org/divorce-law-Georgia.html

Georgia Alimony/Spousal Support Law
- Ga. Ann. Code § 19-6-1
- www.legalaid-ga.org/GA/index.cfm (click Family Law)

Georgia Property Division Law
- www.hg.org/divorce-law-Georgia.html
- www.divorcenet.com/states/georgia/ga_property

Georgia Child Custody Law
- Ga. Ann. Code § 19-9-1
- www.legalaid-ga.org/GA/index.cfm (click Family Law)

Georgia Guardian Ad Litem and Attorney for Child
- Ga. Ann. Code §§ 15-11-9, 15-11-6(b), 15-11-98(a)
- www.childwelfare.gov/systemwide/laws_policies/statutes/represent.pdf

Georgia Child Support Law
- www.georgiacourts.org/csc
- ocse.dhr.georgia.gov/portal/site
- www.supportguidelines.com/links.html
- www.acf.hhs.gov/programs/cse/extinf.html

Georgia Paternity Law
- ocse.dhr.georgia.gov/portal (click Services and then Paternity Establishment)
- www.acf.hhs.gov/programs/cse/pubs/2002/reports/essentials/c8.html

Georgia Legal Definition of Father
- Ga. Ann. Code § 19-8-1
- www.childwelfare.gov/systemwide/laws_policies/statutes/putative.pdf

Georgia Adoption Law
- Ga. Ann. Code §§ 19-8-3 et seq.
- www.legalaid-ga.org/GA/index.cfm (click Family Law)
- laws.adoption.com/statutes/georgia-adoption-laws.html
- law.findlaw.com/state-laws/adoption/Georgia

Georgia Termination of Parental Rights
- Ga. Ann. Code § 15-11-94
- www.law.cornell.edu/wex/table_emancipation
- www.childwelfare.gov/systemwide/laws_policies/statutes/groundtermin.cfm

Georgia Putative Father Registry
- Ga. Ann. Code § 19-11-9
- health.state.ga.us/programs/vitalrecords/fatherreg.asp irreconcilable differences
- laws.adoption.com/statutes/georgia-laws,5.html
- www.courts.state.nh.us/probate/registrylist.pdf

Georgia Emancipation Law
- www.law.cornell.edu/topics/Table_Emancipation
- www.youthrights.net/index.php?title=Georgia_Emancipation_Law

Georgia Age of Majority
- law.findlaw.com/state-laws/minors-and-the-law/georgia
- www.law.cornell.edu/topics/Table_Emancipation

Georgia Child Protection/Protective Services
- dhs.georgia.gov (enter Child Protection in the search box)

Georgia Child Welfare Agencies
- dfcs.dhs.georgia.gov/portal/site/DHS-DFCS

Georgia Juvenile Law
- www.djj.state.ga.us
- www.ncjj.org/State/Georgia.aspx

Georgia Domestic Violence Law
- www.legalaid-ga.org/GA/index.cfm (click Family Law)

Georgia Surrogacy Law
- www.surrogacy.com/legals/article/gaoverv.html
- www.selectsurrogate.com/surrogacy-laws-by-state.html

Georgia Grandparent Rights

- Ga. Ann. Code § 19-7-3
- www.legalaid-ga.org/GA/index.cfm (click Family Law)

Georgia Annulment Law

- Ga. Ann. Code§§ 19-4-1 et seq.

Georgia Family Law Forms

- sca.cobbcountyga.gov/sup_ct_adm_forms.htm
- www.uslegalforms.com/rominger/divorce.htm

Georgia Vital Records (Birth, Marriage, Divorce, Death)

- www.cdc.gov/nchs/w2w.htm
- publicrecords.onlinesearches.com/Georgia.htm

Georgia Self-Help Services in Family Law Cases

- www.georgiacourts.org/aoc/selfhelp
- www.legalaid-ga.org/GA/index.cfm (click Family Law)

Georgia State Legal Research

- www.ll.georgetown.edu/states/georgia.cfm
- www.loc.gov/law/help/guide/states/us-ga.php

Georgia Court Rules

- www.georgiacourts.org/index.php?option=com_content&view=article&id=122&Itemid=82
- www.llrx.com/courtrules-gen/state-Georgia.html

HAWAII FAMILY LAW

Hawaii Family Code/Domestic Relations Code

- www.capitol.hawaii.gov
- www.law.cornell.edu/wex/table_family

Hawaii Marriage Law (formation)

- hawaii.usmarriagelaws.com
- marriage.about.com/cs/marriagelicenses/p/hawaii.htm
- www.law.cornell.edu/wex/table_marriage

Hawaii Common Law Marriage

- topics.law.cornell.edu/wex/table_marriage
- www.buddybuddy.com/common.html

Hawaii Same-Sex Marriage, Domestic Partnership, Civil Union, Defense of Marriage Status (Baby-DOMA)

- en.wikipedia.org/wiki/Recognition_of_same-sex_unions_in_Hawaii
- www.lambdalegal.org/publications/nationwide-status-same-sex-relationships
- www.ncsl.org/issues-research/human-services/civil-unions-and-domestic-partnership-statutes.aspx

Hawaii Divorce Law

- Haw. Rev. Stat. § 580-41
- www.courts.state.hi.us/self-help/divorce/divorce.html
- www.divorcelawinfo.com/states/hi/hawaii.htm

Hawaii Legal Separation Law

- Haw. Rev. Stat. § 580-71

Hawaii Alimony/Spousal Support Law

- Haw. Rev. Stat. § 580-47

Hawaii Property Division Law

- Haw. Rev. Stat. §§ 510-9, 580-47

Hawaii Child Custody Law

- Haw. Rev. Stat. § 571-46
- www.lawhelp.org/hi (click Family and Juvenile)

Hawaii Guardian Ad Litem and Attorney for Child

- Haw. Rev. Stat. § 587A-16
- www.childwelfare.gov/systemwide/laws_policies/statutes/represent.pdf

Hawaii Child Support Law

- hawaii.gov/ag/csea
- hawaii.gov/jud/childpp.htm

- www.state.hi.us/jud/library/childsupport.htm
- www.acf.hhs.gov/programs/cse/extinf.html

Hawaii Paternity Law

- hawaii.gov/ag/csea/main/pis/paternity
- www.acf.hhs.gov/programs/cse/pubs/2002/reports/essentials/c8.html

Hawaii Legal Definition of Father

- Haw. Rev. Stat. § 584-4
- www.childwelfare.gov/systemwide/laws_policies/statutes/putative.pdf

Hawaii Adoption Law

- laws.adoption.com/statutes/hawaii-adoption-laws.html
- law.findlaw.com/state-laws/adoption/hawaii

Hawaii Termination of Parental Rights

- Haw. Rev. Stat. § 571-61
- www.law.cornell.edu/wex/table_emancipation
- www.childwelfare.gov/systemwide/laws_policies/statutes/groundtermin.cfm

Hawaii Putative Father Registry

- laws.adoption.com/statutes/hawaii-laws,5.html
- www.courts.state.nh.us/probate/registrylist.pdf

Hawaii Emancipation Law

- www.law.cornell.edu/topics/Table_Emancipation
- www.supportcollectors.com/resources_hawaii.php#majority

Hawaii Age of Majority

- law.findlaw.com/state-laws/minors-and-the-law/hawaii
- www.law.cornell.edu/topics/Table_Emancipation

Hawaii Child Protection/Protective Services

- hawaii.gov/dhs/social_services/child_welfare

Hawaii Child Welfare Agencies

- hawaii.gov/dhs/protection/social_services/child_welfare

Hawaii Juvenile Law

- www.courts.state.hi.us/self-help/juvenile/juvenile_proceedings.html
- hawaii.gov/ag/cpja/main/jjis
- www.ncjj.org/State/Hawaii.aspx

Hawaii Domestic Violence Law

- Haw. Rev. Stat. § 321-471
- www.hscadv.org

Hawaii Surrogacy Law
- www.hrc.org/laws-and-legislation/entry/hawaii-surrogacy-law
- www.selectsurrogate.com/surrogacy-laws-by-state.html

Hawaii Grandparent Rights
- Haw. Rev. Stat. § 571.46((a)(7)

Hawaii Annulment Law
- Haw. Rev. Stat. § 580-21

Hawaii Parental Liability for Acts of Minors
- Haw. Rev. Stat. § 577.3.5

Hawaii Family Law Forms
- www.courts.state.hi.us/self-help/courts/forms/court_forms.html
- www.uslegalforms.com/rominger/divorce.htm

Hawaii Vital Records (Birth, Marriage, Divorce, Death)
- www.cdc.gov/nchs/w2w.htm
- publicrecords.onlinesearches.com/Hawaii.htm

Hawaii Self-Help Services in Family Law Cases
- www.courts.state.hi.us/self-help/help.html
- www.courts.state.hi.us/self-help/divorce/divorce.html
- www.lawhelp.org/hi (click Family and Juvenile)

Hawaii State Legal Research
- www.ll.georgetown.edu/states/hawaii.cfm
- www.loc.gov/law/help/guide/states/us-hi.php
- www.state.hi.us/jud/library/legalresearch.htm

Hawaii Court Rules
- www.courts.state.hi.us/legal_references/rules/rulesOfCourt.html
- www.llrx.com/courtrules-gen/state-Hawaii.html

IDAHO FAMILY LAW

Idaho Family Code/Domestic Relations Code
- www.legislature.idaho.gov/idstat/TOC/IDStatutesTOC.htm
- www.legislature.idaho.gov
- www.law.cornell.edu/wex/table_family

Idaho Marriage Law (formation)
- usmarriagelaws.com/search/united_states/idaho/index.shtml
- marriage.about.com/cs/marriagelicenses/p/idaho.htm
- www.law.cornell.edu/wex/table_marriage

Idaho Common Law Marriage
- I.C. § 32-201
- topics.law.cornell.edu/wex/table_marriage
- www.buddybuddy.com/common.html

Idaho Same-Sex Marriage, Domestic Partnership, Civil Union, Defense of Marriage Status (Baby-DOMA)
- en.wikipedia.org/wiki/LGBT_rights_in_Idaho
- www.lambdalegal.org/publications/nationwide-status-same-sex-relationships
- www.ncsl.org/issues-research/human-services/civil-unions-and-domestic-partnership-statutes.aspx

Idaho Divorce Law
- Idaho Code Ann. § 32-601
- www.divorcelawinfo.com/states/id/idaho.htm
- www.hg.org/divorce-law-idaho.html

Idaho Legal Separation Law
- www.hg.org/divorce-law-idaho.html

Idaho Alimony/Maintenance/Spousal Support Law
- Idaho Code Ann. § 32-705
- www.hg.org/divorce-law-idaho.html

Idaho Property Division Law
- Idaho Code Ann. § 32-712
- www.hg.org/divorce-law-idaho.html

Idaho Child Custody Law
- Idaho Code Ann. § 32-717

Idaho Guardian Ad Litem and Attorney for Child
- Idaho Code Ann. § 16-1614
- www.isc.idaho.gov/guardian/about-us

- www.childwelfare.gov/systemwide/laws_policies/statutes/represent.pdf

Idaho Child Support Law
- Idaho Code Ann. § 32-706
- www.healthandwelfare.idaho.gov
- www.supportguidelines.com/links.html
- www.acf.hhs.gov/programs/cse/extinf.html

Idaho Paternity Law
- healthandwelfare.idaho.gov (enter Paternity in the search box)
- www.acf.hhs.gov/programs/cse/pubs/2002/reports/essentials/c8.html

Idaho Legal Definition of Father
- Idaho Code Ann. § 16-2002
- www.childwelfare.gov/systemwide/laws_policies/statutes/putative.pdf

Idaho Adoption Law
- laws.adoption.com/statutes/idaho-adoption-laws.html
- law.findlaw.com/state-laws/adoption/hawaii

Idaho Termination of Parental Rights
- Idaho Code Ann. § 16-2002
- www.law.cornell.edu/wex/table_emancipation
- www.childwelfare.gov/systemwide/laws_policies/statutes/groundtermin.cfm

Idaho Putative Father Registry
- Idaho Code Ann. § 16-1513
- laws.adoption.com/statutes/idaho-laws,5.html
- www.courts.state.nh.us/probate/registrylist.pdf

Idaho Emancipation Law
- www.law.cornell.edu/topics/Table_Emancipation
- www.youthrights.net/index.php?title=Idaho_Emancipation_Law

Idaho Age of Majority
- law.findlaw.com/state-laws/minors-and-the-law/idaho
- www.law.cornell.edu/topics/Table_Emancipation

Idaho Child Protection/Protective Services
- healthandwelfare.idaho.gov/Children/AbuseNeglect/tabid/74/Default.aspx

Idaho Child Welfare Agencies

- healthandwelfare.idaho.gov/Children/tabid/57/Default.aspx

Idaho Juvenile Law

- www.ncjj.org/State/Idaho.aspx
- www.idjc.idaho.gov

Idaho Domestic Violence Law

- Idaho Code Ann. § 18-918

Idaho Grandparent Rights

- Idaho Code Ann. § 32-719

Idaho Annulment Law

- Idaho Code Ann. § 32-501

Idaho Family Law Forms

- www.courtselfhelp.idaho.gov
- www.isc.idaho.gov/search/node/forms

- www.idaholegalaid.org/SelfHelp/family
- www.uslegalforms.com/rominger/divorce.htm

Idaho Vital Records (Birth, Marriage, Divorce, Death)

- www.cdc.gov/nchs/w2w.htm
- publicrecords.onlinesearches.com/Idaho.htm

Idaho Self-Help Services in Family Law Cases

- www.courtselfhelp.idaho.gov
- www.idaholegalaid.org/SelfHelp

Idaho State Legal Research

- www.isll.idaho.gov
- www.ll.georgetown.edu/states/idaho.cfm
- www.loc.gov/law/help/guide/states/us-id.php

Idaho Court Rules

- www.isc.idaho.gov/problem-solving/idaho-court-rules
- www.llrx.com/courtrules-gen/state-Idaho.html

ILLINOIS FAMILY LAW

Illinois Family Code/Domestic Relations Code

- www.ilga.gov/legislation/ilcs/ilcs.asp
- www.law.cornell.edu/wex/table_family

Illinois Marriage Law (formation)

- www.usmarriagelaws.com/search/united_states/illinois/marriage_licenses
- marriage.about.com/cs/marriagelicenses/p/illinois.htm
- www.law.cornell.edu/wex/table_marriage

Illinois Common Law Marriage

- topics.law.cornell.edu/wex/table_marriage
- www.buddybuddy.com/common.html

Illinois Same-Sex Marriage, Domestic Partnership, Civil Union, Defense of Marriage Status (Baby-DOMA)

- en.wikipedia.org/wiki/Recognition_of_same-sex_unions_in_Illinois
- www.lambdalegal.org/publications/nationwide-status-same-sex-relationships
- www.ncsl.org/issues-research/human-services/civil-unions-and-domestic-partnership-statutes.aspx

Illinois Divorce Law

- 750 Ill. Comp. Stat. Ann. § 5/401
- www.law.siu.edu/selfhelp/info/divorce/packets.asp
- www.divorcelawinfo.com/states/ill/illinois.htm
- www.hg.org/divorce-law-Illinois.html

Illinois Legal Separation Law

- 750 Ill. Comp. Stat. Ann. § 5/402

Illinois Alimony/Spousal Support/Maintenance Law

- 750 Ill. Comp. Stat. Ann. § 5/504
- www.hg.org/divorce-law-Illinois.html

Illinois Property Division Law

- 750 Ill. Comp. Stat. Ann. § 5/503
- www.hg.org/divorce-law-Illinois.html

Illinois Child Custody Law

- 750 Ill. Comp. Stat. Ann. § 5/602
- www.hg.org/divorce-law-Illinois.html

Illinois Guardian Ad Litem and Attorney for Child

- 705 Ill. Comp. Stat. Ann. §§ 405/2-17, 405/1-5
- www.childwelfare.gov/systemwide/laws_policies/statutes/represent.pdf

Illinois Child Support Law

- www.ilchildsupport.com
- www.supportguidelines.com/links.html
- www.acf.hhs.gov/programs/cse/extinf.html

Illinois Paternity Law

- www.ilga.gov/legislation/ilcs/ilcs3.asp?ActID=2097&ChapterID=59
- www.illinoislegalaid.org/index.cfm?fuseaction=home.dsp_content&contentID=5004#
- www.acf.hhs.gov/programs/cse/pubs/2002/reports/essentials/c8.html

Illinois Legal Definition of Father

- 750 Ill. Comp. Stat. Ann. §§ 45/2, 45/5
- www.childwelfare.gov/systemwide/laws_policies/statutes/putative.pdf

Illinois Adoption Law

- laws.adoption.com/statutes/illinois-adoption-laws.html
- statelaws.findlaw.com/illinois-law/illinois-adoption-laws.html

Illinois Termination of Parental Rights

- 20 Ill. Comp. Stat. Ann. § 505/35.2
- www.law.cornell.edu/wex/table_emancipation
- www.childwelfare.gov/systemwide/laws_policies/statutes/groundtermin.cfm

Illinois Putative Father Registry

- www.putativefather.org/index.aspx
- laws.adoption.com/statutes/illinois-laws,5.html
- www.courts.state.nh.us/probate/registrylist.pdf

Illinois Emancipation Law

- www.law.cornell.edu/topics/Table_Emancipation
- www.youthrights.net/index.php?title=Illinois_Emancipation_Law

Illinois Age of Majority

- law.findlaw.com/state-laws/minors-and-the-law/illinois
- www.law.cornell.edu/topics/Table_Emancipation

Illinois Child Protection/Protective Services

- www.state.il.us/dcfs/child/index.shtml

Illinois Child Welfare Agencies

- www.state.il.us/dcfs/index.shtml

Illinois Juvenile Law

- www.idjj.state.il.us
- www.ncjj.org/State/Illinois.aspx

Illinois Domestic Violence Law

- 750 Ill. Comp. Stat. Ann. § 60/103

Illinois Surrogacy Law

- 750 Ill. Comp. Stat. Ann. § 45/2.5
- 750 Ill. Comp. Stat. Ann. §§ 47/1 et seq.
- www.selectsurrogate.com/surrogacy-laws-by-state.html

Illinois Grandparent Rights

- 750 Ill. Comp. Stat. Ann. § 5/607

Illinois Annulment Law

- 750 Ill. Comp. Stat. Ann. § 5/301

Illinois Parental Liability for Acts of Minors

- 740 Ill. Comp. Stat. Ann. §115/1

Illinois Family Law Forms

- www.illinoislegalaid.org/index.cfm?fuseaction=home.formLibrary
- www.uslegalforms.com/rominger/divorce.htm

Illinois Vital Records (Birth, Marriage, Divorce, Death)

- www.cdc.gov/nchs/w2w.htm
- publicrecords.onlinesearches.com/Illinois.htm

Illinois Self-Help Services in Family Law Cases

- www.illinoislegalaid.org/index.cfm?fuseaction=home.formLibrary
- www.state.il.us/court/default.asp
- www.state.il.us/court/citizen.asp
- www.law.siu.edu/selfhelp

Illinois State Legal Research

- www.ll.georgetown.edu/states/illinois.cfm
- www.loc.gov/law/help/guide/states/us-il.php
- www.findlaw.com/11stategov/il/index.html

Illinois Court Rules

- www.state.il.us/court/supremecourt/rules
- www.llrx.com/courtrules-gen/state-Illinois.html

INDIANA FAMILY LAW

Indiana Family Code/Domestic Relations Code

- www.state.in.us/legislative/ic/code/title31/ar15
- www.state.in.us/legislative/ic/code
- www.law.cornell.edu/wex/table_family

Indiana Marriage Law (formation)

- www.in.gov/legislative/ic/2010/title31/ar11
- www.usmarriagelaws.com/search/united_states/indiana/marriage_licenses
- www.law.cornell.edu/wex/table_marriage

Indiana Common Law Marriage

- topics.law.cornell.edu/wex/table_marriage
- www.buddybuddy.com/common.html

Indiana Same-Sex Marriage, Domestic Partnership, Civil Union, Defense of Marriage Status (Baby-DOMA)

- en.wikipedia.org/wiki/Recognition_of_same-sex_unions_in_Indiana
- www.lambdalegal.org/publications/nationwide-status-same-sex-relationships
- www.ncsl.org/issues-research/human-services/civil-unions-and-domestic-partnership-statutes.aspx

Indiana Divorce Law

- Ind. Code Ann. § 31-15-2-3
- www.divorcelawinfo.com/states/ind/indiana.htm
- www.hg.org/divorce-law-Indiana.html

Indiana Legal Separation Law

- Ind. Code Ann. § 31-15-3-2
- www.hg.org/divorce-law-Indiana.html

Indiana Alimony/Spousal Support/Maintenance Law

- Ind. Code Ann. § 31-15-7-1

Indiana Property Division Law

- Ind. Code Ann. § 31-15-7-4
- www.hg.org/divorce-law-Indiana.html

Indiana Child Custody Law

- Ind. Code Ann. § 31-17-2-8

Indiana Relocation of Child

- Ind. Code Ann. § 31-17-2.2-2

Indiana Guardian Ad Litem and Attorney for Child

- Ind. Code Ann. §§ 31-32-3-1, 31-9-2-43.2, 31-32-3-2
- www.childwelfare.gov/systemwide/laws_policies/statutes/represent.pdf

Indiana Child Support Law

- www.in.gov/dcs/support.htm
- www.in.gov/judiciary/rules/child_support/index.html
- www.supportguidelines.com/links.html
- www.acf.hhs.gov/programs/cse/extinf.html

Indiana Paternity Law

- www.in.gov/dcs/2485.htm
- www.acf.hhs.gov/programs/cse/pubs/2002/reports/essentials/c8.html

Indiana Legal Definition of Father

- Ind. Code Ann. §§ 31-9-2-9, 31-9-2-88, 31-9-2-100
- www.childwelfare.gov/systemwide/laws_policies/statutes/putative.pdf

Indiana Adoption Law

- laws.adoption.com/statutes/indiana-adoption-laws.html
- law.findlaw.com/state-laws/adoption/Indiana

Indiana Termination of Parental Rights

- Ind. Code Ann. § 31-35-2-5
- www.law.cornell.edu/wex/table_emancipation
- www.childwelfare.gov/systemwide/laws_policies/statutes/groundtermin.cfm

Indiana Putative Father Registry

- Ind. Code Ann. § 31-19-5-2
- www.indy.gov/eGov/County/Clerk/Court/Juvenile/Pages/notice-putatitve.aspx

- laws.adoption.com/statutes/indiana-laws,5.html
- www.courts.state.nh.us/probate/registrylist.pdf

Indiana Emancipation Law

- www.law.cornell.edu/topics/Table_Emancipation
- www.youthrights.net/index.php?title=Indiana_Emancipation_Law
- www.in.gov/legislative/ic/code/title31/ar16/ch6.html

Indiana Age of Majority

- law.findlaw.com/state-laws/minors-and-the-law/indiana
- www.law.cornell.edu/topics/Table_Emancipation

Indiana Child Protection/Protective Services

- www.in.gov/dcs/2398.htm

Indiana Child Welfare Agencies

- www.in.gov/core/family.html

Indiana Juvenile Law

- www.doe.in.gov/student-services/attendance/juvenile-justice
- www.ncjj.org/State/Indiana.aspx

Indiana Domestic Violence Law

- Ind. Code Ann. § 34-6-2-34.5

Indiana Surrogacy Law

- Ind. Code Ann. § 31-20-1-1
- www.selectsurrogate.com/surrogacy-laws-by-state.html

Indiana Grandparent Rights

- Ind. Code Ann. § 31-17-5-1

Indiana Annulment Law

- Ind. Code Ann. § 31-11-9-1
- www.in.gov/legislative/ic/2010/title31/ar11

Indiana Family Law Forms

- www.in.gov/judiciary/2684.htm
- www.in.gov/judiciary/selfservice/2333.htm
- www.uslegalforms.com/rominger/divorce.htm

Indiana Vital Records (Birth, Marriage, Divorce, Death)

- www.cdc.gov/nchs/w2w.htm
- publicrecords.onlinesearches.com/Indiana.htm

Indiana Self-Help Services in Family Law Cases

- www.in.gov/judiciary/selfservice
- www.in.gov/judiciary/selfservice/2332.htm

Indiana Family Law Legal Research

- www.in.gov/judiciary/selfservice/2332.htm

Indiana State Legal Research (general)

- www.in.gov/judiciary/selfservice/2358.htm
- www.ll.georgetown.edu/states/indiana.cfm
- www.loc.gov/law/help/guide/states/us-in.php
- www.law.cornell.edu/states/indiana.html

Indiana Court Rules

- www.in.gov/judiciary/2684.htm
- www.llrx.com/courtrules-gen/state-Indiana.html

IOWA FAMILY LAW

Iowa Family Code/Domestic Relations Code

- www2.legis.state.ia.us/IACODE/1999/598
- www.legis.state.ia.us/IowaLaw.html
- www.law.cornell.edu/wex/table_family

Iowa Marriage Law (formation)

- www.usmarriagelaws.com/search/united_states/iowa/marriage_licenses
- statutes.laws.com/iowa/title-15/subtitle-1/chapter-595
- www.law.cornell.edu/wex/table_marriage

Iowa Common Law Marriage

- *In re Dallman's Estate*, 228 N.W.2d 187 (Iowa 1975)
- topics.law.cornell.edu/wex/table_marriage
- www.buddybuddy.com/common.html

Iowa Same-Sex Marriage, Domestic Partnership, Civil Union, Defense of Marriage Status (Baby-DOMA)

- en.wikipedia.org/wiki/Same-sex_marriage_in_Iowa
- www.lambdalegal.org/publications/nationwide-status-same-sex-relationships
- www.ncsl.org/issues-research/human-services/civil-unions-and-domestic-partnership-statutes.aspx

Iowa Divorce Law

- Iowa Code Ann. § 598.5
- www.iowacourtsonline.org/Representing_Yourself/DivorceFamily_Law/Divorce
- www.iowalegalaid.org/IA/index.cfm (click Family and Juvenile)
- www.divorcelawinfo.com/states/ia/iowa.htm
- www.hg.org/divorce-law-Iowa.html

Iowa Legal Separation Law

- www.hg.org/divorce-law-Iowa.html

Iowa Alimony/Spousal Support Law

- Iowa Code Ann. § 598.21A
- www.hg.org/divorce-law-Iowa.html

Iowa Property Division Law

- Iowa Code Ann. § 598.21
- www.hg.org/divorce-law-Iowa.html

Iowa Child Custody Law

- Iowa Code Ann. § 598.41
- www.iowacourtsonline.org/Representing_Yourself/DivorceFamily_Law/Child_Custody
- www.iowalegalaid.org/IA/index.cfm (click Family and Juvenile)
- www.hg.org/divorce-law-Iowa.html

Iowa Relocation of Child

- Iowa Code Ann. § 598.21D

Iowa Guardian Ad Litem and Attorney for Child

- Iowa Code §§ 232.71C, 232.89
- www.childwelfare.gov/systemwide/laws_policies/statutes/represent.pdf

Iowa Child Support Law

- Iowa Code Ann. § 598.21B
- secureapp.dhs.state.ia.us/childsupport/welcome.asp
- www.iowacourtsonline.org/Representing_Yourself/DivorceFamily_Law/Child_Support
- www.acf.hhs.gov/programs/cse/extinf.html

Iowa Paternity Law
- www.iowacourtsonline.org/Representing_Yourself
  /DivorceFamily_Law/Paternity
- www.acf.hhs.gov/programs/cse/pubs/2002/reports/essentials
  /c8.html

Iowa Legal Definition of Father
- Iowa Code § 144.12A
- www.childwelfare.gov/systemwide/laws_policies/statutes
  /putative.pdf

Iowa Adoption Law
- laws.adoption.com/statutes/iowa-adoption-laws.html
- law.findlaw.com/state-laws/adoption/iowa

Iowa Termination of Parental Rights
- Iowa Code Rule 6.201
- www.law.cornell.edu/wex/table_emancipation
- www.childwelfare.gov/systemwide/laws_policies/statutes
  /groundtermin.cfm

Iowa Putative Father Registry
- Iowa Code Ann. § 144.12A
- laws.adoption.com/statutes/iowa-laws,5.html
- www.courts.state.nh.us/probate/registrylist.pdf

Iowa Emancipation Law
- Iowa Code § 232C.1
- www.law.cornell.edu/topics/Table_Emancipation

Iowa Age of Majority
- law.findlaw.com/state-laws/minors-and-the-law/iowa
- www.law.cornell.edu/topics/Table_Emancipation

Iowa Child Protection/Protective Services
- www.dhs.iowa.gov/Consumers/Test/ProtectiveServices.html
- www.dhs.state.ia.us/consumers/safety_and_protection/abuse
  _reporting/childabuse.html

Iowa Child Welfare Agencies
- www.dhs.iowa.gov/Consumers/Test/ProtectiveServices.html

Iowa Juvenile Law
- www.ncjj.org/State/Iowa.aspx
- www.iowalegalaid.org/IA/index.cfm (click Family and Juvenile)

- www.iowacourtsonline.org/Representing_Yourself/Juvenile
  _Court/index.asp
- www.iowacourtsonline.org/Court_Rules_and_Forms/Juvenile_Forms

Iowa Domestic Violence Law
- www.iowacourtsonline.org/Representing_Yourself/Domestic
  _Violence/index.asp
- www.iowalegalaid.org/IA/index.cfm (click Family and Juvenile)

Iowa Surrogacy Law
- Iowa Code § 710.11
- www.selectsurrogate.com/surrogacy-laws-by-state.html

Iowa Grandparent Rights
- Iowa Code Ann. § 600C.1
- www.iowacourtsonline.org/Representing_Yourself
  /DivorceFamily_Law/Grandparent_Visitation

Iowa Annulment Law
- Iowa Code Ann. § 595.19
- www.hg.org/divorce-law-Iowa.html

Iowa Parental Liability for Acts of Minors
- Iowa Code Ann. § 613.16

Iowa Family Law Forms
- www.iowacourtsonline.org/Court_Rules_and_Forms
- www.iowacourtsonline.org/Court_Rules_and_Forms/Juvenile_Forms
- www.uslegalforms.com/rominger/divorce.htm

Iowa Vital Records (Birth, Marriage, Divorce, Death)
- www.cdc.gov/nchs/w2w.htm
- publicrecords.onlinesearches.com/Iowa.htm

Iowa Self-Help Services in Family Law Cases
- www.iowacourtsonline.org/Representing_Yourself
- www.iowalegalaid.org/IA/index.cfm (click Family and Juvenile)

Iowa State Legal Research
- www.ll.georgetown.edu/states/iowa.cfm
- www.loc.gov/law/help/guide/states/us-ia.php

Iowa Court Rules
- www.iowacourtsonline.org/Court_Rules_and_Forms
- www.llrx.com/courtrules-gen/state-Iowa.html

KANSAS FAMILY LAW

Kansas Family Code/Domestic Relations Code
- kansasstatutes.lesterama.org/detailedindex.html
- www.law.cornell.edu/wex/table_family

Kansas Marriage Law (formation)
- kansasstatutes.lesterama.org/Chapter_23/Article_1
- www.usmarriagelaws.com/search/united_states/kansas/marriage
  _licenses
- www.law.cornell.edu/wex/table_marriage

Kansas Common Law Marriage
- *Sullivan v. Sullivan*, 413 P.2d 988 (Kan. 1966)
- topics.law.cornell.edu/wex/table_marriage
- www.buddybuddy.com/common.html

Kansas Same-Sex Marriage, Domestic Partnership, Civil Union, Defense of Marriage Status (Baby-DOMA)
- en.wikipedia.org/wiki/LGBT_rights_in_Kansas
- www.lambdalegal.org/publications/nationwide-status-same-sex
  -relationships

- www.ncsl.org/issues-research/human-services/civil-unions-and
  -domestic-partnership-statutes.aspx

Kansas Divorce Law
- Kan. Stat. Ann. § 23-2802
- www.divorcelawinfo.com/states/ks/kansas.htm
- www.hg.org/divorce-law-Kansas.html

Kansas Legal Separation Law
- www.hg.org/divorce-law-Kansas.html

Kansas Alimony/Spousal Support/ Maintenance Law
- Kan. Stat. Ann. § 23-2701
- www.hg.org/divorce-law-Kansas.html

Kansas Property Division Law
- Kan. Stat. Ann. § 23-2701
- www.hg.org/divorce-law-Kansas.html

Kansas Child Custody Law

- Kan. Stat. Ann. § 23-3203
- www.hg.org/divorce-law-Kansas.html

Kansas Relocation of Child

- Kan. Stat. Ann. §§ 60-1620

Kansas Guardian Ad Litem and Attorney for Child

- Kan. Stat. Ann. § 38-2205
- www.childwelfare.gov/systemwide/laws_policies/statutes
  /represent.pdf

Kansas Child Support Law

- www.srs.ks.gov/services/Pages/CSE.aspx
- www.kscourts.org/Rules-procedures-forms/Child-support
  -guidelines/default.asp
- www.acf.hhs.gov/programs/cse/extinf.html

Kansas Paternity Law

- www.kansaslegalservices.org/legal_library/Family_Law/Paternity
- www.acf.hhs.gov/programs/cse/pubs/2002/reports/essentials/c8.html

Kansas Legal Definition of Father

- Kan. Stat. Ann. §§ 38-1111, 38-1114
- www.childwelfare.gov/systemwide/laws_policies/statutes
  /putative.pdf

Kansas Adoption Law

- laws.adoption.com/statutes/kansas-adoption-laws.html
- public.findlaw.com/LCsearch.html?entry=kansas+adoption+law

Kansas Termination of Parental Rights

- Kan. Stat. Ann. § 38-2269
- www.law.cornell.edu/wex/table_emancipation
- www.childwelfare.gov/systemwide/laws_policies/statutes
  /groundtermin.cfm

Kansas Putative Father Registry

- laws.adoption.com/statutes/kansas-laws,5.html
- www.courts.state.nh.us/probate/registrylist.pdf

Kansas Emancipation Law

- www.law.cornell.edu/topics/Table_Emancipation
- www.youthrights.net/index.php?title=Kansas_Emancipation_Law

Kansas Age of Majority

- law.findlaw.com/state-laws/minors-and-the-law/kansas
- www.law.cornell.edu/topics/Table_Emancipation

Kansas Child Protection/Protective Services

- www.srs.ks.gov/agency/cfs/Pages/ChildProtectiveServices.aspx

Kansas Child Welfare Agencies

- www.srs.ks.gov/Pages/Default.aspx

Kansas Juvenile Law

- www.jja.ks.gov
- www.ncjj.org/State/Kansas.aspx

Kansas Grandparent Rights

- Kan. Stat. Ann. § 23-3301

Kansas Annulment Law

- Kan. Stat. Ann. § 23-102
- kansasstatutes.lesterama.org/Chapter_23/Article_1

Kansas Family Law Forms

- www.kscourts.org/Rules-Procedures-Forms/Legal
  -Forms.asp
- www.kansaslegalservices.org/FreeLegalForms
- www.uslegalforms.com/rominger/divorce.htm

Kansas Vital Records (Birth, Marriage, Divorce, Death)

- www.cdc.gov/nchs/w2w.htm
- publicrecords.onlinesearches.com/Kansas.htm

Kansas Self-Help Services in Family Law Cases

- www.kansaslegalservices.org
- www.kscourts.org/programs/self-help/Legal-Assistance.asp
- www.kscourts.org/programs/self-help/default.asp

Kansas State Legal Research

- www.ll.georgetown.edu/states/kansas.cfm
- www.loc.gov/law/help/guide/states/us-ks.php

Kansas Court Rules

- www.kscourts.org/rules/default.asp

KENTUCKY FAMILY LAW

Kentucky Family Code/Domestic Relations Code

- www.lrc.state.ky.us/KRS/403-00/CHAPTER.HTM
- www.lrc.state.ky.us/index.htm
- www.law.cornell.edu/wex/table_family

Kentucky Marriage Law (formation)

- www.usmarriagelaws.com/search/united_states/kentucky
  /marriage_licenses
- law.findlaw.com/state-laws/marriage-age-requirements
  /kentucky
- www.law.cornell.edu/wex/table_marriage

Kentucky Common Law Marriage

- topics.law.cornell.edu/wex/table_marriage
- www.buddybuddy.com/common.html

Kentucky Same-Sex Marriage, Domestic Partnership, Civil Union, Defense of Marriage Status (Baby-DOMA)

- en.wikipedia.org/wiki/LGBT_rights_in_Kentucky
- www.lambdalegal.org/publications/nationwide-status-same-sex
  -relationships

- www.ncsl.org/issues-research/human-services/civil-unions-and
  -domestic-partnership-statutes.aspx

Kentucky Divorce Law

- Ky. Rev. Stat. §§ 403.140, 403.170
- kyjustice.org/home
- www.divorcelawinfo.com/states/ky/kentucky.htm
- www.hg.org/divorce-law-Kentucky.html

Kentucky Legal Separation Law

- Ky. Rev. Stat. §§ 403.050, 403.140
- www.hg.org/divorce-law-Kentucky.html

Kentucky Alimony/Spousal Support/ Maintenance Law

- Ky. Rev. Stat. § 403.200
- www.hg.org/divorce-law-Kentucky.html

Kentucky Property Division Law

- Ky. Rev. Stat. § 403.190
- www.hg.org/divorce-law-Kentucky.html

Kentucky Child Custody Law

- Ky. Rev. Stat. § 403.270
- kyjustice.org/home
- www.hg.org/divorce-law-Kentucky.html

Kentucky Guardian Ad Litem and Attorney for Child

- Ky. Rev. Stat. § 620.100
- www.childwelfare.gov/systemwide/laws_policies/statutes/represent.pdf

Kentucky Child Support Law

- Ky. Rev. Stat. § 403.212
- chfs.ky.gov/dis/cse.htm
- kyjustice.org/home
- www.acf.hhs.gov/programs/cse/extinf.html

Kentucky Paternity Law

- paternity.uslegal.com/paternity-laws/kentucky-paternity-law
- www.lrc.state.ky.us/krs/406-00/chapter.htm
- www.acf.hhs.gov/programs/cse/pubs/2002/reports/essentials/c8.html

Kentucky Legal Definition of Father

- www.childwelfare.gov/systemwide/laws_policies/statutes/putative.pdf

Kentucky Adoption Law

- laws.adoption.com/statutes/kentucky-adoption-laws.html
- statelaws.findlaw.com/kentucky-law/kentucky-adoption-laws.html

Kentucky Termination of Parental Rights

- Ky. Rev. Stat. § 625-090
- www.law.cornell.edu/wex/table_emancipation
- www.childwelfare.gov/systemwide/laws_policies/statutes/groundtermin.cfm

Kentucky Putative Father Registry

- laws.adoption.com/statutes/kentucky-laws,5.html
- www.courts.state.nh.us/probate/registrylist.pdf

Kentucky Emancipation Law

- www.law.cornell.edu/topics/Table_Emancipation

Kentucky Age of Majority

- law.findlaw.com/state-laws/minors-and-the-law/kentucky
- www.law.cornell.edu/topics/Table_Emancipation

Kentucky Child Protection/Protective Services

- chfs.ky.gov/dcbs/dpp/childsafety.htm

Kentucky Child Welfare Agencies

- chfs.ky.gov/dcbs/dpp

Kentucky Juvenile Law

- djj.ky.gov
- www.ncjj.org/State/Kentucky.aspx

Kentucky Domestic Violence Law

- Ky. Rev. Stat. § 403.720
- kyjustice.org/home

Kentucky Surrogacy Law

- *Surrogate Parenting Assoc. v. Commonw.*, 704 S.W.2d 209 (Ky. 1986)
- www.selectsurrogate.com/surrogacy-laws-by-state.html
- www.surrogacyforall.com/Surrogacy-Law.html

Kentucky Grandparent Rights

- Ky. Rev. Stat. § 405.021

Kentucky Annulment Law

- Ky. Rev. Stat. § 403.120
- www.hg.org/divorce-law-Kentucky.html

Kentucky Family Law Forms

- courts.ky.gov/resources/legalforms/Pages/default.aspx
- www.kyjustice.org/selfhelpforms
- www.uslegalforms.com/rominger/divorce.htm

Kentucky Vital Records (Birth, Marriage, Divorce, Death)

- www.cdc.gov/nchs/w2w.htm
- publicrecords.onlinesearches.com/Kentucky.htm

Kentucky Self-Help Services in Family Law Cases

- kyjustice.org/home
- www.kyjustice.org/selfhelpforms
- www.courtreference.com/Kentucky-Courts-Self-Help.htm

Kentucky State Legal Research

- www.ll.georgetown.edu/states/kentucky.cfm
- www.loc.gov/law/help/guide/states/us-ky.php

Kentucky Court Rules

- government.westlaw.com/linkedslice/default.asp?SP=KYR-1000
- www.llrx.com/courtrules-gen/state-Kentucky.html

LOUISIANA FAMILY LAW

Louisiana Family Code/Domestic Relations Code

- www.legis.state.la.us/lss/tsrssearch.htm
- www.legis.state.la.us
- www.law.cornell.edu/wex/table_family

Louisiana Marriage Law (formation)

- www.usmarriagelaws.com/search/united_states/louisiana/marriage_licenses
- www.law.cornell.edu/wex/table_marriage

Louisiana Common Law Marriage

- topics.law.cornell.edu/wex/table_marriage
- www.buddybuddy.com/common.html

Louisiana Covenant Marriage

- La. Rev. Stats. § 9:272

- www.divorcereform.org/la01.html
- patriot.net/~crouch/cov/index.html

Louisiana Same-Sex Marriage, Domestic Partnership, Civil Union, Defense of Marriage Status (Baby-DOMA)

- en.wikipedia.org/wiki/LGBT_rights_in_Louisiana
- www.lambdalegal.org/publications/nationwide-status-same-sex-relationships
- www.ncsl.org/issues-research/human-services/civil-unions-and-domestic-partnership-statutes.aspx

Louisiana Divorce Law

- La. Stat. Ann. Civil Code Art. 103
- www.lawhelp.org/LA (click Family & Children)
- www.divorcelawinfo.com/states/la/louisiana.htm
- www.hg.org/divorce-law-Louisiana.html

Louisiana Alimony/Spousal Support Law

- La. Stat. Ann. Civil Code Art. 111
- www.lawhelp.org/LA (click Family & Children)
- www.hg.org/divorce-law-Louisiana.html

Louisiana Property Division Law

- La. Stat. Ann. Civil Code Art. 159
- www.hg.org/divorce-law-Louisiana.html

Louisiana Child Custody Law

- La. Stat. Ann. Civil Code Arts. 131, 134
- www.lawhelp.org/LA (click Family & Children)

Louisiana Relocation of Child

- La. Rev. Stats. § 9:355.12

Louisiana Guardian Ad Litem and Attorney for Child

- www.childwelfare.gov/systemwide/laws_policies/statutes/represent.pdf

Louisiana Child Support Law

- www.legis.state.la.us/lss/lss.asp?doc=107373
- dss.louisiana.gov/index.cfm?md=pagebuilder&tmp=home&pid=137
- www.lawhelp.org/LA (click Family & Children)
- www.acf.hhs.gov/programs/cse/extinf.html

Louisiana Paternity Law

- new.dhh.louisiana.gov/index.cfm/page/681/n/237
- www.acf.hhs.gov/programs/cse/pubs/2002/reports/essentials/c8.html

Louisiana Legal Definition of Father

- La. Stat. Ann. Children's Code Art. 116(17)
- www.childwelfare.gov/systemwide/laws_policies/statutes/putative.pdf

Louisiana Adoption Law

- laws.adoption.com/statutes/louisiana-adoption-laws.html
- www.lawhelp.org/LA (click Family & Children)
- law.findlaw.com/state-laws/adoption/louisiana

Louisiana Termination of Parental Rights

- La. Stat. Ann. Children's Code Art. 1015
- www.lawhelp.org/LA (click Family & Children)
- www.law.cornell.edu/wex/table_emancipation
- www.childwelfare.gov/systemwide/laws_policies/statutes/groundtermin.cfm

Louisiana Putative Father Registry

- new.dhh.louisiana.gov/index.cfm/page/646
- laws.adoption.com/statutes/louisiana-laws,5.html
- www.courts.state.nh.us/probate/registrylist.pdf

Louisiana Emancipation Law

- La. Rev. Stats. § 9:101
- La. Stat. Ann. Civil Code Art. 365
- www.law.cornell.edu/topics/Table_Emancipation

Louisiana Age of Majority

- La. Stat. Ann. Civil Code Art. 29
- law.findlaw.com/state-laws/minors-and-the-law/louisiana

Louisiana Child Protection/Protective Services

- www.dcfs.louisiana.gov/index.cfm?md=pagebuilder&tmp=home&pid=109

Louisiana Child Welfare Agencies

- www.dss.state.la.us

Louisiana Juvenile Law

- www.ncjj.org/State/Louisiana.aspx
- www.lawhelp.org/LA (click Family & Children)

Louisiana Domestic Violence Law

- www.lawhelp.org/LA (click Family & Children)
- www.lcadv.org

Louisiana Employment Discrimination Law

- La. Rev. Stats. § 23:301

Louisiana Surrogacy Law

- La. Rev. Stat. Ann. § 9:2713
- www.selectsurrogate.com/surrogacy-laws-by-state.html

Louisiana Grandparent Rights

- La. Stat. Ann. Civil Code Art. 136
- La. Rev. Stats. § 9:344
- www.lawhelp.org/LA (click Family & Children)

Louisiana Annulment Law

- La. Stat. Ann. Civil Code Art. 94
- www.hg.org/divorce-law-Louisiana.html

Louisiana Family Law Forms

- www.familycourt.org/forms.html
- www.uslegalforms.com/rominger/divorce.htm

Louisiana Vital Records (Birth, Marriage, Divorce, Death)

- www.cdc.gov/nchs/w2w.htm
- publicrecords.onlinesearches.com/Louisiana.htm

Louisiana Self-Help Services in Family Law Cases

- www.lawhelp.org/LA (click Family & Children)
- www.courtreference.com/Louisiana-Courts-Self-Help.htm

Louisiana State Legal Research

- www.ll.georgetown.edu/states/louisiana.cfm
- www.loc.gov/law/help/guide/states/us-la.php

Louisiana Court Rules

- www.lasc.org/rules
- www.llrx.com/courtrules-gen/state-Louisiana.html

MAINE FAMILY LAW

Maine Family Code/Domestic Relations Code

- www.mainelegislature.org/legis/statutes/19-A/title19-Ach0sec0.html
- www.maine.gov/legis
- www.law.cornell.edu/wex/table_family

Maine Marriage Law (formation)

- www.usmarriagelaws.com/search/united_states/maine/marriage_licenses
- statutes.laws.com/maine/title19a/title19-Ach23sec0
- www.law.cornell.edu/wex/table_marriage

Maine Common Law Marriage

- www.maine.gov/legis/lawlib/whatis.htm
- topics.law.cornell.edu/wex/table_marriage
- www.buddybuddy.com/common.html

Maine Same-Sex Marriage, Domestic Partnership, Civil Union, Defense of Marriage Status (Baby-DOMA)

- en.wikipedia.org/wiki/Domestic_partnership_in_Maine
- en.wikipedia.org/wiki/LGBT_rights_in_Maine
- en.wikipedia.org/wiki/Same-sex_marriage_in_Maine
- www.lambdalegal.org/publications/nationwide-status-same-sex -relationships
- www.ncsl.org/issues-research/human-services/civil-unions-and -domestic-partnership-statutes.aspx

Maine Divorce Law

- 19-A Me. Rev Stat. Ann. § 902
- helpmelaw.org/library (click Family Law)
- www.divorcelawinfo.com/states/me/maine.htm
- www.hg.org/divorce-law-Maine.html

Maine Legal Separation Law

- 19-A Me. Rev Stat. Ann. § 851
- www.hg.org/divorce-law-Maine.html

Maine Alimony/Spousal Support Law

- 19-A Me. Rev Stat. Ann. § 953
- www.hg.org/divorce-law-Maine.html

Maine Property Division Law

- 19-A Me. Rev Stat. Ann. § 951-A
- www.hg.org/divorce-law-Maine.html

Maine Child Custody Law

- 19-A Me. Rev Stat. Ann. § 1501
- www.hg.org/divorce-law-Maine.html

Maine Guardian Ad Litem and Attorney for Child

- 19-A Me. Rev Stat. Ann. § 1507
- www.childwelfare.gov/systemwide/laws_policies/statutes /represent.pdf

Maine Child Support Law

- www.maine.gov/dhhs/ofi/dser
- helpmelaw.org/library (click Family Law)
- www.hg.org/divorce-law-Maine.html
- www.acf.hhs.gov/programs/cse/extinf.html
- www.maine.gov/legis/lawlib/whatis.htm

Maine Paternity Law

- www.maine.gov/ag/children_families/child_paternity_support .html
- www.maine.gov/dhhs/ofi/dser/paternity/aop.html
- helpmelaw.org/library (click Family Law)
- www.acf.hhs.gov/programs/cse/pubs/2002/reports/essentials/c8.html

Maine Legal Definition of Father

- 18-A Me. Rev Stat. Ann. § 9-102(h)
- 19-A Me. Rev Stat. Ann. § 1601(1)
- www.childwelfare.gov/systemwide/laws_policies/statutes /putative.pdf

Maine Adoption Law

- laws.adoption.com/statutes/maine-adoption-laws.html
- helpmelaw.org/library (click Family Law)
- law.findlaw.com/state-laws/adoption/maine

Maine Termination of Parental Rights

- 22 Me. Rev Stat. Ann. § 4055

- 18-A Me. Rev Stat. Ann. § 9-204
- www.law.cornell.edu/wex/table_emancipation
- www.childwelfare.gov/systemwide/laws_policies/statutes /groundtermin.cfm

Maine Putative Father Registry

- laws.adoption.com/statutes/maine-laws,5.html
- www.courts.state.nh.us/probate/registrylist.pdf

Maine Emancipation Law

- 1 Me. Rev Stat. Ann. § 73
- www.law.cornell.edu/topics/Table_Emancipation
- www.maine.gov/legis/lawlib/whatis.htm
- www.youthrights.net/index.php?title=Maine_Emancipation _Law

Maine Age of Majority

- 1 Me. Rev Stat. Ann. § 73
- law.findlaw.com/state-laws/minors-and-the-law/maine
- www.law.cornell.edu/topics/Table_Emancipation

Maine Child Protection/Protective Services

- www.maine.gov/dhhs/ocfs/cw/abuse.shtml

Maine Child Welfare Agencies

- www.maine.gov/dhhs/ocfs/cw

Maine Juvenile Law

- www.maine.gov/corrections/juvenile/index.htm
- www.ncjj.org/State/Maine.aspx

Maine Domestic Violence Law

- 17-A Me. Rev Stat. Ann. § 207-A
- helpmelaw.org/library (click Family Law)

Maine Employment Discrimination Law

- 5 Me. Rev Stat. Ann. § 4552

Maine Surrogacy Law

- www.surrogacyforall.com/Surrogacy-Law.html
- www.selectsurrogate.com/surrogacy-laws-by-state.html

Maine Grandparent Rights

- www.maine.gov/legis/lawlib/whatis.htm

Maine Annulment Law

- 19-A Me. Rev Stat. Ann. § 752
- www.hg.org/divorce-law-Maine.html

Maine Family Law Forms

- www.courts.state.me.us/fees_forms/forms/index.shtml#fm
- www.courts.state.me.us/fees_forms/forms/index.shtml
- www.uslegalforms.com/rominger/divorce.htm

Maine Vital Records (Birth, Marriage, Divorce, Death)

- www.cdc.gov/nchs/w2w.htm
- publicrecords.onlinesearches.com/Maine.htm

Maine Self-Help Services in Family Law Cases

- helpmelaw.org/library (click Family Law)

Maine State Legal Research

- www.ll.georgetown.edu/states/maine.cfm
- www.loc.gov/law/help/guide/states/us-me.php

Maine Court Rules

- www.courts.state.me.us/rules_adminorders/rules/index.shtml
- www.llrx.com/courtrules-gen/state-Maine.html

MARYLAND FAMILY LAW

Maryland Family Code/Domestic Relations Code
- www.lexisnexis.com/hottopics/mdcode
- www.lexisnexis.com/hottopics/michie
- www.law.cornell.edu/wex/table_family

Maryland Marriage Law (formation)
- www.peoples-law.org/categories/4449/2
- maryland.usmarriagelaws.com
- www.usmarriagelaws.com/search/united_states/maryland /marriage_licenses
- www.law.cornell.edu/wex/table_marriage

Maryland Common Law Marriage
- topics.law.cornell.edu/wex/table_marriage
- www.buddybuddy.com/common.html

Maryland Same-Sex Marriage, Domestic Partnership, Civil Union, Defense of Marriage Status (Baby-DOMA)
- en.wikipedia.org/wiki/Same-sex_marriage_in_Maryland
- www.lambdalegal.org/publications/nationwide-status-same-sex -relationships
- www.ncsl.org/issues-research/human-services/civil-unions-and -domestic-partnership-statutes.aspx

Maryland Divorce Law
- Md. Code Ann. Family Law § 7-103
- www.peoples-law.org/categories/4449/2
- www.divorcelawinfo.com/MD/flc.htm
- www.hg.org/divorce-law-Maryland.html

Maryland Legal Separation Law (Limited Divorce)
- Md. Code Ann. Family Law § 7-102
- www.hg.org/divorce-law-Maryland.html

Maryland Alimony/Spousal Support Law
- Md. Code Ann. Family Law § 11-105
- www.hg.org/divorce-law-Maryland.html

Maryland Property Division Law
- Md. Code Ann. Family Law §§ 8-20 et seq.
- www.hg.org/divorce-law-Maryland.html

Maryland Child Custody Law
- www.peoples-law.org/categories/4449/2
- www.hg.org/divorce-law-Maryland.html

Maryland Relocation of Child
- Md. Code Ann. Family Law § 9-106

Maryland Guardian Ad Litem and Attorney for Child
- Md. Code Ann. Courts & Jud. Proc. § 3-813
- www.peoples-law.org/categories/4449/2
- www.childwelfare.gov/systemwide/laws_policies/statutes/represent.pdf

Maryland Child Support Law
- www.dhr.state.md.us/csea/index.php
- www.peoples-law.org/categories/4449/2
- www.acf.hhs.gov/programs/cse/extinf.html

Maryland Paternity Law
- dhr.maryland.gov/csea/pat.php
- www.acf.hhs.gov/programs/cse/pubs/2002/reports/essentials/c8.html

Maryland Legal Definition of Father
- Md. Code Ann. Est. and Trusts § 1-208
- www.childwelfare.gov/systemwide/laws_policies/statutes/putative.pdf

Maryland Adoption Law
- laws.adoption.com/statutes/maryland-adoption-laws.html
- www.peoples-law.org/categories/4449/2
- statelaws.findlaw.com/maryland-law/maryland-adoption-laws.html

Maryland Termination of Parental Rights
- Md. Code Ann. Family Law § 5-339
- www.law.cornell.edu/wex/table_emancipation
- www.childwelfare.gov/systemwide/laws_policies/statutes /groundtermin.cfm

Maryland Putative Father Registry
- laws.adoption.com/statutes/maryland-laws,5.html
- www.courts.state.nh.us/probate/registrylist.pdf

Maryland Emancipation Law
- www.peoples-law.org/children/emancipation/emancipation%20 home.htm
- www.law.cornell.edu/topics/Table_Emancipation

Maryland Age of Majority
- law.findlaw.com/state-laws/minors-and-the-law/maryland
- www.law.cornell.edu/topics/Table_Emancipation

Maryland Child Protection/Protective Services
- www.dhr.state.md.us/cps

Maryland Child Welfare Agencies
- www.dhr.state.md.us

Maryland Juvenile Law
- www.peoples-law.org/categories/4449/2
- www.djs.state.md.us
- www.ncjj.org/State/Maryland.aspx

Maryland Domestic Violence Law
- Md. Code Ann. Family Law § 4-513
- www.peoples-law.org/categories/4459/2
- www.courts.state.md.us/domesticviolence/index.html

Maryland Surrogacy Law
- Md. Code Ann. Crim. Law § 3-603
- www.selectsurrogate.com/surrogacy-laws-by-state.html

Maryland Grandparent Rights
- Md. Code Ann. Family Law § 9-102
- www.peoples-law.org/categories/4449/2

Maryland Annulment Law
- Md. Code Ann. Family Law § 2-202
- www.peoples-law.org/categories/4449/2
- www.hg.org/divorce-law-Maryland.html

Maryland Family Law Forms
- www.courts.state.md.us/family/forms/index.html
- www.courts.state.md.us/courtforms/index.html
- www.uslegalforms.com/rominger/divorce.htm

Maryland Vital Records (Birth, Marriage, Divorce, Death)
- www.cdc.gov/nchs/w2w.htm
- publicrecords.onlinesearches.com/Maryland.htm

Maryland Self-Help Services in Family Law Cases
- www.peoples-law.org/about
- www.courts.state.md.us/family/selfhelp.html
- www.peoples-law.org

Maryland State Legal Research

- www.ll.georgetown.edu/states/maryland.cfm
- www.loc.gov/law/help/guide/states/us-md.php

Maryland Court Rules

- www.lexisnexis.com/hottopics/michie
- www.llrx.com/courtrules-gen/state-Maryland.html

MASSACHUSETTS FAMILY LAW

Massachusetts Family Code/Domestic Relations Code

- www.malegislature.gov/Laws/GeneralLaws/PartII/TitleIII/Chapter208
- www.malegislature.gov/Laws/GeneralLaws
- www.law.cornell.edu/wex/table_family

Massachusetts Marriage Law (formation)

- www.lawlib.state.ma.us/subject/about/marriage.html
- usmarriagelaws.com/search/united_states/massachusetts/index.shtml
- www.law.cornell.edu/wex/table_marriage

Massachusetts Law on Return of Engagement Rings

- www.lawlib.state.ma.us/subject/about/engagement.html

Massachusetts Common Law Marriage

- topics.law.cornell.edu/wex/table_marriage
- www.buddybuddy.com/common.html

Massachusetts Same-Sex Marriage, Domestic Partnership, Civil Union, Defense of Marriage Status (Baby-DOMA)

- www.lawlib.state.ma.us/subject/about/gaymarriage.html
- www.lambdalegal.org/publications/nationwide-status-same-sex-relationships
- www.ncsl.org/issues-research/human-services/civil-unions-and-domestic-partnership-statutes.aspx

Massachusetts Cohabitation Law

- www.lawlib.state.ma.us/subject/about/unmarried.html

Massachusetts Divorce Law

- Mass. Gen. Laws Ann. Chap. 208, § 1
- www.lawlib.state.ma.us/subject/about/divorce.html
- www.lawlib.state.ma.us/subject/about/modification.html
- www.masslegalhelp.org (click Children and Families)
- www.divorcelawinfo.com/states/ma/massachusetts.htm
- www.hg.org/divorce-law-Massachusetts.html

Massachusetts Legal Separation Law

- www.hg.org/divorce-law-Massachusetts.html

Massachusetts Alimony

- Mass. Gen. Laws Ann. Chap. 208, § 34
- www.lawlib.state.ma.us/subject/about/alimony.html

Massachusetts Property Division Law

- Mass. Gen. Laws Ann. Chap. 208, § 34
- www.hg.org/divorce-law-Massachusetts.html

Massachusetts Child Custody Law

- Mass. Gen. Laws Ann. Chap. 208, §§ 31, 31A
- www.lawlib.state.ma.us/subject/about/custody.html
- www.masslegalhelp.org (click Children and Families)
- www.hg.org/divorce-law-Massachusetts.html

Massachusetts Guardian Ad Litem and Attorney for Child

- Mass. Gen. Laws Ann. Chap. 119, § 39F6
- www.lawlib.state.ma.us/subject/about/guardian.html
- www.childwelfare.gov/systemwide/laws_policies/statutes/represent.pdf

Massachusetts Child Support Law

- Mass. Gen. Laws Ann. Chap. 208, § 28
- www.mass.gov/dor/child-support
- www.lawlib.state.ma.us/subject/about/support.html
- www.lawlib.state.ma.us/subject/about/support18.html
- www.lawlib.state.ma.us/subject/about/modification.html
- www.acf.hhs.gov/programs/cse/extinf.html
- www.masslegalhelp.org (click Children and Families)

Massachusetts Paternity Law

- www.lawlib.state.ma.us/subject/about/paternity.html
- www.masslegalhelp.org (click Children and Families)
- www.acf.hhs.gov/programs/cse/pubs/2002/reports/essentials/c8.html

Massachusetts Legal Definition of Father

- Mass. Gen. Laws Ann. Chap. 209C, § 6
- laws.adoption.com/statutes/massachusetts-laws,5.html
- www.childwelfare.gov/systemwide/laws_policies/statutes/putative.pdf

Massachusetts Adoption Law

- www.lawlib.state.ma.us/subject/about/adoption.html
- www.lawlib.state.ma.us/subject/forms/index.html#adoption
- laws.adoption.com/statutes/massachusetts-adoption-laws.html
- statelaws.findlaw.com/massachusetts-law/massachusetts-adoption-laws.html

Massachusetts Termination of Parental Rights

- Mass. Gen. Laws Ann. Chap. 210, § 3
- www.law.cornell.edu/wex/table_emancipation
- www.childwelfare.gov/systemwide/laws_policies/statutes/groundtermin.cfm

Massachusetts Putative Father Registry

- laws.adoption.com/statutes/massachusetts-laws,5.html
- www.courts.state.nh.us/probate/registrylist.pdf

Massachusetts Emancipation Law

- www.lawlib.state.ma.us/subject/about/emancipation.html
- www.masslegalhelp.org (click Children and Families)
- www.law.cornell.edu/topics/Table_Emancipation

Massachusetts Age of Majority

- law.findlaw.com/state-laws/minors-and-the-law/massachusetts
- www.law.cornell.edu/topics/Table_Emancipation

Massachusetts Child Protection/Protective Services

- www.mass.gov/eohhs/gov/departments/dcf
- www.lawlib.state.ma.us/subject/about/childabuse.html

Massachusetts Child Welfare Agencies

- www.mass.gov/eohhs/gov/departments/dcf

Massachusetts Juvenile Law

- www.lawlib.state.ma.us/subject/about/juvenile.html
- www.mass.gov/courts/courtsandjudges/courts/juvenilecourt/index.html

Massachusetts Domestic Violence Law

- www.lawlib.state.ma.us/subject/about/domviolence.html

Massachusetts Employment Discrimination Law
- Mass. Gen. Laws Ann. Chap. 151B, § 3A

Massachusetts Surrogacy Law
- www.lawlib.state.ma.us/subject/about/surrogate.html
- *Culliton v. Beth Israel*, 756 N.E.2d 1133 (Mass. 2001)
- www.surrogacyforall.com/Surrogacy-Law.html

Massachusetts Grandparent Rights
- Mass. Gen. Laws Ann. Chap. 119, § 26B
- www.lawlib.state.ma.us/subject/about/grandparent.html

Massachusetts Annulment Law
- Mass. Gen. Laws Ann. Chap. 207, §§ 1 et seq.
- www.lawlib.state.ma.us/subject/about/marriage.html
- www.hg.org/divorce-law-Massachusetts.html

Massachusetts Family Law Forms
- www.mass.gov/courts/formsandguidelines/forms.html
- www.lawlib.state.ma.us/subject/forms/index.html
- www.masslegalhelp.org/children-and-families/forms
- www.uslegalforms.com/rominger/divorce.htm

Massachusetts Vital Records (Birth, Marriage, Divorce, Death)
- www.cdc.gov/nchs/w2w.htm
- publicrecords.onlinesearches.com/Massachusetts.htm

Massachusetts Self-Help Services in Family Law Cases
- www.lawlib.state.ma.us/subject/about/index.html
- www.lawlib.state.ma.us/subject/about/prose.html
- www.masslegalhelp.org (click Children and Families)

Massachusetts Family Law Legal Research
- www.lawlib.state.ma.us/subject/about/index.html
- www.lawlib.state.ma.us/subject/forms/index.html

Massachusetts State Legal Research (general)
- www.ll.georgetown.edu/states/massachusetts.cfm
- www.loc.gov/law/help/guide/states/us-ma.php

Massachusetts Court Rules
- www.lawlib.state.ma.us/source/mass/rules
- www.llrx.com/courtrules-gen/state-Massachusetts.html

MICHIGAN FAMILY LAW

Michigan Family Code/Domestic Relations Code
- www.legislature.mi.gov
- www.law.cornell.edu/wex/table_family

Michigan Marriage Law (formation)
- www.usmarriagelaws.com/search/united_states/michigan/marriage_licenses
- www.law.cornell.edu/wex/table_marriage

Michigan Common Law Marriage
- topics.law.cornell.edu/wex/table_marriage
- www.buddybuddy.com/common.html

Michigan Same-Sex Marriage, Domestic Partnership, Civil Union, Defense of Marriage Status (Baby-DOMA)
- en.wikipedia.org/wiki/LGBT_rights_in_Michigan
- www.lambdalegal.org/publications/nationwide-status-same-sex-relationships
- www.ncsl.org/issues-research/human-services/civil-unions-and-domestic-partnership-statutes.aspx

Michigan Divorce Law
- Mich. Comp. Laws § 552.6
- michiganlegalhelp.org/self-help-tools/family
- www.michiganlegalaid.org/library_client (click Family Law)
- www.divorcelawinfo.com/states/mi/michigan.htm
- www.hg.org/divorce-law-Michigan.html

Michigan Separate Maintenance Law
- Mich. Comp. Laws § 552.7
- www.hg.org/divorce-law-Michigan.html

Michigan Alimony/Spousal Support Law
- Mich. Comp. Laws § 552.151
- michiganlegalhelp.org/self-help-tools/search?query=alimony
- www.michiganlegalaid.org/library_client (click Family Law)
- www.hg.org/divorce-law-Michigan.html

Michigan Property Division Law
- Mich. Comp. Laws § 722.23
- www.hg.org/divorce-law-Michigan.html

Michigan Child Custody Law
- Mich. Comp. Laws § 557.212
- michiganlegalhelp.org (click Child Custody)
- www.michiganlegalaid.org/library_client (click Family Law)
- www.hg.org/divorce-law-Michigan.html

Michigan Guardian Ad Litem and Attorney for Child
- Mich. Comp. Laws §§ 722.630, 712A.17d
- www.childwelfare.gov/systemwide/laws_policies/statutes/represent.pdf

Michigan Child Support Law
- michiganlegalhelp.org/self-help-tools/family (click Child Support)
- www.michigan.gov/dhs (click Child Support)
- www.acf.hhs.gov/programs/cse/extinf.html
- www.michiganlegalaid.org/library_client (click Family Law)

Michigan Child Support Specialty Court
- courts.michigan.gov (enter Support Specialty Court in search box)

Michigan Paternity Law
- michiganlegalhelp.org (click Paternity)
- www.michiganlegalaid.org/library_client (click Family Law)
- www.acf.hhs.gov/programs/cse/pubs/2002/reports/essentials/c8.html

Michigan Legal Definition of Father
- Mich. Comp. Laws §§ 722.1002, 722-1003
- www.childwelfare.gov/systemwide/laws_policies/statutes/putative.pdf

Michigan Adoption Law
- laws.adoption.com/statutes/michigan-adoption-laws.html
- www.michiganlegalaid.org/library_client (click Family Law)

Michigan Termination of Parental Rights
- Mich. Comp. Laws § 712A.19b
- www.law.cornell.edu/wex/table_emancipation
- www.childwelfare.gov/systemwide/laws_policies/statutes/groundtermin.cfm

Michigan Putative Father Registry

- laws.adoption.com/statutes/michigan-laws,5.html
- www.courts.state.nh.us/probate/registrylist.pdf

Michigan Emancipation Law

- www.law.cornell.edu/topics/Table_Emancipation
- www.youthrights.net/index.php?title=Michigan_Emancipation _Law

Michigan Age of Majority

- law.findlaw.com/state-laws/minors-and-the-law/michigan
- www.law.cornell.edu/topics/Table_Emancipation

Michigan Child Protection/Protective Services

- www.michigan.gov/dhs/0,4562,7-124-7119---,00.html

Michigan Child Welfare Agencies

- www.michigan.gov/dhs/0,4562,7-124-5452_26744---,00.html

Michigan Juvenile Law

- www.michigan.gov/dhs/0,1607,7-124-5452_34044---,00.html
- www.ncjj.org/State/Michiogan.aspx

Michigan Teen Court

- courts.michigan.gov (enter Teen Court in search box)

Michigan Domestic Violence Law

- Mich. Comp. Laws § 400.1501
- www.michiganlegalaid.org/library_client

Michigan Domestic Violence Specialty Court

- courts.michigan.gov (enter Domestic Violence Specialty Court in search box)

Michigan Surrogacy Law

- Mich. Comp. Laws § 722.851
- www.surrogacyforall.com/Surrogacy-Law.html

Michigan Grandparent Rights

- Mich. Comp. Laws § 722.27

Michigan Annulment Law

- Mich. Comp. Laws § 552.37
- www.hg.org/divorce-law-Michigan.html

Michigan Family Law Forms

- michiganlegalhelp.org
- michiganlegalhelp.org/self-help-tools/family?f[0]=type%3 Acourt_form
- www.uslegalforms.com/rominger/divorce.htm

Michigan Vital Records (Birth, Marriage, Divorce, Death)

- publicrecords.onlinesearches.com/Michigan.htm
- www.cdc.gov/nchs/w2w.htm

Michigan Self-Help Services in Family Law Cases

- michiganlegalhelp.org
- www.michiganlegalaid.org
- www.michiganlegalaid.org/library_client

Michigan State Legal Research

- www.ll.georgetown.edu/states/michigan.cfm
- www.loc.gov/law/help/guide/states/us-mi.php

Michigan Court Rules

- coa.courts.mi.gov/rules
- www.llrx.com/courtrules-gen/state-Michigan.html

MINNESOTA FAMILY LAW

Minnesota Family Code/Domestic Relations Code

- www.revisor.mn.gov/statutes/?id=518
- www.revisor.mn.gov/pubs
- www.law.cornell.edu/wex/table_family

Minnesota Marriage Law (formation)

- www.revisor.mn.gov/statutes/?id=517
- www.usmarriagelaws.com/search/united_states/minnesota /marriage_licenses
- www.law.cornell.edu/wex/table_marriage

Minnesota Common Law Marriage

- topics.law.cornell.edu/wex/table_marriage
- www.buddybuddy.com/common.html

Minnesota Same-Sex Marriage, Domestic Partnership, Civil Union, Defense of Marriage Status (Baby-DOMA)

- www.leg.state.mn.us/lrl/issues/issues.aspx?issue=gay
- en.wikipedia.org/wiki/Recognition_of_same-sex_unions_in _Minnesota
- www.lambdalegal.org/publications/nationwide-status-same-sex -relationships
- www.ncsl.org/issues-research/human-services/civil-unions-and -domestic-partnership-statutes.aspx

Minnesota Divorce Law

- Minn. Stat. Ann. §§ 518.06, 518.10
- www.mncourts.gov/selfhelp/?page=342
- www.lawhelpmn.org/issues/family-law/divorce-dissolution

- www.divorcelawinfo.com/states/minn/minnesota.htm
- www.hg.org/divorce-law-Minnesota.html

Minnesota Legal Separation Law

- Minn. Stat. Ann. §§ 518.06, 518.10
- www.mncourts.gov/selfhelp/?page=341
- www.hg.org/divorce-law-Minnesota.html

Minnesota Alimony/Spousal Maintenance Law

- Minn. Stat. Ann. § 518.552
- www.commissions.leg.state.mn.us/oesw/cola/index.htm
- www.hg.org/divorce-law-Minnesota.html

Minnesota Property Division Law

- Minn. Stat. Ann. § 518.58
- www.hg.org/divorce-law-Minnesota.html

Minnesota Child Custody Law

- Minn. Stat. Ann. § 518.17
- www.mncourts.gov/selfhelp/?page=343
- www.lawhelpmn.org/issues/family-law/custody-and-visitation
- www.hg.org/divorce-law-Minnesota.html

Minnesota Guardian Ad Litem and Attorney for Child

- Minn. Stat. Ann. § 260C.163(3)&(5)
- Minn. Stat. Ann. § 518.165
- www.lawhelpmn.org/issues/family-law/child-abuse-and -protection-chips
- www.childwelfare.gov/systemwide/laws_policies/statutes /represent.pdf

Minnesota Child Support Law

- www.mncourts.gov/selfhelp/?page=344
- www.childsupport.dhs.state.mn.us/Action/Welcome
- www.commissions.leg.state.mn.us/oesw/cola/index.htm
- www.acf.hhs.gov/programs/cse/extinf.html

Minnesota Paternity Law

- www.mncourts.gov/selfhelp/?page=1708
- www.mncourts.gov/selfhelp/?page=1808
- www.lawhelpmn.org/issues/family-law/paternity
- www.acf.hhs.gov/programs/cse/pubs/2002/reports/essentials/c8.html

Minnesota Legal Definition of Father

- Minn. Stat. Ann. §§ 257.52, 257.55
- www.childwelfare.gov/systemwide/laws_policies/statutes/putative.pdf

Minnesota Adoption Law

- www.lawhelpmn.org/issues/family-law/adoption
- laws.adoption.com/statutes/minnesota-adoption-laws.html
- law.findlaw.com/state-laws/adoption/minnesota

Minnesota Termination of Parental Rights

- Minn. Stat. Ann. § 260C.301
- www.law.cornell.edu/wex/table_emancipation
- www.childwelfare.gov/systemwide/laws_policies/statutes/groundtermin.cfm

Minnesota Putative Father Registry

- www.health.state.mn.us/divs/chs/registry/faq.htm
- laws.adoption.com/statutes/minnesota-laws,5.html
- www.courts.state.nh.us/probate/registrylist.pdf

Minnesota Emancipation Law

- www.leg.state.mn.us/lrl/issues/issues.aspx?issue=legalage
- www.law.cornell.edu/topics/Table_Emancipation

Minnesota Age of Majority

- law.findlaw.com/state-laws/minors-and-the-law/minnesota
- www.law.cornell.edu/topics/Table_Emancipation

Minnesota Child Protection/Protective Services

- mn.gov/dhs (click Abuse)
- www.lawhelpmn.org/issues/family-law/child-abuse-and-protection-chips

Minnesota Child Welfare Agencies

- mn.gov/dhs

Minnesota Juvenile Law

- www.mncourts.gov/district/4/?page=372
- www.ncjj.org/State/Minnesota.aspx
- www.lawhelpmn.org/issues/family-law/child-abuse-and-protection-chips

Minnesota Domestic Violence Law

- Minn. Stat. Ann. § 518B.01
- www.lawhelpmn.org/issues/family-law/domestic-violence-spousal-abuse

Minnesota Surrogacy Law

- www.selectsurrogate.com/surrogacy-laws-by-state.html
- www.surrogacyforall.com/Surrogacy-Law.html

Minnesota Grandparent Rights

- Minn. Stat. Ann. § 257C.08
- www.lawhelpmn.org/issues/family-law/relatives-caring-for-children

Minnesota Annulment Law

- Minn. Stat. Ann. § 518.05
- www.mncourts.gov/selfhelp/?page=341
- www.hg.org/divorce-law-Minnesota.html

Minnesota Family Law Forms

- www.mncourts.gov/default.aspx?page=513
- www.uslegalforms.com/rominger/divorce.htm

Minnesota Vital Records (Birth, Marriage, Divorce, Death)

- www.cdc.gov/nchs/w2w.htm
- publicrecords.onlinesearches.com/Minnesota.htm

Minnesota Self-Help Services in Family Law Cases

- www.mncourts.gov/selfhelp
- www.lawhelpmn.org/issues/family-law
- www.lawhelpmn.org (click Family)

Minnesota Family Law Legal Research

- library.law.umn.edu/researchguides/familylaw.html

Minnesota State Legal Research (general)

- www.ll.georgetown.edu/states/minnesota.cfm
- www.loc.gov/law/help/guide/states/us-mn.php
- www.romingerlegal.com/state/minnesota.html

Minnesota Court Rules

- www.mncourts.gov/?page=511
- www.llrx.com/courtrules-gen/state-Minnesota.html

MISSISSIPPI FAMILY LAW

Mississippi Family Code/Domestic Relations Code

- www.mscode.com/free/statutes/toc.htm
- www.lexisnexis.com/hottopics/michie
- www.law.cornell.edu/wex/table_family

Mississippi Marriage Law (formation)

- statutes.laws.com/mississippi/title-93/1
- www.usmarriagelaws.com/search/united_states/mississippi/marriage_licenses
- www.law.cornell.edu/wex/table_marriage

Mississippi Common Law Marriage

- topics.law.cornell.edu/wex/table_marriage
- www.buddybuddy.com/common.html

Mississippi Same-Sex Marriage, Domestic Partnership, Civil Union, Defense of Marriage Status (Baby-DOMA)

- en.wikipedia.org/wiki/LGBT_rights_in_Mississippi
- www.lambdalegal.org/publications/nationwide-status-same-sex-relationships
- www.ncsl.org/issues-research/human-services/civil-unions-and-domestic-partnership-statutes.aspx

Mississippi Divorce Law

- Miss. Code Ann. § 93-5-1
- www.mslegalservices.org/MS/index.cfm (click Family and Juvenile)
- www.divorcelawinfo.com/states/miss/mississippi.htm
- www.hg.org/divorce-law-Mississippi.html

Mississippi Alimony/Spousal Support Law
- Miss. Code Ann. § 93-5-23
- www.hg.org/divorce-law-Mississippi.html

Mississippi Property Division Law
- *Ferguson v. Ferguson*, 639 So. 2d 921 (Miss. 1994).
- www.hg.org/divorce-law-Mississippi.html

Mississippi Child Custody Law
- Miss. Code Ann. § 93-5-24
- www.mslegalservices.org/MS/index.cfm (click Family and Juvenile)
- www.hg.org/divorce-law-Mississippi.html

Mississippi Guardian Ad Litem and Attorney for Child
- Miss. Code Ann. §§ 43-21-121, 43-21-201
- www.childwelfare.gov/systemwide/laws_policies/statutes /represent.pdf

Mississippi Child Support Law
- www.mdhs.state.ms.us/cse.html
- www.mslegalservices.org/MS/index.cfm (click Family and Juvenile)
- www.acf.hhs.gov/programs/cse/extinf.html

Mississippi Paternity Law
- www.mdhs.state.ms.us/cse_asap.html
- www.mscode.com/free/statutes/93/009/0028.htm
- www.mslegalservices.org/MS/index.cfm (click Family and Juvenile)
- www.acf.hhs.gov/programs/cse/pubs/2002/reports/essentials /c8.html

Mississippi Legal Definition of Father
- Miss. Code Ann. § 43-21-105(d)
- www.childwelfare.gov/systemwide/laws_policies/statutes /putative.pdf

Mississippi Adoption Law
- laws.adoption.com/statutes/mississippi-adoption-laws.html
- www.mslegalservices.org/MS/index.cfm (click Family and Juvenile)
- statelaws.findlaw.com/mississippi-law/mississippi -adoption-laws.html

Mississippi Termination of Parental Rights
- Miss. Code Ann. § 93-15-103
- www.mslegalservices.org/MS/index.cfm (click Family and Juvenile)
- www.law.cornell.edu/wex/table_emancipation
- www.childwelfare.gov/systemwide/laws_policies/statutes /groundtermin.cfm

Mississippi Putative Father Registry
- laws.adoption.com/statutes/mississippi-laws,5.html
- www.courts.state.nh.us/probate/registrylist.pdf

Mississippi Emancipation Law
- www.mdhs.state.ms.us/csemdhs.html
- www.law.cornell.edu/topics/Table_Emancipation

Mississippi Age of Majority
- law.findlaw.com/state-laws/minors-and-the-law/mississippi
- www.law.cornell.edu/topics/Table_Emancipation

Mississippi Child Protection/Protective Services
- www.mdhs.state.ms.us/fcs.html

Mississippi Juvenile Law
- www.mslegalservices.org/MS/index.cfm (click Family and Juvenile)
- courts.ms.gov/trialcourts/youthcourt/youthcourt.html
- www.ncjj.org/State/Mississippi.aspx

Mississippi Domestic Violence Law
- Miss. Code Ann. § 93-21-3
- www.mslegalservices.org/MS/index.cfm (click Family and Juvenile)

Mississippi Surrogacy Law
- www.selectsurrogate.com/surrogacy-laws-by-state.html
- www.surrogacyforall.com/Surrogacy-Law.html

Mississippi Grandparent Rights
- Miss. Code Ann. § 93-16-1
- www.mslegalservices.org/MS/index.cfm (click Family and Juvenile)

Mississippi Annulment Law
- Miss. Code Ann. § 93-7-3
- www.hg.org/divorce-law-Mississippi.html

Mississippi Family Law Forms
- courts.ms.gov/forms/forms.html
- www.uslegalforms.com/rominger/divorce.htm

Mississippi Vital Records (Birth, Marriage, Divorce, Death)
- www.cdc.gov/nchs/w2w.htm
- publicrecords.onlinesearches.com/Mississippi.htm

Mississippi Self-Help Services in Family Law Cases
- www.mslegalservices.org/MS/index.cfm (click Family and Juvenile)
- www.courtreference.com/Mississippi-Courts-Self-Help.htm

Mississippi State Legal Research
- www.ll.georgetown.edu/states/mississippi.cfm
- www.loc.gov/law/help/guide/states/us-ms.php
- www.romingerlegal.com/state/mississippi.html

Mississippi Court Rules
- courts.ms.gov/rules/msrules.html
- www.llrx.com/courtrules-gen/state-Mississippi.html

MISSOURI FAMILY LAW

Missouri Family Code/Domestic Relations Code
- www.moga.mo.gov/STATUTES/STATUTES.HTM
- www.moga.mo.gov
- www.law.cornell.edu/wex/table_family

Missouri Marriage Law (formation)
- www.mo.gov/living-in-missouri/marriagedivorce
- www.usmarriagelaws.com/search/united_states/missouri /marriage_licenses
- www.law.cornell.edu/wex/table_marriage

Missouri Common Law Marriage
- topics.law.cornell.edu/wex/table_marriage
- www.buddybuddy.com/common.html

Missouri Same-Sex Marriage, Domestic Partnership, Civil Union, Defense of Marriage Status (Baby-DOMA)

- en.wikipedia.org/wiki/LGBT_rights_in_Missouri
- www.lambdalegal.org/publications/nationwide-status-same-sex-relationships
- www.ncsl.org/issues-research/human-services/civil-unions-and-domestic-partnership-statutes.aspx

Missouri Divorce Law

- Ann. Mo. Stat. § 452.305
- www.lsmo.org/library/family-law
- www.divorcelawinfo.com/states/mo/missouri.htm
- www.hg.org/divorce-law-Missouri.html

Missouri Legal Separation Law

- Ann. Mo. Stat. § 452.305
- www.hg.org/divorce-law-Missouri.html

Missouri Alimony/Spousal Support/Maintenance Law

- Ann. Mo. Stat. § 452.335
- www.hg.org/divorce-law-Missouri.html

Missouri Property Division Law

- Ann. Mo. Stat. § 452.330
- www.hg.org/divorce-law-Missouri.html

Missouri Child Custody Law

- Ann. Mo. Stat. § 452.375
- www.lsmo.org/library/family-law
- www.hg.org/divorce-law-Missouri.html

Missouri Guardian Ad Litem and Attorney for Child

- Ann. Mo. Stat. § 210.160
- www.childwelfare.gov/systemwide/laws_policies/statutes/represent.pdf

Missouri Child Support Law

- Ann. Mo. Stat. § 452.340
- www.dss.mo.gov/cse
- www.lsmo.org/library/family-law
- www.acf.hhs.gov/programs/cse/extinf.html

Missouri Paternity Law

- www.dss.mo.gov/cse/father0705.htm
- www.lsmo.org/library/family-law
- www.moga.mo.gov/statutes/c200-299/2100000826.htm
- www.acf.hhs.gov/programs/cse/pubs/2002/reports/essentials/c8.html

Missouri Legal Definition of Father

- Ann. Mo. Stat. §§ 210.817(4), 210.822
- www.childwelfare.gov/systemwide/laws_policies/statutes/putative.pdf

Missouri Adoption Law

- laws.adoption.com/statutes/missouri-adoption-laws.html
- www.lsmo.org/library/family-law
- statelaws.findlaw.com/missouri-law/missouri-adoption-laws.html

Missouri Termination of Parental Rights

- Ann. Mo. Stat. §211.447
- www.law.cornell.edu/wex/table_emancipation

- www.childwelfare.gov/systemwide/laws_policies/statutes/groundtermin.cfm

Missouri Putative Father Registry

- health.mo.gov/data/vitalrecords/putative.php
- laws.adoption.com/statutes/missouri-laws,5.html
- www.courts.state.nh.us/probate/registrylist.pdf

Missouri Emancipation Law

- www.law.cornell.edu/topics/Table_Emancipation

Missouri Age of Majority

- law.findlaw.com/state-laws/minors-and-the-law/missouri
- www.law.cornell.edu/topics/Table_Emancipation

Missouri Child Protection/Protective Services

- www.dss.mo.gov/cd/rptcan.htm

Missouri Child Welfare Agencies

- www.dss.mo.gov/pr_cs.htm

Missouri Juvenile Law

- www.lsmo.org/library/family-law
- dss.mo.gov/dys
- www.ncjj.org/State/Missouri.aspx

Missouri Domestic Violence Law

- Ann. Mo. Stat. §§ 375.1312, 455.010
- www.lsmo.org/library

Missouri Surrogacy Law

- www.selectsurrogate.com/surrogacy-laws-by-state.html
- www.surrogacyforall.com/Surrogacy-Law.html

Missouri Grandparent Rights

- Ann. Mo. Stat. § 452.402

Missouri Annulment Law (declaration of invalidity)

- Ann. Mo. Stat. §§ 451.030, 452.300(2)
- www.hg.org/divorce-law-Missouri.html

Missouri Family Law Forms

- www.courts.mo.gov/page.jsp?id=525
- www.uslegalforms.com/rominger/divorce.htm

Missouri Vital Records (Birth, Marriage, Divorce, Death)

- www.cdc.gov/nchs/w2w.htm
- publicrecords.onlinesearches.com/Missouri.htm

Missouri Self-Help Services in Family Law Cases

- www.lsmo.org/library
- www.selfrepresent.mo.gov/page.jsp?id=39815

Missouri State Legal Research

- www.ll.georgetown.edu/states/missouri.cfm
- www.loc.gov/law/help/guide/states/us-mo.php
- www.romingerlegal.com/state/missouri.html

Missouri Court Rules

- www.courts.mo.gov/page.jsp?id=46
- www.llrx.com/courtrules-gen/state-Missouri.html

MONTANA FAMILY LAW

Montana Family Code/Domestic Relations Code

- data.opi.mt.gov/bills/mca_toc/index.htm
- leg.mt.gov/css
- www.law.cornell.edu/wex/table_family

Montana Marriage Law (formation)

- statutes.laws.com/montana/40
- www.montanalawhelp.org (click Families and Kids)

- www.usmarriagelaws.com/search/united_states/montana/marriage_licenses
- www.law.cornell.edu/wex/table_marriage

Montana Common Law Marriage
- *Snetsinger v. Montana Univ.*, 104 P.3d 445 (Mont., 2004)
- topics.law.cornell.edu/wex/table_marriage
- www.buddybuddy.com/common.html

Montana Same-Sex Marriage, Domestic Partnership, Civil Union, Defense of Marriage Status (Baby-DOMA)
- en.wikipedia.org/wiki/LGBT_rights_in_Montana
- www.lambdalegal.org/publications/nationwide-status-same-sex-relationships
- www.ncsl.org/issues-research/human-services/civil-unions-and-domestic-partnership-statutes.aspx

Montana Divorce Law
- Mt. Code Ann. § 40-4-107
- www.montanalawhelp.org (click Families and Kids)
- www.divorcelawinfo.com/states/mont/montana.htm

Montana Legal Separation Law
- Mt. Code Ann. § 40-4-104

Montana Alimony/Spousal Support/Maintenance Law
- Mt. Code Ann. § 40-4-203

Montana Property Division Law
- Mt. Code Ann. § 40-4-202

Montana Child Custody Law
- Mt. Code Ann. § 40-4-212
- www.montanalawhelp.org (click Families and Kids)

Montana Guardian Ad Litem and Attorney for Child
- Mt. Code Ann. §§ 41-3-112, 41-3-425, 40-4-205
- www.childwelfare.gov/systemwide/laws_policies/statutes/represent.pdf

Montana Child Support Law
- Mt. Code Ann. § 40-4-204
- www.dphhs.mt.gov/csed/index.shtml
- www.montanalawhelp.org (click Families and Kids)
- www.acf.hhs.gov/programs/cse/extinf.html

Montana Paternity Law
- www.dphhs.mt.gov/csed/paternity
- courts.mt.gov/library/topic/paternity.mcpx
- www.montanalawhelp.org (click Families and Kids)
- www.acf.hhs.gov/programs/cse/pubs/2002/reports/essentials/c8.html

Montana Legal Definition of Father
- Mt. Code Ann. §§ 40-6-102(2), 42-1-103, 42-2-201
- www.childwelfare.gov/systemwide/laws_policies/statutes/putative.pdf

Montana Adoption Law
- Mt. Code Ann. §§ 42-1-103 et seq.
- laws.adoption.com/statutes/montana-adoption-laws.html
- www.montanalawhelp.org (click Families and Kids)
- law.findlaw.com/state-laws/adoption/montana

Montana Termination of Parental Rights
- Mt. Code Ann. § 42-2-607
- www.law.cornell.edu/wex/table_emancipation
- www.childwelfare.gov/systemwide/laws_policies/statutes/groundtermin.cfm

Montana Putative Father Registry
- www.dphhs.mt.gov/csed/paternity
- laws.adoption.com/statutes/montana-laws,5.html
- www.courts.state.nh.us/probate/registrylist.pdf

Montana Emancipation Law
- www.montanalawhelp.org (click Families and Kids)
- www.law.cornell.edu/topics/Table_Emancipation

Montana Age of Majority
- law.findlaw.com/state-laws/minors-and-the-law/montana
- www.law.cornell.edu/topics/Table_Emancipation

Montana Child Protection/Protective Services
- www.dphhs.mt.gov/cfsd/index.shtml

Montana Child Welfare Agencies
- www.dphhs.mt.gov/cfsd/index.shtml

Montana Juvenile Law
- mbcc.mt.gov/JuvenileJustice/JuvJustice.asp
- www.ncjj.org/State/Montana.aspx

Montana Domestic Violence Law
- Mt. Code Ann. § 45-5-206
- doj.mt.gov/victims/domestic-violence

Montana Surrogacy Law
- www.selectsurrogate.com/surrogacy-laws-by-state.html
- www.surrogacyforall.com/Surrogacy-Law.html

Montana Grandparent Rights
- Mt. Code Ann. § 40-4-228
- www.montanalawhelp.org (click Families and Kids)

Montana Annulment Law
- Mt. Code Ann. § 40-1-402

Montana Family Law Forms
- wcc.dli.mt.gov/forms.asp
- courts.mt.gov/library/topic/default.mcpx
- www.uslegalforms.com/rominger/divorce.htm

Montana Vital Records (Birth, Marriage, Divorce, Death)
- www.cdc.gov/nchs/w2w.htm
- publicrecords.onlinesearches.com/Montana.htm

Montana Self-Help Services in Family Law Cases
- courts.mt.gov/library/topic/default.mcpx
- www.montanalawhelp.org (click Families and Kids)

Montana State Legal Research
- www.ll.georgetown.edu/states/montana.cfm
- www.loc.gov/law/help/guide/states/us-mt.php
- www.romingerlegal.com/state/montana.html

Montana Court Rules
- courts.mt.gov/library/montana_laws.mcpx#judicial
- www.llrx.com/courtrules-gen/state-Montana.html

NEBRASKA FAMILY LAW

Nebraska Family Code/Domestic Relations Code
- nebraskalegislature.gov/laws/laws.php
- nebraskalegislature.gov
- www.law.cornell.edu/wex/table_family
- nebraskalegislature.gov/laws/laws.php

Nebraska Marriage Law (formation)
- nebraskaccess.ne.gov/marriagelicense.asp
- www.usmarriagelaws.com/search/united_states/nebraska/marriage_licenses
- www.law.cornell.edu/wex/table_marriage

Nebraska Common Law Marriage
- topics.law.cornell.edu/wex/table_marriage
- www.buddybuddy.com/common.html

Nebraska Same-Sex Marriage, Domestic Partnership, Civil Union, Defense of Marriage Status (Baby-DOMA)
- en.wikipedia.org/wiki/LGBT_rights_in_Nebraska
- www.lambdalegal.org/publications/nationwide-status-same-sex-relationships
- www.ncsl.org/issues-research/human-services/civil-unions-and-domestic-partnership-statutes.aspx

Nebraska Divorce Law
- Neb. Rev. Stats. § 42-361
- www.divorcelawinfo.com/states/ne/nebraska.htm
- www.hg.org/divorce-law-Nebraska.html

Nebraska Legal Separation Law
- www.hg.org/divorce-law-Nebraska.html

Nebraska Alimony/Spousal Support Law
- Neb. Rev. Stats. § 42-365
- www.hg.org/divorce-law-Nebraska.html

Nebraska Property Division Law
- Neb. Rev. Stats. § 42-365
- www.hg.org/divorce-law-Nebraska.html

Nebraska Child Custody Law
- Neb. Rev. Stats. § 42-364
- www.hg.org/divorce-law-Nebraska.html

Nebraska Guardian Ad Litem and Attorney for Child
- Neb. Rev. Stats. §§ 42-358, 43-272, 43-3710
- www.childwelfare.gov/systemwide/laws_policies/statutes/represent.pdf

Nebraska Child Support Law
- dhhs.ne.gov/children_family_services/Pages/cse_cseindex.aspx
- www.supportguidelines.com/links.html
- www.acf.hhs.gov/programs/cse/extinf.html

Nebraska Paternity Law
- dhhs.ne.gov/children_family_services/Pages/cse_patern.aspx
- www.acf.hhs.gov/programs/cse/pubs/2002/reports/essentials/c8.html

Nebraska Legal Definition of Father
- www.childwelfare.gov/systemwide/laws_policies/statutes/putative.pdf

Nebraska Adoption Law
- laws.adoption.com/statutes/nebraska-adoption-laws.html
- statelaws.findlaw.com/nebraska-law/nebraska-adoption-laws.html

Nebraska Termination of Parental Rights
- Neb. Rev. Stats. § 43-292
- www.law.cornell.edu/wex/table_emancipation
- www.childwelfare.gov/systemwide/laws_policies/statutes/groundtermin.cfm

Nebraska Putative Father Registry
- Neb. Rev. Stats. § 43-104.01
- laws.adoption.com/statutes/nebraska-laws,5.html
- www.courts.state.nh.us/probate/registrylist.pdf

Nebraska Emancipation Law
- nebraskaaccess.ne.gov/agemajority.asp
- www.law.cornell.edu/topics/Table_Emancipation

Nebraska Age of Majority
- law.findlaw.com/state-laws/minors-and-the-law/nebraska
- www.law.cornell.edu/topics/Table_Emancipation

Nebraska Child Protection/Protective Services
- dhhs.ne.gov/children_family_services/Pages/jus_jusindex.aspx

Nebraska Child Welfare Agencies
- dhhs.ne.gov/children_family_services/Pages/children_family_services.aspx

Nebraska Juvenile Law
- www.supremecourt.ne.gov/separate-juvenile-court/index.shtml?sub5
- www.ncjj.org/State/Nebraska.aspx

Nebraska Domestic Violence Law
- ndvsac.org

Nebraska Surrogacy Law
- Neb. Rev. Stats. § 25-21,200
- www.surrogacyforall.com/Surrogacy-Law.html

Nebraska Grandparent Rights
- Neb. Rev. Stats. § 43-1801

Nebraska Annulment Law
- www.hg.org/divorce-law-Nebraska.html

Nebraska Family Law Forms
- www.uslegalforms.com/rominger/divorce.htm

Nebraska Vital Records (Birth, Marriage, Divorce, Death)
- www.cdc.gov/nchs/w2w.htm
- publicrecords.onlinesearches.com/Nebraska.htm

Nebraska Self-Help Services in Family Law Cases
- supremecourt.ne.gov/public
- www.supremecourt.ne.gov/self-help/families.html
- www.neequaljustice.org
- www.neequaljustice.org/dir/399

Nebraska State Legal Research

- www.ll.georgetown.edu/states/nebraska.cfm
- www.loc.gov/law/help/guide/states/us-ne.php
- www.romingerlegal.com/state/nebraska.html

Nebraska Court Rules

- www.supremecourt.ne.gov/rules/index.shtml
- www.llrx.com/courtrules-gen/state-Nebraska.html

NEVADA FAMILY LAW

Nevada Family Code/Domestic Relations Code

- www.leg.state.nv.us/NRS/NRS-125.html
- www.leg.state.nv.us
- www.law.cornell.edu/wex/table_family

Nevada Marriage Law (formation)

- www.leg.state.nv.us/nrs/NRS-122.html
- www.usmarriagelaws.com/search/united_states/nevada /marriage_licenses
- www.law.cornell.edu/wex/table_marriage

Nevada Common Law Marriage

- topics.law.cornell.edu/wex/table_marriage
- www.buddybuddy.com/common.html

Nevada Same-Sex Marriage, Domestic Partnership, Civil Union, Defense of Marriage Status (Baby-DOMA)

- en.wikipedia.org/wiki/LGBT_rights_in_Nevada
- www.lambdalegal.org/publications/nationwide-status-same-sex -relationships
- www.ncsl.org/issues-research/human-services/civil-unions-and -domestic-partnership-statutes.aspx

Nevada Divorce Law

- Nev. Rev. Stat. § 125.010
- www.clarkcountycourts.us/shc/Divorce/self_help_choose.htm
- www.divorcelawinfo.com/states/nevada/nevada.htm
- www.hg.org/divorce-law-Nevada.html

Nevada Legal Separation Law

- www.hg.org/divorce-law-Nevada.html

Nevada Alimony/Spousal Support/Maintenance Law

- Nev. Rev. Stat. § 125.150
- www.hg.org/divorce-law-Nevada.html

Nevada Property Division Law

- Nev. Rev. Stat. § 125.150
- www.hg.org/divorce-law-Nevada.html

Nevada Child Custody Law

- Nev. Rev. Stat. § 125.480
- www.hg.org/divorce-law-Nevada.html
- www.nevadalawhelp.org/NV/index.cfm (click Family and Juvenile)
- www.clarkcountycourts.us/shc/Custody/self_help_custody.htm

Nevada Guardian Ad Litem and Attorney for Child

- Nev. Rev. Stat. §§ 432B.500, 432B.420
- www.childwelfare.gov/systemwide/laws_policies/statutes /represent.pdf

Nevada Child Support Law

- www.leg.state.nv.us/NRS/NRS-125B.html
- dwss.nv.gov/index.php?option=com_content&task=view&id=56 &Itemid=129
- www.acf.hhs.gov/programs/cse/extinf.html

Nevada Paternity Law

- www.nevadalawhelp.org/NV/index.cfm (click Family and Juvenile)
- www.clarkcountycourts.us/shc/Paternity/self_help_paternity.htm

- dwss.nv.gov/index.php?option=com_content&task=view&id=65 &Itemid=143
- www.acf.hhs.gov/programs/cse/pubs/2002/reports/essentials/c8.html

Nevada Legal Definition of Father

- Nev. Rev. Stat. §§ 108.016, 127.021, 126.051
- www.childwelfare.gov/systemwide/laws_policies/statutes/putative.pdf

Nevada Adoption Law

- laws.adoption.com/statutes/nevada-adoption-laws.html
- law.findlaw.com/state-laws/adoption/nevada

Nevada Termination of Parental Rights

- Nev. Rev. Stat. § 128.150
- www.law.cornell.edu/wex/table_emancipation
- www.childwelfare.gov/systemwide/laws_policies/statutes /groundtermin.cfm

Nevada Putative Father Registry

- laws.adoption.com/statutes/nevada-laws,5.html
- www.courts.state.nh.us/probate/registrylist.pdf

Nevada Emancipation Law

- www.leg.state.nv.us/nrs/nrs-129.html
- www.law.cornell.edu/topics/Table_Emancipation

Nevada Age of Majority

- law.findlaw.com/state-laws/minors-and-the-law/nevada
- www.law.cornell.edu/topics/Table_Emancipation

Nevada Child Protection/Protective Services

- www.dcfs.state.nv.us/dcfs_childprotectivesvcs.htm

Nevada Child Welfare Agencies

- dcfs.state.nv.us

Nevada Juvenile Law

- www.dcfs.state.nv.us/DCFS_JuvenileJusticeSvcs.htm
- www.clarkcountycourts.us/shc/Juvenile/self_hlep_juvenile.html
- www.ncjj.org/State/Nevada.aspx

Nevada Domestic Violence Law

- Nev. Rev. Stat. § 33.018
- www.nevadalawhelp.org/NV/index.cfm (click Family and Juvenile)

Nevada Surrogacy Law

- Nev. Rev. Stat. § 126.045
- www.surrogacyforall.com/Surrogacy-Law.html
- www.selectsurrogate.com/surrogacy-laws-by-state.html

Nevada Grandparent Rights

- Nev. Rev. Stat. § 125C.050

Nevada Annulment Law

- Nev. Rev. Stat. §§ 125.290 et seq.
- www.hg.org/divorce-law-Nevada.html

Nevada Family Law Forms

- lawlibrary.nevadajudiciary.us/selfHelp/forms.php
- www.uslegalforms.com/rominger/divorce.htm

Nevada Vital Records (Birth, Marriage, Divorce, Death)

- www.cdc.gov/nchs/w2w.htm
- publicrecords.onlinesearches.com/Nevada.htm

Nevada Self-Help Services in Family Law Cases

- www.clarkcountycourts.us/shc
- lawlibrary.nevadajudiciary.us/selfHelp/forms.php
- www.nevadalawhelp.org/NV/index.cfm (click Family and Juvenile)

Nevada State Legal Research

- www.ll.georgetown.edu/states/nevada.cfm
- www.loc.gov/law/help/guide/states/us-nv.php
- www.romingerlegal.com/state/nevada.html

Nevada Court Rules

- www.leg.state.nv.us/courtrules
- www.llrx.com/courtrules-gen/state-Nevada.html

NEW HAMPSHIRE FAMILY LAW

New Hampshire Family Code/Domestic Relations Code

- www.gencourt.state.nh.us/rsa/html/indexes/default.html
- www.law.cornell.edu/wex/table_family

New Hampshire Marriage Law (formation)

- www.usmarriagelaws.com/search/united_states/new_hampshire/index.shtml
- www.law.cornell.edu/wex/table_marriage

New Hampshire Common Law Marriage

- N.H. Rev. Stat. § 457:39
- *Joan S. v. John S.*, 427 A.2d 498 (N.H., 1981)
- topics.law.cornell.edu/wex/table_marriage
- www.buddybuddy.com/common.html

New Hampshire Same-Sex Marriage, Domestic Partnership, Civil Union, Defense of Marriage Status (Baby-DOMA)

- en.wikipedia.org/wiki/LGBT_rights_in_New_Hampshire
- en.wikipedia.org/wiki/Same-sex_marriage_in_New_Hampshire
- www.lambdalegal.org/publications/nationwide-status-same-sex-relationships
- www.ncsl.org/issues-research/human-services/civil-unions-and-domestic-partnership-statutes.aspx

New Hampshire Divorce Law

- NH Rev. Stats. § 458:7
- www.courts.state.nh.us/fdpp/divorce_parenting.htm
- www.divorcelawinfo.com/states/nh/newhampshire.htm
- www.hg.org/divorce-law-NewHampshire.html

New Hampshire Legal Separation Law

- NH Rev. Stats. § 458:26

New Hampshire Alimony/Spousal Support Law

- NH Rev. Stats. § 458:19
- www.hg.org/divorce-law-NewHampshire.html

New Hampshire Property Division Law

- NH Rev. Stats. § 458:16-a
- www.hg.org/divorce-law-NewHampshire.html

New Hampshire Child Custody Law

- NH Rev. Stats. § 461-A:6
- www.courts.state.nh.us/fdpp/divorce_parenting.htm

New Hampshire Guardian Ad Litem and Attorney for Child

- NH Rev. Stats. § 169-C:10
- www.courts.state.nh.us/fdpp/guardianship_of_minors.htm
- www.childwelfare.gov/systemwide/laws_policies/statutes/represent.pdf

New Hampshire Child Support Law

- www.dhhs.nh.gov/dcss/index.htm

- www.supportguidelines.com/links.html
- www.acf.hhs.gov/programs/cse/extinf.html

New Hampshire Paternity Law

- NH Rev. Stats. § 168-A:2
- ocse.acf.hhs.gov/necsrs/pubs/vap_forms/nh_vap.pdf
- www.dhhs.nh.gov/dcss/index.htm
- www.acf.hhs.gov/programs/cse/pubs/2002/reports/essentials/c8.html

New Hampshire Legal Definition of Father

- NH Rev. Stat. Ann. § 170-B:2(X)
- www.childwelfare.gov/systemwide/laws_policies/statutes/putative.pdf

New Hampshire Adoption Law

- NH Rev. Stat. Ann. § 170-B:2
- www.courts.state.nh.us/fdpp/adoption.htm
- laws.adoption.com/statutes/new-hampshire-adoption-laws.html
- law.findlaw.com/state-laws/adoption/new-hampshire

New Hampshire Termination of Parental Rights

- NH Rev. Stats. § 169-C:24-a
- www.courts.state.nh.us/fdpp/terminiation.htm
- www.law.cornell.edu/wex/table_emancipation
- www.childwelfare.gov/systemwide/laws_policies/statutes/groundtermin.cfm

New Hampshire Putative Father Registry

- NH Rev. Stats. § 170-B:6
- laws.adoption.com/statutes/new-hampshire-laws,5.html
- www.courts.state.nh.us/probate/registrylist.pdf

New Hampshire Emancipation Law

- www.law.cornell.edu/topics/Table_Emancipation

New Hampshire Age of Majority

- law.findlaw.com/state-laws/minors-and-the-law/new-hampshire
- www.law.cornell.edu/topics/Table_Emancipation

New Hampshire Child Protection/Protective Services

- www.dhhs.nh.gov/dcyf/index.htm
- www.dhhs.state.nh.us/dcyf/cps/index.htm

New Hampshire Child Welfare Agencies

- www.dhhs.nh.gov/dcyf/index.htm

New Hampshire Juvenile Law

- www.courts.state.nh.us/fdpp/juvenile_delinquency.htm
- www.dhhs.state.nh.us/djjs/index.htm
- www.ncjj.org/State/New-Hampshire.aspx

New Hampshire Domestic Violence Law

- www.courts.state.nh.us/fdpp/dv_petitions.htm
- www.courts.state.nh.us/selfhelp/getting_started.htm

New Hampshire Surrogacy Law
- NH Rev. Stat. Ann. § 168-B:1
- www.surrogacyforall.com/Surrogacy-Law.html

New Hampshire Grandparent Rights
- NH Rev. Stats. § 461-A:6(V)

New Hampshire Annulment Law
- NH Rev. Stats. § 458:1
- www.hg.org/divorce-law-NewHampshire.html

New Hampshire Family Law Forms
- www.courts.state.nh.us/superior/forms/
- www.uslegalforms.com/rominger/divorce.htm

New Hampshire Vital Records (Birth, Marriage, Divorce, Death)
- www.cdc.gov/nchs/w2w.htm
- publicrecords.onlinesearches.com/Newhampshire.htm

New Hampshire Self-Help Services in Family Law Cases
- www.courts.state.nh.us/selfhelp/legal_assistance.htm
- www.courts.state.nh.us
- www.nhlegalaid.org

New Hampshire State Legal Research
- www.ll.georgetown.edu/states/newhampshire.cfm
- www.loc.gov/law/help/guide/states/us-nh.php
- www.romingerlegal.com/state/newhampshire.html

New Hampshire Court Rules
- www.courts.state.nh.us/rules/index.htm
- www.llrx.com/courtrules-gen/state-New-Hampshire.html

NEW JERSEY FAMILY LAW

New Jersey Family Code/Domestic Relations Code
- www.njleg.state.nj.us
- www.law.cornell.edu/wex/table_family

New Jersey Marriage Law (formation)
- www.lsnjlaw.org (click Family and Relationships)
- www.usmarriagelaws.com/search/united_states/new_jersey/marriage_licenses
- marriage.about.com/cs/marriagelicenses/p/newjersey.htm
- www.law.cornell.edu/wex/table_marriage

New Jersey Common Law Marriage
- topics.law.cornell.edu/wex/table_marriage
- www.buddybuddy.com/common.html

New Jersey Same-Sex Marriage, Domestic Partnership, Civil Union, Defense of Marriage Status (Baby-DOMA)
- en.wikipedia.org/wiki/LGBT_rights_in_New_Jersey
- www.lambdalegal.org/publications/nationwide-status-same-sex-relationships
- www.ncsl.org/issues-research/human-services/civil-unions-and-domestic-partnership-statutes.aspx

New Jersey Divorce Law
- NJ Stat. Ann. § 2A:34-2
- www.lsnjlaw.org (click Family and Relationships)
- www.divorcelawinfo.com/NJ/flc.htm
- www.hg.org/divorce-law-NewJersey.html

New Jersey Legal Separation Law
- NJ Stat. Ann. § 2A:34-3
- www.hg.org/divorce-law-NewJersey.html

New Jersey Alimony/Spousal Support Law
- NJ Stat. Ann. § 2A:34-23
- www.lsnjlaw.org (click Family and Relationships)
- www.hg.org/divorce-law-NewJersey.html

New Jersey Property Division Law
- NJ Stat. Ann. § 2A:34-23.1
- www.hg.org/divorce-law-NewJersey.html

New Jersey Child Custody Law
- NJ Stat. Ann. § 9:2-4
- www.lsnjlaw.org (click Family and Relationships)

- www.hg.org/divorce-law-NewJersey.html

New Jersey Guardian Ad Litem and Attorney for Child
- NJ Stat. Ann. § 9:6-8.23
- www.childwelfare.gov/systemwide/laws_policies/statutes/represent.pdf

New Jersey Child Support Law
- www.njchildsupport.org
- www.lsnjlaw.org (click Family and Relationships)
- www.acf.hhs.gov/programs/cse/extinf.html

New Jersey Paternity Law
- www.njchildsupport.org/Article.asp?AID=39
- www.acf.hhs.gov/programs/cse/pubs/2002/reports/essentials/c8.html

New Jersey Legal Definition of Father
- NJ Stat. Ann. §§ 9:3-38, 9:17-39, 9:17-43
- www.childwelfare.gov/systemwide/laws_policies/statutes/putative.pdf

New Jersey Adoption Law
- NJ Stat. Ann. §§ 9:3-38
- laws.adoption.com/statutes/new-jersey-adoption-laws.html
- www.lsnjlaw.org (click Family and Relationships)
- law.findlaw.com/state-laws/adoption/new-jersey

New Jersey Termination of Parental Rights
- NJ Stat. Ann. § 30:4C-15.1
- www.law.cornell.edu/wex/table_emancipation
- www.childwelfare.gov/systemwide/laws_policies/statutes/groundtermin.cfm

New Jersey Putative Father Registry
- laws.adoption.com/statutes/new-jersey-laws,5.html
- www.courts.state.nh.us/probate/registrylist.pdf

New Jersey Emancipation Law
- www.njchildsupport.org/Article.asp?AID=51
- www.law.cornell.edu/topics/Table_Emancipation

New Jersey Age of Majority
- law.findlaw.com/state-laws/minors-and-the-law/new-jersey
- www.law.cornell.edu/topics/Table_Emancipation

New Jersey Child Protection/Protective Services

- www.visitmonmouth.com/page.aspx?ID=2695

New Jersey Child Welfare Agencies

- www.state.nj.us/dcf/index.shtml

New Jersey Juvenile Law

- www.nj.gov/oag/jjc/movingjjc.htm
- www.ncjj.org/State/New-Jersey.aspx

New Jersey Domestic Violence Law

- NJ Stat. Ann. § 2C:25-19
- www.lsnjlaw.org (click Family and Relationships)

New Jersey Surrogacy Law

- *AHW. v. GHB*, 772 A.2d 948 (NJ Super. 2000)
- www.selectsurrogate.com/surrogacy-laws-by-state.html
- www.surrogacyforall.com/Surrogacy-Law.html

New Jersey Grandparent Rights

- NJ Stat. Ann. § 9:2-7.1

New Jersey Annulment Law

- NJ Stat. Ann. § 2A:34-1

New Jersey Family Law Forms

- www.judiciary.state.nj.us/prose/index.htm
- www.uslegalforms.com/rominger/divorce.htm

New Jersey Vital Records (Birth, Marriage, Divorce, Death)

- publicrecords.onlinesearches.com/NewJersey.htm
- www.cdc.gov/nchs/w2w.htm

New Jersey Self-Help Services in Family Law Cases

- www.judiciary.state.nj.us/prose/index.htm
- www.lsnjlaw.org (click Family and Relationships)

New Jersey State Legal Research

- www.ll.georgetown.edu/states/newjersey.cfm
- www.loc.gov/law/help/guide/states/us-nj.php
- www.romingerlegal.com/state/newjersey.html

New Jersey Court Rules

- www.judiciary.state.nj.us/rules/index.html
- www.llrx.com/courtrules-gen/state-New-Jersey.html

NEW MEXICO FAMILY LAW

New Mexico Family Code/Domestic Relations Code

- www.nmlegis.gov/lcs
- www.law.cornell.edu/wex/table_family

New Mexico Marriage Law (formation)

- www.usmarriagelaws.com/search/united_states/new_mexico /marriage_licenses
- marriage.about.com/cs/marriagelicenses/p/newmexico.htm
- www.law.cornell.edu/wex/table_marriage

New Mexico Common Law Marriage

- topics.law.cornell.edu/wex/table_marriage
- www.buddybuddy.com/common.html

New Mexico Same-Sex Marriage, Domestic Partnership, Civil Union, Defense of Marriage Status (Baby-DOMA)

- en.wikipedia.org/wiki/LGBT_rights_in_New_Mexico
- www.lambdalegal.org/publications/nationwide-status-same-sex -relationships
- www.ncsl.org/issues-research/human-services/civil-unions-and -domestic-partnership-statutes.aspx

New Mexico Divorce Law

- NM Stats. Ann. § 40-4-1
- lawhelpnewmexico.org/?q=content/legal-topics (click Family Law)
- www.divorcelawinfo.com/states/nm/newmexico.htm
- www.hg.org/divorce-law-NewMexico.html

New Mexico Legal Separation Law

- www.hg.org/divorce-law-NewMexico.html

New Mexico Alimony/Spousal Support Law

- NM Stats. Ann. § 40-4-7
- www.hg.org/divorce-law-NewMexico.html

New Mexico Property Division Law

- NM Stats. Ann. § 40-4-7
- www.hg.org/divorce-law-NewMexico.html

New Mexico Child Custody Law

- NM Stats. Ann. § 40-4-9
- www.hg.org/divorce-law-NewMexico.html
- lawhelpnewmexico.org/?q=content/legal-topics (click Family Law)

New Mexico Guardian Ad Litem and Attorney for Child

- NM Stat. § 32A-4-10
- www.childwelfare.gov/systemwide/laws_policies/statutes /represent.pdf

New Mexico Child Support Law

- NM Stats. Ann. § 40-4-11.1
- www.hsd.state.nm.us/csed
- lawhelpnewmexico.org/?q=content/legal-topics (click Family Law)
- www.acf.hhs.gov/programs/cse/extinf.html

New Mexico Paternity Law

- NM Stats. Ann. §§ 40-11A-301 et seq
- lawhelpnewmexico.org/?q=content/legal-topics (click Family Law)
- www.acf.hhs.gov/programs/cse/pubs/2002/reports/essentials /c8.html

New Mexico Legal Definition of Father

- NM Stat. § 32A-5-3
- www.childwelfare.gov/systemwide/laws_policies/statutes /putative.pdf

New Mexico Adoption Law

- laws.adoption.com/statutes/new-mexico-adoption-laws.html
- law.findlaw.com/state-laws/adoption/new-mexico

New Mexico Termination of Parental Rights

- NM Stat. § 32A-4-28
- www.law.cornell.edu/wex/table_emancipation
- www.childwelfare.gov/systemwide/laws_policies/statutes /groundtermin.cfm

New Mexico Putative Father Registry

- www.vitalrecordsnm.org/PutFathReg.shtml

- laws.adoption.com/statutes/new-mexico-laws,5.html
- www.courts.state.nh.us/probate/registrylist.pdf

New Mexico Emancipation Law

- www.law.cornell.edu/topics/Table_Emancipation
- law.justia.com/codes/new-mexico/2011/chapter32A/article21/section32A-21-7/

New Mexico Age of Majority

- law.findlaw.com/state-laws/minors-and-the-law/new-mexico
- www.law.cornell.edu/topics/Table_Emancipation

New Mexico Child Protection/Protective Services

- www.cyfd.org/node/26

New Mexico Child Welfare Agencies

- www.cyfd.org

New Mexico Juvenile Law

- www.nmjustice.net/website/controller.php
- www.ncjj.org/State/New-Mexico.aspx

New Mexico Domestic Violence Law

- NM Stat. § 31-12-12
- lawhelpnewmexico.org/?q=content/legal-topics
- www.nmcadv.org

New Mexico Surrogacy Law

- NM Stat. § 32A-5-34

- www.surrogacyforall.com/Surrogacy-Law.html

New Mexico Grandparent Rights

- NM Stats. Ann. § 40-9-2

New Mexico Annulment Law

- NM Stats. Ann. § 40-1-9
- www.hg.org/divorce-law-NewMexico.html

New Mexico Family Law Forms

- www.nmcourts.gov/cgi/prose_lib
- www.uslegalforms.com/rominger/divorce.htm

New Mexico Vital Records (Birth, Marriage, Divorce, Death)

- www.cdc.gov/nchs/w2w.htm
- publicrecords.onlinesearches.com/NewMexico.htm

New Mexico Self-Help Services in Family Law Cases

- lawhelpnewmexico.org
- lawhelpnewmexico.org/?q=content/legal-topics (click Family Law)

New Mexico State Legal Research

- www.ll.georgetown.edu/states/newmexico.cfm
- www.loc.gov/law/help/guide/states/us-nm.php
- www.romingerlegal.com/state/newmexico.html

New Mexico Court Rules

- www.nmcompcomm.us/nmrules/NMRuleSets.aspx
- www.llrx.com/courtrules-gen/state-New-Mexico.html

NEW YORK FAMILY LAW

New York Family Code/Domestic Relations Code

- public.leginfo.state.ny.us/menugetf.cgi?COMMONQUERY=LAWS
- assembly.state.ny.us/leg/?by=k&qs=child+custody
- www.law.cornell.edu/wex/table_family

New York Marriage Law (formation)

- statutes.laws.com/new-york/dom
- www.usmarriagelaws.com/search/united_states/new_york/marriage_licenses
- www.law.cornell.edu/wex/table_marriage

New York Common Law Marriage

- topics.law.cornell.edu/wex/table_marriage
- www.buddybuddy.com/common.html

New York Same-Sex Marriage, Domestic Partnership, Civil Union, Defense of Marriage Status (Baby-DOMA)

- NY Dom. Rel. Law § 10-a (Marriage Equality Act)
- www.lawhelp.org/NY (click Family & Juvenile)
- en.wikipedia.org/wiki/Same-sex_marriage_in_New_York
- www.lambdalegal.org/publications/nationwide-status-same-sex-relationships
- www.ncsl.org/issues-research/human-services/civil-unions-and-domestic-partnership-statutes.aspx

New York Divorce Law

- NY Dom. Rel. Law § 170
- www.lawhelp.org/NY (click Family & Juvenile)
- www.divorcelawinfo.com/states/ny/newyork.htm
- www.hg.org/divorce-law-NewYork.html

New York Legal Separation Law

- NY Dom. Rel. Law § 200
- www.hg.org/divorce-law-NewYork.html

New York Alimony/Spousal Support Law

- NY Dom. Rel. Law § 236
- www.lawhelp.org/NY (click Family & Juvenile)
- www.hg.org/divorce-law-NewYork.html

New York Property Division Law

- NY Dom. Rel. Law § 236
- www.hg.org/divorce-law-NewYork.html

New York Child Custody Law

- NY Dom. Rel. Law § 240
- www.hg.org/divorce-law-NewYork.html

New York Guardian Ad Litem and Attorney for Child

- NY Family Court Act § 1016
- www.childwelfare.gov/systemwide/laws_policies/statutes/represent.pdf

New York Child Support Law

- www.childsupport.ny.gov/dcse/home.html
- www.lawhelp.org/NY (click Family & Juvenile)
- www.supportguidelines.com/links.html
- www.acf.hhs.gov/programs/cse/extinf.html

New York Paternity Law

- newyorkchildsupport.com/dcse/paternity_establishment.html
- www.lawhelp.org/NY (click Family & Juvenile)
- www.acf.hhs.gov/programs/cse/pubs/2002/reports/essentials/c8.html

New York Legal Definition of Father

- NY Soc. Serv. Law § 372-c
- www.childwelfare.gov/systemwide/laws_policies/statutes/putative.pdf

New York Adoption Law

- laws.adoption.com/statutes/new-york-adoption-laws.html

- www.lawhelp.org/NY (click Family & Juvenile)
- law.findlaw.com/state-laws/adoption/new-york

New York Termination of Parental Rights
- NY Soc. Serv. Law § 384-b
- www.law.cornell.edu/wex/table_emancipation
- www.childwelfare.gov/systemwide/laws_policies/statutes/groundtermin.cfm

New York Putative Father Registry
- www.ocfs.state.ny.us/main/publications/Pub5040text.asp
- laws.adoption.com/statutes/new-york-laws,5.html
- www.courts.state.nh.us/probate/registrylist.pdf

New York Emancipation Law
- www.law.cornell.edu/topics/Table_Emancipation

New York Age of Majority
- law.findlaw.com/state-laws/minors-and-the-law/new-york
- www.law.cornell.edu/topics/Table_Emancipation

New York Child Protection/Protective Services
- ocfs.ny.gov/main/cps

New York Child Welfare Agencies
- ocfs.ny.gov/main

New York Juvenile Law
- www.lawhelp.org/NY (click Family & Juvenile)
- www.nyc.gov/html/acs/html/yfj/youth_family_justice.shtml
- www.ncjj.org/State/New-York.aspx

New York Domestic Violence Law
- NY Soc. Serv. Law § 459-a
- www.lawhelp.org/NY (click Family & Juvenile)

New York Surrogacy Law
- NY Dom. Rel. Law § 122

- www.selectsurrogate.com/surrogacy-laws-by-state.html
- www.surrogacyforall.com/Surrogacy-Law.html

New York Grandparent Rights
- NY Dom. Rel. Law § 240
- www.lawhelp.org/NY (click Family & Juvenile)

New York Annulment Law
- NY Dom. Rel. Law § 140
- www.hg.org/divorce-law-NewYork.html

New York Family Law Forms
- www.nycourts.gov/divorce/forms.shtml
- www.courts.state.ny.us/forms/index.shtml
- www.nycourts.gov/divorce/divorce_withoutchildrenunder21.shtml
- www.nycourts.gov/divorce/divorce_withchildrenunder21.shtml#ucdforms
- www.uslegalforms.com/rominger/divorce.htm

New York Vital Records (Birth, Marriage, Divorce, Death)
- www.cdc.gov/nchs/w2w.htm
- publicrecords.onlinesearches.com/NewYork.htm

New York Self-Help Services in Family Law Cases
- www.nycourts.gov/divorce/forms.shtml
- www.lawhelp.org/NY (click Family & Juvenile)

New York Family Law Legal Research
- law.syr.edu/academics/center-and-institutes/family-law-and-social-policy (click Research Guides)

New York State Legal Research
- www.ll.georgetown.edu/states/newyork.cfm
- www.loc.gov/law/help/guide/states/us-ny.php
- www.romingerlegal.com/state/newyork.html

New York Court Rules
- www.courts.state.ny.us/rules/trialcourts/index.shtml
- www.llrx.com/courtrules-gen/state-New-York.html

NORTH CAROLINA FAMILY LAW

North Carolina Family Code/Domestic Relations Code
- www.ncga.state.nc.us/gascripts/Statutes/StatutesTOC.pl?0050
- www.law.cornell.edu/wex/table_family

North Carolina Marriage Law (formation)
- statutes.laws.com/north-carolina/Chapter_51
- www.usmarriagelaws.com/search/united_states/north_carolina/marriage_licenses
- www.law.cornell.edu/wex/table_marriage

North Carolina Common Law Marriage
- topics.law.cornell.edu/wex/table_marriage
- www.buddybuddy.com/common.html

North Carolina Same-Sex Marriage, Domestic Partnership, Civil Union, Defense of Marriage Status (Baby-DOMA)
- en.wikipedia.org/wiki/Recognition_of_same-sex_unions_in_North_Carolina
- www.lambdalegal.org/publications/nationwide-status-same-sex-relationships
- www.ncsl.org/issues-research/human-services/civil-unions-and-domestic-partnership-statutes.aspx

North Carolina Divorce Law
- NC Gen. Stat. §§ 50-5.1, 50-6, 50-13.2
- www.lawhelp.org/NC (click Family and Juvenile)

- www.divorcelawinfo.com/states/nc/northcarolina.htm
- www.hg.org/divorce-law-NorthCarolina.html

North Carolina Legal Separation Law
- NC Gen. Stat. § 50-7
- www.lawhelp.org/NC (click Family and Juvenile)
- www.hg.org/divorce-law-NorthCarolina.html

North Carolina Alimony/Spousal Support Law
- NC Gen. Stat. § 50-16.3A
- www.lawhelp.org/NC (click Family and Juvenile)
- www.hg.org/divorce-law-NorthCarolina.html

North Carolina Property Division Law
- NC Gen. Stat. § 50-20
- www.hg.org/divorce-law-NorthCarolina.html

North Carolina Child Custody Law
- NC Gen. Stat. § 50-13.2
- www.lawhelp.org/NC (click Family and Juvenile)
- www.hg.org/divorce-law-NorthCarolina.html

North Carolina Relocation of Child
- NC Gen. Stat. § 50-13.2

North Carolina Guardian Ad Litem and Attorney for Child
- NC Gen. Stat. § 7B-601

- www.childwelfare.gov/systemwide/laws_policies/statutes/represent.pdf

North Carolina Child Support Law

- www.ncchildsupport.com
- www.lawhelp.org/NC (click Family and Juvenile)
- www.supportguidelines.com/links.html
- www.acf.hhs.gov/programs/cse/extinf.html

North Carolina Paternity Law

- www.ncdhhs.gov/dss/cse/help.htm#P434_35626
- info.dhhs.state.nc.us/olm/manuals/dss/cse/man/CSEcI-02.htm
- www.acf.hhs.gov/programs/cse/pubs/2002/reports/essentials/c8.html

North Carolina Legal Definition of Father

- www.childwelfare.gov/systemwide/laws_policies/statutes/putative.pdf

North Carolina Adoption Law

- laws.adoption.com/statutes/north-carolina-adoption-laws.html
- www.lawhelp.org/NC (click Family and Juvenile)
- law.findlaw.com/state-laws/adoption/north-carolina

North Carolina Termination of Parental Rights

- NC Gen. Stat. § 7B-1111
- www.lawhelp.org/NC (click Family and Juvenile)
- www.law.cornell.edu/wex/table_emancipation
- www.childwelfare.gov/systemwide/laws_policies/statutes/groundtermin.cfm

North Carolina Putative Father Registry

- laws.adoption.com/statutes/north-carolina-laws,5.html
- www.courts.state.nh.us/probate/registrylist.pdf

North Carolina Emancipation Law

- www.law.cornell.edu/topics/Table_Emancipation
- www.ncga.state.nc.us/enactedlegislation/statutes/html/byarticle/chapter_7b/article_35.html

North Carolina Age of Majority

- law.findlaw.com/state-laws/minors-and-the-law/north-carolina
- www.law.cornell.edu/topics/Table_Emancipation

North Carolina Child Protection/Protective Services

- www.ncdhhs.gov/dss/cps/about.htm

North Carolina Child Welfare Agencies

- www.ncdhhs.gov/childrenandyouth/index.htm

North Carolina Juvenile Law

- www.lawhelp.org/NC (click Family and Juvenile)
- www.ncdjjdp.org
- www.ncjj.org/State/North-Carolina.aspx

North Carolina Domestic Violence Law

- NC Gen. Stat. § 50B-1
- www.lawhelp.org/NC (click Family and Juvenile)

North Carolina Surrogacy Law

- NC Gen. Stat. § 48-10-102
- www.surrogacyforall.com/Surrogacy-Law.html

North Carolina Grandparent Rights

- NC Gen. Stat. § 50-13.2

North Carolina Annulment Law

- NC Gen. Stat. § 50-4
- www.hg.org/divorce-law-NorthCarolina.html

North Carolina Family Law Forms

- www.nccourts.org/Forms/FormSearch.asp
- www.uslegalforms.com/rominger/divorce.htm

North Carolina Vital Records (Birth, Marriage, Divorce, Death)

- www.cdc.gov/nchs/w2w.htm
- publicrecords.onlinesearches.com/NorthCarolina.htm

North Carolina Self-Help Services in Family Law Cases

- www.lawhelp.org/NC (click Family and Juvenile)
- www.legalaidnc.org/client/faq.aspx
- www.courtreference.com/North-Carolina-Courts-Self-Help.htm

North Carolina State Legal Research

- www.ll.georgetown.edu/states/northcarolina.cfm
- www.loc.gov/law/help/guide/states/us-nc.php
- www.romingerlegal.com/state/northcarolina.html

North Carolina Court Rules

- www.aoc.state.nc.us/www/public/html/rulesgen.htm
- www.llrx.com/courtrules-gen/state-North-Carolina.html

NORTH DAKOTA FAMILY LAW

North Dakota Family Code/Domestic Relations Code

- www.legis.nd.gov/cencode/t14.html
- www.legis.nd.gov/information/statutes/cent-code.html
- www.legis.nd.gov/index.html
- www.law.cornell.edu/wex/table_family

North Dakota Marriage Law (formation)

- usmarriagelaws.com/search/united_states/north_dakota/index.shtml
- www.legis.nd.gov/cencode/t14.html
- www.law.cornell.edu/wex/table_marriage

North Dakota Common Law Marriage

- topics.law.cornell.edu/wex/table_marriage
- www.buddybuddy.com/common.html

North Dakota Same-Sex Marriage, Domestic Partnership, Civil Union, Defense of Marriage Status (Baby-DOMA)

- en.wikipedia.org/wiki/LGBT_rights_in_North_Dakota
- www.lambdalegal.org/publications/nationwide-status-same-sex-relationships
- www.ncsl.org/issues-research/human-services/civil-unions-and-domestic-partnership-statutes.aspx

North Dakota Divorce Law

- ND Cent. Code § 14-05-03
- www.divorcelawinfo.com/states/nd/northdakota.htm

North Dakota Legal Separation Law

- ND Cent. Code § 14-05-03.1

North Dakota Alimony/Spousal Support Law
- ND Cent. Code § 14-05-24.1

North Dakota Property Division Law
- ND Cent. Code § 14-05-24

North Dakota Child Custody Law
- ND Cent. Code § 14-09-06.2

North Dakota Guardian Ad Litem and Attorney for Child
- ND Cent. Code § 50-25.1-08, ND R. Ct, 8.7
- www.childwelfare.gov/systemwide/laws_policies/statutes/represent.pdf

North Dakota Child Support Law
- www.nd.gov/dhs/services/childsupport
- www.supportguidelines.com/links.html
- www.acf.hhs.gov/programs/cse/extinf.html

North Dakota Paternity Law
- www.nd.gov/dhs/services/childsupport/progserv/paternity
- www.acf.hhs.gov/programs/cse/pubs/2002/reports/essentials/c8.html

North Dakota Legal Definition of Father
- ND Cent. Code §§ 14-20-02, 14-20-10
- www.childwelfare.gov/systemwide/laws_policies/statutes/putative.pdf

North Dakota Adoption Law
- laws.adoption.com/statutes/north-dakota-adoption-laws.html
- law.findlaw.com/state-laws/adoption/north-dakota

North Dakota Termination of Parental Rights
- ND Cent. Code § 27-20-44
- www.law.cornell.edu/wex/table_emancipation
- www.childwelfare.gov/systemwide/laws_policies/statutes/groundtermin.cfm

North Dakota Putative Father Registry
- laws.adoption.com/statutes/north-dakota-laws,5.html
- www.courts.state.nh.us/probate/registrylist.pdf

North Dakota Emancipation Law
- www.law.cornell.edu/topics/Table_Emancipation

North Dakota Age of Majority
- law.findlaw.com/state-laws/minors-and-the-law/north-dakota
- www.law.cornell.edu/topics/Table_Emancipation

North Dakota Child Protection/Protective Services
- www.nd.gov/dhs/services/childfamily/cps

North Dakota Child Welfare Agencies
- www.nd.gov/dhs/services/childfamily

North Dakota Juvenile Law
- www.ncjj.org/State/North-Dakota.aspx
- www.ojp.usdoj.gov/saa/nd.htm

North Dakota Domestic Violence Law
- ND Cent. Code § 14-07.1-01

North Dakota Surrogacy Law
- ND Cent. Code §14-18-05
- www.surrogacyforall.com/Surrogacy-Law.html

North Dakota Grandparent Rights
- ND Cent. Code § 14-09-05.1

North Dakota Annulment Law
- ND Cent. Code § 14-04-01

North Dakota Parental Liability for Acts of Minors
- ND Cent. Code § 32-03-39

North Dakota Family Law Forms
- www.ndcourts.gov/court/forms
- www.legalassist.org/?id=104
- www.uslegalforms.com/rominger/divorce.htm

North Dakota Vital Records (Birth, Marriage, Divorce, Death)
- www.cdc.gov/nchs/w2w.htm
- publicrecords.onlinesearches.com/NorthDakota.htm

North Dakota Self-Help Services in Family Law Cases
- www.ndcourts.gov/court/forms
- www.legalassist.org
- www.courtreference.com/North-Dakota-Courts-Self-Help.htm

North Dakota State Legal Research
- www.ll.georgetown.edu/states/northdakota.cfm
- www.loc.gov/law/help/guide/states/us-nd.php
- www.romingerlegal.com/state/northdakota.html

North Dakota Court Rules
- www.ndcourts.gov/rules
- www.llrx.com/courtrules-gen/state-North-Dakota.html

OHIO FAMILY LAW

Ohio Family Code/Domestic Relations Code
- codes.ohio.gov/orc
- www.law.cornell.edu/wex/table_family

Ohio Marriage Law (formation)
- codes.ohio.gov/orc/3101
- www.usmarriagelaws.com/search/united_states/ohio/marriage_licenses
- www.law.cornell.edu/wex/table_marriage

Ohio Common Law Marriage
- Ohio Revised Code § 3105.12

- *Fitzgerald v. Mayfield*, 584 N.E.2d 13 (Ohio App. 4 Dist., 1990).
- topics.law.cornell.edu/wex/table_marriage
- www.buddybuddy.com/common.html

Ohio Same-Sex Marriage, Domestic Partnership, Civil Union, Defense of Marriage Status (Baby-DOMA)
- en.wikipedia.org/wiki/LGBT_rights_in_Ohio
- www.lambdalegal.org/publications/nationwide-status-same-sex-relationships
- www.ncsl.org/issues-research/human-services/civil-unions-and-domestic-partnership-statutes.aspx

Ohio Divorce Law
- Ohio Rev. Code Ann. § 3105.01
- www.divorcelawinfo.com/states/ohio/ohio.htm
- www.hg.org/divorce-law-Ohio.html

Ohio Legal Separation Law
- Ohio Rev. Code Ann. § 3105.17
- www.hg.org/divorce-law-Ohio.html

Ohio Alimony/Spousal Support Law
- Ohio Rev. Code Ann. §3105.18
- www.ohiolegalservices.org/public/legal_problem (click Family Law)
- www.hg.org/divorce-law-Ohio.html

Ohio Property Division Law
- Ohio Rev. Code Ann. § 3105.171
- www.hg.org/divorce-law-Ohio.html

Ohio Child Custody Law
- Ohio Rev. Code Ann. § 3109.04
- www.ohiolegalservices.org/public/legal_problem (click Family Law)
- www.hg.org/divorce-law-Ohio.html

Ohio Guardian Ad Litem and Attorney for Child
- Ohio Rev. Code Ann. § 2151.281
- www.childwelfare.gov/systemwide/laws_policies/statutes/represent.pdf

Ohio Child Support Law
- jfs.ohio.gov/ocs
- www.ohiolegalservices.org/public/legal_problem (click Family Law)
- www.supportguidelines.com/links.html
- www.acf.hhs.gov/programs/cse/extinf.html

Ohio Paternity Law
- www.oh-paternity.com
- www.ohiolegalservices.org/public/legal_problem (click Family Law)
- www.acf.hhs.gov/programs/cse/pubs/2002/reports/essentials/c8.html

Ohio Legal Definition of Father
- Ohio Rev. Code Ann. §§ 3111.01, 3111.03, 3107.01
- www.childwelfare.gov/systemwide/laws_policies/statutes/putative.pdf

Ohio Adoption Law
- laws.adoption.com/statutes/ohio-adoption-laws.html
- www.ohiolegalservices.org/public/legal_problem (click Family Law)
- law.findlaw.com/state-laws/adoption/ohio

Ohio Termination of Parental Rights
- Ohio Rev. Code Ann. § 2151.414
- www.law.cornell.edu/wex/table_emancipation
- www.childwelfare.gov/systemwide/laws_policies/statutes/groundtermin.cfm

Ohio Putative Father Registry
- jfs.ohio.gov/pfr

- laws.adoption.com/statutes/ohio-laws,5.html
- www.courts.state.nh.us/probate/registrylist.pdf

Ohio Emancipation Law
- www.law.cornell.edu/topics/Table_Emancipation
- www.youthrights.net/index.php?title=Ohio_Emancipation_Law

Ohio Age of Majority
- law.findlaw.com/state-laws/minors-and-the-law/ohio
- www.law.cornell.edu/topics/Table_Emancipation

Ohio Child Protection/Protective Services
- jfs.ohio.gov/families/protective_services/index.stm

Ohio Child Welfare Agencies
- jfs.ohio.gov/families/index.stm

Ohio Juvenile Law
- www.dys.ohio.gov/dnn
- www.ncjj.org/State/Ohio.aspx

Ohio Domestic Violence Law
- Ohio Rev. Code Ann. § 2919.25
- www.ohiolegalservices.org/public/legal_problem

Ohio Surrogacy Law
- Ohio Rev. Code Ann. § 3111.89
- www.selectsurrogate.com/surrogacy-laws-by-state.html
- www.surrogacyforall.com/Surrogacy-Law.html

Ohio Grandparent Rights
- Ohio Rev. Code Ann. § 3109.11

Ohio Annulment Law
- Ohio Rev. Code Ann. § 3105.31
- www.ohiolegalservices.org/public/legal_problem (click Family Law)

Ohio Family Law Forms
- www.ohiolegalservices.org/public/find_local_court_forms_rules
- www.ohiocourtlinks.org
- www.uslegalforms.com/rominger/divorce.htm

Ohio Vital Records (Birth, Marriage, Divorce, Death)
- publicrecords.onlinesearches.com/Ohio.htm
- www.cdc.gov/nchs/w2w.htm

Ohio Self-Help Services in Family Law Cases
- www.ohiolegalservices.org/public/legal_problem

Ohio State Legal Research
- www.ll.georgetown.edu/states/ohio.cfm
- www.loc.gov/law/help/guide/states/us-oh.php
- www.romingerlegal.com/state/ohio.html

Ohio Court Rules
- www.supremecourt.ohio.gov/LegalResources/Rules
- www.ohiocourtlinks.org
- www.llrx.com/courtrules-gen/state-Ohio.html

OKLAHOMA FAMILY LAW

Oklahoma Family Code/Domestic Relations Code
- oklegal.onenet.net/statutes.basic.html
- www.oscn.net/applications/oscn/index.asp?ftdb=STOK&level=1
- www.law.cornell.edu/wex/table_family

Oklahoma Marriage Law (formation)
- statutes.laws.com/oklahoma/Title43
- www.usmarriagelaws.com/search/united_states/oklahoma/marriage_licenses
- www.law.cornell.edu/wex/table_marriage

Oklahoma Common Law Marriage

- *Brooks v. Sanders*, 190 P.3d 357 (Okla. Civ. A p. Div. 4, 2008)
- topics.law.cornell.edu/wex/table_marriage
- www.buddybuddy.com/common.html

Oklahoma Same-Sex Marriage, Domestic Partnership, Civil Union, Defense of Marriage Status (Baby-DOMA)

- 43 Okla. Stat. § 3.1
- en.wikipedia.org/wiki/LGBT_rights_in_Oklahoma
- www.lambdalegal.org/publications/nationwide-status-same-sex-relationships
- www.ncsl.org/issues-research/human-services/civil-unions-and-domestic-partnership-statutes.aspx

Oklahoma Divorce Law

- 43 Okla. Stat. § 101
- oklaw.org (click Family Law)
- www.legalaidok.org (click Free Legal Information and then scroll down to Family)
- www.divorcelawinfo.com/states/ok/oklahoma.htm
- www.hg.org/divorce-law-Oklahoma.html

Oklahoma Legal Separation Law

- 43 Okla. Stat. §§ 103, 129
- www.hg.org/divorce-law-Oklahoma.html

Oklahoma Alimony/Spousal Support Law

- 43 Okla. Stat. § 121
- www.hg.org/divorce-law-Oklahoma.html

Oklahoma Property Division Law

- 43 Okla. Stat. § 121
- www.hg.org/divorce-law-Oklahoma.html

Oklahoma Child Custody Law

- 43 Okla. Stat. § 112
- oklaw.org (click Family Law)
- www.hg.org/divorce-law-Oklahoma.html

Oklahoma Relocation of Child

- 43 Okla. Stat. § 112.3

Oklahoma Guardian Ad Litem and Attorney for Child

- 10A Okla. Stat. § 1-4-102, 1-4-306
- www.childwelfare.gov/systemwide/laws_policies/statutes/represent.pdf

Oklahoma Child Support Law

- www.okdhs.org/divisionsoffices/visd/ocss
- oklaw.org (click Family Law)
- www.supportguidelines.com/links.html
- www.acf.hhs.gov/programs/cse/extinf.html

Oklahoma Paternity Law

- oklaw.org (click Family Law)
- www.okdhs.org/programsandservices/ocss/cssvcs/docs/affidavitpaternity.htm
- www.okdhs.org/programsandservices/ocss/cssvcs/docs/patprocess.htm
- www.acf.hhs.gov/programs/cse/pubs/2002/reports/essentials/c8.html

Oklahoma Legal Definition of Father

- 10A Okla. Stat. § 1-1-105, 10 Okla. Stat. § 7700-102
- www.childwelfare.gov/systemwide/laws_policies/statutes/putative.pdf

Oklahoma Adoption Law

- laws.adoption.com/statutes/oklahoma-adoption-laws.html
- oklaw.org (click Family Law)
- statelaws.findlaw.com/oklahoma-law/oklahoma-adoption-laws.html
- www.legalaidok.org (click Free Legal Information and then scroll down to Family)

Oklahoma Termination of Parental Rights

- 10A Okla. Stat. § 1-4-904
- www.law.cornell.edu/wex/table_emancipation
- www.childwelfare.gov/systemwide/laws_policies/statutes/groundtermin.cfm

Oklahoma Putative Father Registry

- 10 Okl. Stat. Ann. § 7506-1.1
- laws.adoption.com/statutes/oklahoma-laws,5.html
- www.courts.state.nh.us/probate/registrylist.pdf

Oklahoma Emancipation Law

- www.law.cornell.edu/topics/Table_Emancipation

Oklahoma Age of Majority

- law.findlaw.com/state-laws/minors-and-the-law/oklahoma
- www.law.cornell.edu/topics/Table_Emancipation

Oklahoma Child Protection/Protective Services

- www.okdhs.org/programsandservices/cps

Oklahoma Child Welfare Agencies

- www.okdhs.org/divisionsoffices/hsc/cfsd

Oklahoma Juvenile Law

- www.ncjj.org/State/Oklahoma.aspx
- www.ok.gov/oja

Oklahoma Domestic Violence Law

- okdvhelp.com
- oklaw.org (click Family Law)
- www.legalaidok.org (click Free Legal Information and then scroll down to Family)

Oklahoma Surrogacy Law

- 10 Okla. Stat. § 7505-3.2; 21 Okla. Stat. § 866
- www.selectsurrogate.com/surrogacy-laws-by-state.html
- www.surrogacyforall.com/Surrogacy-Law.html

Oklahoma Grandparent Rights

- 43 Okla. Stat. § 109.4

Oklahoma Annulment Law

- 43 Okla. Stat. § 2
- www.legalaidok.org (click Free Legal Information and then scroll down to Family)
- www.hg.org/divorce-law-Oklahoma.html

Oklahoma Family Law Forms

- www.oscn.net/oscn/scrules/scforms.html
- www.uslegalforms.com/rominger/divorce.htm

Oklahoma Vital Records (Birth, Marriage, Divorce, Death)

- www.cdc.gov/nchs/w2w.htm
- publicrecords.onlinesearches.com/Oklahoma.htm

Oklahoma Self-Help Services in Family Law Cases

- oklaw.org (click Family Law)
- www.legalaidok.org (click Free Legal Information and then scroll down to Family)

Oklahoma State Legal Research

- www.ll.georgetown.edu/states/oklamona.cfm
- www.loc.gov/law/help/guide/states/us-ok.php
- www.romingerlegal.com/state/oklahoma.html

Oklahoma Court Rules

- www.oscn.net/applications/oscn/index.asp?ftdb=STOK&level=1
- www.llrx.com/courtrules-gen/state-Oklahoma.html

OREGON FAMILY LAW

Oregon Family Code/Domestic Relations Code
- landru.leg.state.or.us/ors/106.html
- www.leg.state.or.us/ors/home.html
- www.law.cornell.edu/wex/table_family

Oregon Marriage Law (formation)
- www.leg.state.or.us/ors/106.html
- www.usmarriagelaws.com/search/united_states/oregon /marriage_licenses
- www.osbar.org/public/legalinfo/1131_Marriage.htm
- www.law.cornell.edu/wex/table_marriage

Oregon Common Law Marriage
- topics.law.cornell.edu/wex/table_marriage
- www.buddybuddy.com/common.html

Oregon Same-Sex Marriage, Domestic Partnership, Civil Union, Defense of Marriage Status (Baby-DOMA)
- www.hg.org/divorce-law-Oregon.html
- en.wikipedia.org/wiki/Same-sex_marriage_in_Oregon
- www.lambdalegal.org/publications/nationwide-status-same-sex -relationships
- www.ncsl.org/issues-research/human-services/civil-unions-and -domestic-partnership-statutes.aspx

Oregon Divorce Law
- Or. Rev. Stat. Ann. § 107.025
- www.divorcelawinfo.com/states/or/oregon.htm
- www.hg.org/divorce-law-Oregon.html
- www.oregonlawhelp.org/OR/index.cfm (click Family)

Oregon Legal Separation Law
- www.oregonlawhelp.org/OR/index.cfm (click Family)
- www.hg.org/divorce-law-Oregon.html

Oregon Alimony/Spousal Support Law
- Or. Rev. Stat. Ann. §§ 107.105, 107.406
- www.oregonlawhelp.org/OR/index.cfm (click Family)
- www.hg.org/divorce-law-Oregon.html

Oregon Property Division Law
- Or. Rev. Stat. Ann. § 107.105
- www.hg.org/divorce-law-Oregon.html
- www.oregonlawhelp.org/OR/index.cfm (click Family)

Oregon Child Custody Law
- Or. Rev. Stat. Ann. § 107.137
- www.oregonlawhelp.org/OR/index.cfm (click Family)
- www.hg.org/divorce-law-Oregon.html

Oregon Guardian Ad Litem and Attorney for Child
- Or. Rev. Stat. Ann. § 419A.170, 419B.195
- www.childwelfare.gov/systemwide/laws_policies/statutes /represent.pdf

Oregon Child Support Law
- oregonchildsupport.gov
- www.supportguidelines.com/links.html
- www.acf.hhs.gov/programs/cse/extinf.html

Oregon Paternity Law
- oregonchildsupport.gov/services/paternity.shtml
- www.osbar.org/public/legalinfo/1142_Paternity.htm
- www.oregonlawhelp.org/OR/index.cfm (click Family)
- www.acf.hhs.gov/programs/cse/pubs/2002/reports/essentials /c8.html

Oregon Legal Definition of Father
- Or. Rev. Stat. Ann. § 109.070
- www.childwelfare.gov/systemwide/laws_policies/statutes /putative.pdf

Oregon Adoption Law
- laws.adoption.com/statutes/oregon-adoption-laws.html
- statelaws.findlaw.com/oregon-law/oregon-adoption-laws.html
- www.oregonlawhelp.org/OR/index.cfm (click Family)

Oregon Termination of Parental Rights
- Or. Rev. Stat. Ann. § 419B.49B
- www.law.cornell.edu/wex/table_emancipation
- www.childwelfare.gov/systemwide/laws_policies/statutes /groundtermin.cfm

Oregon Putative Father Registry
- laws.adoption.com/statutes/oregon-laws,5.html
- www.courts.state.nh.us/probate/registrylist.pdf

Oregon Emancipation Law
- www.law.cornell.edu/topics/Table_Emancipation
- www.youthrights.net/index.php?title=Oregon_Emancipation _Law

Oregon Age of Majority
- law.findlaw.com/state-laws/minors-and-the-law/oregon
- www.law.cornell.edu/topics/Table_Emancipation

Oregon Child Protection/Protective Services
- www.oregon.gov/DHS/children/abuse/cps/cw_branches .shtml

Oregon Child Welfare Agencies
- www.oregon.gov/DHS/children/index.shtml

Oregon Juvenile Law
- www.oregonlawhelp.org/OR/index.cfm (click Family)
- www.oregon.gov/oya/pages/juvrights.aspx
- www.ncjj.org/State/Oregon.aspx

Oregon Domestic Violence Law
- Or. Rev. Stat. Ann. § 132.586

Oregon Employment Discrimination Law
- Or. Rev. Stat. Ann. §§ 659A.029 et seq.

Oregon Surrogacy Law
- Or. Rev. Stat. Ann. § 163.537(2)(d)
- www.selectsurrogate.com/surrogacy-laws-by-state.html
- www.surrogacyforall.com/Surrogacy-Law.html

Oregon Grandparent Rights
- Or. Rev. Stat. Ann. § 109.332

Oregon Annulment Law
- Or. Rev. Stat. Ann. § 106.020
- www.oregonlawhelp.org/OR/index.cfm (click Family)

Oregon Parental Liability for Acts of Minors
- Or. Rev. Stat. Ann. § 30.765

Oregon Family Law Forms
- courts.oregon.gov/OJD/forms/index.page
- courts.oregon.gov/OJD/forms/pages/index.aspx
- www.uslegalforms.com/rominger/divorce.htm

Oregon Vital Records (Birth, Marriage, Divorce, Death)
- www.cdc.gov/nchs/w2w.htm
- publicrecords.onlinesearches.com/Oregon.htm

Oregon Self-Help Services in Family Law Cases
- courts.oregon.gov/OJD/selfhelp/index.page
- www.oregonlawhelp.org/OR/index.cfm (click Family)
- www.courtreference.com/Oregon-Courts-Self-Help.htm

Oregon State Legal Research
- www.ll.georgetown.edu/states/oregon.cfm
- www.loc.gov/law/help/guide/states/us-or.php
- www.romingerlegal.com/state/oregon.html

Oregon Court Rules
- www.courts.oregon.gov/OJD/programs/utcr/utcrrules.page
- www.llrx.com/courtrules-gen/state-Oregon.html

PENNSYLVANIA FAMILY LAW

Pennsylvania Family Code/Domestic Relations Code
- government.westlaw.com/linkedslice/default.asp?SP=pac-1000
- www.legis.state.pa.us/cfdocs/legis/li/public/cons_index.cfm
- www.law.cornell.edu/wex/table_family

Pennsylvania Marriage Law (formation)
- www.usmarriagelaws.com/search/united_states/pennsylvania/marriage_licenses
- marriage.about.com/cs/marriagelicenses/p/pennsylvania.htm
- www.law.cornell.edu/wex/table_marriage

Pennsylvania Common Law Marriage
- 23 Pa.C.S.A. § 1103
- *Cann v. Cann*, 632 A.2d 322(Pa. Super., 1993).
- topics.law.cornell.edu/wex/table_marriage
- www.buddybuddy.com/common.html

Pennsylvania Same-Sex Marriage, Domestic Partnership, Civil Union, Defense of Marriage Status (Baby-DOMA)
- en.wikipedia.org/wiki/Recognition_of_same-sex_unions_in_Pennsylvania
- www.lambdalegal.org/publications/nationwide-status-same-sex-relationships
- www.ncsl.org/issues-research/human-services/civil-unions-and-domestic-partnership-statutes.aspx

Pennsylvania Divorce Law
- 23 Pa Consol. Stats. Ann. § 3301
- www.divorcelawinfo.com/PA/flc.htm
- www.hg.org/divorce-law-Pennsylvania.html
- www.palawhelp.org/PA/index.cfm (click Children and Families)

Pennsylvania Legal Separation Law
- www.hg.org/divorce-law-Pennsylvania.html

Pennsylvania Alimony/Spousal Support Law
- 23 Pa Consol. Stats. Ann. § 3701
- www.hg.org/divorce-law-Pennsylvania.html

Pennsylvania Property Division Law
- 23 Pa Consol. Stats. Ann. § 3502 (equitable division)
- www.divorcelawinfo.com/PA/papropdiv.htm
- www.hg.org/divorce-law-Pennsylvania.html

Pennsylvania Child Custody Law
- 23 Pa Consol. Stats. Ann. § 5323
- www.palawhelp.org/PA/index.cfm (click Children and Families)
- www.hg.org/divorce-law-Pennsylvania.html

Pennsylvania Relocation of Child
- Lehigh County Rules of Civil Procedure, Rule 1915.4-4

Pennsylvania Guardian Ad Litem and Attorney for Child
- 42 Pa Consol. Stats. Ann. §§ 6311, 6342
- www.childwelfare.gov/systemwide/laws_policies/statutes/represent.pdf

Pennsylvania Child Support Law
- www.humanservices.state.pa.us/csws/home_controller.aspx
- www.supportguidelines.com/links.html
- www.acf.hhs.gov/programs/cse/extinf.html

Pennsylvania Paternity Law
- 23 Pa Consol. Stats. Ann. § 4343
- law.onecle.com/pennsylvania/domestic-relations/00.051.003.000.html
- www.acf.hhs.gov/programs/cse/pubs/2002/reports/essentials/c8.html
- www.palawhelp.org/PA/index.cfm (click Children and Families)

Pennsylvania Legal Definition of Father
- 23 Pa Consol. Stats. Ann. § 5102
- www.childwelfare.gov/systemwide/laws_policies/statutes/putative.pdf

Pennsylvania Adoption Law
- 23 Pa Consol. Stats. Ann. § 2101
- www.palawhelp.org/PA/index.cfm (click Children and Families)
- laws.adoption.com/statutes/pennsylvania-adoption-laws.html
- statelaws.findlaw.com/pennsylvania-law/pennsylvania-adoption-laws.html

Pennsylvania Termination of Parental Rights
- Pa Orphans' Court Rule 15.4
- www.law.cornell.edu/wex/table_emancipation
- www.childwelfare.gov/systemwide/laws_policies/statutes/groundtermin.cfm

Pennsylvania Putative Father Registry
- laws.adoption.com/statutes/pennsylvania-laws,5.html
- www.courts.state.nh.us/probate/registrylist.pdf

Pennsylvania Emancipation Law
- www.nwls.org/emancipation_of_minors.htm
- www.law.cornell.edu/topics/Table_Emancipation
- www.palawhelp.org/PA/index.cfm (click Children and Families)

Pennsylvania Age of Majority
- law.findlaw.com/state-laws/minors-and-the-law/pennsylvania
- www.law.cornell.edu/topics/Table_Emancipation

Pennsylvania Child Protection/Protective Services
- www.pacode.com/secure/data/055/chapter3490/subchapatoc.html
- www.alleghenycounty.us/dhs/childprotection.aspx

Pennsylvania Child Welfare Agencies
- www.dpw.state.pa.us/forchildren/childwelfareservices/index.htm

Pennsylvania Juvenile Law
- www.ncjj.org/State/Pennsylvania.aspx
- www.jcjc.state.pa.us/portal/server.pt/community/jcjc_community/5030
- www.palawhelp.org/PA/index.cfm (click Children and Families)

Pennsylvania Domestic Violence Law

- 23 Pa Consol. Stats. Ann. § 6102
- www.palawhelp.org/PA/index.cfm (click Children and Families)

Pennsylvania Surrogacy Law

- www.selectsurrogate.com/surrogacy-laws-by-state.html
- www.surrogacyforall.com/Surrogacy-Law.html

Pennsylvania Annulment Law

- 23 Pa Consol. Stats. Ann. § 3303
- www.hg.org/divorce-law-Pennsylvania.html

Pennsylvania Parental Liability for Acts of Minors

- www.nwls.org/emancipation_of_minors.htm#III. FAMILY LAW

Pennsylvania Family Law Forms

- www.palawhelp.org/PA/index.cfm (click Children and Families)
- www.uslegalforms.com/rominger/divorce.htm

Pennsylvania Vital Records (Birth, Marriage, Divorce, Death)

- www.cdc.gov/nchs/w2w.htm
- publicrecords.onlinesearches.com/Pennsylvania.htm

Pennsylvania Self-Help Services in Family Law Cases

- www.nwls.org/Resources.htm
- www.palawhelp.org/PA/index.cfm (click Children and Families)
- libguides.law.widener.edu/content.php?pid=159023&sid=2345714

Pennsylvania State Legal Research

- www.ll.georgetown.edu/states/pennsylvania.cfm
- www.loc.gov/law/help/guide/states/us-pa.php
- www.romingerlegal.com/state/pennsylvania.html

Pennsylvania Court Rules

- www.pacode.com/secure/data/231/231toc.html
- www.pacourts.us/T/SpecialCourts/LocalRules.htm
- www.llrx.com/courtrules-gen/state-Pennsylvania.html

RHODE ISLAND FAMILY LAW

Rhode Island Family Code/Domestic Relations Code

- www.rilin.state.ri.us/Statutes/TITLE15/15-5/INDEX.HTM
- www.rilin.state.ri.us/Statutes/Statutes.html
- www.law.cornell.edu/wex/table_family

Rhode Island Marriage Law (formation)

- www.health.ri.gov/records/howto/getamarriagelicense/
- www.usmarriagelaws.com/search/united_states/rhode_island/marriage_licenses
- www.law.cornell.edu/wex/table_marriage

Rhode Island Common Law Marriage

- *Fravala v. City of Cranston...*, 996 A.2d 696 (R.I., 2010)
- topics.law.cornell.edu/wex/table_marriage
- www.buddybuddy.com/common.html

Rhode Island Same-Sex Marriage, Domestic Partnership, Civil Union, Defense of Marriage Status (Baby-DOMA)

- en.wikipedia.org/wiki/Same-sex_marriage_in_Rhode_Island
- www.lambdalegal.org/publications/nationwide-status-same-sex-relationships
- www.ncsl.org/issues-research/human-services/civil-unions-and-domestic-partnership-statutes.aspx

Rhode Island Divorce Law

- RI Gen Laws §§ 15-5-2 et seq.
- www.divorcesource.com/ds/rhodeisland/rhode-island-divorce-laws-713.shtml
- www.divorcelawinfo.com/states/ri/rhodeisland.htm

Rhode Island Legal Separation Law

- RI Gen Laws § 15-5-9

Rhode Island Alimony/Spousal Support Law

- RI Gen Laws § 15-5-16
- www.hg.org/article.asp?id=18172

Rhode Island Property Division Law

- RI Gen Laws § 15-5-16.1

Rhode Island Child Custody Law

- RI Gen Laws § 15-5-16
- www.cse.ri.gov

Rhode Island Guardian Ad Litem and Attorney for Child

- RI Gen Laws § 40-11-14
- www.childwelfare.gov/systemwide/laws_policies/statutes/represent.pdf

Rhode Island Child Support Law

- RI Gen Laws § 15-5-16.2
- www.cse.ri.gov
- www.supportguidelines.com/links.html
- www.acf.hhs.gov/programs/cse/extinf.html

Rhode Island Paternity Law

- www.cse.ri.gov/services/establishment_paternity.php
- www.cse.ri.gov/downloads/An%20Introduction_to_RI_Paternity.pdf
- www.acf.hhs.gov/programs/cse/pubs/2002/reports/essentials/c8.html
- www.ri.gov/search/?q=paternity&Submit=Go

Rhode Island Legal Definition of Father

- RI Gen Laws § 15-8-3
- www.childwelfare.gov/systemwide/laws_policies/statutes/putative.pdf

Rhode Island Adoption Law

- laws.adoption.com/statutes/rhode-island-adoption-laws.html
- law.findlaw.com/state-laws/adoption/rhode-island
- www.ri.gov/search/?q=adoption&Submit=Go

Rhode Island Termination of Parental Rights

- RI Gen Laws § 15-7-7
- www.law.cornell.edu/wex/table_emancipation
- www.childwelfare.gov/systemwide/laws_policies/statutes/groundtermin.cfm

Rhode Island Putative Father Registry

- laws.adoption.com/statutes/rhode-island-laws,5.html
- www.courts.state.nh.us/probate/registrylist.pdf

Rhode Island Emancipation Law

- www.law.cornell.edu/topics/Table_Emancipation
- www.child-advocate.ri.gov/HandbooksandBrochures/ChildAdvocateHandbookindex.php

Rhode Island Age of Majority

- law.findlaw.com/state-laws/minors-and-the-law/rhode-island
- www.law.cornell.edu/topics/Table_Emancipation

Rhode Island Child Protection/Protective Services

- www.dcyf.ri.gov/child_welfare
- www.dcyf.state.ri.us/child_welfare/index.php#reportabuse

Rhode Island Child Welfare Agencies

- www.dcyf.state.ri.us

Rhode Island Juvenile Law

- www.rijustice.state.ri.us/juvenile/index.php
- www.ncjj.org/State/Rhode-Island.aspx
- www.child-advocate.ri.gov/HandbooksandBrochures
  /ChildAdvocateHandbookindex.php

Rhode Island Domestic Violence Law

- RI Gen Laws § 12-29-2
- www.ri.gov/search/?q=domestic+violence&Submit=Go

Rhode Island Employment Discrimination Law

- RI Gen Laws § 28-51-2

Rhode Island Surrogacy Law

- RI Gen Laws §§ 23-16.4-1 et seq.
- www.selectsurrogate.com/surrogacy-laws-by-state.html
- www.surrogacyforall.com/Surrogacy-Law.html

Rhode Island Grandparent Rights

- RI Gen Laws § 15-5-24.3

Rhode Island Annulment Law

- RI Gen Laws §§ 15-1-1 et seq.

Rhode Island Family Law Forms

- www.uslegalforms.com/rominger/divorce.htm

Rhode Island Vital Records (Birth, Marriage, Divorce, Death)

- publicrecords.onlinesearches.com/RhodeIsland.htm
- www.cdc.gov/nchs/w2w.htm

Rhode Island Self-Help Services in Family Law Cases

- www.courts.ri.gov/Self%20Help%20Center/default.aspx
- www.ri.gov/search/?q=self+help&Submit=Go
- www.courts.ri.gov/Pages/Search%20Results.aspx?k=divorce

Rhode Island State Legal Research

- www.ll.georgetown.edu/states/rhodeisland.cfm
- www.loc.gov/law/help/guide/states/us-ri.php
- www.romingerlegal.com/state/rhodeisland.html

Rhode Island Court Rules

- www.llrx.com/courtrules-gen/state-Rhode-Island.html

SOUTH CAROLINA FAMILY LAW

South Carolina Family Code/Domestic Relations Code

- www.scstatehouse.gov/code/statmast.php
- www.law.cornell.edu/wex/table_family

South Carolina Marriage Law (formation)

- statutes.laws.com/south-carolina/title-20/chapter-1
- www.usmarriagelaws.com/search/united_states/south_carolina
  /marriage_licenses
- www.law.cornell.edu/wex/table_marriage

South Carolina Common Law Marriage

- Code 1976 § 20-1-100
- *Callen v. Callen*, 620 S.E.2d 59 (S.C., 2005).
- topics.law.cornell.edu/wex/table_marriage
- www.buddybuddy.com/common.html

South Carolina Same-Sex Marriage, Domestic Partnership, Civil Union, Defense of Marriage Status (Baby-DOMA)

- Code of Laws of So. Car. § 20-1-15
- en.wikipedia.org/wiki/Recognition_of_same-sex_unions_in
  _South_Carolina
- statutes.laws.com/south-carolina/title-20/chapter-1
- www.lambdalegal.org/publications/nationwide-status-same-sex
  -relationships
- www.ncsl.org/issues-research/human-services/civil-unions-and
  -domestic-partnership-statutes.aspx

South Carolina Divorce Law

- Code of Laws of So. Car. § 20-3-10
- www.divorcelawinfo.com/states/sc/southcarolina.htm
- www.hg.org/divorce-law-SouthCarolina.html

South Carolina Legal Separation Law

- www.hg.org/divorce-law-SouthCarolina.html

South Carolina Alimony/Spousal Support Law

- Code of Laws of So. Car. § 20-3-130

South Carolina Alimony/Spousal Support/Maintenance Law

- www.hg.org/divorce-law-SouthCarolina.html

South Carolina Property Division Law

- Code of Laws of So. Car. § 20-3-620
- www.hg.org/divorce-law-SouthCarolina.html

South Carolina Child Custody Law

- Code of Laws of So. Car. § 20-3-160
- www.lawhelp.org/sc (click Family and Juvenile)
- www.hg.org/divorce-law-SouthCarolina.html

South Carolina Guardian Ad Litem and Attorney for Child

- Code of Laws of So. Car. § 63-7-1620
- www.childwelfare.gov/systemwide/laws_policies/statutes
  /represent.pdf

South Carolina Child Support Law

- www.state.sc.us/dss/csed
- www.supportguidelines.com/links.html
- www.acf.hhs.gov/programs/cse/extinf.html

South Carolina Paternity Law

- www.state.sc.us/dss/csed/patest.htm
- www.acf.hhs.gov/programs/cse/pubs/2002/reports/essentials
  /c8.html

South Carolina Legal Definition of Father

- Code of Laws of So. Car. § 63-9-310
- www.childwelfare.gov/systemwide/laws_policies/statutes
  /putative.pdf

South Carolina Adoption Law

- Code of Laws of So. Car. §§ 63-9-10 et seq.
- laws.adoption.com/statutes/south-carolina-adoption-laws .html
- www.lawhelp.org/sc (click Family and Juvenile)
- law.findlaw.com/state-laws/adoption/south-carolina

South Carolina Termination of Parental Rights

- Code of Laws of So. Car. § 63-7-2570
- www.law.cornell.edu/wex/table_emancipation
- www.childwelfare.gov/systemwide/laws_policies/statutes /groundtermin.cfm

South Carolina Responsible Father Registry

- ssl.sc.gov/DSSFatherRegistry/FatherReg/RegIndex.aspx
- laws.adoption.com/statutes/south-carolina-laws,5.html
- www.courts.state.nh.us/probate/registrylist.pdf

South Carolina Emancipation Law

- www.law.cornell.edu/topics/Table_Emancipation

South Carolina Age of Majority

- law.findlaw.com/state-laws/minors-and-the-law/south-carolina
- www.law.cornell.edu/topics/Table_Emancipation

South Carolina Child Protection/Protective Services

- dss.sc.gov/content/customers/protection/index.aspx

South Carolina Child Welfare Agencies

- dss.sc.gov/content/customers/index.aspx

South Carolina Juvenile Law

- www.state.sc.us/djj
- www.ncjj.org/State/South-Carolina.aspx

South Carolina Domestic Violence Law

- Code of Laws of So. Car. § 16-25-20
- www.lawhelp.org/sc (click Domestic Violence)

South Carolina Surrogacy Law

- *Mid-South Ins. Co. v. Doe*, 274 F.Supp.2d 757 (DC 2003)
- www.selectsurrogate.com/surrogacy-laws-by-state.html
- www.surrogacyforall.com/Surrogacy-Law.html

South Carolina Grandparent Rights

- Code of Laws of So. Car. § 63-3-530(A)(33)

South Carolina Annulment Law

- Code of Laws of So. Car. §§ 20-1-80, 20-1-510
- statutes.laws.com/south-carolina/title-20/chapter-1
- www.hg.org/divorce-law-SouthCarolina.html

South Carolina Family Law Forms

- www.judicial.state.sc.us/forms/index.cfm
- www.uslegalforms.com/rominger/divorce.htm

South Carolina Vital Records (Birth, Marriage, Divorce, Death)

- www.cdc.gov/nchs/w2w.htm
- publicrecords.onlinesearches.com/SouthCarolina.htm

South Carolina Self-Help Services in Family Law Cases

- www.judicial.state.sc.us/selfHelp/index.cfm
- www.lawhelp.org/sc (click Family and Juvenile)

South Carolina State Legal Research

- www.ll.georgetown.edu/states/southcarolina.cfm
- www.loc.gov/law/help/guide/states/us-sc.php
- www.romingerlegal.com/state/southcarolina.html

South Carolina Court Rules

- www.judicial.state.sc.us/courtReg
- www.llrx.com/courtrules-gen/state-South-Carolina.html

SOUTH DAKOTA FAMILY LAW

South Dakota Family Code/Domestic Relations Code

- legis.state.sd.us/statutes/index.aspx
- www.law.cornell.edu/wex/table_family

South Dakota Marriage Law (formation)

- doh.sd.gov/vitalrecords/marriage.aspx
- www.usmarriagelaws.com/search/united_states/south_dakota /marriage_licenses
- www.law.cornell.edu/wex/table_marriage

South Dakota Common Law Marriage

- topics.law.cornell.edu/wex/table_marriage
- www.buddybuddy.com/common.html

South Dakota Same-Sex Marriage, Domestic Partnership, Civil Union, Defense of Marriage Status (Baby-DOMA)

- en.wikipedia.org/wiki/LGBT_rights_in_South_Dakota
- www.lambdalegal.org/publications/nationwide-status-same-sex -relationships
- www.ncsl.org/issues-research/human-services/civil-unions-and -domestic-partnership-statutes.aspx

South Dakota Divorce Law

- So. Dak. Codif. Laws § 25-4-2
- www.divorcelawinfo.com/states/sd/southdakota.htm

South Dakota Legal Separation Law

- So. Dak. Codif. Laws § 25-4-17.2

South Dakota Alimony/Spousal Support/Maintenance Law

- So. Dak. Codif. Laws § 25-4-41

South Dakota Property Division Law

- So. Dak. Codif. Laws § 25-4-44

South Dakota Child Custody Law

- So. Dak. Codif. Laws § 25-4-45

South Dakota Guardian Ad Litem and Attorney for Child

- So. Dak. Codif. Laws §§ 63-11-510, 63-11-530, 63-11-540
- www.childwelfare.gov/systemwide/laws_policies/statutes /represent.pdf

South Dakota Child Support Law

- dss.sd.gov/childsupport
- www.supportguidelines.com/links.html
- www.acf.hhs.gov/programs/cse/extinf.html

South Dakota Paternity Law

- dss.sd.gov/childsupport/services/paternityestablishment.asp
- www.acf.hhs.gov/programs/cse/pubs/2002/reports/essentials/c8.html

South Dakota Legal Definition of Father

- So. Dak. Codif. Laws § 25-5A-1
- www.childwelfare.gov/systemwide/laws_policies/statutes/putative.pdf

South Dakota Adoption Law

- laws.adoption.com/statutes/south-dakota-adoption-laws.html
- law.findlaw.com/state-laws/adoption/south-dakota

South Dakota Termination of Parental Rights

- So. Dak. Codif. Laws § 26-8A-26.1
- www.law.cornell.edu/wex/table_emancipation
- www.childwelfare.gov/systemwide/laws_policies/statutes/groundtermin.cfm

South Dakota Putative Father Registry

- laws.adoption.com/statutes/south-dakota-laws,5.html
- www.courts.state.nh.us/probate/registrylist.pdf

South Dakota Emancipation Law

- legis.state.sd.us/statutes/DisplayStatute.aspx?Statute=25-5&Type=Statute
- www.law.cornell.edu/topics/Table_Emancipation

North Dakota Age of Majority

- law.findlaw.com/state-laws/minors-and-the-law/north-dakota
- www.law.cornell.edu/topics/Table_Emancipation

South Dakota Child Protection/Protective Services

- dss.sd.gov/cps

South Dakota Child Welfare Agencies

- dss.sd.gov/cps/index.asp

South Dakota Juvenile Law

- www.ncjj.org/State/South-Dakota.aspx

South Dakota Domestic Violence Law

- www.sdnafvsa.com

South Dakota Surrogacy Law

- www.selectsurrogate.com/surrogacy-laws-by-state.html
- www.surrogacyforall.com/Surrogacy-Law.html

South Dakota Grandparent Rights

- So. Dak. Codif. Laws § 25-4-52

South Dakota Annulment Law

- So. Dak. Codif. Laws §§ 25-3-1 et seq.

South Dakota Family Law Forms

- www.sdjudicial.com/forms/default.aspx
- www.uslegalforms.com/rominger/divorce.htm

South Dakota Vital Records (Birth, Marriage, Divorce, Death)

- www.cdc.gov/nchs/w2w.htm
- publicrecords.onlinesearches.com/SouthDakota.htm

South Dakota Self-Help Services in Family Law Cases

- www.courtreference.com/South-Dakota-Courts-Self-Help.htm
- www.helpsouthdakota.com/resource-library

South Dakota State Legal Research

- www.ll.georgetown.edu/states/southdakota.cfm
- www.loc.gov/law/help/guide/states/us-sd.php
- www.romingerlegal.com/state/southdakota.html

South Dakota Court Rules

- www.sdjudicial.com/sc/scrules.aspx
- www.llrx.com/courtrules-gen/state-South-Dakota.html

TENNESSEE FAMILY LAW

Tennessee Family Code/Domestic Relations Code

- www.lexisnexis.com/hottopics/tncode
- www.law.cornell.edu/wex/table_family

Tennessee Marriage Law (formation)

- Tenn. Code Ann. § 36-3-113
- www.usmarriagelaws.com/search/united_states/tennessee/marriage_licenses
- www.countyclerkanytime.com/marriage/default.htm
- www.law.cornell.edu/wex/table_marriage

Tennessee Common Law Marriage

- topics.law.cornell.edu/wex/table_marriage
- www.buddybuddy.com/common.html

Tennessee Same-Sex Marriage, Domestic Partnership, Civil Union, Defense of Marriage Status (Baby-DOMA)

- en.wikipedia.org/wiki/LGBT_rights_in_Tennessee
- www.lambdalegal.org/publications/nationwide-status-same-sex-relationships
- www.ncsl.org/issues-research/human-services/civil-unions-and-domestic-partnership-statutes.aspx

Tennessee Divorce Law

- Tenn. Code Ann. § 36-4-101
- www.las.org/booklets/family_problems
- www.divorcelawinfo.com/states/tn/tennesee.htm
- www.hg.org/divorce-law-Tennessee.html

Tennessee Legal Separation Law

- Tenn. Code Ann. § 36-4-102

Tennessee Alimony/Spousal Support Law

- Tenn. Code Ann. § 36-5-101
- www.hg.org/divorce-law-Tennessee.html

Tennessee Property Division Law

- Tenn. Code Ann. § 36-4-121
- www.hg.org/divorce-law-Tennessee.html

Tennessee Child Custody Law

- Tenn. Code Ann. § 36-6-106
- www.hg.org/divorce-law-Tennessee.html

Tennessee Relocation of Child

- Tenn. Code Ann. § 36-6-108

Tennessee Guardian Ad Litem and Attorney for Child

- Tenn. Code Ann. §§ 36-4-132, 37-1-149
- www.childwelfare.gov/systemwide/laws_policies/statutes/represent.pdf

Tennessee Child Support Law

- tennessee.gov/humanserv/cs/cs_main.html

- www.supportguidelines.com/links.html
- www.acf.hhs.gov/programs/cse/extinf.html

Tennessee Paternity Law
- Tenn. Code Ann. § 24-7-112
- www.tn.gov/tccy/tnchild/24/24-7-113.htm
- www.acf.hhs.gov/programs/cse/pubs/2002/reports/essentials/c8.html

Tennessee Legal Definition of Father
- Tenn. Code Ann. §§ 36-2-302, 36-2-304(a)
- www.childwelfare.gov/systemwide/laws_policies/statutes/putative.pdf

Tennessee Adoption Law
- laws.adoption.com/statutes/tenne3ssee-adoption-laws.html
- statelaws.findlaw.com/tennessee-law/tennessee-adoption-laws.html

Tennessee Termination of Parental Rights
- Tenn. Code Ann. § 36-1-113
- www.law.cornell.edu/wex/table_emancipation
- www.childwelfare.gov/systemwide/laws_policies/statutes/groundtermin.cfm

Tennessee Putative Father Registry
- www.state.tn.us/tccy/tnchild/36/36-2-318.htm
- laws.adoption.com/statutes/tennessee-laws,5.html
- www.courts.state.nh.us/probate/registrylist.pdf

Tennessee Emancipation Law
- www.law.cornell.edu/topics/Table_Emancipation

Tennessee Age of Majority
- law.findlaw.com/state-laws/minors-and-the-law/tennessee
- www.law.cornell.edu/topics/Table_Emancipation

Tennessee Child Protection/Protective Services
- reportabuse.state.tn.us

Tennessee Child Welfare Agencies
- www.state.tn.us/youth

Tennessee Juvenile Law
- www.tncourts.gov/programs/court-improvement/youth-juvenile-court

- www.state.tn.us/youth/juvenilejustice.htm
- www.ncjj.org/State/Tennessee.aspx

Tennessee Domestic Violence Law
- Tenn. Code Ann. §40-14-109

Tennessee Surrogacy Law
- Tenn. Code Ann. § 36-1-102(48)
- www.selectsurrogate.com/surrogacy-laws-by-state.html
- www.surrogacyforall.com/Surrogacy-Law.html

Tennessee Grandparent Rights
- Tenn. Code Ann. § 36-6-302

Tennessee Annulment Law
- Tenn. Code Ann. § 36-4-119
- www.hg.org/divorce-law-Tennessee.html

Tennessee Family Law Forms
- www.tsc.state.tn.us/forms-publications
- www.tncourts.gov/help-center/court-approved-divorce-forms
- www.uslegalforms.com/rominger/divorce.htm

Tennessee Vital Records (Birth, Marriage, Divorce, Death)
- www.cdc.gov/nchs/w2w.htm
- publicrecords.onlinesearches.com/Tennessee.htm

Tennessee Self-Help Services in Family Law Cases
- www.tncourts.gov/programs/self-help-center
- www.courtreference.com/Tennessee-Courts-Self-Help.htm
- www.las.org/booklets

Tennessee State Legal Research
- www.ll.georgetown.edu/states/tennessee.cfm
- www.loc.gov/law/help/guide/states/us-tn.php
- www.romingerlegal.com/state/tennessee.html

Tennessee Court Rules
- www.tsc.state.tn.us/courts/rules
- www.llrx.com/courtrules-gen/state-Tennessee.html

TEXAS FAMILY LAW

Texas Family Code/Domestic Relations Code
- www.statutes.legis.state.tx.us
- www.statutes.legis.state.tx.us
- www.law.cornell.edu/wex/table_family

Texas Marriage Law (formation)
- Texas Family Code §6.204
- statutes.laws.com/texas/family-code/title-1-the-marriage-relationship
- www.usmarriagelaws.com/search/united_states/texas/marriage_licenses
- www.law.cornell.edu/wex/table_marriage

Texas Common Law (Informal) Marriage
- V.T.C.A., Family Code § 2.401.
- topics.law.cornell.edu/wex/table_marriage
- www.buddybuddy.com/common.html

Texas Same-Sex Marriage, Domestic Partnership, Civil Union, Defense of Marriage Status (Baby-DOMA)
- en.wikipedia.org/wiki/LGBT_rights_in_Texas

- www.lambdalegal.org/publications/nationwide-status-same-sex-relationships
- www.ncsl.org/issues-research/human-services/civil-unions-and-domestic-partnership-statutes.aspx

Texas Divorce Law
- Texas Family Code §§ 6.001 et seq.
- www.texaslawhelp.org/TX/index.cfm (click Family Law)
- www.divorcelawinfo.com/states/texas/texas.htm
- www.hg.org/divorce-law-Texas.html

Texas Legal Separation Law
- www.hg.org/divorce-law-Texas.html

Texas Alimony/Spousal/Maintenance Support Law
- Texas Family Code § 8.051

Texas Property Division Law
- Texas Family Code § 7.001
- statutes.laws.com/texas/family-code/title-1-the-marriage-relationship
- www.hg.org/divorce-law-Texas.html

Texas Child Custody Law

- www.texaslawhelp.org/TX/index.cfm (click Family Law)

Texas Guardian Ad Litem and Attorney for Child

- Texas Family Code §§ 107.001, 107.011, 107.012
- www.childwelfare.gov/systemwide/laws_policies/statutes /represent.pdf

Texas Child Support Law

- www.oag.state.tx.us/cs/index.shtml
- www.supportguidelines.com/links.html
- www.acf.hhs.gov/programs/cse/extinf.html

Texas Paternity Law

- www.oag.state.tx.us/ag_publications/txts/paternity.shtml
- www.texaslawhelp.org/TX/index.cfm (click Family Law)
- www.acf.hhs.gov/programs/cse/pubs/2002/reports/essentials/c8.html

Texas Legal Definition of Father

- Texas Family Code §§ 160.102, 160.204
- www.childwelfare.gov/systemwide/laws_policies/statutes/putative.pdf

Texas Adoption Law

- www.texaslawhelp.org/TX/index.cfm (click Family Law)
- laws.adoption.com/statutes/texas-adoption-laws.html
- law.findlaw.com/state-laws/adoption/texas

Texas Termination of Parental Rights

- Texas Family Code § 161.001
- www.law.cornell.edu/wex/table_emancipation
- www.childwelfare.gov/systemwide/laws_policies/statutes /groundtermin.cfm

Texas Putative Father Registry

- Texas Family Code § 160.401
- laws.adoption.com/statutes/texas-laws,5.html
- www.courts.state.nh.us/probate/registrylist.pdf

Texas Emancipation Law

- www.law.cornell.edu/topics/Table_Emancipation
- www.youthrights.net/index.php?title=Texas_Emancipation_Law

Texas Age of Majority

- law.findlaw.com/state-laws/minors-and-the-law/texas
- www.law.cornell.edu/topics/Table_Emancipation

Texas Child Protection/Protective Services

- www.dfps.state.tx.us
- www.dfps.state.tx.us/child_protection/about_child_protective_services

Texas Child Welfare Agencies

- www.dfps.state.tx.us

Texas Juvenile Law

- Texas Family Code §§ 51.01 et seq.
- www.texaslawhelp.org/TX/index.cfm (click Family Law)
- www.tjjd.texas.gov
- www.ncjj.org/State/Texas.aspx

Texas Domestic Violence Law

- www.tcfv.org

Texas Surrogacy Law

- Texas Fam. Code Ann. §§ 160.754, 160.762
- www.selectsurrogate.com/surrogacy-laws-by-state.html
- www.surrogacyforall.com/Surrogacy-Law.html

Texas Grandparent Rights

- www.texaslawhelp.org/TX/index.cfm (click Family Law)

Texas Annulment Law

- Texas Family Code §§ 6.102 et seq.
- www.hg.org/divorce-law-Texas.html

Texas Parental Liability for Acts of Minors ($25,000)

- Texas Family Code §§ 41.001 et seq.

Texas Family Law Forms

- www.txcourts.gov/pubs/pubs-home.asp
- www.texaslawhelp.org/TX/index.cfm (click Family Law)
- www.uslegalforms.com/rominger/divorce.htm

Texas Vital Records (Birth, Marriage, Divorce, Death)

- publicrecords.onlinesearches.com/Texas.htm
- www.cdc.gov/nchs/w2w.htm

Texas Self-Help Services in Family Law Cases

- www.texaslawhelp.org/TX/index.cfm (click Family Law)
- tarltonguides.law.utexas.edu/content .php?pid=118666&sid=1033690

Texas State Legal Research

- www.ll.georgetown.edu/states/texas.cfm
- www.loc.gov/law/help/guide/states/us-tx.php
- www.romingerlegal.com/state/texas.html

Texas Court Rules

- www.supreme.courts.state.tx.us/rules
- www.llrx.com/courtrules-gen/state-Texas.html

UTAH FAMILY LAW

Utah Family Code/Domestic Relations Code

- le.utah.gov/Documents/code_const.htm
- www.law.cornell.edu/wex/table_family

Utah Marriage Law (formation)

- www.utcourts.gov/howto/marriage
- marriage.about.com/cs/marriagelicenses/p/utah.htm
- www.law.cornell.edu/wex/table_marriage

Utah Common Law Marriage

- Utah Code Ann. § 30-1-4.5
- topics.law.cornell.edu/wex/table_marriage
- www.buddybuddy.com/common.html

Utah Same-Sex Marriage, Domestic Partnership, Civil Union, Defense of Marriage Status (Baby-DOMA)

- en.wikipedia.org/wiki/LGBT_rights_in_Utah
- www.lambdalegal.org/publications/nationwide-status-same-sex -relationships
- www.ncsl.org/issues-research/human-services/civil-unions-and -domestic-partnership-statutes.aspx

Utah Divorce Law

- Utah Code Ann. § 30-3-1
- www.utcourts.gov/howto/divorce
- www.divorcelawinfo.com/states/utah/utah.htm
- www.hg.org/divorce-law-Utah.html

Utah Legal Separation Law

- www.hg.org/divorce-law-Utah.html

Utah Alimony/Spousal Support/Maintenance Law

- Utah Code Ann. § 30-3-5

Utah Property Division Law

- Utah Code Ann. § 30-3-5

Utah Child Custody Law

- Utah Code Ann. § 30-3-10
- www.utcourts.gov/howto/divorce/custody.html

Utah Guardian Ad Litem and Attorney for Child

- Utah Ann. Code §§ 78A-6-902, 78A-2-227
- www.childwelfare.gov/systemwide/laws_policies/statutes /represent.pdf
- www.utcourts.gov/resources/forms
- www.utcourts.gov/howto/seniors/g_and_c.asp

Utah Child Support Law

- www.ors.utah.gov
- www.supportguidelines.com/links.html
- www.acf.hhs.gov/programs/cse/extinf.html

Utah Paternity Law

- www.ors.state.ut.us/faq_paternity.htm
- www.utcourts.gov/resources/forms
- www.acf.hhs.gov/programs/cse/pubs/2002/reports/essentials /c8.html

Utah Legal Definition of Father

- Utah Ann. Code § 78B-15-102
- www.childwelfare.gov/systemwide/laws_policies/statutes /putative.pdf

Utah Adoption Law

- www.utcourts.gov/howto/family/adoption
- laws.adoption.com/statutes/utah-adoption-laws.html
- statelaws.findlaw.com/utah-law/utah-adoption-laws.html

Utah Termination of Parental Rights

- Utah Ann. Code § 62A-4a-203.5
- www.law.cornell.edu/wex/table_emancipation
- www.childwelfare.gov/systemwide/laws_policies/statutes /groundtermin.cfm

Utah Putative Father Registry

- Utah Ann. Code § 78B-6-110
- laws.adoption.com/statutes/utah-laws,5.html
- www.courts.state.nh.us/probate/registrylist.pdf

Utah Emancipation Law

- Utah Code Ann. § 78A-6-805
- www.utcourts.gov/courts/juv/juvyfaq.htm
- www.law.cornell.edu/topics/Table_Emancipation

Utah Age of Majority

- law.findlaw.com/state-laws/minors-and-the-law/utah
- www.law.cornell.edu/topics/Table_Emancipation

Utah Child Protection/Protective Services

- www.dcfs.utah.gov/ReportChildAbuse.htm

Utah Child Welfare Agencies

- www.dcfs.utah.gov

Utah Juvenile Law

- www.utcourts.gov/courts/juv/juvyfaq.htm
- www.jjs.utah.gov
- www.ncjj.org/State/Utah.aspx

Utah Domestic Violence Law

- Utah Code Ann. § 77-36-1
- www.udvac.org/home.htm

Utah Employment Discrimination Law

- Utah Code Ann. § 34A-5-107

Utah Surrogacy Law

- Utah Code Ann. §78B-15-801
- www.selectsurrogate.com/surrogacy-laws-by-state.html
- www.surrogacyforall.com/Surrogacy-Law.html

Utah Grandparent Rights

- Utah Code Ann. § 30-5-2

Utah Annulment Law

- Utah Code Ann. §§ 30-1-1 et seq.
- www.utcourts.gov/howto/divorce/annulment.html

Utah Family Law Forms

- www.utcourts.gov/resources/forms
- www.uslegalforms.com/rominger/divorce.htm

Utah Vital Records (Birth, Marriage, Divorce, Death)

- www.cdc.gov/nchs/w2w.htm
- publicrecords.onlinesearches.com/Utah.htm

Utah Self-Help Services in Family Law Cases

- www.utcourts.gov/selfhelp
- www.utcourts.gov/resources/forms
- www.utcourts.gov/selfhelp/#families
- www.utahlegalservices.org/public/flyers

Utah State Legal Research

- www.ll.georgetown.edu/states/utah.cfm
- www.loc.gov/law/help/guide/states/us-ut.php
- www.romingerlegal.com/state/utah.html

Utah Court Rules

- www.utcourts.gov/resources/rules
- www.llrx.com/courtrules-gen/state-Utah.html

VERMONT FAMILY LAW

Vermont Family Code/Domestic Relations Code

- www.leg.state.vt.us/statutes/chapters.cfm?Title=15
- www.leg.state.vt.us/statutesMain.cfm
- www.law.cornell.edu/wex/table_family

Vermont Marriage Law (formation)

- 15 Vt. Stats. Ann. § 8
- www.sec.state.vt.us/municipal/civil_mar.htm

- www.usmarriagelaws.com/search/united_states/vermont /marriage_licenses
- www.law.cornell.edu/wex/table_marriage

Vermont Common Law Marriage

- topics.law.cornell.edu/wex/table_marriage
- www.buddybuddy.com/common.html

Vermont Same-Sex Marriage, Domestic Partnership, Civil Union, Defense of Marriage Status (Baby-DOMA)

- en.wikipedia.org/wiki/Same-sex_marriage_in_Vermont
- www.lambdalegal.org/publications/nationwide-status-same-sex-relationships
- www.ncsl.org/issues-research/human-services/civil-unions-and-domestic-partnership-statutes.aspx

Vermont Divorce Law

- 15 Vt. Stats. Ann. § 551
- www.vermontjudiciary.org/GTC/Family/Pamphlets.aspx
- www.divorcelawinfo.com/states/vermont/vermont.htm

Vermont Legal Separation Law

- 15 Vt. Stats. Ann. § 555

Vermont Alimony Law

- www.vermontjudiciary.org/GTC/Family/Pamphlets.aspx

Vermont Property Division Law

- 15 Vt. Stats. Ann. §§ 751 et seq.
- www.vermontjudiciary.org/GTC/Family/Pamphlets.aspx

Vermont Child Custody Law

- 15 Vt. Stats. Ann. §§ 665 et seq.

Vermont Guardian Ad Litem and Attorney for Child

- 33 Vt. Stat. Ann. § 5112
- www.childwelfare.gov/systemwide/laws_policies/statutes/represent.pdf

Vermont Child Support Law

- 15 Vt. Stats. Ann. §et seq.654 et seq.
- dcf.vermont.gov/ocs
- www.supportguidelines.com/links.html
- www.vermontjudiciary.org/GTC/Family/Pamphlets.aspx
- www.acf.hhs.gov/programs/cse/extinf.html

Vermont Paternity Law

- 15 Vt. Stats. Ann. §§ 307; 15B Vt. Stats. Ann. 701
- www.acf.hhs.gov/programs/cse/pubs/2002/reports/essentials/c8.html

Vermont Legal Definition of Father

- 15A Vt. Stat. Ann. § 1-101
- www.childwelfare.gov/systemwide/laws_policies/statutes/putative.pdf

Vermont Adoption Law

- laws.adoption.com/statutes/vermont-adoption-laws.html
- statelaws.findlaw.com/vermont-law/vermont-adoption-laws.html

Vermont Termination of Parental Rights

- 15A Vt. Stat. Ann. § 3-504
- www.law.cornell.edu/wex/table_emancipation
- www.childwelfare.gov/systemwide/laws_policies/statutes/groundtermin.cfm

Vermont Putative Father Registry

- laws.adoption.com/statutes/vermont-laws,5.html
- www.courts.state.nh.us/probate/registrylist.pdf

Vermont Emancipation Law

- www.leg.state.vt.us/statutes/fullchapter.cfm?Title=12&Chapter=217
- www.law.cornell.edu/topics/Table_Emancipation
- www.youthrights.net/index.php?title=Vermont_Emancipation_Law

Vermont Age of Majority

- law.findlaw.com/state-laws/minors-and-the-law/vermont
- www.law.cornell.edu/topics/Table_Emancipation

Vermont Child Protection/Protective Services

- dcf.vermont.gov/protectkids

Vermont Child Welfare Agencies

- dcf.vermont.gov

Vermont Juvenile Law

- www.ncjj.org/State/Vermont.aspx

Vermont Domestic Violence Law

- 15 Vt. Stats. Ann. § 1151
- www.vtnetwork.org

Vermont Employment Discrimination Law

- 21 Vt. Stats. Ann. § 495h

Vermont Surrogacy Law

- www.selectsurrogate.com/surrogacy-laws-by-state.html
- www.surrogacyforall.com/Surrogacy-Law.html

Vermont Grandparent Rights

- 15 Vt. Stats. Ann. § 1011

Vermont Annulment Law

- 15 Vt. Stats. Ann. §§ 511 et seq.

Vermont Family Law Forms

- www.vermontjudiciary.org/masterpages/Court-Formsindex.aspx
- www.uslegalforms.com/rominger/divorce.htm

Vermont Vital Records (Birth, Marriage, Divorce, Death)

- www.cdc.gov/nchs/w2w.htm
- publicrecords.onlinesearches.com/Vermont.htm

Vermont Self-Help Services in Family Law Cases

- www.selfhelpsupport.org
- www.vermontjudiciary.org/GTC/Family/Pamphlets.aspx

Vermont State Legal Research

- www.ll.georgetown.edu/states/vermont.cfm
- www.loc.gov/law/help/guide/states/us-vt.php
- www.romingerlegal.com/state/vermont.html

Vermont Court Rules

- www.lexisnexis.com/hottopics/michie
- www.llrx.com/courtrules-gen/state-Vermont.html

VIRGINIA FAMILY LAW

Virginia Family Code/Domestic Relations Code

- leg1.state.va.us/cgi-bin/legp504.exe?000+cod+TOC
- leg1.state.va.us/000/src.htm
- www.law.cornell.edu/wex/table_family

Virginia Marriage Law (formation)

- www.usmarriagelaws.com/search/united_states/virginia/marriage_licenses
- www.vsb.org/site/publications/marriage-in-virginia
- www.law.cornell.edu/wex/table_marriage

Virginia Common Law Marriage

- topics.law.cornell.edu/wex/table_marriage
- www.buddybuddy.com/common.html

Virginia Same-Sex Marriage, Domestic Partnership, Civil Union, Defense of Marriage Status (Baby-DOMA)

- en.wikipedia.org/wiki/LGBT_rights_in_Virginia
- www.lambdalegal.org/publications/nationwide-status-same-sex -relationships
- www.ncsl.org/issues-research/human-services/civil-unions-and -domestic-partnership-statutes.aspx

Virginia Divorce Law

- Va. Code Ann. § 20.91
- www.vsb.org/site/publications/divorce-in-virginia
- www.valegalaid.org/issues/family-and-domestic-and-sexual -violence/divorce
- www.divorcelawinfo.com/VA/flc.htm
- www.hg.org/divorce-law-virginia.html

Virginia Legal Separation Law

- Va. Code Ann. § 20-95
- www.hg.org/divorce-law-virginia.html

Virginia Alimony/Spousal Support Law

- Va. Code Ann. §§ 20-107.1, 20-108.1
- www.hg.org/divorce-law-virginia.html

Virginia Property Division Law

- Va. Code Ann. § 20-107.3
- www.divorcelawinfo.com/VA/marprop/propdiv.htm
- www.hg.org/divorce-law-virginia.html

Virginia Child Custody Law

- Va. Code Ann. §§ 16.1-278.15, 20-124.1 et seq.
- www.hg.org/divorce-law-virginia.html
- www.valegalaid.org/issues/family-and-domestic-and-sexual -violence/custodyvisitation

Virginia Guardian Ad Litem and Attorney for Child

- Va. Code Ann. §§ 16.1-266, 9.1-153
- www.childwelfare.gov/systemwide/laws_policies/statutes /represent.pdf

Virginia Child Support Law

- Va. Code Ann. §§ 20-108.1 et seq.
- www.dss.virginia.gov/family/dcse/index.cgi
- www.supportguidelines.com/links.html
- www.acf.hhs.gov/programs/cse/extinf.html

Virginia Paternity Law

- Va. Code Ann. §§ 210-49.6, 63.2-1913
- www.dss.virginia.gov/pub/pdf/dcse_paternity.pdf
- www.acf.hhs.gov/programs/cse/pubs/2002/reports/essentials /c8.html

Virginia Legal Definition of Father

- Va. Code Ann. §§ 63.2-1249, 63.2-1250
- www.childwelfare.gov/systemwide/laws_policies/statutes /putative.pdf

Virginia Adoption Law

- laws.adoption.com/statutes/virginia-adoption-laws.html
- statelaws.findlaw.com/virginia-law/virginia-adoption-laws.html
- www.valegalaid.org/issues/family-and-domestic-and-sexual -violence/adoption

Virginia Termination of Parental Rights

- Va. Code Ann. § 16.1-283
- www.law.cornell.edu/wex/table_emancipation
- www.childwelfare.gov/systemwide/laws_policies/statutes /groundtermin.cfm

Virginia Putative Father Registry

- www.dss.virginia.gov/family/ap/putative_registry.cgi
- laws.adoption.com/statutes/virginia-laws,5.html
- www.courts.state.nh.us/probate/registrylist.pdf

Virginia Emancipation Law

- www.law.cornell.edu/topics/Table_Emancipation
- www.youthrights.net/index.php?title=Virginia_Emancipation _Law

Virginia Age of Majority

- law.findlaw.com/state-laws/minors-and-the-law/virginia
- www.law.cornell.edu/topics/Table_Emancipation

Virginia Child Protection/Protective Services

- www.dss.virginia.gov/family/cps/index2.cgi

Virginia Child Welfare Agencies

- www.dss.virginia.gov/family/children.html

Virginia Juvenile Law

- www.djj.virginia.gov
- www.ncjj.org/State/Vermont.aspx

Virginia Domestic Violence Law

- www.dss.virginia.gov/community/dv/index.cgi
- www.vsdvalliance.org/secGetHelp/gethelplegal.html

Virginia Surrogacy Law

- Va. Code Ann. § 20-156
- www.selectsurrogate.com/surrogacy-laws-by-state.html
- www.surrogacyforall.com/Surrogacy-Law.html

Virginia Grandparent Rights

- Va. Code Ann. §§ 16.1-278.15, 20-124.1

Virginia Annulment Law

- Va. Code Ann. § 20-89.1
- www.hg.org/divorce-law-virginia.html

Virginia Family Law Forms

- www.courts.state.va.us/forms/home.html
- www.valegalaid.org/self-help-forms
- www.uslegalforms.com/rominger/divorce.htm

Virginia Vital Records (Birth, Marriage, Divorce, Death)

- www.cdc.gov/nchs/w2w.htm
- publicrecords.onlinesearches.com/Virginia.htm

Virginia Self-Help Services in Family Law Cases

- www.valegalaid.org/self-help-forms

Virginia State Legal Research

- www.ll.georgetown.edu/states/virginia.cfm
- www.loc.gov/law/help/guide/states/us-va.php
- www.romingerlegal.com/state/virginia.html

Virginia Court Rules

- www.courts.state.va.us/courts/scv/rules.html
- www.llrx.com/courtrules-gen/state-Virginia.html

WASHINGTON FAMILY LAW

Washington Family Code/Domestic Relations Code
- apps.leg.wa.gov/rcw/default.aspx?Cite=26
- apps.leg.wa.gov/rcw
- www.law.cornell.edu/wex/table_family

Washington Marriage Law (formation)
- www.usmarriagelaws.com/search/united_states/washington/marriage_licenses
- access.wa.gov/living/resources/marriage.aspx
- www.law.cornell.edu/wex/table_marriage

Washington Common Law Marriage
- topics.law.cornell.edu/wex/table_marriage
- www.buddybuddy.com/common.html

Washington Same-Sex Marriage, Domestic Partnership, Civil Union, Defense of Marriage Status (Baby-DOMA)
- www.washingtonlawhelp.org/WA/index.cfm (click Family Law)
- en.wikipedia.org/wiki/Same-sex_marriage_in_Washington
- www.lambdalegal.org/publications/nationwide-status-same-sex-relationships
- www.ncsl.org/issues-research/human-services/civil-unions-and-domestic-partnership-statutes.aspx

Washington Divorce Law
- Wash. Rev. Code §§ 26.09.002 et seq.
- www.washingtonlawhelp.org/WA/index.cfm (click Family Law)
- www.divorcelawinfo.com/states/wash/washington.htm
- www.hg.org/divorce-law-washington.html

Washington Legal Separation Law
- Wash. Rev. Code §§ 26.09.002 et seq.

Washington Alimony/Spousal Support Law
- Wash. Rev. Code § 26.09.090

Washington Community Property Law
- Wash. Rev. Code §§ 26.09.080, 26.16.030 et seq

Washington Child Custody Law
- Wash. Rev. Code § 26.09.181
- www.washingtonlawhelp.org/WA/index.cfm (click Family Law)

Washington Relocation of Child
- Wash. Rev. Code §§ 26.09.410 et seq.
- www.washingtonlawhelp.org/WA/index.cfm (click Family Law)

Washington Guardian Ad Litem and Attorney for Child
- Wash. Rev. Code §§ 26.44.053, 13.34.100, 13.34.102
- www.childwelfare.gov/systemwide/laws_policies/statutes/represent.pdf

Washington Child Support Law
- www.dshs.wa.gov/dcs
- www.washingtonlawhelp.org/WA/index.cfm (click Family Law)
- www.supportguidelines.com/links.html
- www.acf.hhs.gov/programs/cse/extinf.html

Washington Paternity Law
- www.dshs.wa.gov/dcs/services/paternity.asp
- www.acf.hhs.gov/programs/cse/pubs/2002/reports/essentials/c8.html

Washington Legal Definition of Father
- Wash. Rev. Code §§ 26.26.011, 26.26.116
- www.childwelfare.gov/systemwide/laws_policies/statutes/putative.pdf

Washington Adoption Law
- Wash. Rev. Code §§ 26.33.010 et seq.
- laws.adoption.com/statutes/washington-adoption-laws.html
- www.washingtonlawhelp.org/WA/index.cfm (click Family Law)
- law.findlaw.com/state-laws/adoption/washington
- www.dshs.wa.gov/ca/adopt/index.asp

Washington Termination of Parental Rights
- Wash. Rev. Code § 13.34.145
- www.law.cornell.edu/wex/table_emancipation
- www.childwelfare.gov/systemwide/laws_policies/statutes/groundtermin.cfm

Washington Putative Father Registry
- laws.adoption.com/statutes/washington-laws,5.html
- www.courts.state.nh.us/probate/registrylist.pdf

Washington Emancipation Law
- www.courts.wa.gov/forms/?fa=forms.contribute&formID=17
- www.law.cornell.edu/topics/Table_Emancipation

Washington Age of Majority
- Wash. Rev. Code § 26.28.010
- law.findlaw.com/state-laws/minors-and-the-law/washington
- www.law.cornell.edu/topics/Table_Emancipation

Washington Child Protection/Protective Services
- www.dshs.wa.gov/ca/general/index.asp

Washington Child Welfare Agencies
- www.dshs.wa.gov/ca/general/index.asp

Washington Juvenile Law
- www.dshs.wa.gov/ojj
- www.ncjj.org/State/Washington.aspx

Washington Domestic Violence Law
- Wash. Rev. Code §§ 26.50.010 et seq.
- www.wscadv.org/resourcesPublications.cfm

Washington Surrogacy Law
- Wash. Rev. Code §§ 26.26.101, 26.26.210
- www.selectsurrogate.com/surrogacy-laws-by-state.html
- www.surrogacyforall.com/Surrogacy-Law.html

Washington Grandparent Rights
- Wash. Rev. Code § 26.09.240

Washington Annulment Law
- Wash. Rev. Code §§ 26.04.010 et seq.

Washington Family Law Forms
- www.kcll.org/researchhelp/researchguides/familylaw/index.html
- www.uslegalforms.com/rominger/divorce.htm

Washington Vital Records (Birth, Marriage, Divorce, Death)
- www.cdc.gov/nchs/w2w.htm
- publicrecords.onlinesearches.com/Washington.htm

Washington Self-Help Services in Family Law Cases
- www.washingtonlawhelp.org/WA/index.cfm

Washington State Family Law Legal Research
- www.kcll.org/guides/family-law-guide-index

Washington State Legal Research
- www.ll.georgetown.edu/states/washington.cfm

- www.loc.gov/law/help/guide/states/us-wa.php
- www.romingerlegal.com/state/washingtonstate.html

Washington Court Rules
- www.courts.wa.gov/court_rules
- www.llrx.com/courtrules-gen/state-Washington.html

WEST VIRGINIA FAMILY LAW

West Virginia Family Code/Domestic Relations Code
- www.legis.state.wv.us/WVCODE/Code.cfm
- www.law.cornell.edu/wex/table_family

West Virginia Marriage Law (formation)
- www.usmarriagelaws.com/search/united_states/west_virginia/marriage_licenses
- marriage.about.com/cs/marriagelicenses/p/westvirginia.htm
- www.law.cornell.edu/wex/table_marriage

West Virginia Common Law Marriage
- topics.law.cornell.edu/wex/table_marriage
- www.buddybuddy.com/common.html

West Virginia Same-Sex Marriage, Domestic Partnership, Civil Union, Defense of Marriage Status (Baby-DOMA)
- en.wikipedia.org/wiki/LGBT_rights_in_West_Virginia
- www.lambdalegal.org/publications/nationwide-status-same-sex-relationships
- www.ncsl.org/issues-research/human-services/civil-unions-and-domestic-partnership-statutes.aspx

West Virginia Divorce Law
- W.Va. Code §§ 48-5-201 et seq.
- www.lawv.net/taxonomy/term/561
- www.divorcelawinfo.com/states/wva/westvirginia.htm
- www.hg.org/divorce-law-westvirginia.html

West Virginia Alimony/Spousal Support/Maintenance Law
- W.Va. Code §§ 48-1-242 et seq.
- www.hg.org/divorce-law-westvirginia.html

West Virginia Property Division Law
- W.Va. Code §§ 48-6-101, 48-7-101

West Virginia Child Custody Law
- W.Va. Code §§ 48-9-101, 48-20-106
- www.legis.state.wv.us/WVCODE/Code.cfm?chap=48&art=9#09

West Virginia Guardian Ad Litem and Attorney for Child
- W.Va. Code § 49-6-2
- www.childwelfare.gov/systemwide/laws_policies/statutes/represent.pdf

West Virginia Child Support Law
- www.wvdhhr.org/bcse
- www.supportguidelines.com/links.html
- www.acf.hhs.gov/programs/cse/extinf.html

West Virginia Paternity Law
- www.legis.state.wv.us/wvcode/code.cfm?chap=48&art=24
- www.wvdhhr.org/bph/hsc/vital/paternity.asp
- www.acf.hhs.gov/programs/cse/pubs/2002/reports/essentials/c8.html

West Virginia Legal Definition of Father
- W.Va. Code §§ 48-22-105, 109, 110, 113, 114
- www.childwelfare.gov/systemwide/laws_policies/statutes/putative.pdf

West Virginia Adoption Law
- laws.adoption.com/statutes/west-virginia-adoption-laws.html
- law.findlaw.com/state-laws/adoption/west-virginia

West Virginia Termination of Parental Rights
- W.Va. Code § 49-6-7
- www.law.cornell.edu/wex/table_emancipation
- www.childwelfare.gov/systemwide/laws_policies/statutes/groundtermin.cfm

West Virginia Putative Father Registry
- laws.adoption.com/statutes/west-virginia-laws,5.html
- www.courts.state.nh.us/probate/registrylist.pdf

West Virginia Emancipation Law
- www.law.cornell.edu/topics/Table_Emancipation

West Virginia Age of Majority
- law.findlaw.com/state-laws/minors-and-the-law/west-virginia
- www.law.cornell.edu/topics/Table_Emancipation

West Virginia Child Protection/Protective Services
- www.wvdhhr.org/bcf/children_adult/cps

West Virginia Child Welfare Agencies
- www.wvdhhr.org/bcf/cfdirect.asp

West Virginia Juvenile Law
- www.wvdjs.state.wv.us
- www.ncjj.org/State/West-Virginia.aspx

West Virginia Domestic Violence Law
- W.Va. Code §§ 48-27-202 et seq.

West Virginia Surrogacy Law
- W.Va. Code § 48-22-803(e)(3)
- www.selectsurrogate.com/surrogacy-laws-by-state.html
- www.surrogacyforall.com/Surrogacy-Law.html

West Virginia Grandparent Rights
- W.Va. Code §§ 48-10-401 et seq.

West Virginia Annulment Law
- W.Va. Code §§ 48-3-104 et seq.

West Virginia Family Law Forms
- www.courtswv.gov/legal-community/court-forms.html
- www.uslegalforms.com/rominger/divorce.htm

West Virginia Vital Records (Birth, Marriage, Divorce, Death)

- publicrecords.onlinesearches.com/WestVirginia.htm
- www.cdc.gov/nchs/w2w.htm
- www.courtreference.com/West-Virginia-Courts.htm

West Virginia Self-Help Services in Family Law Cases

- www.lawv.net
- www.lawv.net/lawhelp

West Virginia State Legal Research

- www.ll.georgetown.edu/states/westvirginia.cfm
- www.loc.gov/law/help/guide/states/us-wv.php
- www.romingerlegal.com/state/westvirginia.html

West Virginia Court Rules

- www.state.wv.us/wvsca/Rules/ctrules.htm
- www.llrx.com/courtrules-gen/state-West-Virginia.html

WISCONSIN FAMILY LAW

Wisconsin Family Code/Domestic Relations Code

- docs.legis.wisconsin.gov/statutes/prefaces/toc
- legis.wisconsin.gov/rsb/stats.html
- www.law.cornell.edu/wex/table_family

Wisconsin Marriage Law (formation)

- www.usmarriagelaws.com/search/united_states/wisconsin/marriage_licenses
- wilawlibrary.gov/topics/familylaw/marriage.php
- www.law.cornell.edu/wex/table_marriage

Wisconsin Common Law Marriage

- topics.law.cornell.edu/wex/table_marriage
- www.buddybuddy.com/common.html

Wisconsin Same-Sex Marriage, Domestic Partnership, Civil Union, Defense of Marriage Status (Baby-DOMA)

- en.wikipedia.org/wiki/Recognition_of_same-sex_unions_in_Wisconsin
- www.lambdalegal.org/publications/nationwide-status-same-sex-relationships
- www.ncsl.org/issues-research/human-services/civil-unions-and-domestic-partnership-statutes.aspx

Wisconsin Divorce Law

- Wisc. Stat. § 767-315
- wilawlibrary.gov/topics/familylaw/divorce.php
- www.divorcelawinfo.com/states/wiscon/wisconsin.htm
- www.hg.org/divorce-law-wisconsin.html

Wisconsin Legal Separation Law

- Wisc. Stat. § 767-315
- www.hg.org/divorce-law-wisconsin.html

Wisconsin Property Division Law

- Wisc. Stat. § 766-588
- wilawlibrary.gov/topics/familylaw/maritalproperty.php

Wisconsin Child Custody Law

- Wisc. Stat. § 822-06
- wilawlibrary.gov/topics/familylaw/childcustody.php
- www.divorcelawinfo.com/states/wiscon/wisconsin.htm

Wisconsin Relocation of Child

- Wisc. Stat. § 767.481

Wisconsin Guardian Ad Litem and Attorney for Child

- Wisc. Stat. §§ 48.23, 48.235
- wilawlibrary.gov/topics/familylaw/gal.php
- www.childwelfare.gov/systemwide/laws_policies/statutes/represent.pdf

Wisconsin Child Support Law

- dcf.wisconsin.gov/bcs
- wilawlibrary.gov/topics/familylaw/childsupport.php
- www.supportguidelines.com/links.html
- www.acf.hhs.gov/programs/cse/extinf.html

Wisconsin Paternity Law

- wilawlibrary.gov/topics/familylaw/paternity.php
- www.acf.hhs.gov/programs/cse/pubs/2002/reports/essentials/c8.html

Wisconsin Legal Definition of Father/Parent

- Wisc. Stat. §§ 48.02, 891.405
- www.childwelfare.gov/systemwide/laws_policies/statutes/putative.pdf

Wisconsin Child Custody Law

- wilawlibrary.gov/topics/familylaw/childcustody.php

Wisconsin Adoption Law

- laws.adoption.com/statutes/wisconsin-adoption-laws.html
- statelaws.findlaw.com/wisconsin-law/wisconsin-adoption-laws.html

Wisconsin Termination of Parental Rights

- Wisc. Stat. § 48-40
- wilawlibrary.gov/topics/familylaw/tpr.php
- www.law.cornell.edu/wex/table_emancipation
- www.childwelfare.gov/systemwide/laws_policies/statutes/groundtermin.cfm

Wisconsin Putative Father Registry

- laws.adoption.com/statutes/wisconsin-laws,5.html
- www.courts.state.nh.us/probate/registrylist.pdf

Wisconsin Emancipation Law

- www.law.cornell.edu/topics/Table_Emancipation

Wisconsin Age of Majority

- law.findlaw.com/state-laws/minors-and-the-law/wisconsin
- www.law.cornell.edu/topics/Table_Emancipation

Wisconsin Child Protection/Protective Services

- dcf.wisconsin.gov/Children/CPS/cpswimap.htm?ref=hp

Wisconsin Child Welfare Agencies

- dcf.wisconsin.gov

Wisconsin Juvenile Law

- www.wi-doc.com/index_juvenile.htm
- www.ncjj.org/State/Wisconsin.aspx

Wisconsin Domestic Violence Law
- Wisc. Stat. § 905.045

Wisconsin Employment Discrimination Law
- Wisc. Stat. §§ 111.32, 111.321
- www.ncsl.org/documents/employ/
  DiscriminationChart-III.pdf

Wisconsin Surrogacy Law
- Wisc. Stat. § 69.14(h)
- www.selectsurrogate.com/surrogacy-laws-by
  -state.html
- www.surrogacyforall.com/Surrogacy-Law.html

Wisconsin Grandparent Rights
- wilawlibrary.gov/topics/familylaw/grandparents.php
- wilawlibrary.gov/topics/familylaw/childcustody.php

Wisconsin Annulment Law
- Wisc. Stat. § 767.313
- wilawlibrary.gov/topics/familylaw/divorce.php#annul

Wisconsin Parental Liability for Acts of Minors
- Wisc. Stat. § 895.035

Wisconsin Family Law Forms
- www.wicourts.gov/forms1/circuit/index.htm
- www.uslegalforms.com/rominger/divorce.htm

Wisconsin Vital Records (Birth, Marriage, Divorce, Death)
- www.cdc.gov/nchs/w2w.htm
- publicrecords.onlinesearches.com/Wisconsin.htm
- wilawlibrary.gov/topics/records/index.php#VITAL

Wisconsin Self-Help Services in Family Law Cases
- www.wicourts.gov/services/public/selfhelp
- wilawlibrary.gov/topics/shc.php

Wisconsin Family Law Legal Research (general)
- wilawlibrary.gov/topics/familylaw/index.php

Wisconsin State Legal Research
- www.ll.georgetown.edu/states/wisconsin.cfm
- www.loc.gov/law/help/guide/states/us-wi.php
- www.romingerlegal.com/state/wisconsin.html

Wisconsin Court Rules
- wilawlibrary.gov/topics/wisconsinlaw.php#WCC
- www.llrx.com/courtrules-gen/state-Wisconsin.html

WYOMING FAMILY LAW

Wyoming Family Code/Domestic Relations Code
- legisweb.state.wy.us/titles/statutes.htm
- www.law.cornell.edu/wex/table_family

Wyoming Marriage Law (formation)
- marriage.about.com/cs/marriagelicenses/p/wyoming.htm
- www.law.cornell.edu/wex/table_marriage

Wyoming Common Law Marriage
- topics.law.cornell.edu/wex/table_marriage
- www.buddybuddy.com/common.html

Wyoming Same-Sex Marriage, Domestic Partnership, Civil Union, Defense of Marriage Status (Baby-DOMA)
- en.wikipedia.org/wiki/LGBT_rights_in_Wyoming
- www.lambdalegal.org/publications/nationwide-status-same-sex
  -relationships
- www.ncsl.org/issues-research/human-services/civil-unions-and
  -domestic-partnership-statutes.aspx

Wyoming Divorce Law
- www.divorcelawinfo.com/states/wyo/wyoming.htm
- divorce.laws.com/divorce-in-wyoming

Wyoming Judicial Separation Law
- Wyo. Statutes Ann. § 20-2-106

Wyoming Alimony Law
- Wyo. Statutes Ann. § 20-2-114

Wyoming Property Division Law
- Wyo. Statutes Ann. § 20-2-106

Wyoming Child Custody Law
- Wyo. Statutes Ann. § 20-5-301
- www.courts.state.wy.us/DandCS.aspx

Wyoming Guardian Ad Litem and Attorney for Child
- Wyo. Statutes Ann. §§ 14-3-211, 14-6-216
- www.childwelfare.gov/systemwide/laws_policies/statutes
  /represent.pdf

Wyoming Child Support Law
- dfsweb.state.wy.us/child-support-enforcement/index.html
- legisweb.state.wy.us/statutes/titles/Title20/T20CH2AR3.htm
- www.supportguidelines.com/links.html
- www.acf.hhs.gov/programs/cse/extinf.html

Wyoming Paternity Law
- Wyo. Statutes Ann. § 14-2-504 (presumption of paternity)
- Wyo. Statutes Ann. § 14-2-817 (adjudication of paternity)
- paternity.uslegal.com/paternity-laws/wyoming-paternity-law/
- www.acf.hhs.gov/programs/cse/pubs/2002/reports/essentials
  /c8.html

Wyoming Legal Definition of Father
- Wyo. Statutes Ann. § 1-22-101 ("parent" "putative father")
- www.childwelfare.gov/systemwide/laws_policies/statutes
  /putative.pdf

Wyoming Adoption Law
- Wyo. Statutes Ann. §§ 1-22-102 et seq
- wyoming.gov/government.aspx (enter Adoption Child in the
  search box)
- laws.adoption.com/statutes/wyoming-adoption-laws.html
- law.findlaw.com/state-laws/adoption/wyoming

Wyoming Termination of Parental Rights Law
- Wyo. Statutes Ann. § 14-3-431
- legisweb.state.wy.us/statutes/titles/Title14/T14CH2AR3.htm
- www.law.cornell.edu/wex/table_emancipation
- www.childwelfare.gov/systemwide/laws_policies/statutes
  /groundtermin.cfm

Wyoming Putative Father Registry

- Wyo. Statutes Ann. § 1-22-117
- wyoming.gov/government.aspx (enter Putative Father Registry in the search box)
- laws.adoption.com/statutes/wyoming-laws,5.html
- www.courts.state.nh.us/probate/registrylist.pdf

Wyoming Emancipation Law

- Wyo. Statutes Ann. §§ 14-1-101 et seq.
- www.law.cornell.edu/topics/Table_Emancipation
- www.youthrights.net/index.php?title=Wyoming_Emancipation_Law

Wyoming Age of Majority

- Wyo. Statutes Ann. § 14-1-101
- law.findlaw.com/state-laws/minors-and-the-law/wyoming
- www.law.cornell.edu/topics/Table_Emancipation

Wyoming Child Protection/Protective Services

- Wyo. Statutes Ann. §§ 14-3-201 et seq.
- dfs.wy.gov/protective-services/cps/index.html

Wyoming Child Welfare Agencies

- dfsweb.state.wy.us/protective-services/index.html

Wyoming Juvenile Law

- www.ncjj.org/State/Wyoming.aspx
- www.ojp.usdoj.gov/saa/wy.htm

Wyoming Domestic Violence Law

- Wyo. Statutes Ann. §§ 35-21-101 et seq.
- www.aardvarc.org/dv/states/wydv.shtml

Wyoming Employment Discrimination Law

- Wyo. Statutes Ann. § 29-9-102
- www.ncsl.org/documents/employ/DiscriminationChart-III.pdf

Wyoming Surrogacy Law

- www.selectsurrogate.com/surrogacy-laws-by-state.html
- www.surrogacyforall.com/Surrogacy-Law.html

Wyoming Grandparent Rights

- Wyo. Statutes Ann. § 20-7-101
- grandparents.about.com/od/grandparentsrights/qt/Grandparent_Rights_in_Wyoming.htm

Wyoming Annulment Law

- Wyo. Statutes Ann. § 20-2-101
- statutes.laws.com/wyoming/Title20/chapter2

Wyoming Parental Liability for Acts of Minors

- Maximum liability $2,000
- Wyo. Statutes Ann. § 14-2-203

Wyoming Family Law Forms

- www.courts.state.wy.us/DandCS.aspx
- www.uslegalforms.com/rominger/divorce.htm

Wyoming Vital Records (Birth, Marriage, Divorce, Death)

- www.cdc.gov/nchs/w2w.htm
- publicrecords.onlinesearches.com/Wyoming.htm

Wyoming Self-Help Services in Family Law Cases

- www.wyominglawhelp.org/WY/index.cfm
- www.courts.state.wy.us/DandCS.aspx

Wyoming State Legal Research

- www.loc.gov/law/help/guide/states/us-wy.php
- www.ll.georgetown.edu/states/wyoming.cfm
- www.romingerlegal.com/state/wyoming.html

Wyoming Court Rules

- courts.state.wy.us/CourtRules.aspx
- www.llrx.com/courtrules-gen/state-Wyoming.html

Glossary

A

abandonment   Voluntarily leaving a child or ending communication with a child for a specific period or indefinitely without arranging for alternative care and supervision while away. Conduct that constitutes a relinquishing of one's parental responsibilities. See also criminal nonsupport, desertion.

abduction   The unlawful taking away of another.

abduction or enticement of a child   A tort involving serious interference with a parent's custody of his or her child. Also called tortious interference with custody, tortious interference with parental relationships.

abortion   An induced termination of a pregnancy in order to destroy an embryo or fetus. See also therapeutic abortion.

abrogation of adoption   A cancellation or nullification of a decree of adoption.

absolute divorce   A declaration by a court that the marriage is terminated so that the parties can remarry. Also called *complete divorce, divorce a vinculo matrimonii.* See also *divorce.*

abuse   See child abuse, domestic violence.

accounting   See financial statement.

account receivable   A business debt that has not yet been collected.

adjudicate   To decide by judicial process; to judge.

adjusted basis   A property's basis calculated after making allowed adjustments and deductions to the initial capital investment in the property (e.g., an increase in the basis because of a capital improvement). See also basis, tax effect.

adjusted gross income (AGI)   The total income from all of a person's taxable sources less specifically allowed deductions.

adoption   The legal process by which one person (the adoptive parent) becomes the parent of another person (the adoptee).

Adoption and Safe Families Act (ASFA)   A federal statute that requires states to take specific placement action on behalf of children in foster care, such as terminating parental rights in order to facilitate adoption after a designated period of time trying to reunite the child with its biological parents.

adoption by estoppel   See equitable adoption, estopped.

adoptive parent   A person who adopts another person.

ADR   See alternative dispute resolution.

adultery   (1) Voluntary sexual intercourse between a married person and someone other than his or her spouse. (2) Voluntary intimate sexual relations between a spouse and someone other than his or her spouse, irrespective of the specific sexual acts performed, the marital status of the nonspouse, or the gender of the nonspouse.

adversary   (1) An opponent. (2) Involving a dispute between opposing sides who argue their case before a neutral official such as a judge.

adversary proceeding   A proceeding in which both sides appear and argue their positions when court action is requested. See also ex parte proceeding.

adversary system   A method of resolving a legal dispute whereby the parties (alone or through their advocates) argue their conflicting claims before a neutral decision maker.

adverse   Opposed to; harmful, unfavorable.

adverse interest   A goal or claim of one person that is different from or opposed to the goal or claim of another.

AFDC   Aid to Families with Dependent Children, a public assistance program. See Temporary Assistance for Needy Families.

affiant   A person making an affidavit.

affidavit   A written statement containing facts, claims, or other legal positions given under oath or affirmation.

affinity   Relationship by marriage rather than by blood.

affirmative defense   A defense raising facts or arguments that will defeat the opponent's claim even if the opponent's fact allegations in the claim are proven.

agency adoption   An adoption through an agency. See also public agency adoption.

age of majority   The age at which children reach legal adulthood, usually 18, entitling them to many civil rights such as the right to manage their own affairs.

agreed judgment   See separation agreement.

aggrieved   Injured or wronged and thereby entitled to a remedy.

AGI   See adjusted gross income.

AI   See artificial insemination.

alien   A person who was born outside the United States, is still a subject of a foreign nation, and has not been naturalized in the United States.

alienage   The condition of being an alien.

alienation of affections   The tort of causing a diminishment of the marital relationship or interfering with the consortium rights that the plaintiff has with his or her spouse.

alimony   Money or other property paid in fulfillment of a duty to support one's spouse (or ex-spouse) after a legal separation, a divorce, or in some states, an annulment. Also called maintenance, spousal support. Note, however, that the Internal Revenue Service uses a broader definition of alimony for purposes of determining whether it is deductible. See also rehabilitative alimony.

alimony in gross   Alimony in the form of a single (lump sum) payment. Also called lump-sum alimony.

alimony pendente lite   See temporary alimony.

alimony trust   A trust to which a spouse or ex-spouse transfers funds that will be used to meet an alimony obligation.

alleged father   See putative father.

alternate payee   A nonworker who is entitled to receive all or part of the pension or other retirement benefits of a current or former worker pursuant to a qualified domestic relations order (QDRO).

alternative dispute resolution (ADR)   A method or procedure for resolving a legal dispute without litigating the dispute in a court or administrative agency. ADR methods include mediation, arbitration, and Med-Arb.

ambulance chasing   Approaching accident victims (or anyone else who might have a legal problem or claim) to encourage them to hire a particular attorney. If the attorney uses someone else to do the soliciting, the latter is called a *runner.* If this other person uses deception or fraud in the solicitation, he or she is sometimes called a *capper* or a *steerer.*

a mensa et thoro   See divorce a mensa et thoro.

American Bar Association   A voluntary national organization of attorneys.

American Jurisprudence, 2d   A national legal encyclopedia.

American Law Reports   A set of reporters that contain selected opinions from many different courts. In addition, the A.L.R. volumes contain research papers—called *annotations*—that give surveys of the law on particular issues found in the opinions.

amnesty   Forgiveness; a pardon issued by the state.

ancillary   Supplementary; subordinate; auxiliary, aiding.

annotated   Organized by subject matter with research references or other commentary.

annotation   (1) A note or commentary on something. (2) A research paper in one of the sets of American Law Reports.

annuitant   Recipient of an annuity.

annuity   A fixed sum payable periodically for life or for a specific period of time. The recipient of the annuity is called the annuitant.

annulment   A declaration by a court that a valid marriage never existed.

answer   A party's pleading that responds to the petition or complaint of an opposing party. It is the first pleading of the defendant that responds to the plaintiff's claims.

antenuptial agreement   See premarital agreement.

anticontact rule   An advocate should not contact an opposing party without permission of the latter's attorney. If the party is unrepresented, the advocate must not convey the impression that the advocate is *disinterested* (uninvolved).

antimiscegenation law   See miscegenation.

antinepotism   See nepotism.

appearance   Formally going before a court.

appellant   The party bringing an appeal because of disagreement with the decision of a lower tribunal.

appellate brief   A document submitted (filed) by a party to an appellate court (and served on an opposing party) in which arguments are presented as to why the appellate court should affirm (approve), reverse, or otherwise modify what a lower court has done.

appellee   The party against whom an appeal is brought.

appreciation   An increase in the value of property after it is acquired.

arbitration   A method of alternative dispute resolution (ADR) in which the parties avoid litigation by submitting their dispute to a neutral third person (the arbitrator) who renders a decision resolving the dispute.

arm's length   As strangers. Pertaining to how parties would treat each other if they were strangers looking out for their own self-interests with no confidential or other relationship between them that would cause one to expect the other to provide a special advantage or to act with fairness.

arrearages   See arrears.

arrears   Payments that are due but have not been made. Also called arrearages.

ART   See assisted reproductive technology.

artificial insemination (AI)   Inserting sperm into the uterus by a method other than sexual intercourse.

ASFA   See Adoption and Safe Families Act.

assign   To transfer rights or property to someone. The noun is *assignment*. The person who makes the transfer is called the *assignor*. The person who receives the transfer is called the *assignee* or the *assign*.

assignee   The person to whom ownership or rights are transferred. See also assign.

assignment   See assign.

assignor   See assign.

assisted reproductive technology (ART)   Fertility treatment to help a woman become pregnant by procedures such as surgically removing eggs from a woman's ovaries, combining the eggs with sperm in a laboratory, and returning the fertilized eggs to the woman's body or donating them to another woman.

at arm's length   See arm's length.

at common law   During a time in our early history when law was created by court opinions and legislatures, often before it was changed by later legislatures. See also common law.

attachment   (1) A court authorization of the seizure of a person's property so that it can be used to satisfy a judgment against him or her. (2) The seizure of such property as security for such a judgment.

attestation clause   A clause in a document stating that you saw (witnessed) someone sign a document or perform other tasks related to the validity of the document.

attorney-client privilege   A client or a client's attorney can refuse to disclose any confidential (private) communication between them if the purpose of the communication was to facilitate the provision of legal services to the client.

attorney in fact   See power of attorney.

attorney work-product   See work-product rule.

autonomy, right to personal   See right to privacy.

a vinculo matrimonii   See divorce a vinculo matrimonii.

B

baby-buying   See black-market adoption.

basis   One's initial capital investment in property, usually the cost of acquiring the property. Also called cost basis. An *adjusted basis* is calculated after making allowed adjustments and deductions to the initial capital investment (e.g., an increase in the basis because of a capital improvement).

bastard   A child born to parents who are not married to each other and who never legitimated the child. Also called illegitimate child, nonmarital child, child of an informal relationship, child out of wedlock, child with no presumed father.

bastardy   Pertaining to a child born to unmarried parents who never legitimated the child. Also called illegitimacy.

battered woman syndrome   A woman's psychological helplessness or paralysis because of conditions such as financial dependence, loneliness, guilt, shame, and fear of reprisal from her husband or boyfriend who has repeatedly subjected her to physical, sexual, and/or emotional abuse in the past.

battery   An unpermitted and intentional physical contact with a person that is harmful or offensive.

bench trial   A nonjury trial.

beneficial interest   A right to a benefit from property or an estate as opposed to the legal ownership of that property or estate.

beneficiary   The person named in a document such as a will or insurance policy to receive property or other benefit.

bequest   A gift of personal property in a will. (In some states, a bequest can be a gift of personal property or real property in a will.)

best interests attorney (BIA)   An attorney who provides legal representation for a child to protect the child's best interests without being bound by the child's directives or objectives.

best interests of the child   A standard used by a court to decide what would best serve a child's welfare when the court must make custody, visitation, adoption, guardianship, and change-of-name decisions.

BFOQ   See bona fide occupational qualification.

BIA   See best interests attorney.

bias   Prejudice for or against something or someone. A predisposition, inclination, or tendency to think or to act in a certain way. A danger of prejudgment.

bifurcated divorce   A case in which the dissolution of the marriage—the divorce itself—is tried separately from other issues in the marriage such as property division.

bigamy   Marrying while still in a valid, undissolved marriage with someone else.

bilateral divorce   A divorce granted by a court when both the husband and the wife are present before the court.

biological parent   One's parent by blood.

black market adoption An illegal adoption that involves a payment beyond reasonable expenses in order to facilitate the adoption. Also called baby-buying.

boilerplate Standard or often-used language that is commonly found in the same kind of document. Standard verbiage.

bona fide occupational qualification (BFOQ) An employment qualification based on gender, religion, or other characteristic that is reasonably necessary for the normal operation of a particular business and hence is not an illegal requirement under federal employment discrimination laws.

bona fides Good faith. The absence of wrongful intent or desire to take inappropriate advantage of someone.

bond See surety bond.

book value The value at which an asset is carried on the balance sheet.

bridge-the-gap alimony See rehabilitative alimony.

bundled legal services All tasks needed to represent a client on a legal matter; all-inclusive legal services. See also unbundled legal services.

burden of proof The responsibility of proving a fact at trial.

C

canon law Church or ecclesiastical law.

capacity (1) The legal power to do something such as enter a contract or a relationship. Also called legal capacity. (2) The ability to understand the nature and effects of one's actions or inactions.

capital improvements Structural improvements on property, as opposed to ordinary maintenance work.

capper See ambulance chasing.

CAPTA See Child Abuse Prevention and Treatment Act.

caption The heading or introductory part of a pleading or other document that identifies what it is, the names of the parties, the court involved, etc.

caregiver alimony Alimony for an ex-spouse who cannot be self-supporting because of his or her need to care for a disabled child.

CARTWHEEL A research technique designed to help you think of a large variety of words and phrases to check in indexes, tables of contents, and online search engines.

CASA See court appointed special advocate.

case law The body of law found in court opinions.

cause of action (1) A legally acceptable reason for bringing a suit. A rule that constitutes a legal theory for bringing a suit. (2) The facts that give a person a right to judicial relief. When you state a cause of action, you list the facts that give you a right to judicial relief against the wrongdoer.

ceremonial marriage A marriage that is entered in compliance with statutory requirements (e.g., obtaining a marriage license, having the marriage performed by an authorized person before witnesses). A marriage other than a common law marriage. Also called formal marriage, statutory marriage.

certificate of service See proof of service.

chambers A judge's private office.

chancellor A judge in a court of equity.

chattel See personal property.

child abuse Serious physical, emotional, or sexual mistreatment of a child that is not the result of accident or circumstances beyond the control of the parent or guardian.

Child Abuse Prevention and Treatment Act (CAPTA) A federal statute that helps fund state programs for the identification, prevention, and treatment of child abuse and neglect (42 U.S.C. § 5101).

Child in Need of Supervision and Services (CHIPS) See status offense, juvenile delinquent.

child maltreatment An act or failure to act by a parent or caretaker that intentionally or carelessly results in physical or emotional harm to a child or that presents an imminent risk of such harm to a child.

child neglect The failure of a parent or other caregiver to provide the basic needs of a child, including physical needs (e.g., food and shelter), emotional needs, medical needs, and educational needs.

child protective services A state agency that investigates child neglect and abuse, offers assistance to families of children at risk, and administers foster care or other placement programs.

child-support guidelines State-mandated rules for calculating the amount of child support owed by adults obligated to pay such support (obligors).

Chinese Wall Steps taken to prevent a tainted employee (e.g., attorney or paralegal) from having any contact with the case of a particular client because of the conflict of interest the employee has created in that case. A tainted employee shielded by a Chinese Wall becomes a quarantined employee.

CHIPS (Child in Need of Supervision and Services) See status offense, juvenile delinquent.

choice of law A selection of which law to apply when a court is being asked to apply the law of two states or two countries.

choice of venue See venue.

circumstantial evidence Evidence of one fact from which another fact (not personally observed or known) can be inferred. Also called indirect evidence.

civil Pertaining to a private right or matter. Noncriminal; nonmilitary.

civil contempt The refusal of a party to comply with a court order (usually issued for the benefit of another), which can lead to punishment (including incarceration) until the party complies with the order.

civil union A same-sex legal relationship in which the individuals in the relationship have some or all of the same state benefits and responsibilities as individuals in a marriage.

classification (1) A group the government treats differently from another group in that the government discriminates for or against that group. (2) The government's different treatment of one group over another. (3) The identification of property as either separate property or marital property (or community property).

CLE See continuing legal education.

clean hands See dirty hands.

clear and convincing evidence A standard of proof that is met when the evidence demonstrates that the existence of a disputed fact is much more probable than its nonexistence. This standard is stronger than preponderance of the evidence but not as strong as beyond a reasonable doubt.

code A book or set of books that contain rules or laws organized by subject matter. The state code, also called the *state statutory code*, is a collection of statutes written by the state legislature, organized by subject matter.

cohabit To live together in an intimate (usually sexual) relationship in the manner of a husband and wife. The noun is *cohabitation*. Although a married couple cohabits, the word is more often used in reference to unmarried couples.

cohabitation Living together in an intimate (usually sexual) relationship in the manner of a husband and wife. A de facto husband and wife relationship. The verb is *cohabit*. Although a married couple cohabits, the word *cohabitation* is more often used in reference to unmarried couples.

cohabitation agreement A contract by persons in an intimate relationship who are not married to each other (and who intend to stay unmarried indefinitely) that covers financial and related matters while they are living together and upon the end of the relationship by death or separation.

cohabitants Two persons living together in an intimate (usually sexual) relationship.

collaborative law A method of practicing law in which the attorneys and parties seek to resolve their family-law differences without litigation. To encourage settlement, the attorneys refuse to continue representing the parties if litigation becomes necessary; the parties must find other attorneys if the case goes to trial. Collaborative law is a form of *limited-scope representation* and *alternative dispute resolution (ADR)*.

collateral attack A challenge or attack against the validity of a judgment raised in a different proceeding from the one that rendered the judgment.

collusion (1) An agreement to commit fraud. (2) An agreement by spouses that one or both will lie to the court in order to help secure their divorce.

collusive divorce A divorce obtained in a proceeding in which the husband and wife agreed to lie to the court in order to facilitate the granting of the divorce.

comity The court's decision to give effect to the laws and judicial decisions of another state as a matter of deference and mutual respect even if no obligation exists to do so.

commingling Mixing together. (Examples: mixing separate property with marital property; mixing client funds with funds needed to run an office.)

common law (1) Judge-made law in the absence of controlling statutory law or other higher law. (2) Court opinions, all of case law. (3) The legal system of England and of those countries such as the United States whose legal system is based on England's. (4) The case law and statutory law in England and in the American colonies before the American Revolution. See also *at common law*.

common-law marriage A marriage entered without license or traditional ceremony by persons who (a) agree to marry, (b) live together as husband and wife, and (c) hold themselves out as married. A marriage of two people who have not gone through a ceremonial marriage. Called *informal marriage* in Texas.

common-law property Property acquired during the marriage in a state other than a community-property state. (Older definition: Property acquired during the marriage that is owned by the spouse who earned it or who has title to it.)

common representation See multiple representation.

community property Property in which each spouse has a 50 percent interest because it was acquired during the marriage other than by gift, will, or intestate succession (inheritance) to only one of the spouses.

comparative rectitude A comparison of the wrongdoing of two spouses in causing the breakdown of the marriage so that the divorce can be given to the spouse least at fault.

compelling state interest An interest that is of the highest order; an interest that has a clear justification in the necessities of national or community life.

compensatory damages Money paid to restore an injured party to his or her position prior to the injury or other loss.

competent (1) Using the knowledge and skill that are reasonably necessary to represent a particular client. (2) Allowed (having the legal capacity) to give testimony because the person understands the obligation to tell the truth, has the ability to communicate, and has knowledge of the topic of his or her testimony. The noun is *competency*.

complaint (1) A plaintiff's first pleading that states a claim against the defendant. Also called petition. (2) A formal criminal charge.

conclusive presumption An assumption or inference of fact that a party will not be allowed to dispute or rebut.

concurrent estate An estate that is owned by two or more persons at the same time.

concurrent jurisdiction Subject-matter jurisdiction that resides in more than one kind of court in the same judicial system.

condonation An express or implied forgiveness by the innocent spouse of the marital fault committed by the other spouse.

conducive to divorce Tending to encourage divorce.

confidential Pertaining to information that others do not have a right to receive.

confidential marriage A ceremonial marriage entered with fewer technical/procedural requirements and greater privacy than a traditional ceremonial marriage.

confidential relationship See fiduciary relationship.

conflict of interest Divided loyalties that actually or potentially harm (or disadvantage) someone who is owed undivided loyalty.

conflict of laws An inconsistency between the laws of different legal systems such as two states or two countries.

conflicts check A determination of whether a conflict of interest exists that might disqualify a law office from representing a client or from continuing the representation.

Confrontation Clause A clause in the U.S. Constitution stating that a criminal defendant has a right to confront an accusing witness face-to-face and to cross-examine him or her. U.S. Const. amend. VI.

conjugal Pertaining to marriage; appropriate for married persons.

connivance A willingness or a consent by one spouse that a marital wrong be done by the other spouse.

consanguinity Relationship by blood.

consent See informed consent.

conservator A person appointed by the court to manage the affairs of persons who are not competent to do so on their own.

consideration Something of value that is exchanged between parties. It can be an act, a forbearance (not performing an act), a promise to perform an act, or a promise to refrain from performing an act.

consortium A right to the benefits that are naturally expected in a particular family relationship. See also filial consortium, loss of consortium, parental consortium, spousal consortium.

constitution The basic legal document of a government that allocates power among the three branches of the government and that may also enumerate fundamental rights of individuals.

constitutionalization Changes in state law that result from interpretation of the U.S. Constitution by the U.S. Supreme Court and other federal courts.

constructive desertion (1) A spouse's conduct that justifies the other spouse's departure from the home. (2) A spouse's rejection of a sincere offer of reconciliation from the spouse who left the home without justification.

constructive service See substituted service.

constructive trust A trust created by operation of law to prevent unjust enrichment by someone who has improperly obtained property through fraud, duress, abuse of confidence, or other wrongful conduct.

consummation (1) Sexual intercourse for the first time, particularly between spouses. (2) The completion of a marriage by the first act of sexual intercourse.

contact veto A denial of consent to have contact between the adoptee and the biological parent, although permission for the release of identifying information might be given.

contempt Conduct that defies or disrespects the authority of a court or legislative body. When the court is defied or disrespected, it is called *contempt of court*. See also civil contempt, criminal contempt.

contested Challenged; opposed or disputed.

contingency An event that may or may not occur.

contingent Conditional; dependent on something that may or may not happen.

contingent fee A fee that is paid only if the case is successfully resolved by litigation or settlement. (The fee is also referred to as a contingency.)

continuing, exclusive jurisdiction (CEJ) The authority of a court, obtained by compliance with the Uniform Interstate Family Act (UIFA) to make all initial and modifying support decisions in a case to the exclusion of courts in any other state. See also exclusive, continuing jurisdiction.

continuing jurisdiction A court's power (by retaining jurisdiction) to modify its orders after entering judgment.

continuing legal education Training in the law (usually short term) that a person receives after completing his or her formal legal training.

contract A legally enforceable agreement. The elements of most contracts are offer, acceptance, and consideration. Some contracts must be in writing. See also cohabitation agreement, premarital agreement, separation agreement.

contract cohabitation See *cohabitation agreement.*

conversion (1) Changing a legal separation into a divorce after the parties have lived apart for a designated period of time. The time they lived apart becomes a ground for divorce, called a conversion divorce or a convertible divorce. (2) An intentional interference with another's personal property, consisting of an exercise of dominion over it.

conversion divorce, convertible divorce See conversion.

conveyance The transfer of an interest in property. The verb is *convey.*

coparenting Shared responsibility by two adults to raise a child, regardless of the marital status or sexual orientation of the adults.

copulate To engage in sexual intercourse.

corespondent The person who allegedly had sexual relations with a defendant charged with adultery.

corporal punishment Punishment inflicted on the physical body.

corporeal See tangible.

Corpus Juris Secundum (CJS) A national legal encyclopedia.

corroborate To introduce additional evidence of a fact in dispute.

corroboration Additional evidence of a fact in dispute.

cosigner A person who signs a document along with the main signer, usually to agree to pay the debt created by the document in the event that the main signer fails to pay it.

costs See court costs.

counterclaim A claim by one side in a case (usually the defendant) that is filed in response to a claim asserted by an opponent (usually the plaintiff).

court appointed special advocate (CASA) A volunteer appointed by the court to undertake special assignments pertaining to children in the court system.

court costs Charges or fees (paid to and imposed by the court) that are directly related to litigation in that court.

court opinion The written explanation by a court of why it reached a certain conclusion or holding.

covenant A promise or agreement.

covenant marriage A form of ceremonial marriage (a) that is entered upon proof of premarital counseling and a promise to seek marital counseling when needed during the marriage, and (b) that is dissolved upon separation for a designated period or upon proof of marital fault. Also called high-test marriage.

coveture The legal status of a married woman whereby her civil existence for many purposes merged with (was covered up by) that of her husband.

coveture fraction The portion of a pension earned during a marriage if part of the pension of a married worker was earned when the worker was not married.

CP See custodial parent.

credit clouding Notifying a creditor or credit bureau that a debtor is delinquent on certain debts such as child support.

criminal contempt The refusal of a party to comply with a court order, which can lead to punishment (including incarceration) because of the repeated or aggravated nature of the refusal.

criminal conversation The tort that occurs when the defendant has sexual relations with the plaintiff's spouse.

criminal homicide Causing the death of a person without justification or excuse.

criminal law The body of law covering acts declared to be crimes by the legislature for statutory crimes or by the courts for common law crimes.

criminal neglect of family See criminal nonsupport.

criminal nonsupport The willful, repeated, or aggravated failure to pay support for a person that the defendant is obligated to support from available resources. Also called nonsupport, criminal neglect of family, abandonment of children.

cruelty The infliction of serious physical or mental suffering on another.

cryobank See sperm bank.

cryopreservation The storage of cells or whole tissues at sub-zero temperatures for later thawing and use. For example, freezing embryos from an ART cycle for potential use (transfer or implantation) at a later time.

curtesy The right of a husband to the lifetime use (called a *life estate*) of all the land his deceased wife owned during the marriage (if issue were born of the marriage).

custodial parent (CP) The parent with whom the child is living; the parent with physical custody of the child. Also called residential parent. For federal income tax purposes, a custodial parent is the parent with whom the child lived for the greater number of nights. The other parent is the noncustodial parent (NCP).

custodial responsibility See physical custody.

custodian A person or institution in charge of something. A caretaker. Also called guardian.

custody (1) The right to the care and control of a person or thing. (2) The actual care and control that someone has over a person or thing. See also joint legal custody, joint physical custody, legal custody, physical custody, sole legal custody, sole physical custody, split custody.

D

damages Money paid because of a wrongful injury or loss to person or property.

Deadbeat Parents Punishment Act (DPPA) A federal statute that makes it a crime for a parent to repeatedly fail to pay child support for a child living in another state or who crosses state lines to avoid paying child support. (18 U.S.C. § 228.)

debtor One who owes a debt.

decedent The person who has died; the deceased.

decision-making responsibility See legal custody.

declaratory judgment A binding judgment that establishes (declares) rights or duties but does nor order their enforcement.

decree nisi A provisional court decree that will become final within a designated time unless a party files an objection to the decree that the court accepts.

deep pocket (1) An individual, business, or other organization with resources to pay a potential judgment. (2) Sufficient assets for this purpose. The opposite of *shallow pocket.*

de facto adoption See equitable adoption.

de facto marriage A marriage in fact. A relationship of a cohabiting couple that is recognized as a marriage for limited purposes even though the relationship does not meet the requirements of a ceremonial, common law, or putative marriage, despite the fact that the couple has acted in a marriage-like manner.

default divorce A divorce that is granted because of the failure of a party to appear, plead, or otherwise defend the divorce action of the other party.

default judgment A judgment against a party for failure to file a required pleading or otherwise respond to an opponent's claim.

defendant The party against whom a claim is brought at the commencement of litigation.

defense Allegations of fact or legal theories offered to offset or defeat claims or demands.

Defense of Marriage Act (DOMA) A federal statute that says (1) one state is not required to give full faith and credit to a same-sex marriage entered in another state (28 U.S.C. § 1738C), and (2) for federal purposes, only opposite-sex marriage is recognized (1 U.S.C. § 7).

defined-benefit plan (DB) A pension plan that provides a set or defined pension benefit upon retirement, usually based on salary and years of employment.

defined-contribution plan   A pension plan consisting of individual accounts for each worker whose retirement benefit depends on the amount in his or her account.

dependency   (1) The condition of a child who has been placed in the custody of the state because the child has been abused, neglected, or abandoned. (2) Pertaining to a child who lacks basic care through no fault of the parent or guardian.

dependent   (1) Abused, neglected, or abandoned. (2) Lacking basic care through no fault of a parent or guardian.

deponent   A person questioned in a deposition.

deposed   Asked questions in a deposition.

deposition   A discovery device in which one party questions another party (or questions the other party's witness), usually outside the courtroom.

depreciation   A decrease in value of property after it is acquired.

descent   Acquiring property by inheritance rather than by will; acquiring property from a decedent who died intestate.

desertion   The voluntary departure of one spouse from another (without justification or consent) with the intent not to return to resume cohabitation with the spouse. Also called abandonment. See also constructive desertion.

devise   A gift of real property in a will. (In some states, a devise can be a gift of real property or personal property in a will.) The person making the gift of property is the *devisor*. The person receiving it is the *devisee*.

devisee/devisor   See devise.

digest   (1) Set of books containing brief summaries of court opinions arranged by topic and by court or jurisdiction. (2) A summary of a document or a series of documents.

dilatory   Causing delay, usually without merit or justification.

direct attack   A challenge or attack against the validity of a judgment raised in the same proceeding that rendered the judgment (e.g., an appeal).

dirty hands   Wrongdoing or other inappropriate behavior that would make it unfair or inequitable to allow persons to assert a right or a defense they would normally have. Also called *unclean hands*. A person without dirty hands is said to have *clean hands*.

disability   Not having the legal capacity to perform a certain task such as entering a contract.

disaffirm   To repudiate or cancel. To exercise a right to repudiate and refuse to perform one's own contract. (A right enjoyed by minors.)

disbursement   Payment.

discharge   Extinguish; forgive a debt so that it is no longer owed.

discipline   Imposing correction or punishment.

discoverable   Pertaining to information or other materials an opponent can obtain through deposition, interrogatories, or other discovery device.

discovery   (1) Devices used by parties to force information from each other before trial to aid in trial preparation. Examples of such devices include interrogatories and depositions. (2) Devices used by parties to force information from each other after trial to aid in the enforcement of the trial judgment.

discrimination   Treating things or people differently depending on which group they are in. Differential treatment.

disinterested   Not working for one side or the other in a controversy; not deriving benefit if one side of a dispute wins or loses; objective.

dissipation   The improper reduction or waste of marital assets that should have been available for property division upon divorce.

dissolution   A divorce. A court's termination of a marriage for specified grounds. In a few states, however, a divorce is the result of a court proceeding in which one spouse establishes grounds against the other, whereas a dissolution is the result of a joint petition in which both spouses ask the court for the same relief pursuant to the separation agreement that they have negotiated.

diversity of citizenship   The disputing parties are citizens of different states and the amount in controversy exceeds $75,000. This diversity gives subject-matter jurisdiction to a federal trial court—a U.S. District Court. It is called diversity jurisdiction.

divided custody   See split custody.

divided loyalty   Representing a client when a conflict of interest exists. See conflict of interest.

divisible divorce   A divorce judgment or decree that is enforceable only in part. The part of a divorce decree that dissolves the marriage is enforceable (if the plaintiff was domiciled in the state), but the part of the divorce that ordered alimony, child support, or a property division is not enforceable (if the court did not have personal jurisdiction over the defendant).

divorce   A declaration by a court that a validly entered marriage is terminated so that the parties are no longer married to each other. Also called dissolution, marital dissolution, divorce a vinculo matrimonii (divorce from the chains of marriage). See *dissolution* for a distinction between divorce and dissolution in some states.

divorce a mensa et thoro   Divorce from bed and hearth; divorce from bed and board. A legal separation. A declaration by a court that parties can live apart even though they are still married to each other. Also called separation from bed and board.

divorce a vinculo matrimonii   Divorce from the chains of marriage. A declaration by a court that a marriage has been dissolved so that the parties are no longer married to each other. Also called divorce, absolute divorce.

divorce kit   A package of do-it-yourself materials containing standard forms and written instructions on how to obtain a divorce without an attorney.

DNA testing   Genetic testing on deoxyribonucleic acid removed from cells.

doctor-patient privilege   A patient or a patient's doctor can refuse to disclose any confidential (private) communications between them that relate to the patient's medical care.

DOMA   See Defense of Marriage Act.

domestic partners   (1) Two same-sex or opposite-sex legal unmarried individuals who are emotionally and financially interdependent and who have some of the same state benefits and responsibilities as individuals in a marriage. (2) "Two persons of the same sex or opposite-sex, not married to one another, who for a significant period of time share a primary residence and a life together as a couple." American Law Institute, *Principles of the Law of Family Dissolution*, § 6.03 (2000).

domestic partnership   A same-sex or opposite-sex legal relationship of unmarried individuals who are emotionally and financially interdependent and who have some of the same state benefits and responsibilities as individuals in a marriage. See also domestic partners.

domestic-relations exception   Federal courts do not have subject-matter jurisdiction over the granting of divorce, alimony, or child custody even if there is diversity of citizenship among the parties, which will usually give such jurisdiction to a federal court.

domestic tort   See marital tort.

domestic violence (DV)   Actual or threatened injury or abuse of one member of a family or household by another member. Under § 102 of the *Model Code on Domestic and Family Violence*, 1. "Domestic or family violence" means the occurrence of one or more of the following acts by a family or household member, but does not include acts of self-defense: (a) Attempting to cause or causing physical harm to another family or household member; (b) Placing a family or household member in fear of physical harm; or (c) Causing a family or household member to engage involuntarily in sexual activity by force, threat of force, or duress. (National Council of Juvenile and Family Court Judges, www.ncjfcj.org/images/stories/dept/fvd/pdf/modecode_fin_printable.pdf.).

domicile The place where a person has been physically present with the intent to make that place a permanent home (or with no intent to make any other place a permanent home); the place to which one intends to return when away. A residence, on the other hand, is simply the place where you are living at a particular time. A person can have more than one residence, but generally can have only one domicile.

domicile by choice A domicile selected by a person with the legal capacity to choose.

domiciliary One who is domiciled in a particular place.

domiciliary state The state where one has a domicile.

donee The person who receives a gift.

donor The person who gives a gift.

DOS Date of separation.

dower The right of a widow to the lifetime use (called a *life estate*) of one-third of the land her deceased husband owned during the marriage. (Owned means *fee simple*, the most complete form of ownership possible.) For dower to exist, some states imposed the requirement that she die leaving issue capable of inheriting the estate.

DPL See due process of law.

due diligence Reasonable efforts to find and verify factual information needed to carry out an obligation, to avoid harming someone, or to make an important decision (e.g., to locate a parent).

due process of law (DPL) Both procedural due process and substantive due process. See these terms.

durational alimony See rehabilitative alimony.

duress The unlawful use of force or threats that overcomes the will so that a person does something he or she does not want to do. Illegal coercion.

E

ecclesiastical Pertaining to the church. See also canon law.

ecclesiastical court A court that resolves disputes on church or canon law.

ECJ See exclusive, continuing jurisdiction.

EDD See electronic data discovery.

e-discovery See electronic data discovery (EDD).

EEOC See Equal Employment Opportunity Commission.

elective abortion An abortion that is not undertaken to safeguard the mother's life or health.

elective share The percentage of a deceased spouse's estate that the surviving spouse can choose (elect) to receive despite what the will of the deceased spouse provided for the surviving spouse. Also called right of election, statutory share, forced share.

electronic data discovery (EDD) The discovery of data found in e-mails, spreadsheets, databases, and other digital formats. Also called *e-discovery*.

electronic house arrest (EHA) See house arrest.

element A portion of a rule that is a precondition to the applicability of the entire rule.

element in contention The element or portion of a rule about which the parties cannot agree. The disagreement may be over the definition of the element, whether the facts fit within the element, or both.

elevated scrutiny See intermediate scrutiny.

emancipated Legally independent of one's parent or legal guardian. The noun is *emancipation*.

emancipation See emancipated.

embryo An egg that has been fertilized by a sperm in the early stage of development; it has undergone one or more divisions. The product of conception to about the eighth week of pregnancy.

encrypt Convert text into a code that renders it incomprehensible until it is reconverted to a readable format by an authorized recipient.

enjoin To prohibit something through injunction.

Enoch Arden divorce A divorce granted on the ground that a spouse has disappeared for a designated number of years with no explanation.

Enoch Arden presumption A spouse is presumed to be dead after being missing without explanation for a designated number of years despite due diligence in attempting to locate him or her.

enterprise goodwill An asset of a business or practice that exists by virtue of its business location, existing arrangements with suppliers and employees, and anticipated future customer base, but is not dependent on the continued presence of a particular individual in the business or practice.

enticement of a child See abduction or enticement of a child.

enticement of a spouse A tort in which the defendant encourages the plaintiff's spouse to leave or to stay away from the plaintiff.

EPL See equal protection of law.

Equal Employment Opportunity Commission (EEOC) The federal agency that enforces federal laws against employment discrimination (www.eeoc.gov).

equal protection of law (EPL) The constitutional requirement that the government treat one group or class the same as it treats another group or class in like circumstances. Shortened to equal protection.

equitable adoption A child will be considered the adopted child of a person who intended to adopt the child and acted as the child's parent but failed to go through the formal adoption procedures. Also called adoption by estoppel, de facto adoption, virtual adoption.

equitable distribution The just and fair, but not necessarily equal, division of property between spouses upon divorce.

equitable estoppel The voluntary conduct of a person will preclude him or her from asserting rights against another who justifiably relied on the conduct and who would suffer damage or injury if the person is now allowed to repudiate the conduct. Also called estoppel in pais.

equitable remedy A form of relief (e.g., injunction, specific performance, or constructive trust) that may be available when remedies at law (e.g., damages) are not adequate.

escalation clause A provision in a contract or other document that provides for an increase or decrease in the amount to be paid based upon a factor over which the parties do not have complete control.

escrow Property (e.g., money, a deed) delivered to a neutral person (e.g., bank, escrow agent) to be held until a specified condition occurs, at which time the property is to be delivered to a designated person.

essentials test Did the matter go to the heart or essence of the marriage relationship?

estate (1) All of the assets and liabilities of a decedent upon his or her death. (2) The legal entity that exists upon a person's death, consisting of that person's assets and liabilities. (3) An interest in real or personal property. (4) The extent and nature of one's interest in real or personal property. (5) All of the property of whatever kind owned by a person. (6) Land.

estate tax A tax on money or other property that is transferred by someone who dies leaving a valid will (testate) or without such a will (intestate). There is a federal estate tax and some states impose a state estate tax.

estopped Prevented from asserting a right or a defense because it would be unfair or inequitable to allow the assertion. The noun is *estoppel*.

estoppel See estopped.

ethics Rules that embody standards of behavior to which members of an occupation, profession, or other organization are expected to conform.

et ux   And wife.

evidence   Anything offered to establish the existence or nonexistence of a fact in dispute.

exclusive, continuing jurisdiction (ECJ)   The authority of a court, obtained by compliance with the Uniform Child Custody Jurisdiction and Enforcement Act (UCCJEA), to make all initial and modifying custody decisions in a case to the exclusion of courts in any other state. See also continuing, exclusive jurisdiction.

exculpatory agreement   An agreement that relieves a party from liability.

execute   (1) To take needed steps to create a legal document. (2) To perform or carry out according to its terms.

executed   Performed or carried out according to its terms.

execution   (1) A command or writ to a court officer (e.g., sheriff) to seize and sell the property of the losing litigant in order to satisfy the judgment debt. Also called general execution and writ of execution. (2) Carrying out or performing some act to its completion (e.g., the process of carrying into effect the decisions in a judgment). (3) Signing and doing whatever else is needed to finalize a document and make it legal. (4) Implementing a death sentence.

execution of judgment   The process of carrying out or satisfying the judgment of a court. Using a writ of execution, a court officer (e.g., a sheriff) is commanded to seize the property of the losing litigant, sell it, and pay the winning litigant out of the proceeds.

executor   A person designated in a will to carry out the terms of the will and handle related matters. If a female, this person is sometimes called an *executrix*. See also personal representative.

executory   Unperformed as yet.

executory contract   A contract in which the parties bind themselves to future activity. A contract that is not yet fully completed or performed.

executrix   See executor.

exemplary damages   See punitive damages.

ex parte   With only one side present (usually the plaintiff or petitioner) when court action is requested.

ex parte divorce   A divorce rendered by a court when only one of the spouses participates or appears in court. Also called unilateral divorce.

ex parte proceeding   A proceeding in which only one side appears and argues its position when court action is requested. See also adversary proceeding.

expectancy   The bare hope (but more than wishful thinking) of receiving a property interest.

expectation damages   Money to compensate for the loss of what was reasonably anticipated from a contract that was not performed.

expedited procedure   An accelerated procedure achieved by bypassing some of the procedural steps that are normally required.

express   Explicitly stated, rather than merely implied or inferred.

express contract   An agreement or contract whose terms are explicitly stated by the parties.

F

FACE   See Freedom of Access to Clinic Entrances Act.

facilitation of divorce   That which makes a divorce easier to obtain.

fact particularization (FP)   A fact-gathering technique to generate a large list of factual questions (who, what, where, how, when, and why) that will help you obtain a specific and comprehensive picture of all available facts that are relevant to a legal issue.

fair employment practices agency (FEPA)   A state or local government agency that enforces state or local employment discrimination laws, often in coordination with the Equal Employment Opportunity Commission (EEOC), which enforces federal employment discrimination laws.

fair market value   The price that could be obtained in an open market between a willing buyer and a willing seller dealing at arm's length, neither being under any compulsion to buy or sell and both having reasonable knowledge of or access to the relevant facts. See also arm's length.

family-automobile rule   See family purpose doctrine.

family expense act   A state statute that makes spouses jointly liable for the basic support needs of the family. Creditors that extend credit for such needs can reach the property of either spouse.

family law   The body of law that defines relationships, rights, and duties in the formation, ongoing existence, and dissolution of marriage and other family units.

family purpose doctrine   An owner of a car (or a person controlling the use of a car) is liable for the negligence committed by a family member using the car for a family purpose. Also called family automobile rule.

family violence indicator (FVI)   A designation placed on a participant in a child-support case indicating that he or she may be a victim of domestic violence so that access to information about the participant is restricted.

fault grounds   Marital wrongs that will justify the granting of a divorce (e.g., adultery).

federalization   Changes in state law that result from (a) laws written by the federal legislature (Congress) and (b) interpretations of the U.S. Constitution by federal courts.

Federal Parent Locator Service (FPLS)   A program of the U.S. Office of Child Support Enforcement that uses data in federal databases to locate parents for purposes of child-support enforcement. Requests for information from the FPLS go through a state parent locator service (SPLS).

fee-sharing   See fee-splitting.

fee-splitting   (1) Giving a nonlawyer part of the fee of a particular client. The latter is often done as payment for making a referral of the client. (2) A single bill to a client covering the fee of two or more lawyers who are not in the same firm. Also called fee-sharing.

felony   See misdemeanor.

feme covert   (A covered woman.) A married woman.

FEPA   See Fair Employment Practices Agency.

feticide   The unlawful killing of a fetus.

fetus   A developing organism—the unborn offspring—from the eighth week after conception until birth.

FFC   See full faith and credit.

FFCCSOA   See Full Faith and Credit for Child Support Orders Act.

fictive kin   A person who is not related by birth or marriage but who has an emotionally significant, family-like relationship with another.

fiduciary   (1) Pertaining to the high standard of good faith and fair treatment that must be exercised on behalf of another (adjective). (2) A person who owes another good faith and fair treatment in protecting the other's interest (noun).

fiduciary relationship   The relationship that exists when one party (called the *fiduciary*) owes another loyalty, candor, and fair treatment. The fiduciary is required to act in the interest of and for the benefit of the other. Also called a confidential relationship.

filial consortium   The right of a parent to the normal companionship and affection of a child.

filiation   (1) A judicial determination of paternity. (2) The relation of child to a particular parent.

filius nullius   "The son [or child] of no one." The status of an illegitimate child at common law.

financial statement   A report covering the assets (e.g., income, investments) and debts of a person or business as of a particular date or over a designated period. A financial accounting or balance sheet.

first impression Concerning an issue being addressed by a court for the first time.

fixed fee See contingent fee.

flowchart An overview of the step-by-step process by which something is done.

forced share See elective share.

foreign divorce A divorce obtained in another state or country. A divorce that was not obtained in the forum state where the parties are now in litigation. If, for example, you live in Florida and obtain a divorce in Ohio, you have a foreign divorce.

forensic (1) Pertaining to the use of scientific techniques to discover and examine evidence. (2) Belonging to or suitable in courts of law. (3) Concerning argumentation. (4) Forensics (ballistics or firearms evidence).

formal marriage See ceremonial marriage.

formbook A practical treatise or manual containing standard forms along with checklists, summaries of the law, etc. See also treatise.

fornication Voluntary sexual intercourse between unmarried persons.

forum (1) A court. (2) The place where the parties are presently litigating their dispute. (3) A court or tribunal hearing a case.

forum non conveniens The discretionary power of a court to decline the exercise of its jurisdiction when it would be more convenient and the ends of justice would be better served if the action were tried in another court.

forum shopping When more than one court has subject-matter jurisdiction over a claim, choosing the court that is most likely to issue a favorable ruling.

forum state The state in which the case is now being litigated.

foster care A child welfare service that provides shelter and substitute family care when a child's own family cannot provide this care.

foster care adoption See public agency adoption.

foster home A temporary home for children when their own families cannot provide care and when adoption either is not possible at the present time or is under consideration.

IV-D agency A state agency that helps custodial parents enforce child-support obligations.

FPLS See Federal Parent Locator Service.

fraud An intentionally false statement of fact that is material and is made to induce reliance by the plaintiff, and that results in harm because of the reliance. Also called deceit, misrepresentation.

fraudulent transfer A transfer of an asset for little or no payment or consideration that is made to avoid an obligation to a creditor.

Freedom of Access to Clinic Entrances Act (FACE) A federal statute that provides a remedy for victims of assault or other attack suffered while trying to obtain (or provide) reproductive health services (18 U.S.C. § 248(a)(1).)

friendly divorce A divorce proceeding in which the husband and wife are not contesting the dissolution of the marriage, or anything related thereto. An uncontested divorce.

front load Make substantial "alimony" payments shortly after the separation or divorce in an attempt to disguise nondeductible property division as deductible alimony.

full blood Having the same mother and father. *Half* blood is having the same mother or father but not both.

full faith and credit (FFC) The obligation of one state to recognize and enforce the legal decisions of another state. The obligation is based on the U.S. Constitution, which provides that "Full Faith and Credit shall be given in each State to the public Acts, Records, and judicial Proceedings of every other State." Article IV, § 1.

Full Faith and Credit for Child Support Orders Act (FFCCSOA) A federal statute governing when states must give full faith and credit to each other's child-support orders (28 U.S.C. § 1738B).

fundamental right A right that (a) is specifically guaranteed in the U.S. Constitution, (b) is implicit in the concept of ordered liberty, or (c) is deeply rooted in the nation's history and tradition.

G

garnishment A court proceeding by a creditor to force a third party in possession of the debtor's property (e.g., wages) to turn the property over to the creditor to satisfy a debt.

general appearance Coming to court as a party without restrictions and thereby submitting to the full jurisdiction of the court.

gestational carrier (also called a gestational surrogate) A woman who gestates, or carries, an embryo that was formed from the egg of another woman. The gestational carrier usually has a contractual obligation to return the infant to its intended parents.

gestational surrogacy The carrying and delivering of a child for another in which the woman does not use her own egg and is therefore not genetically related to the child.

get A document that grants a Jewish divorce.

gift The voluntary delivery of something with the present intent to transfer title and control, for which no payment or consideration is made. The person making the gift is the *donor*. The person receiving it is the *donee*.

good cause A legally sufficient ground or reason. Also called just cause, sufficient cause.

good faith The absence of wrongful intent or desire to take inappropriate advantage of someone. Also called bona fides.

goodwill The reputation of a business or professional practice that causes it to generate additional customers. The value of a business or practice that exceeds the value of the combined assets used in the business or practice. See also enterprise goodwill, personal goodwill.

grantor A transferor; a person who makes a grant.

gratuitous Performed without expectation of payment.

green-card marriage A marriage of a foreigner with an American citizen that entitles the foreigner to permanent resident status in the United States.

gross income The total amount received or earned before deductions.

grounds Reasons that are legally sufficient to obtain a particular remedy or result.

guarantee A warranty or assurance that a particular result will be achieved.

guardian A person who has legal authority to care for the person or property of another. Also called custodian.

guardian ad litem (GAL) A special guardian (often, but not always, an attorney) appointed by the court to appear in court proceedings on behalf of a person who is a minor, is insane, or is otherwise incapacitated.

guardianship The legal right to the custody of an individual.

H

half blood Having the same mother or father but not both. Full blood is having the same mother and father.

harassment See hostile environment harassment, quid pro quo harassment.

harmless Without injury or damage.

heart-balm action An action based on the loss of love and relationships—on a broken heart (e.g., breach of promise to marry, alienation of affections, and seduction).

heart-balm statute A statute that abolishes heart-balm actions.

heightened scrutiny See intermediate scrutiny.

high-test marriage See covenant marriage.

hold harmless To assume any liability in a transaction and thereby relieve another from responsibility or loss arising out of the transaction. Also called save harmless.

holding A court's answer to one of the legal issues in a case.

holding out Taking steps that will allow others to believe that something exists such as a legal status.

holographic Wholly in the handwriting of a person.

home state The state where the child has lived with a parent (or anyone acting as a parent) for at least six consecutive months immediately before the court proceeding begins or since birth if the child is less than six months old.

homestead One's dwelling house along with adjoining land and buildings.

hostile environment sexual harassment Pervasive unwelcome sexual conduct or sex-based ridicule that unreasonably interferes with an individual's job performance or that creates an intimidating, hostile, or offensive working environment, even if no tangible or economic consequences result.

house arrest The confinement of an accused or convicted person to his or her home except for approved travel such as for employment. If an electronic devise (e.g., a bracelet) is attached to the body to monitor the arrest, it is called Electronic House Arrest (EHA).

husband–wife immunity See interspousal immunity.

husband–wife privilege See marital-communications privilege.

I

ICPC See Interstate Compact on the Placement of Children.

illegitimacy Pertaining to a child born to unmarried parents who never legitimated the child. Also called bastardy.

illegitimate child A child born to parents who are not married to each other and who never took the steps needed to legitimate the child. Also called nonmarital child, child of an informal relationship, child out of wedlock, child with no presumed father, bastard.

illicit cohabitation Sexual intercourse between unmarried persons who are living together. See also cohabitation.

IME See independent medical examination.

imminent Near at hand; coming soon; about to happen; immediate.

immunity A defense that prevents someone from being sued for what would otherwise be wrongful conduct.

impeach To challenge; to attack the credibility of.

impediment A legal obstacle that prevents the formation of a valid marriage or other contract.

implicate (1) May apply or be relevant to. (2) May involve or affect.

implied contract See implied-in-fact contract, implied-in-law contract.

implied-in-fact contract A contract that is not created by an express agreement between the parties but is inferred as a matter of reason and justice from their conduct and the surrounding circumstances. A contract that is manifested by conduct and circumstances rather than by words of agreement. A contract that a reasonable person would infer exists, even though there is no express agreement. Also called an contract implied-in-fact.

implied-in-law contract An obligation created by the law to avoid unjust enrichment in the absence of an express or implied contract creating this obligation. Also called quasi contract.

impotence The inability to engage in sexual intercourse. For males, it is often the inability to achieve or maintain an erection.

imputed disqualification All attorneys in the same firm are ineligible to represent a client because one of the attorneys or other employees in the firm has a conflict of interest with that client. Also called vicarious disqualification.

imputed income Income that will be assumed to be available regardless of whether it is actually available.

in camera In the judge's private chambers; not in open court.

incapacity alimony Alimony, usually long-term, for an ex-spouse unable to be self-supporting because of his or her severe physical or mental incapacity.

incest Sexual relations between two people who are too closely related to each other as defined by law.

inchoate Partial; not yet complete.

incident to Closely connected to something else.

incident to divorce (a) Occurring within one year after the date a marriage ends or (b) relating to the ending of a marriage because it occurs within six years after a marriage ends pursuant to a divorce decree or separation agreement.

income withholding The process whereby an employer is required to deduct some of an employee's income, which will be used to meet the child-support obligations of the employee. (In some states, the deductions can also be used to meet spousal support obligations.)

incompatibility A no-fault ground for divorce that is established when there is such discord between the husband and wife that it is impossible for them to live together in a normal marital relationship.

incorporation and merger The acceptance of the terms of one document (e.g., an agreement) and making the terms become part of another document (e.g., a court decree) so that the former document ceases to exist as a separate entity.

incorporeal See intangible.

incorrigible Habitually disobedient and disruptive.

indemnify To compensate another for any loss or expense incurred.

indemnity The right to have another person pay you the amount you were forced to pay.

independent adoption An adoption that is arranged by the birth parent(s) and the adoptive parent(s) without the involvement of a public agency but often with the assistance of a facilitator or intermediary. Also called private adoption, direct-placement adoption, private-placement adoption, and facilitated adoption.

independent medical examination (IME) A discovery device in which a party obtains a court order for a professional examination of a person whose physical or mental condition is in controversy.

independent professional judgment Advice given by an attorney who is not subject to a conflict of interest. See *conflict of interest*.

indicia of parenthood Conduct that indicates or evidences a parental relationship with a child.

indigent Poor; without means to afford something such as a private attorney or filing fees.

individual property See separate property.

induced abortion See therapeutic abortion.

infancy (1) Minority. (2) The defense of being a minor, which allows the minor to disaffirm a voidable contract.

infant See minor.

infanticide The unlawful killing of a newborn.

infertility The inability to conceive a child. The failure of a couple to conceive in over a year in spite of having sexual relations without contraceptives.

informal marriage A common law marriage in Texas.

in forma pauperis As a poor person who is allowed to proceed without paying certain filing fees and other court costs.

informed consent Agreement to let something happen after obtaining a reasonable explanation of the benefits and risks involved.

inheritance Property received from someone who dies without leaving a valid will. Property received by intestate succession. The state determines which relatives receive such property.

initiating state   The state in which a support case is filed in order to forward it to another state (called the *responding state*) for enforcement proceedings under the Uniform Interstate Family Support Act (UIFSA).

injunction   A court order requiring a person or organization to do or to refrain from doing a particular thing.

in loco parentis   Standing in the place of a parent by assuming some or all parental responsibilities without being a biological or adoptive parent.

innocent spouse relief   A former spouse will not be liable for taxes, interest, and penalties owed on prior joint returns if (a) he or she did not know or have reason to know that the other spouse understated the taxes due and (b) it would be unfair to hold the innocent spouse responsible for the understatement of tax on the return.

in personam jurisdiction   See personal jurisdiction.

in praesenti   At present; now.

in propria persona   See pro se.

in rem jurisdiction   The court's power over a particular *res*, which is a thing (e.g., a car) or a status (e.g., a marriage) that is located within the territory over which the court has authority.

insanity   Mental illness that negates a person's civil or criminal responsibility or capacity. Also called lunacy.

instrument   (1) A formal written document that gives expression to or embodies a legal act or agreement (e.g., contract, will). (2) A means by which something is achieved.

insupportability   The no-fault ground for divorce in Texas consisting of discord or conflict of personalities that destroys the legitimate ends of the marital relationship and prevents any reasonable expectation of reconciliation.

intake memorandum   A written report that summarizes an interview with a new client of the office. It normally contains basic facts on the client and on his or her legal problems. See also interoffice memorandum, memorandum of law.

intangible   Not having a physical form. Also called incorporeal.

intended parent   A person who wants to raise a child as its legal parent and who enters an agreement with a surrogate mother to bear and deliver the child. The person hiring the surrogate mother may or may not be genetically (biologically) related to the child.

intentional infliction of emotional distress   Intentionally causing severe emotional distress by extreme or outrageous conduct.

intentional tort   A tort in which a person either desired to bring about the result or knew with substantial certainty that the result would follow from what the person did or failed to do.

inter alia   Among other things.

intercept program   A procedure by which the government seizes designated benefits owed to a parent in order to cover the latter's delinquent child-support payments.

interest   A legal share or right in something, which can often be sold or transferred.

interference with contract relations   Intentionally encouraging or provoking a breach of contract between two other persons. Also called tortious interference with contractual relations.

interlocutory   Not final; interim.

intermediate scrutiny   The government's action must be substantially related to serve an important state interest. Also called heightened scrutiny, elevated scrutiny.

interoffice memorandum   A written report addressed to someone in the office where you work, usually a supervisor. If the report explains how the law applies to a given set of facts, it is a memorandum of law.

interracial adoption   An adoption of a child whose race is different from the race of the adoptive parents. Also called transracial adoption.

interrogatories   ("rogs") A discovery device in which one party sends written questions to another party.

interspousal   Between or pertaining to a husband and wife.

interspousal immunity   Spouses cannot sue each other for designated categories of torts. Also called husband–wife immunity.

interspousal tort   See marital tort.

interstate central registry   An office in each state that receives and responds to cases involving interstate child-support enforcement.

Interstate Compact on the Placement of Children (ICPC)   A statute that governs adoption of a child born or living in one state who will be adopted by someone in another state.

inter vivos gift   A gift that takes effect while the donor is living.

intestacy   The condition of dying without a valid will.

intestate   (1) Pertaining to someone who dies without a valid will. (2) A person who dies without a valid will.

intestate share   A designated portion of the estate of a person who dies intestate (i.e., without a valid will) to which a specific relative of the deceased is entitled according to state law.

intestate succession   The transfer of a decedent's property to state-designated relatives of the decedent who dies without leaving a valid will. Also called descent and distribution, hereditary succession.

intrafamily tort   A tort committed by one family member against another. See also marital tort.

intrafamily tort immunity   Family members cannot sue each other for designated categories of torts.

in vitro fertilization (IVF)   The surgical removal of a woman's eggs from the ovaries, the fertilization of the eggs with sperm (in the laboratory), and the transfer of the resulting embryos (or pre-embryos) into the uterus through the cervix. An ART method.

irreconcilable differences   A no-fault ground for divorce that is established when there is such discord between the husband and wife that there has been an irremediable breakdown of the marriage.

irremediable breakdown   See irreconcilable differences.

irrevocable   Not capable of being altered or revoked.

issue   (1) A child and anyone else who has descended from a common ancestor. (2) A legal question. See also legal periodical.

IVF   See in vitro fertilization.

J

joint adoption   An adoption by two adults (usually married) who both seek to become adoptive parents of a child.

joint and several liability   Legally responsible together and individually. Each debtor is individually responsible for the entire debt; the plaintiff/creditor can choose to collect the full debt from one debtor or from all of them until the debt is satisfied.

joint custody   See joint legal custody, joint physical custody.

joint legal custody   The right of both parents to make the child-rearing decisions on health, education, religion, discipline, and general welfare. Also called shared legal custody.

joint physical custody   The right of both parents to have the child reside with both for alternating (but not necessarily equal) periods of time. Also called shared physical custody.

joint representation   See multiple representation.

joint tenancy   Ownership of property by two or more persons (called joint tenants) in equal shares, equal rights to possess the whole property, and a right of survivorship. A joint tenancy is sometimes referred to as a joint tenancy with right of survivorship (JTWROS).

joint venture   A business or profit-seeking activity of two or more persons who each participate and control the activity (or who have the right of participation and control).

JTWROS   See joint tenancy.

judgment debtor   The person who loses and therefore must pay a money judgment.

judgment creditor   The person who wins and therefore has a right to collect a money judgment.

judicial review   The power of a court to determine the constitutionality of a statute or other law, including the power to refuse to enforce it if the court concludes that it violates the constitution.

judicial separation   See legal separation.

jurisdiction   (1) The power of a court to act in a particular case to resolve a legal dispute. There are three major kinds of power jurisdiction: subject-matter jurisdiction, in rem jurisdiction, and personal jurisdiction. (2) The geographic area over which a particular court has authority or power. See also concurrent jurisdiction, exclusive jurisdiction, in rem jurisdiction, personal jurisdiction, subject-matter jurisdiction.

juvenile delinquent   A young person under a designated age whose conduct would constitute a crime if committed by an adult. Sometimes called PINS (Person in Need of Supervision), MINS (Minor in Need of Supervision), or CHIPS (Child in Need of Protection and Services).

K

kinship adoption   An adoption in which the adoptive parent is related to the adoptee.

L

last-in-time marriage presumption   If more than one marriage is alleged to exist, the most recent marriage is presumed to be valid.

latchkey child   A child who is at home after school without supervision of adults; a self-care child.

law review   A legal periodical published by a law school. Also called law journal. See also legal periodical.

legal advice   The application of laws or legal principles to the facts of a particular person's legal problem.

legal analysis   The application of one or more rules to the facts of a client's case in order to answer a legal question that will help (1) avoid a legal dispute, (2) resolve a legal dispute that has arisen, or (3) prevent a legal dispute from becoming worse.

legal capacity   See capacity.

legal custody   The right to make the major child-rearing decisions on health, education, religion, discipline, and general welfare. Also called decision-making responsibility.

legal encyclopedia   An alphabetical summary of every important legal topic. The major national legal encyclopedias are published by West Group: *Corpus Juris Secundum* (C.J.S.), available in volumes; and *American Jurisprudence 2d* (Am. Jur. 2d), available in volumes and online on Westlaw and LexisNexis. In addition, several single-state legal encyclopedias exist (e.g., *California Jurisprudence*).

legal issue   A question of law; a question of what the law is, or what the law means, or how the law applies to a set of facts. Also called *issue of law*. If the dispute is over the existence or nonexistence of the alleged facts, it is referred to as a question of fact, a factual issue, or an issue of fact.

legal malpractice   The failure of an attorney to exercise the skills commonly applied by attorneys in the same area of practice under the same circumstances.

legal periodical   A pamphlet on legal topics that is issued at regular intervals. The major examples are law reviews and bar journals. Pamphlets in the same year are often bound in a hard cover.

legal separation   A declaration by a court that parties can live apart even though they are still married to each other. Also called judicial separation, limited divorce, divorce a mensa et thoro, and separation from bed and board.

legal treatise   A book written by a private individual (or by a public official writing as a private citizen) that provides an overview, summary, or commentary on a legal topic. Hornbooks, manuals, and formbooks are treatises.

legislative divorce   A divorce granted by an act of the legislature rather than by the decree of a court.

legitimacy   The status or condition of being born within a lawful marriage. See also presumption of legitimacy.

legitimate child   A child born to parents who are married to each other.

legitimate state purpose   Any government objective that the state has the authority to pursue, such as to provide for the public safety.

legitimation   (1) The declaration that a child is legitimate. The verb is *legitimize*. (2) The steps taken to declare that a child is legitimate.

legitimize   To formally declare that children born out of wedlock are legitimate.

letter of nonengagement   A letter sent by an attorney to a prospective client explicitly stating that the attorney will not be representing this person.

levy   (1) The collection or seizure of property by a public official to satisfy a judgment. (2) An assessment or tax.

Lexis–Nexis   A fee-based legal database for computer research.

lex loci celebrationis   Law of the place where the marriage or other contract was entered.

lex loci contractus   Law of the place where the contract was executed.

liabilities   That which one owes; debts.

liability insurance   Insurance in which the insurer agrees to pay damages that an insured is obligated to pay to a third person because of a legal liability that the insured owes the third person for committing a tort or other wrong covered by the insurance policy.

lien   A security, encumbrance, or claim on property that remains until a debt is paid.

life estate   An interest in property whose duration is limited to the life of an individual. An ownership of property that lasts as long as a designated person is alive. Also called estate for life, life tenancy.

limited divorce   A declaration by a court that parties can live apart although they are still married to each other. Also called legal separation, separation from bed and board, divorce a mensa et thoro.

living apart   A no-fault ground for divorce that is established when spouses live separately for a designated period of consecutive time during which they intended to end the marriage. Also called living separate and apart.

loco parentis   See in loco parentis.

long-arm jurisdiction   The personal jurisdiction that a state acquires over a nonresident defendant because of his or her purposeful contact with the state.

long-arm statute   A statute that allows a state to obtain personal jurisdiction over a nonresident defendant because of the latter's purposeful contact with the state.

Lord Mansfield's rule   The testimony of either spouse is inadmissible on the question of whether the husband had access to the wife at the time of conception if such evidence would tend to bastardize (i.e., declare illegitimate) the child.

loss of consortium   Interference with the companionship, love, affection, sexual relations, and services that a person naturally expects to receive from his or her spouse.

loss of services   Interference with the right of a parent to the services of his or her unemancipated child, such as doing household chores.

lucid interval   A period of time during which a mentally ill or insane person had the mental capacity to understand what he or she was doing before the mental illness or insanity returned.

lump-sum alimony   See alimony in gross.

lump-sum payment   A single payment of an amount of money to fulfill what would otherwise be a continuing obligation.

lunacy   See insanity.

M

maintenance Food, clothing, shelter, and other necessaries of life. See also alimony.

majority See age of majority.

malice (1) The intent to inflict injury or other wrongful harm. (2) Reckless disregard of what is right. (3) Animosity or ill will.

malicious (1) Pertaining to a wrongful act that is done intentionally and without just cause or excuse. (2) Pertaining to conduct that is certain or almost certain to cause harm.

malpractice See legal malpractice.

mandatory reporting Required communication of designated information to a public authority, such as informing the police or child protective services of suspected child abuse or neglect.

manslaughter The unlawful killing of a person that does not constitute murder.

marital-communications privilege A person can refuse to testify and can prevent his or her spouse or ex-spouse from testifying about any confidential communications made between them during the marriage. Also called marital privilege, husband–wife privilege.

marital dissipation See dissipation.

marital privilege See marital-communications privilege.

marital property Any property acquired by either or both spouses during the marriage that is not separate property. See also separate property.

marital separation agreement See separation agreement.

marital tort A tort that one spouse commits against another. Also called domestic tort.

market value See fair market value.

marriage The legal union of two persons as spouses with designated rights and obligations to each other. See also ceremonial marriage, common law marriage.

marriage by estoppel A relationship that is recognized as a marriage because a party is prevented from asserting the invalidity of the marriage even though grounds for its invalidity may exist.

married women's property acts Statutes removing all or most of a woman's legal disabilities on matters such as entering contracts, disposing of her property, and being a party to litigation independent of her husband.

material (1) Important enough to influence the decision that was made. (2) Serious and substantial.

maternal preference See tender years presumption.

matrimonii, a vinculo See divorce.

Med-Arb A method of alternative dispute resolution (ADR) in which the parties first try mediation, and if it does not work, they try arbitration.

mediation A method of alternative dispute resolution (ADR) in which the parties avoid litigation by submitting their dispute to a neutral third person (the mediator) who helps the parties resolve their dispute; he or she does not render a decision resolving it for them.

medical examination See independent medical examination.

mensa et thoro See divorce a mensa et thoro.

MEPA See Multiethnic Placement Act.

meretricious (1) Pertaining to prostitution or unlawful sexual relations. (2) Vulgar or tawdry. (3) In Washington State, a meretricious relationship means a stable, marital-like relationship where both parties cohabit with knowledge that a lawful marriage between them does not exist.

merger See incorporation and merger.

meritorious Having merit; having a reasonable basis to believe that a person's claim or defense will succeed.

metadata Data about data. Data about a computer document that are hidden within the document itself (e.g., earlier versions of the document).

migratory divorce A divorce obtained in a state to which one or both of the spouses traveled before returning to their state of domicile.

mini-DOMA A statute of a state declaring that its strong public policy is not to recognize any same-sex marriage that might be validly entered in another state.

minimum contacts Activities in or connected with a state by a nonresident that are substantial enough so that it can be said that the nonresident has invoked the benefits and protections of the state, thereby making it fair for the state to assert personal jurisdiction over the nonresident.

Minnesota Multiphasic Personality Inventory Test (MMPI) A psychological test designed to assess personality characteristics.

minor A person under age of legal adulthood, often 18. One who has not reached the age of majority. Also called infant.

minority The status of being under age of legal adulthood—under the age of majority.

MINS **(minor in need of supervision)** See status offense, juvenile delinquent.

miscegenation Marriage between persons of different races. A law that forbids marriage between persons of different races is called an antimiscegenation law.

misdemeanor Any crime that is not as serious as a felony. In many states, a misdemeanor is any crime punishable by fine or by detention (often for a year or less) in an institution other than a prison. A *felony* is any crime that is more serious than a misdemeanor. In many states, a felony is any crime punishable by death or imprisonment (often for more than a year).

MMPI See Minnesota Multiphasic Personality Inventory Test.

Model Rules of Professional Responsibility ABA ethics rules.

moot (1) Pertaining to a nonexistent controversy where the issues have ceased to exist from a practical point of view. (2) Subject to debate.

mortgage An interest in land that provides security for the performance of a duty or the payment of a debt.

movant A person making a motion.

Multiethnic Placement Act (MEPA) A federal statute that forbids delay or denial of adoption on the basis of race, color, or national origin. (42 U.S.C. § 1996B.)

multiple representation Representing more than one side in a legal matter or controversy. Also called joint representation, common representation.

murder Killing a person (1) with the intent to kill, (2) with the intent to cause grievous bodily harm, (3) with reckless disregard for human life, or (4) while committing a designated felony.

N

narrowly tailored No more than needed to maintain the effectiveness of a goal; no broader than absolutely necessary.

National Directory of New Hires (NDNH) A national database of wage and employment information used to assist state child-support agencies in locating noncustodial parents in order to establish paternity and enforce child-support obligations.

NCP See noncustodial parent.

NDNH See National Directory of New Hires.

necessaries The basic items needed by family members to maintain a standard of living, particularly food, shelter, and clothing. These items can be purchased and charged to the spouse who has failed to provide them.

ne exeat A writ that forbids a person from leaving or from removing a child or property from the state, country, or jurisdiction of the court.

neglect See child neglect.

negligence The failure to use reasonable care that an ordinary prudent person would have used in a similar situation, resulting in injury or other loss.

negligent entrustment Carelessly allowing the use of a vehicle, tool, or other object by someone who poses an unreasonable risk of harm to others.

negligent supervision   Carelessly monitoring or supervising an incompetent person who poses an unreasonable risk of harm to others.

nepotism   Favoritism shown to relatives. A rule against nepotism is called an antinepotism rule.

net worth   Total assets of a person or business less total liabilities.

neutral evaluation   A method of alternative dispute resolution (ADR) in which both sides hire an experienced attorney or an expert in the area involved in the dispute who will listen to an abbreviated version of the evidence and arguments of each side and offer an evaluation in the hope that this will stimulate more serious settlement discussions. Sometimes called case evaluation.

nisi   Not final; interim.

no-contact order   See stay-away order.

no-fault divorce   A divorce that is granted without having to prove marital wrongs that caused the break-up.

nonaccess   Evidence of the absence of opportunities for sexual intercourse with the mother of a child around the time the child was conceived.

nonage   Below the required minimum age to enter a relationship or perform a task. Minority.

noncustodial parent (NCP)   The parent who is not living with the child; the parent who does not have physical custody of the child. Also called nonresidential parent. For federal income tax purposes, a custodial parent is the parent with whom the child lived for the greater number of nights. The other parent is the noncustodial parent.

nondischargeable   Not eliminated or forgiven by bankruptcy.

nondomiciliary   One who is not domiciled in a particular place.

nonengagement   See letter of nonengagement.

nonmarital child   A child born to parents who are not married to each other and who have not legitimated the child. Also called illegitimate child, child of an informal relationship, child out of wedlock, child with no presumed father, bastard.

nonmolestation clause   A clause in an agreement that the parties will not disturb, annoy, or harass each other.

nonresident   Someone who does not have a residence in a particular place.

nonresidential parent   See noncustodial parent.

nonsupport   See criminal nonsupport.

notarize   To certify or attest to something, e.g., the authenticity of a signature.

nullity   Legally void.

O

objective standard   A standard by which something is measured by comparing (1) what a person actually knew, felt, or did with (2) what a reasonable person would have known, felt, or done under the same circumstances. See also subjective standard.

objectivity   The state of being dispassionate; the absence of a bias.

obligee   One to whom a legal obligation is owed. See also payee.

obligor   One who has a legal obligation to do something, usually to make a payment. See also payor.

officiant   One who leads or performs a ceremony, often a religious service.

open adoption   An adoption in which the biological parent maintains certain kinds of initial and/or ongoing contact with the adoptee, whose adoptive parent(s) may have been selected by the biological parent. The contact might consist of letters or visits.

operation of law   The means by which legal consequences are imposed by law, regardless of (or even despite) the intent of the parties involved.

opinion   See court opinion.

opportunity interest   The right of a father to develop a relationship with his child.

order of protection   See protective order, restraining order.

outstanding   Unpaid; to be collected.

overreaching   Taking unfair advantage of another's naiveté or other vulnerability, especially by deceptive means.

P

palimony   Support payments ordered after the end of a nonmarital relationship (a) if the party seeking support was induced to initiate or stay in the relationship by a promise of support or (b) if ordering support is otherwise equitable.

paralegal   A person with legal skills who works under the supervision of an attorney or who is otherwise authorized to use those skills.

paralegal fee   A fee that an attorney can collect for the nonclerical work of his or her paralegal on a client case.

parens patriae   Parent of the country, referring to the state's role in protecting children and those under disability.

parental alienation syndrome (PAS)   A disorder characterized by a child's obsessive and unjustified denigration of a parent that results both from the child's persistent attacks on the parent and from manipulation (brainwashing) by the other parent of the child's attitude toward the targeted parent.

parental consortium   The right of a child to the normal companionship and affection of a parent.

Parental Kidnapping Prevention Act (PKPA)   A federal statute that requires a state to enforce (give full faith and credit to) child-custody orders of other states (28 U.S.C. § 1738A).

parental-liability law   A statute that imposes vicarious liability (up to a limited dollar amount) on parents for the torts committed by their children. Also called parental-responsibility law.

parental-responsibility law   See parental-liability law.

parenting coordinator (PC)   A professional who assists parents in resolving custody disputes that arise under a parenting plan.

parenting plan   A plan for separated parents that states (1) where and with whom the children will live (physical custody); (2) who will make child-rearing decisions on schooling, discipline, religion, health, and general welfare (legal custody); (3) what the visitation schedule for the noncustodial parent will be; and (4) related matters such as what method the parents will use to resolve future child-rearing disagreements between them.

parenting time   Visitation.

Parent Locator Service   See Federal Parent Locator Service, State Parent Locator Service.

partial-birth abortion   An abortion in which the fetus is destroyed after it is partially extruded from the womb. Intact dilation and evacuation.

partition   The dividing of land held by joint tenants and tenants in common. The division results in individual ownership.

partnership   A voluntary association of two or more persons to place their resources in a jointly owned business or enterprise, with a proportional sharing of profits and losses.

passive appreciation   An increase in the value of property that is due to inflation or market forces rather than to the active efforts of the owner.

passive income   Income that is earned from money or other property without direct involvement or active participation by the earner.

passive registry   A reunion registry that requires both the adoptee and the biological parent to register their consent to release identifying information. When both have registered and a match is made, an agency employee will contact both. Also called mutual consent registry.

paternity   The biological fatherhood of a child.

paternity by estoppel   Paternity that is established when a court does not allow the presumption of paternity to be rebutted even though there is no biological relationship between the presumed (putative) father and the child.

payee   One to whom money is paid or is to be paid.

payor One who makes a payment of money or who is obligated to do so.

PC See parenting coordinator.

PDP See procedural due process.

pecuniary Relating to money. (A pecuniary interest is a financial interest.)

pendente lite Pending the [outcome of the] litigation. See also temporary alimony.

periodic payments Payments to be made over a period of time as opposed to a single (lump-sum) payment.

perjury Making a false statement under oath concerning a material matter with the intent to provide false testimony. Also called false swearing.

permanent alimony Alimony that is awarded periodically (e.g., monthly) until a designated date or indefinitely (without a termination date). Also called traditional alimony.

per se In and of itself. Without additional facts or support.

personal autonomy, right to See right to privacy.

personal goodwill An asset of a business or practice that is dependent on the continued presence of a particular individual because the asset is attributed to that individual's personal skill, training, or reputation.

personal jurisdiction A court's power over a person to determine (adjudicate) his or her personal rights and duties. Also called *in personam jurisdiction*. A court with such jurisdiction is not limited to rulings on property interests or on someone's status. More limited kinds of jurisdiction include the court's power over a person's interest in specific property (*quasi in rem jurisdiction*) or over the property itself (*in rem jurisdiction*).

personal property Property other than land or other than things attached to the land. Also called chattels.

personal protection order (PPO) See restraining order.

personal representative An executor or administrator of the estate of the deceased; someone who formally acts on behalf of the estate of the deceased.

personal service Handing the service-of-process documents to the person who is the target of the service.

Person in Need of Supervision (PINS) See status offense, juvenile delinquent.

petition (1) A complaint. (2) A formal request that the court take some action.

petitioner (1) A party who files a petition or complaint. A plaintiff. (2) A party who files an appeal. Appellant.

physical custody (1) The right of an adult to have a child reside with the adult. Also called residential custody, custodial responsibility. (2) Where the child is actually living.

physical examination See independent medical examination.

PINS **(Person in Need of Supervision) (PINS)** See status offense, juvenile delinquent.

PKPA See Parental Kidnapping Prevention Act (PKPA).

plaintiff The party bringing a claim against another.

plead (1) To file a pleading, a formal document that asserts or responds to claims or defenses. (2) To make a formal assertion or response.

pleadings Formal litigation documents (e.g., a complaint or petition, an answer) filed by parties that state or respond to claims or defenses of other parties.

polyandry The condition or practice of having more than one husband at the same time.

polygamy The condition or practice of having more than one spouse at the same time.

polygyny The condition or practice of having more than one wife at the same time.

posthumous child A child born after the death of a parent.

postnuptial After marriage.

postnuptial agreement A contract between married persons that covers financial and related matters. The spouses may have no intention of separating. If they have this intention, the contract is commonly called a separation agreement.

power of attorney (1) A document that authorizes another to act as one's agent or attorney in fact. (2) The authority itself to act for another as agent or attorney in fact.

PPO (personal protection order) See restraining order.

practice manual See *manual*.

practice of law Using legal skills to assist a specific person in resolving his or her specific legal problem. See also unauthorized practice of law.

praesenti See in praesenti.

prayer A formal request.

precedent A prior decision covering a similar issue that can be used as a standard or guide in a later case.

premarital agreement A contract by persons about to be married that can cover (1) financial and related matters once the marriage occurs and (2) spousal support, property division, and related matters in the event of death, separation, divorce, or annulment. Also called prenuptial agreement ("prenup"), antenuptial agreement.

prenatal tort A tort committed against a fetus.

prenup A prenuptial agreement. See premarital agreement.

prenuptial Before marriage.

prenuptial agreement ("prenup") See premarital agreement.

preponderance of the evidence A standard of proof that is met when the evidence establishes that it is more likely than not that the facts are as alleged. Also called fair preponderance of evidence.

present value The amount of money an individual would have to be given now in order to generate a certain amount of money within a designated period of time through prudent investment, usually at compound interest. Also called present cash value, present worth.

presumed parent A person who, under the Uniform Parentage Act, is presumed to be the natural parent a child if the person receives the child into his or her home and openly holds out the child as his or her natural child. The presumed parent does not have to be biologically related to the child.

presumption An assumption or inference that a certain fact is true once another fact is established. The presumption is *conclusive* if a party is not allowed to introduce evidence to show that the assumption is false. The presumption is *rebuttable* if a party is allowed to introduce evidence to show that the assumption is false.

presumption of legitimacy A child born to a married woman is presumed to be legitimate unless conclusively proven otherwise.

presumption of paternity A man is presumed to be the father of a child (until proven otherwise) if he is married to the mother at the time of conception or birth, he marries the mother after the birth, he formally acknowledges paternity, he allows his name on the birth certificate, he receives the child into his home and holds the child out as his own, or he is obligated to pay child support.

presumptive Created or arising out of a presumption; based on inference.

pretrial conference A meeting of the attorneys and the judge (or magistrate) before the trial to attempt to narrow the issues, secure stipulations, make a final effort to settle the case without a trial, and cover other preliminary matters. Also called a trial management conference.

prima facie case A party's presentation of evidence that will prevail unless the other side offers more convincing counterevidence.

primary authority Any law that a court could rely on in reaching its decision (e.g., a constitutional provision, statute, regulation, ordinance, other court opinion).

primary-caregiver presumption Custody should be granted to the parent who thus far has taken care of most of the daily needs of the child unless this parent is unfit.

privacy See right to privacy.

private judging Arbitration or mediation by a retired judge. Sometimes called *rent-a-judge*.

privilege (1) A special legal benefit, right, exemption, or protection. (2) The right to act contrary to the right of another without being subject to tort or other liability. A defense that authorizes conduct that would otherwise be wrongful.

privileged Protected from disclosure; not discoverable.

privilege for marital communication See marital-communications privilege.

probable cause (1) A reasonable belief that a specific crime has been committed and that the accused committed the crime. (2) A reasonable belief that good grounds exist to bring civil proceedings against someone.

probate A court proceeding at which a will is proved to be valid or invalid.

probation (1) Living in the community (in lieu of institutionalization) so long as there is compliance with court-imposed conditions. (2) A trial or test period.

pro bono Concerning or involving legal services that are provided for the public good (pro bono publico) without fee or compensation. Sometimes also applied to services given at a reduced rate. Shortened to pro bono.

procedural due process The constitutional requirement that the government provide fair procedures such as notice and an opportunity to be heard whenever the government seeks to deprive someone of life, liberty, or property.

procedural fairness Full financial disclosure, adequate opportunity to consult with others, voluntariness, and the absence of duress and fraud. Informed consent.

procedural law The rules that govern the mechanics of resolving a dispute in court or in an administrative agency (e.g., a rule on the time by which a party must respond to a complaint).

process The means (e.g., a summons, writ, or other court order) used by the court to acquire or exercise its power or jurisdiction over a person.

production See request for production.

professional responsibility Standards of ethics.

proof of service A sworn statement (or other evidence) that service of process on a party has been accomplished. Also called certificate of service, return of service.

pro per See pro se.

property See personal property, real property, property division.

property division The allocation and distribution of property between spouses (or ex-spouses) after a legal separation or divorce. Also called property settlement, property distribution.

property tort A tort that damages or interferes with a person's real property or personal property.

pro se (on one's own behalf) Representing oneself; not being represented by an attorney. Also called pro per (in propria persona).

prosecute To commence and proceed with a lawsuit.

prosecution (1) Bringing and processing criminal proceedings against someone. The words *prosecution* and *prosecute* can also refer to bringing and processing civil proceedings against someone, although the words are more commonly used in criminal proceedings. (2) The attorney representing the government in a criminal case. Also called the prosecutor.

pro se divorce A divorce obtained when a party represents himself or herself.

protective order A court order directing a person to refrain from doing something such as harming or harassing another. Also called order of protection.

prove-up The presentation of evidence to support one's claims even if they are unopposed.

provocation Inciting the conduct that constitutes the marital wrong by the other spouse.

proxy marriage A ceremonial marriage in which agents ("stand-ins") take the place of one or both of the prospective spouses because of their absence at the ceremony.

psychological parent An adult who, in a substantial and continuing way, has provided for the physical and emotional needs of a child. The adult can be a biological parent, but most often the term refers to someone other than a biological or adoptive parent.

public agency adoption An adoption that occurs directly through a public agency or through a private agency under contract with a public agency. The public agency usually has legal and physical custody of the child in the foster care system. See also private agency adoption.

public assistance Welfare or other forms of financial help from the government to the poor.

public charge An individual who is primarily dependent on the government for subsistence, as demonstrated by either the receipt of public cash assistance for income maintenance or by institutionalization for long-term care at government expense.

public policy The principles inherent in the customs, morals, and notions of justice that prevail in a state; the foundation of public laws; the principles that are naturally and inherently right and just.

punitive damages Damages that are added to actual or compensatory damages in order to punish malicious, outrageous, or reckless conduct and to deter similar conduct in the future. Also called exemplary damages, smart money, vindictive damages.

purported Claimed or professed, often falsely.

putative Alleged or reputed.

putative father The man believed to be the biological father of a child but who has not yet been medically or legally declared to be the father. Also called alleged father, reputed father.

putative father registry A government office where the father of a child can register so that he can be notified of a proposed adoption of the child.

putative marriage See putative spouse.

putative spouse A person who believes in good faith that he or she entered (and cohabitated in) a valid marriage even though an impediment made the marriage invalid. The marriage with such a spouse is called a *putative marriage*. Under § 209 of the Uniform Marriage and Divorce Act, "Any person who has cohabited with another to whom he is not legally married in the good faith belief that he was married to that person is a putative spouse until knowledge of the fact that he is not legally married terminates his status and prevents acquisition of further rights."

Q

QDRO See qualified domestic relations order.

QMCSO See qualified medical child support order.

qualified domestic relations order (QDRO) A court order that allows a nonworker to reach all or part of the pension or other retirement benefits of a worker or former worker in order to satisfy the worker's support or other marital obligation.

qualified medical child support order (QMCSO) A court order to an employer to extend its group health insurance benefits to the child of one of its workers even if the child does not live with the worker.

quantum meruit "As much as he deserves." An award of the reasonable value of services provided despite the absence of an express or implied agreement to pay for the services.

quasi-community property Personal property acquired during the marriage by the spouses when they lived in a non–community property state before moving to a community property state. If they had acquired it in a community property state, it would have been community property.

quasi contract A contract created by the law to avoid unjust enrichment. See implied-in-law contract.

quasi-suspect class A class based on gender or on a child's legitimacy.

quid pro quo sexual harassment Submission to or rejection of unwelcome sexual conduct used as a basis for employment decisions on promotion or other job-related benefits.

quitclaim A release or giving up of whatever claim or title you have in property. The party who quitclaims the property turns over whatever he or she has, without guaranteeing anything.

R

rape See statutory rape.

ratification Approval of something after it has occurred. Approval retroactively by agreement, conduct, or any inaction that can reasonably be interpreted as an approval. The verb is *ratify*.

rational basis The government's action must be reasonably related to a legitimate state purpose. Also called minimal scrutiny, rational relation.

rational relation The standard used to determine if a restriction or a classification complies with due process or equal protection (and is therefore constitutional); the restriction or the classification must be reasonably related to a legitimate state purpose. Also called rational basis.

real estate See real property.

realize To receive an actual benefit or to suffer an actual loss from something as opposed to a mere potential (paper) benefit or loss.

real property Land and anything attached or affixed to the land, such as buildings, fences, and trees. Also called real estate.

real-time Occurring now; happening as you are watching; able to respond immediately or within milliseconds.

reasonable See unreasonable.

reasonably related Logically connected (pertaining to any means used to achieve a goal that is reasonably likely to be successful).

rebut To attack, dispute, or refute.

rebuttable presumption An assumption or inference of fact that a party will be allowed to try to disprove (rebut) but that will be treated as true if it is not disproved.

recapture The recalculation of a tax liability in order to remove a deduction (or other tax benefit) to which the taxpayer was not entitled. An example is an alimony deduction created by front loading payments that are part of a nondeductible property division. See also front load.

receiver A person appointed by the court to manage property in litigation or in the process of bankruptcy.

recital A preliminary statement in a document covering its background or purpose.

reconciliation The full resumption of the marital relationship.

record (verb) To deposit a document with an official office or body such as a county clerk's office.

recordation Filing a document with a government body so it becomes part of the official record.

recrimination A serious marital wrong committed by the spouse seeking a divorce even though this spouse is charging the other spouse with committing a serious marital wrong.

reformation An equitable remedy to correct a writing so that it embodies the actual intent of the parties.

regional reporter The volumes that contain the full text of opinions from courts within a designated cluster of states.

regulation A law enacted by an administrative agency.

rehabilitative alimony Support payments to an ex-spouse for a limited time to allow him or her to return to financial self-sufficiency through employment or job training. Also called durational alimony, transitional alimony, bridge-the-gap alimony.

reimbursement alimony Alimony that repays an ex-spouse who worked or made other financial contributions during the marriage so that the other spouse could obtain training or otherwise enhance his or her future earning capacity. Also called restitutional alimony.

relation back The rule that an act done at one time is considered by a fiction of the law to have been done at a prior time.

release To formally give up or relinquish (a claim or a right).

rem See in rem jurisdiction.

remedy (1) The means by which a right is enforced or the violation of a right is prevented, compensated for, or otherwise redressed. (2) To correct. The plural is *remedies*.

remise To give up or release.

rent-a-judge See private judging.

reporter (1) A volume (or set of volumes) of court opinions. Also called case reports. An official reporter is printed under the authority of the government, often by a government printing office. An unofficial reporter is printed by a commercial publishing company without special authority from the government. (2) The person in charge of reporting the decisions of a court. (3) The person who takes down and transcribes proceedings such as a deposition or court hearing.

reprimand A form of public discipline by which an attorney's conduct is declared to have been improper but his or her right to practice law is not limited.

request for admissions (RFA) A discovery device in which one party sends a request to another party that the latter agree that a certain fact or legal conclusion is true so that there will be no need to present proof or arguments about such matters during the trial.

request for production (RFP) A discovery device in which one party requests that another party provide access to documents or other tangible things for copying or inspection. The device can also include a request to enter the party's land.

res (1) A thing (e.g., land) or a status (e.g., marriage). (2) The subject matter of a trust.

rescission The cancellation of something.

residence The place where someone is living. See also domicile.

resident Someone who lives at a particular place.

residential custody See physical custody.

residential parent See custodial parent.

res judicata A defense raised to prevent the same parties from retrying a claim that has already been resolved in a prior case or to prevent the litigation of a claim arising out of the same transaction involved in the first case that could have been raised in the first case but was not.

respondeat superior An employer is responsible for the conduct of employees while they are acting within the scope of employment.

respondent (1) The party responding to a position or claim of another party; the defendant. (2) The party against whom an appeal is filed. See also appellee.

responding state The state to which a support case is forwarded for enforcement proceedings under the Uniform Interstate Family Support Act (UIFSA). The case was forwarded by the initiating state.

responsive pleading A pleading that replies to a prior pleading of an opponent.

Restatement of Torts A treatise written by the American Law Institute that articulates or restates the law of torts. The second edition is *Restatement (Second) of Torts*.

restitution An equitable remedy in which a person is restored to his or her original position prior to the loss or injury; restoring to the plaintiff the value of what he or she parted with or lost.

restitutional alimony See reimbursement alimony.

restraining order A form of injunction, initially issued ex parte (with only one side present), to restrain the defendant from doing a threatened act. Also called order of protection, personal protection order (PPO), protection from abuse (PFA). See also ex parte.

restraint of marriage A condition in a contract or gift that a benefit will be lost upon marriage or remarriage.

resulting trust A trust created by operation of law to prevent unjust enrichment when a person transfers property under circumstances that raise the inference that he or she did not intend to transfer a beneficial interest to the person taking or holding the property.

retainer (1) An amount of money (or other property) paid by a client as a deposit or advance against future fees, costs, and expenses of providing services. (2) The act of hiring or engaging the services of someone, usually a professional. The verb is *retain*.

retroactive   Applying to facts that arise before as well as after a particular event or date.

return of service   See proof of service.

reunion registry   A central adoption file that could be used to release identifying information about, and allow contact between, adult adoptees and biological parents. See also active registry, passive registry.

revival   Restoration of what was once inoperative or terminated.

revocable   Susceptible of being revoked, cancelled, or recalled.

RFA   See request for admission.

RFP   See request for production.

right of election   See elective share.

right to privacy   A constitutional right to make personal decisions without undue government interference on matters such as marriage, procreation, family relationships, child rearing and education, contraception, and abortion. The right is implied in specific provisions of the constitution such as the Due Process Clause of the Fourteenth Amendment. Also called right to personal autonomy.

right of survivorship   When one owner dies, his or her share automatically goes to the other owners; it does not go through the estate of the deceased owner.

rogs   See interrogatories.

rules of professional responsibility   Rules of ethics.

runner   See ambulance chasing.

S

safe-haven law   A law that protects a woman from prosecution if she abandons a baby at designated locations such as a hospital or doctor's office where it can receive immediate medical care.

sanction   (1) Penalty or punishment imposed for unacceptable conduct. (2) Permission or authorization.

scienter   Intent to deceive or mislead.

SDNH   See State Directory of New Hires (SDNH)

SDP   See substantive due process.

secondary authority   Any nonlaw that a court could rely on in reaching its decision (e.g., a legal periodical, a legal treatise). Writings that describe or explain, but do not constitute, the law.

second-glance doctrine   To help determine the validity of a document that a party wants to enforce, a court will examine changed circumstances since the time the document was entered (executed). Also called second-look rule.

second-parent adoption   The adoption of a child by an unmarried partner (or cohabitant) of a biological parent who does not give up (relinquish) his or her own parental rights when the adoption occurs.

security   (1) Collateral that guarantees a debt or other obligation. (2) A financial instrument that is evidence of a debt interest (e.g., a bond), an ownership/equity interest, (e.g., a stock) or other specially defined rights (e.g., a futures contract). (3) Surety. (4) The state of being secure.

seduction   (1) The tort of engaging in sexual relations with the plaintiff's minor daughter by force or with the consent of the daughter. (2) Wrongfully inducing another, without the use of force, to engage in sexual relations.

self-defense   The use of reasonable force to prevent harmful or offensive contact to one's person when there is an imminent danger of such contact.

separate maintenance   Court-ordered spousal support while the parties are separated but still married. Also called separate support, alimony without divorce.

separate property   Property acquired by one spouse before marriage and brought into the marriage or any property acquired during the marriage that is not marital or community property.

separate support   See separate maintenance.

separation   See legal separation, separation agreement.

separation agreement   A contract by married persons who have separated (or who are about to separate) that can cover support, custody, property division, and other terms of their separation and possible divorce. Also called marital settlement agreement. Contracts (such as separation agreements) made during a marriage are also called postnuptial contracts. If divorce is contemplated, the more common term is *separation agreement*.

separatizer   The party seeking to prove that designated property (in whole or in part) is separate property rather than marital or community property.

sequester   To remove or hold until legal proceedings or legal claims are resolved. The noun is *sequestration*.

service of process   A formal delivery of notice to a defendant that a suit has been initiated to which he or she must respond. *Process* is the means used by the court to acquire or exercise its power or jurisdiction over a person.

settlor   See *trust*.

severability clause   A clause in an agreement that provides that if any part of the agreement is declared to be invalid, the remaining valid portions of the agreement should be carried out.

severable   Removable without destroying what remains. Something is severable when what remains after it is taken away has legal force and can survive without it. The opposite of severable is *essential* or *indispensable*.

severally   Individually, separately.

sexual harassment   Unwanted and offensive sexual advances, contact, comments, or other interaction. See also hostile environment sexual harassment, quid pro quo sexual harassment.

shallow pocket   See deep pocket.

sham   Pretended, counterfeit. Something false that purports to be genuine.

sham divorce   A divorce sought by parties who do not intend to stay divorced from each other once the divorce is granted.

shared legal custody   See joint legal custody.

shared physical custody   See joint physical custody.

Shariah   Islamic law.

Shepardize   To use the set of law books called *Shepard's Citations* to obtain specific information about a document (e.g., whether an opinion has been overruled or whether a statute has been repealed).

sole custody   See sole legal custody, sole physical custody.

sole legal custody   Only one parent has the right to make the major child rearing decisions on health, education, religion, discipline, and general welfare.

solemnization   Formal steps taken in a public ceremony in order to enter a status or contract. The verb is *solemnize*.

solemnize   To take formal steps in a public ceremony to enter into a status or contract. The noun is *solemnization*.

sole physical custody   Only one parent has the right to have the child reside with him or her.

sole proprietorship   A form of business in which one person owns all the assets.

solicitation   (1) An appeal or request for clients or business. (2) An attempt to obtain something by persuasion or application.

specialization   The development of experience and expertise in a particular area of practice.

specialty certification   Recognition of competency in a particular area of law.

specific performance   A remedy for breach of contract that forces the wrongdoing party to complete the contract as promised.

sperm bank   A facility that collects and stores human sperm from donors who will usually be anonymous to any woman who uses the sperm to become pregnant by artificial insemination. Also called cryobank.

split custody   A custody arrangement in which siblings are in the physical custody of different parents or guardians.

spoliation   Intentionally destroying, altering, or concealing evidence.

SPLS See State Parent Locator Service.

spousal consortium The right of one spouse to the relational benefits naturally expected from the other spouse. The benefits include companionship, love, affection, sexual relations, and services (e.g., cooking, making repairs around the house).

spousal refusal A person's formal declaration that he or she will no longer support his or her ailing spouse so that the latter will qualify for Medicaid or other public benefits.

spousal support See alimony.

spousal-unity rule See unity of person.

stalking (1) Repeatedly following someone, often surreptitiously. (2) A course of conduct consisting of following or loitering around a person, who is thereby placed in reasonable fear of harm.

standard form A frequently used format for a document such as a contract, complaint, or tax return. The form is designed to be used by many individuals, often by filling in blanks that call for specific information commonly needed for such documents.

standing The right to bring a case and seek relief from a court.

State Directory of New Hires (SDNH) A child-support database, maintained by each state, which contains information regarding newly hired employees in the respective state.

State Parent Locator Service (SPLS) A state government program that helps locate parents for purposes of child-support enforcement. See also Federal Parent Locator Service.

status A person's legal condition in which rights and obligations are imposed by law, often without regard to the consent or contract desires of the person involved.

status offense Disruptive behavior by a young person under a designated age that would not be considered illegal by an adult (e.g., leaving home without permission, habitual truancy). The state might refer to a status offender (or a juvenile delinquent) as a PINS (Person in Need of Supervision), MINS (Minor in Need of Supervision), or CHIPS (Child in Need of Protection and Services).

statute An act of the state or federal legislature declaring, commanding, or prohibiting something.

statute of frauds A law requiring some contracts (e.g., one that cannot be performed within a year of its making) to be in writing and signed by the party to be charged by the contract.

statute of limitations A law stating that civil or criminal actions are barred if not brought within a specified period of time. The action is time-barred.

statutory code See code.

statutory marriage See ceremonial marriage.

statutory rape Sexual intercourse with a person under a designated age (e.g., 16) even if the latter consents.

statutory share See elective share.

stay The suspension of a judgment or proceeding.

stay-away order A court order forbidding a person from being in a designated area (e.g., within 200 feet of an alleged domestic-violence victim of the defendant) or from contacting the person except for approved purposes. Also called no-contact order.

steerer See ambulance chasing.

stepparent A person who marries the natural mother or father of a child, but who is not one of the child's biological parents.

sterility Inability to have children; infertility.

stipulate To enter an agreement with an opposing party on a particular matter. The noun is *stipulation*.

stipulation An agreement between opposing parties about a particular matter. The verb is *stipulate*.

strict scrutiny The government's action must be narrowly tailored to serve a compelling state interest.

subjective standard A standard by which something is measured by what a particular person actually knew, felt, or did. See also objective standard.

subject-matter jurisdiction The court's power to resolve a particular type of legal dispute and to grant a particular type of relief.

subpoena (1) To command that someone appear at a certain time and place. (2) A command to appear at a certain time and place.

subpoena duces tecum A command that a witness appear at a certain time and place and bring specified things such as documents or jewelry.

subscribe To sign a document.

subscribed Signed.

subscription (1) A signature. (2) The act of signing one's name.

substantive due process (SDP) The constitutional requirement that the government avoid arbitrary and capricious actions that deprive someone of life, liberty, or property regardless of how fair the government is in the procedures that lead to the deprivation.

substantive fairness Equitable in the sense that the terms are satisfactory and reasonable.

substantive law Nonprocedural laws that define or govern rights and duties.

substituted service An approved method of completing service of process other than by handing the process documents to the defendant (or to the defendant's authorized representative) in person (e.g., service by mail or by publication in a newspaper). Also called constructive service.

summary dissolution A divorce obtained in an expedited manner because of the brevity of the marriage, the minimal amount of marital property, and the lack of controversy between the husband and wife.

summary seizure Taking possession of a person or property without notice or prior hearing.

summons A court notice served on the defendant ordering him or her to appear and answer the allegations of the plaintiff.

sunset Automatic termination or expiration.

supervised visitation Visitation of a child in the presence of another adult (other than the custodial parent).

Supremacy Clause The clause in the U.S. Constitution (art. VI, cl. 2) that has been interpreted to mean that when valid federal law conflicts with state law, federal law controls.

surety bond A bond given as insurance to guarantee that a contract will be completed within the agreed-upon time. An obligation by a guarantor to pay X if Y fails to perform a duty that Y owes X. Also called a performance bond.

surrender A voluntary relinquishment of rights.

surrogacy (1) The carrying and delivering of a child for another. (2) The status or act of being a substitute for another.

surrogate mother A woman who becomes pregnant (usually by artificial insemination or in vitro fertilization) with the semen of a man who is not her husband, with the understanding that she will surrender her legal rights to the baby upon its birth.

survivors benefits A form of life insurance from Social Security in which widows, children, and other designated survivors can receive monthly payments and other benefits upon the death of a worker. Also called survivorship benefits.

survivorship See right of survivorship.

suspect class A class based on race, national origin, or alienage. Alienage is the condition of being an alien. (An alien is a person who was born outside the United States, is still a subject of a foreign nation, and has not been naturalized in the United States.)

T

tacit Understood without being openly stated; implied by silence or conduct.

tainted Having or causing a conflict of interest.

talak "I divorce you." Words spoken by a husband to his wife in a Muslim divorce.

TANF See Temporary Assistance for Needy Families.

tangible   Having a physical form; able to make contact with through touch or other senses. Also called corporeal.

task-based billing   Charging a specific amount for each legal task performed. Also called unit billing, project billing.

tax basis   See basis.

tax effect   (1) To determine the tax consequences of something (verb). (2) The tax consequences of something (noun).

template   A set of formulas used to perform a designated task.

temporary alimony   Alimony awarded on an interim basis before the court makes its final decision on alimony. Also called alimony pendente lite.

Temporary Assistance for Needy Families (TANF)   The federal-state welfare system (42 U.S.C. § 601) that replaced Aid to Families with Dependent Children (AFDC). Unlike AFDC, benefits under TANF are limited to five years.

tenancy by the entirety   A joint tenancy held by a married couple and, in some states, by parties in a civil union or domestic partnership.

tenancy in common (TIC)   Ownership of property by two or more persons (called tenants in common) in shares that may or may not be equal, each person having an equal right to possess the whole property but without a right of survivorship. Also called estate in common.

tender-years presumption   In general, mothers are better suited to raise their young children (usually under five years of age) and should be awarded custody of such children unless the mothers are unfit. Also called maternal preference.

termination of parental rights (TPR)   A judicial declaration that ends the legal relationship between parent and child when this is in the best interests of the child. The parent no longer has any right to participate in decisions affecting the welfare of the child and no longer has any duties toward the child.

testament   A will.

testamentary   Pertaining to a will.

testamentary gift   A gift made in a will.

testate   (1) Pertaining to someone who dies with a valid will. (2) A person who dies with a valid will. Under this definition, also called the testator and, if female, the testatrix.

testator   A man or woman who dies with a valid will. Sometimes called testatrix if a woman.

testatrix   A woman who dies with a valid will. More commonly called testator.

therapeutic abortion   An abortion undertaken in order to safeguard the mother's life or health. Also called induced abortion.

three-pony rule   (No child needs more than three ponies.) Child support for children of parents with very high incomes should be adjusted so that payments do not go beyond what is reasonably and rationally related to the realistic needs of the child.

tickler   A system designed to provide reminders of important dates.

time-barred   Prevented or barred from bringing a civil or criminal action because of the passage of a designated period of time without commencing the action.

timeline   A chronological presentation of significant events, often organized as a straight-line diagram.

tort   A civil wrong (other than a breach of contract) that causes injury or other loss for which our legal system deems it just to provide a remedy such as damages. Injury or loss can be to the person (a personal tort), to movable property (a personal property tort), or to land and anything attached to the land (a real property tort).

tortious interference with custody, tortious interference with parental relationships   See abduction or enticement of a child.

tortious interference with parental relationships   Fraud in concealing the whereabouts of a child or otherwise wrongfully interfering with a parent's relationship with his or her child.

TPR   See termination of parental rights.

tracing   Determining the ownership or characteristics of property from the time it came into existence.

traditional alimony   See permanent alimony.

traditional surrogacy   The carrying and delivering of a child for another in which the woman uses her own egg and is therefore genetically related to the child.

transcribed   Taken down in a word-for-word account.

transcript   A word-for-word account. A written copy of oral testimony.

transferee   The person to whom an interest in property is transferred.

transferor   The person who transfers an interest in property.

transitional alimony   See rehabilitative alimony.

transitory divorce   A divorce granted in a state where neither spouse was domiciled at the time.

transmutation   The voluntary change of separate property into marital property or vice versa (in a common-law state); the voluntary change of separate property into community property or vice versa (in a community-property state).

transracial adoption   An adoption of a child whose race is different from the race of the adoptive parents. Also called interracial adoption.

transsexual   (1) A person who has undergone a sex-change operation. (2) A person who wants to be considered by society as having a gender of the opposite sex.

treatise   See legal treatise.

trespass   Wrongfully intruding on land in possession of another.

trial management conference   See pretrial conference.

trial notebook   A collection of documents, arguments, and strategies that an attorney plans to use during a trial.

triennial cohabitation   A man was presumed to be impotent if his wife remained a virgin after three years of cohabitating together.

trimester   Three months.

truancy   The willful and unjustified failure to attend school by one who is required to attend.

trust   A device or arrangement by which its creator (the *settlor* or *trustor*) transfers property (the *corpus*) to a person (the *trustee*) who holds legal title for the benefit of another (the *beneficiary* or *cestui que trust*).

trustee   The person or company holding legal title to property for the benefit of another.

U

UCCJEA   See Uniform Child Custody Jurisdiction and Enforcement Act.

UIFSA   See Uniform Interstate Family Support Act.

unauthorized practice of law (UPL)   (1) Assistance on a legal matter provided by a person who does not have a license to practice law or other special authorization to provide that assistance. (2) Engaging in legal tasks without attorney supervision and/or without special authorization to engage in such tasks.

unbundled legal services   Discrete task representation as opposed to providing services on all tasks needed by a client on a legal matter. See also bundled legal services.

unclean hands   Someone who has dirty hands. See dirty hands.

unconscionable   Shocking the conscience by heavily favoring one side due to the absence of meaningful choice and the highly unequal bargaining positions of the parties.

uncontested   Unchallenged; without opposition or dispute.

uncontested divorce   A divorce granted to a spouse when the other spouse does not appear or when the other spouse appears but does not dispute any of the other spouse's claims. See also friendly divorce.

undertaking   A promise, engagement, or enterprise.

undue influence   Improper persuasion, coercion, force, or deception.

unemancipated   Legally dependent on one's parent or legal guardian.

unethical conduct   See ethics.

unfit   Demonstrating abuse or neglect that is substantially detrimental to a child.

Uniform Child Custody Jurisdiction and Enforcement Act (UCCJEA)   A model state statute on the enforcement of custody and visitation orders across state lines.

Uniform Interstate Family Support Act (UIFSA)   A state law on establishing and enforcing alimony and child-support obligations against someone who does not live in the same state as the person to whom the alimony and child support is owed.

uniform laws   Laws proposed to state legislatures in areas where uniformity is deemed appropriate. Each state can adopt, modify, or reject the proposals. Sometimes called model acts.

Uniform Marriage and Divorce Act (UMDA)   A model statute on marriage and divorce proposed to the states for adoption.

Uniform Parentage Act (UPA)   A model statute that has been adopted by most states on how paternity or parenthood is determined.

Uniform Premarital Agreement Act (UPAA)   A model statute adopted by many states that governs the legality of premarital agreements.

Uniform Probate Code   A law adopted by some states that covers (1) the probating of wills and (2) the distribution of the estate of persons who die without wills (intestate succession).

Uniform Transfers to Minors Act (UTMA)   A statute adopted by many states that allows transfers of property to minors and allows custodians to manage the property.

unilateral divorce   (1) See ex parte divorce. (2) A divorce that can be granted even though only one party wants to dissolve the marriage.

unity of identity   See unity of person.

unity of person   The now-rejected view that the legal identity of a wife was subsumed into the legal identity of the husband. Also called doctrine of oneness, spousal-unity rule, unity of identity.

unjust enrichment   The receipt of a benefit in the form of goods or services from another when in fairness and equity the recipient should provide restitution for (a return of) the goods or compensation for the services even though there was no express or implied promise to do so. The amount the recipient should pay for services is called *quantum meruit*, the reasonable value of the services provided.

unreasonable   That which is contrary to the behavior of an ordinary, prudent person under the same circumstances.

UPA   See Uniform Parentage Act.

UPAA   See Uniform Premarital Agreement Act.

UPL   See unauthorized practice of law.

UTMA   See Uniform Transfers to Minors Act.

ux (uxor)   Wife. See also *et ux*.

V

venue   The place of the trial. The proper county or geographical area in which a court with jurisdiction may hear a case. When more than one court has subject-matter jurisdiction to hear a particular kind of case, the selection of the court is called *choice of venue*.

verification   A formal declaration that a party has read the pleading and swears that it is true to the best of his or her knowledge.

vested   Fixed so that it cannot be taken away by future events or conditions; accrued so that you now have a right to present or future possession or enjoyment.

viable   Able to live indefinitely outside the womb by natural or artificial support systems.

vicarious liability   Liability imposed on a person because of the conduct of another, based solely on the status of the relationship between the two. The person liable is not the person whose conduct led to the liability.

vinculo matrimonii   See divorce a vinculo matrimonii.

virtual adoption   See equitable adoption.

visitation   (1) The right to have access to a child who resides with another. Some states prefer the phrase "parenting time" when the person "visiting" the child is the noncustodial parent. (2) Actual time spent by a noncustodial parent with his or her child.

vital statistics   Data on major events such as births, deaths, marriages, divorces, and abortions, often kept current by the government for public health and other civic purposes.

void   Of no legal effect; invalid whether or not a court declares it so.

void ab initio   Invalid from the beginning, from the time something started.

voidable   Valid unless cancelled or invalidated.

voidable marriage   A marriage that is valid unless a court declares its invalidity.

void marriage   A marriage that is invalid even if no court ever declares its invalidity.

voir dire   Jury selection.

voluntary   By choice; proceeding from a free and unconstrained will.

voluntary manslaughter   The intentional, unlawful killing of someone but with extenuating circumstances such as provocation. Murder reduced to manslaughter because of the absence of malice or premeditation.

W

waiver   The relinquishment or giving up of a right or privilege because of an explicit rejection of it or because of a failure to take appropriate steps to claim it at the proper time.

ward   A person (e.g., minor) placed by the court under the care or protection of a guardian.

welfare   See public assistance.

will   An instrument (legal document) that specifies the disposition of one's property (and related instructions) upon death.

workers' compensation   A no-fault system of paying for medical care and providing limited wage benefits to a worker for an employment-related injury or illness regardless of who was at fault in causing the injury or illness.

work-product rule   Notes, working papers, memoranda, or similar things prepared by or for an attorney in anticipation of litigation are not discoverable by an opponent, absent a showing of substantial need. They are protected by privilege. Also called attorney work product.

writ of execution   See execution of judgment.

wrongful adoption   An action seeking damages for carelessly stating (or failing to disclose) to prospective adoptive parents available facts on the health or other condition of the adoptee that would be relevant to the decision on whether to adopt.

wrongful birth   An action by parents of an unwanted impaired child for negligence in failing to warn them of the risks that the child would be born with birth defects. The parents seek their own damages.

wrongful death   A death caused by a tort or other wrong.

wrongful life   An action by or on behalf of an unwanted impaired child for negligence that precluded an informed parental decision to avoid the child's conception or birth. The child seeks its own damages.

wrongful pregnancy   An action by parents of an unplanned healthy child for a wrong related to pregnancy such as negligent performance of a vasectomy. The parents seek their own damages. Also called wrongful conception.

Z

zygote   A fertilized egg. A cell produced by the union of a male sex cell and a female sex cell.

Index